Accounting for Governmental and Nonprofit Entities

Accounting for Governmental and Nonprofit Entities

11 EDITION

Earl R. Wilson, Ph.D., CPA
KPMG *Peat Marwick/Joseph A. Silvoso*
  Distinguished Professor
University of Missouri–Columbia

Leon E. Hay, Ph.D., CPA, CGFM
Distinguished Professor Emeritus
University of Arkansas–Fayetteville

Susan C. Kattelus, Ph.D., CPA, CGFM
Associate Professor
Eastern Michigan University

Irwin McGraw-Hill

Boston   Burr Ridge, IL   Dubuque, IA   Madison, WI   New York   San Francisco   St. Louis
Bangkok   Bogotá   Caracas   Lisbon   London   Madrid
Mexico City   Milan   New Delhi   Seoul   Singapore   Sydney   Taipei   Toronto

Irwin/McGraw-Hill

A Division of The **McGraw-Hill** Companies

ACCOUNTING FOR GOVERNMENTAL AND NONPROFIT ENTITIES

This book is printed on acid-free paper.

1 2 3 4 5 6 7 8 9 0 DOC/DOC 9 3 2 1 0 9 8

ISBN 0-256-16872-5

Vice president and editorial director: *Michael W. Junior*
Publisher: *Jeffrey J. Shelstad*
Sponsoring editor: *George Werthman*
Editorial assistant: *Irene Baki*
Senior marketing manager: *Rhonda Seelinger*
Project manager: *Paula M. Buschman*
Production supervisor: *Scott M. Hamilton*
Freelance design coordinator: *JoAnne Schopler*
Supplement coordinator: *Cathy L. Tepper*
Compositor: *GAC Shepard Poorman*
Typeface: *10.5/12 Goudy*
Printer: *R. R. Donnelley & Sons Company*

Library of Congress Cataloging-in-Publication Data

Wilson, Earl Ray
   Accounting for governmental and nonprofit entities / Earl R.
Wilson, Leon E. Hay, Susan C. Kattelus. — 11th ed.
    p. cm.
   Includes index.
   ISBN 0-256-16872-5
   1. Finance, Public—Accounting. 2. Nonprofit organizations—
Accounting. 3. Nonprofit organizations—United States—Accounting.
I. Hay, Leon Edwards, 1923- . II. Kattelus, Susan C.
III. Title.

HJ9733.W48 1999   98-5443
657'.95—dc21   CIP

http://www.mhhe.com

Preface

The first two editions of this text (published in 1951 and 1956) were written by Professor R. M. Mikesell of Indiana University–Bloomington. Dr. Leon Hay, a coauthor of this 11th edition, joined Professor Mikesell as coauthor of the third and fourth editions (1961 and 1969). After Professor Mikesell's death in 1972, Professor Hay prepared the fifth (1974), sixth (1980), seventh (1985), and eighth (1989) editions with the help and suggestions of many good friends, but without a coauthor. Dr. Earl R. Wilson of the University of Missouri–Columbia became a coauthor beginning with the ninth edition of *Accounting for Governmental and Nonprofit Entities*. Dr. Hay and Dr. Wilson also coauthored the 10th edition of the text. Dr. Susan C. Kattelus, an Associate Professor at Eastern Michigan University, has joined as coauthor on this 11th edition. Professor Kattelus brings a broad range of professional and academic experience to the text, particularly in the area of not-for-profit organizations. Her expertise in this area will be obvious as readers use this edition.

Because financial accounting and reporting standards, as well as auditing standards, are expected to continue their rapid change, new editions are expected to be published at least every three years. During the life of this 11th edition, the authors will prepare Update Bulletins as needed to inform adopters of this text of changes in the standards explained and illustrated in the 11th edition, as necessitated by new pronouncements of the Governmental Accounting Standards Board, the Financial Accounting Standards Board, Federal Accounting Standards Advisory Board, U.S. General Accounting Office, the U.S. Office of Management and Budget, and the American Institute of Certified Public Accountants. Users of the text should occasionally check for Update Bulletins at the lead author's web page: http://www.missouri.edu/~accterw. In addition to downloading bulletins from the web page, users can submit technical inquiries about the text and provide the authors with feedback or point out errors and omissions. Your input will be greatly appreciated.

As was true of each previous edition, the authors owe a debt of gratitude to the many professors, students, and governmental financial report users, preparers, and auditors who have shared their knowledge, experience, and views on governmental and not-for-profit organization accounting and financial reporting. In the preparation of this edition the authors are greatly indebted to the standards-setters themselves, especially to Tom L. Allen, Chairman; David Bean, Director of Research; and to all the member of the Governmental Accounting Standards Board and its staff, both current and past.

Many professors who were thanked by name in the Prefaces to earlier editions have continued to give generously of their time and effort in improving explanations in chapters of the text and improving the wording of questions, exercises, problems, answers, and solutions. The authors gratefully acknowledge the following individuals for reviewing drafts of chapters, providing excellent suggestions for improvement, and providing useful materials for inclusion in the text, either in this 11th edition, the preceding edition, or both: Dr. Kenneth W. Brown of Southwest Missouri State University for Chapter 11 on the evaluation of financial performance; Robert Bramlett of the Federal Accounting Standards Advisory Board, Bruce K. Michelson of the U.S. General Accounting Office, and J. Thomas Luter, formerly of the U.S. Department of the Treasury, for Chapter 13 on federal government accounting; Bridget M. Anderson, KPMG Peat Marwick, LLP, and Dr. Zafar Khan, Eastern Michigan University, for Chapter 14 on budgeting and costing; Susan B. Perlin, Plante & Moran, LLP, for Chapter 16 on not-for-profit organizations; Sherwood A. Mitter, CPA, for Chapter 17 on regulatory and taxation issues related to not-for-profit organizations; Dr. Mary L. Fischer of the University of Texas at Tyler, Robert T. Forrester, Coopers & Lybrand, LLP, and David Smarr of the University of Missouri–Columbia for Chapter 18 on colleges and universities; and James L. Birchler, CPA, and Sonja J. Schuster for Chapter 19 on health care organizations. Bobbye S. Hay, CPA, contributed greatly to this and previous editions, both technically and personally. Florence J. Wilson also provided significant administrative assistance as well as much needed moral support. John T. Kattelus also provided much appreciated support. Wei Jin, a graduate assistant at Eastern Michigan University, devoted many hours to helping with the preparation of the text.

The authors appreciate the courtesy of the Government Accounting Standards Board in giving permission to quote their pronouncements and reproduce illustrations from their publications. The Government Finance Officers Association of the United States and Canada generously gave permission to use its published materials. The American Institute of Certified Public Accountants has also been very helpful by allowing use of questions and problems from previous Uniform Certified Public Accountant Examinations and permitting quotations from its publications, particularly in the audit and accounting guide series. The International City/ County Management Association contributed significantly to the material now in Chapter 11 by granting permission for use of its materials on financial analysis. In

Chapter 16, the United Way of America graciously allowed the use of illustrations from *Accounting and Financial Reporting: A Guide for United Ways and Not-for-Profit Human Service Organizations.*

Ancillary materials that accompany this text include:

- Instructor's Guide (revised to include teaching and case analysis tips).
- Power Point lecture presentations (new) which include 20 to 30 slides for each chapter.
- Test Bank
- Computerized Test Bank
- Computerized Continuous Problem/Practice Set.

Although a number of persons helped refine the explanations in the chapters and the wording of the questions, cases, exercises, and problems, it is probable that errors, inconsistencies, and ambiguities remain in this edition. As readers encounter errors of omission or commission in this text, we urge them to let us know so that corrections can be made. Additionally, every user of this edition who has suggestions or comments about the material in the chapters—or the questions, cases, exercises, or problems—is invited to share them with either of the following two coauthors, either by regular mail, e-mail, or Internet.

Dr. Earl R. Wilson
School of Accountancy
University of Missouri-Columbia
Columbia, MO 65211
wilson@bpa.missouri.edu
http://www.missouri.edu/~accterw

Dr. Susan C. Kattelus
Department of Accounting
Eastern Michigan University
Ypsilanti, MI 48197
susan.kattelus@emich.edu
http://www.online.emich.edu/~acc_kattelus

Brief Contents

ix

Contents

CHAPTER 1

Financial Reporting for Governmental and Not-for-Profit Entities

Learning Objectives

After studying this chapter, you should be able to:

- Identify and explain the characteristics that distinguish governmental and not-for-profit entities from for-profit entities.
- Identify the authoritative bodies responsible for setting financial reporting standards for (1) state and local governments, (2) the federal government, and (3) not-for-profit organizations.
- Contrast and compare the objectives of financial reporting for (1) state and local governments, (2) the federal government, and (3) not-for-profit organizations.
- Distinguish the general purpose financial reports of state and local governments from their comprehensive annual financial reports.
- Explain the rationale for the proposed dual perspective reporting model.
- Explain why analysis of the financial performance of governmental and not-for-profit entities differs from that of for-profit entities.

Governmental and not-for-profit organizations are vast in number and diversity. In the United States, governments exist at the federal, state, and local levels and serve a wide variety of functions. The most recent census of governments reports there are 84,955 local governmental units within the 50 states: 3,043 counties, 19,279 municipalities, 16,656 townships, 14,422 independent school districts, and 31,555 special districts.[1]

States, counties, municipalities (for example, cities and villages), and townships are **general purpose governments**—governments that provide many categories of services to their residents (such as police and fire protection; sanitation; construction and maintenance of streets, roads, and bridges; and health and welfare). Independent school districts and special districts are **limited purpose governments**—governments that provide only a single function, or a limited number of functions (such as education, drainage and flood control, irrigation, soil and water conservation, fire protection, and water supply). Limited purpose governments have the power to levy and collect taxes and to raise revenues from other sources as provided by state laws to finance the services they provide.

Not-for-profit organizations also exist in many forms and serve many different functions. Estimates of the number of not-for-profit organizations range from several hundred thousand to more than 1 million.[2] These include private colleges and universities, various kinds of health care entities, libraries, museums, professional and trade associations, fraternal and social organizations, and religious organizations.

Distinguishing Characteristics of Governmental and Not-for-Profit Entities

Governmental and not-for-profit organizations differ in important ways from business organizations. Moreover, as you will soon learn, accounting and financial reporting for governmental and not-for-profit organizations are markedly different from accounting and financial reporting for businesses. An understanding of how governmental and not-for-profit organizations differ from business organizations is essential to understanding the unique accounting and financial reporting principles that have evolved for governmental and not-for-profit organizations.

In its *Statement of Financial Accounting Concepts No. 4,* the **Financial Accounting Standards Board (FASB)** noted the following characteristics that it felt distinguished governmental and not-for-profit entities from business organizations:

---

[1]U.S. Department of Commerce, Bureau of the Census, *1992 Census of Governments*, vol. 1, no. 2 (Washington, DC: U.S. Government Printing Office), p. v.

[2]The U.S. Bureau of the Census (1992 *Census of Service Industries*, SC92-S-1, Table 1b) reports that in 1992 there were 208,911 tax-exempt service organizations. This does not include, however, numerous other not-for-profit organizations such as religious organizations, labor unions, and political organizations. The total of tax-exempt not-for-profits numbers more than 1 million (*1996–97 Nonprofit Almanac: Dimensions of the Independent Sector*, Washington, DC).

Receipts of significant amounts of resources from resource providers who do not expect to receive either repayment or economic benefits proportionate to the resources provided.

Operating purposes that are other than to provide goods or services at a profit or profit equivalent.

Absence of defined ownership interests that can be sold, transferred, or redeemed, or that convey entitlement to a share of a residual distribution of resources in the event of liquidation of the organization.[3]

The **Governmental Accounting Standards Board (GASB)** further distinguishes governmental entities in the United States from not-for-profit entities and from businesses by stressing that governments exist in an environment in which the power ultimately rests in the hands of the people. Voters delegate that power to public officials through the election process; the power is divided among the executive, legislative, and judicial branches of the government so that the actions, financial and otherwise, of governmental executives are constrained by legislative actions; and executive and legislative actions are subject to judicial review. Further constraints are imposed on state and local governments by the existence of the federal system in which higher levels of government encourage or dictate activities by lower levels and finance the activities (partially, at least) by an extensive system of intergovernmental grants and subsidies that require the lower levels to be accountable to the entity providing the resources, as well as to the citizenry. Revenues raised by each level of government come, ultimately, from taxpayers. Taxpayers are required to serve as providers of resources to governments even though they often have very little choice about which governmental services they receive and the extent to which they receive them.

Since governments may have a monopoly on the services they provide to the public, the lack of a competitive marketplace makes it difficult to measure efficiency in the provision of the services. It is also extremely difficult to measure optimal quantity or quality for many of the services rendered by government—for example, how many police are "enough"? The Governmental Accounting Standards Board notes the determination of optimal quantity or quality of government services is complicated by the involuntary nature of the resources provided. "A consumer purchasing a commercial product can determine how much to purchase and may choose among 'good,' 'better,' or 'best' quality and pay accordingly. A group of individuals paying for governmental services (and paying in different proportions for services that some of them may not use or desire) presents a far more complex situation."[4]

---

[3]Financial Accounting Standards Board, *Statement of Financial Accounting Concepts No. 4*, "Objectives of Financial Reporting by Nonbusiness Organizations" (Norwalk, CT, 1980), p. 3. In 1985 the FASB decided to replace the term *nonbusiness* with the term *not-for-profit*. Other organizations use the term *nonprofit* as a synonym for not-for-profit. The terms are used interchangeably in this text.

[4]Governmental Accounting Standards Board, *Codification of Governmental Accounting and Financial Reporting Standards as of June 30, 1997* (Norwalk, CT, 1997), Appendix B, par. 17e.

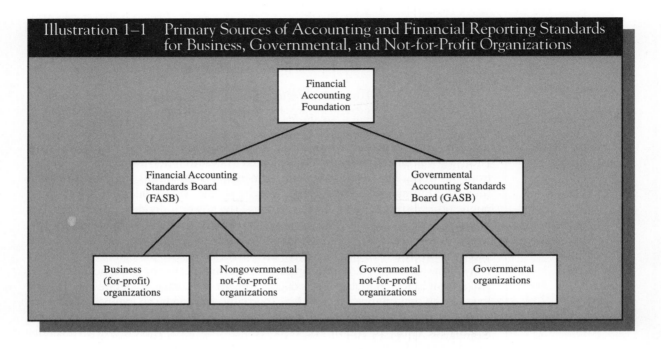

Illustration 1–1   Primary Sources of Accounting and Financial Reporting Standards for Business, Governmental, and Not-for-Profit Organizations

Sources of Financial Reporting Standards

Illustration 1–1 shows the primary sources of accounting and financial reporting standards for business, governmental, and not-for-profit organizations. As shown, the FASB establishes accounting and financial reporting standards for business (for-profit) organizations; the GASB establishes standards for governmental organizations.

Authority to establish accounting principles (accounting and financial reporting standards) for not-for-profit organizations is split between the GASB and the FASB because a sizable number of not-for-profit organizations (particularly colleges and universities, and hospitals) are governmentally related, but many others are independent of governmental units. Accordingly, the GASB has the responsibility for establishing accounting and financial reporting standards for not-for-profit organizations that are considered to be governmental in character. The FASB has the responsibility for establishing accounting and financial reporting standards for nongovernmental not-for-profit organizations.

The GASB and the FASB are parallel bodies under the oversight of the Financial Accounting Foundation. The Financial Accounting Foundation appoints the members of the two boards and supports the operating expenses of the boards by obtaining contributions from business corporations; professional organizations of accountants, financial analysts, and other groups concerned with financial reporting; CPA firms; debt-rating agencies; and state and local governments (for support of the GASB). Because of the breadth of support and the lack of ties to any single organization or governmental unit, the GASB and the FASB are referred to as "independent standards-setting boards in the private sector." Before the creation of the GASB and the FASB, financial reporting standards were set by groups sponsored by professional organizations: The forerunners of the GASB (formed in 1984) were the National Council on Governmental Accounting (1973–84), the National Committee on Governmental Accounting (1948–73), and the National Committee on Municipal Accounting (1934–41). The forerunners of the FASB (formed in 1973) were the Accounting Principles Board (1959–73) and the Committee on Accounting Procedure (1938–59) of the American Institute of Certified Public Accountants.

The American Institute of Certified Public Accountants (AICPA) has formally designated the GASB and the FASB as the authoritative bodies to establish accounting principles for state and local governments and for business organizations and nongovernmental not-for-profit organizations, respectively. "Authority to establish accounting principles" is interpreted in practice to mean "authority to establish accounting and financial reporting standards."

Federal statutes assign responsibility for establishing and maintaining a sound financial structure for the federal government to three officials: the Comptroller General, the Director of the Office of Management and Budget, and the Secretary of the Treasury. In 1990, these three officials created the **Federal Accounting Standards Advisory Board (FASAB)** to recommend accounting principles and standards for the federal government and its agencies. It is understood that, to the maximum extent possible, federal accounting and financial reporting standards will be consistent with those established by the GASB and, where applicable, by the FASB.

Determining Whether a Not-for-Profit Organization Is Governmental

Illustration 1–1 suggests that the kinds of organizations for which the FASB and GASB are responsible for setting standards are clearcut. Unfortunately, this is sometimes not the case. In practice, it may be difficult to determine whether some types of not-for-profits are governmental in nature or not, and thus which standards-setting body to look to for authoritative guidance.

The U.S. Bureau of the Census defines a *government* as:

> An organized entity which, in addition to having governmental character, has sufficient discretion in the management of its own affairs to distinguish it as separate from the administrative structure of any other governmental unit.[5]

This definition, though helpful, provides insufficient guidance because it fails to explain the meaning of "having governmental character." In order to provide additional guidance for auditors on this issue, two audit and accounting guides of the AICPA, with the tacit approval of both the FASB and the GASB, state:

---

[5]U.S. Department of Commerce, Bureau of the Census, *1992 Census of Governments*, vol. 1, no. 1 (Washington, DC: U.S. Government Printing Office), p. ix.

Public corporations and bodies corporate and politic are governmental organizations. Other organizations are governmental organizations if they have one or more of the following characteristics:

a. Popular election of officers or appointment (or approval) of a controlling majority of the members of the organization's governing body by officials of one or more state or local governments,

b. the potential for unilateral dissolution by a government with the net assets reverting to a government, or

c. the power to enact *and* enforce a tax levy.[6]

Furthermore, organizations are presumed to be governmental if they have the ability to issue directly (rather than through a state or municipal authority) debt that pays interest exempt from federal taxation. However, organizations possessing only that ability (to issue tax-exempt debt) and none of the other governmental characteristics may rebut the presumption that they are governmental if their determination is supported by compelling, relevant evidence.

Objectives of Financial Reporting

In its *Concepts Statement No. 1,* "Objectives of Financial Reporting," the Governmental Accounting Standards Board stated that "**Accountability** is the cornerstone of all financial reporting in government . . . Accountability requires governments to answer to the citizenry—to justify the raising of public resources and the purposes for which they are used."[7] The board elaborated:

> Governmental accountability is based on the belief that the citizenry has a "right to know," a right to receive openly declared facts that may lead to public debate by the citizens and their elected representatives. Financial reporting plays a major role in fulfilling government's duty to be publicly accountable in a democratic society.[8]

Financial reports of state and local governments, according to the GASB, are used primarily to (1) compare actual financial results with the legally adopted budget; (2) assess financial condition and results of operations; (3) assist in determining compliance with finance-related laws, rules, and regulations; and (4) assist in evaluating efficiency and effectiveness.

Closely related to the concept of accountability as the cornerstone of governmental financial reporting is the concept the GASB refers to as **interperiod equity.** The concept and its importance are explained as follows:

> The GASB believes that interperiod equity is a significant part of accountability and is fundamental to public administration. It therefore needs to be considered when estab-

---

[6]American Institute of Certified Public Accountants, Audit and Accounting Guide, *Health Care Organizations* (New York, 1997), par. 102c; and American Institute of Certified Public Accountants, Audit and Accounting Guide, *Not-for-Profit Organizations* (New York, 1997), par. 103.
[7]GASB, *Codification,* Appendix B, par. 56.
[8]Ibid.

lishing financial reporting objectives. In short, *financial reporting should help users assess whether current-year revenues are sufficient to pay for services provided that year and whether future taxpayers will be required to assume burdens for services previously provided.* (Emphasis added.)[9]

Accountability is also the foundation for the financial reporting objectives the Federal Accounting Standards Advisory Board (FASAB) has developed for the federal government. The FASAB's *Statement of Accounting and Reporting Concepts Statement No. 1* (Chapter 4) identifies four objectives of federal financial reporting. In brief, the objectives are to assist report users in evaluating budgetary integrity, operating performance, stewardship, and adequacy of systems and controls.

Unlike the FASB and the GASB, which focus their standards on external financial reporting, the FASAB and its sponsors in the federal government are concerned with both internal and external financial reporting. Accordingly, the FASAB has identified four major groups of users of federal financial reports: citizens, Congress, executives, and program managers. Given the broad role the FASAB has been assigned, its standards focus on cost accounting and service efforts and accomplishments measures, as well as on financial accounting and reporting.

Financial reports of not-for-profit organizations—voluntary health and welfare organizations, colleges and universities, hospitals, religious organizations, and others—have similar uses. However, in recognition of the fact that the financial operations of not-for-profit organizations are generally not subject to as detailed legal restrictions as are those of governments, the Financial Accounting Standards Board believes the financial reports for not-for-profit organizations should provide: (1) information useful in making resource allocation decisions; (2) information useful in assessing services and ability to provide services; (3) information useful in assessing management stewardship and performance; and (4) information about economic resources, obligations, net resources, and changes in them.[10]

Note the objectives of financial reporting for governments and not-for-profit entities stress the need for the public to understand and evaluate the financial activities and management of these organizations. All readers must already be aware of the impact on their lives, and on their bank accounts, of the activities of the layers of government they are obligated to support and of the not-for-profit organizations they voluntarily support. Since each of us is vitally affected, it is important that we be able to read intelligently the financial reports of governmental and not-for-profit entities. In order to understand the content of the financial reports it is necessary for the reader to make the effort to learn the accounting and financial reporting standards developed by authoritative bodies. The standards are explained and illustrated in Chapters 2 through 19 of this text. This chapter is intended to set forth the distinguishing characteristics of governmental and not-for-profit entities and to provide an overview of the objectives of accounting and financial reporting for these entities.

---

[9]Ibid., par. 61.
[10]FASB, *Statement of Financial Accounting Concepts No. 4*, pp. 19–23.

Financial Reporting of State and Local Governments

Both the GASB and the FASB issue concepts statements, which are intended to communicate the framework within which the two bodies strive to establish consistent financial reporting standards for entities within their respective jurisdictions. Both the GASB and the FASB are concerned with standards for financial reporting to *external users*—those who lack the authority to prescribe the information they want and who must rely on the information management communicates to them. The boards do not set standards for reporting to managers, administrators, regulatory bodies, or others deemed to have the ability to enforce their demands for information. Financial reports to external users are called *general purpose financial reports*. General purpose financial reporting includes not only financial statements but all other means of communicating information that relates directly or indirectly to the information provided by the accounting system. The GASB specifies that governmental general purpose financial reporting includes "in addition to **general purpose financial statements (GPFS)**, 'popular reports' and comprehensive annual financial reports (CAFRs)." The GPFS of a governmental reporting entity are the statements that an independent certified public accountant audits and on which the CPA expresses the opinion that the statements are (or are not) in conformity with generally accepted accounting principles (GAAP). Popular reports, as such, are not audited but usually contain selected data from the audited financial statements, statistical data, graphic displays, and narrative explanations. Illustration 1–2 shows the GASB's view of the relation of the GPFS to other information financial report users are thought to need to assess accountability and make resource allocation, investment, and other economic, social, and political decisions. The GASB encourages state and local governments to experiment with reporting **service efforts and accomplishments** to provide more complete information about a governmental entity's performance than can be provided by one operating statement, balance sheet, and budgetary comparison statements and schedules. Indicators of service efforts include inputs of nonmonetary resources as well as inputs of dollars. Indicators of service accomplishments include both outputs and outcomes.

Comprehensive Annual Financial Report

Serious users of governmental financial information need much more detail than is found in the audited general purpose financial statements. For state and local governments, much of that detail, as well as the auditor's report and the GPFS, is found in the governmental reporting entity's **comprehensive annual financial report (CAFR)**, which is considered the entity's official annual report published as a matter of public record.

Standards for the content of the CAFR are found in the GASB's *Codification of Governmental Accounting and Financial Reporting Standards*. Each CAFR should contain an introductory section, a financial section, and a statistical section.

Introductory Section. Introductory material includes such items as title page and contents page, the letter of transmittal, and other material deemed appropriate by management.

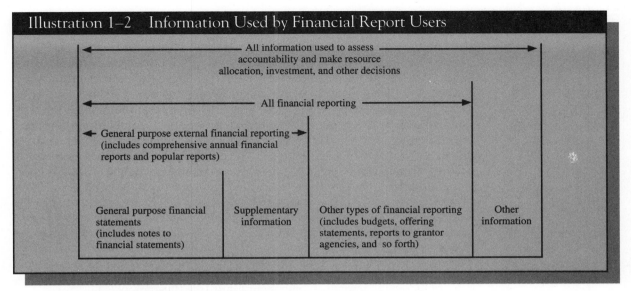

Illustration 1–2   Information Used by Financial Report Users

All information used to assess accountability and make resource allocation, investment, and other decisions

All financial reporting

General purpose external financial reporting (includes comprehensive annual financial reports and popular reports)

General purpose financial statements (includes notes to financial statements)

Supplementary information

Other types of financial reporting (includes budgets, offering statements, reports to grantor agencies, and so forth)

Other information

Source: Adapted from GASB, *Codification,* Appendix B, Figure 1.

The letter of transmittal may be literally that—a letter from the chief finance officer addressed to the chief executive and governing body of the governmental unit—or it may be a narrative over the signature of the chief executive. In either event, the letter or narrative material should cite legal and policy requirements for the report and discuss briefly the important aspects of the financial condition and financial operations of the reporting entity as a whole and of the entity's funds and account groups. Significant changes since the prior annual report and changes expected during the coming year should be brought to the attention of the reader of the report.

Financial Section.   The financial section of a comprehensive annual financial report should include: (1) an auditor's report, (2) general purpose financial statements, and (3) combining and individual fund and account group statements and schedules.

Laws relating to the audit of governmental units vary markedly from state to state. In some states, all state agencies and all governmental units created pursuant to the state law are required to be audited by an audit agency of the state government. In others, local governmental units are audited by independent certified public accountants. In still others, some governmental units are audited by the state audit agency and some by independent certified public accountants. In any event, the auditor's opinion should accompany the financial statements reproduced in the report.

The financial section should contain sufficient information to disclose fully and present fairly the financial position and results of financial operations during the fiscal year. As noted previously, the financial operations of governmental units are constrained in considerable detail by laws of higher jurisdictions and by the actions of the legislative branch of the governmental unit itself. In addition, agreements with creditors and others provide constraints over financial activities and introduce financial reporting requirements. In order to make it possible to determine and demonstrate compliance with laws, regulations, and agreements, governmental units use **fund accounting.** The technical definition of *fund* is given in Chapter 2; the nature of each fund type and account group provided in GASB standards is also explained in Chapter 2. At this point it is sufficient to note that general purpose financial statements of state and local governments are *combined* statements in which financial data are presented in columnar form for each fund type and account group used by the reporting entity. The effects of interfund transactions are not eliminated; therefore the GPFS are *not* properly referred to as *consolidated*. The five combined statements that comprise the GPFS and that must be included in the financial section of a CAFR are:

1. Combined Balance Sheet—All Fund Types, Account Groups, and Discretely Presented Component Units (see Illustration 2–1).
2. Combined Statement of Revenues, Expenditures, and Changes in Fund Balances—All Governmental Fund Types and Discretely Presented Component Units (see Illustration 2–2).
3. Combined Statement of Revenues, Expenditures, and Changes in Fund Balances—Budget and Actual—General and Special Revenue Fund Types (and similar governmental fund types of the primary government for which annual budgets have been legally adopted) (see Illustration 2–3).
4. Combined Statement of Revenues, Expenses, and Changes in Retained Earnings (or Equity)—All Proprietary Fund Types and Discretely Presented Component Units (see Illustration 2–4).
5. Combined Statement of Cash Flows—All Proprietary Fund Types and Discretely Presented Component Units (see Illustration 2–5).

The Notes to the Financial Statements are an integral part of the GPFS and are intended to be read with the GPFS. Accordingly, an independent auditor's report on the GPFS is a report on the five combined statements and on the notes that accompany them. GASB standards allow governments to "lift" the GPFS (including notes and auditor's report) from the CAFR and issue them separately for widespread distribution to users who require less detailed information than is contained in the CAFR. The CAFR must contain the GPFS, however, even if the GPFS are separately issued. Illustrations of the five combined statements, the GPFS, are presented in Chapter 2, as noted in the preceding list of the GPFS.

Governments may have many different funds within each fund type; therefore persons with a depth of interest in the financial condition and financial operations of a governmental reporting entity will wish to refer to the Combining and Individual Fund Statements, which follow the GPFS in the financial section of a CAFR. *Combining* statements are used to aggregate the financial data of all funds within each fund type. (Illustration 5–6 presents an example of a combining balance sheet.) If a reporting entity maintains only one fund within a given fund type it should be obvious that the financial data for that fund would be presented in *individual fund* statements, rather than in combining statements. Individual fund statements may be presented for one or more funds included in a fund-type combining statement where necessary to present prior year or budgetary comparisons. Combining and individual fund statements are not ordinarily audited, but if the reporting entity has need for an auditor's opinion on those statements the audit can be extended to cover the necessary additional work. Unaudited information often presented in the financial section of the CAFR following the combining and individual fund statements includes schedules necessary to demonstrate compliance with finance-related legal and contractual provisions; schedules to present comparative data on such items as tax collections and long-term debt, and schedules to provide greater detail for information reported in the statements.

Statistical Section.   In addition to the introductory section (which presents the highlights of the CAFR) and the financial section (which presents the GPFS, combining and individual fund statements, and supplemental information), a CAFR should contain a statistical section, which presents tables and charts showing social and economic data, financial trends, and the fiscal capacity of the government in detail needed by readers who are more than casually interested in the activities of the governmental unit. The GASB Codification suggests the content of the tables usually considered necessary for inclusion in a CAFR. The statistical section is discussed at greater length in Chapter 10 of this text.

Fund and Account Group Accounting and Reporting

The principles that underlie GASB accounting and financial reporting standards are introduced and discussed briefly in Chapter 2. Chapters 3 through 9 explain and illustrate the standards applicable to each of the fund types and account groups used by state and local governments. Chapter 10 expands the discussion of the treatment of interfund transactions and reviews general purpose financial reporting of a governmental reporting entity. Chapter 11 discusses evaluation of governmental financial condition.

GASB's Proposed Dual Perspective Reporting Model

The GASB has been working since its inception in 1984 on developing a new financial reporting model for state and local governments. After an earlier attempt to require governments to apply the accrual basis of accounting to all funds and subsequent attempts to resolve related balance sheet display issues failed to gain sufficient acceptance from constituents,[11] the GASB issued in June 1995 a *Preliminary Views* (PV) document that presented a *dual perspective* set of basic financial statements.[12] One perspective, the "fund perspective," is similar in most respects to the present fund-type financial statements discussed at length in Chapters 2 through 9 of this text. The other perspective would require entitywide financial statements in which all the activities of a governmental unit would be reported on a full accrual basis, with a flow of economic resources focus—similar to that of the commercial reporting model. This would, of course, represent a major change from the current reporting model discussed in the text. In addition to the basic financial statements, governments would be required to present a **Management's Discussion and Analysis (MD&A)** in which management would provide a brief, objective, and easily readable analysis of the government's financial performance for the year and its financial position at year-end.

Even though subsequent public hearings, written comments, and focus group input revealed continuing disagreement among major constituents (principally state and local government professional organizations and the AICPA), the GASB issued an exposure draft of a proposed standard that will require state and local governments to prepare basic financial statements from both the fund and entitywide perspectives, as well as to provide an MD&A.[13] After additional public hearings and analysis of written comments, the GASB is expected to issue a final statement on the new reporting model in late 1998. If the GASB does adopt the proposed standard, implementation of the new model would not be required until fiscal years beginning after June 15, 2000.[14]

In advocating a dual perspective reporting model the GASB is taking the position that no one set of financial statements can meet the identified objectives of financial reporting, some of which relate to **fiscal accountability** and others which relate to **operational accountability.** The entitywide financial statements are intended to report on operational accountability—information about operating results and financial position from an economic perspective. As such, the entitywide financial statements provide information about both short-term and long-term financial position, and the cost of providing services, broadly summarized for major governmental programs or functions. Fund perspective statements for gov-

---

[11]In 1990 the GASB issued *Statement of Governmental Accounting Standards No. 11*, "Measurement Focus and Basis of Accounting—Governmental Fund Operating Statements," that, upon implementation, would have required the accrual basis of accounting for governmental funds. However, in 1993 the GASB deferred indefinitely the implementation of *Statement No. 11* by issuing *Statement of Governmental Accounting Standards No. 17*, "Measurement Focus and Basis of Accounting—Governmental Fund Operating Statements: Amendment of the Effective Dates of GASB Statement No. 11 and Related Statements."

[12]Governmental Accounting Standards Board, *Preliminary Views*, "Governmental Financial Reporting Model: Core Financial Statements" (Norwalk, CT), June 1995.

[13]Governmental Accounting Standards Board, Exposure Draft, *Proposed Statement of the Governmental Accounting Standards Board*, "Basic Financial Statements—and Management's Discussion and Analysis—For State and Local Governments" (Norwalk, CT), January 1997.

[14]Ibid., par. 140.

ernmental funds continue to emphasize fiscal accountability, that is, current period financial position and budgetary compliance. The GASB has a separate subproject reexamining required note disclosures in light of the new proposed basic financial statements and MD&A.

At many points in Chapters 2 through 9, the proposed new reporting model requirements are contrasted with the current requirements. Chapter 10 discusses at length issues related to the proposed reporting model. Because the final reporting model may yet change from that currently being proposed, this edition emphasizes current accounting and financial reporting requirements. Moreover, as indicated previously, the new standards, if enacted, will not be effective until fiscal periods beginning after June 15, 2000. When the final reporting model standards are issued, the publisher will provide an update bulletin for adopters of this edition. If, as expected, the GASB issues final guidance during 1998, the authors plan to issue the next edition of the text prior to the implementation date to explain fully and illustrate the new reporting model requirements. Meanwhile, we encourage students to contrast and compare the proposed financial statements to those required by current GAAP.

Analysis of Governmental Financial Statements; Independent Auditors' Reports

The characteristics that distinguish governmental and not-for-profit entities from business entities are identified in the section of this chapter headed "Distinguishing Characteristics of Governmental and Not-for-Profit Entities." Consideration of those characteristics should make it obvious that the majority of the ratios used in the analysis of the financial statements of business organizations have no relevance to the analysis of the financial statements of a governmental reporting entity or a not-for-profit entity. Similarly, the section on distinguishing characteristics and the section headed "Objectives of Financial Reporting" should indicate that the objectives of independent audits of governmental financial statements are broader than the objectives of independent audits of profit-seeking businesses. Governmental auditing objectives include reviews of the economy and efficiency with which governmental agencies manage and utilize resources, determination of whether results intended by those who authorized programs or activities are being achieved, as well as audits (similar to those of businesses) to determine whether financial statement presentations are in conformity with generally accepted accounting principles. In all cases auditors of governmental entities should ascertain that the entity has complied with relevant laws and regulations. Chapter 11 discusses financial ratios useful for the analysis of governmental financial statements. Chapter 12 explains government auditing standards established by the Comptroller General of the United States and related publications issued by the AICPA for the guidance of auditors of governmental and not-for-profit entities.

Financial Reporting of the Federal Government and Not-for-Profit Organizations

Accounting and financial reporting standards for the federal government differ significantly from those for state and local governments. An introduction to accounting and reporting standards for the federal government and illustrative financial statements for federal departments or agencies is provided in Chapter 13. Similarly, accounting and financial reporting standards for not-for-profit organizations differ from those for both state and local governments and the federal government. Although logic would suggest that similar entities, such as public and private college and universities, should follow similar accounting and reporting practices, the fact is that their practices are becoming increasingly different.[15] The reason, of course, is the different standards-setting bodies for governmental and nongovernmental not-for-profit organizations, as discussed previously and depicted in Illustration 1–1. Chapters 16 and 17 discuss accounting for not-for-profit organizations and related regulatory and taxation issues. Specific accounting and reporting requirements applicable to colleges and universities and health care organizations are discussed in Chapters 18 and 19.

A Caveat

The first edition of this text was written by the late Professor R. M. Mikesell. Some words of his bear thoughtful rereading from time to time by teachers and students in all fields, not just those concerned with accounting and financial reporting for governmental and not-for-profit entities:

> Even when developed to the ultimate stage of perfection, governmental accounting cannot become a guaranty of good government. At best, it can never be more than a valuable tool for promotion of sound financial management. It does not offer a panacea for all the ills that beset representative government; nor will it fully overcome the influence of disinterested, uninformed citizens. It cannot be substituted for honesty and moral integrity on the part of public officials; it can help in resisting but cannot eliminate the demands of selfish interests, whether in the form of individual citizens, corporations, or the pressure groups which always abound to influence government at all levels.

It is difficult to strike a balance between the pursuit of perfection in a given field in isolation and the effort to improve the total system within which we live (which often involves settling for less than perfection in the elements of the system). The reader is urged to keep in mind the ultimate goal of improving the system in which we live during the time the text is being studied—and thereafter.

---

[15]In March 1997, the GASB issued an exposure draft of a proposed statement on a new reporting model for governmental (public) colleges and universities that, if adopted, will create additional differences between public and private college and university accounting and financial reporting. The proposed statement would establish a dual perspective reporting model for public colleges and universities similar to that proposed for state and local governments. Governmental Accounting Standards Board, Exposure Draft, *Proposed Statement of the Governmental Accounting Standards Board*, "Basic Financial Statements—and Management's Discussion and Analysis—for Governmental Colleges and Universities" (Norwalk, CT), March 1997.

Key Terms*

Accountability,   6

Comprehensive annual financial report
  (CAFR),   8

Federal Accounting Standards Advisory
  Board (FASAB),   5

Financial Accounting Standards Board
  (FASB),   2

Fiscal accountability,   12

Fund accounting,   10

General purpose financial statements
  (GPFS),   8

General purpose governments,   2

Governmental Accounting Standards
  Board (GASB),   3

Interperiod equity,   6

Limited purpose governments,   2

Management's discussion and analysis
  (MD&A),   12

Operational accountability,   12

Service efforts and accomplishments
  (SEA),   8

Questions

1–1. Explain the essential differences between general purpose and limited purpose governments and give several examples of each.

1–2. Name several kinds of not-for-profit organizations.

1–3. What are the principal characteristics that distinguish governmental and not-for-profit organizations from business enterprises?

1–4. Explain which standard-setting bodies have responsibility for establishing accounting and financial reporting standards for: (1) governmental organizations, (2) business organizations, and (3) not-for-profit organizations.

1–5. Explain what distinguishes governmental not-for-profit organizations from nongovernmental not-for-profit organizations. Why is such a distinction necessary?

1–6. GASB and FASB standards are concerned only with *external* financial reporting whereas FASAB standards are concerned with both internal and external financial reporting. Do you agree with this statement? Why or why not?

1–7. Why should persons interested in reading financial reports of governmental and not-for-profit entities be familiar with standards set by the GASB and FASB?

1–8. Explain in your own words why accountability is the cornerstone of all financial reporting in government.

1–9. Why is it more difficult to determine the optimal quantity or quality of services rendered by a government than it is to determine the optimal quantity or quality of the goods or services of a business enterprise?

1–10. Contrast and compare external general purpose financial reporting with all financial reporting.

1–11. In your own words state the primary uses the GASB believes external users have for financial reports of state and local governments. Contrast and compare these with the uses the FASB believes external users have for the financial reports of not-for-profit organizations.

---

*See glossary at the back of the text for a definition of each term and concept.

1–12. What is the significance of the general purpose financial statements (GPFS) to an independent auditor (CPA)?

1–13. What material should be included in the introductory section of a Comprehensive Annual Financial Report (CAFR)?

1–14. What material should be included in the financial section of a CAFR? List the financial statements that should be included in this section.

1–15. What material should be included in the statistical section of a CAFR?

1–16. Explain what is meant by dual perspective financial reporting as set forth in GASB's proposed reporting model?

1–17. Regarding the GASB's proposed reporting model, what kind of accountability is achieved by (1) entitywide financial statements and (2) fund-perspective financial statements?

1–18. What information is the proposed Management's Discussion and Analysis (MD&A) intended to provide?

Cases

1–1. Vinson Pioneer Museum is located in Dodge Valley, a small western city. The museum is open to the general public at no charge; however, signs at the information desk in the entry lobby encourage gifts of $3.00 for adults and $1.00 for children, 12 and under. Many visitors make the recommended contribution, some contribute larger amounts, and some do not contribute at all. Such contributions comprise 40 percent of the museum's total annual revenues, with net proceeds from fund-raising events and governmental grants comprising the remaining 60 percent. The museum shares a building with the local post office, for which it pays fair rental. Except for a part-time director, the museum is staffed exclusively by unpaid volunteers. Duly organized as a tax-exempt not-for-profit organization, the museum is governed by a six-member board of trustees, each appointed for a three-year term. Four of the trustees are appointed by the Dodge Valley City Council, one is appointed by the Dodge County Commission, and one is appointed by the Dodge Arts Commission. The museum's original charter provides that in the event the museum ceases to operate, two-thirds of its net assets will revert to the city and the remaining one-third will revert equally to the county and the Arts Commission.

Although the museum has never been audited, the board of trustees has decided to initiate annual audits. The board wishes to receive an unqualified (clean) audit opinion stating that the museum's financial statements present fairly in conformity with generally accepted accounting principles.

Required:

Assume you have been engaged to conduct this audit. To which standards-setting body (or bodies) would you look for accounting and financial reporting standards to assist you in determining whether the museum's financial statements are in conformity with generally accepted accounting principles? Explain how you arrived at this conclusion.

1–2. **Internet Case.** Use your favorite Internet browser to search for the term "GASB." Browse some of the selected sites as necessary to prepare a brief report about the GASB's mission and structure, its current technical projects, and its current and proposed due-process documents (such as discussion memoranda and exposure drafts). [Note: As of March 1998, the preceding information can be obtained at http://www.rutgers.edu/Accounting/raw/gasb/welcome.htm.]

Exercises and Problems

1–1. Obtain a copy of a recent comprehensive annual financial report (CAFR) of a governmental reporting entity (city, town, or county) and, if possible, the related budget.* Familiarize yourself with the organization of the comprehensive annual financial report—reread Chapter 1 of this text, particularly the section headed "Financial Reporting of State and Local Governments." Note particularly the items suggested below.

A. **Introductory Section.**

Read the *letter of transmittal* or any narrative that accompanies the financial statements. Does this material define the governmental reporting entity and name the primary government and all related component units included in the report? (If the reporting entity is not discussed in the *introductory section*, you should find this information in the Notes to the Financial Statements.) Is the explanation of the reporting entity understandable to you at this time? Does the introductory section discuss the financial condition of the reporting entity at the balance sheet date? Does it discuss the most significant changes in financial condition that occurred during the year? Does it alert the reader to forthcoming changes in financial condition that are not as yet reflected in the financial statements? Do the amounts reported in the letter of transmittal or other narrative agree with amounts in the statements and schedules in the financial section? (Specify any exceptions.) Does the introductory section define the generic fund types and individual funds and account groups included in the CAFR? Does the introductory section include a list of principal officials? An organization chart? Is a reproduction of a Certificate of Achievement for

---

*These may be obtained from the chief financial officer of the city, town, or county. If you do not know the exact title and address, you should write "Director of Finance, City of _____," and address it to the City Hall in the city and state of your choice. It is also acceptable, if you prefer, to obtain a copy of the comprehensive annual financial report of a state government. If you plan on studying Chapter 14 of this text, it would be convenient to request a copy of the most recent available operating budget document as well as the most recent available comprehensive annual financial report. Because some governmental units may not have any report available to send at the time of your request, it may be necessary to write a second or even a third request. The instructor may wish to obtain the reports and budgets before the term starts, or at least approve the selection of governmental units, so that every member of the class has a different report.

Excellence in Financial Reporting from the Government Finance Officers Association (GFOA) included in the introductory section?† Does the introductory section mention that the CAFR has been submitted to the GFOA for consideration for an award of the Certificate of Achievement?

B. Financial Section.

1. *Audit Report.* Are the financial statements in the report audited? By an independent CPA? By state auditors? By an auditor employed by the governmental unit being audited? Does the auditor express an opinion that the statements are (*a*) "in conformity with generally accepted accounting principles," (*b*) "in conformity with generally accepted accounting principles applicable to governmental entities," or (*c*) "in compliance with state laws?" Is the opinion qualified in some manner or disclaimed? Does the auditor clearly indicate the extent of any responsibility taken for other financial section contents? Does the auditor indicate specific responsibility for the general purpose financial statements?

2. *General Purpose Financial Statements.* Does the CAFR contain the five combined statements that must be included: (*a*) Combined Balance Sheet— All Combined Fund Types, Account Groups, and Discretely Presented Component Units; (*b*) Combined Statement of Revenues, Expenditures, and Changes in Fund Balances—All Governmental Fund Types and Discretely Presented Component Units; (*c*) Combined Statement of Revenues, Expenditures, and Changes in Fund Balances—Budget and Actual—General and Special Revenue Fund Types, and similar fund types of the primary government for which annual budgets have been legally adopted; (*d*) Combined Statement of Revenues, Expenses, and Changes in Retained Earnings (or Equity)—All Proprietary Fund Types and Discretely Presented Component Units; and (*e*) Combined Statement of Cash Flows—All Proprietary Fund Types and Discretely Presented Component Units. Does the report contain Notes to the Financial Statements? Notes are an integral part of the GPFS and are intended to be read with the GPFS.

3. *Individual Fund and Combining Financial Statements.* Following the notes to the GPFS, does the CAFR provide combining and individual fund statements? The combining statements should aggregate all the funds of a given fund type. For the general fund and other fund types containing one fund, individual fund statements should be provided.

4. *Management's Discussion and Analysis (MD&A).* Does the CAFR contain an MD&A? If so, where is it located and what does it contain?

C. Statistical Tables.

Become familiar with the material presented in the statistical tables so that you can refer to these tables as needed in subsequent weeks.

---

†The Certificate of Achievement for Excellence in Financial Reporting (Certificate of Achievement) is recognized as the highest award in government financial reporting. The Government Finance Officers Association (GFOA) established the Certificate of Achievement Program in 1945 to encourage government units to publish excellent comprehensive annual financial reports (CAFRs) and to provide peer recognition and educational assistance for the officials preparing CAFRs. (Source: Government Finance Officers Association, 1997.)

CHAPTER 2

Principles of Accounting and Financial Reporting for State and Local Governments

Learning Objectives

After studying this chapter, you should be able to:

~ Explain the nature of the three major activity categories of a state or local government: governmental activities, business-type activities, and fiduciary activities.

~ Describe the 12 principles of accounting and financial reporting, including

- Definition of a *fund*.
- Identification of the seven fund types and the three categories of funds.
- Accounting treatment for fixed assets and long-term liabilities.
- Measurement focus and basis of accounting for each fund type.
- Integration of budgetary control into accounting and financial reporting.
- Interim and annual financial reporting requirements.

~ Explain the distinguishing accounting characteristics of governmental, proprietary, and fiduciary fund types.

Activities of Government

Chapter 1 showed that the characteristics of governmental organizations differ from those of for-profit business organizations. One key difference is that governments are not profit seeking. Rather governments exist to meet citizens' demand for services, consistent with the availability of resources to provide those services. Although the types and levels of services vary from government to government, certain core services are provided by most general purpose governments—those related to protection of life and property (e.g., police and fire protection), public works (e.g., streets and highways, bridges, and public buildings), parks and recreation facilities and programs, and cultural and social services. Governments must also incur costs for general administrative support such as data processing, finance, and personnel. Core governmental services, together with general administrative support, comprise the major part of what GASB *Concepts Statement No. 1* refers to as governmental-type activities.[1] In more recent documents, GASB refers to these activities as simply **governmental activities.** Chapters 3 through 6 of the text focus on various aspects of accounting for governmental activities.

Some readers may be surprised to learn that governments also engage in a variety of **business-type activities**. These include, among others, public utilities (for example, electric, water, gas, and sewer utilities), transportation systems, toll roads and toll bridges, hospitals, parking garages and lots, liquor stores, golf courses, and swimming pools. Many of these activities are intended to be self-supporting by charging users for the services they receive. Operating subsidies from general revenues are not uncommon, however, particularly for transportation systems. Accounting for business-type activities is covered in Chapter 7 of the text.

The final category of governmental activity is **fiduciary activities.** Governments often act in a fiduciary capacity, either as an agent or trustee, for parties outside the government. For example, a government may serve as agent for other governments in the administering and collecting of taxes. Governments serve also as trustees for amounts bequeathed from private citizens for parks and other purposes, as well as for assets being held for employee pension plans. Chapters 8 and 9 cover accounting for fiduciary activities.

Accounting and financial reporting principles for the *governmental activities* category described above have evolved to meet the legal budgetary and financial compliance needs of government—what was termed *fiscal accountability* in Chapter 1. Generally, these principles involve segregating the accounting for the receipt and expenditures of restricted use resources from general use resources. Emphasis is placed on reporting the inflows and outflows of current financial resources. **Current financial resources** are cash or items expected to be converted into cash during the current period, or soon enough thereafter to pay current period liabilities.

---

[1]Governmental Accounting Standards Board, *Codification, of Governmental Accounting and Financial Reporting Standards as of June 30, 1997* (Norwalk, CT, 1997), Appendix B, par. 10.

Accounting and financial reporting principles for the *business-type activities* of a government are quite similar to those for commercial business entities. As in business, if a government intends to charge users for the goods or services they receive, it needs to know the full cost of those goods and services in order to determine appropriate prices. Knowing the full cost is also essential in deciding whether the government should continue to produce or provide particular goods or services, or contract for them with an outside vendor. Thus, as in commercial business accounting, accrual accounting is essential to measuring the full cost of providing governmental business-type services, and reporting on the extent to which each business-type activity is self-sufficient or has to be subsidized. In short, the principles of accounting for business-type activities are intended to measure and report on *operational accountability*, as the term was defined in Chapter 1.

Accounting and reporting for the *fiduciary activities* of a government use the principles for both governmental and business-type activities. Certain fiduciary activities, as will be discussed later in this chapter, bear close resemblance to governmental activities and therefore focus on the measuring and reporting of current financial resources. Other fiduciary activities more closely resemble business-type activities and follow accounting and reporting principles similar to those for business entities.

Summary Statement of Principles

At its inception in 1984, the GASB adopted 12 accounting and financial reporting principles for state and local governments that had been established by its predecessor standards-setting body, the National Council on Governmental Accounting (NCGA). The following overview of the 12 principles from NCGA *Statement No. 1* provides a useful foundation for understanding the unique nature and complexity of governmental accounting and financial reporting, as discussed at length in Chapters 3 through 10 of this text.[2]

1. **Accounting and Reporting Capabilities**
   A governmental accounting system must make it possible both: (*a*) to present fairly and with full disclosure the financial position and results of financial operations of the funds and account groups of the governmental unit in conformity with generally accepted accounting principles; and (*b*) to determine and demonstrate compliance with finance-related legal and contractual provisions.

---

[2]It is assumed the reader of this text is familiar with principles of accounting for business entities, and therefore the text is focused on the differences between accounting for governmental and not-for-profit entities and accounting for business enterprises rather than on the many similarities. Readers who are not familiar with basic accounting should study any contemporary introductory accounting text before attempting to understand the more technical portions of Chapters 3 through 19. Particular attention should be given to the discussion in the introductory text of financial statements and to the explanation of double-entry methodology and the accounting cycle.

Adherence to generally accepted accounting principles (GAAP) is essential to ensuring a reasonable degree of comparability among the general purpose financial reports of state and local governmental units. The American Institute of Certified Public Accountants (AICPA) recognizes the GASB as the designated body to establish accounting principles for state and local governments under the AICPA Ethics Rule 203, *Accounting Principles.*[3]

In some states, however, laws require the state government and the local governments within the state to follow practices (such as cash basis accounting) not consistent with GAAP. In those cases, financial statements and reports prepared in compliance with state law are considered "special reports" or "supplemental schedules" and are *not* the basic general purpose financial statements discussed in Chapter 1. Governmental units may prepare two sets of financial statements: one set in compliance with legal requirements, and one set in conformity with GAAP.

2. Fund Accounting Systems

Governmental accounting systems should be organized and operated on a fund basis. A **fund** is defined as a fiscal and accounting entity with a self-balancing set of accounts recording cash and other financial resources, together with all related liabilities and residual equities or balances, and changes therein, which are segregated for the purpose of carrying on specific activities or attaining certain objectives in accordance with special regulations, restrictions, or limitations. [Emphasis added.]

The definition of *fund* given above is mentioned in Chapter 1. The principle quoted below defines and categorizes the seven fund types that should be used, as needed, by state and local governments, both general purpose and limited purpose such as public school systems.

3. Types of Funds[4]

The following types of funds should be used by state and local governments:

a. **Governmental Funds**

(1) *The General Fund*—to account for all financial resources except those required to be accounted for in another fund.

(2) *Special Revenue Funds*—to account for the proceeds of specific revenue sources (other than expendable trusts or for major capital projects) that are legally restricted to expenditures for specified purposes.

---

[3]American Institute of Certified Public Accountants, *Statement on Auditing Standards No. 69,* "The Meaning of 'Present Fairly in Conformity with Generally Accepted Accounting Principles' in the Independent Auditor's Report" (New York, 1991), par. 12.

[4]As discussed in Chapter 1, the GASB has issued an exposure draft (ED) of a proposed statement that proposes a dual perspective financial reporting model for state and local governments. One proposed change at the "fund perspective" is to add a fourth fund category, "higher education funds," that would be used to report information about public colleges and universities that are part of the primary government. Primary government is defined later in this chapter. See Governmental Accounting Standards Board, Exposure Draft, *Proposed Statement of the Governmental Accounting Standards Board,* "Basic Financial Statements—and Management's Discussion and Analysis—For State and Local Governments" (Norwalk, CT), January 1997, par. 20.

  (3) *Capital Projects Funds*—to account for financial resources to be used for the acquisition or construction of major capital facilities (other than those financed by proprietary funds and trust funds).

  (4) *Debt Service Funds*—to account for the accumulation of resources for, and the payment of, general long-term debt principal and interest.

 b. **Proprietary Funds**

  (5) *Enterprise Funds*—to account for operations (*a*) that are financed and operated in a manner similar to private business enterprises—where the intent of the governing body is that the costs (expenses, including depreciation) of providing goods or services to the general public on a continuing basis be financed or recovered primarily through user charges; or (*b*) where the governing body has decided that periodic determination of revenues earned, expenses incurred, and/or net income is appropriate for capital maintenance, public policy, management control, accountability, or other purposes.

  (6) *Internal Service Funds*—to account for the financing of goods or services provided by one department or agency to other departments or agencies of the governmental unit, or to other governmental units, on a cost-reimbursement basis.

 c. **Fiduciary Funds**

  (7) *Trust and Agency Funds*—to account for assets held by a governmental unit in a trustee capacity or as an agent for individuals, private organizations, other governmental units, and/or other funds. These include (*a*) expendable trust funds, (*b*) nonexpendable trust funds, (*c*) pension trust funds, and (*d*) agency funds. [Authors' note: In 1997, the GASB created an additional fund type: investment trust funds.]

These fund types correspond to the types of activities in which governments engage: Governmental funds are used to account for governmental activities, proprietary funds are used to account for business-type activities, and fiduciary funds are used to account for fiduciary activities. Both the definition of *fund* and the description of each governmental fund type emphasize the segregation of accounting for restricted current financial resources to facilitate reporting on fiscal accountability. Creating a separate self-balancing set of accounts (fund) for each business-type activity permits those activities to be accounted for using accounting principles similar to those of commercial business rather than using the principles for governmental funds. Finally, as mentioned earlier in this chapter, accounting for certain fiduciary funds (expendable trust and agency) follows the principles of accounting for governmental funds. Nonexpendable trust funds and investment trust funds follow principles similar to those for proprietary funds. Although, as explained in Chapter 9, the GASB has issued separate standards for the accounting and reporting of pension trust funds, those standards are similar in most respects to proprietary fund accounting.

Accounting for each of the fund types defined above is explained and illustrated in Chapters 3 through 10. Accounting characteristics common to each of the three categories of fund types—governmental funds, proprietary funds, and fiduciary funds—are set forth in the final section of this chapter.

4. Number of Funds

Governmental units should establish and maintain those funds required by law and sound financial administration. Only the minimum number of funds consistent with legal and operating requirements should be established, however, since unnecessary funds result in inflexibility, undue complexity, and inefficient financial administration.

The importance of the Number of Funds Principle is sometimes overlooked by academicians and, even, independent auditors. *The seven fund types defined in the Types of Funds Principle are to be used if needed by a governmental unit to demonstrate compliance with legal requirements or if needed to facilitate sound financial administration.* In rare instances GASB standards require the use of a certain fund type. If legal requirements, GASB standards, or sound financial administration do not require the use of a given fund type, it should not be used. In the simplest possible situation, a governmental unit could be in conformity with GAAP if it used a single fund, the General Fund, to account for all events and transactions. In addition to that one fund, however, it would need the two account groups for reasons set forth below:

5. Accounting for Fixed Assets and Long-Term Liabilities[5]

A clear distinction should be made between (*a*) fund fixed assets and general fixed assets and (*b*) fund long-term liabilities and general long-term debt.

a. Fixed assets related to specific proprietary funds or trust funds should be accounted for through those funds. All other fixed assets of a governmental unit should be accounted for through the General Fixed Assets Account Group.

b. Long-term liabilities of proprietary funds and trust funds should be accounted for through those funds. All other unmatured general long-term liabilities of the governmental unit, including special assessment debt for which the government is obligated in some manner, should be accounted for through the General Long-Term Debt Account Group.

General long-term obligations are those to be paid from general tax levies, specific debt service tax levies, or special assessments. Accounting and reporting for the General Long-Term Debt Account Group is explained and illustrated in Chapter 6.

General fixed assets include land, buildings, improvements other than buildings, and equipment used by activities accounted for by the four fund types classified as governmental funds. The two principles quoted below establish requirements that relate to fixed asset accounting.

---

[5]Under GASB's proposed dual perspective reporting model (see discussion in Chapter 1), general fixed assets and general long-term liabilities would be reported only at the entitywide level. General fixed assets would be reported in the statement of net assets (i.e., balance sheet) at historical cost less accumulated depreciation. Because general fixed assets and general long-term liabilities would not be reported at the fund perspective, the two account groups currently required would be eliminated (Ibid., paragraphs 33–41). When the GASB issues a final statement, the publisher of this text will distribute to faculty members who have adopted this text an update bulletin describing the effects of the new reporting model.

6. Valuation of Fixed Assets

Fixed assets should be accounted for at cost, or, if the cost is not practicably determinable, at estimated cost. Donated fixed assets should be recorded at their estimated fair value at the time received.

7. Depreciation of Fixed Assets

a. Depreciation of general fixed assets should not be recorded in the accounts of governmental funds. Depreciation of general fixed assets may be recorded in cost accounting systems or calculated for cost-finding analyses; and accumulated depreciation may be recorded in the General Fixed Assets Account Group.

b. Depreciation of fixed assets accounted for in a proprietary fund should be recorded in the accounts of that fund. Depreciation is also recognized in those trust funds where expenses, net income, and/or capital maintenance are measured.

Application of the three preceding principles to the General Fixed Assets Account Group is explained and illustrated in Chapter 5.

8. Accrual Basis in Governmental Accounting

The **modified accrual** or **accrual basis** of accounting, as appropriate, should be utilized in measuring financial position and operating results.

a. *Governmental fund* **revenues** and **expenditures** should be recognized on the modified accrual basis. Revenues should be recognized in the accounting period in which they become **available** and **measurable.**[6] Expenditures should be recognized in the accounting period in which the fund liability is incurred, if measurable, except for unmatured interest on general long-term debt, which should be recognized when due.

b. *Proprietary fund* revenues and **expenses** should be recognized on the accrual basis. Revenues should be recognized in the accounting period in which they are earned and become measurable; expenses should be recognized in the period incurred, if measurable.

c. *Fiduciary fund* revenues and expenses or expenditures (as appropriate) should be recognized on the basis consistent with the fund's accounting measurement objective. Nonexpendable trust and pension trust funds [and investment trust funds] should be accounted for on the accrual basis; expendable trust funds should be accounted for on the modified accrual basis. Agency fund assets and liabilities should be accounted for on the modified accrual basis.

d. *Transfers* should be recognized in the accounting period in which the interfund receivable and payable arise. [Emphasis and identification of new fund type added.]

---

[6]GASB *Statement No. 11*, "Measurement Focus and Basis of Accounting—Governmental Fund Operating Statements," drops the terms *modified accrual* and *available and measurable*. The statement indicates that governmental funds use an accrual basis of accounting, and establishes criteria for the timing of recognition of governmental fund revenues and expenditures. The statement was to have become effective for financial statements for periods beginning after June 15, 1994; but GASB *Statement No. 17* delayed the effective date of *Statement No. 11* until it issues in final form related reporting model statements. If *Statement No. 11* and related statements become effective, an update bulletin will be distributed to faculty members who have adopted this text.

The principle quoted above is not difficult to read, but its importance becomes evident to most students only after they have studied the chapters dealing with each fund type. Briefly, accrual accounting means that (1) revenues should be recorded in the period in which the service is given, although payment is received in a prior or subsequent period, and (2) expenses should be recorded in the period in which the benefit is received, although payment is made in a prior or subsequent period. In business enterprise accounting, the accrual basis is used to obtain a matching of costs against the revenue flowing from those costs, thereby producing a more useful income statement. In governmental entities, however, even for those funds that do attempt to determine net income, only certain trust funds have major interest in the largest possible amount of gain. Internal service and enterprise funds are operated primarily for service; they make use of revenue and expense accounts to promote efficiency of operation and to guard against impairment of ability to render the services desired. For these reasons, operating statements of proprietary funds, nonexpendable trust funds, and pension trust funds are called *statements of revenues and expenses* rather than income statements.

Funds of other types (general funds, special revenue funds, capital projects funds, debt service funds, and expendable trust funds) are not concerned with income determination. As explained in Chapter 3, these funds are concerned with matching *expenditures* of legal appropriations, or legal authorizations, with revenues available to finance expenditures. Accordingly, GASB standards require that the "governmental" funds and expendable trust funds use the "modified accrual" basis. The modified accrual basis requires recognition of revenues in the period in which they become available and measurable. *Measurable* means capable of being expressed in monetary terms; *available* is defined as "collectible within the current period or soon enough thereafter to be used to pay liabilities of the current period."[7] GASB standards currently in effect require the accrual of revenue from property taxes. For other categories of revenue discussed in detail in following chapters, determination of the amount of revenue collectible is ordinarily made at the time of the collection, thus placing the fund partially on the cash basis in respect to revenue recognition.[8] In respect to expenditure recognition, however, the modified accrual basis is almost identical to the accrual basis. Chapter 3 provides complete definitions for the terms *revenues* and *expenditures* in the context of governmental funds.

9. **Budgeting, Budgetary Control, and Budgetary Reporting**
   a. An annual budget(s) should be adopted by every governmental unit.
   b. The accounting system should provide the basis for appropriate budgetary control.
   c. Budgetary comparisons should be included in the appropriate financial statements and schedules for governmental funds for which an annual budget has been adopted.

---

[7]GASB, *Codification*, Sec. 1600.106.

[8]However, sales taxes should be accrued if they have been collected by merchants, but are not yet required to be remitted to the taxing authority at the end of the fiscal year (if measurable by the government), or if held by one government for another at year-end. (Ibid. Sec. 1600.111.)

Part *a* above is not an accounting or financial reporting principle, but it is a necessary precondition to parts *b* and *c*. A budget, when adopted according to procedures specified in state laws, is binding on the administrators of a governmental unit. Accordingly, a distinctive characteristic of governmental accounting resulting from the need to demonstrate compliance with laws governing the sources of revenues available to governmental units, and laws governing the utilization of those revenues, is the formal recording of the legally approved budget in the accounts of funds operated on an annual basis. Chapter 3 explains in appropriate detail the nature and operation of **budgetary accounts.** Briefly, budgetary accounts are opened as of the beginning of each fiscal year and closed as of the end of each fiscal year; therefore, they have no balances at year-end. During the year, however, the budgetary accounts of a fund are integrated with its proprietary (balance sheet and operating statement) accounts. In the governmental sense, **proprietary accounts** include accounts similar to the real and the nominal groups found in accounting for profit-seeking entities—that is, asset, liability, net worth, revenue, and expense (or expenditure) accounts. The nature and use of recommended proprietary accounts are explained in the appropriate chapters. The Combined Statement of Revenues, Expenditures, and Changes in Fund Balances—Budget and Actual, which is listed in Chapter 1 as one of the basic general purpose financial statements, is one of the budgetary comparisons required for conformity with GAAP. Budgetary accounting and budgetary reporting are explained in Chapter 3.

10. Transfer, Revenue, Expenditure, and Expense Account Classifications

  a. Interfund transfers and proceeds of general long-term debt issues should be classified separately from fund revenues and expenditures or expenses.

  b. Governmental fund revenues should be classified by fund and source. Expenditures should be classified by fund, function (or program), organization unit, activity, character, and principal classes of objects.

  c. Proprietary fund revenues and expenses should be classified in essentially the same manner as those of similar business organizations, functions, or activities.

The principle quoted above elaborates on accounting and reporting requirements. The applications of this principle are illustrated and discussed at appropriate points in subsequent chapters.

11. Common Terminology and Classification

A common terminology and classification should be used consistently throughout the budget, the accounts, and the financial reports of each fund.

The Common Terminology and Classification Principle is simply a statement of the commonsense proposition that if the Budgeting, Budgetary Control, and Budgetary Reporting Principle is to be implemented, persons responsible for preparing the budgets and persons responsible for preparing the financial statements and financial reports should work with the persons responsible for designing and operating the accounting system. Agreement on a common terminology and classification scheme is needed to make sure the accounting system produces the information needed for budget preparation and for financial statement and report preparation.

12. **Interim and Annual Financial Reports**
    a. Appropriate interim financial statements and reports of financial position, operating results, and other pertinent information should be prepared to facilitate management control of financial operations, legislative oversight, and, where necessary or desired, for external reporting purposes.
    b. A **comprehensive annual financial report** should be prepared and published, covering all funds and account groups of the **primary government** (including its blended component units) and providing an overview of all discretely presented **component units** of the **reporting entity**—including introductory section, appropriate combined, combining, and individual fund statements; notes to the financial statements; required supplementary information; schedules; narrative explanations; and statistical tables. The reporting entity is the primary government (including its blended component units) and all discretely presented component units presented in accordance with Section 2100, "Defining the Financial Reporting Entity."
    c. **General purpose financial statements** of the reporting entity may be issued separately from the comprehensive annual financial report. Such statements should include the basic financial statements and notes to the financial statements that are essential to the fair presentation of financial position and results of operations (and cash flows of those fund types and discretely presented component units that use proprietary fund accounting). Those statements may also be required to be accompanied by required supplementary information, essential to financial reporting of certain entities.
    d. As discussed in Section 2100, the financial reporting entity consists of (1) the primary government, (2) organizations for which the primary government is financially accountable, and (3) other organizations for which the nature and significance of their relationship with the primary government are such that exclusion would cause the reporting entity's financial statements to be misleading or incomplete. The reporting entity's financial statements should present the fund types and account groups of the primary government (including its blended component units, which are, in substance, part of the primary government) and provide an overview of the discretely presented component units.
    e. The nucleus of a financial reporting entity usually is a primary government. However, a governmental organization other than a primary government (such as a component unit, joint venture, jointly governed organization, or other stand-alone government) serves as the nucleus for its own reporting entity when it issues separate financial statements. For all of these entities, the provisions of Section 2100 should be applied in layers "from the bottom up." At each layer, the definition and display provisions should be applied before the layer is included in the financial statements of the next level of the reporting government. [Emphasis added.]

Interim financial statements of the various fund types are illustrated in the appropriate chapters. Chapter 10 explains the content of a comprehensive interim financial report. The contents of the comprehensive annual financial report (CAFR) and of the general purpose financial statements (GPFS) are discussed briefly in Chapter 1; a more detailed explanation of each is given in appropriate chapters. Illustrations 2–1 through 2–5 present a combined balance sheet, operating statements, and a statement of cash flows prepared in conformity with currently effective GASB standards to display financial data of a primary government and provide summary data for that government's component units.[9] The following section contains explanations of concepts and terminology that readers of this text will encounter in state and local government financial reports. Additional terms used in governmental and not-for-profit accounting are defined in the glossary at the end of this book.

> **Governmental Financial Reporting Entity.**   A governmental reporting entity consists of (*a*) the primary government, (*b*) organizations for which the primary government is financially accountable, and (*c*) other organizations for which the nature and significance of their relationship with the primary government are such that exclusion would cause the reporting entity's financial statements to be misleading or incomplete.[10]

A *primary government* is defined as "a state government or general purpose local government. Also, a special purpose government that has a separately elected governing body, is legally separate, and is fiscally independent of other state or local governments." Note that each fund type and account group of the primary government is reported in a separate column of Illustration 2–1. The column to the right of the Totals—Memorandum Only Primary Government column is headed Component Units. *Component units* are legally separate organizations for which the elected officials of the primary government are financially accountable. In addition, a component unit can be another organization for which the nature and significance of its relationship with the primary government is such that exclusion would cause the reporting entity's financial statements to be misleading or incomplete. Reporting financial data of component units in the manner shown in Illustration 2–1 is called a **discrete presentation.** Discrete presentation should be used unless the financial activities of a component unit are so intertwined with those of the primary government that they are, in substance, the same as the primary government. In such cases the component unit's balances and transactions should be reported in a manner similar to the balances and transactions of the primary government itself; this method of inclusion is known as **blending.** Blending is accomplished by adding financial totals for the component unit's General Fund and special revenue funds to the financial totals for the primary government's special revenue funds, and adding the financial totals for other fund types and account groups of the component unit to the same fund type and account group of the

---

[9]As was discussed in Chapter 1, the GASB exposure draft (ED) on the proposed dual perspective reporting model would substantially change the basic financial statements that would be included in the comprehensive annual financial report. The ED proposes two new statements at the entitywide perspective, a statement of net assets (also called a balance sheet) and a statement of activities. Changes are also proposed for the financial statements at the fund perspective. In particular, the balance sheet shown in Illustration 2–1 would be replaced by three separate balance sheets for the governmental, proprietary, and fiduciary funds, respectively.

[10]GASB, *Codification*, Sec. 2100.111.

Illustration 2–1

NAME OF GOVERNMENTAL UNIT
Combined Balance Sheet–All Fund Types, Account Groups,
and Discretely Presented Component Units
December 31, 1999

| | Primary Government's Fund Types and Account Groups | | | | | |
| | Governmental Fund Types | | | | Proprietary Fund Types | |
	General	*Special Revenue*	*Debt Service*	*Capital Projects*	*Enterprise*	*Internal Service*
Assets:						
Cash	$258,500	$101,385	$ 598,366	$461,917	$ 257,036	$ 29,700
Investments	130,000	37,200	160,990	—	111,800	—
Receivables, net	155,300	77,760	264,666	213,540	161,985	12,000
Investment in joint venture	—	—	—	—	2,300,000	—
Due from component units	65,000	—	—	—	—	—
Lease receivable from primary government	—	—	—	—	—	—
Fixed assets, net	—	—	—	—	4,281,759	103,100
Amount available	—	—	—	—	—	—
Amounts to be provided	—	—	—	—	—	—
Total assets	$608,800	$216,345	$1,024,022	$675,457	$7,112,580	$144,800
Liabilities:						
Accounts payable	$ 50,512	$ 15,380	—	$ 29,600	$ 57,000	$ 15,000
Due to primary government	—	—	—	—	—	—
Lease payable to component unit	—	—	—	—	810,000	—
Revenue bonds payable	—	—	—	—	—	—
Tax-supported bonds payable	—	—	—	—	—	—
Total liabilities	50,512	15,380	—	29,600	867,000	15,000
Equity:						
Investment in general fixed assets	—	—	—	—	—	—
Contributed capital	—	—	—	—	4,103,224	95,000
Retained earnings	—	—	—	—	2,142,356	34,800
Fund balances:						
Reserved	76,000	93,000	—	500,000	—	—
Unreserved	482,288	107,965	$1,024,022	145,857	—	—
Total equity	558,288	200,965	1,024,022	645,857	6,245,580	129,800
Total liabilities and equity	$608,800	$216,345	$1,024,022	$675,457	$7,112,580	$144,800

Source: Based on Example 1, GASB, *Codification*, Sec. 2600.905.

Fiduciary Fund Types	Account Groups		Totals—Memorandum Only Primary Government	Component Units	Totals—Memorandum Only Reporting Entity
Trust and Agency	General Fixed Assets	General Long-Term Debt	December 31, 1999	December 31, 1999	December 31, 1999
$ 216,701	—	—	$ 1,923,605	$ 1,656,960	$ 3,580,565
1,239,260	—	—	1,679,250	893,227	2,572,477
328,855	—	—	1,214,106	87,329	1,301,435
—	—	—	2,300,000	—	2,300,000
—	—	—	65,000	—	65,000
—	—	—	—	810,000	810,000
—	$7,326,500	—	11,711,359	19,191,577	30,902,936
—	—	$1,024,022	1,024,022	—	1,024,022
—	—	5,381,978	5,381,978	193,000	5,574,978
$1,784,816	$7,326,500	$6,406,000	$25,299,320	$22,832,093	$48,131,413
—	—	—	$ 167,492	$ 733,710	$ 901,202
—	—	—	—	65,000	65,000
—	—	—	810,000	—	810,000
—	—	—	—	2,776,000	2,776,000
—	—	$6,406,000	6,406,000	193,000	6,599,000
—	—	6,406,000	7,383,492	3,767,710	11,151,202
—	$7,326,500	—	7,326,500	7,836,545	15,163,045
—	—	—	4,198,224	8,841,640	13,039,864
—	—	—	2,177,156	1,359,581	3,536,737
$1,784,816	—	—	2,453,816	226,617	2,680,433
—	—	—	1,760,132	800,000	2,560,132
1,784,816	7,326,500	—	17,915,828	19,064,383	36,980,211
$1,784,816	$7,326,500	$6,406,000	$25,299,320	$22,832,093	$48,131,413

Illustration 2–2

NAME OF GOVERNMENTAL UNIT

Combined Statement of Revenues, Expenditures, and Changes in Fund Balances—
All Governmental Fund Types and Discretely Presented Component Units
For the Fiscal Year Ended December 31, 1999

| | Primary Government's Fund Types | | | | Fiduciary Fund Type | Totals— Memorandum Only Primary Government December 31, 1999 | Component Units | Totals— Memorandum Only Reporting Entity December 31, 1999 |
| | Governmental Fund Types | | | | | | | |
	General	Special Revenue	Debt Service	Capital Projects	Expendable Trust			
Revenues:								
Taxes	$ 881,300	$ 189,300	$ 380,587	—	—	$1,451,187	$ 675,327	$2,126,514
Intergovernmental	186,500	831,100	41,500	—	—	2,309,100	233,474	2,542,574
Licenses and permits	191,700	—	—	—	—	191,700	13,942	205,642
Miscellaneous	—	—	—	—	$ 2,000	2,000	—	2,000
Total revenues	1,259,500	1,020,400	422,087	1,250,000	2,000	3,953,987	922,743	4,876,730
Expenditures:								
Current:								
General government	1,078,375	—	—	—	—	1,078,375	233,587	1,311,962
Public safety	204,095	534,200	—	—	—	738,295	—	738,295
Highways and streets	—	502,400	—	—	—	502,400	—	502,400
Education	—	—	—	—	—	—	658,923	658,923
Capital outlay	—	—	—	1,437,100	2,000	1,439,100	102,500	1,541,600
Debt service:								
Principal	—	—	315,500	—	—	315,500	33,400	348,900
Interest	—	—	368,420	—	—	368,420	14,800	383,220
Total expenditures	1,282,470	1,036,600	683,920	1,437,100	2,000	4,442,090	1,043,210	5,485,300

	(1)	(2)	(3)	(4)	(5)	(6)	(7)	(8)
Other financing sources (uses):								
Proceeds of general obligation bonds	—	—	—	1,365,500	—	1,365,500	—	1,365,500
Operating transfers in	—	—	77,030	—	—	77,030	—	77,030
Operating transfers from primary government	(74,500)	—	—	—	—	—	100,000	100,000
Operating transfers out	—	—	—	—	—	(74,500)	—	(74,500)
Operating transfers to component units	(200,000)	(75,000)	—	—	—	(275,000)	—	(275,000)
Total other financing sources (uses)	(274,500)	(75,000)	77,030	1,365,500	—	1,093,030	100,000	1,193,030
Excess of revenues and other sources over (under) expenditures and other uses	(297,470)	(91,200)	(184,803)	1,178,400	33,163	604,927	(20,467)	584,460
Net income from golf course operations	—	—	—	—	—	—	2,350	2,350
Fund balance—beginning	855,758	292,165	1,208,825	(532,543)	33,163	1,857,368	1,352,056	3,209,424
(Increase) in reserves	(76,000)	(93,000)	—	(500,000)	—	(669,000)	(226,617)	(895,617)
Fund balance—ending	$ 482,288	$ 107,965	$1,024,022	$ 145,857	$33,163	$1,793,295	$1,107,322	$2,900,617

Source: Based on Example 1, GASB, *Codification*, Sec. 2600.905.

Illustration 2–3

NAME OF GOVERNMENTAL UNIT
Combined Statement of Revenues, Expenditures, and Changes in Fund Balances—Budget and Actual—General and Special Revenue Fund Types of the Primary Government
Non-GAAP Presentation
For the Fiscal Year Ended December 31, 1999

	General Fund			Special Revenue Funds			Totals (memorandum only)		
	Budget	Actual	Actual Over (Under) Budget	Budget	Actual	Actual Over (Under) Budget	Budget	Actual	Actual Over (Under) Budget
Revenues:									
Taxes	$ 882,500	$ 881,300	$ (1,200)	$ 189,500	$ 189,300	$ (200)	$1,072,000	$1,070,600	$ (1,400)
Intergovernmental	200,000	186,500	(13,500)	837,600	831,100	(6,500)	1,037,600	1,017,600	(20,000)
Licenses and permits	195,000	191,700	(3,300)	—	—	—	195,000	191,700	(3,300)
Miscellaneous	—	—	—	—	—	—	—	—	—
Total revenues	1,277,500	1,259,500	(18,000)	1,027,100	1,020,400	(6,700)	2,304,600	2,279,900	(24,700)
Expenditures and encumbrances									
Current:									
General government	1,150,000	1,148,375	(1,625)				1,150,000	1,148,375	(1,625)
Public safety	212,000	210,095	(1,905)	580,000	577,200	(2,800)	792,000	787,295	(4,705)
Highways and streets	—	—	—	555,000	552,400	(2,600)	555,000	552,400	(2,600)
Total expenditures and encumbrances	1,362,000	1,358,470	(3,530)	1,135,000	1,129,600	(5,400)	2,497,000	2,488,070	(8,930)
Other financing sources (uses):									
Operating transfers out	(74,500)	(74,500)	—	—	—	—	(74,500)	(74,500)	—
Operating transfers to component units	(200,000)	(200,000)	—	(75,000)	(75,000)	—	(275,000)	(275,000)	—
Total other financing sources (uses)	(274,500)	(274,500)	—	(75,000)	(75,000)	—	(349,500)	(349,500)	—
Excess of revenues over (under) expenditures, encumbrances, and other uses	(359,000)	(373,470)	(14,470)	(182,900)	(184,200)	(1,300)	(541,900)	(557,670)	(15,770)
Fund balance—beginning	855,758	855,758	—	292,165	292,165	—	1,147,923	1,147,923	—
Fund balance—ending	$ 496,758	$ 482,288	$(14,470)	$ 109,265	$ 107,965	$(1,300)	$ 606,023	$ 590,253	$(15,770)

Source: Prepared by authors in conformity with GASB, *Codification*, Sec. 2600.905.

primary government. Blending ensures that amounts reported for the General Fund of the reporting entity are those of the primary government only—an important point to those who rely on General Fund financial information.

Notes to the Financial Statements should contain a brief description of the component units of the financial reporting entity and their relationships to the primary government. This disclosure should include a brief discussion of the criteria for including the component units and how the component units are reported. Information about individual component units may be presented in condensed financial statements within the notes, or in combining statements. The notes should also include information about how separate financial statements for the individual component units may be obtained.[11]

The notion of financial accountability is basic to the definition of a governmental financial reporting entity. A primary government is, of course, financially accountable for the organizations that make up its legal entity. It is also financially accountable for legally separate organizations if its officials appoint a voting majority of an organization's governing body and either it is able to impose its will on that organization or there is a potential for the organization to provide specific financial benefits to, or to impose specific financial burdens on, the primary government. A primary government may also be financially accountable for governmental organizations that are fiscally dependent on it.

A primary government has the ability to impose its will on an organization if it can significantly influence the programs, projects, or activities of, or the level of services performed or provided by, the organization. A financial benefit or burden relationship exists if the primary government (1) is entitled to the organization's resources; (2) is legally obligated or has otherwise assumed the obligation to finance the deficits of, or provide financial support to, the organization; or (3) is obligated in some manner for the debt of the organization.

Some organizations are included as component units because of their fiscal dependency on the primary government. An organization is fiscally dependent on the primary government if it is unable to adopt its budget, levy taxes or set rates or charges, or issue bonded debt without approval by the primary government.

A Summary of Accounting Characteristics of Fund Types

The 12 principles discussed in the preceding section of this chapter give, in a number of different contexts, information about accounting and financial reporting for governmental funds. The principles also give information pertaining to accounting and financial reporting for proprietary funds and for fiduciary funds. Chapters following this one deal with individual fund types. In order to provide a framework for the student to keep the detailed discussion of fund types in perspective, this section

---

[11]All definitions in this paragraph are quoted or paraphrased from GASB, *Codification*, Sec. 2100.501.

Illustration 2–4

NAME OF GOVERNMENTAL UNIT

Combined Statement of Revenues, Expenses, and Changes in Fund Equity—
All Proprietary Fund Types, Similar Trust Funds, and Discretely Presented Component Units
Year Ended December 31, 1999

| | Primary Government | | | | | | |
| | Proprietary Fund Types | | Fiduciary Fund Types | | Totals—Memorandum Only | | Totals—Memorandum Only |
	Enterprise	Internal Service	Nonexpendable Trust	Pension Trust	Primary Government	Component Units	Reporting Entity
Operating revenues:							
Charges for services	$ 650,333	$109,817	—	$ —	$ 760,150	$1,189,631	$ 1,949,781
Interest	—	—	—	$ 20,150	20,150	—	20,150
Contributions	—	—	—	60,686	60,686	—	60,686
Total operating revenues	650,333	109,817	—	80,836	840,986	1,189,631	2,030,617
Operating expenses:							
Cost of services	357,305	72,999	—	—	430,304	1,018,008	1,448,312
General and administrative	91,226	6,350	—	2,500	100,076	181,856	281,932
Depreciation	123,500	25,050	—	—	148,550	460,102	608,652
Benefit payments	—	—	—	21,000	21,000	—	21,000
Refunds	15,225	—	—	10,520	25,745	—	25,745
Total operating expenses	587,256	104,399	—	34,020	725,675	1,659,966	2,385,641
Operating income (loss)	63,077	5,418	—	46,816	115,311	(470,335)	(355,024)

Nonoperating revenues (expenses):							
Operating grants	55,000	—	—	—	55,000	410,000	465,000
Net income from joint venture	145,000	—	—	—	145,000	—	145,000
Interest revenue	8,830	—	10,790	—	19,620	82,522	102,142
Interest expense and fiscal charges	(62,988)	—	—	—	(62,988)	(248,320)	(311,308)
Tax revenues	—	—	—	—	—	100,000	100,000
Total nonoperating revenue (expenses)	145,842	—	10,790	—	156,632	344,202	500,834
Income (loss) before operating transfers	208,919	5,418	10,790	46,816	271,943	(126,133)	145,810
Operating transfers in	—	65,000	—	—	65,000	—	65,000
Operating transfers from primary government	—	—	—	—	—	175,000	175,000
Operating transfers out	(56,740)	—	(10,790)	—	(67,530)	—	(67,530)
Net income	152,179	70,418	—	46,816	269,413	48,867	318,280
Fund equity—beginning	5,420,735	59,382	296,198	1,408,639	7,184,954	9,445,032	16,629,986
Contributions—capital grants	672,666	—	—	—	672,666	400,000	1,072,666
Fund equity—ending	$6,245,580	$129,800	$296,198	$1,455,455	$8,127,033	$9,893,899	$18,020,932

Source: Based on Example 4, GASB, *Codification*, Sec. 2200.906.

Illustration 2–5

NAME OF GOVERNMENTAL UNIT
Combined Statement of Cash Flows—All Proprietary Fund Types, and Discretely Presented Component Units
Year Ended December 31, 1999

	Primary Government					
	Proprietary Fund Types		Fiduciary Fund Types	Totals—Memorandum Only		Totals—Memorandum Only
	Enterprise	Internal Service	Nonexpendable Trust	Primary Government	Component Units	Reporting Entity
Cash flows from operating activities:						
Cash received from customers	$ 605,000	$110,410	—	$ 715,410	$ 1,220,000	$ 1,935,410
Cash paid to suppliers and employees	(450,000)	(95,000)	—	(545,000)	(1,150,000)	(1,695,000)
Net cash provided by operating activities	155,000	15,410	—	170,410	70,000	240,410
Cash flows from noncapital financing activities:						
Operating grants	55,000	—	—	55,000	410,000	465,000
Operating transfers in from other funds	—	65,000	—	65,000	—	65,000
Operating transfers out to other funds	(56,740)	—	$ (10,790)	(67,530)	—	(67,530)
Operating transfer from primary government	—	—	—	—	175,000	175,000
Net cash provided (used) by (for) noncapital financing activities	(1,740)	65,000	(10,790)	52,470	585,000	637,470
Cash flows from capital and related financing activities:						
Purchase of capital assets	(700,000)	(70,000)	—	(770,000)	(200,000)	(970,000)
Principal payments—capital leases	(81,000)	—	—	(81,000)	—	(81,000)

38

Interest payments—capital leases	(62,988)	—	(62,988)	—	—	(62,988)
Interest payments—revenue bonds	(248,320)	(248,320)	—	—	—	—
Contributions from state government	1,072,666	400,000	672,666	—	—	672,666
Net cash provided (used) by (for) capital and related financing activities	(289,642)	(48,320)	(241,322)	—	(70,000)	(171,322)
Cash flows from investing activities:						
Receipt of interest	102,142	82,522	19,620	10,790	—	8,830
Net income from joint venture	145,000	—	145,000	—	—	145,000
Net cash provided by investing activities	247,142	82,522	164,620	10,790	—	153,830
Net increase (decrease) in cash and cash equivalents	835,380	689,202	146,178	—	10,410	135,768
Cash and cash equivalents at beginning of year	596,656	440,798	155,858	15,300	19,290	121,268
Cash and cash equivalents at end of year	$ 1,432,036	$ 1,130,000	$ 302,036	$ 15,300	$ 29,700	$ 257,036
Reconciliation of operating income to net cash provided by operating activities:						
Operating income (loss)	$ (401,840)	$ (470,335)	$ 68,495	$ -0-	$ 5,418	$ 63,077
Adjustments to reconcile operating income to net cash provided by operating activities:						
Depreciation	608,652	460,102	148,550	—	25,050	123,500
Decrease (increase) in investments	52,303	62,115	(9,812)	—	—	(9,812)
Decrease (increase) in accounts receivable	6,006	29,116	(23,110)	—	(7,795)	(15,315)
Increase (decrease) in accounts payable	(24,711)	(10,998)	(13,713)	—	(7,263)	(6,450)
Total adjustments	642,250	540,335	101,915	-0-	9,992	91,923
Net cash provided by operating activities	$ 240,410	$ 70,000	$ 170,410	$ -0-	$ 15,410	$ 155,000

Source: Format based on GASB, *Codification,* Sec. 2450.901.

presents the accounting characteristics common to each category of fund types: governmental, proprietary, and fiduciary. Illustration 2–6 provides a summary of these characteristics.

Accounting Characteristics Common to Governmental Funds

All funds in any of the four types of funds classified by the GASB as governmental funds (the General Fund, special revenue funds, capital projects funds, and debt service funds) have certain accounting characteristics that differentiate them from proprietary funds and fiduciary funds:

1. Governmental funds are created in accord with legal requirements. Each fund has only those resources allowed by law—a local governmental unit may choose not to use a resource authorized by state law, but it may *not* choose to utilize an unauthorized resource. The resources may be expended only for purposes and in amounts approved by the legislative branch in accord with procedures detailed in laws of component jurisdictions. Therefore, the measurement focus of governmental fund accounting is on the flow of current financial resources (as distinguished from a business organization's focus on the determination of net income). Governmental funds are said to be *expendable;* that is, resources are received and expended, with no expectation that they will be returned through user or departmental charges. Revenues and expenditures (*not* expenses) of governmental funds are recognized on the modified accrual basis of accounting. The meaning of the term *modified accrual* is explained further in Chapter 4.

2. Legal constraints on the raising of revenue and the expenditure of revenue are, in most jurisdictions, set forth in a legally adopted budget. Accordingly, it is a recognized principle of accounting and financial reporting for state and local governmental units that accounting systems of governmental funds should provide the basis for appropriate budgetary control. The nature and operation of budgetary accounts recommended for use by each of the fund types in the governmental funds category is explained in following chapters.

3. Governmental funds account only for current financial resources: cash, receivables, marketable securities, and, if material, prepaid items and supplies inventories. They do not account for plant and equipment.

4. Funds in the governmental category account for only those liabilities to be paid from fund assets.

5. The arithmetic difference between fund assets and fund liabilities is called the **Fund Equity.** Fund Equity may be reserved for reasons discussed in following chapters; the portion of Fund Equity that is not reserved is called **Fund Balance.** Residents of the governmental unit have no legal claim on any portion of the Fund Equity, so it is not equivalent to the capital section of an investor-owned entity.

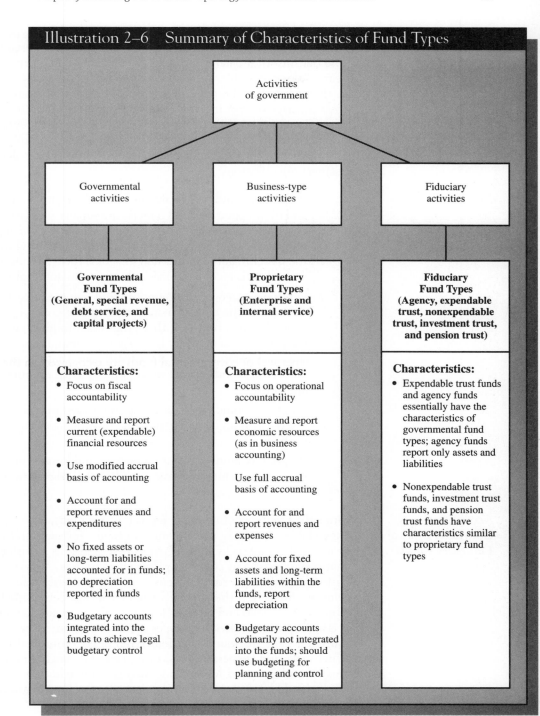

Illustration 2–6   Summary of Characteristics of Fund Types

Accounting Characteristics Common to Proprietary Funds

The definition of *internal service funds*, given in the Types of Funds Principle, states that these funds provide services to users on a "cost-reimbursement basis." The definition of *enterprise funds*, given in the same principle, states that they bear a "close resemblance to investor-owned enterprises" and that they are used in the event that the governmental body desires to compute revenues earned, costs incurred, or net income of certain activities. Proprietary funds are not subject to income taxation, nor do they have owners in the sense that business entities do, but in all other respects it follows that funds properly classified as proprietary funds should adhere to accounting practices deemed appropriate for business organizations:

1. Proprietary funds are established in accord with enabling legislation, and their operations and policies are subject to legislative oversight. Ordinarily, however, the purposes of legislative oversight are served by proprietary fund accounting and financial reporting that focuses on the matching of revenues and expenses (*not* expenditures) on the full accrual basis recommended for business organizations.

2. Funds classified as proprietary should prepare budgets as an essential element in the management planning and control processes. It is generally true, however, that proprietary funds do not have to adopt budgetary documents by law as governmental funds do. Therefore, standards established by the GASB state that accounting systems of proprietary funds do not need to provide for the integration of budgetary accounts.

3. Proprietary funds account for all assets used in fund operations—current assets, plant and equipment, and any other assets considered as belonging to the fund.

4. Proprietary funds account for current and long-term liabilities to be serviced from fund operations and/or to be repaid from fund assets.

Accounting Characteristics of Fiduciary Funds

Since the five types of fiduciary funds (agency funds, expendable trust funds, non-expendable trust funds, investment trust funds, and pension trust funds) all are used to account for assets held by a governmental unit as a trustee or agent, they have that characteristic in common. That characteristic, however, does not provide a basis for specifying a set of accounting characteristics that are appropriate for all fiduciary funds. On the contrary, the GASB has determined that the manner in which *agency funds* and *expendable trust funds* are created and operated is such that it is appropriate for these two types of fiduciary funds to be accounted for in essentially the same manner as the four types of governmental funds. The manner in which *nonexpendable-trust funds*, *investment trust funds*, and *pension trust funds* are created and operated leads the GASB to conclude that these types of fiduciary funds should be accounted for in essentially the same manner as the two types of proprietary funds.

Key Terms

Accrual basis, 25	Fund, 22
Available, 25	Fund Balance, 40
Blending, 29	Fund Equity, 40
Budgetary accounts, 27	General purpose financial statements
Business-type activities, 20	(GPFS), 28
Component unit, 28	Governmental activities, 20
Comprehensive annual financial report	Governmental funds, 22
(CAFR), 28	Measurable, 25
Current financial resources, 20	Modified accrual basis, 25
Discrete presentation, 29	Primary government, 28
Expenditure, 25	Proprietary accounts, 27
Expense, 25	Proprietary funds, 23
Fiduciary activities, 20	Reporting entity, 28
Fiduciary funds, 23	Revenue, 25

Selected References

Governmental Accounting Standards Board. *Codification of Governmental Accounting and Financial Reporting Standards as of June 30, 1997.* Norwalk, CT, 1997.

Questions

2–1. Describe the governmental activities of a state or local government and explain the focus of accounting and financial reporting for these activities.

2–2. Describe the business-type activities of a state or local government and explain the focus of accounting and financial reporting for these activities.

2–3. Describe the fiduciary activities of a state or local government and explain the focus of accounting and financial reporting for these activities.

2–4. What are current financial resources? Why does accounting for governmental activities emphasize measuring and reporting these resources?

2–5. "The primary purpose of an accounting system for a state or a local governmental unit is to make it possible for financial statements to demonstrate compliance with finance-related legal and contractual provisions." Explain why you believe this statement to be correct or incorrect.

2–6. What is the technical meaning of the term *fund* in governmental accounting?

2–7. "In order for the general purpose financial statements of a governmental financial reporting entity to be in conformity with GAAP, the Combined Balance Sheet must provide a column for each of the seven fund types described in the GASB Types of Funds Principle." Do you agree or disagree? Explain the reasons for your answer.

2–8. The Combined Balance Sheet for the City of Briggs shows the following column headings: General Fund, Street and Bridge Fund, Capital Projects Fund, General Asset and Liability Fund, and Utility Fund. In what respects does the City of Briggs appear to follow recommended fund usage, and in what respects does it appear to differ?

2–9. "General fixed assets of a governmental unit should always be reported on the same basis as a business—depreciated historical cost." Do you agree? Why or why not?

2–10. "Governmental fund expenses should be recognized in the accounting period in which the fund liability occurs." Is this statement true or false? Explain your answer.

2–11. "Proprietary funds have as their objective to make a profit; therefore, proprietary funds should use the same accounting principles as a business enterprise." Do you agree or disagree? Why?

2–12. Explain the recognition criteria for revenues and expenditures under the modified accrual basis of accounting. How do these criteria compare with those for recognition of revenues and expenses under the accrual basis used by proprietary funds and business enterprises?

2–13. "Because budgetary accounts are used by governmental units, their financial statements can never be said to be in accord with generally accepted accounting principles." Comment.

2–14. "Interim financial statements are not required by GASB principles." Do you agree? Why or why not?

2–15. Explain in your own words what the term *governmental financial reporting entity* means.

2–16. "If a discrete presentation is used for the financial data of a component unit in the Combined Balance Sheet of a governmental financial reporting entity, there is no need for the component unit to issue a separate financial report." Is this statement true or false? In your answer explain what is meant by the term *discrete presentation*.

2–17. The four types of funds classified by the GASB as governmental funds have certain accounting characteristics in common that differentiate them from proprietary funds and fiduciary funds. In your own words state the accounting characteristics common to governmental funds.

2–18. The two types of funds classified by the GASB as proprietary funds have certain common accounting characteristics that differentiate them from governmental funds and fiduciary funds. In your own words, state the accounting characteristics common to proprietary funds.

2–19. Name the types of fiduciary funds that should be accounted for on the same basis as proprietary funds. Explain why this is the appropriate basis of accounting for those types of funds.

2–20. Name any of the types of funds classified as fiduciary funds that recognize revenues and expenditures on the basis of accounting used by governmental fund types. Explain why this is the appropriate basis.

Exercises and Problems

2–1. Utilizing the CAFR obtained for Exercise 1–1, examine the financial statements included in the Financial Section and answer the following questions.

    a. General Fund. (If necessary refer to the Individual Fund section of the CAFR for the General Fund balance sheet and other information.) What title is given to the fund that functions as the General Fund of the reporting entity? Does the report specify that the General Fund of the reporting entity is the General Fund of the primary government? Does the report state the basis of accounting used for the General Fund? If so, is the financial statement presentation consistent with the stated basis (i.e., some reports claim the modified accrual basis was used but show no receivables in the balance sheet or any other evidence that measurable and available revenues are accrued)? If the basis of accounting is not stated, analyze the statements to determine what basis is used. Is the same basis used for both revenues and expenditures? Is the basis used consistent with GASB standards?

b. *Special Revenue Funds.*   What special revenue funds are included in the report? Are they described as special revenue funds, or only by a title such as "Library Fund," "School Fund," or "Street Fund"? Does the report specify why each special revenue fund was created (is there a reference to a state statute, local government ordinance, or other legislative or administrative action)? Is the basis of accounting for these funds stated, or must it be determined by analysis of the statements? Is the same basis used for all special revenue funds? Is it the same basis as used for the General Fund? If not, does the report explain why each basis is used? Is the basis of accounting for special revenue funds in conformity with GASB standards?

c. *Other Governmental Fund Types.*   List the names of governmental fund types, in addition to the General Fund and special revenue funds, which are included in the combined balance sheet of the reporting entity. Are any governmental fund types included in other combined statements but not included in the balance sheet? If so, determine why.

d. *Proprietary Funds.*   List the names of the proprietary fund types included in the combined balance sheet. Do the balance sheet accounts provide evidence that all proprietary funds are accounted for on the full accrual basis?

e. *Fiduciary Funds.*   List the names of fiduciary fund types included in the combined balance sheet. (You may have to refer to a combining balance sheet for fiduciary funds, or to individual fund balance sheets, to determine the types of fiduciary funds used by this reporting entity.) For each fiduciary fund type identify the basis of accounting used.

f. *Account Groups.*   Does the combined balance sheet include a column for financial data of the General Fixed Assets Account Group? For the General Long-Term Debt Account Group?

g. *Notes to the Financial Statements.*   Read through the Notes to the Financial Statements in order to become generally familiar with their content so that you can refer to the notes as needed in subsequent weeks. At this time determine whether the notes include a summary of significant accounting policies. Do the notes describe the criteria used in determining the scope of the entity for financial reporting purposes? Do the notes disclose which component units were included in the reporting entity and the key decision criteria considered? If there is a component unit disclosed in a separate column as a discrete presentation of the combined financial statements of the reporting entity, do the notes clearly disclose the accounting policies of the component unit and the relationship of the component unit to the primary government? Are there notes that disclose: (1) any material violations of legal provisions, (2) any deficit fund balance or retained earnings of individual funds, or (3) any excess of expenditures over appropriations in individual funds, explanations for the excess, and remedial action planned?

2–2. Write the numbers 1 through 10 on a sheet of paper. Beside each number write the letter corresponding with the *best* answer to each of the following questions:

1. Which of the following is *not* one of the activity categories of government, as described in this chapter?
   a. Fiduciary.
   b. Business-type.
   c. Profit-seeking.
   d. Governmental.

2. An accounting system for a state or local governmental unit must make it possible:
   a. To prepare consolidated statements for the governmental reporting entity in conformity with FASB standards.
   b. To present fairly the financial position and results of financial operations of the funds and account groups in conformity with GAAP and to demonstrate compliance with finance-related legal and contractual provisions.
   c. To prepare financial statements as required by relevant laws.
   d. To demonstrate service efforts and accomplishments.

3. A fund is a (an):
   a. Legal entity created only when authorized or required by law.
   b. Self-balancing set of accounts recording cash and other financial resources, together with all related liabilities and residual equities or balances, and changes therein.
   c. Accounting but not a fiscal entity.
   d. All of the above.

4. The governmental funds category is made up of:
   a. The General Fund, special revenue funds, expendable trust funds, capital projects funds, and debt service funds.
   b. The General Fund, special revenue funds, capital projects funds, debt service funds, and the General Long-Term Debt Fund.
   c. The General Fund, special revenue funds, General Fixed Assets Fund, and the General Long-Term Debt Fund.
   d. The General Fund, special revenue funds, capital projects funds, and debt service funds.

5. Self-supporting activities that provide goods or services to either the public or other departments within the government on a user-charge basis should be accounted for in what fund category?
   a. Governmental.
   b. Governmental Business-Type Fund.
   c. Fiduciary.
   d. Proprietary.

6. Under currently effective GASB standards, governmental funds should recognize revenues and expenditures on the:
   a. Cash basis.
   b. Full accrual basis.
   c. Modified accrual basis.
   d. There is no specific requirement; each government may choose whatever basis it wants, as long as it uses that basis consistently.

7. The proprietary funds category is made up of:
   a. Enterprise funds, nonexpendable trust funds, pension trust funds, and internal service funds.
   b. Internal service funds, special revenue funds, and enterprise funds.
   c. Enterprise funds and internal service funds.
   d. Any of the above, depending on management intent.
8. Currently effective GASB standards require proprietary funds to recognize revenues and expenses on the:
   a. Cash basis.
   b. Full accrual basis.
   c. Modified accrual basis.
   d. There is no specific requirement; each government may choose whatever basis it wants, as long as it uses that basis consistently.
9. The fiduciary funds category is made up of:
   a. Expendable trust funds, agency funds, internal service funds, and general funds.
   b. Expendable trust funds, nonexpendable trust funds, investment trust funds, and debt service funds.
   c. Expendable trust funds, nonexpendable trust funds, agency funds, and special revenue funds.
   d. Expendable trust funds, nonexpendable trust funds, investment trust funds, agency funds, and pension trust funds.
10. Fiduciary funds use which of the following bases of accounting?

	Full Accrual	Modified Accrual
a.	Yes	Yes
b.	Yes	No
c.	No	Yes
d.	No	No

2–3. Write the numbers 1 through 10 on a sheet of paper. Beside each number write the letter corresponding with the *best* answer to each of the following questions:

1. Which of the following funds of a governmental unit should integrate budgetary accounts into the accounting system?
   a. Enterprise.
   b. Special Revenue
   c. Internal Service.
   d. Nonexpendable Trust.
2. One of the differences between accounting for a governmental unit and accounting for a for-profit business is that a government should:
   a. Not record depreciation expense in any of its funds.
   b. Not use full accrual accounting.
   c. Establish and maintain complete self-balancing accounts for each fund.
   d. Use only the cash basis of accounting.
3. Under the modified accrual basis of accounting, revenues should be recognized when they are:
   a. Available and measurable.
   b. Earned and measurable.
   c. Received in cash.
   d. None of the above.

4. Which of the following items would generally be recognized as revenue in a governmental fund type?
   - *a.* Receipts from a city-owned parking structure that is operated on a business basis.
   - *b.* Interest earned on investments held to finance pension payments to retired employees.
   - *c.* Revenues from a city-operated motor pool that is operated on a self-supporting basis.
   - *d.* Property taxes.

5. Which of the following fund types has characteristics most similar to the General Fund of a governmental unit?
   - *a.* Pension trust fund.
   - *b.* Nonexpendable trust fund.
   - *c.* Special revenue fund.
   - *d.* Internal service fund.

6. Fixed assets acquired from the current financial resources of a governmental fund type should be accounted for in:
   - *a.* The governmental fund type.
   - *b.* The General Fixed Assets Account Group.
   - *c.* The General Fixed Assets Fund.
   - *d.* None of the above.

7. The liability for bonds issued to construct a new city hall, which will be repaid from general tax levies, should be accounted for in the (a):
   - *a.* General Long-Term Debt Account Group.
   - *b.* General Fund.
   - *c.* Capital projects fund.
   - *d.* Enterprise fund.

8. A governmental financial reporting entity consists of:
   - *a.* The primary government.
   - *b.* Organizations for which the primary government is financially accountable.
   - *c.* Other organizations for which the nature and significance of their relationship with the primary government are such that exclusion would cause the reporting entity's financial statements to be misleading or incomplete.
   - *d.* All of the above.

9. A *primary government* is defined as:
   - *a.* A state government only.
   - *b.* A state government or a local government with a population of 1 million persons or more.
   - *c.* A state government or a local government designated as a primary government by a state government.
   - *d.* A state government, a general purpose local government, or a special purpose government that has a separately elected governing body, is legally separate, and is fiscally independent of other state or local governments.

10. The arithmetic difference between the assets of a fund and the liabilities of a fund is called the:
    - *a.* Fund balance.
    - *b.* Fund equity.
    - *c.* Fund net investment.
    - *d.* Fund net resources.

2–4. Write the numbers 1 through 10 on a sheet of paper. Beside each number write T if the corresponding statement is true. Write F if the corresponding statement is false. If the statement is false, state what changes should be made to make it true.

1. The General Fund, capital projects funds, and debt service funds are the only fund types that are classified as governmental funds.
2. The measurement focus of governmental funds should be on the flow of current financial resources, rather than on income determination.
3. The accounting system of the General Fund of a governmental reporting entity should incorporate budgetary accounts to assist administrators to achieve budgetary control.
4. The accounting system for proprietary funds should provide for integration of budgetary accounts.
5. Depreciation should be recorded for fixed assets accounted for in the General Fund.
6. A governmental fund accounts for only liabilities to be paid from currently available fund assets.
7. Interfund transfers should be recognized in the period in which the interfund receivable and payable arise.
8. Interfund transfers and proceeds of general long-term debt need not be distinguished from a fund's revenues and expenditures or expenses for financial reporting purposes.
9. Revenues of a proprietary fund type are recognized when earned and measurable.
10. Bonds issued to double the capacity of a city's electric utility (an enterprise fund) and that will be repaid from revenues of the electric utility should be accounted for in the General Long-Term Debt Account Group.

2–5. Write the numbers 1 through 10 on a sheet of paper. Beside each number write T if the corresponding statement is true or F if the corresponding statement is false. If the statement is false, state what changes should be made to make it true.

1. Internal service funds and enterprise funds are the only fund types categorized as proprietary funds.
2. Enterprise fund accounting focuses on matching revenues and expenditures on the full accrual basis.
3. Trust funds appropriate for use by state and local governmental units are classified as expendable trust funds, nonexpendable trust funds, investment trust funds, and pension trust funds.
4. Expendable trust funds are accounted for in essentially the same manner as pension trust funds.
5. Nonexpendable trust funds are accounted for in essentially the same manner as proprietary funds.
6. Since the government has no stockholders, it need not prepare interim financial statements.
7. The combined balance sheet of a governmental financial reporting entity should display in separate columns the financial data for each fund type and account group used by the primary government of the reporting entity.
8. The notion of financial accountability is basic to the definition of a *governmental financial reporting entity*.
9. The method of financial reporting in which the financial information of a component unit is reported in the same manner as those of the primary government, that is, combined with those of similar funds and account groups of the primary government, is referred to as *discrete presentation*.

10. Financial data of component units of a governmental reporting entity are ordinarily not blended with the financial data of the primary government.

2–6. Garden City is financially accountable, as defined in GASB standards, for the Garden City Water Utility, although the administrators of the utility report to the Garden City Water Board.

Required

a. Name the primary government of the Garden City financial reporting entity. Explain your answer.
b. Should the balances of the Garden City Water Utility be blended with the balances of the city, or should the balances of the utility be shown in a discrete presentation? Explain your answer.
c. Should the fixed assets of the utility be reported at cost, or at depreciated cost? Explain.

Continuous Problem

Note: Chapters 3 through 10 of this text deal with specific knowledge needed to understand the accounting for the funds recommended for use by state and local governmental units and with specific aspects of financial management. In order to help the student keep the entire accounting and financial management area in perspective, a series of related problems are presented. This series covers representative activities of the City of Bingham; the problems in this series relate to all funds and account groups; they are designated 2–L, 3–L, 4–L, and so on.

At the option of the instructor, students may be required to solve the City of Bingham problems manually, using journal paper and ledger paper available from college bookstores and from office supply stores, or students may be required to use microcomputers to maintain accounting records and produce financial statements. The instructions accompanying the L problems at the end of this chapter and the following chapters are presented on the assumption that the student is required to prepare solutions manually

2–L. 1. The City of Bingham has the following funds in addition to its General Fund; you are required to classify each in accordance with the types described in the GASB Types of Funds Principle quoted in this chapter.

City Hall Annex Construction Fund. This fund was created to account for the proceeds of the sale of serial bonds issued for the construction and equipping of an annex to the city hall.

Debt Service Fund. Nonactuarially determined contributions and earnings thereon, for the purpose of the payment of interest on and redemption of tax-supported and special assessment long-term debt issued by the City, are accounted for by this fund.

Stores and Services Fund. This fund was established to account for centralized purchasing and management of inventories used by a number of departments of the city government.

Water Utility Fund. The water utility serving the City of Bingham was originally constructed and operated by a private corporation. It was subsequently sold to the City, but it is still operated on a self-supporting basis under the regulations of the State Public Service Commission.

Pass-Through Agency Fund. This fund is used to account for grants, entitlements, and shared revenues, which may be used in more than one fund at the discretion of the City Council of the City of Bingham; or which the City of Bingham receives as the primary recipient of grants, and which must be transmitted in whole or in part to other governmental units.

Employees' Retirement Fund. This fund was established to account for actuarially determined retirement contributions and earnings thereon, and for the payment of retirement annuities.

2. In addition to the funds described above, what account groups should be maintained by the City of Bingham? Why are these called *account groups* rather than *funds*?

3. For each of its funds and account groups, the City of Bingham maintains separate, manually kept books of original entry and ledgers.

Required

a. Open a *general journal* for the General Fund. Allow seven pages of 8½-by-11-inch loose-leaf journal paper, or its equivalent. (Do not open general journals for other funds until instructed to do so in subsequent L problems.) The form you use must allow for entry of subsidiary ledger accounts as well as general ledger accounts, and for entry of adequate explanations for each journal entry. (The form in which journal entries are illustrated in Chapter 3 is appropriate.) You will use the journal as your only posting medium; it should be complete.

b. Open a *general ledger* for the General Fund. Allow three pages of 8½-by-11-inch loose-leaf ledger paper, or its equivalent. On each page allow the number of lines shown below for each account.

Account No.	Title	Lines
1110	Cash	12
1111	Petty Cash	5
1130	Taxes Receivable—Current	5
1131	Estimated Uncollectible Current Taxes	5
1132	Taxes Receivable—Delinquent	5
1133	Estimated Uncollectible Delinquent Taxes	5
1134	Interest and Penalties Receivable on Taxes	5
1135	Estimated Uncollectible Interest and Penalties	5
1140	Advance to Stores and Services Fund	5
1210	Vouchers Payable	10
1211	Tax Anticipation Notes Payable	5
1212	Due to Federal Government	5
1213	Due to Other Funds	5
1300	Estimated Revenues	5
1400	Revenues	8
1500	Appropriations	5
1600	Expenditures—2000	15
1650	Expenditures—1999	5
1700	Encumbrances—2000	5
1800	Reserve for Encumbrances—2000	5
1801	Reserve for Encumbrances—1999	5
1802	Reserve for Advance to Stores and Services Fund	5
1900	Fund Balance	8

c. The trial balance of the General Fund of the City of Bingham as of June 30, 1999, the last day of the fiscal year prior to the year with which the L problems are concerned, is shown below.

(1) Prepare an entry in general journal form to enter the amounts shown in the trial balance in the proper general ledger accounts. Date the entry "July 1, 1999." Note that no subsidiary ledger accounts are affected by this entry.

(2) Post the journal entry to the proper general ledger accounts opened in part *3b* of this problem; each of the amounts entered should be dated "July 1, 1999."

CITY OF BINGHAM
General Fund Trial Balance
As of June 30, 1999

Account No.	Title	Debits	Credits
1110	Cash	$ 45,000	
1132	Taxes Receivable—Delinquent	244,000	
1133	Estimated Uncollectible Delinquent Taxes		$ 24,400
1134	Interest and Penalties Receivable on Taxes	13,376	
1135	Estimated Uncollectible Interest and Penalties		662
1210	Vouchers Payable		187,000
1213	Due to Other Funds		7,000
1801	Reserve for Encumbrances—1999		14,000
1900	Fund Balance		69,314
		$302,376	$302,376

CHAPTER

3

General Funds and Special Revenue Funds—Budgetary Accounting, Classification of Revenues and Expenditures

Learning Objectives

After studying this chapter, you should be able to:

~ Distinguish between proprietary and budgetary accounts used in the General Fund and special revenue funds and describe each type of account and its use.

~ Explain how budgetary accounting contributes to achieving budgetary control over revenues and expenditures, including such aspects as

       Classification of revenues and expenditures.
       Recording of the annual budget.
       Accounting for revenues.
       Accounting for encumbrances and expenditures.

~ Describe the various types of interfund transactions and transfers.

~ Contrast and compare the accounting for proceeds of debt issues and capital lease financings to accounting for General Fund or special revenue fund revenues.

The General Fund of a state or local government unit is the entity that accounts for all the assets and resources used for financing the general administration of the unit and the traditional services provided to the people. General funds are sometimes known as general revenue funds, operating funds, or current funds; the purpose, not the name, is the true test of identity. The typical governmental unit now engages in many activities that for legal and historical reasons are financed by sources other than those available to the General Fund. Whenever a tax or other revenue source is authorized by a legislative body to be used for a specified purpose only, a governmental unit availing itself of that source may create a *special revenue* fund in order to be able to demonstrate that all revenue from that source was used for the specified purpose only. A common example of a special revenue fund is one used to account for state gasoline tax receipts distributed to a local government; many states restrict the use of this money to the construction and maintenance of streets, highways, and bridges. The accounting structure specified for special revenue funds by the Governmental Accounting Standards Board (GASB) is identical with that specified for the General Fund.

In order to avoid excessive repetition of the phrase *General Fund and special revenue funds*, the term **General Fund** is used in this chapter and in following chapters to include both categories of funds. The General Fund and special revenue funds are also referred to generically as revenue funds. According to the GASB Types of Funds Principle, discussed in Chapter 2, the General Fund and special revenue fund types and two other fund types are classified as governmental funds. Chapter 2 presents in brief the essential accounting characteristics common to all governmental funds. This chapter illustrates in greater depth the manner in which the body of generally accepted accounting principles (GAAP) is applied to the General Fund and to special revenue funds.

Proprietary (Balance Sheet and Operating Statement) Accounts

It should be emphasized that the General Fund, special revenue funds, and all other funds classified as governmental funds account for only financial resources (cash, receivables, marketable securities, and, if material, prepaid items and inventories). Assets such as land, buildings, and equipment utilized in fund operations are not accounted for by these funds because they are not normally converted into cash. Similarly, the same categories of funds account for only those liabilities incurred for normal operations that will be liquidated by use of fund assets.[1]

The arithmetic difference between the amount of financial resources and the amount of liabilities recorded in the fund is the **Fund Equity**. Residents of the governmental unit have no legal claim on any excess of liquid assets over current lia-

---

[1]See pp. 11–13 in Chapter 1 for a discussion of the GASB's proposed dual perspective reporting model. This model would result in reporting general fixed assets and general long-term liabilities in the financial statements for governmental activities, but only at the "entitywide" level.

bilities; therefore, the Fund Equity is not analogous to the capital accounts of an investor-owned entity. Accounts in the Fund Equity category of the General Fund and special revenue funds consist of **reserve accounts** established to disclose that portions of the equity are, for reasons explained later, not available for appropriation; the portion of equity available for appropriation is disclosed in an account called **Fund Balance**.

In addition to the Balance Sheet **proprietary accounts** described above, the General Fund and special revenue funds account for financial activities during a fiscal year in proprietary accounts classified as Revenues, Other Financing Sources, Expenditures, and Other Financing Uses. **Revenue** is defined as increases in fund financial resources other than from interfund transfers and debt issue proceeds. Operating transfers to a fund and debt issue proceeds received by a fund are classified as **Other Financing Sources** of the fund. Accounting standards specify that the revenues of all fund types classified as governmental funds (the General Fund, special revenue funds, capital projects funds, and debt service funds) be recognized on an accrual basis, designated in currently effective GASB standards as the modified accrual basis. Because the operations of governmental funds are subject to rather detailed legal restrictions, governmental fund revenues should be recognized in the fiscal year in which they are available to finance expenditures. (In a few jurisdictions laws provide that taxes must be collected in the year before the year in which they are available to finance expenditures. In such jurisdictions, tax collections should be credited to Deferred Revenues when cash is debited; in the following year Deferred Revenues should be debited and Revenues should be credited.)

Expenditure is a term which replaces both the terms *costs* and *expenses* used in accounting for profit-seeking entities. Expenditures are defined as decreases in fund financial resources other than through interfund transfers. Operating transfers out of a fund are classified as **Other Financing Uses**. Under the modified accrual basis an expenditure is recognized in the General Fund, or in special revenue funds, when a liability to be met from fund assets is incurred. It is important to note that an appropriation is considered to be expended in the amount of a liability incurred whether the liability is for salaries (an expense), for supplies (a current asset), or for a long-lived capital asset, such as land, buildings, or equipment.

An example of the use of transfer accounts occurs in those jurisdictions where a portion of the taxes recognized as revenue by the General Fund of a unit is transferred to a debt service fund that will record expenditures for payment of interest and principal of general obligation debt. The General Fund would record the amounts transferred as Operating Transfers Out; the debt service fund would record the amount received as Operating Transfers In. Thus, use of the transfer accounts achieves the desired objective that revenues be recognized in the fund that levied the taxes and expenditures be recognized in the fund that expends the revenue. Other Financing Sources accounts and Other Financing Uses accounts are closed to Fund Balance in a manner identical with the closing of Revenues and Expenditures but are disclosed separately in the Statement of Revenues, Expenditures, and Changes in Fund Balances shown previously in Illustration 2–2.

Budgets and Budgetary Accounts

The fact that budgets are legally binding upon administrators has led to the incorporation of budgetary accounts in the General Fund and in special revenue funds and in other funds for which state laws require the adoption of a budget. GASB standards require that, in addition to the Statement of Revenues, Expenditures, and Changes in Fund Balances shown as Illustration 2–2, which shows only proprietary account balances, a Statement of Revenues, Expenditures, and Changes in Fund Balances—Budget and Actual must be presented. The latter statement, presented in Illustration 2–3, presents information for both proprietary and budgetary accounts. The budgetary comparison statement must include the General Fund, special revenue funds, and all other governmental funds for which a budget has been adopted. In the example shown in Illustration 2–3, it is assumed that legal budgets are required for only the General Fund and all special revenue funds. The amounts in the Actual column of the statement are to be reported on the basis required by law for budget preparation, even if that basis differs from the basis required by GASB financial reporting standards. For example, in some states revenues must be budgeted on the cash basis. If the Budget and Actual columns of the budgetary comparison statement differ from GASB standards, the heading of the statement should so indicate.

Budgetary practices of a government may differ from GAAP accounting practices in respects other than basis. GASB standards identify *timing, entity,* and *perspective* differences. Discussion of these differences is beyond the scope of this text; it is sufficient to emphasize that GASB standards require that the amounts shown in the Actual column of the Budget versus Actual statement conform in all respects with practices used to develop the amounts shown in the Budget column of the statement, so there is a true comparison. Standards further require that either on the face of the Budget versus Actual statement or in the Notes to the Financial Statements the amounts in the Actual column of the Budget versus Actual statement (Illustration 2–3) must be reconciled with the amounts shown in the Combined Statement of Revenues, Expenditures, and Changes in Fund Balances (Illustration 2–2) prepared in conformity with GAAP. Reconciliation of the amounts shown in the two statements is discussed and illustrated in a later section of this chapter.

In order to facilitate preparation of budgets and preparation of the Combined Statement of Revenues, Expenditures, and Changes in Fund Balances—Budget and Actual required for GAAP conformity, accounting systems of funds for which budgets are required by law should incorporate **budgetary accounts**. At a minimum, three general ledger control accounts are needed to provide appropriate budgetary control: **Estimated Revenues, Appropriations,** and **Encumbrances;** all three are supported by subsidiary ledger accounts in whatever detail is required by law or by sound financial administration. Budgeted interfund transfers and debt proceeds may be recorded in **Estimated Other Financing Sources** and **Estimated Other Financing Uses** control accounts supported by subsidiary accounts as needed.

Illustration 3–1 presents a comparison of proprietary and budgetary accounts typically used in the General Fund and in special revenue funds. As shown in Illustration 3–1 and discussed in the preceding section, all balance sheet (or per-

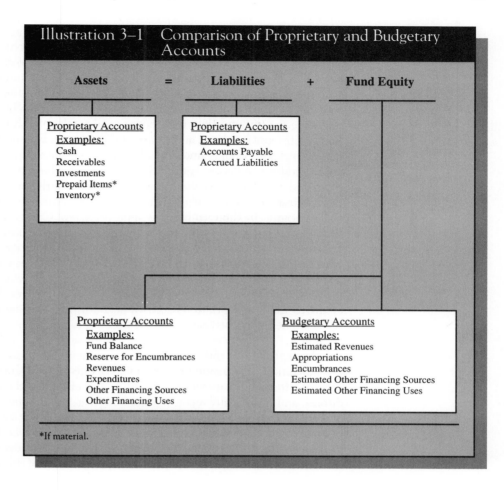

Illustration 3–1 Comparison of Proprietary and Budgetary Accounts

Assets = Liabilities + Fund Equity

Proprietary Accounts
Examples:
Cash
Receivables
Investments
Prepaid Items*
Inventory*

Proprietary Accounts
Examples:
Accounts Payable
Accrued Liabilities

Proprietary Accounts
Examples:
Fund Balance
Reserve for Encumbrances
Revenues
Expenditures
Other Financing Sources
Other Financing Uses

Budgetary Accounts
Examples:
Estimated Revenues
Appropriations
Encumbrances
Estimated Other Financing Sources
Estimated Other Financing Uses

*If material.

manent) accounts are proprietary accounts. Temporary "Sub-Fund Equity" accounts consist of both proprietary and budgetary accounts, as shown. The discerning reader may surmise that comparing revenues proprietary account balances to the corresponding estimated revenues budgetary accounts facilitates budgetary control over revenues. Similarly, comparing actual expenditures and encumbrances (estimated budgetary amounts for goods on order) to budgeted appropriations facilitates budgetary control over expenditures. Budgetary control procedures for both revenues and expenditures are discussed later in this chapter.

Budgetary Accounting

At the beginning of the budget period, the Estimated Revenues control account is debited for the total amount of revenues expected to be recognized, as provided in the Revenues budget. The amount of revenue expected from each source specified in the Revenues budget is recorded in a subsidiary ledger account, so that the total of subsidiary ledger detail agrees with the debit to the control account, and both agree with the adopted budget. If a separate entry is to be made to record the Revenues budget, the general ledger debit to the Estimated Revenues control account is offset by a credit to Fund Balance. Recall that the Fund Balance account, before the budget is recorded, would normally have a credit balance representing the excess of fund assets over the total of liabilities and reserved Fund Equity. (If fund liabilities and reserved Fund Equity exceed fund assets, the Fund Balance account would have a debit balance—referred to as a *deficit*.) After the revenues budget is recorded, Fund Balance represents the excess of fund assets *plus* the estimated revenues and other financing sources for the budget period over liabilities and reserves.[2] The credit balance of the Fund Balance account, therefore, is the total amount available to finance appropriations. Consequently, the accounting entry to record the legally approved appropriations budget is a debit to Fund Balance and a credit to Appropriations for the total amount appropriated for the activities accounted for by the fund. The Appropriations control account is supported by a subsidiary ledger kept in the same detail as provided in the appropriations ordinance, so that the total of the subsidiary ledger detail agrees with the credit to the Appropriations control account, and both agree with the adopted budget. The use of the Encumbrances account is explained in a later section of this chapter.

As explained in the preceding section, the use of budgetary accounts permits comparison of actual revenues and expenditures to budgeted amounts. Budgetary control is further enhanced by clear and logical classification of revenues and expenditures, and by formally recording the budget in the accounts of the General Fund and other funds for which a budget is approved. The use of subsidiary ledgers, which permit recording revenues and expenditures—both actual and budgeted amounts—in the same level of detail as the budget, also helps to achieve sound budgetary control. Each of these topics is discussed in the remainder of this chapter.

Terminology and Classification for Governmental Fund Budgets and Accounts

Budgets as they are incorporated in legal documents and in financial reports required for conformity with GAAP may be described as legally approved plans of financial operations embodying the authorization of expenditures for specified purposes to be made during the budget period and the proposed means of financing them. The sequence of budget preparation in practice is often the same as the sequence in the preceding sentence: Expenditures are planned first; then plans are made to finance the expenditures. For that reason, the discussion in this chapter

---

[2]For simplicity, we assume that a single Fund Balance account is used to record both budgetary (estimated) and actual amounts. In practice, many governments utilize a separate Budgetary Fund Balance account to record the credit amount of estimated revenues and the debit amount of appropriations.

follows the same sequence. Governmental budgeting is discussed in more detail in Chapter 14.

Classification of Appropriations and Expenditures

Recall that an appropriation, when enacted into law, is an authorization to incur on behalf of the governmental unit liabilities for goods, services, and facilities to be used for purposes specified in the appropriation ordinance, or statute, in amounts not in excess of those specified for each purpose. When liabilities authorized by an appropriation have been incurred, the appropriation is said to be expended. Thus budgeted appropriations are often called *estimated expenditures*, and the appropriation budget is called the **Expenditures budget**. According to the GASB Transfer, Revenue, Expenditure, and Expense Account Classifications Principle, expenditures should be classified by (1) fund, (2) function or program, (3) organization unit, (4) activity, (5) character, and (6) object. The GASB Common Terminology and Classification Principle should also be recalled at this time. It provides that a common terminology and classification should be used consistently throughout the budget, the accounts, and the financial reports of each fund.

Classification by Fund

The primary classification of governmental expenditures is by fund, since funds are the basic fiscal and accounting entity of a governmental unit. Within each fund, the other five classifications itemized in the preceding paragraph are used to facilitate the aggregation and analysis of data to meet the objectives of financial reporting set forth in Chapter 1.

Classification by Function or Program

The GASB distinguishes between functions and programs in the following manner:

Functions group related activities that are aimed at accomplishing a major service or regulatory responsibility. **Programs** group activities, operations, or organizational units that are directed to the attainment of specific purposes or objectives.[3] [Emphasis added.]

Examples of functional classifications commonly found are:

General government   Health and welfare
Public safety   Culture and recreation
Highways and streets

In one city in New England, the budget is summarized according to the following program classification:

Policy formulation and   Environmental protection
   administration   Transportation
Protection of persons and   Social enrichment opportunities
   property   Physical resource development

---

[3]GASB, *Codification*, Sec. 1800.117.

Classification by Organization Unit

Classification of expenditures by **organization unit** is considered essential to management control, assuming the organizational structure of a given governmental unit provides clear lines of responsibility and authority. Some examples of organization units that might be found in a city are:

Police Department	City Clerk
Fire Department	Personnel Department
Building Safety Department	Parks and Recreation
Public Works Department	Department
City Attorney	

The key distinction between classification of expenditures by organization unit and classification by program or function is that responsibility for a department is fixed, whereas a number of departments may be involved in the performance of a program or a function. Management control within a department, and rational allocation of resources within the governmental unit, both require much more specific identification of expenditures (and costs and expenses) than is provided by the major classifications illustrated thus far. The next step needed is classification by activity.

Classification by Activity

An **activity** is a specific and distinguishable line of work performed by an organization unit. For example, within the Public Works Department, activities such as the following may be performed:

Solid waste collection—residential.
Solid waste collection—commercial.
Solid waste disposal—landfill.
Solid waste disposal—incineration.

Activity classification is more meaningful if responsibility for the performance of each activity is fixed, performance standards are established, and a good management accounting system is installed to measure input of resources (dollars, personnel time, equipment and facilities used) versus output of services. Such information is useful to those interested in assessing the efficiency of government operations.

The GASB recommends that expenditures also be classified by character.

Classification by Character

Classification by **character,** as defined by the GASB, is based on the fiscal period that benefits from a particular expenditure. A common classification of expenditures by character recognizes three groups:

Current expenditures
Capital outlays
Debt service

Current expenditures are expected to benefit the period in which the expenditure is made. Capital outlays are expected to benefit not only the period in which the capital assets are acquired but as many future periods as the assets provide service. Debt service includes payment of interest on debt and payment of debt principal; if the debt was wisely incurred, residents received benefits in prior periods from the assets acquired by use of debt financing, are receiving benefits currently, and will continue to receive benefits until the service lives of the assets expire.

Character classification of expenditures is potentially of great significance to taxpayers and other citizens. Properly used, it could give them valuable information for appraising the cost of government during a given period. Generally speaking, expenditures for debt service relate to actions incurred by previous administrations. Capital outlays are current expenditures expected to provide benefits in future periods; but the present statement of governmental accounting "principles" does not allow depreciation expense to be recorded in governmental funds in the periods that receive the benefits (see GASB, "Depreciation of Fixed Assets Principle" in Chapter 2). It appears, however, that expenditures in the current expenditures class are the most influential on the public mind, strongly influencing popular attitudes toward responsible officials.

A fourth character class, intergovernmental, is suggested by the GASB for use by governmental units that act as an intermediary in federally financed programs or that transfer "shared revenues" to other governmental units.

Classification by Object

The **object** of an expenditure is the thing for which the expenditure was made. Object classes may be viewed as subdivisions of character classifications. One scheme of object classification includes the following major classes:

Personal services	Capital outlays
Supplies	Debt service
Other services and charges	

Many other object classifications are encountered in practice, generally more detailed than that listed above. Greater detail can, of course, be achieved by the utilization of subclasses under the major titles.[4] Thus personal services may be subdivided on the basis of permanence and regularity of employment of the persons represented; and each subclass may be further subdivided to show whether the services performed were regular, overtime, or temporary. Employee benefits may be recorded in as much detail as desired as subclasses of the personal services class. "Other services and charges" obviously must be subdivided if the class is to provide any useful budgeting and control information. Professional Services, Communication, Transportation, Advertising, Printing and Binding, Insurance, Public Utility Services, Repairs and Maintenance, Rentals, Aid to Other Governments, and Miscellaneous are possible subdivisions.

---

[4]Under an object classification literally followed, the cost of construction of fixed assets by employees of a governmental fund would be dispersed among the personal services, supplies, and other services and charges classes. That is, the cost of salaries, wages, and benefits would be charged to personal services; the cost of materials used, to supplies; the cost of transportation of materials, construction equipment rentals, etc., to other services and charges. From this, the reader can conclude that excessively detailed object classifications should be avoided.

Capital outlays, which is listed as a title under both the character and object classifications, should be subdivided in order to provide information needed in accounting by the General Fixed Assets Account Group for the assets required. Titles such as Land, Buildings, Improvements Other than Buildings, and Machinery and Equipment are useful subclasses of the capital outlays class.

Debt service, also listed as both an object of expenditure and a character class, should be subdivided in as much detail as needed to provide evidence that all interest payments and principal payments that should have been made in a certain fiscal period were actually made (or the appropriate liability recorded).

Classification of Estimated Revenues and Revenues

In order for administrators to determine that proposed expenditures presented in the Appropriations budget can be financed by resources available under the laws of the budgeting jurisdiction and higher jurisdictions, a Revenues budget should be prepared. *Revenue*, in the sense in which it is customarily used in governmental budgeting, includes all financial resource inflows—all amounts that increase the net assets of a fund—interfund transfers and debt issue proceeds, as well as taxes, licenses and permit fees, fines, forfeits, and other revenue sources described in following sections of this chapter.

It should be emphasized that a governmental unit, and the funds thereof, may raise revenues only from sources available to them by law. Often, the law that authorizes a governmental unit to utilize a given revenue source to finance general governmental activities, or specific activities, also establishes the maximum rate that may be applied to a specified base in utilizing the source, or establishes the maximum amount that may be raised from the source during the budget period.

The primary classification of governmental revenue is by *fund*. Within each fund, the major classification is by *source*. Within each major source class, it is desirable to have as many secondary classes as needed to facilitate revenue budgeting and accounting. Secondary classes relating to each major source are discussed below under each source caption. Major revenue source classes commonly used are:

Taxes	Charges for Services
Special Assessments	Fines and Forfeits
Licenses and Permits	Miscellaneous Revenues
Intergovernmental Revenues	

The Revenues budget and the accounting system for each governmental fund should include all revenue sources available to finance activities of that fund. The General Fund of most governmental units will ordinarily need all seven major classes itemized above; in some units, additional major classes may be needed. Each special revenue fund will need to budget and account for only those revenues legally mandated for use in achieving the purpose for which the special revenue fund was created. Similarly, debt service funds budget and account for those sources of revenue that are to be used for payment of interest and principal of tax-supported and special assessment long-term debt. Revenues and other financing sources earmarked for construction or acquisition of general fixed assets are reported as being budgeted and accounted for by capital projects funds.

In order to determine during a fiscal year that revenues are being realized from each budgeted source in amounts consistent with the budget, actual revenues should be accounted for on the same classification system as used in the Estimated Revenues budget.

Taxes

Taxes are of particular importance because (1) they provide a very large portion of the revenue of governmental units on all levels and (2) they are compulsory contributions to the cost of government, whether the affected taxpayer approves or disapproves of the levy.

Ad valorem (based on value) **property taxes** are a mainstay of financing for many units of local government but are not used as a source of revenue by many states or by the federal government. Ad valorem taxes may be levied against real property and personal property. Some property taxes are levied on a basis other than property values, one illustration being the tax on some kinds of financial institutions in relation to the deposits at a specified date. Other kinds of taxes are sales taxes, income taxes, gross receipts taxes, death and gift taxes, and interest and penalties on delinquent taxes.

Ad Valorem Taxes. Revenues from ad valorem taxes should be recognized on the accrual basis in the fiscal period for which the taxes are levied, provided the taxes are due on or before the end of the period. In "available and measurable" terms, tax revenues are available during the period for which they are levied if they may be used to pay liabilities arising from expenditures of that period. Also, the amount of revenue from this source is "measurable" because both the property valuation and the tax rate must be determined in advance of the time the taxes are to be collected.

In the case of property taxes, GASB standards have for many years defined *available* as "due, or past due and receivable within the current period and collected within the current period or expected to be collected soon enough thereafter to be used to pay liabilities of the current period. Such time thereafter shall not exceed sixty days."[5] GASB *Interpretation No. 5* removes the requirement that the property taxes be due within the current period. Under *Interpretation No. 5*, the term *available* means "collected during the current fiscal period or expected to be collected soon enough thereafter to be used to pay liabilities of the current period."[6] The effect of the amendment is to permit property tax installments expected to be collected within 60 days of the end of the current period to be recognized as revenues

---

[5]Governmental Accounting Standards Board, *Interpretation No. 5*, "Property Tax Revenue Recognition in Governmental Funds, an Interpretation of NCGA Statement 1 and an Amendment of NCGA Interpretation 3" (Norwalk, CT, 1997), par. 2.

[6]Ibid., par. 4.

of the current period, even if the installment is not legally due until after the end of the current period. Although *Interpretation No. 5* is not effective until fiscal years beginning after June 15, 2000, early implementation is encouraged.

The valuation of each parcel of taxable real property, and of the taxable personal property owned by each taxpayer, is assigned by a process known as **property assessment**. The assessment process differs state by state, and in some states by jurisdictions within the state. The tax rate is set by one of two widely different procedures: (1) the governmental body simply multiplies the assessed valuation of property in its jurisdiction by a flat rate—either the maximum rate allowable under state law or a rate determined by policy—or (2) the property tax is treated as a residual source of revenue. In the latter event, revenues to be recognized from all sources other than property taxes must be budgeted; the total of those sources must be compared with the total proposed appropriations in order to determine the amount to be raised from property taxes. Illustration 3–2 shows the computation of the total amount of revenues to be raised from property taxes under the assumption that property taxes are a residual source of revenues. The heading of Illustration 3–2 indicates that it is for the Town of Merrill's General Fund. A similar computation would be made for each other fund for which property taxes are levied. It is common for an elected county official to serve as collector for all property taxes levied for all the funds of all of the governmental units within the county (and, of course, for all the funds of the county government itself). As discussed in Chapter 8, in such cases the county official serves as an agent for all funds for which property taxes have been levied; the Taxes Receivable are properly accounted for as assets of the funds for which they are levied, and those funds recognize revenues from the taxes to the extent that the taxes are expected to be collectible.

Note that Illustration 3–2 is a computation of the amount of revenue to be raised from property taxes, which is one step in determining the tax levy for the year. A second step is the determination from historical data and economic forecasts of the percentage of the tax levy expected to be collectible. (Even though property taxes are a lien against the property, personal property may be removed from the taxing jurisdiction and some parcels of real property may not be salable enough for the taxing jurisdiction to recover accumulated taxes against the property.) Therefore, the levy must be large enough to allow for estimated uncollectible taxes. For example, assume the Town of Merrill can reasonably expect to collect only 96 percent of the year 2000 property tax levy for its General Fund. Thus, if tax revenue is to be $3,582,000 (per Illustration 3–2), the gross levy must be $3,582,000 ÷ .96, or $3,731,250.

When the gross levy is known, the tax rate may be computed on the basis of the assessed valuation of taxable property lying within the taxing jurisdiction. The term **taxable property** is used in the preceding sentence in recognition of the fact that property owned by governmental units and property used by religious and charitable organizations are often not taxable by the local government. In addition, senior citizens, war veterans, and others may have statutory exemption from taxation for a limited portion of the assessed valuation of property. Continuing the example, assume the net assessed valuation of property taxable by the General Fund of the Town of Merrill is $214,348,000. In that case, the gross property tax

Illustration 3–2

TOWN OF MERRILL
General Fund
Statement of Amount to Be Raised
by Property Taxes for 2000
July 31, 1999

Requirements:		
Estimated expenditures, August 1–December 31, 1999		$ 4,200,000
Proposed appropriations for 2000		8,460,000
Estimated working balance required for beginning of 2001 . .		510,000
Estimated total requirements		13,170,000
Resources other than tax levy for 2000:		
Actual balance, July 31, 1999	$ 654,000	
Amount to be received from second installment of 1999		
taxes	2,430,000	
Miscellaneous receipts expected during balance of 1999 . . .	1,960,000	
Revenue expected from sources other than property taxes		
during 2000	4,544,000	
Estimated total resources other than property tax levy .		9,588,000
Amount required from property taxes in 2000		$ 3,582,000

levy ($3,731,250) is divided by the net assessed valuation ($214,348,000) to determine the property tax rate. The rate would be expressed as "$1.75 per $100 assessed valuation," or "$17.41 per $1,000 assessed valuation"—rounding up the actual decimal fraction (.017407) to two places to the right of the decimal, as is customary.

Interest and Penalties on Delinquent Taxes.   A **penalty** is a legally mandated addition to a tax on the day it becomes delinquent (generally, the day after the day the tax is due). Penalties should be recognized as revenue when they are assessed. *Interest* at a legally specified rate also must be added to delinquent taxes for the length of time between the day the tax becomes delinquent until the day it is ultimately paid or otherwise discharged; interest revenue should be accrued at the time financial statements are to be prepared.

Sales Taxes, Income Taxes, and Gross Receipts Taxes.   Currently effective GASB standards provide that revenue from sales taxes, income taxes, and gross receipts taxes be recognized, net of estimated refunds, in the accounting period in which they become susceptible to accrual—measurable and available.[7]

Special Assessments   Special assessments differ from ad valorem real property taxes in that the latter are levied against all taxable property within the geographic boundaries of the government levying the taxes, whereas the former are levied against certain properties to

---

[7]See footnote 8 in Chapter 2.

defray part or all of the cost of a specific improvement or service that is presumed to be of particular benefit to the properties against which the special assessments are levied. Briefly, when routine services (street cleaning, snow plowing, and so on) are extended to property owners outside the normal service area of the government, or are provided at a higher level or at more frequent intervals than for the general public, "service-type" special assessments are levied. Service-type special assessments are accounted for by the fund that accounts for similar services rendered to the general public—usually the General Fund or a special revenue fund. Special assessments for capital improvements should be accounted for by a capital projects fund during the construction phase, and by a debt service fund during the debt service phase.

Licenses and Permits   Licenses and Permits include those revenues collected by a governmental unit from individuals or business concerns for various rights or privileges granted by the government. Some licenses and permits are primarily regulatory in nature, with minor consideration to revenue derived, whereas others are not only regulatory but provide large amounts of revenue as well, and some are almost exclusively revenue producers. Licenses and permits may relate to the privilege of carrying on business for a stipulated period, the right to do a certain thing that may affect the public welfare, or the right to use certain public property. Vehicle and alcoholic beverage licenses are found extensively on the state level and serve both regulatory and revenue functions. States make widespread use of professional and occupational taxes for purposes of control. Local governments make extensive use of licenses and permits to control the activities of their citizens; and from some they derive substantial amounts of revenue. Commonly found among licenses and permits are building permits, vehicle licenses, amusement licenses, business and occupational licenses, animal licenses, and street and curb permits.

Regardless of the governmental level or the purpose of a license or permit, the revenue it produces is ordinarily accounted for on a cash basis. Applicable rates or schedules of charges for a future period may be established well in advance, and fairly reliable information may be available as to the number of licenses or permits to be issued, but the probable degree of fluctuation in the latter factor is so great as to prevent satisfactory use of the accrual basis.

Intergovernmental Revenue   Intergovernmental Revenues include grants, entitlements, and shared revenues. As defined by the GASB:

1. A *grant* is a contribution or gift of cash or other assets from another governmental unit to be used or expended for a specified purpose, activity, or facility. *Capital grants* are restricted by the grantor for the acquisition and/or construction of fixed (capital) assets. All other grants are *operating grants*.
2. An *entitlement* is the amount of payment to which a state or local government is entitled as determined by the federal government pursuant to an allocation formula contained in the applicable statutes.

3. A *shared revenue* is a revenue levied by one government but shared on a predetermined basis, often in proportion to the amount collected at the local level, with another government or class of government.[8]

Some kinds of intergovernmental revenues can well be accounted for on the accrual basis while other kinds cannot. Grants by state and federal agencies ordinarily are announced somewhat in advance of their actual distribution, which makes it possible to record the revenue with a debit to Due from State Government or some such title, even to the extent of designating the agency or department from which the grant is forthcoming. Distributions of shared revenues, stating amounts, are frequently announced in advance of the actual disbursements and are obviously adapted to accrual.

Charges for Services

Charges for Services includes revenue from charges for all activities of a governmental unit, except the operations of enterprise funds. A few of the many revenue items included in this category are court costs; special police service; solid waste collection charges; street, sidewalk, and curb repairs; receipts from parking meters; library use fees (not fines); and tuition.

Classification of expenditures by function is discussed in an earlier section of this chapter. The grouping of Charges for Services revenue may be correlated with the functional classification of expenditures. For example, one functional group of expenditures is named General Government, another Public Safety, and so on. A governmental unit, in connection with providing general government service, collects some revenue such as court cost charges, fees for recording legal documents, and zoning and subdivision fees, and should relate the revenues to the expenditures.

Charges for Services should be recognized as revenue when earned, if that is prior to the collection of cash.

Fines and Forfeits

Revenue from Fines and Forfeits includes fines and penalties for commission of statutory offenses and for neglect of official duty; forfeitures of amounts held as security against loss or damage, or collections from bonds or sureties placed with the government for the same purpose; and penalties of any sort, except those levied on delinquent taxes. Library fines are included in this category. If desired, Fines and Forfeits may be the titles of two accounts within this revenue class, or they may be subgroup headings for more detailed breakdowns.

Revenues of this classification should be accrued to the extent practicable. In direct contrast with general property taxes, neither rates nor base or volume may be predetermined with any reasonable degree of accuracy for this type of revenue. Because of these uncertainties, it is often difficult to determine whether all amounts paid by transgressors have been accounted for; therefore, revenues from fines and forfeits may be recognized on the cash basis if accrual is not practicable.

---

[8]Paraphrased from GASB, *Codification*, Sec. G60.501–.514.

Miscellaneous Revenues

Although the word *miscellaneous* is not informative and should be used sparingly, its use as the title of a revenue category is necessary. It (1) substitutes for other possible source classes that might have rather slight and infrequent usage and (2) minimizes the need for forcing some kinds of revenue into source classifications in which they do not generically belong. While Miscellaneous Revenues in itself represents a compromise, its existence aids in sharpening the meanings of other source classes. The heterogeneous nature of items served by the title is indicated by the following listing: interest earnings (other than on delinquent taxes); rents and royalties; sales of, and compensation for loss of, fixed assets; contributions from public enterprises (utilities, airports, etc.); escheats (taking of property in default of legally qualified claimants); contributions and donations from private sources; and "other."

Some items of Miscellaneous Revenues, such as interest earnings on investments, might well be accrued, but mostly they are accounted for on the cash basis.

Proposed Changes in Revenue Recognition

As discussed in Chapter 1, the GASB has proposed an alternative dual perspective financial model in which basic financial statements would display financial information at both the entitywide and fund perspectives. One component of the GASB's reporting model project led to a proposed standard on recognition and measurement criteria for what the GASB calls "nonexchange transactions"—defined as external events in which a government gives (or receives) value without directly receiving (or giving) equal value in exchange.[9] In the proposed standard, nonexchange transactions are further subdivided into four classes: (1) derived tax revenues (examples: income and sales taxes), (2) imposed nonexchange revenues (examples: property taxes and fines and penalties), (3) government-mandated nonexchange transactions (examples: certain education, social welfare, and transportation services mandated and funded by a higher level of government), and (4) voluntary nonexchange transactions (examples: grants and entitlements from higher levels of government and certain private donations).[10]

The proposed standard provides recognition criteria for nonexchange transactions under both the accrual basis—all transactions at the entitywide perspectives and those of proprietary and certain fiduciary funds at the fund perspective—and the modified accrual basis.[11] The latter basis applies to governmental fund nonex-

---

[9]Governmental Accounting Standards Board, Exposure Draft, *Proposed Statement of the Governmental Accounting Standards Board*, "Accounting and Financial Reporting for Nonexchange Transactions" (Norwalk, CT, March 1997), par. 1.

[10]Ibid., par. 7.

[11]Under GASB's proposed reporting model, fiduciary funds would be limited to only those activities for which the government acts as a trustee or agent for individuals or organizations *outside* the government. Most activities currently reported in expendable trust funds would be reported with special revenue funds and most activities currently reported in nonexpendable trust funds would be reported within the proprietary fund category.

change transactions and those of certain fiduciary fund activities under the fund perspective. The complex recognition criteria for each of the four classes of nonexchange transactions under the accrual basis are discussed in Chapter 10. For activities accounted for under the modified accrual basis, the proposed recognition criteria are essentially the same as those discussed in this chapter and Chapter 2; that is, revenues will continue to be recognized when *measurable* and *available*.

Recording the Budget

The use of budgetary accounts is described earlier in this chapter. In order to illustrate entries in journal form to record a budget, assume the amounts in the first money column of Illustration 2–3 are the amounts that have been legally approved as the budget for the General Fund of a certain governmental unit for the fiscal year ending December 31, 1999. As of January 1, 1999, the first day of the fiscal year, the total Estimated Revenues should be recorded in the General Fund general ledger control account, and the amounts expected to be recognized during 1999 from each revenue source specified in the budget should be recorded in subsidiary ledger accounts. An appropriate entry would be:

	General Ledger		Subsidiary Ledger	
	Debits	*Credits*	*Debits*	*Credits*
1. Estimated Revenues	1,277,500			
Fund Balance		1,277,500		
Revenues Ledger:				
Taxes			882,500	
Intergovernmental Revenues			200,000	
Licenses and Permits			195,000	

The total Appropriations and Other Financing Uses legally budgeted for 1999 for the General Fund of the same governmental unit should also be recorded in the General Fund general ledger control accounts, and the amounts appropriated for each function itemized in the budget should be recorded in subsidiary ledger accounts. An appropriate entry would be:

2. Fund Balance	1,636,500			
Appropriations		1,362,000		
Estimated Other Financing Uses		274,500		
Appropriations Ledger:				
General Government				1,150,000
Public Safety				212,000
Other Financing Uses Ledger:				
Operating Transfers Out to				
Other Funds				74,500
Operating Transfers Out to				
Component Units				200,000

It would, of course, be acceptable to combine the two entries illustrated above and make one General Fund entry to record Estimated Revenues, Appropriations, and Estimated Other Financing Uses; in this case there would be a debit to Fund Balance for $359,000 (the amount by which Appropriations and Estimated Other Financing Uses exceed Estimated Revenues). Even if a single combined entry is made in the General Fund general ledger accounts, that entry must provide for entry of the budgeted amounts in each individual subsidiary ledger account as shown in the illustrations of the two separate entries.

Accounting for Revenues

In the preceding section, entries to record the budget in general ledger accounts and in subsidiary ledger accounts are illustrated. During a fiscal year, actual revenues should be recognized in the general ledger accounts of governmental funds by credits to the Revenues account (offset by debits to receivable accounts for revenues that are accrued or by debits to Cash for revenues recognized on the cash basis). The general ledger Revenues account is a control account supported by Revenues subsidiary ledger accounts kept in exactly the same detail as kept for the Estimated Revenues subsidiary ledger accounts. For example, assume the General Fund of the governmental unit for which budgetary entries are illustrated in the preceding section collected revenues in cash during the month of January from Licenses and Permits, $13,200, and Intergovernmental Revenues, $61,900. In an actual case, entries should be made on a current basis and cash receipts should be deposited each working day; however, for the purpose of this chapter, the following entry illustrates the effect on the General Fund accounts of collections during the month of January:

	General Ledger		Subsidiary Ledger	
	Debits	Credits	Debits	Credits
3. Cash	75,100			
Revenues		75,100		
Revenues Ledger:				
Licenses and Permits				13,200
Intergovernmental Revenues				61,900

Comparability between Estimated Revenues subsidiary accounts and Revenues subsidiary accounts is necessary so that periodically throughout the fiscal year actual revenues from each source can be compared with estimated revenues from that source. Material differences between estimated and actual revenues should be investigated by administrators to determine whether (1) estimates were made on the basis of assumptions that may have appeared realistic when the budget was prepared but are no longer realistic (in that event, the budget needs to be revised so that administrators and legislators have better knowledge of revenues to be realized during the remainder of the fiscal year), or (2) action needs to be taken so that revenues estimated with reasonable accuracy are actually realized (i.e., one or more employees may have failed to understand that certain revenue items are to be collected).

Illustration 3–3

NAME OF GOVERNMENTAL UNIT
Revenues Ledger
General Fund

Class: Licenses and Permits

Subclass:

Number: 351.1

Title:

Date	Item	Reference	Estimated Revenues DR.	Revenues CR.	Balance DR. (CR.)
1999 January 1	Budget estimate	J1	$195,000		$195,000
31	Collections	CR6		$13,200	181,800

Illustration 3–3 shows a form of Revenues subsidiary ledger in which the debit column is subsidiary to the Estimated Revenues general ledger control account and the credit column is subsidiary to the Revenues general ledger control account.

A Statement of Actual and Estimated Revenues is illustrated in Chapter 4. Normally, during a fiscal year, the amount of revenue budgeted from each source will exceed the amount of revenue from that source realized to date; consequently, the Balance column will have a debit balance and may be headed Estimated Revenues Not Yet Realized. This amount is a *resource* of the governmental unit—legally and realistically budgeted revenues that will be recognized as assets before the end of the fiscal year.

Accounting for Encumbrances and Expenditures

When enacted into law, an appropriation is an authorization for administrators to incur on behalf of the governmental unit liabilities in the amounts specified in the appropriation ordinance or statute, for the purposes set forth in that ordinance or statute, during the period of time specified. An appropriation is considered *expended* when the authorized liabilities have been incurred. Because penalties are imposed by law on an administrator who incurs liabilities for any amount in excess of that appropriated, or for any purpose not covered by an appropriation, or who incurs liabilities after the authority to do so has expired, prudence dictates that each purchase order and each contract be reviewed before it is signed to determine that a valid and sufficient appropriation exists to which the expenditure can be charged when goods or services are received. If the review indicates that a valid appropriation exists and it has an available balance in excess of the amount of the purchase order or contract being reviewed, the purchase order or contract legally may be issued. When a purchase order or contract has been issued it is important to record the fact that the appropriation has been *encumbered* in the amount of the purchase order or contract. The word *encumbered* is used, rather than the word *expended*, because the amount is only an estimate of the liability that will be incurred when the purchase order is filled or the contract executed. (It is reasonably common for quantities of goods received to differ from quantities ordered, and it is not uncommon for invoice prices to differ from unit prices shown on purchase orders.) The use of appropriation authority is also somewhat tentative inasmuch as some suppliers are unable to fill orders or to perform as stipulated in a contract; in such cases, related purchase orders or contracts must be canceled.

Notice the issuance of purchase orders and/or contracts has two effects: (1) the encumbrance of the appropriation(s) that gave the governmental unit the authority to order goods or services and (2) the starting of a chain of events that will result in the government incurring a liability when the purchase orders are filled and the contracts executed. Both effects should be recorded in order to assist administrators to avoid overexpending appropriations and to plan to be able to pay liabilities on a timely basis. The accounting procedure used to record the two effects is illustrated by Entry 4. The first effect is recorded by the debit to the general ledger account *Encumbrances*. Encumbrances is a control account that is related to the *Appropriations* control account discussed previously and to the *Expenditures* control account discussed in relation to Entries 5a and 5b. In order to accomplish the matching of Appropriations, Expenditures, and Encumbrances necessary for budgetary control, subsidiary account classifications of all three must correspond exactly (see Illustration 3–4). The general ledger account credited in Entry 4, *Reserve for Encumbrances*, is used to record the second effect of issuing purchase orders and contracts—the creation of an expected liability. Reserve for Encumbrances, sometimes called *Outstanding Encumbrances*, is not a control account; the balance of the account at the balance sheet date is reported as a reservation of Fund Equity, as illustrated in Chapter 4.

Entries 4, 5a, 5b, and 6 illustrate accounting for Encumbrances and Expenditures for the General Fund of the governmental unit for which entries are illustrated in previous sections of this chapter. Entry 4 is made on the assumption that early in January purchase orders are issued pursuant to the authority contained in the General Fund appropriations; assumed amounts chargeable to each function for which purchase orders are issued on this date are shown in the debits to the Encumbrances subsidiary accounts.

	General Ledger		Subsidiary Ledger	
	Debits	*Credits*	*Debits*	*Credits*
4. Encumbrances—1999	45,400			
Reserve for Encumbrances—1999 . .		45,400		
Encumbrances Ledger:				
General Government			38,000	
Public Safety			7,400	

When goods or services for which encumbrances have been recorded are received and the suppliers' invoices are approved for payment, the accounts should record the fact that appropriations have been *expended,* not merely encumbered, and that an actual liability, not merely an expected liability, exists. Entry 5a reverses Entry 4 to the extent that purchase orders are filled (ordinarily some of the purchase orders recorded in one encumbrance entry will be filled in one time period, and some in other time periods); it is important to note that since estimated amounts were used when encumbrances were recorded, the reversing entry must also use the estimated amounts. Thus the balance remaining in the Encumbrances control account, and in the Reserve for Encumbrances account, is the *total* estimated dollar amount of purchase orders and contracts outstanding. The estimated dollar amount of purchase orders outstanding against each appropriation is disclosed by the subsidiary accounts, as shown in Illustration 3–4.

5a.	Reserve for Encumbrances—1999	42,000	
	Encumbrances—1999		42,000
	Encumbrances Ledger:		
	General Government		35,000
	Public Safety		7,000
5b.	Expenditures—1999	42,400	
	Vouchers Payable		42,400
	Expenditures Ledger:		
	General Government	35,100	
	Public Safety	7,300	

Expenditures and the liability account must both be recorded at the actual amount the governmental unit agrees to pay the vendors who have filled the purchase orders (see Entry 5b). The fact that estimated and actual amounts differ causes no accounting difficulties as long as goods or services are received in the same fiscal period as ordered. The accounting treatment required when encumbrances outstanding at year-end are filled, or canceled, in a following year is illustrated in Chapter 4.

The encumbrance procedure is not always needed to make sure that appropriations are not overexpended. For example, although salaries and wages of governmental employees must be chargeable against valid and sufficient appropriations in order to give rise to legal expenditures, many governmental units do not find it necessary to encumber the departmental personal services appropriations for estimated payrolls of recurring, relatively constant amounts. Departments having payrolls that fluctuate greatly from one season to another may follow the encumbrance procedure to make sure the personal service appropriation is not overexpended. Entry 6 shows the recording of expenditures of appropriations for salaries and wages not previously encumbered, assuming gross pay is vouchered.

		General Ledger		Subsidiary Ledger	
		Debits	*Credits*	*Debits*	*Credits*
6.	Expenditures—1999	67,600			
	Vouchers Payable		67,600		
	Expenditures Ledger:				
	General Government			57,000	
	Public Safety			10,600	

Illustration 3–4

NAME OF GOVERNMENT UNIT
Appropriations, Expenditures, and Encumbrances Ledger

Code No.: 0607-03
Fund: General
Function: General Government

Year: 1999

Month and Day	Reference	Encumbrances			Expenditures		Appropriations	
		Debits	Credits	Open	Debits	Cumulative Total	Credits	Available Balance
Jan. 2	Budget (Entry 2)						$1,150,000	$1,150,000
3	Purchase orders issued (Entry 4)	$38,000		$38,000				1,112,000
17	Invoices approved for payment (Entries 5a, 5b)		$35,000	3,000	$35,100	$35,100		1,111,900
31	Payrolls (Entry 6)				57,000	92,100		1,054,900

From the foregoing discussion and illustrative journal entries, it should be apparent that administrators of governmental units need accounting systems designed to provide at any given date during a fiscal year comparisons for each item in the legal Appropriations budget of (1) the amount appropriated, (2) the amount of outstanding encumbrances, and (3) the cumulative amount of expenditures to this date. The net of the three items is accurately described as "Unencumbered Unexpended Appropriations" but can be labeled more simply as "Available Appropriations" or "Available Balance." Classification of appropriations, expenditures, and encumbrances was discussed in a preceding section of this chapter. In order to provide needed comparisons, classification of expenditures and encumbrances must agree with the classifications of appropriations mandated by law. In many jurisdictions, good financial management may dictate all three elements be classified in greater detail than required by law.

Illustration 3–4 shows a form of subsidiary ledger that supports all three general ledger control accounts: Appropriations, Expenditures, and Encumbrances.

At intervals during the fiscal year, a Statement of Budgeted and Actual Expenditures and Encumbrances should be prepared to inform administrators and members of the legislative branch of the data contained in the subsidiary ledger records. An example of such a statement is illustrated in Chapter 4 (see Illustration 4–3). Also in Chapter 4, the entry needed at year-end to close budgetary and nominal accounts is illustrated (Entry 22, Chapter 4).

Computerized Accounting Systems

If a computerized accounting system is used, which is typically the case, an account number structure provides for appropriate classification of revenues and expenditures, as well as for the desired classification of assets, liabilities, and fund equities. Many alternative fund accounting software systems are available. Because current information technology makes it feasible to handle large numbers of files and a high transaction volume, the general ledger module of most systems can easily accommodate all the revenue and expenditure detail accounts needed for effective budgetary control. Thus, computerized systems often do not use general ledger control accounts and subsidiary ledgers in the manner of the manual system described in this section.

Instead of using general ledger control accounts and related subsidiary ledgers, computerized systems typically use separate files or ledgers for proprietary and budgetary reporting. For example, the general ledger module of one leading fund accounting software system includes both a general ledger and a budget ledger. Actual revenues and expenditures are posted to the general ledger and budget amounts are posted to the budget ledger. Of course, the same account numbers and titles used in the budget ledger are used in the general ledger to permit budgetary comparison reporting. In addition, the system provides a separate encumbrance ledger to record encumbered amounts and monitor budgetary compliance. Selecting the type of transaction from a menu on the screen determines in which ledger (or ledgers) a particular transaction is posted. All such systems must provide transaction detail reports and other documentation of entries and postings in order to provide an adequate "audit trail."

In a computerized system, the account number structure is an important design feature—one that affects the ease of operation and the ability to prepare useful financial reports. Most account number structures provide for the multiple expenditure classification categories recommended by the GASB, or similar classification. Consider, for example, the following eight-segment account number structure for one eastern city:

$$\text{XXXX - XXXX - XXX - XXXX - XX - X - XX - XXXX}$$
$$\text{(1)} \quad \text{(2)} \quad \text{(3)} \quad \text{(4)} \quad \text{(5)} \; \text{(6)} \; \text{(7)} \quad \text{(8)}$$

The eight segments of numbers represent the following classifications:

Segment	Represents
1	Fund or Account Group
2	Department/Division (or Function)
3	Office/Bureau (or Program)
4	Activity
5	Report Group
6	Account Type
7	Object (Major Object)
8	Line Item (Detailed Object)

Even though these segment names do not agree completely with the classification categories recommended by the GASB and described in this section, their similarity should be apparent. Moreover, it appears that the segments used in this account number provide for at least as much detail as that recommended by GASB.

To illustrate how this account structure appears in practice, an example screen display is presented below for one particular account: an expenditures account for part-time salaries in the Aquatics (swimming pools, etc.) activity of the Customer Relations Program within the Leisure Services Division, accounted for in the General Fund.

```
                     City of Sample

                Display Account Segments

  Fund . . . . . . . . .: 0001 General Fund
  Dept/Div (Function)  .: 0253 Leisure Services
  Office/Bureau (Prog.) : 205  Customer Relations
  Activity (Location)  .: 2531 Aquatics
  Report Group . . . . .: 43   Cultural, Parks, & Rec.
  Account Type . . . . .: 2    Recreation
  Object (Major Obj.)  .: 10   Salaries
  Line Item (Detl. Obj.): 1201 Part-Time
```

All segments of the account number are used for expenditure transactions, but not all segments are needed for revenue and some balance sheet transactions. Segments not needed to record a transaction are left blank. The menu-driven program used by the system makes it relatively simple to move around within the account classification structure. Further, information can be aggregated within any given segment, or groups of segments, to provide a wide variety of custom financial reports, in addition to the financial statements.

Accounting for Allotments

In some jurisdictions, it is necessary to regulate the use of appropriations so only specified amounts may be used from month to month or from quarter to quarter. The purpose of such control is to prevent expenditure of all or most of the authorized amount early in the year, without providing for unexpected requirements arising later in the year. A common device for regulating expenditures is the use of allotments. An **allotment** may be described as an internal allocation of funds on a periodic basis usually agreed upon by the department heads and the chief executive.

Allotments may be formally recorded in ledger accounts. This procedure might begin with the budgetary entry, in which Unallotted Appropriations would replace Appropriations. If this is desired, a combined entry to record the budget would be (using the numbers given in Entries 1 and 2, omitting entries in subsidiary accounts—which would be as illustrated previously, except the subsidiary ledger credits in Entry 2 would be designated as Unallotted Appropriations instead of Appropriations):

	General Ledger		Subsidiary Ledger	
	Debits	*Credits*	*Debits*	*Credits*
Estimated Revenues	1,277,500			
Fund Balance	359,000			
Unallotted Appropriations		1,362,000		
Estimated Other Financing Uses		274,500		

If it is assumed that $342,000 is the amount formally allotted for the first period, the following entry could be made (amounts allotted for each function are shown in the subsidiary ledger entries):

Unallotted Appropriations	342,000			
Allotments		342,000		
Allotments Ledger:				
General Government				289,000
Public Safety				53,000

Expenditures can be recorded periodically as reports are received from using departments or divisions. Under this procedure, Expenditures, Allotments, and Unallotted Appropriations are all closed to Fund Balance at year-end, usually in one combined entry.

Reconciliation of Differences between GAAP and Budgetary Amounts

As previously noted in this chapter, GASB standards require that differences between amounts reported in the GAAP basis operating statement (Illustration 2–2) and those reported in conformity with budgetary practices (Illustration 2–3) be reconciled either on the face of the statements or in the Notes to the Financial Statements. Readers will note that the amounts in the Revenues section of the Actual column of Illustration 2–3 are the same as the revenues reported in Illustration 2–2 because in this example the budget for revenues is prepared on the same basis as is used in the proprietary accounts. The amounts in the Expenditures section of the Actual column of Illustration 2–3 differ from the Expenditures reported in Illustration 2–2; however, because the latter, in conformity with GASB standards, reports expenditures chargeable to the prior year's appropriations as well as expenditures chargeable to 1999 appropriations and does not report encumbrances as expenditures. In contrast, encumbrances outstanding at the end of fiscal year 1999 are added to 1999 expenditures in Illustration 2–3 because both are uses of the 1999 appropriation authority (reported in the Budget column). Expenditures chargeable to the prior year's appropriations are excluded from the budgetary comparison statement (Illustration 2–3) because this statement reports only the 1999 budget and actual amounts. Consequently, the Notes to the Financial Statements should include a reconciliation of the General Fund and special revenue funds Expenditures reported in the two statements illustrated. One form of reconciliation appears below. (The year-end Reserve for Encumbrances in each fund is taken from the Combined Balance Sheet shown as Illustration 2–1.)

	General Fund	Special Revenue Funds
Expenditures of 1999 appropriations, budgetary basis (Illustration 2–3)	$1,358,470	$1,129,600
Less: Increase in Reserve for Encumbrances, December 31, 1999 (Illustration 2–2)	76,000	93,000
Expenditures for 1999, GAAP basis (Illustration 2–2)	$1,282,470	$1,036,600

A second form of reconciliation sometimes found in practice is:

Excess of revenues over (under) expenditures and other uses, budgetary basis (Illustration 2–3)	$ (373,470)	$ (184,200)
Increase in Reserve for Encumbrances (Illustration 2–2)	76,000	93,000
Excess of revenues over (under) expenditures and other uses, GAAP basis (Illustration 2–2)	$ (297,470)	$ (91,200)

Interfund Transactions and Transfers

Quasi-External Transactions

Interfund transactions that would result in the recognition of revenues, expenditures, or expenses if the transactions involved organizations *external* to the governmental unit should be accounted for as revenues, expenditures, or expenses of the funds involved. For example, it is common for enterprise funds to remit to the General Fund a payment in lieu of taxes. If the enterprise had been investor owned, it would have paid taxes to the General Fund. Since taxes are an item of General Fund revenue, the payment in lieu of taxes is also considered General Fund revenue even though from the viewpoint of the governmental unit as a whole there is no increase in net assets because the enterprise fund records an expense equal in amount to the General Fund revenue.

Internal service fund billings to other funds, routine employer contributions from a General Fund to an employee retirement fund, and routine service charges for services provided by a department financed by one fund to a department financed by another fund are additional examples of "quasi-external" interfund transactions that properly result in the recognition of fund revenue, expenditures, or expenses, even though from the viewpoint of the governmental unit as a whole there is no net effect.

Reimbursements

Quasi-external transactions, described above, are the only form of interfund transaction that result in the recognition of revenue by the receiving fund. In certain instances, discussed at greater length in Chapter 10, one fund may record as an expenditure an item that should have been recorded as an expenditure by another fund. When the second fund reimburses the first fund, the first fund should recognize the reimbursement as a reduction of its Expenditures account, not as an item of revenue.

Interfund Transfers

Operating Transfers. Operating transfers are generally periodic, routine transfers. State laws may require that taxes be levied by a General Fund or a special revenue fund to finance an expenditure to be made from another fund (such as a debt service fund). Since the general rule is that revenues should be recorded as such only once, the transfer of tax revenue to the expending fund is recorded by the transferor as Operating Transfers Out and by the transferee as Operating Transfers In. The transferee fund does not recognize the transfer as revenue. Operating transfers are often reported in the Other Financing Sources (Uses) section of the Statement of Revenues, Expenditures, and Changes in Fund Balances. An equally acceptable presentation, however, is to group Other Financing Sources with Revenues, and Other Financing Uses with Expenditures in the Statement of Revenues, Expenditures, and Changes in Fund Balances.

Equity Transfers. Equity transfers are nonroutine transactions often made to establish or liquidate a fund. The creation of a fund by transfer of assets and/or resources from an existing fund to a new fund (remember, a fund is a fiscal entity as well as an accounting entity) does not result in the recognition of revenue by the new fund. Similarly, subsequent return of all or part of the contribution, or transfers of residual balances of discontinued funds, to another fund would not result in the recognition of revenue by the fund receiving the assets or resources. Transfers of equity should be accounted for as such and should be reported in the Changes in Fund Balances section of the Statement of Revenues, Expenditures, and Changes in Fund Balances.

Proceeds of Debt Issues; Capital Leases

The General Fund, special revenue funds, capital projects funds, and debt service funds report only current liabilities to be paid from fund assets. Tax-supported or special assessment capital debt that is not a current liability of these four fund types is reported in the General Long-Term Debt Account Group (GLTDAG). Accordingly, when a fund in any of these four fund types receives the proceeds of general long-term capital debt, it has an increase in assets not offset by an increase in liabilities; therefore, the Fund Equity is increased. An increase in Fund Equity arising from the receipt of proceeds of such debt is considered as an Other Financing Source and reported under that caption in the Statement of Revenues,

Expenditures, and Changes in Fund Balances for the fund. Debt issue proceeds are reported in this manner, rather than as revenue, because the debt is a liability of the governmental unit even though not a liability of the fund.

General fixed assets acquired under capital lease agreements are reported in the General Fixed Assets Account Group (GFAAG); the offsetting liability under the lease is reported in the General Long-Term Debt Account Group. In addition, acquisition of a general fixed asset under a capital lease should be reflected as an expenditure and as an Other Financing Source of a governmental fund, just as if the general fixed asset had been constructed or acquired from debt issue proceeds.

APPENDIX

ACCOUNTING FOR PUBLIC SCHOOL SYSTEMS

As mentioned in Chapter 1, there are more than 14,000 independent public school systems in the United States. Although they are classified as special purpose governments, these school systems follow the same generally accepted accounting principles as state and local governments—the accounting and reporting standards issued by GASB. The approximately 1,500 "dependent" school systems are accounted for as part of their parent general purpose government, either a state, county, municipality, or township. Public school systems, both independent and dependent, often follow specialized accounting and reporting procedures prescribed by a state oversight department or agency. Further, all state oversight departments or agencies collect revenues and expenditures data for all prekindergarten through grade 12 public schools in their state and provide these data to the National Center for Educational Statistics (NCES) so the NCES can prepare the annual "National Public Education Financial Survey."[12] For sake of uniformity, most school systems follow the system of classification for revenues and expenditures recommended by the NCES. This system of classification is discussed next.

Classification of Expenditures of Public School Systems

The NCES system of expenditure classification combines several of the GASB classifications discussed in this chapter. In NCES terminology, a combination of classifications is called a **dimension.** Two groups of dimensions are provided in the expenditure classification system: (1) dimensions essential to meet reporting requirements at the federal level and (2) dimensions optionally available for management use. The dimensions essential to meet federal (and most state) reporting requirements are Program, Function, Object, and Project/Reporting. In the optional group are Level of Instruction, Operational Unit, Subject Matter, Job Classification, and Special Cost Center.

Essential Dimensions. *Program* dimensions provided in the NCES publication include Special Programs (such as Mentally Retarded, Physically Handicapped, or Gifted and Talented), Vocational Programs, Other Instructional Programs—Elementary/Secondary, Nonpublic School Programs, Adult/Continuing Education Programs, Community/Junior College Programs, Community Services Programs, and Enterprise Programs (Food Services, etc.). The *Function* dimension includes Instruction, Support Services such as Guidance Services, Health Services, or Psychological Services, Support Services—Instructional Staff, Support Services—General Administration, Support Services—School Administration, Support Services—Business, Operation and Maintenance of Plant Services, Student Transportation Services, Support Services—Central, Other Support Services, Operation of Non-Instructional Services (Food Services, Other Enterprise Services, Community Services), Facilities Acquisition and Construction Services, and Other Outlays. *Object* classifications of a public school system are Personal Services—Salaries, Personal Services—Employee Benefits, Purchased Professional and Technical Services, Purchased Property

---

[12]An extensive list of NCES reports and resources is available on the Internet at http://www.ed.gov/NCES.

Services, Other Purchased Services, Supplies and Materials, Property, Other Objects (Dues and Fees, Judgments, Interest, etc.), and Other Uses of Funds (Redemption of Principal, Housing Authority Obligations, and Fund Transfers). The *Project/Reporting* code permits school systems to accumulate expenditures to meet a variety of specialized reporting requirements, such as Local Projects, State Projects, and Federal Projects.

Optional Dimensions. The optional dimensions are: Level of Instruction (Elementary, Middle, Secondary, Post-Secondary, and Districtwide); Operational Unit (possibly attendance centers, budgetary units, buildings, or location code for paycheck distribution); Subject Matter (Agriculture, Arts, Business, etc.); Job Classification (this dimension may be used to [1] classify payroll costs for personnel purposes, such as Official, Professional, Technical, Clerical, and [2] segregate certified and noncertified salaries and benefits or accumulate payroll costs by bargaining unit for purposes of labor negotiations); and Special Cost Centers such as Term, Course, Work Order, Bus Route or Vehicle, State Accounting Number, or Federal Common Accounting Number.

Classification of Revenues of Public School Systems

Revenues of public school systems, both those dependent upon a general purpose government and those independent entities, should be classified in the manner prescribed by the National Center for Education Statistics. As is true of the NCES expenditure classification, the NCES revenue classification system provides for a combination of classifications known as a *dimension*. Generally, public school revenues should be classified by fund, source, and project/reporting code. The NCES suggests the following revenue classification:

```
1000  Revenue from Local Sources
        1100  Taxes levied/assessed by the school system
        1200  Revenue from local governmental units other than the school system
        1300  Tuition
        1400  Transportation fees
        1500  Earnings on investments
        1600  Food services
        1700  Student activities
        1800  Community services activities
        1900  Other revenue from local sources
2000  Revenue from Intermediate Sources
        2100  Unrestricted grants-in-aid
        2200  Restricted grants-in-aid
        2800  Revenue in lieu of taxes
        2900  Revenue for/on behalf of the school system
3000  Revenue from State Sources
        3100  Unrestricted grants-in-aid
        3200  Restricted grants-in-aid
        3800  Revenue in lieu of taxes
        3900  Revenue for/on behalf of the school system
4000  Revenue from Federal Sources
        4100  Unrestricted grants-in-aid received directly
        4200  Unrestricted grants-in-aid received through state
        4300  Restricted grants-in-aid received directly
        4500  Restricted grants-in-aid received through state
        4700  Grants-in-aid received through other agencies
        4800  Revenue in lieu of taxes
        4900  Revenue for/on behalf of the school system
```

5000 Other Sources
    5100 Sale of bonds
    5200 Interfund transfers
    5300 Sale or compensation for loss of fixed assets

An additional level of detail provided in the NCES revenue source classification system is not illustrated above. The nature of the detail is readily apparent; for example, revenue account 1100, Taxes, comprehends account 1110, Ad Valorem Taxes levied by local school system; account 1120, Sales and Use Taxes; account 1130, Income Taxes; account 1140, Penalties and Interest on Taxes; and account 1190, other taxes.

"Intermediate" sources of revenue are administrative units or political subdivisions between the local school system and the state. "Grants-in-aid" from intermediate, state, or federal governments are contributions from general revenue sources of those governments, or, if related to specific revenue sources of those units, are distributed on a flat grant or equalization basis. "Revenue in lieu of taxes" analogous to payment from an enterprise fund to the General Fund discussed in Chapter 10 are payments made out of general revenues of intermediate, state, or federal governments to a local school system because the higher governmental units own property located within the geographical boundaries of the local unit that is not subject to taxation. "Revenue for/on behalf of the local school system" includes all payments made by intermediate, state, or federal governments for the benefit of the local system; payments to pension funds, or a contribution of fixed assets, are examples.

Key Terms

Activity, 60
Ad valorem taxes, 63
Allotment, 76
Appropriations, 56
Budgetary accounts, 56
Character, 60
Encumbrances, 56
Estimated other financing sources, 56
Estimated other financing uses, 56
Estimated revenues, 56
Expenditures, 55
Expenditures budget, 59
Function, 59
Fund balance, 55

Fund equity, 54
General Fund, 54
Object, 61
Organization unit, 60
Other financing sources, 55
Other financing uses, 55
Penalty, 65
Program, 59
Property assessment, 64
Proprietary accounts, 55
Reserve accounts, 55
Revenue, 55
Taxable property, 64

Selected References

American Institute of Certified Public Accountants. *Audit and Accounting Guide. Audits of State and Local Governmental Units*. Revised. New York, 1996.

Governmental Accounting Standards Board. *Codification of Governmental Accounting and Financial Reporting Standards as of June 30, 1997*. Norwalk, CT, 1997.

National Center for Education Statistics. *Financial Accounting for Local and State School Systems*. State Educational Records and Reports Series: Handbook II, Revision. Washington, DC: U.S. Government Printing Office, 1990.

Questions

3–1. How should you determine whether the routine activities of a city's Street Department ought to be accounted for in the General Fund or in a special revenue fund?

3–2. Governmental accounting gives substantial recognition to budgets, with those budgets being recorded in the accounts of the governmental unit.
  a. What is the purpose of a governmental accounting system, and why is the budget recorded in the accounts of a governmental unit? Include in your discussion the purpose and significance of appropriations.
  b. Describe when and how a governmental unit records its budget and closes it out.
                                                                    (AICPA)

3–3. Define *fund equity* and explain the kinds of proprietary and budgetary accounts that comprise the fund equity category.

3–4. Distinguish between:
  a. Expenditure and Encumbrance.
  b. Revenues and Estimated Revenues.
  c. Reserve for Encumbrances and Encumbrances.
  d. Reserve for Encumbrances and Fund Balance.
  e. Appropriations and Expenditures.
  f. Expenditure and Expense.

3–5. Explain the potential usefulness of each of the following expenditure classification categories:
  a. By function or program.
  b. By organization unit.
  c. By activity.
  d. By character.
  e. By object.

3–6. On a sheet of paper list the letters (*a*) through (*j*) corresponding to the expenditure items listed below. Beside each letter indicate whether the expenditure item should be classified as a function, program, organization unit, activity, character, or object.
  a. County Treasurer's Office.
  b. Welfare.
  c. Solid waste disposal—landfill.
  d. Accident investigation.
  e. Supplies.
  f. Debt service.
  g. Environmental protection.
  h. Health.
  i. Department of Health.
  j. Personal services.

3–7. On a sheet of paper list the letters (*a*) through (*j*) corresponding to the revenue items listed below. Beside each letter state whether the item should be classified as Taxes, Licenses and Permits, Intergovernmental Revenue, Charges for Services, Fines and Forfeits, or Miscellaneous Revenue.
  a. Sales taxes levied by the governmental units.
  b. Receipts from county in payment for rural library service.
  c. Dog licenses.
  d. Traffic violation penalties.

      e. Federal grant for housing rehabilitation.

      f. Royalties from oil wells on city property.

      g. Charges for solid waste collection and disposal.

      h. Plumbers' registration fees.

      i. City's share of state severance tax.

      j. Charges for pumping basements.

3–8. Define *nonexchange transactions* as discussed in GASB's proposed changes in revenue recognition and describe the four classes of nonexchange transactions. Give an example of each class.

3–9. Why do GASB standards specify that the amounts in the Actual column of a budgetary comparison statement be reported on the basis required by law for budget preparation—even if that basis differs from GAAP?

3–10. Is there any necessity for a governmental unit to use the same expenditure classification system in its General Fund accounting system as in its budget? Why or why not?

3–11. If Estimated Revenues and Estimated Other Financing Sources exceed Appropriations and Estimated Other Financing Uses when the budget of a special revenue fund is recorded, would you expect the balance of Fund Balance to increase, or to decrease, with respect to the balance displayed in the balance sheet of the special revenue fund prepared as of the end of the year preceding the budget year? Explain your answer.

3–12. Explain how legislative appropriations and the use of encumbrance accounting procedures achieve control over governmental fund expenditures. Do budgetary control procedures assure sound financial management? Why or why not?

3–13. Explain how expenditure and revenue classifications for public school systems differ from those for state and local governments.

Cases

3–1. Sara Smith, Chief Accountant for the Town of Woolridge, has several years of experience in corporate accounting, but only recently began her current position. Sara found the manner in which the Town had previously used budgetary accounts to achieve budgetary control as being confusing and stated her opinion that "there are too many accounts to keep up with." Accordingly, for the current year, she prepared a "budgetary spreadsheet" that lists all budgeted revenues and appropriations for the year. Sara explained to the Town Administrator that her budgetary accounting procedures are much simpler than those previously used and will work just as well. At the end of the fiscal year, she will simply compare actual revenues and expenditures to the budgeted amounts and then manually prepare the required Statement of Revenues, Expenditures, and Changes in Fund Balances—Budget and Actual.

Required

Evaluate the appropriateness of the Chief Accountant's new budgetary accounting procedures. Do these procedures conform to GAAP?

3–2. The City of Belmont utilizes a 10-digit account number as part of its computerized accounting system. Its 10-digit account number is organized as follows:

XX-XX-XX-XXXX

The first two positions represent a particular fund or account group, the second two positions represent the organization unit (for example, department), the third two positions represent organization subunit, and the final four positions represent either object class for an expenditure entry or source class for a revenue transaction. (These four positions are also used to represent other transactions such as fixed assets, long-term liabilities, and other financing sources and uses.) Among the several ledgers in the City's accounting system are a general ledger for proprietary accounts, a budget ledger for budgetary accounts, and an encumbrances ledger. There are no subsidiary ledgers per se. Rather, the first two positions of the final four positions in the account number represent a major expenditure/expense or revenue category. For example, the following accounts are found in the City of Belmont's general ledger for the General Fund, Street Department, Supplies and Maintenance (01 represents General Fund, 08 represents Street Department, 0200 represents Supplies, and 0300 represents Maintenance).

Account Number	Account Description
01-08-00-0210	Chemical Supplies
01-08-00-0220	Clothing Supplies
01-08-00-0260	General Office Supplies
01-08-00-0270	Janitorial Supplies
01-08-00-0285	Fuel and Vehicle Supplies
01-08-00-0290	Other Supplies
01-08-00-0302	Building Maintenance
01-08-00-0304	Street Maintenance
01-08-00-0306	Sidewalk Maintenance
01-08-00-0307	Street Sweeping

These same account numbers are utilized in the general ledger, the budget ledger, and the encumbrances ledger, as appropriate. Actual revenues and expenditures are posted from a general journal or special journals to the general ledger accounts, budgeted estimated revenues and appropriations are posted to the budget ledger, and purchase orders placed for goods are posted to the encumbrances ledger.

Required

    a. Discuss whether a system such as that used by the City of Belmont, which does not use the system of general ledger control accounts and subsidiary ledgers discussed in Chapter 3, can achieve the desired level of budgetary control over revenues and expenditures.

    b. What improvements would you recommend in the City of Belmont's system?

3-3. In auditing the Town of Appleton you become aware that the Town's accounting procedures for property taxes may not be in conformity with GAAP. This is the first year Appleton has engaged your firm as auditor. Consistent with options allowed under state law, Appleton levies taxes in December. These taxes are due in two equal installments on January 31 and July 31. The fiscal year ends on June 30. The Town Controller has for several years recorded the total levy as revenues in the fiscal year of the levy. The Controller argues that since the second installment is receivable within 60 days of fiscal year-end, it is properly recognized as revenues of the current fiscal year. Based on audits of other municipalities located in the same state as Appleton, you know that in the same circumstances your previous clients recorded the second installment of the current year levy as deferred revenue in the year of the levy and as revenue of the following year. You believe that if the second installment is not legally due until the next fiscal year, it cannot be recognized as a revenue of the current period. The Controller is strongly opposed to changing the accounting procedures for these taxes.

Required

    a. Who is correct in this situation, you or the client? Explain your answer fully. Base your response on analysis of applicable GASB standards.

    b. Assuming that the two property tax installments are due on March 31 and September 30, and the levy date and fiscal year-end are unchanged, what effect would this have on the recognition of revenue for the second installment of property taxes? Explain fully.

Exercises and Problems

3–1. Utilizing the CAFR obtained for Exercise 1–1, review the combined, combining, and individual governmental fund financial statements and related data. Note particularly the items suggested below:

    a. **Combined Statement of Revenues, Expenditures, and Changes in Fund Balances—All Governmental Fund Types and Discretely Presented Component Units.**

        (1) **Revenues and Other Financing Sources.** What system of classification of revenues is used in the combined, combining, and individual fund statements? Do the major classes used agree with the source classes listed in Chapter 3? If there are differences, are they minor differences of terminology, or major differences in system of classification? Are transfers, proceeds of debt issues, and assets acquired under capital lease agreements identified as described in Chapter 3?

            List the three most important sources of General Fund revenues, and list the most important source of revenue of each special revenue fund. Is the reporting entity dependent upon any single source for as much as one-third of its General Fund revenue? What proportion of revenues is derived from property taxes? Do the notes clearly indicate recognition criteria for primary revenue sources? Do the notes disclose details of the property tax calendar, including lien dates, levy (assessment) dates, due dates, and collection dates?

            Are charts, graphs, or tables included that show the changes over time in reliance on each revenue source? Is the proper distinction made between operating transfers in and equity transfers in? Are operating transfers in reported in the same section of the statement as the revenues, or are they reported in an Other Financing Sources (Uses) section following the Expenditures section? Are proceeds of debt issues, and general fixed assets acquired under capital lease agreements, if any, reported in the same section as operating transfers in? Are equity transfers in reported in the Changes in Fund Balances section of the statement?

(2) **Expenditures and Other Financing Uses.** What system of classification of expenditures is used in the combined, combining, and individual fund statements? If the system of classification is not one discussed in Chapter 3, does it appear to be more or less informative than any of those discussed in the chapter? Are operating transfers out shown in the same section of the statement as expenditures, or are they reported in an Other Financing Sources (Uses) section following the Expenditures section? Are equity transfers out reported in the Changes in Fund Balances section of the statement? List the three categories that caused the largest General Fund expenditures; list the category of the largest expenditure of each of the special revenue funds.

Does the report contain, perhaps in the Introductory Section, any information that would enable the reader to determine what results were achieved for the expenditures?

Are charts, tables, or graphs presented to show the trend of General Fund expenditures, by category, for a period of 10 years? Is expenditure data related to population of the governmental unit, square miles within the governmental unit, or workload statistics (such as tons of solid waste removed and number of miles of street constructed)?

b. **Combined Statement of Revenues, Expenditures, and Changes in Fund Balances—Budget and Actual—General and Special Revenue Fund Types of the Primary Government.**

Note: In addition to reading Chapter 3, read the following before analyzing the budgetary comparisons in the CAFR you are using: The Budget versus Actual statement should include budgetary comparisons for the General Fund, the special revenue fund type, and *all other* fund types for which annual budgets have been legally adopted. The budgets adopted by the reporting entity whose CAFR you are reviewing may differ from the GAAP reporting model as to *basis, timing, perspective,* and *entity.* GASB standards define these differences as:

Basis differences arise through the employment of a basis of accounting for budgetary purposes that differs from the basis of accounting applicable to the fund type when reporting on the operations in accordance with GAAP.

Timing differences that can result in significant variances between budgetary practices and GAAP may include continuing appropriations, project appropriations, automatic reappropriations, and biennial budgeting.

Perspective differences result from the structure of financial information for budgetary purposes. The perspectives used for budgetary purposes include fund structure, organizational structure, or program structure. Additionally, some subsidiary perspective, such as nature of revenue source, special projects, or capital and operating budgets, may also be used. The fund structure and individual fund definitions establish which assets, liabilities, equities, and revenue and expenditure/expense flows are accounted for in a fund. In the traditional view, budgeting, accounting, financial reporting, and auditing would follow the fund perspective.

Entity differences are the fourth possible type of difference. Frequently, an "appropriated budget" may either include or exclude organizations, programs, activities, and functions that may or may not be compatible with the criteria defining the governmental reporting entity.

Actual data presented in budgetary comparison statements should be prepared on the same basis as the budgetary data (which may include encumbrances along with expenditures). If basis, timing, perspective, or entity differences exist between budgetary data and actual data reported in conformity with GAAP, the "actual" data reported in the budgetary comparison statement should be reconciled with the actual data reported in conformity with GAAP; the reconciliation may be made as a part of the budgetary comparison statement or in the Notes to the Financial Statements. If the data reported in the Actual column of the budgetary comparison statement are not in conformity with GAAP, the heading of the statement should make clear that the data are "Non-GAAP."

Questions:

Are any fund types in addition to the General Fund and special revenue funds included in the budgetary comparison statement? If so, list the additional fund types included and attempt to determine whether the inclusion is mandated by state law, local ordinance, or custom.

Is the budgetary comparison presented only in the GPFS (the Combined Statement of Revenues, Expenditures, and Changes in Fund Balances—Budget and Actual), or are there also budgetary comparisons in the combining statements for each fund type, and budgetary comparisons in the individual fund statements? Do budgetary comparison statements show only the budget as originally enacted, the original budget plus or minus budget amendments made during the year, or only the budget as it existed at balance sheet date; or is the report unclear as to which budget is presented? If amendments to the budget are not shown in the financial statement are they shown in the Notes to the Financial Statements, or elsewhere in the CAFR? Is the legal procedure for budget adoption and budget amendment explained in the Notes or elsewhere in the CAFR?

Do the Notes state whether or not appropriations lapse at year-end? Do the Notes disclose the level of control for each budget for which data are presented (the level at which expenditures may not legally exceed appropriations)?

Are the amounts in the Actual column clearly labeled (either in the heading of the statement or in the column heading) as being on the budgetary basis, or does the statement disclose that the budget is on the GAAP basis, or are the bases unclear? Are differences between budgeted amounts and actual amounts shown only in dollars, or are percentage differences shown? Is there any explanation in the Notes to the Financial Statements, the Introductory Section, or elsewhere in the CAFR, of material differences between budget and actual?

If the budget differs from the GAAP reporting model as to *basis, timing, perspective,* or *entity,* are the amounts in the Actual column reconciled with the amounts reported in the Combined Statement of Revenues, Expenditures, and

Changes in Fund Balances (the statement you analyzed in part *a* of this Exercise)? One element that often appears in the reconciliation of Actual on the budgetary basis to Actual on the GAAP basis relates to the fact that encumbrances outstanding at year-end should not be considered as expenditures in GAAP-based statements, but should be added to expenditures in the Actual column of the budgetary comparison statement (unless, by law, encumbrances lapse at year-end). Also, expenditures made during one year that were authorized by appropriations (sometimes called *budgetary expenditures*) of a preceding year may not be distinguished in the GAAP basis statement from expenditures during the year authorized by appropriations for that year; whereas "actual" expenditures reported in the budgetary comparison statement should be only those authorized for the year for which the statement is prepared. Are these and other reconciling items disclosed within the budgetary comparison statement, within the Notes to the Financial Statements, or elsewhere in the CAFR? Is the reconciliation clear and understandable to you, or is it merely confusing?

Do all blended component units use the same budgetary practices as the primary government of the reporting entity? Does the CAFR state this explicitly, or does it indicate that budgetary practices differ by disclosures in the headings of statements, the headings of columns within statements, or by narrative and schedules within the Notes to the Financial Statements?

3–2. Write the numbers 1 through 10 on a sheet of paper. Beside each number write the letter corresponding with the best answer to each of the following questions.

1. Which of the following is *not* a budgetary account?
   a. Appropriations.
   b. Encumbrances.
   c. Reserve for Encumbrances.
   d. Estimated Revenues.

2. Which of the following terms refers to an actual cost rather than an estimate?
   a. Expenditure.
   b. Appropriation.
   c. Budget.
   d. Encumbrance.

3. Which of the following steps in the acquisition of goods and services occurs first?
   a. Appropriation.
   b. Encumbrance.
   c. Disbursement.
   d. Expenditure.

4. An Expenditures account appears in:
   a. The General Fixed Assets Account Group.
   b. The General Long-Term Debt Account Group.
   c. A special revenue fund.
   d. An internal service fund.

5. The Appropriations Control account of a governmental unit is debited when:
   a. Supplies are purchased.
   b. Expenditures are recorded.
   c. The budgetary accounts are closed.
   d. The budget is recorded.

6. Equipment repairs that have been made for a governmental unit, and for which a bill has been received, should be recorded in the General Fund as a debit to an:
   a. Expenditure.
   b. Encumbrance.
   c. Expense.
   d. Appropriation.

7. The City of Hinton incurred $150,000 of salaries and wages for the month ended May 31, 2000. To record this transaction the City of Hinton should debit:
   a. Encumbrances.
   b. Expenditures.
   c. Reserve for Encumbrances.
   d. Both Expenditures and Reserve for Encumbrances.

8. The following balances are included in the subsidiary records of Burwood Village's Parks and Recreation Department at March 31, 2000:

Appropriations—Supplies	$7,500
Expenditures—Supplies	4,500
Encumbrances—Supplies Orders	750

   How much does the Parks and Recreation Department have available for additional purchases of supplies?
   a. $0.
   b. $2,250.
   c. $3,000.
   d. $6,750.

9. The Board of Commissioners of the City of Fulton adopted its budget for the year ending July 31, 2000, which indicated revenues of $1,000,000 and appropriations of $900,000. If the budget is formally integrated into the accounting records, what is the required journal entry?

	Debits	Credits
a. Memorandum entry only		
b. Appropriations	900,000	
General Fund	100,000	
Estimated Revenues		1,000,000
c. Estimated Revenues	1,000,000	
Appropriations		900,000
Fund Balance		100,000
d. Revenues Receivable	1,000,000	
Expenditures Payable		900,000
Fund Balance		100,000

10. Which of the following will decrease the Fund Balance of a governmental unit at the end of the fiscal year?
    a. Appropriations are more than Expenditures and Reserve for Encumbrances—Prior Year.
    b. Appropriations are less than Expenditures and Encumbrances.
    c. Appropriations are more than Estimated Revenues.
    d. Appropriations are more than Expenditures and Encumbrances.

(AICPA. adapted)

3–3. King City has budgeted the following General Fund revenues and appropriations for the fiscal year 1999.

Estimated Revenues:	
Taxes	$6,000,000
Licenses and Permits	1,200,000
Fines and Forfeits	400,000
Intergovernmental Revenues	2,000,000
Total Estimated Revenues	$9,600,000
Appropriations:	
General Administration	$1,700,000
Police	2,000,000
Fire	2,300,000
Health and Welfare	1,800,000
Public Works	1,900,000
Total Appropriations	$9,700,000

a. Assuming a reasonably responsible level of financial management, what is the minimum figure the administration of King City expects to have as the General Fund Fund Balance at the conclusion of fiscal year 1998? Explain.
b. Show in general journal form the entry, or entries, that would be necessary to record the budget, assuming it is legally approved, at the beginning of the budget year, 1999. Show entries in subsidiary ledger accounts as well as general ledger accounts.

3–4. Assume that King City's (Problem 3–3) General Fund received revenues in cash from the following sources during the first month of 1999:

Licenses and Permits	$100,000
Fines and Forfeits	30,000
Intergovernmental Revenues	300,000
Total	$430,000

a. Show the necessary entry in general journal form to record the revenue received. (Show entries in subsidiary ledger accounts as well as in general ledger accounts.)

b. Compute how much revenue King City expects to realize from Licenses and Permits in the remainder of 1999. Does the amount appear reasonable, considering that there are 11 months remaining in 1999?

3–5. Assume purchase orders and contracts in the following estimated amounts were issued by King City (Problem 3–3), chargeable against the 1999 appropriations shown below:

General Administration	$100,000
Police	180,000
Fire	200,000
Public Works	135,000
Total	$615,000

a. Show the necessary entry in general journal form to record the issuance of purchase orders and contracts. (Show entries in subsidiary ledger accounts as well as general ledger accounts.)
b. Explain why GASB standards for state and local governmental units require that the estimated amount of purchase orders issued be recorded in the accounts of governmental fund types, whereas FASB standards for business organizations do not have a similar requirement.

3–6. Assume that purchase orders and contracts issued by King City (see Problem 3–5 for the estimated liability for goods and services ordered) have now been filled and the actual liability of the General Fund is chargeable to the 1999 appropriations as follows:

General Administration	$101,000
Police	180,000
Fire	200,000
Public Works	140,000
Total	$621,000

a. Show the necessary entry or entries in general journal form to record the fact that the purchase orders and contracts have been filled and vouchers payable have been issued in the amount of $621,000.
b. Assuming that King City does not encumber appropriations for salaries of Police Department employees, show the entry needed to record the issuance of vouchers in the amount of $150,000 for salaries chargeable to the Police appropriation.
c. Compute the amount of the Police appropriation available for use during the remainder of 1999, using data given in Problems 3–3, 3–5, and 3–6 as needed.
d. Under what circumstances would you expect a governmental unit to encumber appropriations for wages?

3–7. The common council of the City of Dexter adopted for the City General Fund a budget that is shown below in summary form:

Estimated Revenues:	
Taxes	$11,420,000
Licenses and Permits	2,740,000
Fines and Forfeits	3,790,000
Intergovernmental Revenue	3,010,000
Charges for Services	2,400,000
Total Estimated Revenues	$23,360,000
Appropriations:	
Personal Services	$10,540,000
Contractual Services	2,560,000
Commodities	5,435,000
Capital Outlays	4,639,000
Total Appropriations	$23,174,000

a. Assume that the City of Dexter employs a system of quarterly allotments to enhance expenditure control. Show in general journal form the entry to record the complete budget as of January 1, the first day of the fiscal year, in general ledger and subsidiary ledger accounts.

b. Assume allotments for the first quarter were as follows; make the journal entry as of January 1 to record the allotments in general ledger and subsidiary ledger accounts. Show subsidiary ledger accounts for both unallotted appropriations and allotments.

Personal Services	$2,660,000
Contractual Services	640,000
Commodities	1,350,000
Capital Outlays	1,400,000
Total	$6,050,000

3–8. The printout of the Estimated Revenues and Revenues subsidiary ledger accounts for the General Fund of the City of Salem as of February 28, 2000 appeared as follows:

Property Taxes

Date	Tracer	Estimated Revenues	Revenues	Balance
01 01	45 1	9,600,000		9,600,000
02 28	45 6	(20,000)	9,580,000	–0–

Licenses and Permits

Date	Tracer	Estimated Revenues	Revenues	Balance
01 01	45 1	1,600,000		1,600,000
01 31	27 4		640,000	960,000
02 27	27 7		200,000	760,000

Intergovernmental Revenue

Date	Tracer	Estimated Revenues	Revenues	Balance
01 01	45 1	3,200,000		3,200,000
02 28	27 7		1,500,000	1,700,000

Charges for Services

Date	Tracer	Estimated Revenues	Revenues	Balance
01 01	45 1	600,000		600,000
02 28	27 7		160,000	440,000

Assuming the above printout is correct in all details and that there are no other General Fund revenue classifications, you are to answer the following questions. *Show all necessary computations in good form.*

a. What should be the balance of the Estimated Revenues control account?

b. What was the original approved budget for Estimated Revenues for 2000?

c. (1) Was the FY2000 Estimated Revenues budget adjusted during the year?
   (2) If so, when?
   (3) If so, how much?
   (4) If so, was the original budget increased or decreased?

d. What should be the balance of the Revenues control account?

e. If in the Tracer column of the accounts the numerals 45 stand for General Journal and the numerals 27 stand for Cash Receipts Journal, what is the most likely reason that revenues from Property Taxes are first recognized in a general journal entry, whereas revenues from the other three sources are first recognized in cash receipts journal entries?

3–9. The Director of Finance of the Town of Liberty has asked you to determine whether the appropriation, expenditures, and encumbrances comparison for Office Supplies for a certain year (reproduced below) presents the information correctly.

You determine that the General Fund manual of accounts describes Office Supplies as "tangible items of relatively short life to be used in a business office." You also determine that the transfer of stationery, at cost, to the Town water utility was properly authorized; the Water Utility Fund is to pay the General Fund $330 for the supplies. The transfer of $46,000 from Office Supplies to Personal Services was made by an accounting clerk without knowledge of superiors to avoid reporting that the Personal Services appropriation had been overexpended.

In order to determine whether the comparison shown below is correct you are required to compute each of the following. Organize and label your computations so the Director of Finance can understand them.

a. The final amended amount of the appropriation for Office Supplies for the year.

b. The valid amount of encumbrances outstanding against this appropriation at the end of the year.

c. The net amount of expenditures made during the year that were properly chargeable to this appropriation.

d. The unencumbered unexpended balance of this appropriation.

TOWN OF LIBERTY
General Fund
Appropriation, Expenditures, and Encumbrances
Office Supplies

Purchase No.	Explanation	Appropriations	Encumbrances		Expenditures	Available Balance
			Debits	Credits		
	Budget legally approved	62,200				62,200
350	Purchase order—computer paper		600			61,600
356	Purchase order—stationery			420		62,020
	Refund of prior year expenditure	30				62,050
370	Purchase order—filing supplies		400			61,650
350	Invoice			605	605	61,045
378	Purchase order—microcomputer		3,160			57,885
380	Contract for washing office windows		2,000			55,885
356	Invoice			420	420	55,885
	Cost of stationery issued to Town water utility	330				56,215
	Refund on P.O. 350	10				56,225
370	Invoice			400	425	55,800
380	Invoice				2,000	53,000
385	Purchase order—furniture		7,000			46,000
	Transfer to Personal Services appropriation	(46,000)				–0–

Continuous Problem

3–L. The following budget for the General Fund of the City of Bingham (see Problem 2–L) was legally adopted for the fiscal year ending June 30, 2000.

Estimated Revenues:	
Property Taxes	$3,104,000
Interest and Penalties on Taxes	29,000
Licenses and Permits	443,000
Fines and Forfeits	376,000
Intergovernmental Revenue	531,000
Charges for Services	110,000
Miscellaneous Revenues	70,000
Total Estimated Revenues	$4,663,000
Appropriations:	
General Government	$ 780,000
Public Safety	1,650,000
Public Works	710,000
Health	200,000
Public Welfare	250,000
Recreation	375,000
Contributions to Retirement Funds	344,000
Miscellaneous Appropriations	66,000
Total Appropriations	$4,375,000

Required

a. Record the budget in the general journal. Include the general ledger accounts, subsidiary ledger accounts, and adequate explanations for each entry (and for all journal entries in all L problems).

b. Post the entries to *general ledger* accounts.

c. (1) Open *revenues ledger* accounts for the seven sources of Estimated Revenues listed in the budget for the City of Bingham General Fund. (An appropriate form is illustrated in Chapter 3.) Allow five lines for each account.

   (2) Post to the appropriate revenues ledger accounts the amounts shown in the general journal entry.

d. (1) Open *appropriations ledger* accounts for the eight classifications of appropriations shown in the budget for the General Fund. (An appropriate form is illustrated in Chapter 3.) Allow 10 lines for each account.

   (2) Post the amounts shown in the general journal entry to the proper accounts in the appropriations ledger.

General Funds and Special Revenue Funds— Illustrative Transactions and Financial Statements

Learning Objectives

After studying this chapter, you should be able to:

~ Recognize typical operating transactions for the General Fund and special revenue funds and be able to prepare appropriate journal entries.

~ Distinguish between the form and content of interim financial statements and year-end financial statements.

~ Prepare adjusting entries, including reclassification of property taxes to delinquent status, accrual of interest and penalties for property taxes, and adjustment for inventories.

~ Account for expenditures for goods encumbered in the prior year.

~ Prepare a pre-closing trial balance.

~ Prepare closing journal entries.

~ Account for certain special revenue fund transactions and explain accounting and financial reporting for these funds.

In Chapter 3, the use of general ledger budgetary control accounts (Estimated Revenues, Estimated Other Financing Sources, Appropriations, Estimated Other Financing Uses, and Encumbrances) and related operating statement accounts (Revenues, Other Financing Sources, Expenditures, and Other Financing Uses) was discussed and illustrated. The necessity for subsidiary ledgers, or equivalent computer files or ledgers, supporting the budgetary control accounts and related operating statement accounts was also discussed. In this chapter, common transactions and events in the operation of the General Fund of a hypothetical local governmental unit, the Town of Brighton, are discussed, and appropriate accounting entries and financial statements are illustrated. For the sake of completeness, entries in subsidiary ledger accounts as well as in general ledger accounts are illustrated. The accounting structure illustrated in this chapter is entirely applicable to special revenue funds of state and local governmental units as well to the General Fund.

Illustrative Case

Assume at the end of a fiscal year, 1999, the Balance Sheet shown on the next page is presented for the General Fund of the Town of Brighton.

Flow of Current Financial Resources Focus

Notice that the assets of the General Fund of the Town of Brighton illustrate the flow of current financial resources measurement focus prescribed by GASB standards for all governmental funds. Current financial resources include prepaid items and supplies inventories, if material, and marketable investments, as well as cash and receivables. Land, buildings, and equipment utilized in governmental fund operations are not accounted for by governmental funds because they are not financial resources, as defined by the GASB. Fixed assets used in governmental fund operations are accounted for by the General Fixed Assets Account Group (GFAAG), discussed in Chapter 5.

The arithmetic difference between total financial resources and total liabilities of the fund is the **Fund Equity**. Residents have no legal claim on any excess of liquid assets over current liabilities; therefore, the Fund Equity is not analogous to the Stockholders' Equity of an investor-owned entity. The Town of Brighton's General Fund Balance Sheet illustrates that at December 31, 1999, a portion of Fund Equity is *reserved* because not all of the purchase orders issued in fiscal year 1999 were filled by the end of that year. The liability that will result when goods or services are received in fulfillment of purchase orders outstanding on December 31, 1999, is estimated to total $127,000, as shown by the Reserve for Encumbrances—1999 in the Balance Sheet illustrated below. The portion of Fund Equity not reserved is shown as Fund Balance in the Balance Sheet illustrated. An alternate and more descriptive designation would be "Available for Appropriation" because this amount ($272,900 in the Town of Brighton General Fund Balance Sheet) is the excess of financial resources over actual liabilities and amounts expected to become liabilities when goods and services on order at the balance sheet date are received.

TOWN OF BRIGHTON
General Fund Balance Sheet
As of December 31, 1999

Assets

Cash		$190,000
Taxes receivable—delinquent	$660,000	
Less: Estimated uncollectible delinquent taxes	50,000	610,000
Interest and penalties receivable on taxes	13,200	
Less: Estimated uncollectible interest and penalties	3,300	9,900
Total Assets		$809,900

Liabilities and Fund Equity

Liabilities:		
Vouchers payable	$320,000	
Due to federal government	90,000	
Total Liabilities		$410,000
Fund Equity:		
Reserve for encumbrances—1999	127,000	
Fund balance	272,900	
Total Fund Equity		399,900
Total Liabilities and Fund Equity		$809,900

Recording the Budget

As discussed in detail in Chapter 3, the budget should be recorded in the accounts of each fund for which a budget is legally adopted. Entry 1, below, illustrates an entry to record the budget for the General Fund of the Town of Brighton for fiscal year 2000. (The entry is shown in combined form to illustrate that format. The detail shown is assumed to be the detail needed to comply with laws applicable to the Town of Brighton. Since both Estimated Revenues and Appropriations accounts refer only to the fiscal year 2000 budget and will be closed at the end of the year, it is not necessary to incorporate "2000" in the title of either.)

	General Ledger		Subsidiary Ledger	
	Debits	Credits	Debits	Credits
1. Estimated Revenues..................	3,986,000			
Fund Balance.......................	194,000			
Appropriations..................		4,180,000		
Revenues Ledger:				
Property Taxes.....................			2,600,000	
Interest and Penalties on Delinquent				
Taxes			13,000	
Sales Taxes.........................			480,000	
Licenses and Permits.................			220,000	
Fines and Forfeits....................			308,000	
Intergovernmental Revenue			280,000	
Charges for Services			70,000	
Miscellaneous Revenues			15,000	

	General Ledger		Subsidiary Ledger	
	Debits	*Credits*	*Debits*	*Credits*
Appropriations Ledger:				
General Government				660,000
Public Safety				1,240,000
Public Works				910,000
Health and Welfare				860,000
Parks and Recreation				315,000
Contributions to Retirement and Other Postemployment Benefits Plans				180,000
Miscellaneous Appropriations				15,000

**Tax Anticipation
Notes Payable**

In the December 31, 1999, Balance Sheet of the Town of Brighton, two items, Vouchers Payable and Due to Federal Government, are current liabilities. Assuming there will be a need to pay these in full within 30 days after the date of the Balance Sheet, the Town Treasurer will be forced to do some cash forecasting because the balance of Cash is not large enough to pay the $410,000 debt. In addition to this immediate problem, the Treasurer, and most governmental treasurers, face the problem that cash disbursements during a fiscal year tend to be approximately level month by month, whereas cash receipts from major revenue sources are concentrated in just a few months. For example, property tax collections are concentrated in two separate months, such as May and November, when the installments are due; collections by a local government from the state or federal governments of revenues collected by superior jurisdictions for distribution to a local government are also usually concentrated in one or two months of the year. Therefore, the Treasurer of the Town of Brighton may forecast the need to disburse approximately one-fourth of the budgeted appropriations before major items of revenue are received; one-fourth of $4,180,000 is $1,045,000. This amount plus current liabilities at the beginning of the year, $410,000, equals $1,455,000 expected cash disbursements in the period for which the forecast is made. Experience may indicate that a conservative forecast of collections of delinquent taxes and interest and penalties thereon during the forecast period will amount to $425,000. Further, assume the Treasurer's review of the items in the Estimated Revenues budget indicates that at least $140,000 will be collected in the forecast period. Therefore, total cash available to meet the $1,455,000 disbursements is $755,000 ($190,000 cash as of the beginning of the period, plus the $425,000 and $140,000 items just described), leaving a deficiency of $700,000 to be met by borrowing. The taxing power of the government is ample security for short-term debt; local banks customarily meet the working capital needs of a governmental unit by accepting a **tax anticipation note** from the unit. Additional discussion of cash budgeting is provided in Chapter 15. If the amount of $700,000 is borrowed at this time, the necessary entry is:

(TANs)

	General Ledger		Subsidiary Ledger	
	Debits	*Credits*	*Debits*	*Credits*
2. Cash	700,000			
Tax Anticipation Notes Payable. . .		700,000		

Encumbrance Entry

Purchase orders for materials and supplies were issued in the total amount of $306,450; amounts chargeable against the appropriations for fiscal year 2000 are shown as debits to Encumbrance Ledger accounts. The entry to record the encumbrance for the purchase orders is (since some encumbrance documents issued in 2000 will likely not be filled until the following year, it is convenient to incorporate "2000" in each general ledger account title):

	General Ledger		Subsidiary Ledger	
3. Encumbrances—2000	306,450			
Reserve for				
Encumbrances—2000		306,450		
Encumbrances Ledger:				
General Government.			28,000	
Public Safety.			72,000	
Public Works			160,000	
Parks and Recreation			36,000	
Health and Welfare			10,000	
Miscellaneous Appropriations			450	

Payment of Liabilities as Recorded

Checks were drawn to pay the vouchers payable and the amount due to the federal government as of the end of 1999:

	General Ledger		Subsidiary Ledger	
4. Vouchers Payable	320,000			
Due to Federal Government	90,000			
Cash		410,000		

Notice it is not necessary in the above entry to know what appropriations were affected at the time goods and services giving rise to the liabilities were received, because under the accrual concept, the appropriations were considered expended in 1999 when the goods and services were received.

Payrolls and Payroll Taxes

The gross pay of employees of General Fund departments amounted to $840,000. The Town does not use the encumbrance procedure for payrolls. Deductions from gross pay for the period amount to $72,232 for employees' share of FICA social security and Medicare tax; $84,000 for employees' federal withholding tax; and $16,800 for employees' state withholding tax—the first two will, of course, have to be remitted by the Town to the federal government, and the last item will have to be remitted to the state government. The gross pay is chargeable to the appropriations as indicated by the Expenditures Ledger debits. Assuming the liability for net pay is vouchered, the entry is:

	General Ledger		Subsidiary Ledger	
	Debits	*Credits*	*Debits*	*Credits*
5a. Expenditures—2000	840,000			
Vouchers Payable		666,968		
Due to Federal Government. . . .		156,232		
Due to State Government		16,800		
Expenditures Ledger:				
General Government			116,800	
Public Safety			520,400	
Public Works.			97,200	
Health and Welfare.			63,600	
Parks and Recreation			42,000	

Payment of the vouchers for the net pay results in the following entry:

	General Ledger		Subsidiary Ledger	
5b. Vouchers Payable	666,968			
Cash		666,968		

Inasmuch as the Town is liable for the employer's share of FICA taxes ($72,232) and for contributions to additional retirement plans established by state law (assumed to amount to $18,000 for the pay period ended), it is necessary that the Town's liabilities for its contributions be recorded, as shown in Entry 6. These obligations were provided for in the Appropriations budget under the caption Contributions to Retirement and Other Post-Employment Benefits Plans.

	General Ledger		Subsidiary Ledger	
6. Expenditures—2000	90,232			
Due to Federal Government		72,232		
Due to State Government		18,000		
Expenditures Ledger:				
Contributions to Retirement and				
Other Post-Employment				
Benefits Plans			90,232	

Recording Property Tax Levy

Entry 1 of this chapter shows that the estimated revenue for fiscal year 2000 from property taxes levied for the Town of Brighton General Fund is $2,600,000. If records of property tax collections in recent years, adjusted for any expected changes in tax collection policy and changes in local economic conditions, indicate that approximately 4 percent of the gross tax levy will never be collected, the **gross tax levy** must be large enough so that the collectible portion of the levy, 96 percent, equals the needed revenue from this source, $2,600,000. Therefore, the gross levy of property taxes for the General Fund of the Town of Brighton must be $2,708,333 ($2,600,000 ÷ .96). In an actual situation, property situated in the Town of Brighton also would be taxed for other funds of that Town; for various funds of other general purpose governmental units, such as the township and the county in which the property in the Town of Brighton is located; the various funds of special purpose governmental units that have the right to tax the same property, such as one or more independent school districts or a hospital district; and perhaps the state in which the Town is located.

The gross property tax levies for each fund of the Town of Brighton, and for each other general purpose and special purpose governmental unit, must be aggregated, and the aggregate levy for that unit divided by the assessed valuation of property within the geographical limits of that unit, in order to determine the **tax rate** applicable to property within the unit. In many states, a county official prepares bills for all taxes levied on property within the county; the same official, or another, acts as collector of all property taxes levied for the county and all governmental units within the county. Although the billing and collecting functions may be centralized, the taxes levied for each fund must be recorded as an asset of that fund. If the accounts are to be kept in conformity with generally accepted accounting principles, the portion of the taxes expected to be collectible (.96 of the total levy, in this example) must be recorded as revenues of that fund, and the portion expected to be uncollectible (.04 of the total levy, in this example) recorded in a "contra-asset" account, as illustrated by Entry 7:

	General Ledger		Subsidiary Ledger	
	Debits	Credits	Debits	Credits
7. Taxes Receivable—Current.........	2,708,333			
Estimated Uncollectible Current				
Taxes....................		108,333		
Revenues		2,600,000		
Revenues Ledger:				
Property Taxes				2,600,000

As Entry 7 shows, since the general ledger control account, Revenues, is credited, an entry must also be made in the Revenues subsidiary ledger. Taxes Receivable—Current is also a control account, just as is the Accounts Receivable account of a business entity; each is supported by a subsidiary ledger that shows how much is owed by each taxpayer or customer. Ordinarily, the subsidiary ledger supporting the real property taxes receivable control is organized by parcels of property according to their legal descriptions, since unpaid taxes are liens against the property regardless of changes in ownership. Because of its conceptual similarity to accounting for business receivables, taxes receivable subsidiary ledger accounting is not illustrated in this text.

Recognition of Expenditures for Encumbered Items

When supplies and services ordered during the current year have been received and found to be acceptable, the suppliers' or contractors' invoices should be checked for agreement with purchase orders or contracts as to prices and terms, and for clerical accuracy. If everything is in order, the invoices are approved for payment. If, as is probable, the estimated liability for purchase orders and contracts was recorded in the Encumbrance account and in the appropriate subsidiary accounts, the encumbrance entry must be reversed, and expenditures must be recorded in the control account and appropriate subsidiary accounts in the amount of the actual liability for goods or services received. Assume goods and services ordered during 2000 by departments accounted for by the Town of Brighton General Fund (see Entry 3) are received. Invoices for the items received totaled $269,450; related purchase orders totaled $269,775. (The appropriations assumed to be affected are shown in Entries 8a and 8b.)

	General Ledger		Subsidiary Ledger	
	Debits	*Credits*	*Debits*	*Credits*
8a. Reserve for Encumbrances—2000 . . .	269,775			
Encumbrances—2000		269,775		
Encumbrances Ledger:				
General Government				12,250
Public Safety				72,000
Public Works				150,900
Parks and Recreation				30,000
Health and Welfare				4,175
Miscellaneous Appropriations . . .				450
8b. Expenditures—2000	269,450			
Vouchers Payable		269,450		
Expenditures Ledger:				
General Government			12,300	
Public Safety			72,000	
Public Works			150,600	
Parks and Recreation			30,000	
Health and Welfare			4,100	
Miscellaneous Appropriations			450	

Revenue Recognized on Cash Basis

Revenue from licenses and permits, fines and forfeits, and other sources not previously accrued is recognized on the cash basis. Collections to date in 2000 are assumed to be as shown in Entry 9:

	General Ledger		Subsidiary Ledger	
9. Cash	259,200			
Revenues		259,200		
Revenues Ledger:				
Licenses and Permits				100,000
Fines and Forfeits				151,000
Charges for Services				7,000
Miscellaneous Revenues				1,200

Collection of Delinquent Taxes

Delinquent taxes are subject to interest and penalties that must be paid at the time the tax bill is paid. It is possible for a government to record the amount of penalties at the time the taxes become delinquent. Interest may be computed and recorded periodically to keep the account on the accrual basis; it must also be computed and recorded for the period from the date of last recording to the date when a taxpayer pays delinquent taxes. Assume taxpayers of the Town of Brighton have paid delinquent taxes totaling $440,000, on which interest and penalties of $8,800 had been recorded as receivable at the end of 1999; further assume $600 additional interest was paid for the period from the first day of 2000 to the dates on which the delinquent taxes were paid. Since it is common for the cashier receiving the collections to be permitted to originate source documents that result only in credits to Taxes Receivable—Current, Taxes Receivable—Delinquent, or Interest and Penalties Receivable on Taxes, it is necessary to record the $600 interest earned in 2000 in a separate entry, such as the following:

	General Ledger		Subsidiary Ledger	
	Debits	*Credits*	*Debits*	*Credits*
10a. Interest and Penalties Receivable on Taxes	600			
Revenues		600		
Revenues Ledger:				
Interest and Penalties on Delinquent Taxes..........				600

The collection of delinquent taxes and interest and penalties is summarized in Entry 10b.

10b. Cash...........................	449,400	
Taxes Receivable—Delinquent ..		440,000
Interest and Penalties Receivable on Taxes.................		9,400

Correction of Errors No problems arise in the collection of current taxes if they are collected as billed; the collections are debited to Cash and credited to Taxes Receivable—Current. Sometimes, even in a well-designed and well-operated system, errors occur and must be corrected. If, for example, the assessed valuation of a parcel of property were legally reduced but the tax bill erroneously issued at the higher valuation, the following correcting entry would be made when the error was discovered, assuming the corrected bill to be $364 smaller than the original bill. (The error also caused a slight overstatement of the credit to Estimated Uncollectible Current Taxes in Entry 7, but the error in that account is not considered material and, for that reason, does not require correction.)

11. Revenues	364	
Taxes Receivable—Current		364
Revenues Ledger:		
Property Taxes		364

Postaudit may disclose errors in the recording of expenditures during the current year, or during a prior year. If the error occurred during the current year, the Expenditures account and the proper Expenditures subsidiary account can be debited or credited as needed to correct them. If the error occurred in a prior year, however, the Expenditures account in error has been closed to Fund Balance, so logically the correcting entry should be made to the Fund Balance account. The "all-inclusive income statement" practice that is considered appropriate for profit-seeking entities does not have equal acceptance in governmental accounting because of the greater importance of legal constraints on governmental actions. For example, if a governmental unit collects from a supplier an amount that was erroneously paid in a preceding year, the appropriation for the year of the collection is not increased by the amount collected; it remains as originally budgeted. As a practical matter, collections from suppliers of prior years' overpayments may be budgeted as Miscellaneous Revenues and recorded as credits to the Revenues account.

Interim Financial Statements

Periodically during a year it is desirable to prepare financial statements for the information of administrators and members of the legislative branch of the governmental unit. Illustration 4–1 shows how a Balance Sheet would look for the Town of Brighton if it were prepared in 2000 after the entries numbered 1 through 11 above were made; the date is assumed to be March 31, 2000.

The Interim Balance Sheet, Illustration 4–1, reflects the balances of both proprietary and budgetary accounts. Instead of Assets, which those familiar with accounting for profit-seeking entities would expect, the caption must be Assets and Resources, because the excess of Estimated Revenues over Revenues is not an asset as of balance sheet date but does indicate the amount that will be added to assets when legally budgeted revenues are recognized. Similarly, the caption is not Equities, or Liabilities and Capital, or another title commonly found in financial reports of profit-seeking entities, but Liabilities and Fund Equity. The Liabilities section is consistent with that of profit-seeking entities, but the next section discloses the three subdivisions of the Fund Equity. The first presents the amount appropriated for the year, less the amount of appropriations that have been expended during the year to date, and less the amount of appropriations that have been encumbered by purchase orders and contracts outstanding at balance sheet date; the net is the amount that legally may be expended or encumbered during the remainder of the budget year. In Illustration 4–1 only one item, Reserve for Encumbrances, is shown in the second subdivision. This subdivision discloses the portion of net assets and resources that is not available for appropriation because expected liabilities exist (or because, as discussed later in the Town of Brighton example, certain assets will not be converted into cash in the normal operations of the fund). The remaining subdivision, Fund Balance, discloses that portion of the taxpayers' equity available for appropriation. Accordingly, in financial statement presentation, the word *Unreserved*, or the phrase *Available for Appropriation*, is sometimes used in place of *Fund Balance*. Fund Balance, it should be emphasized, is the excess of the sum of actual assets and budgeted resources over the sum of actual liabilities, available appropriations, and reserves for assets not available for appropriation; in short, it has both proprietary and budgetary aspects.

Interim statements and schedules should be prepared to accompany the interim balance sheet to disclose other information needed by administrators and members of the legislative body; a statement comparing the detail of budgeted and actual revenues is shown as Illustration 4–2, and a statement comparing appropriations, expenditures, and encumbrances in detail is shown as Illustration 4–3. Interim Statements of Revenues, Expenditures, and Changes in Fund Balance are similar to the end-of-the-year statement (Illustration 4–6) on page 122.

Illustration 4–1 Interim Balance Sheet

TOWN OF BRIGHTON
General Fund Balance Sheet
As of March 31, 2000
Assets and Resources

Assets:

Cash		$ 521,632
Taxes receivable—current	$2,707,969	
Less: Estimated uncollectible current taxes	108,333	2,599,636
Taxes receivable—delinquent	220,000	
Less: Estimated uncollectible delinquent taxes	50,000	170,000
Interest and penalties receivable on taxes	4,400	
Less: Estimated uncollectible interest and penalties	3,300	1,100
Total Assets		3,292,368

Resources:

Estimated revenues	3,986,000	
Less: Revenues	2,859,436	1,126,564
Total Assets and Resources		$4,418,932

Liabilities and Fund Equity

Liabilities:

Vouchers payable	$ 269,450	
Due to federal government	228,464	
Due to state government	34,800	
Tax anticipation notes payable	700,000	
Total Liabilities		$1,232,714

Fund Equity:

Appropriations		4,180,000	
Less: Expenditures—2000	$1,199,682		
Encumbrances—2000	36,675	1,236,357	
Available Appropriations		2,943,643	
Reserve for encumbrances—2000		36,675	
Reserve for encumbrances—1999		127,000	
Fund balance		78,900	
Total Fund Equity			3,186,218
Total Liabilities and Fund Equity			$4,418,932

Illustration of Events Subsequent to Date of Interim Statements

Transactions and events such as the collection of revenue and receivables, and the encumbering and expenditure of appropriations, would obviously occur frequently in a governmental unit of any appreciable size. Since entries for the recurring events would be similar to the entries illustrated above, it seems unnecessary to

Illustration 4–2

TOWN OF BRIGHTON
General Fund
Statement of Actual and Estimated Revenues
For the Three Months Ended March 31, 2000

Sources of Revenues	Estimated	Actual	Estimated Revenues Not Yet Realized
Taxes:			
Property taxes	$2,600,000	$2,599,636	$ 364
Interest and penalties on taxes	13,000	600	12,400
Sales taxes	480,000	—	480,000
Total taxes	3,093,000	2,600,236	492,764
Licenses and permits	220,000	100,000	120,000
Fines and forfeits	308,000	151,000	157,000
Intergovernmental revenue	280,000	—	280,000
Charges for services	70,000	7,000	63,000
Miscellaneous revenues	15,000	1,200	13,800
Total General Fund Revenue	$3,986,000	$2,859,436	$1,126,564

Illustration 4–3

TOWN OF BRIGHTON
General Fund
Statement of Budgeted and Actual Expenditures and Encumbrances
For the Three Months Ended March 31, 2000

Function	Appropriations	Expenditures of 2000 Appropriations	Outstanding Encumbrances	Available Appropriations
General government	$ 660,000	$ 129,100	$15,750	$ 515,150
Public safety	1,240,000	592,400	—	647,600
Public works	910,000	247,800	9,100	653,100
Health and welfare	860,000	67,700	5,825	786,475
Parks and recreation	315,000	72,000	6,000	237,000
Contributions to retirement and other postemployment benefits plans	180,000	90,232	—	89,768
Miscellaneous appropriations	15,000	450	—	14,550
Total General Fund	$4,180,000	$1,199,682	$36,675	$2,943,643

present entries for these events in the portion of fiscal year 2000 subsequent to the date of the Interim Balance Sheet shown as Illustration 4–1. Entries for common General Fund transactions and events not previously illustrated are shown in the following sections.

Revision of the Budget

Comparisons of budgeted and actual revenues, by sources, and comparisons of departmental or program appropriations with expenditures and encumbrances, as well as interpretation of information that was not available at the time the budgets were originally adopted, may indicate the desirability or necessity of legally amending the budget during the fiscal year. For example, the Statement of Actual and Estimated Revenues for the three months ended March 31, 2000 (Illustration 4–2), shows that over 70 percent of the revenues budgeted for the General Fund of the Town of Brighton for 2000 have already been realized—almost entirely because revenue from property taxes is recognized on the accrual basis, whereas in this illustrative case revenues from all other sources have been recognized on the cash basis during the three-month period for which entries are illustrated. Consequently, administrators of the Town must review the information shown in Illustration 4–2 and determine whether the budget that was legally approved before the beginning of 2000 appears realistic or whether changes should be made in the Revenues budget in light of current information about local economic conditions; possible changes in state or federal laws relating to grants, entitlements, or shared revenues; or other changes relating to license and permit fees, fines, forfeits, and charges for services. Similarly, revenue collection procedures and revenue recognition policies should be reviewed to determine if changes should be made in the remaining months of the year. Assume the Town of Brighton's General Fund Revenues budget for 2000 has been reviewed as described and the budget is legally amended to reflect that revenues from Charges for Services are expected to be $5,000 more than originally budgeted, and Miscellaneous Revenues are expected to be $10,000 more than originally budgeted; revenues from other sources are not expected to be materially different from the original 2000 budget. Entry 12 records the amendment of the Revenues budget, as well as the amendment of the Appropriations budget, as discussed below.

Information shown in Illustration 4–3 should be reviewed by administrators of the Town of Brighton to determine if the appropriations legally approved before the beginning of 2000 appear realistic in light of expenditures of the 2000 budget incurred in the first three months of 2000 and encumbrances outstanding on March 31 of that year. Illustration 4–3 shows that total cumulative expenditures and outstanding encumbrances exceed 29 percent of the total appropriations by 2000, which can be related to the fact that as of March 31, the year is almost 25 percent over. By function, however, cumulative expenditures and outstanding encumbrances range from 3 percent of the Miscellaneous appropriation to almost 48 percent of the Public Safety appropriation. Therefore, each appropriation should be reviewed carefully in whatever detail is available, in light of current information about expenditures needed to accomplish planned services during the remainder of 2000. Assume the Town of Brighton's General Fund appropriations for 2000 have been reviewed and are legally amended to reflect a $50,000 decrease in the appropriation for Public Works and an $80,000 increase in the appropriation for Public Safety. Entry 12 reflects the legal amendment of appropriations for 2000, as well as the amendment of the Revenues budget. Note the net increase in Appropriations ($30,000) is larger than the net increase in Estimated Revenues ($15,000), requiring a decrease in Fund Balance.

	General Ledger		Subsidiary Ledger	
	Debits	*Credits*	*Debits*	*Credits*
12. Estimated Revenues	15,000			
Fund Balance....................	15,000			
Appropriations		30,000		
Revenues Ledger:				
Charges for Services			5,000	
Miscellaneous Revenues...........			10,000	
Appropriations Ledger:				
Public Works....................			50,000	
Public Safety				80,000

Comparisons of Budget and Actual should be made periodically during each fiscal year. Generally, monthly comparisons are appropriate. In the Town of Brighton case, it is assumed that comparisons subsequent to the ones illustrated disclosed no further need to amend either the Revenues budget or the Appropriations budget for 2000.

Collection of Current Taxes

Collections of property taxes levied in 2000 for the General Fund of the Town of Brighton amount to $2,041,668. Since the revenue was recognized at the time the levy was recorded (see Entry 7), the following entry suffices at this time:

13. Cash	2,041,668	
Taxes Receivable—Current		2,041,668

Repayment of Tax Anticipation Notes

As tax collections begin to exceed current disbursements, it becomes possible for the Town of Brighton to repay the local bank for the money borrowed on tax anticipation notes. Just as borrowing the money did not involve the recognition of revenue, the repayment of the principal is merely the extinguishment of debt of the General Fund and is not an expenditure. Payment of interest, however, must be recognized as the expenditure of an appropriation because it requires a reduction in the net assets of the fund. Assuming the interest to be $13,500, and the amount is properly chargeable to Miscellaneous Appropriations, the entry is:

14. Tax Anticipation Notes Payable.....	700,000	
Expenditures—2000	13,500	
Cash		713,500
Expenditures Ledger:		
Miscellaneous Appropriations		13,500

Procedures of some governmental units would require the interest expenditures to have been recorded as an encumbrance against Miscellaneous

Appropriations at the time the notes were issued, and the liability for the principal and interest to have been vouchered before payment. Even if these procedures were followed by the Town of Brighton, the net result of all entries is achieved by Entry 14.

Encumbrances of Prior Year

As noted under the heading "Flow of Current Financial Resources Focus," purchase orders and other commitment documents issued in 1999 and not filled or canceled by the end of that year total $127,000. This amount is designated as Reserve for Encumbrances—1999 in the December 31, 1999, General Fund Balance Sheet of the Town of Brighton. When the goods or services are received in 2000 their actual cost is considered an Expenditure of the 1999 Appropriations to the extent of the amount encumbered in 1999; any additional amount must be charged to the 2000 Appropriations. The Appropriations account for 1999, however, was closed at the end of that year to Fund Balance, as were the other budgetary accounts for that year. Therefore, when goods or services ordered in 1999 are received in 2000 it is convenient to debit the Expenditures—1999 account when the liability account is credited. When all encumbrance documents outstanding at the end of 1999 have been filled, or canceled, the Expenditures—1999 account is closed to the Reserve for Encumbrances—1999 account, as shown by Entry 21.

Assuming that all goods and services for which encumbrances were outstanding at the end of 1999 were chargeable to the Parks and Recreation appropriation, and that all were received in 2000 at a total invoice cost of $127,250, Entry 15 is necessary. Notice that only the estimated amount, $127,000, may be charged to Expenditures—1999 since this was the amount of the encumbrance against the 1999 appropriation; the difference between the amount encumbered in 1999 and the amount approved for payment in 2000 must be charged against the 2000 appropriation for Parks and Recreation.

	General Ledger		Subsidiary Ledger	
	Debits	*Credits*	*Debits*	*Credits*
15. Expenditures—1999	127,000			
Expenditures—2000	250			
Vouchers Payable		127,250		
Expenditures Ledger:				
Parks and Recreation—1999			127,000	
Parks and Recreation—2000			250	

Interfund Transactions

Water utilities ordinarily provide fire hydrants and water service for fire protection at a flat annual charge. A governmentally owned water utility accounted for by an enterprise fund should be expected to support the cost of its operations by user charges. Fire protection is logically budgeted for as an activity of the fire department, a General Fund department. Assuming the amount charged by the water utility to the General Fund for hydrants and water service is $30,000, and the fire department budget is a part of the Public Safety category in the Town of Brighton example, the General Fund should record its liability as:

	General Ledger		Subsidiary Ledger	
	Debits	*Credits*	*Debits*	*Credits*
16a. Expenditures—2000	30,000			
Due to Other Funds.		30,000		
Expenditures Ledger:				
Public Safety			30,000	

Governmental utility property is not assessed for property tax purposes, but a number of governmental utilities make an annual contribution to the General Fund in recognition of the fact the utility does receive police and fire protection and other services. If the water utility of the Town of Brighton agrees to contribute $25,000 to the General Fund in lieu of taxes, the General Fund entry is:

16b. Due from Other Funds.	25,000			
Revenues		25,000		
Revenues Ledger:				
Miscellaneous Revenues				25,000

Interfund transactions of the nature illustrated by Entries 16a and 16b are called **quasi-external transactions**. That is, transactions that are recognized as revenues and expenditures (or expenses, in the case of proprietary funds) of the funds involved because they would be recognized as revenues and expenditures (or expenses) if the transactions involved organizations external to the governmental unit. In addition to quasi-external transactions, interfund transactions that constitute reimbursements of one fund for expenditures (or expenses) initially recognized by it but that are properly applicable to another fund should be recognized as expenditures (or expenses) by the reimbursing fund and as reductions of the expenditure (or expense) in the fund that is reimbursed. Other types of interfund transactions are classified as transfers, or as interfund loans, and do not, in a strict sense, result in the recognition of revenues, expenditures, or expenses, as explained in Chapter 3.

Adjusting Entries

Physical Inventories.   If a governmental unit is large enough to have sizable inventories of supplies that are used by a number of departments and funds, it is generally recommended that the purchasing function be centralized and the supply activity be accounted for by an internal service fund. For one reason or another, some governments have not created the appropriate internal service fund and account for the supply activity as a part of the General Fund. In either case, accountants would feel better control was provided if perpetual inventory accounts were kept; this procedure is illustrated in Chapter 7. Many small cities, such as the Town of Brighton, not only account for supply activity in the General Fund but do so only on the basis of periodic physical inventories. (If only minor amounts are involved, no accounting records at all may be kept.)

The purchase of supplies must be authorized by an appropriation; therefore, when supplies are received the Expenditures account is debited. If the dollar amount of the physical inventory at the end of a fiscal year is larger than the dollar amount of the inventory at the end of the preceding fiscal year, it is obvious that Expenditures for the year includes the cost of supplies added to inventory. Therefore, the Inventory of Supplies account should be debited and the Expenditures account should be credited for the dollar amount of the increase in physical inventory. (If the dollar amount of the physical inventory at year-end is smaller than the dollar amount of the inventory at the end of the prior year, the Expenditures account should be debited, and the Inventory of Supplies account credited, for the amount of the decrease in inventory.) This procedure is called the **consumption method** of accounting for inventory. Since the inventory will not be converted into cash in the normal operations of a governmental fund, it is not a liquid asset whose carrying cost should be reflected in Fund Balance. Rather, the Inventory account should be offset by a Reserve for Inventory account that is classified for balance sheet purposes in the same manner as discussed for Reserve for Encumbrances under the heading "Interim Financial Statements" in this chapter—both represent elements of Fund Equity not available for appropriation. If a governmental unit uses the consumption method of inventory accounting, the Reserve for Inventory account is credited, and the Fund Balance account is debited, for the increase in the dollar amount of the physical inventory at the time the entries are made in the Inventory and Expenditures accounts. (If the dollar amount of the physical inventory has decreased, Reserve for Inventory should be debited and Fund Balance credited for the amount of the decrease.)

Assuming that the dollar amount of the physical inventory of the Town of Brighton General Fund, as of the end of 2000, is $61,500, and that the inventory at the end of 1999 was such a small amount that it was not recorded, the increase in both the Inventory account and the Reserve for Inventory Account is $61,500. Entry 17 illustrates the consumption method of accounting for inventories (for the sake of simplicity it is assumed that all items in inventory were acquired by expenditure of the Public Works appropriation):

	General Ledger		Subsidiary Ledger	
	Debits	*Credits*	*Debits*	*Credits*
17. Inventory of Supplies	61,500			
Fund Balance.	61,500			
Expenditures—2000		61,500		
Reserve for Inventory				
of Supplies.		61,500		
Expenditures Ledger:				
Public Works.				61,500

An alternative method of accounting for inventories of governmental funds—equally acceptable under present GASB standards—is known as the **purchases method.** Under the purchases method the Expenditures account is *not* credited for the increase in the dollar amount of the physical inventory, nor is the Fund Balance account debited. The only entry required is the debit to the asset account, Inventory, with offsetting credit to the Reserve for Inventory account, for the amount of the increase in the dollar amount of the physical inventory (or the reverse in the event that the dollar amount of the physical inventory decreased).

Write-Off of Uncollectible Delinquent Taxes.   Just as officers of profit-seeking entities should review aged trial balances of receivables periodically in order to determine the adequacy of allowance accounts and authorize the write-off of items judged uncollectible, so should officers of a governmental unit review aged trial balances of taxes receivable and other receivables. Although the levy of property taxes creates a lien against the underlying property in the amount of the tax, accumulated taxes may exceed the market value of the property, or, in the case of personal property, the property may have been removed from the jurisdiction of the governmental unit. When delinquent taxes are deemed uncollectible, the related interest and penalties must also be written off. If the Treasurer of the Town of Brighton receives approval to write off delinquent taxes totaling $26,300 and related interest and penalties of $1,315, the entry would be:

	General Ledger		Subsidiary Ledger	
	Debits	Credits	Debits	Credits
18. Estimated Uncollectible Delinquent Taxes	26,300			
Estimated Uncollectible Interest and Penalties	1,315			
Taxes Receivable—Delinquent. . .		26,300		
Interest and Penalties Receivable on Taxes		1,315		

When delinquent taxes are written off, the tax bills are retained in the files, although no longer subject to general ledger control, because changes in conditions may make it possible to collect the amounts in the future. If collections of written-off taxes are made, it is highly desirable to return the tax bills to general ledger control by making an entry that is the reverse of the write-off entry, so that the procedures described in connection with Entries 10a and 10b may be followed.

Reclassification of Current Taxes.   Assuming all property taxes levied by the Town of Brighton in 2000 were to have been paid before the end of the year, any balance of taxes receivable at year-end is properly classified as **delinquent** rather than *current*. The related allowance for estimated uncollectible taxes should also be transferred to the delinquent classification. An entry to accomplish this, using amounts assumed to exist in the accounts at year-end, is:

19. Taxes Receivable—Delinquent	666,301	
Estimated Uncollectible Current Taxes	108,333	
Taxes Receivable—Current		666,301
Estimated Uncollectible Delinquent Taxes		108,333

Accrual of Interest and Penalties.   Delinquent taxes are subject to interest and penalties, as discussed previously. If the amount of interest and penalties earned in 2000 by the General Fund of the Town of Brighton and not yet recognized is $13,320, but it is expected that only $10,800 of that can be collected, the following entry is necessary:

	General Ledger		Subsidiary Ledger	
	Debits	*Credits*	*Debits*	*Credits*
20. Interest and Penalties Receivable on				
Taxes	13,320			
Estimated Uncollectible Interest				
and Penalties		2,520		
Revenues		10,800		
Revenues Ledger:				
Interest and Penalties on				
Delinquent Taxes				10,800

Pre-Closing Trial Balance

Assuming the illustrated entries for the transactions and events pertaining to the year 2000 for the Town of Brighton have been made and posted, and a number of other entries—not illustrated because they pertain to similar transactions and events—have been made and posted, the trial balance below shows the General Fund general ledger accounts before closing entries:

TOWN OF BRIGHTON
Pre-Closing Trial Balance
As of December 31, 2000

	Debits	Credits
Cash	$ 145,800	
Taxes Receivable—Delinquent	666,300	
Estimated Uncollectible Delinquent Taxes		$ 88,000
Interest and Penalties Receivable on Taxes	3,085	
Estimated Uncollectible Interest and Penalties		1,985
Due from Other Funds	25,000	
Inventory of Supplies	61,500	
Estimated Revenues	4,001,000	
Revenues		4,015,000
Vouchers Payable		396,800
Due to Federal Government		126,520
Due to State Government		39,740
Due to Other Funds		30,000
Expenditures—1999	127,000	
Appropriations		4,210,000
Expenditures—2000	4,069,260	
Encumbrances—2000	70,240	
Reserve for Encumbrances—2000		70,240
Reserve for Encumbrances—1999		127,000
Reserve for Inventory of Supplies		61,500
Fund Balance		2,400
	$9,169,185	$9,169,185

Closing Entries

The essence of the closing process for a governmental fund is the transfer of the balances of the operating statement accounts and the balances of the budgetary accounts for the year to the Fund Balance account. Individual accountants have preferences as to the sequence in which this is done, and as to the combinations of accounts in each closing entry. Any sequence and any combination, however, should yield the same result that closing entries for a profit-seeking entity do: All financial events in the history of the organization are summarized in the balance sheet accounts. This effect is achieved by Entries 21 and 22. Entry 21 is made to close the Expenditures—1999 account and the Reserve for Encumbrances—1999 account since those are the only accounts relating to that year.

	General Ledger		Subsidiary Ledger	
	Debits	*Credits*	*Debits*	*Credits*
21. Reserve for Encumbrances—1999 . . .	127,000			
Expenditures—1999		127,000		
22. Revenues.	4,015,000			
Appropriations	4,210,000			
Estimated Revenues		4,001,000		
Expenditures—2000		4,069,260		
Encumbrances—2000.		70,240		
Fund Balance.		84,500		

Although Entry 22 affects five General Fund general ledger control accounts, it is not considered necessary to make closing entries in their subsidiary ledger accounts because separate subsidiary ledgers are kept for each budget year.

It is important to notice the closing entry has the effect of reversing the entry made to record the budget (Entry 1) and the entry made to amend the budget (Entry 12). Therefore, after the closing entry is posted, the Fund Balance account is purely a balance sheet account and not one in which historical and expected effects are mixed, as is true during a year. That is, it again represents the net amount of financial resources available for appropriation for fund purposes.

Year-End Financial Statements

The Balance Sheet for the General Fund of the Town of Brighton as of the end of 2000 is shown as Illustration 4–4. Since only balance sheet accounts are open, the captions "Assets" and "Liabilities and Fund Equity" are used instead of the captions in the Interim Balance Sheet, Illustration 4–1. The amount due from the Water Utility Fund is offset against the amount due to the same fund, and only the net liability is shown in the balance sheet, in conformity with GASB standards. It should be emphasized that it is *not* acceptable to offset a receivable from one fund against a payable to a different fund. The General Fund balance sheet would be presented in columnar form in the Combined Balance Sheet, one of the five general purpose financial statements required for conformity with generally accepted accounting principles. In addition, GASB standards require disclosures in the notes to the financial statements of a number of details regarding deposits with financial institutions, investments, property taxes, receivables, and other assets.

Illustration 4–4

TOWN OF BRIGHTON
General Fund Balance Sheet
As of December 31, 2000

Assets

Cash		$145,800
Taxes receivable—delinquent	$666,300	
Less: Estimated uncollectible delinquent taxes	88,000	578,300
Interest and penalties receivable on taxes	3,085	
Less: Estimated uncollectible interest and penalties	1,985	1,100
Inventory of supplies		61,500
Total Assets		$786,700

Liabilities and Fund Equity

Liabilities:		
Vouchers payable	$396,800	
Due to federal government	126,520	
Due to state government	39,740	
Due to other funds	5,000	
Total Liabilities		$568,060
Fund Equity:		
Reserve for encumbrances—2000	70,240	
Reserve for inventory of supplies	61,500	
Fund balance	86,900	
Total Fund Equity		218,640
Total Liabilities and Fund Equity		$786,700

A second financial statement that should be presented in the year-end comprehensive annual financial report is a Statement of Revenues, Expenditures, and Changes in Fund Balance (see Illustration 4–5). Illustration 4–5 presents the actual revenues and actual expenditures that resulted from transactions illustrated in this chapter and other transactions not illustrated because they were similar in nature. If the General Fund of the Town of Brighton had had any financial inflows or outflows resulting from operating transfers, the receipt of debt issue proceeds, or other transactions not strictly defined as resulting in revenues or expenditures, their effects should be reported as Other Financing Sources or Other Financing Uses.

The Other Financing Sources (Uses) section in Illustration 4–5 shows a common means of disclosure of nonrevenue financial inflows and nonexpenditure financial outflows. Information shown here as Illustration 4–5 would be presented in columnar form in the Combined Statement of Revenues, Expenditures, and Changes in Fund Balances—All Governmental Fund Types, one of the five general

Illustration 4–5

TOWN OF BRIGHTON
General Fund
Statement of Revenues, Expenditures, and
Changes in Fund Balance
For the Year Ended December 31, 2000

Revenues:		
Property taxes	$2,599,636	
Interest and penalties on delinquent taxes	11,400	
Sales taxes	485,000	
Licenses and permits	213,200	
Fines and forfeits	310,800	
Intergovernmental revenue	284,100	
Charges for services	82,464	
Miscellaneous revenues	28,400	
Total Revenues		$4,015,000
Expenditures:		
2000:		
General government	649,400	
Public safety	1,305,435	
Public works	778,300	
Health and welfare	850,325	
Parks and recreation	292,500	
Contributions to retirement plans	179,100	
Miscellaneous appropriations	14,200	
Expenditures—2000	4,069,260	
1999:		
Parks and recreation	127,000	
Total Expenditures		4,196,260
Excess of Expenditures over Revenues		(181,260)
Other Financing Sources (Uses):		
Operating transfers in	–0–	
Operating transfers out	–0–	
Total Other Financing Sources		–0–
Excess of Expenditures and Other Uses over Revenues and Other Sources		(181,260)
Increase in Reserve for Inventory of Supplies		(61,500)
Decrease in Reserve for Encumbrances during 2000		56,760
Change (Decrease) in Fund Balance for Year		(186,000)
Fund Balance, January 1, 2000		272,900
Fund Balance, December 31, 2000		$ 86,900

purpose financial statements required for conformity with generally accepted accounting principles.

A third statement that should be prepared at year-end is the Statement of Revenues, Expenditures, and Changes in Fund Balance—Budget and Actual (Illustration 4–6). This information should be included in columnar form, as shown in Illustration 2–3, in the Combined Statement of Revenues, Expenditures, and Changes in Fund Balances—Budget and Actual, one of the five general purpose financial statements required for conformity with GAAP.

The amounts in the Revenues section of the Actual column in Illustration 4–6 present the same information as shown in the Revenues section of Illustration 4–5 because in the Town of Brighton example the General Fund revenues budget is on the same basis as the Revenues account. However, the amounts in the Expenditures section of the Actual column of Illustration 4–6 differ from the Expenditures shown in Illustration 4–5 because Illustration 4–5, in order to conform with GASB standards, reports Expenditures chargeable to 1999 appropriations ($127,000) as well as Expenditures of the 2000 appropriations ($4,069,260) and does not report Encumbrances in the Expenditures section of the statement. In contrast, GASB standards require the amounts in the Actual column of Illustration 4–6 to conform with budgetary practices; therefore in that statement Encumbrances outstanding at the end of fiscal 2000 are added to 2000 Expenditures because both are uses of the 2000 appropriation authority. Note that in Illustration 4–6 Expenditures (Public Works) is not adjusted for the inventory of supplies at year-end because the purchase of supplies was a use of 2000 appropriation authority whether or not the supplies were used in 2000. Expenditures for 1999 are excluded from the Budget and Actual statement because that statement relates only to the 2000 budget. GASB standards require differences between the amounts reported in the two statements to be reconciled in the notes to the financial statements if not reconciled on the face of a statement. For example, the notes to the financial statements for the Town of Brighton might include the following reconciliation of General Fund Expenditures reported in the two operating statements illustrated:

Expenditures for 2000, budgetary basis	$4,201,000
Less: Reserve for Encumbrances as of December 31, 2000	(70,240)
Reserve for Inventory of Supplies as of December 31, 2000	(61,500)
Expenditures for 2000, GAAP basis	$4,069,260

The presentation of Reserve for Encumbrances in Illustrations 4–4, 4–5, 4–6, and in the illustrative reconciliation, is based on the assumption that amounts encumbered at year-end do not need to be appropriated for the following year. The amounts shown in Illustration 4–6 in the Expenditures section in the Actual Over (Under) Budget column, however, disclose the portion of each appropriation for 2000 that was neither expended nor encumbered during that year; those amounts, totaling $9,000, are said to *lapse*, that is, become unavailable for expenditure or encumbrance in the year following 2000.

Illustration 4–6

TOWN OF BRIGHTON
General Fund
Statement of Revenues, Expenditures, and
Changes in Fund Balance—Budget and Actual
(Non-GAAP Presentation)
For the Year Ended December 31, 2000

	Budget	Actual	Actual Over (Under) Budget
Revenues:			
Taxes:			
Property taxes	$2,600,000	$2,599,636	$ (364)
Interest and penalties on taxes	13,000	11,400	(1,600)
Sales taxes	480,000	485,000	5,000
Total Taxes	3,093,000	3,096,036	3,036
Licenses and permits	220,000	213,200	(6,800)
Fines and forfeits	308,000	310,800	2,800
Intergovernmental revenue	280,000	284,100	4,100
Charges for services	75,000	82,464	7,464
Miscellaneous revenues	25,000	28,400	3,400
Total Revenues	4,001,000	4,015,000	14,000
Expenditures and Encumbrances:			
General government	660,000	658,850	(1,150)
Public safety	1,320,000	1,318,500	(1,500)
Public works	860,000	859,200	(800)
Health and welfare	860,000	858,650	(1,350)
Parks and recreation	315,000	312,500	(2,500)
Contributions to retirement plans	180,000	179,100	(900)
Miscellaneous appropriations	15,000	14,200	(800)
Total Expenditures	4,210,000	4,201,000	(9,000)
Excess of Expenditures over Revenues	209,000	186,000	(23,000)
Other Financing Sources (Uses)	–0–	–0–	–0–
Decrease in Fund Balance for Year	(209,000)	(186,000)	(23,000)
Fund Balance, January 1, 2000	272,900	272,900	–0–
Fund Balance, December 31, 2000	$ 63,900	$ 86,900	$ 23,000

Special Revenue Funds

As noted in Chapter 2, special revenue funds are needed when legal or policy considerations require separate funds to be created for current purposes other than those served by proprietary or fiduciary funds. An example of a special revenue fund created to demonstrate legal compliance is a Street Fund, which is largely financed by a local government's share of the motor fuel tax levied by the state to be used only for maintenance and construction of streets, roads, and bridges. A second example of a special revenue fund is a Library Operating Fund created to account for a special tax levy or simply the desire of the governing board to have a separate fund to account for an activity that differs from other governmental activities. A third example is a fund to account for grants received from a higher jurisdiction; grant accounting is discussed briefly in the following paragraph.

Accounting for Operating Grants

Grants received by a local government from the state or federal government—or received by a state from the federal government—are often restricted for specified operating purposes.[1] Consequently, revenues of such grants are frequently accounted for by use of a special revenue fund. A number of grants provide that the grantor will pay the grantee on a reimbursement basis. In such instances, GASB standards require that the grant revenue not be recognized until the expenditure has taken place (because the grant revenue has not been "earned" until the terms of the grant have been met through the required expenditure). As an example of appropriate accounting procedures, assume a local government has been awarded a state grant to finance a fine arts program, and a special revenue fund is created. When the grant receivable is recognized, an offsetting credit is made to Deferred Revenues, a liability account, to disclose that no revenue has yet been earned. Therefore, the entry would be:

	General Ledger		Subsidiary Ledger	
	Debits	*Credits*	*Debits*	*Credits*
Grants Receivable—State	150,000			
Deferred Revenues		150,000		

When expenditures for the purposes specified by the grant have taken place, it is appropriate to recognize revenues in the amount of the expenditures, as illustrated by the following entries:

Expenditures	50,000	
Vouchers Payable (or Cash)		50,000
Deferred Revenues	50,000	
Revenues		50,000

Accounting and Financial Reporting

Special revenue fund accounting and financial reporting are exactly parallel to that described for the General Fund in this chapter. Along with the General Fund, the total of the special revenue funds would be included in the Combined Balance Sheet; the Combined Statement of Revenues, Expenditures, and Changes in Fund Balances (All Governmental Fund Types); and the Combined Statement of Revenues, Expenditures, and Changes in Fund Balances—Budget and Actual. In addition, when more than one special revenue fund exists, *combining* balance sheets, operating statements, and budget-actual statements are required for the Comprehensive Annual Financial Report. Combining statements for capital projects funds are illustrated in Chapter 5; combining statements for special revenue funds would be similar.

---

[1] Accounting for capital grants is discussed in Chapter 5, "Accounting for General Fixed Assets and Capital Projects."

Alternatives Sometimes Encountered in General Fund and Special Revenue Fund Accounting

Other Treatments of Encumbrances Outstanding at Year-End

In addition to the method of accounting for encumbrances outstanding at the end of a fiscal year illustrated earlier and assumed to this point, other methods exist in practice. In at least one state, the law requires outstanding encumbrances to be added to the appropriations budgeted for the following year. In this case, the Reserve for Encumbrances account, as well as the Encumbrances account, may be closed at year-end because in essence the encumbered amount is reappropriated for the following year and is not carried forward as a reservation of Fund Balance. Thus at the beginning of the following year it is necessary to debit Encumbrances and credit Reserve for Encumbrances for the amount of purchase orders, contracts, or other commitment documents carried over from the prior year. From that point on no distinction need be made in the accounting records between expenditures arising from encumbrances of the prior year and those arising from encumbrances of the current year.

Cash Basis Recognition of Tax Revenue

Even though taxes become liens on the underlying property, collections in a given period sometimes fall substantially short of the amount levied. If expenditure commitments are based on the amount levied but actual collections fall short of anticipations, the result may be a condition of financial stringency for the taxing unit. Accordingly, *laws of some states require local governments to record all revenue*, including tax revenue, *on the cash basis*. Such laws are, of course, in conflict with GAAP, which require revenues to be recognized on the modified accrual basis. It is possible to keep the accounting system in conformity with GAAP and to adjust the data to the basis required by law when reporting to the state. Alternatively, it is possible to keep the accounting system in compliance with state law and adjust the data to conform with GAAP when preparing general purpose financial statements.

If the cash basis is applied strictly, the receivable from billed taxes cannot be recorded as an asset even though by all accounting criteria it should be. A procedure that permits placing the receivable under accounting control but defers recognition of the revenue until it is collected is illustrated below:

	General Ledger		Subsidiary Ledger	
	Debits	Credits	Debits	Credits
Taxes Receivable—Current	1,000,000			
Estimated Uncollectible Current Taxes		20,000		
Reserve for Uncollected Taxes		980,000		

The entry above records the levy of property taxes assumed to be in the amount of $1,000,000 with 2 percent estimated as uncollectible. The account titles of the debit and the first credit agree with those of Entry 7 above. The second credit, however, is to Reserve for Uncollected Taxes instead of to Revenues. The nature of Reserve for Uncollected Taxes is consistent, under cash basis theory, with that of other reserves discussed earlier. The balance of the Reserve for Uncollected Taxes would be deducted from the net Taxes Receivable on the balance sheet, so that the net noncash item does not add to the asset total (and, obviously, does not add to Fund Equity).

When some of the taxes are collected, the following two entries are necessary (amounts assumed):

	General Ledger		Subsidiary Ledger	
	Debits	*Credits*	*Debits*	*Credits*
Cash	365,000			
Taxes Receivable—Current		365,000		
Reserve for Uncollected Taxes	365,000			
Revenues.....................		365,000		
Revenues Ledger:				
Property Taxes				365,000

The two entries are illustrated because the first one summarizes entries that would be made from source documents originated by the cashier each time taxes are collected. The second entry shows that the Reserve for Uncollected Taxes account must be adjusted periodically to reflect the collection of taxes and the consequent cash basis recognition of revenue.

If financial statements were prepared on the legally required basis after the entries illustrated above, the Statement of Revenues, Expenditures, and Changes in Fund Balance would report revenues from current taxes of $365,000, the amount collected in cash. In the Balance Sheet, full disclosure would be achieved by reporting:

Taxes Receivable—Current		$635,000
Less: Estimated Uncollectible		
Current Taxes	$ 20,000	
Less: Reserve for Uncollected		
Taxes	615,000	635,000

Statements presented on the legally required basis illustrated are, of course, *not* in conformity with GASB standards and would not be considered general purpose financial statements; under AICPA auditing standards they would be considered special reports.

Discounts on Taxes   Some governmental units utilize a cash discount system to encourage early payment of property taxes. Although a small amount of revenue is lost from discounts taken, the practice minimizes the use of short-term borrowing or, another alternative, carrying over a sizable available cash balance from the preceding period. If not prohibited by law, **discounts on taxes** are best accounted for as reductions of the amount of revenue to be derived from a given tax levy. Thus, if a tax levy totals $2,000,000 and the estimated discounts that will be taken amount to $18,000, the latter figure may be subtracted from the amount of the levy, along with the estimated loss from uncollectible taxes, to give the net estimated revenue. Assuming an estimated loss from uncollectible taxes of $31,000, the $2,000,000 levy, with discount provision, would be recorded as follows:

	General Ledger		Subsidiary Ledger	
	Debits	Credits	Debits	Credits
Taxes Receivable—Current	2,000,000			
Estimated Uncollectible Current Taxes		31,000		
Estimated Discounts on Taxes.......		18,000		
Revenues		1,951,000		
Revenues Ledger:				
Property Taxes				1,951,000

Payment of taxes within the discount period requires a debit to the Estimated Discounts on Taxes accounts of the amount earned, in the following manner, using assumed amounts:

Cash	197	
Estimated Discounts on Taxes	3	
Taxes Receivable—Current		200

If discounts are taken in excess of the amount of allowance created, the excess will be debited to Revenues—Property Taxes. Any balance remaining in the allowance after the close of the discount period should be transferred to Revenues—Property Taxes by a credit to that account and a debit to the Estimated Discounts on Taxes account.

As a device for closer control against unwarranted granting of discounts, some governmental units may require discounts on taxes to be covered by an appropriation. Under this method the allowance for discounts is not established when the tax levy is recorded. Discounts granted are debited to Expenditures in the following manner, assuming an entry for one month's collection of taxes:

Cash	23,640	
Expenditures—Discounts on Taxes	360	
Taxes Receivable—Current		24,000

Key Terms

Consumption method,   115
Current financial resources,   100
Delinquent taxes,   116
Discount on taxes,   125
Fund equity,   101

Gross tax levy,   104
Purchases method,   115
Quasi-external transaction,   114
Tax anticipation note,   102
Tax rate,   105

Selected References

American Institute of Certified Public Accountants. Audit and Accounting Guide. *Audits of State and Local Governmental Units*. Revised. New York, 1996.

Governmental Accounting Standards Board. *Codification of Governmental Accounting and Financial Reporting Standards as of June 30, 1997*. Norwalk, CT, 1997.

Questions

4–1. In the preparation of balance sheets for business organizations it is considered essential to classify liabilities as *current* or *long term*. Is it also essential in the balance sheet of a governmental unit General Fund to classify liabilities as current or long term? Why or why not? Would it be essential to classify the liabilities of a special revenue fund? Explain.

4–2. Explain why it is often necessary to reserve a portion of the fund equity of the General Fund or a special revenue fund.

4–3. Explain why a city, even a well-managed one, may find it necessary to issue "tax anticipation notes."

4–4. "Tax anticipation notes" generally require the issuing government to pledge specific assets as security. True or false? Explain.

4–5. If the General Fund of a certain city needs $5,760,000 revenue from property taxes to finance estimated expenditures of the forthcoming year, and historical experience and forecasts indicate 4 percent of the gross levy will not be collected, how much should the gross levy of General Fund property taxes for the forthcoming year be? Show all computations in good form.

4–6. Is it ever permissible to write off uncollectible delinquent property taxes? If so, explain the accounting procedures involved.

4–7. "If the actual liability for goods or services received in one fiscal year but ordered in a prior fiscal year differs from the estimated liability recorded in the prior year, the actual liability should be reported as an Expenditure of the prior year." Do you agree? Why or why not?

4–8. In late 1999 Cato City ordered goods estimated to cost $300. At year-end these goods had not been received and thus were reported as Reserve for Encumbrances—1999 on the City's balance sheet. In early fiscal year 2000 these goods were received at an actual cost of $320. What total amount of expenditures should be reported for these goods on the City's Statement of Revenues, Expenditures, and Changes in Fund Balances for the year 2000? What amount of expenditures is chargeable to the year 2000 appropriation?

4–9. Explain the relationship between proprietary accounts and budgetary accounts in an interim balance sheet prepared for the General Fund.

4–10. "If a budget is prepared on the cash basis, in order to comply with state law, it should be adjusted to the modified accrual basis in order that the budget and actual statement may be prepared in conformity with generally accepted accounting principles." Do you agree? Why or why not?

4–11. State law requires a governmental unit to follow the cash basis of accounting for revenues, yet the finance officer of that unit feels taxes receivable should be placed under accounting control. Suggest a procedure to accomplish both objectives.

4–12. Grant A from the federal government will reimburse the city for allowable costs incurred for authorized operating purposes; grant B is also restricted for a specified operating purpose, but the full amount under the grant is provided to the city at the beginning of the fiscal year in which the grant monies will be used. Explain the difference in revenue recognition procedures for these two grants.

4–13. Since all funds of a governmental unit are part of the same reporting entity, why are certain interfund transactions recorded as Expenditures and liabilities of one fund, and as assets and Revenues of another fund?

4–14. A governmental fund may charge materials and supplies to Expenditures when the items are purchased (the purchases method) or when the items are used (the consumption method). In either case, significant amounts of inventories should be reported in the balance sheet. If administrators are interested in computing and reporting the cost of services rendered, would you recommend the purchases method or the consumption method?

Exercises and Problems

4–1. Utilizing the comprehensive annual financial report obtained for Exercise 1–1, follow the instructions below:

  a. General Fund. What statements and schedules pertaining to the General Fund are presented? In what respects (headings, arrangements, items included, etc.) do they seem similar to the year-end statements illustrated or described in the text? In what respects do they differ?

  What purpose is each statement and schedule intended to serve? How well, in your reasoned opinion, does each statement and schedule accomplish its intended purpose? (After reading the first four chapters of this text carefully and solving assigned problems, you have a much greater understanding of the purposes of General Fund accounting and reporting than most other citizens, and even than nonaccountants in elective or appointive governmental positions.)

  Are any noncurrent or nonliquid assets included in the General Fund balance sheet? If so, are they offset by "Reserve" accounts in the Fund Equity section? Are any noncurrent liabilities included in the General Fund balance sheet? If so, describe them and attempt to determine why they are included in this statement rather than in the Statement of General Long-Term Debt.

  b. Special Revenue Funds. What statements and schedules pertaining to the special revenue funds are presented? Are these only combining statements, or are there also statements for individual special revenue funds?

  Refer to *a* above—answer questions from the perspective of the special revenue funds. Review your answers to Exercises 1–1, 2–1, and 3–1 in light of your study of Chapter 4. If you feel your earlier answers were not entirely correct, change them to conform with your present understanding of GASB financial reporting standards.

4–2. Write the numbers 1 through 10 on a sheet of paper. Beside each number write the letter corresponding with the best answer to each of the following questions:

1. Oro County's Expenditures control account at December 31, 2000, had a balance of $9,000,000. When Oro's books were closed, this $9,000,000 Expenditures control balance should have
   a. Been credited.
   b. Been debited.
   c. Remained open.
   d. Appeared as a contra account.

2. If a city legally adopts its annual General Fund budget on the modified accrual basis of accounting, its estimated revenues should be
   a. Reported as current assets in the General Fund Balance Sheet.
   b. Reported as noncurrent assets in the General Fund Balance Sheet.
   c. Reported on the modified accrual basis of accounting in the General Fund Statement of Revenues, Expenditures, and Changes in Fund Balance— Budget and Actual.
   d. Converted to the cash basis of accounting and reported in the General Fund Statement of Revenues, Expenditures, and Other Changes in Fund Balance—Budget and Actual.

3. At December 31, 2000, Alto Township's encumbered appropriations that had not been expended in 2000 totaled $10,000. Encumbered appropriations do not lapse at year-end. Alto reports on a calendar-year basis. On its December 31, 2000, balance sheet, the $10,000 should be reported as
   a. Fund Balance Reserved for Encumbrances.
   b. Budgetary Fund Balance—Encumbrances.
   c. Vouchers Payable—Prior Year.
   d. Deferred Expenditures.

4. When Rolan County adopted its budget for the year ending June 30, 2000, $20,000,000 was recorded in Estimated Revenues. Actual revenues for the year ended June 30, 2000, amounted to $17,000,000. In closing the budgetary accounts at June 30, 2000,
   a. Estimated Revenues should be debited for $3,000,000.
   b. Revenues should be debited for $3,000,000.
   c. Estimated Revenues should be credited for $20,000,000.
   d. Revenues should be credited for $20,000,000.

5. When equipment was purchased with General Fund resources, an appropriate entry was made in the General Fixed Assets Account Group. Which of the following accounts would have been increased in the General Fund?
   a. Appropriations.
   b. Expenditures.
   c. Due from General Fixed Assets Account Group.
   d. No entry should be made in the General Fund.

6. Property taxes levied in fiscal year 2000 to finance the General Fund budget of fiscal year 2000 should be reported as general fund revenues in 2000:
   a. Regardless of the fiscal year in which collected.
   b. For the amount collected in fiscal year 2000 only.
   c. For the amount collected before the end of fiscal year 2000 or within one year thereafter.
   d. For the amount collected before the end of fiscal year 2000 or within 60 days thereafter.

7. Goods costing $62,000 were received early in 2000. The estimated liability for these goods had been recorded in 1999 as $60,000. The journal entry to record these goods in 2000 will include a:
   a. Debit to Expenditures—1999 in the amount of $62,000.
   b. Debit to Expenditures—1999 in the amount of $60,000.
   c. Debit to Expenditures—2000 in the amount of $62,000.
   d. Debit to Expenditures—2000 in the amount of $60,000.
8. The City of Thomasboro uses the consumption method for recording its inventory of supplies in the General Fund. Physical inventories of supplies were $100,000 and $85,000 at December 31, 1999, and December 31, 2000, respectively. The adjusting journal entry on December 31, 2000, will include a:
   a. Debit to Inventory of Supplies in the amount of $15,000.
   b. Credit to Reserve for Inventory of Supplies in the amount of $85,000.
   c. Debit to Expenditures in the amount of $15,000.
   d. Credit to Expenditures in the amount of $15,000.
9. Gold County received goods that had been approved for purchase but for which payment had not been made. Should the accounts listed below be increased?

	Encumbrances	Expenditures
a.	No	No
b.	No	Yes
c.	Yes	No
d.	Yes	Yes

10. In which of the following fund types of a city government are revenues and expenditures recognized on the same basis of accounting as the General Fund?
    a. Enterprise.
    b. Internal service.
    c. Special revenue.
    d. Nonexpendable trust.

(AICPA, adapted)

4–3. The following is a list of the ledger accounts of the General Fund of Brentwood as of June 30, 1999 (the fiscal year ends on December 31):

Accounts Payable	$ 372,600
Appropriations	2,665,000
Cash	304,600
Encumbrances	120,000
Estimated Revenues	2,700,000
Estimated Uncollectible Current Taxes	75,000
Expenditures—1999	1,398,400
Reserve for Encumbrances—1999	120,000
Revenues	1,480,000
Tax Anticipation Notes Payable	540,000
Taxes Receivable—Current	908,700
Fund Balance	?

Required

    a. Determine the balance of the Fund Balance account as of June 30, 1999, without preparing a balance sheet or closing entries. Show computations.

    b. Prepare in good form an Interim Balance Sheet as of June 30, 1999.

    c. If the only entry recorded in the Fund Balance account during the first six months of 1999 was to record the original budget for the year, compute the balance of the Fund Balance account that would have been reported in the General Fund Balance Sheet as of December 31, 1998.

4–4. As of December 31, 1999, Brentwood's General Fund (see Problem 4–3) had the following account balances:

	Debits	Credits
Accounts Payable		$ 209,700
Appropriations		2,690,000
Cash	$ 152,400	
Encumbrances	35,000	
Estimated Revenues	2,700,000	
Estimated Uncollectible Delinquent Taxes		62,000
Expenditures—1999	2,651,600	
Inventory of Supplies	60,000	
Reserve for Encumbrances—1999		35,000
Reserve for Inventory of Supplies		60,000
Revenues		2,692,100
Taxes Receivable—Delinquent	290,000	
Fund Balance		140,200
	$5,889,000	$5,889,000

Required

    a. The General Fund trial balance shown above is presented as of the last day of the fiscal year of Brentwood. Inspect the trial balance, and the trial balance as of June 30, 1999 (see Problem 4–3), and answer the following questions. Explain the reason for each of your answers. Assume that the purchases method of recording inventories is used.

        (1)   Have closing entries been recorded?

        (2)   Have adjusting entries been recorded?

    b. Have any amendments to the General Fund budget been recorded during the six months ended December 31, 1999? If so, state which budgetary accounts were amended, and whether the amendments represented increases, or decreases, to the budget (state the amount of each increase or decrease). Show in good form all computations needed to support your answers.

4–5. Refer to the December 31, 1999, trial balance of the General Fund of Brentwood (see Problem 4–4) and answer the following questions. Explain each of your answers and show all necessary computations in good form.

a. In the Brentwood General Fund Statement of Revenues, Expenditures, and Changes in Fund Balance for the year ending December 31, 1999, how much should be reported as the Excess of Revenues over Expenditures (or Excess of Expenditures over Revenues, if that is the case)?

b. In the Brentwood General Fund Statement of Revenues, Expenditures, and Changes in Fund Balance—Budget and Actual for the year ended December 31, 1999, how much should be reported as:

(1)   The budgeted Excess of Revenues over Expenditures (or Excess of Expenditures over Revenues)?

(2)   The actual Excess of Revenues over Expenditures (or Excess of Expenditures over Revenues)?

c. Explain why your answer to b(1) differs from your answer to a, if it does.

d. Explain why your answer to b(2) differs from your answer to a, if it does.

e. Compute the Fund Balance that should be reported in the General Fund Balance Sheet for Brentwood as of December 31, 1999. (There are several ways you can compute this amount correctly. It is suggested that you make the computation at least two different ways and prove that the answer is the same in each case.)

4–6. At the end of fiscal year 1999, budgetary and operating statement control accounts in the general ledger of the General Fund of the City of Adams had the following balances: Appropriations, $5,224,000; Estimated Other Financing Uses, $2,776,000; Estimated Revenues, $7,997,000; Encumbrances, $0; Expenditures, $5,182,000; Other Financing Uses, $2,780,000; and Revenues. $8,022,000. Appropriations included an authorization to order a certain item at a cost not to exceed $64,700; this was not ordered during 1999 because it will not be available until late in the following year, 2000. Show in general journal form the entry needed to close all of the accounts listed above that should be closed as of the end of the fiscal year 1999.

4–7. For budgetary purposes the City of Rockton reports encumbrances in the Expenditures section of its Statement of Revenues, Expenditures, and Changes in Fund Balance—Budget and Actual. Expenditures chargeable to a prior year's appropriation are excluded from the current year budgetary comparison statements. From the following information prepare:

a. Entries in general journal form to record the transactions for fiscal year 1999 given below.

b. A Statement of Revenues, Expenditures, and Changes in Fund Balance—Budget and Actual for the General Fund of the City of Rockton for the fiscal year ending December 31, 1999.

(1)   The budget prepared for the fiscal year 1999 was as follows:

Estimated Revenues:	
Taxes	$1,943,000
Licenses and Permits	372,000
Intergovernmental Revenue	297,000
Miscellaneous Revenues	62,000
Total Estimated Revenues	$2,674,000
Appropriations:	
General Government	$ 471,000
Public Safety	786,000
Public Works	650,000
Health and Welfare	600,000
Miscellaneous Appropriations	86,000
Total Appropriations	$2,593,000
Budgeted Increase in Fund Balance	$ 81,000

(2)   Encumbrances issued against the appropriations during the year were as follows:

General Government	$ 58,000
Public Safety	201,000
Public Works	392,000
Health and Welfare	160,000
Miscellaneous Appropriations	71,000
Total	$882,000

(3)   A current-year tax levy of $2,005,000 was recorded; uncollectibles were estimated as $62,000.

(4)   Tax collections from prior years' levies totaled $132,000; collections of the current year's levy totaled $1,459,000.

(5)   Personnel costs during the year were charged to the appropriations shown below in the amounts indicated. Encumbrances were not recorded for personnel costs.

General Government	$ 411,000
Public Safety	584,000
Public Works	254,000
Health and Welfare	439,000
Miscellaneous Appropriations	11,100
Credit to Vouchers Payable	$1,699,100

(6)   Invoices for all items ordered during the prior year were received and approved for payment in the amount of $14,470. Encumbrances had been recorded in the prior year for these items in the amount of $14,000. The amount chargeable to each year's appropriations should be charged to the Public Safety appropriation.

(7) Invoices were received and approved for payment for items ordered in documents recorded as encumbrances in transaction 2 of this problem. The following appropriations were affected:

	Actual Liability	Estimated Liability
General Government	$ 52,700	$ 52,200
Public Safety	187,800	189,700
Public Works	360,000	357,000
Health and Safety	130,600	130,100
Miscellaneous Appropriations	71,000	71,000
	$802,100	$800,000

(8) Revenue other than taxes collected during the year consisted of: licenses and permits, $373,000; intergovernmental revenue, $299,000; and $66,000 of miscellaneous revenues.

(9) Payments on Vouchers Payable totaled $2,475,000.

The General Fund Fund Balance account had a credit balance of $62,700 as of December 31, 1998; no entries other than the entry at the beginning of 1999 to record the budgeted increase have been made in the Fund Balance account during 1999.

4–8. The City of Warren's General Fund had the following after-closing trial balance at April 30, 1999, the end of its fiscal year:

	Debits	Credits
Cash	$ 93,000	
Taxes Receivable—Delinquent	583,000	
Estimated Uncollectible Delinquent Taxes		$189,000
Interest and Penalties Receivable	26,280	
Estimated Uncollectible Interest and Penalties		11,160
Inventory of Supplies	16,100	
Vouchers Payable		148,500
Due to Federal Government		59,490
Reserve for Inventory of Supplies		16,100
Fund Balance		294,130
	$718,380	$718,380

During the six months ended October 31, 1999, the first six months of fiscal year 2000, the following transactions, in summary form, with subsidiary ledger detail omitted, occurred:

1. The budget for fiscal 2000 provided for General Fund estimated revenues totaling $3,170,000 and appropriations totaling $3,100,000.
2. The City Council authorized a temporary loan of $300,000 in the form of a 120-day tax anticipation note. The loan was obtained from a local bank at a discount of 6 percent per annum (debit Expenditures for discount).
3. The property tax levy for fiscal 2000 was recorded. Net assessed valuation of taxable property for the year was $43,000,000, and the tax rate was $5.00 per hundred. It was estimated that 4 percent of the levy would be uncollectible. Classify this tax levy as current.
4. Purchase orders, contracts, and so on, in the amount of $1,027,000 were issued to vendors and others.
5. $1,034,000 of current taxes, $340,000 of delinquent taxes, and interest and penalties of $13,240 were collected. Because of taxpayers' delinquencies in payment of the first installment of taxes, additional penalties of $15,230 were levied but not yet collected.
6. Total payroll during the first six months was $481,070. Of that amount, $36,800 was withheld for employees' FICA tax liability, $61,200 for employees' federal income tax liability, and $20,000 for state taxes; the balance was paid in cash.
7. The employer's FICA tax liability amounted to $36,800.
8. Revenues from sources other than taxes were collected in the amount of $339,000.
9. Amounts due the federal government as of April 30, and amounts due for FICA taxes and state and federal withholding taxes during the first six months of fiscal 2000, were vouchered.
10. Purchase orders and contracts encumbered in the amount of $890,800 were filled at a net cost of $894,900, which was vouchered.
11. $1,099,060 cash was paid on vouchers payable and credit for purchases discount earned was $8,030 (credit Expenditures).
12. The tax anticipation note of $300,000 was repaid.

Required

a. Record in general journal form the effect on the General Fund of the transactions for the six months ended October 31. You need not record subsidiary ledger debits and credits.
b. Prepare a City of Warren General Fund Interim Balance Sheet as of October 31, 1999.

4–9. This problem continues Problem 4–8. During the second six months of fiscal 2000, the following transactions that affected the City of Warren's General Fund occurred:

1. Because of a change in a state law, the City is informed it will receive $100,000 less revenue from the state than was budgeted. Make the entry to amend the Estimated Revenues account accordingly. Do not amend the Appropriations account.
2. Purchase orders and other commitment documents in the amount of $1,032,000 were issued during the six months ended April 30, 2000.
3. Property taxes of $6,500 and interest and penalties receivable of $1,340, which had been written off in prior years, were collected. Additional interest of $270 that had accrued since the write-off was collected at the same time.

4. Personnel costs, excluding the employer's share of the FICA tax, totaled $338,420 for the second six months. Withholdings amounted to $25,890 for FICA; $42,510 for employee's federal income tax liability, and $14,400 for state withholding tax; the balance was paid in cash.

5. The employer's FICA tax of $25,890 was recorded as a liability.

6. The County Board of Review discovered unassessed properties of a total taxable value of $500,000 located within the City boundaries. The owners of these properties were charged with taxes at the City General Fund rate of $5.00 per hundred dollars assessed value. (Do not adjust the Estimated Uncollectible Current Taxes Account.)

7. The following were collected in cash: Current taxes of $927,000; delinquent taxes of $43,270; interest and penalties of $7,330, and revenues of $593,700 from a number of sources. (No part of any of these amounts is included in any other transaction given above.)

8. Accrued interest and penalties, estimated to be 30 percent uncollectible, was recorded in the amount of $23,200.

9. All unpaid current year's taxes became delinquent. The current taxes and related estimated uncollectibles were transferred to the delinquent classification.

10. All amounts due to the federal government and state government were vouchered.

11. Invoices and bills for goods and services that had been encumbered at $1,097,240 were received in the amount of $1,092,670 and were vouchered.

12. Personal property taxes of $39,940 and interest and penalties of $4,180 were written off because of inability to locate the property owners.

13. A physical inventory of materials and supplies at April 30, 2000, showed a total of $19,100. Inventory is recorded on the consumption method.

14. Payments made on vouchers during the second half-year totaled $1,202,600.

Required

a. Record in general journal form transactions for the second half of fiscal 2000.

b. Record in general journal form entries to close the budgetary accounts and operating statement accounts.

c. Prepare a Balance Sheet as of April 30, 2000, for the City of Warren General Fund.

d. Prepare a Statement of Revenues, Expenditures, and Changes in Fund Balance for the fiscal year ended April 30, 2000, in as much detail as is possible from the data given in Problems 4–8 and 4–9.

4–10. Many years ago, Jefferson County accounted for revenue on the accrual basis. After it incurred serious financial difficulty because collections of property taxes fell far short of the amount of revenue shown when the tax levy was recorded, the use of accrual basis for revenue was officially prohibited, but recording of the tax levy as charges against property owners was approved.

At June 30, the end of a fiscal year, Jefferson County's General Fund ledger showed the following names and balances of accounts related to property taxes:

Estimated Uncollectible Taxes—Current Year	$ 30,000
Estimated Uncollectible Taxes—Prior Years	78,000
Estimated Revenues—Current Year's Taxes	835,000
Estimated Revenues—Prior Years' Taxes	58,000
Reserve for Uncollected Taxes—Current Year	56,000
Reserve for Uncollected Taxes—Prior Years	31,000
Revenue—Current Year's Taxes	811,000
Revenue—Prior Years' Taxes	65,000
Taxes Receivable—Current Year	66,000
Taxes Receivable—Prior Years	107,000

It is the practice to transfer at the end of each month the amount collected during the month from Reserve for Uncollected Taxes to Revenue. This had not yet been done at the end of June, as evidenced by the fact that the sum of Reserve for Uncollected Taxes and Estimated Uncollectible Taxes for both this and prior years exceeded the balances of the related taxes receivable accounts.

For the forthcoming year, the town board approved a tax rate that would produce a total levy of approximately $1,000,000 of which 5 percent was expected to be uncollectible.

Required

a. Make all entries required at June 30. Use Fund Balance as the balancing account for the Estimated Revenue and Revenue accounts. Accounts related to the current year's taxes receivable may be transferred to prior years' classification at this time.

b. Record the tax levy for the new fiscal year.

Continuous Problem

4–L. Presented below are a number of transactions of the General Fund of the City of Bingham that occurred during the first six months of fiscal year 2000 for which the budget given in Problem 3–L was prepared, that is, July 1, 1999, through December 31, 1999. You are required to:

a. Record in the general journal the transactions given below. Make any computations to the nearest dollar. For each entry affecting budgetary accounts or operating statement accounts, show subsidiary account titles and amounts as well as general ledger control account titles and amounts.

    (1) A general tax levy in the amount of $3,200,000 was made. It is estimated that 3 percent of the tax will be uncollectible.

    (2) Tax anticipation notes in the amount of $250,000 were issued.

(3)   Purchase orders, contracts, and other commitment documents were issued against appropriations in the following amounts:

General Government	$120,000
Public Safety	162,000
Public Works	342,000
Health	112,000
Public Welfare	105,000
Recreation	114,000
Miscellaneous Appropriations	24,000
Total	$979,000

(4)   The General Fund collected the following in cash: Delinquent Taxes, $212,000; Interest and Penalties Receivable on Taxes, $10,720; Licenses and Permits, $188,000; Fines and Forfeits, $163,000; Charges for Services, $24,500; and Miscellaneous Revenues, $30,000.

(5)   A petty cash fund was established for general operating purposes in the amount of $6,000.

(6)   General Fund payrolls totaled $1,033,000. Of that amount, $147,450 was withheld for employees' income taxes and $79,000 was withheld for employees' FICA tax liability; the balance was paid in cash. The encumbrance system is not used for payrolls. The payrolls were for the following departments:

General Government	$ 316,233
Public Safety	467,771
Public Works	111,732
Health	22,066
Public Welfare	33,653
Recreation	81,545
Total	$1,033,000

(7)   The liability for the City's share of FICA taxes, $79,000, was recorded. The amount was budgeted as part of the Contributions to Retirement Funds appropriation.

(8)   Invoices for some of the services and supplies ordered in transaction (3) were received and approved for payment; departments affected are shown below:

	Actual	Estimated
General Government	$113,500	$113,100
Public Safety	146,375	140,500
Public Works	300,000	298,500
Health	111,700	112,000
Public Welfare	103,100	102,800
Recreation	97,125	99,000
Miscellaneous Appropriations	20,400	20,000
Totals	$892,200	$885,900

(9) Delinquent taxes receivable in the amount of $12,000 were written off as uncollectible. Interest and penalties accrued on these taxes amounting to $600 were also written off.

(10) Collections of the first installment of the current year's taxes totaled $1,632,000.

(11) Payments on General Fund vouchers amounted to $1,060,000.

(12) Collections on delinquent taxes written off in a prior year amounted to $438. Interest and penalties on the taxes written off amounted to $30. Interest accrued since the date of write-off amounted to $14 (this is Revenue of fiscal year 2000). All interest and penalties were collected at the time delinquent taxes were collected.

(13) The General Fund vouchered its required contributions to the Employees' Retirement Fund, $56,490, its liability for employees' income taxes withheld; the total amount of FICA tax liability; and the amount due other funds on July 1. Checks were drawn for all these vouchers.

b. Post each entry to the general ledger accounts and to all subsidiary ledger accounts required. (If you used the subsidiary ledger forms illustrated in Chapter 3, the Revenues ledger debit column supports the Estimated Revenues control account in the general ledger and the credit column supports the Revenues general ledger control account. Similarly, Chapter 3 illustrates how a single account in a subsidiary ledger can support three general ledger control accounts: Appropriations, Encumbrances, and Expenditures. Note the subsidiary ledger form provides only a debit column for Expenditures, so if a general journal entry indicates a credit to Expenditures, the amount must be entered in the subsidiary ledger account as a negative item in the Expenditures debit column. Since only a credit column is provided for Appropriations, if a general journal entry indicates a debit to Appropriations, the amount must be entered as a negative item in the Appropriations credit column of the subsidiary ledger account.)

c. Prepare a trial balance of the General Fund general ledger as of December 31, 1999, the end of the first six months of the fiscal year.

d. Prepare in good form an Interim Balance Sheet for the General Fund as of December 31, 1999. (See Illustration 4–1.)

e. Prepare in good form a Statement of Actual and Estimated Revenues for the six months ended December 31, 1999. (See Illustration 4–2.) Make sure the total Estimated Revenues and total Revenues shown on this statement agree with the same items shown on the December 31 Balance Sheet.

   f. Prepare in good form a Statement of Budgeted and Actual Expenditures and Encumbrances for the six months ended December 31, 1999. (See Illustration 4–3.) Make sure the total Appropriations, Expenditures, and Encumbrances shown on this statement agree with the same items shown on the December 31 Balance Sheet.

   g. Below are described the transactions during January 1–June 30, 2000, the second six months of the fiscal year. Record each in the general journal for the General Fund. For each entry affecting budgetary accounts or operating statement accounts, show subsidiary ledger account titles and amounts as well as general ledger control account titles and amounts.

     (1) In view of the information shown in the Statement of Actual and Estimated Revenues and the Statement of Budgeted and Actual Expenditures and Encumbrances, each for the first six months of the fiscal year, the City Council revised the budgets for the current year as shown below:

	Budget Adjustments Inc. (Dec.)
Estimated Revenues:	
Taxes	$ –0–
Licenses and Permits	3,000
Fines and Forfeits	4,000
Intergovernmental Revenue	(11,000)
Charges for Services	–0–
Miscellaneous Revenue	5,000
Appropriations:	
General Government	60,000
Public Safety	–0–
Public Works	–0–
Health	–0–
Public Welfare	40,000
Recreation	(22,000)
Contributions to Retirement Funds	–0–
Miscellaneous Appropriations	(6,000)

     (2) Purchase orders, contracts, and other commitment documents totaling $842,000 were issued against the following appropriations:

General Government	$ 87,490
Public Safety	416,000
Public Works	120,710
Health	40,000
Public Welfare	104,800
Recreation	52,000
Miscellaneous Appropriations	21,000

(3)   Invoices for services and supplies were received and approved for payment: Actual, $938,730; and Estimated, $918,000.

	Expenditure	Encumbrance
General Government	$ 96,470	$ 94,390
Public Safety	460,450	435,800
Public Works	161,810	160,310
Health	40,000	40,000
Public Welfare	102,000	106,000
Recreation	53,000	56,500
Miscellaneous Appropriations	25,000	25,000

(4)   Payrolls were computed, liabilities for withholdings were recorded, and the net paid in cash, as follows: General Fund—Gross Pay, $1,157,500; Income Tax Withheld, $170,800; and FICA Tax Withheld, $88,500. Payrolls are not encumbered. The distribution was:

General Government	$301,800
Public Safety	551,700
Public Works	132,000
Health	26,000
Public Welfare	50,000
Recreation	96,000

(5)   The City's liability for FICA tax, $88,500, was recorded as an expenditure of the Contributions to Retirement Funds appropriation.

(6)   Collections of the second installment of the current year's taxes were $1,300,000.

(7)   The General Fund collected the following revenue in cash: Licenses and Permits, $259,000; Fines and Forfeits, $220,000; Intergovernmental Revenues, $520,000; Charges for Services, $84,000; and Miscellaneous Revenues, $49,500.

(8)   A taxpayer who had been classified as delinquent proved he had paid general taxes of $8,440 when due. Audit disclosed that a former employee had embezzled $8,440—through oversight of the Treasurer, the employee had not been bonded. Interest and penalties in the amount of $845 had been recorded as receivable on the $8,440 "delinquent" tax bill at the end of the prior year. Since neither the $8,440 taxes nor the $845 interest and penalties are actually receivable, the total of the two, $9,285, was by resolution of the City Council charged as an expenditure of the current year's Miscellaneous Appropriations.

The audit also disclosed that tax bills totaling $2,586 on several pieces of property had been sent to both the present and the prior owner, and no tax bills at all had been prepared for several pieces of property—general taxes of $2,250 should have been charged. (Correct all accounts affected; do not adjust the Estimated Uncollectible Taxes account.)

(9)   Tax anticipation notes issued by the General Fund were paid at maturity at face amount plus interest of $5,000. (Charge Miscellaneous Appropriations for the expenditure.)

(10) Invoices for all items encumbered in the prior year were received and approved for payment in the amount of $14,180. (Charge the amount encumbered in 1999 to Expenditures of Public Works Appropriation. Charge the excess of the amount approved for payment over the Reserve for Encumbrances—1999 balance to Expenditures of the fiscal year 2000 Public Works Appropriation.)

(11) The petty cash fund was reimbursed for $4,810. (Charge General Government for the entire expenditure.)

(12) The General Fund vouchered and paid its liability for employees' income taxes withheld, the total liability for FICA taxes, and the required contribution to the Employees' Retirement Fund, $119,900.

(13) The General Fund recorded its liabilities to other funds for services received during the year, $20,000. ($15,300 should be charged to the Public Safety appropriation and $4,700 to the General Government appropriation.)

(14) The General Fund paid vouchers in the amount of $870,000.

(15) The General Fund made a long-term advance of $30,000 cash to the Stores and Services Fund.

(16) Current taxes receivable and related estimated uncollectibles were transferred to the delinquent category. Interest and penalties accrued on delinquent taxes amounted to $31,240; of this amount it is estimated that $9,360 is uncollectible.

h. Post to the general ledger and prepare a trial balance before adjustment of the accounts of the General Fund. Post to the subsidiary ledgers and make sure the totals of the subsidiary ledger columns agree with the balances of their respective control accounts.

i. Prepare and post the necessary closing entries for the General Fund.

j. Prepare in good form a Balance Sheet as of the end of the fiscal year, June 30, 2000.

k. Prepare in good form a Statement of Revenues, Expenditures, and Changes in Fund Balance for the General Fund for the year ended June 30, 2000. (See Illustration 4–5. Classify 1999 expenditures as Public Works.)

l. Prepare in good form a Statement of Revenues, Expenditures, and Changes in Fund Balance—Budget and Actual for the year ended June 30, 2000. Use the final adjusted budget figures. (See Illustration 4–6.)

CHAPTER

5

Accounting for General Fixed Assets and Capital Projects

Learning Objectives

After studying this chapter, you should be able to:

~ Describe the characteristics of general fixed assets and how they are classified.

~ Account for the acquisition of general fixed assets.

~ Account for the maintenance and disposition of general fixed assets.

~ Prepare a Statement of General Fixed Assets and Schedule of Changes in General Fixed Assets.

~ Explain the purpose of a capital projects fund.

~ Explain the typical sources of financing for capital projects.

~ Prepare journal entries for transactions of a typical capital project.

~ Explain and prepare journal entries for special cases such as

Alternative treatments of residual equities or deficits.

Original issue premiums or discounts and accrued interest on bonds sold.

~ Explain the concepts and accounting procedures for special assessment capital projects.

~ Prepare financial statements for capital projects funds.

Chapters 3 and 4 illustrated that long-lived assets such as office equipment, police cruisers, and other items may be acquired by a governmental unit by expenditure of appropriations of the General Fund or one or more of its special revenue funds. Long-lived assets used by activities accounted for by governmental fund types are called **general fixed assets.** Acquisitions of general fixed assets that require major amounts of money ordinarily cannot be financed from General Fund or special revenue fund appropriations. These general fixed assets usually involve *capital projects.* Capital projects such as the construction of buildings, highways, and bridges often require extensive planning and multiple years to complete. **Capital projects funds** are used to account for financial resources restricted, either legally or morally, for major capital projects and expenditures of these resources for asset construction. Capital projects funds also may be used to account for the acquisition by a governmental unit of general fixed assets under a capital lease agreement.

Illustration 5–1 summarizes the interrelationships among fund types and account groups as they relate to fixed asset acquisition. It shows that general fixed assets may be acquired from expenditures of the General Fund, special revenue funds, and capital projects funds. The cost or other carrying value of general fixed assets is accounted for in the General Fixed Assets Account Group (GFAAG), and long-term debt related to general fixed asset acquisition is accounted for in the General Long-Term Debt Account Group (GLTDAG). Debt service funds are used to account for resources to be used for payment of matured general debt principal and interest.

This chapter focuses on general fixed assets and capital projects funds accounting and financial reporting. Chapters 3 and 4 discussed accounting and financial reporting for the General Fund and for special revenue funds. Accounting for tax-supported general long-term debt and related debt service is explained in Chapter 6.

Accounting for General Fixed Assets

Only enterprise and internal service funds routinely account for property, plant, and equipment used in their operations. Trust funds that use fixed assets for the production of income also account for property, plant, and equipment. All other funds account only for financial resources. Thus, property, plant, and equipment acquired by general, special revenue, and capital projects funds are brought under accounting control by the creation of a General Fixed Assets Account Group.[1]

Accounting control of fixed tangible assets is generally deemed superior to that provided by a record system not formally integrated with the accounting informa-

---

[1]Accounting and financial reporting for capital assets is under study by the GASB at the present time. Some consideration is being given to a number of possible changes in current GASB standards relating to general fixed assets. If standards discussed in this chapter are changed, the publisher will distribute to faculty members who have adopted this text a bulletin describing the effect of the new standards on the explanations and illustrations in this chapter, and in any other chapters affected.

| Illustration 5–1 | Interrelationships among Governmental Fund Types and Account Groups—Fixed Asset Acquisition | |

General Fund and/or Special Revenue Funds	Capital Projects Funds	Debt Service Funds
Account for acquisition of general fixed assets from expenditures of annual appropriations. Cost of assets acquired is recorded in the GFAAG.	Account for acquisition of general fixed assets from expenditures of debt proceeds, capital grants, special assessments, and other sources restricted for fixed asset acquisition. Cost of assets acquired is recorded in the GFAAG. Long-term debt to be serviced from tax revenues, or from special assessments, is recorded in the GLTDAG.	Account for accumulation of resources for, and the payment of, matured debt principal and interest, except that being repaid from revenues of Enterprise Funds. Resources generally include taxes levied for debt service or operating transfers from other funds, accrued interest and premium on tax-supported long-term debt issued, and accrued interest and premium on special assessment long-term debt issued.

General Fixed Assets Account Group	General Long-Term Debt Account Group	
Accounts for cost of general fixed assets acquired by expenditures of the General Fund, special revenue funds, and capital projects funds. Also accounts for GFA acquired under capital leases and for GFA acquired by gift.	Accounts for all unmatured long-term debt except debt being repaid from revenues of enterprise funds. Long-term debt includes present value of rentals under capital leases.	

tion system. Records of individual assets of significant value or groups of assets of lesser unit value should include all information needed for planning an effective maintenance program, preparing budget requests for replacements and additions, providing an adequate insurance coverage, and fixing the responsibility for custody of the assets.

In conformity with generally accepted accounting principles, general fixed assets are recorded at acquisition cost (or fair value at time of receipt if assets are received by donation). If the cost of fixed assets was not recorded when the assets were acquired and is unknown when accounting control over the assets is established, it is acceptable to record them at estimated cost. The General Fixed Assets

Account Group is only an accounting entity, not a fiscal entity (therefore, not a fund). It records no current assets and no liabilities of any kind. The offset to the fixed asset accounts is the set of accounts that indicate the sources from which the fixed assets were acquired. "Investment in General Fixed Assets from Capital Projects Funds—General Obligation Bonds" or "Investment in General Fixed Assets from General Fund Revenues" are examples of typical source accounts of a General Fixed Assets Account Group. Balance sheets of this account group (sometimes called *Statements of General Fixed Assets*) display to interested parties the total cost of each category of general fixed assets and the total amount contributed by each source used for the acquisition of these assets. Customarily, a balance sheet is supplemented by a schedule showing the description of and dollar amount of additions to and deductions from each fixed asset category during the year.

The cost of fixed assets used by funds that are expected to cover their full costs by sale of products or services would be depreciated, just as is done by profit-seeking businesses. General fixed assets are acquired for the production of general governmental services, however, not for the production of services that are sold. Therefore, the GASB Depreciation of Fixed Assets Principle states that:

> Depreciation of general fixed assets should not be recorded in the accounts of governmental funds. Depreciation of general fixed assets may be recorded in cost accounting systems or calculated for cost finding analyses; and accumulated depreciation may be recorded in the General Fixed Assets Account Group.[2]

The provision for the computation of depreciation for unit cost purposes is in recognition of the fact that general fixed assets may be used for activities financed by grants from other governmental units, and that depreciation may be an allowable cost under the terms of the grant. In addition, unit costs stated on an accrual basis, including depreciation on general fixed assets, is considered by some to be useful information to provide administrators and legislators concerned with the allocation of resources to programs, departments, and activities. To a limited extent, a comparison of the accumulated depreciation on an asset with the cost of the asset may be relevant to the process of budgeting of outlays for replacement of capital assets. For these reasons, the GASB sees no objection to recording accumulated depreciation in the General Fixed Assets Account Group and reporting it in the Statement of General Fixed Assets.[3] Since depreciation expense cannot be recorded in the General Fixed Assets Account Group, credits to Accumulated Depreciation accounts must be offset by debits to those Investment in General Fixed Assets accounts that were credited when the depreciating asset was first recorded in the GFAAG.

General fixed assets may be thought of as those not used exclusively in the operations of any one fund nor belonging to any one fund. They include courthouses and city halls, public buildings in general, the land on which they are situated, highways, streets, sidewalks, equipment, and other tangible assets with a life longer than one fiscal year that are not used by an enterprise, non-

---

[2]GASB, *Codification*, Sec. 1100.107.
[3]GASB, *Codification*, Sec. 1400.118.

Illustration 5–2

CITY OF SMALLVILLE
Statement of General Fixed Assets—By Source
June 30, 1999

General Fixed Assets:	
Land	$2,455,033
Buildings	3,549,352
Improvements other than buildings	939,068
Equipment	2,355,114
Total General Fixed Assets	$9,298,567
Investment in General Fixed Assets from:	
Capital projects funds:	
Tax-supported bonds	$1,553,611
Federal grants	942,504
State grants	26,441
General fund revenues	6,679,409
Special revenue fund revenues	96,602
Total Investment in General Fixed Assets	$9,298,567

expendable trust, or internal service fund. Formerly, general fixed assets and general long-term liabilities were sometimes merged in a group under the heading of "Capital Fund" or "General Property Fund," but this practice is not currently allowed. A Statement of General Fixed Assets might appear as shown in Illustration 5–2.

Classification of General Fixed Assets

The asset accounts shown in Illustration 5–2 are those commonly found in Statements of General Fixed Assets. Additional or substitute accounts may be used as needed to present information relating to general fixed assets of a given governmental unit. As in accounting for businesses, cost is the generally accepted basis of accounting for governmental fixed assets. Determination of what constitutes cost of a governmental fixed asset follows the criteria specified in intermediate financial accounting texts for the determination of cost of fixed assets of a profit-seeking entity, except governments are *not* required to capitalize net interest cost during the period of construction of general fixed assets, but may do so if they wish. Similarly, the kinds of items reported in each fixed asset account are the same whether the reporting entity is a governmental body or a profit-seeking entity. Also, as is true in profit-seeking entities, the test of materiality is applied and items costing below an established minimum amount are not recorded in the asset accounts no matter how long their estimated useful lives, but are merely accounted for as expenditures of the acquiring fund. The following paragraphs are presented as a brief review of generally accepted principles of accounting for fixed assets.

Land

The cost of land acquired by a governmental unit through purchase should include not only the contract price but also such other related costs as taxes and other liens assumed, title search costs, legal fees, surveying, filling, grading, drainage, and other costs of preparation for the use intended. Governments are frequently subject to damage suits in connection with land acquisition, and the amounts of judgments levied are considered capital costs of the property acquired. Land acquired through forfeiture should be capitalized at the total amount of all taxes, liens, and other claims surrendered, plus all other costs incidental to acquiring ownership and perfecting title. Land acquired through donation should be recorded on the basis of appraised value at the date of acquisition; the cost of the appraisal itself should not be capitalized, however. Valuation of land obtained by donation is of importance chiefly for report, statistical, and other comparative purposes.

Buildings and Improvements Other than Buildings

The nature of assets to be classified as Buildings is a matter of common knowledge; but if a definition is needed, they may be said to consist of those structures erected above ground for the purpose of sheltering persons or property. "Improvements Other than Buildings" consists of land attachments of a permanent nature, other than buildings, and includes, among other things, roads, bridges, tunnels, walks, walls, and parking lots.

The determination of the cost of buildings and improvements acquired by purchase is relatively simple, although some peripheral costs may be of doubtful classification. The price paid for the assets constitutes most of the cost of purchased items; but legal and other costs, plus expenditures necessary to put the property into acceptable condition for its intended use, are proper additions. The same generalizations may be applied to acquisitions by construction under contract; that is, purchase or contract price, plus positively identified incidentals, should be capitalized. The determination of the cost of buildings and improvements obtained through construction by some agency of the governmental unit (sometimes called **force account** construction) poses slightly more difficulty. In these cases, costs should include not only all the direct and indirect expenditures (including net interest during the period of construction on debt incurred for the purpose of financing construction of fixed assets of proprietary funds—and of general fixed assets if the government chooses to capitalize interest on construction of GFA) of the fund providing the construction but also materials and services furnished by other funds as well. The valuation of buildings and improvements acquired by donation should be established by appraisal. As in the case of land, one reason for setting a value on donated buildings and improvements is to aid in determining the total value of fixed property used by the government, and for reports and comparisons. However, more compelling reasons exist for setting a value on buildings and certain improvements: the need for obtaining proper insurance coverage and the need for being able to substantiate the insurance claim if loss should occur.

Current GASB standards allow governmental units the option of not capitalizing the cost of infrastructure assets such as roads, bridges, curbs and gutters, streets, sidewalks, drainage systems, and lighting systems because such assets are immovable, and generally of value only to the governmental unit. If improvements are omitted from financial statements, the annual report should contain statistical data relative to them that would be of interest to residents, creditors, and other readers of the annual report. It is probable that GASB standards will be changed in the future to require the capitalization of the cost of infrastructure assets.

Equipment, or Machinery and Equipment

Machinery and equipment are most likely acquired by purchase, although construction financed by an internal service fund may be the source in some instances, in which case the same rules will apply as for buildings and improvements constructed by the governmental employees. The cost of machinery and equipment purchased should include items conventional under business accounting practice: purchase price, transportation costs if not included in purchase price, installation cost, and other direct costs of readying for use. Cash discounts on governmental fixed assets purchased should be treated as a reduction of costs. Donated equipment should be accounted for in the same manner, and for the same reasons, as donated buildings and improvements.

Construction Work in Progress

Construction Work in Progress, as an account classification of an enterprise fund, is discussed in Chapter 7. As a fixed asset classification in the General Fixed Assets Account Group, it is needed to account for construction expenditures accumulated as of the balance sheet date on projects financed by capital projects funds. As described later in this chapter, construction expenditures by capital projects funds are ordinarily closed to Fund Balance at the end of each year, but the amounts are not capitalized in the funds doing the construction: The amounts are set up under the caption of Construction Work in Progress in the General Fixed Assets Account Group.

Assets Acquired under Capital Lease Agreements

As explained in some detail in Chapter 6, state and local governmental units generally are subject to constitutional or statutory limits on the amount of long-term debt they may issue. Consequently, it has been customary for governmental units that have reached their legal debt limit, or nearly done so, to acquire the use of capital assets through a lease agreement. A brief example is given below of the computation of the amount to be recorded in a capital projects fund under the provisions of GASB standards if a general fixed asset is acquired under a capital lease. In a governmental fund, usually a capital projects fund, an entry is made to record an expenditure offset by a credit to Other Financing Sources, in the amount of the present value at the inception of the lease of the stream of lease payments.[4] That amount (or the fair value of the leased property, if less) is recorded in the GFAAG as the cost of the leased property.

FASB *SFAS No. 13* defines and establishes accounting and financial reporting standards for a number of forms of leases, only two of which, **operating leases** and **capital leases**, are of importance in governmental accounting. GASB standards accept the *SFAS No. 13* definitions of these two forms of leases and prescribe

---

[4]Intermediate accounting texts generally discuss at length the computation of amounts to be capitalized under capital lease agreements.

accounting and financial reporting for lease agreements of state and local governmental units.[5] If a particular lease meets any *one* of the following classification criteria, it is a *capital* lease.

1. The lease transfers ownership of the property to the lessee by the end of the lease term.
2. The lease contains an option to purchase the leased property at a bargain price.
3. The lease term is equal to or greater than 75 percent of the estimated economic life of the leased property.
4. The present value of rental or other minimum lease payments equals or exceeds 90 percent of the fair value of the leased property less any investment tax credit retained by the lessor.

If none of the criteria is met, the lease is classified as an operating lease by the lessee. Rental payments under an operating lease for assets used by governmental funds are recorded by the using fund as expenditures of the period. In many states, statutes prohibit governments from entering into obligations extending beyond the current budget year. Because of this legal technicality, governmental lease agreements typically contain a "fiscal funding clause," or cancellation clause, which permits governmental lessees to terminate the agreement on an annual basis if funds are not appropriated to make required payments. GASB standards specify that lease agreements containing fiscal funding or cancellation clauses should be evaluated. If the possibility of cancellation is judged remote, the lease should be disclosed in financial statements and accounts in the manner specified for *capital* leases.[6]

As an example of accounting for the acquisition of general fixed assets under a capital lease agreement, assume a governmental unit signs a capital lease agreement to pay $10,000 on January 1, 1999, the scheduled date of delivery of certain equipment to be used by an activity accounted for by a special revenue fund. The lease calls for annual payments of $10,000 at the beginning of each year thereafter; that is, January 1, 2000, January 1, 2001, and so on, through January 1, 2008. There are 10 payments of $10,000 each, for a total of $100,000, but GASB standards require entry in the accounts of the *present value* of the stream of annual payments, not their total. Since the initial payment of $10,000 is paid at the inception of the lease, its present value is $10,000. The present value of the remaining nine payments must be calculated using the rate "the lessee would have incurred to borrow over a similar term the funds necessary to purchase the leased asset."[7] Assuming the rate to be 10 percent, the present value of payments 2 through 10 is $57,590. The present value of the 10 payments is, therefore, $67,590. GASB standards require a

---

[5]GASB, *Codification*, Sec. L20.107.

[6]GASB, *Codification*, Sec. L20.119–122.

[7]Financial Accounting Standards Board, *Statement of Financial Accounting Standards No. 13*, "Accounting for Leases, as Amended and Interpreted through January 1997" (Norwalk, CT, 1997), L10.510.

governmental fund (including, if appropriate, a capital projects fund) to record the following entry at the inception of the capital lease for the present value of the down payment and remaining nine payments:

Expenditures	67,590	
Other Financing Sources—Capital Lease Agreements		67,590

The appropriate entry in the GFAAG is:

Equipment	67,590	
Investment in General Fixed Assets—Capital Leases		67,590

Related entries in the debt service fund and the General Long-Term Debt Account Group are illustrated and discussed in Chapter 6.

Source Accounts or "Investment in General Fixed Assets"

Since the General Fixed Assets Account Group is only a self-balancing set of accounts, not a fiscal entity, the self-balancing feature is achieved by the creation of a series of credit-balance accounts to record the sources from which general fixed assets were acquired. The Investment in General Fixed Assets accounts shown in Illustration 5–2 are examples. If the accounts illustrated do not adequately describe the source of certain general fixed assets of a given governmental reporting entity, other appropriately named accounts should be used.

Cost after Acquisition

Governmental accounting procedures should include clear-cut provisions for classifying cost incurred in connection with fixed assets after the acquisition cost has been established. Outlays closely associated with fixed assets will regularly occur in amounts of varying size, and responsible persons will be charged with deciding whether these should be recorded as additions to assets.

In general, any outlay that definitely adds to a fixed asset or enhances the value of an integral part of it may be classified as a capital item. Thus, drainage of land, addition of a room to a building, and changes in equipment that increase its output or reduce its cost of operation are clearly recognizable as additions to assets. Special difficulty arises in the case of large-scale outlays that are partly replacements and partly additions or betterments. An example would be replacement of a composition-type roof with a roof of some more durable material. To the extent that the project replaces the old roof, outlays should not be capitalized unless cost of the old roof is removed from the accounts; and to the extent that the project provides a better roof, outlays should be capitalized. The distribution of the total cost in such a case is largely a matter for managerial determination. Consistent with policy in recording original acquisition costs, some outlays unquestionably representing increases in permanent values may not be capitalized if the amount is less than some specified minimum or on the basis of any other criterion previously decided on.

Outlays that are partly replacements and partly additions or betterments occasion some accounting difficulty. The distribution of the outlay having been decided on, the estimated amount of addition or betterment might be added to the asset.

Perhaps better results might be obtained by crediting the appropriate asset account for the cost of the replaced part, thus removing the amount, and then debiting the asset account for the total cost of the replacing item.

Reduction of Cost

Reductions in the cost of fixed assets may relate to the elimination of the total amount expended for a given item or items, or they may consist only of removing the cost applicable to a specific part. Thus, if an entire building is demolished, the total cost of the structure should be removed from the appropriate accounts; but if the separation applies only to a wing or some other definitely identifiable portion, the cost eliminated should be the amount estimated as applying thereto. Reductions in the recorded cost of fixed assets may be brought about by sale, retirement from use, destruction by fire or other casualty, replacement of a major part, theft, or loss from some other cause, and possibly other changes. The cost of fixed assets held by a fund or the General Fixed Assets Account Group may sometimes be reduced by the transfer of a unit to another fund or to the General Fixed Assets Account Group.

Accounting for cost reductions consisting of entire units is a relatively simple matter if adequate records have been kept. Entries must be made in both controlling accounts and subsidiary ledger records to show the fact of the reduction. If a separate subsidiary ledger record is kept for the unit in question, that record should be removed from the ledger and stored in a file with other similar inactive records. If the reduction is only partial, the cost as shown by the subsidiary record must be modified to reflect the change, with a complete description of what brought about the change.

Since, under GASB standards, depreciation of general fixed assets does not have to be formally recorded in the general ledger, the removal may be accomplished by crediting the ledger account recording its cost and debiting the source account(s) that were credited when the asset was acquired. If a government follows the option allowed by GASB standards and records accumulated depreciation of general fixed assets, the Accumulated Depreciation account must also be debited to remove the amount related to the disposed asset.

Governments sometimes trade fixed assets for new items. In the general fixed assets accounts, the total cost of the old item should be removed and the total cost (not merely the cash payment) of the new one set up.

Illustrative GFAAG Entries

Acquisition of general fixed assets requires a debit to the appropriate General Fixed Assets general ledger asset account and a credit to an account indicating the source from which the asset was provided. Thus, if office equipment is purchased for the treasurer's office from General Fund resources, the *General Fixed Assets Account Group* entry should be as follows:

Equipment	450	
Investment in General Fixed Assets—General Fund Revenues		450

Although purchased for the immediate use of one department, the equipment belongs to the general government and could, if desired, be transferred to other use. On the *General Fund* books, the foregoing transaction would appear as an appropriation expenditure, which would be recorded as follows, ignoring reversal of the encumbrance.

Expenditures	450	
Vouchers Payable		450

General fixed assets acquired by use of capital projects fund resources would be recorded in the same manner as if acquired from the General Fund, the difference in entries being that the credits should show not only that the Investment in General Fixed Assets came from a capital projects fund but also, to the extent practicable, the specific sources of capital projects fund resources (tax-supported bonds, federal grants, state grants, private gifts, etc.). For example, the set of 15 illustrative entries shown later in this chapter for the Town of Brighton utilizes a capital projects fund to account for the construction of a fire station on land already owned by the Town. Total construction expenditures amounted to $1,493,000; the project was financed by a $1,200,000 bond issue and $300,000 contributed by other governmental units. Of the bond proceeds, $7,000 remained unexpended, or was expended for a noncapitalizable purpose. Assuming the cost of the land on which the fire station was constructed is already recorded in the accounts of the General Fixed Assets Account Group, the required entry in the GFAAG to record the cost of the new fire station is:

Buildings	1,493,000	
Investment in General Fixed Assets—Capital Projects Funds		
—General Obligation Bonds		1,193,000
—Contributions by Other Governmental Units		300,000

If construction of a general fixed asset is in progress at the end of a fiscal year, construction expenditures to the date of the financial report should be capitalized in the General Fixed Assets Account Group. Assuming construction expenditures of $250,000 (financed by a federal grant) had been made on a building project during a given year, the information would be recorded in the General Fixed Assets Account Group by the following entry:

Construction Work in Progress	250,000	
Investment in General Fixed Assets—Capital Projects		
Fund—Federal Grant		250,000

Following through from the foregoing entry, assume the completion of construction in the next year entailed additional expenditures of $275,000 (also provided by a federal grant), which would have been accounted for by the capital projects fund in the normal manner. The additional expenditure would be recorded in the General Fixed Assets Account Group as part of the cost of the completed project; and the previously suspended cost would be converted from its temporary account to the permanent one, as illustrated in the following entry:

Buildings	525,000	
Construction Work in Progress		250,000
Investment in General Fixed Assets—Capital Projects Fund—Federal Grant		275,000

The net effect of the two entries is, of course: Buildings, $525,000; Investment in General Fixed Assets—Capital Projects Fund—Federal Grant, $525,000.

A question arises if fixed assets constructed or acquired by a proprietary fund are later transferred to an activity accounted for by a governmental fund: If the asset is of depreciable nature, at what figure should it be recorded in the accounts of the General Fixed Assets Account Group—book value as shown by the transferor, original cost, or fair value at date of transfer? The answer at present seems to be book value. In the event fair value differs greatly from book value, a minority view is that fair value should be used. Assuming a building carried on the books of a proprietary fund at $200,000 cost less accumulated depreciation of $150,000 is permanently surrendered to the general government, the following entry would be made in the *General Fixed Assets Account Group*:

Buildings	50,000	
Investment in General Fixed Assets—Electric Utility Fund		50,000

The proprietary fund's accounting treatment of this transaction would be as shown below:

Accumulated Provision for Depreciation of Utility Plant	150,000	
Loss on Disposal of Buildings	50,000	
Utility Plant in Service		200,000

Disposal of general fixed assets involves no accounting problem if no cash or other extraneous assets are involved in the liquidation. The requirement is elimination of the fixed asset and reduction of the equity account that records its source. Assuming a building that cost $100,000, provided by a capital projects fund, is retired without revenue or expenditure to the governmental unit, the following entry in the *General Fixed Assets Account Group* would suffice:

Investment in General Fixed Assets—Capital Projects Fund—Federal Grant	100,000	
Buildings		100,000

The subsidiary record or account for the building should receive appropriate notations about the transaction and thereafter be transferred to an inactive file.

In the event cash is disbursed or received in connection with the disposal of general fixed assets, that fact would have no bearing on the entry to be made in the GFAAG. Cash disbursements in connection with the removal of an item from the GFAAG should appear among the transactions of the disbursing fund and be classified according to the nature of the charge. Assuming the General Fund pays $3,000 for the demolition of the building, an entry in the following form should be made on the *General Fund* books:

Expenditures	3,000	
Vouchers Payable (or Cash)		3,000

If cash is received from the disposal of a general fixed asset, some question may arise as to its disposition. Theoretically, it should be directed to the fund that provided the asset; but this may not always be practicable. If the asset was provided by a capital projects fund, the contributing fund may have been liquidated before the sale occurs. Unless prescribed by law, disposition of the results of sale will be handled as decided by the legislative body having jurisdiction over the asset and will be accounted for in the manner required by the accounting system of the recipient fund. Commonly, proceeds of sales of general fixed assets are budgeted as Miscellaneous Revenue by the General Fund. In such cases, when sales actually occur, the General Fund debits Cash (or a receivable) for the selling price and credits Revenues and the appropriate revenues ledger subsidiary account.

Detailed Property Accounts

Governmental organizations should keep both general and subsidiary records for fixed assets owned. General records consist primarily of general ledger accounts operated for control over groups of subsidiary records. Subsidiary records consist of the detailed records kept for individual items of fixed assets.

One or more of a number of purposes are served by the use of adequate fixed property records. The most important of these purposes are as follows:

1. Fixed property records, properly kept, furnish information about the investment that taxpayers and others in the past have made for the benefit of future citizens and other users of government property, in contrast with expenditures for current purposes.
2. They provide a basis for adequate insurance coverage on insurable fixed assets. Although cost is not the major determinant of insurable value, it would be given consideration.
3. Properly kept records, providing for information on care and maintenance, assist in the budgeting of such costs and perhaps in singling out items on which current expenditures are abnormally high or possibly some that require minimum outlays for upkeep and maintenance.
4. They assist in fixing accountability for the custody of individual items and in determining who is responsible for seeing that care and maintenance requirements receive the attention to which they are entitled.
5. Since capital budgets are best developed on a long-term basis, reliable information about fixed assets now owned should be of material assistance in approximating future requirements.
6. Complete fixed assets records are indispensable for proprietary funds as a basis for computing depreciation. For utility funds, they are absolutely essential in establishing the base that should be used in fixing charges for service or in judging the reasonableness of rate schedules already in effect.

The main classifications of fixed assets are shown in Illustration 5–2 and discussed in related paragraphs. The names of these classifications may be used as general ledger account titles; or, more specific account titles may be used, with a code to designate the general classifications to which the account belongs.

Subsidiary ledger accounts for fixed assets may be kept in the form indicated by the data processing system in use. Whatever the form of the subsidiary record, it should provide for showing, among other things, a complete description of the asset, including the formal title and the serial number or other objective information for positive identification of the asset; complete data on increases and decreases in cost, including amounts, dates, and sources from which posted; and provision for memorandum entries related to depreciation, repairs, and maintenance.

Statements of General Fixed Assets

For general fixed assets, the basic exhibit is the Statement of General Fixed Assets or, as it is sometimes captioned, the General Fixed Assets Balance Sheet. Its special contribution is to show the total cost of assets of the various groups in use by the general government and the sources from which they were derived. This statement is shown in Illustration 5–2.

The purposes for which, and by whom, fixed assets were being used at a given date, ordinarily the end of a fiscal period, are set forth in a Schedule of General Fixed Assets classified by functions and activities. Illustration 5–3 is an example of a Schedule of General Fixed Assets—by Function and Activity.

Another schedule that should be of interest to taxpayers and citizens generally shows changes in general fixed assets during a period of time (see Illustration 5–4). The value of this schedule is that it not only accounts systematically for changes between one date and another but also shows the extent to which responsible officials are investing for future requirements, in contrast to spending primarily for current requirements. In addition, the statement of changes serves as a reconcilement or transition between Statements of General Fixed Assets for the ends of consecutive years.

Accounting for Capital Projects

The reason for creating a fund to account for capital projects is the same as the reason for creating special revenue funds: to provide a formal mechanism to enable administrators to ensure revenues dedicated to a certain purpose are used for that purpose and no other, and to enable administrators to report to creditors, and other grantors of capital projects fund resources, that their requirements regarding the use of the resources were met.

Capital projects funds differ from general and special revenue funds in that the latter categories have a year-to-year life, whereas capital projects funds have a project-life focus. In some jurisdictions governments are allowed to account for all capital projects within a single capital projects fund. In other jurisdictions laws are construed as requiring each project to be accounted for by a separate capital projects fund. Even in jurisdictions that permit the use of a single fund, managers may prefer to use separate funds in order to enhance control over each project. In such cases a fund is created when a capital project or a series of related projects is legally authorized; it is closed when the project or series is completed. Budgetary

Illustration 5–3

CITY OF SMALLVILLE
Schedule of General Fixed Assets—By Function and Activity
As of June 30, 1999

Function and Activity	Total	Land	Buildings	Improvements Other than Buildings	Machinery and Equipment
General government:					
Control:					
Legislative	$ 2,825	—	—	—	$ 2,825
Executive	600	—	—	—	600
Judicial	5,070	—	793	—	4,277
Total control	8,495	—	793	—	7,702
Staff agencies:					
Purchasing	10,245	—	—	—	10,245
Finance	3,268	—	—	—	3,268
Data processing	179,875	—	—	—	179,875
Treasurer	1,475	—	—	—	1,475
Recorder	1,366	—	—	—	1,366
Attorney	1,924	—	—	—	1,924
Community development	592,991	$ 237,364	$ 351,888	—	3,739
Taxi	5,300	—	—	—	5,300
Garage	12,188	—	—	—	12,188
Personnel	1,330	—	—	—	1,330
Government buildings	1,640,862	525,113	1,025,569	$ 6,153	84,027
Billing	12,013	—	—	—	12,013
Total staff agencies	2,462,837	762,477	1,377,457	6,153	316,750
Public safety:					
Police department	341,067	—	1,665	676	338,726
Fire department	940,715	—	444,541	92,427	403,747
Total public safety	1,281,782	—	446,206	93,103	742,473
Public works:					
Streets and highways	1,458,257	—	51,463	553,985	852,809
Engineering	93,554	—	—	—	93,554
Planning and zoning	5,050	—	—	—	5,050
Total public works	1,556,861	—	51,463	553,985	951,413
Mosquito abatement	8,588	—	—	—	8,588
Parks	1,872,919	1,612,402	22,299	39,889	198,329
Recreation	2,005,988	66,550	1,619,236	235,416	84,786
Cemetery	20,414	—	—	—	20,414
Library	71,079	4,000	30,320	10,980	25,779
Airport	9,604	9,604	—	—	—
Total General Fixed Assets	$9,298,567	$2,455,033	$3,547,774	$939,526	$2,356,234

Illustration 5–4

CITY OF SMALLVILLE
Schedule of Changes in General Fixed Assets—By Function and Activity
Year Ended June 30, 1999

Function and Activity	General Fixed Assets June 30, 1998	Additions	Deductions	General Fixed Assets June 30, 1999
General government:				
Control:				
Legislative	$ 1,430	$ 1,395	—	$ 2,825
Executive	600	—	—	600
Judicial	5,070	—	—	5,070
Total control	7,100	1,395	—	8,495
Staff agencies:				
Purchasing	10,245	—	—	10,245
Finance	2,493	775	—	3,268
Data processing	67,371	112,504	—	179,875
Treasurer	700	775	—	1,475
Recorder	1,366	—	—	1,366
Attorney	1,924	—	—	1,924
Community development	592,991	—	—	592,991
Taxi	5,300	—	—	5,300
Garage	12,188	—	—	12,188
Personnel	1,330	—	—	1,330
Government buildings	777,814	865,515	$ (2,467)	1,640,862
Billing	12,013	—	—	12,013
Total staff agencies	1,485,735	979,569	(2,467)	2,462,837
Public safety:				
Police department	340,222	39,712	(38,867)	341,067
Fire department	923,056	17,659	—	940,715
Total public safety	1,263,278	57,371	(38,867)	1,281,782
Public works:				
Streets and highways	1,349,142	109,189	(74)	1,458,257
Engineering	89,221	4,333	—	93,554
Planning and zoning	5,050	—	—	5,050
Total public works	1,443,413	113,522	(74)	1,556,861
Mosquito abatement	8,588	—	—	8,588
Parks	1,845,283	28,446	(810)	1,872,919
Recreation	1,981,573	24,415	—	2,005,988
Cemetery	20,414	—	—	20,414
Library	23,191	49,080	(1,192)	71,079
Airport	9,604	—	—	9,604
Total General Fixed Assets	$8,088,179	$1,253,798	$(43,410)	$9,298,567

accounts need not be used because the legal authorization to engage in the project is in itself an appropriation of the total amount that may be obligated for the construction or acquisition of the capital asset specified in the project authorization. Estimated revenues need not be recorded because few contractors will start work on a project until financing is ensured through the sale of bonds or the receipt of grants or gifts. To provide control over the issuance of contracts and purchase orders, which may be numerous and which may be outstanding for several years in construction projects, it is recommended that the encumbrance procedure described in Chapter 3 be used. Since the purpose of the capital projects fund is to account for the acquisition and disposition of revenues for a specific purpose, it (as is true for general and special revenue funds) contains balance sheet accounts for only financial resources and for the liabilities to be liquidated by those resources. Neither the capital assets acquired nor any long-term debt incurred for the acquisition is accounted for by a capital projects fund; the General Fixed Assets Account Group and the General Long-Term Debt Account Group account for these items, as discussed earlier in this chapter and in Chapter 6, respectively.

In some jurisdictions, annual revenues are raised for the expressed purpose of financing major repairs to existing capital assets, or for replacement of components of those assets (e.g., furnaces, air conditioning systems, roofs). Revenues of the nature described are accounted for by a **capital improvements fund,** sometimes called a *cumulative building fund.* The specific repairs and replacements to be undertaken in a given year are not necessarily known at the time the revenues are budgeted. The appropriation process described in previous chapters is used to authorize expenditures from capital improvement funds when the nature and approximate cost of needed repairs and replacements become known. Necessary expenditures that cannot be financed by appropriation of the Fund Balance of a capital improvement fund, nor from the General Fund or special revenue funds, may occasion the establishment of a capital projects fund.

Legal Requirements   Since a governmental unit's power to issue bonds constitutes an ever-present hazard to the welfare of its property owners in particular,[8] and its taxpayers in general, the authority is ordinarily closely regulated by legislation. The purpose of legislative regulation is to obtain a prudent balance between public welfare and the rights of individual citizens. In some jurisdictions, most bond issues must be approved by referendum; in others, by petition of a specified percentage of taxpayers. Not only must bond issues be approved according to law but other provisions, such as method and timing of payments from the proceeds, and determination of validity of claims for payment, must be complied with. A knowledge of all details related to a bond issue is prerequisite to the avoidance of difficulties and complications that might otherwise occur.

---

[8]An issue of bonds to be repaid from tax revenues in essence places a lien on all taxable property within a governmental unit's jurisdiction. Responsibility for payments of principal and interest on general bonded debt provides for no consideration of a property owner's financial condition, and ability or inability to pay.

Participation of state and federal agencies in financing capital acquisitions by local government adds further complications to the process. Strict control of how such grants are used is imperative for ensuring proper use of the funds. This necessitates more or less dictation of accounting and reporting procedures to provide information necessary for proving or disproving compliance with terms of the grants. Details of the fund structure and operation should provide for producing all the required information when it is needed, in the form in which it is needed.

Accomplishment of a capital acquisition project may be brought about in one or more of the following ways:

1. Outright purchase from fund cash.
2. By construction, utilizing the governmental unit's own working force.
3. By construction, utilizing the services of private contractors.
4. By capital lease agreement.

Illustrative Transactions—Capital Projects Funds

GASB standards require use of the same basis of accounting for capital projects funds as for general and special revenue funds. Proceeds of debt issues should be recognized by a capital projects fund at the time the issue is sold, rather than the time it is authorized, because authorization of an issue does not guarantee its sale. Proceeds of debt issues should be recorded as Proceeds of Bonds or Proceeds of Long-Term Notes rather than as Revenues, and they should be reported in the Other Financing Sources section of the Statement of Revenues, Expenditures, and Changes in Fund Balance. Similarly, tax revenues raised by the General Fund, or a special revenue fund, and transferred to a capital projects fund are recorded as Operating Transfers In and reported in the Other Financing Sources section of the operating statement. Taxes raised specifically for a capital projects fund would be recorded as Revenues of that fund, as would special assessments to be used for the construction of assets deemed to be of particular benefit to certain property owners. Grants, entitlements, or shared revenues received by a capital projects fund from another governmental unit are considered Revenues of the capital projects fund, as would be interest earned on temporary investments of the capital projects fund if the interest is available for expenditure by the capital projects fund (if, by law, the interest must be used for service of long-term capital debt the interest should be transferred to the appropriate debt service fund).

In the following illustration of accounting for representative transactions of a capital projects fund, it is assumed the Town Council of the Town of Brighton authorized an issue of $1,200,000 of 6 percent bonds as partial financing of a fire station expected to cost approximately $1,500,000; the $300,000 additional was to be contributed by other governments. The project, to utilize land already owned by the Town, was done partly by a private contractor and partly by the Town's own working force. Completion of the project was expected within the current year. Transactions and entries were as shown below, all of which are assumed to occur in fiscal year 1999. For economy of time and space, vouchering of liabilities will be omitted, as will entries in subsidiary ledger accounts.

The $1,200,000 bond issue, which had received referendum approval by taxpayers, was officially approved by the town council.

> No formal entry is required by GASB standards. A memorandum entry may be made to identify the approved project and the means of financing it.

The sum of $50,000 was borrowed from the National Bank for defraying engineering and other preliminary expenses. Security for this note is the expectation that the approved bond issue can be sold.

1. Cash	50,000	
Bond Anticipation Notes Payable		50,000

The receivable from the other governments was recorded:

2. Due from Other Governmental Units	300,000	
Revenues		300,000

Total purchase orders and other commitment documents issued for supplies, materials, items of minor equipment, and labor required for the part of the project to be performed by the Town's employees amounted to $443,000. (Since the authorization is for the *project*, not for a budget year, it is unnecessary to include "1999," or any other year, in the account titles.)

3. Encumbrances	443,000	
Reserve for Encumbrances		443,000

A contract was let for certain work to be done by a private contractor in the amount of $1,005,000.

4. Encumbrances	1,005,000	
Reserve for Encumbrances		1,005,000

Special engineering and miscellaneous costs that had not been encumbered were paid in the amount of $48,000.

5. Construction Expenditures	48,000	
Cash		48,000

When the project was approximately half finished, the contractor submitted billing for a payment of $495,000.

6a. Reserve for Encumbrances	495,000	
Encumbrances		495,000
6b. Construction Expenditures	495,000	
Contracts Payable		495,000

(This entry records conversion of an estimated liability to a firm liability, eligible for payment upon proper authentication. Contracts Payable records the status of a claim under a contract between the time of presentation and verification for vouchering or payment.)

Payment in full was received from the other governmental units that had agreed to pay part of the cost of the new fire station.

| 7. Cash .... | 300,000 | |
| Due from Other Governmental Units .... | | 300,000 |

The National Bank Loan was repaid with interest amounting to $1,000.

8. Interest Expenditures	1,000	
Bond Anticipation Notes Payable	50,000	
Cash		51,000

The bond issue was sold at par, on June 15, 1999, the date of the bonds.

| 9. Cash .... | 1,200,000 | |
| Proceeds of Bonds .... | | 1,200,000 |

The contractor's initial claim was fully verified and paid.

| 10. Contracts Payable .... | 495,000 | |
| Cash .... | | 495,000 |

Total disbursements for all costs encumbered in Transaction 3 amounted to $440,000.

| 11a. Reserve for Encumbrances .... | 443,000 | |
| Encumbrances .... | | 443,000 |

| 11b. Construction Expenditures .... | 440,000 | |
| Cash .... | | 440,000 |

Billing for the balance due on the contract was received from the contractor.

| 12a. Reserve for Encumbrances .... | 510,000 | |
| Encumbrances .... | | 510,000 |

| 12b. Construction Expenditures .... | 510,000 | |
| Contracts Payable .... | | 510,000 |

Inspection revealed only minor imperfections in the contractor's performance, and on correction of these, the bill was paid.

| 13. Contracts Payable .... | 510,000 | |
| Cash .... | | 510,000 |

All requirements and obligations related to the project having been fulfilled, the operating statement accounts were closed.

14. Revenues	300,000	
Proceeds of Bonds	1,200,000	
Construction Expenditures		1,493,000
Interest Expenditures		1,000
Fund Balance		6,000

Since the project has been completed, it is appropriate to close the capital projects fund. The only asset of the fund remaining after the 14 transactions illustrated is Cash in the amount of $6,000. State laws customarily require that assets no longer needed in a capital projects fund be transferred to the fund that will service the debt incurred for this project, a debt service fund. Transfers of this nature are called **Equity Transfers** and are reported in the Changes in Fund Balance section of the Statement of Revenues, Expenditures, and Changes in Fund Balance as shown in Illustration 5–5. The entries to record the transfer and the closing of the capital projects fund accounts are:

15a. Equity Transfer Out	6,000	
Cash		6,000
15b. Fund Balance	6,000	
Equity Transfer Out		6,000

The cost of the fire station constructed by the Town of Brighton is recorded in the General Fixed Assets Account Group; the necessary entry was illustrated earlier in this chapter. The liability for the bonds sold for the benefit of this fund is recorded in the General Long-Term Debt Account Group, as illustrated in Chapter 6.

Illustration 5–5

TOWN OF BRIGHTON
Fire Station Capital Projects Fund
Statement of Revenues, Expenditures, and
Changes in Fund Balance
For the Year Ended December 31, 1999

Revenues:		
From other governmental units		$ 300,000
Expenditures:		
Construction	$1,493,000	
Interest on short-term debt	1,000	
Total Expenditures		1,494,000
Excess of Revenues over (under) Expenditures		(1,194,000)
Other Financing Sources (Uses):		
Proceeds of bonds		1,200,000
Excess of Revenues and Other Financing Sources over Expenditures		6,000
Fund Balance, January 1, 1999		–0–
Equity transfer out		(6,000)
Fund Balance, December 31, 1999		$ –0–

Illustrative Financial Statements for a Capital Projects Fund

Inasmuch as all balance sheet accounts of the Town of Brighton Fire Station Capital Projects Fund are closed in the case illustrated in the preceding section of this chapter, there are no assets, liabilities, or fund equity to report in a balance sheet. The operations of the year, however, should be reported in a Statement of Revenues, Expenditures, and Changes in Fund Balance, as shown in Illustration 5–5.

Consistent with the illustrative entries for this case, it is assumed the Town of Brighton is not required to adopt a legal budget for this, or any other, capital projects fund. Accordingly, GASB standards do not require the inclusion of a Statement of Revenues, Expenditures, and Changes in Fund Balance—Budget and Actual for the capital projects fund type.

Alternative Treatment of Residual Equity or Deficits

In the example presented above, a modest amount of cash remained in the capital projects fund after the project had been completed and all liabilities of the fund liquidated. If necessary expenditures and other financing uses are planned carefully, and controlled carefully so that actual does not exceed plans, revenues and other financing sources of the capital projects fund should equal, or slightly exceed, the expenditures and other financing uses, leaving a residual equity. If, as in the example presented above, long-term debt had been incurred for the purposes of the capital projects fund, the residual equity is ordinarily transferred to the fund that is to service the debt. If the residual equity were deemed to have come from grants or shared revenues restricted for capital acquisitions or construction, legal advice may indicate that any residual equity must be returned to the source(s) of the restricted grants or restricted shared revenues.

In some situations, in spite of careful planning and cost control, expenditures and other financing uses of a capital projects fund may exceed its revenues and other financing sources, resulting in a negative Fund Balance, or deficit. If the deficit is a relatively small amount, the legislative body of the governmental unit may be able to authorize transfers from one or more other funds to cover the deficit in the capital projects fund. If the deficit is relatively large, and/or if intended transfers are not feasible, the governmental unit may seek additional grants or shared revenues from other governmental units to cover the deficit. If no other alternative is available, the governmental units would need to finance the deficit by issuing debt in whatever form is legally possible and salable under market conditions then existing.

Bond Premium, Discount, and Accrued Interest on Bonds Sold

Governments that issue bonds, or long-term notes, to finance the acquisition of capital assets commonly sell the entire issue to an underwriter, or a syndicate of underwriters, on the basis of bids. The underwriters then "retail" the bonds or notes to institutions or individuals. Statutes of approximately half of the states prohibit the initial sale of an issue of local government bonds at a discount. Accordingly, it is usual to set the interest rate high enough to enable the underwriters to pay the issuer at least the par, or face, value of the bonds; it is not unusual for underwriters to pay issuers an amount in excess of par, known as premium. State statutes, local ordinances, or bond indentures often require that premiums be used for debt service. In such cases only the par value of the bonds is considered as an Other

Financing Source of the capital projects fund; the premium is considered as an Other Financing Source of the debt service fund. Therefore, the sale of bonds at a premium would require an entry in the capital projects fund for the face of the bonds (as shown in Entry 9 of this chapter) and an entry in the debt service fund· for the premium. Similarly, when bonds are sold between interest payment dates the amount of accrued interest is included in the total selling price. Conceptually, accrued interest sold is an offset to the interest expenditure on the first interest payment date following the sale of the bonds. Generally, in practice, however, accrued interest sold is recorded as a Revenue of the debt service fund.

It may happen that the issuing government receives one check from the underwriters for the total amount of the par plus the premium. If procedures of that government indicate that it is desirable to record the entire amount in the capital projects fund, the following entry is currently considered to be appropriate (using assumed amounts):

Cash	1,509,000	
Proceeds of Bonds		1,500,000
Due to Debt Service Fund		9,000

The entry accounts for bond premium as a liability of the capital projects fund because it must be remitted to the debt service fund. Some accountants use Premium on Bonds as the liability account title, rather than Due to Debt Service Fund; the accounting treatment is the same, however. (In the event that the entire proceeds of the bond sale are, in fact, available for expenditure for construction, the amount of premium should be included in the credit to Proceeds of Bonds.)

In those jurisdictions in which it is legal for bonds to be sold initially at a discount, using the amounts assumed in the entry above, the entry might be:

Cash	1,491,000	
Discount on Bonds	9,000	
Proceeds of Bonds		1,500,000

Crediting Proceeds of Bonds for $1,500,000 carries the implication that, if necessary, the discount is expected to be counterbalanced at a future date by receipt of money from another source. When money from another source has been provided, or it has been determined that no money from another source will be provided, the discount would be written off against Proceeds of Bonds. When it is known in advance that the discount will not be made up by transfers from other sources, a debit to Cash and a credit to Proceeds of Bonds, each for par value less discount, would suffice.

Profit-seeking entities amortize bond premium and accumulate bond discount in order to state bond interest expense at its "true" amount (as defined in generally accepted accounting principles). Capital projects funds are concerned with accounting for the receipt and expenditure of financial resource inflows designated for the construction or purchase of capital facilities; they are not concerned with income determination. Accordingly, bond premium is *not* amortized and bond discount is not accumulated by capital projects funds. Other funds and account groups affected by the bond sale and debt service are discussed in Chapter 6; none of these funds or groups record amortization of premium or accumulation of discount on tax-supported bonds payable or special assessment bonds payable.

Sale of bonds to finance a capital project is sometimes avoided, in whole or in part, through an agreement by the contractor to accept bonds in full or part payment for services. This arrangement is common in some states and unused in others. It forces the financing onto the contractor. Not being a specialist in finance, a contractor's costs are likely to be above those of an expert, thus increasing the amount that must be bid on the project.

Retained Percentages   It is common to require contractors on large-scale contracts to give performance bonds, providing for indemnity to the governmental unit for any failure on the contractor's part to comply with terms and specifications of the agreement. Before final inspection of a project can be completed, the contractor may have moved its working force and equipment to another location, thus making it difficult for the contractor to remedy possible objections to its performance. Also, the shortcoming alleged by the governmental unit may be of a controversial nature, with the contractor unwilling to accede to the demands of the governmental unit; and results of legal action in such disagreements are not predictable with certainty.

To provide more prompt adjustment on shortcomings not large or convincing enough to justify legal action, and not recoverable under contractor's bond, as well as those the contractor may admit but not be in a position to rectify, it is common practice to withhold a portion of the contractor's remuneration until final inspection and acceptance have come about. The withheld portion is normally a contractual percentage of the amount due on each segment of the contract.

In the Town of Brighton illustration, the contractor submitted a bill for $495,000, which, on preliminary approval, was recorded in Entry 6 as:

Construction Expenditures	495,000	
Contracts Payable		495,000

Assuming the contract provided for retention of 5 percent, current settlement on the billing would be recorded as follows:

Contracts Payable	495,000	
Cash		470,250
Contracts Payable—Retained Percentage		24,750

Alternatively, the intention of the government to retain the percentage stipulated in the contract could be recorded at the time the progress billing receives preliminary approval. In that event, the credit to Contracts Payable in the first entry in this section would be $470,250, and the credit to Contracts Payable—Retained Percentage in the amount of $24,750 is made at that time. The second entry, therefore, would be a debit to Contracts Payable and a credit to Cash for $470,250.

On final acceptance of the project, the retained percentage is liquidated by a payment of cash. In the event the governmental unit that made the retention finds it necessary to spend money on correction of deficiencies in the contractor's performance, the payment is charged to Contracts Payable—Retained Percentage.

*Claims and
Judgments Payable*

Claims and judgments often, although not always, relate to construction activities of a government. If a claim has been litigated and a judicial decision adverse to the governmental unit has been rendered, there is no question as to the amount of the liability that should be recorded. If claims have not been litigated, or judgments have not been made, as of the balance sheet date, liabilities may be estimated through a case-by-case review of all claims, or the application of historical experience to the outstanding claims, or a combination of these methods.[9]

GASB standards currently specify that the amount of claims and judgments recognized as expenditures and liabilities of governmental funds is limited to the amount that would normally be liquidated with expendable resources then in the fund; any liability for claims and judgments payable that exceeds the amount recognized in the governmental fund must be recognized in the General Long-Term Debt Account Group. (Accounting and financial reporting for the GLTDAG is illustrated in Chapter 6.)

*Bond Anticipation
Notes Payable
and the Problem
of Interest
Expenditures*

Bond Anticipation Notes Payable is a liability resulting from the borrowing of money for temporary financing before issuance of bonds. Delay in perfecting all details connected with issuance of bonds and postponement of the sale until a large portion of the proceeds is needed are the prevailing reasons for preliminary financing by use of **bond anticipation notes.** The "bond anticipation" description of the debt signifies an obligation to retire the notes from proceeds of a proposed bond issue. The account is increased and decreased for the same reasons and in the same manner employed for Tax Anticipation Notes Payable, discussed in Chapter 4.

Interest almost always must be paid on Bond Anticipation Notes Payable. Both practical and theoretical problems are involved in the payment of interest on liabilities. Practically, payment of interest by the capital projects fund reduces the amount available for construction or acquisition of the assets, so the administrators of the capital projects fund would wish to pass the burden of interest payment to another fund. Logically, the debt service fund set up for the bond issue should bear the burden of interest on bond anticipation notes, and possibly on judgments, but at the time this interest must be paid the debt service fund may have no assets. It would also appeal to the capital projects fund's administrators that interest on the bond anticipation notes and judgments should be paid by the General Fund (or any other fund with available cash). If such interest payments had been included in the appropriations budget by the General Fund (or other fund), the payment would be legal; if not, the legislative body might authorize the other fund to pay the interest.

If the capital projects fund bears the interest on bond anticipation notes or other short-term debt, either initially or ultimately, an expenditure account must

---

[9]GASB standards (GASB, *Codification*, Sec. C50.110–.111) require governmental units to use the criteria of FASB *SFAS No. 5* as guidelines for recognizing a loss liability. That is, if information available prior to issuance of the financial statements indicates it is probable that an asset has been impaired or a liability has been incurred at the date of the financial statements and the amount of the loss can be estimated with a reasonable degree of accuracy, the liability should be recognized.

be debited. In Entry 8 in the series of capital projects fund entries illustrated earlier in this chapter, interest paid on bond anticipation notes was debited to Interest Expenditures rather than to Construction Expenditures. The illustrated procedure would be used by governmental units that choose not to capitalize interest payments by capital projects funds. GASB standards allow each governmental unit to choose whether or not it wishes to capitalize net interest incurred in the construction or acquisition of *general* fixed assets as a part of the cost of the asset, as long as the policy is consistently applied and is disclosed in the notes to the financial statements.[10] If a governmental unit chooses to capitalize interest on short-term debt of the Capital Projects Fund, it is logical to debit that item to Construction Expenditures and not create a separate Interest Expenditures account.

If any governmental fund other than a capital projects fund pays interest on bond anticipation notes, it is simpler for the governmental unit to choose not to capitalize the interest, otherwise the accountants will have to analyze all the funds in order to determine the amount of interest to be capitalized. Similarly, since debt service funds routinely pay interest on long-term debt incurred on capital projects, the interest on long-term debt during the period of construction presents the same problem as interest on short-term debt. GASB standards provide that interest expenditures for short-term debt or for long-term debt incurred for the construction or acquisition of general fixed assets should be offset by any interest earned by the governmental unit on investment by a capital projects fund of debt proceeds. (In some jurisdictions, any such revenue may not be used by the capital projects fund but must be transferred to a debt service fund.) The provisions of the relevant standards are more complex than is appropriate for discussion here. Since capitalization of net interest is optional in the case of general fixed assets, the great majority of governmental units choose the simpler option: noncapitalization.

Depreciation on general fixed assets is not recorded by state and local governments, and there is no determination of governmental net income for financial reporting or for federal income tax purposes; therefore, the inclusion or exclusion of interest as an element of asset cost is largely a matter of theoretical concern at this time.

Investments

Interest rates payable by governmental units on general long-term debt have been lower than interest rates the governmental units can earn on temporary investments of high quality, such as U.S. Treasury bills and notes, bank certificates of deposit, and government bonds with short maturities. Consequently, there is considerable attraction to the practice of selling bonds as soon as possible after a capital project is legally authorized, and investing the proceeds to earn a net interest income. (This practice also avoids the problems and costs involved in financing by Bond Anticipation Notes Payable, described in the preceding section.) Arbitrage rules under the Internal Revenue Code, particularly after the Tax Reform Act of

---

[10]GASB, *Codification*, Sec. 1400.111.

1986 became effective, constrain the investment of bond proceeds to securities whose yield does not exceed that of the new debt. Application of these rules to state and local governmental units is subject to continuing litigation and legislative action, so competent legal guidance must be sought by governmental units wishing to invest bond proceeds in a manner that will avoid difficulties with the Internal Revenue Service (IRS). Violation of the arbitrage rules may require the governmental unit to pay excess investment earnings to the IRS. This is referred to as an **arbitrage rebate.** Moreover, violation of arbitrage rules may also result in the IRS disallowing income tax exemption for the interest on the bond issue.

Interest earned on temporary investments is available for use by the capital projects fund in some jurisdictions; in others, laws or local practices require the interest income to be transferred to the debt service fund or to the General Fund. If interest income is available to the capital projects fund, it should be recognized on the accrual basis as a credit to Revenues. If it will be collected by the capital projects fund but must be transferred, the credit for the income earned should be to Due to Other Funds; if the interest will be collected by the debt service fund, or other fund that will recognize it as revenue, no entry by the capital projects fund is necessary.

Multiple-Period and Multiple-Project Bond Funds

Thus far, discussion of capital projects fund accounting has proceeded on the tacit assumption that initiation and completion of projects occur in the same fiscal year. Many projects large enough to require a capital projects fund are started in one year and ended in another. Furthermore, a single comprehensive authorization may authorize two or more purchase or construction projects as segments of a master plan of improvements. Both multiple-period and multiple-project activities require some deviations from the accounting activities that suffice for one-period, one-project accounting.

The first difference appears in the budgeting procedure. Whereas for a one-period operation a single authorization might adequately cover the project from beginning to end, annual budgets, in one form or another, may be desirable or even required for those extending into two or more periods. This practice is resorted to as a means of keeping the project under the legislative body's control and preventing the unacceptable deviations that might result from lump-sum approval, in advance, of a long-term project. Likewise, a large bond issue, to be supplemented by grants from outside sources, may be authorized to cover a number of projects extending over a period of time but not planned in detail before initiation of the first project. Such an arrangement requires the fund administration to maintain control by giving final approval to the budget for each project only as it comes up for action.

For a multiple-projects fund, it is necessary to identify encumbrances and expenditures in a way that will indicate the project to which each encumbrance and expenditure applies, in order to check for compliance with the project budget. This can be accomplished by adding the project name or other designation (e.g., "City Hall," or "Project No. 75") to the encumbrance and expenditure account titles. This device is almost imperative for proper identification in the recording of transactions, and it facilitates preparation of cash and expenditure statements for multiproject operations.

In accounting for encumbrances for multiperiod projects, there is some difference of opinion as to the desirable procedure to follow in relation to encumbrances outstanding at the end of a period. In the management of a General Fund, for example, operations in terms of amounts of revenues and expenditures during a specified standard period of time (quarter, half year, etc.) provide measures of accomplishment. Because capital projects are rarely of the same size and may be started and ended at any time of year, periodic comparisons are of little significance. Furthermore, although the personnel of a legislative body may change at the beginning of a year during which a capital project is in progress, the change is unlikely to affect materially the project's progress. Although the operations of a capital projects fund are project-completion oriented, with slight reference to time, GASB standards require Encumbrances, Expenditures, Proceeds of Bonds, and Revenues accounts to be closed to Fund Balance at year-end in order to facilitate preparation of capital projects fund financial statements for inclusion in the governmental unit's annual report on a basis consistent with year-end statements of other funds.

The required procedure does produce year-end capital projects fund balance sheets that appear similar to those of general and special revenue funds illustrated in preceding chapters. The similarity of appearance and terminology may be misleading, however. The Fund Balance account of a general or special revenue fund represents net financial resources available for appropriation, whereas the Fund Balance account of a multiple-period capital projects fund represents net assets already set aside for the acquisition of specified capital facilities. The Fund Balance of a multiple-period capital projects fund is comparable to the unexpended unencumbered appropriation item on an interim balance sheet of a general or special revenue fund; it is *not* comparable to the year-end Fund Balance of such funds.

Reestablishment of Encumbrances

The year-end closing procedure required by GASB standards for use by capital projects funds artificially chops the Construction Expenditures pertaining to each continuing project into fiscal-year segments, rather than allowing the total cost of each project to be accumulated in a single Construction Expenditures account. Similarly, closing the Encumbrance account of each project to Fund Balance at year-end creates some procedural problems in accounting in the subsequent year. The procedure illustrated for general and special revenue funds (using separate Encumbrances, Reserve for Encumbrances, and Expenditures accounts for each year) could be followed. The procedure illustrated for general and special revenue funds is logical in that case because each appropriation expires at year-end, and yearly Expenditure and Encumbrance accounts are needed to match with the yearly Appropriations account. The authorization (appropriation) for a capital project, however, does not expire at the end of a fiscal year but continues for the life of the project. Accordingly, it appears desirable to reestablish the Encumbrance account at the beginning of each year in order to facilitate accounting for expenditures for goods and services ordered in one year and received in a subsequent year.

Reestablishment of the Encumbrance account may be accomplished as shown by the following entry (amount assumed):

Encumbrances	210,000	
Fund Balance		210,000

If the Encumbrance account is reestablished, subsequent receipt of goods or services entered as encumbrances in a prior year may be accounted for in the same manner as if they had been ordered in the current year:

Reserve for Encumbrances	210,000	
Construction Expenditures	210,000	
Vouchers Payable		210,000
Encumbrances		210,000

Capital Projects Financed by Special Assessments

Another source of financing major acquisitions of general fixed assets is by issuance of long-term debt to be repaid by special assessments. A **special assessment** is a compulsory levy made against certain property to defray part or all of the cost of a specific improvement or service that is presumed to be of general benefit to the public and of particular benefit to the property against which the special assessment is levied. Special assessment financing is allowed under the laws of many states. Generally, a majority of owners of the property that will be assessed must agree to the formation of a special assessment district, sometimes called a *local improvement district*. A special assessment district may be an independent special purpose governmental unit created under the laws of the state in which it is located; or it may be a component unit of a county, city, or other general governmental unit; or in some cases, special assessment transactions are administered directly by a general governmental unit.

If a special assessment district is an independent special purpose governmental unit it will need to account for the construction phase of a capital project in the manner described in this chapter, the debt service phase of the project in the manner described in Chapter 6, and the resulting fixed assets and related long-term debt as described earlier in this chapter and Chapter 6, respectively. The same observations apply to a special assessment district that is a component unit of a primary government, which should be reported in a discrete presentation in the general purpose financial statements of the governmental financial reporting entity, as discussed in relation to Illustration 2–1.

If the financial activities of a special assessment district are so intertwined with those of the primary government that the balances and transactions meet the criteria for blending (see discussion related to Illustration 2–1), it is logical that special assessment transactions be administered directly by the primary government. In that event the accounting and reporting standards set forth in this chapter apply to capital projects financed in whole, or in part, by special assessments, with the following modifications and additions:

The total dollar amount of a capital project to be financed by special assessments must be paid by owners of real property within the special assessment district. Accordingly, the portion of the total to be borne by each parcel of property within the district must be determined in whatever manner is specified by laws of the relevant jurisdiction. It is often true that the amount to be paid by each owner is large enough that laws will provide that the total special assessment against each parcel may be paid in equal installments over a specified period of years. Commonly, the first installment is due within a relatively short period of time (say, 60 days after the assessment is levied) and, if paid by the due date, is noninterest bearing. The remainder of the installments are due annually thereafter, and are interest bearing. Assume, for example, that the final installment is due five years after the levy of the special assessment. Contractors cannot be expected to wait five years to be paid for work done on the project; therefore, an issue of long-term debt is authorized in the amount of installments due in future years. The first installment and the proceeds of the long-term debt would be used to finance the capital project and would be accounted for by a capital projects fund. GASB standards provide that the first installment should be recognized as Revenue of the capital projects fund at the time of the levy—providing, of course, for any estimated uncollectibles.

Long-term debt proceeds would be considered an Other Financing Source—Proceeds of Bonds (or Notes) of the capital projects fund if the primary government has an obligation to assume debt service in the event that collections of remaining installments are insufficient. If the primary government has *no* obligation for debt service and the creditors are payable solely from collections of the special assessment installments and interest thereon, the proceeds of special assessment long-term debt should be credited to a capital projects fund equity account such as Contribution from Property Owners, rather than as Proceeds of Bonds (or Notes).

Installments of special assessments and interest thereon, which are to be used to service long-term debt, and are not available for expenditure by a capital projects fund, should be accounted for as described in Chapter 6, "Accounting for General Long-Term Debt and Debt Service." General fixed assets financed wholly or partially through collections of special assessments are accounted for in the same manner as any other general fixed assets; special assessment long-term debt accounting is discussed in Chapter 6.

Combining Financial Statements for Capital Projects Funds

To give protection against unintended uses of their grants for capital improvements, it is common practice for state and federal governmental agencies to require reports of how their money is being used. Required reports may be conventional financial statements or reports in a form specified by the grantor. Some grantors require the statements or reports to be accompanied by the opinion of an independent Certified Public Accountant, or by the report of auditors employed by a state audit agency. In other instances, the statements or reports need not be accompanied by an auditor's opinion but are merely subject to audit by the grantor agency or its designated auditors.

As noted in Chapter 1, the general purpose financial statements of a state or local government reporting entity are combined statements in which the financial data for each fund type used by the primary government are shown in separate columns. If, as is usually true except for the General Fund, the governmental unit has several funds within each type, it is necessary to present a *combining* statement for each fund type. In a combining statement, the financial data for each fund within that type are shown in columnar form. The data displayed in the Total column of the *combining* statement should be identical with the data shown in the column for that fund type in the *combined* statement. If the combining statement does not present sufficient information to make the statements not misleading, financial statements for individual funds within the fund type must be included in the government's comprehensive annual financial report. Illustration 5–6 shows the

Illustration 5–6

SOUTHWESTERN CITY
All Capital Projects Funds
Combining Balance Sheet
As of September 30, 2000
With Comparative Totals for September 30, 1999
(in thousands of dollars)

	Parks	Streets and Drainage	Buildings	Neighborhood Projects	Totals 9/30/00	Totals 9/30/99
Assets						
Cash and certificates of deposit	$9,499	$34,482	$14,526	$9,411	$67,918	$63,526
Due from other funds	—	—	243	—	243	300
Notes receivable—current	—	1,350	—	35	1,385	—
Total Assets	$9,499	$35,832	$14,769	$9,446	$69,546	$63,826
Liabilities and Fund Balances						
Current Liabilities:						
Accounts payable	$ 203	$ 767	$ 264	$ 127	$ 1,361	$ 1,600
Due to other funds	14	62	454	—	530	380
Total Current Liabilities	217	829	718	127	1,891	1,980
Fund Balances:						
Encumbered	3,362	14,641	3,319	2,338	23,660	20,440
Not encumbered	5,920	20,362	10,732	6,981	43,995	41,406
Total Fund Balances	9,282	35,003	14,051	9,319	67,655	61,846
Total Liabilities and Fund Balances	$9,499	$35,832	$14,769	$9,446	$69,546	$63,826

Combining Balance Sheet for all capital project funds of a certain southwestern city. Illustration 5–7 presents the accompanying Combining Statement of Revenues, Expenditures, and Changes in Fund Balances. In this case, disclosure is deemed sufficient, so individual fund statements are not presented. It should be noted that although the statements are year-end statements in terms of the fiscal year of the city, they are interim statements in terms of the life of the capital project.

The statements illustrated present adequate detail for published reports. For internal management purposes, and for external review of project management, additional information is needed as to whether the work accomplished to statement date is commensurate with expenditures to date and whether the remaining work can be accomplished with the available assets and resources.

Illustration 5–7

SOUTHWESTERN CITY
All Capital Projects Funds
Combining Statement of Revenues, Expenditures, and Changes in Fund Balances
For the Year Ended September 30, 2000
With Comparative Totals for the Year Ended September 30, 1999
(in thousands of dollars)

	Parks	Streets and Drainage	Buildings	Neighbor- hood Projects	Flood Control	Totals 9/30/00	Totals 9/30/99
Revenues:							
Federal grants	—	$ 300	—	—	—	$ 300	$ 2,000
Interest earned	$ 581	1,834	$ 788	$ 538	—	3,741	2,390
Other	19	1,312	54	11	—	1,396	400
Total Revenues	600	3,446	842	549	—	5,437	4,790
Expenditures:							
Capital outlays	4,437	17,068	4,150	635	$ 45	26,335	20,510
Excess of Revenues over (under) Expenditures	(3,837)	(13,622)	(3,308)	(86)	(45)	(20,898)	(15,720)
Other Financing Sources (Uses):							
Proceeds of bonds	3,600	17,610	4,490	800	—	26,500	8,000
Operating transfers in	—	—	243	—	—	243	500
Total Other Financing Sources	3,600	17,610	4,733	800	—	26,743	8,500
Excess of Revenue and Other Sources over (under) Expenditures and Other Uses	(237)	3,988	1,425	714	(45)	5,845	(7,220)
Fund Balances, October 1	9,519	31,015	12,626	8,605	81	61,846	69,066
Residual Equity Transfer to Debt Service Fund	—	—	—	—	(36)	(36)	—
Fund Balances, September 30	$9,282	$35,003	$14,051	$9,319	$ —	$67,655	$61,846

Selected References

Financial Accounting Standards Board. *Statement of Financial Accounting Standards No. 5,* "Accounting for Contingencies." Norwalk, CT, 1975.

_____ . *Statement of Financial Accounting Standards No. 13,* "Accounting for Leases as Amended and Interpreted through January 1990." Norwalk, CT, 1990.

Governmental Accounting Standards Board. *Codification of Governmental Accounting and Financial Reporting Standards as of June 30, 1997.* Norwalk, CT, 1997.

Key Terms

Arbitrage rebate,   169

Bond anticipation note,   167

Capital improvements fund,   159

Capital leases,   149

Capital projects funds,   144

Equity transfers,   163

Force account,   148

General fixed assets,   144

Operating leases,   149

Special assessments,   171

Questions

5–1. Explain how an accountant or administrator would be able to determine whether the cost of a certain piece of equipment purchased by a governmental unit should be recorded in the General Fixed Assets Account Group or in an enterprise fund.

5–2. What sources are often used to finance the acquisition of general fixed assets of governments?

5–3. Below are stated three major expenditures relating to the Town of Renton's general fixed assets. Which expenditures should be debited to asset accounts of the General Fixed Assets Account Group? Which should not? Explain your answers.

a. Replaced an old boiler in the Town Hall with a new model having twice the capacity of the old model.

b. Added a new wing to the Town Hall.

c. Renovated the Town Council Chambers (replaced carpeting, painted walls, and upgraded the sound system).

5–4. GASB standards do not allow depreciation of general fixed assets to be recorded in the accounts of any governmental fund, but do allow accumulated depreciation to be recorded in the General Fixed Assets Account Group. (*a*) Explain how accumulated depreciation can be recorded if depreciation expense cannot. (*b*) Explain why it is *not* in conformity with GASB standards to record depreciation in the accounts of governmental funds.

5–5. Below are stated several transactions related to fixed assets of a governmental unit. Which should be debited to asset accounts of the General Fixed Assets Account Group? Which should not? Explain your answers.

a. Contract price of land purchased for the use of a government-owned utility.

    b. Cost of land title abstract (paid by the utility for the land referred to in item *a* above).

    c. Cost of securing an easement for right-of-way over an adjoining property for a new entrance to the employees' parking lot next to City Hall.

    d. Cost of demolishing and removing an old building from a site to be used for construction of a new City Hall.

    e. Contract price of new building constructed for use as a fire station.

    f. Interest during the period of construction on money borrowed for construction of the new City Hall.

    g. Cost of a set of building plans followed in construction of the new City Hall.

    h. Cost of assembling and testing a piece of complicated machinery purchased for a government-owned utility.

    i. Freight on equipment purchased for use by the Street Department.

    j. Mowing grass and weeds, and other care and maintenance activities, for the grounds around City Hall.

5–6. Under what conditions should a state or local governmental unit utilize the capital projects fund type? If a unit does utilize the capital projects fund type, should it create a separate capital projects fund for each project? Why or why not?

5–7. How does an outlay for a capital *project* differ from a capital outlay of a general or special revenue fund? Give an example of a capital project and an example of a capital outlay.

5–8. How does a *capital projects* fund differ from *general* and *special revenue* funds?

5–9. Should interest expenditures during the period of construction be capitalized as a part of the cost of general fixed assets? Explain your answer.

5–10. Why is encumbrance accounting recommended for capital projects funds even though it is not considered necessary to record Estimated Revenues or Appropriations?

5–11. If a capital project is incomplete at the end of a fiscal year, why is it considered desirable to close Encumbrances and all operating statement accounts at year-end? If these accounts are closed, why is it desirable to reestablish the Encumbrances account as of the first day of the following year?

5–12. "If general fixed assets are acquired under a capital lease agreement, no entry at all needs to be made in any governmental fund at the inception of the lease." Do you agree or disagree? Explain.

5–13. If one capital projects fund is used to account for multiple capital projects, how can adequate control and accountability for individual projects be maintained?

5–14. "If all the capital projects funds of a governmental reporting entity have no assets, no liabilities, and no fund equity at balance sheet date, no columns need be provided for the capital projects fund type in any of the general purpose financial statements." Explain why you agree, or disagree, with this statement.

5–15. How should the residual equity or deficit existing at the completion of a capital project be treated?

Cases

5–1. The statement and two schedules shown in the annual report of Plains City for the year ended June 30, 1999, which present information about general fixed assets, are shown below.

PLAINS CITY
Statement of General Fixed Assets
June 30, 1999
(000 omitted)

General Fixed Assets

Land	$13,186
Building and improvements	17,492
Machinery and equipment	2,384
Streets, sidewalks, and other infrastructure	7,692
Total General Fixed Assets	$40,754

Investment in General Fixed Assets

General obligation bonds	$19,700
Special assessment bonds	4,625
General Fund revenues	12,829
Capital leases	3,600
Total Investment in General Fixed Assets	$40,754

PLAINS CITY
Schedule of General Fixed Assets—By Function and Activity
June 30, 1999
(in thousands)

Function	Total	Land	Buildings	Machinery and Equipment	Streets and Other
General Government Equipment	$10,076			$2,384	$7,692
General Government Buildings	19,492	$ 2,000	$17,492		
Parks and Recreation	11,186	11,186			
Total General Fixed Assets	$40,754	$13,186	$17,492	$2,384	$7,692

PLAINS CITY
Schedule of Changes in General Fixed Assets—By Function and Activity
For the Year Ended June 30, 1999
(in thousands)

	General Fixed Assets 6/30/98	Additions	Deductions	General Fixed Assets 6/30/99
General Government Equipment	$ 9,135	$1,172	$231	$10,076
General Government Buildings	19,057	502	67	19,492
Parks and Recreation	10,425	761		11,186
Total General Fixed Assets	$38,617	$2,435	$298	$40,754

Required

a. To what extent does the information about general fixed assets satisfy the information needs of (1) a new member of the City Council, and (2) a resident interested in the financial management of fixed assets of the city?

b. If you were a CPA auditing the city, should you give a clean (unqualified) opinion on the statements as they exist? If not, are there any changes that the client could make that would enable you to give a clean opinion?

5–2. The case described here illustrates how political factors can be as important as, or even more important than, economic factors in planning and financing major capital projects. Often the political dimension clouds the issues and makes it difficult for even knowledgeable citizens to determine the best course of action. After reading the case, you will be asked to "cast your vote" on the proposed financing plan and explain why you voted as you did. Although the names of the governments described in the case are fictitious, the case is adapted from an actual case that came to the authors' attention. Similar jurisdictional tax disputes are not uncommon.

Background.   Brown County is a rural county with a well-diversified economy, mainly institutional (educational and medical), commercial and light manufacturing, and agricultural. The County has a population of about 125,000, which for the last decade has been growing at nearly 5 percent a year. The County's largest city and the County Seat is Brownville, with a population of about 75,000. The County is governed by three elected commissioners and most key County functions are managed by elected officials. The City has a Council-Manager form of government under which the Chief Executive Officer, the City Manager, is appointed by and serves at the pleasure of the City Council. The governments are "overlapping" in the sense that taxpayers who reside in Brownville pay property and sales taxes to both the City and County. However, except for the court system, the County mainly provides services for persons who live outside incorporated cities and towns. Historically, relationships between the County and City governments have been strained, with each government being suspicious of the motives of the other. As a result, regional planning has generally suffered and agreements, when they have occurred, have related to narrow issues or projects rather than long-range plans.

Situation and Facts.   To cope with rapid population growth, the County has developed a five-year plan that includes paving and upgrading 55 miles of heavily traveled roads at a cost of $7,000,000; upgrading about 150 miles of substandard roads using "chip-and-seal overlay," $2,000,000; eliminating 10 "safety hazard areas," $210,000; and acquiring right of way, $500,000; for a total estimated cost of $9,710,000 over five years. Financing for the plan would come from the following sources:

Half-cent sales tax	$5,400,000
Increase in property tax of 5 cents per $100 of assessed valuation	400,000
Gasoline taxes	500,000
Motor vehicle sales tax	200,000
Annual Revenues	$6,500,000

The gasoline taxes and motor vehicle sales taxes are already being collected and distributed to localities by the state government. The property tax increase requires no special approval since the Road and Bridge property taxes are currently below the limit imposed by state statutes. The half-cent sales tax, however, requires approval by a simple majority of registered voters in the County, including those who reside in Brownville and other incorporated cities and towns. Accordingly, a special election has been called to schedule a vote on the proposed sales tax.

Even a casual look at the financing plan shows that $6,500,000 × 5 years will produce at least $32,500,000 in revenues (excluding probably investment earnings) whereas the required capital outlay will be only $9,710,000 over the five years. The remainder is intended to provide for expanded operations of the County Road and Bridge Department.

In the weeks before the special election, the Brownville City Council and Finance Director have strongly opposed the proposed sales tax on the grounds that it is unfair to expect taxpayers in the cities and towns to pay for road improvements that mainly benefit rural county residents. They argue that special assessment debt financing should be used, with the debt to be repaid by residents receiving the benefit. They further complain that the County's planning process was flawed and that joint planning with the City is needed to coordinate the five-year plan of both governments. City officials are also concerned that the County's proposed sales tax increase would eliminate the City's ability to raise sales taxes during the next five years if a need should arise. To mute some of the opposition, the County has amended the original plan and proposes to cut in half the Road and Bridge property taxes paid by taxpayers in the cities and towns. The property tax rollback would reduce revenues from $32,500,000 to about $27 million over the next five years. However, since property in that state is assessed at different levels for different classes of property (32 percent of market value for commercial and manufacturing property, 19 percent for residential property, and 12 percent for agricultural property), only the larger (mainly commercial and manufacturing) property owners stand to gain if the proposed sales tax increase is approved. For most taxpayers the sales tax increase will still be greater than the property tax decrease. Thus, while some large property owners might now support the sales tax, the majority of Brownville voters view the proposed rollback as regressive and only worsening the inequity for most property owners in the cities and towns.

Advocates for the sales tax argue that the cities and towns will benefit from improved transportation throughout the County. Further, nearly a quarter of the people who work in Brownville live in the unincorporated subdivisions surrounding the City. Advocates also point out that Brownville is a regional shopping center that draws shoppers from a 50-mile radius. Thus, one attractive feature of the proposed sales tax is that it would be borne, in part, by people who neither live nor work in the County.

Required

After weeks of heavy media coverage, both for and against the proposed sales tax, voters have become extremely interested in this issue but thoroughly confused. Election day has finally arrived and turnout is expected to be heavy. Imagine yourself as a voter in the City of Brownville and answer the following questions.

a. Would you vote *yes* for the proposed half-cent sales tax or *no* in opposition? Explain the rationale for your vote, being sure to analyze factors pertinent to your voting decision.

b. Would your vote have changed under different assumed scenarios (e.g., if you were a large commercial or manufacturing property owner versus a residential or agricultural property owner, or renter)?

c. Do you think special assessment financing would be more appropriate than general sales taxes for the proposed projects? Explain.

d. Are there any significant accounting issues related to the financing alternatives? Explain.

Exercises and Problems

5–1. Utilizing the CAFR obtained for Exercise 1–1, follow the instructions below:

General Fixed Assets:

a. Reporting of Fixed Assets. Does the Combined Balance Sheet contain a column reporting the General Fixed Asset Account Group data? Are fund fixed assets reported only in appropriate columns (Enterprise, Internal Service, and Trust and Agency Fund Types and the General Fixed Assets Account Group)? Is a Statement of General Fixed Assets included in the Individual Funds section? Does this statement, or one or more schedules, disclose the function or activity that uses the assets? What categories of fixed assets are shown in the statement? Are Improvements Other than Buildings separately disclosed and described? Do the Notes describe the accounting treatment accorded general fixed assets and fixed assets accounted for by proprietary funds? If donated fixed assets are reported, are they stated at their fair value on the date donated? Are purchased fixed assets stated at historical cost, if known, or estimated historical cost if actual cost is unknown? Has the government refrained from using terms like *appraised values* or *estimated values* without indicating whether they involve historical cost, replacement cost, or market value appraisals or estimates? Do the Notes specify capitalization policies for "public domain" (infrastructure) fixed assets? Are commitments under capital leases and operating leases disclosed? Are assets being acquired under capital leases reported in the GFAAG as specified in this chapter? (See also Exercise 5–1, Capital Projects Funds, part *e*, for related questions relating to assets acquired under capital leases.)

b. Sources of Fixed Asset Financing. Does the Statement of General Fixed Assets disclose the sources from which acquisitions or construction of fixed assets were financed? If not, is the information disclosed elsewhere in the report? If so, are the sources for all general fixed assets disclosed, or only those assets acquired since a certain date? Do the source accounts agree with those discussed in Chapter 5? What three sources account for the major portion of fixed asset acquisitions? What percentage of the total cost, or other carrying value, of fixed assets is accounted for by each of the three major sources?

c. Changes in General Fixed Assets. Does the report contain a Schedule (or Statement) of Changes in General Fixed Assets? If so, does the schedule disclose the sources from which fixed asset acquisitions and construction were financed? Does the schedule disclose changes by function and activity, or merely by asset category?

d. *Other.* Compare the general fixed asset information disclosed in the report with related information disclosed in statements of general and special revenue funds, capital projects funds, or elsewhere in the report. Is the accumulated cost of construction work in progress recorded as an asset in the GFAAG? If not, is the information disclosed adequately, in your opinion? Is net interest during the period of construction on debt incurred to finance construction capitalized? Is this true for just tax-supported debt, or for both tax-supported debt and special assessment debt? Which fund, or funds, account for cash received, or receivables created, from sales of general fixed assets? Which fund, or funds, account for cash received, or receivables created, as a result of charging depreciation on general fixed assets as a cost of grants?

Capital Projects Funds:

a. *Title and Content.* What title is given the funds that function as capital projects funds, as described in Chapter 5? (Bond Funds and Capital Improvement Funds are common titles.) Does the report state the basis of accounting used for capital projects funds? If so, is the financial statement presentation consistent with the stated basis? (That is, the report may state that the modified accrual basis was used, but no receivables are shown, or there is a "Reserve for Receivables," or the report refers to "disbursements" rather than "expenditures.") If the basis of accounting is not stated, analyze the statements to determine which basis is used—full accrual, modified accrual, or cash basis. Is the same basis used for both revenues and expenditures? Is the basis used consistent with GASB standards discussed in Chapter 5? Are there separate capital projects funds for each project; or are there several funds, each of which accounts for related projects; or is only one fund used for all projects?

b. *Statements and Schedules.* What statements and schedules pertaining to capital projects funds are presented? In what respects (headings, arrangement, items included, etc.) do they seem similar to statements illustrated or described in the text? In what respects do they differ? Are any differences merely a matter of terminology or arrangement, or do they represent significant deviations from GASB accounting and reporting standards for capital projects funds?

c. *Financial Resource Inflows.* Describe the nature of the financial resource inflows utilized by the capital projects funds. If tax-supported bonds, or special assessment bonds, are a source, have any been sold at a premium? At a discount? If so, what was the accounting treatment of the bond premium or discount?

d. *Fund Expenditures.* How much detail is given concerning capital projects fund expenditures? Is the detail sufficient to meet the information needs of administrators? Legislators? Creditors? Grantors? Interested residents? For projects that are incomplete at the date of the financial statement, does the report compare the percentage of total authorization for each project expended to date with the percentage of completion? For those projects completed during the fiscal year does the report compare the total expenditures for each project with the authorization for each project? For each cost overrun, how was the overrun financed?

e. *Assets Acquired under Capital Leases.* Were any general fixed assets acquired by the primary government or one or more component units under a capital lease agreement during the year for which you have statements? If so, was the present value of minimum lease rentals recorded as an Expenditure and as an Other Financing Source in a capital projects fund (or in any other governmental fund)? If the primary government or one or more component units leased assets from another component unit, how are the assets, related liabilities, expenditures, and other financing sources reported in the general purpose financial statements, or in another section of the CAFR of the reporting entity?

5–2. Write the numbers 1 through 10 on a sheet of paper. Beside each number write the letter corresponding with the best answer to each of the following questions:

1. Fixed assets donated to a governmental unit should be recorded
   a. At estimated fair value when received.
   b. At the lower of donor's carrying amount or estimated fair value when received.
   c. At the donor's carrying amount.
   d. As a memorandum entry only.

2. The following are Boa City's fixed assets:

Fixed assets used by proprietary fund activities	$1,000,000
Fixed assets used by expendable trust funds	1,800,000
Fixed assets used by governmental funds	9,000,000

What aggregate amount should Boa account for in the General Fixed Assets Account Group?
   a. $ 9,000,000.
   b. $10,000,000.
   c. $10,800,000.
   d. $11,800,000.

3. The General Fixed Assets Account Group is:
   a. An accounting entity.
   b. A fiscal entity.
   c. A legal entity.
   d. All of the above.

4. Accumulated depreciation of general fixed assets:
   a. Should be recorded in the accounts of governmental funds.
   b. May optionally be recorded in the accounts of governmental funds.
   c. May optionally be recorded in the accounts of the General Fixed Assets Account Group.
   d. Either b or c is permitted by GASB standards.

5. General fixed assets should be recorded at:
   a. Cost.
   b. Estimated cost, if cost is not practically determinable.
   c. Fair value, if the fixed assets were donated.
   d. Either a, or b, or c, as appropriate.

6. One feature of state and local government accounting and financial reporting is that fixed assets used for general government activities
   a. Do not depreciate as a result of such use.
   b. Often are not expected to contribute to the generation of revenues.
   c. Are acquired only when direct contribution to revenues is expected.
   d. Should not be maintained at the same level as those of businesses so that current financial resources can be used for other government services.
7. Old equipment, which is recorded in the General Fixed Assets Account Group, is sold for less than its carrying amount. The sale reduces the Investment in General Fixed Assets balance by the

   Carrying value only

   a. Difference between the cost of the equipment and the sales price.
   b. Difference between the carrying amount of the equipment and the sales price.
   c. Selling price of the equipment.
   d. Carrying amount of the equipment.
8. If $2,200,000 of the proceeds from the sale of tax-supported bonds were expended by a capital projects fund during the fiscal year 1999 on a street-paving project not complete at the end of that year, the General Fixed Assets Account Group should:
   a. Make no entry until the project is complete.
   b. Make no entry at all; infrastructure assets are never capitalized.
   c. Debit Construction Work in Progress, $2,200,000; credit Investment in General Fixed Assets—Capital Projects Funds—Tax-Supported Bonds, $2,200,000.
   d. Debit Improvements Other than Buildings, $2,200,000; credit Investments in General Fixed Assets—Capital Projects Funds, $2,200,000.
9. General fixed assets acquired under a capital lease:
   a. Should be capitalized under the same rules as proprietary fund fixed assets acquired under an operating lease.
   b. Should be capitalized at the lesser of (1) the present value of rental and other minimum lease payments, or (2) the fair value of the leased property.
   c. Should not be capitalized.
   d. Should be capitalized at the lower of cost or market.
10. Since general fixed assets are not assets of any fund, generally accepted accounting principles provide that:
    a. They need not be reported at all in any of the general purpose financial statements, or in the notes to the financial statements.
    b. The carrying value of the GFAAG should be disclosed in the notes to the financial statements, but not on the face of any of the statements.
    c. A column should be provided in all general purpose financial statements to report GFAAG financial data.
    d. A column should be provided in the Combined Balance Sheet, but not in any other of the combined statements, to report GFAAG financial data.

   (Items 1, 2, 6, and 7, AICPA, adapted.)

5–3. Write the numbers 1 through 10 on a sheet of paper. Beside each number write the letter corresponding with the best answer to each of the following questions.
1. A capital projects fund of a municipality is an example of what type of fund?
   a. Fiduciary.
   b. Governmental.
   c. Internal Service.
   d. Proprietary.

2. On July 1, 1999, the Town of Dalton borrowed $1,000,000 as temporary financing for construction of a new Town Hall building until bonds could be issued for the project. On October 1, 1999, the Town repaid the short-term notes for temporary financing, including interest of $15,000, which was paid from resources of the capital projects fund. The journal entry to record repayment of the note and interest should include debits to:

a. Bond Anticipation Notes Payable and Construction Expenditures.

b. Bond Anticipation Notes Payable and Interest Expenditures.

c. Construction Expenditures and Interest Expenditures.

d. Either a or b, depending on whether the interest is to be capitalized.

3. In 1999, Menton City received $5,000,000 of bond proceeds to be used for capital projects. Of this amount, $1,000,000 was expended in 1999. Expenditures for the $4,000,000 balance were expected to be incurred in 2000. These bond proceeds should be recorded in capital projects funds for

a. $5,000,000 in 1999.

b. $5,000,000 in 2000.

c. $1,000,000 in 1999 and $4,000,000 in 2000.

d. $1,000,000 in 1999 and in the General Fund for $4,000,000 in 1999.

4. When Calumet City realized $2,020,000 from the sale of a $2,000,000 bond issue, the entry in its capital projects fund was:

Cash	2,020,000	
Proceeds of Bonds		2,000,000
Premium on Bonds		20,000

Recording the transaction in this manner indicates that:

a. A safety factor is being set to cover possible contract defaults on the construction.

b. The nominal rate of interest on the bonds is below the market rate for bonds of such term and risk.

c. The full $2,020,000 can be used by the capital projects fund to accomplish its purpose.

d. The $20,000 cannot be used for the designated purpose of the fund but must be transferred to another fund.

Items 5 and 6 are based on the following:

On December 31, 1999, Vane City paid a contractor $3,000,000 for the total cost of a new municipal annex built in 1999 on city-owned land. Financing was provided by a $2,000,000 general obligation bond issue sold at face amount on December 31, 1999, with the remaining $1,000,000 transferred from the General Fund.

5. What account and amount should be reported in Vane's 1999 financial statements for the General Fund?

a. Other Financing Uses control, $1,000,000.

b. Other Financing Sources control, $2,000,000.

c. Expenditures control, $3,000,000.

d. Other Financing Sources control, $3,000,000.

6. What accounts and amounts should be reported in Vane's 1999 financial statements for the capital projects fund?

a. Other Financing Sources control, $2,000,000; General Long-Term-Debt, $2,000,000.

    b. Revenues control, $2,000,000; Construction Expenditures control, $2,000,000.

    c. Other Financing Sources control, $3,000,000; Construction Expenditures control, $3,000,000.

    d. Revenues control, $3,000,000; Construction Expenditures control, $3,000,000.

7. In what fund type should the proceeds from special assessment bonds issued to finance construction of sidewalks in a new subdivision be reported? Assume that the city agreed to pay debt service if collections of assessments are insufficient.

    a. Agency fund.

    b. Capital projects fund.

    c. Enterprise fund.

    d. Special revenue fund.

8. As of the first day of a fiscal year it is normally desirable to enter in a capital projects fund account:

    a. The amounts of bonds expected to be sold during the year.

    b. The amount of grants expected to be received during the year.

    c. The reestablishment of Encumbrances closed to Fund Balance as of the end of the preceding year.

    d. All of the above.

9. Final inspection of a construction site revealed minor discrepancies that were corrected by employees of the Town of Quincy. An adequate amount had been retained from contractor billings to cover this contingency. The costs of correcting these discrepancies should be recorded in the capital projects fund as a debit to:

    a. Construction Expenditures.

    b. General Fixed Assets.

    c. Reserve for Encumbrances.

    d. Contracts Payable—Retained Percentage.

10. If general fixed assets are acquired by a governmental unit under a lease agreement, it is appropriate to record in a capital projects fund as an Expenditure and as an Other Financing Source:

    a. The lesser of the present value of the rental and other minimum lease payments, or the fair value of the leased property, if the lease agreement meets all of the criteria for capital leases set forth in FASB's *SFAS No. 13.*

    b. The amount recorded at the inception of a capital lease agreement as a liability in the General Long-Term Debt Account Group.

    c. The amount of lease rentals or other minimum lease payments due during the year under operating lease agreements.

    d. The amount of lease rentals or other minimum lease payments paid during the year under capital lease agreements.

            (Items 1 and 3 through 7, AICPA, adapted)

5–4. Below are described a number of transactions, each of which had an effect on the General Fixed Assets Account Group of a certain city. You are required to make an entry or entries for each transaction as it should have been recorded in the General Fixed Assets Account Group.

1. During the year, a capital projects fund completed a building project initiated in the preceding year. The total cost of the project was $6,780,000, of which

$4,130,000 had been expended in the two preceding years. Current-year expenditures on the project were reported to have consisted of $650,000 from a federal grant, with the balance coming from proceeds of a tax-supported bond issue.

2. A tract of land held for future development as a city park was, by resolution of the City Council, transferred to the City Water Utility. The Utility agreed to pay the City General Fund $200,000 for the land, which was carried in the GFAAG at its estimated cost of $50,000. The land had been purchased from General Fund revenues.

3. An electric typewriter was traded in on a personal computer. List price of the personal computer was $3,500; $100 allowance was received for the old machine. The old typewriter had been purchased from General Fund revenue for $500. Cash for the new computer was furnished by a special revenue fund.

4. A piece of heavy equipment was purchased by the Street Fund, a special revenue fund. Catalog price of the equipment was $150,000. Terms of payment quoted by the manufacturer were 2/10, n/30. Payment for the equipment was made within the cash discount period.

5. The cost of remodeling of the interior of the City Hall was $514,700; $38,400 of this amount was classified as maintenance rather than improvement. In the remodeling process, walls, partitions, floors, and so on, estimated to have cost $76,600 were removed and replaced. Cost of the remodeling was financed by a current appropriation of the General Fund. The original construction had been financed by a tax-supported bond issue accounted for by a capital projects fund.

6. A subdivision annexed by the City contained privately financed streets and sidewalks and a system of sewers. The best available information showed a cost of $1,400,000 for the sewer system and $1,550,000 for the streets and sidewalks, of which $150,000 was the estimated cost of the land. Both types of improvements were provided by the developers. The City *does* record infrastructure assets in the GFAAG.

5–5. Information in the CAFR of the Town of Centralia reported general fixed assets in the following amounts as of April 30, 1999:

Land	$1,326,780
Buildings	7,282,680
Improvements other than buildings	3,027,790
Equipment	1,733,820
Construction work in progress	401,130

During fiscal year 2000 the following changes in general fixed assets took place:

1. A project started during fiscal 2000 was being financed by a tax-supported bond issue of $3,000,000 sold at par during the year and a federal grant of $1,000,000, both accounted for through a capital projects fund. By the end of fiscal 2000, $80,000 of the federal grant had been received and expended for planning and engineering for a project in progress. Bond proceeds expended during the year totaled $900,000 ($300,000 for land, and $600,000 for the building under construction).

2. Records of capital projects funds reported that construction work in progress at the end of fiscal 1999 was completed during fiscal 2000 at a total cost of $799,066, all financed from special assessment bonds. All of the construction resulted in additions to Improvements Other than Buildings.
3. Special revenue fund expenditures during the year added equipment costing $152,700.
4. General Fund expenditures during the year for equipment amounted to $416,000.
5. Annexation added buildings for which the estimated cost was $301,600, and land for which the estimated cost was $75,000.
6. Land having an appraised value of $750,000 was donated to the City, and additional land with an appraised value of $15,000 was received in settlement of delinquent General Fund property taxes.
7. Land acquired at an estimated cost of $12,000, on which an $80,000 building was located, was sold to the State Highway Department for a right-of-way at a price of $119,700.
8. Construction activities during fiscal 2000 required demolition of a building that had cost $33,600 and a bridge for which the estimated cost was $119,200. Equipment that had cost $19,300 could not be located and was presumed to have been stolen.

Required

Prepare in good form a Schedule of Changes in General Fixed Assets during the fiscal year ended April 30, 2000. Show the sources of assets acquired and the causes of reduction.

5–6. At June 30, 1999, the fixed property schedule of the City of Glezen was as follows:

General Government:	
Land	$ 110,320
Buildings	1,070,000
Improvements other than buildings	263,500
Equipment	718,570
Fire protection:	
Land	60,500
Buildings	310,000
Equipment	501,850
Police protection:	
Equipment	245,000
Recreation:	
Land	618,770
Buildings	62,000
Improvements other than buildings	281,500
Equipment	109,000
Health and Welfare Department:	
Land	115,930
Buildings	92,410
Improvements other than buildings	301,250
Equipment	64,980

Purchases of equipment during the year ended June 30, 2000, were as follows:

General Government	$ 29,020
Fire Department	407,300
Police Department	81,700
Recreation Department	48,000
Health and Welfare Department	18,020

Also, during the year ended June 30, 2000:

1. A piece of equipment appraised at $57,100 was received from a federal agency for general governmental use.
2. The cost of equipment sold during the year included $10,800 of equipment used by the General Government; $39,000 by the Fire Department; and $2,100 by Health and Welfare. Equipment traded in during the year included $4,700 of equipment used by the Police Department; and $680, by the Health and Welfare Department.
3. Buildings demolished during the year had cost $4,120 (assigned to the Recreation Department), and $12,860 (assigned to the Health and Welfare Department).
4. Reductions from abandonment on account of obsolescence (all equipment) were $18,640 by the General Government; $9,200 by the Fire Department; $4,300 by the Police Department; $2,700 by the Recreation Department; and $1,310 by the Health and Welfare Department.

Required

Prepare in good form a schedule for the year ended June 30, 2000, showing the beginning balance of each class of fixed assets, the causes of change (purchases, received from other governmental units, sales, demolition and abandonment, trade-ins), and the amounts thereof, and the ending balance. Show totals for each function, considering fire protection and police protection as separate functions.

5–7. The post-closing trial balance of the City of Pineville's Capital Projects Fund, as of December 31, 1999, listed Fund Balance in the amount of $1,500,000.

The project had been authorized early in 1999 in the total amount of $5,000,000, to be financed $800,000 by the federal government, $200,000 by the state government, and the remainder by a bond issue. Most of the work was to be done by various private contractors.

Cash from the state grant was received in full during 1999. The entire bond issue was sold at par early in 1999. The federal government is expected to pay its grant in full before March 1, 2000. Cash not disbursed during 1999 was invested on December 31, 1999.

   a. Assuming GASB standards discussed in Chapter 5 were followed:
   (1) How much Revenue was recognized by the Capital Projects Fund in 1999? How much should this fund report as Other Financing Sources for 1999?
   (2) How much did 1999 expenditures total?
   (3) What was the balance of the Investments account on December 31, 1999, assuming all 1999 expenditures were paid in cash?

b. During 2000, the following events occurred:
   (1) Expenditures of the fund totaled $1,350,000 on construction contracts.
   (2) Interest on temporary investments totaled $16,000.

Prepare a Statement of Revenues, Expenditures, and Changes in Fund Balance for the City of Pineville's Capital Projects Fund for the year ended December 31, 2000.

5–8. The following information pertains to Eden Township's construction and financing of a new administration center:

Estimated total cost of project	$9,000,000
Project financing:	
State grant	3,000,000
General obligation bonds:	
Face amount	6,000,000
Stated interest rate	6%
Issue date	December 1, 1999
Maturity date	December 1, 2029

During Eden's year ended June 30, 2000, the following events occurred that affect the Capital Projects Fund established to account for this project:

July 1, 1999—The Capital Projects Fund borrowed $300,000 from the General Fund for preliminary engineering and planning costs.

July 9, 1999—Engineering and planning costs of $200,000, for which no encumbrance had been recorded, were paid to Napp Associates.

December 1, 1999—The bonds were sold at 101. Total proceeds were retained by the Capital Projects Fund. (The premium is available for expenditure for the project.)

December 1, 1999—The grant was formally approved by the state. The grant was to be used only for financing construction of the new administration center.

April 30, 2000—A $7,000,000 contract was executed with Caro Construction Corp., the general contractors, for the major portion of the project. The contract provides that Eden will withhold 4 percent of all billings pending satisfactory completion of the project.

May 9, 2000—$1,000,000 of the state grant was received.

June 10, 2000—The $300,000 borrowed from the General Fund was repaid.

June 30, 2000—Progress billing of $1,200,000 was received from Caro.

Eden uses encumbrance accounting for budgetary control.

Required

  a. Prepare journal entries in the Administration Center Capital Projects Fund to record the foregoing transactions.

  b. Prepare the June 30, 2000, closing entries for the Administration Center Capital Projects Fund.

  c. Prepare the Administration Center Capital Projects Fund balance sheet at June 30, 2000.

(AICPA, adapted)

5–9. The proceeds of the sale of special assessment bonds issued to finance the acquisition of capital facilities amounted to $5,080,000. The face amount of the bond issue was $5,000,000; $25,000 of the proceeds represented interest accrued on the bonds to date of sale.

    a. Assuming both the premium on bonds sold and the interest accrued on the bonds to date of sale must be recorded directly in a debt service fund, show in general journal form the entry made by the capital projects fund for the receipt of the $5,000,000 face amount.

    b. If several months are expected to elapse between receipt of bond proceeds and payment for the capital assets being acquired, what action should be taken by the governmental finance officer?

    c. What are the accounting and financial implications of the course of action you recommended in part *b*?

5–10. During fiscal year 1999, the voters of the Town of Winston approved the construction and equipping of a recreation center to be financed by tax-supported bonds in the amount of $3,000,000. During 1999, the following events and transactions occurred:

    1. Preliminary planning and engineering expenses were incurred in the amount of $75,000. No money was immediately available for paying these costs (credit Vouchers Payable).

    2. Supplies to be used by the town's own working force in connection with the project were ordered in the amount of $30,000.

    3. A contract was let under competitive bids for a major segment of the construction project in the amount of $2,500,000.

    4. All the supplies referred to in item 2 were received at a net cost of $30,500. This amount was approved for payment.

    5. An interfund invoice (not encumbered) was received from the Street Fund for work done on the project in the amount of $40,000. The invoice was approved for payment.

    6. An invoice for $1,600,000 was received from a contractor for a portion of work that had been completed under the general contract.

    7. The bond issue was sold at par plus accrued interest of $30,000 (the accrued interest was deposited in the fund that will service the bonded debt).

    8. The amount due the Street Fund was paid.

    9. The contractor's bill, less a 4 percent retention, was vouchered for payment.

    10. All vouchers payable, except $1,300 (about which there was some controversy), were paid.

    11. Cash in the amount of $1,300,000 was invested in short-term marketable securities.

    12. Fiscal year-end closing entries were prepared.

Required

    a. Prepare journal entries to record the above information in the general ledger accounts of the Recreation Construction Fund (you may omit subsidiary ledger accounts.)

    b. Prepare a Town of Winston Recreation Center Construction Fund Balance Sheet for the year ended December 31, 1999.

     c. Prepare a Recreation Center Construction Fund Statement of Revenues, Expenditures, and Changes in Fund Balance for the year ended December 31, 1999.

5–11. In 1999, Wye City began the work of improving certain streets, to be financed by a bond issue supplemented by a federal grant. Estimated total cost of the project was $3,000,000; $2,500,000 was to come from the bond issue, and the balance from a federal grant. The capital projects fund to account for the project was designated as the Street Improvement Fund.

The following transactions occurred in 1999:

1. Issued $80,000 of 6 percent bond anticipation notes maturing in 180 days.
2. The federal grant was recorded as receivable; half of the grant is to be paid to Wye City in 1999, and the remainder late in 2000.
3. A contract was let to Rogers Construction Company for the major part of the project on a bid of $2,700,000.
4. An invoice received from the City's Stores and Services Fund for supplies provided to the Street Improvement Fund in the amount of $40,000 was approved for payment. (This amount had not been encumbered.)
5. Preliminary planning and engineering costs of $59,000 were paid to the Midwest Engineering Company. There had been no encumbrance for this cost.
6. A voucher payable was recorded for a $14,500 billing from the local telephone company for the cost of moving some of its underground properties necessitated by the street project.
7. An invoice in the amount of $1,000,000 was received from Rogers for progress to date on the project. The invoice was consistent with the terms of the contract and a liability was recorded in the amount of $1,000,000.
8. Cash received during 1999 was as follows:

From federal government	250,000
From sale of bonds at par	2,500,000

9. Repaid bond anticipation notes and interest thereon (see Transaction 1). Interest is an expenditure of the capital projects fund and is not intended to be capitalized as part of the cost of street improvements.
10. The amount billed by the contractor (see Transaction 7), less 5 percent retainage was paid.
11. Temporary investments were purchased at a cost of $1,700,000.
12. Closing entries were prepared as of December 31, 1999.

Required

     a. Prepare journal entries to record the above information in the general ledger accounts of the Street Improvement Fund.

     b. Prepare a Balance Sheet as of December 31, 1999.

     c. Prepare a Statement of Revenues, Expenditures, and Changes in Fund Balance for the period, assuming the date of authorization was July 1, 1999.

5–12. This problem presents the transactions of the Wye City Street Improvement Fund (see Problem 5–11) for fiscal year 2000.

1. Encumbrances in effect on December 31, 1999, were reestablished on January 1, 2000.
2. The City Board of Works decided on further street improvements and, after necessary legal actions, awarded the addition to the original contractor at $500,000. Additional bonds were authorized in that amount.
3. An additional billing submitted by the contractor in the amount of $1,700,000 was recorded as a liability.
4. Investments were disposed of for cash totaling $1,732,000, which included $32,000 accrued interest sold (all of which is revenue of the Street Improvement Fund).
5. Bonds authorized this year were sold at 102, but the premium was paid directly in the Street Improvement Debt Service Fund.
6. The contractor's second billing, less 5 percent retention, was paid.
7. The contractor reported the project completed, including the work authorized in 1999, subject to final inspection and approval by the supervising engineers, and submitted an invoice for the balance of the contract. The final invoice was recorded as a liability.
8. The balance due from the federal government was received.
9. The amount due on the contractor's last billing, less 5 percent retained, was paid.
10. The vouchers payable and the amount due to the Stores and Services Fund was paid.
11. On final inspection, a defect was discovered and reported to the contractor. Having moved a working force and equipment to another job, he authorized correction of the defect at a cost not to exceed $50,000. The correction was made at a cost of $49,700, which was paid from the project Cash account.
12. The balance due to the contractor was paid.
13. All operating statement accounts were closed.
14. The balance of cash was transferred to the Street Improvement Debt Service Fund (debit Equity Transfer Out, then close that account to Fund Balance) on December 31, 2000.

Required

a. Prepare journal entries to record the above information in the general ledger accounts of the Street Improvement Fund.
b. Prepare a Statement of Revenues, Expenditures, and Changes in Fund Balance for inclusion in the City's Financial Report for the year ended December 31, 2000.
c. What is the total cost of the street improvement projects for which data are given in Problems 5–11 and 5–12? Show computations. Is this amount reported in any of the financial statements prepared for Problems 5–11 or 5–12? Explain why or why not.
d. Compare the total cost computed in requirement *c* with estimated cost of the projects (the estimated cost was the basis for bond issues and grant applications). If Transaction 14 had not been given above, explain what alternative disposition might have been made of the cash remaining in the fund after all liabilities had been paid.

Continuous Problem

5–L. Part 1. Capital Projects Fund.　　The voters of the City of Bingham approved the issuance of 8 percent tax-supported bonds in the face amount of $3,000,000 for the construction and equipping of an annex to the City Hall. The bonds are to mature in blocks of $150,000 each year over a 20-year period commencing July 1, 2000.

Required

a. Open a general journal for the City Hall Annex Construction Fund. Record the transactions below, as necessary. Use account titles listed under requirement *b*.

  (1)　On the first day of the fiscal year (July 1, 2000), the bond issue was sold at 101. Cash in the face amount of the bonds, $3,000,000, was deposited in the City Hall Annex Construction Fund; the premium was deposited in the Debt Service Fund, as required by state law.

  (2)　The City Hall Annex Construction Fund purchased land needed for the site for the annex for $165,000; this amount was paid.

  (3)　Legal and other costs of the bond issue were paid in the amount of $40,000.

  (4)　Architects were engaged at a fee of 6 percent of the bid of the contractors. It is estimated that the architect's fee will be $150,000.

  (5)　Preliminary plans were received, and the architects were paid $10,000.

  (6)　The detailed plans and specifications were received, and a liability in the amount of $100,000 to the architects was recorded.

  (7)　Advertisements soliciting bids on the construction were run at a cost of $500. This amount was paid.

  (8)　Construction bids were opened and analyzed. A bid of $2,400,000 was accepted, and the contract let.

  (9)　The contractor requested a partial payment of $1,400,000. This amount was vouchered for payment.

  (10)　Vouchers payable to the contractor and to the architects were paid.

  (11)　Furniture and equipment for the annex were ordered at an estimated total cost of $247,000.

  (12)　The contractor completed the construction and requested payment of the balance due on the contract. After inspection of the work, the amount was vouchered and paid.

  (13)　Furniture and equipment were received at a total actual installed cost of $248,560. Invoices were approved for payment.

  (14)　The remainder of the architect's fee was approved for payment.

  (15)　The City Hall Annex Construction Fund paid all outstanding liabilities on June 30, 2000.

b. Open a general ledger for the City Hall Annex Construction Fund. Use the account titles shown below. Allow five lines unless otherwise indicated. Post the entries to the City Hall Annex Construction Fund general ledger.

  Cash—12 lines
  Proceeds of Bonds
  Vouchers Payable—12 lines
  Construction Expenditures—15 lines

Encumbrances—18 lines
Reserve for Encumbrances—18 lines
Equity Transfers Out
Fund Balance

c. Prepare a City Hall Annex Construction Fund trial balance as of June 30, 2000.
d. The City Hall Annex Construction Fund was closed. Remaining assets were transferred to the debt service fund. Record the proper journal entries in the City Hall Annex Construction Fund and post to its general ledger. All transactions and events were as of June 30, 2000.
e. Prepare a Statement of Revenues, Expenditures, and Changes in Fund Balance for the year ended June 30, 2000.

Part 2. General Fixed Assets Account Group.   The Controller of the City of Bingham assigned you, and other top staff personnel, to audit the General Fixed Assets Account Group—a task that had not been done in many years. The bookkeeper had been a marketing major at the university but had never succeeded in getting his grade average high enough to allow him to graduate. He was able to show you the records he had been keeping but was not able to give a very clear explanation as to why he kept them that way. The auditors found the following General Fixed Assets control account balances as of the audit cutoff date, June 30, 2000. (No source amounts had been kept.)

Land	$ 600,000
Buildings	5,200,000
Improvements Other than Buildings	16,560,000
Equipment and Miscellaneous	3,930,000
Fund Balance	$26,290,000

Required

a. Open a general journal for the General Fixed Assets Account Group and make the entries necessary to state the accounts in accord with GASB standards. Additional information disclosed by your audit is presented below:
(1)   Analysis of the Land account disclosed that the balance was comprised of: (a) An amount of $100,000 entered in 1978 when the General Fixed Assets group was established; this amount was the estimated cost of the City Hall site, the fire station sites, and city park land. The unimproved park land had been acquired as a gift from a citizen and was estimated in 1978 to be worth $12,000; the building sites had been acquired from the proceeds of tax-supported bond issues. (b) An amount of $160,000 entered in 1988 as the cost of two houses and lots. The houses were torn down, and an addition to City Hall was erected on one lot; the remainder was used as a parking lot for city-owned cars and for the private cars of city employees. This amount was financed under a grant from the federal government. (c) An amount of $240,000, dated 1994, which was financed by tax-supported bonds issued for

the purchase of land used as a public park. The former property owners received $200,000; the Mayor, who was a real estate dealer, $20,000 commission for arranging the transaction; and the Mayor's brother, an attorney, $20,000 for handling the legal details. (*d*) An amount of $100,000 entered in 1995 as the cost of land purchased by the Water Utility from current operating funds; the land is being held by the Water Utility as the site of a projected new pumping station.

(2)   Analysis of the Buildings account disclosed that the balance was comprised of: (*a*) An amount of $2,600,000 entered in 1987 as the estimated cost of City Hall and the fire stations, constructed from the proceeds of tax-supported bond issues. (*b*) Charges of $16,000 for demolishing the houses purchased in 1988, and grading the land to the level of City Hall; $1,200,000 for the addition to City Hall; and $104,000 for paving the parking lot—all of which were financed from a grant by the federal government. (*c*) $400,000 for a golf clubhouse in the park, constructed from part of the proceeds of a tax-supported bond issue. (The golf course is not operated as an enterprise fund.) (*d*) $880,000 for a 240-acre estate to be used as a park. The mansion was appraised at $400,000; the unimproved land at $960,000; and the gardens, artificial lakes, and other improvements at $2,000,000. The entire purchase price was charged to Buildings; the amount had been paid over three years out of General Fund appropriations for public works. The City's independent auditors agreed that Land, Buildings, and Improvements Other than Buildings should be recorded at appraised amounts and the source accounts should recognize that the former owner had made a substantial gift to the city.

(3)   The following items had been entered in the Improvements Other than Buildings account: (*a*) Estimated cost of streets, curbs, and sidewalks as of July 1, 1978, $5,250,000—$2,250,000 had been financed from annual General Fund appropriations during the years; the balance had been financed from various special assessment funds. (*b*) $600,000, the cost of constructing a municipal golf course on city park land, financed from a tax-supported bond issue. (*c*) An aggregate of $10,710,000 spent for street paving and widening, curbs, sidewalks, bridges, and culverts—$5,350,000 of this was from the General Fund appropriations, and the remainder from special assessment funds.

(4)   (*a*) "Equipment and Miscellaneous" supporting data were in such an incomplete and obviously inaccurate state that the auditors secured permission to have an appraisal made. The cost of the appraisal was charged to a supplemental appropriation made under the General Government classification of the General Fund. The appraisal cost $30,000; it was a thorough job and showed location, and condition, as well as appraised value of items classifiable as "Equipment and Miscellaneous." The total appraised value of owned equipment and miscellaneous was $6,300,000. The auditors could identify the sources of financing for only a portion of the equipment; therefore, it was decided to assume the sources to have contributed the following percentages of appraised value: General Fund, 65 percent; special revenue funds, 15 percent; capital projects funds, 5 percent; special assessment funds, 5 percent; and grants from the federal government, 10 percent. (*b*) In addition to equipment owned by the City of Bingham,

certain equipment was held under capital lease agreements. The present value of lease rentals, not previously capitalized, amounted to $948,000. The fair value of the leased equipment as of June 30, 2000, was $960,000.

b. None of the information presented in Problems 2–L through 4–L has been recorded by the General Fixed assets bookkeeper. Record the applicable information in the General Fixed Assets general journal. (Expenditures of the City Hall Annex Construction Fund for Land and for Equipment were given previously in this problem; assume the expenditures of that fund for Improvements Other than Buildings amount to $80,260, and the remainder of expenditures are proper charges to Buildings. Interest on City Hall annex bonds during the period of construction is not to be capitalized.)

c. Open a general ledger for the General Fixed Assets Account Group and post your journal entries.

d. Prepare a Statement of General Fixed Assets as of June 30, 2000.

CHAPTER 6

Accounting for General Long-Term Debt and Debt Service

Learning Objectives

After reading this chapter, you should be able to:

~ Explain what kinds of debt are classified as general long-term liabilities.

~ Make journal entries in the General Long-Term Debt Account Group (GLTDAG) to record the issuance and repayment of general long-term liabilities.

~ Prepare a schedule of changes in general long-term debt.

~ Describe the reasons for and nature of statutory debt limits and explain the meaning of debt margin and overlapping debt.

~ Explain the purpose and types of debt service funds, and determine how many funds are to be used.

~ Describe the budgeting requirements for debt service funds.

~ Make appropriate journal entries to account for debt service transactions.

~ Describe the required fair value reporting of investments held by debt service funds.

~ Describe the accounting procedures and make appropriate journal entries for special debt service transactions.

The use of long-term debt is a traditional part of the fiscal policy of state and local governments. Although some governments have issued taxable debt, the interest earned on most debt issued by state and local governments is exempt from federal taxation and, in some states, from state taxation. The tax-exempt feature enables governments to raise large amounts of capital at relatively low cost. For example, in 1996 total long term tax-exempt borrowing amounted to $185 billion at an average interest rate of 5.76 percent for 20-year bonds.[1] Because of the relative ease with which governments can issue debt, most states have acted in the public interest to impose statutory limits on the debt that can be incurred by state and local governments. Consequently, effective management of state and local governmental debt requires good legal advice and a sound understanding of public finance.

This chapter describes the kinds of debt that are reported in the General Long-Term Debt Account Group (GLTDAG) and the concepts of debt limit and debt margin. It also provides illustrative journal entries for the GLTDAG. In addition, the chapter explains the nature and types of debt service funds and debt service accounting for various kinds of general long-term debt, as well as accounting for refunding of debt. In studying this chapter, the reader should recall that the governmental fund types (general, special revenue, capital projects, and debt service) account for only short-term debt to be paid from assets of those funds. Although, as described in Chapter 5, the proceeds of long-term debt may be placed in one of these fund types (usually a capital projects fund), the long-term liability itself must be recorded in the GLTDAG. Enterprise funds, internal service funds, and nonexpendable trust funds account for both long-term debt serviced by the fund and short-term debt to be repaid from assets of these funds.

General Long-Term Debt

Debt instruments backed by the "full faith and credit" of a governmental unit are known as **general obligation debt**; they are obligations of the unit and not of the individual funds. In order to bring such debt under accounting control, the General Long-Term Debt Account Group (GLTDAG) was created. Since the creation of the account group, it has become common for governments to issue debt secured by a pledge of the collections of a certain specified tax (called **limited obligation debt**), or even a certain portion of a tax—for example, 1 cent of a 5-cent sales tax levied by a government (called *tax increment debt*). All debt secured by pledges of tax revenues is known as **tax-supported debt.** In addition to tax-supported long-term debt, GASB standards currently provide that the GLTDAG account for debt backed by special assessments (if the general government is obligated to assume debt service in the event that collections of special assessments are not sufficient to pay debt service); time warrants; notes having a maturity of more than one year

---

[1]Data reported in "Fiscal and Economic Indicators," *Government Finance Review*, October 1997, p. 41.

Illustrative Case

At the end of fiscal year 1998, the Town of Brighton had outstanding two issues of long-term debt that would properly have been reported in the Statement of General Long-Term Debt (the name generally given to the GLTDAG balance sheet). These two issues are reported in the Statement of General Long-Term Debt presented as Illustration 6–1.

Entries in General Long-Term Debt accounts may be made on a current basis throughout the fiscal period as long-term debt is issued, as it is repaid, and as assets are added to debt service funds; or, all the events of the period may be cumulated and appropriate entries made at period-end for the net effect of all events. The latter procedure appears more common. Note that the GLTDAG is concerned only with the principal of general long-term debt, not with transactions involving interest on that debt.

For the sake of the reader's convenience, the effect on the GLTDAG of entries in the three debt service funds of the Town of Brighton is shown separately for each of the three funds for the year 1999.

Regular Serial Bond Issue.   As of June 15, 1999, regular serial bonds in the amount of $1,200,000 were sold at par as partial financing for construction of a fire station. At that time, the entry in the *capital projects fund* was:

Cash	1,200,000	
Proceeds of Bonds		1,200,000

The corresponding entry in the *General Long-Term Debt Account Group* should be:

Amount to Be Provided for Payment of Regular Serial Bonds	1,200,000	
Regular Serial Bonds Payable		1,200,000

During 1999 no assets were provided to the *Regular Serial Bonds Debt Service Fund* for payment of the principal of these bonds; accordingly, no further entry in the GLTDAG is needed in 1999.

Deferred Serial Bond Issue.   The deferred serial bonds reported in the Town of Brighton Statement of General Long-Term Debt (Illustration 6–1) were issued on January 1, 1989. The first installment of principal of the these bonds in the amount of $2,000,000 matured on January 1, 1999. Appropriate entries are made in the Deferred Serial Bond Debt Service Fund to record the matured liability and subsequent payment. Those entries are shown later in this chapter. The effect on the GLTDAG of recording the liability in the debt service fund, and extinguishing the liability, is:

Deferred Serial Bonds Payable	200,000	
Amount Available in Debt Service Fund for Payment of		
Deferred Serial Bonds		200,000

Revenues of the Deferred Serial Bonds Debt Service Fund for 1999 are $262,000 from taxes and $98,250 from interest on investments, a total of $360,250. Since $190,000 was raised for the payment of interest, the remainder, $170,250, was dedicated for bond repayment. The effect on the *GLTDAG* of the Deferred Serial Bonds Debt Service Fund activity is:

Amount Available in Debt Service Fund for Payment of Deferred
   Serial Bonds 170,250
        Amount to Be Provided for Payment of Deferred Serial Bonds .   170,250

The net effect of the two GLTDAG entries illustrated above is a $29,750 decrease in Amount Available in Debt Service Funds for Payment of Deferred Serial Bonds, which agrees with the decrease in the Fund Balance of that fund (shown in Illustrations 6–9 and 6–10).

Term Bond Issue.   Information given later in this chapter with regard to the *Term Bonds Debt Service Fund* discloses that Revenues totaling $120,145 were raised during 1999, and $75,000 was expended for interest; the difference between the two ($45,145) should be reported in the *GLTDAG*, as shown below:

Amount Available in Debt Service Fund for Payment of Term Bonds   45,145
        Amount to Be Provided for Payment of Term Bonds   45,145

The increase in Amount Available shown in the above entry agrees with the increase in the Fund Balance of the Term Bonds Debt Service Fund, as reported in Illustrations 6–9 and 6–10.

The status of the GLTDAG as of December 31, 1999, is reported in Illustration 6–2.

Notice that the Amount Available in each debt service fund reported in Illustration 6–2 agrees with the Fund Balance of the respective debt service fund reported in Illustrations 6–8, 6–9, and 6–10, later in this chapter. This agreement would be true in all cases, unless assets dedicated only for the payment of interest were held by a debt service fund; in that event, *only* the net assets available for payment of debt principal by the debt service fund would be reported by the GLTDAG as an Amount Available.

Changes in Long-Term Debt

The reasons why the amounts of the items in Illustration 6–2 are not the same as the amounts of the same items in Illustration 6–1 are clear to those who have access to the underlying records (here illustrated in journal entry form), but readers of the Annual Report of the Town of Brighton would not have access to the underlying records and should be furnished with a schedule summarizing the reasons for the changes during the year. In the illustrative case, all changes in General Long-Term Debt result from activities summarized in capital projects fund and debt service fund statements; therefore, adequate disclosure may be made by reference to those statements. In any given year, it is common for debt issues to be authorized, for previously authorized debt to be issued, and for older issues to be retired. When a combination of events takes place, a schedule detailing changes in long-term debt is desirable.

Illustration 6–2

TOWN OF BRIGHTON
Statement of General Long-Term Debt
As of December 31, 1999

Amount Available and to Be Provided for Payment
of General Long-Term Debt

Regular serial bonds:		
Amount to be provided		$1,200,000
Deferred serial bonds:		
Amount available in debt service fund	$1,127,625	
Amount to be provided	672,375	
Total deferred serial bonds		1,800,000
Term bonds:		
Amount available in debt service fund	85,529	
Amount to be provided	1,414,471	
Total term bonds		1,500,000
Total available and to be provided		$4,500,000

General Long-Term Debt Payable

Regular serial bonds	$1,200,000
Deferred serial bonds	1,800,000
Term bonds	1,500,000
Total General Long-Term Debt Payable	$4,500,000

Illustration 6–3 presents a schedule reported in the Notes to the Financial Statements of the City of Sunnyville that summarizes, by cause, the changes in Long-Term Debt for the year ended on the date shown. Note that, consistent with current GASB standards, Sunnyville reports both the liability for compensated absences and for capital lease obligations payable from resources to be provided in years subsequent to the balance sheet date.

Schedule of Future Debt Service Requirements

In addition to the Statement of General Long-Term Debt (Illustration 6–2) and the summary of changes in general long-term debt shown in Illustration 6–3, information about the amount of debt principal and interest falling due in future years is useful information to financial managers, bond analysts, and others having an interest in assessing a governmental unit's requirements for future debt service expenditures. One form of such a schedule, taken from the Notes to the Financial Statements for the city of Sunnyville, is shown in Illustration 6–4. The reader should note that the interest portion of the scheduled future debt service payments is *not* a present liability and should not be presented as such. To do so would not be in conformity with generally accepted accounting principles.

Illustration 6–3

CITY OF SUNNYVILLE
Notes to Financial Statements
September 30, 2000

NOTE 4—Long-Term Debt

A summary of changes in long-term debt for the year follows:

	Balances 10/01/99	Additions	Deletions	Balances 09/30/00
General Obligation Bonds	$ 510,000	$ —	$ 140,000	$ 370,000
Public Improvement Revenue Certificates 1985	250,000	—	250,000	0
Public Improvement Revenue and Refunding Bonds 1991	9,940,000	—	580,000	9,360,000
State Financing Commission Loan 1991	520,000	—	75,000	445,000
State Financing Commission Loan 1992	410,000	—	410,000	0
State Financing Commission Loan 1993	—	15,830,000	—	15,830,000
Promissory Note	213,016	—	17,917	195,099
Capital Leases	155,084	41,702	76,047	120,739
Compensated Absences	1,296,122	77,864	—	1,373,986
TOTAL GENERAL LONG-TERM DEBT	13,294,222	15,949,566	1,548,964	27,694,824
ENTERPRISE LONG-TERM DEBT:				
Utility Revenue Bonds	356,053,692	134,920,000	67,017,331	423,956,361
Utility Notes	71,361,000	—	1,700,000	69,661,000
	427,414,692	134,920,000	68,717,331	493,617,361
Less unamortized discount	(7,024,095)	(2,357,438)	—	(9,381,533)
TOTAL ENTERPRISE LONG-TERM DEBT	420,390,597	132,562,562	68,717,331	484,235,828
INTERNAL SERVICE LONG-TERM DEBT:				
Capital Leases	—	54,110	—	54,110
TOTAL LONG-TERM DEBT	$433,684,819	$148,566,238	$70,266,295	$511,984,762

General Long-Term Debt Arising from Capital Lease Agreements

In Chapter 5, under the heading "Assets Acquired under Capital Lease Agreements," a brief example is given of the computation of the present value of rentals under a capital lease agreement. The entry necessary in a governmental fund at the inception of the lease is illustrated in Chapter 5. The corresponding entry in the General Fixed Assets Account Group is also illustrated in Chapter 5, and the entries required in a debt service fund for payment of annual lease rentals in the same example are illustrated and discussed later in this chapter. At the inception of a capital lease for a general fixed asset, it is necessary to record a lease obligation in the GLTDAG at the present value of the stream of annual payments. Continuing the example given in Chapter 5, the entry needed in the GLTDAG on January 1, 1999, is:

Amount to Be Provided for Payment of Capital Lease Obligations	57,590	
Capital Lease Obligations Payable		57,590

Illustration 6–4

CITY OF SUNNYVILLE
Notes to Financial Statements
September 30, 2000

Aggregate annual debt service requirements (excluding the Commercial Paper Notes) including maturities of principal and payment of current interest are as follows:

| Fiscal Year(s) | Debt Service Requirements | | | |
	General	Enterprise*	Internal Service	Total
2001	$ 2,815,299	$ 30,499,026	$22,273	$ 33,336,598
2002	2,838,305	34,499,804	22,273	37,360,382
2003	2,751,053	36,805,138	14,849	39,571,040
2004	2,693,201	39,340,417	—	42,033,618
2005	2,698,904	39,344,076	—	42,042,980
2006–2010	12,294,623	195,959,406	—	208,254,029
2011–2015	11,306,314	203,342,022	—	214,648,336
2016–2020	11,308,384	244,763,213	—	256,071,597
2021–2025	4,115,205	109,164,138	—	113,279,343
2026–2030	—	28,912,475	—	28,912,475
	52,821,288	962,629,715	59,395	1,015,510,398
Less Interest	26,500,450	538,673,354	5,285	565,179,089
Total Principal	$26,320,838	$423,956,361	$54,110	$ 450,331,309

*Excludes principal of $69,661,000 and undeterminable amount of interest. See prior description of the Utility System Commercial Paper Notes.

Included in the above tabulation are debt service requirements for the City's capital lease obligations as follows:

Fiscal year-end September 30:

2001	65,577	
2002	64,016	
2003	54,955	
2004	15,632	
Net minimum lease payments	$200,180	
Less amount representing interest	(25,331)	
Present value of net minimum lease payments	$174,849	

The entry on the preceding page is appropriate because, in this particular example, $10,000 is paid on January 1, 1999, all of which was applied to the principal of the obligation; therefore, only the present value of payments 2 through 10 need be recorded in the GLTDAG.

On January 1, 2000, the second lease rental payment of $10,000 is made. As the table given later in this chapter (page 227) shows, only $4,241 of that payment applies to the principal of the lease obligation, so the following entry is required:

Capital Lease Obligations Payable	4,241
Amount to Be Provided for Payment of Capital Lease	
Obligations	4,241

The credit in the entry above would have been to Amount Available in Debt Service Funds if that account had been debited and the Amount to Be Provided account had been credited when resources were made available in a debt service fund for payment of the lease rental.

Debt Limit and Debt Margin

The debt statements already illustrated in this chapter are primarily useful for the information of administrators, legislative bodies, and others concerned with the impact of long-term debt on the financial condition and activities of the governmental unit, particularly with reference to the resulting tax rates and taxes. Another matter of importance is the legal limit on the amount of long-term indebtedness that may be outstanding at a given time, in proportion to the assessed value of property within the jurisdiction represented. This type of restriction is of importance as a protection of taxpayers against possible confiscatory tax rates. Even though tax-rate limitation laws may be in effect for a governmental unit, the limitation on bonded indebtedness is usually needed because the prevailing practice is to exempt the claims of bondholders from the barrier of tax-rate restrictions. This is to say that, even though a law establishing maxima for tax rates is in the statutes, it will probably exclude debt service requirements from the restrictions of the law. This exclusion would be reiterated, in effect, in the bond indentures.

Before continuing a discussion of debt limitation, it seems well to clarify the meaning of the terms *debt limit* and *debt margin*. **Debt limit** means the total amount of indebtedness of specified kinds that is allowed by law to be outstanding at any one time. The limitation is likely to be in terms of a stipulated percentage of the assessed valuation of property within the government's jurisdiction. It may relate to either a gross or a net valuation. The latter is logical, but probably not prevalent, because debt limitation exists as a device for protecting property owners from confiscatory taxation. For that reason, tax-paying property *only* should be used in regulating maximum indebtedness. In many governmental jurisdictions, certain property is legally excluded even from *assessment*. This includes property owned by governments, churches, charitable organizations, and some others, depending on state laws. Exemptions, which apply to property subject to assessment, are based on homestead or mortgage exemption laws, military service, economic status, and possibly some others. Both exclusions and exemptions reduce the amount of tax-paying property.

Debt margin, sometimes referred to as *borrowing power*, is the difference between the amount of debt limit calculated as prescribed by law and the net amount of outstanding indebtedness subject to limitation. The net amount of outstanding indebtedness subject to limitation differs from total general long-term indebtedness because certain debt issues may be exempted by law from the limitation, and the amount available in debt service funds for debt repayment is deducted from the outstanding debt in order to determine the amount subject to the legal debt limit. Total general long-term indebtedness must, in some jurisdictions, include debt serviced by special assessment funds and by enterprise funds if such debt was issued with covenants that give the debt tax-supported status in the event that collections of special assessments or enterprise fund revenues are insufficient to meet required interest or principal payments. Debt authorized but not issued as of the end of a fiscal year should be added to outstanding debt because it may be sold at any time. Although it would be in keeping with the purpose of establishing a legal debt limit to include the present value of capital lease obligations along with bonded debt in the computation of legal debt margin, state statutes at present generally do not specify that the liability for capital lease obligations is subject to the legal debt limit. The computation of legal debt margin for the City of Sunnyville is shown in Illustration 6–5.

Overlapping Debt

Debt limitation laws ordinarily establish limits that may not be exceeded by each separate governmental unit affected by the laws. This means the county government may incur indebtedness to the legal limit, a township within that county may do likewise, and a city within the township may become indebted to the legal limit, with no restriction because of debt already owed by larger territorial units in which it is located. As a result, a given parcel of real estate or object of personal property may be the basis of debt beyond the so-called legal limit and also may be subject at a given time to assessments for the payment of taxes to retire bonds issued by two or more governmental units. When this situation exists, it is described as **overlapping debt.**

The extent to which debt may overlap depends on the number of units represented within an area that are authorized to incur long-term indebtedness. These may include the state, county, township, city, school board, library board, hospital board, and probably others. To show the total amount of fixed debt against property located within a given jurisdiction, a statement of direct and overlapping debt should be prepared. To this direct debt are added amounts owing by other units and authorities that levy taxes against the same property on which the direct debt is based. A Statement of Direct and Overlapping Debt is shown in Illustration 6–6. Notes included as a part of Illustration 6–6 disclose the relation of direct debt and overlapping debt to assessed valuation of real property within the City of Sunnyville.

Information shown in this chapter as Illustrations 6–3, 6–4, 6–5, and 6–6 may be disclosed in the Notes to the Financial Statements or in supplementary schedules. GASB standards require that the following be disclosed for long-term debt in whatever manner the issuer deems to be the most meaningful presentation:

1. Description of individual bond issues and leases outstanding.
2. Changes in general long-term debt.
3. Summary of debt service requirements to maturity.
4. Disclosure of legal debt margin.
5. Bonds authorized but unissued.
6. Synopsis of revenue bond covenants.

Illustration 6–5

CITY OF SUNNYVILLE
FY2000 Comprehensive Annual Financial Report
Statistical Section
Legal Debt Margin and
Ratio of City's Gross Bonded Debt to Taxable Value
and Bonded Debt per Capita

Legal Debt Margin

Taxable Value = $1,591,052,836

Legal Debt Limit = None (1)

NOTE: (1) Chapter 200.181, State Statutes, allows unrestricted Ad Valorem tax rate levies for debt service requirements for General Obligation Bonds approved by voter referendum.

Tax Roll Year	Taxable Value (January 1)	Bonded Debt (September 30)	Bonded Debt Ratio	City Population (April 1)	Bonded Debt per Capita
1991	$ 928,103,688	$1,885,000	0.20%	81,614	23.10
1992	1,003,863,526	1,305,000	0.13%	82,124	15.89
1993	1,068,009,730	1,210,000	0.11%	82,882	14.60
1994	1,190,125,000	1,110,000	0.09%	83,060	13.36
1995	1,256,295,392	1,005,000	0.07%	83,980	11.97
1996	1,281,612,508	890,000	0.06%	84,815	10.49
1997	1,307,412,913	770,000	0.06%	85,663	8.99
1998	1,349,653,947	645,000	0.05%	84,770	7.61
1999	1,345,552,130	510,000	0.04%	84,544	6.03
2000	1,591,052,836	370,000	0.02%	85,587	4.32

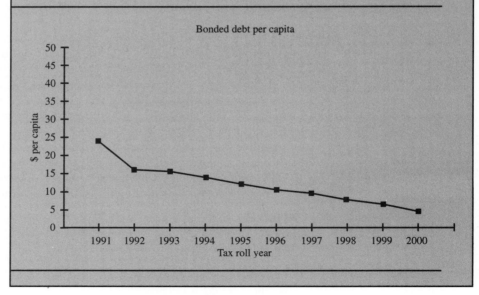

Bonded debt per capita

Illustration 6–6

CITY OF SUNNYVILLE
FY2000 Comprehensive Annual Financial Report
Statistical Section
Statement of Direct and Overlapping Bonded Debt (5)

Taxing Authority	Taxable Property Value (2)	General Obligation Bonded Debt (3)	Percent of Debt Applicable to City	City's Share of Debt (4)
City of Sunnyville	$1,591,052,836	$ 370,000	100.00%	$ 370,000
Sunny County	3,478,806,917	16,930,000	45.74	7,743,782
Sunny County Schools	3,478,806,917	69,723,480	45.74	31,891,520
		$87,023,480	45.97%	$40,005,302

NOTES:
(1) The above information on Bonded Debt does not include Self-Supporting and Non-Self-Supporting Revenue Bonds, Certificates, and Notes as follows (Reserves and/or Sinking Fund balances have *not* been deducted).
(2) As of January 1, 1991, homestead property of certain qualified residents is eligible for up to $25,000 value exemption.
(3) Reserves and Sinking Fund Balances have *not* been deducted.
(4) Chapter 200.181, State Statutes, allows unrestricted Ad Valorem Tax rate levies for debt service for General Obligation Bonds approved by citizen referendum.
(5) Includes $14,735,000 in Sunny County Library District Serial & Term Bonds.

Taxing Authority	Self-Supporting	Non-Self-Supporting	Totals
Sunny County	$ 60,220,000	$ —	$ 60,220,000
Sunny County Schools	—	—	—
City of Sunnyville:			
Utilities	423,956,361	—	423,956,361
Other Than Utilities	—	16,275,000	16,275,000
	$ 484,176,361	$16,275,000	$500,451,361

Debt Service Funds

Long-term debt incurred to provide money to pay for the construction or purchase of fixed assets, or for any other purposes, can be repaid only from revenue raised in subsequent years to service the debt. The Accounting for Fixed Assets and Long-Term Liabilities Principle, discussed briefly in Chapter 2, provides that long-term liabilities to be serviced from the revenues of a proprietary fund should be accounted for by that proprietary fund and the service of such debt is also accounted for by the proprietary fund. *Debt service* includes both the payment of interest and the repayment of principal when due. Long-term debt serviced by tax levies, or by special assessments, however, is accounted for by the General Long-Term Debt Account Group. Revenue raised from taxes or from special assessments for debt service, and expenditures for debt service, are commonly accounted for by use of a *debt service fund*, the subject of this section of the chapter.

Types of Debt Service Funds

Earlier in this century, governmental issues of long-term debt commonly matured in total on a given date. In that era, bond indentures often required the establishment of a "sinking fund," sometimes operated on an actuarial basis. Some sinking fund term bond issues are still outstanding, but they are dwarfed in number and amount by serial bond issues, in which the principal matures in installments. Four types of serial bond issues are found in practice: regular, deferred, annuity, and irregular. If the total principal of an issue is repayable in a specified number of equal annual installments over the life of the issue, it is a **regular serial bond issue.** If the first installment is delayed for a period of more than one year after the date of the issue, but thereafter installments fall due on a regular basis, the bonds are known as **deferred serial bonds**. If the amount of annual principal repayments is scheduled to increase each year by approximately the same amount that interest payments decrease (interest decreases, of course, because the amount of outstanding bonds decreases) so that the total debt service remains reasonably level over the term of the issue, the bonds are called **annuity serial bonds. Irregular serial bonds** may have any pattern of repayment that does not fit the other three categories.

Budgeting for Debt Service

Whether or not additions to debt service funds are required by the bond indenture to be approximately equal year by year, good politics and good financial management suggest that the burden on the taxpayers be spread reasonably evenly rather than lumped in the years that issues or installments happen to mature. If taxes for payment of interest and principal on long-term debt are to be raised directly by the debt service fund, they are recognized as *Revenues* of the debt service fund. If the taxes are to be raised by another fund and transferred to the debt service fund, they must be included in the Revenues budget of the fund that will raise the revenue (often the General Fund) and also budgeted by that fund as *operating transfers* to the debt service fund, and reported as an Other Financing Use by the General Fund. The operating transfers are reported as Other Financing Sources by the debt service fund. Since the debt service fund is a budgeting and accounting entity, it should prepare a Revenues and Other Financing Sources budget that includes operating transfers from other funds as well as revenues it will raise directly or earn on its investments. Although the items may be difficult to budget accurately, debt service funds can often count on receiving premiums on debt issues sold and accrued interest on debt issues sold. Accrued interest on debt sold is considered Revenues of the recipient debt service fund; premium on debt sold is an Other Financing Source. Similarly, as illustrated in Chapter 5, if capital projects are completed with expenditures less than revenues and other financing sources, the residual equity is ordinarily transferred to the appropriate debt service fund. Persons budgeting and accounting for debt service funds should seek competent legal advice on the permissible use of both premium on debt sold and residual equity transfers-in. In some cases, one or both of these items must be held for eventual debt repayment and may not be used for interest payments; in other cases, both premiums and residual equity transfers-in may be used for interest payments.

The Appropriations budget of a debt service fund must provide for the payment of all interest on general long-term debt that will become legally due during the budget year, and for the payment of any principal amounts that will become legally due during the budget year. GASB standards currently require debt service fund accounting to be on the same basis as is required for general and special revenue funds. One peculiarity of the modified accrual basis used by governmental fund types (which is not discussed in Chapter 3 because it relates only to debt service funds) is that interest on long-term debt is not accrued. For example, if the fiscal year of a governmental unit ends on December 31, 1999, and the interest on its bonds is payable on January 1 and July 1 of each year, the amount payable on January 1, 2000, would not be considered a liability in the balance sheet of the debt service fund prepared as of December 31, 1999. The rationale for this recommendation is that the interest is not legally due until January 1, 2000. (See Illustration 6–7.) The same reasoning applies to principal amounts that mature on the first day of a fiscal year; they are not liabilities to be recognized in statements prepared as of the day before. In the event 1999 appropriations include January 1, 2000, interest and/or principal payment, the appropriation and expenditures (and resulting liabilities) should be recognized in 1999.

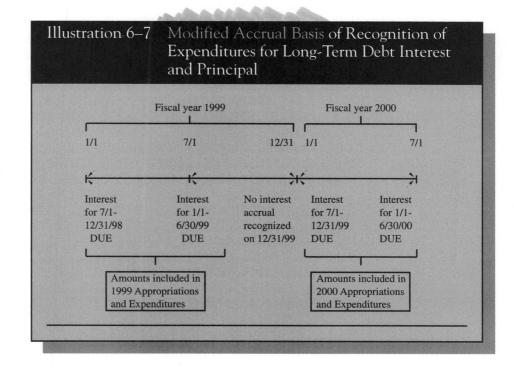

Illustration 6–7 Modified Accrual Basis of Recognition of Expenditures for Long-Term Debt Interest and Principal

Bearer Bonds and
Registered Bonds

Federal law requires tax-exempt bonds issued after June 30, 1983, to be *registered* instead of being *bearer* bonds, as the vast majority of issues were until that date. Many issues of bearer bonds are still outstanding and will continue to be for a number of years—for example, the final maturity of bonds issued as of June 30, 1983, may be June 30, 2013. Bearer bonds have some advantage for issuers in that bondholders receive payment for interest by presenting to their local banks (or other paying agent) on the interest payment date the coupon dated that day. Since the interest payment date may fall on a Saturday, Sunday, or holiday, even an alert bondholder may not collect the interest until two or more days after it is due. On any given interest payment date, some bondholders may not find it convenient to clip their coupons or may forget about it. Even if the coupons are paid on the due date by banks where bondholders reside, bondholders may live in locations distant from the issuing government, so coupons take a number of days to work their way through banking channels to the issuer's paying agent. The same is true of matured bearer bonds; they may not actually be presented to the issuer's paying agent for payment until long after maturity. Consequently, issuers of bearer bonds, and their paying agents, often have the use of a portion of their cash designated for interest and bond redemption long enough after maturity of coupons and bonds to earn significant amounts of interest.

Issuance of bonds that are registered as to interest and principal, however, requires the issuer, or its agent, to write a check as of each interest payment date, and as of the date of maturity of the bonds, to the registered owner of the bonds. Checks are commonly put in the mail in time to be delivered to the payee by the payment date. The fact that checks are written and mailed in advance of the interest or bond payment date makes it prudent for governmental units to raise and collect revenues in one fiscal year in the amount of interest and bonds that will legally be payable early in the next fiscal year. Failure to pay interest, or matured bonds, when due is called a *default*. A default would be viewed seriously by all creditors of the governmental unit or agency that defaulted, not just the bondholders who did not receive the amount of interest and principal when due. News of defaults reaches debt-rating agencies and newspapers and television financial reporters rapidly. Even if the default is cured promptly there is damage to the reputation of the defaulter, and probably to the ratings of all its debt issues, which will make it more difficult and more expensive for that government to borrow in the future. Of more immediate concern, however, is the fact that bond indentures commonly provide that the entire principal of the issue would be deemed to mature at the time any interest payment is defaulted. The prospect of having to pay in the current period the holders of all outstanding bonds of that issue should impress even the least financially knowledgeable administrators with the need for being meticulous about paying interest when due, as well as paying the principal of debt at maturity.

Registered bonds may be issued in much the same form as bearer bonds (i.e., engraved on paper of bank note quality to make it difficult for counterfeiters to issue spurious bonds), or they may be in "book entry" form. In the latter case, issuers deposit a single certificate for each issue of term bonds, or each maturity of serial bonds, with a designated depository. Purchasers of bonds receive only a confirmation of the purchase and periodic statements of their accounts. Similarly, when a bondholder sells one or more bonds, the seller receives a confirmation of the sale, and the new owner receives a confirmation of the purchase.

Number of Debt Service Funds

In addition to term bonds and serial bonds, debt service funds may be required to service debt arising from the use of notes or warrants having a maturity more than one year after date of issue. In addition, debt service funds may be used to make periodic payments required by capital lease agreements. Although each issue of long-term or intermediate-term debt is a separate obligation and may have legal restrictions and servicing requirements that differ from other issues, GASB standards provide that, if legally permissible, a single debt service fund be used to account for the service of all issues of tax-supported and special assessment debt. Subsidiary records of that fund can provide needed assurance that restrictions and requirements relating to each issue are properly budgeted and accounted for. If legal restrictions do not allow the service of all issues of tax-supported and special assessment debt to be accounted for by a single debt service fund, as few additional debt service funds as is consistent with applicable laws should be created. In this chapter, a separate debt service fund for each bond issue is illustrated simply as a means for helping the reader focus on the different accounting procedures considered appropriate for each kind of bond issue encountered in practice.

Use of General Fund to Account for Debt Service

In some jurisdictions, laws do not require the debt service function to be accounted for by a debt service fund. Unless the debt service function is very simple, it may be argued that good financial management would dictate the establishment of a debt service fund even though not required by law. If neither law nor sound financial administration require the use of debt service funds, the function may be performed within the accounting and budgeting framework of the General Fund. In such cases, the accounting and financial reporting standards discussed in this chapter should be followed for the debt service activities of the General Fund.

Debt Service Accounting for Regular Serial Bonds

Accounts recommended for use by debt service funds created to account for revenues to be used for the payment of interest and principal of serial bond issues are similar to those recommended for use by general and special revenue funds, but not exactly the same. Serial bond debt service funds should record the budget in Estimated Revenues and Appropriations control accounts and subsidiary accounts (and Estimated Other Financing Sources and Estimated Other Financing Uses control accounts and subsidiary accounts, if needed) just as general and special revenue funds should, but their operations do not involve the use of purchase orders and contracts for goods and services, so the Encumbrance account is not needed. Proprietary accounts of a serial bond debt service fund include Revenues and Expenditures control and subsidiary accounts (and Other Financing Sources and Other Financing Uses control and subsidiary accounts, if needed); and liquid asset, current liability, and Fund Balance accounts. Liquid assets of a serial bond debt service fund are held for the purpose of paying interest on outstanding bonds and retiring the principal installments as they fall due; for the convenience of bondholders, the payment of interest and the redemption of matured bonds is ordinarily handled through the banking system. Usually the government designates a bank as Paying Agent or Fiscal Agent, to handle interest and principal payments for each issue whether the issue is in registered or bearer form. The assets of a debt service fund may, therefore, include "Cash with Paying Agent," and the appropriations, expenditures, and liabilities may include amounts for the service charges of paying agents. Investment management may be performed by governmental employees or by banks, brokers, or others who charge for the service; investment management fees are a legitimate charge against investment revenues.

Accounting for debt service of regular serial bonds furnishes the simplest illustration of recommended debt service fund accounting. Assume the bonds issued by the Town of Brighton as partial financing for the fire station construction project (discussed in Chapter 5, under the heading "Illustrative Transactions—Capital Projects Fund Accounting") are regular serial bonds maturing in equal annual amounts over 20 years and are registered as to interest and principal. The total face value of the issue was $1,200,000; all bonds in the issue bear interest of 6 percent per year, payable semiannually on June 15 and December 15. The bonds were dated June 15, 1999, and sold on that date at par. During 1999 the only expenditure the debt service fund will be required to make will be the interest payment due December 15, 1999, in the amount of $36,000 ($1,200,000 $\times$ 0.06 $\times \frac{1}{2}$ year). Assuming revenues to pay the first installment of bonds due on June 15, 2000, and both interest payments due in 2000, will be raised in 2000, the budget for 1999 need only provide revenues in the amount of the 1999 expenditure. The entry to record the budget for the year ended December 31, 1999 would be:

1. Estimated Revenues	36,000	
Appropriations		36,000

If revenues in the amount of $30,000 were collected in cash from various sources available for debt service, the entry would be:

2. Cash	30,000	
Revenues		30,000

As illustrated in Chapter 5, the $6,000 residual equity of the Fire Station Capital Projects Fund was transferred to the debt service fund. The entry required in the latter fund is:

3. Cash	6,000	
Equity Transfer In		6,000

On December 15, 1999, when the first interest payment is legally due, the debt service fund records the expenditure of the appropriation:

4. Expenditures—Bond Interest	36,000	
Interest Payable		36,000

Checks totaling $36,000 are written to the registered owners of these bonds:

5. Interest Payable	36,000	
Cash		36,000

As of December 31, 1999, the debt service fund has no assets and no liabilities, therefore no need to prepare a balance sheet; but the budgetary and operating statement accounts have balances, which are closed by the following entry:

6. Revenues	30,000	
Appropriations	36,000	
Fund Balance	6,000	
Estimated Revenues..................................		36,000
Expenditures—Bond Interest		36,000

The Equity Transfer In must be reported in the Changes in Fund Balance section of the operating statement. Accordingly, it is closed in the following manner:

7. Equity Transfer In	6,000	
Fund Balance		6,000

The Regular Serial Bonds Debt Service Fund Statement of Revenues, Expenditures, and Changes in Fund Balance for the year ended December 31, 1999, and the budgetary comparison statement for this fund for the year are illustrated in the combining statements for all debt service funds, Illustrations 6–9 and 6–10.

Debt Service Accounting for Deferred Serial Bonds

If a government issues bonds other than regular serial bonds, debt service fund accounting is somewhat more complex than that illustrated above. In the entries below, it is assumed the Town of Brighton issued a total of $2,000,000 face value of deferred serial bonds on January 1, 1989. Each installment is in the amount of $200,000. The first installment matures on January 1, 1999; the final installment on January 1, 2008. Interest is payable on January 1 and July 1 of each year at the nominal annual rate of 10 percent. Debt service is financed from taxes levied by the debt service fund and from net earnings on debt service fund investments. Taxes for this debt service fund are levied in an amount equal to interest to be paid during the budget year, plus a level amount of $80,000 to be invested by the debt service fund and used for principal repayment when the principal installments fall due. The trial balance of the Town of Brighton's Deferred Serial Bonds Debt Service Fund at the end of the 10th year (1998) following the date of the deferred serial bond issue showed:

	Debits	Credits
Cash	$ 300,000	
Investments	830,625	
Interest Receivable	26,750	
Fund Balance	—	$1,157,375
Totals	$1,157,375	$1,157,375

Notice the trial balance shows Cash in the exact amount of interest on this bond issue due on January 1, 1999 ($2,000,000 × .10 × ½ year = $ 100,000), plus $200,000 for the bonds that mature on January 1, 1999. As noted in a preceding section of this chapter, checks totaling $300,000, dated January 1, 1999, have been written and are in the mail to the registered bondholders; since the checks are dated the day after balance sheet date, they will not be credited to Cash until that date. Similarly, the $300,000 liability does not legally exist until January 1, 1999; therefore, it is not reported in the December 31, 1998, trial balance.

The budget for this fund for fiscal 1999 includes the appropriations for payment of the interest of $100,000 on January 1, the payment of matured bonds of $200,000 on January 1, and the payment of interest of $90,000 on bonds outstanding on July 1, 1999 ($1,800,000 × .10 × ½ year). It is assumed, for the sake of simplicity, that the Town will not incur any fees for paying agents or for investment management; therefore, the total of the *Appropriations budget* for 1999 is $390,000. As noted in the description of this deferred serial bond issue, taxes are levied each year to allow for collection of cash in the amount of interest checks to be written that year, plus an amount of $80,000 to be invested for use for bond principal payment; earnings on the investments are also accumulated for bond principal repayment. Therefore, the *Revenues budget* for 1999 for this fund for revenues from taxes totals $260,000 ($90,000 for the interest payment due July 1, 1999; $90,000 for the interest payment due January 1, 2000; and the $80,000 level amount to be invested); revenues from earnings on investments during 1999 are budgeted at $98,600. Total Estimated Revenues for 1999, therefore, amounts to $358,600. The entry to record the 1999 budget is:

1. Estimated Revenues	358,600	
Fund Balance	31,400	
Appropriations		390,000

Subsidiary records, as needed, would be kept in the manner illustrated in Chapters 3 and 4. Since the records, and their use, are the same, they are omitted from this chapter.

Also, as of January 1, 1999, the bond payment and interest payment due on that date should be recognized as expenditures of 1999 appropriations (Entry 2a), and the fact that checks dated January 1, 1999, have been issued in payment of the interest and bond principal should be recorded (Entry 2b):

2a. Expenditures—Bond Principal	200,000	
Expenditures—Bond Interest	100,000	
Interest Payable		100,000
Bonds Payable		200,000
2b. Interest Payable	100,000	
Bonds Payable	200,000	
Cash		300,000

In an actual case it would, of course, simplify the accounting to make one entry for the net effect of Entries 2a and 2b: a debit to Expenditures and a credit to Cash.

As shown in Illustrations 6–9 and 6–10, however, the expenditures for bond interest and the expenditures for the redemption of matured bonds should be separately reported in the operating statements.

Taxes levied for debt service on the deferred serial bond issue are levied in the amount of $268,000; $8,000 of the levy is expected to be uncollectible:

3. Taxes Receivable—Current	268,000	
Estimated Uncollectible Current Taxes		8,000
Revenues		260,000

Entry 4a summarizes the collection of taxes during the first half-year (assumed to amount to $120,000), the collection of interest receivable as of December 31, 1998 ($26,750, per the trial balance), and the collection of $49,250 interest earned during the first half-year on investments of this fund. Cash in the amount of $106,000 was promptly invested, as shown by Entry 4b.

4a. Cash	196,000	
Taxes Receivable—Current		120,000
Interest Receivable on Investments		26,750
Revenues		49,250
4b. Investments	106,000	
Cash		106,000

Interest payable July 1 is recorded as an expenditure, and checks are written and mailed in the amount of interest payable July 1:

5a. Expenditures—Bond Interest	90,000	
Interest Payable		90,000
5b. Interest Payable	90,000	
Cash		90,000

Tax collections during the second half of 1999 totaled $138,000; interest earnings received in cash during that period amounted to $24,000. Cash in the amount of $162,000 was invested:

6a. Cash	162,000	
Taxes Receivable—Current		138,000
Revenues		24,000
6b. Investments	162,000	
Cash		162,000

Taxes not collected during 1999 must be classified as delinquent, as required by the laws of the state in which the Town of Brighton is located. Administrators estimate that at least $4,000 of taxes levied in 1999 will be collected early in 2000, and the remainder of that levy, $6,000, will be uncollectible. Since the original estimate of uncollectible taxes was $8,000 ($2,000 too much), Revenues should be credited for $2,000. Entry 7 accomplishes the necessary reclassifications:

7. Taxes Receivable—Delinquent 10,000
   Estimated Uncollectible Current Taxes 8,000
       Taxes Receivable—Current 10,000
       Estimated Uncollectible Delinquent Taxes 6,000
       Revenues 2,000

Bonds in the amount of $200,000 will mature on January 1, 2000, and interest in the amount of $90,000 will be payable on that date. Investments in the amount of $290,000 are converted to cash as of December 31, 1999, so that checks dated January 1, 2000, may be mailed.

8. Cash 290,000
       Investments 290,000

Interest receivable on investments accrued at year-end is computed as $25,000; this accrual is recorded:

9. Interest Receivable on Investments 25,000
       Revenues 25,000

Budgetary and operating statement accounts for 1999 are closed:

10. Revenues 360,250
    Appropriations 390,000
        Estimated Revenues 358,600
        Expenditures—Bond Interest 190,000
        Expenditures—Bond Principal 200,000
        Fund Balance 1,650

After recording the entries for 1999, the Town of Brighton Deferred Serial Bonds Debt Service Fund Balance Sheet would be as presented in Illustration 6–8; the Combining Balance Sheet for all debt service funds of the Town of Brighton. In addition to the Balance Sheet, the revenues, expenditures, and changes in fund balance during the fiscal period should be reported for each debt service fund. Illustration 6–9 presents the Combining Statement of Revenues, Expenditures, and Changes in Fund Balances for the Town of Brighton Deferred Serial Bonds Debt Service Fund for the year ended December 31, 1999, and all other debt service funds of the Town. Since the funds are assumed to operate under legally required budgets, a Combining Statement of Revenues, Expenditures, and Changes in Fund Balances—Budget and Actual for the year is required. Illustration 6–10 presents the budgetary comparison for all debt service funds of the Town of Brighton

Debt Service Accounting for Term Bonds

Term bond issues mature in their entirety on a given date, in contrast to serial bonds, which mature in installments. Required revenues of term bond debt service funds may be determined on an "actuarial" basis or on less sophisticated bases designed to produce approximately level contributions during the life of the issue. If an actuarial basis is not used, accounting procedures and statements illustrated for the deferred serial bond issue of the Town of Brighton are appropriate for use by term bond debt service funds. In order to illustrate the differences that exist when an actuarial basis is used, the following example is based on the assumption that the Town of Brighton has a term bond

Illustration 6–8

TOWN OF BRIGHTON
Debt Service Funds
Combining Balance Sheet
As of December 31, 1999

	Deferred Serial Bonds	Term Bonds	Total Debt Service Funds
Assets			
Cash	$ 290,000	$ 613	$ 290,613
Investments	808,625	83,316	891,941
Taxes receivable, net	4,000	1,600	5,600
Interest receivable	25,000	–0–	25,000
Total Assets	$1,127,625	$85,529	$1,213,154
Fund Equity			
Fund Equity			
Fund Balance	$1,127,625	$85,529	$1,213,154
Total Fund Equity	$1,127,625	$85,529	$1,213,154

Illustration 6–9

TOWN OF BRIGHTON
Debt Service Funds
Combining Statement of Revenues, Expenditures,
and Changes in Fund Balances
For the Year Ended December 31, 1999

	Regular Serial Bonds	Deferred Serial Bonds	Term Bonds	Total Debt Service Funds
Revenues:				
Taxes	$ –0–	$ 262,000	$117,000	$ 379,000
Miscellaneous sources	30,000	–0–	–0–	30,000
Interest on investments	–0–	98,250	3,145	101,395
Total Revenues	30,000	360,250	120,145	510,395
Expenditures:				
Interest on bonds	36,000	190,000	75,000	301,000
Redemption of matured bonds	–0–	200,000	–0–	200,000
Total Expenditures	36,000	390,000	75,000	501,000
Excess of Revenues over (under) Expenditures	(6,000)	(29,750)	45,145	9,395
Fund Balance, January 1, 1999	–0–	1,157,375	40,384	1,197,759
Equity Transfer In	6,000	–0–	–0–	6,000
Fund Balance, December 31, 1999	$ –0–	$1,127,625	$ 85,529	$1,213,154

Illustration 6–10

TOWN OF BRIGHTON
Debt Service Funds
Combining Statement of Revenues, Expenditures,
and Changes in Fund Balances—Budget and Actual
For the Year Ended December 31, 1999

	Regular Serial Bonds			Deferred Serial Bonds			Term Bonds			Total Debt Service Funds		
	Budget	Actual	Actual over (under) Budget	Budget	Actual	Actual over (under) Budget	Budget	Actual	Actual over (under) Budget	Budget	Actual	Actual over (under) Budget
Revenues:												
Taxes	$ -0-	$ -0-	$ -0-	$ 260,000	$ 262,000	$2,000	$114,787	$117,000	$2,213	$ 374,787	$ 379,000	$ 4,213
Miscellaneous sources	36,000	30,000	(6,000)	-0-	-0-	-0-	-0-	-0-	-0-	36,000	30,000	(6,000)
Interest on investments	-0-	-0-	-0-	98,600	98,250	(350)	3,056	3,145	89	101,656	101,395	(261)
Total Revenues	36,000	30,000	(6,000)	358,600	360,250	1,650	117,843	120,145	2,302	512,443	510,395	(2,048)
Expenditures:												
Interest on bonds	36,000	36,000	-0-	190,000	190,000	-0-	75,000	75,000	-0-	301,000	301,000	-0-
Redemption of bonds	-0-	-0-	-0-	200,000	200,000	-0-	-0-	-0-	-0-	200,000	200,000	-0-
Total Expenditures	36,000	36,000	-0-	390,000	390,000	-0-	75,000	75,000	-0-	501,000	501,000	-0-
Excess of Revenues over (under) Expenditures	-0-	(6,000)	(6,000)	(31,400)	(29,750)	1,650	42,843	45,145	2,302	11,443	9,395	(2,048)
Fund Balance, January 1, 1999	-0-	-0-	-0-	1,157,375	1,157,375	-0-	40,384	40,384	-0-	1,197,759	1,197,759	-0-
Equity Transfer In	-0-	6,000	6,000	-0-	-0-	-0-	-0-	-0-	-0-	-0-	6,000	6,000
Fund Balance, December 31, 1999	$ -0-	$ -0-	$ -0-	$1,125,975	$1,127,625	$1,650	$ 83,227	$ 85,529	$2,302	$1,209,202	$1,213,154	3,952

issue amounting to $1,500,000 with a 20-year life. The term bonds bear semiannual interest with a nominal annual rate of 5 percent, payable on January 1 and July 1. Revenues and other financing sources of this particular debt service fund are assumed to be taxes levied directly for this debt service fund and earnings on investments of the debt service fund. The amount of the tax levy is computed in accord with annuity tables on the assumption that revenues for principal repayment will be invested and will earn 6 percent per year, compounded semiannually. (Actuaries are usually very conservative in their assumptions because they are concerned with a long time span.) Using either the annuity tables found in most intermediate accounting texts or a calculator, the future amount of an annuity of $1 invested at the end of each period will amount to $75.4012597 at the end of 40 periods, if the periodic compound interest is 3 percent (as specified in the Town of Brighton example). Since the amount needed for bond repayment at the end of 40 six-month periods is $1,500,000, the tax levy for bond principal repayment must yield $1,500,000 ÷ 75.4012597, or $19,893.57 at the end of each six-month period throughout the life of the bonds. Revenue for each bond interest payment must be $37,500 ($1,500,000, the face of the bonds, × 5 percent, the annual nominal interest rate, × $\frac{1}{2}$ year).

Assuming the bonds were issued on January 1, 1998, and actual additions and actual earnings were both exactly as budgeted, and the revenues to cover interest payments were exactly $75,000, while only the interest due on July 1, 1998, was made during FY 1998, the Town of Brighton Term Bonds Debt Service Fund would have the following trial balance as of December 31, 1998:[2]

	Debits	Credits
Cash	$37,500.00	—
Investments	$40,383.95	—
Fund Balance	—	$77,883.95
Totals	$77,883.95	$77,883.95

---

[2]The computation is:

Year	Period	Addition at End of Period	3 Percent Interest per Period	Balance at End of Period
1998	1	$19,893.57	$ –0–	$19,893.57
	2	19,893.57	596.81	40,383.95
1999	3	19,893.57	1,211.52	61,489.04
	4	19,893.57	1,844.67	83,227.28

The balance at the end of period 2 is the total of Investments, and the total of Fund Balance, in this case since actuarial assumptions were met exactly in 1998.

The sum of the interest for period 3 and period 4 is $3,056.19, the required earnings for the second year.

For every year of the life of the issue, the budget for the Term Bonds Debt Service Fund of the Town, reflecting the conditions described above, will include two required additions of $19,893.57 each for investment for eventual principal repayment, and two amounts of $37,500 each for interest payment, for a total of $114,787.14. The budget will also include earnings on debt service fund investments computed in accord with actuarial requirements. For 1999, the second year of the Term Bonds Debt Service Fund's operation, the actuarial assumption is that the fund will earn 6 percent per year, compounded semiannually; the required earnings for the year amount to $3,056.19.[3] Therefore, Estimated Revenues is debited for $117,843.33 ($114,787.14 + $3,056.19). The Appropriations budget would include only the amounts becoming due during the budget year, $75,000 (two interest payments, each amounting to $37,500). The entry to record the budget is shown below.

1. Estimated Revenues	117,843.33	
Fund Balance		42,843.33
Appropriations		75,000.00

If the debt service fund is to accumulate the amount needed to retire the term bond issue at maturity, both additions and earnings must be received, and invested, in accord with the actuarial assumptions. Therefore, the tax levy for this fund must yield collections in the first six months totaling $57,393.57, at least, so that $19,893.57 can be invested and $37,500 interest paid to bondholders, both as of the end of the first six-month period. Collections during the second six months must also total $57,393.57, for the same reason. In the real world it is unlikely that collections would ever total $57,393.57, to the penny, in either six-month period. If collections are less than that amount in either period, it should be obvious that this fund would have to borrow enough to make the required investments—there is no question that the interest would have to be paid when due, as discussed in an early section of this chapter. Assuming collection experience of the Town of Brighton indicates that a tax levy in the amount of $120,000 is needed in order to be reasonably certain that collections during each six-month period will equal the needed amount, the entry to record the levy and the expected uncollectibles amounting to $3,000 is:

2. Taxes Receivable—Current	120,000.00	
Estimated Uncollectible Current Taxes		3,000.00
Revenues		117,000.00

If actual collections during the first six months of 1999 were $57,400, Entry 3 records that fact.

3. Cash	57,400.00	
Taxes Receivable—Current		57,400.00

Entry 4 records the investment of the required $19,893.57 and the payment of interest of $37,500.

---

[3]See footnote 2 for the computation.

4. Expenditures—Bond Interest	37,500.00	
Investments	19,893.57	
Cash		57,393.57

Entry 5 records the addition of interest on June 30 in the amount of $1,261.99 to the investments of $40,383.95 invested for the entire first six months of 1999. Note the actual interest for this period is $50.47 greater than the required earnings of $1,211.52 for the period, because the actual rate was slightly greater than the rate used in actuarial computations.

| 5. Investments | 1,261.99 | |
| Interest Earnings | | 1,261.99 |

During the second six months, tax collections for the Term Bonds Debt Service Fund totaled $58,000 (Entry 6a). The required addition to the Investment account was made, and interest of $37,500 was paid, both actions as of December 31, 1999 (Entry 6b).

| 6a. Cash | 58,000.00 | |
| Taxes Receivable—Current | | 58,000.00 |

6b. Expenditures—Bond Interest	37,500.00	
Investments	19,893.57	
Cash		57,393.57

Interest earnings during the last six months on the $61,539.51 invested since July 1, 1999, totaled $1,883.10; this amount was added to the Investment account:

[handwritten: Increase Fund Balance]

| 7. Investments | 1,883.10 | |
| Interest Earnings | | 1,883.10 |

Taxes levied for 1999 but not collected during the year are recorded as delinquent; the amount in the related Estimated Uncollectible account is reviewed and determined to be reasonable.

8. Taxes Receivable—Delinquent	4,600.00	
Estimated Uncollectible Current Taxes	3,000.00	
Taxes Receivable—Current		4,600.00
Estimated Uncollectible Delinquent Taxes		3,000.00

As of December 31, 1999, the budgetary accounts and operating statement accounts were closed.

9. Appropriations	75,000.00	
Revenues	117,000.00	
Interest Earnings	3,145.09	
Estimated Revenues		117,843.33
Expenditures—Bond Interest		75,000.00
Fund Balance		2,301.76

Assets, liabilities, and Fund Balance of the Term Bonds Debt Service Fund as of December 31, 1999 (all rounded to the nearest dollar), are shown in one column of the Combining Balance Sheet of all debt service funds of the Town of Brighton,

Illustration 6–8. Similarly, revenues, expenditures and changes in fund balance of the Term Bonds Debt Service Fund are shown in the Combining Statement of Revenues, Expenditures, and Changes in Fund Balances, Illustration 6–9, and the Budget and Actual comparison in Illustration 6–10.

Disclosures in Notes to the Financial Statements

Any information in addition to the financial statements shown as Illustrations 6–8, 6–9, and 6–10 that would be helpful to administrators, members of the legislative body, interested residents, creditors, or any other category of person who uses the financial reports of a governmental reporting entity should, of course, be provided. GASB standards require disclosure in the notes to the financial statements (the notes are an integral part of the general purpose financial statements and are covered by the auditor's report) of specific data about deposits with financial institutions and investments. Disclosures are required for the entity as a whole, not just for debt service funds. However, since the Town of Brighton's debt service funds hold almost $1.2 million in cash and investments, it is appropriate to mention required note disclosures at this point.

GASB standards require disclosure in the notes of the types of deposits and investments authorized by legal and contractual provisions (see also Chapter 15 on cash and investments). Any significant violations during the period of legal or contractual provisions should, of course, be disclosed. If bank balances as of balance sheet date are entirely insured or collateralized with securities held by the entity or its agent in the entity's name, that fact should be mentioned. If not, the amount of the total bank balance should be classified and reported in the three categories of credit risk specified in the standards. Similarly, the carrying amount and fair value of investments as of balance sheet date should be disclosed in total and for each type of investment.[4] The disclosure of carrying amounts by type of investment should be classified in the three categories of credit risk specified in the standards.[5]

GASB standards apply to all state and local governmental reporting entities' financial reports that are intended to conform with generally accepted accounting principles. A number of states have established by law reporting requirements for the state government itself and for local governments within the state. It is common for financial reports prepared in compliance with state laws to include a list of the amounts on deposit in named banks; a list of securities held, their cost, and their market value as of balance sheet date; and, perhaps, a schedule of realized gains and losses on investments sold during the year. Supplementary schedules presented in order to conform with laws, or presented because administrators feel the disclosures should be made, are not covered by the independent auditor's report unless the audit engagement specifically extends the scope of the audit to the supplementary schedules.

---

[4]GASB standards define **fair value** as "the amount at which a financial instrument could be exchanged in a current transaction between willing parties, other than in a forced or liquidation sale." GASB, *Codification*, Sec. 150.105. See Chapter 15 for additional discussion.

[5]GASB, *Codification*, Sec. 150.125–132.

**Debt Service
Fund Investments**

As shown in the Deferred Serial Bond Debt Service Fund and the Term Bond Debt Service Fund examples in this chapter, financial resources typically are accumulated in these types of debt service funds for eventual repayment of principal. Such resources should be invested prudently until they are needed for principal repayment. Interest earnings on investments in bonds and other securities purchased at a premium or discount generally would *not* be adjusted for amortization of any premiums or discounts. As noted in footnote 5, current GASB standards require fair value accounting and reporting for most investments, except for certain money market investments with maturities of less than one year. The latter *may* be accounted for at amortized cost (interest earnings adjusted for amortization of premium or discount).[6] Often, however, premiums and discounts are not amortized for short-term investments. All long-term investments in debt and equity securities held for repayment of general long-term debt principal are reported at fair value in the debt service fund balance sheet. All *changes* in the fair value of investments during the period, both realized and unrealized, are reported as revenue in the Statement of Revenues, Expenditures, and Changes in Fund Balances.

**Debt Service
Accounting
for Special
Assessment Debt**

Special assessment projects, as discussed in Chapter 5, typically follow the same pattern as transactions of other capital projects. Specifically, construction activities are usually completed in the first year or so, using either interim financing from the governmental unit or proceeds of special assessment debt issuances (bonds or notes) to pay construction costs to contractors. Either at the beginning of the project or, more commonly, when construction is completed, assessments for debt service are levied against property owners in the defined special benefit district. Annual assessment installments receivable, and interest on deferred installments, usually approximate the amount of debt principal and interest payable during the same year. If the governmental unit is obligated in some manner to make the debt service payments in the event amounts collected from benefited property owners are insufficient, the debt should be recorded in the General Long-Term Debt Account Group (GLTDAG) and a debt service fund should be used to account for debt service activities. If the governmental unit is not obligated in any manner for special assessment debt, the debt should *not* be recorded in the GLTDAG. In the latter case, which is relatively rare, debt service transactions should be accounted for in an *agency fund*, as explained in Chapter 8.

Assume that special assessment bonds, secondarily backed by the general taxing authority of the City of X, were issued to complete a street-widening project. Upon completion of the project the City levied assessments amounting to $480,000, payable in 10 equal installments with 5 percent interest on deferred installments, on owners of properties fronting on the improved streets. As shown

---

[6]The reader should note this discussion refers to amortization of premium and discount on investments purchased with the expectation of holding them until maturity. Premium or discount on bonds payable sold by a governmental unit is *not* amortized; premium on bonds sold is considered as an Other Financing Source of the debt service fund if it must be used for debt service, as discussed in Chapter 5. Accrued interest sold should be recorded as revenue of the debt service fund.

by Entry 1, all receivables are recorded at the time of the levy, but Revenues is credited only for the amount expected to be collected within one year from the date of the levy; Deferred Revenues is credited for the amount of deferred installments. Required budgetary entries, as shown earlier in this chapter for serial bond and term bond debt service funds, are omitted for the sake of brevity.

1.	Assessments Receivable—Current	48,000	
	Assessments Receivable—Deferred	432,000	
	Revenues		48,000
	Deferred Revenues		432,000

All current assessments receivable, due at year-end, were collected along with interest of $24,000 (see Entry 2). Any amounts not collected by the due date should be reclassified by a debit to Assessments Receivable—Delinquent and a credit to Assessments Receivable—Current.

2.	Cash	72,000	
	Assessments Receivable—Current		48,000
	Revenues		24,000

Matured special assessment bond principal in the amount of $48,000 and matured bond interest of $24,000 payable were recorded and paid on schedule.

3a.	Expenditures—Bond Principal	48,000	
	Expenditures—Bond Interest	24,000	
	Bonds Payable		48,000
	Interest Payable		24,000
3b.	Bonds Payable	48,000	
	Interest Payable	24,000	
	Cash		72,000

The second installment of assessments receivable was reclassified from the Deferred category to the Current category. A corresponding amount of Deferred Revenues was reclassified as Revenues.

4a.	Assessments Receivable—Current	48,000	
	Assessments Receivable—Deferred		48,000
4b.	Deferred Revenues	48,000	
	Revenues		48,000

This pattern of journal entries will be repeated during each of the remaining nine years until all special assessment bonds are retired.

Use of Debt Service Funds to Record Capital Lease Payments

In Chapter 5, under the heading "Assets Acquired under Capital Lease Agreements," an example is given of the computation of the amount to be recorded in a governmental fund, usually a capital projects fund, at the inception of a capital lease. The example illustrates the entry required in the General Fixed Assets Account Group when an asset is acquired by a capital lease agreement. The example presented in Chapter 5 specified that the first payment of $10,000 was due on

January 1, 1999, the inception of the lease. Governmental units commonly use a Debt Service Fund to record capital lease payments because the annual payments are merely installment payments of general long-term debt. The first payment, since it is on the first day of the lease, is entirely a payment on the principal of the lease obligation. Accordingly, the payment would be recorded as:

Expenditures—Principal of Capital Lease Obligation	10,000	
Cash		10,000

The Expenditures detail record would show that the entire amount of the first payment was a payment on the principal. The payment due on January 1, 2000, and the payment due each year thereafter, however, must be considered a partial payment on the lease obligation and a payment of interest on the unpaid balance of the lease obligation. GASB standards are consistent with the FASB's *SFAS No. 13*; both specify that a constant periodic rate of interest must be used. In the example started in Chapter 5, the present value of the obligation is computed using the rate of 10 percent per year. It is reasonable to use the same interest rate to determine what part of the annual $10,000 payment is payment of interest, and what part is payment of principal. The following table shows the distribution of the annual lease rental payments:

Payment Date	Amount of Payment	Interest on Unpaid Balance at 10 Percent	Payment on Principal	Unpaid Lease Obligation
				$67,590
1/1/99	$10,000	$ –0–	$10,000	57,590
1/1/00	10,000	5,759	4,241	53,349
1/1/01	10,000	5,335	4,665	48,684
1/1/02	10,000	4,868	5,132	43,552
1/1/03	10,000	4,355	5,645	37,907
1/1/04	10,000	3,791	6,209	31,698
1/1/05	10,000	3,170	6,830	24,868
1/1/06	10,000	2,487	7,513	17,355
1/1/07	10,000	1,736	8,264	9,091
1/1/08	10,000	909	9,091	–0–

As shown by the table above, although the total expenditure recorded each year, January 1, 1999, through January 1, 2008, is $10,000, the detail records for each year should show how much of the expenditure was for interest on the lease obligation and how much was payment on the obligation itself. As noted earlier in this chapter, the unpaid balance of the capital lease obligation is carried in the General Long-Term Debt Account Group.

Accounting for Debt Refunding

If debt service fund assets accumulated for debt repayment are not sufficient to repay creditors when the debt matures, or if the interest rate on the debt is appreciably higher than the governmental unit would have to pay on a new bond issue, or if the covenants of the existing bonds are excessively burdensome, the governmental unit may issue refunding bonds.

The proceeds of refunding bonds issued at the maturity of the debt to be refunded are accounted for as Other Financing Sources of the debt service fund that is to repay the existing debt. The appropriation for debt repayment is accounted for as illustrated in the Town of Brighton Deferred Serial Bond Debt Service Fund example (see Entries 1, 2a, and 2b).

If a governmental unit has accumulated no assets at all for debt repayment, it is probable that no debt service fund exists. In such a case, a debt service fund should be created to account for the proceeds of the refunding bond issue and the repayment of the old debt. When the debt is completely repaid, the debt service fund relating to the liquidated issue should be closed, and a debt service fund for the refunding issue should be created and accounted for as described in this chapter. If the refunding bond issue is not sold but is merely given to the holders of the matured issue in an even exchange, the transaction would not require entries in a debt service fund but could be disclosed adequately in statements and schedules prepared for the General Long-Term Debt Account Group (discussed earlier in this chapter) and in the Notes to the Financial Statements.

Advance Refunding of Debt

Advance refundings of tax-exempt debt are common during periods when interest rates are falling sharply. Complex accounting and reporting issues have surfaced relating to legal questions such as, "Are both issues still the debt of the issuer?" "If the proceeds of the new issue are to be held for the eventual retirement of the old issue, how can the proceeds be invested to avoid conflict with the Internal Revenue Service over the taxability of interest on the debt issue?" (Compliance with the arbitrage rules under Section 148 of the Internal Revenue Code, and related regulations, is necessary for the interest to be exempt from federal income tax and, possibly, from state and local taxes.) Full consideration of the complexities of accounting for advance refundings resulting in defeasance of debt is presented in the GASB Codification Section D20. Defeasance of debt can be either "legal" or "in substance." **Legal defeasance** occurs when debt is legally satisfied based on certain provisions in the debt instrument even though the debt is not actually paid. **In-substance defeasance** occurs when debt is considered defeased for accounting and financial reporting purposes even though legal defeasance has not occurred. GASB *Codification* Section D20.103 sets forth in detail the circumstances for in-substance defeasance. Briefly, the debtor must irrevocably place cash or other assets in trust with an escrow agent to be used solely for satisfying scheduled payments of both interest and principal of the defeased debt. The amount placed in escrow must be sufficiently large so that there is only a remote possibility that the debtor will be required to make future payments on the defeased debt. The trust is restricted to owning only monetary assets that are essentially risk-free as to the amount, timing, and collection of interest and principal.

To illustrate accounting for advance refundings resulting in defeasance of debt reported in the GLTDAG, assume the proceeds from the sale of the refunding issue amount to $2,000,000, and assume debt to be defeased amounted to $2,500,000. The proceeds are recorded in the fund receiving the proceeds (normally, a *debt service fund*) by an entry such as:

Cash	2,000,000	
Other Financing Source—Proceeds of Refunding Bonds		2,000,000

Payments to the escrow agent from resources provided by the new debt should be recorded in the debt service fund as an Other Financing Use; payments to the escrow agent from other resources are recorded as debt service expenditures. Therefore, assuming $500,000 has previously been accumulated in the debt service fund for payment of the $2,500,000 bond issue, the entry to record the payment to the escrow agent would be:

Other Financing Use—Payment to Refunded Bond Escrow Agent	2,000,000	
Expenditures—Payment to Refunded Bond Escrow Agent	500,000	
Cash		2,500,000

Disclosures about Advance Refundings

The *disclosure* guidance on debt refunding in GASB *Codification* Section D20 is applicable to state and local governments, public benefit corporations and authorities, public employee retirement systems, and governmental utilities, hospitals, colleges and universities, and to all funds of those entities.

Detailed disclosure guidance is set forth in Section D20.111–.114. Briefly, all entities subject to GASB jurisdiction are required to provide in the notes to the financial statements in the year of the refunding a general description of any advance refundings resulting in defeasance of debt. At a minimum the disclosures must include (1) the difference between the cash flows required to service the old debt and the cash flows required to service the new debt and complete the refundings, and (2) the economic gain or loss resulting from the transaction. Economic gain or loss is the difference between the *present value* of the old debt service requirements and the *present value* of the new debt service requirements, discounted at the effective interest rate and adjusted for additional cash paid. Section D20.901–.915 provides examples of effective interest rate and economic gain calculations and of note disclosures.

Key Terms

Selected References

American Institute of Certified Public Accountants. Audit and Accounting Guide. *Audits of State and Local Governmental Units*. Revised. New York, 1996.

Governmental Accounting Standards Board. *Codification of Governmental Accounting and Financial Reporting Standards as of June 30, 1997*. Norwalk, CT, 1997.

Questions

6–1. Describe the interrelationship between a debt service fund and the General Long-Term Debt Account Group. What is the relationship between a capital projects fund that receives the proceeds of tax-supported bonds and the General Long-Term Debt Account Group?

6–2. Under current GASB standards, long-term debt that is due the day after the date of the statement may properly be shown in the Statement of General Long-Term Debt. What is the rationale for this situation?

6–3. *a.* When general obligation bonds are issued at a premium that is recorded in a debt service fund and is to be used for eventual retirement of that bond issue, what is the effect on the amount of liability to be shown in the Statement of Long-Term Debt?

    b. If a general obligation bond issue were sold at a premium that is required to be set aside for payment of bond interest, what is the effect upon the accounts in the General Long-Term Debt Account Group?

6–4. Explain the nature and purpose of the debit balance accounts used in the GLTDAG. Are these accounts informative to financial statement users?

6–5. If a bond ordinance provides for regular and recurring payments of interest and principal payments on a general obligation bond issue of a certain government to be made from earnings of an enterprise fund, and these payments *are* being made by the enterprise fund, how should the bond liability be disclosed in the comprehensive annual financial report of the government?

6–6. Why should a governmental annual report include a Schedule of Changes in Long-Term Debt?

6–7. The calculation of debt margin should take into account the amount of bonds authorized but not issued. This reduces borrowing power at a given date. What is the most logical reason for including authorized but unissued bonds?

6–8. "Debt service funds are established to account for long-term debt issued by state or local governments and for assets held to pay interest and matured debt principal." Is this statement true or false? Explain.

6–9. What revenue sources and other financing sources are commonly utilized for service of types of debt discussed in this chapter?

6–10. What basis of accounting is used for expenditures of a debt service fund? What exception is usually followed in recognizing expenditures for matured bond principal and interest?

6–11. "If a certain city has six tax-supported bond issues and three special assessment bond issues outstanding, it would be preferable to operate nine separate debt service funds or, at a minimum, one debt service fund for tax-supported bonds and one for special assessment bonds." Do you agree? Explain.

6–12. It is conceivable that a debt service fund for an issue of regular serial bonds might have no assets or liabilities and, necessarily, no fund balance at the ends of some fiscal years. If this is true why should the fund be created at all? Explain your answer.

6–13. What asset and liability accounts would you expect to find in the statements for a deferred serial bond debt service fund? Why would you expect deferred serial bonds to create a more complex accounting situation than regular serial bonds?

6–14. "Premiums and discounts on bond investments of the Debt Service Fund should not be amortized since the Debt Service fund is not a profit-seeking entity." Do you agree or disagree? Explain your answer.

6–15. During periods of low interest rates, governmental units often refund outstanding bonds in advance of their maturity. Explain the different ways of treating advance refundings that will permit, under GASB standards, removal of the liability for the refunded bonds from the General Long-Term Debt Account Group.

Cases

6–1. Northeast City is a medium-sized city with a population of 200,000. Because of the closing of the City's major employer, ACME Manufacturing Corporation, nearly 10 percent of the City's population has moved out of the City during the last two years to seek employment elsewhere. Northeast City's debt burden is quite heavy, with total debt amounting to 95 percent of the statutory debt limit. Moreover, the City's taxpayers are being taxed for the relatively heavy debt service of Northeast Township, Northeast Public Schools, and several other taxing authorities.

Northeast City's Debt Service Fund Combining Balance Sheet and Combining Statement of Revenues, Expenditures, and Changes in Fund Balances are shown on the following pages. Study these statements and answer the following questions.

Required:

    a. Assume you are considering the purchase of $1 million of Northeast City's general obligation bonds from an existing bondholder. Do the City's combined debt service fund financial statements provide all the information you need to make your decision? If not, what additional information would you like to have in order to better assess the City's financial condition?

    b. What is your assessment of the quality of the City's administration of debt service?

    c. To date, the major bond rating services have not downgraded the City's bond ratings, but both agencies are actively reviewing the appropriateness of the investment grade rating currently assigned to the City's general obligation debt. What is your assessment of the probability that the City may have its rating downgraded? What is your assessment of the probability that the City may default on its general obligation debt? How does your assessment of the probability of a rating downgrade or default affect your decision regarding purchase of the City's bonds?

NORTHEAST CITY
Combining Balance Sheet—All Debt Service Funds
June 30, 2000

	General Obligation Bonds	Urban Renewal Tax Increment Notes	Totals June 30, 2000	Totals June 30, 1999
Assets				
Cash and pooled cash investments	$ 12,000	$ 50,580	$ 62,580	$ 995,640
Taxes receivable	164,976	426,995	591,971	499,735
Total Assets	$176,976	$477,575	$654,551	$1,495,375
Liabilities and Fund Balances				
Liabilities:				
Warrants payable	$ —	$494,493	$494,493	$ 872,846
Matured bonds payable	5,000	—	5,000	50,000
Matured interest payable	167,171	—	167,171	167,034
Total Liabilities	172,171	494,493	666,664	1,089,880
Fund Balance:				
Unreserved:				
Designated for debt service	4,805	(16,918)	(12,113)	405,495
Total Fund Balance	4,805	(16,918)	(12,113)	405,495
Total Liabilities and Fund Balance	$176,976	$477,575	$654,551	$1,495,375

NORTHEAST CITY
Combining Statement of Revenues, Expenditures, and Changes in Fund Balances—
Budget and Actual—All Debt Service Funds
For the Fiscal Year Ended June 30, 2000

	General Obligation Bonds			Urban Renewal Tax Increment Notes			Totals Memorandum Only		
	Budget	Actual	Variance— Favorable (Unfavorable)	Budget	Actual	Variance— Favorable (Unfavorable)	Budget	Actual	Variance— Favorable (Unfavorable)
Revenues:									
Taxes	$6,216,292	$6,054,601	$(161,691)	$677,121	$573,170	$(103,951)	$6,893,413	$6,627,771	$(265,642)
Expenditures:									
Principal retirement	4,439,000	4,379,000	60,000	249,901	249,901	—	4,688,901	4,628,901	60,000
Interest and fiscal charges	2,025,292	1,989,258	36,034	427,220	427,220	—	2,452,512	2,416,478	36,034
Total Expenditures	6,464,292	6,368,258	96,034	677,121	677,121	—	7,141,413	7,045,379	96,034
Excess of Revenues over (under) Expenditures	(248,000)	(313,657)	(65,657)	—	(103,951)	(103,951)	(248,000)	(417,608)	(169,608)
Fund Balance—July 1, 1999	357,170	318,462	(38,708)	—	87,033	87,033	357,170	405,495	48,325
Fund Balance—June 30, 2000	$ 109,170	$ 4,805	$(104,365)	$ —	$(16,918)	$ (16,918)	$ 109,170	$ (12,113)	$(121,283)

Exercises and Problems

6–1. Utilizing the CAFR obtained for Exercise 1–1, follow the instructions below:

 a. *Disclosure of Long-Term Debt.* Does the report contain evidence that the governmental unit maintains a General Long-Term Debt Account Group? What evidence is there? If the unit does not have a General Long-Term Debt Account Group, does the report specify that no such debt is outstanding, or does the report include a list of outstanding tax-supported debt issues; capital lease obligations; claims, judgments, and compensated absence payments to be made in future years; and the unfunded pension obligations?

 If the report contains a Statement of General Long-Term Debt, do the amounts shown in this statement as being available for payment of long-term debt agree with amounts of Fund Balance held for repayment of debt principal reported in statements of funds that perform the debt service function? If not, can you reconcile the differences?

 How does the "amount available" for payment of each issue relate to the "amount to be provided" for payment of each issue? How does the total amount available relate to the total amount to be provided? Has the government refrained from reporting nonasset "other debits" on fund-type balance sheets? (They should be reported only in the General Long-Term Debt Account Group.) Are all nonasset "other debits" referred to as "amounts available" and/or "amounts to be provided," so that it is clear that they do not represent assets? Has the government refrained from reporting interest payable in future years in the Combined Balance Sheet and the Statement of General Long-Term Debt? (It may properly be reported on a schedule such as the one shown as Illustration 6–4.)

 Refer to the Enterprise Funds balance sheets as well as to the Statement of General Long-Term Debt (or list of general debt outstanding): Are any enterprise debt issues backed by the full faith and credit of the general governmental unit? If so, how are the primary liability and the contingent liability disclosed?

 b. *Changes in Long-Term Debt.* How are changes in long-term debt during the year disclosed? If there is a schedule of changes, does the information in that schedule agree with the statements presented for capital projects funds and debt service funds?

 Are interest payments and principal payments due in future years disclosed? If so, does the report relate these future payments with resources to be made available under existing debt service laws and covenants?

 c. *Debt Limitations.* Does the report contain information as to legal debt limit and legal debt margin? If so, is the information contained in the report explained in enough detail so that an intelligent reader (you) can understand how the limit is set, what debt is subject to it, and how much debt the governmental unit might legally issue in the year following the date of the report?

 d. *Overlapping Debt.* Does the report disclose direct debt and overlapping debt of the reporting entity? What disclosures are made of debt of the primary government in distinction to debt of component units? Is debt of component units reported as "direct" debt of the reporting entity, or as "overlapping debt"?

e. *Debt Service Function.* How is the debt service function for tax-supported debt and special assessment debt handled—by the General Fund, by a special revenue fund, or by one or more debt service funds? If there is more than one debt service fund, what kinds of bond issues or other debt instruments are serviced by each fund? Is debt service for bonds to be retired from enterprise revenues accounted for by enterprise funds?

Does the report state the basis of accounting used for debt service funds? If so, is the financial statement presentation consistent with the stated basis? If the basis of accounting is not stated, analyze the statements to determine which basis is used—full accrual, modified accrual, or cash basis. Is the basis used consistent with the standards discussed in Chapter 6?

f. *Investment Activity.* Compare the net assets of each debt service fund at balance sheet date with the amount of interest and the amount of debt principal the fund will be required to pay early in the following year (you may find debt service requirements in supplementary schedules following the individual fund and account group statements in the Financial Section of the CAFR). If debt service funds have accumulated assets in excess of amounts needed within a few days after the end of fiscal year, are the excess assets invested? Does the CAFR contain a schedule or list of investments of debt service funds? Does the report disclose increases or decreases in the fair value of investments realized during the year? Does the report disclose net earnings on investments during the year? What percentage of revenue of each debt service fund is derived from earnings on investments? What percentage of the revenue of each debt service fund is derived from taxes levied directly for the debt service fund? What percentage is derived from transfers from other funds? List any other sources of debt service revenue and other financing sources, and indicate the relative importance of each source.

Are estimated revenues for term bond debt service budgeted on an actuarial basis? If so, are revenues received as required by the actuarial computations?

g. Considering the debt maturity dates as well as the amount of debt, and apparent quality of debt service fund investments, does the debt service activity appear to be properly managed? Does the report disclose whether investments are managed by a corporate fiduciary, another outside investment manager, or by governmental employees? If outside investment managers are employed, is the basis of their fees disclosed? Are the fees accounted for as additions to the cost of investments, or as expenditures?

Is one or more paying agents, or fiscal agents, employed? If so, does the report disclose if the agents keep track of the ownership of registered bonds, write checks to bondholders for interest payments and matured bonds (or, in the case of coupon bonds, pay matured coupons and matured bonds presented through banking channels)? If agents are employed, does the Balance Sheet, or Notes to the Financial Statements, disclose the amount of cash in their possession? If so, does this amount appear reasonable in relation to interest payable and matured bonds payable? Do the statements, schedules, or narratives disclose for how long a period of time debt service funds carry a liability for unpresented checks for interest on registered bonds, for matured but unpresented interest coupons, and for matured but unpresented bonds?

If agents are employed, do they charge fees? If so, is the basis of the fee disclosed? What percentage of interest and principal payments is the fiscal agent's fee? Are fees accounted for as expenditures of debt service fund appropriations? If not, how are they accounted for, and by which fund?

h. *Capital Lease Rental Payments.* If general fixed assets are being acquired under capital lease agreements, are periodic lease rental payments accounted for as expenditures of a debt service fund (or by another governmental fund)? If so, does the report disclose that the provisions of *SFAS No. 13* are being followed (see the "Use of Debt Service Funds to Record Capital Lease Payments" section of this chapter) to determine the portion of each capital lease payment considered as interest and the portion considered as payment on the principal.

 6–2. Write the numbers 1 through 10 on a sheet of paper. Beside each number write the letter corresponding with the best answer to each of the following questions.

1. The following obligations were among those reported by Fern Village at December 31, 1999:

Vendor financing with a term of 10 months when incurred, in connection with a capital asset acquisition that is not part of a long-term financing plan	$ 150,000
Long-term bonds for financing of capital asset acquisition	3,000,000
Bond anticipation notes due in six months, issued as part of a long-term financing plan for capital purposes	400,000

What aggregate amount should Fern report as general long-term debt at December 31, 1999?

a. $3,000,000.
b. $3,150,000.
c. $3,400,000.
d. $3,550,000.

Items 2 through 4 are based on the following:

On March 2, 1999, Finch City issued 10-year general obligation bonds at face amount, with interest payable March 1 and September 1. The proceeds were to be used to finance the construction of a civic center over the period April 1, 1999, to March 31, 2000. During the fiscal year ended June 30, 1999, no resources had been provided to the Debt Service Fund for the payment of principal and interest.

2. On June 30, 1999, Finch's Debt Service Fund should include interest payable on the general obligations bonds for
a. 0 months.
b. 3 months.
c. 4 months.
d. 6 months.

3. Proceeds from the general obligation bonds should be recorded in the
a. General Fund.
b. Capital Projects Fund.
c. General Long-Term Debt Account Group.
d. Debt Service Fund.

4. The liability for the general obligation bonds should be recorded in the
a. General Fund.
b. Capital Projects Fund.
c. General Long-Term Debt Account Group.
d. Debt Service Fund.

5. The General Long-Term Debt Account Group should be used to account for:
   a. All tax-supported bonds and government-commitment special assessment bonds and notes not yet legally due; the noncurrent portion of claims, judgments, and compensated absences; and the unfunded liability for pensions.
   b. General obligation bonds and notes that will mature in more than one year from balance sheet date.
   c. All bonds and notes that will mature in more than one year from balance sheet date.
   d. General obligation bonds and notes not yet legally due.
6. Interest expenditures relating to tax-supported bonds payable should be recorded in a debt service fund:
   a. At the end of the fiscal period if the interest due date does *not* coincide with the end of the fiscal period.
   b. When bonds are issued.
   c. When the interest is legally payable.
   d. When the interest checks are written.
7. Debt service funds may be used to account for:
   a. Lease payments under capital lease agreements.
   b. Repayment of bond principal.
   c. The proceeds of refunding bond issues.
   d. All of the above.
8. Which of the following accounts is *least* likely to appear in a debt service fund?
   a. Estimated Revenues.
   b. Encumbrances.
   c. Appropriations.
   d. Matured Bonds Payable.
9. A debt service fund should be used to account for the payment of interest and principal on:
   a. Debt recorded in the General Long-Term Debt Account Group.
   b. Debt secured by the revenues of a governmentally owned enterprise.
   c. Debt recorded as a liability of the General Fund.
   d. All of the above.
10. Debt service fund financial statements that should be included in the Comprehensive Annual Financial Report of a state or local governmental unit are:
    a. Combining Balance Sheet; Combining Statement of Revenues, Expenditures, and Changes in Fund Balances; and Schedule of Investments.
    b. Combining Balance Sheet; Combining Statement of Revenues, Expenditures, and Changes in Fund Balances; and Combining Statement of Revenues, Expenditures, and Changes in Fund Balances—Budget and Actual for all Debt Service Funds for which annual budgets have been legally adopted.
    c. Combining Balance Sheet; Combining Statement of Cash Flows, and Combining Statement of Revenues and Expenses.
    d. The following statements for each individual Debt Service Fund: Balance Sheet; Statement of Revenues, Expenditures, and Changes in Fund Balances; and Statement of Revenues, Expenditures, and Changes in Fund Balances—Budget and Actual.

(Items 1–4, 6, AICPA, adapted)

6–3. Below are stated a number of unrelated transactions for Culver County, some of which affect a General Long-Term Debt Account Group; none of the transactions have been recorded in that group.

(1) The tax levy for the General Fund included $650,000 to be transferred to the debt service fund; $400,000 of this amount is designated for eventual retirement of outstanding serial bonds; the remainder is to be expended for interest on long-term debt. The transfer was made as planned, and the interest was paid.

(2) A $5,000,000 issue of serial bonds to finance a capital project was sold at 102, plus accrued interest in the amount of $50,000. The accrued interest was recorded as revenues of the debt service fund and the premium was recorded as an Other Financing Source. Accrued interest on bonds sold must be used for interest payments; premium is designated by state law for eventual payment of bond principal.

(3) A summary of debt service fund operations during the year showed receipt of interest on investments in the amount of $180,000; this amount is to be used for payment of interest on long-term debt.

(4) $2,800,000 par value of tax-supported serial bonds were issued in cash to permit partial refunding of a $3,500,000 par value issue of term bonds. The difference was settled with $700,000 that had been accumulated in prior years in a debt service fund.

Required

a. Prepare in general journal form the necessary entry in the General Long-Term Debt Group for each transaction. Explanations may be omitted.

b. Prepare in general journal form all necessary entries in each fund (including budgetary entries to the extent information is available in this problem), and/or in the GFAAG, for each transaction. For each entry you prepare name the fund or account group in which the entry should be made.

6–4. The Town of Preston has agreed to acquire a new fire truck under a capital lease agreement. At the inception of the lease a payment of $50,000 is to be made; nine annual lease payments, each in the amount of $50,000, are to be made at the end of each year after the inception of the lease. The total amount to be paid under this lease, therefore, is $500,000. The Town could borrow this amount for 9 years at the annual rate of 8 percent; therefore, the present value of the lease at inception, including the initial payment, is $362,345. Assume that the fair value of the fire truck at the inception of the lease is $370,000.

a. Show the entry that should be made in a *capital projects fund* at the inception lease.

b. Show the entry that should be made at the inception of the lease in the GFAAG.

c. Show the entry that should be made at the inception of the lease in the GLTDAG.

d. Show the entry that should be made in the *debt service fund* at the end of the first year after the inception of the lease.

6–5. In preparation for a proposed bond sale the city manager of the City of Collinsville requested you to prepare a statement of legal debt margin for the City as of December 31, 1999. You ascertain that the following bond issues are outstanding on that date:

Convention Center bonds	$3,600,000
Electric utility bonds	2,700,000
General obligation serial bonds	3,100,000
Tax increment bonds	2,500,000
Water utility bonds	1,900,000
Transit authority bonds	2,000,000

Other information obtained by you included the following items:
1. Assessed valuation of real and taxable personal property in the City totaled $240,000,000.
2. The rate of debt limitation applicable to the City of Collinsville was 8 percent of total real and taxable personal property valuation.
3. Electric utility, water utility, and transit authority bonds were all serviced by enterprise revenues, but each carries a full-faith-and-credit contingency provision and by law is subject to debt limitation.
4. The Convention Center bonds and tax increment bonds are subject to debt limitation.
5. The amount of assets segregated for debt retirement at December 31, 1999, is $1,800,000.

6–6. At April 30, 1999, all property inside the limits of the City of Marksville was situated within four additional governmental units, each authorized to incur long-term debt. At that date, net long-term debt of the five was as follows:

Florence County	$40,000,000
Florence Library District	2,000,000
City of Marksville	8,000,000
Marksville School District	17,000,000
Marksville Hospital District	13,600,000

Assessed values of property at the same date were: County and Library District, $900,000,000; City, $360,000,000; School District, $450,000,000; and Hospital District, $720,000,000.

Required

a. Prepare a statement of direct and overlapping debt for the City of Marksville. (Carry percentages to tenths.)
b. Compute the actual ratio (in percent carried to tenths) of total debt applicable to the City of Marksville property to assessed value of property within the city limits.
c. Compute the share of the City's direct and overlapping debt that pertained to the Reliable Manufacturing Company, having assessed valuation of $3,600,000 at April 30, 1999.

6–7. You have just accepted accounting responsibility for the City of Litton. As of the end of the preceding fiscal year, your predecessor had prepared the following trial balance:

CITY OF LITTON
General Long-Term Debt Account Group
Trial Balance, December 31, 1999

	Debits	Credits
Amount Available in Debt Service Fund for Payment of Term Bonds	$ 850,000	
Amount to Be Provided for Payment of Term Bonds	11,000,000	
Amount to Be Provided for Payment of Special Assessment Bonds ...	75,000	
6% Term Bonds Payable		$ 6,000,000
7% Term Bonds Payable		5,600,000
4% Term Bonds Payable		250,000
10% Special Assessment Bonds Payable		75,000
	$11,925,000	$11,925,000

Required

a. Prepare in general journal form an entry for each of the following events that occurred in 2000 to record the effects on the accounts of the General Long-Term Debt Account Group.

   (1) $300,000 par value of the 6 percent term bonds were purchased on February 1, 2000, and retired. The retirement was accomplished with a cash payment of $300,000 from the amount available in the Debt Service Fund.

   (2) A $3,000,000 issue of five-year notes payable was sold on March 1. The rate of interest was 7 percent, payable March 1 and September 1.

   (3) $2,000,000 par value of serial bonds were sold at par. The date of issue was May 1, 2000, with final retirement on May 1, 2020. The rate of interest was 6.5 percent per year, payable November 1 and May 1.

   (4) $3,000,000 par value of serial bonds were issued on October 1, 2000; $600,000 par value of the issue was scheduled to mature each year beginning October 1, 2001. Interest at 7 percent per year on the issue is payable semiannually on April 1 and October 1.

   (5) Records of the City Treasurer showed additions of $1,050,000 to debt service funds during 2000, of which $830,000 was for principal of term bonds and the remainder for interest.

b. Prepare a Statement of General Long-Term Debt as of December 31, 2000.

c. Prepare a Schedule of Changes in Long-Term Debt for the year ended December 31, 2000.

6–8. The Town of Shropshire Serial Bond Debt Service Fund Balance Sheet as of December 31, 1999, is presented below:

TOWN OF SHROPSHIRE
Serial Bond Debt Service Fund—Balance Sheet
As of December 31, 1999

Assets		Fund Equity	
Cash	$ 1,500	Fund Balance	$514,000
Investments	500,000		
Interest receivable on			
investments	12,500		
Total Assets	$514,000	Total Fund Equity	$514,000

Required

a. Prepare debt service fund entries in general journal form to reflect, as necessary, the following information:
   (1) The Revenues budget for serial bond debt service for fiscal year 2000 consists of estimated revenues of $330,000 to be raised from a debt service tax levy, and estimated revenues of $30,000 from earnings on investments. The Appropriations budget consists of bond interest to be paid on January 1, $100,000, and bond interest to be paid on July 1, $100,000.
   (2) Taxes receivable in the amount of $340,000 and estimated uncollectible taxes in the amount of $10,000 are recorded.
   (3) Half of the gross levy of taxes is collected in cash.
   (4) Checks are written and mailed for the interest payment due on January 1, 2000.
   (5) Cash in the amount of $70,000 is invested.
   (6) Interest receivable as of December 31, 1999, is collected and invested.
   (7) Taxes in the amount of $160,000 are collected in cash.
   (8) Checks are written and mailed for the interest payment due on July 1, 2000.
   (9) Interest on investments is received in cash in the amount of $15,000; cash in the amount of $75,000 is invested.
   (10) Accrued interest receivable on investments at year-end is computed as $13,000.
   (11) Budgetary and operating statement accounts are closed, and Taxes Receivable and the related Estimated Uncollectible accounts are designated as Delinquent.
b. Prepare a Balance Sheet for the Town of Shropshire Serial Bond Debt Service Fund as of December 31, 2000.
c. Prepare a Statement of Revenues, Expenditures, and Changes in Fund Balance for the fund for the year ended December 31, 2000.
d. Prepare a Statement of Revenues, Expenditures, and Changes in Fund Balance—Budget and Actual for the year ended December 31, 2000.

6–9. The City of Hampton had outstanding 5 percent term bonds, scheduled to mature July 1, 1999, in the amount of $5,000,000. Early in 1999, only $1,000,000 had been accumulated in a Term Bonds Debt Service Fund to apply on retirement of the bonds so a proposal was made to refund the remainder with 6 percent serial bonds, to mature at the rate of $1,000,000 every year, beginning July 1, 2000. Interest on the new issue is to be paid semiannually—on January 1 and July 1. Present term bondholders are to accept the 6 percent serial bonds in exchange for $4,000,000 of term bonds. Enough of the present bondholders accepted the proposal to make it feasible, and the budget for the fiscal year ending June 30, 2000, was set up to pay all the semiannual interest due on July 1 and $1,000,000 to bondholders. The $1,000,000 in the Term Bonds Debt Service Fund was in a noninterest-bearing Cash account.

a. The following transactions occurred in the Term Bonds Debt Service Fund during the year ended June 30, 2000. Record them in general journal form.

(1) The Revenues budget for the year provided for an operating transfer from the General Fund in the amount of the interest due July 1 on the entire $5,000,000 worth of term bonds. The Appropriations budget authorized the July interest payment and the payment of $1,000,000 for bonds to be redeemed. Record the budget.

(2) The General Fund transferred enough cash to the Term Bonds Debt Service Fund to pay interest due July 1 on the entire $5,000,000 worth of term bonds.

(3) The $1,000,000 worth of bonds to be redeemed and the interest due on July 1 were recorded as liabilities.

(4) Interest for the year and the bond liability were paid.

(5) All remaining open accounts were closed.

b. A Serial Bond Debt Service Fund was created to account for debt service activities related to the new issue. During the year ended June 30, 2000, the following transactions occurred. Record them in general journal form:

(1) The budget for the year was recorded. Estimated revenues, to be raised from taxes levied directly for this fund, were in the amount of one year's interest payments and the first serial bond repayment. Appropriations were budgeted only for the interest legally due during the fiscal year.

(2) Taxes receivable were levied to yield the amount of estimated revenues, assuming 3 percent of the taxes would be uncollectible. Round computation of the levy to the nearest $10.

(3) Ninety percent of the gross levy of taxes was collected. The remainder of the taxes receivable and the related Estimated Uncollectible Current Taxes Account were classified as delinquent.

(4) Cash in the amount of the January 1, 2000, interest payment was paid to bondholders; remaining cash was invested.

(5) Interest on investments collected in cash during the year totaled $10,500; interest on investments accrued at year-end was $3,100. Interest and penalties receivable on taxes totaled $3,040, of which $600 is estimated to be uncollectible.

(6) Budgetary and operating statement accounts for the year were closed.

c. Prepare a Serial Bond Debt Service Fund Balance Sheet as of June 30, 2000.

d. Prepare a Serial Bond Debt Service Fund Statement of Revenues, Expenditures, and Changes in Fund Balance for the year ended June 30, 2000.

e. Prepare a Serial Bond Debt Service Fund Statement of Revenues, Expenditures, and Changes in Fund Balance—Budget and Actual for the year ended June 30, 2000.

6–10. Comprehensive Capital Assets/Capital Liabilities Problem. Following are transaction data for related capital assets and capital liabilities of the City of Stevens. Utilizing worksheets formatted as shown at the end of the problem, prepare all necessary journal entries for these transactions in the City's capital projects fund, debt service fund, General Fixed Assets Account Group, and General Long-Term Debt Account Group. You may ignore related entries in the General Fund. Round all amounts to the nearest whole dollar.

   a. On July 1, 1999, the first day of its fiscal year, the City of Stevens issued at par $2,000,000 of 6 percent term bonds to construct a new City office building. The bonds mature in five years on July 1, 2004. Interest is payable semiannually on January 1 and July 1. A sinking fund is to be established with equal semiannual additions made on June 30 and December 31, with the first addition to be made on December 31, 1999. Cash for the sinking fund additions and the semiannual interest payments will be transferred from the General Fund shortly before the due dates. Assume a yield on sinking fund investments of 6 percent per annum, compounded semiannually. Investment earnings are added to the investment principal. Based on this information:

      (1) Prepare a schedule in good form showing the required additions to the sinking fund, the expected semiannual earnings, and the end-of-period balance in the sinking fund for each of the 10 semiannual periods. (Note: The future amount of an ordinary annuity of $1 for 10 periods at 3 percent per period is $11.4638793.)

      (2) Record the issuance of the bonds. (Utilize worksheets formatted as shown at the end of the problem.)

      (3) Create a Term Bond Debt Service Fund and record its budget for the fiscal year ended June 30, 2000. An appropriation should be provided only for the interest payment due on January 1, 2000. Also, record an accrual for all operating transfers to be received from the General Fund during the year.

   b. On July 17, 1999, the City entered into a construction contract with Jones Construction Company for $1,950,000 to construct the new City Office Building.

   c. On December 28, 1999, the General Fund transferred $234,461.01 to the Debt Service Fund. The addition to the sinking fund was immediately invested in 6 percent certificates of deposit.

   d. On December 28, 1999, the City issued checks to bondholders for the interest payment due on January 1, 2000.

   e. On June 1, 2000, Jones Construction billed the City in the amount of $1,000,000 for construction work to date on the City office building project.

   f. On June 15, 2000, the City paid the $1,000,000 partial billing from Jones Construction, except for 5 percent that was retained pending final inspection at the conclusion of the project.

   g. On June 27, 2000, the General Fund transferred $234,461.01 to the Debt Service Fund. The addition for the sinking fund was invested immediately in 6 percent certificates of deposit.

   h. Actual interest earned on sinking fund investments at year-end (June 30, 2000) was the same as the amount budgeted [see *a*(1) and *a*(3) above]. This interest adds to the sinking fund balance.

   i. All appropriate closing entries were made at June 30, 2000.

j. On July 1, 2000, the City paid the interest payment due that date. (Note: As discussed in this chapter, it is important that all principal and interest be paid by the due date. Usually a City does not directly pay the bondholders but instead uses a paying (fiscal) agent to pay the bondholders of record. Further, the use of electronic funds transfer permits same day transfer of cash to the fiscal agent.)

k. On July 1, 2000, the encumbrances were reestablished in the Capital Projects Fund.

l. The budgetary entry for fiscal year 2001 was recorded on July 1, 2000.

m. On September 10, 2000, Jones Construction completed the City office building project and billed the City for the remaining $950,000 due on the contract.

n. On September 14, 2000, the City paid the $950,000 partial billing from Jones, except for 5 percent which was retained pending final inspection at the conclusion of the project.

o. Following final inspection, the City incurred $125,000 for additional exterior and interior refinishing and site cleanup. Public Works (General Fund) employees were used for the refinishing and cleanup, which was completed on October 1, 2000. On October 5, 2000, the $125,000 due to the City's General Fund was paid.

p. The balance of cash in the Capital Projects Fund was transferred to the Term Bond Debt Service Fund. This amount was deemed available for eventual repayment of the principal of the 6 percent term bonds and was invested immediately in 6 percent CDs. Record the transfer and close all accounts in the capital projects fund.

q. Ignoring all other transactions in fiscal years 2001 and those for 2002 and 2003, prepare the journal entries in the Term Bond Debt Service fund for the transfer of cash from the General Fund on June 27, 2004. None of this amount is invested.

r. On June 30, 2004, all sinking fund investments in the Term Bond Debt Service Fund were redeemed for cash in the amount of $1,825,538.99. Of this, amount $99,712.04 represented interest earned during fiscal 2004. $46,540.98 of the interest earned was previously recorded on December 31, 2003.

s. Prepare the closing entry for the Term Bond Debt Service Fund at the end of fiscal year 2004.

t. Prepare the budgetary entry for the Term Bond Debt Service Fund at July 1, 2004, the beginning of fiscal year 2005.

u. Record the payment of bond principal and interest on July 1, 2004. Close all accounts of the Term Bond Debt Service Fund.

Capital Projects Fund		Capital Projects Fund	General Fixed Assets Account Group
Example:			
Cash	2,000,000		
OFS—Proceeds of			
Bonds	2,000,000		

Debt Service Fund	Debt Service Fund	Debt Service Fund

General Long-Term Debt Account Group	General Long-Term Debt Account Group	(Label this column as needed)

Continuous Problem

6–L. Part 1. Debt Service Fund. The City of Bingham utilizes a single debt service fund to account for the service of all issues of tax-supported and special assessment long-term debt. As of June 30, 1999, one issue of tax-supported serial bonds and one issue of special assessment term bonds were outstanding. The post-closing trial balance of the debt service fund as of June 30, 1999, is shown below.

The issue of tax-supported serial bonds outstanding on June 30, 1999, amounted to $6,000,000; bonds of this issue in the amount of $300,000 mature on July 1, 1999, and on each July 1 thereafter. This bond issue bears interest at the annual rate of 6 percent, payable on January 1 and July 1 of each year. The cash balance of the debt service fund on June 30, 1999, is to be used for the repayment of tax-supported bonds maturing on July 1, 1999, and for the interest on those bonds due on July 1, 1999.

The issue of special assessment term bonds outstanding on June 30, 1999, amounted to $600,000; it bears interest at the annual rate of 8 percent, payable on January 1 and July 1 of each year. The bonds will mature on July 1, 2009. As of June 30, 1999, investments in the amount of $260,000 are being held for payment of the special assessment bonds at maturity.

CITY OF BINGHAM
Debt Service Fund
Trial Balance
As of June 30, 1999

	Debits	Credits
Cash	$ 505,000	
Taxes Receivable—Delinquent	42,000	
Estimated Uncollectible Delinquent Taxes		$ 38,000
Special Assessments Receivable—Current	66,000	
Special Assessments Receivable—Deferred	594,000	
Investments for Special Assessment Bond Payment	260,000	
Deferred Revenues		594,000
Fund Balance		835,000
Totals	$1,467,000	$1,467,000

In order to add to investments held to pay the bonds at maturity and to pay interest due in fiscal year 2000, the City of Bingham Debt Service Fund must budget revenues from special assessments during fiscal year 2000 in the amount of $66,000.

Capital lease obligations outstanding have a present value on June 30, 1999, of $1,020,000. Collections of delinquent taxes receivable plus revenues to be raised in fiscal year 2000 will be used to make required lease payments during fiscal year 2000.

On July 1, 1999, the City of Bingham sold an issue of tax-supported serial bonds to finance the construction and equipping of an annex to City Hall. As described in Problem 5–L, the total amount of bonds sold on that date was $3,000,000. The issue bears interest at the annual rate of 8 percent, payable on January 1 and July 1 of each year; bonds in the amount of $150,000 will mature on July 1, 2000, and each July 1 thereafter.

In addition to the accounts listed in the trial balance, general ledger accounts provided for the debt service fund are:

> Investments—Temporary
> Taxes Receivable—Current
> Estimated Uncollectible Current Taxes
> Interest and Penalties Receivable
> Estimated Uncollectible Interest and Penalties
> Estimated Revenues
> Estimated Other Financing Sources
> Revenues
> Appropriations
> Expenditures—2000
> Equity Transfer In

Subsidiary ledger accounts for the debt service fund are:

Revenues—Subsidiary Ledger Accounts
> Property Taxes
> Interest and Penalties on Taxes
> Special Assessments
> Interest on Investments

Other Financing Sources—Subsidiary Ledger Accounts
> Proceeds of Bonds—Premium on Bonds Sold

Appropriations and Expenditures—Subsidiary Ledger Accounts
> Interest on Bonds Payable
> Principal of Matured Bonds
> Interest on Capital Lease Obligations
> Principal of Capital Lease Obligations

Required

    a. Prepare general journal entries to record the following transactions in the general ledger accounts and in subsidiary ledger accounts.

        (1) From the data given about the two bond issues outstanding on June 30, 1999, and the bond issue sold on July 1, 1999, record the adoption of the legal budget for the fiscal year ended June 30, 2000. (The budget provided estimated revenues or estimated other financing sources from property taxes, $1,182,000; from special assessments, $66,000; from premium on bonds sold, $30,000; and from earnings on investments, $28,000. Appropriations were provided for the payment of bonds maturing on July 1, 1999, for bond interest payments due on July 1, 1999, for bond interest payments due on January 1, 2000; $108,000, for interest payments on capital lease obligations, and $72,000 for payments on the principal of capital lease obligations.)

        (2) Taxes were levied by the debt service fund in the amount of $1,218,000. Of this amount, $36,000 was expected to be uncollectible.

(3) Cash in the amount of the premium on the bonds sold on July 1, 1999 (see Problem 5–L, requirement *a*, Transaction 1) was received and deposited by the debt service fund. The premium is not to be amortized; credit Other Financing Sources—Proceeds of Bonds—Premiums on Bonds Sold for the entire $30,000.

(4) Temporary investments in the amount of $30,000 were purchased.

(5) Checks were written and mailed to pay holders of bonds maturing on July 1, 1999, and to pay all bond interest due that day.

(6) Delinquent taxes receivable were collected in the amount of $4,000. Taxes Receivable—Current were collected in the amount of $620,000. Special Assessments in the amount of $66,000 were collected.

(7) Investments to be held for repayment of special assessment bonds at maturity were purchased in the amount of $18,000. Temporary investments in the amount of $610,000 were purchased.

(8) Information was received that interest in the amount of $9,300 had been added to investments held for repayment of special assessment bonds. Interest on temporary investments was received in cash in the amount of $8,000.

(9) Temporary investments amounting to $425,000 were sold at par.

(10) Checks were written and mailed to holders of all three issues of bonds for the interest payments due January 1, 2000. Payments on capital lease obligations totaled $180,000—$108,000 interest and $72,000 on the principal.

(11) Current taxes receivable were collected in the amount of $550,000. The balance of taxes receivable, and the related estimated uncollectible account, were classified as delinquent.

(12) Information was received that interest in the amount of $8,800 had been added to investments held for repayment of special assessment bonds. Interest on temporary investments was received in cash in the amount of $4,600.

(13) Cash to close the City Hall Annex Construction Fund was received (see Problem 5–L, Part 1, requirement *d*).

(14) Special assessments receivable in the amount of $66,000 were transferred from the deferred category to the current category; an equivalent amount was transferred from Deferred Revenues to Revenues.

(15) Interest and penalties on delinquent taxes as of year-end were computed as $9,200, of which $4,200 was expected to be uncollectible.

(16) All temporary investments were converted into cash.

(17) Budgetary and operating statement accounts for the year were closed.

b. Prepare a Balance Sheet for the Debt Service Fund as of June 30, 2000.

c. Prepare a Statement of Revenues, Expenditures, and Changes in Fund Balance for the Debt Service Fund for the year ended June 30, 2000.

d. Prepare a Statement of Revenues, Expenditures, and Changes in Fund Balance—Budget and Actual for the year ended June 30, 2000.

Part 2. General Long-Term Debt Account Group. The June 30, 1999, trial balance of the City of Bingham General Long-Term Debt Account Group follows.

CITY OF BINGHAM
General Long-Term Debt Account Group
Trial Balance
As of June 30, 1999

	Debits	Credits
Amount Available in DSF—6% Tax-Supported Serial Bonds	$ 300,000	
Amount to Be Provided—6% Tax-Supported Serial Bonds	5,700,000	
Amount Available in DSF—8% Special Assessment Term Bonds	260,000	
Amount to Be Provided—8% Special Assessment Term Bonds	340,000	
Amount to Be Provided—Capital Lease Obligations	1,020,000	
Tax-Supported Serial Bonds Payable—6%		$6,000,000
Special Assessment Term Bonds Payable—8%		600,000
Capital Lease Obligations Payable		1,020,000
Totals	$7,620,000	$7,620,000

In addition to the accounts listed in the trial balance, general ledger accounts provided for the GLTDAG are (subsidiary ledger accounts are not required for this problem):

Amount Available in DSF—8% Tax-Supported Serial Bonds
Amount to Be Provided—8% Tax-Supported Serial Bonds
Tax-Supported Serial Bonds Payable—8%

Required

a. Prepare general journal entries to record in the General Long-Term Debt Account Group the sale of 8 percent tax-supported serial bonds on July 1, 1999, in the amount of $3,000,000 as described in Problems 5–L and in 6–L, Part 1.

b. Review your solutions to Problems 2–L through 6–L, Part 1 and prepare general journal entries to record in the GLTDAG all information that should affect the accounts of the General Long-Term Debt Account Group. (Recall that assets held by the Debt Service Fund to be used to pay interest due on July 1, 2000, are *not* reported as "Amount Available in Debt Service Funds for Retirement of Bonds.")

c. Prepare a Statement of General Long-Term Debt as of June 30, 2000.

CHAPTER 7

Accounting for the Business-Type Activities of State and Local Governments

Learning Objectives

After reading this chapter, you should be able to:

- Distinguish between the purposes of internal service funds and enterprise funds.
- Describe the characteristics of proprietary funds.
- Explain the financial reporting requirements, including the similarities and differences between the cash flow statement requirements of FASB and GASB standards.
- Describe the characteristics, accounting procedures, and termination of internal service funds.
- Prepare journal entries and financial statements for an internal service fund.
- Describe the characteristics and specialized accounting procedures for enterprise funds.
- Prepare journal entries and financial statements for an Enterprise Fund.

Proprietary Funds

All of the funds discussed in previous chapters (general, special revenue, capital projects, and debt service funds) owe their existence to legal constraints placed on the raising of revenue and/or the use of resources for the provision of services to the public or segments thereof, and for the acquisition of facilities to aid in the provision of services. As governmental units became more complex, it became apparent that efficiency should be improved if services used by several departments or funds, or even several governmental units, were combined in a single administrative unit. Purchasing is a common example, as is a motor pool. A logical name for a fiscal and accounting entity created to account for resources used for providing centralized services is *internal service fund*. Traditionally, the reason for the creation of funds in this category was to improve the management of resources. In recent years, large numbers of governmental units have experienced a shortfall of revenues with an increase in the demand for governmental services. Consequently, many governmental units have turned to user charges as a means of financing operations formerly financed by tax revenues and intergovernmental revenues. In order to determine whether user charges are commensurate with operating costs, and to improve the ability of administrators and governing bodies to determine that costs are reasonable in relation to benefits, it is desirable for the activities to be operated and accounted for on a business basis. Thus many activities formerly operated on a purely noncommercial basis and accounted for by governmental funds are now accounted for by proprietary funds: *enterprise funds* and *internal service funds*. Activities that produce goods or services to be sold to the general public are accounted for by enterprise funds. Activities that produce goods or services to be provided to departments or agencies of a governmental unit, or to other governmental units, on a cost-reimbursement basis are accounted for by internal service funds. (Internal service funds are also called *intragovernmental service funds, working capital funds, revolving funds*, and other similar names.)

The phrase *cost-reimbursement basis* is to be interpreted broadly. User charges need not cover the full cost of providing the goods or services; transfers from other funds or units to subsidize in part the operations of an internal service fund do not negate the use of this fund type.

Proprietary funds are accounted for in a manner similar to investor-owned business enterprises. Accordingly, such funds recognize revenues and *expenses* (*not expenditures*) on the accrual basis. They account for all fixed assets used in their operations and for long-term debt to be serviced from revenues generated from their operations, as well as for all current assets and current liabilities. Distinction should be made in the equity accounts of proprietary funds between equity contributed to the fund and retained earnings resulting from operations of the fund. Also, as is true of businesses, proprietary funds differ from governmental fund types discussed in preceding chapters in that proprietary funds are not required by GASB standards to record their budgets in their accounting systems. (Although a few states do require all funds of all local governments within the state to operate under legally adopted budgets. In such cases, GASB standards allow the integration of budgetary accounts in the manner described in Chapters 3 and 4 for general and special revenue funds.)

Financial Reporting Requirements

Because proprietary funds account for the business-type activities of state and local governments, it should not be surprising that they prepare essentially the same financial statements that business entities do—that is, a Balance Sheet, an operating statement, and a Statement of Cash Flows. The operating statement, though it reports revenues and expenses, is called a *Statement of Revenues, Expenses, and Changes in Retained Earnings* rather than an Income Statement. Although both proprietary funds and business entities provide a cash flows statement, the statement formats and contents prescribed by GASB standards differ substantially from those prescribed by FASB standards, as explained later in this chapter. Illustrative financial statements for the Town of Brighton Supplies Fund (an internal service fund) are displayed in Illustrations 7–2, 7–3, and 7–4, later in this chapter. The corresponding financial statements for the Town of Brighton Water Utility Fund (an enterprise fund) are provided in Illustrations 7–8, 7–9, and 7–10.

Internal Service Funds

Although the reason for the establishment of an internal service fund is to improve financial management of scarce resources, it should be stressed that a fund is a fiscal entity as well as an accounting entity; consequently, establishment of a fund is ordinarily subject to legislative approval. The ordinance, or other legislative action, that authorizes the establishment of an internal service fund should also specify the source, or sources, of financial resources to be used for fund operations. The original allocation of resources to the fund may be derived from a transfer of assets of another fund, such as the General Fund or an Enterprise Fund, intended as a *contribution* not to be repaid, or a transfer in the nature of a long-term *advance* to be repaid by the internal service fund over a period of years. Alternatively, or additionally, the resources initially allocated to an internal service fund may be acquired from the proceeds of a tax-supported bond issue or transfer from other governmental units that anticipate utilizing the services to be rendered by the internal service fund. Since internal service funds are established to improve the management of resources, it is generally considered that they should be operated, and accounted for, on a business basis. Application of this general truth to a specific case can lead to conflict between managers who wish the freedom to operate the fund in accord with their professional judgment, and legislators who wish to exercise considerable control over the decisions of the internal service fund managers.

For example, assume that administrators request the establishment of a fund for the purchasing, warehousing, and issuing of supplies used by a number of funds and departments. At the time of the request, since no internal service fund exists, each fund or department must include in its budget its requested appropriation for supplies, its requested appropriation for salaries and wages of personnel engaged in purchasing and handling the supplies, and its requested appropriation for any operating expense or facility costs associated with the supply function. Accordingly, legislators tend to feel that through their control over budgets they are controlling the investment in supplies and the use of supplies by each fund and department. Legislators may feel that if they approved the establishment of an internal service fund that had authority to generate operating revenues sufficient to perpetuate the fund without annual appropriations, the supply function would no longer be subjected to annual legislative budget review, and the legislature would "lose control" after the initial allocation of resources to the fund. Administrators are more likely to feel that if an internal service fund did not have authority to generate operating revenues sufficient to perpetuate the fund, and to spend those revenues at the discretion of fund management rather than at the discretion of persons possibly more concerned with reelection than with financial management, there would be little gained by establishment of the internal service fund.

The two opposing views should be somewhat balanced by the fact that, as shown in Illustration 7–1, the customers of an internal service fund are, by definition, other funds and departments of the governmental entity, or of other governmental entities; therefore, each using fund and department must include in its Appropriations budget request justification for the amount to be spent (i.e., paid to the internal service fund) for supplies, so the legislative branch continues to exercise budgetary review over the amount each fund and department budgets for supplies. As shown in Illustration 7–1, departments and programs that require legislative appropriations to expend resources for goods and services should account

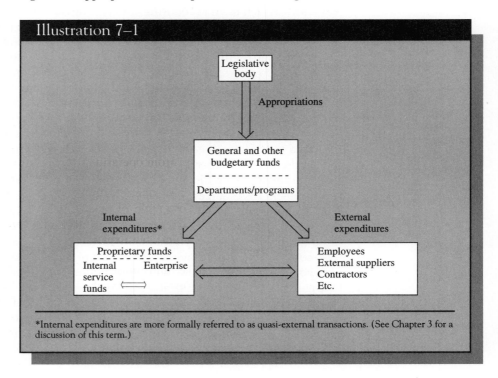

Illustration 7–1

*Internal expenditures are more formally referred to as quasi-external transactions. (See Chapter 3 for a discussion of this term.)

for purchases of goods or services from internal suppliers (i.e., internal service funds or enterprise funds) in essentially the same manner as goods and services purchased from external suppliers. If the legislative branch were to set pricing policies for the service fund, and policies governing the use of current earnings, and retention of earnings, and require the submission of periodic financial statements to evidence that its policies were followed, the legislature would be able to maintain considerable control over the function performed by the service fund, yet leave the fund managers freedom to operate at their discretion within the policies set by the legislative branch.

One of the more difficult problems to resolve to the satisfaction of persons with opposing views is the establishment of a pricing policy. "Cost" is obviously an incomplete answer: Historical cost of the supplies themselves, whether defined as FIFO, LIFO, average, or specific identification, will not provide sufficient revenue to replace supplies issued if replacement prices have risen since the last purchase, or to increase the inventory quantities if the scale of governmental operations is growing. Payroll and other cash operating expenses of the internal service fund must be met; and if the internal service fund has received a loan from another fund or another governmental unit, prices must be set at a level that will generate cash needed for debt retirement. If the internal service fund is to be operated on a true business basis, it must also be able to finance from its operations replacement, modernization, and expansion of plant and equipment used in fund operations. Prices charged by the internal service fund, however, should be less than the using funds and departments would have to pay outside vendors for equivalent products and services, if the existence and continued operation of the internal service fund is to be justified.

Because of the considerations mentioned in preceding paragraphs, many different approaches to internal service fund operations may be found in practice. Since accounting systems should give appropriate recognition to operating policies, as well as to legal requirements, practices vary from those of profit-seeking businesses at one extreme, to those discussed in this text in the chapters relating to general and special revenue funds at the other extreme. In the illustrations given in following sections of this chapter, it is assumed the financial objective of an internal service fund is to recover from operating revenues the full cost of operations, with enough net income to allow for replacement of inventories in periods of rising prices, and enough increase in inventory quantities to meet the needs of using funds and departments whose scale of operations is increasing. Similarly, it is assumed net income should be sufficient to allow for replacement of fixed assets used by the internal service fund, but expansion of the facilities must be financed through contributions from other funds authorized in their Appropriations budgets. Managers of internal service funds must prepare operating plans—budgets—as a management tool. In the illustrations it is assumed budgets of internal service funds are submitted to the legislative body, or bodies, and to the public for information but not for legal action, and therefore the budget is not formally recorded in internal service fund accounts. Similarly, managers of businesses must be kept informed of the status of outstanding purchase orders and contracts, but encumbrances need not be recorded in the accounts in order to accomplish this.

Accounting for an internal service fund concerned with the functions of purchasing, warehousing, and issuing supplies is illustrated in the following section of this chapter.

Illustrative Case—Supplies Fund

Assume that the administrators of the Town of Brighton obtain approval from the Town Council to centralize the purchasing, storing, and issuing functions as of January 1, 2000, and to administer and account for these functions in a Supplies Fund. The town's General Fund is to transfer to the new fund its December 31, 1999, inventory of supplies ($61,500) and $30,000 in cash to be used for working capital; these transfers are intended as contributions to the Supplies Fund and are *not* to be repaid. Transfers of this nature are initially accounted for by the recipient fund as *equity transfers in*, as shown in Entry 1. The Equity Transfers In account is closed at the end of the fiscal period to an appropriately named Fund Equity account—Contribution from General Fund, in this case—and reported in the Changes in Fund Equity section of the operating statement. General Fund entries for the transfer out of cash and inventory are illustrated in Chapter 10.

1.	Cash	30,000	
	Inventory of Supplies	61,500	
	Equity Transfers In		91,500

In order to provide cash to be used for acquisition of a building and equipment needed to handle the supply function efficiently, the town's Water Utility Fund is to advance $130,000 to the Supplies Fund. The advance is to be repaid by the Supplies Fund in 20 equal annual installments. Entry 2 illustrates the entry to be made by the Supplies Fund for the receipt of the advance; Water Utility Fund entries for this transaction are illustrated later in this chapter.

2.	Cash	130,000	
	Advance from Water Utility Fund		130,000

Assume that a satisfactory warehouse building is purchased for $95,000; $25,000 of the purchase price is considered a cost of the land. Necessary warehouse machinery and equipment is purchased for $25,000. Delivery equipment is purchased for $10,000. If the purchases are made for cash, the acquisition of the assets would be recorded in the books of the Supplies Fund as:

3.	Land	25,000	
	Building	70,000	
	Machinery and Equipment—Warehouse	25,000	
	Equipment—Delivery	10,000	
	Cash		130,000

Additional supplies would need to be ordered to maintain inventories at a level commensurate with expected usage. Encumbrances need not be recorded for purchase orders issued, and so information about the dollar value of purchase orders is omitted from this illustration. During 2000, it is assumed supplies are received and related invoices are approved for payment in the amount of $192,600; the entry needed to record the asset and the liability is:

4.	Inventory of Supplies	192,600	
	Vouchers Payable		192,600

The General Fund of the Town of Brighton (see Chapter 4) accounted for supplies on the physical inventory basis. The Supplies Fund, however, should account for its inventories on the perpetual inventory basis since the information is needed for proper performance of its primary function. Accordingly, when supplies are issued, the inventory account must be credited for the cost of the supplies issued. Since the using fund will be charged an amount in excess of the inventory carrying value, the receivable and revenue accounts must reflect the selling price. The markup above cost should be determined on the basis of budgeted expenses and other items to be financed from net income, in relation to expected requisitions by using funds. If the budget for the Town of Brighton's Supplies Fund indicates a markup of 35 percent on cost is needed, issues to General Fund departments of supplies costing $185,000 would be recorded by the following entries:

5a	Cost of Supplies Issued	185,000	
	Inventory of Supplies		185,000
5b.	Due from General Fund	249,750	
	Billings to Departments		249,750

If collections from the General Fund during 2000 totaled $231,000, the entry should be:

6.	Cash	231,000	
	Due from General Fund		231,000

Assuming that payrolls and fringe benefits during the year were all paid in cash and were distributed to the functional expense accounts in the amounts shown below, Entry 7 is appropriate.

7.	Administrative Expenses	11,000	
	Purchasing Expenses	19,000	
	Warehousing Expenses	12,000	
	Delivery Expenses	13,000	
	Cash		55,000

If payments on vouchers during the year totaled $164,000, the entry is:

8.	Vouchers Payable	164,000	
	Cash		164,000

The advance from the Water Utility Fund is to be repaid in 20 equal annual installments; repayment of one installment at the end of 2000 is recorded as:

9.	Advance from Water Utility Fund	6,500	
	Cash		6,500

It is assumed the building used as a warehouse was estimated at the time of purchase to have a remaining useful life of 20 years; the warehouse machinery and equipment was estimated to have a useful life of 10 years, and the delivery equipment to have a useful life of 5 years. If the administrative and clerical office space occupies 10 percent of the area of the warehouse, 10 percent of the depreciation of the warehouse, $350, may be considered administrative expense; similarly, if the purchasing office occupies 10 percent of the space in the warehouse building, 10 percent of the building depreciation, $350, may be considered purchasing expense. The remainder of the building is devoted to warehousing; therefore, 80 percent of the total building depreciation, $2,800, is to be charged to warehousing expense. The latter account is also charged $2,500 for machinery and equipment depreciation expense. Delivery expense is charged $2,000 for depreciation of equipment during the year.

10.	Administrative Expenses	350
	Purchasing Expenses	350
	Warehousing Expenses	5,300
	Delivery Expenses	2,000
	Allowance for Depreciation—Building	3,500
	Allowance for Depreciation—Machinery and Equipment—Warehouse	2,500
	Allowance for Depreciation—Equipment-Delivery	2,000

Organizations that keep perpetual inventory records must adjust the records periodically to reflect shortages, overages, or out-of-condition stock disclosed by physical inventories. Adjustments to the Inventory account are also considered adjustments to the warehousing expenses of the period. In this illustrative case, it is assumed no adjustments were found necessary at year-end.

Assuming all revenues and expenses applicable to 2000 have been properly recorded by the entries illustrated above, the operating statement accounts should be closed as of December 31, 2000:

11.	Billings to Departments	249,750	
	Cost of Supplies Issued		185,000
	Administrative Expenses		11,350
	Purchasing Expenses		19,350
	Warehousing Expenses		17,300
	Delivery Expenses		15,000
	Excess of Net Billings to Departments over Costs		1,750

Excess of Net Billings to Departments over Costs (or Excess of Costs over Net Billings to Departments, if operations resulted in a loss) is the account title generally considered more descriptive of the fund's results than Income Summary or Current Earnings—the titles commonly found in profit-seeking businesses. Whatever title is used for the account summarizing the results of operations for the period, the account should be closed at year-end. The title of the account that records earnings retained in an internal service fund is the same as the title commonly used for profit-seeking businesses: Retained Earnings.

12.	Excess of Net Billings to Departments over Costs	1,750	
	Retained Earnings		1,750

The Equity Transfer In account represents contributed equity and should be closed to an appropriately named account:

13.	Equity Transfer In	91,500	
	Contribution from General Fund		91,500

Illustrative Statements

Balance Sheets.   As one would expect of funds accounted for in a manner similar to profit-seeking businesses, balance sheets of proprietary funds are *classified*; that is, current assets are segregated from fixed assets and other assets, and current liabilities are segregated from long-term debt. The Balance Sheet of the Supplies Fund of the Town of Brighton as of December 31, 2000, is shown as Illustration 7–2.

Illustration 7–2

TOWN OF BRIGHTON
Supplies Fund
Balance Sheet as of December 31, 2000
Assets

Current Assets:			
Cash			$ 35,500
Due from General Fund			18,750
Inventory of supplies, at average cost			69,100
Total Current Assets			123,350
Fixed Assets:			
Land		$25,000	
Building	$70,000		
Less: Allowance for depreciation	3,500	66,500	
Machinery and equipment—warehouse	25,000		
Less: Allowance for depreciation	2,500	22,500	
Equipment—delivery	10,000		
Less: Allowance for depreciation	2,000	8,000	
Total Fixed Assets			122,000
Total Assets			$245,350

Liabilities and Fund Equity

Current Liabilities:	
Vouchers payable	$ 28,600
Total Current Liabilities	28,600
Long-Term Debt:	
Advance from water utility	123,500
Total Liabilities	152,100
Fund Equity:	
Contribution from General Fund	91,500
Retained earnings	1,750
Total Fund Equity	93,250
Total Liabilities and Fund Equity	$245,350

Operating Statements.   The results of operations of an internal service fund should be reported periodically in a Statement of Revenues, Expenses, and Changes in Retained Earnings, which is the equivalent of an income statement for a profit-seeking entity. Illustration 7–3 presents a Statement of Revenues, Expenses, and Changes in Retained Earnings for the year ended December 31, 2000, for the Town of Brighton Supplies Fund. Inasmuch as there was a change in the Contributed Equity during the year, this change is disclosed in the same statement.

Statement of Cash Flows.   GASB financial reporting standards require the preparation of a Statement of Cash Flows as a part of a full set of financial statements for all proprietary funds and nonexpendable trust funds and governmental entities that use proprietary fund accounting (hospitals, utilities, and public benefit corporations and authorities). Categories of cash flows provided by FASB *Statement No. 95* were deemed insufficient to meet the needs of users of governmental financial reports. Consequently, GASB standards provide four categories of cash flows: Operating, Noncapital Financing, Capital and Related Financing, and Investing. In each category, the term *cash* includes **cash equivalents** (defined as short-term, highly liquid investments).

Cash flows from *operating activities* include receipts from customers, receipts from quasi-external operating transactions with other funds, payments to suppliers of goods or services, payments to employees for services, payments for quasi-

Illustration 7–3

TOWN OF BRIGHTON
Supplies Fund
**Statement of Revenues, Expenses, and Changes
in Retained Earnings and Contributed Equity**
For the Year Ended December 31, 2000

Billings to departments		$249,750
Less: Cost of supplies issued		185,000
Gross Margin		64,750
Less: Purchasing expenses	$19,350	
Administrative expenses	11,350	
Warehousing expenses	17,300	
Delivery expenses	15,000	
Total Operating Expenses		63,000
Excess of Net Billings to Departments over Costs for the Year		1,750
Retained Earnings, January 1, 2000		–0–
Retained Earnings, December 31, 2000		1,750
Equity Transfer In from General Fund		91,500
Contributed Equity, January 1, 2000		–0–
Contributed Equity, December 31, 2000		$ 91,500

external operating transactions with other funds (including payments in lieu of taxes), and other operating cash receipts and payments. The transactions of the Town of Brighton's Supplies Fund recorded in Entries 6, 7, and 8 are classified as operating activities and are reported in the first section of the Statement of Cash Flows (see Illustration 7–4). As required by GASB standards the Statement of Cash Flows is accompanied by a reconciliation of operating income (called Excess of Net Billings to Departments over Costs for the Year in Illustration 7–3) with the net cash flow from operating activities.

Illustration 7–4

TOWN OF BRIGHTON
Supplies Fund
Statement of Cash Flows
For the Year Ended December 31, 2000

Cash flows from operating activities:			
Cash received from customers		$231,000	
Cash paid to employees for services		(55,000)	
Cash paid to suppliers		(164,000)	
Net cash provided by operating activities			$ 12,000
Cash flows from noncapital financing activities:			
Equity transfer from General Fund		30,000	
Net cash provided by noncapital financing activities			30,000
Cash flows from capital and related financing activities:			
Advance from Water Utility Fund		130,000	
Partial repayment of advance from Water Utility Fund		(6,500)	
Acquisition of capital assets		(130,000)	
Net cash used for capital and related activities			(6,500)
Net Increase in Cash and Cash Equivalents			35,500
Cash and Cash Equivalents, 1/1/2000			–0–
Cash and Cash Equivalents, 12/31/2000			$ 35,500

Reconciliation of Excess of Net Billings to Departments over Costs to Net Cash Provided by Operating Activities

Excess of Net Billings to Departments over Costs		$ 1,750
Adjustments:		
Depreciation expense		8,000
Increase in receivables from other funds		(18,750)
Increase in inventory	$ 69,100	
Less contributed inventory	61,500	(7,600)
Increase in vouchers payable		28,600
Net Cash Provided by Operating Activities		$ 12,000

Cash flows from *noncapital financing* activities include proceeds from debt not clearly attributable to acquisition, construction, or improvement of capital assets; receipts from grants, subsidies, or taxes other than those specifically restricted for capital purposes or those for specific operating activities; payment of interest on, and repayment of principal of, noncapital financing debt; grants or subsidies paid to other governments, funds, or organizations, except payments for specific operating activities of the grantor government. The contribution from the General Fund to the Supplies Fund of the Town of Brighton (see Entry 1) is reported in the cash flows from noncapital financing activities section of the Statement of Cash Flows (Illustration 7–4).

Cash flows from *capital and related financing* activities include proceeds of debt and receipts from special assessments and taxes specifically attributable to acquisition, construction or improvement of capital assets; receipts from capital grants; receipts from the sale of capital assets; proceeds of insurance on capital assets that are stolen or destroyed; payments to acquire, construct, or improve capital assets; payment of interest on, and repayment or refunding of, capital and related financing debt. The transactions of the Town of Brighton's Supplies Fund recorded in Entries 2, 3, and 9 are classified as capital and related financing activities and are reported in that section of the Statement of Cash Flows (Illustration 7–4).

Cash flows from *investing* activities include receipts from collection of loans; interest and dividends received on loans, debt instruments of other entities, equity securities, and cash management and investment pools; receipts from the sales of debt or equity instruments; withdrawals from investment pools not used as demand accounts; disbursements for loans; payments to acquire debt or equity instruments; and deposits into investment pools not used as demand accounts. None of the transactions of the Town of Brighton's Supplies Fund during 2000 are in the nature of investing activities.

*Combining
Statements*

If a reporting entity operates more than one internal service fund, it is necessary to present a Combining Balance Sheet; a Combining Statement of Revenues, Expenses, and Changes in Retained Earnings; and a Combining Statement of Cash Flows for all internal service funds in order to disclose the detail supporting the Internal Service Funds column in the combined statements.

*Acquisition of Assets
by Contributions
or Grants*

The fixed assets used by the Supplies Fund of the Town of Brighton were purchased for that fund from cash advanced by the Water Utility Fund. In other situations, the fixed assets themselves may have been contributed to the Supplies Fund (or any other internal service fund) by another fund of the same governmental unit or by another governmental unit, may have been purchased from one or more capital grants, or may have been purchased from revenues generated by operations of the internal service fund. Fixed assets purchased for an internal service fund from operating revenues would be accounted for and depreciated in the same manner as illustrated for the Town of Brighton Supplies Fund. If fixed assets are contributed to an internal service fund (or enterprise fund) or are acquired from the proceeds of a capital grant, some accounting questions arise, as discussed below.

Fixed assets acquired as a gift, or contribution, should be capitalized at fair value at date of receipt; the offsetting credit is to an appropriately named Fund Equity account, such as Contributions from City or Contributions from Private Citizens. Similarly, grants, entitlements, or shared revenues that are restricted for capital acquisitions or construction by an internal service fund or an enterprise fund are reported as additions to a Fund Equity account, such as Contributions from State. (Note that the preceding sentence refers to capital grants to proprietary funds. GASB standards provide that operating grants to proprietary funds and grants that may be used for either operations or capital outlays of the proprietary fund should be recognized as nonoperating revenues on the accrual basis, not as contributed equity. In comparison, *all* grants to governmental funds should be recognized as *revenue*, on the accrual basis used by governmental fund types.)[1] Fixed assets acquired from proceeds of capital grants, entitlements, or shared revenues are recorded at cost.

Depreciation of Contributed Assets or Assets Acquired from Capital Grants

The accounting treatment of depreciation of fixed assets contributed to an internal service fund, or assets constructed or acquired by an internal service fund from capital grants, need not differ from the accounting treatment of depreciation illustrated in the Town of Brighton Supplies Fund case. However, GASB standards allow the option of closing the depreciation expense on contributed assets or assets acquired from capital grants to the appropriate contributed equity account, rather than to Retained Earnings. If that option is elected, the Statement of Revenues, Expenses, and Changes in Retained Earnings would be presented as shown in Illustration 7–5, and the equity section of the Internal Service Fund Balance Sheet would be presented as shown in Illustration 7–6. Both illustrations are taken from the GASB *Codification*.

Assets Acquired under Lease Agreements

The acquisition of general fixed assets under lease agreements is discussed in Chapter 5. Assets for use by proprietary funds may also be acquired under lease agreements. The criteria set forth in FASB *SFAS No. 13* (these criteria are itemized in Chapter 5) are used to determine whether the lease is an operating lease or a capital lease.

Assets acquired under an operating lease belong to the lessor and not to the internal service fund; accordingly, the annual lease payment is recorded as a rental

---

[1]As discussed in Chapter 1 and noted in several other chapters, the GASB has issued an exposure draft (ED) of a proposed new dual perspective reporting model. One proposal in the ED would require governmental units to report capital contributions to proprietary funds as nonoperating revenues rather than direct additions to contributed equity. The ED also proposes to report proprietary fund Fund Equity in one section rather than in the two separate sections, Contributed Capital and Retained Earnings, discussed in this chapter. When a final standard is issued for the reporting model, the publisher will provide an update bulletin to all adopters of the 11th edition of the text. For additional information see, Governmental Accounting Standards Board, Exposure Draft, *Proposed Statement of the Governmental Accounting Standards Board*, "Basic Financial Statements—and Management's Discussion and Analysis—For State and Local Governments" (Norwalk, CT, January 1997).

Illustration 7–5

Statement of Revenues, Expenses, and Changes in Retained Earnings
For the Fiscal Year Ended (Date)

Operating Revenues:	
(Detailed)	$XX
Operating Expenses:	
(Detailed—includes depreciation on *all* depreciable fixed assets)	(XX)
Operating Income (Loss)	XX
Nonoperating Revenues (Expenses):	
(Detailed—nonoperating revenues include grants, entitlements, and shared revenues received for operations and/or such resources that may be used for either operations or capital outlay at the discretion of the recipient)	XX
Income (Loss) before Operating Transfers	XX
Operating Transfers:	
(Detailed)	XX
Net Income (Loss)	XX
Add depreciation on fixed assets acquired by grants, entitlements, and shared revenues externally restricted for capital acquisitions and construction that reduces contributed capital [Optional]	XX
Increase (Decrease) in Retained Earnings	XX
Retained Earnings—Beginning of Period	XX
Retained Earnings—End of Period	$XX

Source: GASB, *Codification*, Sec. G60.118.

Illustration 7–6

Proprietary Fund Balance Sheet
Equity Section

Fund Equity:			
Contributed capital:			
Capital grants	$XX		
Less amortization [Optional]	XX	$XX	
Government's contribution		XX	$XX
Retained earnings			XX
Total Fund Equity			$XX

Source: GASB, *Codification*, Sec. G60.116.

expense of the internal service fund,[2] and there is no depreciation expense on the assets acquired under an operating lease agreement. Assets acquired under a capital lease agreement by an internal service fund, or an enterprise fund, should be capitalized by that fund (*not* by the General Fixed Assets Account Group, as is true of assets acquired under a capital lease for use by any of the governmental funds). The amount to be recorded by a proprietary fund as the *cost* of the asset acquired under a capital lease, and as the related liability, is the lesser of (*a*) the present value of the rental and other minimum lease payments or (*b*) the fair value of the leased property. The amount recorded as the cost of the asset is amortized in a manner consistent with the government's normal depreciation policy for owned assets of proprietary funds. The amortization period is restricted to the lease term, unless the lease (*a*) provides for transfer of title or (*b*) includes a bargain purchase option, in which case the economic life of the asset becomes the amortization period.

During the lease term, each minimum lease payment by an internal service fund is to be allocated between a reduction of the obligation under the lease and as interest expense in a manner that produces a constant periodic rate of interest on the remaining balance of the obligation. This allocation and other complexities that arise in certain events are described and illustrated in various paragraphs of *SFAS No. 13* and in many intermediate accounting texts. These complexities are beyond the scope of this text.

Internal Service Funds with Manufacturing Activities

The Supplies Fund of the Town of Brighton, for which journal entries and statements are illustrated in a preceding section of this chapter, is responsible for purchasing, storing, and issuing supplies used by other funds and departments of the town. Many states and local governmental units have funds similar to that of the Town of Brighton. It is also common to find printing shops, asphalt plants, or other service units that produce a physical product to be used by funds and departments, or that facilitate the operations of the other funds and units by performing maintenance or repair jobs, or even perform a temporary financing function.

If an internal service fund performs a continuous process manufacturing operation, its accounting system should provide process cost accounts. If a service fund performs a manufacturing, maintenance, or repair operation on a job-order basis, the fund's accounting system should provide appropriate job-order cost accounts. To the extent that operations, processes, or activities are capable of being standardized, cost standards for materials, direct labor, and overhead should be established; in such cases, the accounting system should provide for the routine measurement and reporting of significant variances from the standards. Cost determination for governmental and nonprofit entities is discussed in Chapter 14 of this text.

Internal Service Funds as Financing Devices

Governmental units may utilize internal service funds as devices to finance risk management, equipment purchases and operations (including centralized computer operations), and other functions that are facilitated by generating revenues from

---

[2]GASB, *Codification*, Sec. L20.109–.112 establishes measurement criteria and recognition criteria for revenues and expenditures/expenses relating to operating leases with scheduled rent increases. This situation is beyond the scope of this text.

user charges to cover costs and expenses computed on a full accrual basis. In the case of funds to finance equipment purchases and operations, including the operations of computers owned by the governmental unit, an internal service fund can include depreciation and, perhaps, expected increases in the cost of replacing assets, in the charge to the using funds—thus incorporating these costs in current appropriations of governmental funds, rather than budgeting the estimated cost of equipment expected to be replaced. If internal service funds are used to finance equipment purchases and operations, therefore, the appropriations and expenditures of governmental funds more nearly approximate costs that would be reported by entities using full accrual accounting than is true under the procedures discussed in Chapters 3 and 4.

GASB has issued accounting and financial reporting standards for risk financing and related insurance activities.[3] Government entities that use internal service funds to account for risk financing activities are required to recognize revenues and claims expenses and liabilities in essentially the same manner as public entity risk pools (cooperative groups of governmental entities joined together to finance risks of loss to property, workers' compensation, employee health care, and similar risks or exposures). Briefly, the internal service fund should recognize claims expense and liability when a claim is asserted, it is probable that an asset has been impaired or a liability has been incurred, and the amount of the loss is reasonably estimable; or if an estimable loss has been incurred and it is probable that a claim will be asserted. Reasonably possible (but not probable) loss contingencies, probable losses that are not reasonably measurable, and loss exposure in excess of the accrued liability should be disclosed in the Notes to the Financial Statements. The disclosure should explain the nature of the contingency and an estimate of the possible loss or range of the loss, or a statement that the amount is not estimable.

Internal service fund charges to other funds for risk financing activities should be sufficient to recover the total amount of claim expenses recognized for the period or, alternatively, may be based on an actuarial method so that internal service fund revenues and expenses over time are approximately equal. Charges to other funds may also include a reasonable provision for expected future catastrophe losses. Internal service fund charges to other funds are recognized as revenues by the internal service fund and as expenditures by governmental funds or expenses by proprietary and nonexpendable trust funds. Internal service fund charges in excess of the full cost amount determined as above should be reported as an other financing source by the internal service fund and an other financing use by the other funds. If the internal service fund fails to recover the full cost of claims over a reasonable period of time, the accumulated fund deficit should be charged to the other funds and reported by the other funds as an expenditure or expense, as appropriate.

Dissolution of an Internal Service Fund

When an internal service fund has completed the mission for which it was established, or when its activity is terminated for any other reason, dissolution must be accomplished. Liquidation may be accomplished in any one of three ways or in

---

[3]GASB, *Codification*, Sec. Po20.

combinations thereof. The three ways are: (1) transfer of the fund's assets to another fund that will continue the operation as a subsidiary activity, for example, a supply fund becoming a *department* of the General Fund; (2) distribution of the fund's assets in kind to another fund or to another governmental unit; (3) conversion of all its noncash assets to cash and distribution of the cash to another fund or other funds. Dissolution of an internal service fund, as for a private enterprise, would proceed by prior payments to outside creditors, followed by repayment of long-term advances not previously amortized, and, finally, liquidation of Residual Equity. The entire process of dissolution should be conducted according to pertinent law and the discretion of the appropriate legislative body. Fund Equity contributed by another fund or governmental unit logically would revert to the contributor fund or governmental unit, but law or other regulations may dictate otherwise. If fund equity has been built up out of charges in excess of costs, then liquidation will follow whatever regulations may govern the case; and if none exist, then the appropriate governing body must decide on the recipient or recipients.

Enterprise Funds

Enterprise funds and internal service funds are both classified by the GASB as proprietary funds. Internal service funds, discussed earlier in this chapter, are used to account for services provided by one department or agency of a governmental unit *to other departments* or agencies, *or to other governmental units* on a user charge basis. Enterprise funds are used by governmental units to account for services provided *to the general public* on a user charge basis. Enterprise funds may also be used to account for any operations "where the governing body has decided that periodic determination of revenues earned, expenses incurred, and/or net income is appropriate for capital maintenance, public policy, management control, accountability, or other purposes."[4] From this description, and from the fact that the word *enterprise* is often used as a synonym for business, it may be apparent that enterprise funds should use full accrual accounting and account for all assets used in the production of goods or services offered by the fund. Similarly, if long-term debt is to be serviced by the fund, it is accounted for by the fund. Distinction should be made in fund equity accounts between equity contributed to the fund and earnings resulting from operations of the fund.

The most common examples of governmental enterprises are public utilities, notably water and sewer utilities. Electric and gas utilities, transportation systems, airports, ports, hospitals, toll bridges, produce markets, parking lots, parking garages, liquor stores, and public housing projects are other examples frequently found. Services of the kinds mentioned are generally accounted for by enterprise funds because they are intended to be largely self-supporting. However, they are properly accounted for by a general or special revenue fund by those governments

---

[4]GASB, *Codification*, Sec. 1100.103b(1).

that support the activities largely from general or special revenue sources other than user charges and are not concerned with measuring the costs of the activities.

Almost every kind of enterprise operated by a government has its counterpart in the private sector. In order to take advantage of the work done by regulatory agencies and trade associations to develop useful accounting information systems for the investor-owned enterprises, *it is recommended that governmentally owned enterprises use the accounting structures developed for investor-owned enterprises of the same nature.*[5] Budgetary accounts should be used only if required by law. Debt service and construction activities of a governmental enterprise are accounted for within the enterprise fund, rather than by separate debt service and capital projects funds. Thus, the financial statements of enterprise funds are self-contained; and creditors, legislators, or the general public can evaluate the performance of a governmental enterprise on the same bases as they can the performance of investor-owned enterprises in the same industry.

By far the most numerous and important enterprise services rendered by local governments are public utilities. In this chapter, therefore, the example used is that of a water utility fund.

Illustrative Case—Water Utility Fund

The Balance Sheet as of December 31, 1998, for the Town of Brighton Water Utility Fund is shown in Illustration 7–7. While the Balance Sheet appears fairly conventional, terminology peculiar to utilities warrants discussion prior to proceeding to the illustrative transactions for the year ending December 31, 1999.

Current and Accrued Assets

Cash and Materials and Supplies shown in Illustration 7–7 in the Current and Accrued Assets section are not peculiar to utilities and need not be discussed here.

---

[5]GASB *Statement No. 20* provides interim guidance on business-type accounting and financial reporting for proprietary activities until GASB addresses these issues more fully as part of its reporting model project. Interim guidance is needed to clarify the authoritative status of FASB pronouncements in determining generally accepted accounting principles (GAAP) for proprietary activities given the GAAP hierarchy provided for in *Statement on Auditing Standards No. 69*, "The Meaning of 'Present Fairly in Conformity with Generally Accepted Accounting Principles' in the Independent Auditor's Report" (AICPA, 1992). GASB *Statement No. 20* gives governments an option between two accounting and financial reporting approaches for proprietary funds. The first approach requires consistent use of all GASB pronouncements and applicable pronouncements of FASB and its predecessors (Accounting Principles Board and Committee on Accounting Procedure) issued on or before November 30, 1989, unless those pronouncements conflict with or contradict GASB pronouncements. The second approach requires consistent use of all GASB pronouncements and all applicable pronouncements (both before and after November 30, 1989) of FASB and its predecessors, unless those pronouncements conflict with or contradict GASB pronouncements. Thus, under the first approach, unless GASB directs otherwise, governments are not required to change their accounting procedures if FASB issues a standard that supersedes or amends a standard issued on or before November 30, 1989. This date (November 30, 1989) is significant as the date the Financial Accounting Foundation resolved a conflict over jurisdiction of the FASB and GASB.

Illustration 7–7

TOWN OF BRIGHTON
Water Utility Fund
Balance Sheet
As of December 31, 1998

Assets

Current and Accrued Assets:			
Cash		$ 126,000	
Customer accounts receivable	$ 69,000		
Less: Accumulated provision for uncollectibles	2,900	66,100	
Accrued utilities revenues		14,800	
Materials and Supplies		28,700	
Total Current and Accrued Assets			$ 235,600
Restricted Assets:			
Cash		6,600	
Investments		556,000	562,600
Utility Plant:			
Utility plant in service		3,291,825	
Less: Accumulated depreciation		440,325	
Utility Plant—Net		2,851,500	
Construction work in progress		125,000	
Net Utility Plant			2,976,500
Total Assets			$3,774,700

Liabilities and Fund Equity

Current Liabilities:			
Accounts payable	$ 33,200		
Customers advances for construction	21,000		
Total Current Liabilities			$ 54,200
Liabilities Payable from Restricted Assets:			
Customer Deposits			23,700
Long-Term Debt:			
Revenue bonds payable (net of unamortized			
discount of $5,300)			1,744,700
Total Liabilities			1,822,600
Fund Equity:			
Contribution from Town		$1,000,000	
Contributions from customers		252,000	
Retained Earnings:			
Reserved for payment of revenue bonds	538,900		
Unreserved	161,200	700,100	
Total Fund Equity			1,952,100
Total Liabilities and Fund Equity			$3,774,700

The other two asset accounts in this section—Customer Accounts Receivable and Accrued Utilities Revenues—are related. The former represents billings to customers that are outstanding at year-end (and are reduced, as one would expect, by an Accumulated Provision for Uncollectibles). The latter results from the fact that utilities generally prepare billings to customers on the basis of meter readings, and it is not practical for utilities to read all meters simultaneously at year-end and bill all customers as of that time. Utilities that meter their service make extensive use of cycle billing, which, in substance, consists of billing part of their customers each day, instead of billing by calendar months. Under this plan, meter reading is a continuous day-by-day operation, with billings following shortly after the filing of the meter readers' reports. Individual meters are read on approximately the same day each month, or every other month, in order that each bill cover approximately the same number of days usage. Cycle billing eliminates the heavy peak load of accounting and clerical work that results from uniform billing on a calendar month basis. It does, however, result in a sizable amount of unbilled receivables on any given date, thus requiring accrual of unbilled receivables (Accrued Utilities Revenues, in regulatory terminology) as of financial statement date in order to state assets and sales properly.[6]

Restricted Assets

The section below Current and Accrued Assets in Illustration 7–7 is captioned Restricted Assets, the caption most commonly used when the use of assets is restricted by contractual agreements or legal requirements. Some governments that use regulatory terminology report restricted assets of utilities under the broader caption, Other Property and Investments. Other Property and Investments may include, in addition to restricted assets, the carrying value of property not being used for utility purposes or being held for future utility use.

Cash and Investments are the only two items reported under the Restricted Assets caption of the balance sheet shown in Illustration 7–7. Those items are restricted for return of customer deposits and for retirement of revenue bonds pursuant to the bond covenants. The amount of assets segregated, $562,600, is offset by liabilities currently payable from restricted assets (in the case of the Town of Brighton, Customer Deposits of $23,700) and reservations of Retained Earnings (in this case, Reserved for Repayment of Revenue Bonds, $538,900). This *funds within a fund* approach permits segregation of assets, related liabilities, and reserved fund equity within a single enterprise fund. Retained earnings should be reserved in the amount of the net assets of each restricted "fund" within the Enterprise Fund, as shown in Illustration 7–7. Other items commonly reported in Restricted Assets include assets set aside to fund depreciation for capital improvements or grants and contributions restricted for capital acquisition or improvement.

---

[6]Many governments use the same or similar chart of accounts for utilities as those of regulated profit-seeking enterprises in the same industry. The principal regulatory bodies are the National Association of Regulatory Utility Commissioners (NARUC), an association of state regulatory utility commissioners, and the Federal Energy Regulatory Commission (FERC), which has jurisdiction over utilities in interstate commerce.

Utility Plant

Utility Plant in Service is a control account, supported in whatever detail is required by regulatory agencies and by management needs. For example, water utilities commonly have six subcategories of plant assets: intangible plant, source of supply plant, pumping plant, water treatment plant, transmission and distribution plant, and general plant. Each of the six subcategories is supported by appropriate subsidiary accounts. For example, intangible plant consists of the costs of organization, franchises and consents, and any other intangible costs "necessary and valuable in the conduct of utility operations." Source of supply plant consists of land and land rights; structures and improvements; collecting and impounding reservoirs; lake, river, and other intakes; wells and springs; infiltration galleries and tunnels; supply mains; and other water source plant. Each of the accounts within each subcategory is supported by necessary subsidiary records for each individual asset detailing its description, location, cost, date of acquisition, estimated useful life, salvage value, depreciation charges, and any other information needed for management planning and control, regulatory agency reports, financial statements, or special reports to creditors.

Construction Work in Progress.   The other Utility Plant item shown on the Balance Sheet, Illustration 7–7, is Construction Work in Progress. This account represents the accumulated costs of work orders for projects that will result in items reportable as Utility Plant when completed and is, of course, supported by the work orders for projects in progress. Each work order, in turn, is supported by documents supporting payments to contractors and to suppliers, or supporting charges for materials, labor, and overhead allocable to the project.

The Uniform System of Accounts for water, sewer, gas, and electric utilities published by NARUC all contain a section on Utility Plant Instructions that, among other items, specifies the components of construction cost. Generally, the components are in agreement with those listed in any intermediate accounting text. One item long recognized in utility accounting but only recently specifically accepted by the FASB is the Allowance for Funds Used During Construction (AFUDC).[7]

AFUDC includes the net cost for the period of construction of borrowed funds used for construction purposes *and a reasonable rate on other funds so used.* Thus, interest paid, accrued, or imputed during the period of construction of a utility plant asset is included as a cost of the asset. Interest paid or accrued, known as the *debt component* of AFUDC, is deducted from Interest on Long-Term Debt in the Other Income and Deductions section of the utility's operating statement (see Illustration 7–9). This practice accomplishes two things: (1) it discloses to financial statement readers the amount of interest that was capitalized during the year, and (2) it reduces the reported interest expense, thus increasing reported net

---

[7]Financial Accounting Standards Board, *Statement of Financial Accounting Standards No. 71,* "Accounting for the Effects of Certain Types of Regulation" (Norwalk, CT, 1982), par. 15, as amended by *Statement of Financial Accounting Standards No. 90* (Norwalk, CT, 1986), par. 8, and *Statement of Financial Accounting Standards No. 92* (Norwalk, CT, 1987), pars. 8 and 9.

income for the period (presumably slowing down utilities' requests for rate increases). If construction is financed, in part, by use of resources generated by operations of the utility, regulatory authorities allow interest to be imputed on these "equity" funds and capitalized. Since imputed interest is not viewed by accountants as an expense, it is offset by reporting the *equity component* of AFUDC as nonoperating income.

Current Liabilities

Items commonly found in the Current Liabilities section of a Utility Balance Sheet are shown under that caption in Illustration 7–7. Accounts Payable needs no comment here. The other item, **Customers Advances for Construction**, results from the practice of utilities of requiring customers to advance to the utility a sizable portion of the estimated cost of construction projects to be undertaken by the utility at the request of the customer. If the advances are to be refunded, either wholly or in part, or applied against billings for service rendered after completion of the project, they are classified as shown in Illustration 7–7. When a customer is refunded the entire amount to which he or she is entitled according to the agreement or rule under which the advance was made, the balance, if any, is transferred to Contributions from Customers, a Fund Equity account. Other items commonly reported under Current Liabilities include accrued expenses, amounts due to other funds, and current portions of long-term liabilities. Some governments also report customer deposits under the Current Liabilities caption.[8]

Liabilities Payable from Restricted Assets

Liabilities payable from restricted assets should be displayed separately from current liabilities as shown in Illustration 7–7. In addition to customer deposits, the current portion of revenue bonds payable, if any, would be reported here since restricted assets have been set aside for that purpose. The Town of Brighton follows the common practice of most utilities and requires all new customers to deposit a sum of money with the utility as security for the payment of bills. In many, but not all, jurisdictions utilities are required to pay interest on customer deposits at a nominal rate. Regulatory authorities or local policy may require utilities to refund the deposits, and interest, after a specified period of time if the customer has paid all bills on time. The utility may be required, as was the Town of Brighton Water Fund, to segregate cash or investments in an amount equal to the liability for Customer Deposits. Customers Advances for Construction are contractually different from Customer Deposits and are less likely to be reported separately as restricted assets and liabilities, unless agreements with developers make it necessary to restrict assets for this purpose.

---

[8]Generally, customer deposits should be reported as Liabilities Payable from Restricted Assets, a special category of current liabilities, as explained in the following section. Although customer deposits may be held for an extended period, possibly for as long as customers receive metered service, the AICPA Audit and Accounting Guide, *Audits of State and Local Governmental Units* states (par. 13.13): "Customer deposits remain in current liabilities until applied against billings or refunded to customers." Reporting customer deposits in this manner seems overly conservative since only a small portion are likely to be refunded in any given year.

Long-Term Debt

Bonds are the customary form of long-term debt. Bonds issued by a utility are usually secured by the pledge of certain portions of the utility's revenue, the exact terms of the pledge varying with individual cases; bonds of this nature are called **revenue bonds**. Some utility bonds are secured not only by a pledge of a certain portion of the utility's revenues but also by an agreement on the part of the town's or city's general government to subsidize the utility in any year in which its normal revenue is inadequate for compliance with the terms of the bond indenture. Other utility bonds carry the pledge of the governmental unit's full faith and credit, although the intent is to service them from utility revenues rather than general taxes. The latter are, therefore, technically **general obligation bonds**. GASB standards provide that general obligation bonds intended to be serviced from utility revenues be reported as a liability of the enterprise fund. Similarly, special assessment debt may be assumed by an enterprise fund if the assets constructed by special assessment financing are used in enterprise fund operations. The General Long-Term Debt Account Group should disclose the contingent liability by note rather than in the body of the Statement of General Long-Term Debt. An example of such a note is presented in Chapter 6 of this text.

Governmentally owned utilities may have received advances from the government's General Fund or other funds. Also, enterprises may acquire assets under a capital lease arrangement. The portion of advances, required lease payments, or bond or other debt issues to be paid within one year from balance sheet date should be reported as a current liability; the remainder is properly reported in the Long-Term Debt section of the Utility Balance Sheet. Long-term bonds payable should be reported net of unamortized discount or premium, as shown in Illustration 7–7, or else unamortized discount or premium can be reported as an offset against bonds payable at par on the Balance Sheet.

Fund Equity

Contributed Equity.　The equity of an enterprise fund consists of **contributed equity** and **retained earnings**. Equity that results from the contribution of assets by a governmental unit requires no explanation here, although readers should recall that the proceeds of capital grants are to be recorded as contributed equity, as are the proceeds of debt that is to be repaid from tax revenue or special assessment revenue rather than from enterprise revenues.

In the case of utilities, equity may also be contributed by customers, as noted in the discussion of Customers Advances for Construction in the section on Current Liabilities. The treatment of Contributions from Customers as an item in Fund Equity is consistent with the uniform system of accounts published by the National Association of Regulatory Utility Commissioners. Utilities in interstate commerce, which are subject to regulation by the Federal Energy Regulatory Commission (FERC), are required to account for contributions from customers as credits to the *asset* accounts that were charged for the cost of such construction. From a regulatory viewpoint, the prescribed treatment reduces the carrying value of the assets to the cost borne by the utility and, therefore, presumably lowers the rate base. From an accounting viewpoint, the FERC requirement results in an understatement of both the costs of the assets and the amount of contributed equity.

Retained Earnings   Although it is generally true that governmental units own utilities in order to have the capacity to render services to residents, rather than as a device to earn revenues, it is obviously in the best interests of taxpayers that the utility be self-supporting. Operating revenues, therefore, must be set at a level expected to cover operating expenses, provide for debt service, and finance routine capital projects. For these reasons, it is customary for governmentally owned utilities to accumulate retained earnings just as investor-owned utilities do—although perhaps not to the same extent.

Illustrative Accounting for a Water Utility Fund

The discussion in preceding pages of the balance sheet accounts of a water utility includes by implication the essential characteristics of accounting necessary for both governmentally owned utilities and investor owned utilities. In this section, accounting for characteristic transactions of a utility fund is illustrated in general journal entry format for the year following the balance sheet presented in Illustration 7–7.

It is assumed the Town of Brighton is located in a state that permits enterprise funds to operate without formal legal approval of their budgets. Utility, or other enterprise, management must prepare operating budgets and capital expenditure budgets as management tools. For the illustrative case, it is assumed the budgets are submitted to the Town administrators, to the Town legislative body, and to the public, for information, not for legal action. Accordingly, the budget is not formally recorded in enterprise fund accounts. Similarly, utility management must be informed periodically of the status of outstanding construction contracts and purchase orders, but encumbrances need not be recorded in the accounts in order to accomplish this.

The nature of the Accrued Utilities Revenues account is explained above in the section on Current and Accrued Assets. In the year following the one for which the balance sheet is shown, it is not feasible when customers' bills are prepared to determine whether a portion of the bill has been accrued and, if so, how much. The simplest procedure, therefore, is to reverse the accrual entry as of the start of the new fiscal year. Assuming the entire December 31, 1998, Town of Brighton Water Utility Fund revenues accrual has been credited to Sales of Water, the following entry is appropriate as of January 1, 1999:

1. Sales of Water	14,800	
Accrued Utility Revenues		14,800

When utility customers are billed during the year, appropriate revenue accounts are credited. Assuming during 1999 the total bills to nongovernmental customers amounted to $696,000, bills to the Town of Brighton General Fund amounted to $30,000, and all revenue was from sales of water, the following entry summarizes the events:

2. Customer Accounts Receivable   696,000
   Due from General Fund   30,000
      Sales of Water   726,000

If collections from nongovernmental customers totaled $680,000 for water billings, Entry 3 is needed:

3. Cash   680,000
     Customer Accounts Receivable   680,000

Materials and supplies in the amount of $138,000 were purchased during the year by the Water Utility Fund. The liability is recorded as:

4. Materials and Supplies   138,000
     Accounts Payable   138,000

Materials and supplies chargeable to the accounts itemized in the entry below were issued during the year.

5. Source of Supply Expenses   18,000
   Pumping Expenses   21,000
   Water Treatment Expenses   24,000
   Transmission and Distribution Expenses   13,000
   Construction Work in Progress   66,000
     Materials and Supplies   142,000

Payrolls for the year were chargeable to the accounts shown in the entry below. Tax Collections Payable is the account provided in the NARUC and FERC systems to report "the amount of taxes collected by the utility through payroll deductions or otherwise pending transmittal of such taxes to the proper taxing authority." Taxes Accrued is the account provided in the NARUC and FERC systems to report the liability for taxes that are the expense of the utility, such as the employer's share of social security taxes. In the entry below, it is assumed that the employer's share of social security taxes is charged to the same accounts that the employees' gross earnings are; it is also assumed that checks have been issued for employees' net earnings.

6. Source of Supply Expenses   8,200
   Pumping Expenses   15,700
   Water Treatment Expenses   17,500
   Transmission and Distribution Expenses   76,250
   Customer Accounts Expenses   96,550
   Sales Expenses   17,250
   Administrative and General Expenses   83,150
   Construction Work in Progress   30,400
     Taxes Accrued   13,800
     Tax Collections Payable   51,750
     Cash   279,450

Bond interest in the amount of $105,000 was paid; the bonds were issued to finance the acquisition of utility plant assets. Amortization of debt discount and expense amounted to $530.

7. Interest on Long-Term Debt	105,000	
Amortization of Debt Discount and Expense	530	
Unamortized Debt Discount and Expense		530
Cash		105,000

Bond interest in the amount of $12,900 was properly capitalized as part of construction work in progress during the year. (The Town of Brighton does not impute interest on its own resources during construction.)

8. Construction Work in Progress	12,900	
Allowance for Funds Used During Construction		12,900

Construction projects on which costs totaled $220,000 were completed and the assets placed in service:

9. Utility Plant in Service	220,000	
Construction Work in Progress		220,000

Collection efforts were discontinued on bills totaling $3,410. The customers owing the bills had paid deposits to the water utility totaling $2,140; the deposits were applied to the bills, and the unpaid remainder was charged to Accumulated Provision for Uncollectible Accounts (Entry 10a). Restricted assets (cash) is reduced by $2,140, the amount of the decrease in Customer Deposits (Entry 10b).

10a. Customer Deposits	2,140	
Accumulated Provision for Uncollectible Accounts	1,270	
Customer Accounts Receivable		3,410
10b. Cash	2,140	
Cash—Customer Deposits		2,140

Customers deposits amounting to $1,320 were refunded by check to customers discontinuing service (see Entry 11a). Deposits totaling $2,525 were received from new customers (see Entry 11b).

11a. Customer Deposits	1,320	
Cash—Customer Deposits		1,320
11b. Cash—Customer Deposits	2,525	
Customer Deposits		2,525

Customers advances for construction in the amount of $14,000 were applied to their water bills; in accord with the agreement with the customers and NARUC recommendations, the remainder of the advances were transferred to Contributions from Customers.

12. Customers Advances for Construction	21,000	
Customer Accounts Receivable		14,000
Contributions from Customers		7,000

Payments of Accounts Payable for materials and supplies used in operations totaled $67,200, and payment of Accounts Payable for materials used in construction totaled $66,000. Payments of Taxes Accrued amounted to $13,500, and payments of Tax Collections Payable amounted to $50,000.

13. Accounts Payable	133,200	
Taxes Accrued	13,500	
Tax Collections Payable	50,000	
Cash		196,700

The Water Utility Fund agreed to pay $25,000 to the Town General Fund as a contribution in lieu of property taxes. The entry in the General Fund is illustrated in Chapter 4 (see Chapter 4, illustrative Entry 16b). The following entry records the event in the accounts of the Water Utility Fund:

14. Contribution in Lieu of Taxes	25,000	
Due to General Fund		25,000

During the year interest in the amount of $44,500 was received in Cash on restricted investments. The amount of $1,375 is allocable to investments of customer deposit assets and is unrestricted as to use; the remaining $43,125 adds to the amount restricted for revenue bond repayment.

15a. Cash	1,375	
Cash—Bond Repayment	43,125	
Interest and Dividend Income		44,500
15b. Unreserved Retained Earnings	43,125	
Retained Earnings Reserved for Bond Repayment		43,125

At year-end, entries to record depreciation expense, the provision for uncollectible accounts, and unbilled customers accounts receivable should be made as illustrated by Entry 16. In accord with regulatory terminology, Customer Accounts Expense, instead of Bad Debts Expense, is debited for the amount added to Accumulated Provision for Uncollectible Accounts. Amounts are assumed.

16. Depreciation Expense	102,750	
Customer Accounts Expenses	3,980	
Accrued Utility Revenues	15,920	
Accumulated Provision for Depreciation of Utility Plant ..		102,750
Accumulated Provision for Uncollectible Accounts		3,980
Sales of Water		15,920

In accord with the revenue bond indenture, $100,000 unrestricted cash was invested in U.S. Government Securities for eventual retirement of revenue bonds. Retained earnings is reserved in an amount equal to the increase in restricted assets. In addition, investments from restricted cash for bond repayment amounted to $40,000.

17a. Investments—Bond Repayment	140,000	
Cash		100,000
Cash—Bond Repayment		40,000
17b. Unreserved Retained Earnings	100,000	
Retained Earnings Reserved for Bond Repayment		100,000

Nominal accounts for the year were closed:

18. Sales of Water 727,120
    Allowance for Funds Used During Construction 12,900
    Interest and Dividend Revenue 44,500
        Source of Supply Expenses 26,200
        Pumping Expenses 36,700
        Water Treatment Expenses 41,500
        Transmission and Distribution Expenses 89,250
        Customer Account Expenses 100,530
        Sales Expenses 17,250
        Administrative and General Expenses 83,150
        Interest on Long-Term Debt 105,000
        Amortization of Debt Discount and Expense 530
        Contribution in Lieu of Taxes 25,000
        Depreciation Expense 102,750
        Unreserved Retained Earnings 156,660

Illustrative Statements

Balance Sheet.   The Balance Sheet for a water utility, and definitions of certain balance sheet categories and items peculiar to regulated utilities, are explained at length in the sections of this chapter preceding the illustrative entries. The Balance Sheet of the Town of Brighton Water Utility Fund as of December 31, 1999, is shown as Illustration 7–8. Note the amount due to the General Fund is offset against the amount due from that fund, and only the net amount of the receivable, $5,000, is shown as an asset.

Operating Statement.   The results of the operations of the Town of Brighton's Water Utility Fund for the year ended December 31, 1999, are shown in Illustration 7–9, the Statement of Revenues, Expenses, and Changes in Retained Earnings. The classifications used in the statement are consistent with NARUC and FERC recommendations.

Statement of Cash Flows.   GASB standards require that a Statement of Cash Flows be prepared for all proprietary funds as a part of a full set of annual financial statements. As discussed at length earlier in this chapter, GASB standards for preparation of a cash flow statement differ from FASB standards; the main difference being that GASB standards specify four major categories of cash flows rather than three. The Statement of Cash Flows for the Town of Brighton for the year ended December 31, 1999 (Illustration 7–10) utilizes only three of the four categories of cash flows since the Town had no cash flows from noncapital financing activities. *Cash flows from operating activities* (Illustration 7–10) were provided by receipts from customers (Entry 3) and the net increase in refundable customer deposits (Entries 11a and 11b). Note that the application of customer deposits to pay overdue bills (Entries 10a and 10b) has no effect on total cash and cash equivalents. Cash from operating activities was used to pay employees (Entries 6 and 13). As suggested in the GASB *Implementation Guide* on reporting cash flows,[9] all

---

[9]Governmental Accounting Standards Board, *Implementation Guide*, "Guide to Implementation of GASB Statement 9 on Reporting Cash Flows of Proprietary and Nonexpendable Trust Funds and Governmental Entities That Use Proprietary Fund Accounting," (Norwalk, CT, 1992), p. 23.

Illustration 7–8

TOWN OF BRIGHTON
Water Utility Fund
Balance Sheet
As of December 31, 1999

Assets

Current and Accrued Assets:			
Cash		$ 128,365	
Customer accounts receivable	$ 67,590		
Less: Accumulated provision for uncollectibles	5,610	61,980	
Accrued utilities revenues		15,920	
Due from General Fund		5,000	
Materials and supplies		24,700	
Total Current and Accrued Assets			$ 235,965
Restricted Assets:			
Cash		8,790	
Investments		696,000	704,790
Utility Plant:			
Utility plant in service		3,511,825	
Less: Accumulated depreciation		543,075	
Utility Plant—Net		2,968,750	
Construction work in progress		14,300	
Net Utility Plant			2,983,050
Total Assets			$3,923,805

Liabilities and Fund Equity

Current Liabilities:			
Accounts payable		$ 38,000	
Taxes accrued		300	
Tax collection payable		1,750	
Total Current Liabilities			$ 40,050
Liabilities Payable from Restricted Assets:			
Customer deposits			22,765
Long-Term Debt:			
Revenue bonds payable (net of unamortized discount of $4,770)			1,745,230
Total Liabilities			1,808,045
Fund Equity:			
Contribution from Town		1,000,000	
Contributions from customers		259,000	
Retained Earnings:			
Reserved for repayment of revenue bonds	$682,025		
Unreserved	174,735	856,760	
Total Fund Equity			2,115,760
Total Liabilities and Fund Equity			$3,923,805

Illustration 7–9

TOWN OF BRIGHTON
Water Utility Fund
Statement of Revenues, Expenses, and Changes in Retained Earnings
For the Year Ended December 31, 1999

Utility Operating Revenue:		
Sales of water		$727,120
Operating Expenses:		
Source of supply expenses	$ 26,200	
Pumping expenses	36,700	
Water treatment expenses	41,500	
Transmission and distribution expenses	89,250	
Customer account expenses	100,530	
Sales expenses	17,250	
Administrative and general expenses	83,150	
Depreciation expense	102,750	
Contribution in lieu of taxes	25,000	
Total Operating Expenses		522,330
Utility Operating Income		204,790
Other Income and Deductions:		
Interest and dividend revenue	(44,500)	
Interest on long-term debt	105,000	
Amortization of debt discount and expense	530	
Allowance for funds used during construction	(12,900)	
Total Other Income and Deductions		48,130
Net Income		156,660
Unreserved Retained Earnings, January 1, 1999		161,200
Total		317,860
Less: Reservations of Retained Earnings		143,125
Unreserved Retained Earnings, December 31, 1999		$174,735
Reserved Retained Earnings, January 1, 1999		$538,900
Add: Reserved during Year		143,125
Reserved Retained Earnings, December 31, 1999		$682,025

employee-related items (in this case Taxes Accrued and Tax Collections Payable) have been added to the amount actually paid to employees. Payroll taxes and fringe benefits may be included in a separate line "cash payments for taxes, duties, fines, and other fees or penalties," if significant in amount. "Cash paid to employees for services" in the amount of $312,550 is calculated as the net cash paid directly to employees, $279,450, less $30,400 capitalized as Construction Work in Progress (Entry 6) plus $63,500 paid for Taxes Accrued and Tax Collections Payable (Entry 13). Finally cash from operating activities was used to pay suppliers (Entry 13). Although suppliers were paid $133,200 in total, only $67,200 of this amount applied to operating activities.

Illustration 7–10

TOWN OF BRIGHTON
Water Utility Fund
Statement of Cash Flows
For the Year Ended December 31, 1999

Cash flows from operating activities:

Cash received from customers	$680,000
Cash provided from customer deposits	1,205
Cash paid to employees for services	(312,550)
Cash paid to suppliers	(67,200)
Net cash provided by operating activities	301,455

Cash flows from capital and related financing activities:

Acquisition and construction of capital assets	(96,400)
Interest paid on long-term bonds	(105,000)
Net cash used for capital and related financing activities	(201,400)

Cash flows from investing activities:

Interest and dividend income	44,500
Purchases of restricted investments	(140,000)
Net cash used for investing activities	(95,500)
Net increase in cash and cash equivalents	4,555
Cash and cash equivalents, January 1, 1999	132,600
Cash and cash equivalents, December 31, 1999	$137,155

Reconciliation of Cash and Cash Equivalents
to the Balance Sheet

	End of Year	Beginning of Year
Cash and cash equivalents in current and accrued assets	$128,365	$126,000
Restricted cash and cash equivalents	8,790	6,600
Total cash and cash equivalents	$137,155	$132,600

Reconciliation of Utility Operating Income
to Net Cash Provided by Operating Activities

Utility operating income		$204,790
Adjustments:		
Depreciation expense	$102,750	
Increase in accounts payable	4,800	
Increase in accrued liabilities	2,050	
Decrease in customer deposits	(935)	
Decrease in inventories	4,000	
Increase in interfund receivables	(5,000)	
Increase in accrued receivables	(1,120)	
Decrease in customer accounts receivable	4,120	
Customer advances applied to customer receivables	(14,000)	
Total adjustments		96,665
Net cash provided by operating activities		$301,455

Cash flows from capital and related activities in Illustration 7–10 show two uses of cash. The first item, acquisition and construction of capital assets, is calculated as the sum of $30,400 (Entry 6) and $66,000 (Entry 13). The other item, interest paid on long-term bonds, reflects bond interest in the amount of $105,000 paid in cash (Entry 7).

Cash flows from investing activities show cash provided by interest and dividend income (Entry 15a) and cash used by purchase of investments (Entry 17a).

As shown in Illustration 7–10, two reconciliations are required. The first reconciliation is necessary because the Town of Brighton's Statement of Cash Flows reports changes in *total* cash and cash equivalents, whereas the Balance Sheet shows two components of cash and cash equivalents: that included in Current and Accrued Assets and that included in Restricted Assets, respectively.[10] GASB standards also require a reconciliation of operating income to net cash provided by operating activities.

Combining Statements

If a reporting entity operates more than one enterprise fund, it is necessary to present a Combining Balance Sheet; a Combining Statement of Revenues, Expenses, and Changes in Retained Earnings; and a Combining Statement of Cash Flows for all Enterprise Funds in order to disclose the detail supporting the Enterprise Funds column in each of the Combined Statements. An illustrative Combining Balance Sheet for the enterprise funds of the City of Rock Island, Illinois, is shown as Illustration 7–11.

Events in Following Year

Earlier in this chapter, the establishment of a Supplies Fund by the Town of Brighton as of January 1, 2000, is illustrated. The Water Utility Fund advanced $130,000 to the Supplies Fund as a long-term loan. The entry by the Supplies Fund is illustrated in Entry 2 in the "Illustrative Case—Supplies Fund" section earlier in this chapter; the corresponding entry in the Water Utility Fund would be:

Long-Term Advance to Supplies Fund	130,000	
Cash		130,000

Toward the end of 2000, the Supplies Fund paid its first installment of $6,500 to the Water Utility Fund as a partial repayment of the long-term advance. Entry 9 of the illustrative entries for the Supply Fund shown earlier in this chapter illustrates the effect on the accounts of the Supplies Fund. The effect on the accounts of the Water Utility Fund is recorded by the following entry:

Cash	6,500	
Long-Term Advance to Supplies Fund		6,500

Regulatory Accounting Principles (RAP)

Investor-owned utilities, and governmentally owned utilities in some states, are required to report in a prescribed manner to state regulatory commissions. Electric and certain other utilities subject to the Federal Power Act must also file reports with the FERC. As mentioned at several points in this chapter, both NARUC and

---

[10]Ibid, p. 28.

FERC prescribe charts of accounts and uniform financial statement formats for reporting to regulatory agencies. Even though the Town of Brighton follows GAAP rather than **regulatory accounting principles** (RAP) in preparing its financial statements, the Town uses the chart of accounts and some of the financial statement captions provided for in regulatory publications. The illustrative financial statements shown earlier in this chapter are typical of those for water funds included in comprehensive annual financial reports.

For utilities that are required to report to a state rate regulatory commission or the FERC, accounting and reporting procedures under RAP are quite different from GAAP. Because plant assets and long-term debt are customarily a dominant share of the total assets and total debt of utilities, and current assets and current liabilities are relatively insignificant in amount, the regulatory balance sheet format displays plant assets before current assets and long-term debt before current liabilities. In Illustration 7–7, for example, Net Utility Plant amounts to almost 79 percent of total assets, and long-term debt is almost 96 percent of total debt.

Under regulatory reporting Utility Plant in Service is stated at original cost. Original cost is a regulatory concept that differs from historical cost, a concept commonly used in accounting for assets of nonregulated businesses. In essence, **historical cost** is the amount paid for an asset by its present owner. In contrast, **original cost** is *the cost to the owner who first devoted the property to public service.* When a regulated utility purchases plant assets from another utility, it must record in its accounts the amounts shown in the accounts of the seller for the Utility Plant purchased and for the related accumulated depreciation. Any premium paid by the present owner over and above such cost less depreciation is in the general nature of payments for goodwill by nonutility enterprises. But utilities enjoy monopoly privileges and are subject to corresponding restrictions. One of the restrictions is that earnings shall not exceed a fair rate of return. Since goodwill is the capitalized value of excess earnings, utilities can have no goodwill (in the accounting sense). Premium on plant purchased is therefore accounted for as **Utility Plant Acquisition Adjustments**. The amount of acquisition adjustment capitalized is amortized over a period of time determined by the appropriate regulatory body; accumulated amortization is disclosed in the Accumulated Provision for Amortization of Utility Plant Acquisition Adjustments account.

Other asset sections of balance sheets prepared in the regulatory format are Other Property and Investments and Deferred Debits. One item usually reported in the former section is Special Funds, which is similar to the Restricted Assets section of the GAAP-format balance sheets shown in Illustrations 7–7 and 7–8. Thus, as mentioned previously, Other Property and Investments is broader in scope than Restricted Assets and may contain items other than restricted assets. One item typically reported under the Deferred Debits caption is Unamortized Debt Discount and Expense, which under GAAP is reported as an offset to the related long-term debt.

Accounting for Nonutility Enterprises

Early in this chapter it was stressed that each governmentally owned enterprise should follow the accounting and financial reporting standards developed for investor-owned enterprises in the same industry. Generally, the standards

Illustration 7–11

CITY OF ROCK ISLAND, ILLINOIS
Enterprise Funds
Combining Balance Sheet
March 31, 1997

	Century Woods Assisted Housing Fund	Sunset Marina Fund
Assets		
Current Assets:		
Cash and investments	$ 974,326	$ 198,071
Receivables, net of allowance for collection losses:		
Accounts	2,036	251,101
Estimated unbilled usage	—	—
Current portion of notes receivable	—	—
Accrued interest	—	—
Other	10,000	—
Due from other funds	—	—
Inventories	—	5,000
Prepaid expenses	—	—
Total current assets	986,362	454,172
Long-Term Assets:		
Long-term notes receivable (net of current portion, net of allowance for uncollectible of $1,030,829)	—	—
Bond issuance costs	—	—
Total long-term assets	—	—
Property and Equipment:		
Land	—	—
Buildings and improvements	7,279,017	—
Equipment	59,860	—
Waterworks system	—	—
Wastewater system	—	—
Bridge and approaches	—	—
Marina facilities	—	2,145,045
Construction in progress	—	40,572
Accumulated depreciation	(79,508)	(1,245,672)
Net property and equipment	7,259,369	939,945
Total Assets	$8,245,731	$1,394,117

developed by the Financial Accounting Standards Board, and its predecessors, have been accepted by the GASB as applying to Internal Service Funds and Enterprise Funds.[11] Consequently, many sections earlier in this chapter, which discuss gener-

---

[11]See Footnote 5.

Waterworks Fund	Wastewater Treatment Fund	Motor Vehicle Parking System Fund	Rock Island Centennial Bridge Fund	Housing and Community Development Loan Fund	Total
$ 1,374,489	$ 1,058,721	$ —	$ 3,630,302	$ 30,892	$ 7,266,801
245,010	153,561	1,422	427	—	653,557
403,293	270,731	—	—	—	674,024
—	2,398	21,487	—	764,371	788,256
—	—	—	13,221	—	13,221
—	2,838	—	—	—	12,838
—	—	14	—	1,479,070	1,479,084
—	—	—	3,000	—	8,000
—	—	—	34,473	—	34,473
2,022,792	1,488,249	22,923	3,681,423	2,274,333	10,930,254
—	30,151	35,867	—	2,539,689	2,605,707
—	—	—	62,883	—	62,883
—	30,151	35,867	62,883	2,539,689	2,668,590
41,976	94,450	1,050,068	2,714,607	—	3,901,101
—	—	3,390,663	—	—	10,669,680
152,482	22,106	16,893	—	—	251,341
16,448,113	—	—	—	—	16,448,113
—	24,206,361	—	—	—	24,206,361
—	—	—	14,167,506	—	14,167,506
—	—	—	—	—	2,145,045
1,771,289	601,639	—	13,701,686	—	16,115,186
(12,205,753)	(13,674,753)	(1,678,552)	(9,743,509)	—	(38,627,747)
6,208,107	11,249,803	2,779,072	20,840,290	—	49,276,586
$ 8,230,899	$12,768,203	$2,837,862	$24,584,596	$4,814,022	$62,875,430

ally accepted accounting principles applicable to Internal Service Funds (such as the sections captioned "Acquisition of Assets by Contributions or Grants," "Depreciation of Contributed Assets or Assets Acquired from Capital Grants," and "Assets Acquired under Lease Agreements"), apply equally to enterprise funds accounting for activities other than utilities.

Illustration 7–11 (concluded)

CITY OF ROCK ISLAND, ILLINOIS
Enterprise Funds
Combining Balance Sheet
March 31, 1997

	Century Woods Assisted Housing Fund	Sunset Marina Fund
Liabilities and Fund Equity		
Current Liabilities:		
Accounts and contracts payable	$ 18,581	$ 2,121
Accrued liabilities	121,428	20,011
Due to other funds	875,455	624
Current portion of capital lease obligation	—	—
Current portion of bonds payable	420,597	54,024
Total current liabilities	1,436,061	76,780
Long-Term Liabilities:		
Capital lease obligation	—	—
Bonds payable	5,485,767	377,843
	5,485,767	377,843
Total liabilities	6,921,828	454,623
Fund Equity:		
Contributed capital	—	116,353
Retained earnings	1,323,903	823,141
Total fund equity	1,323,903	939,494
Total Liabilities and Fund Equity	$8,245,731	$1,394,117

Accounting for Municipal Solid Waste Landfills

According to Environmental Protection Agency (EPA) estimates there are approximately 6,000 municipal solid waste landfills (MSWLFs) in the United States, of which about 80 percent are owned by state or local general purpose or special purpose governments.[12] An EPA Rule, "Solid Waste Disposal Facility Criteria" (40 *Code of Federal Regulations*, parts 257 and 258), establishes certain closure requirements for MSWLFs and imposes stringent criteria for location, design, and operation of landfills, groundwater monitoring and corrective action, postclosure care, and financial assurance. State governments are assigned primary responsibility for implementing and enforcing the EPA rule, and may increase or reduce its provisions based on site conditions existing within their states.

---

[12]Governmental Accounting Standards Board, *Statement of Governmental Accounting Standards No. 18*, "Accounting for Municipal Solid Waste Landfill Closure and Postclosure Costs" (Norwalk, CT, 1993), par. 24.

Waterworks Fund	Wastewater Treatment Fund	Motor Vehicle Parking System Fund	Rock Island Centennial Bridge Fund	Housing and Community Development Loan Fund	Total
$ 81,391	$ 125,055	$ 2,143	$ 31,677	$ 28,524	$ 289,492
99,023	122,222	13,115	73,207	3,998	453,004
30	—	172,104	27,394	30,558	1,106,165
—	—	—	53,546	—	53,546
71,733	245,564	130,949	292,670	—	1,215,537
252,177	492,841	318,311	478,494	63,080	3,117,744
—	—	—	120,214	—	120,214
860,085	1,644,387	—	3,509,148	—	11,877,230
860,085	1,644,387	—	3,629,362	—	11,997,444
1,112,262	2,137,228	318,311	4,107,856	63,080	15,115,188
2,188,371	9,975,121	2,458,173	2,090,000	4,115,136	20,943,154
4,930,266	655,854	61,378	18,386,740	635,806	26,817,088
7,118,637	10,630,975	2,519,551	20,476,740	4,750,942	47,760,242
$8,230,899	$12,768,203	$2,837,862	$24,584,596	$4,814,022	$62,875,430

MSWLFs owners and operators may incur a variety of costs, both during the period of operation and after closure. These costs include the cost of equipment and facilities (including final covering of the MSWLF upon closure) and cost of services for such items as postclosure maintenance and monitoring for a period of 30 years after closure. The EPA requires owners and operators to estimate in detail the current dollar cost of hiring a third party to close the largest area of an MSWLF expected to require a final cover and to care for the MSWLF over the 30-year postclosure period. Each year the closure and postclosure cost estimates must be adjusted for inflation and revised as necessary to reflect changes in plans or conditions. Owners and operators of MSWLFs must provide assurances that adequate financial resources will be available to cover the estimated costs of closure, postclosure care, and remediation or containment of environmental hazards when the landfill has been filled to capacity. Several forms of financial assurance are acceptable, including third-party trusts, surety bonds, letters of credit, insurance, or state-sponsored plans.

GASB standards provide guidance both for measuring and reporting estimated total closure and postclosure costs. Although the detailed cost estimation procedures are beyond the scope of this chapter, reporting requirements for MSWLFs that use proprietary fund accounting are described briefly. An expense and liability should be recognized each period for a portion of the estimated total current cost of MSWLF closure and postclosure care. The portion of total cost to be recognized is based on the units of production method so that estimated total current cost is assigned to periods on the basis of landfill usage rather than the passage of time. Recognition begins in the period in which the MSWLF first accepts solid waste and continues each period until closure. Estimated total closure and postclosure costs should be reevaluated each year during operation of the landfill and the cumulative effect of changes in the estimated costs, if any, should be reported in the period of the change. Costs of equipment, facilities, services, or final cover acquired during the period are reported as a reduction of the accrued liability and not as capital assets. Equipment and facilities installed prior to commencement of operation of the landfill should be fully depreciated by the closure date.

Assets held by third-party trustees or in surety standby trusts to meet financial assurance requirements should be reported as "amounts held by trustee" in the restricted assets section of the balance sheet and as reservations of retained earnings. Earnings on such investments should be reported as revenue.

GASB standards also provide guidance for reporting of MSWLFs in governmental fund types or by other entities such as colleges and universities. Accounting for MSWLFs in the General Fund, for example, requires that an expenditure and fund liability be reported for the current closure and postclosure costs to the extent that an accrued liability would be settled with available fund resources; any remaining liability would be reported in the General Long-Term Debt Account Group discussed in Chapter 6. Regardless of the fund type or entity reporting the MSWLF activities, GASB standards require the following note disclosures.[13]

1. The nature and source of landfill closure and postclosure care requirements (federal, state, or local laws or regulations).
2. That recognition of a liability for closure and postclosure care costs is based on landfill capacity used to date.
3. The reported liability for closure and postclosure care at the Balance Sheet date (if not apparent from the financial statements) and the estimated total current cost of closure and postclosure care remaining to be recognized.
4. The percentage of landfill capacity used to date and approximate remaining landfill life in years.
5. How closure and postclosure care financial assurance requirements, if any, are being met. Also, any assets restricted for payment of closure and postclosure care costs (if not apparent from the financial statements).

---

[13]GASB, *Codification*, Sec. L10.116.

6. The nature of the estimates and the potential for changes due to inflation or deflation, technology, or applicable laws or regulations.

While municipal solid waste landfills may seem to be a dull topic, the costs of improving landfills to meet increased EPA standards, providing financial assurance, and complying with accounting and reporting requirements may be significant for many governmental units.

Required Segment Information

Revenue bonds and other debt instruments are secured by the revenues of individual enterprise funds, not by the aggregate revenues of all enterprise funds. Similarly, rate regulatory bodies and other oversight bodies require information about individual enterprises, rather than aggregated information for all enterprise funds.

GASB standards require, therefore, that general purpose financial statements include certain "segment information for major non-homogeneous enterprise funds." The presentation of segment information in the Notes to the Financial Statements section of the annual report is considered preferable, although some of the information may be included in the body of the combined statements or in the combining statements if the latter are included with the combined statements as part of the General Purpose Financial Statements. Segment information that should be presented for enterprise funds is that deemed essential to make the General Purpose Financial Statements not misleading. The following types of information are specified:

a. Material *inter*governmental operating subsidies to an enterprise fund.
b. Material *intra*governmental operating subsidies to or from an enterprise fund.
c. Material enterprise fund tax revenues.
d. A material enterprise fund *operating* income or loss.
e. A material enterprise fund *net* income or loss.

Materiality should be evaluated in terms of the individual enterprise funds, not in terms of the total enterprise fund type taken as a whole.

Illustration 7–12 presents an example of suggested segment information disclosure.

Key Terms

Cash equivalents,   258
Contributed equity,   271
Customer advances for construction,   270
General obligation bonds,   271
Historical cost,   281

Original cost,   281
Regulatory accounting principles,   281
Retained earnings,   271
Revenue bonds,   271
Utility plant acquisition adjustment,   281

Illustration 7–12

Illustrative Segment Information Disclosure

.601   The following example of Notes to the Financial Statements disclosure of segment information is presented for illustrative purposes only. Alternative presentation formats may be acceptable. This illustration assumes that there were no other material facts necessary to make the GPFS not misleading.

Note (X)—Segment Information for Enterprise Funds

The City maintains five Enterprise Funds which provide water, sewer, airport, golf and parking services. Segment information for the year ended December 31, 19x2, was as follows:

	Water Fund	Sewer Fund	Airport Fund	Other Enterprise Funds	Total Enterprise Funds
Operating Revenues	300,000	20,000	300,000	52,150	672,150
Depreciation, Depletion, and Amortization Expense	70,000	10,000	60,000	4,100	144,100
Operating Income or (Loss)	130,000	5,000	(35,000)	7,970	107,970
Operating Grants, Entitlements, and Shared Revenues	—	—	55,000	—	55,000
Operating Transfers:					
In	—	20,000	—	—	20,000
Out	(30,000)	—	—	—	(30,000)
Tax Revenues	—	10,000	—	—	10,000
Net Income or Loss	42,822	10,000	10,000	15,990	78,812
Current Capital:					
Contributions	682,666	—	—	—	682,666
Transfers	(10,000)	—	—	—	(10,000)
Plant, Property and Equipment:					
Additions	180,000	25,000	125,000	24,453	354,453
Deletions	(30,000)	—	—	—	(30,000)
Net Working Capital	167,491	35,812	43,187	41,773	288,263
Bonds and Other Long-Term Liabilities:					
Payable from Operating Revenues	1,598,000	—	—	—	1,598,000
Payable from Other Sources	200,000	—	—	—	200,000
Total Equity	2,900,000	150,000	400,000	110,002	3,560,002

Source: GASB, *Codification*, Sec. 2500.901.

Selected References

American Institute of Certified Public Accountants. Audit and Accounting Guide. *Audits of State and Local Governmental Units*. Revised. New York, 1996.

Financial Accounting Standards Board. *Statement of Financial Accounting Standards No. 71*, "Accounting for the Effects of Certain Types of Regulation." Norwalk, CT, 1982.

Governmental Accounting Standards Board. *Codification of Governmental Accounting and Financial Reporting Standards as of June 30, 1997*. Norwalk, CT, 1997.

Questions

7–1. Explain how internal service funds and enterprise funds are similar and how they are different.

7–2. Explain the generally accepted accounting principles utilized by proprietary funds.

7–3. What are the benefits of establishing internal service funds? What kinds of activities are typically accounted for in internal service funds?

7–4. "Since the reason for the establishment of internal service funds is to facilitate management of resources, and not primarily to demonstrate compliance with law, they may be established at the discretion of governmental administrators." Comment.

7–5. Since internal service funds are expected to cover the cost of their operations by charges to departments or agencies using their services, they should use the accrual basis of accounting for both revenue recognition and expenditure recognition. Discuss.

7–6. What are some of the more important considerations in establishing a pricing policy for an internal service fund?

7–7. The Supplies Fund of Springfield is an internal service fund. It issues supplies to other funds of the city on a cost-reimbursement basis, as described in this chapter. During a certain year, billings to departments totaled $850,740. The same year, the operating statement showed a loss of $787. Based on those facts, was the fund, in your opinion, well managed? Explain your answer.

7–8. The laws in some states require all funds of local governmental units within those states to be operated under legal budgets. GASB accounting and financial reporting standards specify that internal service funds should be accounted for in the same manner as business organizations—which neither incorporate budgetary accounts in their accounting systems, nor present budget versus actual operating statements. Should a city in a state that requires all funds to be operated under a legal budget include the internal service fund type in its Combined Statement of Revenues, Expenditures, and Changes in Fund Balances in its GPFS? Explain your answer.

7–9. In general, how may an administrator or accountant determine the accounting and financial reporting standards applicable to a nonregulated governmental enterprise? A governmental enterprise in a regulated industry?

7–10. What is the purpose of the Restricted Assets section of an Enterprise Fund Balance Sheet used to account for a utility? Provide examples of items that might be reported in the Restricted Assets section.

7–11. What is the meaning of *Allowance for Funds Used During Construction*? What does this term include that is not includable as an element of the cost of fixed assets constructed by a nonutility enterprise?

7–12. If a governmental unit issues tax-supported bonds or special assessment bonds that are to be serviced by enterprise fund revenues, what treatment should be given to the bonds in the Enterprise Fund Balance Sheet? In the GPFS?

7–13. What is the meaning of *original cost* as used in public utility accounting? In your answer make clear how *original cost* differs from *historical cost*.

7–14. Explain what should be recorded in the Utility Plant Acquisition Adjustments account of a regulated utility, and why this account is used rather than a Goodwill account.

7–15. What are the categories of cash flows required in a proprietary fund statement of cash flows prepared in conformity with GASB standards? What kinds of transactions are reported in each category?

7–16. Explain why utilities customarily need to present an Accrued Utilities Revenues account in their Balance Sheet. How should the amount of the accrual be determined?

7–17. What is meant by "segment information for enterprise funds"? To what source should persons concerned with governmental financial report preparation go to determine the required disclosures?

7–18. Explain how the expense and liability of a period for the estimated current cost for closure and postclosure of a municipal solid waste landfill accounted for in a proprietary fund should be determined. Does this appear rational? Explain.

7–19. What disclosures are required in the Notes to the Financial Statements for a municipal solid waste landfill, regardless of the fund type or entity used to account for it?

7–20. Name the financial statements required in the governmental entity's CAFR if more than one enterprise fund is used.

Cases

7–1. The formal financial objectives and funding policies for the internal service funds of the City of Columbia, Missouri, are presented below and on the next page. Read these policies and respond to the questions that follow.

A Resolution
establishing a formal policy with respect to the financial objectives for internal service funds; and establishing a policy regarding generation of funds required for capital outlay.

BE IT RESOLVED BY THE COUNCIL OF THE CITY OF COLUMBIA, MISSOURI AS FOLLOWS:

SECTION 1. That internal service funds such as Data Processing, Vehicle Maintenance, Utilities Accounts and Billing, Public Buildings, and Printing are funds whose financial objective should be to only recover the complete cost of operations without producing any significant amount of profit in excess of the fund's requirements.

SECTION 2. That Section 1 is consistent with practices of "Governmental Accounting, Auditing, and Financial Reporting."

SECTION 3. That in computing an internal service funds revenue requirement for rate setting purposes, the rate base should include such items as debt expense, interest expense, operating expense, prorated reserve (accumulated over time to allow for purchase option under lease/purchase arrangements), and either depreciation expense or estimated capital outlay, either of which are usually financed 100% internally through rates.

SECTION 4. That since working capital in different funds varies because of many factors it should be reviewed more closely with the budgetary process to assure captive users that the cash account is not a result of billings in excess of revenue requirements.

(continued)

SECTION 5. That if it appears that cash buildup has occurred in excess of reasonable revenue requirements, rates should be adjusted in the budgetary process cost recoveries either over or under, should be rolled forward.

SECTION 6. That generation of funds for capital outlay be allowed either 100% internally through rates or through budgeted depreciation expense when lease/purchase agreements are used, in which case, an amount should be included in the rate base for a prorated reserve which, accumulated over time, will enable purchase of such capital outlay at some future date.

Allowable costs used in determining revenue requirements for the City of Columbia's internal service funds are diagrammed in the next box.

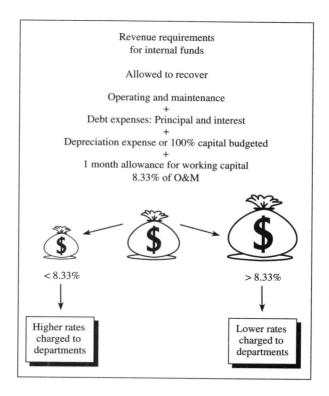

Revenue requirements
for internal funds

Allowed to recover

Operating and maintenance
+
Debt expenses: Principal and interest
+
Depreciation expense or 100% capital budgeted
+
1 month allowance for working capital
8.33% of O&M

< 8.33% > 8.33%

Higher rates charged to departments

Lower rates charged to departments

Required

    a. Do the City of Columbia's financial objectives and funding policies appear to promote sound resource management?

    b. Evaluate the reasonableness of the factors used to determine billing rates/revenue requirements from the viewpoint of

        (1) A City Council member.

        (2) The Mayor or City Manager.

        (3) A department head.

c. Is having a uniform policy for all internal service funds optimal, or would it be better to tailor the revenue requirements to the needs of each individual fund? Explain.

7–2. The Balance Sheet and Statement of Revenues, Expenditures, and Changes in Fund Balance for the Building Maintenance Fund, an internal service fund of Coastal City, are reproduced below. No further information about the nature or purposes of this fund is given in the annual report.

COASTAL CITY
Building Maintenance Fund
Balance Sheet
As of December 31, 1999
Assets

Assets:	
Cash and investments	$152,879
Accounts receivable	2,116
Inventory	779,000
Prepaid expenses	19,854
Total Assets	$953,849

Liabilities and Fund Equity

Liabilities:	
Accounts payable	$ 35,675
Other accrued liabilities	109,099
Accrued annual leave	227,369
Total Liabilities	372,143
Fund equity:	
Fund balance	581,706
Total Liabilities and Fund Equity	$953,849

COASTAL CITY
Building Maintenance Fund
Statement of Revenues, Expenditures, and
Changes in Fund Balance
Year Ended December 31, 1999

Revenues:	
Billings to Departments	$10,774,781
Miscellaneous	100,344
Total Billings	10,875,125
Expenditures:	
Salaries and employee benefits	3,353,413
Supplies	3,409,096
Operating services and charges	495,143
Maintenance and repairs	3,536,443
Total expenditures	10,794,095
Excess of Revenues over Expenditures	81,030
Fund Balance, January 1, 1999	500,676
Fund Balance, December 31, 1999	$ 581,706

Required

    a. Judging from the information presented, does the Building Maintenance Fund appear to be accounted for and operated, financially, as an internal service fund should be?

    b. If you were the manager of a City department that uses the services of the Building Maintenance Fund, what would you want to know in addition to the information disclosed in the financial statements?

7–3. The City of Dixon operates a mass transit system (DTS) consisting of a network of bus and trolley routes. The following information is provided about the operations and financing of the mass transit system.*

    1. Operating revenues for the most recent fiscal year amounted to $549,420; operating expenses for the same year amounted to $1,011,843. Operating revenues have covered only 45 to 50 percent of operating expenditures since DTS was established five years ago.

    2. The operating deficit (from part 1) of $462,423 was financed jointly by $362,423 from the City's General Fund and $100,000 in operating grants from the Urban Mass Transit Administration (UMTA). Capital contributions over the past five years have amounted to $3,334,286 divided about evenly between the City and capital grants from the UMTA.

    3. Transit system managers have been pressured at times by City officials to increase bus and trolley fares but are strongly opposed because they believe DTS ridership would drop significantly. Advocates for disadvantaged groups have also lobbied hard to keep the current fares. Thus, for at least the next several years, the City plans to provide an annual operating subsidy to DTS to cover its operating deficit, less any operating grants received from UMTA or other sources.

    4. Until now DTS has been accounted for and reported as an enterprise fund of the City. The City Finance Director and the head of the mass transit system would like to continue to use enterprise fund accounting; however, influential members of the Finance Committee of the City Council are insisting that, since DTS is never expected to break even, it should be accounted for and reported as a special revenue fund, Changing to a special revenue fund also means that DTS will require Council-approved appropriations for its expenditures.

Required

Based on the information provided for the City of Dixon mass transit system, should the activities of DTS be accounted for in an enterprise fund or as a special revenue fund? Explain fully.

Exercises and Problems

7–1. Utilizing the annual report obtained for Exercise 1–1, follow the instructions on next page:

---

*The authors are indebted to Charles M. Hicks for providing the information from which this case was adapted.

Part 1. Internal Service Funds.

a. *Use of Funds.* What activities of the governmental unit are reported as being administered by internal service funds (working capital funds, revolving funds, rotary funds, industrial funds, and intragovernmental service funds are other names used for funds of the type discussed in Chapter 7)? If internal service funds are not used by the reporting entity, does the report disclose how activities such as purchasing, motor pools, printing, data processing, and other activities commonly used by more than one fund are financed and accounted for? Does the report state the basis of accounting used for the internal service funds? (Are all funds in this category accounted for on the same basis?) If so, is the financial statement presentation consistent with the stated basis? If the basis of accounting is not stated, analyze the statements to determine which basis is used—full accrual, modified accrual, or cash basis. Is the basis used consistent with the standards discussed in Chapter 7?

b. *Fund Disclosure.* In the balance sheet(s) of the internal service fund(s), are assets classified in accord with practices of profit-seeking businesses, or are current, fixed, and other assets not separately displayed? If there are receivables other than from other funds or other governmental units, are allowances for estimated uncollectibles provided? Are allowances for depreciation deducted from related fixed-asset accounts?

Are current liabilities and long-term debt properly distinguished in the balance sheet? Are long-term advances from other funds properly distinguished from capital contributions received from other funds? Are retained earnings (or deficits) from operations clearly distinguished from contributed equity?

Are budgetary accounts (Estimated Revenues, Appropriations, Encumbrances) used by the internal service funds? From what sources were revenues actually obtained by each internal service fund? How are costs and expenses of each fund classified: by character, object, function, or activity (see Chapter 3 for definitions of these terms)? Are noncash expenses, such as depreciation, separately disclosed? Do the revenues of each fund exceed the costs and expenses of the period? Compute the net income (or net loss) of each fund in this category as a percentage of its operating revenue for the period. Does the net income (or net loss) for any fund exceed 5 percent of operating revenues? If so, do the statements, or the accompanying text, explain what the excess is being used for, or how the deficiency is being financed?

c. *Statement of Cash Flows.* Is a Statement of Cash Flows presented for internal service funds? If so, how does the cash provided by operations shown in this statement relate to the revenues and expenses shown in the Statement of Revenues, Expenses, and Changes in Retained Earnings? Are cash flows from financing activities presented separately for noncapital- and capital-related activities? Is there a section for cash flows from investing activities?

Part 2. Enterprise Funds.

a. *Use of Funds.* What activities of the governmental unit are reported as being administered by enterprise funds? Does the governmental unit own and operate its water utility? Electric utility? Gas utility? Transportation system? Are combining statements presented for all enterprise funds, or are separate statements presented for each enterprise fund? Are all enterprise funds accounted for on the full accrual basis? Are all funds in this category earning revenues at least equal to costs and expenses? If not, how is the operating deficit being financed? What sources furnished the original investment in fund assets? Do the notes include segment information on individual enterprise funds where applicable (see "Required Segment Information" section of Chapter 7)?

Are sales to other funds or other governmental units separately disclosed? Are there receivables from other funds? Other governmental units? How are receivables from component units, if any, disclosed? Is there any evidence that enterprise funds contribute amounts to the General Fund in lieu of taxes to help support services received by the enterprise? Is there any evidence that enterprise funds make excessively large contributions to the General Fund or any other funds?

b. *Utility Funds.* Is it possible to tell from the report whether utilities of this governmental unit are subject to the same regulations as investor-owned utilities in the same state? (If the utility statements follow the format of the NARUC and the FERC, as described in Chapter 7, there is a good chance the governmentally owned utilities are subject to at least some supervision by a regulatory agency.) What rate of return on sales (or operating revenues) is being earned by each utility fund? What rate of return on total assets is being earned by each utility fund?

Is depreciation taken on utility plant? Are accounting policies and accounting changes properly disclosed? If so, what method of depreciation is being used? Is the *original cost* basis used for plant assets—is a plant acquisition adjustment account shown? If so, over what period is the acquisition being amortized?

Does each utility account for its own debt service and construction activities in the manner described in Chapter 7? What Special Funds, or Restricted Assets, are utilized by each utility? Is Retained Earnings reserved in an amount equal to or exceeding Special Funds, or Restricted Assets?

c. *Nonutility Enterprise Funds.* Are nonutility enterprise funds accounted for in the same manner as investor-owned enterprises in the same industries? (In order to answer this, you may need to refer to publications of trade associations or to handbooks or encyclopedias of accounting systems found in business libraries.) If you cannot find information about investor-owned counterparts of the governmental nonutility enterprise funds, do the statements of the latter evidence that generally accepted accounting principles devised for profit-seeking businesses were used?

7–2. Write the numbers 1 through 10 on a sheet of paper. Beside each number write the letter corresponding with the best answer to each of the following questions:

1. Which of the following is *not* an appropriate reason to establish an internal service fund?
   a. To improve the management of resources.
   b. To develop a cash reserve to meet future contingencies.
   c. To determine whether user charges are sufficient to cover operating costs.
   d. To determine whether costs are reasonable in relation to benefits.

2. Which of the following is a correct statement of the role of budgeting in proprietary funds?
   a. Fund managers should have discretion to operate within a flexible budget, consistent with pricing and other policies established by the legislative body.
   b. Expenditures from proprietary fund resources require legislative appropriations.

expenses

No encumbrances

c. To ensure appropriations are not overspent, all proprietary funds should use encumbrance procedures.

d. Proprietary fund managers should ensure that goods and services are not provided to other funds or departments unless a valid appropriation exists for the goods or services ordered.

3. An equity transfer from the General Fund to a proprietary fund will be reported in the balance sheet of the fund as a (an):

   a. Contributed item in the Fund Equity section.

   b. Retained earnings item in the Fund Equity section.

   c. Long-term liability.

   d. None of the above. It would only be reported in the bottom section of the operating statement.

4. Watt County operates a centralized data processing center as an internal service fund to provide services to other funds and departments. In 1999, this fund billed the Parks and Recreation Fund $75,000 for data processing services. What account should Wood's internal service fund credit to record the billing to the Parks and Recreation Fund?

   a. Interfund Exchanges.

   b. Billings to Departments.

   c. Operating Transfers In.

   d. Data Processing Expenses.

5. If an internal service fund is intended to operate on a cost-reimbursement basis, then user charges should:

   a. Cover the full costs, both direct and indirect, of operating the fund.

   b. Cover at a minimum the direct costs of operating the fund.

   c. Cover the full costs of operating the fund *and* provide for future expansion and replacement of fixed assets.

   d. Any of the above could be an appropriate basis for establishing user charges, depending on the policy followed by a particular government.

6. During 1999 Bell City reported the following operating receipts from self-sustaining activities paid for by users of the services rendered:

Operations of water supply plant	$5,000,000
Operations of transit system	900,000

What amounts should be reported as operating revenues of Bell's enterprise funds?

   a. $0.

   b. $900,000.

   c. $5,000,000.

   d. $5,900,000.

7. Interest capitalized as a part of the cost of assets constructed by a governmentally owned utility properly consists of:

   a. Net interest paid and accrued during the period of construction on money borrowed for construction purposes.

   b. Net interest paid and accrued during the period of construction on money borrowed for construction purposes, and interest imputed on other money used for construction.

    c. Only net interest actually paid during the period of construction.

    d. None of the above.

8. The proceeds of tax-supported bonds issued for the benefit of an enterprise fund and being serviced by a debt service fund:

    a. Should not be reported by the enterprise fund at all.

    b. Should be reported in the notes to enterprise fund statements, but not in the body of any of the statements.

    c. Should be reported in the enterprise fund as Long-Term Debt.

    d. Should be reported in the enterprise fund as Contributed Equity.

9. Under current GASB standards fixed assets received by gift or contribution by a proprietary fund, or acquired from grants, entitlements, and shared revenues restricted for acquisition of fixed assets, should:

    a. Not be depreciated.

    b. Be depreciated in the normal manner.

    c. Be depreciated or not be depreciated at the option of the governmental unit, provided a consistent policy is followed.

    d. Be depreciated in the normal manner, but Depreciation Expense may optionally be closed to a contributed equity account rather than Retained Earnings.

10. The financial statements required by current GASB standards for a proprietary fund are:

    a. A Balance Sheet and a Statement of Revenues, Expenditures, and Changes in Fund Balance.

    b. A Balance Sheet, Statement of Revenues, Expenditures, and Changes in Fund Balance, and a Statement of Cash Flows.

    c. A Balance Sheet, Statement of Revenues, Expenses, and Changes in Retained Earnings, and a Statement of Cash Flows.

    d. A Balance Sheet and a Statement of Revenues, Expenses, and Changes in Retained Earnings.

7–3. Your examination of the accounts of your new client, the City of Delmas, as of June 30, 1999, revealed the following:

1. On December 31, 1998, the City paid $115,000 out of General Fund revenues for a central garage to service its vehicles, with $67,500 being applicable to the building, which has an estimated life of 25 years; $14,500 to land; and $33,000 to machinery and equipment, which has an estimated life of 15 years. A $12,200 cash contribution was received by the garage from the General Fund on the same date.

2. The garage maintains no records, but a review of deposit slips and canceled checks revealed the following:

Collections for services to General Fund departments	$30,000
Office salaries	6,000
Utilities	700
Mechanics' wages	11,000
Materials and supplies	9,000

3. The garage had uncollected billings of $2,000, accounts payable for materials and supplies of $500, and an inventory of materials and supplies of $1,500 at June 30, 1999.

Required

Prepare journal entries that should be made to establish an Internal Service Fund for the City of Delmas and to record the events for the period given. Also prepare any necessary adjusting and closing entries as of June 30, 1999, the end of the fiscal year.

(AICPA, adapted)

7–4. The City of Ashville operates a central garage through an Internal Service Fund to provide garage space and repairs for all city-owned-and-operated vehicles. The Central Garage Fund was established by a contribution of $300,000 from the General Fund on July 1, 1997, at which time the land and building were acquired. The after-closing trial balance at June 30, 1999, was as follows:

	Debits	Credits
Cash	$110,000	
Due from Other Funds	20,000	
Inventory of Materials and Supplies	90,000	
Land	50,000	
Building	250,000	
Allowance for Depreciation—Building		$ 20,000
Machinery and Equipment	65,000	
Allowance for Depreciation—Machinery and Equipment		12,000
Vouchers Payable		42,000
Contribution from General Fund		325,000
Retained Earnings		186,000
	$585,000	$585,000

The following information applies to the fiscal year ended June 30, 2000:

1. Materials and supplies were purchased on account for $92,000; the perpetual inventory method is used.
2. The cost of materials and supplies used during the year ended June 30, 2000, was $110,000. A physical count taken as of that date showed materials and supplies on hand totaled $72,000 at cost.
3. Salaries and wages paid to employees totaled $235,000, including related costs.
4. A billing was received from the Enterprise Fund for utility charges totaling $30,000, and was paid.
5. Depreciation of the building was recorded in the amount of $10,000; depreciation of the machinery and equipment amounted to $9,000.
6. Billings to other departments for services rendered to them were as follows:

General Fund	$270,000
Water and Sewer Fund	87,000
Special Revenue Fund	40,000

7. Unpaid interfund receivable balances at June 30, 2000, were as follows:

General Fund	$10,000
Special Revenue Fund	17,000

8. Vouchers payable at June 30, 2000, were $16,000.
9. Closing entries for the Central Garage Fund at June 30, 2000, were prepared.

Required

    a. Prepare journal entries to record all of the transactions for this period in the Central Garage Fund accounts.

    b. Assuming that the City of Ashville has no other internal service funds, name the general purpose financial statements in which the financial data of the Central Garage Fund should be reported.

7–5. As of the beginning of a certain year, the Automotive Service Fund of the City of Clarkton had the following post-closing trial balance as of September 30, 1999:

	Debits	*Credits*
Cash	$ 11,000	
Due from Other Funds	20,200	
Service Supplies Inventory	35,300	
Machinery and Equipment	90,000	
Allowance for Depreciation—Machinery and Equipment		$ 18,000
Buildings	210,000	
Allowance for Depreciation—Buildings		70,000
Land	37,000	
Due to Federal Government		1,500
Due to Other Funds		800
Accounts Payable		12,700
Contribution from General Fund		250,000
Retained Earnings		50,500
	$403,500	$403,500

During the fiscal year ended September 30, 2000, the following transactions (summarized) occurred:

    1. Employees were paid $290,000 wages in cash; additional wages of $43,500 were withheld for federal income and social security taxes. The employer's share of social security taxes amounted to $23,375.

    2. Cash remitted to the federal government during the year for withholding taxes and social security taxes amounted to $65,500.

    3. Utility bills received from the City's Utility Fund during the year amounted to $23,500.

    4. Office expenses paid in cash during the year amounted to $10,500.

    5. Service supplies purchased on account during the year totaled $157,500.

6. Parts and supplies used during the year totaled $152,300 (at cost).
7. Charges to departments during the fiscal year were as follows:

General Fund	$294,000
Street Fund	266,000

8. Unpaid balances at year-end were as follows:

General Fund	$10,000
Street Fund	20,000

9. Payments to the Utility Fund totaled $21,800.
10. Accounts Payable at year-end amounted to $13,250.
11. Annual depreciation is recorded at the following rates:

Machinery and Equipment	10%
Buildings	3

12. Revenue and expense accounts for the year were closed.

Required

a. Prepare a Statement of Revenues, Expenses, and Changes in Retained Earnings for the year. Classify expenses as to direct and indirect costs. Wages and payroll taxes are considered to be 90 percent direct and 10 percent indirect. Utility services are estimated to be 80 percent direct and 20 percent indirect. Parts and supplies used, and depreciation of machinery and equipment are considered direct costs; all other costs are considered indirect costs.
b. Comment on the evident success of the pricing policy of this fund, assuming that user charges are intended to cover all operating expenses, including depreciation, but are not expected to provide a net income in excess of 3 percent of billings to departments.
c. Prepare a Balance Sheet for the Automotive Service Fund as of September 30, 2000.
d. Prepare a Statement of Cash Flows for the Automotive Service Fund for the year ended September 30, 2000.

7–6. The City of Dalton operates an Internal Service Fund to manage and contract for the various kinds of insurance carried by the City. It pays all premiums to the insurers; then, as premiums expire, they are charged to the specific funds to which they pertain. Operating costs, consisting of personnel, rent, utilities, and miscellaneous other expenses, are charged to the insured funds by adding an "operating charge" to expired premium charges. For the current year, the operating charge is 10 percent of premium expirations billed. Operating surpluses or deficits are usually small in amount and are closed at year-end to Retained Earnings. Insurers pay directly to insured funds and all losses are borne by the applicable funds; neither are recorded in the Insurance Fund. At June 30, 1999, the trial balance of the Insurance Fund was as follows:

Cash	$ 5,650	
Due from Other Funds	30,000	
Prepaid Insurance Premiums	236,945	
Vouchers Payable		$105,945
Contribution from General Fund		120,000
Contribution from Water Fund		45,000
Retained Earnings		1,650
	$272,595	$272,595

During the year ended June 30, 2000, the following transactions, in summary form, occurred:

1. The fund was billed by insurance companies for $132,625 premiums falling due on insurance coverage for the various funds of the city.

2. A total of $216,700 was charged to various funds on account of premiums that expired during the year in the amount of $197,000 and $19,700 of operating charges thereon.

3. Operating Expenses paid in cash during the year were:

Salaries and Wages	$12,400
Rent	5,200
Utilities	860
Miscellaneous	800
Total	$19,260

The rent and the utilities were paid to other funds; Miscellaneous was paid to external suppliers.

4. A total of $4,000 was received from insurance companies as premium adjustments during the year. This amount, plus $300 billed previously for operating charges, was credited to the amount owed by various funds for the current year's expirations.

5. $127,000 was paid on amounts owed to insurance companies, for the benefit of funds and agencies of the City of Dalton.

6. Additional permanent financing for the fund was received in the form of a $75,000 contribution of cash from the General Fund.

7. $170,500 was collected from the various funds. Of this amount, $155,000 was for expirations of premiums and $15,500 was for the related operating charge, both previously billed.

Required

    a. State what you consider to be the justification for operation of a separate fund for accounting for insurance premium payments and expirations.

    b. In the fund described above there are no transactions related to settlement of losses. State the reason why.

    c. Is the use of the account Retained Earnings appropriate for this fund? Why or why not?

    d. Prepare entries in general journal form to record the transactions of the Insurance Fund, including closing entries, for the fiscal year ended June 30, 2000.

    e. Prepare a Balance Sheet as of June 30, 2000.

    f. Prepare a Statement of Revenues, Expenses, and Changes in Retained Earnings for the fiscal year ended June 30, 2000.

    g. Prepare a Statement of Cash Flows for the fiscal year ended June 30, 2000.

7–7. Webster City issued bonds for the construction of an addition to its utility plant that totaled $9,000,000 and bore interest at the rate of 6 percent per year. The bonds were sold at par on January 15, 1999, the day the construction contract was signed; proceeds were invested on that date at the rate of 6 percent per year. On March 15, investments in the face amount of $1,500,000 plus accrued interest, were sold, in order to make a progress payment to the contractor. Investments in the face amount of $1,500,000, plus accrued interest, were sold on May 15 in order to make the second progress payment to the contractor. On July 15, semiannual bond interest due was paid. Also on July 15, semiannual interest on investments on hand on that date was collected, then investments in the face amount of $3,000,000 were sold in order to make a progress payment to the contractor. On September 15, investments in the face amount of $3,000,000, plus accrued interest, were sold in order to make a progress payment to the contractor. On November 15, 1999, cash in the amount of $3,000,000 derived from operations of the utility was used for the final payment to the contractor; the utility plant addition was deemed completed on that date.

Required

    a. From the information above:

        (1) Compute the bond interest paid or accrued during the period of construction, January 15–November 15.

        (2) Compute interest earned during the period of construction on the investment of the bond proceeds.

        (3) Show in general journal form the entry to capitalize the net interest cost as a part of the cost of the plant addition, as required by GASB standards.

    b. Assuming the amount of interest on utility resources generated from operations and used for construction that is to be capitalized as a part of the cost of the addition to the utility plant is $202,250, show in general journal form the entry to capitalize the imputed interest.

    c. State, or illustrate, how the debt component of the Allowance for Funds Used During Construction (see your answer to part *a* (3) of this problem) should be reported in the utility's operating statement for the fiscal year ended December 31, 1999.

d. State, or illustrate, how the equity component of the Allowance for Funds Used During Construction (see your answer to part *b* of this problem) should be reported in the utility's operating statement for the fiscal year ended December 31, 1999.

7–8. The Council of the City of Templeton directed that $1,000,000 cash be transferred from the City's General Fund as a permanent contribution to a newly created Water Utility Fund. The Water Utility Fund is *not* regulated by any regulatory agency. The cash is intended to cover the purchase price of the Southland Water Company, plus an additional amount to serve as initial working capital for the new activity. At June 30, 1999, the effective date of purchase, the Southland Company had the following after-closing trial balance:

	Debits	Credits
Utility Plant in Service	$2,195,000	
Allowance for Depreciation—Utility Plant		$1,357,000
Cash	29,000	
Accounts Receivable	64,000	
Estimated Uncollectible Receivables		26,000
Materials and Supplies	66,000	
Vouchers Payable		99,000
Miscellaneous Accruals		28,000
Capital Stock		1,000,000
Retained Earnings	156,000	
	$2,510,000	$2,510,000

The acquisition occurred as follows:

1. The General Fund contribution was received on June 27, 1999.
2. As of June 30, 1999, the City of Templeton Water Utility Fund acquired the assets of the Southland Water Company, excluding cash. Receivables were purchased at half of their face value. When the purchased assets were recorded, the allowance for uncollectible receivables was increased to establish the new book value of receivables. The vendor's liabilities were assumed. A cash payment of $900,000 was made for the net assets of the water utility. (Hint: Record Accounts Receivable, Materials and Supplies, Accounts Payable, and Miscellaneous Accruals at the amounts shown in the trial balance. Increase Estimated Uncollectible Receivables to $32,000. Amounts shown for Southland Water Company's Cash, Capital Stock, and Retained Earnings accounts should not be recorded by the Water Utility Fund.)

Required

a. Record in general journal form the entries that should be made in the Water Utility Fund for the events of June 27 and June 30, 1999.
b. Prepare in conformity with GAAP a balance sheet for the City of Templeton Water Utility Fund as of June 30, 1999.

7–9. This problem continues the preceding problem. During the year ended June 30, 2000, the following transactions and events occurred in the City of Templeton Water Utility Fund:

1. On July 1, 1999, to finance needed plant improvements, the Water Utility Fund borrowed $500,000 from a local bank on notes secured by a pledge of water utility revenues. The notes mature in five years and bear interest at the annual rate of 8 percent.

2. Accrued expenses at June 30, 1999, were paid in cash.

3. Billings to nongovernmental customers for water usage during the year totaled $632,000; billings to the General Fund totaled $40,000.

4. Liabilities for the following were recorded during the year:

Materials and supplies	$ 88,000
Source of supply expenses	32,000
Pumping expenses	40,500
Water treatment expenses	51,500
Transmission and distribution expenses	68,000
Customer accounts expenses	93,000
Administrative and general expenses	76,000
Construction work in progress	357,000
Total	$806,000

5. Materials and supplies were used by the following departments in the following amounts: Source of Supply, $10,800; Pumping, $6,500; Treatment, $34,500; Transmission and Distribution, $32,200; total, $84,000.

6. On July 2, 2000, utility plant assets that had a historical cost of $25,000 were sold for $15,000 cash.

7. $28,000 of old accounts receivable were written off.

8. During fiscal 2000, the utility instituted a program of deposits to reduce meter damage and customer defaults on water bills. Cash amounting to $15,000 was collected during the year (debit Cash—Customer Deposits).

9. Accounts receivable collections totaled $460,000 for the fiscal year from nongovernmental customers and $38,000 from the General Fund.

10. $800,000 of accounts payable were paid in cash.

11. $500 was recorded as interest expense accumulated on customers' deposits (credit Customer Deposits).

12. Depreciation expense for the year of $47,050 was recorded.

13. Bills for materials and supplies, $7,000, were received and approved for payment on June 30, 2000.

14. One year's interest on notes payable was paid.

15. Interest on long-term notes was charged to Construction Work in Progress.

16. The provision for uncollectible accounts was increased by an amount equal to 1 percent of the sales of water to nongovernmental customers for the year.

17. Cash in the amount of $100,000 was transferred to Restricted Assets—Cash for eventual redemption of five-year notes. As required by the loan agreement, retained earnings in the same amount was reserved.

18. Operating statement accounts for the year were closed.

Required

    a. Record the transactions for the year in general journal form.
    b. Prepare a Balance Sheet as of June 30, 2000.
    c. Prepare a Statement of Revenues, Expenses, and Changes in Retained Earnings for the year ended June 30, 2000.

7–10. *a.* From your solutions to Problems 7–8 and 7–9, prepare a Statement of Cash Flows for the City of Templeton Water Utility Fund for the fiscal year ended June 30, 2000, assuming that cash outflows for operating activities included $310,000 for wages and salaries.

    b. On the basis of your analysis of the financial statements prepared for Problems 7–8, 7–9, and 7–10, comment on any matters that should be brought to the attention of the management of the City of Templeton Water Utility Fund. What actions do you suggest management should take?

Continuous Problem

7–L. *Part 1. Internal Service Fund.* The City of Bingham established a Stores and Services Fund to be operated as an internal service fund to improve purchasing procedures and facilitate inventory management.

Required

    a. Open a general journal for the Stores and Services Fund; enter the following transaction:

        In June 2000, the Stores and Services Fund recorded the receipt of the advance from the General Fund (see Transaction 15 of part *g* of Problem 4–L).

    b. Although no further transactions took place in the year ended June 30, 2000, the Stores and Services Fund was required to prepare (1) a Balance Sheet as of that date and (2) a Statement of Cash Flows for the year ended June 30, 2000, for inclusion in the City of Bingham's annual report.

    c. In order to put the Stores and Services Fund on a completely self-sustaining basis, it was decided to charge using departments for the stores plus a markup sufficient to recover expected cash expenses plus depreciation of equipment. Stores issues for one year were forecast to be $300,000 at cost. Compute the markup rate based on cost from the following information:

        In addition to rent of $500 per month, the estimated expenses were $3,600 a year for utilities; $46,800 for salaries and fringe benefits; and $2,400 a year for operation and maintenance of warehouse equipment. The warehouse equipment was in the basement of City Hall; nobody was quite clear as to when it had been purchased, for what purpose, by whom, or how much it had cost. It was usable, however; and after it was cleaned and minor repairs were made by the Department of Public Works employees, the equipment was turned over to the Stores and Services Fund. The fair value of the equipment is estimated to be $12,000; its remaining useful life is estimated at 10 years.

d. Record in the Stores and Services Fund general journal all of the following transactions, which took place in July 2000. Use account titles and practices illustrated in Chapter. 7.

(1) Warehouse and office space was not available in city-owned buildings; space was rented in a privately owned building for $500 a month. Five percent of the space is assigned to Purchasing, 5 percent to Administration, and 90 percent to Warehousing. Six months' rent was paid in advance. (Charge Prepaid Rent.)

(2) Record the fair value of the equipment contributed to the Stores and Services Fund. Assume the General Fund was given credit for the contribution.

(3) Invoices for stores received were approved for payment in the amount of $30,000.

(4) Vouchers amounting to $20,000 were paid, as was payroll totaling $3,600. (For the payroll, charge Purchasing Expenses, $800; Administrative Expenses, $800; and Warehousing Expenses, $2,000.)

(5) Invoices for utilities for the month were approved for payment in the amount of $300. (Charge to Warehousing Expenses.)

(6) Stores costing $25,000 were issued to the General Fund; an interfund invoice in the proper amount was prepared.

(7) Expenses for operation and maintenance of warehouse equipment totaled $200. This amount was approved for payment.

(8) The Stores and Services Fund used stores of its own that had cost $100. (Charge Administrative Expenses.)

(9) Adjusting and closing entries were recorded as of the end of the first month of operations.

e. Prepare a Statement of Revenues and Expenses and Changes in Retained Earnings of this fund for July 2000.

Part 2. Enterprise Fund. The city water utility is owned and operated by the City of Bingham. The water utility was originally constructed and operated by a private corporation, but it was sold to the City 30 years before the year for which transactions are given. The post-closing trial balance of the Water Utility Fund, as of June 30, 1999, is shown below and on the next page.

CITY OF BINGHAM
Water Utility Fund
Trial Balance
As of June 30, 1999

	Debits	Credits
Cash	$ 144,952	
Customer Accounts Receivable	77,720	
Accumulated Provision for Uncollectible Accounts		$ 2,360
Due from Other Funds	7,000	
Inventory of Supplies	47,073	
Restricted Cash—Customer Deposits	27,638	
Utility Plant in Service	9,500,695	
Accumulated Depreciation—Utility Plant		2,006,139
Property Held for Future Use	100,000	

Construction Work in Progress	594,700	
Accounts Payable		39,210
Matured Interest		217,050
Customer Deposits		27,638
Revenue Bonds Payable, 6%		7,235,000
Unamortized Bond Discount	32,600	
Contributions from Customers		163,210
Contributions from City		425,000
Retained Earnings		416,771
Totals	$10,532,378	$10,532,378

You will need the following additional information about accounts shown on the June 30, 1999, trial balance:

Matured Interest represents six months' accrual of interest on the 6 percent Revenue Bonds. Interest is payable annually on January 1 of each year. Unamortized Bond Discount is credited once a year for the amortization applicable to the year. Amortization is computed by the straight-line method, The balance of $32,600 is to be amortized over 20 years commencing July 1, 1999.

Required

a. Open a general journal for the Water Utility Fund and enter the transactions shown, as necessary. All transactions occurred during the year ended June 30, 2000. Use the account titles shown in this chapter.

   (1) Billings to nonmunicipal customers for water service for the year totaled $1,468,368. Billings to the City of Bingham for water service totaled $20,000.
   (2) Collections from customers totaled $1,445,568; from the City, $7,000.
   (3) Construction work authorized amounted to $234,000. As a part of this, a contract for $112,000 was signed with a private firm; the remainder of the work was to be done by water utility employees.
   (4) Materials and supplies in the amount of $260,800 were ordered. All of these were received during the period. The invoices agreed with the purchase orders and receiving reports and were approved for payment. A perpetual inventory system is used for all materials and supplies.
   (5) Payrolls totaling $289,765 for operations; $83,210 for maintenance; and $36,000 for construction were paid.
   (6) Materials and supplies issued during the period amounted to $120,000 for operations; $52,000 for maintenance; and $84,000 for construction.
   (7) All bond interest due during the year was paid. Debt discount was amortized on the straight-line basis.
   (8) Interest of $14,500 was charged to Construction Work in Progress.
   (9) A progress billing for $56,000 was received from the construction contractor and paid.
   (10) Certain assets under construction at the start of the year and certain of those started during the year were completed and placed in service. The costs incurred on this construction totaled $456,350.
   (11) The water utility paid $178,342 to the general fund as a contribution in lieu of property taxes.

(12) Collection efforts were discontinued on bills amounting to $1,965; the customers owing the bills had paid deposits and interest to the water utility in the amount of $672.

(13) Customer deposits and interest thereon amounting to $1,274 were applied to the final bills of customers discontinuing service. Additional deposits and interest amounting to $1,510 were refunded by check to customers discontinuing service. Deposits totaling $3,427 were received from new customers.

(14) Accounts payable paid during the year amounted to $167,600 for operating supplies, and $84,000 for materials used in construction.

(15) Interest on deposits amount to $628 (charge Operation Expense). Depreciation on utility plant was 2 percent of the beginning balance (round charge to the nearest dollar). The Accumulated Provision for Uncollectible Accounts should equal $2,910 at year-end. Make these and all other adjusting and closing entries necessary at year-end, including the entry for accrual of six months' interest on bonds payable.

b. Prepare a Balance Sheet for the Water Utility Fund as of the end of the year, June 30, 2000.

c. Prepare a Statement of Revenue, Expenses, and Changes in Retained Earnings for the Water Utility Fund for the year ended June 30, 2000.

d. Prepare a Statement of Cash Flows for the Water Utility Fund for the year ended June 30, 2000.

CHAPTER 8

Accounting for Fiduciary Activities—Agency Funds and Cash and Investment Pools

Learning Objectives

After reading this chapter, you should be able to:

~ Explain the purposes of fiduciary funds and distinguish among agency funds and trust funds (expendable, nonexpendable, investment, and pension).

~ Describe the uses for and characteristics of agency funds.

~ Explain the operations of and accounting for commonly used agency funds, including those for:

Special assessment debt service.
Property tax billing and collection.
"Pass-through" intergovernmental monies.

~ Explain the creation and operation of cash and investment pools and accounting and financial reporting requirements for such pools.

Fiduciary funds are used to account for assets held by a governmental unit acting as a trustee or agent for individuals, organizations, other governmental units, or other funds of the same governmental unit. For that reason, fiduciary funds are often identified in governmental financial reports as Trust and Agency Funds. In law, there is a clear distinction between an agency relationship and a trust relationship. In accounting practice, the legalistic distinctions between trust funds and agency funds are not of major significance. The important and perhaps the sole consideration from an accounting standpoint is: What can and what cannot be done with the fund's assets in accordance with the laws and other pertinent regulations?

The name of a particular fund is not a reliable criterion for determining the correct accounting basis for trust and agency funds. Merely calling a fund by one name or another has no influence on the transactions in which it may engage. In fact, the words *trust* and *agency* are frequently omitted from the titles of funds in this classification. Examples are "public employees' retirement system" and "condemnation and grading fund": the former a trust fund, the latter an agency fund, each classified according to the circumstances under which its assets are held. It is sometimes said that a practical basis for distinguishing between the two types is the length of time specific assets are held. But this is not a wholly reliable guide, since there is no generally recognized pronouncement stating the maximum time restriction for holding assets to constitute an agency fund; nor is there a minimum time to constitute a fund of the trust variety. As suggested earlier, if not explicitly stated, the exact name or designation of a given fund is of little significance in establishing its accounting procedures and limitations; these depend on the enactment that brought about creation of the fund, plus all other regulations under which it operates. Regulations include pertinent statutes, ordinances, wills, trust indentures, and other instruments of endowment, resolutions of the governing body, statements of purposes of the fund, kinds and amounts of assets held, and others. This aggregate of factors, or such as are applicable to a given fund, determines the transactions in which it may and should engage.

In this chapter, several important agency relationships appropriately accounted for as agency funds are discussed. Chapter 9 discusses accounting for expendable trust funds, nonexpendable trust funds, investment trust funds, and pension trust funds.

Agency Funds

GASB standards provide *agency funds* as one of the five types of fiduciary funds. **Agency funds** are used to account for assets held by a governmental unit acting as agent for one or more other governmental units, or for individuals or private organizations. Similarly, if a fund of a governmental unit regularly receives assets that are to be transmitted to other funds of that unit, an agency relationship exists. Assets accounted for in an agency fund belong to the party or parties for which the governmental unit acts as agent. Therefore, *agency fund assets are offset by liabilities equal in amount; no fund equity exists.* GASB standards require agency fund assets and liabilities to be recognized on the modified accrual basis used by governmental funds. In the typical case, revenues, expenditures, and expenses are not recognized in the accounts of agency funds.

Unless use of an agency fund is mandated by law, by GASB standards, or by decision of the governing board of a governmental unit, an agency relationship may be accounted for within governmental and/or proprietary funds. For example, local governmental units must act as agent of the federal and state governments in the collection of employees' withholding taxes, retirement contributions, and social security taxes. In the absence of contrary legal requirements or administrative decisions, it is perfectly acceptable to account for the withholdings, and the remittance to federal and state governments, within the funds that account for the gross pay of the employees, as is shown by the illustrative entries in Chapter 4. In general, if an agency relationship is incidental to the primary purposes for which a given fund exists, the relationship is ordinarily discharged on a rather current basis, and the amounts of assets held as agent tend to be small in relation to fund assets, there is no need to create an agency fund unless required by law or administrative decision.

Agency Fund for Special Assessment Debt Service

Readers of Chapters 5 and 6 of this text should recall that GASB standards specify that a governmental unit that has *no* obligation to assume debt service on special assessment debt in the event of property owners' default, but does perform the functions of billing property owners for the assessments, collecting installments of assessments and interest on the assessments, and *from the collections* paying interest and principal on the special assessment debt, should account for those activities by use of an agency fund.

To illustrate *agency fund* accounting for special assessment debt service activities, assume the same information used in Chapter 6 for the City of X except that the governmental unit is not obligated in any manner for the special assessment debt. When the assessments in the amount of $480,000, payable in 10 equal installments, were levied on benefited property owners, the following journal entry was made in the agency fund.

1. Assessments Receivable—Current	48,000	
Assessments Receivable—Deferred	432,000	
Due to Special Assessment Bondholders—Principal		480,000

All current assessments receivable were collected (see Entry 2) along with $24,000 interest (5 percent on the previous unpaid principal). As indicated in Chapter 6, any amounts not collected by the due date should be reclassified as Assessments Receivable—Delinquent.

2. Cash	72,000	
Assessments Receivable—Current		48,000
Due to Special Assessment Bondholders—Interest		24,000

Special assessment bond principal in the amount of $48,000 and interest in the amount of $24,000 were paid during the current year.

3. Due to Special Assessment Bondholders—Principal	48,000	
Due to Special Assessment Bondholders—Interest	24,000	
Cash		72,000

The second installment of assessments receivable was reclassified at year-end from the Deferred category to the Current category.

4. Assessments Receivable—Current	48,000	
Assessments Receivable—Deferred		48,000

This pattern of journal entries will be repeated during each of the remaining nine years until all special assessment bonds are retired.

Tax Agency Funds

An agency relationship that does, logically, result in the creation of an agency fund is the collection of taxes, or other revenues, by one governmental unit for several of the funds it operates and for other governmental units. State governments commonly collect sales taxes, gasoline taxes, and many other taxes that are apportioned to state agencies and to local governmental units within the state. At the local government level, it is common for an elected county official to serve as collector for all property taxes owed by persons or corporations owning property within the county. Taxes levied by all funds and units within the county are certified to the County Collector for collection. The County Collector is required by law to make periodic distributions of tax collections for each year to each fund or unit in the proportion the levy for that fund or unit bears to the total levy for the year. In many jurisdictions, the law provides that units may request advances or "draws" from the tax agency fund prior to regular distributions; advances are usually limited by law to a specified percentage, often 90 percent, of collections for the period from the last distribution until the date of the advance.

Tax agency fund accounting would be quite simple if all taxes levied for a given year were collected in that year. It is almost always true, however, that collections during any year relate to taxes levied in several prior years as well as taxes levied for the current year, and sometimes include advance collections of taxes for the following year. In many jurisdictions, not only does the total tax rate vary from year to year but the proportion that the rate of each unit (and each fund) bears to the total rate also varies from year to year. Additionally, interest and penalties on delinquent taxes must be collected at statutory rates or amounts at the time delinquent taxes are collected; interest and penalties collected must be distributed to participating funds and units in the same manner that tax collections are distributed.

Illustration of Composition of Total Tax Rates

Assume that the County Collector of Campbell County is responsible for collecting the taxes due in 1999 for the funds and units located within the County. Ordinarily, the taxes levied for each fund and unit within the County are shown in columnar form in a newspaper advertisement as legal notice to taxpayers. In order to keep the illustrations in this text legible and comprehensible, Illustration 8–1 shows two columns of such a legal advertisement. Real property tax statements are prepared for each parcel of property located within the jurisdiction for which a tax agency fund is operated. Whether each statement discloses the amount of tax that will be distributed to all of the entities that levy taxes on that parcel, or whether the statement shows only the total tax payable to the County Collector, the Collector's Office must be able to compute and distribute all taxes collected to the appropriate units and funds.

Illustration 8–1

COMPOSITION OF TAXES TO BE COLLECTED
By County Collector of Campbell County
For Certain Units within the County
For the Year 1999

	Washington Township	City of Washington
Total State Rate	$0.01	$ 0.01
County Funds:		
General	1.08	1.08
Capital Projects	0.09	0.09
Debt Service	0.20	0.20
Welfare	0.11	0.11
Total County Rate	1.48	1.48
Library Fund	0.25	0.25
Township Funds:		
General	0.07	0.07
Fire Protection	0.23	—
Total Township	0.30	0.07
School Funds:		
General	4.50	4.50
Capital Projects	0.18	0.18
Debt Service	0.38	0.38
Total School Rate	5.06	5.06
City Funds:		
General		2.53
Street		0.33
Pension		0.25
Debt Service		0.08
Total City Rate		3.19
Total Tax Rates per $100 Assessed Valuation	$7.10	$10.06

For example, Illustration 8–1 shows that a parcel of property located in Washington Township outside the City of Washington would be taxed at the rate of $7.10 per $100 of assessed valuation; whereas if the parcel were inside the city limits, the tax rate would be $10.06. Therefore, if a parcel of property located in Washington Township outside the City had an assessed valuation of $10,000, the total real property tax payable in 1999 would be $710, but a parcel with the same assessed valuation located within the City would be taxed at $1,006. The total of each of these tax statements is comprised of the taxes levied for each unit, as shown in Illustration 8–1. In turn, the taxes levied for each unit are comprised of the taxes levied for funds of that unit, as also shown in Illustration 8–1. The relationship between direct and overlapping dept is discussed in Chapter 6. Note that

Illustration 8–1 shows that a person or organization owning property within the City of Washington is required to pay 66 cents of the total rate for debt service (20 cents to Campbell County, 38 cents to the school district, and 8 cents to the City of Washington). Illustration 8–2 summarizes the composition of each tax statement by governmental unit.

In those states in which taxes are levied on personal property, the funds and units that levy the personal property taxes are generally assumed to be the ones that levy taxes on the residence of the owner, unless there is convincing evidence that the situs of the personal property is at another location. Inasmuch as the tax rate levied for each unit and each fund often varies from year to year, it is necessary that all tax collections be identified with the year for which the taxes were levied as well as with the particular parcels for which taxes were collected.

Operation of the Collector's Office often requires the use of substantial administrative, clerical, and computer time and provision of extensive building and computer facilities. Accordingly, it is common for the Collector to be authorized to withhold a certain percentage from the collections for each unit, and to remit to the County General Fund (or other fund bearing the expenditures for operating the Tax Agency Fund) the total amount withheld from the collections of other funds.

Accounting for Tax Agency Funds

Taxes levied each year should be recorded in the accounts of each fund of each governmental unit in the manner illustrated in preceding chapters. Although an allowance for estimated uncollectible current taxes would be established in each fund, the *gross* amount of the tax levy for all funds should be recorded in the Tax Agency Fund as a receivable. Note the receivable is designated as belonging to other funds and units, and the receivable is offset in total by a liability. Assuming total real property taxes certified for collection during 1999 amounted to $10,516,400, the Tax Agency Fund entry would be:

Illustration 8–2

1999 TAXES PAYABLE
To Campbell County Collector for
Parcel with Assessed Valuation of $10,000

| | Parcel Located | |
Amount Levied by	Outside City	In City
State	$ 1.00	$ 1.00
County	148.00	148.00
Library	25.00	25.00
Township	30.00	7.00
School.	506.00	506.00
City.	—	319.00
Total	$710.00	$1,006.00

1. Taxes Receivable for Other Funds
    and Units—Current 10,516,400
        Due to Other Funds and Units   10,516,400

It would be necessary, of course, for the County Collector to keep records of the total amount of 1999 taxes to be collected for each of the funds and units that participate in the Tax Agency Fund in order to distribute tax collections properly. Assume that the 1999 taxes were levied for the following units (in order to reduce the detail in this example, a number of the units are combined):

State	$ 10,400
Campbell County	1,480,000
Washington School Corporation	5,060,000
City of Washington	2,400,000
Other units (should be itemized)	1,566,000
	$10,516,400

If collections of 1999 taxes during a certain portion of the year amounted to $5,258,200, the Tax Agency Fund entry would be:

2. Cash 5,258,200
        Taxes Receivable for Other Funds and
            Units—Current   5,258,200

The tax collections must in an actual case be identified with the parcels of property against which the taxes were levied, because the location of each parcel determines the governmental units and funds that should receive the tax collections. Assuming for the sake of simplicity that the collections for the period represent collections of 50 percent of the taxes levied against each parcel in Campbell County, and that the County General Fund is given 1 percent of all collections for units other than the County as reimbursement for the cost of operating the Tax Agency Fund, the distribution of the $5,258,200 collections would be:

	Taxes Collected (50% of Levy)	Collection Fee (Charged) Received	Cash to Be Distributed
State	$ 5,200	$ (52)	$ 5,148
Campbell County	740,000	45,182	785,182
Washington School Corporation	2,530,000	(25,300)	2,504,700
City of Washington	1,200,000	(12,000)	1,188,000
Other units (should be itemized)	783,000	(7,830)	775,170
	$5,258,200	$ –0–	$5,258,200

If cash is not distributed as soon as the above computation is made, the entry by the Tax Agency Fund to record the liability would be:

3. Due to Other Funds and Units 5,258,200
     Due to State 5,148
     Due to Campbell County 785,182
     Due to Washington School Corporation 2,504,700
     Due to City of Washington 1,188,000
     Due to Other Units 775,170

If, as is likely, collections during 1999 include collections of taxes that were levied for 1998, 1997, and preceding years, computations must be made to determine the appropriate distribution of collections for each tax year to each fund and unit that levied taxes against the property for which collections have been received.

When cash is distributed by the Tax Agency Fund, the liability accounts shown in Entry 3 should be debited and Cash credited. If cash is advanced to one or more governmental units or funds prior to a regular periodic distribution, the debits to the liability accounts may precede the credits. By year-end, all advances should be settled, all distributions computed and recorded, and all cash distributed to the units and funds for which the Tax Agency Fund is being operated. Therefore, if all those events have taken place, the year-end Balance Sheet for the Tax Agency Fund would consist of one asset: Taxes Receivable for Other Funds and Units—Delinquent; and one liability: Due to Other Funds and Units.

Required Financial Statement

GASB standards require that the comprehensive annual financial report of a governmental unit include a Combining Statement of Changes in Assets and Liabilities—All Agency Funds. This statement is shown as Illustration 8–3. Note the agency fund combining statement is not an operating statement; it is a required part of the CAFR, however, because it discloses changes in the government's custodial responsibilities.

Entries Made by Funds and Units Participating in Tax Agency Funds

Each unit that receives a distribution must record the appropriate portion of it in each of the funds it maintains. In each fund it must also record the fact that cash received differs from the amount of taxes collected by the fee paid to the County General Fund. The fee paid is, of course, recorded as an Expenditure. For example, the computation for the entries to be made by the various funds of Washington School Corporation would be (using the rates shown in Illustration 8–1):

	1999 Rate	Collections of 1999 Taxes	Collection Fee Paid	Cash Received
School Funds:				
General	$4.50	$2,250,000	$22,500	$2,227,500
Capital Projects.	0.18	90,000	900	89,100
Debt Service	0.38	190,000	1,900	188,100
Total	$5.06	$2,530,000	$25,300	$2,504,700

From the computations it can be seen that the entry made in the Washington School Corporation General Fund for the 1999 collections distributed should be:

Illustration 8–3

NAME OF GOVERNMENTAL UNIT
Combining Statement of Changes in Assets and
Liabilities—All Agency Funds
For Fiscal Year Ended December 31, 1999

	Balance January 1, 1999	Additions	Deductions	Balance December 31, 1999
SPECIAL PAYROLL FUND				
Assets				
Cash	$ 6,000	$ 40,900	$ 43,550	$ 3,350
Liabilities				
Vouchers payable	$ 6,000	$ 40,900	$ 43,550	$ 3,350
PROPERTY TAX FUND				
Assets				
Cash	$ 25,800	$ 800,000	$ 725,000	$100,800
Taxes receivable	174,200	1,205,800	800,000	580,000
Total Assets	$200,000	$2,005,800	$1,525,000	$680,800
Liabilities				
Due to other taxing units:				
County	$180,000	$1,085,220	$ 652,500	$612,720
Special District	20,000	120,580	72,500	68,080
Total Liabilities	$200,000	$1,205,800	$ 725,000	$680,800
STUDENT ACTIVITY FUND				
Assets				
Cash	$ 1,600	$ 1,900	$ 1,650	$ 1,850
Liabilities				
Due to student groups	$ 1,600	$ 1,900	$ 1,650	$ 1,850
TOTALS—ALL AGENCY FUNDS				
Assets				
Cash	$ 33,400	$ 842,800	$ 770,200	$106,000
Taxes receivable	174,200	1,205,800	800,000	580,000
Total Assets	$207,600	$2,048,600	$1,570,200	$686,000
Liabilities				
Vouchers payable	$ 6,000	$ 40,900	$ 43,550	$ 3,350
Due to other taxing units	200,000	1,205,800	725,000	680,800
Due to student groups	1,600	1,900	1,650	1,850
Total Liabilities	$207,600	$1,248,600	$ 770,200	$686,000

Source: GASB, *Codification*, Sec. 2200.910.

Cash	2,227,500	
Expenditures	22,500	
Taxes Receivable—Current		2,250,000

Similar entries would be made in the other two funds of the Washington School Corporation and in all the funds of units that paid a tax collection fee to the County General Fund. Collection by the County General Fund of taxes collected for it and the fee collected for it is computed as follows.

	1999 Rate	Collections of 1999 Taxes	Collection Fee	Cash Received
County Funds:				
General	$1.08	$540,000	$45,182	$585,182
Capital Projects.......................	.09	45,000	–0–	45,000
Debt Service	.20	100,000	–0–	100,000
Welfare	.11	55,000	–0–	55,000
Total	$1.48	$740,000	$45,182	$785,182

The entry to be made in the General Fund of Campbell County for the 1999 collections distributed should be:

Cash	585,182	
Taxes Receivable—Current		540,000
Revenues		45,182

"Pass-Through" Agency Funds

Grants, entitlements, or shared revenues from the federal or a state government often pass through a lower level of government (primary recipient) before distribution to a secondary recipient. Accounting for such "pass-through" grants depends on whether the primary recipient government is deemed to have *administrative involvement* or *direct financial involvement* in the grants. According to GASB standards:

> A recipient government has administrative involvement if, for example, it (a) monitors secondary recipients for compliance with program-specific requirements, (b) determines eligibility of secondary recipients or projects, even if using grantor-established criteria, or (c) has the ability to exercise discretion in how the funds are allocated. A recipient government has direct financial involvement if, for example, it finances some direct program costs because of a grantor-imposed matching requirement or is liable for disallowed costs.[1]

More often than not, the criteria for administrative or direct financial involvement are met, in which case the primary recipient government must recognize

---

[1]GASB, *Codification*, Sec. G60.107.

a revenue for the receipt and an expenditure or expense for the transfer in a governmental trust fund, or proprietary fund. If, however, neither administrative nor financial involvement are deemed to exist, then a "Pass-Through" Agency Fund must be used and no revenue or expenditure/expense is recognized. An agency fund should be used also when it is uncertain which funds of a recipient government will be utilizing a grant or other financial assistance from a grantor government. When the determination has been made, revenues and expenditures or expenses will be recognized in the recipient funds. Any assets held temporarily in an agency fund pending determination of the funds to receive the financial assistance should be reported in the notes to the financial statements.[2]

To illustrate accounting for a "Pass-Through" Agency Fund, assume that $5 million of federal financial assistance is received by a state government from the federal government, the full amount of which must be passed to local governments according to predetermined eligibility requirements and in amounts according to a predetermined formula. Since the state government is serving merely as a "cash conduit" in this case, the use of a Pass-Through Agency Fund is deemed appropriate. The entry to record receipt of the $5 million in the Pass-Through Agency Fund would be:

Cash	5,000,000	
Due to Other Units		5,000,000

Assuming all monies were disbursed to the secondary recipients during the current fiscal year, the Pass-Through Agency Fund entry would be:

Due to Other Units	5,000,000	
Cash		5,000,000

The receipt of Cash or other assets from a Pass-Through Agency Fund should be accounted for by the recipient in conformity with GASB standards discussed previously: Governmental fund types are to recognize all grants as revenue when the grant proceeds are available for use for the purposes of the fund. If grant proceeds are available immediately, the Revenues account is credited; if some action prescribed by the conditions of the grant must be taken, the Deferred Revenues account should be credited at the time the grant proceeds are recognized as assets, and amounts transferred from Deferred Revenues to Revenues as grant conditions are met. Proprietary fund types recognize as nonoperating revenues the proceeds of grants for operating purposes, or that may be expended at the discretion of the recipient government; if the terms of the grant restrict the use of the proceeds to the acquisition or construction of capital assets, the proceeds must be recorded as contributed equity.

Cash and Investment Pools

Effective management of cash and investments often is enhanced by placing the cash and investments of the funds in a pool under the control of the Treasurer

---

[2]Ibid., Sec. G60.108.

of the governmental unit or other official. If the cash and investment pool is an **internal investment pool,** (participating funds are all within the same governmental unit), the cash and investments in the pool may properly be placed under accounting control by use of an agency fund. However, each participating fund is required for financial reporting purposes to report its proportionate share of pooled cash and investments as fund assets and assets and liabilities of the agency fund are not reported in the governmental unit's external financial statements.[3] For internal management purposes, it may be more useful for participating funds to use the account title Equity in Pooled Cash and Investments, the account title used in the illustrative agency fund journal entries shown later in this section.

If a cash and investment pool has *external* participants (for example, other governmental units), GASB standards require that an **investment trust fund** be established to account for the **external investment pool.**[4] Investment trust funds are accounted for using an economic resources measurement focus and the full accrual basis of accounting. Accounting and financial reporting requirements for investment trust funds are discussed in more detail in Chapters 9 and 15.

Creation of a Cash and Investment Pool

Earnings on pooled investments and unrealized and realized gains or losses are allocated to the funds having an equity in the pool in proportion to their relative contributions to the pool. To ensure an equitable division of earnings, gains, and losses, and to conform to GASB standards on investment accounting, it is necessary to revalue all investments in the pool, and all investments being brought into the pool or removed from the pool, to their **fair value** as of the time that investments are being brought into or removed from the pool.[5] Each fund that contributes investments to the pool should debit Equity in Pooled Cash and Investments for the fair value of the investments as of the date the pool is being created, credit the Investments account for the carrying value (cost or fair value at the date the investments were previously marked to fair value), and credit or debit Revenues—Change in Fair Value of Investments, depending on whether the current fair value is higher than or lower than carrying value, respectively. Note that a net debit balance in the Revenues—Change in Fair Value of Investments would be reported as a contra-revenue item in the governmental funds operating statement, as a component of investment income, and not as an expenditure.

Illustration 8–4 presents the condition of the newly created Cash and Investment Pool of Drew County as of March 31, 1999. As discussed previously, for an *internal* cash and investment pool, the agency fund assets are allocated back to the participating funds for financial reporting purposes and the agency fund is not reported in the external financial statements. Nevertheless, if the pool is being

---

[3] Ibid., Sec. 150.112.

[4] Ibid., Sec. 150.116.

[5] GASB standards define *fair value* as the amount at which a financial instrument could be exchanged in a current transaction between willing parties, other than in a forced liquidation sale. GASB, *Codification,* Sec. 150.105.

Illustration 8–4

DREW COUNTY
Cash and Investment Pool
Balance Sheet
As of March 31, 1999
(before admission of Capital Projects Fund)

Assets		*Liabilities*	
Cash	$ 1,000,000	Due to General Fund	$ 9,900,000
Investments:		Due to Debt Service Funds	14,850,000
U.S. Treasury Bills	9,545,000	Due to Enterprise Funds	4,950,000
U.S. Agency Obligations	16,385,000		
Repurchase Agreement	2,060,000		
Accrued Interest	710,000		
Total Assets	$29,700,000	Total Liabilities	$29,700,000

accounted for in an agency fund, a balance sheet such as that shown in Illustration 8–4 may be useful for internal management purposes.

On March 31, 1999, Drew County sold tax-supported bonds in the amount of $15,000,000 to finance the construction of roads and bridges. The proceeds of the bonds are added to the pool for investment until such time as they are needed for capital projects fund disbursements. As of March 31, 1999, the U.S. Treasury bills in the pool have a current fair value of $9,535,000 ($10,000 less than the carrying value reported in the balance sheet shown in Illustration 8–4), and the U.S. Agency Obligations in the pool have a fair value of $16,695,000 ($310,000 more than the carrying value reported in the balance sheet); the current fair value of the repurchase agreement is the same as reported in the balance sheet. Therefore, total assets of the pool revalued to fair value as of March 31, 1999, amount to $30,000,000 (a net increase of $300,000 over the carrying values previously reported). The increase in carrying value of assets should be credited to the liability accounts in proportion to the equity of each fund as of March 31 before asset revaluation. The liability to the General Fund, therefore, is increased by $100,000 ($300,000 × $9,900/$29,700); the liability to the debt service funds is increased by $150,000 ($300,000 × $14,850/$29,700); and the liability to the Enterprise Funds is increased by $50,000 ($300,000 × $4,950/$29,700). Note that the equity of each of the funds in the pool remains proportionately the same (i.e., the amount due to the General Fund is $10,000,000 after revaluing the investments to current fair value; total liabilities of the pool are $30,000,000; $10,000/$30,000 = $9,900/$29,700, etc.).

After revaluation of investments in the pool and receipt of $15,000,000 cash from proceeds of bonds sold to finance road and bridge construction, the Balance Sheet of the Cash and Investment Pool, again shown only for illustrative purposes, is shown in Illustration 8–5.

Illustration 8–5

DREW COUNTY
Cash and Investment Pool
Balance Sheet
As of March 31, 1999
(after admission of Capital Projects Fund)

Assets		Liabilities	
Cash	$16,000,000	Due to General Fund	$10,000,000
Investments:		Due to Capital Projects Fund	15,000,000
U.S. Treasury Bills	9,535,000	Due to Debt Service Funds	15,000,000
U.S. Agency Obligations	16,695,000	Due to Enterprise Funds	5,000,000
Repurchase Agreement	2,060,000		
Accrued Interest	710,000		
Total Assets	$45,000,000	Total Liabilities	$45,000,000

Operation of a Cash and Investment Pool

Although the capital projects fund invested $15,000,000 cash in the pool, upon admission to the pool that Fund no longer has a specific claim on the cash of the pool; rather, it (and each other Fund that is a member of the pool) has a proportionate interest in each of the assets of the pool, and will share in earnings, gains, and losses of the pool in that proportion. Ordinarily, it is inconvenient and unnecessary to apportion to liability accounts for each receipt of dividends or interest and each revaluation of the portfolio to fair value (some pools revalue to fair value daily). It is simpler to accumulate the earnings in an *Undistributed Earnings on Pooled Investments* account and the unrealized and realized gains and losses in a *Reserve for Change in Fair Value of Pooled Investments* account (both of these accounts are liability accounts), and to make periodic distributions from these accounts to the specific liability accounts for pool participants.

The frequency of distributions depends on whether all cash of all funds is pooled, or whether each fund retains an operating cash account. In the former case, the pool would have frequent receipts attributable to collections of revenues and receivables of the funds, and would have daily disbursements on behalf of the funds; in this case, the interest of each fund in the pool would have to be recomputed each day. If, however, a working cash balance is retained in each active fund, the receipts and disbursements of pool cash would be much less frequent, and the distribution of gains and losses, and earnings, and recomputation of the interest of each fund in the pool could be correspondingly less frequent.

As an example of accounting for earnings on investments of a pool, assume the pool shown in Illustration 8–5 collects interest of $1,610,000, including $710,000 accrued as of March 31, 1999. An appropriate entry would be:

Cash	1,610,000	
Accrued Interest		710,000
Undistributed Earnings on Pooled Investments		900,000

By the time the earnings are to be distributed, the fair value of all investments may have changed. Even if this is true, the proportionate interest of each fund will not have changed because each fund bears gains and losses proportionately. Therefore, in this example, when earnings are distributed, the shares apportioned to the funds are: General Fund, 10/45 or 2/9; capital projects fund, 15/45 or 3/9; debt service funds, 15/45 or 3/9; and enterprise funds, 5/45 or 1/9. The *agency fund* entry to distribute $900,000 earnings would be:

Undistributed Earnings on Pooled Investments	900,000	
Due to General Fund		200,000
Due to Capital Projects Fund		300,000
Due to Debt Service Funds		300,000
Due to Enterprise Funds		100,000

After the distribution, each fund has the same proportionate interest in the assets of the pool as it had before the distribution.

As noted previously, internal management of the pool is enhanced if each fund that is a member of the pool maintains an asset account with a title such as Equity in Pooled Cash and Investments. The balance of this account in each member fund should be the reciprocal of the Agency fund account that reports the Pool's liability to that member fund. Thus, in the Drew County example, the Drew County General Fund's Equity in Pooled Cash and Investments had a debit balance amounting to $10,000,000 as of March 31, 1999. At the time the distribution of earnings on pooled investments was made, the following entry should be made in the *General Fund* accounts:

Equity in Pooled Cash and Investments	200,000	
Revenues—Investment Earnings		200,000

Interest and dividends earned on pooled investments would, of course, increase the equity of the funds that are members of the pool, as would realized gains on the sales of investments (excess of fair value on date of sale over carrying price) and unrealized gains resulting from periodic revaluation of the pooled investment portfolio to fair value in times of rising market values of securities held in the portfolio. Realized losses on securities sold (deficit of fair value at prior revaluation date compared with fair value at the sale date), and unrealized losses resulting from periodic revaluation of the portfolio in times of falling market values, both decrease the equity of funds that are members of the pool. In the Drew County Cash and Investments Pool example, each member fund maintains an operating cash account. Consequently, the pool does not need to distribute gains and losses daily, so it accumulates realized and unrealized gains and losses in a *Reserve for Change in Fair Value of Pooled Investments* account. This procedure allows a netting of gains and losses in each account, so that only the net realized and unrealized gain (or loss) need be distributed to the member funds, thus saving some clerical or computer time.

GASB standards require that realized and unrealized gains and losses be reported as a single amount, "Change in Fair Value of Investments," as a component of investment income, rather than being reported as separate amounts in the financial statements. However, realized and unrealized gains and losses can be disclosed in the notes to the financial statements, if desired.[6] If a governmental unit intends to disclose realized and unrealized gains or losses, or needs such information for internal management purposes, it may be useful to maintain a separate *Allowance for Changes in Fair Value of Pooled Investments* (a contra-asset account) to record all changes in fair value rather than increasing and decreasing the balance of the investment accounts. This technique permits the investment accounts to be carried at cost.

Assuming that during a certain time period the realized gains on sales of pooled investments of the Drew County Cash and Investments Pool, all credited to the Reserve for Change in Fair Value of Pooled Investments, amounted to $235,000 (measured as excess of fair value at the sale dates over prior fair value). During the same period, realized losses, all debited to the Reserve account totaled $50,000 (measured as the deficit of fair value at the sale dates under prior fair value). Thus, there was a net credit of $185,000 for realized gains and losses for the period. Similarly, assume the net effect of marking the portfolio to fair value is an unrealized gain of $265,000, which is credited to the Reserve account. Assuming no funds have joined the pool or withdrawn from the pool, and the four funds that have continued to be members of the pool have not transferred additional assets to the pool, nor withdrawn any, the realized and unrealized net gains should be distributed to the member funds in the proportions used for the distribution of earnings (2/9, 3/9, 3/9, and 1/9). The distribution is shown in the following *agency fund* entry:

Reserve for Change in Fair Value of Pooled Investments	450,000	
Due to General Fund		100,000
Due to Capital Projects Fund		150,000
Due to Debt Service Funds		150,000
Due to Enterprise Funds		50,000

If all earnings, gains, and losses have been accounted for by the entries illustrated, the interests of the fund are the same as previously:

General Fund	$10,300,000, or 2/9 of total
Capital Projects Fund	15,450,000, or 3/9 of total
Debt Service Funds	15,450,000, or 3/9 of total
Enterprise Funds	5,150,000, or 1/9 of total
Total	$46,350,000

Withdrawal from Pool

If distributions from a pool are not in proportion to the interest of each fund in the pool, the proportionate shares of each fund will change because there is, in effect, a partial withdrawal from the pool of the fund or funds receiving a larger than proportionate distribution. Therefore, prior to such a distribution there should be an

[6]GASB, *Codification*, Sec. 1600.113. If the entity opts, however, to disclose realized gains and losses, they must be measured independently of the basis used for accounting recognition in the pool. That is, the realized gains and losses reported in the notes must be measured as the fair value at the sale date of the investments over (under) cost, rather than over (under) fair value at the prior revaluation date.

apportionment of earnings, gains, and losses to date. The same is true in the event of complete withdrawal of one or more funds from the pool.

Continuing with the Drew County Cash and Investment Pool example, assume the Debt Service Funds need to withdraw $5,000,000 from the pool to retire matured bonds. The entry in the agency fund for the withdrawal would be:

Due to Debt Service Funds	5,000,000	
Cash		5,000,000

After withdrawal of $5,000,000 by the Debt Service Funds, the interests become:

General Fund	$10,300,000, or 24.9% of total
Capital Projects Fund	15,450,000, or 37.3% of total
Debt Service Funds	10,450,000, or 25.3% of total
Enterprise Funds	5,150,000, or 12.5% of total
Total	$41,350,000

This chapter has discussed accounting and financial reporting for one type of fiduciary fund: agency funds. The remaining fiduciary funds—expendable trust funds, nonexpendable trust funds, investment trust funds, and pension trust funds—are the subjects of Chapter 9.

Key Terms

Agency fund,   310
External investment pool,   320
Fair value,   320

Internal investment pool,   320
Investment trust fund,   320

Selected References

Governmental Accounting Standards Board. *Codification of Governmental Accounting and Financial Reporting Standards as of June 30, 1997.* Norwalk, CT, 1997.

Questions

8–1. Explain the distinction(s) between *agency funds* and *trust funds*.

8–2. Why *are fiduciary funds* used by governmental units?

8–3. Must an agency fund be used to account for withholding taxes, retirement contributions, and (if applicable) social security taxes of general fund employees?

8–4. Why do agency funds have no fund equity?

8–5. Under what circumstances should a governmental unit use an agency fund to account for special assessment debt service? What is the rationale for using an agency fund for these transactions?

8–6. What are the most important factors that cause tax agency fund accounting to be complex?

8–7. Why is it considered reasonable for a governmental unit that operates a tax agency fund to charge other governmental units a fee for collecting their taxes, if state law permits such a charge?

8–8. What is a Pass-Through Agency Fund? How does such a fund differ from a Tax Agency Fund?

8–9. What information is shown in a Combining Statement of Changes in Assets and Liabilities—All Agency Funds? Why should that statement be included in the comprehensive annual financial report for a state or local governmental unit?

8–10. Why would an agency fund be created to account for pooled cash and investments?

8–11. Why would pooled investments be revalued to fair value when a fund is added to the pool, or when a fund withdraws from the pool?

8–12. Explain the financial reporting requirements when an agency fund is used for an *internal investment pool*.

Exercises and Problems

8–1. Utilizing the annual report obtained for Exercise 1–1, follow the instructions below:

   a. *Agency Funds.* Are employees' and employer's FICA tax contributions and contributions to other retirement funds accounted for by the General Fund, by an agency fund, or in some other manner (describe)?

   Does the governmental unit operate a tax agency fund? Participate in a tax agency fund operated by another governmental unit?

   Does the government act as agent for owners of property within a special assessment district, and for the creditors of those property owners? Do the Notes to the Financial Statements disclose the agency relationship clearly and fully?

   Does the governmental unit operate one or more pass-through agency funds? If so, describe. If not, is there any evidence that the governmental unit received grants, entitlements, or shared revenues that might properly have been accounted for by a pass-through agency fund?

   b. *Cash and Investment Pools.* Does the governmental unit operate, or participate in, a cash and investments pool? If so, is the pool accounted for as an agency fund? If there is a cash and investment pool and it is not accounted for as an agency fund, how is it accounted for? Explain.

   c. *Financial Statements.* Are agency funds properly disclosed in combined and combining financial statements? Explain the reasons for your answer.

8–2. Write the numbers 1 through 10 on a sheet of paper. Beside each number write the letter corresponding with the best answer to each of the following questions:

1. Which of the following accounts of an agency fund is (are) closed at the end of the fiscal year?
   a. The budgetary accounts.
   b. The operating statement accounts.
   c. Both *a* and *b*.
   d. None of the above.
2. Currently effective GASB standards require each state and local governmental unit to display in agency fund financial statements:
   a. Investment transactions of internal investment pools.
   b. Investment transactions of external investment pools.
   c. Collections of special assessments and interest thereon, and from those collections payment of interest on and principal of special assessment debt for which the government has no obligation.
   d. All of the above.
3. Taxes collected by the County Collector for distribution to other Funds of the County and/or to governmental units within the County should be accounted for in an:
   a. Enterprise Fund.
   b. Internal Service Fund.
   c. Expendable Trust Fund.
   d. Agency Fund.
4. Taxes certified to the County Collector of Leigh County by other County Funds and by other governmental units within the County should be recorded by the Collector by a debit to:
   a. Taxes Receivable—Current and a credit to Revenues.
   b. Taxes Receivable—Current and a credit directly to Fund Balance.
   c. Taxes Receivable for Other Funds and Units—Current and a credit to Due to Other Funds and Units.
   d. Taxes Receivable—Current and a credit to Due to County General Fund.
5. Agency Fund financial data should be displayed in the GPFS in:
   a. The same combined operating statements as the governmental funds of the primary government.
   b. The same combined operating statements as the proprietary funds of the primary government.
   c. The same combined operating statements as the Account Groups of the primary government.
   d. None of the combined operating statements.
6. Changes in agency fund assets and liabilities during a fiscal year should be displayed in the CAFR in the:
   a. Combined Statement of Changes in Assets and Liabilities—All Agency Funds.
   b. Combining Statement of Changes in Assets and Liabilities—All Agency Funds.
   c. Individual statements of each agency fund.
   d. Statistical section of the CAFR.

Items 7 through 10 relate to the following information:

The City Council of the City of Haysville decided to pool the investments of its General Fund, debt service fund, and capital projects fund, each of which carried its investments at fair value as of the prior balance sheet date. All investments are revalued to current fair value at the date of the creation of the pool. At that date, the prior and current fair value of the investments of each of the three funds were as follows:

	Investments	
	Prior Fair Value	Current Fair Value
General Fund	$ 600,000	$ 590,000
Debt Service Fund	3,600,000	3,640,000
Capital Projects Fund	1,800,000	1,770,000
Total	$6,000,000	$6,000,000

7. At the date of the creation of the pool each of the three funds should:
   a. Debit its Fund Balance account and credit its Investments account for the prior fair value of the assets transferred to the pool.
   b. Debit or credit its Investments account as needed to adjust its carrying value to current fair value. The offsetting entry in each fund should be to Fund Balance.
   c. Debit Equity in Pool for the current fair value of investments pooled, credit Investments for the prior fair value of investments pooled, and credit or debit Revenues—Change in Fair Value of Investments for the difference.
   d. Make a memorandum entry only.
8. At the date of creation of the pool, the City of Haysville should account for all the pooled investments in:
   a. An agency fund at fair value at the date the pool is created.
   b. An agency fund at fair value as of the prior balance sheet date.
   c. Its General Fund at fair value at the date the pool is created.
   d. Its General Fund at fair value as of the prior balance sheet date.
9. One day after creation of the pool, investments that had belonged to the Capital Projects Fund were sold for $1,760,000.
   a. The loss of $40,000 is borne by each underlying fund in proportion to its equity in the pool.
   b. The loss of $10,000 is borne by each underlying fund in proportion to its equity in the pool.
   c. The loss of $40,000 is considered to be a loss borne by the Capital Projects Fund.
   d. The loss of $10,000 is considered to be a loss borne by the Capital Projects Fund.
10. One month after creation of the pool, earnings on pooled investments totaled $59,900. It was decided to distribute the earnings to the underlying funds, rounding the distribution to the nearest dollar. The Debt Service Fund should receive:
    a. $36,000.
    b. $35,940.
    c. $36,339.
    d. $37,000.

8–3. For the three years indicated, the rates applicable to real property within the Town of Truxton were as shown below (rates are in terms of dollars and cents per $100 assessed valuation):

Fund or Unit	1998	1999	2000
Town General Fund	$3.12	$ 3.18	$3.30
Town Debt Service Fund	0.44	0.50	0.60
Total Town Rate	3.56	3.68	3.90
Truxton School Corp.	4.70	4.90	5.00
Canton County Library	0.13	0.20	0.30
Canton County	1.54	1.65	1.80
Total Rate	$9.93	$10.43	$11.00

Taxes on all real property located within Canton County are collected by the County Collector, who then distributes collections to the County Funds and to governmental units located within the County. Collections during the second half of 2000 totaled $6,800,000 from property located within the Town of Truxton, which represented collections of the following levies in the following amounts:

From 1998 levy	$ 72,000
From 1999 levy	360,000
From 2000 levy	6,368,000

Required

a. Assuming state law prohibits the County Collector from charging funds and units for the collection service, how much of the $6,800,000 collected in the second half of 1998 should be remitted by the County Collector to the Truxton Town Treasurer? Show computations in good form.

b. How much of the Town's share of collections of the 2000 levy, as computed in part *a* of this problem, should be remitted to the Town's Debt Service Fund? Show computations in good form.

8–4. The County Collector of Springer County is responsible for collecting all property taxes levied by funds and units within the boundaries of the County. In order to reimburse the County for estimated administrative expenses of operating the Tax Agency Fund, the agency fund deducts 1 percent from the collections for the Town, the School District, and the townships. The total amount deducted is added to the collections for the County and remitted to the County General Fund.

The following events occurred in 1999:

1. Current-year tax levies to be collected by the agency fund were:

County General Fund	$1,420,000
Town of Cronan General Fund	2,287,100
Springer Co. Consolidated	
School District	3,920,000
Various Townships	960,000
Total	$8,587,100

2. $15,100 was charged back to the Town of Cronan because of errors in the computation of that unit's current taxes.
3. $4,190,000 of current taxes were collected during the first half of 1999.
4. Liabilities to all funds and units as the result of the first half-year collections were recorded. (A schedule of amounts collected for each participant, showing amount withheld for the County General Fund and net amounts due the participants, is recommended for determining amounts to be recorded for this transaction. Round computation of the final amounts to the nearest dollar.)
5. All money in the Tax Agency Fund was distributed.

Required

a. Make journal entries for each of the foregoing transactions that affected the Tax Agency Fund.
b. Make journal entries for each of the foregoing transactions that affected the County General Fund. Begin with the tax levy entry, assuming 3 percent of the gross levy will be uncollectible.
c. Make journal entries for each of the foregoing entries that affected the Town of Cronan General Fund. Begin with the tax levy entry, assuming 3 percent of the gross levy will be uncollectible.

8–5. The City of Fayette agreed to bill each owner of each parcel of property within Special Assessment District No. 21 for each installment of the owner's share of the total assessment for the construction project being undertaken by that Special Assessment District. The City agreed to collect the installments and interest thereon, and agreed to use the collections to pay interest and principal due on debt incurred for the construction project, although the City is not obligated in any manner for the special assessment debt.

Required

a. Name the fund type that should be used by the City of Fayette to record the activities described above. Explain the reason for your answer.
b. If the total assessment for the project to be undertaken by the Special Assessment District is $3,600,000, to be collected in three equal annual installments, show in general journal form the entry that should be made for the total assessment, assuming all installments are to be used for service of debt incurred for this project.
c. Show in general journal form the entry that should be made for collections from owners of property within Special Assessment District No. 21 of the first installment amounting to $1,276,000 ($1,160,000 for principal and $116,000 for interest).
d. Show in general journal form the entry that should be made to record the payment of interest amounting to $110,000 and principal amounting to $1,150,000 on debt incurred for the Special Assessment District No. 21 project.
e. Assuming all transactions described above occurred in the fiscal year ended June 30, 1999 and the City of Fayette had no other transactions during that year with the property owners or creditors of Special Assessment District No. 21:
(1) Name the general purpose financial statement, or statements, of the City of Fayette in which the results of the transactions described above should be reported, and state which information about the transactions should be reported in each statement you name.

(2) If the effects of the transactions described above should be reported in a statement included in the CAFR, but not in the GPFS, name the statement and describe its purpose.

8–6. Marshall County customarily receives from various federal government agencies resources that are designated for the use of the governmental units within the County. These resources are accounted for by the County in a Pass-Through Agency Fund.

Required

a. Show in general journal form the entries in the Pass-Through Fund for the following events and transactions, which occurred in 1999.
   (1) The County received in cash a grant of $40,000,000, which is to be distributed to various units within the County in a manner not yet specified.
   (2) Official notice was received that $17,000,000 of the above grant is to be distributed to the City of Pittsfield for public improvements. The distribution was made.
   (3) Official notice was received that $16,000,000 was to be distributed to the County Road and Bridge Fund. The distribution was made. Remaining cash was invested in marketable securities.
   (4) The County received in cash a grant of $3,000,000, to be distributed to law enforcement agencies throughout the County in a manner yet to be specified. The cash was invested in marketable securities.

b. Show in general journal form the entries that should be made in a Capital Projects Fund of the City of Pittsfield for the following:
   (1) $17,000,000 was received from the Marshall County Pass-Through Agency Fund.
   (2) A construction contract in the amount of $7,000,000 was signed.

c. Assuming Marshall County operated a Federal Payroll Tax Agency Fund in addition to the Pass-Through Agency Fund, and the cash balance of the Federal Payroll Tax Agency Fund on January 1, 1999 was $125,800, additions during the year were $850,000, disbursements during the year were $815,500, and the ending balance was held in Cash, prepare a Combining Statement of Changes in Assets and Liabilities—All Agency Funds for Marshall County for the year ended December 31, 1999.

8–7. The City Council of the City of Liberty decided to pool the investments of its General Fund, its Capital Projects Fund, and its Debt Service Fund, each of which had accounted for its investments at fair value as of the end of the last fiscal year. At the date of the creation of the pool, the current fair value of the investments of each of the three funds were as follows:

	Investments	
	Prior Fair Value	Current Fair Value
General Fund	$ 800,000	$ 790,000
Capital Projects Fund	4,600,000	4,740,000
Debt Service Fund	3,000,000	3,060,000
Total	$8,400,000	$8,590,000

Required

a. Show the entry that should be made by (1) the General Fund, (2) the Capital Projects Fund, and (3) the Debt Service Fund, to do the following: open a new asset account, Equity in Investment Pool, in the amount of the current fair value of the investments transferred to the pool; close the existing Investments account; and debit or credit the Revenues account of each fund as needed to balance the entry.

b. Show in general journal form the entries to be made in the accounts of the Investments Pool Agency Fund to record the following transactions of the first year of its operations:

   (1) Record at current fair value the investments transferred to the pool; assume the investments of the General Fund were in U.S. Treasury bills, and the investments of both the Capital Projects Fund and the Debt Service Fund were in certificates of deposit.

   (2) Certificates of deposit that had been recorded at a fair value of $1,000,000 matured. The pool received $1,050,000 in cash ($1,000,000 for the face of the CDs and $50,000 interest). The entire amount was reinvested in a new issue of certificates of deposit.

   (3) Interest on Treasury bills was collected in the amount of $50,000, and interest on certificates of deposit was collected in the amount of $300,000. These amounts were reinvested in Treasury bills.

   (4) Interest on certificates of deposit accrued at year-end amounted to $28,250.

   (5) At the end of the year, it was decided to compute and record the pool's liability to each of the three member funds for its proportionate share of earnings on the pooled investments. Carry your computation of each fund's proportionate share to four decimal places. Round the amount of the distribution to each fund to the nearest dollar.

c. Record in each of the three member funds the increase in its Equity in Investment Pool.

8–8. This problem continues the City of Liberty Investment Pool Agency Fund (Problem 8–7).

Required

Show in general journal form the entries for the following transactions by the investments pool in the second year of its existence.

   (1) It was decided that the Debt Service Fund should withdraw $2,000,000 from the investment pool because of the imminent need for cash to redeem matured bonds. Accordingly, the investments of the pool were revalued at current fair value—U.S. Treasury bills, $1,200,000; and certificates of deposit, $7,900,000. The current fair values are recorded by the investment pool, and the liability to each of the three funds for its proportionate share of the unrealized increase in the fair values of investments is recorded.

   (2) Cash in the amount of interest accrued at the end of the prior year is received.

   (3) U.S. Treasury bills carried at the amount of $500,000 are sold for $500,000. Certificates of deposit in the amount of $1,500,000 matured, and the face amount was collected in cash.

   (4) The amount the Debt Service Fund wished to withdraw, $2,000,000, is paid in cash.

(5) Interest collected in cash during the remainder of the year amounted to $26,000;. $3,840 of interest was accrued at year-end.

(6) At the end of the year, it was decided to compute and record the liability to each member fund for its shares of earnings on pooled investments for the second year. (Compute the distribution on the basis of the proportionate share of each fund in the pool after the Debt Service Fund's withdrawal of $2,000,000.)

Continuous Problem

8–L. The City of Bingham utilizes a Pass-Through Agency Fund to account for grants, entitlements, and shared revenues that may be used in more than one fund pending determination by the City Council of the City of Bingham, or which the City of Bingham receives as primary recipient of grants, and that must be transmitted, without discretion of the City of Bingham, to other governmental units.

The Pass-Through Agency Fund had disbursed all cash received during the fiscal year ended June 30, 1999, and had no assets or liabilities on that date.

Required

a. Open a general journal for the City of Bingham Pass-Through Agency Fund and record the following events and transactions that occurred during the fiscal year ended June 30, 2000:

(1) The City of Bingham is designated as the primary recipient of a grant from a federal agency. The City must remit 30 percent of the grant proceeds to the Bingham School Corporation and 10 percent of the grant proceeds to Bingham Township, both of which are governmental units independent of the City of Bingham. The remaining 60 percent of the grant proceeds may be spent by the City of Bingham for "ordinary and necessary maintenance and operating expenses," with distribution to City funds to be determined by the City of Bingham City Council. In January 2000, the grantor agency informed the City of Bingham that the total amount of the grant is to be $800,000; the entire amount is to be paid to the City within 60 days of notification.

(2) The City receives cash in the full amount of the grant, $800,000.

(3) The City remits the amounts due to the secondary recipients of the grant: Bingham School Corporation and Bingham Township. Remaining cash is invested in short-term certificates of deposit until the City Council determines the proper disposition of the City's share of the grant.

(4) The certificates of deposit matured and were converted into cash. Interest in the amount of $4,000 is received in cash on the certificates of deposit; this amount must, under terms of the grant, be added to the amount of the grant to be used at the discretion of the City Council.

(5) The City Council determined that the entire amount of the City's share of the grant should be expended by the General Fund for purposes included in

General Fund appropriations recorded in Problem 3–L, as amended in Problem 4–L. (You may assume the City's share of grant proceeds, plus interest, is included in transaction 7 of Problem 4–Lg, as a part of Intergovernmental Revenue.)

b. Prepare a Statement of Changes in Assets and Liabilities for the Pass-Through Agency Fund for the year ended June 30, 2000. You may use the form shown as Illustration 8–3.

CHAPTER 9

Accounting for Fiduciary Activities—Trust Funds and Pension Plans

Learning Objectives

After studying this chapter, you should be able to:

~ Describe the characteristics of each of the following fund types:

Expendable trust funds.

Nonexpendable trust funds.

Investment trust funds.

Pension trust funds and similar funds for post-employment benefits administered by a pension plan.

~ Account for and explain the financial reporting requirements for each of the preceding fund types as well as employer accounting and financial reporting for pensions.

In addition to agency funds discussed in Chapter 8, the fiduciary fund classification includes expendable trust funds, nonexpendable trust funds, investment trust funds, and pension trust funds (also referred to as public employee retirement systems).

Trust funds differ from agency-funds principally in degree: Frequently a trust fund is in existence over a longer period of time than an agency fund; it represents and develops vested interests to a greater extent; and it involves more complex administrative and financial problems. In both trust and agency funds, the governmental unit has a fiduciary relationship with the creators and beneficiaries of the trust or agency. A historically important reason for the creation of a trust fund is the acceptance by a governmental unit of trusteeship over assets to be invested to produce income to be used for specified purposes (generally cultural or educational). The fair value of the assets placed in trust under such an agreement is referred to as the *principal*, or *corpus*, of the trust. Since the principal of this form of trust must be held intact in order to produce income, the trust is called *nonexpendable*. Nonexpendable trust funds are often called **endowment funds.** The income from the assets of a nonexpendable trust may be used only for the purposes specified by the trustor; therefore, the income is *expendable*. Separate funds should be established to account for expendable and nonexpendable assets. Nonexpendable trust funds should be accounted for in essentially the same manner as proprietary funds (Internal Service Funds and Enterprise Funds, discussed in Chapter 7). Expendable trust funds should be accounted for in essentially the same manner as the governmental funds discussed in Chapters 3 through 6.

GASB standards issued in 1997 created a new type of trust fund: the *investment trust fund*.[1] This fund is used to account for external investment pools. **External investment pools** are centrally managed investment portfolios (pools) that manage the investments of participants (for example, other governmental units and not-for-profit organizations) outside the reporting entity of the government that administers the pool. Typically, the sponsoring government also participates in the pool; however, its equity in the pool is considered *internal* and is not reported in the financial statements of the investment trust fund. As discussed in Chapter 8, the assets representing the internal portion of the pool are reported on the balance sheet of each of the participating funds of the sponsoring government. Thus, only the portion of the pooled investments representing the equity of the *external* participants is reported in the financial statements of the investment trust fund. Investment Trust Funds should be accounted for in essentially the same manner as nonexpendable trust funds and proprietary funds, but their financial statements are more similar to those of pension trust funds (discussed later in this chapter) than those of nonexpendable funds and proprietary funds. Similar to pension trust funds, investment trust funds are not required to provide a Statements of Cash Flows. Further discussion of investment trust funds is beyond the scope of this text.

GASB standards previously required governments that operated deferred compensation plans for their employees under Internal Revenue Code (IRC) Section

---

[1]GASB, *Codification*, Sec. 150.116.

457 to account for such plans in an agency fund. That treatment was consistent with then existing law, which permitted such assets to remain in the control of the employer government "until made available to the plan participants or beneficiaries."[2] Effective August 20, 1996, the laws governing IRC Section 457 plans required that the assets and income from the assets of new plans be held in trust for employees.[3] Existing plans have until January 1, 1999, to comply with the new law. Accordingly, GASB issued new standards in 1997 that require, effective for periods beginning after December 31, 1998, that IRC Section 457 plans be reported as an expendable trust fund, rather than as an agency fund.[4] Plan investments should be reported at fair value.

Accounting for Trust Funds—General Recommendations

The rules of law pertaining to testamentary and intervivos trusts are applicable to trusts in which a government acts as trustee; trust fund accounting information systems are therefore constrained by the trust laws of the states. A primary problem is the distinction between transactions that affect the trust principal, or corpus, and transactions that relate to trust income. A case in point is the accounting treatment of depreciable assets. Governmental funds discussed in Chapters 3 through 6 do not account for fixed assets. However, if fixed assets are included in the principal of a trust fund, they obviously must be accounted for. Therefore, GASB standards specify that nonexpendable trust funds follow the accounting practices recommended for proprietary funds discussed in Chapter 7. However, under the older rules of trust law that still govern some trusts, cash basis accounting is assumed, which means the principal of the fund would record the fair value of the fixed assets at date of creation of the trust and carry that value until the assets were disposed of; no depreciation during that time would be recognized, nor would any difference between par and the fair value of securities held as part of the principal be amortized.

Trust laws adopted in many states make it possible for a trustor to specify that the income of the fund be computed on the accrual basis. If that is done, depreciation would be recognized as an expense and cash retained in the nonexpendable fund, or transferred to it, in the amount of depreciation and amortization taken—thus maintaining the fund principal at its original dollar amount. Accrual accounting, accompanied by "funding the depreciation" (as the retention of cash to offset depreciation expense is called), enables the administrators to maintain the principal intact, in the sense of maintaining the original dollar amount, which the older rules of trust law and cash basis accounting do not do. More important than

---

[2]Governmental Accounting Standards Board, *Statement No. 32*, "Accounting and Financial Reporting for Internal Revenue Code Section 457 Deferred Compensation Plans" (Norwalk, CT, 1997), par. 1.

[3]IRC Section 457 (g)(1).

[4]GASB, *Statement No. 32*, par. 4.

maintaining fund principal at its original dollar amount is maintaining or enhancing the earning power of the assets placed in trust. Cash basis accounting offers no help in the measurement of the degree of success of trust fund administrators in maintaining or improving the earning power of the assets comprising the fund principal. Accordingly, GASB standards require nonexpendable trust funds to be kept on the full accrual basis.

Although some states still adhere to the old law of trust, in which gains and losses serve to increase or decrease the principal of the trust rather than affect the distributable income, most states have adopted some version of the Uniform Management of Institutional Funds Act (UMIFA) which dates back to the 1970s and some have adopted the Uniform Prudent Investors Act (1994). These Acts set standards for portfolio management and delegation of investment authority. The effect of the legislative trend has been to liberalize the amount of portfolio gains that can be considered income, while retaining a prudent portion of gains in the principal to permit it to stay abreast of inflation.

Budgetary Accounts

Budgetary accounts generally are not needed for nonexpendable trust funds because transactions of the fund result in changes in the fund principal only incidentally; by definition, the principal cannot be appropriated or expended. Expendable trust funds, on the other hand, may be required by law to use the appropriation procedure to ensure adequate notice to affected parties as to the expenditure of fund assets. If the appropriation procedure is required, the use of budgetary accounts by expendable trusts is recommended for reasons discussed at length in preceding chapters of this text.

Illustrative Case—Nonexpendable Trust Funds and Expendable Trust Funds

As an illustration of the nature of accounting for nonexpendable and expendable trust funds, assume on November 1, 1999, James Smith died, having made a valid will that provided for the gift of various securities to the City of Columbia to be held as a nonexpendable trust. Net income from the securities is to be computed on the full accrual basis, in conformity with generally accepted accounting principles. The will specifies that investment income (dividends and interest) received in cash, as well as accrued investment income, is to be used to partially finance operations of the Columbia Library. To facilitate accounting for the receipt and expenditure of endowment income, City officials created a Library Operating Fund, which is to be accounted for as an expendable trust fund. According to the provisions of the will, all gains and losses, both realized and unrealized, are to be retained in Fund Balance and are not considered available for use by the Library Operating Fund. In this jurisdiction, the latter fund is operated as a budgetary fund on the modified accrual basis described in Chapters 3 and 4. The gift was accepted by the City of Columbia and a Library Endowment Fund was established to account for the nonexpendable trust. The following securities were received by the Library Endowment Fund:

	Interest Rate per Year	Maturity Date	Face Value	Fair Value as of 11/1/99
Bonds:				
AB Company	10%	1/1/04	$330,000	$340,000
C & D Company	9	7/1/01	110,000	112,000
D & G Company	9	1/1/19	200,000	200,000
Total			$640,000	$652,000

	Number of Shares	Fair Value as of 11/1/99
Stocks:		
M Company, common	2,400	$126,000
S Company, common	10,000	96,000
K Company, common	3,000	129,000
GF Company, common	2,000	145,000
Total		$496,000

Illustrative Entries—
Nonexpendable
Trust Fund

The receipt of the securities by the Library Endowment Fund is properly recorded at the fair value of the securities as of the date of the gift because this is the amount the trustees are responsible for. Although the trustees will receive the face value of the bonds at maturity (if the bonds are held until maturity), GASB standards require that investments in bonds maturing more than one year from receipt must be reported at fair value on the balance sheet date. Further, amortization of the difference between fair value of the bonds and their face value (discount or premium) is *not* permitted.[5] For investment management purposes, it may be prudent to retain the original fair value at receipt of the gift in the Investment account and utilize an Allowance for Change in Fair Value of Investments contra-asset account to account for all changes in fair value. For simplicity, in this example, changes in fair value are recorded directly in the investment accounts. Assuming that accrued interest on the bonds received by gift (payable on January 1 and July 1 each year) is to be recorded as part of the corpus or principal of the trust, the entry in the Library Endowment Fund to record the receipt of the securities as of November 1, 1999, is:

1. Investment in Bonds	652,000	
Investment in Stocks	496,000	
Accrued Interest Receivable	20,300	
Fund Balance		1,168,300

[Interest accrued is AB ($330,000 × 10% × 4/12 = $11,000), C&D ($110,000 × 9% × 4/12 = $3,300) and D&G ($200,000 × 9% × 4/12 = $6,000).]

---

[5]Ibid., Sec. 150.111.

As of January 1, 2000, interest is received on all bonds—$16,500 from AB Company; $4,950 from C&D Company; and $9,000 from D&G Company; however, only two months of this interest (one-third of the total) is earned investment revenue that can be transferred to the Library Operating Fund. The entry for the receipt of bond interest on January 1, 2000, and the revenue earned for transfer to the Library Operating Fund is:

2. Cash	30,450	
Accrued Interest Receivable		20,300
Revenues—Bond Interest		10,150

Dividends on stock do not accrue. They become a receivable only when declared by the corporation issuing the stock. Ordinarily the receivable is not recorded because it is followed in a reasonably short time by issuance of a dividend check. Assuming dividends on the stock held by the Library Endowment Fund were received early in January 2000, in the amount of $9,800, Entry 3 is appropriate:

3. Cash	9,800	
Revenues—Dividends		9,800

The Library Endowment Fund has sufficient cash to pay the amount owed to the Library Operating Fund for bond interest during the two months since the bond interest and stock dividends were received in cash. Assuming cash is transferred as of January 3, 2000, Entry 4 is:

4. Operating Transfers Out	19,950	
Cash		19,950

On the advice of an investment manager, 1,000 shares of GF Company stock were sold for $78,750; this amount and cash of $19,000 were invested in 2,000 shares of LH Company common stock. The GF Company stock sold was half the number of shares received when the trust was established; therefore, it was recorded at its fair value then of $72,500; the difference between its book value and the proceeds is considered in this trust to belong to the corpus and does not give rise to gain or loss that would be transferred to the Library Operating Fund. Therefore, the sale of GF Company stock and the purchase of LH Company stock should be recorded in the Library Endowment Fund as shown in Entries 5a and 5b:

5a. Cash	78,750	
Investment in Stocks		72,500
Change in Fair Value of Investment in Stocks		6,250
5b. Investment in Stocks	97,750	
Cash		97,750

Assuming there were no further purchases or sales of stock and that dividends received on April 1, 2000, amounted to $9,920, Entry 6a is necessary, as well as Entry 6b to make the required operating transfer to the Library Operating Fund.

6a. Cash	9,920	
Revenues—Dividends		9,920

6b. Operating Transfers Out	9,920	
Cash		9,920

Interest accrued on June 30, 2000, amounted to $30,450, the same amount received early in January 2000. The fair value of the Library Endowment Fund investments as of June 30, 2000, is given below.

		Fair Value as of 11/1/99	Fair Value as of 6/30/00	Change in Fair Value
Bonds:				
AB Company		$340,000	$360,000	$20,000
C & D Company		112,000	108,000	(4,000)
D & G Company		200,000	206,000	6,000
Total		$652,000	$674,000	$22,000
Stocks:	*No. of Shares*			
M Company	2,400	$126,000	$132,000	$ 6,000
S Company	10,000	96,000	98,000	2,000
K Company	3,000	129,000	122,000	(7,000)
GF Company	1,000	72,500	75,500	3,000
LH Company	2,000	97,750	96,450	(1,300)
Total		$521,250	$523,950	$ 2,700

Entry 7a records the accrual of interest earned for transfer to the Library Operating Fund. Entry 7b records the adjusting entry to record the change in fair value during the fiscal year, as required by GASB standards. Entry 7c records the liability to the Library Operating Fund.

7a. Accrued Interest Receivable	30,450	
Revenues—Bond Interest		30,450
7b. Investment in Bonds	22,000	
Investment in Stocks	2,700	
Change in Fair Value of Investments		24,700
7c. Operating Transfers Out	30,450	
Due to Library Operating Fund		30,450

The closing entry at fiscal year-end, 6-30-00, is shown in Entry 8.

8. Revenues—Bond Interest	40,600	
Revenues—Dividends	19,720	
Change in Fair Value of Investment	30,950	
Operating Transfers Out		60,320
Fund Balance		30,950

*Illustrative Financial
Statements—
Nonexpendable
Trust Fund*

At June 30, the end of the City of Columbia's fiscal year, the Library Endowment Fund should prepare financial statements for inclusion in the City's annual report, although the fund was created on November 1, 1999 and has been in operation only eight months. No adjustments in addition to Entries 7a, 7b, and 7c are necessary as of June 30 because dividends on stock are not accrued. The financial statements required for this nonexpendable trust fund for inclusion in the City's report for the period ended June 30, 2000, are shown in Illustrations 9–1, 9–2, and 9–3.

Illustration 9–1

CITY OF COLUMBIA
Library Endowment Fund
Balance Sheet
As of June 30, 2000

Assets		*Liabilities and Fund Equity*	
Cash	$ 1,300	Due to Library Operating Fund	$ 30,450
Accrued interest receivable	30,450	Fund Balance	1,199,250
Investments:			
Bonds, at fair value	674,000		
Stock, at fair value	523,950		
		Total Liabilities and	
Total Assets	$1,229,700	Fund Equity	$1,229,700

Illustration 9–2

CITY OF COLUMBIA
Library Endowment Fund
Statement of Revenues, Expenses, and Changes in Fund Balance
Eight Months Ended June 30, 2000

Revenues:	
Interest on bonds	$ 40,600
Dividends on stock	19,720
Net increase in fair value of investments	30,950
Total Revenues	91,270
Expenses:	–0–
Income before operating transfers	91,270
Other financing sources (uses):	
Operating transfers to Library Operating Fund	(60,320)
Net increase (decrease) in fund balance	30,950
Fund balance received from Executor, November 1, 1999	1,168,300
Fund Balance, June 30, 2000	$1,199,250

Illustration 9–3

CITY OF COLUMBIA
Library Endowment Fund
Statement of Cash Flows
For Eight Months Ended June 30, 2000

Cash flows from investing activities:	
Interest and dividends on investments	$50,170
Proceeds of sale of investments	78,750
Purchase of investments	(97,750)
Net cash provided by investing activities	31,170
Cash flow from noncapital financing activities:	
Operating transfers to expendable trust	(29,870)
Net increase in cash and cash equivalents	1,300
Cash and cash equivalents, November 1, 1999	–0–
Cash and cash equivalents, June 30, 2000	$ 1,300

**Reconciliation of Net Increase in Fund Balance to Net Cash
Provided by Investing and Noncapital Financing Activities**

Net increase in fund balance	$30,950
Adjustments:	
Increase in accrued interest receivable	(10,150)
Excess of purchases of investments over sales of investments	(19,000)
Increase in unrealized fair value of investments	(24,700)
Realized gain on sale of investments	(6,250)
Increase in interfund liability	30,450
Total adjustments	(29,650)
Net cash provided by investing and noncapital financing activities	$ 1,300

Investments are displayed in the balance sheet (Illustration 9–1) at fair value on the balance sheet date, in conformity with GASB standards. Note that the equity account of a nonexpendable trust fund is called Fund Balance instead of Contribution from Trustor, although the fund is said to be accounted for in a manner similar to proprietary funds. Since no earnings are retained by the non-expendable trust fund, there is no need for a Retained Earnings account, and the name given to the single equity account is moot.

**Illustrative Entries—
Expendable Trust
Fund**

In the case of the gift of James Smith to the City of Columbia, the trust corpus, or principal, was nonexpendable. Accounting for the nonexpendable trust fund, the Library Endowment Fund, which was established to account for the gift, is illustrated in the preceding sections. By the terms of James Smith's will, endowment income (interest and dividends) is to be transferred to the City's Library to help finance library operations. As noted previously, recognized changes in fair value of investments increase or decrease the fund balance of the nonexpendable trust fund and do not affect income that can be distributed to the Columbia Library. In many cases, a city library is operated as a special revenue fund of the city. Endowment fund income in such cases can be transferred to the special revenue fund. In this case, however, City officials deemed it necessary to create a separate Library Operating Fund to be accounted for as an expendable trust fund. Accounting for an expendable trust fund is similar in nature to accounting for general and special revenue funds described in Chapters 3 and 4.

Since the Library Operating Fund was not created until November 1, 1999, and the City's fiscal year 2000 started on July 1, 1999, the income from Mr. Smith's endowment was not foreseen when the City Council approved the budget for fiscal year 2000. After the securities were transferred to the Library Endowment Fund and an estimate could be made of the revenues to be made available to the Library Operating Fund, the City Council approved the Library Director's recommended operating budget for the Library Operating Fund. The budget provided for estimated revenues of $60,000 and appropriations for subscriptions to periodicals of $9,000 and purchases of books of $50,000. Entry 1 is required to record the budget of the Library Operating Fund (subsidiary ledger detail should be recorded, as described in Chapters 3 and 4; the detail is omitted from the illustration in this chapter):

1. Estimated Revenues	60,000	
Appropriations		59,000
Fund Balance		1,000

The Library Operating Fund received $19,950 from the Library Endowment Fund:

2. Cash	19,950	
Operating Transfers In		19,950

The Library Operating Fund ordered subscriptions for periodicals expected to cost $7,000 and ordered books expected to cost $12,000:

3. Encumbrances—2000	19,000	
Reserve for Encumbrances—2000		19,000

The Library Operating Fund received $9,920 from the Library Endowment Fund. It also received and approved for payment invoices from magazine publishers ($7,100) and book publishers ($12,160), fulfilling all purchase orders recorded in Entry 3.

4a. Cash	9,920	
Operating Transfers In		9,920
4b. Reserve for Encumbrances—2000	19,000	
Expenditures—2000	19,260	
Encumbrances—2000		19,000
Vouchers Payable		19,260

The Library ordered books expected to cost $37,000 in anticipation of receiving further distributions from the Library Endowment Fund.

5. Encumbrances—2000	37,000	
Reserve for Encumbrances—2000		37,000

The Library Operating Fund recorded a receivable in the amount of $30,450 from the Library Endowment Fund for bond interest earned.

6. Due from Library Endowment Fund	30,450	
Operating Transfers In		30,450

Although in an actual situation the entries illustrated above would be incorporated with entries recording other transactions and events affecting the Library Operating Fund, for the purposes of this chapter only the effect of illustrated entries on the closing process is shown below:

7. Appropriations	59,000	
Operating Transfers In	60,320	
Estimated Revenues..................................		60,000
Expenditures—2000		19,260
Encumbrances—2000		37,000
Fund Balance		3,060

Financial statements prepared for the Library Operating Fund for inclusion in the City of Columbia's annual report for the period ending June 30, 2000, would be similar in content and format to those illustrated in Chapters 3 and 4. Thus, no financial statements for the Library Operating Fund are presented here.

Pension Accounting

Assets held by public pension plans at December 31, 1996, amounted to over $1 trillion.[6] Thus, it is not surprising that the GASB has devoted substantial effort to improving accounting and financial reporting for pension plans. This chapter provides an overview of the accounting and reporting requirements for pension plans, as well as the governmental employers that sponsor such plans.

Pension plans are of two general types, *defined contribution plans* and *defined benefit plans*. A **defined contribution plan** specifies the amount or rate of contribution, often a percentage of covered salary, that the employer and employees must contribute to the members' accounts in the pension plan. The level of benefits payable upon retirement is determined by the total amount of contributions to a member's account, earnings on investments, and allocations of forfeited contributions of other members credited to the account.[7] Because future benefits are neither formula-based nor guaranteed, the risk associated with defined contribution plans rests primarily with employees; the employer's responsibility essentially ends once the required contribution is made. Such plans ordinarily are *not* administered on an actuarial basis; therefore, accounting and financial reporting requirements for both the plan and the employer are straightforward and present few complications. Essentially, the plan reports the fair value of pension assets and any liability for

---

[6]U.S. Bureau of the Census, *Quarterly Public Employment Survey*, Table 1.
[7]GASB, *Codification*, Sec. Pe5.525.

accrued plan benefits; the employer reports expenditures/expenses for the amount contributed to plan. Both the plan and the employer are required to provide in the Notes to the Financial Statements a brief description of the plan, classes of employees covered, plan provisions, contribution requirements, significant accounting policies for the plan, and concentrations of investments in any one organization that exceed 5 percent or more of plan net assets.[8]

A **defined benefit plan** provides a specified amount of benefits based on a formula that may include such factors as age, salary, and years of employment.[9] Determining the present value of projected pension benefits involves numerous factors, such as employee mortality, employee turnover, salary progression, and investment earnings. To ensure that plan assets will be adequate to cover future benefits, professional actuaries are engaged to calculate the present value of benefits and the required contributions that must be made by employers and, in some cases, employees. Of course, the basic assumptions underlying actuaries' projections may change over time, giving rise to periodic revisions in the required contributions. Because of the need to rely extensively on actuaries' estimates, it is not surprising that accounting for defined benefit plans is much more complex than for defined contribution plans. The remainder of this section provides a summary overview of the accounting and financial reporting requirements for defined benefit pension plans; a complete discussion of these plans is considerably beyond the scope of this text.

The illustrative transactions for defined benefit pension plan accounting discussed in this section are based on a "single-employer plan," that is, a single plan administered by a single governmental employer. Readers should be aware, however, that many governments sponsor multiple pension plans for different classes of employees (for example, a plan for general employees and one or more separate and usually more generous plans for public safety employees). Further, in some states, some or all local government employees participate in a statewide defined benefit pension plan, rather than one sponsored by the local government itself. Such plans or groups of plans are often referred to as **Public Employee Retirement Systems (PERS)**. The GASB standards that apply to a single-employer plan apply as well to multiple-employer plans, although accounting and reporting for multiple-employer plans are more complex.

Some pension plans are accounted for in pension trust funds of the sponsoring government, and their financial data are included in the combined financial statements and in the combining financial statements prepared for fiduciary funds of the sponsoring government. Other plans are administered as legally separate entities that publish "stand-alone" financial statements.

Until 1996, governments had considerable latitude regarding the choice of accounting method for pension plans. GASB *Statement No. 1*, issued in 1984, permitted governments to follow either the pension accounting and reporting

---

[8]Ibid., Sec. Pe6.104.
[9]Ibid., Sec. Pe5.524.

standards set forth in the NCGA *Statement 1*, NCGA *Statement 6*, or in FASB *Statement No. 35*, pending the issuance by the GASB of a statement or statements on pension accounting and financial reporting. GASB *Statement No. 5*, "Disclosure of Pension Information by Public Employee Retirement Systems and State and Local Governmental Employers," issued in late 1986, superseded the disclosure requirements of NCGA *Statement 1*, NCGA *Statement 6*, and FASB *Statement No. 35*. Those disclosures were very extensive, often resulting in more than 10 pages of pension-related disclosures in the Notes to the Financial Statements. After several years of effort, the GASB issued three new standards that collectively provide comprehensive guidance on pension accounting and financial reporting. These standards provide accounting and reporting guidance for defined benefit pension plans (GASB *Statement No. 25*), postemployment healthcare plans administered by defined benefit pension plans (GASB *Statement No. 26*), and the sponsor/employer (GASB *Statement No. 27*). Complete texts of these standards can be found in the GASB's *Codification of Governmental Accounting and Financial Reporting Standards*, Sections Pe5, Po50, and P20, respectively. Most observers agree that the new standards have helped to achieve more uniform reporting of governmental pension plans. Moreover, required note disclosures have been reduced substantially under the new standards.

Required Financial Reporting for Defined Benefit Pension Plans

GASB standards establish a financial reporting framework for defined benefit pension plans that includes both required financial statements and required schedules of historical trend information. The schedules are *required supplementary information* that must follow immediately after the financial statements.[10] Two financial statements and two supplementary schedules of historical trend data are required. These requirements are described as:

a. A *statement of plan net assets* showing plan assets, liabilities, and net assets. Plan assets should be reported at fair value. (See Illustration 9–4 for an example of a PERS that administers three defined benefit pension plans.)

b. A *statement of changes in plan net assets* showing additions to plan net assets, deductions from plan net assets, and net increase (decrease) in plan net assets. (See Illustration 9–5.)

c. A *schedule of funding progress* showing historical trend data about the actuarially determined status of plan funding "from a long-term, ongoing perspective and the progress made in accumulating sufficient assets to pay benefits when due." (See Illustration 9–6.)

d. A *schedule of employer contributions* showing historical trend data about the *annual required contributions of the employer* (ARC) and employer contributions in relation to ARC.[11] (See Illustration 9–7.)

---

[10]Ibid., Sec. Pe5.111.
[11]Ibid.

Illustration 9–4

COLUMBINE RETIREMENT SYSTEM
Statements of Plan Net Assets
As of June 30, 19X2, and 19X1
(in thousands)

	State Employees	School Districts	Municipal Employees	19X2 Total	19X1 Total
Assets					
Cash and short-term investments	$ 66,129	$ 116,988	$ 27,014	$ 210,131	$ 440,146
Receivables:					
Employer	16,451	18,501	2,958	37,910	45,770
Employer—long-term		986		986	1,088
Interest and dividends	33,495	48,299	4,951	86,745	81,183
Total receivables	49,946	67,786	7,909	125,641	128,041
Investments at fair value:					
U.S. Government obligations	541,289	780,541	80,001	1,401,831	1,571,404
Municipal bonds	33,585	48,416	4,969	86,970	86,417
Domestic corporate bonds	892,295	1,217,251	191,801	2,301,347	1,961,288
Domestic stocks	1,276,533	1,784,054	183,893	3,244,480	3,230,446
International stocks	461,350	665,269	68,187	1,194,806	1,187,703
Mortgages	149,100	209,099	24,453	382,652	319,745
Real estate	184,984	266,748	27,350	479,082	420,806
Venture capital	26,795	38,638	3,960	69,393	37,120
Total investments	3,565,931	5,010,016	584,614	9,160,561	8,814,929
Properties, at cost, net of accumulated depreciation of $5,164 and $4,430, respectively	6,351	8,924	1,040	16,315	16,093
Total Assets	3,688,357	5,203,714	620,577	9,512,648	9,399,209
Liabilities					
Refunds payable and other	4,212	1,849	429	6,490	37,211
Net assets held in trust for pension benefits	$3,684,145	$5,201,865	$620,148	$9,506,158	$9,361,998

Source: GASB, *Codification*, Sec. Pe5.901, Illustration 1.

In addition, the plan is required to provide notes to the financial statements *and* notes to the required schedules. The notes to the financial statements should disclose the following information:

a. Plan description, including:
1. Identification of the type of plan.
2. Classes of employees covered.

Illustration 9–5

COLUMBINE RETIREMENT SYSTEM
Statements of Changes in Plan Net Assets
For the Years Ended June 30, 19X2, and 19X1
(in thousands)

	State Employees	School Districts	Municipal Employees	19X2 Total	19X1 Total
Additions:					
Contributions:					
Employer	$ 137,916	$ 157,783	$ 19,199	$ 314,898	$ 284,568
Employer—long-term		102		102	102
Plan member	90,271	117,852	16,828	225,651	216,106
Total contributions	228,887	275,737	36,027	540,651	500,776
Investment income					
Net appreciation (depreciation) in fair value of investments	(241,408)	(344,429)	(35,280)	(621,117)	788,913
Interest	157,371	225,446	23,098	405,915	422,644
Dividends	123,953	177,654	18,191	319,798	560,848
Real estate operating income, net	10,733	15,383	1,575	27,691	25,296
	50,649	74,054	7,584	132,287	1,797,701
Less investment expense	54,081	61,872	7,529	123,482	500,674
Net investment income	(3,432)	12,182	55	8,805	1,297,027
Total additions	225,455	287,919	36,082	549,456	1,797,803
Deductions:					
Benefits	170,434	172,787	18,073	361,294	325,881
Refunds of contributions	15,760	13,200	3,671	32,621	38,406
Administrative expense	4,984	5,703	694	11,381	12,681
Total deductions	191,168	191,690	22,438	405,296	376,968
Net increase	34,287	96,229	13,644	144,160	1,420,835
Net assets held in trust for pension benefits:					
Beginning of year	3,649,858	5,105,636	606,504	9,361,998	7,941,163
End of year	$3,684,145	$5,201,865	$620,148	$9,506,158	$9,361,998

Source: GASB, *Codification*, Sec. Pe5.901, Illustration 1.

    3. Brief description of benefit provisions.
  b. Summary of significant accounting policies.
  c. Description of contributions and reserves, including:
    1. The authority under which contributions are made.
    2. Funding policies.
    3. Required contribution rates of active plan members.

Illustration 9–6   Required Supplementary Information

Schedules of Funding Progress
(dollar amounts in thousands)

Actuarial Valuation Date	Actuarial Value of Assets (a)	Actuarial Accrued Liability (AAL) –Entry Age (b)	Unfunded AAL (UAAL) (b − a)	Funded Ratio (a/b)	Covered Payroll (c)	UAAL as a Percentage of Covered Payroll ((b − a)/c)
SEPP						
12/31/W6	$2,005,238	$2,626,296	$621,058	76.4%	$ 901,566	68.9%
12/31/W7	2,411,610	2,902,399	490,789	83.1	956,525	51.3
12/31/W8	2,709,432	3,331,872	622,440	81.3	1,004,949	61.9
12/31/W9*	3,001,314	3,604,297	602,983	83.3	1,049,138	57.5
12/31/X0	3,366,946	3,930,112	563,166	85.7	1,093,780	51.5
12/31/X1	3,658,323	4,284,961	626,638	85.4	1,156,346	54.2
SDEPP						
12/31/W6	$2,888,374	$3,499,572	$611,198	82.5%	$1,205,873	50.7%
12/31/W7	3,473,718	3,867,483	393,765	89.8	1,279,383	30.8
12/31/W8	3,902,705	4,439,761	537,056	87.9	1,344,151	40.0
12/31/W9*	4,323,137	4,802,700	479,563	90.0	1,403,255	34.2
12/31/X0	4,849,798	5,236,922	387,124	92.6	1,462,965	26.5
12/31/X1	5,269,502	5,709,764	440,262	92.3	1,546,650	28.5
MEPP						
12/31/W6	$301,305	$342,842	$41,537	87.9%	$163,508	25.4%
12/31/W7	362,366	378,885	16,519	95.6	173,476	9.5
12/31/W8	407,117	434,949	27,832	93.6	182,258	15.3
12/31/W9*	450,975	470,512	19,537	95.8	190,272	10.3
12/31/X0	505,714	513,044	7,330	98.6	198,368	3.7
12/31/X1	549,696	559,367	9,671	98.3	209,715	4.6

*Revised economic and noneconomic assumptions due to experience review.
Source: GASB, *Codification*, Sec. Pe5.901, Illustration 1.

4. Brief description of any long-term contracts for contributions.
5. Balances of the plan's legally required reserves at the reporting date.[12]

The notes to the required schedules should provide:

a. Identification of actuarial methods used and significant actuarial assumptions for the most recent year covered by the required supplementary schedules.

b. Factors such as changes in benefit provisions, employees covered by the plan, or actuarial methods or assumptions used, that significantly affect the trends reported in the schedules.[13]

---

[12]Ibid., Sec. Pe5.124.
[13]Ibid., Sec. Pe5.132.

Illustration 9–7

SCHEDULES OF EMPLOYER CONTRIBUTIONS
(dollar amounts in thousands)

Employer Contributions

Year Ended June 30	SEPP Annual Required Contribution	Percentage Contributed	SDEPP Annual Required Contribution	Percentage Contributed	MEPP Annual Required Contribution	Percentage Contributed
19W7	$100,729	100%	$115,935	100%	$15,042	100%
19W8	106,030	100	122,682	100	15,959	100
19W9	112,798	100	129,822	100	16,768	100
19X0	118,735	100	137,378	100	17,505	100
19X1	124,276	100	142,347	100	18,049	100
19X2	137,916	100	157,783	100	18,653	100

Source: GASB, *Codification*, Sec. Pe5.901, Illustration 1.

Statement of Plan Net Assets

Illustration 9–4, reproduced from the GASB *Codification*, presents the statements of plan net assets for the hypothetical Columbine Retirement System, a public employee retirement system (PERS). Columbine administers three pension plans: the state employees' plan, the school districts' plan, and the municipal employees' plan. As shown, plan investments should be reported at fair value (last reported sales price) for all investments in securities that trade on active exchanges. Investments in mortgages should be based on the discounted present value of future interest and principal payments to be received. Investments in real estate should be reported at fair value based on independent appraisals. All other investments should be reported at estimated fair value, including institutional price quotes for debt securities for which trade prices are unavailable.

Depreciable assets of a PERS, that is, assets held as property, plant, and equipment for use by the PERS, should be reported at cost less accumulated depreciation. Cash and short-term investments (reported at cost), and receivables typically represent a minor part of the total assets of a PERS. An astute reader will note also the assets of a PERS are not classified as current and fixed; the distinction not being important since short-term liabilities typically are immaterial in relation to available plan assets. PERS liabilities, usually short term (e.g., benefits due but unpaid, refunds for terminated employees, vouchers payable, accrued expenses, and payroll taxes payable), are reported as a deduction from PERS assets; the difference is captioned "Net assets held in trust for pension benefits."

Statement of Changes in Plan Net Assets

The *Statements of Changes in Net Plan Assets* for the Columbine Retirement System is presented in Illustration 9–5. This statement reports employer and employee contributions and investment income as **additions** to net assets rather than as revenues. Similarly, benefits paid, refunds of contributions, and administrative expense are reported under the caption **deductions** from net assets rather than as expenses. The net increase (decrease) in net assets is added to beginning-of-period net assets to calculate end-of-period net assets. Additions and deductions are recognized on the accrual basis.

Schedule of Funding Progress

An example *Schedules of Funding Progress* is presented in Illustration 9–6. This schedule shows funding progress of the plan in relation to *actuarial* requirements. A key measure of how well the plan is funded is the *funded ratio*. The **funded ratio** is the ratio of *actuarial value of assets* to *actuarial accrued liability* (AAL). **Actuarial value of assets** is the value of plan assets used by the actuary; the methods of determination for the various assets should be disclosed in the notes.[14] **Actuarial accrued liability** is determined by using any of several generally accepted actuarial methods (consistently applied, of course)—in this case, the Entry Age method—and is the present value of projected benefits, other than normal costs (benefits earned from current and future employee service). Thus, AAL arises primarily from past unfunding and ad hoc changes in plan provisions. Both the Schedule of Funding Progress and the other required schedule, the Schedule of Employer Contributions, should present information for the current year and as many prior years for which comparable data can be provided. By the sixth and subsequent years after implementation of GASB *Statement No. 25*, information should be provided for the current and five prior years (six years in total).

Schedule of Employer Contributions

The key information the reader should note in the *Schedules of Employer Contributions* shown in Illustration 9–7 is the *annual required contribution* (ARC) and what percentage of the ARC the employer has contributed. **Annual required contribution** is an actuarially determined amount that the employer should contribute each year to ensure full actuarial funding of the plan. Calculation of the ARC is discussed later in the section headed "Employer's Pension Accounting."

Alternative Reporting and Disclosure

The two financial statements and two schedules discussed previously, and related note disclosures, are those required in the stand-alone statements of a plan or PERS. If a plan is administered directly by the employer government, the financial information and note disclosures required would be reported in the employer government's combined and combining financial statements in its CAFR. In this case, however, the difference between plan assets and liabilities would be captioned "Fund balance reserved for employee pension benefits," rather than "Net assets held in trust for pension benefits."[15]

---

[14]The definitions paraphrased here and following are based on those provided in GASB, *Codification*, Sec. Pe5.A-1 and A-3.

[15]GASB, *Codification*, Sec.Pe5.119, note 10.

Illustrative Transactions for a Defined Benefit Pension Plan

Assume the Johnson County Employee Retirement Plan started the fiscal year beginning July 1, 1999, with the Statement of Plan Net Assets presented in Illustration 9–8. During fiscal year 2000, the following transactions occurred that require journal entries as shown.

Accrued interest receivable as of June 30, 1999, was collected:

1. Cash	2,507,612	
Accrued Interest Receivable		2,507,612

Member contributions in the amount of $8,009,400 and employer contributions in the amount of $14,126,292 were received in cash:

2. Cash	22,135,692	
Additions—Member Contributions		8,009,400
Additions—Employer Contributions		14,126,292

Annuity benefits in the amount of $3,134,448 and disability benefits in the amount of $287,590 were recorded as liabilities:

3. Deductions—Annuity Benefits	3,134,448	
Deductions—Disability Benefits	287,590	
Accounts Payable and Accrued Expenses		3,422,038

Accounts payable and accrued expenses paid in cash amounted to $3,571,969:

4. Accounts Payable and Accrued Expenses	3,571,969	
Cash		3,571,969

Illustration 9–8

JOHNSON COUNTY EMPLOYEE RETIREMENT SYSTEM
Statement of Plan Net Assets
June 30, 1999

Assets

Cash	$	28,569
Accrued interest receivable		2,507,612
Investments (at fair value):		
Bonds		71,603,976
Common stocks		31,957,205
Commercial paper and repurchase agreements		12,570,401
Properties, at cost, net of accumulated		
depreciation of $17,673		22,644
Total assets		118,690,407

Liabilities

Accounts payable and accrued expenses		401,581
Net assets held in trust for pension benefits		$118,288,826

Terminated employees whose benefits were not vested were refunded $2,057,265 in cash:

5. Deductions—Refunds to Terminated Employees	2,057,265	
Cash		2,057,265

Investment income received in cash amounted to $9,440,769; $4,882,076 interest income was accrued at year-end. In addition, the fair value of investments in bonds decreased during the year by $5,626,382 and the fair value of investments in common stocks increased by $3,427,600.

6a. Cash	9,440,769	
Accrued Interest Receivable	4,822,076	
Additions—Investment Income		14,262,845
6b. Investment in Common Stock	3,427,600	
Deductions—Change in Fair Value of Investments	2,198,782	
Investment in Bonds		5,626,382

Commercial paper and repurchase agreements carried at a cost of $1,354,568 matured, and cash in that amount was received:

7. Cash	1,354,568	
Commercial Paper and Repurchase Agreements		1,354,568

Common stocks carried at fair value of $6,293,867 were sold for that amount; $1,536,364 was reinvested in common stocks and the remainder in bonds. An additional amount of $29,229,967 was also invested in bonds:

8a. Cash	6,293,867	
Investment in Common Stocks		6,293,867
8b. Investment in Bonds	33,987,470	
Investment in Common Stocks	1,536,364	
Cash		35,523,834

Administrative expenses for the year totaled $568,219 all paid in cash:

9. Deductions—Administrative Expenses	568,219	
Cash		568,219

Equipment costing $11,059, on which depreciation in the amount of $5,000 had accumulated, was sold for $6,059 cash:

10. Accumulated Depreciation—Equipment	5,000	
Cash	6,059	
Equipment		11,059

Equipment costing $15,000 was purchased:

11. Equipment	15,000	
Cash		15,000

Depreciation expenses for the year amounted to $12,000 (charge to Administrative Expenses):

12. Deductions—Administrative Expenses	12,000	
Accumulated Depreciation—Equipment		12,000

Nominal accounts for the year were closed:

13. Additions—Member Contributions	8,009,400	
Additions—Employer Contributions	14,126,292	
Additions—Investment Income	14,262,845	
Deductions—Annuity Benefits		3,134,448
Deductions—Disability Benefits		287,590
Deductions—Refunds to Terminated Employees		2,057,265
Deductions—Administrative Expenses		580,219
Deductions—Change in Fair Value of Investments		2,198,782
Net Assets Held in Trust for Pension Benefits		28,140,233

Entries 1 through 13 result in the financial statements shown as Illustrations 9–9 and 9–10, when applied to the accounts existing at the beginning of the period as shown in Illustration 9–8.

Employer's Pension Accounting

GASB standards for the employer's accounting for defined benefit pension plans provide guidance for measurement, recognition, and display of the employer's pension information. In addition to general purpose government employers, the

---

Illustration 9–9

JOHNSON COUNTY EMPLOYEE RETIREMENT SYSTEM
Statement of Plan Net Assets
June 30, 2000

Assets

Cash	$ 30,849
Accrued interest receivable	4,822,076
Investments (at fair value):	
Bonds	99,965,064
Common stocks	30,627,302
Commercial paper and repurchase agreements	11,215,833
Properties, at cost, net of accumulated	
depreciation of $24,673	19,585
Total assets	146,680,709

Liabilities

Accounts payable and accrued expenses	251,650
Net assets held in trust for pension benefits	$146,429,059

Illustration 9–10

JOHNSON COUNTY EMPLOYEE RETIREMENT SYSTEM
Statement of Changes in Plan Net Assets
For the Fiscal Year Ended June 30, 2000

Additions:	
Contributions:	
Employer	$ 14,126,292
Plan members	8,009,400
Total contributions	22,135,692
Investment income:	
Net decrease in fair value of investments	(2,198,782)
Interest and dividends	14,262,845
Total investment income	12,064,063
Total additions	34,199,755
Deductions:	
Annuity benefits	3,134,448
Disability benefits	287,590
Refunds to terminated employees	2,057,265
Administrative expenses	580,219
Total deductions	6,059,522
Net increase	28,140,233
Net assets, July 1, 1999	118,288,826
Net assets, June 30, 2000	$146,429,059

standards apply also to governmental public benefit corporations and authorities, utilities, hospitals, and other healthcare providers, colleges and universities, and, if they are employers, to public employee retirement systems.

Many of the note and statistical disclosures applicable to defined benefit pension plans, discussed in the preceding paragraphs, apply as well to the employer. If the plan (or PERS) is deemed to be part of the government's reporting entity, then many of the employer's required disclosures are redundant of those required of the plan (a pension trust fund). In this case, the employer need not make disclosures that would duplicate those made by the plan. If the plan issues a stand-alone financial report, however, the employer will have to make many of the same disclosures in the CAFR that the plan makes in its stand-alone report. Because of the similarity of the disclosures and supplementary information required of the employer to those enumerated previously for the plan, the reader is referred to GASB *Codification*, Sec. P20.117, for specific disclosure requirements applicable to the employer.

Whether a government employer accounts for payroll in a governmental fund or proprietary fund, or both, there are three primary measures to be calculated and

Illustration 9–11

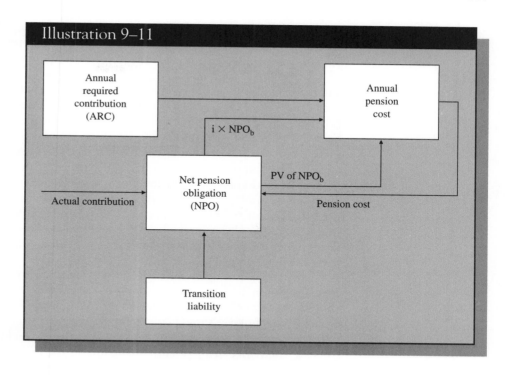

reported: (1) *annual required contribution* (ARC), (2) *annual pension cost*, and (3) *net pension obligation* (NPO).

Calculation of Annual Pension Cost and Net Pension Obligation.　*Annual pension cost* must be calculated and disclosed in the notes to the employer's financial statements. As shown in Illustration 9–11, the *annual required contribution* (ARC) is the starting point for understanding the calculation of annual pension cost. A discussion of the detailed procedures for calculating ARC is well beyond the scope of this text; therefore, only identification of the components of ARC is discussed here.

ARC is calculated in accordance with certain parameters provided in GASB standards. The parameters require that for financial reporting purposes an actuarial valuation be performed at least biennially and that ARC be based on an actuarial valuation as of a date not more than 24 months prior to the beginning of the current fiscal year. A component of ARC is the **actuarial present value of total projected benefits**, allowing for projected salary increases and additional statutory or contractual agreements such as ad hoc cost-of-living increases and other types of postemployment benefit increases.

The parameters used to calculate ARC also provide broad guidance regarding actuarial and economic assumptions, even though any of six actuarial methods are permitted, subject to the limitation that in most cases the same actuarial method should be used both for funding and financial reporting purposes. Further, both the plan and the employer should use the same actuarial method.

An employer's ARC should include **normal cost** (i.e., the actuarial present value of benefits allocated to the current year by the actuarial cost method being used) and amortization of any **unfunded actuarial liability** (same as *unfunded actuarial accrued liability* defined previously in the discussion of the required Schedule of Funding Progress). The provision for amortization can be determined using either level dollar amounts each year or a level percentage of the projected payroll. The amortization period must fall between defined maximum and minimum amortization periods. The maximum amortization period for the first 10 years after June 15, 1996, the effective date of GASB *Statement No. 25*, is 40 years. After the first 10 years the maximum period is 30 years. If there is a significant decrease in the total unfunded actuarial liability caused by a change in actuarial cost method or a change in asset valuation method, the decrease must be amortized over a period of not less than 10 years.

Once ARC has been calculated, it becomes an input to the calculation of annual pension cost (see Illustration 9–11). If there were no *net pension obligation* (NPO), the annual pension cost would be the same as ARC, and that would be the amount the employer should contribute during the period to the plan in order to fully fund current-period accrued benefits. If the employer has undercontributed in the past, then ARC will contain an amount for the amortization of the unfunded actuarial liability. Moreover, if actual contributions have been less than annual pension cost, NPO will have a positive balance. Thus, annual pension cost will be affected by the existence of an NPO, in addition to ARC. Before discussing the precise calculation of annual pension cost in the presence of an NPO, it will be useful to first examine the components of NPO.

Net pension obligation.   **Net pension obligation** (NPO) has two components: (1) the transition pension liability (or asset), if any, existing at the date GASB *Statement No. 27* is implemented and (2) the cumulative difference from the implementation date of *Statement 27* to the current balance sheet date between annual pension cost (the amount that should be contributed) and the employer's actual contributions. These inputs to NPO (actual contribution, annual pension cost, and transition liability) are shown clearly in Illustration 9–11.

Annual pension cost.   When an employer has an NPO, **annual pension cost** is equal to: (1) the ARC, plus (2) one year's interest on the beginning-of-year NPO, and minus or plus (3) an adjustment for any amounts already included in ARC for past amortization of contribution deficiencies or excess contributions. The adjustment is minus if the beginning balance of NPO is positive (contribution deficiencies) and plus if NPO is negative (excess contributions). As shown in Illustration 9–11, the adjustment to ARC is approximated by deducting an amount equal to the present value of the beginning balance of NPO. Illustration 9–12 provides a

Illustration 9–12	Calculation of Annual Pension Cost and Net Pension Obligation

Annual required contribution (ARC)	$165,485
Interest on net pension obligation (i × NPO$_b$)	5,070
Adjustment to annual required contribution (PV of NPO$_b$)	(3,692)
Annual pension cost	166,863
Contributions made during the year	(157,982)
Increase in net pension obligation	8,881
Net pension obligation, January 1, 1999	67,594
Net pension obligation, December 31, 1999	$ 76,475

Source: Based on example shown in GASB, *Codification*, Sec. P20.902.

numerical example of how annual pension cost and NPO are related and how each is calculated.

Employer Reporting of Pension Expenditure/Expense

Referring to Illustrations 9–11 and 9–12, a governmental employer that reports pension expenditures in a governmental or expendable trust fund should recognize the expenditures on the modified accrual basis. Thus, the amount recognized will be the actual amount contributed to the plan during the year. If the amount of pension expenditures for the year is less than annual pension cost, the difference should be added to NPO. If the expenditures amount is greater than annual pension cost, the difference should be deducted from NPO. Any cumulative positive balance of NPO, including a transition liability, should be reported in the General Long-Term Debt Account Group. A negative NPO balance should be used to reduce any other liability to the plan to zero, but should not be reported as a fund asset. Annual pension cost should be disclosed in the Notes to the Financial Statements. Under- or overfunding by a proprietary fund employer should be reported in the same manner except the NPO should be reported in the Balance Sheet of the proprietary fund. The amount of pension expense recognized in the proprietary fund should be the same as the annual pension cost.

Required Disclosures for Other Postemployment Benefits (OPEB)

Since unfunded other postemployment benefits (OPEB) may represent a material liability, GASB standards require certain disclosures by governmental employers that provide OPEB. If the OPEB plan is administered by a defined benefit pension plan, the OPEB follows the standards set forth in GASB *Statement No. 26* and codified in GASB *Codification*, Sec. Po50. Those standards impose financial reporting and disclosure requirements on the OPEB plan that are very similar to those for defined benefit pension plans, and thus do not need to be elaborated on here.

For OPEB plans that are not administered as part of a defined benefit pension plan, GASB standards provide disclosure standards only; financial display issues relating to such OPEB plans are being examined in a separate project by the GASB.[16] The Notes to the Financial Statements should provide, at a minimum, the following disclosures, either separately for each OPEB or in the aggregate for all OPEB provided:

a. Description of the OPEB; employee groups covered; eligibility requirements; and the employer and participant obligations to contribute, quantified in some manner.

b. Description of the statutory, contractual, or other authority under which OPEB provisions and obligations to contribute are established.

c. Description of the accounting and financing or funding policies followed.

d. Expenditure/expense information. If OPEB are financed on a pay-as-you-go basis, the employer should disclose expenditures/expenses recognized during the period by the employer (net of participant contributions) and the number of participants currently eligible to receive benefits. If OPEB are advance funded on an actuarially determined basis, the employer should disclose the number of active plan participants, the employer's actuarially required and actual contributions for the period (net of participant contributions), the amount of net assets available for the OPEB, and the actuarial accrued liability and unfunded actuarial accrued liability.

e. Description (and dollar effect, if measurable) of any significant matters that affect the comparability of the disclosures with those for the previous period.

f. Any additional information that the employer believes will help users assess the nature and magnitude of the cost of the employer's commitment to provide OPEB.

Employers that advance fund an OPEB through a pension plan have the option of following required employer pension disclosures, discussed previously in this chapter, or the OPEB disclosures just listed.

Illustrative Combined Financial Statements

The five combined financial statements required by GASB standards are listed in Chapter 1. A Combined Balance Sheet—All Fund Types and Account Groups and Discretely Presented Component Units is presented in Illustration 2–1. Combined Statements of Revenues, Expenditures, and Changes and Fund Balances, both

---

[16]Ibid., Sec. P50.105. If the GASB should issue new standards on recognition and measurement for postemployment benefits other than pension benefits, the publisher will provide an update to adopters of this edition of the text.

GAAP basis and budget and actual, for governmental funds (and expendable trust funds), are also illustrated in Chapter 2 (Illustrations 2–2 and 2–3). The two required combined financial statements for proprietary funds and nonexpendable trust funds are the Combined Statement of Revenues, Expenses, and Changes in Fund Equity—All Proprietary Fund Types, Similar Trust Funds, and Discretely Presented Component Units (Illustration 2–4), and the Combined Statement of Cash Flows—All Proprietary Fund Types, and Discretely Presented Component Units (Illustration 2–5). The GASB's requirement that proprietary and certain trust funds report their operating activities and cash flows in the statements shown in Illustrations 2–4 and 2–5 is consistent with FASB standards that require similar business enterprises to provide an Income Statement and a Statement of Cash Flows. It will be noted that pension funds are included along with nonexpendable trust funds in the combined operating statement (Illustration 2–4) but are excluded from the Statement of Cash Flows (Illustration 2–7). GASB standards do not require PERS to present a Statement of Cash Flows, but do not preclude them from doing so.[17]

Key Terms

Actuarial accrued liability, 352
Actuarial present value of total projected
   benefits, 357
Actuarial value of assets, 352
Additions (to net assets), 351
Annual pension cost, 358
Annual required contributions, 352
Deductions (from net assets), 352
Defined benefit pension plan, 346

Defined contribution pension, 345
Endowment Funds, 336
External investment pool, 336
Funded ratio, 352
Net pension obligation, 358
Normal cost, 358
Public Employee Retirement
   System, 346
Unfunded actuarial liability, 358

Selected References

American Institute of Certified Public Accountants. Audit and Accounting Guide, *Audits of State and Local Governmental Units*, revised. New York, 1996.
Governmental Accounting Standards Board. *Codification of Governmental Accounting and Financial Reporting Standards as of June 30, 1997*. Norwalk, CT, 1997.

Questions

9–1. Five types of funds are classified as fiduciary funds.

   (*a*) Two of the five are to be accounted for in a manner similar to governmental funds. Name these two fund types, and explain why the modified accrual basis is appropriate for their use.

---

[17]GASB, *Codification*, Sec. 2450.102.

(*b*) Three of the five are to be accounted for on the full accrual basis in a manner similar to proprietary funds. Name these three fund types, and explain why the full accrual basis is appropriate for their use.

9–2. If Nonexpendable Trust Funds are accounted for in a manner similar to proprietary funds, why is the Fund Balance account used as the equity account rather than the Contributions from Trustor and Retained Earnings accounts?

9–3. Why are assets received by a governmental unit to be held as the principal, or corpus, of a nonexpendable trust recorded at fair value rather than historical cost?

9–4. Why is it not appropriate to classify a public employee retirement system (PERS) as either a nonexpendable trust fund or an expendable trust fund?

9–5. "Budgetary accounts generally are needed for both expendable and nonexpendable trust funds." Do you agree or disagree? Why?

9–6. Explain why Internal Revenue Code Section 457 deferred compensation plans are now accounted for as *expendable trust funds* rather than as *agency funds*, which was the prior requirement under GASB standards.

9–7. Explain the required valuation for nonexpendable trust fund investments and how they are reported in the fund's financial statements.

9–8. Explain the essential differences between a *defined benefit pension plan* and a *defined contribution pension plan*. Which involves the more complex accounting and reporting requirements? Why?

9–9. What are the required financial statements and supplementary schedules that must be reported by a defined benefit pension plan in its stand-alone financial report, or in the CAFR of the employer (sponsor government), if applicable?

9–10. Describe the disclosures a defined benefit plan is required to make in the notes to its required financial statements and the notes to the required supplementary schedules.

9–11. Explain why the amount of required *employer* disclosures depends on whether the *plan* publishes a stand-alone financial report or publishes its financial information in a pension trust fund of the employer.

9–12. How is annual pension cost calculated? How does an employer government's pension expenditure or expense relate to annual pension cost?

9–13. Explain how *net pension obligation* (NPO) is calculated, and how it should be reported/disclosed in the employer's financial report.

9–14. Explain how financial reporting requirements differ between other postemployment benefits (OPEB) plans administered by a defined benefit pension plan and those that are not administered by a pension plan.

9–15. Describe the required disclosures for a postemployment benefit plan that is *not* administered by a defined benefit pension plan.

Case

9–1. Selected financial statements for Boise City, Idaho's fiduciary funds for the fiscal year ended September 30, 1996, are reproduced on the following pages. Read these statements closely and answer the following questions.

Required

a. The description of the Dedicated Trust Funds indicates only that the interest is used for current operations. Is this practice consistent with the older law of trust still applicable in some states, or with the revised laws of many states that permit the use of net realized gains and a prudent portion of unrealized gains for specified operating purposes?

b. In your judgment, is the Housing Rehabilitation Fund properly accounted for as a nonexpendable trust? Explain fully.

c. From the limited information provided, are the items reported in the Boise City Trust Fund financial statements accounted for as an agency fund?

d. Do the financial statements appear to conform with generally accepted accounting principles? If not, explain any deficiencies you believe exist.

e. Based on the limited information provided, do the fiduciary funds of the City appear to be soundly managed?

Boise City, Idaho

Fiduciary Funds

Nonexpendable Trust Funds

Dedicated Trust Funds: to account for monies which are dedicated for a specific purpose. The principal must remain intact; only the interest income is used for current operations.

Housing Rehabilitation Fund: to account for several revolving loan funds that provide low interest loans for housing. Various federal grants were used to establish the existing fund balance. The collection of the loans are used to run the program and make new loans to qualified citizens.

Agency Funds

Boise City Trust Fund: to account for items which must be held in trust for any reason. The major items accounted for in this fund are the City's deferred compensation plan and Boise Improvement District payments.

BOISE CITY, IDAHO
Combining Balance Sheet—All Fiduciary Funds September 30, 1996
With Comparative Totals for September 30, 1995

	Nonexpendable Trust Funds		Agency Fund	Totals	
	Dedicated Trust Funds	Housing Rehabilitation	Boise City Trust	1996	1995
Assets					
Cash	—	—	—	—	$ 13,348
Investments	$1,420,384	$ 1,042,021	$ 50,683	$ 2,513,088	1,832,109
Accounts and interest receivable	4,423	583,711	—	588,134	582,639
Grants receivable	—	—	—	—	10,659
Mortgage loans receivable	—	6,377,020	—	6,377,020	6,134,516
Mortgage loans in process	—	77,575	—	77,575	497,261
Due from other funds	2,465	11,593	44,363	58,421	28,763
Prepaid expenses	—	53	—	53	72
Restricted assets:					
Cash and investments	—	—	10,247,076	10,247,076	8,137,745
Total current assets	1,427,272	8,091,973	10,342,122	19,861,367	17,237,112
Other receivables	—	100,000	—	100,000	100,000
Other assets	—	1,064,162	—	1,064,162	1,050,686
Property, plant and equipment:					
Land	—	592,967	—	592,967	592,967
Buildings	—	4,412,300	—	4,412,300	4,311,802
Automobiles and trucks	—	18,400	—	18,400	—
Machinery and equipment	—	32,615	—	32,615	32,615
	—	5,056,282	—	5,056,282	4,937,384
Less allowance for depreciation	—	351,266	—	351,266	182,301
	—	4,705,016	—	4,705,016	4,755,083
Construction in progress	—	—	—	—	50,494
	—	4,705,016	—	4,705,016	4,805,577
Total assets	$1,427,272	$13,961,151	$10,342,122	$25,730,545	$23,193,375
Liabilities and Fund Equity					
Liabilities:					
Deficit in cash	—	—	$ 41,445	$ 41,445	—
Accounts and interest payable	$ 541	$ 69,792	—	70,333	$ 101,106
Other accrued liabilities	—	118,889	25,316	144,205	185,407
Due to other funds	76,041	21,389	28,285	125,715	262,445
Deferred revenues	—	—	—	—	1,630
Deferred compensation	—	—	10,247,076	10,247,076	8,137,745
Total liabilities	76,582	210,070	10,342,122	10,628,774	8,688,333
Fund Equity:					
Contributed capital:					
Grants and developer contributed	—	2,103,322	—	2,103,322	2,049,272
	—	2,103,322	—	2,103,322	2,049,272
Fund balance:					
Reserved for loans	—	11,647,759	—	11,647,759	11,209,410
Reserved for dedicated purposes	1,350,690	—	—	1,350,690	1,246,360
	1,350,690	11,647,759	—	12,998,449	12,455,770
Total fund equity	1,350,690	13,751,081	—	15,101,771	14,505,042
Total liabilities and fund equity	$1,427,272	$13,961,151	$10,342,122	$25,730,545	$23,193,375

BOISE CITY, IDAHO
Combining Statement of Revenues, Expenses, and Changes in Fund Balance—All Nonexpendable Trust Funds
For the Fiscal Year Ended September 30, 1996
With Comparative Totals for the Fiscal Year Ended September 30, 1995

	Dedicated Trust Funds	Housing Rehabilitation	Totals 1996	Totals 1995
Operating revenues:				
Charges for services	$ 90,260	—	$ 90,260	$ 136,498
Interest	—	$ 357,070	357,070	342,508
Miscellaneous revenues	—	463,515	463,515	559,867
Total revenues	90,260	820,585	910,845	1,038,873
Operating expenses:				
Personal services	—	106,931	106,931	158,633
Contractual services and utilities	541	474,634	475,175	329,722
Supplies and materials	—	112	112	467
Depreciation	—	150,566	150,566	119,606
Total operating expenses	541	732,243	732,784	608,428
Operating income	89,719	88,342	178,061	430,445
Nonoperating revenues:				
Operating grants	—	326,178	326,178	45,621
Interest revenue	90,652	61,050	151,702	93,415
Total nonoperating revenues	90,652	387,228	477,880	139,036
Income before operating transfers	180,371	475,570	655,941	569,481
Operating transfers in	—	101,148	101,148	436,510
Operating transfers out	(76,041)	(184,816)	(260,857)	(102,345)
	(76,041)	(83,668)	(159,709)	334,165
Net income	104,330	391,902	496,232	903,646
Add depreciation on fixed assets acquired by grants externally restricted for capital acquisition and construction that reduces contributed capital	—	46,447	46,447	22,493
Increase in fund balance	104,330	438,349	542,679	926,139
Fund balance at beginning of year	1,246,360	11,209,410	12,455,770	11,529,631
Fund balance at end of year	$1,350,690	$11,647,759	$12,998,449	$12,455,770

BOISE CITY, IDAHO
Combining Statement of Cash Flows
All Nonexpendable Trust Funds
For the Fiscal Year Ended September 30, 1996 and 1995

	Dedicated Trust Funds	Housing Rehabilitation	Totals 1996	1995
Cash flows from operating activities:				
Operating income	$ 89,719	$ 88,342	$ 178,061	$ 430,445
Adjustments to reconcile operating income to net cash provided by operating activities:				
Depreciation	—	150,566	150,566	119,605
Loss on disposal of fixed assets	—	50,494	50,494	—
Change in assets and liabilities:				
(Increase) decrease in accounts receivable	(435)	(2,601)	(3,036)	30,835
(Increase) in mortgage loans receivable	—	(242,504)	(242,504)	(859,274)
(Increase) decrease in mortgage loans in process	—	419,686	419,686	(205.460)
(Increase) decrease in due from other funds	(2,465)	(6,826)	(9,291)	4,775
Decrease in prepaid expenses	—	19	19	131
(Increase) decrease in other assets	—	(13,476)	(13,476)	108,764
(Decrease) in accounts payable	(45)	(29,755)	(29,800)	(396,803)
Increase in other accrued liabilities	—	32,882	32,882	24,102
(Decrease) increase in due to other funds	20,195	(87,373)	(67,178)	106,449
(Decrease) in deferred revenue	—	—	—	(537)
Total adjustments	17,250	271,112	288,362	(1,067,413)
Net cash provided by (used for) operating activities	106,969	359,454	466,423	(636,968)
Cash flows from noncapital financing activities:				
Principal paid on long-term debt	—	—	—	—
Operating grants received	—	336,342	336,342	74,531
Operating transfers in	—	123,176	123,176	465,165
Operating transfers out	(76,041)	(201,268)	(277,309)	(66,736)
Advances to other funds	—	—	—	10,000
Net cash provided by (used for) noncapital financing activities	(76,041)	258,250	182,209	482,960
Cash flows from capital and related financing activities:				
Acquisition and construction of capital assets	—	(100,499)	(100,499)	(964,344)
Capital grants received	—	100,992	100,992	323,818
Net cash provided by (used for) capital and related financing activities	—	493	493	(640,526)
Cash flows from investing activities:				
Purchase of investment securities	(2,791,795)	(4,481,790)	(7,273,585)	(4,088,921)
Proceeds from sale and maturities of investment securities	2,668,899	3,805,394	6,474,293	4,743,656
Interest on investments	91,144	58,099	149,243	97,323
Net cash provided by (used for) investing activities	(31,752)	(618,297)	(650,049)	752,058
Net decrease in cash	(824)	(100)	(924)	(42,476)
Cash at beginning of year	824	100	924	43,400
Cash at end of year	–0–	–0–	–0–	$ 924

BOISE CITY, IDAHO
Combining Statement of Changes in Assets and Liabilities
All Agency Funds
For the Fiscal Year Ended September 30, 1996

	Balance October 1, 1995	Additions	Deductions	Balance September 30, 1996
Boise City Trust Fund				
Assets				
Cash	$ 10,794	$2,501,749	$2,512,543	—
Investments	8,306,741	3,918,541	1,927,523	$10,297,759
Due from other funds	1,968	44,363	1,968	44,363
Total assets	$8,319,503	$6,464,653	$4,442,034	$10,342,122
Liabilities				
Deficit in cash	—	$ 41,445	—	$ 41,445
Accounts and interest payable	973	122,429	123,402	—
Other accrued liabilities	99,400	533,651	607,735	25,316
Due to other funds	81,385	690,070	743,170	28,285
Deferred compensation	8,137,745	2,109,331	—	10,247,076
Total liabilities	$8,319,503	$3,496,926	$1,474,307	$10,342,122
Housing Rehabilitation Fund				
Assets				
Cash	$ 1,630	—	$ 1,630	—
Total assets	$ 1,630	—	$ 1,630	—
Liabilities				
Deferred revenues	$ 1,630	—	$ 1,630	—
Total liabilities	$ 1,630	—	$ 1,630	—
Totals—All Agency Funds				
Assets				
Cash	$ 12,424	$2,501,749	$2,514,173	—
Investments	8,306,741	3,918,541	1,927,523	$10,297,759
Due from other funds	1,968	44,363	1,968	44,363
Total assets	$8,321,133	$6,464,653	$4,443,664	$10,342,122
Liabilities				
Deficit in cash	—	$ 41,445	—	$ 41,445
Accounts and interest payable	$ 973	122,429	$ 123,402	—
Other accrued liabilities	99,400	533,651	607,735	25,316
Due to other funds	81,385	690,070	743,170	28,285
Deferred revenues	1,630	—	1,630	—
Deferred compensation	8,137,745	2,109,331	—	10,247,076
Total liabilities	$8,321,133	$3,496,926	$1,475,937	$10,342,122

Exercises and Problems

9–1. Utilizing the annual report obtained for Exercise 1–1, follow the instructions below and on the next page.

a. *General.* Are all fiduciary funds shown in a single combining statement in the annual report, or are nonexpendable trust funds and retirement systems reported with proprietary funds and other fiduciary funds reported with governmental funds?

Does the report state the basis of accounting used for trust and agency funds? Are all funds in this category accounted for on the same basis? If so, is the financial statement presentation consistent with the stated basis? If the basis is not stated, analyze the statements to determine which basis is used—full accrual, modified accrual, or cash basis. Are the bases used consistent with those required by GASB standards discussed in the text? Are nonexpendable assets and expendable assets accounted for in separate funds? If not, are Fund Balance accounts for each category kept separate? Does the report include an investment trust fund? If so, is the fund accounted for on the accrual basis?

b. *Trust Funds.* Does the report contain a schedule or list of investments of trust funds? Are the investments identified as belonging to specific trust funds or merely to Trust Funds? Are investments reported at fair value? Is the net increase (decrease) in the fair value of investments reported separate from interest and dividend income?

If nonexpendable trust funds own depreciable assets, is depreciation taken? If so, is depreciation considered a charge against principal or against income? Are any trust funds operated as profit-seeking businesses? If so, does the annual report contain income statements for the businesses?

c. *Pension Trust Funds*, or PERS. Are the government employees covered by a Retirement Fund operated by a local government, by the state, by the federal Social Security Administration, or by two or more of these?

If the government operates one or more Retirement Funds, or retirement systems, are the Retirement Fund financial statements accompanied by a separate audit report, or are they included in the auditor's opinion accompanying the other funds? Are the Retirement Fund statements accompanied by an actuary's report? If not, is reference made to the actuary's report in the Balance Sheet, in Notes to the Financial Statements, or in the Auditor's Report? Does the Retirement Fund have an "actuarial deficiency" or an "unfunded actuarial liability"? If so, is this condition explained in the notes accompanying the statement? Is a net pension obligation (NPO) reported in the GLTDAG and/or in a proprietary fund?

Are the financial statements in the format shown in Illustrations 9–8, 9–9, and 9–10? Is all the pension information specified in GASB standards and discussed in Chapter 9 presented in the Notes to the Financial Statements? Are the required supplementary schedules and related notes to the schedules reported in the comprehensive annual financial report?

9–2. Write the numbers 1 through 10 on a sheet of paper. Beside each number write the letter corresponding with the best answer to each of the following questions.

1. Which of the following is *not* a fiduciary fund?
   a. Nonexpendable Trust Fund.
   b. Expendable Trust Fund.
   c. Internal Service Fund.
   d. Pension Trust Fund.

2. Which of the following trust funds requires a careful distinction between principal (or corpus) and income in accounting for investment income and gains and losses?
   a. Expendable Trust Funds.
   b. Nonexpendable Trust Funds.
   c. Pension Trust Funds.
   d. All of the above.

3. Which of the following fiduciary fund types is most likely to require formal legislative approval (appropriation procedures) for expenditures?
   a. Expendable Trust Funds.
   b. Nonexpendable Trust Funds.
   c. Pension Trust Funds.
   d. Investment Trust Funds.

4. A Statement of Cash Flows is required by current GASB standards for which of the following fiduciary fund types?
   a. Investment Trust Funds.
   b. Expendable Trust Funds.
   c. Pension Trust Funds.
   d. Nonexpendable Trust Funds.

5. An Investment Trust Fund is used to report the net assets available to the:
   a. Sponsoring government only.
   b. External participants only.
   c. Financial institution that acts as custodian for the fund's investments.
   d. All of the above.

6. Arkmo City has a single pension plan for its employees, all of whose salaries and wages are paid from the General Fund. Ordinarily, the City's General Fund should report an expenditure for its annual pension contribution to a defined benefit plan in an amount equal to the:
   a. Annual required contribution.
   b. Annual pension cost.
   c. Net pension obligation.
   d. Actual contribution.

7. GASB's pension standards require defined benefit pension plans to provide which of the following statements and schedules?
   a. Balance Sheet, Statement of Revenues and Expenses, Cash Flow Statement, and a Schedule of Actual and Required Contributions.
   b. Balance Sheet, Statement of Revenues and Expenditures, and a Schedule of Funding Progress.
   c. Statement of Plan Net Assets, Statement of Changes in Plan Net Assets, Schedule of Funding Progress, and a Schedule of Employer Contributions.
   d. Balance Sheet, Statement of Pension Activities, Schedule of Funding Progress, and a Statement of Plan Assets and Projected Pension Benefits—Funded and Unfunded.

8. Regarding financial reporting by governmental employers and defined benefit pension plans, which of the following is a correct statement?
   a. Expenditures and/or expenses incurred by governmental employers need not be reported separately in governmental and proprietary funds if the pension plan is determined to be a part of the governmental reporting entity.
   b. Expenditures and/or expenses incurred by governmental unit employers, and other pension-related financial information pertaining to employers, should be distinguished from financial information required to be reported by the pension plan.
   c. When a pension plan is considered to be part of a governmental reporting entity, its financial information need not be reported in the Fiduciary Funds column of the Combined Balance Sheet.
   d. Disclosure of pension plan financial information is required only when there is a positive net pension obligation.

Items 9 and 10 are based on the following information:

Elm City contributes to and administers a single-employer defined benefit pension plan on behalf of its covered employees. The plan prepares its own stand-alone financial report and is not accounted for in a pension trust fund. The annual pension cost and actual contributions made for the past three years, along with the percentage of annual covered payroll, were as follows:

	Actual Contribution		Annual Pension Cost	
	Amount	Percent	Amount	Percent
2000	$25,000	26	$25,000	26
1999	7,500	12	15,000	24
1998	–0–	—	9,000	20

9. What account should be credited by the pension plan to record the year 2000 employer contribution of $25,000?
   a. Revenues—Employer Contributions.
   b. Other Financing Sources—Operating Transfers In.
   c. Due from General Fund.
   d. Additions—Employer Contributions.

10. To record the year 2000 pension contribution of $25,000, what account would be debited in the General Fund for the employer pension contributions?
    a. Other Financing Uses—Operating Transfers Out.
    b. Expenditures.
    c. Pension Expense.
    d. Due to Pension Fund.

9–3. The City of Westwood has three fiduciary funds: Cemetery Trust Endowment Fund, Cemetery Trust Operating Fund, and City Employees' Retirement Fund. Below are several paragraphs of financial information as of June 30, 1999, about the funds:

1. Total cash and temporary investments of the three funds totaling $697,918 were distributed: $178,667 to the Cemetery Trust Endowment Fund; $475,492 to

City Employees' Retirement Fund; and $43,759 to the Cemetery Trust Operating Fund.

2. The City Employees' Retirement Fund was owed contributions from members in the amount of $62,401.

3. Various City funds owed the Retirement Fund contributions in the amount of $89,078.

4. The City Employees' Retirement Fund owned U.S. Treasury bonds of $8,998,000 at fair value as of June 30, 1999; a decrease of $49,600 from the previous carrying value for these bonds.

5. U.S. Treasury notes having a fair value on June 30, 1999, of $4,899,462, owned by the funds, were distributed: $2,861,026 to the City Employees' Retirement Fund; $1,992,003 to the Cemetery Trust Endowment Fund; and the remainder to the Cemetery Trust Operating Fund. The previous carrying value for these notes had been $4,762,382.

6. Accrued interest receivable at June 30, 1999, consisted of $469 for the Cemetery Trust Operating Fund; $46,942 for the Cemetery Trust Endowment Fund; and $161,918 for the City Employees' Retirement Fund. The accrued interest of the Cemetery Trust Endowment Fund is due to the Cemetery Trust Operating Fund.

7. Annuities payable by the City Employees' Retirement Fund to members and beneficiaries totaled $52,875.

8. The Cemetery Trust Operating Fund had Vouchers Payable of $60,161.

Required

    a. Prepare a trial balance for each of the funds at June 30, 1999. The Fund Balance of each fund will have to be derived. (Note: When a pension plan, such as the City Employees' Retirement Fund, is accounted for as a fiduciary fund of the employer, the difference between plan assets and liabilities is called Fund Balance Reserved for Employees' Pension Benefits rather than Net Assets.) If desired, all trial balances may be shown in combined columnar form.

    b. Explain why recording accrued interest receivable in the accounts of the Cemetery Trust Operating Fund is consistent with GAAP.

9–4. The Town of Benton received a cash contribution in the amount of $500,000 from Annabelle Benton, great-granddaughter of the town's founder, Alex Benton, which is to be held as a nonexpendable trust. Under terms of the agreement, the Town must invest and conserve the principal in perpetuity. Earnings, measured on the full accrual basis, must be used to maintain Alex Benton Town Park, including Alex Benton's gravesite, in an "attractive manner." Gains or losses realized on sale of Endowment Fund investments must be used to adjust the fund balance of the Endowment Fund and do not affect earnings. Information pertaining to transactions of the funds for the fiscal year ended June 30, 2000, is given as follows:

1. The contribution of $500,000 was received and recorded on December 31, 1999.

2. On December 31, 1999, bonds having a face value of $400,000 were purchased for $406,300, plus accrued interest of $6,000. A certificate of deposit with a face

and fair value of $70,000 was also purchased on this date. Bonds mature on October 1, 2008, and pay interest of 6 percent per annum semiannually on April 1 and October 1. The certificate of deposit pays interest of 4 percent per annum payable on March 31, June 30, September 30, and December 31.

3. On January 2, 2000, the Town Council approved a budget for the Benton Park Expendable Trust Fund for estimated other financing sources of $13,400 and appropriations of $12,900.

4. On March 31, 2000, interest on the certificate of deposit was received and transferred in cash to the Expendable Trust Fund.

5. The April 1, 2000, bond interest payment was received and transferred in cash to the Expendable Trust Fund.

6. On June 30, 2000, interest on the certificate of deposit was received and transferred cash to the Expendable Trust Fund.

7. For the year ended June 30, 2000, maintenance expenditures from the Expendable Trust Fund amounted to $2,700 for materials and contractual services, and $10,150 for wages and salaries. All expenditures were paid in cash except for $430 of accounts payable as of June 30, 2000. Inventories of materials are deemed immaterial.

8. On June 30, 2000, bonds with face value of $100,000 were sold for $102,000, plus accrued interest of $1,500. On the same date, 2,000 shares of ABC Corporation's stock were purchased at $52 per share. Appropriate adjusting and closing entries were made in order to prepare financial statements as of the end of the town's fiscal year. The amount due to the Expendable Trust Fund for accrued bond interest was paid in advance on June 30, 2000.

Required

a. Prepare in general journal form the entries required in the Benton Park Endowment Fund to record the transactions occurring during the fiscal year ending June 30, 2000.

b. Prepare in general journal form the entries required in the Benton Park Expendable Trust Fund to record the transactions above.

c. Prepare for the Benton Park Endowment Fund:
   (1) Balance Sheet as of June 30, 2000.
   (2) A Statement of Revenues, Expenses, and Changes in Fund Balance for the fiscal year ended June 30, 2000.
   (3) A Statement of Cash Flows for the year ended June 30, 2000.

d. Prepare for the Benton Park Expendable Trust Fund:
   (1) A Balance Sheet as of June 30, 2000.
   (2) A Statement of Revenues, Expenditures, and Changes in Fund Balance for the fiscal year ended June 30, 2000.

9–5. The City of Malcolm has a recreation center that is partially supported by the earnings from a nonexpendable trust, the Joshua Malcolm Endowment Fund (named after its benefactor). The principal of the trust consists largely of an office building. By terms of the trust, all cash operating expenses, necessary maintenance, and improvements to keep the building attractive to desirable tenants, depreciation, and debt service are deducted from gross rentals to determine the net income to be transferred to the Recreation Center Operating Fund. The fiscal year of the City ends on March 31; the Balance Sheet of the nonexpendable trust fund as of March 31, 1999, was as follows:

CITY OF MALCOLM
Joshua Malcolm Endowment Fund
Balance Sheet
As of March 31, 1999

Assets

Current Assets:			
Cash		$ 20,000	
Rents receivable		40,000	
Total Current Assets			$ 60,000
Property and Equipment:			
Land		240,000	
Building	$2,600,000		
Less: Accumulated depreciation	300,000	2,300,000	
Equipment	60,000		
Less: Accumulated depreciation	5,000	55,000	
Total Property and Equipment			2,595,000
Total Assets			$2,655,000

Liabilities and Fund Equity

Liabilities:		
Current Liabilities:		
Due to recreation center operating fund	$ 17,000	
Accrued supplies expenses	11,000	
Deferred rent revenue	30,000	
Current portion of mortgage payable	46,000	
Total Current Liabilities		$ 104,000
Long-Term Debt:		
Mortgage payable		1,254,000
Total Liabilities		1,358,000
Fund Equity:		
Fund balance		1,297,000
Total Liabilities and Fund Equity		$2,655,000

During fiscal year 2000, the following transactions and events, stated in summary form, occurred.

1. Rentals collected in cash during the year totaled $480,000 ($40,000 of the total represented collection of rents receivable as of April 1, 1999; $48,000 of the total represented rentals applicable to fiscal year 2001). Rentals amounting to $30,000 that had been collected in fiscal 1999 were earned in fiscal 2000. In addition, rents amounting to $20,000 that should have been collected in fiscal 2000 were still receivable at year-end.

2. The accrued expenses as of April 1, 1999, were paid in cash. Other cash disbursements during the year were for wages and salaries expense, $105,000; supplies and other operating expenses, $78,000 (all paid to external suppliers);

and payments to the Recreation Center Operating Fund, $66,000 (this included the liability as of April 1, 1999, and an advance on anticipated net income for fiscal 2000). Payment was made during the year for mortgage interest (8% per annum) in the amount of $104,000 and mortgage principal in the amount of $46,000. Inventories of supplies are deemed immaterial and thus are not reported.

3. Accrued as of March 31, 2000, were supplies and other operating expenses of $14,000. Depreciation on the building amounted to $78,000; depreciation on the equipment amounted to $5,000.

4. Closing entries were made in order to determine the liability to Recreation Center Operating Fund for net income for fiscal 2000. An entry was also made to reclassify the current portion of Mortgage Payable as a current liability, assuming the total payment for Principal and interest in fiscal 2001 will be $150,000—the same as fiscal 2000.

Required

a. Prepare the financial statements as of March 31, 2000, and for the year then ended for the Joshua Malcolm Endowment Fund. Prepare all statements required for conformity with generally accepted accounting principles, assuming the City of Malcolm has no other nonexpendable trust funds.

b. If you were Director of the Recreation Center, would you be satisfied with the net income earned by the Joshua Malcolm Endowment Fund? Explain. If you think you would be satisfied, what criteria did you use for determining adequacy of income? If you would not be satisfied, what questions would you raise with the Endowment Fund administrator or City chief executive?

9–6. The Town of Dover accepted a gift of cash and securities to be held as a nonexpendable trust; the net income from the trust investments is to be computed on the full accrual basis. Income received in cash or accrued on fixed-income securities, is to be transferred to an expendable trust fund operated on a budgetary basis for the purchase of works of art for display in public buildings. The nonexpendable trust fund, to be known as the Art Endowment Fund, received the following as trust principal on July 1, 1999: cash, $525,000; XY bonds (face value, $1,000,000; fair value on July 1, 1999, $1,040,000; interest rate 8 percent per year payable on March 1 and September 1); and one certificate of deposit ($100,000 face and 7 percent per year payable on August 1, November 1, February 1, and May 1). Accrued interest receivable on XY bonds, $26,667; accrued interest receivable on certificate of deposit, $1,167.

Required

a. Show in general journal form the entries required in the Art Endowment Fund to record the following:
   (1) The receipt of the trust principal on July 1, l999, as itemized above.
   (2) On July 1, 1999, the following common stocks were purchased: LM Company, 2,000 shares, cost $255,000; NO, Inc., 1,000 shares, cost $65,000; PQ Company, 800 shares, cost $200,000.
   (3) The August 1, 1999, interest on the certificate of deposit was received. The portion that was accrued when the Endowment Fund was

established is retained; the portion subsequently earned is transferred in cash to the Artworks Expendable Trust Fund.

(4) The September 1, 1999, interest payment on XY bonds was received. Interest accrued at date of establishment of the Endowment Fund was retained in the Endowment Fund; the remainder was transferred in cash to the Artworks Expendable Trust Fund.

(5) On October 1, cash dividends were received from LM Company common stock, $5,000; NO, Inc., common stock, $1,500; and PQ Company common stock, $2,000. All cash received was transferred to the Artworks Expendable Trust Fund.

(6) On November 1, interest on the certificate of deposit was received and transferred to the Artworks Expendable Trust Fund.

(7) In order to prepare financial statements as of the end of the City's fiscal year, December 31, 1999, appropriate adjusting and closing entries were made. As of December 31, 1999, the fair value of bonds was $1,040,000 and the fair value of stocks was $518,600.

b. Show in general journal form the entries required in the Artworks Expendable Trust Fund to record the following:

(1) On July 1, 1999, a budgetary entry was made to record as Estimated Other Financing Sources six months' interest on the XY bonds; six months' interest on the certificate of deposit; and an estimated amount of $8,300 from dividends on common stock. It was decided that Appropriations for the period should be $27,000.

(2) Cash transferred from the Art Endowment Fund on August 1, 1999, was received.

(3) Cash transferred from the Art Endowment Fund on September 1, 1999, was received.

(4) A portrait of the Mayor was commissioned on September 15; the artist is receive $6,800 when the portrait is completed. He was given an advance $1,900 cash.

(5) Cash transferred from the Art Endowment Fund on October 1, 1999, was received.

(6) Cash transferred from the Art Endowment Fund on November 1, 1999, was received.

(7) The accrued interest receivable from the Art Endowment Fund was recorded as of December 31, 1999.

(8) In order to prepare financial statements as of year-end, December 31, 1999, appropriate closing entries were made.

c. Prepare for the Art Endowment Fund:

(1) A Balance Sheet as of December 31, 1999.

(2) A Statement of Revenues, Expenses, and Changes in Fund Balance for the six months ended December 31, 1999.

(3) A Statement of Cash Flows for the six months ended December 31, 1999.

d. Prepare for the Artworks Expendable Trust Fund:

(1) A Balance Sheet as of December 31, 1999.

(2) A Statement of Revenues, Expenditures, and Changes in Fund Balance for the six months ended December 31, 1999.

9–7. The Village of Vandover administers a defined benefit pension plan for its police and fire personnel. Employees are not required to contribute to the plan. The Village received from the actuary and other sources the following information about the Public Safety Employees' Pension Fund as of December 31, 1999.

Item	Amount
Annual required contribution	$ 49,600
Net pension obligation, 1/1/99	147,300
Present value of net pension obligation as of 1/1/99	12,400
Interest rate applicable to beginning net pension obligation	8%
Transition liability	–0–

Required

Assuming the Village of Vandover contributes $45,000 cash to the plan on December 31, 1999, calculate the employer's

a. Annual pension cost.

b. Net pension obligation, as of December 31, 1999.

9–8. The State of Arkoma operates a Public Employee Retirement System for all employees of the state. The trial balance of the PERS as of June 30, 1999, follows (in thousands of dollars):

	Debits	Credits
Cash	$ 6,254	
Accrued Interest Receivable	32,955	
Investments, at fair value	1,961,986	
Equipment and Fixtures	15,200	
Accumulated Depreciation— Equipment and Fixtures		$ 3,110
Accounts Payable and Accruals		33,396
Net Assets Held in Trust for Pension Benefits, July 1, 1998		1,647,748
Member Contributions		112,126
Employer Contributions		197,768
Interest and Dividend Income		199,679
Change in Fair Value of Investments	92,600	
Annuity Benefits	43,882	
Disability Benefits	4,026	
Refunds to Terminated Employees	28,801	
Administrative Expenses	8,123	
Totals	$2,193,827	$2,193,827

Required

a. Prepare a Statement of Changes in Net Plan Assets for the State of Arkoma Public Employee Retirement System for the year ended June 30, 1999, in as much detail as possible.

b. Prepare a Statement of Net Plan Assets as of June 30, 1999, for the State of Arkoma Public Employee Retirement System.

Continuous Problem

9–L. The City of Bingham (see Problems 2-L through 8–L) has had an Employees' Retirement Fund for many years. The fund is financed by actuarially determined contributions from the City's General Fund; the employees make no contribution. Administration of the Retirement Fund is handled by General Fund employees, and the Retirement Fund does not bear any administrative expenses.

The Balance Sheet of the Employees' Retirement Fund (a pension trust fund) as of the end of the fiscal year prior to the one with which this problem is concerned is shown below:

CITY OF BINGHAM
Employees' Retirement Fund
Statement of Plan Net Assets
As of June 30, 1999

Assets

Cash	$ 8,360
Accrued interest receivable	15,000
Investments, at fair value	750,840
Total Assets	$774,200

Liabilities

Accounts payable and accrued expenses	6,000
Net Assets Available for Benefits	$768,200

Required

a. Record in the general journal for the Employees' Retirement Fund the following events and transactions, which occurred during the year ended June 30, 2000:
  (1) The interest receivable on investments as of the beginning of the year was collected in cash.
  (2) A liability for annuities payable was recorded in the amount of $75,000.
  (3) Contributions from the General Fund in the amount of $176,390 were received in cash.
  (4) Interest earnings received in cash amounted to $30,000; additional interest earnings were accrued in the amount of $16,000.
  (5) Accounts Payable for Annuities in the amount of $78,000 were paid.
  (6) Investments held at June 30, 1999, increased in fair value during the year by $32,600.
  (7) Additional investments were purchased at a cost of $150,000.
  (8) Nominal accounts for the year were closed.
b. Prepare a Statement of Plan Net Assets as of June 30, 2000, for the Employee's Retirement Fund.
c. Prepare a Statement of Changes in Plan Net Assets for the year ended June 30, 2000.

[Note: When the statements prepared in parts *b* and *c* are included in the City's Combined Balance Sheet—All Fund Types and Account Groups, the assets and liabilities reported in the Statement of Plan Net Assets will be reported in the Assets and Liabilities sections of the Combined Balance Sheet, respectively. Net Assets Held in Trust for Pension Benefits reported in the Statement of Plan Net Assets will be reported in the Fund Equity section of the Combined Balance Sheet under the caption "Fund Balance Reserved for Employee's Pension Benefits." When the plan is reported in the City's Combined Statement of Revenues, Expenses, and Changes in Fund Equity—All Proprietary Fund Types and Similar Trust Funds, items reported as additions and deductions in the Statement of Changes in Plan Net Assets will be reported in the Revenues and Expenses of the City's combined operating statement. The Net Increase (Decrease) in Net Assets amount will be reported as a net increase (decrease) in fund equity.]

CHAPTER

10

Review and Financial Reporting of State and Local Governments

Learning Objectives

After studying this chapter, you should be able to:

~ Recall and describe the funds used in state and local government accounting, the characteristics of each fund type, and the objectives of financial reporting of state and local governments.

~ Explain the key concepts and terms used in describing the governmental reporting entity.

~ Apply the GASB criteria used to determine whether a potential component unit should be included in the reporting entity, and the manner of reporting component units.

~ Identify and describe the contents of interim and annual financial reports.

~ Explain contemporary financial reporting issues, including:

The GASB's proposed financial reporting model.
Service efforts and accomplishments (SEA) reporting.
Popular reporting.

Chapters 2 through 9 present extended discussions of the nature of fund types and account groups provided in Governmental Accounting Standards Board pronouncements. The reasons why each fund type and account group exists are set forth and the essential characteristics of accounting for typical transactions of the funds and groups are discussed in those chapters. In the first section of this chapter, the nature, purposes, and accounting characteristics of each fund type and account group are summarized and interfund transactions are reviewed. The second section of this chapter presents a brief discussion of the complexities of defining the governmental reporting entity. The third section reviews and describes general purpose financial statements and the comprehensive annual financial report. The final section discusses recent developments in financial reporting and unresolved reporting issues.

Summary of the Nature and Accounting Characteristics of Funds and Account Groups

A fund is an independent fiscal and accounting entity with a self-balancing set of accounts recording assets and resources, and related liabilities, reserves, and equities, segregated for the purpose of carrying on specific activities or attaining certain objectives in compliance with legal restrictions or agreements. Fund types are classified in three major categories—governmental funds, proprietary funds, and fiduciary funds—and two account groups. Four types of funds are classified as *governmental funds*: general funds, special revenue funds, capital projects funds, and debt service funds. Internal service funds and enterprise funds are classified as *proprietary funds*. *Fiduciary funds* is the generic name for all trust and agency funds. The two account groups are the General Fixed Assets Account Group and the General Long-Term Debt Account Group.

Classification of funds by major category is helpful because the principal accounting recommendations differ by category: *Governmental* fund revenues and expenditures should be recognized on the **modified accrual basis** of accounting. Governmental fund operating statements have a flow of financial resources measurement focus. Governmental funds do not account for fixed assets used in their operations, nor for long-term debt. *Proprietary* fund revenues and expenses should be recognized on the **full accrual basis**. Proprietary fund operating statements have an income determination focus. Proprietary funds account for fixed assets used in their operations and for long-term debt serviced by revenues from their operations. *Fiduciary* funds consist of investment trust funds, nonexpendable trust funds, and pension trust funds, all of which are accounted for in a manner similar to proprietary funds; and Expendable Trust Funds and Agency Funds, both of which are accounted for in a manner similar to governmental funds. The two account groups exist to account for fixed assets and long-term debt not accounted for by the governmental funds. Illustration 10–1 presents a comparison of the principal accounting characteristics of funds and account groups provided for use by state and local governmental units by GASB standards. The following sections of this chapter summarize the nature, purposes, and accounting characteristics of each fund and group.

Governmental Funds

General Funds and Special Revenue Funds. The *General Fund* is the name given to the entity that accounts for all of the assets and resources used for financing the general administration of the governmental unit and the traditional services provided to its residents. Operating funds and current funds are names sometimes given to funds that function as a General Fund.

The typical governmental unit now engages in many activities financed by revenues designated by law for a particular operating purpose. In order to demonstrate compliance with such laws, it is recommended that a *special revenue fund* be used to account for the receipt and use of each such restricted category of revenue.

Both general funds and special revenue funds are sometimes known as *revenue funds*. In terms of accounting characteristics, both types are alike. The effect of the budget when it becomes a legal document is recorded in the accounts of each type. Estimated Revenues, a control account for all sources of revenues available to the fund and to be utilized during the budget period, is debited for the total amount of revenues expected to be recognized during the budget period; Estimated Other Financing Sources, a control account for all sources of financial resource inflows not classified by the GASB as revenues, is debited for the total other financing sources expected to be recognized during the budget period. Appropriations, a control account for all categories of expenditures authorized in the legally approved budget, is credited; Estimated Other Financing Uses, a control account for all categories of financial resource outflows not classified by the GASB as expenditures, is credited for the total other financing uses authorized for the budget period. Fund Balance, the account that is similar to a capital account of a profit-seeking entity, is debited or credited for the difference between Estimated Revenues plus Estimated Other Financing Sources less Appropriations and Estimated Other Financing Uses.

Accounting for general and special revenue funds differs from accounting for profit-seeking entities in more respects than just the obvious one of formally recording the budget in the accounts. Two principal differences are:

1. Expenditures are made for the purposes specified in the Appropriations Budget and are not made in the hope of generating revenue (as is true of profit-seeking entities); therefore, income determination, which is the principal focus of accounting for profit-seeking entities, is of no concern in accounting for general and special revenue funds.

2. The sources and amounts of revenues and other financing sources relate to a budget for a particular time period, generally one year, so general and special revenue funds can be said to have a year-to-year life rather than an indefinite life, as is true of a profit-seeking entity. Thus, the going-concern assumption that is basic to accounting for profit-seeking entities is not applicable to accounting for revenue funds; flow of financial resources is the focus of general and special revenue funds.

| Illustration 10–1 | Comparison of Characteristics of Funds and Account Groups of State and Local Governmental Units under Currently Effective GASB Standards |

	Governmental Funds			
Characteristic	General	Special Revenue	Capital Projects	Debt Service
Focus	Liquidity	Liquidity	Liquidity	Liquidity
Length of Life	Year to year	Year to year	From approval of project until completion	From issue of general debt until final liquidation
Balance Sheet Accounts:				
Current Assets	Yes	Yes	Yes	Yes
Fixed Assets	No	No	No	No
Assets Available and to Be Provided	—	—	—	—
Current Liabilities	Yes	Yes	Yes	Yes
Fixed Liabilities	No	No	No	No
Fund Equity:				
Fund Balance—Reserved	Yes	Yes	Yes	No
Fund Balance—Available	Yes	Yes	Yes	Yes
Contributed Capital	—	—	—	—
Retained Earnings	—	—	—	—
Invested in G.F.A.	—	—	—	—
Operating Statement Accounts—Basis of Recognition:				
Revenues	Modified Accrual	Modified Accrual	Modified Accrual	Modified Accrual
Expenditures	Full Accrual	Full Accrual	Full Accrual	Modified Accrual
Expenses	—	—	—	—
Budgetary Accounts:				
Estimated Revenues	Yes	Yes	No	Yes
Appropriations	Yes	Yes	No	Yes
Encumbrances	Yes	Yes	Yes	No

Notes: 1. An Agency Fund recognizes, on the modified accrual basis, assets to be collected on behalf of the funds and units that are parties to the agency relationship. Since all assets belong to other funds and units, the assets are offset by liabilities to other funds and units.
2. Long-term debt of an Internal Service Fund is usually owed to another fund rather than to external creditors.
3. Accumulated depreciation may be recorded in this group; related expense should not be recorded in any governmental fund.

Source: Adapted from a comparative chart prepared by Professor W. David Brooks, CPA, of Chemeketa Community College, Salem, Oregon.

| | Fiduciary Funds | | Proprietary Funds | | Account Groups | |
Agency	Expendable Trust	Nonexpendable, Investment, and Pension Trust	Internal Service	Enterprise	General Fixed Assets	General Long-Term Debt
Liquidity Duration of agency	Liquidity Duration of trust	Going concern Duration of trust	Going concern Decision of governing board	Going concern Decision of governing board	— As long as general fixed assets exist	— As long as unmatured long-term general debt exists
(Note 1)	Yes	Yes	Yes	Yes	No	No
No	No	Yes	Yes	Yes	Yes	No
—	—	—	—	—	—	Yes
(Note 1)	Yes	Yes	Yes	Yes	No	No
No	No	Yes	(Note 2)	Yes	No	Yes
—	Yes	No	—	—	—	—
—	Yes	Yes	—	—	—	—
—	—	—	Yes	Yes	—	—
—	—	—	Yes	Yes	—	—
—	—	—	—	—	Yes	—
—	Modified Accrual	Full Accrual	Full Accrual	Full Accrual	—	—
—	Full Accrual	—	—	—	—	—
—	—	Full Accrual	Full Accrual	Full Accrual	(Note 3)	—
—	Yes	—	—	—	—	—
—	Yes	—	—	—	—	—
—	Yes	—	—	—	—	—

Legally approved appropriations are authorizations to incur liabilities for specified purposes in specified amounts during a specified time period. Penalties provided by law may be imposed on governmental administrators who expend governmental resources in a manner in any way contrary to that authorized in appropriation ordinances or statutes. For that reason, it is recommended that Encumbrances, a control account supported by the appropriations expenditures subsidiary ledger, be debited, and Reserve for Encumbrances, a Fund Equity account, be credited when purchase orders, contracts, or other commitment documents are issued. When goods or services have been received, a liability is incurred and an appropriation is deemed to have been expended (under accrual accounting theory); thus, if the appropriation has previously been encumbered, it is necessary to reverse the encumbrance entry at the time the Expenditure account is debited and the liability account is credited.

Revenues of a general or special revenue fund are to be recognized on the modified accrual basis. That is, those items of revenue that are "susceptible to accrual" (measurable and available), such as property taxes, are recorded on the accrual basis; other items of revenue are generally recorded on the cash basis. Revenues and Expenditures are operating statement accounts and are closed to Fund Balance at the end of a fiscal period. Estimated Revenues, Estimated Other Financing Sources, Appropriations, Estimated Other Financing Uses, and Encumbrances, all referred to as *budgetary* accounts, are also closed to Fund Balance at the end of a fiscal period. Therefore, when budgetary and operating statement accounts have been closed, the balance sheet accounts remain open and their balances are reported in a balance sheet for the General Fund and in a combining balance sheet for the special revenue fund type. The balance sheet accounts of a general or special revenue fund consist of accounts for financial resources available for fund operations, current liabilities to be paid from fund assets, and Fund Equity. If prepaid items and/or inventories of materials and supplies are owned by a revenue fund, they should be included as an asset, but Fund Equity should be *reserved* in an equivalent amount. Unreserved Fund Balance, therefore, represents the net amount of financial resources available for appropriation and expenditure for legally approved purposes or for authorized other financing uses.

Capital Projects Funds.   The receipt and disbursement of all monies from the sale of tax-supported or special assessment bonds issued for the construction or acquisition of capital facilities, along with the receipt and disbursement of all monies from other sources (such as grants from governmental units, special assessments, transfers from other funds, or gifts from citizens for the construction or acquisition of capital facilities), are accounted for by capital projects funds. The acquisition of general fixed assets under a capital lease is also recorded in a governmental fund, usually a capital projects fund.

A capital projects fund exists because certain resources are dedicated to a given capital purpose; all activities of the fund have the objective of accomplishing that purpose. Therefore, it is not considered necessary for budgetary accounts other than Encumbrances to be used. Encumbrances and Reserve for

Encumbrances are considered desirable because of the large number of commitment documents that are issued for a typical governmental capital project. The encumbrance entry is reversed and Construction Expenditures of a capital projects fund are recognized when goods and services are received and the corresponding liability is recorded. Revenues of a capital projects fund are recognized on the same accrual basis as general and special revenue funds. The life of a capital projects fund is the length of time from legal approval of the project until completion of the project and formal acceptance of the capital assets by the governmental unit. The life of a capital projects fund generally does not coincide with a fiscal period; therefore, operating statement accounts and encumbrances are ordinarily closed at year-end to facilitate preparation of annual statements. Neither the fixed assets nor any long-term liabilities resulting from the project are accounted for by a capital projects fund. Only assets that will be converted into cash and disbursed for the project are to be accounted for by a fund of this type. Similarly, only liabilities that are to be paid out of fund assets are accounted for by capital projects funds. Fund Balance of a capital projects fund represents the excess of current assets over the sum of current liabilities and expected liabilities (Reserve for Encumbrances) or, therefore, the amount available for expenditure for the approved purposes of the fund.

Debt Service Funds. Tax-supported long-term debt issued and the interest thereon must be serviced primarily from revenue raised in years subsequent to the issue. Special assessment long-term debt for which a general government is obligated in some manner is expected to be serviced from collections of assessments and interest thereon. Laws of superior jurisdictions and bond indentures commonly require local governmental units to establish funds to account for debt service revenue.

It is recommended that debt service funds record Estimated Revenues and Appropriations (and Estimated Other Financing Sources and Estimated Other Financing Uses, if needed). Encumbrance accounting is ordinarily not needed for debt service funds because the only appropriations for these funds are for the payment of interest and the payment of principal of matured debt.

Although a major portion of the revenues of a debt service fund for tax-supported bonds arises from taxes, a portion of the revenues arises from interest on investments. Special assessments against property benefited by a special assessment project, and interest on the assessments, furnish revenues for debt service of special assessment bonds. Since the fund must stay in existence until all general long-term debt is repaid, in most cases the fund may be said to have an unlimited life.

The accrual basis of accounting specified for debt service funds has the same meaning for the revenues of debt service funds as it has for general and special revenue funds, but whereas the expenditures of a general or special revenue fund are to be accounted for on the full accrual basis, the expenditures of a debt service fund for interest and matured bonds are to be accounted for in the fiscal year in which appropriations for the payment of interest and principal are made—generally, the year in which the items become due.

As is true of general and special revenue funds and capital projects funds, a regular serial bond debt service fund accounts for only current assets and current liabilities (matured interest and matured principal payments), and the Fund Balance represents the excess of current assets available for fund purposes. A term bond debt service fund or a deferred serial bond debt service fund ordinarily is expected to accumulate assets over the life of the bonds; it is prudent for the assets to be held in the form of high-quality investments that are readily marketable or that will mature by the time cash is needed. The debt to be retired by the debt service fund is recorded by the general long-term debt group, not the debt service fund (until maturity).

Proprietary Funds

Internal Service Funds.   If governmental resources are segregated for the purpose of providing services to several departments or funds of the same governmental unit or to other governmental units, the resources are accounted for by an internal service fund. The internal service fund type may be operated under many different levels of legislative supervision; in this summary it is assumed the financial objective of the fund is to recover through user charges the full cost of operations and to earn enough net income to allow for replacement of inventories and facilities in periods of rising prices. Accordingly, although budgets should be prepared for managerial use, it is not necessary to record the budget in the accounting system. Full accrual accounting should be used for revenues and for *costs* and *expenses* (these terms are used rather than *expenditures* because the latter refers to appropriation accounting). The life of an internal service fund is indefinite, so the going-concern assumption should be applied to accounting decisions. Current assets and fixed assets used in internal service fund operations should be accounted for by the internal service fund. Long-term debt to be repaid from earnings of the fund should also be accounted for by the internal service fund, as should all other liabilities to be paid from fund assets. Since net income is retained in the fund, a Retained Earnings account is needed as well as accounts that disclose the amount and source of the permanent equity of the fund.

Enterprise Funds.   In contrast with internal service funds, resources utilized by a governmental unit to provide services on a user-charge basis to the general public are accounted for by an Enterprise Fund. Governmentally owned utilities are common examples of activities accounted for by enterprise funds. Almost any form of business engaged in by individuals, partnerships, and corporations may also be owned and operated by a governmental unit, however, and would be accounted for by an enterprise fund. Utilities or other enterprises that would be regulated if they were investor-owned should use the charts of accounts and accounting and statistical definitions required of investor-owned enterprises in the same industry. Other governmentally owned enterprises should use charts of accounts and definitions established by trade associations for the appropriate industry. In general, principles of accounting established for profit-seeking entities apply. Differences between regulatory accounting and accounting for nonregulated industries are discussed in Chapter 7.

In addition to operations financed primarily through user charges, the enterprise fund structure may be used to account for any other operations for which the governing body of the governmental unit desires a periodic determination of revenues earned, expenses incurred, and/or net income.

The life of an enterprise is assumed to be indefinite. Full accrual accounting is used. All assets used in fund operations and all debt to be serviced from fund earnings are included in enterprise fund accounts. A Retained Earnings account as well as accounts that disclose the amount and source of the contributed equity of the fund are utilized.

Fiduciary Funds

Trust and agency funds are used to account for assets held by a state or local government in a fiduciary capacity. A governmental unit that collects taxes for other units would have need for an agency fund, for example. Employees' retirement plans, also referred to as *Public Employee Retirement Systems* (PERS), are often accounted for in pension trust funds. However, some PERS are organized as separate legal entities and therefore publish their own stand-alone financial statements, rather than report as a pension trust fund.

Agency Funds. An agency relationship may be accounted for satisfactorily within the accounting structure of the General Fund, or other fund, if the amounts collected pursuant to the agency are small in relation to total fund assets, and if the amounts are remitted to the owner without an appreciable lapse of time. If the amounts collected are relatively large, however, or if they are held for an appreciable time, or if the law or GASB standards (discussed in Chapter 8) require it, agency funds should be established. A very simple set of proprietary accounts ordinarily suffices for an agency fund because all fund assets are held as agent and are entirely offset by a liability to the owner. At year-end, if all assets have been collected and have been remitted to the owner, the agency fund would have no balances to report in the annual statements. GASB standards provide that agency fund assets and liabilities are to be accounted for on the basis used by governmental fund types.

Trust Funds. Trust funds differ from agency funds in that a trust fund generally holds assets and manages them for the beneficiaries over a substantial period of time. As discussed in Chapter 9, trust fund accounting problems often relate to the distinction between trust principal and trust income, and to the distinction between expendability and nonexpendability. *Expendable trust funds*, in general, are those that are created to account for trust income expendable for purposes specified by the trustor. Thus, expendable trust funds are similar in nature to special revenue funds, and GASB standards provide that the measurement focus and basis of accounting for expendable trust funds be the same as for governmental funds.

Nonexpendable trust funds are created to account for trust principal, or corpus, held for purposes specified by the trustor—often, the generation of net income to be transferred to an expendable trust. If the generation of net income is the objective of a trust fund, it seems obvious that accounting principles derived for profit-seeking entities and proprietary funds are applicable. Thus, fixed assets given by the donor as a part of the trust principal, or acquired in pursuit of the trust objectives, and long-term debt related to trust assets are accounted for by the trust fund, as well as current assets and current liabilities of the trust.

Investment Trust Funds are used to account for external investment pools, those which invest the monies of governmental and not-for-profit organizations *external* to the government that administers the pool. The assets of such pools must be reported at fair value as of the balance sheet date. Investment trust funds are accounted for on the full accrual basis, similar to the accounting for proprietary funds and nonexpendable trust funds.

Pension Trust Funds are accounted for as explained in Chapter 9. Since this type of trust fund generally has an objective of maximizing earnings from its investments (although the nature of investments that may be held is usually subject to legal restriction), GASB standards require that pension trusts be accounted for in a manner similar to proprietary funds.

Account Groups

General Fixed Assets. Only proprietary funds and fiduciary funds similar to proprietary funds routinely account for property, plant, and equipment used in their operations. All other funds account only for assets that will be turned into cash during the regular operations of the fund. Thus, property, plant, and equipment acquired by governmental funds and fiduciary funds similar to governmental funds are brought under accounting control by the creation of a General Fixed Assets Account Group. No other assets are recorded in the General Fixed Assets Account Group. No liabilities at all are recorded in the accounts of this group. The credit-balance accounts that offset the fixed assets accounts to create a self-balancing group show the source of the investment in general fixed assets.

Depreciation of general fixed assets is not recorded by any fund. It is permissible, but not required, for depreciation to be recorded in the General Fixed Assets Account Group as a deduction from the Investment in General Fixed Assets accounts. Accumulated depreciation accounts would then be deducted from related assets in the Statement of General Fixed Assets.

General Long-Term Debt. Debt instruments backed by the taxing power of a governmental unit are obligations of the governmental unit as a whole and not of the individual funds. The General Long-Term Debt Account Group (GLTDAG) was created to account for such debt. The GLTDAG is also used to account for special assessment long-term debt for which the government is obligated in some manner; the present value of capital lease payments; the noncurrent portions of claims, judgments, and compensated absences to be paid when due by use of the resources of governmental funds; and any unfunded liability for pensions of employees of activities accounted for by governmental funds. No assets are recorded in the group. The amount of long-term (and intermediate-term) debt is offset by accounts entitled Amounts Available in Debt Service Funds for Payment of _____ and Amounts to Be Provided for Payment of _____ .

Summary of Interfund Transactions

Transactions, or events, that affect the accounts of more than one fund or account group of a single governmental unit have been noted in the discussions and illustrative entries of preceding chapters. A brief review of interfund transactions and events at this point should aid the reader in reinforcing his or her understanding of the relationships that exist among the funds and groups.

Each fund is (1) a fiscal entity, (2) an accounting entity and, in a sense, (3) a legal entity. Each account group is only an accounting entity, not a fiscal entity nor, in any sense, a legal entity. Events and transactions that must be recognized in more than one accounting entity of a single governmental unit may be classified in the following manner:

I. Transactions and Transfers between Funds
    A. Interfund loans and advances
    B. Transactions that would be treated as revenues, expenditures, or expenses if they involved organizations external to the governmental unit (quasi-external transactions)
    C. Transactions that reimburse a fund for expenditures made by it on behalf of another fund
    D. Recurring periodic transfers made primarily for the purpose of shifting resources from one fund to another (operating transfers)
    E. Nonrecurring transfers made in compliance with special statutes or ordinances that do not qualify as revenues or expenditures to the receiving or disbursing funds (equity transfers)
II. Events Requiring Recognition in More than One Accounting Entity
    A. Acquisition of general fixed assets
    B. Creation of tax-supported and special assessment long-term debt, or repayment of principal of such long-term debt

Examples of each of the seven classes of interfund events or transactions, and entries that record them in each affected fund or group, are illustrated in the following paragraphs.

Transactions and Transfers between Funds

Interfund Loans and Advances.   The terms *loans* and *advances* are used to indicate amounts that are temporarily transferred from one fund to another but that will have to be repaid in due time.

Since each fund is a fiscal entity, the interfund receivables and payables resulting from loans and advances must be disclosed in a Combined Balance Sheet. They may not be eliminated, as would be proper in the preparation of consolidated statements for parent and subsidiary profit-seeking corporations.

Interfund loans and advances are discussed and illustrated in Chapter 7. The Supplies Fund of the Town of Brighton received a $130,000 long-term advance from the Water Utility Fund of the Town. (The Supplies Fund also received a contribution from the General Fund, which is reviewed below under the Nonrecurring Transfers heading.) The effect of the advance on each fund is:

Supplies Fund

Cash	130,000	
Advance from Water Utility Fund		130,000

Water Utility Fund

Long-Term Advance to Supplies Fund	130,000	
Cash		130,000

Partial repayment of the advance was made at year-end:

Supplies Fund

Advance from Water Utility Fund	6,500	
Cash		6,500

Water Utility Fund

Cash	6,500	
Long-Term Advance to Supplies Fund		6,500

Transactions to Be Reported as Revenues and Expenditures. Interfund transactions that would result in the recognition of revenues, expenditures, or expenses if one of the parties were external to the governmental unit are called **quasi-external transactions**. One of the most common examples of this type of interfund transaction, which properly results in the recognition of revenue by one fund and the recording of an expenditure by another fund, is the provision to the General Fund of fire hydrants and water for fire protection by a municipally owned water utility; illustrative entries are given in Chapters 4 and 7 for this type of interfund transaction. The effect on the general ledger accounts of the Town of Brighton's General Fund and Water Utility Fund for fire protection service provided by the utility is:

General Fund

Expenditures	30,000	
Due to Other Funds		30,000

Water Utility Fund

Due from Other Funds	30,000	
Sales of Water		30,000

The Water Utility Fund of the Town of Brighton received services from General Fund departments, as is also common. The entries to record the resulting expense and revenues, as given in Chapters 4 and 7, are:

General Fund

Due from Other Funds	25,000	
Revenues		25,000

Water Utility Fund

Contribution in Lieu of Taxes	25,000	
Due to Other Funds		25,000

The net effect of the transactions between the two funds of the Town of Brighton is that the General Fund owes the Water Utility Fund $5,000. It is considered proper for the Balance Sheet of each fund, and the Combined Balance Sheet for all funds, to display this net amount as a receivable or payable. It should be stressed, however, that it is *not* acceptable to offset a receivable from one fund against a payable to a different fund.

Transactions in the Nature of Reimbursements of Expenditures.   If one fund performs services for another fund on an incidental rather than recurring basis, administrators and accountants may consider it more reasonable for the fund receiving the services to reimburse the fund rendering the services for their cost (or estimated cost) rather than to treat the transaction as a quasi-external transaction in the manner described above. For example, if the city engineers' office, a General Fund department, performed services of an incidental nature for the Street Fund (assumed to be a special revenue fund in this example), the following entries would reflect the reimbursement given to the General Fund by the Street Fund (assuming $2,600 is thought to reflect fairly the expenditure the city engineers' office incurred for the benefit of the Street Fund):

General Fund

Cash	2,600	
Expenditures		2,600

Street Fund

Expenditures	2,600	
Cash		2,600

Similarly, it is not uncommon for an amount to be recorded as an expenditure, or expense, of one fund which, in fact, should have been recorded as an expenditure, or expense, of another fund. This may occur because of incorrect account coding, data entry error, or lack of adequate information at the time the transaction was recorded. Since the general rule is that revenues, expenditures, and expenses should be reported as such only once, it is considered proper for the fund that should have borne the expenditure, or expense, to debit the appropriate expenditure, or expense, account when it recognizes its liability to the fund that first recorded the expenditure. Similarly, the fund that erroneously recorded the expenditure should debit a receivable from the fund that should have recognized the expenditure, or expense, and should credit the expenditure, or expense, account originally debited.

Recurring Periodic Shifts of Resources (Operating Transfers).   A common example of a transfer of resources that would occur at regular periodic intervals, but that would not result in a true expenditure to the fund raising the revenue, or true revenue to the fund receiving the transfer, is the situation in which revenue to be used for debt service is raised by the General Fund and transferred to a debt service fund. The entry in the General Fund for the shift of resources from the General Fund to the debt service fund would be (amount assumed):

General Fund

Operating Transfers Out	128,000	
Cash		128,000

The corresponding entry in the Debt Service Fund would be:

Debt Service Fund

Cash	128,000	
Operating Transfers In		128,000

The transfer illustrated above also has an effect on the General Long-Term Debt Account Group if a portion of the transfer is to be used for payment of debt principal. Assuming $50,000 of the $128,000 is to be used for debt principal payment, the entry in the GLTDAG would be:

General Long-Term Debt Account Group

Amount Available in Debt Service Fund for Payment of Regular Serial Bonds	50,000	
Amount to Be Provided for Payment of Regular Serial Bonds		50,000

Nonrecurring Transfers Made in Compliance with Special Statutes (Equity Transfers)[1].   In Chapter 7, the first entry in the illustrative case of the Town of Brighton Supplies Fund reflects the transfer of inventory and cash from the General Fund of that town as a contribution of working capital that is not expected to be repaid. This transfer would have to have been authorized by appropriate legal action and therefore is an example of a nonrecurring transfer made in compliance with special statutes or ordinances that does not result in revenues or expenditures to the receiving or disbursing fund. The transfer is stated to have taken place in the year following the year for which illustrative entries are shown for the Town of Brighton General Fund, so the entries in that fund are not shown in Chapter 4. The entries to be made by both funds at the time of the transfer are:

General Fund

Equity Transfers Out*	91,500	
Cash		30,000
Inventory of Supplies		61,500

Supplies Fund

Cash	30,000	
Inventory of Supplies	61,500	
Equity Transfers In†		91,500

*In the General Fund the Equity Transfers Out account would be closed to Fund Balance; the Reserve for Inventory of Supplies account would also be closed to Fund Balance since the General Fund no longer accounts for the inventory.
†In the Supplies Fund the Equity Transfers In account would be closed to the Contribution from General Fund account.

An example similar to the one discussed above is the contribution of equity by a General Fund to a utility fund. The return of part or all of such contributions

---

[1]The GASB *Codification* continues the use of the NCGA's term *residual equity transfer,* which is appropriate to describe the transfer of the residual equity of a capital projects fund to a debt service fund (illustrated in Chapters 5 and 6, respectively) but not appropriate to describe equity transfers in general.

would also be a transfer of the nature comprehended in this category. A further example would be the transfer of residual equity balances of discontinued funds to general or debt service funds, normally required by statute.

Events Requiring Recognition in More Than One Accounting Entity

Acquisition of General Fixed Assets. Preceding discussions of the General Fixed Assets Account Group emphasized that the group was created to place under accounting control assets acquired through expenditures of General Funds, special revenue funds, and capital projects funds, none of which account for fixed assets. Chapter 5 illustrates several sets of entries in funds financing the acquisition of general fixed assets and corresponding entries in the General Fixed Assets Account Group. For review purposes, one set of entries involving the purchase of office equipment by the General Fund of a state or local governmental unit is shown below:

General Fund

Expenditures	1,450	
Vouchers Payable		1,450

General Fixed Assets Account Group

Equipment	1,450	
Investment in General Fixed Assets—General Fund Revenues		1,450

The acquisition of general fixed assets by use of a capital lease agreement results in three sets of entries at the inception of the lease: the assets must be recorded in the General Fixed Assets Account Group, the related liability must be recorded in the General Long-Term Debt Account Group, and an Expenditure and an Other Financing Source must be recorded in a governmental fund (including, if appropriate, a capital projects fund). Entries at the inception of one hypothetical capital lease are illustrated in Chapters 5 and 6.

Creation or Repayment of General Long-Term Debt. One event that must be recorded in both a fund and in the General Long-Term Debt Account Group is the issuance of tax-supported bonds so that the proceeds may be used for the acquisition of capital facilities. In the Town of Brighton case presented in Chapter 6, the town has outstanding a deferred serial bond issue in the amount of $2,000,000. At the time the bonds were sold, assuming they were sold at par for the acquisition of capital facilities, the following entries were necessary:

Capital Projects Fund

Cash	2,000,000	
Proceeds of Bonds		2,000,000

General Long-Term Debt Account Group

Amount to Be Provided for Payment of Deferred Serial Bonds	2,000,000	
Deferred Serial Bonds Payable		2,000,000

Later, after cash for bond repayment has been received by the debt service fund and the GLTDAG has recorded that amount in the Amount Available account, and removed it from the Amount to Be Provided account, assume the first

$200,000 of bonds matures and the liability is transferred from the General Long-Term Debt Account Group to the debt service fund for payment, as shown in the following entries:

Debt Service Fund

Expenditures—Bond Principal	200,000	
Bonds Payable		200,000

General Long-Term Debt Account Group

Deferred Serial Bonds Payable	200,000	
Amount Available in Debt Service Fund for Payment of		
Deferred Serial Bonds		200,000

General long-term debt arising from a capital lease agreement is recorded at the inception of the lease, as noted in the section above. The payment of rentals during the term of the lease requires entries in a governmental fund (ordinarily a debt service fund) and in the General Long-Term Debt Account Group, as illustrated in Chapter 6.

The Governmental Reporting Entity

The objectives of accounting and financial reporting for governmental units set forth in the GASB's *Concepts Statement No. 1* are discussed in Chapter 1. *Concepts Statement No 1* does not deal with the practical problem of deciding what a "governmental unit" is. The average citizen—including accountants whose only experience has been with business organizations—has only a vague knowledge, and little understanding, of the overlapping layers of general purpose and limited-purpose governmental organizations that have some jurisdiction over us wherever we may live and work. Illustration 8–1 indicates the layers of general purpose governments that levy taxes on property. The School Funds in that illustration show that taxes are also levied by limited-purpose governmental units (an independent school district, in that illustration). Omitted from that illustration, for the sake of brevity, are taxes levied by any special districts. Special districts are defined by the Bureau of the Census as "independent limited-purpose governmental units (other than school districts) that exist as separate entities and have substantial administrative and fiscal independence from general purpose local governments."[2] Over 37 percent of the local governments in the United States are classified as special districts.[3]

Although the Census definition stresses the independence of special districts, in many instances they were created to provide a vehicle for financing services demanded by residents of a general purpose governmental unit that could not be financed by the general purpose unit because of constitutional or statutory

---

[2]U.S. Department of Commerce, Bureau of the Census, *1992 Census of Governments* 1, no. 2 (Washington, DC: U.S. Government Printing Office, 1993), p. B–2.

[3]Ibid., 1, No. 2., p. v.

limits on the rates or amounts it could raise from taxes, other revenue sources, and debt. Building authorities are an example of special districts created as a financing vehicle.

In addition to special districts, defined by the Bureau of the Census as independent entities, but whose financial activities are often closely related to those of one or more general governmental units, it is common for certain governmental activities to be carried on by commissions, boards, and other agencies that are not considered as independent of a general governmental unit by the Bureau of the Census but that may have some degree of fiscal and administrative independence from the governing board of the general governmental unit. In past years, some governments have included in their annual reports the financial statements of such semi-independent boards and commissions, and even certain of the special districts, whereas other governments have excluded from their reports the financial data of semi-independent and independent entities.

In order to reduce disparity in reporting and to promote the preparation of financial reports consistent with GASB *Concepts Statement No. 1,* GASB *Codification* Section 2100 provides authoritative guidance on defining the reporting entity, and Section 2600 presents guidance on reporting entity and component unit presentations and disclosure.

Entity Definition Criteria

GASB *Codification* Section 2100 notes that all government organizations are ultimately responsible to elected governing officials at the federal, state, or local level. Elected officials of the primary government are accountable to the citizens for those organizations that are financially dependent on the primary government, or for which the primary government can impose its will. Thus, Section 2100 takes the position that governmental financial reporting should report the elected officials' accountability for such organizations. It should be emphasized that Section 2100 deals only with criteria for defining a governmental reporting entity; it does not establish standards for the incorporation of financial data of component units in the financial statements of the reporting entity. Standards for the incorporation of financial data are set forth in Section 2600.

Definitions of key terms and concepts needed to understand and apply reporting entity criteria are given in Section 2100.501, from which selected terms and concepts are provided here:

Financial Reporting Entity.   A primary government, organizations for which the primary government is financially accountable, and other organizations for which the nature and significance of their relationship with the primary government are such that exclusion would cause the reporting entity's financial statements to be misleading or incomplete. The nucleus of a financial reporting entity usually is a primary government. However, a governmental organization other than a primary government (such as a component unit, a joint venture, a jointly governed organization, or other stand-alone government) serves as the nucleus for its own reporting entity when it issues separate financial statements.

Primary Government.   A state government or general purpose local government. Also, a special purpose government that has a separately elected governing body, is legally separate, and is fiscally independent of other state or local governments.

Component Units.   Legally separate organizations for which the elected officials of the primary government are financially accountable. In addition, a component unit can be another organization for which the nature and significance of its relationship with a primary government is such that exclusion would cause the reporting entity's financial statements to be misleading or incomplete.

Blending (Blended).   The method of reporting the financial data of a component unit that presents the component unit's balances and transactions in a manner similar to the presentation of the balances and transactions of the primary government.

Discrete Presentation (Discretely Presented).   The method of reporting financial data of component units in a column(s) separate from the financial data of the primary government. An integral part of this method of presentation is that individual component unit supporting information is required to be provided either in condensed financial statements within the notes to the reporting entity's financial statements, or in combining statements in its general purpose financial statements (GPFS).

Financial Accountability (Financially Accountable).   The level of accountability that exists if a primary government appoints a voting majority of an organization's governing board and is either able to impose its will on that organization or there is a potential for the organization to provide specific financial benefits to, or impose specific financial burdens on, the primary government. A primary government may also be financially accountable for governmental organizations with a separately elected governing board, a governing board appointed by another government, or a jointly appointed board that is fiscally dependent on the primary government.

Jointly Governed Organizations.   A regional government or other multigovernmental arrangement that is governed by representatives from each of the governments that create the organization, but that is not a joint venture because the participants do not retain an ongoing financial interest or responsibility.

Joint Venture.   A legal entity or other organization that results from a contractual arrangement and that is owned, operated, or governed by two or more participants as a separate and specific activity subject to joint control, in which the participants retain (*a*) an ongoing financial interest or (*b*) an ongoing financial responsibility.

Legally Separate Organization (Separate Legal Standing).   An organization created as a body corporate or a body corporate and politic or otherwise possessing similar corporate powers. An organization that has separate legal standing has an identity of its own as an "artificial person" with a personality and existence distinct from that of its creator and others.

Other Stand-Alone Government. A legally separate governmental organization that (*a*) does not have a separately elected governing body and (*b*) does not meet the definition of a component unit. Other stand-alone governments include some special purpose governments, joint ventures, jointly governed organizations, and pools.

The definition of the reporting entity is based primarily on the notion of financial accountability. A primary government is financially accountable for the organizations that make up its legal entity. It is also financially accountable for legally separate organizations if its officials appoint a voting majority of an organization's governing body and either it is able to impose its will on that organization or there is a potential for the organization to provide specific financial benefits to, or to impose specific financial burdens on, the primary government.

A primary government has the ability to impose its will on an organization if it can significantly influence the programs, projects, or activities of, or the level of services performed or provided by, the organization. A financial benefit or burden relationship exists if the primary government (*a*) is entitled to the organization's resources; (*b*) is legally obligated or has otherwise assumed the obligation to finance the deficits of, or provide financial support to, the organization; or (*c*) is obligated in some manner for the debt of the organization.

Some organizations are included as component units because of their fiscal dependency on the primary government. An organization is fiscally dependent on the primary government if it is unable to adopt its budget, levy taxes, or set rates or charges, or issue bonded debt without approval by the primary government.[4]

The flowchart in Illustration 10–2 shows the decision process for inclusion or exclusion of a potential component unit (PCU) and how the PCU should be presented in the financial statements or the notes thereto. *Codification* Section 2100.902–920 provides several examples of the application of the reporting entity criteria in specific circumstances.

GASB standards require that most component units be **discretely presented** (as defined previously) since they are legally separate organizations.[5] If, however, a component unit is, in substance, a part of the primary government, **blended** reporting is required. An example of the latter is a building authority established to finance and construct public facilities for the primary government, with debt service provided by lease payments made by the primary government. Blended reporting is accomplished by including component units' financial data for particular fund types and account groups with that for the same fund types and account groups of the primary government (e.g., special, revenue fund data of the

---

[4]GASB, *Codification*, Sec. 2100.
[5]GASB, *Codification*, Sec. 2600, 107–114.

Illustration 10–2   Decision Process for Inclusion or Exclusion of PCU

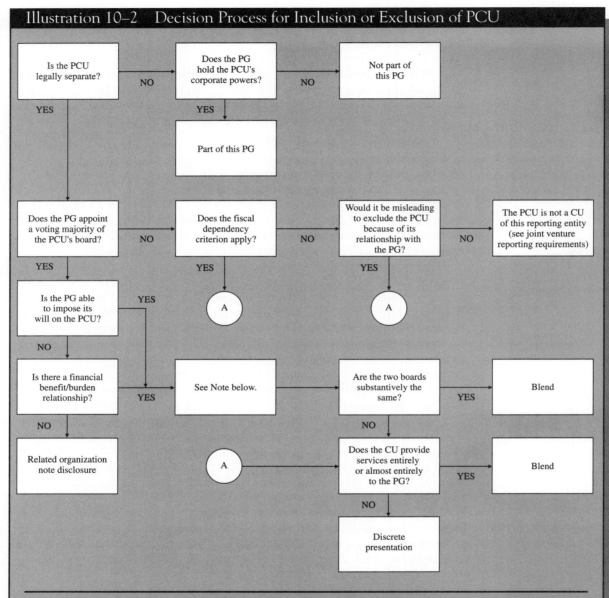

Note: A potential component unit (PCU) for which a primary government (PG) is financially accountable may be fiscally dependent on another government. An organization should be included as a component unit (CU) of only one reporting entity. Professional judgment should be used to determine the most appropriate reporting entity. A primary government that appoints a voting majority of the governing board of a component unit of another government should make the disclosures required for related organizations.

Source: GASB, *Codification*, Sec. 2100.901.

component unit included along with that of the primary government in the Special Revenue Funds column of combined financial statements). One exception in blended reporting is that component unit General Fund data is included in the Special Revenue Funds column of combined financial statements rather than the General Fund column.[6] Thus, the General Fund column presents only the data for the primary government's General Fund.

Governmental Financial Reports

Once the reporting entity has been determined in accord with the criteria discussed in the preceding section, persons responsible for preparing financial reports for the reporting entity should follow the guidance given in currently effective authoritative literature to determine the content of financial reports to be issued for external users. Chapter 2 contains a summary of the standards the GASB *Codification* sets forth for the content of the comprehensive annual financial report (CAFR) of a state or local governmental reporting entity. Chapters 3 through 9 elaborate on the application of those standards to accounting and financial reporting for each of the fund types and account groups provided in the GASB *Codification* and subsequent GASB Statements and Interpretations. Although much of the discussion in preceding chapters is concerned with general purpose external financial reporting, the needs of administrators. legislators, and other users not properly classifiable as "external" have been given some attention. In the following paragraphs, the discussion in preceding chapters is briefly summarized and placed in perspective.

Need for Periodic Reports

Persons concerned with the day-to-day operations and activities accounted for by governmental funds and groups should be familiar with much of the data processed by the accounting information system because it results from the events and transactions with which they are involved. It is easy for these persons to become overconfident of the intuitive "feel" they develop from their daily involvement. Past events were not always as remembered, and the relative significance of events changes over time. Similarly, administrators at succeedingly higher levels in the organization may feel that participation in decision making and observation of the apparent results of past decisions obviate the necessity for periodic analysis of accounting and statistical reports prepared objectively and with neutrality. However, the memory and perceptions of administrators at higher levels are also subject to failure. Therefore, it is generally agreed that it is useful for financial reports to be prepared and distributed at intervals throughout a fiscal period as well as at period-end.

Interim Financial Reports

Administrators of a governmental unit have greatest need for interim financial reports, although members of the legislative branch of the governmental unit (particularly those on its finance committee) should also find them of considerable use.

---

[6]GASB, *Codification*, Sec. 2600.117.

Other users of interim reports are news media and residents who are particularly concerned with aspects of the financial management of the unit.

A complete interim financial report should include at least the following statements and schedules:

1. Statement of Actual and Estimated Revenue (for the general and special revenue funds and each other fund type for which budgets have been legally adopted).
2. Statement of Actual and Estimated Expenditures (for the general and special revenue funds and for each other fund type for which budgets have been legally adopted).
3. Comparative Statement of Revenue and Expense (for each enterprise and internal service fund and for similar fiduciary funds).
4. Combined Statement of Cash Receipts, Disbursements, and Balances—All Funds.
5. Forecast of Cash Positions—All Funds.

Statements and schedules in addition to those listed above are needed by governmental units with varied and complex activities. A statement of investments held and their cost and market values is an example of an additional statement that is of wide utility.

Schedules of past-due receivables from taxes, special assessments, and utility customers may also be needed at intervals.

Complete interim reports should be prepared and distributed at regular intervals throughout a fiscal period, generally monthly, although small governmental units that have little financial activity may find a bimonthly or quarterly period satisfactory. Partial interim reports dealing only with those items of considerable current importance should be prepared and distributed as frequently as their information would be of value. For example, reports of market values of investments and of purchases and sales may be needed by a relatively small number of users on a daily basis during certain critical periods.

Annual Financial Reports

Governmental annual financial reports are needed by the same individuals and groups who should receive interim reports. They are also often required to be distributed to agencies of higher governmental jurisdictions and to major creditors. Other users include financial underwriters; debt insurers; debt rating agencies; debt analysts; libraries; other governmental units; associations of governmental administrators, accountants, and finance officers; and college professors and students.

A comprehensive annual financial report should be prepared and published by each state and local governmental unit as a matter of public record. The comprehensive annual financial report is the governmental unit's official annual report prepared and published as a matter of public record. GASB standards make it clear that a primary government is the nucleus of a financial reporting entity for which a CAFR is prepared. However, a governmental organization other than a primary government (e.g., a component unit, joint venture, jointly governed organization, or other stand-alone government) serves as the nucleus of its own reporting entity. The separately issued financial statements of such a reporting entity should follow the same reporting entity standards as those for a primary government and its component units. Specifically, *Codification* Section 1100.112 requires that the Section 2100 criteria for defining a reporting entity be applied in layers "from the bottom up." For each layer, reporting entity definition and display requirements must be applied before the layer is included in the financial statements for the next higher layer.

In addition to the general purpose financial statements (GPFS, in GASB nomenclature), the CAFR should contain introductory material, schedules necessary to demonstrate legal compliance, and statistical tables.

Introductory Section. The introductory section of a CAFR should include the title page and contents page, the letter of transmittal, and other material deemed appropriate by management.

The letter of transmittal may be a letter from the chief finance officer addressed to the chief executive and governing body of the governmental unit, or it may be a narrative over the signature of the chief executive. In either event, the letter or narrative material should cite legal and policy requirements for the report and discuss briefly the important aspects of the financial condition and financial operations of the governmental unit as a whole and of the unit's funds and account groups. Significant changes since the prior annual report and changes expected during the coming year should be brought to the attention of the reader of the report.

Financial Section. The financial section of a comprehensive annual financial report should include: (1) an auditor's report, (2) general purpose financial statements, or component unit financial statements, (3) required supplementary information, and (4) combining and individual fund and account group statements and schedules.

Laws relating to the audit of governmental units vary markedly from state to state. In some, all state agencies and all governmental units created pursuant to the state law are required to be audited by an audit agency of the state government. In others, local governmental units are audited by independent Certified Public Accountants. In still others, some governmental units are audited by the state audit agency and some by independent Certified Public Accountants. In any event, the auditor's report should accompany the financial statements reproduced in the CAFR. Chapter 12 illustrates auditors' reports and explains their significance.

The financial section should contain sufficient information to disclose fully and present fairly the financial position and results of financial operations during the fiscal year. GASB *Codification* Section 2200.108 lists the five combined statements that are the basic general purpose financial statements of a state or local government and stresses that these statements and notes thereto are required for conformity with GAAP. The GPFS, therefore, consists of the:

1. Combined Balance Sheet—All Fund Types, Account Groups, and Discretely Presented Component Units. (See Illustration 2–1.)
2. Combined Statement of Revenues, Expenditures, and Changes in Fund Balances—All Governmental Fund Types and Discretely Presented Component Units. (See Illustration 2–2.)
3. Combined Statement of Revenues, Expenditures, and Changes in Fund Balances—Budget and Actual—General and Special Revenue Fund Types (and similar governmental fund types of the primary government for which annual budgets have been legally adopted). (See Illustration 2–3.)
4. Combined Statement of Revenues, Expenses, and Changes in Retained Earnings (or Equity)—All Proprietary Fund Types, Similar Trust Funds, and Discretely Presented Component Units. (See Illustration 2–4.)
5. Combined Statement of Cash Flows—All Proprietary Fund Types and Discretely Presented Component Units. (See Illustration 2–5.)
6. Notes to the Financial Statements.

The general purpose financial statements are a necessary part of an official comprehensive annual financial report, but GASB standards specifically provide that the GPFS may also be issued separately for widespread distribution to users requiring less detailed information than is contained in the complete CAFR. A Combined Statement of Revenues, Expenditures, and Changes in Fund Balances—Budget and Actual—General and Special Revenue Fund Types is illustrated in Chapter 2 (see Illustration 2–3) as a means of introducing the reader to budgetary accounting and reporting. Each subsequent chapter illustrates individual fund and account group statements and combining statements needed to support the fund-type column in combined statements when a reporting entity has more than one fund in a given fund type.

Statistical Tables. In addition to the output of the accounting information system presented in the financial section of the governmental annual report, statistical tables reflecting social and economic data, financial trends, and the fiscal capacity of the government are needed by the reader who is more than casually interested in the activities of the governmental unit. Tabulations required by the GASB for inclusion in a CAFR are:

1. General Governmental Expenditures by Function—Last Ten Fiscal Years.
2. General Revenues by Source—Last Ten Fiscal Years.
3. Property Tax Levies and Collections—Last Ten Fiscal Years.
4. Assessed and Estimated Actual Value of Taxable Property—Last Ten Fiscal Years.
5. Property Tax Rates—All Overlapping Governments—Last Ten Fiscal Years.
6. Special Assessment Billings and Collections—Last Ten Fiscal Years (if the government is obligated in some manner for related special assessment debt).

7. Ratio of Net General Bonded Debt to Assessed Value and Net Bonded Debt per Capita—Last Ten Fiscal Years.
8. Computation of Legal Debt Margin (if not presented in the financial section).
9. Computation of Overlapping Debt (if not presented in the financial section).
10. Ratio of Annual Debt Service for General Bonded Debt to Total General Expenditures—Last Ten Fiscal Years.
11. Revenue Bond Coverage—Last Ten Fiscal Years.
12. Demographic Statistics.
13. Property Value, Construction, and Bank Deposits—Last Ten Fiscal Years.
14. Principal Taxpayers.
15. Miscellaneous Statistics.

Classification of governmental expenditures by function, classification of revenues by source, and other meaningful classifications of revenues and expenditures are discussed at some length in Chapter 3. Assessment of property and the levy and collection of property taxes are discussed in Chapter 4 and in subsequent chapters as appropriate. Reporting of the ratio of net general bonded debt to assessed valuation and the ratio per capita, as well as the computation of legal debt limit, legal debt margin, and direct and overlapping debt and future debt service requirements, are all illustrated and discussed in Chapter 6. Information about investments held for the various funds is often presented in the statistical section of a CAFR, although, as shown in Chapter 6, the information may also be presented in other sections of the report. Additional information listed by the GASB as desirable for presentation in the statistical section of the CAFR is generally self-explanatory. The demographic statistics and miscellaneous statistics often presented are those that are of interest to debt insurers, debt rating agencies, creditors and potential creditors, and organizations considering locating in the area included in the reporting entity, such as population, per capita income, unemployment rate, average education of the work force, fire protection data, police protection data, information about public schools and colleges and universities, recreation and cultural facilities, and parking facilities. Additionally, it seems to be common for state laws to require local governments to list administrators and their salaries, and to list property, casualty, and fidelity insurance coverage carried by the reporting entity.

Developments in Financial Reporting and Unresolved Issues

GASB reporting objectives emphasize the role of accountability in external financial reporting. Indeed, accountability is considered to be "the paramount objective from which all other objectives must flow."[7] GASB *Concepts Statement No. 1*

---

[7]GASB, *Codification*, Appendix B, *Concepts Statement No. 1*, par. 76.

expands the definition of accountability beyond the traditional notion of accountability for expenditures of financial resources in conformity with the legally adopted budget. GASB's concept of accountability includes also accountability for the efficient and effective use of resources in providing government services and for interpersonal equity, or the extent to which current-year revenues are sufficient to pay for current-year services.[8] It follows that the boundaries of external general purpose financial reporting may need to be expanded to meet the objectives implied by the broader concept of accountability. The GASB, accordingly, has established several projects aimed at meeting these broader objectives. Not all constituents agree with the objectives GASB has established and their implications for financial reporting. Thus, some projects have been highly controversial. Some of GASB's key financial reporting projects are discussed briefly in the following paragraphs.

Measurement Focus and Basis of Accounting— Governmental Fund Types (MFBA)

In May 1990, after extensive due process, the GASB issued *Statement No. 11 "Measurement Focus and Basis of Accounting—Governmental Fund Operating Statements,"* which was to have become effective for fiscal years beginning after June 15, 1994. This *Statement* would have shifted the measurement focus for governmental fund revenues and expenditures from flow of *available* financial resources to the flow of financial resources, regardless of when cash is received or paid. Thus, revenues and expenditures would have been recognized on an accrual basis (revenues when earned or demanded and expenditures when incurred) rather than on the modified accrual basis required by current GAAP. GASB believed that use of the accrual basis for governmental funds would achieve better reporting on interperiod equity by including in governmental fund operating statements changes in noncurrent assets and noncurrent liabilities relating to operating activities. Early implementation of *Statement No. 11* was not permitted since the *Statement* dealt only with measurement, recognition, and display of operating statement accounts; subsequent guidance on balance sheet display was to have been provided prior to implementation as part of GASB's financial reporting project.

Some constituent organizations strongly opposed issuance of *Statement No. 11* prior to resolving related financial reporting (especially balance sheet display) issues. Their opposition continued after *Statement No. 11* was issued, perhaps encouraged by inability of the GASB Board Members to reach agreement on a reporting model and the manner of reporting long-term accruals and operating debt in balance sheets, among other unresolved reporting issues. In 1992 GASB issued a Preliminary Views document designed to gather constituents' reactions to alternative views within the GASB about implementation of *Statement No. 11*. A majority of the Board, the "preliminary view," believed that operating debt and long-term accrued obligations related to operations should be reported as liabilities of governmental funds. The minority, or "alternative view," held that, pending completion of the full financial reporting model project, such liabilities should continue to be reported in the GLTDAG. Subsequent hearings found no consensus

---

[8]Ibid., par. 77.

among constituents for either approach. After further due process input indicated that a number of constituents opposed implementation of *Statement No. 11*, as scheduled, prior to completion of the financial reporting model project, GASB issued *Statement No. 17* in June 1993 that delayed indefinitely the implementation of *Statement No. 11*. The GASB, however, issued a standard that requires accrual recognition of revenues from taxpayer-assessed taxes (such as income and sales taxes) when the amount is known or reasonably determinable.

Financial Reporting Model

Since its inception in 1984, the GASB has had a project on its agenda to develop a new financial reporting model for state and local governments. As discussed in the preceding sections, after its earlier attempt to require governments to apply the accrual basis of accounting to all funds failed to gain sufficient acceptance from constituents, the GASB issued proposals for a new "dual perspective" reporting model.[9] One perspective, the "fund perspective," is similar in most respects to the present fund-type financial statements discussed at length in Chapters 2 through 9 of this text. The other perspective would require entitywide financial statements to be reported using an economic resource focus—similar to the commercial accounting model, including recognition of revenues and expenses on the full accrual basis. This would, of course, represent a major change from the current reporting model discussed in the text.

In addition to the basic financial statements, governments would be required to present a Management Discussion and Analysis (MD&A) section. Similar to the MD&A that the Securities and Exchange Commission requires of publicly traded corporations, the MD&A would consist of a narrative summary prepared by management giving a brief, objective, and easily readable analysis of the government's financial performance for the year and its financial position at year-end.

In advocating a dual perspective reporting model the GASB is taking the position that no *one* set of financial statements can meet the identified objectives of financial reporting, some that are related to **fiscal accountability** and others that are related to **operational accountability**. The entitywide financial statements are intended to report on operational accountability—information about operating results and financial position from an economic perspective. As such, the entitywide financial statements would provide information about both short-term and long-term financial position, and the cost of providing services, broadly summarized for activities of the government. Fund perspective statements for the governmental funds would continue the emphasis on fiscal accountability. Thus, for governmental activities, the fund perspective statements would continue to focus on current-period financial position and budgetary compliance.[10]

---

[9]Governmental Accounting Standards Board, *Preliminary Views*, "Governmental Financial Reporting Model: Core Financial Statements" (Norwalk, CT, June 1995). GASB, Exposure Draft, *Proposed Statement of the Governmental Accounting Standards Board*, "Basic Financial Statements—and Management's Discussion and Analysis—For State and Local Governments" (Norwalk, CT, January 1997).

[10]GASB, Exposure Draft, par. 140.

In March 1997, the GASB issued an exposure draft on accounting and financial reporting for nonexchange transactions, a subproject of its overall reporting model project.[11] The exposure draft identifies four classes of nonexchange transactions: (1) derived tax revenues such as sales and income taxes; (2) imposed revenues other than derived tax revenues (for example, property taxes and fines); (3) government-mandated revenues, such as those from federal programs that state and local governments are mandated to perform; and (4) voluntarily provided revenues, such as certain grants and private donations. The GASB also has a separate subproject to reexamine required note disclosures in light of the new proposed basic financial statements and MD&A.

Public hearings, written comments, and focus group research subsequent to issuance of the reporting model exposure draft have revealed continuing strong disagreement among major constituents (particularly among state and local government professional organizations and the AICPA). Nevertheless, the GASB is proceeding with analysis of public input and deliberations about issues surrounding the reporting model. Although the GASB is expected to issue a final statement on the new reporting model by late 1998, implementation of the new model would not be required until fiscal years beginning after June 15, 2000, and perhaps later.[12]

Because the continuing controversy could lead to further changes to the reporting model from those currently being proposed, this edition of the text has emphasized *current* accounting and financial reporting requirements. When final reporting model standards are issued, the publisher will provide an update bulletin for adopters of this edition. Moreover, prior to the implementation date for any new reporting model standards, the authors plan to issue the next edition of the text to fully explain and illustrate the requirements of whatever new model the GASB may prescribe.

Service Efforts and Accomplishments (SEA)

GASB, as mentioned previously, has expanded the accountability reporting objective to include reporting on the efficient and effective use of resources. GASB *Codification* Section 100.177c states:

> Financial reporting should provide information to assist users in assessing the service efforts, costs, and accomplishments of the governmental entity.

The lack of a bottom-line measure of performance for a governmental entity, such as profit for a for-profit entity, means that *nonfinancial* measures of **service efforts and accomplishments** (SEA), and related costs, are necessary for informed decision making by citizens, elected officials, appointed officials, investors and creditors, and

---

[11]Governmental Accounting Standards Board, Exposure Draft, *Proposed Statement of the Governmental Accounting Standards Board*, "Accounting and Financial Reporting for Nonexchange Transactions" (Norwalk, CT, March 1997).

[12]As noted in the discussion in the following paragraphs, the current status of the proposed reporting model is somewhat tenuous and may change from what is being proposed. For that reason, we do not devote any space in this edition of the text to illustrative proposed financial statements. For readers interested in such statements, a copy of the reporting model exposure draft and illustrative financial statements can be obtained from the GASB.

others having an interest in the government's performance. Advances in information technology, the growing number of highly qualified public managers, and increasing public demand for accountability now make feasible more sophisticated performance measurement and reporting systems than in the past. Thus, the GASB has sponsored and conducted extensive research on SEA measures for several service areas, including, among others, elementary and secondary education, higher education, fire departments, police departments, hospitals, public health, mass transit, road maintenance, and sanitation collection and disposal.

Based on the research to date, GASB issued in 1994 *Concepts Statement No. 2,* which identified three broad categories of SEA measures: (1) measures of service efforts, (2) measures of service accomplishments, and (3) measures that relate efforts to accomplishments.[13] Measures of service efforts, or **input measures,** relate to the amount of financial and nonfinancial resources (such as money and materials) used in a program or process.[14] Measures of service accomplishments are of two types: outputs and outcomes. **Output measures** are quantity measures that reflect either the quantity of a service provided, such as the number of lane-miles of road repaired, or the quantity of service provided that meets a specified quality requirement, such as the number of lane-miles of road repaired to a specified minimum condition. **Outcome measures** gauge accomplishments, or the results of services provided, such as the percentage of lane-miles of road in excellent, good, or fair condition. Such measures are particularly useful when compared with established objectives or norms, or with results from previous years. Finally, measures that relate efforts to accomplishments are essential to assessing efficiency and effectiveness. **Efficiency measures** relate the quantity or cost of resources used to unit of output (e.g., cost per lane-mile of road repaired). Measures that relate resource costs to outcomes are useful in evaluating how effectively service objectives are being met and at what cost (e.g., the cost per lane-mile of road maintained in excellent, good, or fair condition). Additional quantitative and narrative explanation may be necessary to help users fully assess the entity's performance.

The authors believe that some form of SEA reporting, possibly as required supplemental disclosure in the CAFR, or perhaps in a separately issued "performance" report, will eventually be required by GASB. However, there is currently little consensus as to what kinds of measures should be reported, and even whether setting standards for SEA reporting is within the scope of GASB's mandate. Thus, considerable experimentation and deliberation will be required before GASB can issue a standard on SEA reporting.

Other Reporting Issues

GASB has established a number of other projects on reporting issues. These include accounting for postemployment benefits other than pensions, definition and

---

[13]Governmental Accounting Standards Board, *Concepts Statement No. 2,* "Service Efforts and Accomplishments Reporting" (Norwalk, CT, April 1994).

[14]The discussion of SEA measures in this paragraph is paraphrased from the discussion in *Concepts Statement No. 2,* pars. 50–53.

measurement focus for the government's business-type activities, and accounting for government-owned or affiliated colleges and universities.[15] It should be obvious from the preceding discussion that governmental accounting has changed rapidly in recent years. Developments in this area are expected to continue at a rapid pace for the forseeable future.

Popular Reporting

Although the CAFR has evolved to meet the diverse information needs of financial report users (i.e., citizens, legislative and oversight bodies, and investors and creditors), it is widely recognized that most citizens are unable to read and comprehend the CAFR. Indeed, only a relatively few sophisticated analysts with taxpayer associations, citizen watchdog groups, and the media find the CAFR to be useful. To better communicate financial results to citizens. a growing number of governments prepare and distribute **popular reports** that provide highly condensed financial information, budget summaries, and narrative descriptions. They are usually short in length and employ a variety of graphical techniques to enhance understandability. Popular reports are intended to supplement the CAFR, not replace it. Since they do not present minimum data required for complete and fair presentation, popular reports are considered "summary data" and are unaudited.[16] Both GASB and the Government Finance Officers Association (GFOA), however, recognize the value of popular reports. GASB has published a commissioned research report on popular reporting,[17] and the GFOA has established an award program for excellence in popular reporting. As citizens continue to demand greater accountability from their elected and appointed officials, popular reporting is likely to become more common.

Persons concerned with decision making for governmental bodies, auditors, bond analysts and investors, and others have a need to understand and evaluate both financial and nonfinancial information not incorporated in the comprehensive annual financial report. Chapter 11 explains how to use financial statements in evaluating the financial condition of governments. Chapter 14 introduces the subject of budgeting as a means of aiding administrators and legislators in evaluating alternative plans and, after plans are decided on, in evaluating whether activities are conducted according to plan.

Chapter 15 introduces the important topics of cash budgeting and cash management. It also discusses accounting and reporting requirements for deposits with financial institutions and investments.

---

[15]As standards are issued in these areas, the publisher will provide updates to adopters of this edition of the text.

[16]Audit standards issued by the American Institute of Certified Public Accountants permit auditors to express their opinion that a popular report (and other forms of summary data) is fairly stated in relation to the general purpose financial statements from which it is derived. Current AICPA guidance does not permit auditors to express an opinion on popular reports that they are fairly presented in conformity with GAAP.

[17]Frances H. Carpenter and Florence C. Sharp, *Research Report*, "Popular Reporting: Local Government Financial Reports to the Citizenry" (Norwalk, CT: GASB, 1992).

Key Terms

Blended presentation,   396, 397

Component unit,   396

Discrete presentation,   397

Efficiency measures,   407

Financial reporting entity,   395

Fiscal accountability,   405

Full accrual basis,   380

Input measures,   407

Modified accrual basis,   380

Operational accountability,   405

Outcome measures,   407

Output measures,   407

Popular reports (or reporting),   408

Primary government,   396

Quasi-external transaction,   390

Service efforts and accomplishments,   406

Selected References

American Institute of Certified Public Accountants, Audit and Accounting Guide. *Audits of State and Local Governmental Units*. Revised, New York, 1996.

Governmental Accounting Standards Board. *Codification of Governmental Accounting and Financial Reporting Standards as of June 30, 1997*. Norwalk, CT, 1997.

Questions

10–1. *a.* State the principal reasons for the use of funds in accounting for governmental units.

b. List five kinds of funds frequently found in the accounting system of a municipality, and briefly discuss the content of each.

10–2. What is the minimum number of funds a government could keep if it were attempting to adhere to GASB standards? Explain.

10–3. Identify and describe the five classes of interfund transactions or transfers between funds. How do interfund loans and advances differ from the other four categories of interfund transactions?

10–4. The Mayor of a city contends that since he is the elected head of all city activities, he has authority to transfer assets from one fund to another on a temporary basis because "it is all in the family." What is the merit, if any, of the Mayor's contention?

10–5. William Bates is executive vice president of Mavis Industries, Inc., a publicly held industrial corporation. Bates has just been elected to the City Council of Gotham City. Prior to assuming office as a member of the City Council, he asks you as his CPA to explain the major differences that exist in accounting and financial reporting for a large city when compared to a large industrial corporation.

Required

a. Describe the major differences that exist in the purpose of accounting and financial reporting and in the types of financial reports of a large city when compared to a large industrial corporation.

    b. Why are inventories often ignored in accounting for local governmental units? Explain.

    c. Under what circumstances should depreciation be recognized in accounting for local governmental units? Explain.

                                    (AICPA)

10–6. What are the three major sections of a CAFR and what are the contents of each?

10–7. A single balance sheet in which like items of all funds are consolidated into single figures has the valuable attribute of being very compact. Why, then, does the GASB require a combined balance sheet, rather than a consolidated balance sheet, in the GPFS?

10–8. Listed below are four independent transactions or events that relate to a local government.

1. $25,000 was disbursed from the General Fund (or its equivalent) for the cash purchase of new equipment.
2. An unrestricted cash gift of $100,000 was received from a donor.
3. Listed common stocks with a total carrying value of $100, 000 were sold by an endowment fund for $105,000, before any dividends were declared on these stocks. There are no restrictions on the gain.
4. General obligation bonds with a face amount of $1,000,000 were sold at par, with the proceeds required to be used solely for construction of a new building. This building was completed at a total cost of $1,000,000, and the total amount of bond issue proceeds was disbursed in connection therewith. Disregard interest capitalization.

Required

For each of the above-listed transactions or events, prepare journal entries, without explanations, specifying the affected funds and account groups and showing how these transactions or events should be recorded by a local government whose debt is serviced by general tax revenues.

10–9. Explain the criteria currently prescribed by GASB standards for determining whether an organization is a primary government and whether it is financially accountable for another organization. Assuming a decision has been made to include a component unit in the reporting entity, how does one determine whether to report the component unit by discrete presentation or by blending?

10–10. Explain the essential features of GASB's proposed dual perspective reporting model.

Cases

10–1. The following example of application of reporting entity criteria is based on an example contained in GASB *Codification* Section 2100.

The Greater Metropolis Urban Development Authority (GMUDA) was authorized as a nonprofit corporation by the state legislature and created by the City of Metropolis Council to attract new industry and participate in long-range planning of the City. Although the City Council appoints GMUDA's governing board, the Board has complete authority to hire management and all other employees. The City has no role in monitoring or participating in the day-to-day operating activities of GMUDA.

Per its state charter, GMUDA has separate taxing powers and levies taxes on all commercial and industrial properties located within the designated development district. GMUDA's tax levies are completely independent of the City's, other than they are levied on some of the same taxpayers. GMUDA performs some services for the Chamber of Commerce and other local business organizations for a fee. However, its primary source of revenues is property taxes. GMUDA receives no financial subsidies of any kind from the City and the City is not obligated in any manner for the authority's debt. Even though GMUDA does not require the City's approval of its operating budget, it routinely sends the budget to the City Council for review. The City Attorney has ruled that the City Council has no option but to approve the budget as submitted.

Required

a. Using the reporting entity flow chart presented in Illustration 10–2, and the reporting entity definitions and criteria discussed in Chapter 10, determine whether or not the Greater Metropolis Urban Development Authority should be included in the reporting entity of which the City of Metropolis is the primary government? If so, should GMUDA be reported by blending or by discrete presentation? Explain your rationale for the inclusion/exclusion decision and, if applicable, method of display.

b. Assume the same facts as in Part *a* above except that the City Council has the power to remove members of GMUDA's board for cause. Also, the City must approve all debt issuances and all expenditures in excess of $100,000. Do your conclusions made in Part *a* above change in light of the different facts in Part *b*? Explain fully.

10–2. The letter of transmittal to the Mayor and Council accompanying the annual financial statements of the Town of Stevens is presented below. (Note: This case is based on an actual letter of transmittal and financial statements received by one of the authors quite some time ago; however, the name of the Town and certain other facts have been changed.)

LETTER OF TRANSMITTAL

To the Honorable Mayor and Town Council
Town of Stevens

Gentlemen:

We are attaching the financial report for the Town of Stevens for the year 19--. The statements and organization of this report are designed to conform to generally accepted principals [sic] and standards of government accounting and reporting. A review of this report will reveal much information about the financial position and movements of the Town, some of which it is hoped will be valuable and some of which we fear will be tiresome and redundant.

Plans and performance for 19-- did not exactly match. Hopes for major street repair and water line replacement on Castle Avenue were frustrated by the need to follow the county engineering and road department on its Jones Street relocation project. This meant relocating 300 feet of 6-inch main line, the rebuilding of two laterals, 12 services and the digging out and adjusting of 10 valve covers a number of times. This work, which was not anticipated, occupied most of the summer and partly explained why the water line maintenance cost was $97,418 for 19-- as compared with $46,554 for last year. It is hoped that this deferred work can be accomplished next year.

For the first time in a number of years the streets were hand-cleaned of old dirt and the remains of the winter debris. Although a new and richer layer of gum wrappers, beer cans, and cigarette packs corrected this condition, the Town's purchase of a Wayne sweeper in August puts the Town temporarily one up in its long struggle for clean streets. An additional help is that a tough antilitter ordinance was passed.

The new Town Hall was purchased on a contract for $90,900 payable at $30,000 per year, the first installment of which was met in 19--. We thus own outright the Town Hall from the front door to the west end of the fireplace. A new roof was installed and arrangements made to have part of the interior repaired next year.

At the moment the Town's financial position is not too grim. This may be changed in attempting to solve the remaining problems of sewage disposal and providing additional water to the areas the Town is required to serve.

/s/ Treasurer-Clerk

THE TOWN OF STEVENS
General Fund

Balance Sheet—December 31, 19--	Form A–1
Assets:	
Petty cash	500.00
Cash on deposit with treasurer	(16,404.70)
Temporary investments (S–9)	100,000.00
Inventory of supplies	3,800.00
Total Assets	87,895.30
Liabilities, reserves, and surplus:	
Warrants payable	8,586.70
Contract payable—new town hall	60,900.00
Cumulative reserve fund	53,298.80
Deficit (A–2)	(34,890.20)
	87,895.30

Analysis of Changes in Fund Balance   Form A–2

	Estimated	Actual	Excess or Deficiency
Surplus—Jan. 1, 19--	43,030.90	43,030.90	
Add: Revenues (A–3)	288,200.00	303,879.50	15,679.60
Total	331,230.90	346,910.40	15,679.50
Less: Town hall contract		90,900.00	(90,900.00)
Expenditures (A–4)	310,200.00	290,900.60	19,299.40
Deficit—Dec. 31, 19--	21,030.90	(34,890.20)	55,921,10

Statement of Revenues—Estimated and Actual			Form A–3
	Estimated	Actual	Difference
General property tax	140,000.00	94,635.60	45,364.40
Special tax—utilities	33,000.00	31,400.00	1,600.00
Licenses and permits	10,000.00	8,145.60	1,854.40
Fines and penalties	9,000.00	21,275.00	(12,275.00)
Rental income	7,200.00	6,700.00	500.00
Revenue from other agencies:			
Aid to Cities	7,000.00	23,457.40	(16,457.40)
State liquor tax	39,000.00	38,795.30	204.70
Motor vehicle excise tax	35,000.00	38,373.90	(3,373.90)
Expense sharing—Fire district 2	8,000.00	4,852.70	3,147.30
Interest income		4,750.00	(4,750.00)
Other income		31,494.00	(31,494.00)
	288,200.00	303,879.50	15,679.50

THE TOWN OF STEVENS
General Fund
Statement of Expenditures Compared with Authorizations   Form A–4

	Appropriated	Expended	Actual Under (Over) Estimate
Police:			
Salaries	123,000.00	123,482.20	(482.20)
FICA tax	5,500.00	5,495.30	4.70
Retirement	7,400.00	7,228.80	171.20
Industrial insurance	3,000.00	1,666.70	1,333.30
Hospital insurance	3,000.00	2,644.30	355.70
Vehicle care	1,500.00	4,763.10	(3,263.10)
Police bond	700.00	550.00	150.00
Motor fuel	8,000.00	11,641.10	(3,641.10)
Supplies	2,000.00	2,892.80	(892.80)
Total	154,100.00	160,364.30	(6,264.30)
Clerk:			
Salaries	21,000.00	21,335.40	(335.40)
FICA tax	1,000.00	1,067.40	(67.40)
Retirement	2,300.00	2,345.40	(45.40)
Hospital	1,200.00	527.60	672.40
Bond	150.00	140.00	10.00
Office supplies	2,500.00	2,997.70	(497.70)
Total	28,150.00	28,413.50	(263.50)

	Appropriated	Expended	Actual Under (Over) Estimate
Fire Department:			
Salaries	12,000.00	8,120.00	3,880.00
Pensions	6,000.00	2,655.00	3,345.00
Hydrant rental	12,000.00	12,000.00	–0–
Vehicle care	2,000.00	240.80	1,759.20
Equipment repair		511.80	(511.80)
Heat and lights		5,102.20	(5,102.20)
Motor fuel	1,500.00	272.80	1,227.20
Supplies	1,000.00	1,252.80	(252.80)
Total	34,500.00	30,155.40	4,344.60
General Government:			
Census	1,000.00	897.00	103.00
Elections	800.00		800.00
Attorney fees	10,000.00	1,500.00	8,500.00
Police judge	9,000.00	6,000.00	3,000.00
Councilmen:			
Salaries (Ord. #581)		3,666.30	(3,666.30)
Retirement		374.40	(374.40)
FICA tax		171.60	(171.60)
Heat and lights	8,000.00	4,762.10	3,237.90
Telephone	1,500.00	1,687.10	(187.10)
Building repair	5,000.00	6,356.30	(1,356.30)
Audit fee	4,000.00		4,000.00
Printing	2,000.00	302.50	1,697.50
Advertising	2,850.00	2,256.10	593.90
Postage	500.00	468.80	31.20
Surety bonds and insurance	15,000.00	12,850.00	2,150.00
Janitor service	1,800.00	1,440.40	359.60
Library	19,000.00	15,110.00	3,890.00
Travel and subsistence	2,000.00	1,975.20	24.80
Association dues	2,000.00	1,875.10	124.90
Planning commission	3,000.00		3,000.00
Miscellaneous	3,500.00	3,948.40	(448.40)
Supplies	1,000.00	1,030.90	(30.90)
Household supplies	1,500.00	525.20	974.80
Driver education		4,770.00	(4,770.00)
Total	93,450.00	71,967.40	21,482.60
Combined totals—General Fund	310,200.00	290,900.60	19,299.40

Required

The remainder of the report deals with other funds and account groups of the Town of Stevens; those statements are not reproduced because they are similar to the General Fund statements above. On the basis of the material given you, prepare a written evaluation of the information produced by the Town's accounting system from the standpoint of its usefulness to:

   a. Town administrators.

   b. The Town Council (the legislative body).

   c. Taxpayers and citizens of the town.

   d. Creditors of the town.

Exercises and Problems

10–1. Utilizing the CAFR obtained for Exercise 1–1 and your answers to the question asked in Exercise 1–1, and the corresponding exercises in Chapters 2 through 9, comment on the following:

  a. *Analysis of Introductory Section.* Does the report contain all introductory material specified by the GASB (see Chapter 10). Is the introductory material presented in such a manner that it communicates significant information effectively—do you understand what they are telling you and why they are telling it to you? On the basis of your study of the entire report, list any additional information you feel should have been included in the introductory section and explain why you feel it should have been included. On the basis of your study of the entire report, do you think the introductory material presents the information fairly? Comment on any information in the introductory section you feel is superfluous, and explain why.

  b. *Analysis of Financial Statements.*

    1. Do the statements, notes, and schedules in the financial section present the information required by the GASB (see Chapter 10)? Are Total columns provided in the combined statements and schedules for the primary government and the reporting entity? If so, are the Total columns for the current year compared with Total columns for the prior year? Are the combined statements, combining statements, and notes cross-referenced to each other? Are they cross-referenced to the statements and schedules of individual funds and account groups?

    2. Review your answers to the questions asked in Exercises 3–1 and 4–1 in light of your study of subsequent chapters of the text and your analysis of all portions of the annual report. If you feel your earlier answers were not entirely correct, change them in accord with your present understanding of generally accepted accounting principles and proper disclosure of the financial position and financial operations of a governmental reporting entity.

    3. Review your answers to Exercise 5–1 and all subsequent exercises in this series in light of knowledge you have gained since you prepared the answers. If any of your earlier answers should be changed, change them.

  c. *Analysis of Statistical Section.* Are statistical tables presented in the annual report in conformity with GASB standards (see Chapter 10)? Make note of any data omitted. Make note of any additional data presented. If data have been omitted, to what extent does each omission impair your ability to understand the report? To what extent does each additional table, chart, graph, or other statistical presentation add to your understanding of the governmental reporting entity, its problems, its financial position, past and probable future changes in its financial position, financial operations, or past and probable future changes in financial operations?

d. GFOA *Certificate of Achievement.* Does the report include a copy of a GFOA Certificate of Achievement for Excellence in Financial Reporting or refer to the fact that the governmental unit has received one? If the report has been awarded a certificate, does your review indicate it was merited? If the report has not been awarded a certificate, does your review indicate that the report should be eligible for one?

e. *Service Potential of the CAFR.* Specify the most important information needs that a governmental annual report should fulfill for each of the following:
   (1) Administrators.
   (2) Members of the legislative branch.
   (3) Interested residents.
   (4) Creditors or potential creditors.
   In what ways does the CAFR you have analyzed meet the information needs you have specified for each of the four groups, assuming members of each group make an effort to understand reports equivalent to the effort you have made? In what way does the report fail to meet the information needs of each of the four groups?

f. Does your CAFR present any service efforts and accomplishments (SEA) data in the introductory section, statistical section, or elsewhere in the CAFR? If so, are measures provided for both service efforts and service accomplishments? From the data and/or narrative provided can you infer whether major service functions of the governmental unit were carried out efficiently and economically, and that program activities are having the desired effects?

10–2. Write the numbers 1 through 10 on a sheet of paper. Beside each number write the letter corresponding with the best answer to each of the following questions:

1. One of the differences between accounting for a governmental unit and accounting for a business is that a government should:
   a. Use only the cash basis of accounting.
   b. Not record depreciation expense in any of its funds.
   c. Use only the modified accrual basis of accounting.
   d. Always establish and maintain complete self-balancing accounts for each fund.

2. Which of the following funds of a governmental unit integrates budgetary accounts into the accounting system?
   a. Special Revenue.
   b. Enterprise.
   c. Internal Service.
   d Nonexpendable Trust.

3. Which of the following items would generally be recognized as revenue in the General Fund of a governmental unit?
   a. Receipts from a city-owned parking structure that is operated on a business basis.
   b. Property taxes.
   c. Interest earned on investments held to finance pension payments to retired employees.
   d. Revenues from internal service funds.

4. Cook County received goods that had been approved for purchase but for which payment had not yet been made. Should the accounts listed below be increased?

	Encumbrances	Expenditures
a.	No	No
b.	No	Yes
c.	Yes	No
d.	Yes	Yes

5. Proceeds of General Obligation Bonds is an account of a governmental unit that would be included in the:
   a. Enterprise Fund.
   b. Nonexpendable Trust Fund.
   c. Capital Projects Fund.
   d Debt Service Fund.

6. What journal entry should be made at the end of the fiscal year to close Encumbrances?
   a. Debit Fund Balance and credit Encumbrances.
   b. Debit Encumbrances and credit Reserve for Encumbrances.
   c. Debit Reserve for Encumbrances and credit Encumbrances.
   d. None. The account is only closed when no encumbrance documents are outstanding.

7. Which of the following funds ordinarily should account for the payment of interest and principal on revenue bond debt?
   a. Debt Service.
   b. Capital Projects.
   c. Expendable Trust.
   d. Enterprise.

8. The Appropriations Control account of a governmental unit is debited when:
   a. Supplies are purchased.
   b. Expenditures are recorded.
   c. The budgetary accounts are closed.
   d The budget is recorded.

9. Equipment in general governmental service that had been constructed 10 years before by the Capital Projects Fund was sold. The receipts were accounted for as unrestricted revenue. Entries are necessary in the:
   a. General Fund and Capital Projects Fund.
   b. General Fund and General Fixed Assets Account Group.
   c. General Fund, Capital Projects Fund, and Enterprise Fund.
   d. General Fund, Capital Projects Fund, and General Fixed Assets Account Group.

10. The members of the Library Board of the City of Fayetteville are appointed by the City Council of the City of Fayetteville, and the City Council has agreed to finance any operating deficits of the Library. Under these conditions:
    a. The Library is a primary government.
    b. The City is a primary government.
    c. Financial data of the Library should be included in the financial statements of the reporting entity, in the manner specified in GASB standards.
    d. Both *b* and *c*.

(AICPA, adapted)

10–3. Write the numbers 1 through 10 on a sheet of paper. Beside each number write the letter corresponding with the best answer to each of the following questions:

1. Self-supporting activities provided to the public on a user-charge basis are accounted for in what fund type?
   a. Agency.
   b. Enterprise.
   c. Internal Service.
   d. Special Revenue.

Items 2 through 5 are based on the following information:

The following related entries were recorded in sequence in the General Fund of a city:

1. Encumbrances	12,000	
Reserve for Encumbrances		12,000
2. Reserve for Encumbrances	12,000	
Encumbrances		12,000
3. Expenditures	12,350	
Vouchers Payable		12,350

2. The sequence of entries indicates that:
   a. An adverse event was foreseen, and a reserve of $12,000 was created; later the reserve was canceled, and a liability for the item was acknowledged.
   b. An order was placed for goods or services estimated to cost $12,000; the actual cost was $12,350, for which a liability was acknowledged on receipt.
   c. Encumbrances were anticipated but later failed to materialize and were reversed. A liability of $12,350 was incurred.
   d. The first entry was erroneous and was reversed; a liability of $12,350 was acknowledged.

3. Entries similar to those for the General Fund may also appear on the books of the City's:
   a. General Fixed Assets Account Group.
   b. General Long-Term Debt Account Group.
   c. Nonexpendable Trust Fund.
   d. Special Revenue Fund.

4. Assuming GASB standards were followed, the entries:
   a. Occurred in the same fiscal period.
   b. Did not occur in the same fiscal period.
   c. Could have occurred in the same fiscal period.
   d. Reflect the equivalent of a "prior period adjustment" had the entity concerned been operated for profit.

5. Immediately after Entry 1 was recorded, the city had a balanced General Fund budget for all transactions. What would be the effect of recording Entries 2 and 3?
   a. Not change the balanced condition of the budget.
   b. Cause the city to show a surplus.
   c. Cause the city to show a deficit.
   d. Not affect the current budget but would affect the budget of the following fiscal period.

6. What would be the effect on the General Fund Fund Balance in the current fiscal year of recording a $15,000 purchase for a new automobile out of General

Fund resources, for which a $14,600 encumbrance had been recorded in the General Fund in the previous year?

a. Reduce the Fund Balance $15,000.

b. Reduce the Fund Balance $14,600.

c. Reduce the Fund Balance $400.

d. Have no effect on the Fund Balance.

7. The activities of a central data processing department that offers data processing services at a discount to other departments of a certain city should be accounted for in:

a. An Enterprise Fund.

b. An Internal Service Fund.

c. A Special Revenue Fund.

d. The General Fund.

8. The initial contribution of cash from the General Fund in order to establish an Internal Service Fund would require the General Fund to credit Cash and debit:

a. Accounts Receivable—Internal Service Fund.

b. Equity Transfers Out.

c. Operating Transfers Out.

d. Long-Term Advance to Internal Service Fund.

9. The premium received at the time an issue of general obligation bonds is sold is usually considered an other financing source of what fund or account group?

a. Debt Service.

b. General Long-Term Debt.

c. General.

d. Special Revenue.

10. Brockton City's Debt Service Fund (for term bonds) recorded estimated other financing sources and estimated revenues for the current fiscal year of $15,000 and $7,000, respectively. The actual transfers in and interest earnings for future repayment of principal were $16,000 and $6,500, respectively. What are the necessary amounts to record the year's actual transfers and earnings in the Debt Service Fund and in the General Long-Term Debt Account Group, respectively?

a. $22,500 and $22,000.

b. $22,000 and $22,000.

c. $22,500 and $22,500.

d. $22,500 and no entry.

(AICPA, adapted)

10–4. Write the numbers 1 through 10 on a sheet of paper. Beside each number write the letter corresponding with the best answer to each of the following questions:

1. Which of the following is an appropriate basis of accounting for a proprietary fund of a governmental unit?

	Cash Basis	Accrual Basis
a.	Yes	Yes
b.	Yes	No
c.	No	No
d.	No	Yes

2. The budget of a governmental unit, for which the appropriations exceed the estimated revenues, was adopted and recorded in the general ledger at the beginning of the year. During the year, expenditures and encumbrances were less than appropriations; whereas revenues equaled estimated revenues. The Budgetary Fund Balance account is:
   a. Credited at the beginning of the year and debited at the end of the year.
   b. Credited at the beginning of the year and *not* changed at the end of the year.
   c. Debited at the beginning of the year and credited at the end of the year.
   d. Debited at the beginning of the year and *not* changed at the end of the year.
3. Which of the following amounts are included in a General Fund's Encumbrance account?
   I. Outstanding vouchers payable amounts.
   II. Outstanding purchase order amounts.
   III. Excess of the amount of a purchase order over the actual expenditure for that order.
       a. I only.
       b. I and III.
       c. II only.
       d. II and III.
4. Property taxes levied in fiscal year 1999 to finance the General Fund budget of fiscal year 2000 should be reported as General Fund revenues in fiscal year 2000:
   a. Regardless of the fiscal year in which collected.
   b. For the amount collected in fiscal year 2000 only.
   c. For the amount collected before the end of fiscal year 2000 only.
   d. For the amount collected before the end of fiscal year 2000 or shortly thereafter.
5. Repairs that have been made for a governmental unit, and for which a bill has been received, should be recorded in the General Fund as a debit to an:
   a. Expenditure.
   b. Encumbrance.
   c. Expense.
   d. Appropriation.
6. Brockton City serves as collecting agency for the local independent school district and for a local water district. For this purpose, Brockton has created a single Agency Fund and charges the other entities a fee of 1 percent of the gross amounts collected. (The service fee is treated as General Fund revenue.) During the latest fiscal year, a gross amount of $268,000 was collected for the independent school district and $80,000 for the water district. As a consequence of the foregoing, Brockton's General Fund should:
   a. Recognize receipts of $384,000.
   b. Recognize receipts of $344,520.
   c. Record revenue of $3,480.
   d. Record encumbrances of $344,520.

Items 7 and 8 are based on the following information:
   During the year ended December 31, 1999, Leyland City received a state grant of $500,000 to finance the purchase of buses and an additional grant of $100,000 to aid in the financing of bus operations in 1999. Only $300,000 of the capital grant was used in 1999 for the purchase of buses, but the entire operating grant of $100,000 was spent in 1999.

7. If Leyland's bus transportation counted for as part of the City's General Fund, how much should Leyland report as grant revenues for the year ended December 31, 1999?
   a. $100,000.
   b. $300,000.
   c. $400,000.
   d. $500,000.
8. If Leyland's bus transportation system is accounted for as an Enterprise Fund, how much should Leyland report as grant revenues for the year ended December 31, 1999?
   a. $100,000.
   b. $300,000.
   c. $400,000.
   d. $500,000.
9. The comprehensive annual financial report (CAFR) of a governmental reporting entity should contain a Combined Statement of Revenues, Expenses, and Changes in Retained Earnings for:

	Governmental Funds	Proprietary Funds
a.	No	Yes
b.	No	No
c.	Yes	No
d.	Yes	Yes

10. The comprehensive annual financial report (CAFR) of a governmental reporting entity should contain a Combined Statement of Cash Flows for:

	Governmental Funds	Account Groups
a.	Yes	No
b.	Yes	Yes
c.	No	Yes
d.	No	No

(AICPA, adapted)

10–5. The following transactions represent practical situations frequently encountered in accounting for state and local governments. Each transaction is independent of the others.

1. The City Council of Bernardville adopted a budget for the general operations of the government during the new fiscal year. Revenues were estimated at $695,000. Legal authorizations for budgeted expenditures were $650,000.
2. Taxes of $160,000 were levied for the Special Revenue Fund of Millstown. One percent was estimated to be uncollectible.
3. a. On July 25, 1999, office supplies estimated to cost $2,390 were ordered for the City Manager's office of Bullersville. Bullersville, which operates on the calendar year, does not maintain an inventory of such supplies.
   b. The supplies ordered July 25 were received on August 9, 1999, accompanied by an invoice for $2,500.
4. On October 10, 1999, the General Fund of Washingtonville repaid to the Utility Fund a loan of $1,000 plus $40 interest. The loan had been made earlier in the fiscal year.

5. A prominent citizen died and left 10 acres of undeveloped land to Harper City for a future park site. The donor's cost of the land was $55,000. The fair value of the land was $85,000 at the time its ownership was transferred to the City.

6. *a.* On March 6, 1999, Dahlstrom City issued 9 percent special assessment bonds payable March 6, 2004, at face value of $90,000. Interest is payable annually. Dahlstrom City, which operates on the calendar year, will use the proceeds to finance a curbing project. In case of default by property owners, the City agreed to assume debt service.

   b. On October 29, 1999, the full $84,000 cost of the completed curbing project was recorded as a liability. Also, appropriate closing entries were made with regard to the project. Cash in the amount of the residual equity was transferred to the Debt Service Fund to be used for interest payments.

7. *a.* Conrad Thamm, a citizen of Basking Knoll, donated common stock valued at $22,000 to the City under a trust agreement. Under the terms of the agreement, the principal amount is to be kept intact; use of revenue from the stock is restricted to financing academic college scholarships for needy students.

   b. On December 14, 1999, dividends of $1,100 were received on the stock donated by Mr. Thamm.

8. *a.* On February 23, 1999, the Town of Lincoln, which operates on the calendar year, issued 9 percent general obligation bonds with a face value of $3,000,000 payable February 23, 1999, to finance the construction of an addition to the city hall. The bonds were sold for $3,080,000. The premium was recorded directly in the Debt Service Fund and is to be held for bond repayment at maturity.

   b. On December 31, 1999, the addition to the city hall was officially approved, the full cost of $2,970,000 was paid to the contractor, and appropriate closing entries were made with regard to the project. (Assume no entries have been made with regard to the project since February 23, 1999.) The residual equity of the Construction Fund was transferred to the Debt Service Fund to be held for bond repayment at maturity.

Required

For each transaction, prepare the necessary journal entries for *all* of the funds and account groups involved. No explanation of the journal entries is required. Use the following headings for your workpaper:

Transaction Number	Journal Entries	Dr.	Cr.	Fund or Account Group

In the far right column, indicate in which fund or account groups each entry is to be made, using the coding below:

Funds:
General	G
Special Revenue	SR
Capital Projects	CP
Debt Service	DS
Enterprise	E
Internal Service	IS
Nonexpendable Trust	NT
Expendable Trust	ET

Account Group:
    General Fixed Assets   GFA
    General Long-Term Debt   LTD

(AICPA, adapted)

10–6. The Village of Dexter was recently incorporated and began financial operations on July 1, 1999, the beginning of its fiscal year.

The following transactions occurred during this first fiscal year, July 1, 1999, to June 30, 2000:

1. The Village Council adopted a budget for general operations during the fiscal year ending June 30, 2000. Revenues were estimated at $2,000,000. Legal authorizations for budgeted expenditures were $1,970,000.
2. Property taxes were levied in the amount of $1,950,000; it was estimated that 2 percent of this amount would prove uncollectible. These taxes are available as of the date of levy to finance current expenditures.
3. During the year, a resident of the Village donated marketable securities valued at $250,000 to the Village under the terms of a trust agreement. The terms of the trust agreement stipulated that the principal amount is to be kept intact; use of revenue generated by the securities is restricted to financing college scholarships for needy students. Revenue earned and received on these marketable securities amounted to $27,500 through June 30, 2000.
4. A General Fund transfer of $100,000 was made to establish an Internal Service Fund to provide for a permanent investment in inventory.
5. The Village decided to install lighting in a subdivision of the Village; a special assessment project was authorized to install the lighting at a cost of $375,000. Assessments were levied for $360,000; the Village's share of cost was $15,000. All assessments were collected during the year, as was the transfer from the Village's General Fund.
6. A contract for $375,000 was let for the installation of the lighting. At June 30, 2000, the contract was completed. The contractor was paid all but 5 percent, which was retained to ensure compliance with the terms of the contract. Encumbrance accounting is used.
7. During the year, the Internal Service Fund purchased various supplies at a cost of $95,000.
8. Cash collections recorded by the General Fund during the year were as follows:

    Property taxes $1,930,000
    Licenses and permits   35,000

9. The Village Council decided to build a village hall at an estimated cost of $2,500,000 to replace space occupied in rented facilities. In order to finance the project, 6 percent bonds were sold at their face value of $2,500,000. No contracts have been signed for this project, and no expenditures have been made.
10. A purchase order in the amount of $100,000 was issued for a truck for use by the street department, a General Fund department. The truck was received, and a voucher in the amount of $102,500 was approved and paid.

Required

Prepare journal entries to properly record each of the above transactions in the appropriate fund(s) or group of accounts of Dexter Village for the fiscal year ended June 30, 2000. Use the following funds and account groups, as necessary:

General Fund
Capital Projects Fund
Internal Service Fund
Nonexpendable Trust Fund
Scholarship Fund
General Long-Term Debt Account Group
General Fixed Assets Account Group

Each journal entry should be numbered to correspond with the transactions described above. Do *not* prepare closing entries for any fund.

Your answer sheet should be organized as follows:

Transaction Number	Fund or Account Group	Account Title and Explanation	Debits	Credits

(AICPA, adapted)

10–7. You have been engaged by the Town of Rego to examine its June 30, 1999, balance sheet. You are the first CPA to be engaged by the Town and find that employees of the Town are unaware of governmental accounting and financial reporting standards. The Town clerk stated that the books had not been closed and presented the following preclosing trial balance of the General Fund as of June 30, 1999:

	Debits	Credits
Cash	$ 550,000	
Taxes Receivable—Current Year	159,200	
Estimated Losses—Current-Year Taxes Receivable		$ 18,000
Taxes Receivable—Prior Year	28,000	
Estimated Losses—Prior-Year Taxes Receivable		30,200
Estimated Revenues	1,310,000	
Appropriations		1,348,000
Donated Land	127,000	
Expenditures—Building Addition Constructed	250,000	
Expenditures—Serial Bonds Paid	56,000	
Other Expenditures	1,005,000	
Special Assessment Bonds Payable		500,000
Revenues		1,354,000
Accounts Payable		126,000
Fund Balance		109,000
	$3,485,200	$3,485,200

Additional Information

1. The estimated losses of $18,000 for current-year taxes receivable were determined to be a reasonable estimate.
2. Included in the Revenues account is a credit of $127,000 representing the value of land donated by the state to be used for a town park.
3. The Expenditures—Building Addition Constructed account balance is the cost of an addition to the Town Hall building. This addition was constructed and completed in June 1999. The General Fund recorded the payment as authorized.
4. The Expenditures—Serial Bonds Paid account reflects the annual retirement of general obligation bonds issued to finance the construction of the Town Hall. Interest payments of $24,000 for this bond issue are included in the Other Expenditures account.
5. Operating supplies ordered in the prior fiscal year and chargeable to that year were received, recorded, and consumed in July 1998. The outstanding purchase orders for these supplies, which were not recorded in the accounts at June 30, 1998, amounted to $28,800. The vendors' invoices for these supplies totaled $30,400. Appropriations lapse one year after the end of the fiscal year for which they are made.
6. Outstanding purchase orders at June 30, 1999, for operating supplies totaled $10,100. These purchase orders were not recorded on the books.
7. The special assessment bonds were sold in June 1999 to finance a street paving project. No contracts have been signed for this project, and no expenditures have been made.
8. The balance in the Revenues account includes credits for $100,000 for a note issued to a bank to obtain cash in anticipation of tax collections and for $5,000 for the sale of scrap iron from the Town's water plant. The note was still outstanding at June 30, 1999. The operations of the water plant are accounted for in the Water Fund.

Required

a. Prepare the formal adjusting and closing journal entries for the General Fund for the fiscal year ended June 30, 1999. Assume capital projects and debt service legally may be accounted for in the General Fund.
b. The foregoing information disclosed by your examination was recorded only in the General Fund even though other funds or account groups were involved. Prepare the formal adjusting journal entries for any other funds or account groups involved, assuming that financial statements are to be prepared in conformity with GAAP.

(AICPA, adapted)

Continuous Problem

10–L. *a.* Assemble all statements and schedules prepared for your solutions to Problems 2–L through 9–L.

    b. From your solutions to Problems 2–L through 9–L, prepare:

      (1) A Combined Balance Sheet for All Funds and Account Groups of the City of Bingham as of June 30, 2000.

      (2) A Combined Statement of Revenues, Expenditures, and Changes in Fund Balances—All Governmental Fund Types for the fiscal year ended June 30, 2000.

      (3) A Combined Statement of Revenues, Expenditures, and Changes in Fund Balance—Budget and Actual for the General Fund and the Debt Service Fund for the year ended June 30, 2000.

      (4) A Combined Statement of Revenues, Expenses, and Changes in Retained Earnings/Fund Balances—All Proprietary Fund Types and Similar Fiduciary Funds for the year ended June 30, 2000.

      (5) A Combined Statement of Cash Flows—All Proprietary Fund Types and Nonexpendable Trust Funds for the year ended June 30, 2000. (Note: The City of Bingham is a primary government and has no other organizations for which it is accountable as component units.)

CHAPTER

Analysis of Governmental Financial Performance

Learning Objectives

After studying this chapter, you should be able to:

~ Explain the importance of evaluating governmental financial performance.

~ Distinguish and describe key financial performance concepts, such as:

Financial position.
Financial condition.
Interperiod equity.

~ Explain the relationships among environmental factors, organizational factors, and financial factors in determining governmental financial condition.

~ Identify, calculate, and interpret key economic and financial ratios that measure financial condition.

~ Describe how financial performance is related to the operating performance of a governmental entity.

The Need to Evaluate Financial Condition

Over the past three decades, numerous financial crises have underscored the need for an effective system to provide taxpayers, creditors, managers, legislative and oversight bodies, and others with an *early warning* of impending financial difficulty. Municipalities that have experienced financial crises during this period include such highly publicized cases as Boston; Bridgeport, Connecticut; Cleveland; Miami; New York City; Orange County, California; and Washington, DC. The most recent cases are Orange County, which filed for bankruptcy in 1994 after suffering investment losses estimated variously from $1.5 to $2.1 billion,[1] and the cities of Miami, Florida, and Washington, DC. Because of their current financial crises, both Miami and Washington, DC, are (as of January 1998) in a state of public *receivership*—the financial management of both cities has been handed over to public boards until fiscal integrity has been restored.[2]

By far, the fiscal crisis with the greatest impact was that of New York City. In the aftermath of the City's default on several billion of short-term debt in 1975, deficient financial reporting was singled out as one of the contributing factors.[3] Indeed, several published studies following the New York City crisis found widespread deficiencies in municipal financial reporting. For example, a joint Coopers and Lybrand/University of Michigan study of 46 municipalities conducted in 1976 found the following percentages of noncompliance with required disclosures: accounting policies for pensions, 63 percent; accrued vacation and sick leave pay, 84 percent; overlapping debt, 50 percent; lease obligations, 93 percent; description of significant accounting policies, 46 percent; annual report issued within 90 days of fiscal year-end, 61 percent; and preparation of interim financial reports for the general and special revenue funds, 39 percent and 63 percent, respectively.[4] Another study conducted for the National Council on Governmental Accounting (NCGA), the standards-setting body that preceded the GASB, noted that:

> In many instances, the financial reports of those [financially distressed] jurisdictions did not permit the general public to appreciate their precarious situation until it was too late. In response to pressures brought by lenders, these jurisdictions have had to alter materially and improve their reporting practices.[5]

---

[1]"Bitter Fruit: Orange County, Mired in Investment Mess, Files for Bankruptcy, *The Wall Street Journal*, December 7, 1994, pp. A1, A4.

[2]James Seemuth, "Gloom Over Miami: City Government Projects $68 Million Deficit in Its Budget for 1997," *Florida Trend* 39, no. 9 (January 1997), p. 26; and Katherine Barrett and Richard Greene, "Capital of Bad Management (Washington, D.C., A Special Report Ranking the Cities)" *Financial World*, no. 164 (March 14, 1995), pp. 50–55.

[3]Soybel (1992) summarizes the City's serious accounting deficiencies, including those identified in the SEC's study of the default. See Virginia E. Soybel, "Municipal Financial Reporting and the General Obligation Bond Market: New York City, 1961–1975," *Journal of Accounting and Public Policy* 2, no. 3 (Fall 1992), pp. 207–32.

[4]Coopers & Lybrand and the University of Michigan, *Financial Reporting Practices of the American Cities, A Public Report* (New York: Coopers & Lybrand, 1976.)

[5]W. D. Haseman and R. P. Strauss, "The Quality of Financial Reporting by General Purpose Local Governments," in *Objectives of Accounting and Financial Reporting for Governmental Units: A Research Study*, vol. II (Chicago: NCGA, 1981), p. 2-1.

As the foregoing quotation suggests, the widespread financial distress of many cities in the 1970s, particularly the default of New York City, was a double-edged sword. Although, it created consternation and hardship for the cities involved (as well as for the municipal credit markets), it unleashed forces that transformed the quality of governmental financial management and financial reporting nationwide. Strong pressure from the credit markets and the effective leadership of national professional organizations such as the Government Finance Officers Association (GFOA) (then known as the Municipal Finance Officers Association) and the National Association of State Auditors, Comptrollers, and Treasurers (NASACT) were major factors in the rapid improvement of both financial reporting standards and compliance with those standards. Because of these improvements, deteriorating financial performance is much more likely to be detected now than in the past.

New York City's default led also to considerable research on measuring financial condition. In 1980, the International City Management Association (ICMA) (since renamed the International City and County Management Association) published a series of five handbooks that dealt with evaluating financial condition, implementing a financial trend monitoring system, identifying unsound financial practices, setting long-range financial goals, and identifying tools for improving financial decisions.[6] These handbooks resulted from a three-year research project funded by a National Science Foundation grant. Some local governments that participated in field testing, as well as other governments, continue to use the financial trend monitoring system developed in the handbooks to monitor their financial condition. The third-edition ICMA handbook (see footnote 6), together with various publications of the municipal credit market, remain the main sources of guidance for monitoring and evaluating governmental financial condition, including how to use financial and other information for these purposes.

Despite the widespread improvements in financial management over the past 20 years, instances of poor financial management continue to crop up. As mentioned earlier, three recent examples are Orange County, California, and the cities of Miami, Florida, and Washington, DC. Orange County officials issued billions of dollars in short-term, reverse-repurchase debt instruments to leverage the acquisition of interest rate–sensitive derivative investments known as *inverse floaters*. When interest rates were low, the County's investment pool earned well above normal returns; however, when interest rates increased in 1994, the derivative investments lost significant value, triggering a default on the short-term debt and forcing the County, traditionally one of the wealthiest and most conservative in the nation, to declare bankruptcy.[7]

---

[6]In 1986, the ICMA published a revised, single handbook, *Evaluating Financial Condition: A Handbook for Local Government*, which integrates and updates information from all the handbooks. The third edition of this handbook was published in 1994. Sanford M. Groves and Maureen G. Valente, *Evaluating Financial Condition: A Handbook for Local Government*, 3rd ed. (Washington, DC: ICMA, 1994).

[7]Laura Jaweski, "Orange County Borrowed $1 Billion Even as Its Investment Losses Piled Up," *The Wall Street Journal*, December 5, 1994, pp. A3–A4.

In 1996, an FBI investigation known as Operation Green Palm uncovered massive payoffs, kickbacks, and other financial wrongdoing in Miami, involving, among other officials, a City Commission member, the City Manager, and the City's Finance Director. City officials were also accused of using funds designated for pensions, capital projects, and other purposes to hide a $68 million operating budget deficit that threatened to force the City into bankruptcy.[8] To avoid bankruptcy and restore fiscal integrity, the Governor of Florida appointed a *Financial Emergency Oversight Board.* As a result, the City has made substantial progress toward recovery. Miami voters narrowly defeated a measure on September 4, 1997, that would have abolished the City of Miami as a separate entity and turned its governance over to Dade County.

A 1995 survey of major U.S. cities by Barrett and Greene for *Financial World* ranked Washington, DC, worst among 30 cities surveyed in terms of financial management. Unlike Miami, the reason for Washington, DC's poor showing relates primarily to economic factors and serious mismanagement, rather than corruption. In commenting on the City's mismanagement, which had created a projected $722 million budget deficit for fiscal 1995, Barrett and Greene note:

> It's midyear 1993, Sharon Pratt Kelly, then the mayor of Washington, D.C., is short of revenues to balance her books. Money isn't coming in as quickly as expected. Expenses are up. The mayor's plans to cut staff dramatically have been torn to shreds by the unions and city agencies. So the mayor simply adds a fifth quarter to 1993. This moves the income scheduled to come in from property tax in the first quarter of 1994 to 1993. No more cash actually pours into her coffers. But on paper it does give her about $180 million. The Monopoly money gets spent just as if it were real cash.[9]

These current financial crises illustrate an ongoing need to monitor the financial well-being of governments. Moreover, increasing demands for services in the face of a growing unwillingness of taxpayers to pay higher taxes have created a nationwide movement, at all levels of government, to develop performance measurement systems to enhance the efficient and effective delivery of services. Whereas such systems may not have been feasible 10 or 20 years ago because of limited data collection and processing capabilities, recent technological developments, such as computer networking, the Internet, shared databases, and data warehousing, now make such systems not only feasible but necessary, especially for larger governments.

Evaluating Financial Condition

Preventing financial crises such as those discussed earlier in this chapter requires an early warning system to identify trends or practices that may adversely impact financial condition. Ensuring that the government has the financial capacity to

---

[8]Linda Robinson, "The Drive to Abolish the City of Miami: Charges of Corruption Would Be Thigh-Slapping Entertainment if the Place Weren't Going Broke," *U.S. News and World Report* 121, no. 22 (December 2, 1996), pp. 39–40.

[9]Barrett and Greene, "Capital of Bad Management," p. 50.

sustain desired services is the primary reason for internal managers to monitor financial condition. Bond investors and creditors have a similar interest in evaluating financial condition, namely, to assess the government's ability to make future interest and principal payments, even in the face of adverse economic trends or other events (for example, natural disasters). Knowledge that internal managers are employing a system to track financial trends provides investors and creditors with added confidence in the quality of the government's financial management, particularly if such trend data are shared with credit analysts. Credit analysts also have more than a passing interest in the government's ability to provide services in the long run since experience has shown that, in times of fiscal crisis, expenditures for vital services often take priority over debt service payments.

Legislative bodies have responsibility for helping formulate sound fiscal policies for the government they serve, whereas oversight bodies have responsibility for monitoring, and in some cases establishing, the fiscal policies of governmental units for which they have oversight responsibility. Some states, for example, impose uniform financial accounting and reporting systems that all municipalities within the state must follow. Municipalities may also be required to submit annual financial reports to a state oversight body. Finally, legislative and oversight bodies typically have responsibilities to monitor executives' compliance with laws and regulations.

Although citizens should have an interest in the government's overall financial condition, often their interests lie more narrowly with a particular program or with rising tax rates or service fees. Moreover, citizens' interests usually are represented through intermediaries such as the media, taxpayer *watchdog* groups, special interest groups, and groups that serve the public interest, such as the League of Women Voters. Thus, citizen groups typically have little interest or involvement in evaluating the overall financial condition of government, even though they may suffer severe cutbacks in governmental services in the event of a financial crisis.

The remainder of this chapter focuses on the ICMA financial trend monitoring system that *internal managers* may use to monitor and evaluate the financial condition of their government and similar methods used by *investors and creditors* to assess financial condition, or, more specifically, general obligation creditworthiness. Presumably, these methods can be useful as well for legislative and oversight bodies and citizen groups.

As mentioned earlier in this chapter, the *financial trend monitoring system* was developed by the ICMA in the wake of the New York City default for financial managers to use in tracking the financial performance of their own governments. Credit market analysts, particularly analysts with the major rating agencies, have developed proprietary (in-house) approaches for evaluating the general obligation creditworthiness of governmental units that issue bonds. Although evaluation objectives differ slightly between internal and external evaluation systems, and among the approaches used by external users, both types focus on many of the same kinds of factors. Prior to examining systems for evaluating financial condition, it is important to distinguish between the key terms *financial position* and *financial condition*.

Financial Position versus Financial Condition

Various definitions have been developed for the terms *financial position* and *financial condition*. A GASB research study notes that **financial position** "tends to be a shorter-run concept compared with financial condition."[10] The GASB study further notes that "*financial position* for governmental funds focuses on assets and liabilities that require cash or are normally converted to cash in the near future and can generally be determined from the financial statements alone.[11] Thus, *financial position* is closely related to the concept of liquidity. By contrast, the GASB study defines **financial condition** as:

> The probability that a government will meet both its financial obligations to creditors, consumers, employees, taxpayers, suppliers, constituents, and others as they become due and its service obligations to constituents, both currently and in the future.[12]

Similarly, the ICMA handbook summarizes *financial condition* as "a local government's ability to finance its services on a continuing basis."[13] The handbook notes more specifically that *financial condition* "refers to a government's ability to (1) maintain existing service levels, (2) withstand local and regional economic disruptions, and (3) meet the demands of natural growth, decline, and change."[14] Definitions of both the GASB study and the ICMA handbook make it clear that *financial condition* is similar to the common accounting term *solvency*. The ability to maintain existing or provide increasing service levels is related also to the accountability concept of *interperiod equity*, a term the GASB defines as determining "whether current-year revenues are sufficient to pay for the services provided that year and whether future taxpayers will be required to assume burdens for services previously provided.[15] Excessive shifting of the burden to pay for current services to future taxpayers may threaten the government's ability to sustain the current level of services or to expand services to meet future population growth.

Internal Financial Trend Monitoring

Both the GASB study and the revised ICMA Handbook point out that financial condition is a complex, multidimensional concept whose measurement requires analysis of a multitude of factors. The GASB study identifies the major categories of factors as economy and demographics; revenue base; current and capital expenditures; debt, pensions and other postemployment benefits; internal resources; management capabilities; infrastructure; and willingness to raise revenues and to provide needed public services.[16] Perusal of this list suggests that evaluation of some categories such as management capabilities, infrastructure, and willingness to raise

---

[10]Robert Berne, *Research Report*, "The Relationship Between Financial Reporting and the Measurement of Financial Condition," (Norwalk, CT: GASB, 1992), pp. 16–17.

[11]Ibid., p. 17.

[12]Ibid.

[13]Groves and Valente, *Evaluating Financial Condition*, p. 2.

[14]Ibid.

[15]Governmental Accounting Standards Board, *Concepts Statement No. 1*, "Objectives of Financial Reporting" (Norwalk, CT: GASB, 1987), par. 61.

[16]Berne, *Research Report*, p. 25.

revenues and provide services are largely qualitative judgments. Thus, unlike the rather straightforward evaluation of the financial condition of a business entity based on analysis of profitability and well-understood financial ratios, evaluation of governmental financial condition involves subjective judgments about the interplay of complex environmental, organizational, and financial factors.

Illustration 11–1 shows the framework developed by the ICMA for internal managers to use in evaluating financial condition. Environmental factors such as community needs and resources, economic conditions, political culture, intergovernmental constraints, and natural disasters and emergencies largely determine revenue capacity and demand for services. How fiscal policy within the governmental unit responds to environmental demand and changes in the environment is a major factor determining how environmental factors are translated into financial factors. Financial factors (identified in Illustration 11–1 as revenues, expenditures, operating position, debt structure, unfunded liabilities, and condition of capital plant) are the result of management and legislative policies in response to environmental demands and resources. Measures of financial condition include ratios consisting of one financial amount divided by another financial amount (such as fund balance divided by revenues) and ratios consisting of financial amounts divided by demographic or economic measures (such as debt divided by population).

Although identifying financial indicators and interpreting them is more of an art than a science, the ICMA provides a large number of potentially useful indicators grouped into 12 categories or factors corresponding to the environmental, organizational, and financial dimensions shown in Illustration 11–1. Examining changes in indicators over time and relationships among indicators can yield useful information on financial issues, such as whether revenue trends are adequate to meet expenditure trends, the adequacy of financial reserves to withstand revenue shortfalls or unforeseen expenditure requirements, current debt burden and future debt capacity, future service demands and ability of the governmental unit to meet those demands, adequacy of enterprise fund revenues to meet debt covenant requirements, and what portions of operating costs could be met by user charges rather than by taxes. However, making a reasonable judgment about the financial condition of a particular entity requires a sound understanding of how environmental factors influence the demand for and capacity to supply services, how organizational factors influence fiscal policy given a particular level or trend in the demand for and capacity to supply services, and how to measure the financial outcomes of the entity's fiscal policy. Each of these sets of factors is discussed at some length prior to moving to the identification, calculation, and interpretation of financial ratios.

Environmental Factors

Community needs and resources (see Illustration 11–1) determine in part the kinds and levels of services that are needed and the capacity to provide those services. Other environmental factors such as the legal and fiscal constraints under which the government operates, the kinds of major disruptions to which the government is susceptible, and the political culture of the government also affect the demand for services and the government's capacity to provide services.

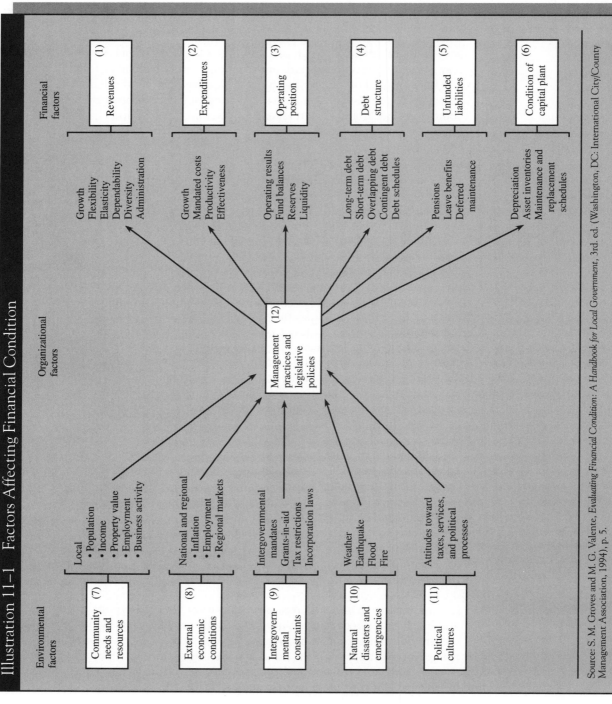

Illustration 11–1   Factors Affecting Financial Condition

Source: S. M. Groves and M. G. Valente, *Evaluating Financial Condition: A Handbook for Local Government*, 3rd. ed. (Washington, DC: International City/County Management Association, 1994), p. 5.

Community Needs and Resources. This category consists of factors (see Illustration 11–1) that determine the demand for services such as population demographics (growth, density, and composition), median age, and percentage of households below the poverty level, as well as the capacity to provide services, such as personal income per capita, property values, employment (level, diversity, and types), and level of business activity. Some indicators affect both the demand for and capacity to provide services, for example a low personal income per capita generally is correlated with both high demand and low capacity, whereas high personal income is correlated with low demand and high capacity. The reason for this two-sided effect may be that personal income itself is the result of other factors such as the employment base, educational level, and median age. Thus, even when evaluating factors within a single category, the factors are often interrelated, making it difficult to assess any single factor in isolation. These difficulties notwithstanding, the more diversified and stable is the employment base, the higher are property values and personal income, and the more robust is business activity (for example, building permits, bank deposits, and retail sales), the lower will be demand for services and the higher the capacity to provide services. Population and related demographics such as growth, composition by age and race, housing patterns, and location (urban, rural, or suburban) also may strongly affect the demand for and capacity to provide services. A constant enigma in public finance is that the greater the need for services, the lower is the capacity to provide them, and vice versa.

Illustration 11–2 presents the trend, description, and analysis of one of the City of Columbia, Missouri's business activity indicators: Indicator 36-B, Retail Sales. This information is taken from its Financial Trend Monitoring System for the years 1991 through 1996. The City of Columbia was a test city for the ICMA financial condition research project in the late 1970s and has since continued to use the trend monitoring system to monitor its financial condition. Based on the City's own analysis, it appears that retail sales have been growing at a satisfactory rate.

External Economic Conditions. Obviously, no local or state government operates independently of the regional and national economy. Regional economic activity affects local business activity, employment, and income, by influencing the demand for manufactured, agricultural, and service products, and the levels of wholesale and retail sales. Similarly, inflation at the national level influences regional and local prices, including wages and the cost of debt financing. Although consideration of external economic conditions is essential to assessing the local economy, the linkages are generally difficult to pinpoint and quantify.

Intergovernmental Constraints. Most local governments operate under various legal constraints imposed by the state government. Moreover, the federal government imposes constraints as a condition for receiving federal financial assistance. Among the state-imposed constraints may be legal limitations on the ability of local governments to raise revenues and issue debt. If such limitations exist, the current levels of revenues and debt subject to such limits should be compared to the authorized limits. Of particular importance is considering the extent to which

Illustration 11–2   Indicator 36-B—Business Activity: Retail Sales

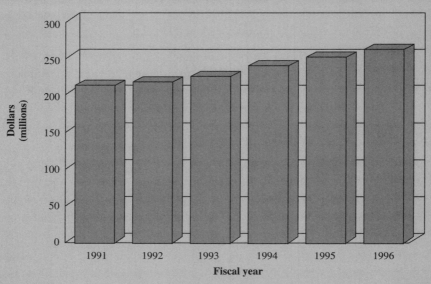

Warning Trend:

Decline in Business Activity as Measured by Retail Sales (constant dollars)

Formulation:

Retail Sales (constant dollars)

	Fiscal Year					
	1991	*1992*	*1993*	*1994*	*1995*	*1996*
Estimated retail sales	854,964,300	907,706,900	964,032,600	1,056,384,400	1,133,710,600	1,207,907,000
Consumer price index	411.1	423.2	434.7	447.5	459.0	470.4
Retail sales in constant dollars	207,969,910	214,486,508	221,769,634	236,063,553	246,995,773	256,782,951

Description:

The level of retail sales can affect the City's financial condition in two ways. First, it directly affects revenue yields to the extent that they are reliant on sales tax receipts. And second, the affect is indirect to the extent that changes in retail sales affect other demographic and economic areas such as employment base, personal income, and so on. This in turn can create further declines in such business activity.

Analysis:

Constant dollar retail sales increased 23.47 percent from FY 91 to FY 96. The FY 91 figure is $207,969,910 and increased to $256,782,951 in FY 96. This reflects well on the ability of the business sector to maintain and increase future retail sales growth. The growth in sales tax has ranged from approximately 6 percent to 9 percent for the past six years. Any constant dollar decline in retail sales may need to be monitored closely in the future. However, there has been a positive trend for the period studied.

Source: City of Columbia, Missouri, *Financial Trend Monitoring System*, 1991–1996, pp. 104–105.

legal limits may impede needed acquisition of capital assets and future growth in services.

Natural Disasters and Emergencies. The need to consider and plan for natural disasters is incumbent on all top governmental officials. Certainly, no place is immune from such events, although some locations are more vulnerable than others. The question that should be asked is What would happen if a major earthquake or hurricane were to strike? Related questions that need to be asked are (1) Does the City have sufficient insurance and reserves to cover possible losses? and (2) Does the government have sufficient resources (and a plan) for evacuation, protection against looting, and cleanup?

Political Culture. This perhaps is the most difficult of all factors to measure, but certainly critically important to determining how the administration will react to the other environmental factors in shaping the government's fiscal policy. Political culture includes such factors as form of government (e.g., mayor-council—weak or strong, council-manager, commission) and the entity's economic, political, and social history. The entity's history may reveal underlying community philosophies regarding willingness to support higher taxes, issuances of long-term debt, and increased social services.

Organizational Factors

Management Practices and Legislative Policies. As indicated by their pivotal location in Illustration 11–1, *management practices and legislative policies* play a crucial role in determining fiscal policy in response to the environmental factors just discussed. Sound financial management and the political will to resist easy solutions can minimize financial problems that might otherwise result from such factors as economic downturns, plant closings, or natural disasters. Financial crises often build over a number of years during economic recessions. Politicians may be either unwilling or unable to curtail expenditures for services in response to revenue shortfalls. Results of past policies, such as heavy reliance on debt or an excessive labor force, may make it difficult or infeasible to reduce expenditures sufficiently in the short run. Short-run solutions, such as deferring needed maintenance, curtailing capital expenditures, or underfunding pensions, may lead to even greater problems in the future. Thus, sound financial management means planning for adverse environmental conditions or events and devising long-run solutions when problems do occur. Although management practices and legislative policies are critical determinants of financial condition, they are among the most difficult factors to measure. Among indicators that credit analysts use to assess management quality are the legal and political relationship between a local government and the state government, growth of services relative to capacity, background and experience of key government managers, accounting and budgeting practices, debt management, and tax policies.[17] Evidence of mismanagement or deficient fiscal policies may include deferral of maintenance; underfunding pensions; declining tax collection rates; use of

---

[17]Standard & Poor's, *Municipal Finance* Criteria (New York: Standard & Poor's, 1995), pp. 23–24.

one-time revenues, long-term reserves, debt proceeds, or the proceeds from the sale of assets to balance the operating budget; and accounting gimmickry.[18]

Financial Factors   Examples of governmental fund financial ratios typically used in assessing financial condition in the ICMA trend monitoring system are shown in Illustration 11–3. Although the ratios contained in Illustration 11–3 represent what the authors consider key ratios, they are not intended to represent all the ratios that might be useful in evaluating financial condition. In fact, the ICMA handbook provides for a total of 27 financial indicators. The 13 ratios given in Illustration 11–3 cover each of the financial factors shown on the right-hand side of Illustration 11–1, except for condition of capital plant. Currently, most governmental entities do not include information on the condition of capital plant in their CAFR. Descriptive information on miles of street, miles of sewer, number of fire and police stations, number of employees, and so on, are often provided, but seldom is any information provided about the *condition* of capital plant. Although the lack of such disclosures creates problems for *external* analysts, internal users can obtain information on maintenance effort and condition of equipment from the Public Works Department. Such information when combined with information on maintenance expenditures and capital outlay can provide useful indicators of the condition of capital plant.[19]

The data to calculate the 13 financial ratios shown in Illustration 11–3 are readily obtainable from most CAFRs. Except for population, which is usually disclosed in the statistical section, data for the first 8 ratios and ratio 11 can be obtained from the Combined Statement of Revenues, Expenditures, and Changes in Fund Balances—All Governmental Fund Types and Discretely Presented Component Units (see Illustration 2–2) and the Combined Balance Sheet—All Fund Types and Account Groups (see Illustration 2–1). Data for the remaining ratios usually can be found in the Notes to the Financial Statements.

In calculating ratios 1 through 8, some analysts prefer to utilize General Fund data only, whereas others will utilize combined data for all governmental fund types. This decision will depend, in part, on how large the General Fund is relative to all governmental fund types. In calculating operating revenues, capital project fund revenues should be excluded since the capital project fund is not an operating fund. For purposes of calculating revenues and expenditures in these ratios, other financing sources are often added to revenues and other financing uses are often added to expenditures.

Using Financial Reports in Evaluating Financial Condition

Given the complex analytical framework just discussed, one might question the usefulness of the Comprehensive Annual Financial Report in evaluating financial

---

[18]Groves and Valente, *Evaluating Financial Condition*, pp. 146–51.

[19]The GASB has a project to develop standards for reporting of capital assets, including asset condition. If the GASB issues standards for capital assets, the publisher will provide an update to adopters of this text.

Illustration 11–3   Financial Ratios Based on CAFR Governmental Funds Information

Financial Ratios	Explanation for Ratio
Revenue measures:	
1. $\dfrac{\text{Total revenues}}{\text{Population}}$	Indicates demand for resources and the entity's ability and willingness to provide resources. Over time shows how revenues are changing relative to population changes. A high ratio, and increasing trend, in relation to ratio 3 below, is desirable. However, a high ratio may also suggest less flexibility for obtaining additional revenues.
2. $\dfrac{\text{Own source revenues}}{\text{Total revenues}}$	Indicates extent of fiscal self-reliance; a high ratio is viewed as a positive characteristic.
Expenditure measures:	
3. $\dfrac{\text{Total expenditures}}{\text{Population}}$	Indicates cost of providing services per capita. Over time it reflects changes in expenditures relative to changes in population. A high ratio may indicate inefficiency or that cost of services may eventually exceed residents' ability to pay for services.
4. $\dfrac{\text{Operating expenditures}}{\text{Total expenditures}}$	Operating expenditures = Total expenditures − Capital expenditures. A high ratio may indicate inadequate financial capacity to maintain infrastructure. Capital expenditures are often one of the first discretionary expenditures cut when fiscal stress occurs. Deferred capital expenditures create a need for increased capital expenditures in the future.
Operating position liquidity measures:	
5. $\dfrac{\text{Total revenues}}{\text{Total expenditures}}$	Indicates relationship of inflow from revenues to outflow for expenditures; a high ratio is viewed as a positive characteristic.
6. $\dfrac{\text{Unreserved fund balance(s)}}{\text{Operating revenues}}$	Indicates availability of "financial reserves" to meet unforeseen contingencies and for appropriation for future operations. A ratio below 5 percent is often regarded by the debt rating agencies as a red flag indicating probable fiscal stress.
7. $\dfrac{\text{(Cash + Short-term investments)}}{\text{Current liabilities}}$	Indicates liquidity or "cash position"; a ratio of less than one is considered as a negative factor, particularly if it occurs in consecutive years.
8. $\dfrac{\text{Current liabilities}}{\text{Operating revenues}}$	Indicates the ability of the government to meet its current liabilities.
Debt structure measures:	
9. $\dfrac{\text{Net tax-supported long-term debt}}{\text{Net assessed valuation}}$	Net tax-supported debt is direct tax-supported debt less amount available in debt service funds. Indicates the government's ability to repay its net general long-term debt; a ratio of 10 percent or more is viewed as a negative factor. This may not be a valid benchmark in states that have extremely low assessment ratios, such as Missouri, which averages 24 percent.
10. $\dfrac{\text{Net tax-supported long-term debt}}{\text{Population}}$	An alternative indicator measure of general long-term debt burden is debt per capita. A debt burden greater than $1,200 per capita or level of debt exceeding 90 percent of amount authorized by law may be considered a warning signal.
11. $\dfrac{\text{Debt service}}{\text{Operating revenues}}$	Indicates extent of the government's fixed costs for paying principal and interest on its direct tax-supported debt. A ratio of 20 percent or more is considered a warning signal; 10 percent or below is considered good.
Unfunded liabilities:	
12. $\dfrac{\text{Unfunded pension liability}}{\text{Net assessed valuation}}$	When compared with ratio 9 above, this ratio indicates the level of unfunded liabilities relative to net tax-supported bonded debt. Other useful ratios would be unfunded "other postemployment benefits" or unfunded accrued vacation and sick leave divided by net assessed valuation.
13. $\dfrac{\text{Pension plan assets}}{\text{Benefits paid}}$	Indicates the amount of accumulated cash and investments relative to annual benefits paid. Over time, a decline in this ratio may indicate serious problems in the management or design of the pension plan.

Source: These ratios are adapted from S. M. Groves and M. G. Valente, *Evaluating Financial Condition: A Handbook for Local Government*, 3rd ed. (Washington, DC: International City/County Management Association, 1995).

439

condition. A common complaint is that the fund-based financial statements in the typical CAFR do not portray a clear picture of the governmental entity's financial condition. In fact, many trained analysts find the introductory and statistical sections of the CAFR, and the Notes to the Financial Statements, to be more useful than the financial statements for assessing financial condition. This is not surprising since the introductory and statistical sections of the CAFR and the Notes to the Financial Statements provide important information on environmental and organizational factors (such as those shown in Illustration 11–1), and how they relate to financial factors. Moreover, as discussed in Chapters 1 and 10, the fund-based financial statements prepared by state and local governments focus on short-term *financial position*, rather than long-term *financial condition*. Many governments further enhance the understandability of their CAFR by providing excellent narrative and graphical explanation of economic and financial factors, including trend data, comparisons with other governments, and forecasts in the introductory section.

In the authors' view, the fact that many find the introductory and statistical sections to be as useful as financial statements for evaluating financial condition is a reflection of the complex nature of financial condition rather than an indictment of financial statements. These complexities and the lack of a "bottom-line" performance measure (profit) may also explain why the CAFR has evolved to its present form, and provides justification for publishing a complete CAFR rather than just general purpose financial statements. From this perspective, the combined general purpose financial statements (illustrated in Chapter 2) are not useless; they provide useful information for calculating financial ratios essential to understanding the entity's financial position, an important component of financial condition.

Use of Benchmarks to Aid Interpretation

Regardless of how the ratios are calculated, the more difficult task is how to interpret the ratios to make an informed judgment about financial condition. Checking each ratio against the applicable "red-flag" level shown in Illustration 11–3 may provide early warning signals about low liquidity, over-reliance on intergovernmental revenues, an imbalance between revenues and expenditures, excessive debt burden, and poor management of retirement plans. Five or 10-year trends in these ratios are essential in pinpointing emerging or existing problem areas.

In addition to comparing ratios to established red-flag levels, **benchmarking** can be a very useful tool. For internal trend monitoring purposes, comparing current-period ratios to those of prior years provides useful information, particularly when the data are displayed in graphs. Illustration 11–4 shows the use of time-series trend monitoring by the City of Columbia, Missouri, along with credit industry benchmarking, to display data for the years 1991 through 1996 for Indicator 16, Excess of Revenues over Expenditures (of the General Fund). (See Illustration 11–6.) Besides showing the time-series data in both graphical and tabular form, the City explains the manner of formulating the indicator, and provides a narrative description and interpretation of the indicator. In addition, the City provides both time-series warning trend and credit industry benchmark information and a complete analysis of the trend information that is provided.

Illustration 11–4   Indicator 16—Excess of Revenues over Expenditures: General Fund

Warning Trend:

Increasing Amount of General Fund Operating Deficits as a Percent of Operating Revenues and Transfers

Formulation:

General Fund operating (deficits) surpluses

Operating revenues and transfers

	Fiscal Year					
Fiscal Year	1991	1992	1993	1994	1995	1996
General Fund operating surplus (deficit)*	124,821	1,077,666	1,296,056	742,880	(122,256)	1,122,324
Operating revenues and transfers†	27,549,255	29,653,277	32,156,759	34,412,828	36,945,336	38,794,027
General Fund operating surpluses (deficits) as a percentage of operating revenues and transfers	0.45%	3.63%	4.03%	2.16%	−0.33%	2.89%

*Not including encumbrances.

†Operating revenues and transfers: General Fund revenues plus operating transfers from other funds and increase in obligations under capital leases and appropriated Fund Balance where applicable.

Description:

An operating deficit will occur as operating expenditures exceed operating revenues. However, this does not necessarily mean the budget will be out of balance. Reserves (fund balances) and transfers are sometimes used to cover the

(continued)

Illustration 11–4   *(concluded)*

difference. Continuing use of reserves and the unjustifiable transfer of funds to balance the deficit may indicate a revenue/expenditure problem.

The existence of an operating deficit in one year is not cause for concern, but frequent and increasing deficits can indicate that current revenues are not supporting current expenditures, and that serious problems may lie ahead.

Credit Industry Benchmarks:

A current year operating deficit would be considered a minor warning signal, and the reasons and manner of funding would be carefully examined before it was even considered a negative factor. However, the following situations would be looked at with considerably more attention and would probably be considered negative factors:

1. Two consecutive years of operating fund deficits.
2. A current year deficit greater than the previous year's deficit.
3. A current operating fund deficit in two or more of the last five years.
4. An abnormally large deficit (5% to 10% of operating revenues) in any one year.

Analysis:

FY 95 shows a deficit percentage of −0.33%, the first deficit in 10 years. This is not cause for alarm as we have not experienced any other deficits in the period shown and FY 96 reflects a 2.89% surplus percentage of Operating Revenues and Transfers. The adopted budget for FY 97 reflects a balanced budget with $150,000 Contingency and $20,501 for the City Council to allocate to programs or projects during the fiscal year. The FY 97 budget provides for increases in personnel and capital costs. Management and City Council are addressing avenues for increasing the City's revenue base.

Operating Revenues and Transfers increase primarily due to increases in sales tax, intragovernmental revenues, fees and service charges, operating transfers, public safety, health and environment, and appropriation of prior year fund balance. For six years the General Fund has appropriated amounts from the prior year's fund balance ranging from $1,013,000 to $1,929,001. The appropriated fund balance for FY 96 is $1,437,707.

Source: City of Columbia, Missouri, *Financial Trend Monitoring System*, 1991–1996, pp. 42–43.

Internal managers and external analysts can also compare specific ratios to national and state medians published by Moody's Investors Service,[20] or to comparative ratios published by Dr. Kenneth Brown of Southwest Missouri State University for both cities and counties.[21] Dr. Brown's benchmark data are grouped by state, Census Bureau region, and population range and are based on annual financial data collected by the GFOA. His publication provides comparative ratio data for the 25th, 50th, and 75th percentiles, by group, for ratios 1 and 2, 4 through 8, and 10 and 11 of the 13 ratios shown in Illustration 11–3. Dr. Brown's ratios are based mainly on General Fund financial data. For readers who may have forgotten their statistics, the 50th percentile corresponds to the median.

Illustration 11–5 presents Dr. Brown's comparative ratios for 419 cities located in the U.S. Census Bureau's Midwest Region. The column headed *Best* indicates

---

[20]Moody's Investor's Service, Inc., [year] *Medians: Selected Indicators of Municipal Performance* (New York: Moody's, annual).

[21]Kenneth W. Brown, *Dr. Kenneth W. Brown's Comparative Ratios for Cities: Developed for Analyses of FY 1996 Financial Statements* (Springfield, MO: Solstice Productions, 1997).

Illustration 11–5

FY 1996 COMPARATIVE RATIOS FOR CITIES
Comparison Group—Cities by U.S. Census Region
(U.S. Census Region = Midwest States)

Ratio	Number	Best	25%	50%	75%
1 Total Revenues to Population	419	High	$492.61	$607.64	$733.69
2 Local GF Revenues to Total GF Revenues	419	High	0.711	0.868	0.958
3 Operating Transfers In to Total GF Revenues and Operating Transfers In	419	Low	0.051	0.012	0.000
4 Operating Expenditures to Total Expenditures	419	Low	0.935	0.856	0.771
5 Total Revenues to Total Expenditures	419	High	0.854	0.951	1.038
6 Unreserved GF Balance to GF Revenues	419	High	0.151	0.276	0.436
7 Total GF Cash to GF Liabilities	419	High	0.796	1.590	3.850
8 Total GF Liabilities to GF Revenues	419	Low	0.279	0.155	0.083
9 Direct General Long-Term Debt to Population	419	Low	$574.40	$281.26	$72.66
10 Debt Service to Total Revenues	419	Low	0.164	0.091	0.045

Source: Reprinted by Permission of Dr. Kenneth W. Brown. Kenneth W. Brown, *Comparative Ratios for Cities: Developed for Analyses of FY 1966 Financial Statements* (Springfield, MO: Solstice Productions, 1997).

whether a high or low measure is preferred. Comparing the 25th and 75th percentile values shows the values for some ratios are highly variable across cities. This fact should also be kept in mind when comparing a city's ratios to ratios from a comparison group.

How should financial condition be evaluated and interpreted? After each indicator (ratio) is calculated, it should be compared with the same indicator from prior years, as well as against any credit market or other *red flags*. If available, each indicator can be compared with a comparative benchmark value, such as those from Moody's Medians (see footnote 20) or those published by Dr. Brown. A table can then be prepared listing each indicator and showing whether the indicator is positive ($+$) or negative ($-$). Such a table for the City of Columbia, Missouri, showing 36 indicators (for all financial factors plus community needs and resources) is shown in Illustration 11–6. Alternative measures are calculated for some indicators. Further, the City of Columbia calculates the 10 ratios contained in Dr. Brown's database and compares them to the comparison ratios. Calculation of the 10 ratios and comparison to the comparison ratios are shown in Illustration 11–7. The 10-point test is based on instructions in Dr. Brown's publication. Scores should be interpreted as follows: For each ratio, if the City of Columbia's ratio is in the first quartile (below the 25th percentile comparison ratio), score -1; if in the second quartile (at or above the 25th percentile but below the 50th percentile), score 0; if

Illustration 11–6   Columbia Financial Trend Monitoring System: Summary 1991–1996

| | | State of Indicator | | |
| | | General Fund/ Government Funds | Enterprise/Internal Service Funds | Community Needs and Resources |
Indicator	*Description of Indicator*			
Chart A	Columbia Financial Trend Monitoring System: Warning Trends/Factors			
Revenues:				
Chart B	Impact of Inflation on City Revenues	+		
1	Revenues per Capita: General Fund	+		
2-A	Restricted Revenues: Governmental Funds	+		
2-B	Restricted Revenues: Enterprise Funds		+	
3	Intergovernmental Revenues: General Fund	+		
4	Elastic Tax Revenues: General Fund	+		
5	Operating Transfers from Other Funds: General Fund	+		
6	Temporary Revenues: Governmental Funds	+		
7	Property Tax Revenues: General Fund	+		
8	Uncollected Property Taxes: General Fund	+		
9	Service Charges Coverage: General Fund	+		
10	Revenues—Budgeted versus Actual: General Fund	+		
Expenditures:				
Chart C	Impact of Inflation on City Expenditures	+	+	
11-A	Expenditures per Capita: General Fund	+		
11-B	Expenses per Capita: Enterprise Funds		+	
12-A	Employees per Capita: General Fund	+		
12-B	Employees per Capita: Enterprise Funds and Internal Service Funds		+	
13	Fixed Costs: All Funds	Monitor	Monitor	
14	Fringe Benefits	+	+	
15	Expenditures: General Fund over/under Budget	+		
Operating Position:				
16	Excess of Revenues over Expenditures: General Fund	+		
17	Enterprise Retained Earnings/Loss		+	
18	General Fund Balances	+		
19-A	Liquidity: General Fund	+		
19-B	Liquidity: Enterprise Funds		+	
20-A	Revenues to Expenditures: Governmental Funds & Expendable Trust Funds	+		
20-B	Revenues to Expenses: Proprietary Funds & Non-expendable Trust Funds		+	
21-A	Current Liabilities: General Fund	+		
21-B	Current Liabilities: Enterprise Fund		+	
22-A	General Obligation Long-Term Debt: per Assessed Valuation	+		
22-B	General Obligation Long-Term Debt: per Capita	+		
23-A	Debt Service: General Obligation Bonds	+		
23-B	Debt Service: Revenue Bonds		+	

(continued)

Illustration 11–6 (concluded)

Indicator	Description of Indicator	General Fund/ Government Funds	Enterprise/Internal Service Funds	Community Needs and Resources
		State of Indicator		
Unfunded Liabilities:				
24	Pension Assets	+	+	
25	Accumulated Employee Leave	+	+	
26-A	Maintenance Effort: Streets & Sidewalks	+		
26-B	Maintenance Effort: Water & Electric Utilities		+	
27	Capital Outlay: General, Internal Service, & Enterprise Funds	Monitor	Monitor	
28	Depreciation: Enterprise & Internal Service Funds		+	
Community Needs & Resources:				
29	Population			+
30	Median Age			+
31	Household Effective Buying Income			+
32	Public Assistance Recipients			Monitor
33	Property Value			+
34	Residential Development			+
35	Employment Base			+
36-A	Business Activity: Business License Accounts			+
36-B	Business Activity: Retail Sales			+

Source: City of Columbia, Missouri, *Financial Trend Monitoring System*, 1991–1996, pp. 106–7.

in the third quartile (at or above the 50th percentile, but below the 75th percentile), score +1; and if in the fourth quartile (at or above the 75th percentile), score +2. The total score for each column is interpreted as follows:

Score	Percentile	Relation to Score of Other Cities
14	99th	Only 1% scored higher
12	95th	Only 5% scored higher
10	90th	Only 10% scored higher
8	75th	Only 25% scored higher
5	50th	50% scored higher
2	25th	75% scored higher
0	10th	90% scored higher
−2	5th	95% scored higher
−4	1st	99% scored higher

Since the City of Columbia's total scores ranged from 6 to 10, depending on which comparison group was used, it scored quite well on these benchmarks.

Illustration 11–7 City of Columbia Ratios Using Ten-Point Test of Financial Condition: FY 1996

Calculation	Favorable	1996 Numbers	1996 Ratio	By City Size: 50,000–99,999 Quartile	Score	By Census Region: Midwest Quartile	Score	By Census Region and City Size Quartile	Score	By State: Missouri Quartile	Score
1. Total revenues / Population	High	48,116,463 / 75,561	636.79	3	1	3	1	3	1	4	2
2. Total GF revenues from own sources / Total General Fund revenues	High	29,876,965 / 31,574,238	0.946	3	1	3	1	3	1	3	1
3. GF sources from other funds / Total General Fund sources	Low	535,515 / 32,109,753	0.017	3	1	3	1	3	1	2	0
4. Operating expenditures / Total expenditures	Low	42,189,985 / 45,455,711	0.928	2	0	2	0	2	0	3	1
5. Total revenues / Total expenditures	High	48,116,463 / 45,455,711	1.059	4	2	4	2	4	2	3	1
6. Unreserved GF balance / Total General Fund revenues	High	9,985,694 / 31,574,238	0.316	4	2	3	1	3	1	3	1
7. Total GF cash and investments / Total General Fund liabilities	High	16,163,531 / 5,352,900	3.020	3	1	3	1	4	2	3	1
8. Total General Fund liabilities / Total General Fund revenues	Low	5,352,900 / 31,574,238	0.170	2	0	2	0	3	1	1	−1
9. Direct long-term debt / Population	Low	3,816,215 / 75,561	$50.51	4	2	4	2	4	2	3	1
10. Debt service / Total revenues	Low	6,463,148 / 48,116,463	0.134	2	0	2	0	2	0	1	−1
Total score					10		9		11		6
Percentile					90%		75%		90%		50%

Further, the large number of + signs included in Illustration 11–6 suggests that the City is in sound financial condition.

A caveat to keep in mind in using benchmarks from other states is that local government organizational structures differ significantly from state to state, and these differences may have a large effect on some ratios. A good example is that in a few states local school districts are legally part of the government of the city in which they are located, whereas in most states the school districts are independent governmental units. In those states in which schools are part of the city government, per capita measures such as ratios 1, 3, and 10 may be much larger than in the other states.

In addition to analyzing ratios, one should evaluate the stability, flexibility, and diversity of revenue sources; budgetary control over revenues and expenditures; adequacy of insurance protection; level of overlapping debt; and growth of unfunded employee-related benefits. Socioeconomic and demographic trends should also be analyzed, including trends in employment, real estate values, retail sales, building permits, population, personal income, and welfare. Much of this information is contained in the statistical section of the CAFR; the remainder can be obtained from the U.S. Bureau of the Census publications available in most university libraries.

Despite the complexity of evaluating governmental financial condition, there are recognizable signals of fiscal stress.[22] These include: (1) a decline or inadequate growth in revenues relative to expenditures, (2) declining property values, (3) declining economic activity (such as increasing unemployment, declining retail sales, and declining building activity), (4) erosion of capital plant, particularly infrastructure, (5) increasing levels of unfunded pension and other postemployment obligations, and (6) inadequate capital expenditures. Warning signals such as these, particularly if several exist simultaneously, may indicate a potential fiscal crisis unless the government takes action to increase revenues or decrease spending.

Credit Analyst Models

As discussed earlier in this chapter, credit analysts are concerned with assessing a government's ability to pay interest and principal when due. Credit analysts typically examine the same kinds of information that internal managers use in evaluating financial condition. Of course, internal managers have access to *all* information generated by the government, for as far back as data are retained, whereas credit analysts have access only to what management provides or what they require from management. Thus, internal managers have an informational advantage with respect to their own government. Credit analysts with the major bond rating agencies (Moody's Investors Service and Standard & Poor's), or with companies that insure bonds against default, may have an informational advantage

---

[22]See, for example, Groves and Valente, *Evaluating Financial Condition*, Part 2; and J. R. Miller and M. H. Granof, *Governmental Accounting and Auditing Update 1*, no. 3 (Boston, MA: Warren, Gorham & Lamont, March 1990).

with respect to *benchmark* information, in that they have data from thousands of entities whose bonds are rated or insured. Moreover, these analysts develop extensive multiple-year libraries, including budgets and CAFRs, for the entities whose bonds are rated or insured, and they often visit the entity for discussions with management. Analysts with investment firms (underwriters and brokers) tend to collect and process much less information than do bond rating and insurer organizations. Rather, these analysts rely in part on agency ratings to help them properly determine the credit risk of municipal bonds.

Both Moody's and Standard & Poor's examine factors in the following four groups: (1) economic, (2) financial, (3) debt, and (4) administrative/political.[23] Moody's is known to emphasize debt factors in its analyses, whereas Standard & Poor's emphasizes the issuer's economic base.[24] Nevertheless, both agencies thoroughly examine factors in each of the four groups. Although little is known about which specific factors are examined in each group, or how factors are weighted in assigning ratings, the bond market literature suggests the agencies examine many, if not most, of the same factors that are considered for internal financial trend monitoring. Thus, there is little need to describe the credit analysis models, beyond this basic discussion. One should note, however, that the ratings themselves are often viewed, particularly by investors, as crude indicators of long-term financial condition. For example, a Moody's Aaa rating indicates a city is likely in better financial condition than a city with a Baa rating (the lowest *investment grade* rating). Further, ratings assigned to general obligation (GO) bonds often apply to all GO bonds of the same issuer. This is not necessarily the case, however. For example, GO bonds issued with state credit backing or other credit enhancement may carry a higher rating than the ordinary GO bonds of the same issuer. Insured bonds and certain defeased[25] bonds are automatically assigned the top rating category by both Moody's and Standard & Poor's.

Relation of Financial Performance to Operating Performance

This chapter describes the evaluation of financial condition. Continued sound financial condition is an indication of quality financial management and good financial performance. Achieving strong financial performance, however, does not ensure efficient and effective operating performance. Although it is difficult to provide an adequate level of services without sufficient financial resources, achieving efficient and effective use of *productive* resources requires innovative budgeting and management techniques. We defer discussion of these techniques until Chapter 14. In reading Chapter 14, one should keep in mind the importance of maintaining sound financial condition if service levels are to be sustained.

---

[23]Robert Lamb and Stephen P. Rappaport, *Municipal Bonds*, 2nd ed. (New York: McGraw-Hill, 1987), pp. 40–44.

[24]Ibid.

[25]See Chapter 6 for a discussion of defeased bonds.

Key Terms

Benchmarking, 440
Financial condition, 432

Financial position, 432

Selected References

Berne, Robert. *Research Report*, "The Relationship Between Financial Reporting and the Measurement of Financial Condition." Norwalk, CT: GASB, 1992.

Brown, Kenneth W. *Comparative Ratios for Cities*. Springfield, MO: Solstice Publications, 1997.

————— . "The 10-Point Test of Financial Condition: Toward an Easy-to-Use Assessment Tool for Smaller Cities." *Government Finance Review*, December 1993, pp. 21–26.

Governmental Accounting Standards Board. *Concepts Statement No. 1*, "Objectives of Financial Reporting." Norwalk, CT: GASB, 1987.

Groves, Sanford M., and Maureen G. Valente. *Evaluating Financial Condition: A Handbook for Local Government*, 3rd ed. Washington, DC: ICMA, 1994.

Lamb, Robert, and Stephen P. Rappaport. *Municipal Bonds*, 2nd ed. New York: McGraw-Hill, 1987.

Public Securities Association. *Fundamentals of Municipal Bonds*, 4th ed. New York: PSA, 1990.

Questions

11–1. Explain why a city government needs an effective system to monitor and evaluate financial condition.

11–2. Discuss and compare the quality of governmental financial reporting now and that at the time of the New York City default (mid-1970s). How does the quality of financial reporting affect the ability to evaluate financial condition?

11–3. Explain some typical causes of municipal financial crises.

11–4. How do the objectives of evaluating financial condition differ between internal managers and credit analysts? How are their objectives similar?

11–5. "Citizens have a strong interest in evaluating their city's financial condition." Do you agree with this statement? Why or why not?

11–6. Distinguish *financial position* from *financial condition*.

11–7. How is *interperiod equity* related to *financial condition*?

11–8. Why are management practices and legislative policies considered to be critically important in evaluating financial condition?

11–9. Explain how environmental factors influence a city's fiscal policy.

11–10. "Financial statements are virtually useless in evaluating a city's financial condition." Do you agree with this statement? Why or why not?

Cases

11–1. The Combined Balance Sheet—All Fund Types, Account Groups, and Discretely Presented Component Units; Combined Statement of Revenues, Expenditures, and Changes in Fund Balances—All Governmental Fund Types and Expendable Trust Funds; selected demographic statistics; and information on general bonded debt and assessed valuations of taxable property for the City of Marshall are provided on pages 452–461.

Required

a. Using the financial statements and other information provided, calculate the 10 ratios for which Dr. Kenneth Brown's comparative ratios for Midwest states are provided in Illustration 11–5 of this chapter.

Calculate ratios as follows: (Note: Use all revenues and expenditures as reported; do not include operating transfers in and out.) (GF = General Fund, SRF = special revenue funds, DSF = debt service funds, CPF = capital projects funds)

Ratio No.	Numerator	Denominator
1.	Total governmental fund revenues (GF + SRF + DSF + CPF)	Population
2.	GF Revenues minus GF Inter-governmental Revenues	GF Revenues
3.	GF Operating Transfers In	GF Revenues plus GF Intergovernmental Revenues
4.	GF Expenditures + SRF Expenditures + DSF Expenditures	GF Expenditures + SRF Expenditures + DSF Expenditures + CPF Expenditures
5.	Same as ratio 1	Same as ratio 4
6.	Unreserved Fund Balance of the GF (both designated and undesignated)	GF Revenues
7.	GF Cash + GF Investments	GF Total Liabilities
8.	GF Total Liabilities	GF Revenues
9.	Direct Debt (Use Total Debt)	Population
10.	Total Debt Service Expenditures	Same as numerator of ratios 4 and 5

b. Compare each ratio calculated in part *a* above to the comparative ratios provided in Illustration 11–5. Prepare a 10-point test of financial condition for FY 1997 (even though the comparative data are intended for FY 1996) and interpret the City's financial condition. (See explanation in text about scoring method.)

c. Provide an overall assessment of the City's financial condition using all information, both financial and nonfinancial, provided.

11–2. Comprehensive Case. (Different city for each student. Works well as a term or semester project.)

Objective and General Requirements: The objective of this case is to help you obtain a better understanding of how to use financial and nonfinancial information to assess the current and long-term financial condition of a city of your choice, or one assigned by your instructor. You should write or call the city to obtain their CAFR, or, alternatively, your instructor may provide you with a CAFR. It is recommended that you use a city with a population of at least 25,000 to increase the chances of obtaining a complete usable CAFR. Be sure to specify that you need the full CAFR. Be prepared to contact two or three cities if necessary to ensure you receive at least one.

You will use the information provided in the city's CAFR, as well as data from the U.S. Census Bureau and other data sources you may locate, to assess the current financial position and long-term financial condition or solvency of the city. Your conclusions must, of course, be based on an in-depth analysis of all information provided in the CAFR, as well as your other sources. Because evaluation of municipal financial condition is more of an art than a science, you may have to be creative and resourceful to do a good job.

Overview: For purposes of this project, financial condition is broadly defined as the ability of a city to provide an adequate range of services on a continuing basis. Specifically, it refers to a city's ability to (1) maintain existing service levels, (2) withstand major economic disruptions, and (3) meet the demands of a changing society in a changing economy. *Current* financial position can be assessed to some extent by examining the relationship between financial inflows and outflows, the adequacy of fund balances, level of short-term debt (relative to cash, investments, and receivables), and management's comments in the introductory section of the CAFR. As discussed in the text, assessment of *financial condition* is more complicated, however. An assessment of financial condition requires estimates of the dynamic balance between the probable levels of service demand and the capacity of the city to continue to provide those services. To make such an assessment one must therefore consider critical social and economic factors that may impact on the demand for services or the capacity to provide services, or both. Additional guidance, largely gleaned from the discussion in this chapter, follows. (Note: Not all these items will apply in every case.)

Assessing Financial Condition:

1. Analysis of revenues and revenue sources.
   a. How stable and flexible are the city's revenue sources in the event of adverse economic conditions?
   b. Is the revenue base well diversified or is the city heavily reliant on one or two major sources?
   c. Has the city been relying on intergovernmental revenues for an excessive portion of its operating expenditures?
2. Analysis of reserves.
   a. Are the levels of financial reserves (i.e., fund balances and contingency funds) adequate to meet unforeseen operational requirements or catastrophic events?
   b. Is insurance protection adequate to cover losses due to lawsuits or damage to property?
   c. Is an adequate amount of cash and securities on hand, or could the city borrow quickly to cover short-term obligations?   (*continued* on p. 462)

CITY OF MARSHALL
Combined Balance Sheet—All Fund Types, Account Groups, and
Discretely Presented Component Units
June 30, 1997

	Governmental Fund Types				Proprietary Fund Types	
	General	*Special Revenue*	*Debt Service*	*Capital Projects*	*Enterprise*	*Internal Service*
Assets and Other Debits						
Assets:						
Cash and pooled cash investments	$ 592,976	$ 282,360	$ 36,177	$ 619,283	$ 320,031	$ 78,798
Cash and pooled cash investments— nonexpendable trust	—	—	—	—	—	—
Investments	103,526	3,800,299	150,000	6,453,100	3,506,055	777,808
Investments held by deferred compensation plan administrators—Note 9	—	—	—	—	—	—
Receivables:						
Property tax	44,583	12,608	24,350	—	—	—
Accounts and unbilled usage (net of allowance for uncollectibles)	23,709	7,153	—	634	748,789	—
Special assessments	—	2,657	—	6,810	—	—
Interest	8,992	25,215	420	7,189	70,577	9,926
Due from other funds—Note 3	34,787	1,921	—	—	1,807	—
Due from component unit—Note 3	—	—	—	—	148,663	—
Advance to other funds—Note 3	—	65,603	—	108,272	19,667	—
Due from other governments	93,949	233,712	—	265,328	1,238	175
Inventories, at cost	41,837	—	—	—	41,973	—
Prepaid items	205,046	7,135	—	—	59,999	6,150
Deferred charges	—	83,855	—	—	—	—
Restricted assets:						
Cash	—	—	—	—	—	—
Investments	—	—	—	—	911,445	—
Land and improvements—Note 4	—	—	—	—	3,081,964	—
Buildings and structures—Note 4	—	—	—	—	5,936,704	—
Equipment and vehicles—Note 4	—	—	—	—	10,910,421	2,795
Sanitary sewers and lift stations	—	—	—	—	5,480,786	—
Construction in progress—Note 4	—	—	—	—	1,005,484	—
Accumulated depreciation	—	—	—	—	(9,492,366)	(2,795)
Other Debits:						
Amount available in debt service fund	—	—	—	—	—	—
Amount to be provided for retirement of general long-term debt	—	—	—	—	—	—
Total Assets and Other Debits	$1,149,405	$4,522,518	$210,947	$7,460,616	$22,753,237	$872,857

Fiduciary Fund Type	Account Groups		Totals Primary Government (Memorandum Only)	Component Units		Totals Reporting Entity (Memorandum Only)
Trust and Agency	General Fixed Assets	General Long-Term Debt		Water Works	Convention and Visitors Bureau	
$ 106,590	—	—	$ 2,036,215	$ 183,995	$51,992	$ 2,272,202
2,517	—	—	2,517	—	—	2,517
147,445	—	—	14,938,233	450,000	—	15,388,233
2,352,314	—	—	2,352,314	—	—	2,352,314
—	—	—	81,541	—	—	81,541
—	—	—	780,285	151,090	—	931,375
—	—	—	9,467	—	—	9,467
940	—	—	123,259	5,471	—	128,730
—	—	—	38,515	—	—	38,515
—	—	—	148,663	—	—	148,663
—	—	—	193,542	—	—	193,542
—	—	—	594,402	—	—	594,402
—	—	—	83,810	1,877	—	85,687
607	—	—	278,937	45,711	643	325,291
—	—	—	83,855	—	—	83,855
—	—	—	—	323,329	—	323,329
—	—	—	911,445	—	—	911,445
—	$ 1,007,674	—	4,089,638	737,224	—	4,826,862
—	4,215,180	—	10,151,884	4,845,306	—	14,997,190
—	7,048,018	—	17,961,234	1,415,294	57,745	19,434,273
—	—	—	5,480,786	6,864,798	—	12,345,584
—	—	—	1,005,484	—	—	1,005,484
—	—	—	(9,495,161)	(4,961,978)	(32,050)	(14,489,189)
—	—	$196,004	196,004	—	—	196,004
—	—	17,852,743	17,852,743	—	—	17,852,743
$2,610,413	$12,270,872	$18,048,747	$69,899,612	$10,062,117	$78,330	$80,040,059

(continued)

CITY OF MARSHALL
Combined Balance Sheet—All Fund Types, Account Groups, and Discretely Presented Component Units
June 30, 1997
(continued)

	Governmental Fund Types				Proprietary Fund Types	
	General	Special Revenue	Debt Service	Capital Projects	Enterprise	Internal Service
Liabilities, Equity, and Other Credits						
Liabilities:						
Accounts payable	$120,564	$138,873	—	$399,605	$ 241,110	$181,952
Accrued payroll and payroll benefits	153,000	3,668	—	—	23,359	—
Compensated absences payable—Note 5	111,680	7,389	—	—	97,219	—
Retainage payable	—	17,651	—	83,083	19,043	—
Advantage from other funds—Note 3	—	19,667	—	—	173,875	—
Deferred revenues	10,236	58,362	$ 235	7,228	232	—
Due to other governments	—	192,030	—	—	10,506	—
Due to other funds—Note 3	—	28,186	—	3,608	684	—
Due to primary government—Note3	—	—	—	—	—	—
Due to employees	—	—	—	—	—	—
Due to general public	—	—	—	—	—	—
Matured interest payable	—	—	14,708	—	—	—
Liabilities payable from restricted assets:						
Customers' deposits	—	—	—	—	—	—
Accrued interest payable	—	—	—	—	27,917	—
Current portion of revenue bonds (net of $1,313 unamortized discounts)	—	—	—	—	48,687	—
General obligation bonds and notes payable—Note 5	—	—	—	—	—	—
Urban renewal tax increment revenue bonds—Note 5	—	—	—	—	—	—
Revenue bonds payable (net of $68,572 unamortized discounts)—Note 5	—	—	—	—	5,851,428	—
Total Liabilities	395,480	465,826	14,943	493,524	6,494,060	181,952

Fiduciary Fund Type	Account Groups		Totals Primary Government (Memorandum Only)	Component Units		Totals Reporting Entity (Memorandum Only)
Trust and Agency	General Fixed Assets	General Long-Term Debt		Water Works	Convention and Visitors Bureau	
$ 5,465	—	—	$ 1,087,569	$139,228	$ 744	$ 1,227,541
75,404	—	—	255,431	14,983	1,462	271,876
—	—	$ 608,747	825,035	47,302	—	872,337
—	—	—	119,777	—	—	119,777
—	—	—	193,542	—	—	193,542
—	—	—	76,293	—	—	76,293
1,045	—	—	203,581	—	—	203,581
6,037	—	—	38,515	—	—	38,515
—	—	—	—	148,663	—	148,663
2,352,576	—	—	2,352,576	—	—	2,352,576
36,048	—	—	36,048	—	—	36,048
—	—	—	14,708	—	—	14,708
—	—	—	—	70,849	—	70,849
—	—	—	27,917	—	—	27,917
—	—	—	48,687	—	—	48,687
—	—	16,945,000	16,945,000	—	—	16,945,000
—	—	495,000	495,000	—	—	495,000
—	—	—	5,851,428	—	—	5,851,428
2,476,575	—	18,048,747	28,571,107	421,025	2,206	28,994,338

(continued)

CITY OF MARSHALL
Combined Balance Sheet—All Fund Types, Account Groups, and Discretely Presented Component Units
June 30, 1997
(concluded)

	Governmental Fund Types				Proprietary Fund Types	
	General	Special Revenue	Debt Service	Capital Projects	Enterprise	Internal Service
Liabilities, Equity, and Other Credits						
Fund Equity and Other Credits:						
Contributed capital—Note 6	—	—	—	—	7,433,430	—
Investment in general fixed assets	—	—	—	—	—	—
Reserved retained earnings:						
Reserved for bond and interest payments	—	—	—	—	661,445	—
Reserved for improvements	—	—	—	—	250,000	—
Reserved for advance to other funds	—	—	—	—	19,667	—
Unreserved retained earnings	—	—	—	—	7,894,635	690,905
Reserved fund balances:						
Reserved for endowments	—	—	—	—	—	—
Reserved for inventories	41,837	—	—	—	—	—
Reserved for prepaid items	205,046	7,135	—	—	—	—
Reserved for employees retirement systems	—	2,115,078	—	—	—	—
Reserved for advance to other funds	—	65,603	—	108,272	—	—
Reserved for debt service	—	—	196,004	—	—	—
Unreserved fund balances:						
Designated for future equipment and capital maintenance	35,732	—	—	—	—	—
Designated for future cash flow	59,475	—	—	—	—	—
Undesignated	411,835	1,868,876	—	6,858,820	—	—
Total Fund Equity and Other Credits	753,925	4,056,692	196,004	6,967,092	16,259,177	690,905
Total Liabilities, Equity, and Other Credits	$1,149,405	$4,522,518	$210,947	$7,460,616	$22,753,237	$872,857

See Notes to Financial Statements.

Fiduciary Fund Type	Account Groups		Totals Primary Government (Memorandum Only)	Component Units		Totals Reporting Entity (Memorandum Only)
Trust and Agency	General Fixed Assets	General Long-Term Debt		Water Works	Convention and Visitors Bureau	
—	—	—	7,433,430	—	—	7,433,430
—	12,270,872	—	12,270,872	—	—	12,270,872
—	—	—	661,445	—	—	661,445
—	—	—	250,000	—	—	250,000
—	—	—	19,667	—	—	19,667
—	—	—	8,585,540	9,641,092	76,124	18,302,756
2,521	—	—	2,521	—	—	2,521
—	—	—	41,837	—	—	41,837
—	—	—	212,181	—	—	212,181
8,359	—	—	2,123,437	—	—	2,123,437
—	—	—	173,875	—	—	173,875
—	—	—	196,004	—	—	196,004
—	—	—	35,732	—	—	35,732
—	—	—	59,475	—	—	59,475
122,958	—	—	9,262,489	—	—	9,262,489
133,838	12,270,872	—	41,328,505	9,641,092	76,124	51,045,721
$2,610,413	$12,270,872	$18,048,747	$69,899,612	$10,062,117	$78,330	$80,040,059

CITY OF MARSHALL
Combined Statement of Revenues, Expenditures, and Changes in Fund Balances—
All Governmental Fund Types and Expendable Trust Funds
For the Fiscal Year Ended June 30, 1997

		Governmental Fund Types			Fiduciary Fund Type	Totals Primary Government
	General	Special Revenue	Debt Service	Capital Projects	Expendable Trust	(Memorandum Only)
Revenues:						
Property tax	$4,778,343	$1,349,285	$2,651,407	—	—	$ 8,779,035
Tax increment financing revenues	—	92,028	—	—	—	92,028
Other city taxes	236,954	3,461	6,668	—	—	247,083
Use of money and property	156,570	158,039	49,392	$ 251,374	$ 5,363	620,738
Licenses and permits	196,185	—		—	—	196,185
Intergovernmental	971,061	2,637,743	—	818,715	—	4,427,519
Charges for services	302,446	—	—	1,079	40,372	343,897
Special assessments	—	2,658	—	1,530	—	4,188
Miscellaneous	281,714	73,270	—	22,374	60,713	438,071
Total Revenues	6,923,273	4,316,484	2,707,467	1,095,072	106,448	15,148,744
Expenditures:						
Current:						
Community Protection Program	5,048,950	369,780	—	—	10,062	5,428,792
Human Development Program	1,532,342	59,748	—	—	72,338	1,664,428
Home and Community Environment Program	1,245,616	2,053,088	—	—	—	3,298,704
Policy and Administration Program	882,488	2,127	—	—	—	884,615
Total Current Expenditures	8,709,396	2,484,743	—	—	82,400	11,276,539
Capital outlay	—	—	—	4,752,596	—	4,752,596
Debt Service:						
Principal	13,839	73,333	2,055,000	—	—	2,142,172
Interest and other fiscal charges	—	—	725,779	—	—	725,779
Other debt service costs	—	—	2,407	—	—	2,407
Total Debt Service	13,839	73,333	2,783,186	—	—	2,870,358
Total Expenditures	8,723,235	2,558,076	2,783,186	4,752,596	82,400	18,899,493
Excess (Deficiency) of Revenues Over (Under) Expenditures	(1,799,962)	1,758,408	(75,719)	(3,657,524)	24,048	(3,750,749)
Other Financing Sources (Uses):						
Sale of general fixed assets	2,687	—	—	—	—	2,687
Proceeds of general obligation bonds	—	—	—	8,736,155	—	8,736,155
Proceeds of general obligation capital loan notes	250,000	—	—	—	—	250,000
Operating transfers in	2,063,770	2,375	56,000	608,320	—	2,730,465
Operating transfers out	(189,057)	(2,300,935)	—	(435,394)	—	(2,925,386)
Total Other Financing Sources (Uses)	2,127,400	(2,298,560)	56,000	8,909,081	—	8,793,921
Excess (Deficiency) of Revenues and Other Financing Sources Over (Under) Expenditures and Other Financing Uses	327,438	(540,152)	(19,719)	5,251,557	24,048	5,043,172
Fund balances at beginning of year	427,894	4,596,844	215,723	1,715,535	98,910	7,054,906
Decrease in reserve for inventory	(1,407)	—	—	—	—	(1,407)
Fund balances at end of year	$ 753,925	$4,056,692	$ 196,004	$6,967,092	$122,958	$12,096,671

CITY OF MARSHALL
Demographic Statistics
(Unaudited)

Year	Population	Median Age (Zip 50158)	Retail Sales	Number of Businesses	School Enrollment Public	School Enrollment Private	Unemployment Rate
1987	26,938	N/A	$183,882,515	3,287	4,999	287	6.20
1988	26,938	28.8	199,298,854	3,327	5,007	300	4.10
1989	26,938	N/A	214,882,189	3,312	4,990	305	3.90
1990	25,178	36.7	225,091,244	3,314	4,869	307	3.70
1991	25,178	N/A	238,200,615	3,326	4,883	301	4.00
1992	25,178	N/A	242,596,231	3,362	4,891	304	4.50
1993	25,178	37.1	257,104,537	3,489	4,782	285	4.30
1994	25,178	37.2	288,619,825	3,519	4,872	304	3.30
1995	25,178	37.2	289,608,208	3,513	4,958	285	3.60
1996	25,178	37.8	298,889,577	3,480	4,995	285	3.80

Marshall County

Year	Per Capita Income	Median Household Income	Median Age	Retail Sales	Number of Businesses	Unemployment Rate
1987	$14,305	N/A	N/A	$204,248,849	4,764	6.10
1988	14,706	$25,263	33.3	218,790,354	4,779	4.10
1989	15,915	26,634	33.6	233,427,717	4,726	3.80
1990	17,280	27,114	36.7	244,137,122	4,668	3.70
1991	17,894	N/A	N/A	258,648,375	4,631	4.00
1992	18,814	N/A	N/A	262,118,716	4,608	4.30
1993	18,844	31,456	37.1	272,526,510	4,669	4.10
1994	20,748	33,091	37.2	304,752,174	4,683	3.20
1995	N/A	29,479	37.4	306,775,790	4,607	3.40
1996	N/A	35,810	37.9	315,917,997	4,531	3.60

CITY OF MARSHALL
Ratio of General Bonded Debt to Assessed Values
and General Bonded Debt per Capita
Last Ten Fiscal Years
(Unaudited)

Fiscal Year	General Obligation Bonded Debt	TIF Debt	Total Bonded/ TIF Debt	Assessed Value of Property*[1]
1987–88	$13,550,000	—	$13,550,000	$543,435,685
1988–89	13,615,000	—	13,615,000	545,498,178
1989–90	12,655,000	—	12,655,000	545,372,168
1990–91	11,710,000	—	11,710,000	551,921,255
1991–92	11,050,000	—	11,050,000	576,216,321
1992–93	9,805,000	—	9,805,000	585,744,670
1993–94	13,375,000	$ 515,000	13,890,000	614,238,646
1994–95	11,710,000	515,000	12,225,000	638,734,005
1995–96	9,955,000	515,000	10,470,000	729,253,341
1996–97	13,045,000	4,395,000	17,440,000	738,087,652

Fiscal Year	Population[2]	Ratio of Bonded/TIF Debt to Assessed Value	Bonded/TIF Debt per Capita
1987–88	26,938	2.49%	$503.01
1988–89	26,938	2.50	505.42
1989–90	26,938	2.32	469.78
1990–91	25,178	2.12	465.09
1991–92	25,178	1.92	438.88
1992–93	25,178	1.67	389.43
1993–94	25,178	2.26	551.67
1994–95	25,178	1.91	485.54
1995–96	25,178	1.44	415.84
1996–97	25,178	2.36	692.67

*Sources: Assessed value includes the addition of regular realty and tax increment financing (TIF).
[1]County Auditor's Office and City Assessor.
[2]United States Census Bureau.

CITY OF MARSHALL
Computation of Direct and Overlapping Debt
As of June 30, 1997
(Unaudited)

Name of Governmental Unit	Debt Outstanding[1]	Percentage Applicable to City of Marshall[2]	City of Marshall Share of Debt
City of Marshall	$17,440,000	100.00%	$17,440,000
Green Valley Schools	12,705,000	54.90	6,975,045
Marshall Schools	195,000	0.08	156
Marshall Community School District	2,010,000	83.62	1,680,762
Marshall County	—	54.30	—
Total direct and overlapping debt	$32,350,000		$26,095,963

Sources:
[1]Individual units.
[2]Marshall County Auditor's Office.

CITY OF MARSHALL
Ratio of Annual Debt Service Expenditures
for General Debt to Total General Expenditures:
General, Special Revenue, and Debt Service Funds
Last Ten Fiscal Years
(Unaudited)

Fiscal Year	Principal	Interest and Other Fiscal Charges	Total Debt Service*	Total General Expenditures[†]	Ratio of Debt Service to Total Expenditures
1987–88	$ 775,000	$1,038,661	$1,813,661	$ 9,500,890	19.09%
1988–89	811,250	990,201	1,801,451	9,506,113	18.95
1989–90	892,500	1,015,896	1,908,396	10,177,688	18.75
1990–91	1,006,396	1,012,734	2,019,130	11,661,441	17.31
1991–92	1,146,204	906,275	2,052,479	11,809,777	17.38
1992–93	2,775,819	898,607	3,674,426	12,994,768	28.28
1993–94	1,500,362	856,064	2,356,426	12,547,004	18.78
1994–95	1,759,609	799,144	2,558,753	12,499,729	20.47
1995–96	1,848,173	709,173	2,557,346	13,020,476	19.64
1996–97	2,142,172	728,186	2,870,358	14,046,846	20.43

*General obligation debt paid from property taxes.
[†]Expenditures do not include transfers out.

(continued from page 451)

3. Analysis of expenditures.
   a. Are there any components of expenditures that exhibit sharp growth?
   b. Is adequate budgetary control being exercised over expenditures?
   c. How does the growth pattern of operating expenditures over the past 10 years compare with that of revenues?

4. Analysis of debt burden.
   a. What has been the 10-year trend in general obligation long-term debt relative to population trend and trends in revenue capacity?
   b. Are there significant debts of other governmental units being supported by the same taxable properties (e.g., a school district, a county)? What has been the trend for this "overlapping" debt?
   c. Are there significant levels of short-term operating debt? If so, has it shown indications of growth?
   d. Are there any significant quasi-debts (e.g., lease obligations, unfunded pension liabilities, accrued employee benefits) or contingent liabilities?
   e. Are there any risky investments such as derivatives disclosed in the notes to the financial statements? Are the types of investments adequately explained and are their risks adequately disclosed?

5. Socioeconomic factors.
   What have been the trends in demographic and economic indicators such as real estate values, building permits, retail sales, population, income per capita, percent of population below the poverty level, average age, average educational level, employment and unemployment, and business licenses? (Note: Many of these items and other potentially useful information can be obtained from the *City and County Data Book* published by the U.S. Bureau of the Census. This book is available in the reference area of most university libraries. Selected data can be obtained from the Census Bureau's Internet site also at http://www.census.gov.)

6. Potential "red flags" or warning signs.
   a. Decline in revenues.
   b. Decline in property tax collection rate.
      (1) Less than 92 percent of current levy collected?
      (2) Property taxes greater than 90 percent of legal tax limit?
      (3) Decreasing tax collections in two of the last three years?
   c. Expenditures increasing more rapidly than revenues.
   d. Declining balances of liquid resources and fund balances.
      (1) General fund deficit in two or more of the last five years?
      (2) General fund balance less than 5 percent of general fund revenues and operating transfers in?
   e. Growing debt burden.
      (1) Short-term debt greater than 5 percent of operating revenues?
      (2) Two-year trend of increasing short-term debt?
      (3) Short-term interest and current-year debt service on general obligation debt greater than 20 percent of operating revenue?
      (4) Debt per capita ratio 50 percent higher than four years ago?

(continued)

(Case 11–2 *concluded*)

   f. Growth of unfunded pension and other employee-related benefits such as compensated absences and postemployment health care benefits.

   g. Deferral of needed maintenance on capital plant.

   h. A decrease in the value of taxable properties, retail sales levels, or disposable personal income.

   i. Decreasing revenue support from federal or state government.

   j. Increasing unemployment.

   k. Unusual climatic conditions or the occurrence of natural disasters.

   l. Ineffective management and/or dysfunctional political circumstances.

As part of evaluating the foregoing factors, it is recommended that you compute as many of the ratios shown in Illustration 11–3 of the text as you can, consistent with data availability in your CAFR. For ratios 1 through 5 you may wish to use total governmental funds operating revenues and expenditures, as usually reported among the first tables in the statistical section of the CAFR. You may wish to show these computations in an appendix to your paper.

Required

Using the information in your CAFR and other sources as discussed above, prepare a report providing the results of your analysis. Your instructor will provide specific guidance, but it is recommended that the report be about eight (8) pages of text, double-spaced, typed with 12-point font size. The report should have an appendix providing a few graphs and/or tables to provide support for your analysis. In particular, graphs showing general revenues and expenditures in the same graph for the past 10 years, key debt ratios for the past 10 years, and selected demographic and socioeconomic trends are particularly helpful. You should carefully decide what data is most relevant to your study and include only that data in your graphs and/or tables. Using headings in the report corresponding to each major area in the preceding outline may help focus your report.

11–3. Internet Case. Use any of the several Internet search engines to locate the homepage for Moody's Investors Service and Standard & Poor's (Spell precisely as shown. You may wish also to visit the homepage of a third rating service: Fitch Investors Service.) Locate and print their bond-rating categories. Do they provide any information on how they perform municipal (tax-backed) bond-rating evaluations? If so, summarize those procedures and compare them to the procedures described in this chapter.

Exercises and Problems

11–1. Utilizing the CAFR obtained for Exercise 1–1, and used in Chapters 2 through 10, calculate insofar as possible the 13 financial ratios shown in Illustration 11–3. Evaluate the ratios in terms of the red flags and benchmarks provided in Illustration 11–3 and long-term trend data for each ratio, if available. In your opinion, is the governmental entity whose CAFR you have analyzed in sound financial condition? Explain your conclusions.

11–2. Write the numbers 1 through 10 on a sheet of paper. Beside each number write the letter corresponding with the best answer to each of the following questions:

1. Which of the following groups or parties generally has the *least* incentive to evaluate the financial condition of a city?
   a. Credit market analysts.
   b. Citizens.
   c. Internal managers.
   d. Legislative and oversight bodies.

2. Which of the following improvements was *not* influenced by the default of New York City in 1975?
   a. Improvements in financial reporting standards.
   b. Improvements in the quality of financial reporting in terms of reporting in conformity with GAAP.
   c. Improvements in the quality of municipal elections.
   d. Improvements in the quality of financial management.

3. Which of the following terms or concepts focuses primarily on assets and liabilities that require cash, or are normally converted to cash or require the use of cash in the near future, and can generally be determined from fund-based financial statements alone?
   a. Interperiod equity.
   b. Financial condition.
   c. Solvency.
   d. Financial position.

4. The concept of *financial condition* refers to a governmental unit's ability to:
   a. Maintain existing service levels.
   b. Withstand local and regional economic disruptions.
   c. Meet the demands of natural growth, decline, and change.
   d. All of the above.

5. Which of the following environmental factors primarily determines a city's demand for services and its capacity to provide those services?
   a. Intergovernmental constraints.
   b. Community needs and resources.
   c. Political culture.
   d. Management policies and legislative policies.

6. The group of factors that largely determines how fiscal policy is influenced by environmental factors are:
   a. Natural disasters and emergencies.
   b. Unfunded liabilities.
   c. External economic conditions.
   d. Management practices and legislative policies.

7. Which of the following would *not* be an effective means of *benchmarking*?
   a. Comparing key ratios of the city to those of special purpose governments in the area.
   b. Comparing current-period ratios to those of prior periods.
   c. Comparing current-period ratios to *early warning* or *red flag* levels.
   d. Comparing current-period ratios to published medians of the same ratios for similar size cities or cities in the same geographic region.

8. Which of the following conditions may signal impending fiscal stress?
   a. Increasing unemployment.
   b. Increasing property values.
   c. Increasing retail sales.
   d. All of the above.

9. Credit rating agencies such as Moody's and Standard & Poor's examine factors in which of the following four major groups in assessing creditworthiness for purposes of rating tax-supported bonds?
   a. Economic, scope of services, financial, and debt.
   b. Economic, financial, debt, and administrative/political.
   c. Economic, financial, administrative/political, and education.
   d. Economic, financial, debt, and education.

10. Which of the following statements is correct regarding the relationship between *financial condition* and *operating performance*?
    a. Sound financial condition ensures efficient and effective operating performance.
    b. Sound financial condition may be a necessary but not sufficient condition for achieving efficient and effective operating performance.
    c. Efficient and effective operating performance ensures sound financial condition.
    d. Both *a* and *c*.

11–3. Write the numbers 1 through 10 on a sheet of paper. Beside each number write a "+" if a high or increasing value of the item is generally associated with *stronger* financial condition, a "−" if a high or increasing value of the item is generally associated with a *weaker* financial condition, and "NE" if the item generally has *no effect* on financial condition or the direction of the effect cannot be predicted.

   1. Personal income per capita.
   2. Inflation rate.
   3. Percentage of households below the poverty level.
   4. Bank deposits.
   5. Property values.
   6. Population growth.
   7. Political party of the mayor.
   8. Unfunded pension liability.
   9. Level of overlapping debt.
   10. Reserves for self-insurance.

11–4. The City of Calloway is a small city located in the Midwest Region, as defined by the U.S. Census Bureau. The City Finance Director desires to compare ratios for the City to the 10 benchmark ratios produced by Dr. Kenneth Brown, as discussed in this chapter. The results of her calculations, along with the median (50th percentile) values for all cities in the same size group (10,000–24,999) located in the Midwest Region, are shown below:

Ratio No.	City of Calloway	Brown's Median
1	$435.78	$617.08
2	0.760	0.860
3	0.051	0.013
4	0.680	0.839
5	0.823	0.952
6	0.184	0.312
7	1.432	1.836
8	0.192	0.192
9	$299.64	$207.37
10	0.102	0.081

Required

Prepare the 10-point test of financial condition shown in Illustration 11–7 and explained in this chapter. Prepare a brief analysis of how the City's financial condition compares with similar size cities in the Midwest Region.

Continuous Problem

11–L. After calculating the financial ratios presented in Illustration 11–3 and examining the financial statements and schedules prepared for 10–L *a* and *b*, prepare a letter of transmittal to accompany the general purpose financial statements and the individual fund and account group statements. Your letter of transmittal should be addressed to the Honorable Mayor, City Council, and City Manager of the City of Bingham and should inform them of the accounting and budgeting policies employed by the City and explain in some detail which financial statements and schedules are enclosed. Your letter should also summarize the financial condition of the City and its funds, and, in general, note significant changes since the end of the prior year. (Trial balances and balance sheets as of June 30, 1999, given at the beginning of each "L" problem, as needed, give you information about the financial condition of funds at the end of the prior year.)

CHAPTER

Audits of Governmental and Not-for-Profit Organizations

Learning Objectives

After studying this chapter, you should be able to:

~ Explain the essential characteristics of financial audits by independent CPAs, including:

The objective(s) of financial audits.

The source and content of generally accepted auditing standards (GAAS).

The types of audit reports that can be rendered.

The contents of an unqualified and a qualified audit report.

~ Explain what is meant by generally accepted government auditing standards (GAGAS), the source of GAGAS, and why GAGAS are much broader than GAAS.

~ Distinguish between financial audits and performance audits conducted under GAGAS and explain the objectives of each.

~ Explain the characteristics of a single audit, including

The purpose.

Which entities must have a single audit.

What auditing work is required.

How major programs are selected for audit.

What reports must be rendered, when and to whom.

Financial statements of governmental entities, colleges and universities, hospitals and other health care organizations, voluntary health and welfare organizations, and other not-for-profit organizations are the representations of the officials responsible for the financial management of the entity. In order for users of the financial statements to have the assurance that the statements are prepared in conformity with accounting and financial reporting standards established by authoritative bodies, and that all material facts are disclosed, the statements should be accompanied by the report of an independent auditor. Audits for this purpose are called *financial audits*, or attest audits. Other audits discussed in this chapter focus on determining whether managers of an organization are using resources entrusted to them efficiently and effectively in accomplishing organizational objectives, or whether program goals are being attained. These audits are called *performance audits*.

Financial Audits by Independent CPAs

The auditor's objective in performing a financial audit is to render a report expressing his or her opinion that the financial statements present fairly the financial position, results of operations, and where appropriate, cash flows of the organization. "Present fairly" means in conformity with generally accepted accounting principles. Auditing standards prescribe standard wording of audit reports to ensure that report users clearly understand the responsibilities of management and those of the auditor, what was audited, the scope of audit, and the nature of the audit opinion.

Audits of State and Local Governments

In the case of state and local government units, audits may be performed by independent certified public accountants (CPAs) or by state or federal audit agencies. In performing audits, auditors are professionally and ethically obligated by Rule 202 of the American Institute of Certified Public Accountants' (AICPA) *Code of Professional Conduct* to follow **generally accepted auditing standards (GAAS)**— standards set by the AICPA and promulgated in *Statements on Auditing Standards*. GAAS have been summarized by the AICPA in the three general standards, three standards of field work, and four standards of reporting shown in Illustration 12–1. These 10 standards are amplified by numerous *Statements on Auditing Standards* published in codified form in the AICPA's *Professional Standards*. Failure to follow GAAS can result in severe sanctions, including, in some instances, loss of the auditor's license to practice as a CPA and expulsion from the AICPA. It is the auditor's duty to adhere to auditing standards, and it is his or her technical qualifications and independence from the entity being audited that add credibility to reported financial information and increase financial statement users' confidence in the information.

In addition to the obligation to follow GAAS, auditors must follow **generally accepted government auditing standards (GAGAS)** for audits of state and local government and not-for-profit organizations that expend $300,000 or more from federal sources. The Comptroller General of the United States establishes these standards. For certain of these audits, the auditor is also required to follow audit guidance published by the federal Office of Management and Budget (OMB) or program-specific audit guides issued by individual federal departments or agencies. Audits conducted under GAGAS and other federal guidance are discussed later in this chapter.

Types of Audit Reports

Illustration 12–2 shows the standard audit report wording for an unqualified audit opinion on the general purpose financial statements (GFPS) of a state or local government. The first paragraph of the auditor's report is called the *opening paragraph*. In the first sentence of that paragraph, the auditor specifies the financial statements on which the opinion is being expressed. Since 1986, GASB standards (Codification Section 2200.134) have stated that the general purpose financial

---

Illustration 12–1   Generally Accepted Auditing Standards— AICPA

General Standards

1. The audit is to be performed by a person or persons having adequate technical training and proficiency as an auditor.
2. In all matters relating to the assignment, an independence in mental attitude is to be maintained by the auditor or auditors.
3. Due professional care is to be exercised in the performance of the audit and the preparation of the report.

Standards of Field Work

1. The work is to be adequately planned and assistants, if any, are to be properly supervised.
2. A sufficient understanding of the internal control structure is to be obtained to plan the audit and to determine the nature, timing, and extent of tests to be performed.
3. Sufficient competent evidential matter is to be obtained through inspection, observation, inquiries, and confirmations to afford a reasonable basis for an opinion regarding the financial statements under audit.

Standards of Reporting

1. The report shall state whether the financial statements are presented in accordance with generally accepted accounting principles.
2. The report shall identify those circumstances in which such principles have not been consistently observed in the current period in relation to the preceding period.
3. Informative disclosures in the financial statements are to be regarded as reasonably adequate unless otherwise stated in the report.
4. The report shall either contain an expression of opinion regarding the financial statements, taken as a whole, or an assertion to the effect that an opinion cannot be expressed. When an overall opinion cannot be expressed, the reasons therefore should be stated. In all cases where an auditor's name is associated with financial statements, the report should contain a clear-cut indication of the character of the auditor's work, if any, and the degree of responsibility the auditor is taking.

Source: *AICPA Professional Standards*, AU 150.02.

Illustration 12–2 Unqualified Opinion on General Purpose Financial Statements Submitted Together with Combining and Individual Fund and Account Group Financial Statements and Supporting Schedules as Supplementary Data

Independent Auditor's Report

We have audited the accompanying general purpose financial statements of City of Example, Any State, as of and for the year ended June 30, 19X1. These general purpose financial statements are the responsibility of City of Example, Any State, management. Our responsibility is to express an opinion on these general purpose financial statements based on our audit.

We conducted our audit in accordance with generally accepted auditing standards. Those standards require that we plan and perform the audit to obtain reasonable assurance about whether the general purpose financial statements are free of material misstatement. An audit includes examining, on a test basis, evidence supporting the amounts and disclosures in the general purpose financial statements. An audit also includes assessing the accounting principles used and significant estimates made by management, as well as evaluating the overall general purpose financial presentation. We believe that our audit provides a reasonable basis for our opinion.

In our opinion, the general purpose financial statements referred to above present fairly, in all material respects, the financial position of City of Example, Any State, as of June 30, 19X1, and the results of its operations and cash flows of its proprietary fund types and nonexpendable trust funds for the year then ended in conformity with generally accepted accounting principles.

Our audit was made for the purpose of forming an opinion on the general purpose financial statements taken as a whole. The combining and individual fund and account group financial statements and schedules listed in the table of contents are presented for purposes of additional analysis and are not a required part of the general purpose financial statements of City of Example, Any State. Such information has been subjected to the auditing procedures applied in the audit of the general purpose financial statements and, in our opinion, is fairly presented in all material respects in relation to the general purpose financial statements taken as a whole.

[Signature]

[Date]

Source: American Institute of Certified Public Accountants, Audit and Accounting Guide: *Audits of State and Local Governmental Units* (New York: AICPA, 1996), App. A, Example A.2. Copyright © 1996 by the American Institute of Certified Public Accountants, Inc.

statements (GPFS—illustrated and discussed in Chapters 2, 3, and 9) are the statements that must be presented for conformity with generally accepted accounting principles (GAAP). The comprehensive annual financial report (CAFR) should include combining and individual fund and account group financial statements, as well as the general purpose financial statements; but in the auditor's report shown in Illustration 12–2, the auditor accepts responsibility only for the combined statements, not for the combining statements or for the individual fund and account group financial statements. This is also clear from the second sentence of the fourth paragraph of the auditor's report. Inasmuch as combined statements are prepared from combining and individual fund and account group statements, the auditor would apply auditing procedures to financial data reported in combining and individual fund and account group statements from which the combined statements were derived. If the auditor is expressing an opinion on the GPFS, and they are issued separately from a CAFR, then the fourth paragraph is not required. If the government officials desire an audit report on combining statements, or an individual fund or account group statements, that fact should be made explicit, in writing, before the start of the audit so the auditor can modify the scope of the examination appropriately. The opening paragraph also states that the financial statements are the responsibility of the entity's management.

The first sentence of the second or *scope paragraph* of the auditor's report (Illustration 12–2) states that the examination was made "in accordance with generally accepted auditing standards." That phrase has a definite meaning to professional auditors—a meaning they have been trying for many years to communicate to clients, bankers, judges, legislators, and every other group with a need to understand what an auditor's report means.

The scope paragraph also includes a statement that GAAS require that the auditor plan and perform the audit to obtain reasonable assurance as to whether the financial statements are free of material misstatements. In addition, the scope paragraph includes a statement that an audit includes: (1) examining, on a test basis, evidence supporting the amounts and disclosures in the financial statements, (2) assessing the accounting principles used and significant estimates made by management, and (3) evaluating the overall financial statement presentation. Finally, the scope paragraph includes a statement that the auditor believes that the audit provides a reasonable basis for the opinion rendered.[1]

The third paragraph of the auditor's report (Illustration 12–2) is referred to as the *opinion paragraph.* In that paragraph, the financial statements on which the auditor is expressing an opinion are identified as presenting fairly in conformity with generally accepted accounting principles the financial position of the reporting entity as of a certain date; the results of its operations for the fiscal year ended on that date; and, in the case of proprietary fund types and nonexpendable trust funds, cash flows during the fiscal year. The auditor states a professional opinion that the financial statements described in the report are fairly presented in conformity with GAAP.

The introductory, scope, and opinion paragraphs would be sufficient if the independent auditor's report accompanied separately issued GPFS. If the auditor's report is associated with the GPFS in the financial section of a CAFR, however, as is customary, a fourth paragraph known as the *explanatory paragraph* is added. The purpose of the explanatory paragraph is to explain that the combining, individual

---

[1] American Institute of Certified Public Accountants, Inc., *Professional Standards* AU 508.08 (New York: AICPA, 1996).

fund, and individual account group financial statements and schedules are not a required part of the GPFS, but that such information has been subjected to auditing procedures applied in the audit of the GPFS, and, in the auditor's opinion, is fairly presented in all material respects in relation to the GPFS taken as a whole.

If the auditor determines the financial statements contain a departure from GAAP, the effect of which is material or there has been a material change between periods in accounting principles, or in the method of their application, the auditor may not express an unqualified opinion.

One example that precludes an unqualified opinion is a stand-alone consolidated report that some governments have issued on an experimental basis. If an audit opinion is to be rendered on such a report it must be an *adverse opinion* stating the report does not present fairly in conformity with GAAP.[2] It is also possible that the auditor cannot express an unqualified opinion because the scope of the examination was affected by conditions that precluded the application of one or more auditing procedures the auditor considered necessary in the circumstances. If it is not appropriate for the auditor to express an unqualified opinion, the auditor should consult relevant authoritative pronouncements to determine if a *qualified opinion* (see Illustration 12–3) should be issued, or if an opinion should be *disclaimed*. Expanded discussion of the nature of each of these types of opinions, and the conditions that would warrant the use of each, is beyond the scope of this text. Interested readers are referred to current collegiate auditing texts and to the pronouncements of the AICPA.[3]

Before any audit work is done, there should be a clear understanding of the scope of each engagement by all interested parties. A written memorandum of the engagement, or engagement letter, specifying the scope of the work to be done should be prepared in advance and copies retained by both the auditor and auditee. A written record of the agreement is essential for the protection of both parties. Independent public accountants have had the need for specific, written memorandums of the scope of engagements forcefully pointed out to them by a number of well-known liability cases.

Governmental units often engage more than one audit firm to conduct annual audits. Some component units such as airports, hospitals, and utilities may have their own governing boards and select their own auditor, yet meet the criteria discussed in Chapters 2 and 10 for inclusion in the governmental reporting entity. The principal auditor for the governmental unit (the auditor of the General Fund

---

[2] Because consolidated reports are based on different accounting principles than are used for certain fund types of the GPFS, the auditor must render an adverse opinion. Auditors may, however, issue a restrictively worded report that certain summary information of the type published by some governments in "popular reports" is fairly presented in relation to the GPFS from which it has been derived. The auditor must have audited the GPFS and must refer to that audit in the "in relation to" report on the summary information. Source: American Institute of Certified Public Accountants, Audit and Accounting Guide, *Audits of State and Local Governmental Units* (New York: AICPA, 1996), pars. 18.23–18.32.

[3] A convenient source of information on currently effective pronouncements is a publication of the American Institute of Certified Public Accountants: *AICPA Professional Standards*.

Illustration 12–3   Qualified Opinion on General Purpose Financial Statements that Omit One or More, but Not All, Component Units of the Reporting Entity*

Independent Auditor's Report

We have audited the accompanying general purpose financial statements of City of Example, Any State, as of and for the year ended June 30, 19X1. These general purpose financial statements are the responsibility of City of Example, Any State, management. Our responsibility is to express an opinion on these general purpose financial statements based on our audit.

We conducted our audit in accordance with generally accepted auditing standards. Those standards require that we plan and perform the audit to obtain reasonable assurance about whether the general purpose financial statements are free of material misstatement. An audit includes examining, on a test basis, evidence supporting the amounts and disclosures in the general purpose financial statements. An audit also includes assessing the accounting principles used and significant estimates made by management, as well as evaluating the overall general purpose financial statement presentation. We believe that our audit provides a reasonable basis for our opinion.

The general purpose financial statements referred to above do not include financial activities of the *(identify the component unit[s] omitted)*, which should be included in order to conform with generally accepted accounting principles. If the omitted component unit(s) had been included,[†] the assets and revenues of the *[identify fund types(s)—for example, special revenue fund type—or component column(s)]* would have been increased by \$XXX,XXX and \$XXX,XXX, respectively, there would have been an excess of expenditures over revenues in that fund type *[or component unit(s)]* of \$XXX,XXX for the year, and the *[identify fund type(s) or discretely presented component column(s)]* fund balance would have been a deficit of \$XXX,XXX.

In our opinion, except for the effects on the financial statements of the omission described in the preceding paragraph, the general purpose financial statements referred to above present fairly, in all material respects, the financial position of City of Example, Any State, as of June 30, 19X1, and the results of its operations and cash flows of its proprietary fund types and nonexpendable trust funds for the year then ended in conformity with generally accepted accounting principles.

[Signature]

[Date]

---

*There may be circumstances when, based on professional judgment, the auditor may determine that an adverse opinion on the general purpose financial statements is appropriate. In such a case, a separate explanatory paragraph should state all the substantive reasons for the adverse opinion and the principal effects of those matters. If an adverse opinion is to be rendered, the last two paragraphs of this report should be replaced with the following paragraphs:

The general purpose financial statements referred to above do not include financial activities of the *[identify the component unit(s) omitted]*, which should be included in order to conform with generally accepted accounting principles.

Because of the departure from generally accepted accounting principles identified above, as of June 30, 19X1, the assets and revenues of the *[identify fund type(s)]—for example, special revenue fund type—or component column(s)]* would have increased by \$XXX,XXX and \$XXX,XXX, respectively, there would have been an excess of expenditures over revenues in the fund type *[or component unit(s)]* for the year of \$XXX,XXX and the *[identify fund type(s) or component unit(s)]* fund balance would have been a deficit of \$XXX,XXX.

In our opinion, because of the effects of the matters discussed in the preceding paragraphs, the general purpose financial statements referred to above do not present fairly, in conformity with generally accepted accounting principles, the financial position of City of Example, Any State, as of June 30, 19X1, or the results of its operations or the cash flows of its proprietary fund types or nonexpendable trust funds for the year then ended.

†If the amounts applicable to the omitted component unit have not been audited, insert the phrase *based on unaudited information*.

Source: American Institute of Certified Public Accountants, Audit and Accounting Guide, *Audits of State and Local Governmental Units* (New York: AICPA, 1996), Appendix A, Example A.5 Copyright © 1996 by the American Institute of Certified Public Accountants, Inc.

of the primary government) must in this case decide whether to make reference to the other auditor in his or her audit report or to assume responsibility for the work performed by the other auditor without reference in the audit report. If reference is made to the other auditor, the principal auditor's report should disclose the magnitude of the portion of the financial statements audited by the other auditor. An audit report making reference to another auditor is not a qualified report, unless some other reason exists for qualification.

Auditing procedures deemed particularly applicable to audits of state and local governments by independent CPAs are published in the AICPA Audit and Accounting Guide, *Audits of State and Local Governmental Units*. The Audit Guide and other authoritative auditing literature provide guidance to all auditors, not just independent CPAs, whose function it is to examine financial statements, and the underlying records, for the purpose of determining whether the statements present fairly the financial position as of a certain date, and the results of operations and cash flows for a fiscal period, in conformity with generally accepted accounting principles.

The audit guide emphasizes the importance of testing for compliance with laws and regulations that may have a material effect on the determination of financial statement amounts. The guide notes that:

> The auditor should design the audit to provide reasonable assurance that the financial statements are free of material misstatement resulting from violations of laws and regulations that have a direct and material effect on the determination of financial statement amounts. This responsibility exists for all audits conducted in accordance with GAAS.[4]

Audits conducted under the government auditing standards issued by the U.S. General Accounting Office place even greater emphasis on testing and reporting on compliance with laws and regulations. These standards are discussed next.

Government Auditing Standards

Audit standards that are to be followed by auditors of federal organizations, programs, activities, functions, and federal funds received by contractors, state and local governmental organizations, and nonprofit organizations are much broader in scope than the audits discussed in the first section of this chapter. The General Accounting Office under the direction of the Comptroller General of the United States has developed government auditing standards. Government auditing standards are set forth and explained in the publication *Government Auditing Standards*—because of the color of its cover, the document is generally referred to as the yellow book. Generally accepted auditing standards (GAAS), shown in Illustration 12–1, were used as a basis for federal auditing standards. Reasons why the standards established by the AICPA were deemed to be too narrow in scope for audits of governmental entities are expressed in the Introduction of the yellow book:

---

[4]American Institute of Certified Public Accountants, Audit and Accounting Guide, *Audits of State and Local Governmental Units*, Revised (New York: AICPA, 1996), par. 5.08.

Our system of managing public programs today rests on an elaborate structure of relationships among all levels of government. Officials and employees who manage these programs must render an account of their activities to the public. While not always specified by law, this accountability concept is inherent in the governing processes of this Nation.

The need for accountability has caused a demand for more information about government programs and services. Public officials, legislators, and citizens want and need to know whether *government funds are handled properly and in compliance with laws and regulations*. They also want and need to know whether government *organizations, programs, and services are achieving their purposes and whether these organizations, programs, and services are operating economically and efficiently.* [Emphasis added.][5]

Types of Audits

As the italicized phrases in the preceding quote suggest, the scope of audits conducted under *Government Auditing Standards* is much broader than that of audits of business entities. In fact, the term *audit* in the yellow book refers to both financial and performance audits. **Financial audits** are intended to provide an auditor's opinion that financial statements present fairly, in all material respects, an entity's financial position, results of operations, and, where appropriate, cash flows, in conformity with GAAP, or that financial reports comply with other finance-related criteria. **Performance audits** are intended to provide an auditor's independent determination (but not an opinion) of the extent to which government officials are efficiently, economically, and effectively carrying out their responsibilities, or of whether governmental programs are producing the desired results. The yellow book provides that, in any given audit, auditors may perform a combination of financial statement, finance-related, and economy, efficiency, and program results audits. Accordingly, *Government Auditing Standards* place on those who authorize or plan governmental audits the responsibility to provide audit coverage that is sufficiently broad to fulfill the reasonable needs of potential users of audit reports.[6] Illustration 12–4 contrasts and compares the objectives and characteristics of financial and performance audits.

Generally Accepted Government Auditing Standards. The first edition (1972) of the yellow book presented a single set of auditing standards that were similar to the AICPA statement of generally accepted auditing standards (GAAS) shown in Illustration 12–1. Subsequent revisions of the yellow book in 1981 and 1994, however, have developed a progressively broader set of standards, reflecting the need to provide standards for performance audits in addition to financial audits. The broader standards also reflect the unique auditing and operating environments of government and not-for-profit organizations. Government auditing standards now differ so much from GAAS that the term *generally accepted government auditing standards (GAGAS)* is typically used to distinguish the yellow book standards from

---

Illustration 12–4   Types of Government Audits

Financial Audits

1. Financial statement audits provide reasonable assurance about whether financial statements of an audited entity present fairly the financial position, results of operations, and cash flows in conformity with generally accepted accounting principles, or in conformity with any of several other bases of accounting discussed in auditing standards issued by the AICPA.
2. Finance-related audits include determining whether (*a*) financial information is presented in accordance with established or stated criteria, (*b*) the entity has adhered to specific financial compliance requirements, or (*c*) the entity's internal control structure over financial reporting and/or safeguarding assets is suitably designed and implemented to achieve the control objectives.

Performance Audits

1. Economy and efficiency audits include determining (*a*) whether the entity is acquiring, protecting, and using its resources (such as personnel, property, and space) economically and efficiently; (*b*) the causes of inefficiencies or uneconomical practices; and (*c*) whether the entity has complied with laws and regulations concerning matters of economy and efficiency.
2. Program audits include determining (*a*) the extent to which the desired results or benefits established by the legislature or other authorizing body are being achieved; (*b*) the effectiveness of organizations, programs, activities, or functions; and (*c*) whether the entity has complied with significant laws and regulations applicable to the program.

Source: *Government Auditing Standards* (Washington, DC: U.S. General Accounting Office, 1994), pp. 12–14.

GAAS.[7] GAGAS, as presented in the yellow book, consist of four general standards, plus nine field work standards for financial audits, five field work standards for performance audits, nine reporting standards for financial audits, and five reporting standards for performance audits. Thus, GAGAS consist of 32 standards, compared with 10 for GAAS.

The four general standards presented in *Government Auditing Standards* consist of, in paraphrased and expanded form, the three GAAS general standards shown in Illustration 12–1 and one additional general standard on quality control. In explaining the first general standard relating to adequacy of professional proficiency, the yellow book states:

> This standard places responsibility on the audit organization to ensure that each audit is conducted by staff who collectively have the knowledge and skills necessary for that audit. They should also have a thorough knowledge of governmental auditing and of the specific or unique environment in which the audited entity operates, relative to the nature of the audit being conducted.[8]

---

[7]Another acronym often used to denote government auditing standards is GAS, which is the abbreviation for the publication *Government Auditing Standards*. These terms are used interchangeably; however, the term GAGAS is used in this text.

[8]*Government Auditing Standards*, p. 18.

To ensure that auditors conducting audits under GAGAS maintain adequate technical proficiency, the yellow book requires that each auditor responsible for planning, directing, conducting, or reporting on audits under GAGAS complete at least 80 hours of continuing education (CE) and training every two years.[9] At least 20 hours of the 80 hours of CE must be completed in each year of the two-year period, and at least 24 of the 80 hours must be on subjects directly related to the government or not-for-profit environment and to government or not-for-profit auditing. To further ensure the quality of such audits, the fourth general standard requires each audit organization to have an "appropriate internal control system" and undergo an external quality control review at least once every three years by an audit organization not affiliated with the audit organization being reviewed.[10]

The nine field work standards for financial audits contained in GAGAS emphasize the importance of audit follow-up on prior audit findings; detection and reporting of irregularities, illegal acts, and other instances of noncompliance with laws and regulations; and understanding and testing of internal controls. Of the nine GAGAS field work standards, six are also required by GAAS, either by the three field work standards listed in Illustration 12–1 or by various *Statements on Auditing Standards*.

Similarly, the nine GAGAS reporting standards for financial audits incorporate the four GAAS reporting standards shown in Illustration 12–1. Additional reporting standards cover reporting on compliance, required communications, and report distribution.

The GAGAS field work and reporting standards for performance audits overlap to a small degree those of GAAS, but largely are unique in recognition that the objective of performance audits is to provide evidence to assess performance of a governmental organization, program, activity, or function, rather than to render a professional opinion. Thus, testing for compliance with laws and regulations, though of critical importance in a financial audit, may be relatively less so if the audit objective in a performance audit is to assess the efficiency and effectiveness of a program, and there are no laws and regulations that would have a material effect on the program.

Single Audit

Federal grants-in-aid to state and local governments grew from $2.2 billion in 1950 to $227.8 billion in 1996. Although grants-in-aid originate from more than 1,000 different programs administered by more than 50 federal departments and agencies, over 92% of the grants-in-aid in 1996 were made by five departments: the Department of Health and Human Services (56.7%), Department of Transportation (11.4%), Department of Housing and Urban Development (9.4%), Department of Agriculture (7.5%), and the Department of Education (7.1%).

---

[9]Ibid., p. 19.
[10]Ibid., pp. 28–29.

Until the mid-1980s each agency established accounting, reporting, and auditing requirements for each program it administered, and these requirements differed from agency to agency. The requirements for programs administered by a given agency also often differed from program to program and from year to year. Furthermore, each agency had the right to make on-site audits of grant funds, and often did. Since even a relatively small local governmental unit might have during any given fiscal year several dozen active federal grants (each with different accounting, reporting, and auditing requirements), the amount of time spent keeping track of conflicting requirements, and providing facilities for a succession of different groups of auditors, became extremely burdensome. Efforts were made in the 1960s to standardize grant accounting, reporting, and auditing requirements, but with only modest success. In 1979, the Office of Management and Budget (OMB) issued Attachment P, *Audit Requirements*, OMB Circular A-102, *Uniform Administrative Requirements for Grants-in-Aid to State and Local Governments*. Attachment P was intended to ensure that audits were made on an organization-wide basis, rather than on a grant-by-grant basis. This concept is called the **single audit**.

Single Audit Act of 1984

Experience with Attachment P led to the enactment of the Single Audit Act of 1984. The purposes of the act were to:

(1) Improve the financial management of state and local governments with respect to federal financial assistance programs,
(2) Establish uniform requirements for audits of federal financial assistance provided to state and local governments,
(3) Promote the efficient and effective use of audit resources, and
(4) Ensure that federal departments and agencies, to the maximum extent practicable, rely upon and use audit work done pursuant to chapter 75 of title 31, United States Code (as added by this Act).

In 1985, OMB issued Circular A-128, *Audits of State and Local Governments*, to provide administrative guidance to federal program managers, state and local government recipients of federal financial assistance, and auditors in implementing and complying with the Single Audit Act. Each state and local government that received federal financial assistance equal to or in excess of $100,000 in any of its fiscal years was required to have an audit made for such fiscal year in accordance with the provisions of the Single Audit Act and OMB Circular A-128. The 1984 Act applied only to state and local governments, even though a large amount of federal assistance was also being provided to not-for-profit organizations, particularly institutions of higher education. In order to extend the benefits of the single audit to not-for-profit organizations, the OMB issued in 1990 Circular A-133, *Audits of Institutions of Higher Education and Other Nonprofit Institutions*, which administratively required single audits for institutions of higher education and other not-for-profit organizations.

Subsequent studies by the U.S. General Accounting Office found that the Single Audit Act of 1984 had improved accountability over federal assistance, strengthened the financial management of state and local governments and not-for-profit organizations, and reduced the overall audit burden. In evaluating benefits relative to costs, however, it was apparent that thousands of single audits were being imposed on small entities that in aggregate accounted for only a small percentage of total federal assistance.

Recognizing the need to further improve the Single Audit Act, Congress passed the Single Audit Act Amendments of 1996 (P.L. 104–156). The purposes of the amendments are essentially the same as the four purposes of the Single Audit Act of 1984, listed above, plus one additional purpose: to reduce [audit] burdens on state and local governments, Indian tribes, and nonprofit organizations.

The 1996 Act:

1. Raises the threshold for a single audit from $100,000 to $300,000, thus exempting thousands of smaller entities from the single audit requirement.
2. Extends the statutory requirement for single audit coverage to not-for-profit organizations as well as state and local governments.
3. Establishes a risk-based approach for selecting programs for audit testing, ensuring greater audit coverage for high-risk programs.
4. Improves the contents and timeliness of single audit reporting.
5. Increases administrative flexibility by giving OMB the authority to revise certain audit requirements periodically without seeking further amendments to the Single Audit Act.

In June 1997, OMB issued a revised Circular A-133, *Audits of States, Local Governments, and Non-Profit Organizations*, which provides administrative guidance in implementing both the Single Audit Act of 1984 and the Single Audit Act Amendments of 1996 (although the 1996 amendments essentially replace the 1984 act). The revised Circular A-133 provides uniform guidance for administering and conducting *all* single audits and thus replaces Circular A-128, which previously covered only single audits of state and local governments. Moreover, Circular A-133 amends the previous A-133, which covered only not-for-profit organizations.

Who Must Have a Single Audit?

Illustration 12–5 provides a flowchart to determine if an entity must have a single audit or other type of audit. As Illustration 12–5 shows, nonfederal entities that *expend* $300,000 or more in a year in federal awards must have a single audit or a **program-specific audit** for that year. The election of a program-specific audit applies when an auditee expends federal awards under only one program, or a cluster of related programs, and the program's (cluster's) laws, regulations, or grant agreements do not require an entitywide financial statement audit. A program-specific audit is usually performed on the financial statements of the particular program and examines matters related to the program such as internal controls and compliance with pertinent laws, regulations, and agreements. In many cases a program-specific audit guide will be available to provide detailed audit guidance for conducting the program-specific audit.

Illustration 12–5 shows that nonfederal entities that expend less than $300,000 of federal awards during the fiscal year generally are exempt from federal audit

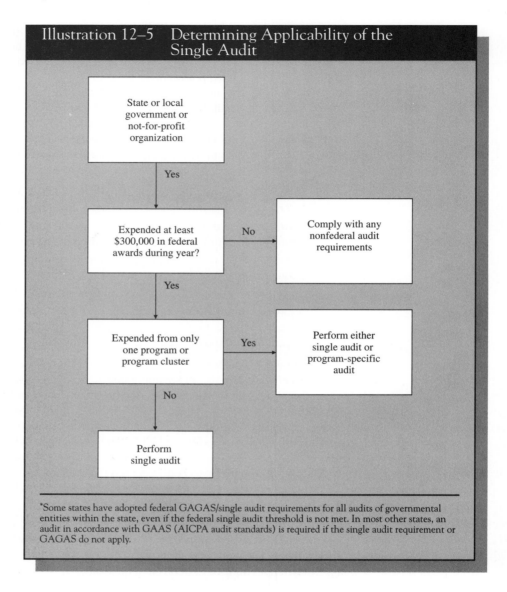

Illustration 12–5   Determining Applicability of the Single Audit

State or local government or not-for-profit organization

Yes

Expended at least $300,000 in federal awards during year?

No → Comply with any nonfederal audit requirements

Yes

Expended from only one program or program cluster

Yes → Perform either single audit or program-specific audit

No

Perform single audit

*Some states have adopted federal GAGAS/single audit requirements for all audits of governmental entities within the state, even if the federal single audit threshold is not met. In most other states, an audit in accordance with GAAS (AICPA audit standards) is required if the single audit requirement or GAGAS do not apply.

requirements for that year. Nonetheless, any federal awarding agency may conduct or arrange for additional audits it deems necessary. Such additional audits should be rare, should build upon work performed for other audits, and should be paid for by the federal agency conducting or requesting the audit. The footnote to Illustration 12–5 points out that some states have voluntarily adopted federal GAGAS and single audit requirements that may apply under state audit mandates, even if federal awards expended are less than $300,000 and no other federal audit requirement exists. In other states that do not mandate their own requirements for GAGAS audits or single audits, annual audits of local governments and not-for-profit organizations, when required, will be performed in conformity with AICPA GAAS, discussed earlier in this chapter.

The foregoing discussion raises two terminology questions. First, what kinds of entities are included in the term *nonfederal entities?* Circular A-133 defines a nonfederal entity as a state or local government, or nonprofit organization. Second, what is meant by the term *federal awards?* A-133 defines federal awards as:

> Federal financial assistance [defined by OMB as grants, loans, loan guarantees, property, cooperative agreements, interest subsidies, insurance, food commodities, direct appropriations, and other assistance] and federal cost-reimbursement contracts that nonfederal entities receive directly from federal awarding agencies or indirectly from pass-through entities. It does not include procurement contracts, under grants or contracts, used to buy goods or services from vendors. Any audits of such vendors shall be covered by the terms and conditions of the contract. Contracts to operate federal government owned, contractor operated facilities are excluded from the requirements of this part, as are payments for Medicare services provided.[11]

An important change made by the 1996 amendments is that the required audit threshold is now based on federal awards *expended* rather than *received,* as was previously the case. Unfortunately, calculating federal awards expended is not as straightforward as it might seem. The basic rule is that a federal award has been expended at the point in time when the awarding agency has become at risk and the nonfederal recipient has become accountable for how the award is being used. Risk exposure and a duty of accountability normally arise when activity occurs that requires the nonfederal entity to begin complying with laws, regulations, or contractual provisions relating to the award. Typical examples are expenditure/expense transactions (such as incurring labor costs, purchasing or using supplies, and paying utility bills) associated with grants, cost-reimbursement contracts, cooperative agreements, and direct appropriations; disbursement of funds by a pass-through entity to a subrecipient; the receipt of property; the receipt or use of program income (such as charges to program beneficiaries for services rendered and rental from program facilities); and the distribution or consumption of food commodities.[12] Amounts expended would normally be determined using the entity's basis of accounting. Thus, either an expenditure or expense may enter into the calculation of federal awards expended. Federal noncash assistance received such as free rent (if received by a nonfederal entity to carry out a federal program), food stamps, commodities, and donated property should be valued at fair value at the time of receipt or the assessed value provided by the awarding federal agency.

If federal awards involve loan, loan guarantee, and insurance programs, the federal award expended is the amount to which the federal government is at risk for

---

[11]Office of Management and Budget, OMB Circular No. A-133, *Audits of States, Local Governments, and Non-Profit Organizations* (Washington, DC, OMB, 1996), par. ___ .105.
[12]Ibid., par. ___ .205(a).

the loans. Generally this will be the amount of loans made (or received) during the year, plus any loan balances from previous years for which the federal government imposes continuing compliance requirements, plus any interest subsidy, cash, or administrative cost allowance received.[13] To the extent new and previously issued loans may have been repaid during the year, adjustments would need to be made. This is because the federal awards expended under a loan or insurance program are the highest amount of risk exposure of the federal government during the year. Thus, if the total loan balance varies during the year, the highest loan balance outstanding at any point during the year is the amount of federal awards expended.

Illustration 12–6 provides an example of how federal awards expended would be calculated for a hypothetical direct loan program administered by a local government or not-for-profit organization. Although neither the beginning nor ending loan balances exceed the $300,000 single audit threshold, it is assumed that at one point during the year the loan balance reached $320,000. Because at that point in time the federal government was at risk for $320,000, and the nonfederal entity had compliance duties for the $320,000 in loans outstanding, federal awards are deemed to have been expended in the same amount. If this was the only federal program for which awards were received during the year, the entity would have the option of having a single audit or a program-specific audit.

What Does the Single Audit Require?

The 1996 Amendments to the Single Audit Act of 1984 mandate the following audit requirements for the single audit:

1. An annual audit must be performed encompassing the nonfederal entity's financial statements and schedule of expenditures of federal awards. (Note: A biennial audit is permissible under certain restrictive conditions provided for in the 1996 amendments.)

2. The audit must be conducted by an independent auditor in accordance with generally accepted government auditing standards (GAGAS) and cover the operations of the entire nonfederal entity. Alternatively, a series of audits that cover departments, agencies, and other organizational units is permitted if the series of audits encompasses the financial statements and schedule of expenditures of federal awards for each such department, agency, or other organizational unit, which in aggregate are considered to be a nonfederal entity. *Independent auditor* means an external state or local auditor who meets the GAGAS independence standards or an independent public accountant.

3. The auditor must determine whether the financial statements are presented fairly in all material respects with GAAP and whether the schedule of federal financial awards is presented fairly in relation to the financial statements taken as a whole.

4. For each major program, the auditor must obtain an understanding of the internal controls pertaining to the compliance requirements for the

---

[13]Ibid., par. ____ .205(b).

Illustration 12–6   Determining Federal Awards Expended for a Hypothetical Direct Loan Program

Loan Activity	Amounts	Highest Balance
Balance, beginning of year	$200,000	
New loans during year	150,000	
		$320,000*
Loans repaid during year	(100,000)	
Balance, end of year	$250,000	

*$320,000 is assumed to have been the highest loan balance outstanding at any point during the year. Because the federal government was at risk at one point during the year for $320,000, that is the amount of federal awards deemed to have been expended.

program, assess control risk and perform tests of controls, unless the controls are deemed to be ineffective. (Note: OMB Circular A-133 requires the auditor to obtain an understanding of and conduct testing of internal controls to support a low assessed level of control risk; that is, as if high reliance will be placed on the internal controls). In addition, for each major program the auditor shall determine whether the nonfederal entity has complied with laws, regulations, and contract or grant provisions pertaining to federal awards of the program. In auditing compliance auditors test compliance with the requirements listed for each program in the A-133 *Compliance Supplement* published by the OMB. The *Compliance Supplement* details compliance auditing requirements for many federal programs, listed by *Catalog of Federal Domestic Assistance* (CFDA) title and number.

5. The audit assigns certain responsibilities to federal awarding agencies and nonfederal entities that act as "pass-through" agents in passing federal awards to subrecipient nonfederal entities.

Compliance Audits.   As noted in item (4) above, Circular A-133 requires the auditor to express an opinion that the auditee complied with laws, regulations, and grant or contract provisions that could have a direct and material effect on each major program. To gather sufficient evidence to support his or her opinion in such **compliance audits,** the auditor tests whether each major program was administered in conformity with administrative requirements contained in OMB Circular A-102, *Uniform Administrative Requirements for Grants and Cooperative Agreements to State and Local Governments* or OMB Circular A-110, *Uniform Administrative Requirements for Grants and Cooperative Agreements with Institutions of Higher Education, Hospitals, and Other Nonprofit Organizations*, as appropriate. The auditor also tests for compliance with the detailed compliance requirements for major programs provided in the A-133 *Compliance Supplement* or other guidance provided by federal awarding agencies. Many compliance requirements are generic and thus apply to compliance audits of most federal programs. The *Compliance Supplement* identifies 14 generic compliance requirements, although not all the requirements apply to every major program. Moreover, there are additional compliance requirements specified for some programs. Detailed discussion of the 14 compliance requirements is beyond the scope of this text. In general, however, they relate to such matters as allowed and unallowed activities; allowed and unallowed costs; eligibility of program beneficiaries; responsibilities of the nonfederal entity regarding matching, level of effort, and earmarking; management of equipment and real property acquired from federal awards; and required reporting.

Auditee Responsibilities.   OMB Circular A-133 also details the responsibilities of auditees (nonfederal entities). Auditees are responsible to identify in the accounts all federal awards received and expended, and the federal programs under which they were received. Identification of the federal program includes the CFDA title and number, award number and year, and name of the federal agency. In addition, auditees are responsible for maintaining appropriate internal controls and systems to ensure compliance with all laws, regulations, and contract or grant provisions applicable to federal awards. Finally, auditees must prepare appropriate financial statements and the schedule of expenditures of federal awards, ensure that audits are properly performed and submitted when due, and follow up and take appropriate corrective action on audit findings. The latter requirement includes preparation of a summary schedule of prior audit findings and a corrective action plan for current year audit findings.

How Are Program Selected for Audit?

Illustration 12–7 shows the procedures and criteria for selecting major programs for audit. A **major program** is a federal award program selected for audit using the procedures described below and shown in Illustration 12–7, or by request of a federal awarding agency. Use of a **risk-based approach** for selecting major programs for audit ensures that audit effort is concentrated on the highest risk programs. The risk-based approach is applied as follows:

1. Identify the "larger" federal programs and analyze them according to the Type A criteria. Programs not meeting Type A criteria are identified as Type B programs. Type A programs are determined using the following sliding scale:

Federal Awards Expended	Threshold for Type A Program
$300,000 to $100 million	Larger of $300,000 or 3% of total federal awards expended
More than $100 million to $10 billion	Larger of $3 million or .3% (.003) of total federal awards expended
More than $10 billion	Larger of $30 million or .15% (.0015) of total federal awards expended

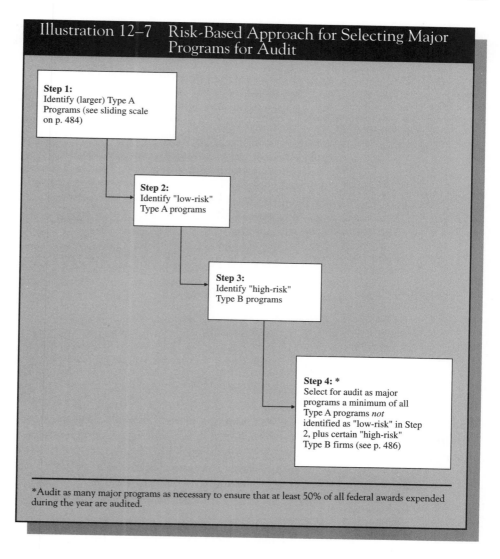

Illustration 12–7   Risk-Based Approach for Selecting Major Programs for Audit

Step 1:
Identify (larger) Type A Programs (see sliding scale on p. 484)

Step 2:
Identify "low-risk" Type A programs

Step 3:
Identify "high-risk" Type B programs

Step 4: *
Select for audit as major programs a minimum of all Type A programs *not* identified as "low-risk" in Step 2, plus certain "high-risk" Type B firms (see p. 486)

*Audit as many major programs as necessary to ensure that at least 50% of all federal awards expended during the year are audited.

2. Identify low-risk Type A programs: programs previously audited in at least one of the two most recent audit periods as a major program, with no audit findings in the most recent audit period; programs with no significant changes in personnel or systems that would have significantly increased risk; and programs that, in the auditor's professional judgment, are low risk, after considering such factors as the inherent risk of the program, the level of oversight exercised by federal awarding agencies and pass-through agencies, and the phase of a program in its life cycle. New programs, for example, tend to be more risky than more mature programs.

3. Identify Type B programs that, based on the auditor's professional judgment and criteria discussed above, are high risk. The auditor is not expected to perform risk assessments on relatively small federal programs. Risk assessments are performed only for those Type B programs that are (a) $100,000 or .3% (.003) of total federal awards expended when total federal awards expended are less than or equal to $100 million or (b) $300,000 or .03% (.0003) of total federal awards expended when total federal awards expended are more than $100 million.

4. At a minimum, audit as major programs all Type A programs *not* identified as low risk and certain high-risk Type B programs, using one of the following options: (a) Audit at least half of the high-risk Type B programs; but not required to audit more Type B than Type A programs identified as low risk; or (b) audit one high-risk Type B program for each Type A program identified as low risk.

5. *Percentage of coverage rule*: As many major programs as necessary must be audited to ensure that at least 50% of total federal awards expended are audited.

In addition to the possibility of reduced audit coverage resulting from individual Type A programs being classified as low risk, A-133 also provides that the auditee itself can be classified as low risk and thereby receive even greater reduction in audit coverage. An auditee that meets the rather stringent criteria prescribed in Circular A-133 to be a low-risk auditee needs only to have audited a sufficient number of major programs to encompass 25% of total federal awards expended.

What Reports Are Required for the Single Audit?

The 1996 amendments require that all auditors' reports for the single audit be submitted to the federal clearinghouse designated by the OMB within the earlier of 30 days after receipt of the auditor's report(s), or nine months after the end of the audit period. Both the auditee and auditor have responsibilities for particular reports that comprise the reporting package.

The reporting package consists of:

1. Financial statements and schedule of expenditures of federal awards.
2. Summary schedule of prior audit findings.
3. Auditors' reports.
4. Corrective action plan.

The auditee is responsible for preparing all the documents described in items (1), (2), and (4) above. The auditor is responsible for preparing the various auditors' reports in item (3) and for following up on prior year audit findings, including testing the accuracy and reasonableness of the summary schedule of prior audit findings. In addition, both the auditee and auditor have responsibilities for completing and submitting the comprehensive data collection form that accompanies the reporting package to the clearinghouse. A complete description of the numerous data elements that must be provided on the data collection form is beyond the scope of this text. In general, however, the form provides for extensive descriptive data about the auditee, the auditor, identification of types and amounts of federal awards and major programs, types of reports issued by the auditor, and whether the auditor identified internal control deficiencies or significant noncompliance with laws, regulations, and grant provisions. Both a senior-level representative of the auditee and auditor must sign the data collection form, certifying its accuracy and completeness.

Auditor's Reports.   OMB Circular A-133 specifies several reports that the auditor must submit for each single audit engagement. These reports can be in the form of separate reports for each requirement or a few combined reports. The auditor's report on the financial statements should indicate that the audit was conducted in accordance with GAAS and GAGAS. Other auditor's reports required by the single audit should indicate the audits were conducted in accordance with GAAS, GAGAS, and provisions of Circular A-133. The required single audit reports, whether made as separate reports or combined, must include:

1. An opinion (or disclaimer of opinion) as to whether the financial statements are presented fairly in conformity with GAAP and whether the schedule of expenditures of federal awards is presented fairly in relation to the financial statements taken as a whole.
2. A report on internal controls related to the financial statements and major programs.
3. A report on compliance with laws, regulations, and provisions of grant or contract agreements that could have a material effect on the financial statements. The report must also include an opinion on compliance matters related to major programs audited (see Illustration 12–7 and related discussion for selection criteria) that could have a direct and material effect on each major program. Where applicable, include findings of noncompliance in the separate schedule of findings and questioned costs, described in item (4) below.
4. A schedule of findings and questioned costs, containing the following:
   (*a*) A summary of the auditor's results, including such information as type of opinion rendered on the financial statements, reportable conditions relating to internal control weaknesses, material noncompliance affecting the financial statements, major programs audited, type of opinion on compliance for major programs and reportable conditions in internal control affecting major programs, and a statement as to whether the auditee qualified as low risk.
   (*b*) Findings related to the audit of the financial statements required to be reported by the yellow book (GAGAS). These relate primarily to the auditor's responsibility to ensure adequate communication of material irregularities and illegal acts.
   (*c*) Audit findings and questioned costs. Audit findings are discussed next.

Reporting Audit Findings.   As listed in item (4) above auditors must prepare a schedule of findings and questioned costs. **Audit findings** reported in the schedule provide detail on such matters as internal control weaknesses, instances of noncompliance, questioned costs, fraud, and material misrepresentations (by the auditee) in the schedule of prior audit findings.

Regarding reporting on internal controls, item (4a) above uses the term **reportable condition**. This term is used in AICPA authoritative audit publications and adopted in the yellow book and Circular A-133. In the context of GAGAS audits, a reportable condition is a significant deficiency in the design or operation of the internal control structure that could adversely affect the entity's ability to administer a federal award program in accordance with laws and regulations. A **material weakness** is a reportable condition of such magnitude that the internal control structure elements do not reduce the risk of material noncompliance to an acceptably low level.

A **questioned cost** arises from an audit finding, generally relating to noncompliance with a law, regulation, or agreement, where the costs are either not supported by adequate documentation or appear unreasonable. Cost principles to be followed by nonfederal entities in the administration of federal awards are prescribed by (1) OMB Circular A-21, *Cost Principles for Educational Institutions*, (2) OMB Circular A-87, *Cost Principles for State, Local, and Indian Tribal Governments*, and (3) OMB Circular A-122, *Cost Principles for Non-Profit Organizations*. The circulars define concepts such as direct and indirect costs, allowable and unallowable costs, and methods for calculating indirect cost rates.

The cost principles in these circulars are similar, but differ to meet the unique environment of each type of organization. Recovery of indirect costs (such as depreciation, general administrative costs, library costs, and interest expense) is based on rates approved by the federal government in cost allocation plans (state, local, and Indian tribal governments only) or indirect cost rate proposals (all other nonfederal agencies). Unallowable costs are generally consistent across the three circulars. Bad debt expenses and political/lobbying costs are generally unallowable. Some costs, such as advertising and public relations costs, are allowable, subject to certain restrictions. The auditing of program costs is inherently complex and professional judgment is often required to determine the appropriate classification of costs. This is particularly true in auditing institutions of higher education. Individuals who audit federal awards must be familiar with the applicable cost circular and ascertain that the methods of charging costs to cost pools and federal programs conform to approved cost allocation plans or indirect cost rate proposals.

Circular A-133 requires that *known questioned costs* greater than $10,000, identified in auditing a major program, be reported in the schedule of findings and questioned costs. A known questioned cost is one that the auditor has specifically identified in performing audit procedures. In evaluating the impact of a known questioned cost, the dollar impact also includes a best estimate of "likely questioned costs." Thus the auditor must also report known questioned costs if the likely questioned costs exceed $10,000, even if the known dollar amount is zero. Nonmajor programs are not normally audited for compliance (except for audit follow-up of a program that was previously audited as a major program); however, if the auditor becomes aware of a known questioned cost in a nonmajor program, he or she must also report it in the schedule of findings and questioned costs.

Other Single Audit Requirements

Audit Working Papers. The 1994 revision to the yellow book (GAGAS) requires that auditors make their audit working papers available to other auditors and to oversight officials from federal awarding agencies and cognizant agents for quality review purposes. The 1996 amendments to the Single Audit Act are even more explicit in requiring independent auditors to provide access to federal oversight officials. Federal agency access also includes the right to obtain copies of the working papers. Circular A-133 reemphasizes this requirement and the GAGAS requirement that auditors retain all working papers and reports for a minimum of three years.

Cognizant Agents. OMB Circular A-133 provides that a **cognizant agency for audit responsibilities** will be designated for each nonfederal entity expending more than $25 million a year in federal awards. The cognizant agency will be the federal awarding agency that provides the predominant amount of direct funding unless the OMB specifically designates a different cognizant agency. Among the cognizant agency's responsibilities are providing technical audit advice and liaison to auditees and auditors, obtaining or conducting quality control reviews of selected audits made by nonfederal auditors, communicating to affected parties deficiencies identified by quality control reviews (including, when necessary, referral of deficiencies to state licensing agencies and professional bodies for possible disciplinary action), and promptly communicating findings of irregularities and illegal acts to affected federal agencies and appropriate federal law enforcement agencies. Nonfederal entities expending less than $25 million in federal awards are assigned an **oversight agency**. The oversight agency is the agency that makes the predominant amount of direct funding to the nonfederal entity. An oversight agency has responsibilities similar to a designated cognizant agency, but less extensive.

Audit Committees

An **audit committee** is typically a committee of the governing board whose function it is to help select the auditor, monitor the audit process, review results of the audit, assist the governing board in understanding the results of the audit, and participate with both management and the independent auditor in resolving internal control or other deficiencies identified during the audit. Audit committees usually consist of selected members of the governing board (e.g., the city council or school board) and sometimes outside members in order to increase the independence of the committee.

Audit committees, when properly organized and utilized, can provide substantial benefit to all concerned parties. The audit committee can strengthen the stewardship reporting function of the governing board; it can also improve communications between the independent auditor and management and enhance the auditor's independence by serving as an objective buffer between the auditor and management. For taxpayers and creditors, audit committees help ensure maximum value and benefit from the audit.

Although most major corporations now consider an audit committee to be an important aspect of corporate governance, governmental units have been slow to establish audit committees. Perhaps, as the benefits of having an audit committee become apparent, we can anticipate greater use of these committees in the future.

Key Terms

Audit committee,   489
Audit findings,   488
Cognizant agency for audit
  responsibilities,   489
Compliance audit,   483
Generally accepted auditing standards
  (GAAS),   468
Generally accepted government auditing
  standards (GAGAS),   468
Financial audits,   475

Major programs,   484
Material weakness,   488
Oversight agency,   489
Performance audits,   475
Program-specific audit,   479
Questioned cost,   488
Reportable condition,   488
Risk-based approach,   484
Single audit,   478

Selected References

American Institute of Certified Public Accountants. Audit and Accounting Guide. *Audits of State and Local Governmental Units*. Revised. New York: AICPA, 1996.
_____ . *Statement on Auditing Standards, No. 1*, et seq. New York, 1973 to date.
Comptroller General of the United States. *Government Auditing Standards*. Washington, DC: Superintendent of Documents, U.S. Government Printing Office, 1994 revision.
Office of Management and Budget. *Circular A-133*, "Audits of Institutions of Higher Education and Other Nonprofit Organizations." Washington, DC: Superintendent of Documents, U.S. Government Printing Office, 1997.
_____ . *Compliance Supplement for Single Audits of State and Local Governments*. Washington, DC. Superintendent of Documents, U.S. Government Printing Office, 1997.
[Note: AICPA documents must be ordered from the AICPA; all others can be downloaded at no charge by following website links at http://www.financenet.gov.]

Questions

12–1. What assurance does the independent auditor provide users of financial statements of governmental and nonprofit entities?

12–2. What information is contained in the *opening paragraph* of an auditor's report prepared in conformity with the AICPA's standard wording?

12–3. What is the meaning of the term *scope paragraph* (of an auditor's report prepared in conformity with the AICPA's standard wording)? The term *opinion paragraph*?

12–4. The standard report used by certified public accountants sets forth that the financial statements are presented in conformity with "generally accepted accounting principles." How may an auditor determine the meaning of this phrase in the case of a state or local government?

12–5. What is the meaning of the term *unqualified opinion* as used in auditing literature?

12–6. Define GAGAS. How do GAGAS differ from GAAS?

12–7. What are the two major types of audits described in the General Accounting Office's *Government Auditing Standards* (the yellow book), and how do they differ?

12–8. GAGAS consists of 32 standards compared to only 10 for GAAS. Why is this the case?

12–9. Describe briefly the single audit concept set forth in the Single Audit Act of 1984, the 1996 amendments, and OMB Circular A-133.

12–10. Explain the key provisions of the 1996 amendments to the Single Audit Act of 1984.

12–11. Which nonfederal entities are required to have a single audit? Explain.

12–12. What audit work is required for a single audit?

12–13. Explain how federal award programs are selected for audit under the risk-based approach.

12–14. Discuss some of the *auditee's* responsibilities under the Single Audit Act.

12–15. Distinguish between the terms *reportable condition* and *material weakness* in reporting internal control findings.

12–16. Define the term *questioned cost*. What criteria does an auditor use to determine whether a questioned cost must be reported?

12–17. What documents comprise the single audit reporting package that must be sent to the federal clearinghouse?

12–18. Describe the audit reports the auditor must submit upon completion of a single audit.

12–19. Which nonfederal entities are assigned a cognizant agency for audit responsibilities? What are the cognizant agency's responsibilities?

12–20. What are the benefits of having an audit committee?

Cases

12–1. Background.   Mountain Lake Mental Health Affiliates, a nongovernmental not-for-profit organization, has contacted Bill Wise, CPA, about conducting an annual audit for their first year of operations. The governing board wishes to obtain an audit of the financial statements and, having received favorable information about Mr. Wise's ability to conduct such audits, has decided not to issue a request for proposals from other audit firms. Cybil Civic, president of the board, heard from a friend associated with a similar organization that $5,000 is an appropriate price for such an audit and has offered Mr. Wise the audit for that price. Although Mr. Wise agrees that $5,000 would be reasonable for a typical financial statement audit of an organization of Mountain Lake's type and size, he refuses to contract for the audit at that price until he is able to estimate the extent of audit work that would be involved.

Facts.   In discussions with Mountain Lake's controller, Mr. Wise obtains the following information about the organization for the year just ended:

1. Mountain Lake received a $200,000 grant from the City of Mountain Lake, of which 50 percent was stated as being from federal sources. $150,000 was expended during the year, ratably from federal and nonfederal sources.
2. Unrestricted gifts of $50,000 were received from private donors; $40,000 was spent during the year.
3. The organization received $300,000 from Medicare for mental health services rendered during the year.
4. A building owned by the U.S. Department of Health and Human Services is occupied by Mountain Lake for rent of $1 per year. The fair value of the rental has been appraised at $30,001.
5. Mountain Lake carried out a program with the Federal Bureau of Prisons to provide alcohol and drug abuse counseling services for prisoners at a nearby federal prison. Services are provided on a "units of service" reimbursement basis. Each unit of services is reimbursed at the rate of $100 and the contract provides for maximum reimbursement of $200,000. Actual units of service for the year were 2,200. Direct costs incurred for these services amounted to $150,000 in total.

Required

a. Based on the foregoing facts, is Mountain Lake Mental Health Affiliates required to have a single audit? Explain your answer.
b. Should Mr. Wise accept the audit engagement for a $5,000 fee? Why or why not?

(Note: The authors are indebted to James Brown, a partner with Baird, Kurtz & Dobson in Joplin, Missouri, for providing the example on which Case 12–1 is based.)

12–2. The City of Salem expended federal awards from the following programs during its most recent fiscal year.

Program	Amount Expended
1. Community Service Block Grants	$ 400,000
2. Solid Waste Management Assistance	300,000
3. Emergency Federal Law Enforcement Assistance	250,000
4. Low Income Home Energy Assistance	200,000
5. Community Economic Adjustment Planning Assistance	150,000
6. Air Pollution Control Program	50,000
Total	$1,350,000

Other Information

The auditor has rendered an unqualified report on the financial statements and found no reportable conditions or material weaknesses in internal control at the financial statement level. In addition, the auditor has given an unqualified opinion on the Schedule of

Expenditures of Federal Awards, from which the preceding information was obtained. Next the auditor must determine which major federal award programs require internal control evaluation and compliance testing.

Following the risk-based approach, the auditor, with the concurrence of the oversight agency, has classified programs 2 and 4 as low risk. Program 6 was not assessed as to risk due to its small size.

Required

    a. Which programs should the auditor audit as major programs for the year just ended? Explain your rationale.

    b. How would your answer to requirement *a* differ if program 2 had not been classified as low risk?

12–3. Internet Case. The Town of Grandview Health Department receives pass-through funds from the State Department of Social Services to assist in administering the federally funded Special Supplemental Nutrition Program for Women, Infants, and Children (WIC). At the request of the State Department of Social Services, the town of Grandview has engaged you to perform a program-specific audit of its expenditures of federal awards for the WIC program. Although you are unfamiliar with this particular program, you have extensive experience in governmental auditing and have audited many other federal programs.

Required: Utilize the Internet to answer the following question about this program.

    a. What is the Catalog of Federal Domestic Assistance (CFDA) number for this program? (Relevant website is: http://www.gsa.gov/. Use the index at that site to search for the catalog.

    b. Describe the purpose of this program.

    c. Who are the eligible beneficiaries of the program?

    d. Which of the 14 compliance items listed in the A-133 *Compliance Supplement* are applicable to auditing compliance for this program? (Hint: Access Parts 2, 3, and 4 of the *Compliance Supplement* at website http://www.whitehouse.gov/WH/EOP/OMB/Grants/A-133_compliance/. If you find this site is not directly accessible, you can access it by first opening http://www.whitehouse.gov/, then selecting sequentially "The President & Vice President," "Executive Office of the President," "White House Offices and Agencies," "Office of Management and Budget," "Grants Management," and "A-133 Compliance Supplement.")

    e. Depending on your instructor's preference, either print the compliance audit requirements for this program from Part 4 of the compliance supplement (about nine pages) or summarize them in a brief report.

12–4. For its most recent fiscal year Jeffcoat County expended $900,000 in federal awards from various federal programs. In each of the last three years, Jeffcoat County received a single audit from a large, national accounting firm. Until last year the County had always received unqualified audit opinions and had received no reportable conditions or significant findings of noncompliance. Last year, however, the accounting firm rendered a qualified opinion for its audit of financial statements. In additional, it identified many reportable conditions in its evaluation of internal controls related to the financial statements and major programs, three of which were reported as material weaknesses. Several findings of noncompliance with laws, regulations, and grant agreements were also identified, resulting in a qualified opinion on the compliance report for major programs.

Jeffcoat County's Director of Finance, who had been hired early last year, expressed strong disagreement with the qualified opinions and reported findings and vowed to switch auditors for the current year's single audit. Accordingly, the County solicited bids for the current year audit and received bids ranging from $6,000 to $59,000 to conduct the audit. By mutual agreement, the incumbent audit firm did not tender a bid. The $6,000 bid was received from Mary Benson, CPA, a local accountant, who 20 years earlier had conducted grant audits for local governmental and not-for-profit organizations. Ms. Benson had not done an audit of federal awards during the past 20 years, nor had she received any continuing professional education or peer evaluation for such audits. She had bid on the County audit in the hope of using it as a springboard for building a practice in federal program auditing to replace declining revenues from tax services. Given current budget constraints, Ms. Benson received strong support from a majority of the County Commissioners. Commissioners noted the fact that she held a valid CPA license from the state and had relevant experience. Furthermore, the Director of Finance felt that a local auditor would be less critical of the County's financial management and reporting practices. Based on these considerations, Ms. Benson was selected to perform the single audit for the current year.

Required

(Note: For guidance in answering the following questions you may wish to access OMB Circular A-133. Conduct your search at http://www.financenet.gov.)

a. Is Ms. Benson qualified to conduct the single audit for Jeffcoat County? Why or why not?

b. What are some of the potential ramifications of selecting Ms. Benson to conduct this year's audit?

Exercises and Problems

12–1. Write the numbers 1 through 10 on a sheet of paper. Beside each number, write the letter corresponding with the best answer to each of the following questions:

1. The scope paragraph of an independent auditor's report on a financial audit of a local governmental unit:
   a. States that generally accepted auditing standards require that the auditor plan and perform the audit to obtain reasonable assurance as to whether the financial statements are free of material misstatement.
   b. Identifies the financial statements on which the auditor is expressing an opinion.
   c. States whether, in the auditor's opinion, the financial statements present fairly in conformity with generally accepted accounting principles the financial position of the reporting entity.
   d. All of the above.

2. An unqualified opinion paragraph of an independent auditor's report on a financial audit of a local government unit:
   a. States that, in the auditor's opinion, the combined financial statements present fairly the financial position, results of operations, and cash flows in conformity with generally accepted accounting principles.
   b. States that, in the auditor's opinion, the financial statements of the individual funds and account groups accurately present the financial

condition as of a certain date, and the results of operations for the year then ended.

   c. States that the combining financial statements fairly present the financial condition as of a certain date, and the results of operations for the year then ended.

   d. None of the above.

3. Which of the following is *not* one of the types of opinions an auditor may render in accordance with GAAS?

   a. Unqualified.

   b. Qualified.

   c. Satisfactory.

   d. Adverse.

4. Which of the following *best* describes the relationship between GAAS and GAGAS?

   a. GAAS do not apply to audits conducted in accordance with the yellow book.

   b. GAAS apply to independent CPA auditors; GAGAS apply to governmental auditors.

   c. Audits done in accordance with GAGAS must also be done in accordance with GAAS.

   d. Audits of state and local governmental units always require that the audit be conducted in accordance with both GAAS and GAGAS.

5. Financial audits, as defined in the GAO's *Government Auditing Standards*, may include determining

   a. Whether the financial statements present fairly the entity's financial position, results of operations, and cash flows in conformity with GAAP.

   b. Whether financial information is presented in accordance with established or stated criteria.

   c. Whether the entity has adhered to specific financial compliance requirements.

   d. All of the above.

6. Performance audits, as defined in the GAO's *Governmental Auditing Standards:*

   a. Provide a basis for an auditor's opinion as to whether the entity is acquiring, protecting, and using its resources economically and efficiently.

   b. Include determining whether or the extent to which government officials are efficiently, economically, and effectively carrying out their responsibilities.

   c. Provide assurance that operations are in compliance with *all* applicable laws and regulations that may have a material effect on the financial statements.

   d. Are performed by the internal audit staff to assist the entity's independent auditor.

7. When performing an audit of a city that is subject to the requirements of the Single Audit Act of 1984 and the 1996 amendments, an auditor should adhere to:

   a. Governmental Accounting Standards Board's *General Standards*.

   b. Governmental Finance Officers Association's *Governmental Accounting, Auditing, and Financial Reporting Principles*.

   c. General Accounting Office's *Government Auditing Standards*.

   d. Securities and Exchange Commission's *Regulation S-X*.

8. When engaged to audit a governmental entity in accordance with *Government Auditing Standards*, an auditor prepares a written report on the internal control structure:
   a. In all audits, regardless of circumstances.
   b. Only when the auditor has noted reportable conditions.
   c. Only when requested by the governmental entity being audited.
   d. Only when requested by the federal government funding agency.
9. Kent is auditing an entity's compliance with requirements governing a major federal financial assistance program in accordance with the Single Audit Act. Kent detected noncompliance with requirements that have a material effect on that program. Kent's report on compliance should express a (an):
   a. Unqualified opinion with a separate explanatory paragraph.
   b. Qualified opinion or an adverse opinion.
   c. Adverse opinion or a disclaimer of opinion.
   d. Limited assurance on the items tested.
10. What is an auditor's responsibility for supplementary information required by GASB that is placed outside the basic financial statements?
   a. Label the information as unaudited and expand the auditor's report to include a disclaimer on the information.
   b. Add an explanatory paragraph to the auditor's report and refer to the information as "required supplementary information."
   c. Apply limited procedures to the information and report deficiencies in, or the omission of, the information.
   d. Audit the required supplementary information in accordance with generally accepted government auditing standards.

(Items 7–10, AICPA, adapted)

12–2. On September 23, 1998, the CPA firm of Green and Jones completed its audit of the City of Deerfield's general purpose financial statements (GPFS) for the year ended June 30, 1998. The City presents its financial position, results of operations, and cash flows using the financial statements prescribed by generally accepted accounting principles. However, Green and Jones believe that the Deerfield Cultural Center, a theater for the performing arts and financially subsidized by the City, meets the criteria specified by GASB for inclusion as a component unit in Deerfield's GPFS. Deerfield's finance director has steadfastly refused to include the cultural center in Deerfield's GPFS on the basis that it would cause the financial statements to be misleading. Green and Jones feel compelled to issue an "except for" qualified audit opinion to bring attention to this departure from GAAP, although they believe the financial statements present fairly in all other respects. Green and Jones have determined that the effect of including the cultural center in Deerfield's GPFS would have been to increase the reported assets and revenues of the enterprise funds by $450,000 and $127,000, respectively, and increase the excess of revenues over expenses in that fund type by $5,200 for the year ended June 30, 1998.

Required

Prepare the qualified audit report that Green and Jones, CPAs, should render on the City of Deerfield's GPFS for the year ended June 30, 1998.

12–3. Jones and Todd, a local CPA firm, received an invitation to bid for the audit of a local, federally assisted program. The audit is to be conducted in accordance with generally accepted government auditing standards (GAGAS) published by the General Accounting Office (GAO). Jones and Todd has become familiar with GAGAS and recognizes that GAGAS are not inconsistent with generally accepted auditing standards (GAAS) issued by the AICPA. GAGAS, unlike GAAS, are concerned with more than the financial aspects of an entity's operations. GAGAS are broader because they provide standards for two types of audits, financial audits and performance audits. Jones and Todd has been engaged to perform the following specific audits, encompassing both a financial and a performance audit for the program:

1. An examination of whether (*a*) financial transactions, accounts, and reports are presented in accordance with the criteria stated in the program; (*b*) the entity has complied with applicable financial compliance requirements specified by the program; and (*c*) the entity's internal control structure achieves control objectives.
2. A review of efficiency and economy in the use of resources, such as personnel and equipment, including compliance with applicable laws and regulations concerning economy and efficiency.
3. A review to determine whether desired results are effectively achieved (program results), including compliance with laws and regulations applicable to the program.

Required

a. Jones and Todd should perform sufficient audit work to satisfy the financial and compliance element of the GAO standards. What should such audit work determine?
b. After making appropriate review and inquiries, what uneconomical practices or inefficiencies should Jones and Todd be alert to in satisfying the efficiency and economy element encompassed by the GAO standards?
c. After making appropriate review and inquiries, what should Jones and Todd consider to satisfy the program results element encompassed by the GAO standards?

(AICPA, adapted)

12–4. The City of Granville receives grants from various state agencies as well as grants from several federal government agencies.

The City engaged Hall & Hall, CPAs, to audit its financial statements for the year ended July 31, 1999, in accordance with *Government Auditing Standards*. Accordingly, the auditor's reports are to be submitted by the City of Granville to granting government agencies, which make the reports available for public inspection.

The auditor's separate report on compliance with laws and regulations that was drafted by a staff accountant of Hall & Hall at the completion of the engagement contained the statements below. It was submitted to the engagement partner who reviewed matters thoroughly and properly concluded that no material instances of noncompliance were identified.

1. A statement that the audit was conducted in accordance with generally accepted auditing standards and with *Government Auditing Standards* issued by the Comptroller General of the United States.
2. A statement that the auditor's procedures included tests of compliance.
3. A statement that the standards require the auditors to plan and to perform the audit to detect all instances of noncompliance with applicable laws and regulations.
4. A statement that management is responsible for compliance with laws, regulations, contracts, and grants.
5. A statement that the auditor's objective was to provide an opinion on compliance with the provisions of laws and regulations equivalent to that to be expressed on the financial statements.
6. A statement of negative assurance that, with respect to items tested, nothing came to the auditor's attention that caused the auditors to believe that the entity had not complied, in all material respects, with the provisions of laws, regulations, contracts, and grants.
7. A statement that the report is intended only for the information of the specific legislative or regulatory bodies, and that this restriction is intended to limit the distribution of the report.

Required

For each of above statements indicate whether each is an appropriate or inappropriate element within the report on compliance with laws and regulations. If a statement is *not* appropriate, explain why.

(AICPA, adapted)

12–5. The report of the independent auditors that appeared in an annual financial report for Plains City is reproduced below.

Required

Compare this report with the ones shown in Illustrations 12–2 and 12–3 and discuss the likely reasons for the different wording. What type of opinion is rendered in this report? (The exhibits and tables referred to in the report are not included here.)

Independent Auditors' Report

The Honorable Mayor and Members of the City Council, Plains City

We have audited the general purpose financial statements of Plains City as of and for the year ended December 31, 1998. These general purpose financial statements are the responsibility of Plains City management. Our responsibility is to express an opinion on these general purpose financial statements based on our audit.

We conducted our audit in accordance with generally accepted auditing standards. Those standards require that we plan and perform the audit to obtain reasonable assurance about whether the general purpose financial statements are free of material misstatement. An audit includes examining, on a test basis, evidence supporting the amounts and disclosures in the general purpose financial statements. An audit also includes assessing the accounting principles used and significant estimates made by management, as well as evaluating the overall general purpose financial statement presentation. We believe that our audit provides a reasonable basis for our opinion.

The general purpose financial statements referred to above do not include the general fixed assets account group, which should be included in order to conform with generally accepted accounting principles. The amount that should be recorded in the general fixed assets account group is not known as Plains City does not maintain records of general fixed assets.

In our opinion, except for the effect on the financial statements of the omission described in the preceding paragraph, the general purpose financial statements referred to above present fairly, in all material respects, the financial position of Plains City at December 31, 1998, and the results of its operations and cash flows of its proprietary fund types and nonexpendable trust funds for the year then ended, in conformity with generally accepted accounting principles.

Our audit was made for the purpose of forming an opinion on the general purpose financial statements of Plains City taken as a whole. The combining and individual fund and account group financial statements and schedules listed in the table of contents and the schedule of expenditures of federal awards are presented for purposes of additional analysis and are not a required part of the general purpose financial statements of Plains City. Such information has been subjected to the auditing procedures applied in the audit of the general purpose financial statements and, in our opinion, is fairly presented in all material respects in relation to the general purpose financial statements taken as a whole.

[*Signature*]
[*Date*]

12–6. Tri-States Community Service Agency expended federal awards during their most recent fiscal year in the following amounts for the programs shown:

Program 1	$ 450,000
Program 2	350,000
Program 3	140,000
Program 4	60,000
Total	$1,000,000

Additional information: Programs 1 and 2 were audited as major programs in each of the two preceding fiscal years, with no audit findings reported. Although neither Program 1 nor 2 is considered inherently risky, a new manager, recently graduated from the state university, was appointed during the current year to manage activities related to Program 2.

Required
> *a.* Assuming the auditor classifies Programs 2 and 3 as high risk and Program 1 as low risk, which programs would be audited as major programs? Explain.
> *b.* Explain what audit work would be required to audit the major programs.

12–7. You are auditing the accounts of the clerk-treasurer of the Town of Belton. You find, in the ledger, accounts for a General Fund, a Street Fund, and a Capital Projects Fund. The legally approved budget for the Street Fund for the year you are examining consisted of the following three appropriations only:

Labor	$60,000
Materials	66,000
Equipment	24,000

In the appropriation and disbursement ledger accounts, you find the record of transactions for the Street Fund shown as follows:

LABOR ACCOUNT

Date	Description	Warrant	Appropriation	Disbursements	Appropriation Balance
Jan. 1	From advertised budget		$60,000		$60,000
31	Street labor	115–142		$ 6,000	54,000
Feb. 28	Street labor	219–241		7,000	47,000
Mar. 31	Street labor	252–263		6,000	41,000
Apr. 30	Street labor	274–294		5,000	36,000
June 30	Labor on municipal parking lots	371–388		8,000	28,000
Aug. 31	Street labor	400–424		10,000	18,000
Oct. 31	Street labor	510–523		10,000	8,000
Dec. 31	Street labor	600–621		8,000	–0–

MATERIALS ACCOUNT

Date	Description	Warrant	Appropriation	Disbursements	Appropriation Balance
Jan. 1	From advertised budget		$66,000		$66,000
20	Asphalt mix for street repair	109		$ 6,000	60,000
Feb. 21	Repair of truck used on streets	217		2,000	58,000
Mar. 12	Purchased used truck for street department	268		12,000	46,000
Apr. 15	Auditor of State, gasoline tax distribution		4,920		50,920
May 31	Gas and oil for street trucks	301		3,000	47,920
June 6	Tile	367		4,000	43,920
July 14	Concrete for building fireplaces in park	425		6,900	37,020
Aug. 7	Street lights (utility bill)	451		7,220	29,800
Sep. 29	Refund received on tile purchased by warrant No. 367		100		29,900
Oct. 18	Labor on streets	524–532		12,000	17,900
Nov. 2	Reimbursement for cutting weeds on private property		640		18,540
Dec. 11	To contractor for paving street	622		20,000	(1,460)
Dec. 31	Additional appropriations as advertised on this date		1,460		–0–

EQUIPMENT ACCOUNT

Date		Description	Warrant	Appropriation	Disbursements	Appropriation Balance
Jan.	1	From advertised budget		$24,000		$24,000
	9	Grading equipment			$16,000	8,000
Feb.	10	Fire hydrants	189		6,000	2,000
	19	Shovels, picks, and hand tools	208		1,420	580

Required

    a. Comment on whether accounting for the Street Fund appears in conformity with generally accepted accounting principles. Explain fully.

    b. As the auditor, would you be able to render an unqualified opinion on the financial statements of the Town of Belton? Would your answer depend on whether you are engaged to report on the financial statements at the individual fund level rather than at the combined level (general purpose financial statements)?

12–8. The City of Clayton's Balance Sheet as of December 31, 1998, is shown below. The *Annual Report for 1998* also includes a Statement of Changes in Cash for that year and an operating statement for that year. No Auditor's Report is associated with these three financial statements. Assuming you made an audit for 1998 and found no material errors in the amounts presented in the statements, could you express the opinion that the statements present fairly the financial position of the City at December 31, 1998, and the results of its operations for the year then ended in conformity with generally accepted accounting principles? Why or why not? Be explicit.

CITY OF CLAYTON
Balance Sheet
As of December 31, 1998
Assets

Cash	$ 155,155	
Accounts receivable		
Current-year property taxes	58,792	
Prior-year property taxes	2,921	
Other taxes	514	
Municipal services—usage	71,861	
Municipal services—tap fees	9,077	
Toll bridges	30,598	
School district	5,242	
Other	173	
Total current assets		$ 334,333
Property, plant, and equipment:		
Library—building and equipment	$ 16,550	
Storage shed	14,742	
Public Safety Dept.—building and equipment	266,317	
Municipal Services Dept.—land, building, and equipment	2,325,893	
Highway Department	28,755	
Cemetery	21,595	

Town office—equipment	4,369	
Land	12,000	
Toll bridges	22,500	
Total property, plant, and equipment	2,712,721	
Less: Accumulated depreciation	(283,357)	2,429,364
Total assets		$2,763,697

Liabilities and Equity

Accounts payable	$ 1,725	
Tax anticipation notes	250,000	
Current portion—long-term debt:		
Bonds	85,000	
Notes	84,304	
Due school district	46,089	
Total current liabilities	467,118	
Long-term debt:		
Bonds	1,395,000	
Notes	373,416	
Total liabilities		$2,235,534
Equity	850,421	
Less: Wind recovery costs	(322,258)	528,163
Total liabilities and equity		$2,763,697

Continuous Problem

12–L. *a.* Prepare the audit report you believe would be appropriate for a certified public accountant to provide on the general purpose financial statements of the City of Bingham (see 10–L *a* and *b*). Explain the rationale for the nature of the audit report (qualified or unqualified) rendered.

CHAPTER 13

Accounting and Reporting for Federal Government Agencies

Learning Objectives

After studying this chapter, you should be able to:

- Describe the financial management structure applicable to the federal government.
- Describe the structure for establishing accounting and financial reporting standards for federal agencies.
- Explain the concepts underlying federal agency accounting and financial reporting.
- Contrast and compare budgetary accounting with proprietary accounting.
- Describe the hierarchy of budgetary accounts and the flow of budgetary authority through the accounts.
- Make budgetary and proprietary journal entries applicable to federal agencies.
- Identify and prepare financial statements required of federal agencies.

An accounting structure has been provided for the federal government of the United States of America by statutes since 1789. The professional accounting consultants to the first and second Hoover Commissions generally are given credit for being among the first to provide direction to the effort to improve federal government accounting. Recent years have seen major institutional change that is providing the impetus for even greater change in federal accounting. Among these changes are the Chief Financial Officers Act of 1990, the creation of the Federal Accounting Standards Advisory Board (FASAB) in 1990, the Government Performance and Results Act of 1993 (GPRA), and the Federal Financial Management Improvement Act of 1996. Federal accounting standards are similar in some respects to those used by private sector entities, and in other respects are like those developed for state and local governments, as discussed in Chapters 1–11 of this text. Important differences do exist, however. This chapter focuses on the unique aspects of accounting for federal agencies.

Federal Government Financial Management Structure

The United States Code (31 U.S.C. 3512) requires the head of each executive agency to establish, evaluate, and maintain adequate systems of accounting and internal control. Despite this requirement, many federal agencies have been slow to establish effective financial management systems. To help ensure that federal agencies correct their deficient accounting and reporting systems, Congress enacted the **Federal Financial Management Improvement Act of 1996 (FFMIA).** The Act states:

> To rebuild the accountability and credibility of the Federal Government, and restore public confidence in the Federal Government, agencies must incorporate accounting standards and reporting objectives established for the Federal Government into their financial management systems so that all the assets and liabilities, revenues, and expenditures or expenses, and the full costs of programs and activities of the Federal Government can be consistently and accurately recorded, monitored, and uniformly reported throughout the Federal Government.[1]

The Federal Financial Management Improvement Act further requires that each agency "shall implement and maintain financial management systems that comply substantially with federal financial management systems requirements, applicable federal accounting standards, and the United States Government Standard General Ledger at the transaction level."[2] The Act also requires that each audit of a federal agency's financial statements shall report whether the agency is in compliance with the preceding requirement. If not in compliance, the agency must establish a remediation plan that will ensure compliance no later than three years after the date of determination of noncompliance.

---

[1]Public Law 104-208, 104th Congress, Federal Financial Management Improvement Act of 1996, Sec. 802(a)(5).

[2]Ibid., Sec. 803(a).

Federal statutes assign responsibility for establishing and maintaining a sound financial management structure for the federal government as a whole to three principal officials: the Comptroller General, the Secretary of the Treasury, and the Director of the Office of Management and Budget (OMB). Responsibilities assigned to each of these officials and the Director of the Congressional Budget Office are discussed briefly, after which recent cooperative efforts of these officials to enhance the quality of federal financial management under the auspices of the Joint Financial Management and Improvement Program (JFMIP) will be examined.

Comptroller General

The Comptroller General of the United States is the head of the General Accounting Office (GAO), an agency of the legislative branch of the government. The Comptroller General is appointed by the President with the advice and consent of the Senate for a term of office of 15 years. Since 1950, the United States Code (31 U.S.C. 3511) has assigned to the Comptroller General responsibility for prescribing the accounting principles, standards, and related requirements to be observed by each executive agency in the development of its accounting system. The executive branch has never acknowledged the constitutional authority of the Comptroller General to set accounting standards for the executive branch. Moreover, the Chief Financial Officers Act of 1990 assigns significant responsibility for establishing policies and procedures for approving and publishing accounting principles and standards (particularly as regards agency financial reporting) to the Director of the Office of Management and Budget. Thus, both under the law and in fact, the responsibility for prescribing accounting principles and standards is now a joint responsibility.

Just as the appropriational authority of state and local governments rests in their legislative bodies, the appropriational authority of the federal government rests in the Congress. The Congress is, therefore, interested in determining that financial and budgetary reports from executive, judicial, and legislative agencies are reliable; that agency financial management is intelligent, efficient, and economical; and that legal requirements have been met by the agencies. Under the assumption that the reports of an independent audit agency would aid in satisfying these interests of the Congress, the General Accounting Office was created as the audit agency of the Congress itself. The standards of auditing followed by the GAO are discussed in some detail in Chapter 12. Briefly, the standards are set forth in the publication, *Government Auditing Standards,* often referred to as the "yellow book," and are usually followed by independent CPAs when auditing federal government funds, as well as by state audit agencies, programs, activities, and functions.

Secretary of the Treasury

The Secretary of the Treasury is the head of the Department of the Treasury, a part of the executive branch of the federal government. The Secretary of the Treasury is a member of the Cabinet of the President, appointed by the President with the advice and consent of the Senate to serve an indefinite term of office. The Department of the Treasury was created in 1789 to receive, keep, and disburse monies of the United States, and to account for them. From the beginning, the word *receive* was construed as *collect,* and the Internal Revenue Service, Bureau of

Customs, and other agencies active in the enforcement of the collections of revenues due the federal government are parts of the Department of the Treasury, as are the Bureau of the Mint, the Bureau of Engraving and Printing, the Bureau of Public Debt, the Office of Treasurer of the United States, and the Bureau of Government Financial Operations. Although there is no complete centralized accounting system for the federal government at this time, the Secretary of the Treasury, in coordination with the Director of OMB and the Comptroller General, has for 21 years published prototype consolidated financial statements for the United States Government as a whole. Beginning with Fiscal Year 1997, the consolidated financial statements are no longer prepared on a prototype basis; they are now an official report of the federal government.

The Secretary of the Treasury is responsible for the preparation of reports that will inform the President, the Congress, and the public on the financial condition and operations of the government (31 U.S.C. 3513). An additional responsibility of the Secretary of the Treasury is the maintenance of a system of central accounts of the public debt and cash to provide a basis for consolidation of the accounts of the various executive agencies with those of the Department of the Treasury.

Statutes provide that the reports of the Secretary of the Treasury shall include financial data needed by the Office of Management and Budget, and that the Department of the Treasury system of central accounting and reporting shall be consistent with the principles, standards, and related requirements prescribed for federal agency accounting systems. Instructions and requirements relating to central accounting, central financial reporting, and various other fiscal matters have been codified by the Department of the Treasury in the *Treasury Financial Manual* for guidance of departments and agencies.

The Department of the Treasury (Financial Management Service) also provides support for the interagency Standard General Ledger Board, which maintains the *U.S. Government Standard General Ledger,* subject to the approval of the OMB. The *Standard General Ledger* was developed by an interagency task force under the direction of the OMB and was originally published by the OMB in 1986. The *Standard General Ledger* is intended to (1) provide an accounting structure that will standardize financial information accumulation and processing, (2) enhance financial control, and (3) support budget reporting and external financial reporting. Implementation of the *Standard General Ledger* has enhanced the ability of central agencies to more accurately consolidate accounting data derived from individual agency accounting records. The chart of accounts presented in the *Standard General Ledger* is based on a standardized coding system for asset, liability, equity, budgetary, revenue, expense, and "gains/losses/extraordinary items, etc." accounts and provides flexibility so that agency-specific accounts may be incorporated. In addition to the chart of accounts, the *Standard General Ledger* publication provides account descriptions; illustrates the manner in which accounting transactions should be recorded; discusses data elements, subaccounts, and definitions; and illustrates crosswalks to external reports. Accounting for typical transactions of a federal agency illustrated in a later section of this chapter is based on the *Standard General Ledger* structure.

Director of the Office of Management and Budget

The Director of the Office of Management and Budget is appointed by the president and is a part of the Executive Office of the President. As the direct representative of the President with the authority to control the size and nature of appropriations requested of each Congress, it is obvious that the Director of the Office of Management and Budget is an extremely powerful figure in the federal government.

Congressional requirements for the budget have a number of accounting implications in addition to the explicit historical comparisons that necessitate cooperation among the Office of Management and Budget, the Department of the Treasury, and the General Accounting Office. Implicit in the requirements for projections of revenues and receipts is the mandate that the Office of Management and Budget coordinate closely with the Council of Economic Advisers in the use of macroeconomic (the study of the economic system in its aggregate) and macroaccounting (accounting for the economy in the aggregate) forecasts. Macroaccounting is beyond the scope of this text, yet the subject is of great, and increasing, importance in the financial management of the federal government.

The OMB is assigned major responsibilities under the Chief Financial Officers Act of 1990 for establishing policies and procedures for approving and publishing financial accounting principles and standards to be followed by executive branch agencies. Pursuant to the Act, an Office of Federal Financial Management has been established within the OMB, headed by a controller appointed by the President. The Act also authorizes each major department or agency of the federal government to have a Chief Financial Officer (CFO) and a deputy CFO. Under the Act, the Director of the OMB is required to prepare and update each year a five-year financial plan for the federal government.

Director of the Congressional Budget Office

The Congressional Budget and Impoundment Control Act of 1974 established House and Senate budget committees, created the Congressional Budget Office (CBO), structured the congressional budget process, and enacted a number of other provisions to improve federal fiscal procedures. The Director of the CBO is appointed for a four-year term by the Speaker of the House of Representatives and the President pro tempore of the Senate. The CBO gathers information for the House and Senate budget committees with respect to the budget (submitted by the executive branch), appropriation bills, and other bills providing budget authority or tax expenditures.[3] The CBO also provides the Congress with information concerning revenues, receipts, estimated future revenues and receipts, changing revenue conditions, and any related information-gathering and analytic functions assigned to the CBO; its Director is responsible for working with the Comptroller General, the Secretary of the Treasury, and the Director of the Office of Management and Budget in developing central files of data and information to meet the recurring requirements of the Congress.

---

[3]A *tax expenditure* is a revenue loss attributable to provisions of federal tax laws that allow special exclusion, exemption, or deduction from gross income, or that provide a special credit, a preferential rate of tax, or a deferral of tax liability.

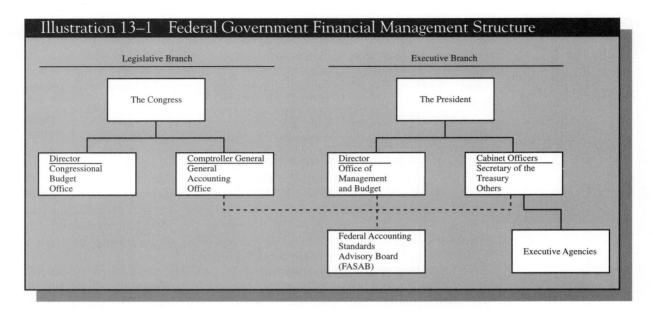

Illustration 13–1   Federal Government Financial Management Structure

Illustration 13–1 shows in chart form the interrelationships among the officials and organizations whose accounting and financial management responsibilities are discussed above.

Structure for Establishing Accounting and Financial Reporting Standards for Federal Agencies

As noted previously, the three officials or "principals" of the Joint Financial Management Improvement Program (JFMIP)—the Comptroller General, the Director of OMB, and the Secretary of the Treasury—have joint statutory responsibilities for improving financial management in the federal government. Although accounting principles and standards were prescribed for many years by *Title 2* of the *General Accounting Office Policy and Procedures Manual for Guidance of Federal Agencies*, not all federal agencies complied with the guidance contained in *Title 2*. The diverse financial systems used among and within federal departments and agencies made it difficult to achieve uniform financial reporting and to educate and train federal financial managers.

To establish an improved, and more generally accepted, structure for setting accounting principles and standards, the three principal sponsors of the JFMIP signed a memorandum of understanding in October 1990 creating the **Federal Accounting Standards Advisory Board (FASAB).** The nine-member board utilizes a due process similar to that of FASB and GASB. The new board is comprised of one member from each of the three principal sponsors; one member from each of the following federal constituencies: the Congressional Budget Office, defense and international agencies, and civilian agencies; and three members from the nonfederal "general financial community" (defined as the accounting and auditing community and academia). According to OMB *Circular A-134*, "Financial Accounting Principles and Standards" (par. 2):

> The role of the FASAB is to deliberate upon and make recommendations to the Principals on accounting principles and standards for the Federal Government and its agencies. The MOU [memorandum of understanding] states that if the Principals agree with the recommendations, the Comptroller General and the Director of OMB will publish the accounting principles and standards.

During its first six years, the FASAB has issued nine Statements of Federal Financial Accounting Standards (SFFASs) and two statements of recommended concepts that collectively provide general and specific accounting and financial reporting standards on a variety of topics, including assets; liabilities; inventory and related property; property, plant, and equipment; revenues and other financial sources; direct loans and loan guarantees; managerial cost accounting concepts; and supplementary stewardship reporting. This chapter provides only an overview of these initial basic standards; detailed discussion of the many complex issues covered by these standards is beyond the scope of this text.[4] The authoritative status of SFFASs is made clear by OMB *Circular A-134*, issued in 1993:

> SFFASs shall be considered generally accepted accounting principles (GAAP) for Federal agencies.[5] Agencies shall apply the SFFASs in preparing financial statements in accordance with the requirements of the Chief Financial Officers Act of 1990. Auditors shall consider SFFASs as authoritative references when auditing financial statements. (par. 5.b)

Hierarchy of Accounting Principles and Standards

OMB *Bulletin 97-01* acknowledges that federal agencies may engage in transactions that are not addressed by the SFFASs issued to date. Thus, the Bulletin establishes the following hierarchy of generally accepted accounting principles for the federal government:

1. Individual standards (SFFASs) agreed to by the Director of OMB, the Controller General, and the Secretary of the Treasury and published by OMB and the General Accounting Office.
2. Interpretations related to the SFFASs issued by OMB in accordance with the procedures outlined in OMB *Circular A-134*, "Financial Accounting Principles and Standards."
3. Requirements contained in OMB's Form and Content Bulletin in effect for the period covered by the financial statements [currently OMB *Bulletin 97-01*].

---

[4]The FASAB continues to deliberate on possible additional standards that may extend or modify the initial basic statements that have been issued to date. Students who desire information about current FASAB projects, including exposure drafts of possible new standards, should consult FASAB's Internet site at http://www.financenet.gov/fasab.htm.

[5]The American Institute of CPAs has not yet accorded Rule 203 recognition to federal government standards as generally accepted accounting principles. Thus, federal government standards are currently considered by auditors as a lower level of GAAP than the standards issued by the FASB and the GASB.

4. Accounting principles published by other authoritative standard-setting bodies and other authoritative sources (a) in the absence of other guidance in the first three parts of this hierarchy, and (b) if the use of such accounting principles improves the meaningfulness of the financial statements.[6]

Conceptual Framework

Accounting standards recommended by the FASAB, and issued by the Comptroller General and the OMB for federal agencies, are intended to be consistent with a conceptual framework the FASAB is developing. In this respect, the FASAB is following the general pattern established by the FASB, which attempts to issue standards consistent with its several Statements of Financial Accounting Concepts; and the GASB, which looks to its *Concepts Statement No. 1,* "Objectives of Financial Reporting" (see Chapter 1 of this text). To date, the FASAB has issued two concepts statements: *Statement of Federal Financial Accounting Concepts (SFFAC) No. 1,* "Objectives of Federal Financial Reporting," and *SFFAC No. 2,* "Entity and Display." *SFFAC No. 1* is considerably broader in scope than either the FASB's or GASB's concepts statements on objectives. The FASAB, for example, intends to set standards for internal management accounting and performance measurement, as well as for external financial reporting. The FASAB objectives are described briefly in the next section.

Objectives

SFFAC No. 1 identifies four objectives of federal financial reporting, all of which rest on the foundation of accountability. The objectives in brief are to assist report users in evaluating *budgetary integrity, operating performance, stewardship,* and adequacy of *systems and controls. Budgetary integrity* pertains to accountability for raising monies through taxes and other means in accordance with appropriate laws, and expenditures of these monies in accordance with budgetary authorization. Accountability for *operating performance* is accomplished by providing report users information on service efforts and accomplishments—how well resources have been managed in providing services efficiently and economically, and effectively, in attaining planned goals. *Stewardship* relates to the federal government's accountability for the general welfare of the nation. To assess stewardship, report users need information about the "impact on the country of the government's operations and investments for the period and how, as a result, the government's and the nation's financial conditions have changed and may change in the future" (par. 134). Finally, financial reporting should help users assess whether financial management *systems and controls* (internal accounting and administrative controls) "are adequate to ensure that (1) transactions are executed in accordance with budgetary and

---

[6] OMB, *Bulletin 97-01,* "Formats and Instructions for the Form and Content of Agency Financial Statements" (Washington, DC: October 1996), par. VIII.

financial laws and other requirements, are consistent with the purposes authorized, and are recorded in accordance with federal accounting standards, (2) assets are properly safeguarded to deter fraud, waste, and abuse, and (3) performance measurement information is adequately supported" (par. 146).

Unlike the FASB and the GASB, which focus their standards on external financial reporting, the FASAB and its sponsors are concerned with both internal and external financial reporting. Accordingly, the FASAB has identified four major groups of users of federal financial reports: citizens, Congress, executives, and program managers. Given the broad role the FASAB has been assigned, future standards recommended by the Board may focus on cost accounting systems and controls, and the use of financial information in service efforts and accomplishments measures, as well as on financial accounting and reporting. The Memorandum of Understanding among the sponsors provides, however, that FASAB jurisdiction does not extend to agency budgetary accounting and the manner of controlling expenditures of budgetary resources.

SFFAC No. 2, "Entity and Display," provides additional conceptual guidance for federal agency financial reporting. SFFAC No. 2:

a. Specifies the types of entities that should provide financial reports.

b. Establishes guidelines for defining each type of reporting entity.

c. Identifies the types of financial statements each type of reporting entity should provide.

d. Suggests the types of information each type of statement should convey.[7]

Reporting Entity

Defining the reporting entity is important because it communicates to the users of the financial statements which organizational subunits' or separate organizations' financial information is included as part of the reporting entity and which is not. As discussed in Chapter 10 for state and local governments, accountability reporting is facilitated by including as part of the reporting entity all separate entities for which there is financial accountability or financial interdependence.

SFFAC No. 2 discusses three perspectives from which the federal government can be viewed for accounting and reporting purposes: organizational, budget, and program. From the *organizational perspective*, the government is viewed as a collection of departments and agencies that provide governmental services. From the *budget perspective*, the government is viewed as a collection of expenditure (appropriations or funds) or receipt budget accounts. **Budget accounts** are generally quite broad in scope and are not the same as the Standard General Ledger accounts used for accounting purposes. A budget account may cover an entire organization or a group of budget accounts may aggregate to cover an organization. A budget account may also aggregate to form federal or trust funds as discussed later in this

---

[7]Paraphrased from FASAB, *Report Number 1, Reporting Relevant Financial Information,* "Overview of Federal Accounting Concepts and Standards" (as of September 30, 1996) (Washington, DC: 1996), p. 11.

chapter. From the *program perspective* the government is viewed as an aggregation of programs (or functions) and activities.

As *SFFAC No. 2* (pars. 25–26) points out, most programs are financed by more than one budget account and some programs are administered by more than one organization. Similarly, some organizations administer multiple programs. Thus, in defining the reporting entity, it is necessary to consider the interacting nature of the perspectives. *SFFAC No. 2* provides three criteria that an entity must meet in order to be considered a reporting entity:

1. There is a management responsible for controlling and deploying resources, producing outputs and outcomes, executing the budget or a portion thereof (assuming that the entity is included in the budget), and held accountable for the entity's performance.
2. The entity's scope is such that its financial statements would provide a meaningful representation of operations and financial condition.
3. There are likely to be users of the financial statements who are interested in and could use the information in the statements to help them make resource allocation and other decisions and hold the entity accountable for its deployment and use of resources (par. 29).

Although these criteria provide general guidance for identifying a reporting entity, there can still be uncertainty in applying the criteria in specific cases. Most of the reporting entities (for example, departments and agencies) identified will be component units of a larger entity: the federal government. Thus, the major uncertainty is in identifying the lower level reporting entities.

To reduce uncertainty, *SFFAC No. 2* presents two additional kinds of criteria to use in deciding what to include in the reporting entity. First is a *conclusive criterion,* which is an inherent conclusion that an organization should be included in the reporting entity. As noted in *SFFAC No. 2,* "Appearance in the Federal budget section currently entitled 'Federal Program by Agency and Account' is a conclusive criterion. Any organization, program, or budget account . . . should be considered part of the U.S. Federal Government, as well as part of the organization with which it appears" (par. 42). Second are *indicative criteria,* which either individually or collectively may indicate that an organization should be included in the reporting entity. These criteria, listed below, are similar to those established by the GASB and discussed in Chapter 10.

1. It exercises any sovereign power of the government to carry out Federal functions.
2. It is owned by the Federal Government, particularly if the ownership is of the organization and not just the property.
3. It is subject to the direct or continuing administrative control of the reporting entity, as revealed by such features as (1) the ability to select or remove the governing authority or the ability to designate management, particularly if there is to be a significant continuing relationship with the governing authority or management with respect to carrying out

important public functions (in contrast to selections and designations in which there is little continuing communication with, or accountability to, the appointing official); (2) authority to review and modify or approve budget requests, budgetary adjustments, or amendments or rate or fee changes; (3) ability to veto, overrule, or modify governing body decisions or otherwise significantly influence normal operations; (4) authority to sign contracts as the contracting authority; (5) approval of hiring, reassignment, and removal of key personnel; (6) title to, ability to transfer title to, and/or exercise control over facilities and property; and (7) right to require audits that do more than just support the granting of contracts. (SFFAC No. 2, par. 44)

SFFAC No. 2 addresses also the nature of the financial statements that should be included in the financial report of a reporting entity and the recommended format and content of the financial statements. Thus, it provides clear and strong direction to the FASAB and its three sponsoring agencies in setting accounting and reporting standards for the federal government, and leaves little discretion to go down a different path.

Funds Used in Federal Accounting

FASAB's standards do not focus on fund accounting, but Congress regularly passes laws that create, define, and modify funds for various purposes. Fund accounting is needed for federal agencies to demonstrate compliance with requirements of legislation for which federal funds have been appropriated or otherwise authorized to carry out specific activities, and also for financial reporting.

Two general types of funds are found in federal government accounting: (1) those used to account for resources derived from the general taxation and revenue powers or from business operations of the government and (2) those used to account for resources held and managed by the government in the capacity of custodian or trustee. Six kinds of funds are specified within the two general types:

1. Funds derived from general taxing and revenue powers and from business operations.
   a. General fund accounts.
   b. Special fund accounts.
   c. Revolving fund accounts.
   d. Management fund accounts.
2. Funds held by the government in the capacity of custodian or trustee.
   a. Trust fund accounts.
   b. Deposit fund accounts.

General Fund. The General Fund is credited with all receipts that are not dedicated by law and is charged with payments out of appropriations of "any money in the Treasury not otherwise appropriated" and out of general borrowings.

Strictly speaking, there is only one General Fund in the entire federal government. The Bureau of Government Financial Operations of the Department of the Treasury accounts for the centralized cash balances (the cash is under the control of the Treasurer of the United States; cash accounts subsidiary to those of the Bureau of Government Financial Operations are maintained by the Treasurer), the appropriations control accounts, and unappropriated balances. On the books of an agency, each appropriation is treated as a fund with its own self-balancing group of accounts; these agency "appropriation funds" are subdivisions of *the* General Fund.

Special Funds. Receipt and expenditure accounts established to account for receipts of the government that are earmarked by law for a specific purpose, but that are not generated from a cycle of operations for which there is continuing authority to reuse such receipts (as is true for revolving funds), are classified as *special fund accounts* in federal usage. The term and its definition are very close to that of the classification "special revenue funds" used in accounting for state and local governments.

Revolving. A revolving fund is credited with collections, primarily from other agencies and accounts, that are earmarked by law to carry out a cycle of business-type operations, in which the government is the owner of the activity. This type of fund is quite similar to internal service funds.

Management (including Working Funds). These are funds in which there are merged monies derived from two or more appropriations, in order to carry out a common purpose or project, but not involving a cycle of operations. Management funds include consolidated working funds that are set up to receive (and subsequently disburse) advance payments, pursuant to law, from other agencies or bureaus.

Trust Funds. Trust funds are established to account for receipts that are held in trust for use in carrying out specific purposes and programs in accordance with agreement or statute. In distinction to revolving funds and special funds, the assets of trust funds are frequently held over a period of time and may be invested in order to produce revenue. For example, the assets of the Federal Old Age and Survivors Insurance Trust Fund are invested in U.S. securities.

The corpus of some trust funds is used in business-type operations. In such a case, the fund is called a *trust revolving fund*. The term "trust fund" is used by Congress to describe some funds that in state and local governmental accounting would be called special revenue funds. An example is the Highway Trust Fund. Other federal trust funds, such as those used to account for assets that belong to Native Americans, are true trust funds.

Deposit Funds. Combined receipt and expenditure accounts established to account for receipts held in suspense temporarily and later refunded or paid to some other fund, or receipts held by the government as a banker or agent for others and paid out at the discretion of the owner, are classified within the federal government as deposit fund accounts. They are similar in nature to the agency funds established for state and local governmental units.

Required Financial Reporting

OMB *Bulletin 97-01* specifies the form and content of financial statements for 24 major executive departments and agencies that have been designated as reporting entities. OMB *Bulletin 97-01* specifies that the *annual financial statement* of a reporting entity is comprised of "(1) an overview of the reporting entity, (2) principal statements and related notes, (3) required supplemental stewardship information, and (4) required supplemental information" (par. VI). These requirements are discussed briefly in the following paragraphs.

Overview of Reporting Entity

OMB *Bulletin 97-01* requires a brief narrative overview of the reporting entity, which should provide a "clear and concise description of the reporting entity and its mission, activities, program and financial results, and financial condition" (p. 11). The overview is also referred to as the Management Discussion and Analysis (MD&A). This requirement is intended to assist in the governmentwide implementation of the Government Performance and Review Act (GPRA), which becomes effective in fiscal year 1999. Accordingly, the overview should provide information on the reporting entity's mission and organizational structure, its performance goals and results, and limitations of its financial statements.

Financial Statements

OMB *Bulletin 97-01* specifies essentially the same financial statements recommended by *SFFAC No. 2*. It also provides detailed descriptions and instructions for completing each part of each statement. These statements include a (1) Balance Sheet, (2) Statement of Net Cost, (3) Statement of Changes in Net Position, (4) Statement of Budgetary Resources, (5) Statement of Financing, and (6) Statement of Custodial Activity. Each of these statements is discussed briefly in the following paragraphs.

Balance Sheet. An example Balance Sheet from OMB *Bulletin 97-01* is presented in Illustration 13–2. *Bulletin 97-01* permits agencies considerable latitude regarding the level of aggregation to be used in preparing the financial statements. Agencies can use either a single-column (consolidated) format or a multicolumn format displaying financial information for component units or lines of business. If consolidated reporting is used, *Bulletin 97-01* (p. 9) requires a separate column presenting the intraentity transactions (for example, eliminations of intercomponent unit receivables and payables) in the *consolidating* statements underlying the consolidated statements. If consolidated financial information is provided, comparative totals for the prior year must be presented for the Balance Sheet, the Statement of Budgetary Resources, and the Statement of Custodial Activity.

Assets. As shown in Illustration 13–2, *entity* assets are reported separately from *nonentity* assets and *intragovernmental* assets are reported separately from *governmental* assets. These are the asset classifications specified in *Statement of Federal Financial Accounting Standards (SFFAS) No. 1*. **Entity assets** are those the reporting entity has authority to use in its operations, whereas **nonentity assets** are

Illustration 13–2

DEPARTMENT/AGENCY REPORTING ENTITY
Consolidated Balance Sheet
As of September 30, 19xx
(In dollars/thousands/millions)

	19xx	19xx
Assets		
Entity Assets:		
Intragovernmental:		
Fund Balance with Treasury (Note 2)	$ xxx	$ xxx
Investments (Note 4)	xxx	xxx
Accounts receivable, net (Note 5)	xxx	xxx
Interest receivable (net)	xxx	xxx
Other assets (Note 6)	xxx	xxx
Governmental:		
Investments (Note 4)	xxx	xxx
Accounts receivable, net (Note 5)	xxx	xxx
Interest receivable (net)	xxx	xxx
Credit program receivables and related foreclosed property, net (Note 7)	xxx	xxx
Cash and other monetary assets (Note 3)	xxx	xxx
Inventory and related property, net (Note 8)	xxx	xxx
General property, plant, and equipment, net (Note 9)	xxx	xxx
Other assets (Note 6)	xxx	xxx
Total Entity Assets	xxx	xxx
Nonentity Assets:		
Intragovernmental:		
Fund Balance with Treasury (Note 2)	xxx	xxx
Accounts receivable, net (Note 5)	xxx	xxx
Interest receivable (net)	xxx	xxx
Other assets (Note 6)	xxx	xxx
Governmental:		
Accounts receivable, net (Note 5)	xxx	xxx
Interest receivable (net)	xxx	xxx
Cash and other monetary assets (Note 3)	xxx	xxx
Other assets (Note 6)	xxx	xxx
Total Nonentity Assets	x,xxx	x,xxx
Total Assets	$x,xxx	$x,xxx

held by the entity but are not available for the entity to spend. An example of a nonentity asset is federal income taxes collected by the Internal Revenue Service for the U.S. government. **Intragovernmental assets (liabilities)** are claims by (against) a reporting entity that arise from transactions between that entity and other reporting entities. **Governmental assets (liabilities)** arise from transactions of the federal government or an entity of the federal government with nonfederal entities.

Illustration 13–2 (concluded)

	19xx	19xx
Liabilities		
Liabilities Covered by Budgetary Resources:		
Intragovernmental liabilities:		
Accounts payable	$ xxx	$ xxx
Interest payable	xxx	xxx
Other intragovernmental liabilities (Note 11)	xxx	xxx
Governmental liabilities:		
Accounts payable	xxx	xxx
Interest payable	xxx	xxx
Liabilities for loan guarantees (Note 7)	xxx	xxx
Lease liabilities (Note 12)	xxx	xxx
Pensions, other retirement benefits and other postemployment benefits (Note 13)	xxx	xxx
Insurance liabilities (Note 14)	xxx	xxx
Other governmental liabilities (Note 11)	xxx	xxx
Total Liabilities Covered by Budgetary Resources	x,xxx	x,xxx
Liabilities Not Covered by Budgetary Resources:		
Intragovernmental liabilities:		
Accounts payable	xxx	xxx
Debt (Note 10)	xxx	xxx
Other intragovernmental liabilities (Note 11)	xxx	xxx
Governmental liabilities:		
Accounts payable	xxx	xxx
Debt (Note 10)	xxx	xxx
Lease liabilities (Note 3)	xxx	xxx
Pensions, other retirement benefits and other postemployment benefits (Note 13)	xxx	xxx
Insurance liabilities (Note 14)	xxx	xxx
Other governmental liabilities (Note 11)	xxx	xxx
Total Liabilities Not Covered by Budgetary Resources	x,xxx	x,xxx
Total Liabilities	$x,xxx	$x,xxx
Net Position		
Unexpended Appropriations (Note 15)	$xxx	$xxx
Cumulative Results of Operations	xxx	xxx
Total Net Position	xxx	xxx
Total Liabilities and Net Position	$x,xxx	$x,xxx

Note: This statement is shown as presented in OMB *Bulletin 97-01*. Notes to Financial Statements are not provided.
Source: OMB, *Bulletin 97-01*, pp. 15–17.

SFFAS No. 1 provides specific standards relating to Cash, Fund Balance with Treasury, Accounts Receivable, Interest Receivable, and various other asset categories. In most federal agencies *Fund Balance with Treasury* is used rather than *Cash* to indicate that the agency has a claim against the U.S. Treasury on which it may draw to pay liabilities. Only a few large federal departments and agencies, such as the Department of Defense, are authorized to write and issue checks directly against their balances with the Treasury. Most departments and agencies must request that the Treasury issue checks to pay their liabilities. If a federal agency does have the right to maintain one or more bank accounts, bank balances would be reported as *Cash*.

Consistent with the manner in which business entities report inventories, *SFFAS No. 3*, "Accounting for Inventory and Related Property," distinguishes inventory from consumable supplies. Inventory is defined as "tangible personal property that is (1) held for sale, (2) in the process of production for sale, or (3) to be consumed in the production of goods for sale or in the provision of services for a fee" (p. 4). Inventory may be valued at either historical cost or latest acquisition cost. Supplies to be consumed in normal operations are reported as *operating materials and supplies*. *SSFAS No. 3* also defines several additional types of inventory or related property: (1) stockpile materials, (2) seized and forfeited property, (3) foreclosed property, and (4) goods held under price support and stabilization programs. Discussion of these other types is beyond the scope of this text.

SSFAS No. 6, "Accounting for Property, Plant, and Equipment" establishes standards for several categories of property, plant, and equipment (PP&E).

1. **General PP&E.** PP&E used to provide general government goods and services.
2. **Federal mission PP&E.** PP&E such as military weapon systems and space exploration equipment or PP&E that exhibits other characteristics set by the FASAB.[8]
3. **Heritage assets.** PP&E such as the Washington Monument that possess educational, cultural, or natural characteristics.
4. **Stewardship land.** Land other than that included in general PP&E (for example, national parks).

Categories (2), (3), and (4) are collectively referred to as **stewardship PP&E.** *SSFAS No. 6* provides that for these assets, acquisition, replacement, construction, reconstruction, and improvements will be reported as a cost (i.e., expense) in the period incurred. They are not reported on the Balance Sheet and are not depreciated. Category (1) PP&E are capitalized at acquisition cost and, except for land, are depreciated over their useful lives.

Liabilities.   SSFAS No. 1 provides specific accounting standards for Accounts Payable, Interest Payable, and Other Current Liabilities. OMB *Bulletin 97-01* provides additional guidance on reporting liabilities. For example, it requires separate

---

[8]The FASAB has issued an exposure draft of a standard that would amend SFFAS 6. The proposed standard would restrict use of the federal mission category to certain national defense assets. FASAB, *Exposure Draft*, "Amendments to Accounting for Property, Plant, and Equipment." (FASAB, Washington, DC, February 1998).

Balance Sheet reporting of liabilities covered by budgetary resources (funded) and liabilities not covered by budgetary resources (unfunded). *Liabilities covered by budgetary resources* are those for which monies have been made available either through Congressional appropriations or current earnings of the entity. *Liabilities not covered by budgetary resources* result from the receipt of goods or services in the current or prior periods but for which monies have not yet been made available through Congressional appropriations or current earnings of the entity. Examples of the latter are liabilities for accrued leave, capital leases, and pensions.

SFFAS No. 5, "Accounting for Liabilities of the Federal Government" establishes standards for liabilities not covered in *SFFAS No. 1* and *No. 2*. The Statement defines a *liability* as "a probable future outflow or other sacrifice of resources as a result of past transactions or events" (par. 19). *SFFAS No. 5* provides the following recognition criteria for liabilities arising from the transactions or events indicated:

1. *Exchange transactions.* Recognize the liability when one party receives goods or services in exchange for a promise to provide money or other resources in the future.

2. *Nonexchange transactions* (for example, grants and entitlements). Recognize a liability for any unpaid amounts due at the end of the fiscal period.

3. *Government-related events* (nontransactions-based events that involve interaction between federal entities and their environment; for example, damage to private property). Recognize a liability when the event occurs if the future outflow of resources is probable and measurable.

4. *Government-acknowledged events* (events for which the government *chooses* to acknowledge responsibility. For example, damage from a natural disaster). Recognize liability when the government formally acknowledges responsibility for an event and a nonexchange or exchange transaction has occurred.

5. *Contingencies.* Generally disclosed in the notes or, in some cases such as contingencies related to government-acknowledged events, not disclosed at all.

6. *Capital leases.* Criteria for a capital lease are essentially the same as those specified by the FASB for commercial entities and the GASB for state and local governmental entities (see Chapter 5 of this text). A liability should be recognized in the amount of the present value of the rental and other minimum lease payments.

7. *Federal debt* (for example, U.S. Treasury bonds). Recognize a liability when an exchange transaction occurs between involved parties. Original issue premiums and discounts are amortized using the effective interest method.

8. *Pensions, other retirement benefits, and other postemployment benefits.* Recognize an expense at time employees' services are rendered. Any unfunded portion of cost calculated using the "Aggregate Entry Age Normal Cost" method should be reported as a liability.

9. *Insurance and guarantee programs* (other than social insurance and loan guarantee programs). Recognize a liability for unpaid claims incurred as a result of insured events that have already occurred. (Note: Loan guarantee program liabilities are covered by *SFFAS No. 2*. Reporting of social insurance programs, such as, social security, is covered in *SFFAS No. 8*, "Supplementary Stewardship Reporting.")

SFFAS No. 5 also requires disclosure in the Notes to the Financial Statements of the condition and estimated cost to remedy deferred maintenance on PP&E. In addition, it provides standards for measurement and recognition of expenses and liabilities related to environmental cleanup and closure costs from removing general PP&E from service.

Net Position.   OMB *Bulletin 97-01* requires that the fund balances of the entity's funds be reported in the Balance Sheet as **Net Position.** The components of net position are (1) **Unexpended Appropriations,** the amount of unexpended budget authority appropriated by Congress, both available and unavailable, and (2) **Cumulative Results of Operations,** the net difference between expenses/losses and financing sources, including appropriations, revenues, and gains, since the inception of the activity. Effective with fiscal year 1998, Cumulative Results of Operations also includes the net investment of the government in the reporting entity. The net investment of the government in the reporting entity includes the acquisition cost of capitalized fixed assets financed by appropriations; the additional investment in a revolving fund to commence operations or begin a new activity; less the reduction in investment due to depreciation, amortization, sales or exchanges, donations, other disposals, the return of initial investment to an investor, or transfer to another entity or revolving fund. Cumulative Results of Operations would also include any other items that would affect the net position, including, for example, the fair market value of donated assets, plus any costs incurred to place the donated assets in use, and assets (net of liabilities) transferred to or from other federal entities without reimbursement.

Statement of Net Cost.   Illustration 13–3 presents an example Consolidating Statement of Net Cost. This statement is intended to show the components of the net cost of the reporting entity's operations, both for the entity as a whole and for each of its responsibility centers or segments. If the reporting entity has a complex organizational structure, it may need to provide supporting schedules in the Notes to the Financial Statements to provide net cost information for its major programs and activities.[9]

---

[9] Because of inadequate cost accounting systems, federal agencies sought a two-year delay in implementation of *SFFAS No. 4* to permit them time to upgrade their cost accounting systems. After deliberation, the FASAB issued *SSFAS No. 9*, which deferred implementation of *SFFAS No. 4* by one year until periods beginning after September 30, 1997.

Illustration 13–3

REPORTING ENTITY
DEPARTMENT/AGENCY
Consolidating Statement of Net Cost
For the year ending September 30, 19xx
(in dollars/thousands/millions)

	Suborganization A	Suborganization B	Suborganization C	Intraagency Eliminations	Consolidated Totals
Costs:					
Crosscutting Programs:					
Program A:					
Intragovernmental	$xxx	—	$ xx	$(xx)	$xxx
With the public	xxx	—	—	—	xxx
Total	xxx	—	xx	(xx)	xxx
Less earned revenues	(xx)	—	(xx)	xx	(xx)
Net program costs	xxx	—	xx	(xx)	xxx
Other programs (Note XX):					
Program B:	—	xx	—	—	xx
Program C:	—	xx	—	—	xx
Program D:	—	xx	—	—	xx
Program E:	—	—	xx	—	xx
Program F:	—	—	xx	—	xx
Program G:	xx	—	—	—	xx
Program H:	xx	—	—	—	xx
Other programs:	—	—	xx	—	xx
Cost not assigned to programs	xx	xx	xx	—	xx
Less earned revenues not attributed to programs	—	—	(xx)	—	xx
Deferred maintenance (Note X)					
Net Cost of Operations	$xxx	$xxx	$xxx	$(xx)	$xxx

Source: OMB, *Bulletin 97-01*, p. 25.

Statement of Changes in Net Position. An example Consolidating Statement of Changes in Net Position is shown in Illustration 13–4. The purpose of this statement is to communicate all changes in the reporting entity's net position, as well as that for major responsibility segments (organizational subunits or major programs and activities). Net cost of operations is obtained from the bottom line of the Statement of Net Cost (see Illustration 13–3) and includes gross costs less exchange (earned) revenues. The net cost of operations less nonexchange (nonearned) financing sources provides the *net results from operations*— the equivalent of net income. Further additions or deductions, as appropriate, of prior-period adjustments (due to material errors or accounting changes), change

Illustration 13–4

**DEPARTMENT/AGENCY
REPORTING ENTITY**
Consolidating Statement of Changes in Net Position
For the years ended September 30, 19xx
(in dollars/thousands/millions)

	Suborganization A	Suborganization B	Suborganization C	Intraagency Eliminations	Consolidated Totals
Net Cost of Operations	$xxx	$xxx	$xxx	$xxx	$xxx
Financing Sources (other than exchange revenues):					
Appropriations Used	xxx	xxx	xxx	xxx	xxx
Taxes (and other nonexchange revenues)	xxx	xxx	xxx	xxx	xxx
Donations (nonexchange revenue)	xxx	xxx	xxx	xxx	xxx
Imputed financing	xxx	xxx	xxx	xxx	xxx
Transfers-in	xxx	xxx	xxx	xxx	xxx
Transfers-out	(xxx)	(xxx)	(xxx)	(xxx)	(xxx)
Net Results of Operations	xxx	xxx	xxx	xxx	xxx
Prior-Period Adjustments	xxx	xxx	xxx	xxx	xxx
Net Change in Cumulative Results of Operations	xxx	xxx	xxx	xxx	xxx
Increase (Decrease) in Unexpended Appropriations	xxx	xxx	xxx	xxx	xxx
Change in Net Position	xxx	xxx	xxx	xxx	xxx
Net Position—Beginning of Period	xxx	xxx	xxx	xxx	xxx
Net Position—End of Period	$xxx	$xxx	$xxx	$xxx	$xxx

Source: OMB, *Bulletin 97-01*, p. 30.

in cumulative results of operations, and unexpended appropriations comprise the total change in net position.

Statement of Budgetary Resources.   The Statement of Budgetary Resources (see Illustration 13–5) presents the availability of budgetary resources and the status of those resources at year-end. OMB *Circular A-34,* "Instructions on Budget Execution," provides the definitions and guidance for budgetary accounting and reporting. As shown in Illustration 13–5, the equation for this statement is Budgetary resources = Status of budgetary resources. Available **Budgetary Resources** includes new budgetary authority for the period plus unobligated budgetary authority carried over from the prior period and offsetting collections, if any, and plus/minus any budgetary adjustments. The *Status of Budgetary Resources* section consists of obligations incurred (that is, budget authority expended and

Illustration 13–5

**DEPARTMENT/AGENCY
REPORTING ENTITY**
Statement of Budgetary Resources
For the years ended September 30, 19xx
(in dollars/thousands/millions)

	19xx	*19xx*
Budgetary Resources:		
Budget authority (line 1)	$ xxx	$ xxx
Unobligated balances—beginning of period (line 2A)	xxx	xxx
Spending authority from offsetting collections (line 3)	xxx	xxx
Adjustments (lines 4–6)	xxx	xxx
Total budgetary resources (line 7)	$ xxx	$ xxx
Status of Budgetary Resources:		
Obligations incurred (line 8)	$ xxx	$ xxx
Unobligated balances—available (line 9)	xxx	xxx
Unobligated balances—not available (line 10)	xxx	xxx
Total, status of budgetary resources (line 11)	$ xxx	$ xxx
Outlays:		
Obligations incurred (line 8)	$ xxx	$ xxx
Less: Spending authority from offsetting collections and adjustments (lines 3A, B, D, & 4A)	(xxx)	(xxx)
Obligated balance, net—beginning of period (line 12)	xxx	xxx
Obligated balance transferred, net (line 13)	xxx	xxx
Less: Obligated balance, net—end of period (line 14)	(xxx)	(xxx)
Total outlays (line 15)	$ xxx	$ xxx

Source: OMB, *Bulletin 97-01*, p. 33.

amounts reserved for undelivered orders) plus any current budgetary authority that is still available to finance operations of the current period (Unobligated balances—available, line 9 in Illustration 13–5) or those of prior periods (Unobligated balances—not available, line 10). The lower portion of the Statement of Budgetary Resources reconciles obligations incurred during the period to total budgetary outlays for the period, after adjusting for offsetting collections and budgetary adjustments, and the change during the year in obligations carried forward.

Statement of Financing. Another required statement is the Statement of Financing (see Illustration 13–6). This statement reconciles the budget-based information in the Statement of Budgetary Resources to the accrual-based *net cost of operations* information in the Statement of Net Costs. Total budgetary and nonbudgetary resources available to fund current-period operations are reported in the

Illustration 13–6

DEPARTMENT/AGENCY
REPORTING ENTITY
Statement of Financing
For the year ended September 30, 19xx
(in dollars/thousands/millions)

Obligations and Nonbudgetary Resources:		
Obligations incurred	$ xxx	
Less: Spending authority for offsetting collections and adjustments	xxx	
Donations not in the budget	xxx	
Financing imputed for cost subsidies	xxx	
Transfers-in (out)	xxx	
Exchange revenue not in the budget	xxx	
Other	xxx	
Total Obligations, as Adjusted, and Nonbudgetary Resources		$ xxx
Resources That Do Not Fund Net Cost of Operations:		
Change in amount of goods, services, and benefits ordered but not yet received or provided	(xxx)	
Costs capitalized on the Balance Sheet	(xxx)	
Financing sources that fund costs of prior periods	(xxx)	
Other	(xxx)	
Total Resources That Do Not Fund Net Cost of Operations		(xxx)
Costs That Do Not Require Resources:		
Depreciation and amortization	xxx	
Revaluation of assets and liabilities	xxx	
Other	xxx	
Total Costs That Do Not Require Resources		xxx
Financing Sources Yet to Be Provided		xxx
Net Cost of Operations		$ xxx

Source: OMB, *Bulletin 97-01*, p. 35.

upper section captioned *Obligations and Nonbudgetary Resources*. The *Resources That Do Not Fund Net Cost of Operations* section essentially deducts items that were included in sources or uses of budgetary resources, but were not included as part of the *net cost of operations* on the accrual basis. The third section, *Costs That Do Not Require Resources*, are items that would have been included in the measurement of the net cost of operations but that did not require financing. The final section, *Financing Sources Yet to Be Provided*, would typically be required for an increase in unfunded liabilities, such as unfunded annual leave. An accrual for annual leave would have been included in the net cost of operations, but not as an obligation incurred for budgetary purposes. Of course, this item would be deducted in a future period when the leave is funded as *financing sources that fund costs of prior periods* in the third section.

Statement of Custodial Activity. OMB *Bulletin 97-01* requires entities that "collect nonexchange revenue for the General Fund of the Treasury, a trust fund, or other recipient entities" (p. 39) to prepare a Statement of Custodial Activity (see Illustration 13–7). This statement usually would be required of agencies that collect taxes or duties, such as the Internal Revenue Service or the U.S. Customs Service (OMB *Bulletin 97-01*, p. 39). As shown in Illustration 13–7, the Statement of Custodial Activity essentially reports on the agency's fiduciary responsibility to account for how much has been collected and accrued, and how the monies were distributed.

Required Supplemental Information

SFFAS No. 8, "Supplementary Stewardship Reporting," requires that information on *Stewardship Property, Plant, and Equipment* (heritage assets, federal mission PP&E, and stewardship land, described earlier in this chapter) be disclosed to "highlight their long-term-benefit nature and to demonstrate accountability over them" (*SFFAS No. 8*, Summary). OMB *Bulletin 97-01* requires that the costs related to stewardship PP&E be recognized on the face of the Statement of Net

---

Illustration 13–7

DEPARTMENT/AGENCY REPORTING ENTITY
Statement of Custodial Activity
For the years ended September 30, 19xx
(in dollars/thousands/millions)

	19xx	19xx
Sources of Collections:		
Cash collections (by type of tax or duty)	$ xxx	$ xxx
Less refunds and other payments	(xxx)	(xxx)
Net collections	xxx	xxx
Accrual adjustment	xxx	xxx
Total revenue	xxx	xxx
Disposition of Collections:		
Transferred to others net of refunds (by recipient)	xxx	xxx
Increase (decrease) in amounts to be transferred	xxx	xxx
Retained by the entity	xxx	xxx
Total disposition of revenue	xxx	xxx
Net Custodial Activity	$ 0	$ 0

Source: OMB, *Bulletin 97-01*, p. 38.

Costs or be disclosed in the Notes to the Financial Statements. Disclosures are also required about deferred maintenance for both general and stewardship PP&E.

Information about *stewardship investments*, such as the amount of annual investments and description of major programs related to these investments, must also be disclosed. **Stewardship investments** are beneficial investments of the government in such items as nonfederal physical property (property financed by the federal government but owned by state or local governments), human capital, and research and development. In addition, pursuant to applicable federal accounting standards, *Bulletin 97-01* discusses the required disclosures about environmental cleanup costs, detail of budgetary resources and obligations, and incidental amounts of custodial collections and distributions that may not warrant separate reporting in a Statement of Custodial Activity.

Two-Track Accounting System

Financial reports of federal agencies must be based on historical costs to indicate whether an entity has complied with laws and regulations (e.g., 31 U.S.C. 1341). Congressional policy, as expressed in 31 U.S.C. 3512 and the Federal Financial Management Improvement Act of 1996, calls for using cost information in budgeting and in managing operations. This law also provides for using cost-based budgets, at such time as may be determined by the President, in developing requests for appropriations. This law has not been implemented because of deficient cost accounting systems. Federal agencies are struggling to implement SFFAS 4 (see footnote 9) and the Government Performance Review Act, both of which require more cost information than some agencies currently produce. All departments and agencies, therefore, should have budget and accounting systems that have the capability to produce cost-based budgets. In this context, cost is the value of goods and services used or consumed by a government agency within a given period, regardless of when they were ordered, received, or paid for. In any given year, the obligations incurred may be less than, equal to, or greater than the costs recognized for that period, due to changes in inventories, obligations, and so on. At the completion of a program, however, obligations and costs are identical.

The accounting system of a federal agency must provide information needed for financial management as well as information needed to demonstrate that agency managers have complied with budgetary and other legal requirements. Accordingly, federal agency accounting is based on a *two-track system;* one track being a self-balancing set of *proprietary* accounts intended to provide information for agency management, and the other track being the self-balancing set of *budgetary* accounts needed (1) to assure that available budgetary resources and authority are not overexpended or overobligated and (2) to facilitate standardized budgetary reporting requirements. The two-track system is not likely to change in the near future since the FASAB's role specifically excludes budgetary accounting. Illustration 13–8 summarizes key differences between budgetary and proprietary track accounting in terms of the timing of the recognition of events and transactions. The use of the two-track system is illustrated in the next section, "Illustrative Transactions and Entries."

Illustration 13–8	**Summary of Key Differences between Budgetary and Proprietary Accounting in Recognition of Events Which Constitute Transactions**

Budgetary Accounting	*Proprietary Accounting*
Entries are made for commitment of funds in advance of preparing orders to procure goods and services.	Entries are not made for commitments.
Entries are made for obligation of funds at the time goods and services are ordered.	Entries are not made for obligations.
Entries are made to expend appropriations when goods and services chargeable to the appropriation are received, regardless of when they are used and regardless of when they are paid for.	Goods and services that will last more than a year and otherwise meet the criteria to qualify as assets are capitalized and expensed when consumed, regardless of what appropriation funded them and when they are paid for.
Entries are only made against an appropriation for transactions funded by the appropriation.	Goods and services consumed in the current period for which payment is to be made from one or more subsequent appropriations is recognized as an expense in the current period.
Entries are not made against an appropriation for transactions not funded by the appropriation.	Goods and services consumed in the current period but paid for in prior periods are expensed in the current period.

Source: U.S. General Accounting Office, *GAO Accounting Guide: Basic Topics Relating to Appropriations and Reimbursables* (Washington, DC: GAO, 1990), p. 3–2.

Illustrative Transactions and Entries[10]

The basic budgetary authority for a federal agency can come from many different sources. Only one of those sources is illustrated here—basic operating appropriations. The flow of budgetary authority generally follows a sequence of events described as follows:

1. The Congressional **appropriation** is enacted into law and provides budget authority to fund an agency's operations for the year.
2. An **apportionment,** usually quarterly, is approved by the Office of Management and Budget which may be used by the agency to procure goods and services for the quarter.

[10] The illustrative journal entries shown in this section are modeled on the account titles prescribed by the U.S. Government Standard General Ledger, except that we have added fiscal year designations after certain accounts for instructional purposes. The financial statements that follow are based on those specified by OMB *Bulletin No. 97-01.*

3. The head of the agency or his designee authorizes an **allotment** of the apportionment for procurement of goods and services.

4. Authorized agency employees reserve allotted budget authority in the estimated amount of an order as a **commitment** prior to the actual ordering of goods and services.

5. **Obligation** of the allotment occurs when a formal order is placed for acquisition of goods and services, charging the allotment with the latest estimate of the cost of goods or services ordered.

6. An **expended appropriation** occurs when goods or services have been received.

It should be noted that the term *expended appropriation* means the budget authority has been used and is no longer available to provide for goods and services. It does not necessarily mean that cash has been disbursed; it may be that only a liability has been incurred. A *commitment* (item 4 above) does not legally encumber an appropriation, but its use is recommended for effective planning and fund control. Some agencies, however, use commitments only for certain spending categories.[11]

As shown in Illustration 13–9, the full amount of an agency's appropriation for the year is reported as a budgetary resource that, at a given point during the period, is distributed among the budgetary accounts shown under "Status of Resources." As discussed above, and in the following illustrative transactions, budgetary authority normally flows down the accounts, culminating ultimately in the expending of authority.

If the agency whose September 30, 1999, Post-Closing Trial Balance is shown in Illustration 13–10 receives from Congress a one-year appropriation for fiscal year 2000 (FY2000) in the amount of $2,500,000, the Treasury's Bureau of Government Financial Operations would prepare a formal notice to the agency after the appro-

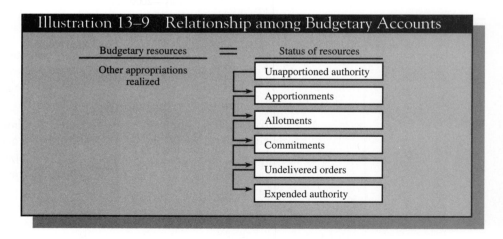

Illustration 13–9   Relationship among Budgetary Accounts

Budgetary resources	=	Status of resources
Other appropriations realized		Unapportioned authority
		Apportionments
		Allotments
		Commitments
		Undelivered orders
		Expended authority

---

[11]For a discussion of these commitments, see U.S. General Accounting Office, *GAO Accounting Guide: Basic Topics Relating to Appropriations and Reimbursables* (Washington, DC: GAO, 1990), p. 2–3.

Illustration 13–10

FEDERAL AGENCY
Post-Closing Trial Balance
As of September 30, 1999

	Debits	Credits
Proprietary Accounts:		
Fund Balance with Treasury—1999	$ 675,000	
Operating Materials and Supplies	610,000	
Equipment	3,000,000	
Accumulated Depreciation on Equipment		$ 600,000
Accounts Payable		275,000
Unexpended Appropriations—1999		400,000
Cumulative Results of Operations		3,010,000
	$4,285,000	$4,285,000
Budgetary Accounts:		
Other Appropriations Realized—1999	$ 400,000	
Undelivered Orders—1999		$ 400,000
	$ 400,000	$ 400,000

---

priation act has been signed by the President. The following entries would be made in the agency accounts:

1a. *Budgetary:*

Other Appropriations Realized—2000	2,500,000	
Unapportioned Authority—2000		2,500,000

1b. *Proprietary:*

Fund Balance with Treasury—2000	2,500,000	
Unexpended Appropriations—2000		2,500,000

The *Other Appropriations Realized* account is used in the U.S. Standard General Ledger to distinguish basic operating appropriations from specific appropriation authority that earmarks appropriations for specific purposes.

When the Office of Management and Budget approves the quarterly apportionment, the agency would be notified. Assuming the OMB approved apportionments of $2,500,000 during FY 2000, the agency would record the apportionments as follows:[12]

2. *Budgetary:*

Unapportioned Authority—2000	2,500,000	
Apportionments—2000		2,500,000

---

[12]OMB ordinarily does not have authority to withhold apportionments. If OMB does withhold a portion of an apportionment, special accounts would be used. This requirement is beyond the overview scope of our coverage here.

If, during FY 2000, the agency head allotted to subunits within the agency the entire apportionment, the event would be recorded in the agency accounts in the following manner:

3. *Budgetary:*
Apportionments—2000 2,500,000
    Allotments—2000 2,500,000

All three entries—for the annual appropriation, for the apportionment by the OMB, and for the agency allotments—would be made as of October 1, the first day of fiscal year 2000, although in some years the appropriation bill might not have been actually enacted by that date. Fiscal year 2000 runs through September 30, 2000. The substance of the three entries is that agency managers had obligational spending authority for the year totaling $2,500,000 to finance agency operations. As discussed in Chapters 3 and 4 for state and local government accounting, federal agencies are legally constrained to manage the activities of the agency so they do not exceed their obligational authority. It should also be noted that if the OMB should withhold any portion of the annual appropriations, that amount would not be available to the agency. Further, for single-year appropriations, any apportionments and allotments not expended or obligated ordinarily must be returned to the U.S. Treasury at the end of the fiscal year.

Operations of the example agency for FY 2000 are summarized in the following journal entries:

Commitments were recorded during FY 2000 in the amount of $1,150,000.

4. *Budgetary:*
Allotments—2000 1,150,000
    Commitments—2000 1,150,000

Purchase orders and contracts for goods and services were issued in the amount of $1,144,000 during the year.

5. *Budgetary:*
Commitments—2000 1,144,000
    Undelivered Orders—2000 1,144,000

Checks for Accounts Payable as of October 1 were requested from the Treasury. The Accounts Payable were for materials received in fiscal year 1999 in the amount of $90,000 and equipment received in the amount of $185,000. This event does not reduce the agency's Fund Balance with Treasury until the checks are actually issued by the Treasury. Instead, most agencies would credit the account *Disbursements in Transit* until notified by the Treasury that the requested checks have been issued. Disbursements in Transit is a current liability account since liabilities to vendors and creditors cannot be considered settled until the checks have actually been issued. If this agency had been one of the few with authority to issue checks directly, then Fund Balance with Treasury would have been credited immediately. Since this agency is not assumed to have check-writing authority, the following entry would be made:

6. *Proprietary:*
Accounts Payable 275,000
    Disbursements in Transit—1999 275,000

The agency received notification from the Treasury that the checks requested in Transaction 6 had been issued. This notification would be recorded as:

7. *Proprietary:*

Disbursements in Transit—1999	275,000	
Fund Balance with Treasury—1999		275,000

Goods and equipment ordered in FY 1999 (prior fiscal year) are reported in Illustration 13–10 in the Net Position account, Unexpended Appropriations—1999, a proprietary account, as amounting to $400,000. A budgetary account Undelivered Orders—1999 also exists in the same amount, as does its offsetting account Other Appropriations Realized—1999. (All other budgetary accounts for 1999 were closed at the end of that fiscal year because all unobligated appropriation authority expired at year-end.) Assuming all the goods and equipment ordered in 1999 were received during the first quarter of FY 2000, one entry is necessary in the budgetary accounts to show that fiscal 1999 obligations are now liquidated and that the prior-year appropriation is expended in the same amount. Entries in proprietary accounts are required to record the debit to Unexpended Appropriations—1999 and the offsetting credit to the Appropriations Used account,[13] and debits to asset accounts and a credit to Accounts Payable. These entries are:

8a. *Budgetary:*

Undelivered Orders—1999	400,000	
Expended Authority—1999		400,000

8b. *Proprietary:*

Operating Materials and Supplies	150,000	
Equipment	250,000	
Accounts Payable		400,000
Unexpended Appropriations—1999	400,000	
Appropriations Used		400,000

Operating materials and supplies were received from suppliers during FY 2000 at an actual cost of $1,010,000, for which Undelivered Orders—2000 had been recorded in the estimated amount of $1,005,000. Budgetary track and proprietary track entries for these transactions are shown in Entries 9a and 9b. Because the actual cost of materials and supplies exceeded the estimated amount recorded previously as Undelivered Orders—2000, the $5,000 excess must be debited to Allotments—2000 to record the additional expenditure of obligational authority.

9a. *Budgetary:*

Undelivered Orders—2000	1,005,000	
Allotments—2000	5,000	
Expended Authority—2000		1,010,000

9b. *Proprietary:*

Operating Materials and Supplies	1,010,000	
Accounts Payable		1,010,000

---

[13]Until FY 1998, such capitalized amounts would have been reported in Invested Capital. These amounts, as well as the net effects of operations, are now reported in the net position account, Cumulative Results of Operations, the account to which Appropriations Used is closed at fiscal year-end. Use of the Invested Capital account has been discontinued.

Unexpended Appropriations—2000	1,010,000	
Appropriations Used		1,010,000

Payrolls for FY 2000 amounted to $1,188,000. Utilities in the amount of $120,000 were also approved for payment during the year. (The agency does not record commitments for payrolls and other recurring operating expenses.) Checks totaling $1,308,000 were requested from the Treasury for these expenses. The debit in the first proprietary track entry is to the control account Operating/Program Expenses. Obviously, each agency would have a subsidiary expense ledger or more detailed expense accounts in their general ledger tailored to its specific needs. The required entries are:

10a. *Budgetary:*

Allotments—2000	1,308,000	
Expended Authority—2000		1,308,000

10b. *Proprietary:*

Operating/Program Expenses	1,308,000	
Disbursements in Transit—2000		1,308,000
Unexpended Appropriations—2000	1,308,000	
Appropriations Used		1,308,000

Materials and supplies used in the operating activities during FY 2000 amounted to $1,620,000. The entries would be:

11. *Proprietary:*

Operating/Program Expenses	1,620,000	
Operating Materials and Supplies		1,620,000

Accounts Payable in the amount of $1,410,000 (see Entries 8b and 9b) were approved for payment and checks were requested from the Treasury. Of this amount, $400,000 will be charged against the FY 1999 Fund Balance with Treasury and $1,010,000 against the FY 2000 Fund Balance with Treasury. The required entry is:

12. *Proprietary:*

Accounts Payable	1,410,000	
Disbursements in Transit—1999		400,000
Disbursements in Transit—2000		1,010,000

The agency was notified by the Treasury that checks in the amount of $2,718,000 (including $400,000 for Accounts Payable arising from fiscal 1999—see Entry 12) had been issued during FY 2000. Of the $2,318,000 charged against the FY 2000 Fund Balance with Treasury, $1,010,000 was for operating materials and supplies (see Entry 9b), $1,188,000 was for payrolls, and $120,000 was for utilities expense.

13. *Proprietary:*

Disbursements in Transit—1999	400,000	
Disbursements in Transit—2000	2,318,000	
Fund Balance with Treasury—1999		400,000
Fund Balance with Treasury—2000		2,318,000

Adjusting Entries   In order to prepare accrual-based financial statements, the following items were taken into account: (1) payroll accrued for the last week of the fiscal year is computed to be $27,000 and (2) invoices or receiving reports for goods received, but for which payment has not yet been approved, totaled $105,000, of which $36,000 worth has been used in operations and $69,000 is in ending inventory. Because the obligations for the items in (1) and (2) have become certain in amount and relevant expense accounts or inventory accounts can be charged, as illustrated below, the amounts should be shown in the financial statements as current liabilities. It is assumed that the goods received had been previously obligated in the amount of $105,000, but no commitment or obligation had been recorded for the accrued payroll. The required entries are:

14a. *Budgetary:*

Allotments—2000	27,000	
Undelivered Orders—2000	105,000	
Expended Authority—2000		132,000

14b. *Proprietary:*

Operating/Program Expenses	63,000	
Operating Materials and Supplies	69,000	
Accounts Payable		105,000
Accrued Funded Payroll and Benefits		27,000
Unexpended Appropriations—2000	132,000	
Appropriations Used		132,000

Depreciation of equipment was computed as $300,000 for FY 2000. Inasmuch as depreciation is not an expense chargeable against the appropriation, the accrual of depreciation expense does not affect any of the appropriation, allotment, or obligation accounts. However, it is recorded as in business accounting to measure the cost of activities on an accrual basis. The debit to Accumulated Depreciation reduces the book value of the equipment.

15. *Proprietary:*

Depreciation and Amortization	300,000	
Accumulated Depreciation on Equipment		300,000

Although not illustrated here, federal agencies also accrue some expenses such as accrued annual leave that will be funded by future-period appropriations. These unfunded accrued expenses require entries in the proprietary track, but require no entries in the budgetary track. The effect of these unfunded expenses is to reduce the balance of Cumulative Results of Operations since the expenses are not offset by a financing source.

Illustrative Financial Statements

After entries illustrated above have been made, the federal agency Balance Sheet at the end of fiscal year 2000 and the other required statements can be prepared. As discussed earlier in this chapter, OMB *Bulletin 97-01* prescribes the form and content of financial statements required to be prepared under the Chief Financial Officers (CFO) Act of 1990 and the Federal Financial Management Improvement Act of 1996 by most executive agencies and departments. The content of each agency's *annual financial statement* and examples of the basic financial statements were provided as Illustrations 13–2 through 13–7, earlier in this chapter.

Basic financial statements are shown in Illustrations 13–12 through 13–15 for the simple federal agency whose transactions were just discussed. These statements are a Balance Sheet, Statement of Changes in Net Position, Statement of Budgetary Resources, and a Statement of Financing. Since the example federal agency used in this chapter had no material custodial activities, no Statement of Custodial Activities is needed. Also, no supplemental financial and management information are provided. In the case of an actual federal entity, such as the Department of Defense, for example, there would be numerous funds, programs, and organizational units, and thus a need for consolidating and consolidated financial statements, as well as required supplemental information.

Prior to preparing the illustrative financial statements, as of and for the fiscal year ended September 30, 2000, lapsed budgetary authority should be closed and a pre-closing general ledger trial balance should be prepared such as that presented in Illustration 13–11. Note that it is standard practice to prepare the U.S. Standard General Ledger

Illustration 13–11

FEDERAL AGENCY
Pre-Closing Trial Balance
As of September 30, 2000

	Debits	Credits
Proprietary Accounts:		
Fund Balance with Treasury—2000	$ 166,000	
Operating Materials and Supplies	219,000	
Equipment	3,250,000	
Accumulated Depreciation on Equipment		$ 900,000
Disbursements in Transit—2000		0
Accounts Payable		105,000
Accrued Funded Payroll and Benefits		27,000
Unexpended Appropriations—2000		34,000
Cumulative Results of Operations		3,010,000
Appropriations Used—1999		400,000
Appropriations Used—2000		2,450,000
Operating/Program Expenses	2,991,000	
Depreciation and Amortization	300,000	
	$6,926,000	$6,926,000
Budgetary Accounts:		
Appropriations Realized But Withdrawn—2000	$16,000	
Other Appropriations Realized—2000	34,000	
Unapportioned Authority—2000	0	
Apportionments—2000	0	
Allotments—2000		$ 0
Commitments—2000		0
Undelivered Orders—2000		34,000
Restorations, Writeoffs, and Withdrawals—2000		16,000
	$ 50,000	$ 50,000

pre-closing trial balance after the expended and withdrawn budgetary authority accounts have been closed, but before the other temporary proprietary accounts are closed. Closing of expended and withdrawn budgetary authority is discussed below.

Total credits to the Expended Authority—2000 account (Entries 9a, 10a, and 14a) amounted to $2,450,000. Thus, the total *unexpended* budgetary authority at the end of FY 2000 is $50,000 ($2,500,000 − $2,450,000). Of the $50,000 unexpended amount, $34,000 is *reserved* in the Undelivered Orders—2000 for goods or services still on order at year-end. However, the $6,000 balance in Commitments—2000 and $10,000 in Allotments—2000 have not been reserved and must be returned to Treasury. The following journal entries are needed to record the lapse of obligational authority for the $16,000 not obligated or reserved by fiscal year-end. As the first entry in Entry 16a shows, unused commitments and allotments (as well as apportionments if there had been a year-end balance) are closed to Other Appropriations Realized—2000, as is the amount of appropriations that was expended. In addition, the $400,000 balance in Expended Authority—1999 is closed to Other Appropriations Realized—1999, which also has a $400,000 balance prior to closing. In order to establish a record of withdrawn appropriations, the second budgetary entry shown below should also be made. In addition, temporary proprietary accounts would be closed as shown in 16b.

16a. *Budgetary:*

Commitments—2000	6,000	
Allotments—2000	10,000	
Expended Authority—1999	400,000	
Expended Authority—2000	2,450,000	
Other Appropriations Realized—1999		400,000
Other Appropriations Realized—2000		2,466,000
Appropriations Realized But Withdrawn—2000	16,000	
Restorations, Write-Offs, and Withdrawals—2000		16,000

16b. *Proprietary:*

Unexpended Appropriations—2000	16,000	
Fund Balance with Treasury—2000		16,000

Accounting procedures also exist to reverse the second entry under Entry 16a to the extent the actual cost of goods or services received early in FY 2001 exceeds the $34,000 estimated in Undelivered Orders. Essentially, a portion of the budgetary authority that was withdrawn in Entry 16a would be *restored* in this case. These accounting procedures are well beyond the scope of the limited coverage presented in this chapter. (For additional information, see the source cited in footnote 8.)

Temporary proprietary accounts should be closed to update the Net Position accounts so the end-of-period balance sheet can be prepared. The necessary closing entry would be:

17. *Proprietary:*

Appropriations Used	2,850,000	
Cumulative Results of Operations	441,000	
Operating/Program Expenses		2,991,000
Depreciation and Amortization		300,000

The balance sheet for the example federal agency whose pre-closing trial balance is shown in Illustration 13–11 is presented in Illustration 13–12. In more complex agencies, a consolidated balance sheet like the one shown in Illustration 13–2 is usually prepared. The example federal agency is assumed to have only entity assets (those that can be used for the agency's operations) and, except for Fund Balance with Treasury, the remaining assets are governmental. All liabilities (Accounts Payable and Accrued Funded Payroll and Benefits) are assumed to be governmental. Further, all liabilities are covered by budgetary resources. As discussed earlier in this chapter, the *net position* consists of only two items, unexpended appropriations ($34,000 reserved for goods and services on order at year-end) and Cumulative Results of Operations.

A Consolidating Statement of Net Cost for a major federal agency was presented in Illustration 13–3. Because the federal agency used in our example is assumed to have a simple organizational structure and no earned revenues, its Statement of Net Cost would be very simple; net cost would be the same as gross cost. Moreover, since the agency's net suborganization or program costs are

Illustration 13–12

FEDERAL AGENCY
Balance Sheet
As of September 30, 2000

Assets

Entity Assets:	
Intragovernmental:	
Fund Balance with Treasury	$ 166,000
Governmental:	
Operating materials and supplies	219,000
Equipment (net of accumulated depreciation of $900,000)	2,350,000
Total Entity Assets	$2,735,000

Liabilities

Liabilities Covered by Budgetary Resources:	
Governmental liabilities:	
Accounts payable	$ 105,000
Accrued funded payroll and benefits	27,000
Total Liabilities Covered by Budgetary Resources	132,000

Net Position

Unexpended Appropriations	34,000
Cumulative Results of Operations	2,569,000
Total Net Position	2,603,000
Total Liabilities and Net Position	$2,735,000

Illustration 13–13

FEDERAL AGENCY
Statement of Changes in Net Position
For the year ended September 30, 2000

	Suborganization A	Suborganization B	Consolidated Totals
Net Cost of Operations (Note A)	$1,316,400	$1,974,600	$3,291,000
Financing Sources:			
Appropriations Used	1,140,000	1,710,000	2,850,000
Net Results from Operations	(176,400)	(264,600)	(441,000)
Prior-Period Adjustments	0	0	0
Net Change In Cumulative Results of Operations	(176,400)	(264,600)	(441,000)
Decrease in Unexpended Appropriations	(146,400)	(219,600)	(366,000)
Change in Net Position	(322,800)	(484,200)	(807,000)
Net Position—Beginning of Year	1,364,000	2,046,000	3,410,000
Net Position—End of Year	$1,041,200	$1,561,800	$2,603,000

Note A: These amounts are taken from the bottom line of the Statement of Net Costs, which is not included here for sake of brevity.

reported on the first line of the Statement of Changes in Net Position presented in Illustration 13–13, a Statement of Net Cost would convey little additional information. Therefore, we do not include one here.

For illustrative purposes, the agency whose Statement of Changes in Net Position is shown in Illustration 13–13, is assumed to have two suborganizations, A and B, and there are no interorganization transactions that require eliminations. Further, 40 percent of total net cost is assigned to suborganization A and 60 percent to B. Since the only financing source for this agency is annual appropriations, the Statement of Changes in Net Position is quite simple, but informative nonetheless.

The example federal agency would also have to prepare a Statement of Budgetary Resources (see Illustration 13–14). The astute reader will note that the equation applicable to this statement is Budgetary resources = Status of budgetary resources. Budgetary resources in this case is $2,884,000, consisting of current-year appropriations of $2,500,000 less expired appropriations of $16,000, plus $400,000 carried forward from prior-year appropriations to cover undelivered orders at the end of the prior year. Since there are no unobligated appropriations that can be carried forward at year-end, the *status of budgetary resources* in this case is simply the amount of budgetary resources expended ($2,850,000) plus $34,000 obligated for goods on order at the end of FY 2000 that had not yet been expended. Outlays are reported in the bottom section of the Statement of Budgetary Resources and are the same as the total amount expended during the year, or $2,850,000 ($2,450,000

Illustration 13-14

FEDERAL AGENCY
Statement of Budgetary Resources
For the year ended September 30, 2000 (Note A)

Budgetary resources:	
Budgetary authority (Note B)	$2,484,000
Status of Budgetary Resources:	
Obligations incurred (Note C)	$2,484,000
Total status of budgetary resources	$2,484,000
Outlays:	
Obligations incurred (Note C)	$2,484,000
Obligated balance, net—beginning of period	400,000
Less obligated balance, net—end of year	(34,000)
Total outlays	$2,850,000

Note A: Comparative totals should also be presented for the prior year. Those totals are omitted in this example.
Note B: Total budgetary resources were $2,500,000 appropriation, less $16,000 of expired appropriation at year-end.
Note C: Expended authority of current year of $2,450,000, plus $34,000 obligated budgetary authority for undelivered goods at year-end.

chargeable to the current-year appropriation and $400,000 chargeable to the prior-year appropriation).

The final statement presented for the simple federal agency illustrated in this chapter is the Statement of Financing (see Illustration 13–15). This statement is intended to reconcile the budgetary basis expenditure or obligation of budgetary resources (obligations incurred) with the accrual basis net cost of operations. As shown in Illustration 13–15, there are certain resources that affect budgetary resources but do not affect the net cost of operations. These include the net change in the amount of goods, services, or benefits ordered (in this case, the change in Undelivered Orders from the beginning to the end of the year) and the net change in assets capitalized on the balance sheet. As explained in Note C to the statement, $250,000 of equipment purchases were capitalized during the year, but the balance of Operating Materials and Supplies decreased by $391,000, resulting in a net decrease in capitalized assets of $141,000. The lower section of the statement shows an addition for depreciation expense, since it had not been included in obligations incurred but is a part of the net cost of operations.

Summary of Accounting and Reporting for Federal Government Agencies

Illustration 13–16 provides a summary comparison of budgetary and proprietary accounting procedures for state and local governments as compared with federal

Illustration 13–15

FEDERAL AGENCY
Statement of Financing
For the year ended September 30, 2000

Obligations and Nonbudgetary Resources:	
Obligations incurred (Note A)	$2,484,000
Resources That Fund Net Cost of Operations:	
Change in amount of goods, services, and benefits ordered but not yet received or provided (Note B)	366,000
Costs capitalized on the balance sheet (Note C)	141,000
Total Resources That Fund Net Cost of Operations	507,000
Costs That Do Not Require Resources:	
Depreciation and amortization	300,000
Net Cost of Operations	$3,291,000

Note A: Obligations incurred consist of $2,450,000 expended from the FY 2000 appropriation plus $34,000 obligated for goods on order at the end of FY 2000.
Note B: The change in goods and services on order is a decrease of $366,000 ($400,000 − $34,000).
Note C: Equipment acquisition capitalized at $250,000 minus a net decrease in operating materials and supplies of $391,000. Thus, there was a net *decrease* in capitalization of $141,000, so this amount should be added in reconciling the use of budgetary resources to the net cost of operations.

agencies. Although some similarities exist, there are areas specific to each level of government. As shown in Illustration 13–16, state and local governments do not account for apportionments and most do not account for allotments. Federal agency accounting takes into consideration certain accruals (supplies used and depreciation) generally ignored in state and local government accounting, although as mentioned in several earlier chapters, changes in the reporting model being considered by the GASB may lead to greater use of accrual accounting by state and local governments.

The head of each agency in the executive branch of the federal government has the statutory responsibility for the establishment and maintenance of systems of accounting and internal control in conformity with principles, standards, and requirements established by the Comptroller General, the Secretary of the Treasury, and the Director of the OMB. Federal agency accounting is directed at providing information for intelligent financial management of agency activities and programs to the end they may be operated with efficiency and economy, as well as providing evidence of adherence to legal requirements. As emphasized by the headings of Illustration 13–16, and by the discussions in earlier chapters, accounting for governmental funds is presently focused on legal compliance. The focus of federal agency accounting, in contrast, is broadened to include information needed for the management of agency resources (the *proprietary* track) as well as for compliance with fund control requirements (the *budgetary* track).

Illustration 13–16 Comparison of Accounting for State and Local Governmental Fund Types and Accounting for Federal Agencies (journal entries)

Item	State and Local Government Funds Compliance Track Only	Federal Agency	
		Budgetary Track	Proprietary Track
1. Passage of appropriations (and for state and local governments, revenue) bills	Estimated Revenues Appropriations Fund Balance	Other Appropriations Realized Unapportioned Authority	Fund Balance with Treasury Unexpended Appropriations
2. Revenues accrued (at expected collectible amount)	Taxes Receivable Estimated Uncollectible Taxes Revenues	No equivalent for taxes; user charges, if any, recognized as billed	No entry*
3. Apportionment by OMB	No equivalent	Unapportioned Authority Apportionments	No entry
4. Allotment by agency head	No equivalent†	Apportionments Allotments	No entry
5. Budget authority reserved prior to ordering goods or services	No equivalent	Allotments Commitments	No entry
6. Goods or services ordered	Encumbrances Reserve for Encumbrances	Commitments Undelivered Orders‡	No entry
7. Goods or services received	Reserve for Encumbrances Encumbrances Expenditures Accounts Payable	Undelivered Orders Expended Authority	Expense or asset account Accounts Payable Unexpended Appropriations Appropriations Used
8. Liability paid (expenditure recorded in 7 above)	Accounts Payable Cash	No entry	Accounts Payable Fund Balance with Treasury§

9. Supplies used	No entry	No entry	Operating/Program Expenses Inventory for Agency Operations
10. Physical inventory (consumption method assumed for state and local governments)	Inventory Expenditures Fund Balance Reserve for Inventory	No entry	Entry for (7) assumes perpetual inventory; would need entry for (10) if physical inventory and book inventory differed
11. Depreciation computed	No entry (computation used for cost reimbursements and management information)	No entry (Not an expenditure of appropriations; will never require a check to be drawn on U.S. Treasury)	Depreciation and Amortization Accumulated Depreciation (on general property, plant, and equipment, but not certain military assets and stewardship assets)
12. Closing entries	Appropriations Revenues Estimated Revenues Encumbrances Expenditures Fund Balance	Expended Authority Other Appropriations Realized; (Also must close any budgetary accounts associated with expired budget authority)	Cumulative Results of Operations Operating/Program Expenses Appropriations Used Cumulative Results of Operations

* Prototype consolidated financial statements of federal government do include an accrual for taxes, fines, and other revenue categories.

† As discussed in Chapter 3, some local governmental units utilize allotment accounting. In such cases, the credit in Entry 1 would be to Unallotted Appropriations, and an Entry 4 would be necessary to record the debit to that account and the credit to Allotments.

‡ As illustrated by Entry 4 earlier in this chapter, and by entry 5, some agencies opt to use the interim account Commitments to improve planning for procurement of goods and services. If commitments are not recorded in advance of placing orders the debit for the budgetary track would be "Allotments."

§ As indicated in this chapter, the account credited here might be Disbursements in Transit rather than Fund Balance with Treasury.

Key Terms

Allotment,   528
Apportionment,   527
Appropriation,   527
Budget accounts,   511
Budgetary resources,   522
Commitment,   528
Cumulative results of operations,   520
Entity assets,   515
Expended appropriation (authority),   528
Federal Accounting Standards Advisory
   Board (FASAB),   508
Federal Financial Management
   Improvement Act,   504
Federal mission property, plant, and
   equipment,   518

General property, plant, and equipment,
   518
Governmental assets (liabilities),   516
Heritage assets,   518
Intragovernmental assets (liabilities),   516
Net position,   520
Nonentity assets,   515
Obligation,   528
Stewardship investments,   526
Stewardship land,   518
Stewardship property, plant, and
   equipment,   518
Unexpended appropriations,   520

Selected References

General Accounting Office. *Accounting Guide: Basic Topics Relating to Appropriations and Reimbursables.* 1990.
Office of Management and Budget. *U.S. Government Standard General Ledger,* 1997.
———. *Bulletin 97-01,* "Form and Content of Agency Financial Statements." 1996.
———. *Circular A-134,* "Financial Accounting Principles and Standards." 1993.

Questions

13–1. Identify which of the following are part of the legislative branch of the federal government and which are part of the executive branch:

  a. Secretary of the Treasury.
  b. Director of the Office of Management and Budget.
  c. Director of the Congressional Budget Office.
  d. Comptroller General.

13–2. Describe the institutional framework for establishing accounting and financial reporting standards for the federal government.

13–3. Discuss the conceptual framework of accounting for federal agencies and compare it to the conceptual framework established by the GASB for state and local governments.

13–4. What are the objectives of financial reporting identified in *Statement of Federal Financial Accounting Concepts No. 1*?

13–5. Describe the criteria developed in *Statement of Federal Financial Accounting Concepts No. 2* for defining the federal reporting entity.

13–6. Describe the two-track system used in federal agency accounting.

13–7. Identify the budgetary accounts used in federal agency accounting and explain the sequential flow of budgetary authority through the accounts.

13–8. Distinguish between a commitment and an obligation in budgetary track accounting for a federal agency.

13–9. What accounts are used to describe the net position of a federal agency?

13–10. Name the financial statements that should be prepared for each federal agency in conformity with OMB *Bulletin 97-1*.

Cases

13–1. **Internet Case** The Consolidated Statement of Financial Position and Consolidated Statement of Operations for the U.S. Department of Transportation are provided on the following pages. After reading and evaluating these financial statements, use the Internet to answer the following questions or provide the requested information. [You may wish to access the Department of Transportation's Internet homepage at http://www.dot.gov/, then at that site locate a link to "Budget and Financial." The specific homepage for the Department's 1996 Consolidated Financial Statements was http://ostpxweb.dot.gov/budget/cfs.htm. Because this information may change over time, you may need to navigate the Department's homepage as necessary to find the required information.]

   a. What organizations comprise the Department of Transportation reporting entity?

   b. Were these consolidated financial statements prepared in conformity with FASAB and OMB guidance applicable in FY 1996?

   c. How does the Net Position section of the Statement of Financial Position compare with the Net Position section of the balance sheet required by OMB *Bulletin 97-01*, as shown in Illustration 13–2 and as discussed in this chapter?

   d. What amount of operations was funded by appropriations during FY 1996?

   e. Referring to the Statement of Operations, does the fact that total expenses exceeded revenues and financing sources by slightly over $1.3 billion indicate unlawful activity or lack of budget compliance for the year?

13–2. **Internet Case** At the cutoff date for publication of this edition of the text, nine Statements of Federal Financial Accounting Standards (SFFASs) had been issued. In addition, as of the cutoff date, OMB *Bulletin 97-01* provided authoritative guidance for the form and content of federal agency financial statements.

Required

Using the Internet [we recommend you search FASAB and OMB links from http://www.financenet.gov], determine if:

   a. There have been any additional SFFACs issued. If so, list them by name and provide their effective date.

   b. Has the OMB replaced *Bulletin 97-01* with a later Bulletin? If so, how do the financial statements required by the later Bulletin compare to those required by *Bulletin 97-01*, as described and illustrated in Chapter 13? [Note: The preceding OMB *Bulletin* on form and content of agency financial statements was OMB *Bulletin 94-01*. Thus, the OMB may not intend to make frequent changes in its reporting guidance.]

U.S. DEPARTMENT OF TRANSPORTATION
Consolidated Statement of Financial Position
As of September 30, 1996
(Dollars in thousands)

	1996 Total
Assets	
Entity Assets:	
Intragovernmental Assets:	
Fund Balance with Treasury (Note 2)	$10,551,357
Investments (Note 3)	30,200,289
Accounts Receivable, Net (Note 4)	388,075
Interest Receivable	412,128
Advances and Prepayments	40,100
Other (Note 5)	223,072
Governmental Assets:	
Investments (Note 3)	27
Accounts Receivable, Net (Note 4)	70,183
Credit Program Receivables and Related Foreclosed Property, Net (Note 6)	143,107
Interest Receivable	249
Advances and Prepayments	197,875
Other (Note 5)	1,004
Cash and Other Monetary Assets	10,926
Inventory, Net (Note 7)	46,795
Operating Materials and Supplies, Net (Note 8)	1,366,426
Property and Equipment, Net (Note 9)	24,342,033
Total Entity Assets	67,993,656
Nonentity Assets:	
Intragovernmental Assets:	
Fund Balance with Treasury (Note 2)	(4,735)
Other (Note 5)	13,781
Governmental Assets:	
Accounts Receivable, Net (Note 4)	18,663
Total Nonentity Assets	27,709
Total Assets	$68,021,365

	1996 Total
Liabilities	
Liabilities Covered by Budgetary Resources:	
Intragovernmental Liabilities:	
Accounts Payable	$ 177,311
Debt (Note 10)	129,105
Other (Note 11)	313,104
Governmental Liabilities:	
Accounts Payable	1,315,696
Liabilities for Loan Guarantees (Note 12)	80,068
Other (Note 11)	376,830
Total Liabilities Covered by Budgetary Resources	2,392,114
Liabilities Not Covered by Budgetary Resources:	
Intragovernmental Liabilities:	
Debt (Note 10)	21
Other (Note 11)	301,035
Governmental Liabilities:	
Lease Liabilities (Note 12)	110,989
Pensions and Other Actuarial Liabilities (Note 13)	18,704,672
Other (Note 11)	35,013,554
Total Liabilities Not Covered by Budgetary Resources	54,130,271
Total Liabilities	$56,522,385
Net Position (Note 14)	
Balances:	
Unexpended Appropriations	$13,675,298
Invested Capital	27,964,391
Cumulative Results of Operations	24,099,251
Other	(109,689)
Future Funding Requirements	(54,130,271)
Total Net Position	11,498,980
Total Liabilities and Net Position	$68,021,365

[Notes not provided here]

U.S. DEPARTMENT OF TRANSPORTATION
Consolidated Statement of Operations
For the Period Ended September 30, 1996
(Dollars in thousands)

	1996 Total
Revenues and Financing Sources:	
Appropriated Capital Used	$ 38,914,060
Revenues from Sales of Goods and Services:	
To the Public	1,338,881
Intragovermental	1,048,870
Interest and Penalties, Nonfederal	59,072
Interest, Federal	2,108,675
Taxes (Note 15)	27,056,763
Other Revenues and Financing Sources (Note 16)	1,084,218
Less: Taxes and Receipts Transferred to the Treasury or Other Agencies	(30,030,224)
Total Revenues and Financing Sources	41,580,315
Expenses:	
Program or Operating Expenses (Note 17)	41,142,980
Cost of Goods Sold:	
To the Public	11,123
Intragovernmental	778,312
Depreciation and Amortization	22,638
Bad Debts and Writeoffs	33,610
Interest:	
Federal Financing Bank/Treasury Borrowing	3,240
Other	7,637
Other Expenses (Note 18)	820,277
Total Expenses	42,819,817
Excess (Shortage) of Revenues and Financing Sources over Total Expenses before Extraordinary Items	(1,239,502)
Plus (Minus) Extraordinary Items (Note 19)	(61,141)
Excess (Shortage) of Revenues and Financing Sources over Total Expenses	(1,300,643)
Change in Net Position:	
Net Position, Beginning Balance, as Previously Stated	53,162,694
Adjustments (Note 19)	(4,240,061)
Net Position, Beginning Balance, as Restated	48,922,633
Excess (Shortage) of Revenues and Financing Sources over Total Expenses	(1,300,643)
Plus (Minus) Nonoperating Changes (Note 20)	(36,123,010)
Net Position, Ending Balance	$ 11,498,980

[Notes not provided here]

Exercises and Problems

13–1. Write the numbers 1 through 10 on a sheet of paper. Beside each number write the letter corresponding with the best answer to each of the following questions.

1. Federal statutes assign responsibility for establishing and maintaining a sound financial structure for the federal government to the:
   a. Comptroller General.
   b. Director of the OMB.
   c. Secretary of the Treasury.
   d. All of the above.

2. Which of the following is a true statement about the process of setting accounting standards for the federal government?
   a. The FASAB authorizes the issuance of accounting standards.
   b. The FASAB recommends accounting standards.
   c. The GASB has primary responsibility for issuing federal government accounting standards; the FASAB has secondary responsibility for federal standards.
   d. Each federal agency is responsible for setting its own accounting standards; those standards take precedence over standards developed by the FASAB.

3. In the GAAP hierarchy for federal agency accounting and financial reporting, the highest level GAAP is (are):
   a. The *Treasury Financial Manual*.
   b. Interpretations of the U.S. General Accounting Office.
   c. Statements of Federal Financial Accounting Standards (SFFASs).
   d. OMB *Bulletin 97-01*, "Form and Content of Agency Financial Statements."

4. Which of the following is *not* one of the principals of the Joint Financial Management Improvement Project?
   a. Executive Director of the FASAB.
   b. Comptroller General.
   c. Director of the OMB.
   d. Secretary of the Treasury.

5. Which of the following is *not* an objective of federal financial reporting?
   a. Assist report users in evaluating budgetary integrity.
   b. Assist report users in evaluating operating performance.
   c. Assist report users in evaluating the reliability of financial information.
   d. Assist report users in evaluating stewardship.

6. When closing entries are made, the Cumulative Results of Operations account will be decreased by which of the following transactions or events that occurred during the year?
   a. Expiration of budget authority.
   b. Purchase of property, plant, and equipment.
   c. Depreciation of property, plant, and equipment.
   d. Both *b* and *c*.

7. Assuming that an agency's unused appropriations expire at year-end, but appropriations continue in effect for obligated amounts (purchase orders, etc.), which of the following budgetary accounts would likely be found in the agency's post-closing trial balance at year-end?

    a. Commitments and Other Appropriations Realized.

    b. Expended Authority and Undelivered Orders.

    c. Commitments and Undelivered Orders.

    d. Undelivered Orders and Other Appropriations Realized.

8. Which of the following is a correct mathematical relationship among proprietary account balances?

    a. Fund Balance with Treasury equals Unexpended Appropriations.

    b. Net Position equals Total Assets minus Total Liabilities.

    c. Cumulative Results of Operations equals Revenues and Financing Sources minus Operating/Program Expenses.

    d. Disbursements in Transit equals Fund Balance with Treasury minus Accounts Payable and Other Current Liabilities.

9. Which of the following is *not* a component of the changes in net position reported in a federal agency's annual Statement of Changes in Net Position?

    a. Appropriations used during the period.

    b. Change in Cumulative Results of Operations.

    c. Prior-period adjustments.

    d. Commitments.

10. In a Statement of Budgetary Resources prepared in conformity with OMB *Bulletin 97-01*, the amount shown for Total Outlays in the lower section of the statement represents the amount of:

    a. Expended budgetary authority for the current period.

    b. Expenditures accrued but unpaid at the end of the period.

    c. Amount of cash paid for all purposes during the period.

    d. Total reduction in Fund Balance with Treasury during the period.

13–2. One amount is missing in the following trial balance of proprietary accounts and one amount is missing from the trial balance of budgetary accounts of a certain agency of the federal government. The debits are not distinguished from the credits.

Required

a. Compute each missing amount in the pre-closing trial balance below.

FEDERAL AGENCY
Pre-Closing Trial Balance
September 30, 1999

Proprietary Accounts:

Accounts Payable	$ 300,000
Accumulated Depreciation—Plant and Equipment	2,600,000
Appropriations Used	4,000,000
Fund Balance with Treasury—1999	?
Operating Materials and Supplies	1,000,000
Cumulative Results of Operations—10/1/98	6,600,000
Operating/Program Expenses	3,150,000
Depreciation and Amortization	150,000
Plant and Equipment	8,900,000
Unexpended Appropriations—1999	1,500,000

Budgetary Accounts:

Other Appropriations Realized—1999	?
Expended Authority—1999	4,000,000
Undelivered Orders—1999	1,500,000

        b. Compute the net additions to assets other than Fund Balance with Treasury during fiscal year 1999. Clearly label your computations and show all work in good form.

13–3. Using the data from Problem 13–2:

        a. Prepare in general journal form entries to close the budgetary accounts as needed, and to close the operating statement proprietary accounts.

        b. Prepare in good form a Balance Sheet for the Federal Agency as of September 30, 1999. [Note: Assume that all assets are *entity assets*, Fund Balance with Treasury is an *intragovernmental asset*, and all other assets are *governmental*. Assume also that all liabilities are covered by budgetary resources.]

        c. Prepare in good form a Statement of Changes in Net Position of the Federal Agency for the year ended September 30, 1999, assuming Unexpended Appropriations, as of October 1, 1998, amounted to $1,300,000, and that there are no material suborganizations or programs to be separately reported.

13–4. The Balance Sheet for the Rural Assistance Agency of the federal government for the year ended September 30, 1999 is provided as follows:

RURAL ASSISTANCE AGENCY
Balance Sheet
As of September 30, 1999
(thousands)

Assets

Entity Assets:	
Intragovernmental:	
Fund Balance with Treasury	$2,164
Governmental:	
Property, plant, and equipment, net of	
accumulated depreciation of $1,790	6,835
Operating materials and supplies	325
Total Assets	$9,324

Liabilities

Liabilities Covered by Budgetary Resources:	
Accounts payable	$240
Accrued funded payroll and benefits	55
Total Liabilities Covered by Budgetary Resources	295
Liabilities Not Covered by Budgetary Resources:	
Accrued unfunded liabilities	340
Total Liabilities	635

Net Position

Unexpended Appropriations	1,869
Cumulative results of operations	6,820
Total Net Position	8,689
Total Liabilities and Net Position	$9,324

Additional Information:

1. Total Appropriations for the fiscal year ending September 30, 2000, totaled $15,513,000.
2. Accounts Payable reported on the Balance Sheet as of September 30, 1999, in the amount of $240,000 were paid early in fiscal year 2000.
3. Materials and supplies ordered in fiscal 1999 were received in early fiscal year 2000 in the amount of $1,869,000, the same amount as reported for Unexpended Appropriations on the Balance Sheet as of September 30, 1999. All materials and supplies are credited to Accounts Payable upon receipt.
4. Additional materials and supplies were ordered and received during fiscal year 2000 in the amount of $2,050,000. Property, Plant, and Equipment in the amount of $400,000 was also purchased during fiscal year 2000. Upon the agency's request the Treasury paid $400,000 for the Property, Plant, and Equipment. (Note: The $2,050,000 for purchases of materials and supplies was credited to Accounts Payable.)
5. Operating/program expenses for fiscal year 2000 totaled $15,076,000. This amount excluded depreciation expense of $450,000 on Property, Plant, and Equipment, but included accruals at fiscal year-end in the amounts of $60,000 for accrued payroll and benefits and $10,000 for accrued annual leave. [Credit Accrued Unfunded Liabilities for the accrued leave. Note that accrued annual leave is unfunded and therefore does not reduce the balance of Unexpended Appropriations nor does it increase Appropriations Used. The total FY 2000 appropriations used amounted to $11,162,000: $15,076,000 for FY 2000 expenses minus $3,904,000 of materials and supplies consumed minus $10,000 for expenses that will be funded in future years.] Except for materials and supplies in the amount of $3,904,000 consumed in operations and the two accrued items, all other operating/program expenses were paid by checks drawn on the Treasury during the fiscal year.
6. Accounts payable in the amount of $3,654,000 were paid during the year. Of this amount, checks in the amount of $1,869,000 were drawn against Fund Balance with Treasury—1999; the remainder against Fund Balance with Treasury—2000. In addition, early in FY 2000, the $55,000 reported as accrued funded payroll and benefits on the September 30, 1999, Balance Sheet was paid by charging against Fund Balance with Treasury—1999.
7. There was no property, plant, and equipment sold or otherwise disposed of during fiscal year 2000.

Required

a. Prepare all necessary *proprietary* journal entries only for the Rural Assistance Agency (ignore *budgetary* entries) for fiscal year 2000.
b. Prepare a Comparative Balance Sheet for the Rural Assistance Agency as of September 30, 1999, and 2000.
c. Prepare a Statement of Changes in Net Position for the Rural Assistance Agency for the year ended September 30, 2000.

13–5. The trial balance of the Federal Science Administration, as of August 31, 1999, is shown below:

	Debits	Credits
Proprietary Accounts		
Fund Balance with Treasury—1999	$1,635,772	
Operating Materials and Supplies.	1,184,186	
Plant and Equipment	7,651,633	
Accumulated Depreciation—Plant and Equipment		$ 2,332,628
Construction Work in Progress.	581,818	
Accounts Payable		328,123
Advances from Other Federal Agencies.		43,518
Appropriations Used.		2,630,724
Unexpended Appropriations		1,264,131
Cumulative Results of Operations—10/1/98		6,842,823
Operating/Program Expenses	2,388,538	
Total Proprietary Accounts.	$13,441,947	$13,441,947
Budgetary Accounts:		
Other Appropriations Realized—1999.	$ 3,894,855	
Unapportioned Authority—1999.		$ 100,000
Apportionments—1999		150,000
Allotments—1999		600,000
Commitments—1999.		50,000
Undelivered Orders—1999.		364,131
Expended Authority—1999		2,630,724
Total Budgetary Accounts	$ 3,894,855	$ 3,894,855

Required

a. Prepare a Balance Sheet for the Federal Science Administration, as of August 31, 1999.

b. Prepare a Statement of Changes in Net Position for the 11 months ended August 31, 1999, assuming the balance, as of September 30, 1998, for the Unexpended Appropriations—1998 account was $1,210,210.

c. Prepare a Statement of Budgetary Resources for the 11 months ended August 31, 1999, assuming goods on order at the end of the prior year amounted to $1,210,210.

13–6. The Statement of Financial Position of the Throttlebottom Commemorative Commission, of the United States Department of Culture, is given as follows:

THROTTLEBOTTOM COMMEMORATIVE COMMISSION
Balance Sheet
September 30, 1999

Assets

Entity Assets:		
Intragovernmental:		
Fund Balance with Treasury—1999		$1,650,000
Operating Materials and Supplies		365,000
Equipment	$600,000	
Less: Accumulated Depreciation	60,000	540,000
Total Assets		$2,555,000

Liabilities

Liabilities Covered by Budgetary Resources:		
Accounts Payable		$ 850,000
Total Liabilities Covered by Budgetary Resources		850,000

Net Position

Unexpended Appropriations		800,000
Cumulative Results of Operations		905,000
Total Net Position		1,705,000
Total Liabilities and Net Position		$2,555,000

Required

a. Prepare entries in general journal form for the following transactions, which summarize all financial transactions for fiscal year October 1, 1999–September 30, 2000. Use the account titled *Operating/Program Expenses* for all expense items, realizing, of course, that in an actual accounting system, either additional general ledger detail or an expense subsidiary ledger would be used.

(1) An appropriation for FY 2000 in the amount of $12,000,000 is authorized by Congress, and the bill is signed by the President.

(2) The Office of Management and Budget apportioned $11,000,000 to the agency and withheld $1,000,000.

(3) The agency head allotted $11,000,000 to subordinates.

(4) Commitments are recorded in the amount of $10,300,000.

(5) Obligation documents totaling $10,000,000 are recorded for those commitments that had been previously recorded.

(6) Goods and services were received and liabilities recorded for: Payroll, $6,500,000; equipment, $600,000; and materials and supplies, $2,000,000. The equipment and $200,000 worth of the materials and supplies had been ordered in the prior year; the remainder of the materials and the payroll relate to obligations of the current year.

(7) Materials and supplies issued during the period and used in operations, $1,200,000.

(8) Liabilities paid totaled $8,950,000, of which $1,650,000 was paid from Fund Balance with Treasury—1999.

(9) Depreciation is recorded at the rates of 10 percent on the beginning balance and 5 percent on the additions during the year.

(10) Accruals as of September 30, 2000, are recorded for payroll, $350,000; and materials and supplies, $68,000. Obligations had been previously recorded for these amounts.

(11) The withheld and unobligated portions of the appropriation lapsed at year-end.

  b. Prepare a trial balance as of September 30, 2000.

  c. Prepare closing entries as of September 30, 2000.

  d. Prepare a Balance Sheet as of September 30, 2000, in the format used for the September 30, 1999, Balance Sheet.

  e. Prepare a Statement of Changes in Net Position for 2000.

13–7. The Flood Control Commission was authorized by Congress to start operations on October 1, 1999.

Required

 a. Record the following transactions in general journal form as they should appear in the accounts of the Flood Control Commission. Record all expenses in the "Operating/Program Expenses" account.

(1) The Flood Control Commission received official notice that the one-year appropriation passed by Congress and signed by the President amounted to $7,000,000 for operating expenses.

(2) The Office of Management and Budget notified the Commission of the following schedule of apportionments: first quarter, $2,000,000; second quarter, $2,000,000; third quarter, $1,500,000; and fourth quarter, $1,500,000.

(3) The Flood Control Commissioner allotted $1,000,000 for the first month's operations.

(4) Obligations were recorded for salaries and fringe benefits, $400,000; furniture and equipment, $270,000; materials and supplies, $250,000; rent and utilities, $50,000. The Flood Control Commission does not record commitments prior to recording obligations.

(5) Payroll for the first two weeks in the amount of $170,000 was paid.

(6) Invoices approved for payment totaled $395,000; of the total, $180,000 was for furniture and equipment, $175,000 for materials and supplies, and $40,000 for rent.

(7) Liability was recorded for the payroll for the second two weeks, $160,000; and for the employer's share of FICA taxes for the four weeks, $23,000. [Credit Accrued Funded Payroll and Benefits.]

(8) Accounts payable totaling $189,000 were paid, which included liabilities for materials and supplies, $149,000, and Rent, $40,000. Accrued Funded Payroll and Benefits were paid in the amount of $183,000.

(9) Accruals recorded at month-end were salaries, $30,000, and utilities, $10,000. Materials and supplies costing $60,000 were used during the month. Depreciation of $2,500 was recorded on furniture and equipment for the month. [Note: In practice, this would likely be done in worksheet form for monthly reporting purposes.]

(10) Necessary closing entries were prepared as of October 31, 1999.
[Again, for monthly statements, this would be a worksheet entry only.]

b. Prepare a Balance Sheet for the Flood Control Commission as of October 31, 1999, assuming that all of the Commission's assets are entity assets, that Fund Balance with Treasury is intragovernmental, and that all other assets are governmental. Further, all liabilities are covered by budgetary resources.

c. Prepare a Statement of Changes in Net Position for the Flood Control Commission for the month ended October 31, 1999.

d. Prepare a Statement of Budgetary Resources for the Flood Control Commission for the month ended October 31, 1999.

e. Prepare a Statement of Financing for the Flood Control Commission for the month ended October 31, 1999.

13–8. The following trial balances were prepared for a federal agency at the end of its first month of existence by a new accountant, whose only prior experience had been as a bookkeeper in the accounting department of a large city.

INTERSTATE PARKS COMMISSION
Trial Balance
October 31, 1999

	Debits	Credits
General Fund:		
Accounts Payable		$1,200,000
Allotments		1,600,000
Due from U.S. Treasury	$3,140,000	
Encumbrances	50,000	
Estimated Revenues	3,500,000	
Expenditures	1,410,000	
Fund Balance	50,000	
Inventory of Supplies	50,000	
Reserve for Encumbrances		50,000
Reserve for Inventory		50,000
Revenues		3,400,000
Unallotted Appropriations		1,900,000
	$8,200,000	$8,200,000
General Fixed Assets Account Group:		
Buildings	$ 720,000	
Equipment	180,000	
Improvements Other than Buildings	45,000	
Investment in General Fixed Assets—General Fund Revenues		$1,000,000
Land	55,000	
	$1,000,000	$1,000,000

Early in the second month of the agency's existence (before any transactions of the second month have been posted), you are sent to the agency to see how the new accountant is getting along. After looking over the trial balances, you ask to see the underlying accounts. (These are reproduced below. Related debits and credits are indicated by the same number. Explanations appear with the debit member of each entry.)

<u>General Fund Accounts</u>

Accounts Payable

Checks requested from U.S. Treasury	(7)	260,000		(5)	1,150,000
				(6)	310,000

Allotments

				(3)	1,600,000

Due from U.S. Treasury

OMB Apportionment	(2)	3,400,000		(7)	260,000

Encumbrances

Option to purchase land, building, and equipment, 1,000,000; supplies ordered, 200,000	(4)	1,200,000		(5)	1,150,000

Estimated Revenues

Congressional appropriation	(1)	3,500,000	

Expenditures

Title taken to land, etc., 1,000,000; supplies received, 150,000	(5)	1,150,000		(8)	50,000
Salaries and wages	(6)	310,000			

Fund Balance

To set up Reserve for inventory	(8)	50,000	

Inventory of Supplies

Month-end physical inventory	(8)	50,000	

Reserve for Encumbrances

See explanation in Expenditures account	(5)	1,150,000		(4)	1,200,000

Reserve for Inventory

| | | (8) | 50,000 |

Revenues

| | | (2) | 3,400,000 |

Unallotted Appropriations

| Allotment for July | (3) 1,600,000 | (1) | 3,500,000 |

General Fixed Assets Account Group

Buildings

| See GF entry (5); expected life, 30 years | (5) | 720,000 | |

Equipment

| See GF entry (5); expected life, 10 years | (5) | 180,000 | |

Improvements Other than Buildings

| See GF entry (5); expected life, 15 years | (5) | 45,000 | |

**Investment in General Fixed Assets—
General Fund Revenues**

| | | (5) | 1,000,000 |

Land

| See GF entry (5) | (5) | 55,000 | |

Required

a. Prepare entries in general journal form to state the accounts of the Interstate Parks Commission correctly as of October 31, 1999.
b. Prepare a Balance Sheet for the Interstate Parks Commission as of October 31, 1999, assuming that all of the Commission's assets are entity assets, that Fund Balance with Treasury is intragovernmental, and that all other assets are governmental. Further, all liabilities are covered by budgetary resources.
c. Prepare a Statement of Changes in Net Position for the Interstate Parks Commission for the month ended October 31, 1999.

CHAPTER 14

Budgets and Cost Determination

Learning Objectives

After studying this chapter, you should be able to:

~ Explain the objectives of budgeting and cost determination in relation to measuring performance.

~ Explain the differences among various budgeting approaches.

~ Identify the procedures involved in specific types of budgets including appropriation budgets, revenue budgets, and capital budgets.

~ Describe budgeting for performance:

Total quality management (TQM).
Service efforts and accomplishments (SEA).

~ Explain unique aspects of costing government services:

Federal contracts and grants.
Activity-based costing (ABC).
Cost accounting and expenditure accounting.

~ Describe the unique budget and cost issues in a nongovernmental, nonprofit organization.

The 1990s brought a renewed interest in measuring the performance of organizations in the public and nonprofit sectors, as well as in the private sector. The budget has always played a unique role in governmental entities because it is a legal document. Cost determination has long been a critical task in complying with requirements accompanying federal funds. What appears to be new is the pervasive acceptance across entities that assessing outcomes and accomplishments is key to being accountable to resource providers and remaining viable and competitive as an organization. A challenge is to integrate the functions of management, budgeting, and costing into the accounting information system so that performance can be continuously monitored and improved.

The analysis of government financial performance was discussed in Chapter 11. In this chapter, the roles of budgets, cost determination, and accounting information systems in that process are examined. The concepts and tools are discussed primarily from the perspective of a state or local government or public entity, such as a public university or public hospital; however, many of the issues apply equally well to nongovernmental, not-for-profit organizations.

Objectives of Budgeting

The GASB *Budgeting, Budgetary Control, and Budgetary Reporting* Principle provides that:

a. An annual budget(s) should be adopted by every governmental unit.
b. The accounting system should provide the basis for appropriate budgetary control.
c. Budgetary comparisons should be included in the appropriate financial statements and schedules for governmental funds for which an annual budget has been adopted.

The *Budgeting* Principle is directly related to the *Accounting and Reporting Capabilities* Principle, which specifies that a governmental accounting system must make it possible for a governmental unit (1) to prepare financial reports in conformity with generally accepted accounting principles (GAAP) and (2) to determine compliance with finance-related legal provisions. Chapter 3 is concerned with budgets as legal documents binding on the actions of administrators and with budgetary accounting needed to make it possible to prepare budgetary reports to demonstrate legal compliance. It is also concerned with budgetary comparisons required for inclusion in general purpose financial statements in conformity with GASB standards.

Budgeting is also an important tool for achieving efficient and effective management of resources. Because of growing public demand for improved government performance, innovative performance measurement systems are being developed at all levels of government. In 1993, for example, the U.S. Congress passed the Government Performance and Results Act, which mandates the development of strategic plans, performance measures, annual performance plans, and performance reporting for all federal agencies.[1]

In November 1997, the National Advisory Council on State and Local Budgeting, a cooperative of organizations, issued a draft document that describes nearly 60 *best* budget practices covering the planning, development, adoption, and execution phases of the budget process.[2] This document recognizes that budgeting is one of the most important activities undertaken by state and local governments in allocating scarce resources to programs and services. A final report is expected after public comment and due process. Over the years, governments have experimented with various approaches to budgeting. These approaches are described in the next section.

Rational Budgeting Approaches

The legalistic view is that a budget is a plan of financial operation embodying an estimate of proposed expenditures for a given period of time and the proposed means of financing them. In a much more general sense, budgets may be regarded as devices to aid management to operate an organization more effectively. In the general sense, budgets are the financial expression of plans prepared by managers for operating an organization during a time period and for changing its physical facilities and its capital structure.

Incremental Budgeting. A simplistic, and often used, approach to budgeting is called **incremental budgeting**. In essence, an incremental budget is derived from the current year's budget by adding amounts expected to be required by salary and wage increases and increases in the cost of supplies and equipment to be purchased; decreases would result from shrinkage in the scale of operations forced by pressures such as spending limitations mandated by the electorate (for example, California's Proposition 13 in 1978) or cuts in capital equipment purchases. Incremental budgeting focuses largely on resource inputs and typically uses the *line-item* budget format in which the focus is on departmental expenditures for specified purposes, or objects, such as personnel, supplies, equipment, and travel.

---

[1] Progress on implementation of "The Results Act" is reported on this web page— http://www.npr.gov/. Federal agencies were required to submit their strategic plans to Congress by September 30, 1997.

[2] The founding organizations are the Association of School Business Officials International (ASBO), Council of State Governments (CSG), Government Finance Officers Association (GFOA), International City/County Management Association (ICMA), National Association of Counties (NACo), National Conference of State Legislatures (NCSL), National League of Cities (NLC), and the U.S. Conference of Mayors (USCM). Membership also includes representatives from academic institutions, public employee organizations, and the public finance industry. The report can be obtained from any of these organizations' Internet homepages, for example, http://www.gfoa.org.

Incremental budgeting is often contrasted with *rational* budgeting approaches, which stress the relation of inputs to outputs (quantities of work accomplished) and outcomes (impacts on goals and objectives). Rational budgeting approaches, as they have evolved, attempt to identify fundamental objectives of the governmental unit, estimate future-year costs and benefits, and systematically analyze alternative ways of meeting the governmental unit's objectives. Three approaches commonly described as rational are performance/program budgeting, planning-programming-budgeting system, and zero-based budgeting. These approaches are discussed next.[3]

Performance Budgeting.   The evolution of the concept of a budget from "an estimate of proposed expenditures and the proposed means of financing them" to an "operating plan" was a natural accompaniment to the development of the concept of professional management. In public administration, as in business administration, the concept of professionalism demanded that administrators, or managers, attempt to put the scarce resources of qualified personnel and money to the best possible uses. The legal requirement that administrators of governmental units and agencies submit appropriate requests to the legislative bodies in budget format provided a basis for adapting required budgetary estimates of proposed expenditures to broader management use. The legislative appropriation process has traditionally required administrators to justify budget requests. A logical justification of proposed expenditures is to relate the proposed expenditures of each governmental subdivision to the programs and activities to be accomplished by that subdivision during the budget period. The type of budgeting in which input of resources is related to output of services is sometimes known as **performance budgeting**. Performance budgeting is linked conceptually with *performance auditing* as defined in Chapter 12 of this text. Performance budgeting is a plan for relating resources inputs to the efficient production of outputs; performance auditing is the subsequent evaluation to determine that resources were in fact used efficiently and effectively in accordance with the plan.

Program budgeting is another term sometimes used synonymously with performance budgeting. However, the term is more generally used to refer to a budget format that discloses the full costs of programs or functions without regard to the number of organizational units that might be involved in performing the various aspects of the program or functions. Performance budgeting, at least in its earlier forms, focuses on the relation between inputs and outputs of each organizational unit rather than programs.

The use of performance budgeting in governmental units received significant impetus from the work of the first Hoover Commission for the federal government. The report of this Commission, presented to the Congress in 1949, led to the

---

[3]More details about these specific budgeting techniques and their application to industries, such as service, nonprofit, higher education, and health care can be found in Robert Rachlin and H. W. Allen Sweeny, *Handbook of Budgeting,* 3rd ed. with 1997 Cumulative Supplement (New York: John Wiley & Sons, 1997).

adoption in the federal government of budgets then known as *cost-based budgets* or *cost budgets*. The use of these designations suggests that a governmental unit desiring to use performance budgeting must have an accrual accounting system, rather than a cash accounting system, in order to routinely ascertain the costs of programs and activities. The recommendations of the second Hoover Commission led to the statutory requirement of both accrual accounting and cost-based budgeting for agencies of the executive branch of the federal government. Federal statutes also require the synchronization of budgetary and accounting classifications and the coordination of these with the organizational structure of the agencies. Subsequently it was realized that the planning and programming functions of federal agencies were not performed by the same organizational segments that performed the budgeting and accounting functions and that plans and programs were thus often not properly related to appropriation requests.

Planning-Programming-Budgeting System.   The integration of planning, programming, budgeting, and accounting has considerable appeal to persons concerned with public administration because an integrated system should, logically, provide legislators and administrators with much better information for the management of governmental resources than has been provided by separate systems. In the late 1960s, there was a concentrated effort to introduce a **planning-programming-budgeting system**, called PPBS, throughout the executive branch of the federal government, and to adapt the concept to state and local governmental units and to other complex organizations.

Zero-Based Budgeting.   In the 1970s, the wave of interest in PPBS receded and was replaced by widespread discussion of another approach to wedding the legally required budget process to a rational process of allocating scarce resources among alternative uses: The approach was called **zero-based budgeting** or ZBB. As the name indicates, the basic concept of ZBB is that the very existence of each activity be justified each year, as well as the amounts of resources requested to be allocated to each activity.

Many governmental units of various sizes have experimented with performance budgeting, program budgeting, PPBS, ZBB, and mixed approaches to rational budgeting.[4] Successful implementation of these approaches, particularly PPBS, requires formulation of the governmental unit's fundamental objectives and identification and evaluation of alternative ways of achieving the objectives. Techniques used to evaluate alternatives are sometimes referred to as *systems analysis, cost/benefit analysis*, and *cost-effectiveness analysis*. Techniques for "productivity measurement" or "productivity evaluation" are also often utilized by administrators who use the budgeting process as an aid in the allocation of scarce resources among competing demands for services. Quantitative techniques such as model building and

---

[4]See Daniel E. O'Toole, James Marshall, and Timothy Grewe, "Current Local Government Budgeting Practices," *Government Finance Review*, December 1996, pp. 25–29 for the results of a survey of budgeting practices of members of the Government Finance Officers Association.

simulation studies are utilized as aids in evaluating alternative allocations of governmental resources just as they are for evaluating business alternatives.

However simple or however sophisticated the methods used to develop information to aid in the resource allocation process, any method can produce useful output only if the data input are sufficiently reliable. Chapters 2 through 10 are intended to provide the reader with the background needed to understand data produced in conformity with GASB standards. Modifications that would facilitate rational budgeting are discussed later in this chapter.

Interrelation of Policysetting, Service Delivery, and Evaluation Activities

Illustration 14–1 is a graphic representation of the interrelations among the processes of policysetting, service delivery, and evaluation in one city. Illustration 14–1 shows that budget preparation is constrained by evaluation of prior years' action plans and accomplishments, generation of data about the city, and adjustment of goals and policies. Not specifically presented in the chart is the necessity of recognizing the impact on the city's action plans of changes in federal and state policies, programs, and revenues and expenditures structures. Note that this city uses the term "corporate" as governments are public corporations.

Budgeting Procedures

Budgeting Governmental Appropriations

Appropriations budgets are an administration's requests for authorization to incur liabilities for goods, services, and facilities for specified purposes. In practice, the preparation of appropriations budgets for any one year is related to the administration's budget of revenues since the revenues budget is the plan for financing the proposed appropriations. If the program, or performance, budget concept is followed, appropriations budgets are prepared for each existing and continuing work program or activity of each governmental subdivision; for each program authorized or required by action of past legislative bodies but not yet made operative; and for each new program the administration intends to submit to the legislative body for approval.

In business budgeting, each ongoing program should be subjected to rigorous management scrutiny at budget preparation time to make sure there is a valid reason for continuing the program at all: This is the fundamental idea of zero-based budgeting. If the program should be continued, then management must decide whether the prior allocation of resources to the program is optimal, or whether changes should be made in the assignment of personnel, equipment, space, and money. In a well-managed governmental unit, the same sort of review is given to each continuing program. The mere fact that the program was authorized by a past legislative body does not mean the administration may shirk its duty to recommend discontinuance of a program that has ceased to serve a real need. If the program should be continued, in the judgment of the administration, the appropriate level of activity and the appropriate allocation of resources must be determined; this determination takes far more political courage and management skill than the common practice of simply extrapolating the trend of historical activity and historical cost.

Illustration 14–1 Integrated Budgeting Planning System

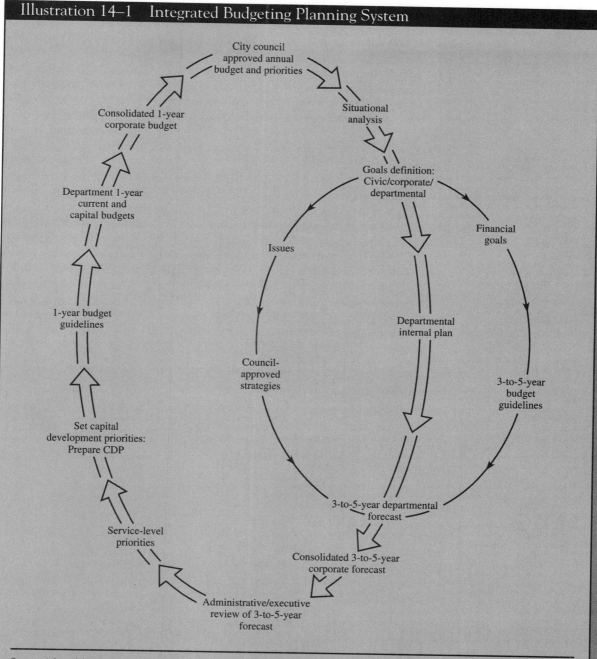

City council
approved annual
budget and priorities

Consolidated 1-year
corporate budget

Situational
analysis

Department 1-year
current and
capital budgets

Goals definition:
Civic/corporate/
departmental

Issues

Financial
goals

1-year budget
guidelines

Departmental
internal plan

Council-
approved
strategies

3-to-5-year
budget
guidelines

Set capital
development priorities:
Prepare CDP

Service-level
priorities

3-to-5-year departmental
forecast

Consolidated 3-to-5-year
corporate forecast

Administrative/executive
review of 3-to-5-year
forecast

Source: Adapted from Peter P. Fernandes and Myriam P. Laberge, "Setting Local Government Priorities through the Budget Process," *Government Finance Review*, April 1986, p. 23. Reprinted with permission of the Government Finance Officers Association.

If the administration is convinced that a program should be continued and the prior allocation of resources is relatively appropriate, the preparation of the appropriations budget is delegated to the persons in charge of the program. In the case of a new program, the administration states the objectives of the program and sets general guidelines for the operation of the program, then delegates budget preparation to individuals who are expected to be in charge of the program when legislative authorization and appropriations are secured. State laws or local ordinances typically require that certain steps be followed in the budgeting process and may prescribe dates by which each step must be completed. These requirements are referred to as the **budget calendar**. A budget calendar for a small city is presented in Illustration 14–2.

In order to ensure that administrative policies are actually used in budget preparation and that the budget calendar and other legal requirements are met, it is customary to designate someone in the central administrative office as budget officer. In addition to the responsibilities enumerated, the **budget officer** is responsible for providing technical assistance to the operating personnel who prepare the budgets. The technical assistance provided may include clerical assistance with budget computations as well as the maintenance of files for each program containing: (1) documents citing the legal authorization and directives, (2) relevant administrative policies, (3) historical cost and workload data, (4) specific factors affecting program costs and workloads, and (5) sources of information to be used in projecting trends.

Illustration 14–2

SAMPLE CITY
Budget Calendar
Year Ending September 30

Date	Event	Requirement or Action
July 20	1st Budget Workshop	Draft budget and documentation.
August 4	2nd Budget Workshop	Draft budget and documentation.
August 11	Regular Council Meeting/ 3rd Budget Workshop	Long-term GF projections, capital outlay and analysis of budget increases.
August 25	Regular Council Meeting/ 4th Budget Workshop	Budget presentations by County Health District, Chamber of Commerce, and other organizations.
September 1	Special Council meeting/ 5th Budget Workshop	Water/Sewer budget presentation. Call for public hearing to be held September 8.
September 3	Newspaper Publication	Publish notice of public hearing on budget to be held on September 8.
September 8	Regular Council Meeting	Public hearing on proposed budget.
September 15	Special Council Meeting	First reading of budget ordinance.
September 22	Regular Council Meeting	Second reading and vote on adoption of budget ordinance.

Budgets prepared by departmental administrators should be reviewed by the central administration before submission to the legislative branch because the total of departmental requests frequently exceeds the total of estimated revenues, and it is necessary to trim the requests in some manner. Central review may also be necessary to make sure enough is being spent on certain programs. Good financial management of the taxpayers' dollars is a process of trying to determine the optimum dollar input to achieve the desired service output, not a process of minimizing input. Even though the appropriations budget is a legally prescribed document, the administration should not lose sight of its managerial usefulness.

It should be emphasized that governmental budgets submitted to the legislative branch for action must be made available for a certain length of time for study by interested citizens, and one or more public hearings must be held before the legislative branch takes final action. Ordinarily, few citizens take the trouble to study the proposed budgets in detail; however, newspaper and television reporters often publicize proposed appropriations, especially those for programs, activities, and functions deemed particularly newsworthy. News reporters also publicize increases in taxes and fees proposed to finance budgeted appropriations. Representatives of such organizations as the state or local Chamber of Commerce and League of Women Voters analyze the budgets in detail and furnish analyses to their members, the public, and news media. Generally, such broadly based organizations attempt to be even-handed in their budget analyses. In many instances, however, members of special interest groups also sift through the proposed budget to determine the proposed allocation of resources to the programs, activities, and functions of interest to the groups they represent; budget analyses of special interest groups are not intended to be even-handed. If the proposed budget does not meet the interests of the group as well as they think they can expect realistically, the groups may be counted on to attempt to influence the votes of the members of the legislative branch to change the budget before it is enacted into law. Thus it is evident that the governmental process involves political and social considerations and, at higher levels of government, aggregate economic considerations, all of which may be more important to many voters, administrators (bureaucrats), and legislators (politicians) than financial considerations. The relationship among these stakeholders is presented graphically in Illustration 14–3. Governmental budgeting considerations are consistent with the overall goal of governmental accounting and financial reporting, discussed in Chapter 1.

Comparable considerations exist for business enterprises. A profit-seeking business will succeed in the long run only if it serves the needs of its customers and of society in general: The financial managers of a business must budget within this framework. In business budgeting, revenues and expenses of any year are interrelated; expenses are incurred in the effort to produce revenue, and the production of revenue enables the further incurring of expenses and the further production of revenue. Revenues and expenses are interdependent variables in business budgeting.

Business budgeting concepts are appropriate for governmental activities run on a business basis. A similar interrelationship may be said to exist at the federal government level in the cases of certain General Fund expenditures made in order to

Illustration 14–3   The Governmental Budget Decision Process

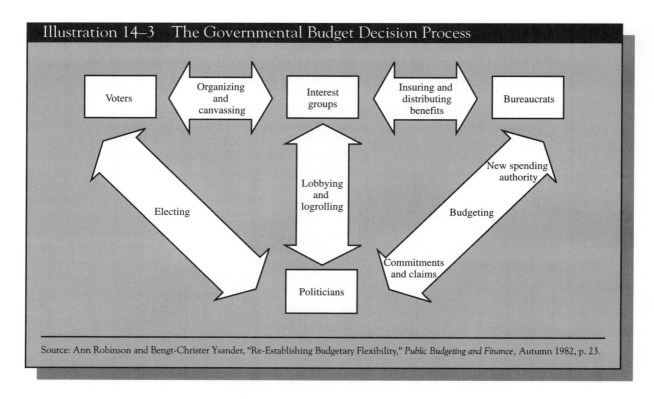

Source: Ann Robinson and Bengt-Christer Ysander, "Re-Establishing Budgetary Flexibility," *Public Budgeting and Finance*, Autumn 1982, p. 23.

stimulate segments of the economy; the costs of increasing economic activity tend to be recouped by increased tax revenue. For general governmental activities, however, revenues and expenditures are not interdependent variables. Expenditures are made in order to render a service to the citizens, and not in order to generate revenue. Similarly, although revenues may vary from month to month, the variation of revenues has little direct effect on the incurring of expenditures.

Budgeting Governmental Revenues

Although governmental revenues and expenditures are not interdependent variables as business revenues and expenses are, the availability of revenues is a necessary prerequisite to the incurring of expenditures. Some states and local governments may operate at a deficit temporarily, but it is generally conceded that they may not do so indefinitely. Thus, wise financial management calls for the preparation of revenues budgets, at least in rough form, prior to the preparation of detailed operating plans and finalizing appropriations budgets.

Revenues is a term that has a precise meaning in governmental accounting. The GASB states that the term *revenues* "means increases in (sources of) fund financial resources other than from interfund transfers and debt issue proceeds."[5]

---

[5]GASB, *Codification*, Sec. 1800, 114.

For purposes of budgeting inflows of financial resources of a fund, it does not seem particularly valuable to distinguish among revenues, as defined by the GASB, interfund transfers, and debt issue proceeds, other than to keep budgeting terminology consistent with accounting and financial reporting terminology.

Sources of revenue and other financial inflows available to a given local governmental unit are generally closely controlled by state law; state laws also establish procedures for the utilization of available sources and may impose ceilings on the amount of revenue a local government may collect from certain sources. Sources generally available for financing routine operations include property taxes, sales taxes, income taxes, license fees, fines, charges for services, grants or allocations from other governmental units, and revenue from the use of money or property. Chapter 3 of this text describes revenue sources and discusses revenue accounting in some detail. The present discussion is, therefore, limited to the broad aspects of governmental revenue budgeting.

Within the framework set by legal requirements and subject to the approval of the legislative body (which, in turn, reacts to the electorate), the determination of revenue policy is a prerogative of the administration. Major considerations underlying the policy formulation are set forth in the preceding section of this chapter. After policies are established, the technical preparation of the revenues budget is ordinarily delegated to the budget officer. In order to facilitate budget preparation, experienced budget officers generally keep for each revenue source a file containing (1) a copy of legislation authorizing the source and any subsequent legislation pertaining to the source; (2) historical experience relative to collections from the source, including collections as a percentage of billings, where applicable; (3) relevant administrative policies; and (4) specific factors that affect the yield from the source, including for each factor the historical relationship of the factor to revenue procedures to be used in projecting the trend of factors affecting yield, and factors affecting collections. Graphic presentations of these factors are also frequently included in the file. Finance officers of large governmental units use more sophisticated statistical and econometric methods of revenue forecasting, particularly to evaluate alternative assumptions, but the method described here is generally used for preparation of a legal revenues budget.

Budgeting Capital Expenditures

Accounting principles for business enterprises and for proprietary funds of governmental units require the cost of assets expected to benefit more than one period to be treated as a balance sheet item, rather than as a charge against revenues of the period. No such distinction exists for governmental fund types. Expenditures for long-lived assets to be used in the general operations of a governmental unit are treated in the appropriations process in the same manner as are expenditures for salaries, wages, benefits, materials, supplies, and services to be consumed during the accounting period. Accounting control over long-lived assets used in general operations is established, however, as described in Chapter 5 of this text.

Effective financial management requires the plans for any one year to be consistent with intermediate- and long-range plans. Governmental projects such as the construction or improvement of streets; construction of bridges and buildings;

acquisition of land for recreational use, parking lots, and future building sites; and urban renewal all may require a consistent application of effort over a span of years. Consequently, administrators need to present to the legislative branch and to the public a multiyear capital improvements program, as well as the budget for revenues, operating expenditures, and capital outlays requested for the forthcoming year.

Effective financial management also requires nonfinancial information such as physical measures of capital assets, their service condition, and their estimated replacement cost. Nonfinancial information of these types is useful for purposes of forecasting future asset repair and replacement schedules, repair and replacement costs, and financing requirements. The GASB has established a project on nonfinancial service condition reporting for governmental capital assets and may prescribe disclosures.

Budgeting for Performance

During the 1980s and 1990s, growth in service demands and cutbacks in unrestricted federal funding forced numerous state and local governments to increase taxes and user fees. Meanwhile, taxpayers have become increasingly more frustrated with paying higher taxes for what they perceive as bloated, inefficient government bureaucracies. Fiscal reform has thus become a popular platform for politicians aspiring to key elective offices. Even though, as discussed previously in this chapter, many governments have experimented with so-called rational budgeting approaches, most of these experiments seem to have had little real impact on improving the efficiency and effectiveness of service delivery. Given their limited success with prior budgeting approaches, political leaders have had little choice but to experiment with recent management innovations in the private sector that might improve the efficiency of government operations and reduce the need for higher taxes.

Many state and local governments are well along in their efforts to budget for performance goals. For example, the Government Finance Officers Association (GFOA) has recognized the cities of Sunnyvale, California; Indianapolis, Indiana; and Glendale, Arizona; (among others) with the GFOA's Distinguished Budget Presentation Award for excellence in budgeting for legal compliance and performance.[6] Some states have passed legislation that requires performance measures, both financial and nonfinancial, to be reported by local governments and public institutions, such as colleges and universities. Two innovations being employed by many governments to measure the results or performance of the organization are total quality management and service efforts and accomplishments.

---

[6]Amy Chan and Dan Rich, "Sunnyvale's Outcome Management: Taking Performance Budgeting One Step Further," *Government Finance Review*, December 1996, pp. 13–17.

Total Quality Management

Total quality management (TQM) is attractive to many government officials because it links customer (taxpayer and other resource provider) satisfaction to improvements in the operating systems and processes used to provide goods and services. TQM seeks to continuously improve the government's ability to meet or exceed customer demands, where the customer might be external, such as taxpayers and service recipients, or internal, such as the customers of an internal service fund. Central to TQM is using customer data to identify and correct problems. Individual governments have tailored their TQM structures to meet their unique requirements, but most incorporate a majority of the following elements:

1. Support and commitment of top-level officials.
2. Customer orientation.
3. Employee involvement in productivity and quality improvement efforts.
4. Employees rewarded for quality and productivity achievement.
5. Training provided to employees in methods for improving productivity and quality.
6. Reduction of barriers to productivity and quality improvement.
7. Productivity and quality measures and standards that are meaningful to the governmental unit.
8. Written vision or mission statements that are linked directly to team-established targets or goals.[7]

The elements of TQM are obviously consistent with those of the rational budgeting approaches (particularly PPBS) previously discussed. Thus governments that have implemented one of the rational budgeting approaches, or a mixed approach, may find it less costly to implement a TQM structure. On the other hand, few governments possess adequate data on customer satisfaction. Moreover, the traditional emphases of government on line-item budgeting, rigid personnel classifications, restrictive procurement regulations, and so on, tend to reduce management autonomy, and thus may be inconsistent with the need under TQM to empower employees to be "entrepreneurial" in improving processes and meeting customer demand. It should also be noted that the objective of TQM is not necessarily to reduce cost but rather to increase "value for the dollar." Insofar as a TQM program successfully adds value, it has the potential to improve the public perception of government, in addition, of course, to improving service delivery.

Element 7 from the preceding list of TQM elements requires that the governmental unit develop meaningful standards for and measures of performance in terms of productivity and quality. In the government and nonprofit context, the analogous performance terms more typically used, are *efficiency* and *effectiveness*, the former relating efforts (resource inputs) to outputs of a service process and the latter relating efforts to outcomes or the results produced by service.

---

[7]Adapted from James J. Kline, "Total Quality Management in Local Government," *Government Finance Review*, August 1992, p. 7.

Service Efforts and Accomplishments

Because of growing public demand for greater accountability, a number of governments currently report some **service efforts and accomplishments** (SEA) measures for selected service functions, although there are no generally accepted standards to guide selection of the measures to report. The GASB has conducted and commissioned research into appropriate SEA measures for a variety of service functions, including, among others, police departments, fire departments, mass transit, public assistance programs, road maintenance, and colleges and universities.[8]

As discussed in Chapter 10, SEA measures fall into three broad categories: (1) service efforts (resources used), (2) service accomplishments (outputs and outcomes), and (3) those that relate service efforts to service accomplishments (efficiency measures and cost-outcome measures). Illustration 14–4 shows recommended SEA indicators for police departments. As shown in Illustration 14–4 the input measures indicate quantities and dollar amounts of resources used in providing police services. The output and outcome indicators collectively indicate service accomplishments, where outputs indicate quantities of work done on particular activities (such as patrol, responding to calls, and investigations) and outcomes indicate the results of activities in achieving desired objectives (such as reduction of deaths, bodily injury, and property loss). SEA measures for key programs or service functions are essential for measuring entity performance and can provide much of the data needed for implementation of a TQM system.

Development of sophisticated rational budgeting approaches and TQM systems requires sophisticated cost accounting systems to determine the full cost of programs or functions. Better managed state and local governmental units are therefore actively developing improved cost accounting systems. One innovative costing approach being implemented by some governments, which can be implemented in tandem with TQM or other performance measurement systems, is activity-based costing (ABC), discussed later in this chapter.

Fortunately, many governments have improved their budgeting practices over the past decade. A major impetus for this improvement has been the Government Finance Officers Association's Distinguished Budget Presentation Awards Program. Voluntary applications for this award increased from 113 in 1984, the year the program was initiated, to 851 in 1997. About 80 percent of the applicants have received the award and many of the unsuccessful applicants received confidential reviewer suggestions that permitted them to subsequently qualify for the award.

Costing of Government Services

The explosive increase in demand for government services, relative to the increase in resources, has forced the adoption of the techniques of good financial management, including cost accounting. The use of cost as a measure of the input of

---

[8]Governmental Accounting Standards Board, Research Report, *Service Efforts and Accomplishments Reporting: Its Time Has Come* (Norwalk, CT: GASB, 1990).

resources into a program, as an element of the budget, and as a basis to assess performance has been discussed earlier in this chapter. This section discusses the role of costs in a system that integrates management, budgeting, and costing for a governmental or not-for-profit organization.

Illustration 14–4	**Recommended SEA Indicators for Police Departments***

Indicator	*Rationale for Selecting Indicator*
Inputs:	
Budget expenditures	To provide a measure of financial resources used to provide services.
Equipment, facilities, vehicles	To provide a measure of nonpersonnel resources used to provide services.
Number of personnel or hours expended	To provide a measure of the size of the organization and the human resources used to provide services.
Outputs:	
Hours of patrol	To provide a measure of the quantity of patrol service provided; patrol is generally regarded as a primary product of police efforts.
Responses to calls for service	To provide a measure of the quantity of response service provided.
Crimes investigated	To provide a measure of the quantity of services provided by investigation units.
Number of arrests	To provide a measure of the success of police efforts in apprehending criminal offenders.
Persons participating in crime-prevention activities	To provide a measure of the quantity of service provided by crime-prevention units.
Outcomes:	
Deaths and bodily injury resulting from crime	To provide a measure of the effectiveness of police efforts in reducing the incidence of personal harm attributed to criminal activity.
Value of property lost due to crime	To provide a measure of the effectiveness of police efforts in reducing the incidence of property loss due to criminal activity.
Crimes committed per 100,000 population	To provide a measure of the effectiveness of police efforts in reducing criminal activity.
Percentage of crimes cleared	To provide a measure of the effectiveness of police efforts in detection of criminal activity and apprehension of criminal offenders.
Response time	To provide a measure of the quality of police response to calls.
Citizen satisfaction	To provide a measure of the overall effectiveness of police efforts in meeting citizen needs.
Efficiency:	
Cost per case assigned; cost per crime cleared	To provide an indication of the cost efficiency of police efforts.
Personnel-hours per crime cleared	To provide an indication of the productivity of personnel in providing police services.

(continued)

Illustration 14–4   (concluded)

Indicator	Rationale for Selecting Indicator
Explanatory variables: Population by age group Unemployment rate Number of households; number of business firms Percentage of population below poverty level Land area Dollar value of property within jurisdiction Demand: Calls for service Cases assigned	To provide information on factors that are likely to affect the incidence and effects of criminal activity so that measures of output, outcome, and efficiency may be viewed in proper context.

*The recommended indicators presented in this exhibit are illustrative. They are intended to serve as a starting point for use in the development of a comprehensive set of SEA indicators for external reporting of an entity's results of operation.

This exhibit does not provide illustrations of indicator disaggregation or of comparison data such as trends, targets, or other comparable entities. Both disaggregation and comparison data are important aspects of SEA reporting.

Source: Government Accounting Standards Board, Research Report, *Service Efforts and Accomplishments Reporting: Its Time Has Come* (Norwalk, CT: GASB, 1990), Exhibit 8–1.

Cost accounting, as discussed in standard college texts, is obviously applicable to business operations of governments and health care entities; but its application to nonbusiness activities of a government, not-for-profit organizations, or colleges and universities is not as immediately obvious. However, the same tasks of segregating direct from indirect costs, variable from fixed costs, standard from actual costs, and incremental from sunk costs are as important in capturing the total cost of delivering governmental or not-for-profit program services, as they are in private-sector companies. Another similarity with traditional cost accounting in the context of for-profit organizations is that **job order cost** accounting may be appropriate for some tasks (i.e., recording costs chargeable to specific grants, programs, projects, activities, or departments), and for others **process cost** accounting is more appropriate (i.e., recording continuous activities of governmental units, health care entities, and universities for a time period). In any organization, predetermination of overhead rates involves budgeting the overhead costs that should be incurred at the level of activity chosen as a basis for determination of the rate. Governments and not-for-profit organizations can use **flexible budgeting** to budget costs at different levels of activity and then compare costs that were actually incurred in a period with costs that should have been incurred to achieve that level of output.

Cost determination, the recasting of data derived from fund accounting to obtain desired cost information, is often a necessary task for governmental and not-for-profit organizations given the poor state of many such organizations' cost accounting systems. Cost determination procedures may be considered statistical if they are done apart from the accounting information system, and may be done at regular intervals or only on a special study basis. This section presents two other cost accounting issues with special significance to governmental and not-for-profit organizations. The first, acceptance of federal grants and sponsored agreements, brings with it the duty to comply with particular regulations on allowable costs and methods of spending. The second, activity-based costing, has been adopted by some governments as a key element of performance evaluation systems. Such systems are enhanced by designing accounting systems to provide as much activity-based cost data as possible, even though the need for some statistical cost data outside of the accounting system is inevitable.

Federal Grants and Sponsored Agreements

State and local governmental units and nonprofit entities, particularly colleges and universities, have found grants from and sponsored agreements with the federal government important, although diminishing, sources of financing. The United States Office of Management and Budget has issued a series of Circulars to set forth *cost principles* to govern payments by the federal government under grant programs, contracts, and other agreements, to state and local governments (OMB *Circular A-87*), educational institutions (OMB *Circular A-21*), and other nonprofit organizations (OMB *Circular A-122*).[9] The wording of all three Circulars is similar in many respects. They provide that the total cost of a program or contract is the sum of the allowable direct costs incident to its performance, plus its allocable portion of allowable indirect costs, less applicable credits. The terms *allowable costs*, *direct costs*, and *indirect costs*, among others, are defined in the Circulars.

Administrative requirements describing *how* federal expenditures are made are also detailed in OMB Circulars (for example, maintaining a financial management system and competitive bidding for procuring supplies and property). Illustration 14–5 shows the relationship of these Circulars to the organizations they cover. Just as the OMB combined *Circulars A-128* and *A-133* (as discussed in Chapter 12), there is a movement towards a combined circular for cost principles and another for administration requirements covering all types of organizations receiving federal funds. Of course, even with one Circular for educational institutions and nonprofit agencies (OMB *Circular A-110*), only 12 federal agencies have adopted *A-110* without major changes. Seven agencies, including the Departments of Education, Health and Human Services, and Housing and Urban Development, have made major changes to the version of *A-110* that applies to grants they make. An organization accepting federal funds must follow *all* relevant OMB Circulars.

---

[9]In addition, the Cost Accounting Standards Board (CASB) has instituted 19 standards since its inception in 1970 that apply to federal government contractors.

Illustration 14–5	OMB Grants Management Circulars	
	Cost Principles	*Administrative Requirements*
State and local governments	*Circular A-87* "Cost Principles for State, Local and Indian Tribal Governments" (revised 1995, amended 8/29/97)	*Circular A-102* "Grants and Cooperative Agreements with State and Local Governments" known as "The Common Rule" (revised 1994, amended 8/29/97)
Educational institutions	*Circular A-21* "Cost Principles for Educational Institutions" (revised 1996, amended 8/29/97)	*Circular A-110* "Uniform Administrative Requirements for Grants and Other Agreements with Institutions of Higher Education, Hospitals, and Other Non-Profit Organizations" (revised 1993, amended 8/29/97*)
Nonprofit organizations	*Circular A-122* "Cost Principles for Non-Profit Organizations" (revised 5/8/97, amended 8/29/97)	*Circular A-110* (same as above)

*Specific agencies implemented OMB *Circular A-110* (some with changes) from 1994 through 1996.
Source: All Circulars are available from the Office of Management and Budget (Washington, DC: Superintendent of Documents, U.S. Government Printing Office).

Allowable Costs.   To be an **allowable cost**, the cost must meet the following general criteria:

a. Be necessary and reasonable for proper and efficient performance and administration of federal awards. (A cost is reasonable if it does not exceed that which would be incurred by a prudent person under the circumstances prevailing at the time the decision was made to incur the cost.)

b. Be allocable to federal awards under provisions of *Circular A-87*.

c. Be authorized or not prohibited under state or local laws or regulations.

d. Conform to any limitations or exclusions, federal laws, terms and conditions of the federal award, or other governing regulations as to types or amounts of cost items.

e. Be consistent with policies, regulations, and procedures that apply uniformly to both federally assisted and other activities of the governmental unit.

f. Be accorded consistent treatment. Consequently, a cost may not be assigned to a federal award as a direct cost if any other cost incurred for the same purpose has been allocated to the federal award as an indirect cost.

g. Except as otherwise provided for, be determined in accordance with generally accepted accounting principles.

  h. Not be included as a cost or used to meet cost sharing or matching requirements of any other federal award in either the current or a prior period, except as specifically provided by federal law.

  i. Be determined net of all applicable credits (e.g., purchase discounts; rebates or allowances; recoveries or indemnities on losses; sale of publications and scrap; income from personal or incidental services; insurance refunds or rebates; earnings or imputed earnings on reserves; and adjustments of overpayments or erroneous charges).

  j. Be adequately documented.[10]

Each Circular provides standards for determining the allowability of selected items of cost. Certain items of cost are generally allowable whether or not mentioned specifically in a grant, contract, or other agreement document. Certain other cost items are allowable only if specifically approved by the grantor agency, and certain other cost items are unallowable. *Circular A-87* lists 42 cost items ranging alphabetically from Accounting to Underrecovery of Costs under Federal Agreements. Of the 42 cost items, 31 are allowable whether direct or indirect to the extent they pertain to specific grants or to the overall management of all grant programs. Depreciation and use allowances are included in the 31 allowable cost items. As explained in Chapter 5, even though governmental funds do not record depreciation expense, depreciation may be computed for purposes of claiming it as an allowable cost under federal grants and contracts. Similarly, public (governmentally owned) colleges and universities ordinarily do not record depreciation in their Current Funds for buildings and equipment, although private colleges and universities are required to do so by Financial Accounting Standards Board (FASB) standards. Public colleges and universities may find it useful, however, to report depreciation in Plant Fund accounts in order to compute depreciation charges for work under federal grants and contracts.

  Several of the 31 allowable items are allowable under highly restrictive conditions, and generally require the explicit approval of the grantor agency. An example is advertising costs that are allowable only for such items as recruitment of personnel, procurement of goods and services, and disposal of scrap or surplus materials related to the performance of federal assistance programs. Eleven of the 42 cost items are *unallowable*, including such items as alcoholic beverages, bad debt expenses, contributions and donations, fund-raising and investment management costs, entertainment, general expenses of the state or local government (e.g., salaries of the chief executive, legislatures, judicial department officials), and lobbying. Similar prohibitions apply to colleges and universities under the provisions of *Circular A-21*.

Direct Costs.   **Direct costs** are those that can be identified specifically with a particular cost objective. A **cost objective,** in federal terminology, is an organizational unit, function, activity, project, cost center, or pool established for the accumulation of costs. A final, or ultimate, cost objective is a specific grant, project,

---

[10]OMB, *Circular A-87*, Attachment A, C-1.

contract, or other activity (presumably one of interest to the federal agency that provides resources for the activity under a grant, contract, or other agreement). A cost may be direct with respect to a given function or activity but indirect with respect to the grant or other final cost objective of interest to the grantor or contractor. Typical direct costs chargeable to grant programs include compensation of employees for the time and efforts devoted specifically to the execution of grant programs; cost of materials acquired, consumed, or expended specifically for the purpose of the grant; and other items of expense incurred specifically to carry out the grant agreement. If approved by the grantor agency, equipment purchased and other capital expenditures incurred for a certain grant or other final cost objective would be considered direct costs.

Indirect Costs.   **Indirect costs**, according to *Circular A-87*, are those (*a*) incurred for a common or joint purpose benefiting more than one cost objective, and (*b*) not readily assignable to the cost objectives specifically benefited, without effort disproportionate to the results achieved. The term *indirect costs* applies to costs originating in the grantee department, as well as to those incurred by other departments in supplying goods, services, and facilities to the grantee department. To facilitate equitable distribution of indirect expenses to the cost objectives served, it may be necessary to establish a number of "pools" of indirect cost within the grantee department. Indirect cost pools should be distributed to benefited cost objectives on bases that produce an equitable result in consideration of relative benefits derived. In certain instances, grantees may negotiate annually with the grantor a predetermined fixed rate for computing indirect costs applicable to a grant, or a lump-sum allowance for indirect costs, but generally grantees must prepare a cost allocation plan that conforms with instructions issued by the U.S. Department of Health and Human Services. Cost allocation plans of local governments will be retained for audit by a designated federal agency. (Audit of federal grants is discussed in some detail in Chapter 12 of this text.)

Activity-Based Costing

Activity-based costing (ABC) was developed for use by manufacturing companies when it became apparent that traditional cost accounting systems were producing distorted product costs. Thus, some products that were thought to be profitable were, on closer inspection, found to be unprofitable, and vice versa. Two Harvard University professors, Robin Cooper and Robert S. Kaplan, made convincing arguments that typical cost accounting systems often understate profits on high-volume products and overstate profits on low-volume specialty items.[11] This problem is attributable, in part, to greater product diversity, shorter product life cycles, shift in production technology from labor to automation, more diverse distribution channels, and greater quality demands, all of which are driven by need to more effectively compete in the global marketplace. The net effect of these trends (which are also applicable to government, at least to some extent) is to create a

---

[11]Robin Cooper and Robert S. Kaplan, "Measure Costs Right: Make the Right Decisions," *Harvard Business Review*, September–October 1988, pp. 96–103.

larger infrastructure of "production support" activities, and thus to shift costs from direct cost categories to indirect cost, or overhead, categories. As a larger proportion of these costs is allocated to products, product cost distortions become a larger problem and may result in poor product decisions.

ABC essentially attempts to determine the cost of specific process-related activities, the "drivers" of those costs (e.g., labor-hours, machine-hours, or units of material), and the consumption of cost drivers in producing outputs of goods or services. Emphasis is placed on tracing the specific activities performed to specific outputs of goods or services, rather than on allocating average costs to units of output as done in conventional cost accounting systems. A publication of the Institute of Management Accountants explains the advantage of the ABC approach relative to traditional cost accounting allocations:[12]

> In traditional systems, financial controllers usually create elaborate, step-down, sequential allocations that distribute service department cost to production work centers based on percentage estimates. These allocations are often flawed because they assume arbitrary relationships; for example, using square feet or head count. These measures do not reflect disproportionate resource consumption. Such burden-averaging techniques are convenient for accountants but are not of service to users of information.
>
> With ABC, resource cost drivers replace the step-down allocations with cause-and-effect relationships at the activity level. (p. 13)

Determining the amount of each activity that is consumed in each product or service utilizes materials usage records, observation, and timekeeping systems, but is often augmented with estimates obtained through employee interviews and other means. The cost of designing a system that totally eliminates the need for overhead allocation is likely to be prohibitive. If allocation of "residual" unassigned costs is not potentially distortive, it may be more cost effective to focus ABC design on major activities and cost drivers, and then allocate remaining costs on an appropriate basis.

State-of-the-art approaches, such as total quality management (TQM) and service efforts and accomplishments (SEA) measures, implemented by some governments to improve performance require timely information on the full cost of resources consumed in providing service outputs. To calculate the full cost of services, however, requires careful allocation of indirect costs such as the clerical and administrative costs of general government functions (e.g., chief executive's office, finance department, legal department). The use of inappropriate allocation bases may produce distorted cost estimates for some service outputs in much the same manner that conventional cost systems produce distorted product costs. It is not surprising then that some governments have adopted ABC for key service functions. An article by Bridget Anderson explains the objectives of ABC in a governmental environment as follows:[13]

---

[12]Gary Cokins, Alan Stratton, and Jack Helbling, *An ABC Manager's Primer: Straight Talk on Activity-Based Costing* (Montvale, NJ: Institute of Management Accountants, 1993).

[13]Bridget M. Anderson, "Using Activity-Based Costing for Efficiency and Quality," *Government Finance Review*, June 1993, pp. 7–9.

The objectives of ABC are to preserve, at a minimum, the present quality and availability of core services but to acknowledge that some of the forces for greater expenditures have not been controlled. It seeks to reduce the costs of service outcomes by:

- reducing the number of service units through program redesign,
- finding lower cost alternatives,
- making volume increases dependent on cost reductions, and
- understanding and controlling the delivery/program design interaction.

A simplified diagram of an ABC cost model used by the City of Indianapolis to identify activity-based costs for snow control and patching chuckholes is shown in Illustration 14–6. Total activities cost for one particular district of the City for the two functions (snow control and chuckhole patching) is $2,600 as displayed in the leftmost table of Illustration 14–6. The five activities are C labor, D labor, salt, SAD (a type of truck), and central service overhead. The drivers identified in Illustration 14–6 are direct labor-hours of C and D labor, tons of salt, SAD (vehicle usage) hours, and total labor-hours for C and D combined to allocate overhead to units of output. The Consumption table shows the driver units of each activity that were consumed for each of the two service functions. Finally, as shown in the Cost per Output table, driver units consumed are multiplied by cost per driver unit

Illustration 14–6   Identification of Activity-Based Costs

Activities

Activity Name	Total Dollars
C labor	$1,000
D labor	600
Salt	400
SAD truck	400
Central service O/H	200
Total	$2,600

Activities and Related Drivers

Activity Name	Driver
C labor	C hours
D labor	D hours
Salt	Tons of salt
SAD truck	SAD hours
Central serv O/H	Total labor-hours

Consumption

Drivers	Snow Control	Patch Chuckhole	Total
C hours	50	50	100
D hours	10	20	30
Tons of salt	500	0	500
SAD hours	80	70	150
Total labor-hours	60	70	130

Cost per Output

Activities	Snow Control	Patch Chuckhole	Total
C labor	$ 500	$ 500	$1,000
D labor	200	400	600
Salt	400	0	400
SAD truck	213	187	400
Central serv O/H	92	108	200
Total	$1,405	$1,195	$2,600
12 miles of road	$117.08		
14 tons of mix		$85.36	

Source: Bridget M. Anderson, "Using Activity-Based Costing for Efficiency and Quality," *Government Finance Review,* June 1993, p. 8. Reprinted with permission of the Government Finance Officers Association.

and aggregated to determine the total cost of providing snow control and patching chuckholes. The cost for the current period for clearing snow from 12 miles of road was $1,405 or $117.08 per mile. Similarly, the cost of 14 tons of mix for patching chuckholes was $1,195 or $85.36 per ton.

Actual snow removal costs per mile for five geographic cost centers of the City of Indianapolis are presented in Illustration 14–7. As shown in this illustration, the cost per mile for snow removal ranged from $39.96 for 1,846 miles of road in the Southeast cost center to $117.59 for 1,000 miles of road in the Southwest cost center. Subsequent cost analysis by the City's Department of Transportation revealed that the Southwest cost center was using excessive amounts of salt per mile and was

Illustration 14–7   Cost Analysis of Snow Removal

Activity	Geographic Cost Center				
	Northwest	*Northeast*	*Center*	*Southwest*	*Southeast*
C labor	0.89	1.19	3.08	0.14	0.42
D labor	7.27	11.76	25.29	13.21	7.73
E labor	5.09	5.84	5.59	2.77	1.17
Supervisors	2.27	2.69	3.81	6.10	1.81
T supervisors	2.60	5.10	2.13	2.06	2.08
Personnel Costs	**18.12**	**26.58**	**39.90**	**24.28**	**13.21**
Calcium	0.86			4.86	
Salt	36.18	9.25	20.78	43.96	5.24
Sand				0.14	
Direct Materials Costs	**37.04**	**9.25**	**20.78**	**48.96**	**5.24**
Central Services	9.35	13.29	19.74	18.63	7.47
Facilities	1.84	3.81	0.94	0.59	0.66
Fixed assets	0.14	0.08	0.05	0.07	0.05
Administration	3.18	4.30	4.98	3.77	2.34
Overhead Costs	**14.51**	**21.48**	**25.71**	**23.06**	**10.52**
Crewcab pickup	0.01				
Loader	8.24	3.83	1.43	4.25	0.77
Mini pickup	6.11				
SAD 90	6.24	6.12	0.50	6.51	2.73
SADA 85	1.17	1.93	0.88	4.02	1.67
Sedan	3.31				
TAD 90	2.87	0.79	3.72	2.98	1.89
TADA	10.41	4.25	1.73	2.98	2.85
Dump truck	0.01	0.02			
Unused equipment	0.48	0.55	0.13	0.55	1.08
Rolling Stock Costs	**38.85**	**17.49**	**8.39**	**21.29**	**10.99**
TOTAL	**$108.52**	**$74.80**	**$94.78**	**$117.59**	**$39.96**
Miles plowed	1,100	1,000	900	1,000	1,846

Source: Bridget M. Anderson, "Using Activity-Based Costing for Efficiency and Quality," *Government Finance Review*, June 1993, p. 9. Reprinted with permission of the Government Finance Officers Association.

not using an optimal mix of equipment. The Center geographic cost center was using excessive labor. This analysis led to reallocation of both personnel and equipment between cost centers thus resulting in improved efficiency without loss of quality.[14]

Clerical and Administrative Costs.   A very large part of governmental expenditures are incurred for services of a general nature (such as the costs of the chief executive's office, costs of accounting and auditing, or costs of boards and commissions), which are somewhat remote from the results any given subdivision is expected to accomplish. Furthermore, in smaller units of government, many offices or departments perform such a variety of services that separating their costs is practically impossible under their present schemes of organization.

Given the importance and magnitude of key administrative offices, government officials should attempt to measure the efficiency and effectiveness of the activities of these offices just as it would other service activities. The primary difference is that many of these activities, such as those of the finance and legal departments for example, mainly serve customers within the government rather than the general public. Activity-based costing would seem to be a useful tool for measuring the cost of such activities. Possible activities and cost drivers for selected offices are provided below.

Office	Activities	Cost Drivers
Tax Collector	Preparing tax bills.	Number of bills prepared.
	Collecting tax bills.	Number of bills collected.
	Preparing receipts.	Number of receipts prepared.
	Mailing receipts.	Number of receipts mailed.
	Preparing deposits.	Number of deposits prepared.
Accounting	Recording revenues.	Number of revenue transactions.
	Recording expenditures.	Number of expenditure transactions.
	Processing payroll.	Number of employees.
	Recording purchase orders.	Number of orders.
Public Recorder	Recording documents	Number of documents or number of lines.

This table is intended to be illustrative of the kinds of activities and cost drivers that might apply to certain administrative offices. Obviously, the list is incomplete, but, insofar as the activities and drivers are appropriate for a particular office, costs accumulated by activity could be useful both for internal performance review and pricing services to other offices. As an example of pricing services rendered, the costs of accounting services could be priced to other departments on the basis of the amount of accounting activities they consume. For example, assume that the Public Works Department generates 30 percent of all purchase requisitions processed by

---

[14]Ibid., p. 8.

the Accounting Department. Arguably, it should then be charged for 30 percent of the total cost of recording purchase orders in the accounting function. Similarly, the costs of recording expenditures could be charged to departments proportionate to the expenditures they make. Although an activity-based costing approach to costing central services seems technologically feasible, much additional research is needed to determine whether the benefits would warrant the considerable costs involved.

Limitations on the Use of Unit Costs.   It has been said that *no* unit costs are better than inaccurate ones, the reason being that unless they are reliable they may lead to unwarranted and erroneous conclusions on the part of administrators, taxpayers, and the public, generally. Corollary to this, it may be said that crude unit costs, although both theoretically and technically correct, may be almost as misleading as inaccurate ones. No unit cost figure, especially in government, should be used as the basis for decisive action or opinions without careful evaluation in light of all pertinent facts. Such influences as regional variations in personnel costs, differences in climate and other physiographic conditions, size of the organization represented, and density of population in the area served are some of the factors that must be recognized if they are present and given due weight in appraising differences in unit costs. The establishment of standard costs that take into account all local circumstances and conditions has been recommended as one method for obviating the effect of comparisons with figures that are not entirely analogous. Historical costs compiled by other governmental units may not be entirely acceptable as a standard of comparison. This is true because one or more factors that affect costs in one jurisdiction may be decidedly more or less influential, or even not present. Finally, the quality of service represented by the unit of product must never be lost sight of in reaching a judgment as to the reasonableness of unit costs. Even such objective units as gallons of water and kilowatts of electricity have intangible qualities such as purity, taste, pressure, reliability, attention to complaints, and other service factors. For administrative government, on the other extreme, the possibilities for variance are far greater. At best, therefore, unit cost accounting in government and nonprofit entities is not an automatic process for turning out a standardized product, but only a means for helping to accomplish a desired end. Recent focus on activities for management, budgeting, and costing can also help minimize problems arising from the use of unit costs for decision making.[15]

Cost Accounting and Expenditure Accounting

Accounting for proprietary funds and nonexpendable trust funds of state and local governments, and for health care and many kinds of nonprofit entities, focuses on costs and expenses, as business accounting does; therefore, a cost accounting system is relatively easily installed. Accounting for governmental funds of state and local governments, and for colleges and universities, however, focuses on expenditures rather than on costs and expenses, and it is necessary to translate the legalistic

---

[15]Wayne K. Simpson and Michael J. Williams, "Activity-Based Costing, Management and Budgeting," *Government Accountants Journal*, Spring 1996, pp. 26–28.

concept of expenditures into the business concept of cost before a cost accounting system can be implemented.

Expenditures for Materials or Supplies. An expenditure occurs when a liability is created. Since a liability is created when personal or contractual services are received, expenditures for service fit the accrual definition of cost. However, when materials or supplies are received, an appropriation is expended, but there is no "cost" until the materials or supplies are used. If the inventory of materials or supplies at the end of a period is approximately the same as at the beginning of a period, expenditures for these items during the period may be a reasonably close approximation of cost during the period. Although reasonably level inventories in total may be common, there is no assurance that the usage of supplies for each program, or grant, during a period corresponds to expenditures for supplies for each program, or grant, during that period. If the supply cost of a given program is small in relation to total costs of that program, again expenditure accounting may provide a reasonable approximation of cost. If inventories fluctuate widely, or if some programs are heavy users of expensive supplies while other programs are light users of inexpensive supplies, accounting for governmental funds (which provides for the use of inventory accounts) must be supplemented by a system to provide for routine reporting of supply usage by programs.

Depreciation. As is true in the case of the purchase of materials and supplies, an appropriation is expended when a capital asset is acquired or constructed. By definition, a capital asset has a service life expected to extend over more than one fiscal period. The process of allocating the cost of a capital asset to the periods during which the asset is used is called *depreciation* accounting. The basis of accounting presently required by the GASB does not allow for the recording of depreciation of general fixed assets as an expense of the governmental fund that finances the department using the fixed asset (although the standards specifically provide for recording of depreciation by Enterprise Funds and other businesslike activities). The GASB standards further complicate the determination of depreciation expense by programs in that they require general fixed assets to be accounted for by the General Fixed Assets Account Group (GFAAG), not by the fund entity that accounts for the operations of the department or activity using the long-lived assets in the provision of services (nor even the fund entity that expended an appropriation in order to acquire the asset).

Recommended records of the General Fixed Assets Account Group provide enough information (cost of each asset, its estimated useful life, its location, or the department to which it is assigned) to enable depreciation to be computed in a system divorced from the currently recommended accounting system. The cost system may selectively focus only on those programs or activities, or grants, for which depreciation would be a significant element of cost.

It is fairly apparent that the assignment of depreciation expense as a program, activity, or grant cost is not difficult if the asset being depreciated is used for only one program, activity, or grant. If an asset benefits more than one program or activity (such as a building occupied by several departments), an equitable and clerically feasible basis for allocation of the total depreciation expense must be found. Presently recommended records of the General Fixed Assets Account Group would not necessarily provide the appropriate information, but it would not be difficult to supplement existing records by statistical studies and estimates of knowledgeable personnel to provide depreciation expense chargeable to each program or activity in all instances in which depreciation is a significant element of cost. (The designers of accounting systems for agencies of the federal government of the United States have provided for routine recording of depreciation expense and other program expenses as well as the recording of appropriation expenditures, as explained in Chapter 13.)

Measurement of Costs *Ex Ante*.   Underlying the discussion in the preceding section on translating expenditures into costs is the assumption that cost is being measured *ex post* (after the fact). The observations in that section would hold true in developing program costs *ex ante* (before the fact), but only in the rather near future for which costs will result from activities that may be planned with a reasonable degree of certainty. The costs of proposed programs, however, must often be projected for many years into the future (as much as 100 years in the case of natural resources programs). Capital budgeting techniques widely advocated for use by both profit-seeking businesses and governmental bodies—and actually used to some extent by both—provide for discounting future costs to their value at the time the decision to accept or reject the project is to be made. Economists argue among themselves as to the correct discount rate to use in these computations. The answer is probably easier for state and local governmental projects than for projects proposed for the federal government; at least there appears to be some agreement that the rate paid on tax-exempt state and local governmental bonds would be appropriate. This conclusion is an oversimplification, however, because it is logical to allow for opportunity costs and political and social costs as well as accounting costs, that is: (1) If available general obligation bonding power is used to finance one given proposed project, no general obligation bonding power would be available for present alternative projects or for future alternative projects until the growth of assessed valuation and the retirement of debt allowed new bond issues; therefore, other financing sources, probably bearing higher rates, would have to be used. So, should all projects be discounted at the higher rates? (2) If the proposed construction of new freeways would split neighborhoods, isolating people from accustomed schools, churches, or shopping centers, as well as cause the condemnation of homes and the forced relocation of numerous residents (who also need to be thought of as voters), what *are* the costs that should be charged to the project? Even if the cost factors can be identified, with what degree of certainty can they be measured?

Measurement of Benefits.   In contrast to the problem of measurement of costs of governmental programs, which can be solved *ex post* at least by a reorientation of traditional accounting and the supplementation of it by additional statistical data, traditional government accounting offers little help in the solution of the problem of measurement of benefits. Nor does traditional business accounting offer much help. Determination of the existence or absence of a benefit of a governmental program is a subjective matter rather than the objective one faced by businesses, which can define a benefit in terms of earnings. Both direct benefits and spillover benefits may be claimed by proponents of a proposed program. Some benefits, of both categories, may be measurable in monetary units; some may be quantifiable but not in monetary terms; and some may be expressed in terms of increased cultural or recreational opportunities or other values of doubtful quantifiability. Further, each of the above categories can be subdivided on the basis of the expected timing of the occurrence of benefits (the range is from immediately on approval of the project to possibly 100 years in the future); on the basis of the degree of certainty of the occurrence of the benefits (ranging from reasonably certain to highly conjectural); and on the basis of dependence of the occurrence of the benefits on events external to the program under consideration (the range is from independent to highly dependent; the occurrence of the external events themselves may be of varying probabilities). Nonetheless, in spite of all the difficulties, rational allocation of resources requires the best available information as to benefits expected to result from a proposed program to be matched with the best available information as to costs of the same program. Before a purported benefit can be identified as a true benefit, the objectives of the government and the objectives of the proposed program must be identified. Relative to this, Hinrichs points out:

> The student of government decision making must not always assume that obscure and obfuscated objectives are totally lacking in function. Many times objectives are uncertain, changing, conflicting; this may not be the time for total inaction but instead a time of discovering and discussing objectives in the very process of moving in a general direction. Objectives often are a result of a feed-back process in getting the job underway and in working toward broader goals.[16]

Equally pragmatic, and equally relevant to the present discussion, is a comment by Hatry on the problem of expressing benefits in monetary items:

> Realistically most governmental problems involve major objectives of a nondollar nature. Not only is it very difficult for analysts to assign dollar "values" to such nondollar objectives, but it is also questionable whether it would be desirable even if it could be done. Thus, questions of the value of such effects as reducing death rates, reducing illness incidences and severities, improving housing conditions, and increasing recreational opportunities should not become simply a problem of estimating the dollar values of these things.
>
> The analysts should rather concentrate upon the estimation and presentation, for each alternative, of full information as the actual dollar effects and the effects upon the nonmonetary criteria. *This is the primary function of program analysis.*[17] [Emphasis added]

---

[16]Harley M. Hinrichs and Graeme M. Taylor, *Program Budgeting and Benefit-Cost Analysis* (Santa Monica, CA: Goodyear Publishing, 1969), p. 13.
[17]Ibid., p. 101.

If the anticipated benefits from a program cannot be stated in quantitative terms, they must be stated verbally. In order to be of value in the management process, the statement must be explicit and in operational terms, not "God and Motherhood" generalities.

Budgeting in Nongovernmental Not-for-Profit Organizations

The budgeting and costing issues of not-for-profit organizations, such as voluntary health and welfare organizations (VHWOs) differ from those in governmental entities, in part, because VHWOs rely on grants and contributions in the operation of distinct programs, rather than on taxes or user charges. Grants may be received from governmental entities, other not-for-profit organizations, or foundations; and contributions come from individual donors. Either type of funding may be given to support specified programs or the organization as a whole. Grants are characterized by proposed budgets, authorized direct and indirect costs, grant periods, and periodic reports to the grantor by the recipient agency. The accounting challenge is to capture total costs of each program and to match actual to budgeted costs for each grant. Difficulties arise because shared costs must be allocated across programs, grantors have different fiscal years, and terminology often differs across granting sources. For example, federal government grants may approve *telephone and printing* costs, while a local government grant covers *communication* costs. Further complications come when there are multiple grantors for one program, and multiple programs supported by one grantor.

Accounting Information Systems

Even small organizations have computerized accounting systems. At issue is whether the entity will use a relatively inexpensive commercial package designed for business entities, or higher priced software designed for not-for-profit entities. Whatever the decision, the creation of a chart of accounts is a critical step that must be done at the beginning stages of the organization, and revised each time the agency changes software or has other structural changes in its operation. The chart of accounts provides the framework used to classify transactions that affect programs as well as granting sources. Decision makers who are expected to use the reports generated by the accounting information system (for example, management, program directors, the Board of Directors, grantors, and donors) should all be considered in the process of creating the chart of accounts so that the accounting system captures information that is useful, relevant, and reliable.

Illustration 14–8 shows a simple chart of accounts for a VHWO that advocates for school-age students at-risk. The agency has seven programs funded, in part, by 12 grantors. Natural expenses (i.e., objects of expenditures or line items) are called *costs* when associated with programs and *expenses* when related to general and administrative or fund-raising activities.

In order to report on activities effectively for various decision makers, the chart of accounts must allow for costs to be characterized by program and grant, as well as natural line item. Some accounting software facilitates this reporting by

Illustration 14–8   Chart of Accounts for a Nongovernmental, Not-for-Profit Organization

Type of Account X	Object XX	Program X	Funding Source XX
1 = Assets	10 = Cash 20 = Accounts receivable 30 = Inventory 40 = Prepaid expenses 50 = Investments 60 = Property, plant, and equipment 70 = Accumulated depreciation	A = Community Impact B = Youth Commission C = Juvenile Court Advocacy D = Student Outreach E = Safe Schools F = Parent Effectiveness Training G = Advocacy	01 = Federal grant 02 = Community development block grant 21 = State grant 22 = County grant 23 = City grant 24 = City Housing Commission grant 30 = Ford Foundation grant 31 = Kellogg Foundation grant 32 = Smith Foundation grant 33 = Brown Foundation grant 43 = Universal Church 50 = United Way
2 = Liabilities	10 = Accounts payable 20 = Accrued payroll 30 = Other accrued liabilities		
3 = Net assets	10 = Unrestricted net assets 20 = Unrestricted, designated net assets 30 = Temporarily restricted net assets 40 = Permanently restricted net assets		
4 = Revenues	10 = Contributions 20 = Grants 30 = Charges for services 40 = Dues 50 = Investment income 60 = Special events 70 = Miscellaneous		
5 = Cost of programs 6 = Expenses (General and administrative; fund-raising)	11 = Salaries and wages 12 = Fringe benefits and payroll taxes 20 = Travel 30 = Supplies, phone, postage, printing 40 = Occupancy costs 60 = Equipment maintenance 61 = Depreciation 70 = Legal and professional services 80 = Miscellaneous		

allowing reports to be prepared based on a range of account numbers in which fields of the account number are *masked* to focus on the distinguishing field in the account number. For the example agency in Illustration 14–8, which has a six-digit account number, a report for the Community Impact program could be generated by printing all revenues and costs for the A program; that is, the range of accounts used in the report would be 4**A** and 5**A** where the * is used as a *wild card* to indicate all numbers. Similarly, if the agency wants a report on the Federal grant, they select 4***01 and 5***01 accounts. Other software may produce the same result by allowing each revenue or cost to be characterized, and consequently sorted, by another item; for example, programs may be considered *classes or jobs* and funding sources may be treated as *customers*. Not surprisingly, more expensive software programs written specifically with nonprofit agencies and their needs in mind may be more efficient in producing specialized reports.

Conclusion

An entity that integrates its strategic planning, budgeting, and cost/benefit analysis with the management of the resources with which it is entrusted can more effectively document performance than if these financial management functions stand alone. The statement of anticipated benefits from a proposed program, activity, or grant should follow from a statement of objectives for it. The statement of objectives should be expanded into a plan of action to achieve the objectives, which in turn serves as a basis for planning costs to be incurred. Unless this course is followed, administrators and legislators will not be able to allocate resources of the governmental unit wisely, nor will administrators be able to manage resources committed to approved programs. Legislators and the public have a right to expect this integration of long-range analysis and fiscal period planning, so that they may evaluate the actions of the administrators in following the plan as well as the success of the programs in achieving the stated objectives. Cost accounting takes on an even more important role in long-range fiscal planning as organizations evaluate the benefits of privatizing and out-sourcing traditional functions.

Key Terms

Activity-based costing (ABC), 576	Indirect costs, 576
Allowable costs, 574	Performance budgeting, 560
Budget calendar, 564	Process cost, 572
Budget officer, 564	Program budgeting, 560
Cost determination, 573	Planning-programming-budgeting system ·
Cost objective, 575	(PPBS), 561
Direct costs, 575	Service efforts and accomplishments, 570
Flexible budgeting, 572	Total quality management, 569
Job order cost, 572	Zero-based budgeting, 561
Incremental budgeting, 559	

Questions

14–1. Explain the interrelation among the processes of policy setting, service delivery, evaluation, and budgeting that should exist in a governmental unit.

14–2. If governmental budgets should be prepared to facilitate management of resources, why should the budget documents be subjected to study by individual taxpayers, reporters, and public interest groups, as well as by legislative bodies?

14–3. Explain the costs and benefits of performance budgeting compared with incremental budgeting.

14–4. "Every rational budgeting approach that has been experimented with by governments has been a failure." Do you agree or disagree with this statement? Explain fully.

14–5. What advantages does total quality management (TQM) offer compared with rational budgeting approaches? Is it fundamentally a budgeting approach?

14–6. What are some of the factors to be taken into account in preparing revenue estimates for inclusion in a budget?

14–7. Assuming the typical governmental budget is a collection of departmental budgets, each of which shows only the department's requested appropriation for personal services, materials and supplies, and capital outlays, specify the advantages and disadvantages each of the following groups should find if a city were to convert to a program budget:

a. The city's central administration.
b. The city's departmental administrators.
c. The city's legislative body.
d. The city's taxpayers.

14–8. Why is a good cost accounting system an important component of rational budgeting?

14–9. If governmental units, educational institutions, and nonprofit health care entities exist in order to provide services needed by the public, or a segment of the public, and are not concerned with the generation of net income, why should they be interested in the determination of costs? Explain your answer.

14–10. The Finance Officer of a small city has heard that certain items of cost may be allowable under federal grants and contracts, even though they were not incurred specifically for the grant or contract. To what source could the Finance Officer go to determine what costs are allowable under federal grants and contracts?

14–11. Explain in your own words what indirect costs are. For what reason would the administrator of a governmental unit or nonprofit organization want indirect costs allocated to cost objectives?

14–12. What criteria should be applied to the selection of a basis for the allocation of indirect expenses? Explain.

14–13. Below are listed a number of activities and work units often used in measuring output of the activities for purposes of relating cost to output or determining unit costs. For each one, state one or more factors that might make it difficult to evaluate performance of the activity.

Street cleaning—linear mile	Servicing of parking meters—each
Sweeping and collection of leaves—square yard	School bus operation—student-day
Billing of taxes—bill	
Earth excavation—cubic yard	Solid waste collection—ton
Snow and ice removal—cubic yard	Recording documents—document
Laying of mains—linear foot	

14–14. Explain why conventional cost accounting systems have become less useful in both the business and government setting. How does activity-based costing (ABC) reduce the problems created by conventional cost accounting systems?

Cases

14–1. The Frumerville Hospital has always determined the full cost of serving patients by accounting for the direct and indirect costs of all hospital operations. The hospital uses the step-down method of allocating indirect costs: The costs of nonrevenue producing departments are allocated in sequence to departments they serve, whether or not these produce revenue; once the costs of a department have been allocated, the costing process for that department is closed, and it receives no further charges. A new CFO has recently joined the Hospital after a distinguished career in the manufacturing industry. In that capacity, he initiated activity-based costing (ABC), which resulted in a documented savings to the business. As an accounting assistant, you have been asked to meet with the CFO to discuss the issues involved in implementing ABC in this Hospital. A copy of the Hospital's most recent Step-Down Expense Distribution is presented here.

FRUMERVILLE HOSPITAL
Step-Down Method—Expense Distribution
Year Ended April 30, 19—

	Direct Costs	Mainte-nance of Plant	Opera-tion of Plant	House-keeping	Laundry and Linen	Cafe-teria	Adminis-tration	Medical Supplies	Medical Records	Nursing Service	Dietary	Total Costs
General Services:												
Maintenance of plant	$ 252,000	$(252,000)	—	—	—	—	—	—	—	—	—	—
Operation of plant	354,600	113,400	$(468,000)	—	—	—	—	—	—	—	—	—
Housekeeping	357,000	2,520	2,340	$(361,860)	—	—	—	—	—	—	—	—
Laundry and linen service	216,000	10,080	16,848	7,236	$(250,164)		—	—	—	—	—	—
Cafeteria	23,640	756	14,508	7,236	1,251	$(47,391)	—	—	—	—	—	—
Administration	844,800	7,560	28,548	25,332	249	6,918	$(913,407)	—	—	—	—	—
Medical supplies	480,000	2,520	6,084	1,809	501	1,707	39,276	$(531,897)	—	—	—	—
Medical records	132,000	2,520	4,680	10,857	—	1,137	25,575	—	$(176,769)	—	—	—
Nursing service	1,800,000	1,764	7,020	2,532	6,504	20,709	466,752	—	—	$(2,305,281)	—	—
Dietary	657,000	10,080	19,188	10,857	3,003	4,596	103,215	—	—	—	$(807,939)	—
Special Services:												
Operating rooms	482,460	25,200	28,548	3,618	41,778	3,459	77,640	79,785	—	—	—	$ 742,488
Delivery rooms	141,000	15,120	14,508	10,857	21,015	1,422	31,968	53,190	—	—	—	289,080
Radiology	300,000	10,080	14,508	14,475	3,003	1,707	29,276	—	—	—	—	383,049
Laboratory	381,000	7,560	16,848	14,475	3,003	3,459	77,640	—	—	—	—	503,985
Blood bank	219,000	2,016	3,744	5,427	249	570	12,789	—	—	—	—	243,795
Cost of medical supplies sold	—	—	—	—	—	—	—	265,947	—	—	—	265,947
Routine Services:												
Medical and surgical	144,000	25,200	219,024	218,202	138,339	—	—	79,785	137,880	1,959,489	807,939	3,729,858
Nursery	13,500	3,024	23,868	7,236	18,762	—	—	26,595	8,838	345,792	—	447,615
Outpatient clinic	192,000	12,600	47,736	21,711	12,507	1,707	39,276	26,595	30,051	—	—	384,183
Totals	$6,990,000	$ 0	$ 0	$ 0	$ 0	$ 0	$ 0	$ 0	$ 0	$ 0	$ 0	$6,990,000

Required

In preparation for the meeting, answer the following questions by examining the Expense Distribution:

   a. What "activities" do you consider most appropriate in describing the operations of the Hospital?
   b. What are the cost drivers of these programs?
   c. What particular problems do you expect to face in implementing ABC in this Hospital?

14–2. As a cost reimbursement accountant in a large public research university, you are aware that federal agencies have increased auditing efforts in the area of federal research grants to higher education institutions. In particular, OMB *Circular A-21* detailing allowable costs for colleges and universities receiving federal funds has been revised. The administration has asked you whether it is appropriate to include certain overhead costs in the pool of indirect costs (facilities and administrative costs) that are recovered in most federal research awards. Items include: (1) holiday lights put on the President's university-owned home, (2) library books in the research section of the undergraduate library, (3) cost of a large boat used by the higher administration in meeting with faculty and outside researchers for social events, (4) advertising new graduate programs in the large urban newspaper, (5) clerical salaries in the academic departments where a large amount of research is conducted, and (6) utility bills in the research wing of one of the buildings.

Required

Write a short businesslike memo to the administration giving your opinion about whether these costs would be allowable "indirect costs" to be recovered in part by federal research grants. Defend your position.

14–3. **Internet Case.** Use the Internet to list as many governments as you can (in the state in which the college or university you are attending is located) that have received the Government Finance Officers Association Distinguished Budget Award since its inception in 1984 until today. Information may be available on the GFOA's own homepage (http://www.gfoa.org) or the individual city's homepages, or by searching the Internet using key words such as *governmental budgeting*. Identify the particular strengths of their budgets for which they were recognized.

Exercises and Problems

14–1. Obtain a copy of a recent operating budget document of a governmental unit.* Familiarize yourself with the organization of the operating budget document; read the letter of transmittal or any narrative that accompanies the budgets.

---

*The footnote of Exercise 1–1 suggested that you attempt to obtain an operating budget document from the entity whose CAFR you analyzed for Exercises 1–1 through 11–1. If this was not possible, write the Budget Officer of the city, town, or county of your choice and request a copy of the most recent available operating budget document.

Budgetary practices may differ from the GAAP reporting model as to *basis, timing, perspective,* and *entity.* GASB standards (*Codification,* Section 2400. 113–.122) define these differences as:

1. *Basis* differences arising through the employment of a basis of accounting for budgetary purposes that differs from the basis of accounting applicable to the fund type when reporting on the operations in accordance with GAAP.
2. *Timing* differences that can result in significant variances between budgetary practices and GAAP may include continuing appropriations, project appropriations, automatic reappropriations, and biennial budgeting.
3. *Perspective* differences resulting from the structure of financial information for budgetary purposes. The perspectives used for budgetary purposes include fund structure, and organizational structure, or program structure. In addition, some subsidiary perspective, such as nature of revenue source, special projects, or capital and operating budgets, may also be used. The fund structure and individual fund definitions establish which assets, liabilities, equities, and revenue and expenditure/expense flows are accounted for in a fund. In the traditional view, budgeting, accounting, financial reporting, and auditing would follow the fund perspective.
4. *Entity* differences are the fourth possible type of difference. Frequently, an "appropriated budget" may either include or exclude organizations, programs, activities, and functions that may or may not be compatible with the criteria defining the governmental reporting entity.

Answer the following questions, which aid in assessing the quality of the budget document you are reviewing.[†]

Policy Document: Does the operating budget you are reviewing include a coherent statement of organizationwide financial and programmatic policies and goals that address long-term concerns and issues? Does the operating budget document describe the organization's short-term financial and operational policies that guide budget development for the upcoming year? Does the budget document include a coherent statement of goals and objectives of organizational units (e.g., departments, divisions, offices, or programs)? Does the document include a budget message that articulates priorities and issues for the budget for the new year and describes significant changes in priorities from the current year, and the factors producing those changes?

Financial Plan: Does the operating budget document include and describe all funds that are subject to appropriation? Does the document present a summary of major revenues and expenditures, as well as other financing sources and uses? Does the document include summaries of revenues, and other resources, and of expenditures for prior-year actual, current-year budget and/or estimated current-year actual, and proposed budget year? Are major revenue sources described? Are the underlying assumptions for revenue estimates and significant revenue trends explained? Does the document include projected changes in fund balances for governmental funds included in the budget presentation, including all balances potentially available for appropriation?

[†]These questions are paraphrased from the awards criteria established by the Government Finance Officers Association for its Distinguished Budget Presentation Awards Program. Questions are arranged under the four key categories included in the award criteria: **Policy Document, Financial Plan, Operations Guide,** and **Communication Device.**

Does the budget document include budgeted capital expenditures and a list of major capital projects (even if these are authorized in a separate capital budget)? Does the document describe if, and to what extent, capital improvements or other major capital spending will impact the entity's current and future operating budget? Are financial data on current debt obligations provided, describing the relationship between current debt levels and legal debt limits, and explaining the effects of existing debt levels on current and future operations? Is the basis of budgeting explained for all funds, whether GAAP, cash, modified accrual, or some other basis?

Operations Guide: Does the operating budget document describe activities, services, or functions carried out by organizational units? Are objective methods (quantitative and/or qualitative) of measurement of results provided by unit or program? (Information on results should be provided for prior-year actual, current-year budget, and/or estimate, and budget year.) Does the budget document include an organizational chart for the entire organization? Is a schedule(s) or summary table(s) provided giving personnel or position counts for prior, current, and budget years, including descriptions of significant changes in levels of staffing or reorganizations planned for the budget year?

Communication Device: Does the operating budget document provide summary information, including an overview of significant budgetary issues, trends, and resource choices? Does the budget document explain the effect, if any, of other planning processes (e.g., strategic plans, long-range plans, capital improvement plans) upon the budget and budget process? Is the process used to prepare, review, adopt, and amend the budget explained? If a separate capital budget is prepared, is a description provided of the process by which it is prepared and how it relates to the operating budget? Are charts and graphs used, where appropriate, to highlight financial and statistical information? Is narrative information provided when the messages conveyed by the charts and graphs are not self-evident? Does the document provide narrative, tables, schedules, crosswalks, or matrices to show the relationship between different revenue and expenditure classifications (e.g., funds, programs, organization units)? Is a table of contents provided to make it easy to locate information in the document? Is there a glossary to define terms (including abbreviations and acronyms) that are not readily understood by a reasonably informed lay reader? Does the document include statistical and supplemental data that describe the organization and the community of population it serves, and provide other pertinent background information related to services provided? Finally, is the document printed and formatted in such a way as to enhance understanding and utility of the document to a lay reader? Is it attractive, consistent, and oriented to the reader's needs?

14–2. Write the numbers 1 through 10 on a sheet of paper. Beside each number write the letter corresponding with the best answer to each of the following questions.

1. The GASB *Budgeting, Budgetary Control, and Budgetary Reporting* Principle provides that:
   a. An annual budget should be adopted for every *governmental* fund type of a governmental unit.
   b. An annual budget should be adopted by every governmental unit.
   c. Budgetary comparisons should be included in the appropriate financial statements and schedules for governmental funds for which an annual budget has been adopted.
   d. Both *b* and *c* are correct.

2. Which of the following is *not* considered a "rational" budgeting approach?
    a. Incremental budgeting.
    b. Performance budgeting.
    c. Program budgeting.
    d. PPBS.
3. Which of the following budgeting approaches focuses mainly on relating work activity outputs to resource inputs?
    a. Incremental (line-item) budgeting.
    b. Performance budgeting.
    c. Program budgeting.
    d. PPBS.
4. Which of the following budgeting approaches requires formulation of the governmental unit's fundamental objectives and identification and evaluation of alternative ways of achieving objectives?
    a. Incremental (line-item) budgeting.
    b. Performance budgeting.
    c. Program budgeting.
    d. PPBS.
5. Which of the following steps would *not* usually be part of the budgeting process?
    a. Heads of operating departments prepare budget requests.
    b. Budget officer and other central administrators review and make adjustments to departmental requests.
    c. One or more public budget hearings are held.
    d. The Chief Executive (Mayor or City Manager, as appropriate) formally adopts the budget, thus giving it the force of law.
6. Which of the following kinds of information is useful for effective capital budgeting?
    a. A multiple-year forecast of needed capital improvements and proposed means of financing them.
    b. Physical measures of the service condition of plant assets.
    c. Estimated replacement costs to replace plant assets.
    d. All of the above are useful for capital budgeting.
7. Which of the following budgeting approaches is most consistent with total quality management (TQM)?
    a. Incremental (line-item) budgeting.
    b. Performance budgeting.
    c. Program budgeting.
    d. PPBS.
8. Measurement of *efficiency* requires that:
    a. Inputs be related to outputs.
    b. Inputs be related to outcomes.
    c. Outputs be related to outcomes.
    d. Dollar cost of inputs be related to quantities of inputs.
9. Which of the following is the central focus of a TQM system?
    a. Measuring productivity and quality improvement.
    b. Rewarding employees for productivity and quality achievement.
    c. Obtaining the support and commitment of top-level officials.
    d. Continuously meeting or exceeding customer expectations.

10. Measures of service accomplishments include:
    a. Input measures.
    b. Output measures.
    c. Outcome measures.
    d. Both *b* and *c*.

14–3. Write the numbers 1 through 10 on a sheet of paper. Beside each number write the letter corresponding with the best answer to each of the following questions.

1. Cost principles established by the federal Office of Management and Budget (OMB) apply to which of the following types of entities?
   a. State and local governments.
   b. Colleges and universities.
   c. Nonprofit organizations such as museums.
   d. All of the above.

2. Which of the following is *not* a general criterion for a cost item to be an "allowable" cost?
   a. Be necessary and reasonable for proper and efficient performance and administration of the federal financial assistance program.
   b. Be approved by the Cost Accounting Standards Board.
   c. Be determined in accordance with generally acceptable accounting principles.
   d. Be authorized or not prohibited under state or local regulations.

3. Which of the following is an example of an applicable credit?
   a. Purchase discount.
   b. Advertising expense.
   c. A fund equity item that is reserved for capital construction with the permission of the grantor agency.
   d. All of the above.

4. Which of the following cost items would be unallowable by a federal grantor agency?
   a. Depreciation on buildings and equipment.
   b. Advertising expense.
   c. Alcoholic beverages for a Christmas party.
   d. All of the above.

5. Which of the following ordinarily would *not* be classified as a direct cost of a particular grant?
   a. Depreciation on buildings and equipment.
   b. Compensation of employees for time spent working on the specific federal assistance programs.
   c. Materials consumed in performance of the specific federal assistance programs.
   d. None of the above.

6. Costs that are incurred for a common or joint purpose benefiting more than one cost objective and that are not readily assignable to the cost objectives specifically benefited, without effort disproportionate to the results achieved, are referred to as:
   a. Pseudo costs.
   b. Indirect costs.
   c. Direct costs.
   d. Activity-based costs.

7. Which of the following statements about activity-based costing is true?
   a. It is intended to reduce the probability of distorted unit costs that may adversely affect management decisions.
   b. It eliminates the need for allocation of indirect costs.
   c. It permits measuring the true cost of every unit of output (i.e., cost measures that are free from subjective estimates).
   d. All of the above.
8. In activity-based costing, the amount of activity-related cost that is consumed in producing goods or service is measured by the consumption of units of particular allocation bases referred to as:
   a. Activities.
   b. Cost objects.
   c. Activity cost drivers.
   d. Unit costs.
9. A good cost accounting system facilitates a kind of budgeting in which the costs associated with different levels of activity are planned for. Such a form of budget is referred to as:
   a. Incremental budgeting.
   b. Fixed budgeting.
   c. Rational budgeting.
   d. Flexible budgeting.
10. Determining the cost of depreciation related to the general fixed assets of a governmental unit for purposes of charging the cost to a federal grant, or for internal costing of services, is complicated by which of the following factors?
    a. The method of depreciation used does not correspond with actual patterns of asset consumption.
    b. Some fixed assets are used for many activities and typically no records of such use are maintained.
    c. Depreciation is not recorded in any governmental fund type for such assets, nor is depreciation usually recorded in the General Fixed Assets Account Group.
    d. Both *b* and *c* are correct.

14–4. A portion of the General Fund operating budget for Southwest City's Street Department is shown below and on the following two pages.

Required

After reading and evaluating the budget information for the Street Department of Southwest City, answer the following questions:
   a. Does the City appear to be using program budgeting? If not, what form of budgeting is the City using?
   b. Does the budget provide information useful for evaluating the performance of the Street Department's management?
   c. Do the goals established for the Street Department appear appropriate? How could they be improved?

SOUTHWEST CITY
ANNUAL BUDGET
FY 1999–2000

GENERAL FUND
DESCRIPTION
STREETS

DEPARTMENT DESCRIPTION

The Street Department is responsible for maintaining all City-owned streets, alleys and parking lots, keeping them in serviceable condition to ensure the safety and welfare of the public. Activities include repairing damage caused by waterline breaks; repairing potholes and patching utility cuts; repairing base failures; preparing street driving surfaces for annual seal coating program; reconstructing streets to upgrade driving surface and drainage to meet increased traffic volumes; cleaning and repairing drainage ditches and structures; inspecting and making repairs to City bridges and sidewalks; performing annual crack sealing to prevent water damage to driving surface of streets; performing traffic counts on an as-needed basis; installing and maintaining traffic control signs and paving markings; responding to emergency conditions by barricading, sandbagging, clearing of fallen trees and debris from streets and drainage structures, and sanding of streets during icing conditions; mowing rights-of-way and maintaining street and alley shoulders; installing and maintaining street name signs; and assisting other departments as needed.

Expenditure Summary

Classification	97–98 Actual	98–99 Budget	98–99 Estimated	99–2000 Budget
Personnel	$206,135	$226,748	$227,273	$250,000
Supplies	10,649	11,714	11,818	13,000
Maintenance	70,624	77,686	66,367	73,000
Services	73,768	81,145	60,909	67,000
Capital Outlay	31,927	2,500	34,000	3,000
Total	$393,103	$399,793	$400,367	$406,000

Staffing

Position	Number
Superintendent	1
Assistant superintendent	1
Crew leader	2
Equipment operator	6
Total	10

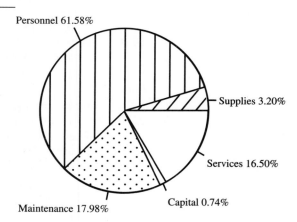

Personnel 61.58%
Supplies 3.20%
Services 16.50%
Capital 0.74%
Maintenance 17.98%

SOUTHWEST CITY
ANNUAL BUDGET
FY 1999–2000 *(continued)*

GENERAL FUND
DEPARTMENTAL GOALS
STREETS

Department Goals

Increase the number of repairs for old utility cuts, upgrade the street driving surface, and prevent future water damage.

Pursue an aggressive weed and grass control program within street gutters, rights-of-way, and behind curbs.

Increase miles of street shoulder repairs to prevent pavement breaking and erosion.

Replace existing noncompliance yield signs with stop signs.

Increase work-hours spent on trimming overhanging limbs and brush in and over streets.

Indicators

Measurement	97–98 Actual	98–99 Estimated	99–2000 Proposed
Traffic and street signs	84	159	175
Miles of streets maintained	66	70	70
Square yards of seal coating	42,500	44,800	42,500
Number of utility cuts	136	155	250
Miles of right-of-way mowing	34	172	172
Tons of asphalt for potholes	84	102	175
Tons of asphalt for street leveling	66	40	100
Feet of drainage ditches cleared	3,350	3,750	4,250
Feet of street shoulder bladed	4,150	5,275	6,000
Square yards of sidewalks repaired	40	65	150
Feet of weed control on streets	12,500	16,750	18,000
Miles of streets cleaned	10	19	76

Streets

Account Number	Account Description	FY98 Actual	FY99 Budget	FY99 Estimated	FY2000 Budget
02-13-00-0101	Salaries—Administrative	$ 4,827.90	$ 4,910.00	$ 4,910.00	$ 4,910.00
02-13-00-0102	Salaries—Operations	27,445.47	29,834.00	29,834.00	36,617.00
02-13-00-0103	Salaries—Supervisory	67,951.32	70,081.00	59,231.00	58,577.00
02-13-00-0104	Salaries—Skilled	42,957.99	42,944.00	55,175.00	69,443.00
02-13-00-0107	Salaries—Overtime	6,584.77	6,854.00	7,604.00	6,500.00
02-13-00-0108	Part-time and hourly	0	1,800.00	0	0
02-13-00-0116	TMRS retirement	12,159.21	11,847.00	12,169.00	11,665.00
02-13-00-0117	Employer's FICA	11,249.99	1,581.00	11.208.00	11,707.00
02-13-00-0118	Hospitalization insurance	12,203.21	13,532.00	13,090.00	15,544.00
02-13-00-0119	Workers' compensation	20,351.76	32,987.00	33,941.00	33,941.00
02-13-00-0120	Unemployment compensation	403.38	378.00	111.00	1,096.00
	Total Personnel	$206,135.00	$226,748.00	$227,273.00	$250,000.00
02-13-00-0210	Chemical supplies	$ 760.95	$ 250.00	$ 0	$ 1,500.00
02-13-00-0220	Clothing supplies	1,638.28	2,164.00	1,520.00	1,600.00
02-13-00-0260	General office supplies	14.79	50.00	6.00	25.00
02-13-00-0270	Janitorial supplies	143.43	50.00	72.00	75.00

SOUTHWEST CITY
ANNUAL BUDGET
FY 1999–2000 (concluded)

GENERAL FUND
EXPENDITURES
STREETS

Account Number	Account Description	FY98 Actual	FY99 Budget	FY99 Estimated	FY2000 Budget
02-13-00-0280	Minor tools	609.32	300.00	496.00	400.00
02-13-00-0285	Fuel and vehicle supplies	6,938.49	8,500.00	8,861.00	8,900.00
02-13-00-0290	Other supplies	543.74	400.00	863.00	500.00
	Total Supplies	$ 10,649.00	$ 11,714.00	$ 11,818.00	$ 13,000.00
02-13-00-0302	Building maintenance	$ 0	$ 50.00	$ 93.00	$ 50.00
02-13-00-0304	Street maintenance	17,520.75	20,950.00	20,950.00	18,950.00
02-13-00-0305	Seal coating and overlays	37,457.21	35,488.00	24,481.00	35,275.00
02-13-00-0306	Sidewalks	5,085.75	1,048.00	1,048.00	1,000.00
02-13-00-0307	Street sweeping	0	10,500.00	10,500.00	9,575.00
02-13-00-0401	Heating and air conditioning maintenance	60.00	50.00	225.00	50.00
02-13-00-0420	Machine tools maintenance	1,928.05	1,500.00	1,978.00	1,500.00
02-13-00-0430	Motor vehicle maintenance	5,000.00	5,000.00	5,000.00	3,500.00
02-13-00-0460	Radio maintenance	0	100.00	0	100.00
02-13-00-0480	Signs	3,572.24	3,000.00	2,092.00	3,000.00
	Total Maintenance	$ 70,624.00	$ 77,686.00	$ 66,367.00	$ 73,000.00

14–5. The police chief of the Town of Meridian submitted the following budget request for the Police Department for the forthcoming budget year 2000–01.

Item	Actual FY99	Budget FY00	Forecast FY00	Budget FY01
Personnel	$1,051,938	$1,098,245	$1,112,601	$1,182,175
Supplies	44,442	61,971	60,643	64,450
Maintenance	47,163	45,310	46,139	47,422
Miscellaneous	34,213	36,272	32,198	37,723
Capital outlay	65,788	69,433	67,371	102,210
Totals	$1,243,544	$1,311,231	$1,318,952	$1,433,980

Upon questioning by the newly appointed Town Manager, a recent Masters of Public Administration graduate from a nearby university, the Police Chief explained that he had determined the amounts in the budget request by multiplying the prior year's budget amount by 1.04 (to allow for the expected inflation rate of 4 percent). In addition, the personnel category includes a request for a new uniformed officer at an estimated $40,000 for salary, payroll expenses, and fringe benefits. Capital outlay includes a request for a new patrol vehicle at an estimated cost of $30,000. The amount of $300 was added to the Maintenance category for estimated maintenance on the new vehicle. The Police Chief is strongly resisting instructions from the Town Manager that he justify not only the need for the new uniformed position and additional vehicle but also the need for the *existing* level of resources in each category. The Town Manager has stated she will not request any increase in the Police Department's budget unless adequate justification is provided.

Required

    a. Evaluate the strengths and weaknesses of the Police Chief's argument that his budget request is reasonable.

    b. Are the Town Manager's instructions reasonable? Explain.

    c. Would the Town Council likely support the Town Manager or the Police Chief in this dispute, assuming the Police Chief might take his case directly to the Town Council?

    d. What other improvements could be made to the Town's budgeting procedures?

14–6. Compensation for personal services rendered during the period of performance under the grant agreement is an allowable cost under OMB *Circular A-87,* as are employee benefits such as vacation leave, sick leave, or employer's contributions to retirement and health plans, and so on, if "the cost thereof is equitably allocated to all related activities, including grant programs."

    During 1999, Jane Anderson, an employee of Oak City, was paid an annual salary of $56,000. She took three weeks' paid vacation plus one-week paid sick leave. The employer's contributions to retirement and health plans amounted to 25 percent of Anderson's annual salary. During 1999, Anderson worked 12 weeks on HHS Grant No. 9227. Compute the appropriate charge to that grant for Anderson's salary and fringe benefits (round to the nearest dollar).

14–7. On the basis of the following data, prepare a statement for the Town of Chippewa for the year ended June 30, 2000, showing the total cost of solid waste removal and the cost per ton of residential solid waste removed, or cubic yard of commercial solid waste removed (carry unit costs to three decimal places).

	Residential	*Commercial*
By town employees:		
Salaries and wages	$702,000	$481,000
Materials and supplies	$ 39,000	$ 36,090
Equipment use	$300,840	$201,470
Tons collected	165,000	—
Cubic yards collected	—	248,000
Labor-hours	90,000	68,000
By contractors:		
Cost	$ 78,900	$ 48,000
Tons collected	23,000	—
Cubic yards collected	—	30,000

Overhead for town force collection of residential solid waste is $0.948 per labor-hour; for commercial solid waste collection, $0.924 per labor-hour. Overhead for contract residential solid waste collection, 20 percent of cost (exclusive of overhead); for commercial solid waste collection, 15 percent of cost (exclusive of overhead).

14–8. The City of Lakeville operates a Shop and Maintenance Department and accounts for its activities by means of an internal service fund. In order to charge the using departments on an equitable basis for work orders filled, the Shop and Maintenance Department uses job order costing. Direct labor, materials used, and any other costs readily identifiable with a specific work order are charged to that work order, and overhead is allocated to each work order at the predetermined rate of 50 percent of direct labor dollars charged to the work order.

As of the end of fiscal year 1999, four work orders were being worked on; costs charged to each during 1999 were:

Work Order No.	Direct Labor	Direct Materials	Overhead	Total
871	$1,720	$ 770	$ 860	$3,350
875	240	660	120	1,020
876	860	750	430	2,040
877	380	630	190	1,200
Totals	$3,200	$2,810	$1,600	$7,610

During January 2000, direct labor cost was incurred for the following orders in the amount shown:

Work Order No.	Amount
871	$1,200
875	3,600
876	4,400
877	700
878	800
879	1,280
880	360
881	540

During January 2000, materials were used for the following orders in the dollar amounts shown:

Work Order No.	Amount
875	$2,600
876	570
877	120
878	440
879	680
880	600
881	1,210
882	80
883	120

The following orders were completed during January for departments accounted for by the funds shown:

Work Order No.	Fund
871	Capital Projects Fund (CPF)
875	General Fund (GF)
876	Enterprise Fund (EF)
878	Special Revenue Fund (SRF)

Required:

    a. Show in good form your computation of the total costs charged to each work order completed in January 2000.

    b. Assuming the department requesting work order 875 had estimated the cost to be $8,500, and the department requesting work order 876 had estimated the cost to be $9,000, show the entries each of these funds should make to record the approval of the invoice received from the Shop and Maintenance Department for the completed work order.

14–9. When the County Commission of Copper County questioned the County Treasurer about his request for additional appropriations, he claimed the large number of tax bills prepared and collected was responsible for the heavy expenses of his office. Since the duties of the Treasurer's office are rather uniform and of limited range, it was decided to attempt a cost study in an effort to determine the reasonableness of the Treasurer's request. As tax bills are numbered serially, it is possible to determine accurately the number prepared and collected. It was decided to divide the activities of the office into general administration, billing, and collecting. General administration consists of supervising the office and providing information to taxpayers, attorneys, and others. It would be measured on the basis of thousands of dollars of collections. Preparing bills and collecting would be measured on the basis of number of bills prepared and collected, respectively. The following information is available about the costs of the office:

1. The salary of the Treasurer is $4,000 per month. His time is devoted to general administration, except that during approximately three months of each year he spends practically all his time on collections.
2. Two regular deputies each receive $1,800 per month. Their time is divided approximately four months to billing, four months to collections, and the remainder to general administration.
3. During the year, the office spent $12,000 for extra help, of which two-thirds was chargeable to billing and one-third to collecting.
4. The office collected $240,000 of delinquent taxes, interest, and penalties during the year, of which the Treasurer retained 4 percent, to be credited equally to administration and collection.
5. Utility bills, stationery and stamps, repairs to office equipment, and retirement contributions, and so on, totaled $81,480 for the year. This was distributed to administration, billing, and collection on the basis of total salaries chargeable to those operations, except $20,600 spent for stamped envelopes was chargeable in total to collections.
6. The number of tax bills prepared during the year was 51,280, of which 740 were unpaid at the end of the year. The $240,000 of delinquent taxes collected during the year was on 625 bills.
7. Collection of current taxes during the year amounted to $3,000,000.

Required

a. Prepare a schedule to show the allocation of the Treasurer's office costs to general administration, billing, and collecting.
b. Prepare a schedule to show the computation of the unit costs for each activity. (The basis for measuring each activity is given above. Carry unit costs to the third decimal place.)

14–10. Activity-based costing data for various activities relating to signs, one of many responsibilities of the Department of Transportation for the City of Indianapolis, is provided on the following pages. Cost data relating to manufacturing, installation, removal, and other activities pertaining to highway signs and showing the level of accomplishment in terms of labor-hours expended for each activity and the total number of signs for each type of activity are provided below.

Required

    a. How does this method of accumulating costs compare with a typical cost accounting system that allocates many indirect costs on a predetermined overhead rate basis? Have you learned anything from this data that would not have been provided by a conventional costing system? Explain fully.

    b. Can you envision any problems with the ABC approach used here in terms of cost versus benefit analysis?

    c. Name some additional service programs that might benefit from a similar costing approach.

Total Costs for Signs

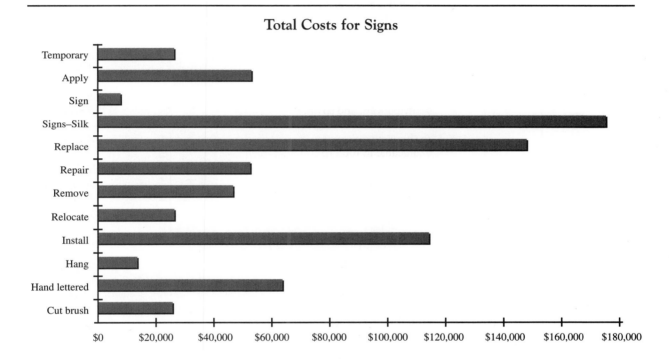

Total Costs for Signs (concluded)

Activity	Cut Brush	Hand-Lettered Signs	Hang Banners	Install Signs	Relocate Signs	Remove Signs	Repair Signs	Replace Signs	Signs—Silk Screen	Sign Cover	Apply Sign Face	Temporary Installation	Total
Personnel Costs:													
Operations administration	$ 735	$ 3,923	$ 538	$ 2,882	$ 339	$ 1,473	$ 1,787	$ 4,002	$ 5,560	$ 478	$ 2,295	$ 1,077	$ 25,089
Section administration	627	3,348	459	2,460	290	1,257	1,525	3,416	4,746	408	1,959	919	21,416
Section administration OT	3	16	2	12	1	6	7	16	23	2	9	4	103
Sign installation TECH I	2,871	0	838	9,310	0	3,684	5,817	13,286	0	0	0	2,363	38,169
Sign installation TECH II	7,364	0	1,866	26,707	0	12,836	14,173	38,711	0	0	0	8,423	110,080
Sign manufacturer	0	20,965	0	0	0	0	0	0	30,547	814	11,442	0	63,768
Warehouse	0	2,304	2,304	2,304	2,304	2,304	2,304	2,304	2,304	2,304	2,304	2,304	25,344
Total Personnel Costs	11,600	30,556	6,008	43,676	2,934	21,560	25,614	61,735	43,181	4,006	18,009	15,091	283,969
Direct Material Costs:													
Aluminum blank signs	0	0	0	0	0	0	0	0	0	0	7,072	0	7,072
Aluminum	0	4,290	0	0	0	0	0	0	35,450	0	0	0	39,739
Black ink	0	4	0	0	0	0	0	0	85	0	0	0	88
Face cover	0	0	0	0	0	0	0	0	0	0	13,559	0	13,559
Lettering	0	141	0	0	0	0	0	0	218	0	0	0	360
Red ink	0	15	0	0	0	0	0	0	44	0	0	0	59
Sheeting—ENG	0	2,193	0	0	0	0	0	0	10,132	0	0	0	12,324
Sheeting—HI	0	1,625	0	0	0	0	0	0	51,699	0	0	0	53,324
U iron	0	0	0	16,105	0	0	0	16,937	0	0	0	0	33,042
Total Direct Material Costs	0	8,267	0	16,105	0	0	0	16,937	97,628	0	20,630	0	159,567
Overhead Costs:													
Facility	2,138	0	543	7,769	0	3,734	4,123	11,264	0	0	0	2,450	32,021
Fixed assets	403	0	102	1,463	0	703	777	2,122	0	0	0	462	6,032
Central services	1,348	7,191	986	5,284	622	2,701	3,276	7,337	10,194	877	4,207	1,975	45,996
Supplies	3,184	16,989	2,330	12,484	1,469	6,380	7,738	17,333	24,082	2,071	9,939	4,665	108,664
Total Overhead Costs	7,073	24,180	3,961	27,000	2,091	13,518	15,913	38,056	34,276	2,948	14,146	9,552	192,713
Rolling Stock Costs:													
Unused equipment	477	0	121	1,733	0	833	920	2,513	0	0	0	547	7,145
Aerial van 28	883	0	1,980	6,931	0	2,060	1,124	6,850	0	0	0	642	20,471
Crewcab	0	0	0	1,555	0	11	0	0	0	0	0	0	1,566
Double bucket	0	0	0	0	0	0	0	0	0	0	0	797	797
Sign truck	4,171	0	0	10,948	0	6,801	8,334	20,549	0	0	0	3,905	54,709
VL aerial truck	0	0	0	5,664	0	1,122	393	673	0	0	0	1,346	9,197
Total Rolling Stock Costs	5,531	0	2,101	26,831	0	10,827	10,771	30,586	0	0	0	7,236	93,884
Total	$24,204	$63,003	$12,070	$113,611	$5,025	$45,906	$52,298	$147,315	$175,084	$6,954	$52,785	$31,879	$730,133

Signs—Unit Costs and Accomplishments

Activity	Cut Brush	Hand-Lettered Signs	Hang Banners	Install Signs	Relocate Signs	Remove Signs	Repair Signs	Replace Signs	Signs—Silk Screen	Sign Cover	Apply Sign Face	Temporary Installation	Total
Personnel Costs:													
Operations administration	1.42	1.60	1.42	0.75	1.42	1.42	1.42	0.89	0.99	1.42	1.86	1.42	16.03
Section administration	1.21	1.37	1.21	0.64	1.21	1.21	1.21	0.76	0.84	1.21	1.59	1.21	13.68
Section administration OT	0.01	0.01	0.01	0.01	0.01	0.01	0.01	0.00	0.00	0.01	0.01	0.01	0.07
Sign installation TECH I	5.54	0.00	2.21	2.43	0.00	3.55	4.62	2.94	0.00	0.00	0.00	3.11	24.41
Sign installation TECH II	14.22	0.00	4.92	6.97	0.00	12.37	11.26	8.57	0.00	0.00	0.00	11.10	69.40
Sign manufacturer	0.00	8.57	0.00	0.00	0.00	0.00	0.00	0.00	5.43	2.41	9.29	0.00	25.70
Warehouse	0.00	0.94	6.08	0.60	9.64	2.22	1.83	0.51	0.41	6.84	1.87	3.04	33.97
Total Personnel Costs	22.40	12.49	15.85	11.40	12.28	20.76	20.35	13.67	7.67	11.89	14.62	19.89	183.26
Direct Material Costs:													
Aluminum blank signs	0.00	0.00	0.00	0.00	0.00	0.00	0.00	0.00	0.00	0.00	5.74	0.00	5.74
Aluminum	0.00	1.75	0.00	0.00	0.00	0.00	0.00	0.00	6.30	0.00	0.00	0.00	8.05
Black ink	0.00	0.01	0.00	0.00	0.00	0.00	0.00	0.00	0.02	0.00	0.00	0.00	0.03
Face cover	0.00	0.00	0.00	0.00	0.00	0.00	0.00	0.00	0.00	0.00	11.01	0.00	11.01
Lettering	0.00	0.06	0.00	0.00	0.00	0.00	0.00	0.00	0.04	0.00	0.00	0.00	0.10
Red ink	0.00	0.01	0.00	0.00	0.00	0.00	0.00	0.00	0.01	0.00	0.00	0.00	0.01
Sheeting—ENG	0.00	0.90	0.00	0.00	0.00	0.00	0.00	0.00	1.80	0.00	0.00	0.00	2.70
Sheeting—HI	0.00	0.66	0.00	0.00	0.00	0.00	0.00	0.00	9.19	0.00	0.00	0.00	9.85
U iron	0.00	0.00	0.00	4.20	0.00	0.00	0.00	3.75	0.00	0.00	0.00	0.00	7.95
Total Direct Material Costs	0.00	3.39	0.00	4.20	0.00	0.00	0.00	3.75	17.36	0.00	16.75	0.00	45.44
Overhead Costs:													
Facility	1.81	2.05	1.81	0.96	1.81	1.81	1.81	1.13	1.26	1.81	2.38	1.81	20.45
Fixed assets	0.34	0.39	0.34	0.18	0.34	0.34	0.34	0.21	0.24	0.34	0.45	0.34	3.86
Central services	2.60	2.94	2.60	1.38	2.60	2.60	2.60	1.62	1.81	2.60	3.41	2.60	29.38
Supplies	6.15	6.95	6.15	3.26	6.15	6.15	6.15	3.84	4.28	6.15	8.07	6.15	69.41
Total Overhead Costs	10.90	12.33	10.90	5.78	10.90	10.90	10.90	6.80	7.59	10.90	14.31	10.90	123.10
Rolling Stock Costs:													
Unused equipment	0.92	0.00	0.32	0.45	0.00	0.80	0.73	0.56	0.00	0.00	0.00	0.72	4.50
Aerial van 28	1.70	0.00	5.22	1.81	0.00	1.99	0.89	1.52	0.00	0.00	0.00	0.85	13.98
Crewcab	0.00	0.00	0.00	0.41	0.00	0.01	0.00	0.00	0.00	0.00	0.00	0.00	0.42
Double bucket	0.00	0.00	0.00	0.00	0.00	0.00	0.00	0.00	0.00	0.00	0.00	1.05	1.05
Sign truck	8.05	0.00	0.00	2.86	0.00	6.55	6.62	4.55	0.00	0.00	0.00	5.14	33.78
VL aerial truck	0.00	0.00	0.00	1.48	0.00	1.08	0.31	0.15	0.00	0.00	0.00	1.77	4.79
Total Rolling Stock Costs	10.67	0.00	5.54	7.01	0.00	10.43	8.55	6.78	0.00	0.00	0.00	9.53	58.52
Total	43.97	28.21	32.29	28.39	23.18	42.09	39.81	31.00	32.62	22.79	45.67	40.33	—
Accomplishment	518 hours	2,446 signs	379 hours	3,832 signs	239 hours	1,038 hours	1,259 hours	4,517 signs	5,628 signs	337 hours	1,232 signs	759 hours	

605

CHAPTER

Planning and Control of Cash and Investments

Learning Objectives

After studying this chapter, you should be able to:

- Explain the objectives of cash management in a nonbusiness entity.
- Discuss cash planning and budgeting techniques.
    - Cash receipts budgeting.
    - Cash disbursements budgeting.
    - Forecasting monthly cash surplus or deficits.
- Describe internal controls over cash.
- Explain management of transfers between the federal, state, and local governments.
- Describe management of deposits and investments.
- Discuss other considerations in cash and investment management including arbitrage and the impact of technology.

The evolution of rational budgeting approaches and, more recently, governments' experimentation with total quality management (TQM) and service efforts and accomplishments (SEA) reporting, were discussed in Chapter 14. Motivating these experiments, of course, is the objective of improving government performance through better management of resources. Efficient and effective management of cash and investments is an important aspect of improving overall resource management. Sound cash management ensures maximum availability of cash to meet operating liquidity needs and reduces the need for short-term borrowing. Sound management of investments maximizes investment yield consistent with acceptable risk. Cash management and investment management are closely related activities, with cash representing both the input and output of the investment process. Both activities involve considerable risks that require well-designed policies and operating procedures to safeguard and protect cash and investments. Key aspects of managing cash and investments, as well as internal control procedures for safeguarding cash and investments, are discussed in this chapter. The focus will be on governments, although these concepts apply equally well to nongovernmental not-for-profit organizations, especially those that receive grants from governmental sources.

Objectives of Cash Management

Cash flows of a governmental entity arise from its operating activities, its investing activities, and its financing activities. This chapter focuses on the government's operating activities, represented by its operating cycle, and investing activities. As shown in Illustration 15-1, the **operating cycle** involves forecasting cash flows, collecting revenues, making disbursements for various purposes, and monitoring, evaluating, and auditing cash flows.

The cash management system should be designed to operate within the context of the overall financial management and operating systems of the government. As such, objectives for the cash management system should be consistent with program objectives and contribute to their attainment. Objectives for cash management are usually stated as (1) maximizing available cash to meet liquidity needs, (2) maximizing investment return or yield, and (3) protection of principal. Availability of minimum balances may be expressed as average days of cash on hand or percentage of budgeted cash outflows for a period such as a month. Expected or budgeted yield or return on investments of idle cash is determined, in part, by the governmental entity's policies for short-term investment of idle cash and its contractual arrangements with depository financial institutions (see Illustration 15-1). Actual yields for a period may be contractually fixed for investments such as deposits with depository institutions and repurchase agreements, but vary with market yields for other investments such as U.S. Government securities. Finally, effective policies for cash collections and disbursements are required to ensure revenues and other monies are collected as quickly as legally permissible and that obligations are paid when due but not before that date, except to take advantage of cash discounts for early payment.

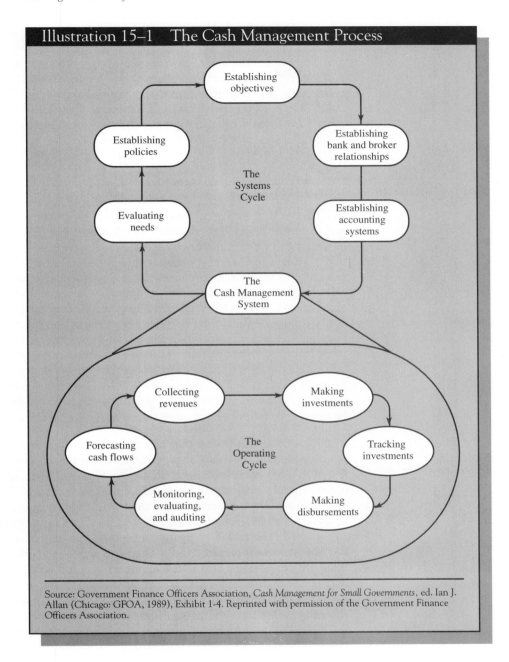

Illustration 15–1 The Cash Management Process

Source: Government Finance Officers Association, *Cash Management for Small Governments*, ed. Ian J. Allan (Chicago: GFOA, 1989), Exhibit 1-4. Reprinted with permission of the Government Finance Officers Association.

In a typical city, the elected City Council is responsible for establishing the city's cash management policy, and the City Manager, Mayor, Finance Director, Treasurer, and/or Cash Manager share responsibility for implementing it. The Data

Processing Manager and legal counsel are also key players in the cash management function. There is an increasing need for financial management expertise on the part of these people due to fluctuating interest rates and earnings in the financial markets, more-complex financial instruments, increasingly sophisticated computer technology, and limitations on the amount of taxes that can be levied due to tax-payer revolts in the 1970s and 80s. Public accountability is more important than ever in the face of the bankruptcy of the wealthiest county in the nation due to the unsound practices of its investment manager.[1]

Cash Planning and Budgeting

In Chapters 3, 4, and 14, it was assumed that, for the purposes described, Revenues and Expenditures budgets would best be prepared on the same basis as the accounts and financial reports: modified accrual, in the case of governmental funds—particularly general funds and special revenue funds. Although it is highly desirable for persons concerned with the financial management of governmental units (or any other organization) to foresee the effects of operating plans and capital improvement plans on receivables, payables, inventories, and facilities, it is absolutely necessary to foresee the effects on cash. An organization must have sufficient cash to pay employees, suppliers, and creditors amounts due at the times due, or it risks labor troubles, an unsatisfactory credit rating, and consequent difficulties in maintaining its capacity to render services at acceptable levels to its residents. An organization that maintains cash balances in excess of needs fails to earn interest on temporary investments; therefore, it is raising more revenues than would otherwise be needed, or failing to offer services.

Cash Receipts Budgeting

In Chapter 4 it was noted, that in a typical governmental unit, cash receipts from major sources of revenues of general funds and special revenue funds are concentrated in a few months of each fiscal year, whereas cash disbursements tend to be approximately level month by month. Under the heading "Tax Anticipation Notes Payable" in Chapter 4, reference is made to cash forecasting done by the Treasurer of the Town of Brighton in order to determine the amount of **tax anticipation notes** to be issued. The cash forecasting method illustrated in that chapter is quite crude but often reasonably effective if done by experienced persons. Sophisticated cash budgeting methods used in well-managed governmental units require additional data, such as historical records of monthly collections from each revenue source including percentage of billings, where applicable. In addition to the historical record of collections, the budget files should contain analyses of the factors affecting the collections from each source, so that adjustments to historical patterns may be made, if needed, for the budget year. For example, in the Town of Brighton illustrative case in Chapter 4, the revenue budget of the General Fund for FY2000 is:

---

[1]"As Orange County Blames Others, Guess Where Latest Report Points," *The Wall Street Journal*, September 7, 1995.

Property taxes	$2,600,00
Interest and penalties on delinquent taxes	13,000
Sales taxes	480,00
Licenses and permits	220,000
Fines and forfeits	308,000
Intergovernmental revenue	280,000
Charges for services	70,000
Miscellaneous revenues	15,000
Total	$3,986,000

As illustrated in Chapter 4, the revenues budget is currently prepared on the modified accrual basis: Those revenues susceptible to accrual are budgeted on the accrual basis. Property taxes, interest and penalties on delinquent taxes, and some items in the miscellaneous category are to be recognized as revenue when billed; the same would be true (although not specifically illustrated in Chapter 4) of regularly billed charges for inspection or other routinely provided services. Most intergovernmental revenues also may become measurable and available prior to collection; therefore, they may be accrued. Sales taxes and income taxes also may be accrued in instances in which taxpayer liability has been established and collectibility can be estimated with reasonable accuracy. Revenues expected from licenses and permits, fines and forfeits, charges for services, and items in the miscellaneous revenue category are usually budgeted (and recognized as revenue during the year) on the cash basis because the items ordinarily are not measurable in advance of collection. The only problem presented by the latter group of revenue sources in converting the revenues budget to a cash receipts budget is the forecast of how much revenue from each source will be collected during each month of the budget year. That is the primary problem presented by converting the accrual-based estimated revenues to the cash basis for cash budgeting purposes.

Additional problems arise in forecasting how much of the billed receivables will be collected in the year(s) following the one in which they are to be recognized as revenue, and how much of the billed receivables will probably never be collected. For example, in Chapter 4 (see Transaction 7) it is estimated that 4 percent of the property taxes billed will never be collected; therefore, in order to realize revenue of $2,600,00 it is necessary to levy taxes totaling $2,708,333. Assuming the tax bills are mailed to the taxpayers in March of each year, and taxpayers are required to pay half of their taxes no later than the first Monday in May and the remaining half no later than the first Monday in November, the historical collection experience, adjusted for economic conditions expected to affect owners of property in the Town of Brighton in FY2000, gives the following expected pattern of collection of taxes billed in 2000 (note that approximately 1 percent of the tax bills are paid in February before the bills are prepared and mailed; it is common for a few people who expect to be out of town during the late spring to have the Treasurer compute their bills early so they can pay their taxes before they leave):

January 2000	0.0%	August 2000	1.5%
February 2000	1.0	September 2000	1.5
March 2000	2.0	October 2000	5.0
April 2000	10.0	November 2000	22.0
May 2000	30.0	December 2000	3.0
June 2000	1.0	January 2001 and later	18.0
July 2000	1.0	Uncollectible	4.0

In accord with the above schedule, collections from the gross levy of $2,708,333 would be budgeted as (rounded to the nearest hundred dollars):

January 2000	$ 0	August 2000	$40,600
February 2000	27,100	September 2000	40,600
March 2000	54,200	October 2000	135,400
April 2000	270,800	November 2000	595,800
May 2000	812,500	December 2000	81,200
June 2000	27,100	January 2001 and later	487,600
July 2000	27,100	Total collectible	$2,600,000

In addition to collections of FY2000 revenues, the monthly cash budget of the Town of Brighton should include anticipated collections of receivables existing at the beginning of 2000 (Taxes Receivable—Delinquent, $660,000; and Interest and Penalties Receivable on Taxes, $13,200). Therefore, the total monthly Cash Receipts budget would be the sum of the amount expected to be collected each month from receivables as of the beginning of the year, revenues budgeted on the accrual basis, and revenues budgeted on the cash basis.

Property taxes are often the largest recurring cash receipt in a government; however, all other expected cash receipts must be included in the cash budget. More difficult to project are self-assessed taxes, such as income taxes; nonrecurring receipts, such as those from the sale of assets; and income earned on **sweep accounts,** arrangements where a bank automatically "sweeps" cash that exceeds the target balance into short-term cash investments.

Cash Disbursements Budgeting

Except for special provisions regarding expenditures of debt service funds, the expenditures of all other governmental funds (and of all proprietary funds) are to be recognized and budgeted on the full accrual basis. Therefore, the conversion of the approved appropriations budget (which is the legal authorization to incur liabilities for purposes and amounts specified in the appropriations bill or ordinance) into a cash disbursements budget involves a knowledge of personnel policies, purchasing policies, and operating policies and plans, which should govern the timing of expenditures of appropriations, and the consequent payment of liabilities. Information as to current and previous typical time intervals between the ordering of goods and contractual services, their receipt, and the related disbursements should be available from the appropriation expenditures ledgers and cash disbursement records. In the case of salaries and wages of governmental employees, the cash disbursements budget for each month is affected by the number of paydays that fall in the month, rather than that number of working days in the month.

As an example of cash disbursements budgeting, in the Town of Brighton illustrative case in Chapter 4 the FY2000 appropriation for Public Safety is $1,240,000. No further detail is given in Chapter 4 as to the organization units, functions, activities, or other classifications of expenditures authorized under the Public Safety heading. Assume detail provided in the appropriation ordinance includes the Fire Department under the Public Safety heading and specifically authorizes the Fire Department to incur expenditures in 2000 for the following object classes in the amounts given:

	Budget for 2000
Personal services	$408,960
Contractual services	44,400
Supplies	36,720
Capital outlays	118,640
Total Fire Department	$608,720

The appropriations budget may have provided for additional personnel to be added on completion of a new fire station, or on some other event expected to occur during the budget year, for promotions, retirements, changes in base pay, or a number of other events that need to be provided for in the legal appropriations but may not actually cause cash outlays during the budget year in the authorized amounts. The cash disbursements budget is a management tool, not a legal document; therefore, it should be prepared on the basis of what is actually expected to happen. If the Town of Brighton Fire Department is expected to be fully staffed with persons at the ranks and salaries specified in the appropriation, and if the personnel are paid every two weeks (26 paydays per year), the monthly cash disbursements for personal services would be $31,460 for each month in which two paydays occur, but $47,190 for each month in which three paydays occur—ignoring such real-world complications as the fact that withholding taxes and other deductions from gross pay may not need to be remitted to the state and federal government in the same months in which paychecks are issued.

The cash disbursements budgets for contractual services, supplies, and capital outlays for the Town of Brighton Fire Department depend on when goods, services, and equipment are expected to be ordered, received, and paid for. Assume the plans of the Department, purchasing agents, and others concerned produce the following pattern of disbursements, in total, for the remaining three object classes of the Fire Department appropriation (contractual services, supplies, and capital outlays):

	Total		Total
January 2000	$ 6,400	July 2000	$ 5,300
February	5,600	August	6,300
March	5,800	September	114,200
April	7,200	October	5,400
May	16,460	November	6,200
June	5,300	December	6,600

Cash disbursements budgets must, of course, allow for the provision of cash required to pay liabilities expected to exist at the beginning of the budget year that will mature during the year; offsetting the payment of liabilities incurred prior to the budget year is the fact that not all goods and services ordered in the budget year will be received during that year, and some of those received are purchased under terms that will not require payment until the year following the budget year.

Forecasting Monthly Cash Surplus or Deficits

After monthly cash receipts budgets are prepared for all sources of revenues of each fund and cash disbursements budgets are prepared for all organization units, and so forth, it is possible, and desirable, to match the two in order to determine when and for how long cash balances will rise to unnecessarily high levels, or fall to levels below those prudent management would require (or even to overdraft positions). Note the preceding sentence is concerned with cash receipts and disbursements of all funds of a governmental unit, not a single fund. There is no reason for bank accounts and fund cash accounts to agree, except in total. Effective cash planning and control suggests that *all* cash be put under control of the Treasurer of the governmental unit. To illustrate this cash management concept, assume cash budgets of all funds of the Town of Brighton indicate that receipts and disbursements of 2000 may be expected to have the relationships shown in Illustration 15-2, which appear to be self-explanatory. The operation of cash and investment pools is discussed in detail in Chapter 8.

As shown in Illustration 15–2, cash receipts for the Town of Brighton are highest in April, May, and November, presumably when taxes are collected. Disbursements are fairly constant across the year, except for January, which may be when capital assets are acquired. The pattern of short-term borrowing, repayment, and investment in Illustration 15–2 seems to indicate that the City's cash and investment policies include: (1) a target monthly cash balance of at least $425,000, (2) new borrowing made in increments of $5,000, and (3) cash exceeding the target used to repay short-term borrowing; any remaining excess is invested.

The preceding illustrations are based on the assumption that cash receipts and cash disbursements should be budgeted for each month of the budget year. A very small governmental unit that has few receipts and infrequent disbursements may be able to plan temporary investments and short-term borrowings on the basis of cash budgets for periods longer than one month, perhaps quarterly or semiannually. Conversely, a governmental unit with considerable cash activity involving large

Illustration 15–2

TOWN OF BRIGHTON
Budgeted Cash Receipts and Disbursements for 2000
(000 omitted)

	January	February	March	April	May	June	July	August	September	October	November	December
Balance first of month	$ 610	$425	$425	$425	$ 425	$425	$425	$427	$427	$427	$ 427	$425
Expected receipts during month	165	250	295	570	1,096	134	280	370	285	270	892	116
Cash available	775	675	720	995	1,521	559	705	797	712	697	1,319	541
Expected disbursements during month	1,050	240	280	325	320	320	508	325	315	335	320	455
Provisional balance at end of month	(275)	435	440	670	1,201	239	197	472	397	362	999	86
Less: Temporary investments purchased	—	—	—	—	346	—	—	—	—	—	454	—
Less: Repayment of short-term borrowings	—	10	15	245	430	—	—	45	—	—	120	—
Add: Temporary investments sold	—	—	—	—	—	186	160	—	—	—	—	340
Add: Short-term borrowings	700	—	—	—	—	—	70	—	30	65	—	—
Balance at end of month	$ 425	$425	$425	$425	$ 425	$425	$427	$427	$427	$427	$ 425	$426

sums might need to budget cash receipts and cash disbursements on a daily basis to maintain adequate, but not excessive, cash balances.

Budgeting, by definition, involves planning on the basis of assumptions about economic conditions, salary levels, numbers of employees at each salary level, prices of supplies and capital acquisitions, and other factors that cannot be foreseen with great accuracy. Accordingly, it is necessary at intervals throughout the year to compare actual receipts with budgeted receipts, source by source; and actual disbursements with budgeted disbursements for each organizational unit, function and object; not only for the sake of control (cash control is discussed in the next section of this chapter) but for the sake of evaluating the budget and, if necessary, revising the budget in light of new knowledge about economic conditions, salary, and price levels, and other factors affecting collections and disbursements.

Internal Controls

Because of its high state of liquidity and ease of transfer, cash occupies a preeminent position in the attention of accountants and auditors. Its usefulness to the rightful owners and its attractiveness to others cause it to be widely sought by means usually fair but sometimes foul. Furthermore, possibilities for honest mistakes are numerous in the receipt, custody, and disbursement of cash. Administrators, accountants, and auditors must be constantly alert in their endeavors that only fair or legal methods be used and that loss through error be reduced to a minimum. These observations are no less true of governmental cash than of that belonging to private individuals or enterprises. In fact, the greater separation in government of the ones who pay and the ones who spend, and the need for protection of those by whom government is financed, may constitute an even greater obligation for safeguarding public cash. Although parts of the following discussion are applicable to cash in general, special reference is intended to cash of governments and not-for-profit organizations.

Requirements for Adequate Cash Accounting

Some elements of desirable cash procedure pertain strictly to cash in one or another of its forms. Other elements may relate not only to cash but also to other financial aspects of the governmental unit concerned. As one example, some cash accounting procedures are closely related to accounting for revenue and expenditures, others to the reduction of noncash assets. It may be said that, in general, adequate cash control procedures must include the following:

1. Provision for determining, insofar as is reasonably possible, that the government receives all the cash to which it is legally entitled.
2. Accurate and complete accounting for cash received.
3. Adequate protection of cash between the time of receipt and the time of disbursement.

4. Provision for determining that the government disburses cash for all just debts when due.
5. Accurate and complete accounting for cash disbursed.

An indispensable element of good cash procedure, whatever other safeguards may exist, is a carefully planned and diligently applied system of internal control of the kind discussed in earlier chapters. In addition to the main scheme of internal control, numerous other techniques—such as the bonding of all employees handling cash and regular annual audits—serve to prevent or reveal irregularities; but detailed discussion of these precautions is not appropriate here.

Determining Whether All Cash that Ought to Be Received Is Received

One situation permitting a definite, clear-cut comparison between cash that should be received and cash actually received is found in the case of certain governmental revenue accounted for on the accrual basis. If one or more units or departments of government are charged with ascertaining and billing a given kind of revenue, whereas another department accounts for collection, the division of labor represents a very desirable form of control over cash. The best illustration of a situation such as the one described above is the prevailing practice and plan of handling the assessment, billing, and collection of property taxes. In one state, for example, assessing and billing are functions of the assessors' and auditors' offices, and collection rests with the treasurer. Because of direct and indirect checks on taxes reported as unpaid, the possibilities for the diversion of cash collected from taxpayers, without disclosure, is reduced to a minimum. Unfortunately, this control device cannot overcome defects in the assessment procedure that may undervalue property or entirely omit it from the basic inventory. However, this latter deficiency is more of a revenue problem than a cash problem.

Other forms of governmental revenue activity that lend themselves to the use of an accrual basis are utility services, some kinds of licenses and permits, revenue from the use of money and property, and revenue from other agencies. Utility services are furnished on a contractual basis; and with the proper use of service, billing, and collection forms, a close degree of correlation between the amount due and the amount received is possible. Many kinds of licenses and permits are granted for privileges to operate at specified locations or within given areas, and failure to obtain a license or permit is readily ascertainable. Assuring that fees arising from licenses and permits will be accounted for is largely a matter of using prenumbered authorization forms, for which strict accounting must be made. Money and property are of such tangible nature that accrual of income for their use and receipt of cash from that source are readily ascertainable through record-keeping and the exercise of reasonable care. Also subject to exact verification are receipts from the sale of bonds, from the issuance of notes, and from special assessment levies.

Some forms of revenue do not lend themselves to the use of accrual accounting; but once having reached the realization stage, accurate accounting for the cash to be received is largely a matter of well-organized and well-administered procedures. Thus it is not possible to determine accurately the amounts of income or gross receipts taxes that each taxpayer should pay; but once the taxpayer has acknowledged his liability by filing a return, or his employer has filed an information return, there can be close correlation between amounts of cash that should be received and amounts actually finding their way into the treasury. On the local governmental level, there is no practicable way of accruing revenue from parking meters; but once the money has been placed in the meter, determination of whether it gets into the bank account is a matter of establishing recognized safeguards around its movement from meter to bank account, that is, at least one control procedure at every stage.

For some kinds of revenue or receipts it is difficult to determine whether they have been collected and, if so, in what amount. In this category are fines, forfeitures, and penalties; some kinds of fees; refunds on disbursements; collection of receivables previously written off; and miscellaneous transactions not formally recorded until cash is received. Advance determination of amounts that should be received from each major revenue source, as discussed in the cash receipts budgeting section of this chapter, provides a basis for determining the reasonableness of amounts actually reported as collected.

In summary, to ensure that cash collected will be fully accounted for:

1. The accrual basis of accounting should be used wherever possible in order to establish liability of some employee or department to account formally for realization into cash of the asset recorded by the accrual.
2. Wherever possible, prenumbered forms should be used as a sort of receipt to be issued to the payor; every one of the numbered forms should be strictly accounted for; and payors should be encouraged to demand a formal, written receipt.
3. A system of internal control or check should be developed with the smallest possible number of weaknesses under the prevailing conditions and circumstances.
4. Cash receipts from all major revenue sources should be budgeted for each month of the fiscal year; actual collections should be compared with budgeted collections; and significant differences investigated.

After receipt of cash has been made a matter of record, the next step is proper and complete reporting. Since a government unit usually operates several funds, it is important to determine with certainty and to report the one to which each receipt belongs. Ownership of most cash is ascertainable without difficulty, but some collections may be of such miscellaneous nature that their classification should be settled by someone with recognized authority to decide doubtful cases. Within each fund, it is imperative to indicate the exact credit to be reported for the cash received. These credits may be to receivables, to revenue accounts for income not previously accrued, to liability accounts, to asset accounts for investments or properties sold, to expenditures accounts for refunds, and to others. Reporting of collections should be done in some prescribed form with supporting documents arranged in a predetermined manner, the entire arrangement devised to accomplish accurate and speedy recording of the transactions represented. Cash receipts should be delivered or deposited in total, without reductions for disbursements; but this admonition is sometimes ignored for convenience.

Classification by Fund

Techniques and rules for recording cash received by a governmental unit are primarily responsibilities of the accounting department. It is charged with ensuring that receipts are distributed to the various funds or activities to which they pertain. This means the accounting department must see that each fund or activity gets the cash to which it is rightfully entitled. Concerning the other side of the transaction, the sources from which cash is received must be recorded with accuracy. If it came from individuals or others to whom some charge had been made on a prior occasion, its recording must provide for properly crediting the accounts of those who had previously been charged. If no formal charge had been made, the credit will indicate the revenue or other source from which the collection originated, in order that statements and other financial reports may be prepared.

Media for the recording of cash receipts by the accounting department will normally consist of duplicate copies of receipts, stubs of licenses, and so forth issued, but sometimes they will consist of only classified summaries of departmental collections. These media may originate in departments, in special cashiers' offices, or in the main office of the treasury itself. Preferably, media and records for cash collections submitted to the accounting department should include not only copies or portions of the underlying document for each transaction but also a formal summarization showing sources and ownership of cash collected. These evidences may be accompanied by one or more copies of a bank deposit slip if the collection was deposited directly by the collecting agency, or by the collectors themselves.

Going a step further in control, some procedures may require formal permission by the controller before the collections may be presented to the treasurer. This permission may be in the form of a document known as a **deposit warrant, pay-in warrant,** or order, which is basically a formal acknowledgment that the collections and records thereof are accepted and an authorization to the treasury to receive them.

Custody and Protection of Cash

As mentioned previously, one device used to protect against loss is the bonding of all employees entrusted with handling cash. To make this safeguard protective to the fullest extent, daily or other frequent checks must be made on cash in the custody of the individuals bonded. A common practice contributing to this end is the preparation of daily or other periodic cash statements accounting for beginning balances, increases, decreases, and ending balances. Wherever possible, increase and decrease totals should be properly substantiated by documentary evidence—for example, copies of paid **warrants for disbursements**. A disbursement warrant is essentially a formal certification of the validity of a debt, with authorization or direction to a financial agent to pay the debt. A warrant, therefore, advances a claim one step beyond a voucher in the payment process.

Under some circumstances, variations may exist between cash as shown by the accounting department and cash according to the treasurer's records. Certain transactions may have been recorded by one and not by the other. Accounting for warrants payable is a common source of difference between the two sets of records. Assume the accounting department credits Cash to record warrants drawn on the treasury, whereas the treasurer credits Cash only when a check is issued or when the warrant is countersigned and issued, if the warrant serves as a bill of exchange after signature by the treasurer. At a given time, warrants issued by the accounting department but not yet covered by payments in the treasurer's office would cause the records of cash in the two offices to differ. On the other hand, the accounting department may treat warrants as liability instruments and not credit Cash (and debit Warrants Payable) until evidence of disbursement has been received from the treasurer's office. In this event, warrant payments that have not yet been taken up on the controller's books would cause variance between the two Cash accounts. Thus, in governmental accounting, cash reconciliations must recognize not only deposits in transit, outstanding checks, and other similar causes of difference found in reconciling individual and commercial bank accounts, but also another set of differences in the form of variances between accounting and treasury records. To be complete, governmental cash reconciliations must be extended to incorporate both sets of variations.

The selection of depositories of public funds must be made with extreme care to provide a maximum of safety. Some states, if not all, have enacted statutes regulating deposits of public funds. In some states, public funds are given priority of settlement over private deposits in the liquidation of banks. In others, certain standards of safety are prescribed, such as classification as a national bank or protection by the Federal Deposit Insurance Corporation (FDIC), or both. However, the maximum direct insurance provided by FDIC protection is only $100,000 except for some very special types of Trust Funds in the custody of the governmental unit. Another common form of protection is the requirement that the depository of public funds must give security in excess of the amount of deposits of public funds that it holds. At least one state requires banks to enter into a formal contract with the governmental unit to cover their extra liability as public depositories. Recall that GASB standards require disclosure in the Notes to the Financial Statements of the types of deposits authorized by legal and contractual provisions, as discussed later in this chapter and also in Chapter 6.

How many bank accounts should a governmental unit maintain? Should it have a separate bank account (not necessarily in separate banks) for each fund, bearing in mind that some states and local governments may have a multiplicity of funds? To this question no one answer will satisfactorily cover all situations. One argument favoring numerous bank accounts is that it is thus simpler to correlate the cash of each fund with the bank balance that belongs to it than if cash of several funds is mingled in one account. A second argument favoring separate bank accounts for each fund is that unauthorized interfund borrowing through fund overdrafts is made more difficult. If cash of two or more funds is deposited in one bank account, the cash of one fund may be overdrawn without showing as a bank overdraft, because of being covered by cash belonging to the other fund. Favoring a limited number of bank accounts are the arguments that fewer bank reconciliations are necessary at the end of each month and that consolidation of fund cash into a small number of accounts gives more substantial balances, minimizes overdrafts and service charges that might result from numerous small balances, and facilitates investment of amounts of cash not needed for disbursement. Also, as discussed in Chapter 8, pooling of cash and investments helps achieve improved investment of idle cash balances and contributes to improved cash management as well.

In determining the number of bank accounts to be used, convenience and details of the situation must be weighted carefully before making a decision. If only a few funds exist, a separate bank account for each one may be desirable and feasible. If the government unit has many funds, some consolidation would probably be advisable or even necessary. In any event, timely reconciliation of monthly bank statements to general ledger cash accounts and detailed journals is a critical internal control over cash, and, in the authors' opinion , the one most often neglected.

Large cities and states have the problem of accounting for cash that is collected in regional, district, or departmental offices and that cannot well be delivered to the main treasury for acknowledgment and deposit. A sound and convenient method for handling such collections is to require them to be deposited daily to the credit of the governmental unit to which they belong. This reduces the danger of loss and also makes the collection promptly available for use by the fund to which it belongs.

Cash Records

The form of records used to account for cash in the control of a governmental finance officer is subject to numerous variations; however, at least two requirements are fundamental:

1. The finance officer's (treasurer's) records must show exactly the amount of cash in his or her custody. This must include both bank balances and undeposited receipts.
2. The finance officer's records must show the ownership of all the cash in his or her custody, that is, the amount belonging to each fund and organizational unit.

Charges to the finance officer's cash accounts and credits to the equity accounts will derive largely from collections turned over for the credit of the funds. Credits to the cash accounts and charges to equity accounts will derive principally from disbursement documents, probably either a warrant for payment presented by the controller, countersigned by the treasurer, and issued to the creditor, or a check based on a warrant presented by the controller. Another type of charge may be an interfund transfer based on a transfer warrant and not requiring a disbursement document; however, some governmental units require even interfund settlements to be accomplished by a disbursement warrant or check. Although records of the treasurer's office are likely to be more or less simple in form, they must provide for the ultimate in accuracy and be of such nature as to facilitate frequent providing and reporting of funds on hands.

Two kinds of situations may complicate record-keeping for the treasury. One of these is the receipt of uncollectible checks and counterfeit money, and the other is shortages and overages. To provide a measure of protection against uncollectible checks, some governmental units require a notation on each check to show the number of the receipt or other document issued for the check. This facilitates correlating the check with the transaction and allows it to be charged back, sometimes with an additional penalty charge, if it was for payment of a receivable, or allows cancellation of the license, permit, or other privilege represented. To minimize the danger of loss from accepting counterfeit money, special memoranda, usually involving identification of the payor, may be required on all currency exceeding a given denomination. Cashiers or other collecting agents may be held chargeable for counterfeits accepted. To reduce disruption of regular procedures on account of uncollectible checks, governmental units operate a special cash revolving fund from which to finance uncollectible checks. Exact details of this plan may vary, but one common characteristic is that restitution is made directly to the revolving fund when the delayed item is collected.

Cash shortages and overages are unavoidable in handling large amounts of cash. Practices in accounting for these conditions vary extensively in the field of governmental accounting. Every reasonable effort should be made to determine the cause of each shortage and to correct it. If the effort is unsuccessful, the responsible cashier may be charged with the amount of the shortage; or it may be classified and accounted for as an additional disbursement. Shortages of large amounts that arise from misappropriation or other gross irregularities should be recovered from the cashier's bondsman. Causes of overages, likewise, should be carefully investigated and corrections made, if possible. Unadjusted overages should be credited to a revenue or other balance account. Some governmental units operate a Cash Short or Over account for recording shortages and overages for which adjustments or corrections have not been possible. One thoroughly reprehensible practice in handling cash overages and shortages is to make no record of them but to operate an unofficial fund into which overages are placed and from which shortages are made up. On the contrary, every individual overage and shortage should be made a matter of record, for administrative use. Employees experiencing a high frequency of shortages and overages should be relieved of cashier duties.

Accounting for Disbursements

Although custody of governmental cash is primarily a responsibility of the finance officer, general accounting for disbursements, as well as for collections, may be principally a duty of the chief accountant. In addition to making sure that all disbursements are properly classified as to the account or accounts to be charged, he or she must also be on guard that only legal, authorized purposes shall be served; that all laws, rules, and regulations governing the form, manner, and method of disbursing have been complied with; and that the amount and timing of payments are correct. Use of a well-developed voucher system is one of the best ways of making sure that a claim for payment receives regular, methodical scrutiny before final approval. Having been approved for payment, and a full record of the liability and related accounting facts having been made, the liability is passed to the finance officer in the form of a warrant or order for payment. Unlike the related voucher, the payment warrant will ordinarily cover only a few points, although an extra copy of the voucher might be utilized as a warrant. Among those points are the name of the fund to which the payment is to be charged; the amount ordered to be paid; identification of the claim, preferably by number, to which the warrant pertains; and authentication by the accounting officer. Payment warrants are of two general types. If the document is to be exclusively an order to pay, the actual disbursement still requires the writing of a check in many systems; however, a rapidly increasing number of governments are moving toward a sharp reduction in the amount of paper used by means of electronic funds transfers directly to banks.

If prescribed accounting procedures entail some delay between the issuance and payment of warrants, they may require accounting recognition as very current liabilities during the interval. Vouchers Payable would be debited and Warrants Payable credited by the accounting department to record this advancement of the claim toward payment. On receipt of official advice that payment has been made, Warrants Payable would be debited. If payment of the warrant promptly follows presentation to the finance department, it may be the practice to classify the issuance as a disbursement, with a debit to the liability account and a credit to Cash. Because of these variances in practice, a warrant is sometimes merely a form of liability and at other times a cash disbursement medium.

Cash Statements

Some cash statements serve the primary purpose of internal control, whereas others are chiefly instruments for general administration and guidance. In the former category are daily cash statements and periodic reconciliations, to mention the more common ones. In the latter are periodic statements setting forth receipts and disbursements by source and purpose and by funds, or in some less detailed form; detailed statements along other lines for individual funds or groups of funds; statements for a year to date, with projection into the future to forecast the probability of having to borrow; and others.

Treasurer's Daily Cash Statement. Statements of this type may serve two purposes:

1. They provide a constant check on the treasurer's records as a means of detecting irregularities and normal errors.
2. They provide daily information on the amount of money available for use.

If some collections and disbursements are handled outside the main offices, the validity of the treasurer's daily statements requires immediate reports of these extramural transactions in order that they may be incorporated in the summary report without undue delay to its preparation and issuance. Insofar as possible, the treasurer's daily report (see Illustration 15-3) should be supported by documentary evidence of changes included therein.

At the end of each month, daily cash reports may be recapitulated in a monthly cash report of the same form. Daily cash reports aid the treasurer in detecting irregularities that may have occurred in his or her department, either in handling or in reporting cash; and they are useful also to the controller as a constant check on the treasurer's activity. Both daily and monthly reports may be expanded to show transfers in and transfers out, or any other form of information that may

Illustration 15–3

COUNTY OF RANDOLPH
All Funds
Treasurer's Daily Report
December 18, 1999

Explanation	General Fund	Library Fund	Trust Funds	Agency Funds	Total
Balance, preceding day	$15,000	$9,000	$82,000	$13,000	$119,000
Receipts for today	4,200	160		4,100	8,460
Total	19,200	9,160	82,000	17,100	127,460
Disbursements for today	14,300	6,280		600	21,180
Closing balance, today	$ 4,900	$2,880	$82,000	$16,500	$106,280

contribute to more effective control. Whether subsidiary to the daily cash report shown in Illustration 15-3 or in addition to it, the treasurer may be required to submit a daily list of disbursements.

Other Cash Reports.   At the end of each month, the treasurer may be called on to submit, in addition to the summary described above, an analysis of cash balances, including both bank deposits and actual cash, subdivided by funds—that is, a simple cash balance sheet for each fund.

For inclusion in the published annual report, it may be desirable to provide a somewhat more elaborate statement, including the following:

1. A summary of cash transactions by funds for the year, with an indication of fund equities in the closing balances.
2. A statement showing the composition of the total ending balance.
3. The treasurer's certification.

It is desirable that summaries of bank balances be supplemented by information to indicate that these balances are fully protected in the event the depository should experience financial difficulty. The information may be given in various forms.

The last treasurer's statement to be mentioned here is a bank reconciliation in which the treasurer accounts for differences between ending bank balances per his or her records and ending bank balances per bank statements. This statement has the usual purposes of bank reconciliations: first, to explain normal differences between the two sets of figures; and second, to bring to light possible variances requiring investigation and possibly other action, such as corrections or adjustments.

Cash reconciliations should also be prepared by the controller. Prior to preparation of the reconciliations, the controller should be provided with a copy of the

Illustration 15-4

CITY OF SPRINGDALE
Reconciliation of Bank Statements, Treasurer's Books, and
Controller's Books with Actual Cash Balances
May 31, 1999

	Bank	Treasurer	Controller
Balances, per books	$117,131	$115,260	$112,600
Add: Unrecorded deposits	3,200		
Interest credited by bank		903	903
Warrants not countersigned			2,660
Totals	120,331	116,163	116,163
Deduct: Outstanding warrants	4,186		
Bank charges		18	18
Actual cash balance	$116,145	$116,145	$116,145

treasurer's reconciliation and with reports of bank balances obtained directly from the depositories themselves. A standard certificate form may be furnished to the banks for supplying this information, or copies of bank statements in the conventional form may be utilized. Reconciliations by the controller will likely be somewhat more complex than those prepared by the treasurer because the former must bring into agreement not two balances but three: the controller's , the treasurer's, and the bank's. Illustration 15-4 is an example of the statement reconciling bank balances with balances per controller's records and per treasurer's records.

Management of Cash Transfers between the Federal and State Governments

Annual cash transfers between the federal and state governments amounted to nearly $150 billion in 1994. Dating back to the rapid expansion of federally funded programs during the 1960s, federal agencies have voiced concern that the federal government is losing interest earnings because states frequently "draw down" federal monies in advance of the time they are needed for program purposes. States, on the other hand, have complained about losing interest earnings from having to use their own funds for federal program purposes pending reimbursement by the federal government. To ensure greater efficiency, effectiveness, and equity in the exchange of monies between the federal government and the states, the U.S. Congress passed Public Law 101-453 known as the **Cash Management Improvement Act (CMIA) of 1990**. The Act requires the Secretary of the Treasury to regulate and enforce timely disbursement by federal agencies and to negotiate and monitor agreements with the states to achieve the efficient transfer of monies. CMIA's provisions apply as well to state-chartered colleges and universities, and all other organizations included within the GAAP definition of the state's reporting entity.

CMIA requires states to pay interest on federal monies received in advance of need when paying such interest is not inconsistent with program purposes. Exceptions are provided for programs that are below the "major program" threshold (see Chapter 12 for definition) or when interest earned is authorized to be spent for program purposes, or the state is legally required to retain the interest. Even in these exceptional cases, CMIA provides that state and federal agencies must minimize the time between the transfer of monies from the U.S. Treasury and the time the monies are needed for program purposes. A negotiated periodic transfer schedule method, such as monthly or bimonthly, is acceptable for certain programs. An example of the latter is **block grants** for which no matching requirements exist.

CMIA generally requires electronic funds transfer (EFT) of monies from the federal government to state governments. States can claim reimbursement from the Treasury for allowable direct costs relating to development of compliance systems and calculation of interest. CMIA also requires each state to prepare an annual report for submission to the Financial Management Services (FMS) agency within the U.S. Department of the Treasury. The annual report must include, at a minimum, the federal interest liability for each program and in total for all programs administered by the state; the state interest liability for each program and in total for all programs; the net total interest owed by the state or federal government; and, for information purposes only, the actual interest earnings on and the related banking costs for all monies drawn from the state's accounts with the Unemployment Trust Fund. The net interest payable to or by a state for its most recently completed fiscal year will be paid no later than March 1.

The General Accounting Office (GAO) reported that in 1994, the first year of implementation of the Act, governments acknowledged a heightened awareness of cash management. The GAO complimented the key agents (the FMS, federal program agencies, and states and territories) on the substantial progress made in achieving the Act's purpose of equitable, timely funds transfers. In fact, the cumulative net state interest liability due to the federal government was approximately $34 million in 1994, a small percent of the $150 billion of cash transfers between the federal and state governments.[2] The FMS published regulation and implementation guides, streamlined the transfer and reporting process, and generally allowed for greater variation in funding techniques by eliminating the four funding techniques prescribed in the original Act Amendments. The revised Compliance Supplement for the Single Audit Act of 1996 includes guidance for auditors in testing for compliance with CMIA requirements.

The CMIA represents a major step forward in the management of cash flows between the federal and state governments. It consummates many years of joint efforts by federal and state officials to improve the efficiency, effectiveness, and equity of cash transfers between governments. As such it serves as a good example of how taxpayers can benefit from better intergovernmental cooperation.

---

[2]General Accounting Office, *Financial Management: Implementation of the Cash Management Improvement Act* (Washington, DC: Government Printing Office, January 8, 1996), GAO/AIMD-96-4.

Management of Deposits and Investments

Management of cash resources, as discussed previously in this chapter, requires that cash be deposited with designated financial institutions to meet payrolls and other obligations of the government. In addition, legal and contractual provisions, as well as sound financial management, dictate investment of cash to meet various objectives. Investment activities of governmental entities range from overnight investments of idle cash to long-term investment of pension and sinking fund assets. Regardless of the type of deposit or investment, it is imperative that they be made and managed in conformity with applicable statutes, ordinances, local policies, and contractual agreements. Even without legal or contractual restriction, however, a prudent policy for deposits and investments should be followed. Such a policy would include, at a minimum, the following items:[3]

1. A written policy approved by the governing board.
2. Knowledge of and compliance with legal authority.
3. Proper organization structure and effective internal controls.
4. A written procedures manual for managing deposits and investments.
5. Skilled, trained staff.
6. An up-to-date cash budget.
7. Consideration of the security for each investment and collateral for deposits.
8. Analyses of risks and rewards (returns or yields).
9. Well-maintained records and documentation.
10. Careful monitoring of portfolio performance.
11. Periodic reporting to management and elected officials.
12. Internal and external audits.

Generally speaking, sound management of deposits and investments requires close attention to the security of the deposits and investments, meeting liquidity needs, and achieving target rates of return or yield consistent with an acceptable level of risk. Although there are several types of risk that affect deposits and investments, the two major risks are credit risk and market risk.[4] **Credit risk** relates to the probability of loss due to nonpayment of principal or interest, either on investment securities or on securities pledged as collateral. Thus, credit risk relates to the financial viability and dependability of issuers of securities, depository financial institutions, and custodians of securities or collateral. **Market risk** is the risk of loss arising from increases in market rates of interest or other factors that reduce market value of securities. Market risk can be managed by careful attention to the average term

---

[3] The following list is adapted from Judith K. Welch and J. Dwight Hadley, "Cash and Investment Management," in *Handbook of Governmental Accounting & Finance*, ed. Nicholas G. Apostolou and D. Larry Crumbley, 2nd ed. (New York: John Wiley & Sons, 1992), p. 18.10.

[4] GASB, *Codification*, Sec. 150.511.

to maturity of debt securities and matching maturities to forecasted liquidity needs. Credit risk is the primary concern of statutory provisions, and the main focus of the following section.

Security of Deposits

Statutes often impose restrictions on the governmental entity's deposit and investment procedures. Such laws, policies, and agreements usually prescribe permissible types of deposits and investments, methods for selecting depository financial institutions, minimum balances in liquid deposits and investments, and security requirements in terms of collateral for deposits. Restrictions such as these are intended to limit the level of risk to which public deposits and investments are exposed.

Demand deposits (checking) and time deposits (savings accounts and certificates of deposits) are generally insured by the Federal Deposit Insurance Corporation (FDIC) up to $100,000 for each governmental entity and are classified as **deposits** rather than investments. Statutes typically require that deposits in excess of FDIC insurance coverage be **collateralized**, either partially or fully, by low-risk securities. Qualifying securities that may be pledged ordinarily include obligations of the federal government, the state, or local governments or political subdivisions within the state.[5] The credit risk associated with such collateral depends on who is holding the security, in whose name the collateral is being held, the depositor's access to the collateral, and the depositor's rights to the collateral in the event the financial institution defaults.[6] The level of credit risk is lower if collateral is being held by the depositor or an independent third-party agent rather than by the financial institution or its agent. Similarly, the risk is lower if the collateral is held by the pledging financial institution, or by a trust department or agent of the institution, in the name of the depositor government rather than not in the depositor's name. Finally, if the depositor holds a *perfected security interest* (pursuant to the Uniform Commercial Code) in the collateral, risk is lower than if no perfected security interest is held in the collateral.

Accounting for Investments

Governments invest in securities or other assets primarily for the purpose of obtaining income or profit.[7] Governmental entities can choose from a wide array of **investments.** The nature of the investment chosen will depend on what is allowable under state and local law, specific investment objectives, liquidity needs, market conditions, experience of the chief financial officer, past practices, and other factors. Among the most commonly used investment securities are obligations of the federal government and its agencies or instrumentalities (e.g., U.S. Treasury bills, bonds, and notes, and obligations issued by the Farmers Home Administration), repurchase agreements, bankers' acceptances, commercial paper, money market funds, and state and local bonds and investment pools. Pension fund assets

---

[5]Welch and Hadley, "Cash and Investment Management," p. 18.13.
[6]GASB, *Codification*, Sec. I50.119.
[7]GASB, *Codification*, Sec. I50.525.

are often invested in corporate debt and securities, and even foreign debt and equity securities, as well as U.S. government securities.

Of the investments listed above **repurchase agreements**, or repos as they are often called, have been both the most popular and the most risky. Repos involve the transfer of excess cash by a governmental entity (buyer-lender) to a financial institution or broker-dealer (seller-borrower) in exchange for U.S. government or other securities. The seller-borrower promises to repay the cash, with interest, in exchange for the *same* securities.[8] Repos provide a flexible, relatively high-yield investment, ostensibly backed by high-quality U.S. government securities. Unfortunately, repos can also have very high-credit risk, as explained in a cash management publication of the Government Finance Officers Association (GFOA):

> Throughout the 1970s and 1980s repos revolutionized the world of local government finance. Even small jurisdictions found it possible to obtain high overnight rates of return using instruments that were secured by government securities. For ten years, the repo instrument was used without incident, and helped banks to avoid reserve requirements which detracted from their earnings and yields. Likewise, government securities dealers found repos an attractive way to finance their growing inventories of government securities. Meanwhile, local governments earned attractive interest rates and maintained considerable liquidity. Unfortunately, the collapse of several government securities dealers in the early and mid-1980s stunned the public markets and left numerous municipalities holding worthless paper.[9]

As a result of the collapse of the repos market, numerous reforms have been implemented to avoid similar problems in the future, including:

1. Thorough investigation of the counterparty bank or security dealer's creditworthiness.
2. Use of an independent custodian to hold collateral securities.
3. Adoption of the delivery versus payment procedure for settling repo transactions.
4. Marking collateral to market daily, so that price fluctuations do not undermine the value of the protective collateral.
5. Overcollateralization to provide a safe margin for error and possible price fluctuation.

Governments that continue to use repos should be advised to use a master repo agreement detailing the responsibilities of all parties, and to follow the steps listed above.

Fair Value Accounting. The GASB follows the lead of the Financial Accounting Standards Board by requiring governments to report their investments at fair value, rather than cost, amortized cost, or lower of cost or market.[10] Although

---

[8]GASB, *Codification*, Sec. 150.933.

[9]Government Finance Officers Association, *Cash Management for Small Governments*, ed. Ian J. Allen (Chicago: GFOA, 1989), p.131.

[10]GASB, *Codification*, Sec. 150.

there are differences, the objective of all three of these statements (GASB *Statement No. 31* for governments, *SFAS No. 115* for for-profit entities, and *SFAS No. 124* for not-for-profit organizations) is to provide users with more relevant information about an entity's investments and the effects of its investment practices. **Fair value** is the amount at which a financial instrument could be exchanged in an arms'-length transaction between willing parties. At acquisition, the fair value of an investment is its cost, which includes the agreed-upon purchase price plus every outlay required to obtain a clear title to the assets including any fees, such as legal, brokerage, or commissions.

Investment income and changes in the fair value of the investments are reported as revenue in the operating statement. The change in the fair value of investments, including realized gains and losses, should be captioned *net increase (decrease) in the fair value of investments*.[11] Sec. I50 of the GASB *Codification* applies to these investments held by a government: (1) participating interest-earning investment contracts, (2) external investment pools, (3) open-end mutual funds, (4) debt securities, and (5) equity securities, option contracts, stock warrants, and stock rights that have readily determinable values. Participating investment contracts are those whose redemption value is affected by market or interest rate changes.

Governmental entities may report certain money market investments, those with remaining maturities of one year or less at the time of purchase, at amortized cost. If debt investments are purchased between interest payment dates, then, just like for-profit entities, the accrued interest purchased must be calculated separately from the cost of the investment and reported as interest receivable. Accounting for the purchase and sale of debt instruments is discussed more fully in intermediate accounting textbooks and is not repeated here.

External Investment Pools.   A government may establish or participate in an **external investment pool** that commingles monies of more than one legally separate entity and invests in a portfolio. GASB requires that *all* investments held by an external investment pool be reported at fair value in the Balance Sheet and all investment income, including changes in the fair value of investments, as revenue in the operating statement. One exception is that if the pool is a 2a7-like pool it may report its investments at amortized cost. A **2a7 pool** is one that is not registered with the Securities and Exchange Commission as an investment company, but has a policy that it will, and does, operate in a manner consistent with the SEC's Rule 2a7 of the Investment Company Act of 1940.

Required Financial Statement Disclosures

To assist users of financial statements in assessing the risks of a governmental entity's deposits and investments, GASB standards require the following disclosures in the Notes to the Financial Statements.[12]

---

[11]GASB, *Codification*, Sec. I50.111.
[12]GASB, *Codification*, Sec. I50.120–132.

1. A description of the types of investments authorized by legal or contractual provisions. Material differences between the authorized investments of specific funds, fund types, or component units and those of the combined entity.
2. Significant violations of legal or contractual provisions for deposits and investments.
3. Whether or not the bank balances of deposits as of the balance sheet date are entirely insured or collateralized with securities held by the entity or by its agent in the entity's name. If not, the following disclosures should be made:
   a. Reported amount of total deposits, if not separately displayed on the Balance Sheet.
   b. Total bank balance classified in the following categories of credit risk:
      (1) Insured or collateralized with securities held by the entity or by its agent in the entity's name.
      (2) Collateralized with securities held by the pledging financial institution's trust department or agent in the entity's name.
      (3) Uncollateralized, including collateralized with securities held by the pledging financial institutions's trust department or agent but *not* in the entity's name.
4. Reported amount and fair value of investments (including repurchase agreements) as of the balance sheet date, in total and for each type of investment, classified in the following three categories of credit risk:
   a. Insured or registered, or securities held by the entity or its agent in the entity's name.
   b. Uninsured or unregistered, with securities held by the counterparty's trust department or agent in the entity's name.
   c. Uninsured or unregistered, with securities held by the counterparty or its trust department or agent, but *not* in the entity's name.
5. The types of investments made during the period but not owned as of the balance sheet date.
6. Losses recognized during the period due to default by counterparties to deposit or investment transactions and amounts recovered from prior-period losses if not separately displayed on the operating statement.

In addition to the disclosures stated above, GASB *Statement No. 31* requires that the following be disclosed in the Notes to the Financial Statements:

1. The methods and significant assumptions used to estimate the fair value of investments, if anything other than quoted market prices.
2. The policy for determining which investments, if any, are reported at amortized cost.
3. A brief description of regulatory oversight for any investments in external investment pools that are not SEC registered.
4. Any involuntary participation in an external investment pool.

5. The methods used and significant assumptions made in determining the fair value of an investment in a pool when the pool sponsor does not provide that information.

6. Any income from investments associated with one fund that is assigned to another fund.[13]

A good example of the required disclosures for investments is provided in Illustration 15-5, which presents the disclosures from the Notes to the Financial Statements of the City of Seattle, Washington. According to Illustration 15-5, deposits in excess of FDIC insurance are collateralized by a multiple financial institution collateral pool administered by the Public Deposit Protection Commission (PDPC). At the balance sheet date, about 16 percent of the City of Seattle's deposits were collateralized by this PDPC collateral. The City of Seattle's investments are classified into the three categories specified by GASB standards. As shown in Illustration 15-5, all of the City's investments are held by the City's agents in the City's name, and are classified in category 1, the lowest of the three risk categories. Thus, the City of Seattle's investments appear quite safe, although financial statement users may want to know more about the riskiness of some investments, such as the repurchase agreements, bankers' acceptances, and foreign entity securities. The City's disclosures for deposits and investments appear to conform to those required by GASB standards.

Other Considerations in Investment Management

Arbitrage.   As discussed briefly in Chapter 5, the Internal Revenue Code (Sec. 148), particularly after the Tax Reform Act of 1986, significantly limits the ability of a governmental entity to realize **arbitrage** earnings by investing tax-exempt bond proceeds in higher yielding taxable securities. Interest earnings in excess of those permitted by current federal tax regulations must be rebated to the federal government. Penalties for not rebating the excess interest earned may include a 50 percent penalty or loss of the tax-exempt status of the debt issue. The rules governing arbitrage are exceedingly complex and thus are beyond the scope of this text. Nevertheless, arbitrage considerations should be a standard part of investment policy for investments of bond proceeds.

Impact of Technology.   Computer technology has automated routine aspects of cash management, sped up the transfer of funds through electronic funds transfers (EFT), and generally expanded the range of investments available to cash managers. An increasingly higher level of expertise is required of the manager in charge of meeting the government's cash and investment goals. Software exists to aid in the collection of information, development of investment reports, and calculation of investment yields to ensure that the monies received by government are put to the best possible use. Along with the advantages of speed that computer technology offers comes increased risk.[14]

---

[13]GASB, *Codification*, Sec. 150.119.

[14]W. Paul Zorn, "Cash Management Technology,"in *Cash Management for Small Governments*, ed. Ian J. Allan (Chicago: GFOA, 1989).

Illustration 15–5

CITY OF SEATTLE, WASHINGTON
Notes Disclosures for Cash and Investments
For Year Ended December 31, 1996

The Federal Deposit Insurance Corporation (FDIC) insures the City's deposits up to $100,000. All deposits not covered by FDIC insurance are covered by the Public Deposit Protection Commission (PDPC) of the State of Washington. The PDPC is a statutory authority established under RCW Chapter 39.58. It constitutes a multiple financial institution collateral pool. In the case of a loss by any public depository in the State, each public depository is liable for an amount up to 10 percent of its public deposits. Provisions of RCW Chapter 39.58, Section 60 authorize the PDPC to make pro-rata assessments in proportion to the maximum liability of each such depository as it existed on the date of loss. Therefore, PDPC protection is of the nature of collateral, not insurance. At the end of 1996, approximately 16 percent of the City's deposits would have been covered by this collateral.

Note 1 describes the investment policies of the City. Banks or trust companies acting as the City's agents hold most of the City's investments in the City's name. These investments are classified risk category 1. In some cases, the trust department of the City's depository bank holds City investments in the City's name. These investments are classified risk category 2. Certain investments are uninsured and held by the trust department of the City's agent in the agent's name. These are classified risk category 3. The City currently has no investments in categories 2 and 3.

INVESTMENTS BY RISK CATEGORY AND TYPE

Investments in the City's Name	Carrying Amount	Fair Value
Category 1		
Treasury Residual Investments:		
Commercial paper	$ 24,707,703	$ 24,700,678
Bankers' acceptances	24,628,757	24,621,435
Treasuries	60,025,316	59,060,156
Agencies	225,977,283	221,660,820
Repurchase agreement	60,500,000	60,500,000
	395,839,059	390,543,089
Securities Held for Dedicated Funds:		
Treasuries	17,933,527	19,029,034
Agencies	26,593,710	27,140,720
Gross unrealized holding gain (loss)	(197,849)	—
	44,329,388	46,169,754
Employee's Retirement System Investments:		
U.S. Government bonds	120,971,129	125,047,856
Foreign government bonds	131,213,164	132,235,973
Corporate bonds	61,727,767	65,280,852
Common stock	339,079,205	391,326,067
International stock	185,375,985	185,375,985
	838,367,250	899,266,733
Total Investments in Risk Category 1	1,278,535,697	1,335,979,576
Investments Not Subject to Credit Risk		
Mortgages	131,724,151	132,383,270
Realty equities	29,216,116	29,216,116
Venture capital	5,082,731	5,082,469
Short-term investment fund	100,679,748	100,679,748
	266,702,746	267,361,603
Total Investments	$1,545,238,443	$1,603,341,179

Illustration 15–5 (concluded)

CASH AND EQUITY IN POOLED INVESTMENTS
Combined Balance Sheet (From Exhibit 1)
(in thousands)

Cash and equity in pooled investments	$364,583
Cash with fiscal agent	325
Restricted cash and equity in pooled investments:	
Revenue bond reserve accounts	23,375
Construction accounts	14,830
Customer deposits	663
Rate stabilization fund	5,800
Total—DECEMBER 31, 1996	**$409,576**
Composition:	
Cash in banks	$719
Cash held by Treasurer	62
Warrant clearing account	6,250
Residual investments—at amortized cost	395,760
Total Treasurer's Cash and Investments	402,791
Cash with fiscal agent	325
Trustee accounts:	
Municipal Courts	628
Retainage on public works contracts in escrow	5,734
DCLU refund account not booked	9
Petty cash and revolving funds held by departments	89
Total Cash and Equity in Pooled Investments	**$409,576**

It should be apparent that the increasing professionalism of investment management in government and improved technology have been a double-edged sword. Although many governmental entities have benefited from computers and the use of new and innovative investment instruments, some instruments (e.g., repurchase agreements) have exposed governmental entities to added credit risk. GASB standards require that the entity specifically evaluate those risks and communicate them to interested financial statement users.

Summary

Efficient and effective management of cash, deposits, and investments is an important aspect of improving the overall performance of government. This chapter discusses the processes by which sound cash and investment management can be achieved. By their nature, cash and investments require special attention to ensure public monies are protected and safeguarded. Thus, the emphasis in this chapter was on cash planning, well-designed operating procedures, and effective internal controls. Similarly, the primary focus of the discussion on management of deposits and investments was on assessing and reporting credit risks and compliance with legal and contractual requirements. Nevertheless, it is management's responsibility to invest all idle cash and to achieve the highest rate of return consistent with an acceptable level of risk. As new and innovative financial instruments continue to evolve, assessment and management of credit and market risk are likely to become more and more challenging.

Key Terms

Arbitrage, 632	Market risk, 627
Block grants, 626	Operating cycle, 608
Collateralized, 628	Pay-in warrant, 619
Credit risk, 627	Repurchase agreements, 629
Deposits, 628	Sweep accounts, 612
Deposit warrant, 619	Tax anticipation note, 610
External investment pool, 630	Warrants for disbursements, 619
Fair value, 630	2a7 pool, 630
Investment, 628	

Selected References

Government Accounting Office. "Financial Management: Implementation of the Cash Management Improvement Act, " AIMD-96-4. Washington, DC: GAO, January 8, 1996.

Governmental Accounting Standards Board. *Codification of Governmental Accounting and Financial Reporting Standards as of June 30, 1997*. Norwalk, CT: 1997.

Government Finance Officers Association. *Cash Management for Small Governments.* Edited by Ian J. Allan. Chicago: GFOA, 1989.

_____ . *An Introduction to Treasury Management Practices*. Chicago: GFOA, 1997.

Miller, Girard. *Investing Public Funds*. 2nd ed. Chicago: GFOA, 1998.

Welch, Judith K., and J. Dwight Hadley. "Cash and Investment Management." In *Handbook of Governmental Accounting & Finance*. 2nd ed. Ed. Nicholas G. Apostolou and D. Larry Crumbley. New York: John Wiley & Sons, 1992, chap. 18.

Questions

15–1. How does cash and investment management contribute to improving overall resource management?

15–2. Explain what is meant by the *operating cycle* and how it relates to the cash management system.

15–3. "The purpose of budgeting cash receipts month by month is to provide a means for determining that the government receives all the cash to which it is legally entitled." Do you agree? Why or why not?

15–4. Describe briefly the relationship between budgeting cash receipts and disbursements and planning short-term borrowing and/or investments.

15–5. Sometimes a governmental unit with a limited amount of cash will endeavor to "window-dress" its liabilities at the end of the fiscal period by writing and recording checks in payment of the liabilities, but holding the checks until a later date, thus avoiding a bank overdraft. Would you consider such checks as outstanding in preparing a bank reconciliation? It you were an outside auditor charged with preparing correct financial statements of the governmental unit, what would you do about the situation described?

15–6. What are the objectives of the Cash Management Improvement Act of 1990?

15–7. What is required, at a minimum, for a prudent management policy for deposits with financial institutions and investments?

15–8. Describe accounting for investments for state and local governments under generally accepted accounting principles.

15–9. What are the two major risks that affect the security of deposits and investments? Briefly define each of the two risks.

15–10. Explain the three risk categories into which a government entity's investments must be classified for financial reporting purposes.

Cases

15–1. Orange County, California, one of the wealthiest counties in the United States, filed for bankruptcy in 1994 after losing $1.64 billion on its $7.4 billion investment portfolio. The County managed an external investment pool that included itself and 200 other governmental agencies and school districts. The Former County Treasurer pleaded guilty to felony charges of misleading investors, and the County sued its investment brokers for promoting a highly risky investment strategy for a public fund. As a CPA and newly elected County Commissioner of a large county, you want to make sure that what happened in Orange County does not happen in your county.

Required

  a. What caused the large loss in the investment portfolio of Orange County, California, in 1994? How did derivatives contribute to the catastrophe?
  b. Did the audited annual financial statements disclose the riskiness of these investments?
  c. What changes in generally accepted accounting principles since 1994 may make it less likely that the public is surprised by a huge loss in a government's investments?

15–2. Joanne McGuire is the New Finance Director for the City of Superior. As her first official duty, she must present the audited annual financial statements to the City Council, and she is concerned that the Council will raise questions about the following note:

Note 3.   Deposits

At year-end, the fair value of the City's cash and time deposits was $10,866,499 and the bank deposit balance was $11,490,261. Of the bank balance, $1,455,592 was covered by federal depository insurance. The remainder was uncollateralized and uninsured.

Required

 a   Determine if this note to the financial statements on deposits discloses adequate information for decision makers. What other information might be useful?

 b. Do you think Joanne should make a recommendation to the Council regarding the deposits? If so, what?

15–3. Internet Case. What kind of resources are available to help a small government develop policies for cash and investment management? Go to the homepages of associations whose mission it is to assist financial managers of governments and see what publications are available. For example, look at the homepages of the Government Finance Officers Association (http:///www.gfoa.org), the Association of Governmental Accountants (http://www.aga.org), and the National Association of State Auditors, Comptrollers and Treasurers (http:www.nasact.org). What publications do they produce? Which books would you purchase if you were a newly hired City Finance Director with experience in business, but not government, and had a limited publication budget of $100?

Exercises and Problems

15–1. Write the numbers 1 through 10 on a sheet of paper. Beside each number write the letter corresponding with the best answer to each of the following questions:

 1. Which of the following is *not* a universal rule for achieving strong internal control over cash?

   a. Separate the cash-handling and record-keeping functions.

   b. Have bank reconciliations performed by employees independent with respect to handling cash.

   c. Deposit each day's cash receipts by the end of the day.

   d. Decentralize the receiving of cash as much as possible.

 2. Under which of the following circumstances would an auditor be most likely to intensify an examination of a $500 imprest pretty cash fund?

   a. Reimbursement vouchers are *not* prenumbered.

   b. Reimbursement occurs twice each week.

   c. The custodian occasionally uses the cash fund to cash employee checks.

   d. The custodian endorses reimbursement checks.

 3. An unrecorded check issued during the last week of the year would most likely be discovered by the auditor when the:

   a. Check register for the last month is reviewed.

   b. Cut-off bank statement is reconciled.

   c. Bank confirmation is reviewed.

   d. Search for unrecorded liabilities is performed.

4. The auditor's count of the client's cash should be coordinated to coincide with the:
   a. Study of the system of internal controls with respect to cash.
   b. Close of business on the balance sheet date.
   c. Count of marketable securities.
   d. Count of inventories.

5. When counting cash on hand, the auditor must exercise control over all cash and other negotiable assets to prevent:
   a. Theft.
   b. Irregular endorsement.
   c. Substitution.
   d. Deposits-in-transit.

6. Which one of the following would the auditor consider an incompatible operation if the cashier received remittances from the mailroom?
   a. The cashier posts the receipts to the accounts receivable subsidiary ledger cards.
   b. The cashier makes the daily deposit at a local bank.
   c. The cashier prepares the daily deposit.
   d. The cashier endorses the checks.

7. Which of the following statements regarding the Cash Management Improvement Act of 1990 is *not* true?
   a. For all federal assistance programs (major and minor), state governments are required to pay interest to the federal government if federal monies are received in advance of need.
   b. For *major* federal assistance programs only, state governments are required to pay interest to the federal government if federal monies are received in advance of need.
   c. If a federal agency requires a state government to use state monies for federal program purposes and request subsequent reimbursement, the federal government must pay interest to the state government.
   d. The net interest payable to or by a state for its most recently completed fiscal year must be paid no later than March 1.

8. Which of the following organizational units would be subject to the provisions of the Cash Management Improvement Act of 1990?
   a. State governments.
   b. A mental hospital supported by state appropriations.
   c. A state-chartered public college or university.
   d. All of the above.

9. The risk of loss from the insolvency of a financial institution acting as custodian of a local government's cash deposits is properly termed:
   a. Market risk.
   b. Call risk.
   c. Credit risk.
   d. Depositor's risk.

10. Which of the following risk categories represents the *least* amount of risk to a governmental depositor?
    a. Deposits insured or collateralized with securities held by the entity or by its agent in the entity's name.

b. Deposits collateralized with securities held by the pledging financial institution's trust department or agent in the entity's name.

c. Uncollateralized, including collateralized with securities held by the pledging financial institution's trust department or agent but not in the entity's name.

d. A checking account with overdraft protection.

(Items 1 through 6, AICPA)

15–2. Given the following information about the City of Dalton General Fund, prepare a Cash Receipts budget for each month of fiscal year 1999. Round each calculation to the nearest $1,000.

The following are balances expected as of the end of the fiscal year 1998:

Taxes receivable—delinquent	$360,000
Interest and penalties receivable on taxes	40,000
Due from other funds	25,000
Due from state government	450,000

The Estimated Revenues budget for 1999 consisted of:

Property taxes	$1,600,000
Licenses and permits	300,000
Fines and forfeits	200,000
Intergovernmental revenue	400,000

Additional information

1. Delinquent taxes and interest and penalties on taxes are expected to be collected as follows (for purposes of cash budgeting, the two items may be added together):

January 1999	5%	August 1999	2%
February	10	September	2
March	35	October	10
April	5	November	5
May	2	December	5
June	2	In following years	5
July	2	Uncollectible	10

2. The amount due from other funds is expected to be collected in full in January 1999; the amount due from the state is expected to be collected in full in February 1999.

3. Property taxes budgeted for 1999 are expected to be collected as follows:

January 1999	0%	August 1999	2%
February	0	September	2
March	2	October	30
April	10	November	5
May	30	December	2
June	5	In following years	8
July	2	Uncollectible	2

4. Licenses and permits, and fines and forfeits budgeted for 1999 are expected to be collected as follows (for purposes of cash budgeting, the two items may be added together):

January 1999	8%	July 1999	8%
February	8	August	8
March	8	September	8
April	8	October	8
May	10	November	8
June	10	December	8

5. Intergovernmental revenue budgeted for 1999 is expected to be collected as follows:

March 1999	25%	September 1999	25%
June	25	December	25

15–3. Given the following information about the City of Dalton's General Fund, prepare a Cash Disbursements budget for each month of fiscal year 1999.

The following are balances expected as of the end of fiscal year 1998:

Vouchers payable	$360,00
Tax anticipation notes payable	280,000
Due to other funds	40,000

The Appropriations budget for 1999 consisted of:

	Personal Services	Supplies	Capital Outlays
General government	$ 240,000	$ 25,000	$ 20,000
Public safety	510,000	70,000	120,000
Public works	400,000	100,000	60,000
Health, welfare, and recreation	670,000	150,000	40,000
Totals	$1,820,000	$345,000	$240,000

Additional information

1. Vouchers payable and the amount due to other funds on December 31, 1998, are to be paid in full in January 1999.
2. Tax anticipation notes as of December 31, 1998, plus interest of $22,000, are to be paid in February 1999.
3. The City of Dalton pays all employees every two weeks. Each month in 1999 will have two paydays, except June and December will have three paydays. You may assume all items included in the Personal Services budget are paid by the General Fund on paydays.
4. Items included in the Supplies budget are expected to result in cash disbursements in the following months:

January 1999	$12,000	July 1999	$36,000
February	25,000	August	30,000
March	32,000	September	25,000
April	31,000	October	22,000
May	32,000	November	18,000
June	36,000	December	17,000
		Unpaid	29,000

5. Items included in the Capital Outlays budget are expected to result in cash disbursements in the following months:

February 1999	$ 8,000	June 1999	$60,000
April	48,000	September	50,000
May	52,000	December	22,000

15–4. From your solutions to Problems 15–2 and 15–3, prepare a Statement of Budgeted Cash Receipts and Disbursements for fiscal year 1999 for the City of Dalton's General Fund. It is suggested that you follow the format in Illustration 15–2.

The cash balance on January 1, 1999, is expected to be $80,000. The policy of the City Treasury is to issue 60-day tax anticipation notes in amounts of $100,000 or multiples thereof, as needed, in any month in which the provisional balance is expected to be negative. The notes bear interest at the rate of 1 percent per month. If payment of notes and interest could cause a negative cash balance, the policy is to issue a refunding note with the same terms as described.

15–5. The Village of Longford had poor internal control over its cash transactions. The facts about its cash position at April 30, 2000, were as follows:

The cash books showed a balance of $29,101.62, which included cash on hand. A credit of $200 on the bank's record did not appear on the books of the town. The balance per the bank statement was $25,750; and outstanding checks were No. 62 for $116.25. No. 183 for $150, No. 284 for $253.25, No. 7121 for $190.71, No. 7122 for $206.80, and No. 7128 for $145.28.

The Treasurer removed all the cash on hand in excess of $3,794.41 and then prepared the following reconciliation:

Balance per books, April 30, 2000		$29,101.62
Add: Outstanding checks:		
No. 7121	$190.71	
No. 7122	206.80	
No. 7128	145.28	442.79
		29,544.41
Deduct: Cash on hand		3,794.41
Balance per bank, April 30, 2000		25,750.00
Deduct: Unrecorded credit		200.00
True cash, April 30, 2000		$25,550.00

Required

    a. How much did the Treasurer remove, and how did he attempt to conceal his theft?

    b. Name two specific features of internal control that were apparently missing.

    c. If the Treasurer's March 31 reconciliation is known to be in order and the audit is started on May 5 for the year ended April 30, what procedures would uncover the fraud?

15–6. Two sets of cash records are kept for the City of Fordham Recreation Center, one by the County Treasurer and one by the Director of the center.

    The cash balance on the Treasurer's books at January 1, 1999 was $5,060. The Director's books showed $3,040. The difference was due to a payment received from a state agency on December 31, 1998, and recorded by the Treasurer on that date but not recorded by the Director until the next year.

    On the Director's record, 1999 receipts totals were $179,940, and total disbursements were $172,440. Among the receipts were $360 from the sale of certain recreational items that had not been reported to the City Treasurer by the end of the year. The sum of $1,600 cash contributed to the center by an anonymous donor was first reported to the City Treasurer in January 2000. Disbursements not of record on the Treasurer's books until 2000 were $610 paid by the Director for Christmas presents for underprivileged children and $500 for a Christmas party. Another cause of difference was $200 underfooting of disbursements by the Director.

    At the end of December, the Treasurer had paid $100 for supplies and paid $1,040 for recreational equipment, neither of which was reported to the Director until the next month. The Treasurer showed a December receipt of $2,800 for the facility from a state agency, but this was not entered in the Director's records until the following month. As of December 31, 1999, the Treasurer's books showed a balance of $11,150.

Required

    a. Determine the cash balance shown on the Director's books as of December 31, 1999.

    b. Determine the correct cash balance as of December 31, 1999.

    c. Prepare any correcting or adjusting entries the Treasurer would need to make as of December 31, 1999.

15–7. All disbursements of the Village of Yarbey are made on the authority of warrants issued by the Controller and countersigned by the Treasurer. The Controller records all disbursements as credits to Cash at the time the warrants are issued. Since the warrants become bills of exchange on being countersigned, the Treasurer records cash disbursements as such at the time she countersigns the warrants.

On June 30, 2000, the Treasurer's books showed the following balances:

Explanation	First National Bank
General Fund	$115,260
Internal Service Fund	11,462
Capital Projects Fund	98,327
Debt Service Fund	13,500

The balances according to the Controller's books were as follows:

General Fund	$110,480
Internal Service Fund	11,300
Capital Projects Fund	94,300
Debt Service Fund	13,500

One back account is kept for all funds. The bank statement showed the following balance on June 30:

First National Bank	$250,387

The following deposits, made on June30, did not appear on the bank statement:

General Fund	$3,200
Debt Service Fund	2,000

The Treasurer reports that the following countersigned warrants have not been returned by the bank:

Explanation	First National Bank	
General Fund:		
No. 1702	$ 937	
1712	489	
1714	1,825	
1717	715	
1718	220	
Total		$4,186
Internal Service Fund:		
No. 2431	42	
2440	125	
2442	283	
2443	94	
Total		544

Explanation	First National Bank	
Capital Projects Fund:		
No. 3674	3,500	
3680	740	
3684	1,285	
3686	375	
3687	1,460	
Total		7,360
Debt Service Fund:		
No. 4128	820	
4131	392	
4133	540	
4134	260	
Total		2,012
Grand Total		$14,102

The following warrants have been issued by the Controller but have not been countersigned by the Treasurer:

General Fund:		
No. 1720	$3,800	
1721	900	
1722	80	
Total		$4,780
Internal Service Fund:		
No. 2444	75	
2445	87	
Total		162
Capital Projects Fund:		
No. 3688	1,450	
3689	870	
3690	1,707	
Total		4,027
Grand Total		$8,969

An interest credit in the amount of $2,964 on the bank statement had not been recorded on the books; bank charges in the amount of $28 on the bank statement had not been recorded on the books. The Treasurer and Controller agreed that these amounts should be allocated to the funds as follows:

Explanation	First National Bank
Interest credited by the bank:	
General Fund	$1,450
Internal Service Fund	135
Capital Projects Fund	1,224
Debt Service Fund	155
Bank charges:	
General Fund	21
Internal Service Fund	7

Required

　　a. Reconcile the balance per Treasurer's books for each fund to the actual cash balance for each fund. Reconcile the balance per Controller's books for each fund to the actual cash balance for each fund.

　　b. Reconcile the balance per bank statement to the total actual cash balance of all funds.

15–8. The State Department of Corrections of a midwestern state is responsible for administering the state's penal system and its parole board and probation network. The Department of Corrections has developed an unusually effective rehabilitation system for yourthful offenders, which is based on the military "boot camp" concept. The major source of funding for the Youth Rehabilitation Program (YRP) is a grant from the Federal Department of Justice. For the year ended June 30, 1999, which was prior to implementation of the Cash Management Improvement Act, the YRP received a special grant in the amount of $500,000 for purchase of military-style clothing for program participants. The $500,000 was received in cash during January 1999, but, as of June 30, 1999, only $150,000 of this amount had been expended. The unspent portion has been invested in the state's cash and investment pool where it has earned interest at 7 percent per annum.

　　In addition to the $500,000 for uniforms, the YRP received a grant for operations from the Department of Justice in the amount of $4,000,000. However, cash can only be drawn against this amount at the end of each month, after filing the required documentation showing amounts expended during the month for allowable purposes.

Required

Answer the following questions and explain your answers fully.

　　a. In what respects are these grants inequitable to:

　　　(1) The Federal Government?

　　　(2) The State Government?

　　b. How would the Cash Management Improvement Act improve the efficiency and equity of cash flows between the federal government and the Youth Rehabilitation Program?

15–9. Note 3 from the Notes to the Financial Statements for the City of Chicago, Illinois, for the year ended December 31, 1996, is provided below.

Required

Evaluate the City of Chicago's note disclosure for cash and investments and comment on the extent to which it conforms or does not conform to GASB standards. What questions would you like to ask the City Treasurer about the City's Investments?

CITY OF CHICAGO, ILLINOIS
Notes to Combined Financial Statements
Year Ended December 31, 1996

Note 3: Cash and Investments (continued)

(b) **Investments** are categorized indicating the level of credit risk. Category 1 includes investments that are insured or registered in the City's name or securities that are held by the City or its agent in the City's name. Category 2 includes uninsured and unregistered investments for which the securities are held by the counterparty's trust department or its agent in the City's name. Category 3 includes uninsured and unregistered investments for which the securities are held by the financial institution or counterparty, or by its trust department or agent, but not in the City's name. The following table provides a summary of the book and market values for all funds at December 31, 1996 (dollars in millions):

	Category			Book Value	Market Value
	1	2	3		
City Funds					
U.S. Government Obligations	$2,338.6	$48.1	—	$2,386.7	$2,387.9
Repurchase Agreements	8.1	—	—	8.1	8.1
Commercial Paper	13.1	—	—	13.1	13.1
Total	$2,359.8	$48.1	—	2,407.9	2,409.1
Investments Not Categorized:					
Mutual and Pooled Funds				454.5	453.8
Deferred Compensation				951.5	951.5
Total City Funds				$3,813.9	$3,814.4
Pension Trust Funds					
Bonds	$ 734.1	—	$1,808.2	$2,542.3	$2,573.6
Stocks	860.4	—	1,886.6	2,747.0	3,803.4
Repurchase Agreements	—	—	5.6	5.6	5.6
Commercial Paper	2.5	—	—	2.5	2.5
Other	—	—	57.8	57.8	57.8
Total	$1,597.0	—	$3,758.2	5,355.2	6,442.9
Investments Not Categorized:					
Pooled Funds				1,638.5	1,908.1
Real Estate				260.8	216.0
Other				185.3	205.0
Total Pension Trust Funds				$7,439.8	$8,772.0

The following schedule summarizes cash and investments reported in the Combined Balance Sheet (dollars in millions):

Per Note 3:	
Cash and Certificates of Deposit	$ 220.0
Investments—City	3,813.9
Investments—Pension Funds	7,439.8
	$11,473.7
Per Financial Statements:	
Cash and Cash Equivalents	$ 874.6
Investments	8,816.3
Cash and Investments with Escrow Agent	55.4
Restricted Assets—Cash and Cash Equivalents	796.6
Restricted Assets—Investments	930.8
	$11,473.7

(c) Other Investments.   In 1992 the City entered into a six-year, $200 million notional value fixed-receiver interest rate swap agreement approved by the City Council. The City was paid a fixed rate of interest of 5.45 percent in exchange for a floating interest rate paid to a counterparty. In 1993 the counterparty exercised its option to reverse the swap. The City has no intention to reset the terms of the agreement.

Individuals

Provide

CHAPTER 16

Accounting for Nonprofit Organizations

Learning Objectives

After studying this chapter, you should be able to:

~ Distinguish not-for-profit organizations (NPOs) from entities in the governmental and commercial sectors of the U.S. economy.

~ Identify the authoritative standards-setting body for establishing GAAP for nongovernmental NPOs.

~ Explain financial reporting and accounting for NPOs.

   Accounting for revenue, gains, and support.
   Accounting for expenses.
   Accounting for assets.

~ Describe optional fund accounting.

~ Identify the unique accounting issues of financially interrelated organizations.

~ Prepare financial statements using *SFAS No. 117*.

Defining the Not-for-Profit Sector

In the United States there are more than 1 million entities in the not-for-profit sector that receive several hundred billions of dollars in revenues and support each year.[1] This diverse sector includes organizations that may be tax-exempt or taxable; charitable or mutually beneficial; a public charity or a private foundation. Not-for-profit organizations (NPOs) are characterized by the absence of owners and dependence on contributions,[2] dues, and charges for services rather than taxes as their source of revenues. The definition of a **not-for-profit organization** recently articulated by the AICPA and FASB is an entity that possesses the following characteristics that distinguish it from a business enterprise.[3,4]

1. Contributions of significant amounts of resources from resource providers who do not expect commensurate or proportionate pecuniary return.
2. Operating purposes other than to provide goods or services at a profit.
3. Absence of ownership interests like those of business enterprises.

Not-for-profit organizations have the preceding characteristics in varying degrees. NPOs include **voluntary health and welfare organizations (VHWO)** or **human service organizations** (those which receive contributions from the public at large and provide health and welfare services for a nominal or no fee), such as the American Cancer Society, Girl Scouts, and Boy Scouts. There are a variety of other not-for-profit organizations, such as cemetery organizations, civic organizations, fraternal organizations, labor unions, libraries, museums, cultural institutions, performing arts organizations, political parties, private schools, professional and trade associations, social and country clubs, research and scientific organizations, and religious organizations. These organizations are classified more or less by Internal Revenue Code Sections (discussed further in Chapter 17). Illustration 16–1 shows various organizational forms that comprise the not-for-profit sector of the U.S. economy.

---

[1]Independent Sector, *Nonprofit Almanac: Dimensions of the Independent Sector 1996–97* (San Francisco, CA: Jossey-Bass, 1996), p. 25, reports that in 1992 there were 1.03 million organizations in the independent, voluntary, not-for-profit sector. The Internal Revenue Service's Pub. 78 (Rev. 11-96) lists almost 500,000 tax-exempt entities in 1993 to which charitable contributions were deductible by individuals.

[2]The AICPA prefers the term *not-for-profit organizations.* A Texas statute states that "nonprofit corporation" is equivalent to "not-for-profit corporation." Howard L. Oleck and Martha E. Stewart *Nonprofit Corporations, Organizations & Associations,* (Englewood Cliffs, NJ: Prentice Hall, 1994) p. 12. Abbreviations for nongovernmental, not-for-profit entities include NPO, NFP entity, ONPO (other nonprofit organizations), and NGO (nongovermental organizations, a term used in an international context). The abbreviation NPO is used in this chapter, and the terms nonprofit and not-for-profit are used interchangeably.

[3]American Institute of Certified Public Accountants, Audit and Accounting Guide, *Not-for-Profit Organizations* (New York, 1996), par. 1.01.

[4]Financial Accounting Standards Board, *Statement of Financial Accounting Standards No. 116,* "Accounting for Contributions Received and Contributions Made" (Norwalk, CT, 1993), App. D.

Illustration 16–1   Organizational Forms

For-Profit	Not-for-Profit
(investor owned)	(absence of ownership interests)

Commercial
Business sector

Non-governmental
Not-for-profit sector

Governmental
Public sector
(e.g., governments and
governmental NPOs)

Taxable NPOs
(e.g., those with a political agenda)

Tax-exempt NPOs

Mutual nonprofits
Sec. 501(c)5 — 23
Sec. 521(a)
(e.g., professional
associations,
co-operatives)

Social welfare
organizations
Sec. 501(c)4
(e.g., civic leagues,
local employee
associations)

Charitable,
educational,
scientific
Sec. 501(c)3

Religious
communities
Sec. 501(d)

Public charities, such as

Private schools (pre-K through 12)
Nonprofit health care organizations
Private colleges and universities
Voluntary health and welfare
organizations
Community foundations
Other nonprofit organizations

Private foundations
Sec. 509(a)

Operating or nonoperating;
Independent or corporate

Organizations that provide dividends, lower costs, or other economic benefits directly and proportionately to their owners, members, or participants (e.g. mutual insurance companies, credit unions, farm and rural electric cooperatives, and employee benefit plans) are nonprofit because they do not have residual interest owners; however, they do not meet the criteria stated previously for a not-for-profit organization.[5] They operate essentially as commercial businesses and are covered under separate Industry Audit Guides.

There are also "governmental" not-for-profit organizations that may receive tax revenue or be controlled by a government,[6] but are not governments.[7] Examples of entities that receive special tax revenue include libraries and transportation authorities. Governments often control museums, cemeteries, development authorities, housing authorities, public hospitals, public colleges and universities, and other public benefit corporations. Some such organizations are reported as a department or unit of a general purpose government.

Not-for-profit entities are first organized as nonprofit corporations or charitable trusts under a state statute so that they are legally separate from the incorporators. The NPO may then choose to apply to the Internal Revenue Service for tax-exempt status. The IRS, together with the Independent Sector,[8] developed a National Taxonomy of Exempt Entities (NTEE) that divides that largest set of tax-exempt entities, Internal Revenue Code Sec. 501(c)(3) organizations, into 10 functional categories (arts, culture, and humanities; education; environment/animals; health; human services; international/foreign affairs; public/society benefit; religion related; mutual/membership benefit; and others) and 26 major group areas. See Chapter 17 for more discussion of regulation over tax-exempt entities.

GAAP for Nongovernmental NPOs

The FASB assumed primary responsibility for providing guidance on generally accepted accounting principles for nongovernmental not-for-profit entities in 1979.[9] The GASB is responsible for governmental organizations including governmental not-for-profit organizations (see Illustration 1–1, p. 5).[10] Governmental

---

[5]Ibid.

[6]The terms *public* and *private* are problematic; for example, *public* charities are in the not-for-profit sector, *public* schools are in the governmental sector, and *publicly* traded companies are in the for-profit sector of our economy. Distinguishing between for-profit, not-for-profit, and governmental/nongovernmental is more useful.

[7]See p. 6 for the definition of a governmental entity.

[8]The Independent Sector is a nonprofit coalition of corporate, foundation, and voluntary organization members with national interest and impact in philanthropy and voluntary action based in Washington, DC.

[9]Financial Accounting Standards Board, *Statement of Financial Accounting Standards No. 32,* "Specialized Accounting and Reporting Principles in AICPA Statements of Position and Guides on Accounting and Auditing Matters" (New York, 1979).

[10]American Institute of Certified Public Accountants, *Statement of Auditing Standards (SAS) No. 69,* "The Meaning of 'Present Fairly in Conformity with Generally Accepted Accounting Principles' in the Independent Auditor's Report" (New York, 1992). The FASB rescinded *SFAS No. 32* upon the issuance of this guidance.

not-for-profit organizations that have applied the principles in AICPA guidance for VHWOs and certain other nonprofit organizations may continue to do so until the GASB completes its financial reporting project (discussed in Chapter 1), or may change to the current governmental financial reporting model illustrated in Chapters 2 through 10. They are not permitted to adopt FASB's standards applicable to nongovernmental NPOs. This chapter focuses on nongovernmental not-for-profit entities.[11]

There has been a concerted effort recently among the AICPA, the FASB, and the federal Office of Management and Budget (OMB) to standardize the accounting, financial reporting, and auditing rules for the diverse set of entities in the not-for-profit sector and reduce the inconsistencies across segments of this sector. The AICPA's 1996 revised Audit and Accounting Guide, *Not-for-Profit Organizations* superseded three audit guides (Voluntary Health and Welfare Organizations, Colleges and Universities, and Certain Not-for-Profit Organizations) and four statements of Position (*SOPs 74-8, 78-10, 87-2,* and *94-2*). The FASB has completed four of its five not-for-profit agenda items designed to reduce inconsistencies across NPOs: depreciation (*SFAS No. 93*), contributions (*SFAS No. 116*), financial reporting display (*SFAS No. 117*), and investments (*SFAS No. 124*). The remaining item is on financially interrelated entities, and is integrally tied to the for-profit project on consolidations and related matters. Each of these statements is discussed in this chapter. Congress revised the Single Audit Act in 1996 to cover both governmental and not-for-profit entities, and the OMB issued a revision of *Circular A-133* (see Chapter 12)[12] that includes governments, not-for-profit organizations, and health care entities.

Financial Reporting and Accounting

As stated in Chapter 1, the FASB's objectives of financial reporting for not-for-profit agencies are to provide information useful in (1) making resource allocation decisions, (2) assessing services and ability to provide services, (3) assessing management stewardship and performance, and (4) assessing economic resources, obligations, net resources, and changes in them.[13] Users of not-for-profit financial statements include donors, grantors, members, creditors, and others who provide resources to NPOs.

Financial Reporting   FASB *Statement No. 117* requires NPOs to present financial statements showing an aggregate view of the entity.[14] This revolutionary approach effectively moved not-for-profit financial reporting away from the disaggregated, traditional method of

---

[11]Governmental Accounting Standards Board, *Statement No. 29*, "The Use of Not-for-Profit Accounting and Financial Reporting Principles by Governmental Entities" (Norwalk, CT, 1996).

[12]Office of Management and Budget, *Circular A-133*, "Audits of Not-for-Profit Organizations Receiving Federal Awards" (Washington, DC, 1997).

[13]FASB, *Concepts Statement No. 4*, pp. 19–23.

[14]Financial Accounting Standards Board, *Statement of Financial Accounting Standards No. 117* "Financial Statements for Not-for-Profit Organizations" (Norwalk, CT, 199?).

fund-based reporting and more toward the commercial for-profit model of financial reporting. Not all users welcomed this change and the impacts of this controversial change will take several years to be assessed.[15]

FASB *Statement No. 117* established minimum standards for general purpose external financial statements for NPOs by requiring a Statement of Financial Position, Statement of Activities, and Statement of Cash Flows, along with Notes to the Financial Statements. Voluntary health and welfare organizations must also present a Statement of Functional Expenses. Although the information specified by *SFAS No. 117* is to be presented for the entity as a whole, the statement permits additional display of disaggregated information, such as fund-based information that may be useful for management of the entity and accountability to donors and others. Comparative statements are encouraged, but not required. Illustrative financial statements for the Community Family Service Agency, Inc., a VHWO, are presented in Illustrations 16–2 through 16–5, although alternative financial statement formats are allowed by *SFAS No. 117*. The amounts shown in the financial statements reflect the illustrative transactions and journal entries presented later in this chapter.

— balance sheet

Statement of Financial Position.   This statement shows total assets, total liabilities, and the difference, **net assets,** for the organization as a whole. As seen in Illustration 16–2, net assets for this VHWO are categorized into the three classes required by *SFAS No. 117:* unrestricted net assets, temporarily restricted net assets, and permanently restricted net assets. **Unrestricted net assets** arise from contributions that either have no donor restrictions or the restrictions have expired, revenues for services provided, and most investment income. Unrestricted net assets can be further segregated into Board-designated and residual available for operations. **Board-designated net assets** are those unrestricted net assets appropriated or set aside by the governing board rather than an external donor and are sometimes subtitled "investments" and "net equity in fixed assets."

Temporarily restricted net assets result from contributions in which the donor imposes restrictions as to purpose (how the asset is used) or time (when the asset is used). When the restrictions are met, these net assets are "released" and reported as unrestricted net assets. **Permanently restricted net assets** are assets for which the donor stipulates that the assets be held in perpetuity, but allows the organization to spend the income. These gifts are also called **endowments** and are nonexpendable. Endowments may take the form of *pure* endowments, *term* endowments, or *quasi-*endowments. Term endowments are classified as temporarily restricted net assets because as the term expires, the assets can be used at the discretion of the NPO. Quasi-endowments are those in which the Board designates that funds be set aside; however, since the Board can reverse that decision, this form of endowment is classified as an unrestricted net asset. Permanently restricted net assets may also be in the form of artwork, land, or other assets that must be used for a certain purpose

like a nonexpendable trust fund

---

[15]See Robert N. Anthony, "The Not-for-Profit Accounting Mess," and Robert H. Northcutt, "Observations on Professor Anthony's Commentary," *Accounting Horizons*, June 1995, pp. 44–55.

Illustration 16–2

COMMUNITY FAMILY SERVICE AGENCY, INC.
Statement of Financial Position
December 31, 2000, and 1999

	2000	1999
Assets:		
Cash	$ 28,953	$ 58,711
Short-term investments, at fair value	22,000	22,000
Accounts receivable (net)	1,150	2,350
Contributions receivable (net)	6,061	5,165
Supplies, at lower of cost or market	19,100	23,095
Prepaid expense	3,600	3,917
Assets restricted to investment:		
For land, buildings, and equipment:		
Investments, at fair value	15,000	20,000
Contributions receivable (net)	982	10,182
For endowment:		
Investments, at fair value	230,000	230,000
Land, buildings, and equipment, less allowance for accumulated		
depreciation of $17,961 and $13,776	104,763	103,948
Long-term investments	17,000	17,000
Total assets	$448,609	$496,368
Liabilities and net assets:		
Accounts payable and accrued expenses	$ 44,147	$ 25,911
8 1/4% mortgage payable, due 2015	48,500	55,000
Total liabilities	92,647	80,911
Net assets:		
Unrestricted	29,627	97,302
Temporarily restricted	96,335	88,155
Permanently restricted	230,000	230,000
Total net assets	355,962	415,457
Total liabilities and net assets	$448,609	$496,368

and may not be sold. Information on temporarily and permanently restricted net assets can be reported on the face of the Statement of Financial Position or in the Notes to the Financial Statements.

SFAS No. 117 recommends that assets and liabilities be listed in their order of liquidation similar to the manner in which they are listed by business enterprises. The nature of assets and any restrictions should be disclosed. In general, restrictions apply to net assets, not to specific assets. However, if cash or other assets received are designated for long-term purposes or have donor-imposed restrictions that limit their use, they should be segregated on the financial statement, as seen in Illustration 16–2. An alternative form of the Statement of Financial Position is displayed at the end of this chapter.

— Income Statement

Statement of Activities.   The Statement of Activities presents, in aggregated fashion, all changes in unrestricted net assets, temporarily restricted net assets, permanently restricted net assets, and total net assets for the reporting period. These changes take the form of revenues, gains, expenses, and losses. As seen in Illustration 16–3, there is also a section titled "Net assets released from restrictions" that indicates the reclassification of temporarily restricted support to unrestricted support in the year in which the donor stipulations were met. Reclassifications are made for (1) satisfaction of program or purpose restrictions, (2) satisfaction of equipment acquisition restrictions, in the form of depreciation expense, and (3) satisfaction of time restrictions, either actual donor or implied restrictions.

NPOs have considerable flexibility in presenting financial information as long as it is useful and understandable to the reader. *SFAS No. 117* does not preclude the NPO from using additional classifications, such as operating and nonoperating, expendable and nonexpendable, earned and unearned, and recurring and nonrecurring. An alternative format is presented later in the chapter.

In the absence of any donor restrictions, contributions including unconditional promises to give are shown as revenue or support increasing unrestricted net assets. Unconditional promises to give that will not be received until future periods must be reported among the temporarily restricted net assets unless explicit donor stipulations or the circumstances surrounding the promise make it clear that the donor intended the contribution to support activities of the current period. If the provisions of a temporarily restricted contribution are met in the period of the gift, then the revenue and expenses *may* be reported in the unrestricted category. If events simultaneously increase one asset class and decrease another, they should be reported as separate items.

Although some NPOs may use the cash basis as a simple method of accounting internally, external financial statements must be prepared on the accrual accounting basis in order to be in conformity with GAAP. In general, all revenues and expenses should be reported at their gross amounts. Exceptions include activities peripheral to the entity's central operations and investment revenue, which may be reported net of related expenses, if properly disclosed. Although revenues are categorized into three classes, all expenses are reported as reductions of unrestricted net assets. In addition, expenses must be reported by their functional classification (e.g., program or supporting) either in this statement or in the Notes to the Financial Statements. Gains and losses on investments and other assets are reported as changes in unrestricted net assets unless their use is temporarily or permanently restricted.

Statement of Cash Flows.   *SFAS No. 117* requires a Statement of Cash Flows by amending *SFAS No. 95* to extend its coverage to not-for-profit organizations as well as for-profit entities.[16] As Illustration 16–4 shows, cash flows are reported in three categories: operating, investing, and financing. The direct or indirect method may be used. If the direct method is used, a reconciliation showing the change in total net assets from the Statement of Activities to net cash used for operating activities must be prepared.

---

[16]Financial Accounting Standards Board, *Statement of Financial Accounting Standards No. 95*, "Statement of Cash Flows" (Norwalk, CT, 1987).

Illustration 16–3

COMMUNITY FAMILY SERVICE AGENCY, INC.
Statement of Activities
Year Ended December 31, 2000

Changes in unrestricted net assets:	
Revenues and gains:	
Contributions	$388,196
Program service fees	55,250
Membership dues	1,000
Sales to public (net)	100
Investment income	15,680
Miscellaneous	1,500
Total unrestricted revenues and gains	461,726
Net assets released from restrictions:	
Satisfaction of program requirements	27,400
Satisfaction of equipment acquisition restrictions	4,185
Expiration of time restrictions	5,125
Total net assets released from restrictions	36,710
Total unrestricted revenues, gains, and other support	498,436
Expenses and losses:	
Program services:	
Counseling	185,513
Adoption	69,560
Foster home care	172,531
Special outreach project	62,870
Total program services	490,474
Supporting services:	
Management and general	53,085
Fund-raising	13,978
Total supporting services	67,063
Payments to affiliated organizations	8,574
Total expenses and losses	566,111
Decrease in unrestricted net assets	(67,675)
Changes in temporarily restricted net assets:	
Contributions	43,500
Investment income	1,390
Net assets released from restrictions	(36,710)
Increase in temporarily restricted net assets	8,180
Change in permanently restricted net assets	–0–
Decrease in net assets	(59,495)
Net assets, December 31, 1999	415,457
Net assets, December 31, 2000	$355,962

Illustration 16–4

COMMUNITY FAMILY SERVICE AGENCY, INC.
Statement of Cash Flows
Year Ended December 31, 2000

Cash flows from operating activities:	
Cash received from contributors	$349,440
Cash collected on contributions receivable	68,500
Cash received from service recipients	57,200
Cash collected from members	1,000
Investment income	15,680
Miscellaneous receipts	1,750
Cash paid to employees and suppliers	(530,164)
Cash paid to affiliated organizations	(8,574)
Interest paid	(4,540)
Net cash used for operating activities	(49,708)
Cash flows from investing activities:	
Purchase of property and equipment	(5,000)
Proceeds from sale of securities	5,000
Net cash used by investing activities	–0–
Cash flows from financing activities:	
Proceeds from contributions restricted for:	
Investment in plant	8,660
Future operations	16,400
Other financing activities:	
Interest and dividends restricted for plant acquisition	1,390
Repayment of long-term debt	(6,500)
Net cash provided by financing activities	19,950
Net increase (decrease) in cash	(29,758)
Cash, December 31, 1999	58,711
Cash, December 31, 2000	$ 28,953
Reconciliation of Changes in Net Assets to Net Cash	
Used for Operating Activities:	
Change in net assets	$ (59,495)
Adjustments to reconcile changes in net assets to net cash provided	
by operating activities:	
Depreciation	4,185
Decrease in accounts receivable, net	1,200
Decrease in contributions receivable, net	8,304
Decrease in supplies	3,995
Decrease in prepaid expenses	317
Increase in accounts payable and accrued expenses	18,236
Gifts, grants, and bequests restricted for long-term investment	(25,060)
Interest restricted for long-term investment	(1,390)
Cash used for operating activities	$ (49,708)

Donor-imposed restrictions are not separately reported in the cash flows statement; however, the statement does have some unique aspects. Unrestricted gifts are included with the operating activities; purchases or sales of long-term assets, including investments, are reported in the investing activities section; and the receipt of temporarily and permanently restricted net assets given for long-term purposes are included in the financing activities section, with the related income. The financing activities section also includes the issuance and repayment of long-term debt. Noncash gifts or in-kind contributions (discussed later) are disclosed as noncash investing and financing activities in a separate section.

Notes to the Financial Statements. As with all entities, the notes are an integral part of the financial statements of NPOs. Disclosures include principles applicable to for-profit entities, unless there is a specific exemption for not-for-profit organizations. Examples of required disclosures are those relating to financial instruments; commitments; contingencies; extraordinary items; prior-period adjustments; changes in accounting principles; employee benefits; and credit risks. In addition, the nature and amounts of unrestricted, temporarily restricted, and permanently restricted net assets must be disclosed if not displayed on the face of the financial statements. Notes are encouraged to report the detail of reclassifications, investments, and promises to give. Policy statements regarding whether restricted gifts received and expended in the same period are reported first as temporarily restricted must also be disclosed.

Statement of Functional Expenses. VHWOs must prepare a Statement of Functional Expenses along with their other financial statements. Illustration 16–5 shows a format with functional expenses reported in the columns and the natural classification of expenses shown as rows. The functional expenses are those that relate to the program or mission of the organization as opposed to the management and general and fund-raising expenses required to operate the programs. The natural classification of expenses, or object of expense, includes salaries, supplies, occupancy costs, interest, and depreciation, among other categories the organization considers useful to the readers. The ratio of program expenses to total expenses is often used by watchdog agencies, donors, and others as a measure of an NPO's performance. According to the National Charities Information Bureau, the ratio of program expenses to total expenses should be greater than 60 percent. Natural expenses that apply to more than one function must be allocated across program, general and administrative, and fund-raising using a systematic method. Allocation of fund-raising costs is discussed later in this chapter.

Accounting for Revenues, Gains, and Support

Not-for-profit organizations have traditionally distinguished between revenues, gains, and support. **Revenues** represent increases in net assets arising from bilateral **"exchange transactions"** in which the other party to the transaction is presumed to receive direct tangible benefit commensurate with the resources provided. Examples are membership dues, program service fees, sales of supplies and services, and investment income. **Gains,** such as realized gains on investment transactions

Illustration 16–5

COMMUNITY FAMILY SERVICE AGENCY, INC.
Statement of Functional Expenses
Year Ended December 31, 2000
(with comparative totals for 1999)

	Program Services					Supporting Services			Total Program and Supporting Services Expenses	
	Counseling	Adoption	Foster Home Care	Special Outreach Project	Total	Management and General	Fund-Raising	Total	2000	1999
Salaries	$ 87,720	$36,559	$ 83,610	$13,738	$221,627	$35,153	$ 8,220	$43,373	$265,000	$232,170
Employee benefits	16,882	7,036	16,091	2,644	42,653	6,765	1,582	8,347	51,000	47,035
Payroll taxes	6,720	2,801	6,405	1,051	16,977	2,693	630	3,323	20,300	11,400
Total salaries and related expenses	111,322	46,396	106,106	17,433	281,257	44,611	10,432	55,043	336,300	290,605
Professional fees	25,107	3,929	11,643	18,143	58,822	1,178	—	1,178	60,000	54,600
Supplies	4,049	2,167	4,747	3,950	14,913	790	592	1,382	16,295	8,500
Telephone	3,897	1,430	3,350	190	8,867	600	333	933	9,800	9,610
Postage and shipping	2,840	1,073	2,402	908	7,223	684	210	894	8,117	6,750
Occupancy	8,772	1,415	8,078	2,586	20,851	2,468	581	3,049	23,900	24,600
Rental and maintenance of equipment	3,669	1,520	3,511	—	8,700				8,700	8,750
Printing and publications	2,761	1,420	1,352	1,462	6,995	940	1,565	2,505	9,500	7,200
Travel	7,700	1,500	7,500	5,000	21,700	300	—	300	22,000	24,000
Conferences, conventions, meetings	3,450	887	4,436	4,436	13,209	591	—	591	13,800	13,700
Specific assistance to individuals	9,000	1,000	16,100	3,900	30,000	—	—	—	30,000	28,500
Membership dues	234	187	93	93	607	93	—	93	700	677
Awards and grants to National Headquarters	—	5,500	—	—	5,500	—	—	—	5,500	5,000
Miscellaneous	1,744	843	1,891	4,144	8,622	118	—	118	8,740	5,200
Total before depreciation	184,545	69,267	171,209	62,245	487,266	52,373	13,713	66,086	553,352	487,692
Depreciation of buildings and equipment	968	293	1,322	625	3,208	712	265	977	4,185	4,200
Total expenses	$185,513	$69,560	$172,531	$62,870	$490,474	$53,085	$13,978	$67,063	$557,537	$491,892

and gains on sale or disposal of equipment, are increases in net assets that relate to peripheral or incidental transactions of the entity and often are beyond the control of management. **Support** is an increase in net assets arising from contributions of resources of **"nonexchange transactions"** and include only amounts for which the donor derives no tangible benefits from the recipient agency. Membership dues may be part revenue and part contribution if the value received by the member is less than the dues payment. A government grant is usually considered unrestricted support, unless it is essentially a purchase of services, in which case the recipient is considered a vendor and the grant is classified as revenue. Often organizations present one section in the Statement of Activities for revenues, gains, and support, in which case these distinctions are less important. All revenues, gains, and support should be recognized on the accrual basis and reported at gross amounts to be in conformity with GAAP. Revenue that is restricted by an agreement, such as fees or dues dedicated for a specific purpose, is reported in unrestricted net assets because it does not arise from a restricted gift by a donor.

Contributions.　　Not-for-profit organizations, in particular voluntary health and welfare organizations, depend on contributions for their operations. A **contribution** is an unconditional transfer of cash or other asset to the entity (or a settlement or cancellation of its liabilities) in a voluntary, nonreciprocal transfer by another entity acting other than as an owner. *SFAS No. 116* provides guidance on contributions where the reporting entity is a donor or donee; however, it does not apply to exchange transactions; those in which the entity is acting as an agent, trustee, or intermediary; or to tax exemptions, incentives, or abatements.[17] Donors may restrict the period in which the gift can be used or its purpose, or make the contribution without restrictions. In general, *SFAS No. 116* requires recognition of both unrestricted and restricted gifts as support at fair value at the time of the gift. Restricted support increases either temporarily or permanently restricted net assets, depending on whether the restriction is temporary or permanent. In the absence of donor-imposed restrictions, unrestricted net assets are increased.

Promises to give assets to an organization (commonly called *pledges*) can be conditional or unconditional. A **conditional promise to give** depends on the occurrence of a specified future and uncertain event to bind the promissor, such as, obtaining matching gifts by the recipient. A conditional promise to give is *not* recognized as support until the conditions on which it depends are substantially met.

An **unconditional promise to give** depends only on the passage of time or demand by the promisee for performance. These promises are recorded as support in the year made. Unconditional pledges payable in the future, or multiyear promises, are treated as temporarily restricted support, then reclassified to the unrestricted net asset class when the period arrives or the donor stipulation is met. The contribution is measured at the present value of future cash flows. Any difference in previously recorded temporarily restricted support and the current value when the period arrives is recorded as contribution revenue, not interest income.

---

[17]FASB, *SFAS No. 116*, par. 4.

Promises may require the establishment of an allowance for estimated un-collectible pledges, inasmuch as pledges may not be enforceable under law. A description of promises and their terms must be disclosed in the Notes to the Financial Statements. Pledges or intentions to give are not recorded until they have the characteristics of an unconditional promise to give, for example, a written document, partial payment, or a public announcement by the donor.

These *nonexchange* transactions can take the form of cash, securities, capital assets, materials, or services. Cash contributions require that a strong system of internal controls over the safeguarding of this asset be in place; however, they pose no unusual accounting or reporting problems. Donated securities may be received for any purpose, although generally they are received as a part of the principal of an endowment. They are recorded at their fair value at the date of the gift, and the same valuation rule is applied to capital assets received either as a part of an endow-ment or for use in the operations of the organization. Donations of capital assets, such as land, buildings, or works of art, may be temporarily or permanently restricted. If the donor does not stipulate how the asset should be used, then the gift is classified as unrestricted. If the donor does impose restrictions, such as how long the asset must be used as a building, or if the NPO has a policy implying a time restriction over the useful life of the asset, then the contribution is classified as tem-porarily restricted. For buildings and equipment, an amount equal to annual depre-ciation expense is reclassified from temporarily restricted to unrestricted each year.

Donated Materials and Services.   One of the basic characteristics that distin-guishes not-for-profit organizations from commercial organizations is their reliance on noncash contributions or **gifts in kind.** Sheltered workshops for handicapped persons often depend heavily on donations of clothing and furniture, and health agencies may obtain contributions of drugs from pharmaceutical houses. Office space may be furnished rent free; and television, radio, and periodicals may publi-cize fund drives, special events, or the general work of NPOs at no charge. *SFAS No. 116* requires that all unconditional gifts, including material amounts of donated materials, be reported as both a contribution, measured at fair value on the date of the gift, and as an expense. An objective, clearly measurable basis for fair value can be established by proceeds from resale by the organization, price lists, market quotations, or appraisals.[18] Donated materials used or consumed in render-ing services should be reported as part of the cost of the services rendered.

The services of unpaid workers may well make the difference between an effec-tive organization and one that fails to achieve its objectives. Voluntary health and welfare organizations typically rely on the efforts of volunteer workers to supple-ment the efforts of paid employees. *SFAS No. 116* requires recognition of con-tributed services at their fair value if the services received (1) create or enhance nonfinancial assets; or (2) require specialized skills, are provided by individuals pos-sessing those skills, and typically would need to be purchased if not provided by

---

[18]*SFAS No. 116,* par. 19.

donation (e.g., accountants or secretaries). Although *SFAS No. 116* does not provide an example of the first criterion, a logical example would be recognition of support for donated architectural, legal, or carpentry services related to construction of a building addition. In this example, a capital asset account, rather than a program or support expense, would be debited. In general, nonfinancial assets are assets other than cash and assets readily convertible into cash, such as consumable supplies and fixed assets. The second criterion is quite restrictive and results in many donated services not being recognized.

Split-Interest Gifts. Donors may arrange to split the interest in a gift among several beneficiaries, including an NPO. These complex legal agreements, often involving trusts, as well as deferred giving programs and gifts of life insurance, are beyond the scope of this book.

Special Events. Special events are fund-raising activities in which "something of tangible value is offered to donor participants or designees for a payment which includes a contribution" adequate to yield revenue for the sponsoring agency over and above direct expenses. Dinners, dances, golf outings, bazaars, card parties, fashion shows, and sales of candy cookies, cakes, or greeting cards are typical "special events." The special events category of support is reserved for those events sponsored by the voluntary organization or by an organization over which it has control. If a completely independent organization sponsors an event for the voluntary agency's benefit, the amount given to the agency should be reported as contributions.

Special events may give rise to incidental revenue, such as advertising of programs; incidental revenue is properly reported in the special events category of support. NPOs have traditionally netted direct costs of special events (such as the cost of dinner, rental of ballroom, or cost of prizes) against the gross proceeds of the special event. FASB *Statement No. 117,* par. 138, requires that all special event revenue and direct costs, except those of a peripheral or incidental nature, be reported at their gross amounts. In the Statement of Activities presented in Illustration 16–3 in this chapter, special events support is included as part of the "Contributions" rather than as a separate amount. If desired, NPOs can provide more detailed reporting of support categories, either on the face of the Statement of Activities or in the Notes to the Financial Statements.

Expenses of promoting and conducting special events, such as expenses of printing tickets and posters, mailings, fees and expenses of public relations and fund-raising consultants, and salaries of employees of the voluntary agency attributable to planning, promoting, and conducting special events, are treated as fund-raising expenses and are not charged against special events support.

Accounting for Expenses

Generally accepted accounting principles require that all expenses of NPOs be measured on the accrual basis and be reported as decreases in unrestricted net assets on the Statement of Activities. Depreciation of fixed assets, including contributed capital assets, used in the operation of the organization is required by *SFAS No. 93*.[19] Depreciation of art and historical collections is discussed later in this chapter.

Functional Expenses.   NPOs have long been required to report some degree of functional expenses; that is, segregation of expenses incurred for operating the *programs* from expenses incurred for *supporting* the programs (e.g., fund-raising or management and general expenses). Depreciation expense should be allocated to programs as well as to support function expenses. Illustration 16–6 presents a chart from the United Way of America's book, *Accounting and Financial Reporting: A Guide for United Ways and Not-for-Profit Human Service Organizations* that shows the relationship between functional and natural or object classifications of expenses. The human service organization used in the illustration is a United Way of America agency operating three programs: adoption, foster home care, and counseling. A local fund-raising organization, such as the United Way, that is intended to allocate most of its inflows to participating agencies rather than to engage directly in offering program services to the public may find it desirable to present "allocating and agency relations" or "planning and evaluation" as well as management and general and fund-raising.

Allocation of Costs with a Fund-Raising Appeal.   AICPA *Statement of Position 98-2* revises *SOP 87-2* on joint costs and makes it more difficult to allocate "educating the public" or "advocacy" costs to program expenses. *SOP 98-2* provides:

1. The costs of all materials and activities that include a fund-raising appeal should be reported as fund-raising costs (including costs that are otherwise clearly identifiable with program or management and general functions) unless a bona fide program or management and general function has been conducted in conjunction with the appeal for funds.

2. Costs that are clearly identifiable should be charged to program, management and general, or fund-raising. The joint costs of a bona fide program or management and general function should be allocated between those cost objectives and fund-raising.

3. Criteria of purpose, audience, and content must be met in order to conclude that a bona fide program or management and general function has been conducted in conjunction with the appeal for funds.

4. Certain information must be disclosed if joint costs are allocated.[20]

This statement goes beyond *SOP 87-2* by covering total costs, not just joint costs, and applying to state and local governmental entities, as well as to NPOs.

---

[19]Financial Accounting Standards Board, *Statement of Financial Accounting Standards No. 93* "Recognition of Depreciation by Not-for-Profit Organizations" (Norwalk, CT, 1987).

[20]AICPA, *SOP 98-2*, "Accounting for Costs of Activities of Not-for-Profit Organizations and State and Local Governmental Entities that Include Fund-Raising" (New York, 1998) is effective for years beginning on or after December 15, 1998.

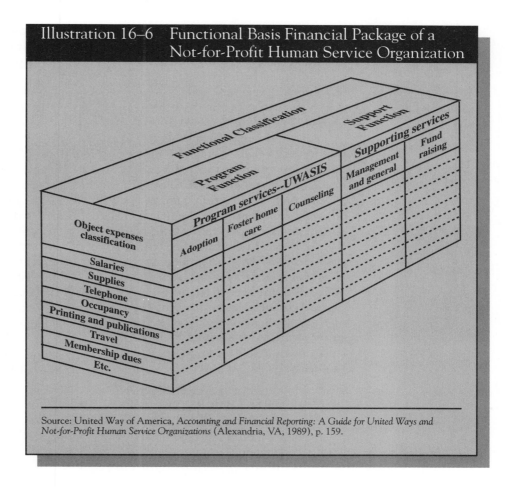

Illustration 16–6   Functional Basis Financial Package of a Not-for-Profit Human Service Organization

Source: United Way of America, *Accounting and Financial Reporting: A Guide for United Ways and Not-for-Profit Human Service Organizations* (Alexandria, VA, 1989), p. 159.

Expenses incurred for multiple purposes should be allocated to program services and to fund-raising, if allocation bases that are both equitable and clerically feasible are available. Management and general expenses include the cost of publicity and public relations activities designed to keep the organization's name before prospective contributors. Costs of informational materials that contain only general information regarding the health or welfare problem and the costs of informational materials distributed to potential contributors, but not as a part of a fund drive, are considered management and general expenses. The costs of budgeting, accounting, reporting, legal services, office management, purchasing, and similar activities are examples of expenses properly classifiable as management and general expenses.

Fund-raising expenses include the costs of television and radio announcements that request contributions, including the costs of preparing the announcements and purchasing or arranging for the time; the costs of postage, addressing, and maintenance of mailing lists and other fund drive records; the costs of preparing or purchasing fund-raising materials; the costs of public meetings to "kick off" a fund drive; and an appropriate portion of the salaries of personnel who supervise fund-raising activities or keep records of them.

Accounting for Assets

Assets that have different treatment in NPOs than in for-profit entities include investments and collection items.

Investments. *SFAS No. 124* provides guidance to NPOs on accounting for investments in a manner similar to *SFAS No. 115* for businesses, and removes the inconsistencies in investment accounting across the various audit guides for nongovernmental not-for-profit entities.[21] *SFAS No. 124* requires that not-for-profit organizations mark all investments in equity securities that have readily determinable values and all debt securities to market or *fair value*, rather than reporting them at original cost, amortized cost, or lower of cost or market. This statement is simpler than *SFAS No. 115* in that there is no requirement that NPOs classify their investments into trading, available-for-sale, and held-to-maturity categories. It does not apply to investments in securities accounted for under the equity method; consolidated subsidiaries; or investments with no readily determinable market value, such as real estate mortgages, oil and gas interests, and limited partnerships without a publicly traded market value.

Gains and losses are measured as the changes in fair value of the investments. Fair values are determined by quoted market prices, if available; selling price of similar securities; or valuation techniques, such as discounted cash flows. All realized and unrealized gains and losses on investments, as well as investment income (i.e., interest and dividends) are reported in the current period's Statement of Activities. Income and gains and losses are reported as increases in unrestricted net assets, unless their use is restricted by the donor or legally restricted by state law.[22] If restrictions on income exist, then income is reported as an increase in either temporarily or permanently restricted net assets, depending on the nature of the restriction; and gains and losses are reported in the same way as the income. When the restriction is satisfied in the same period the income or gain is earned, then the investment income and gains may be reported as increases in unrestricted net assets as long as the organization has a similar policy for reporting contributions received, reports consistently from period to period, and discloses its accounting policy.

Endowments, gifts that the donor requires be held permanently, pose some additional accounting problems. If the donor requires that a specific investment security

---

[21]Financial Accounting Standards Board, *Statement of Financial Accounting Standards No. 124*, "Accounting for Certain Investments Held by Not-for-Profit Organizations" (Norwalk, CT, 1995), and *Statement of Financial Accounting Standards No. 115*, "Accounting for Certain Investments in Debt and Equity Securities" (Norwalk, CT, 1994).

[22]Most states have adopted some version of the Uniform Management of Institutional Funds Act (UMIFA) (1970s) and some have adopted the Uniform Prudent Investors Act (1994), which describes standards of care, portfolio theory, and delegation of investment authority.

be held into perpetuity, then gains and losses on that security are also permanently restricted. However, if the NPO can choose suitable investments, then gains on those investments are reported as increases in unrestricted net assets, unless the income was restricted. The donor may stipulate that part of the net appreciation value (unrealized gain) is restricted, most often done to protect the endowment from the effects of inflation. In this case, gains are reported as permanently restricted net assets until the required net appreciation value is reached, then the remainder is reported as unrestricted. Losses on endowments are more complicated, in part, because the donor is often silent regarding any loss. *SFAS No. 124* requires that endowment losses reduce unrestricted net assets if the net appreciation requirement has been reached; otherwise, endowment losses decrease temporarily restricted net assets. In subsequent years, gains that restore the fair value of the endowment assets to the required level are reported as increases in unrestricted net assets.

SFAS No. 124 also requires extensive disclosures such as:

1. Composition of investment return, including investment income, net realized gains and losses on investments reported at other than fair value, and net gains and losses on investments reported at fair value.

2. A reconciliation of investment return to amounts reported in the Statements of Activities, if investment return is separated into operating and nonoperating amounts, together with a description of the policy used to determine the amount that is included in the measure of operations, and a discussion of circumstances leading to any change in that policy.

3. The aggregate carrying amount of investments by major types (e.g., equity securities, U.S. Treasury securities, mutual funds, corporate, debt securities, real estate).

4. The basis for determining the carrying amount for investments not covered by this standard.

5. The method(s) and significant assumptions used to estimate the fair values of investments other than financial instruments, if those other investments are reported at fair value.

6. The aggregate amount of deficiencies for all donor-restricted endowment funds for which the fair value of the investment at the reporting date is less than the level required by donor stipulation or law.

7. The nature of and carrying amount for each individual investment or group of investments that represents a significant concentration of market risk.

NPOs must follow the disclosure guidance in *SFAS Nos. 105, 107,* and *109.*[23]

---

[23]Financial Accounting Standards Board, *Statement of Financial Accounting Standards No. 105,* "Disclosure of Information about Financial Instruments with Off-Balance Sheet Risk and Financial Instruments with Concentrations of Credit Risk" (Norwalk, CT, 1990); *SFAS No. 107,* "Disclosures about Fair Value of Financial Instruments" (1991); and *SFAS No. 119,* "Disclosures about Derivative Financial Instruments and Fair Value of Financial Instruments" (1994).

Collection Items.   Certain not-for-profit organizations, particularly museums and libraries, have significant collections. *SFAS No. 116* defines **collections** as works of art, historical treasures, or similar assets that are:

1. Held for public exhibition, education, or research in furtherance of public service rather than financial gain.
2. Protected, kept unencumbered, cared for, and preserved.
3. Subject to an organizational policy that requires the proceeds of items that are sold to be used to acquire other items for collection.[24]

An NPO may adopt a policy of recognizing collections as assets, or not recognizing them; however, selective capitalization is not allowed. Implementation of *SFAS No. 116* required organizations to either retroactively capitalize their collections, prospectively capitalize the collection, or not capitalize at all.

If an NPO capitalizes its collections, then it should recognize them as assets in the period in which they are acquired, either at cost or fair market value, if contributed. If contributed, collections should be recorded in the appropriate net asset category depending on any restrictions placed on the contribution by the donor. If the organization chooses not to capitalize, then it should provide note disclosure of its collections.

SFAS No. 93 states that works of art or historical treasures do not need to be depreciated so long as their economic benefit is used up so slowly that their estimated useful lives are extraordinarily long. This characteristic exist if (1) the assets individually have cultural, aesthetic, or historic value that is worth preserving perpetually, and (2) the holder has the technological and financial ability to protect and preserve essentially undiminished the service potential of the asset and is doing that.[25]

Optional Fund Accounting

Fund accounting was defined and illustrated in Chapters 1 through 10 for governments as a method of segregating assets, liabilities, and fund balances into separate accounting entities associated with specific activities, donor-imposed restrictions, or obligations. This system makes it possible to determine compliance with laws, regulations, and agreements; and demonstrate that the NPO is meeting its stewardship responsibility to resource providers. Many NPOs still use this accounting method for internal management purposes. As mentioned previously, *SFAS No. 117* permits not-for-profit organizations to also present disaggregated data classified by fund groups, as long as the aggregated net asset statements are also presented.

---

[24]AICPA, Audit and Accounting Guide, *Not-for-Profit Organizations*, par. 7.05; and FASB, *SFAS No. 116*, Appendix D.
[25]FASB, *SFAS No. 93*, par. 6.

Fund categories described in the AICPA Audit and Accounting Guide, *Not-for-Profit Organizations*, are:

- Unrestricted current funds (or unrestricted operating or general funds).
- Restricted current funds (or restricted operating or specific purpose funds).
- Plant funds (or land, building, and equipment funds).
- Loan funds. University
- Endowment funds.
- Annuity and life income funds (or split-interest funds).
- Agency funds (or custodian funds).[26]

All NPO funds are self-balancing sets of accounts that are both accounting entities and fiscal entities accounted for on the full accrual basis, except the Agency Fund, which is comprised only of assets and liabilities. The residual difference between total assets and total liabilities in a fund is labeled Fund Balance. Net assets also represent residual interests, but net assets are not the same as fund balances.

Unrestricted current funds are used to account for all resources that may be used at the discretion of the governing Board for carrying on the operations of the organization, including assets designated by the Board for specific purposes. Restricted current funds account for resources that may be used for operations, but have been *restricted* by the stipulations of donors or grantors. Current liabilities are recorded in the appropriate fund depending on which funds will be used to pay them.

Plant funds are used to account for land, buildings, and equipment used by not-for-profit organizations in the conduct of their operations; liabilities relating to the acquisition or improvement of plant assets; and cash, investments, or receivables contributed specifically for acquiring, replacing, or improving plant. Loan funds account for loans made to students, employees, and other constituents; consequently, they appear most often in accounting for colleges and universities (see Chapter 18).

The principal amounts of gifts and bequests that must, under the terms of agreements with donors, be maintained intact in perpetuity, or until the occurrence of a specified event or for a specified time period, are accounted for as endowment funds. Other gifts may take the form of split interests in which donors retain some of the gift (either the income or principal) for a period of time, sometimes until their death. Annuity funds are used when the donor specifies an amount of income to be paid to the donor or to a designated third party for a specified period. A life income fund is used when the donor stipulates that all income will be paid to the donor or a designated third party, with the principal reverting to the NPO upon the donor's death, or some other specified time.

Agency or custodian funds are established to account for assets received by an organization to be held or disbursed only on instructions of the person or organization from whom they were received. Assets accounted for by a custodian fund are

---

[26]AICPA, Audit and Accounting Guide, *Not-for-Profit Organizations*, par. 16.01–16.20.

assets of the donors, not assets of the organization; income generated from the assets is added to the appropriate liability account. For these reasons, neither the receipt of assets to be held in custody nor the receipt of income from those assets should be reported by the not-for-profit organization as revenue or support. Assets of custodian funds and the offsetting liabilities should not be combined with assets and liabilities of other funds.

NPOs that use fund accounting recognize revenues and expenses for all categories of funds except custodian funds. This practice makes it relatively easy for NPOs to prepare the aggregated entitywide financial statements required by FASB *Statement No. 117*. Unrestricted current fund balance is reported as unrestricted net assets; restricted current fund balances as temporarily restricted net assets, and *pure* endowment fund balance as permanently restricted net assets. The remaining fund balances can contain elements of each category, and the terms of their existence must be examined for donor restrictions. All interfund receivables and payables must be eliminated in preparing entitywide statements. Fund accounting for not-for-profit entities is not illustrated in this chapter.

Financially Interrelated Entities

Not-for-profit organizations may *have control over* or be *financially interrelated with* another entity, such as a for-profit entity or another NPO. At issue is whether the financial statements of the two entities should be combined and what disclosures will provide the decision maker with the fairest picture of the overall organization. AICPA *SOP 94-3* provides guidance to NPOs on reporting affiliated entities and makes uniform the previous guidance in the three former industry audit guides (Colleges and Universities, VHWO, and Certain Not-for-Profit Organizations).[27] In general, the nature of the relationship between the entities should drive the decision to consolidate financial information of two entities and the extent of disclosures if statements are not consolidated.

Investments in For-Profit Entities

If an NPO has a controlling financial interest through direct or indirect ownership of a majority voting interest in a for-profit entity, it should consolidate that entity's financial information with its own, if conditions of *ARB No. 51* and *SFAS No. 94* are met, and the control is not expected to be temporary.[28] If an entity owns less than a controlling interest, but has significant influence over a for-profit entity, it should use the equity method to report investments in that entity if the guidelines

---

[27]American Institute of Certified Public Accountants, Statement of Position 94-3, *Reporting of Related Entities by Not-for-Profit Organizations* (New York, 1994), effective for fiscal years beginning after December 15, 1994, and one year later for smaller organizations.

[28]*Accounting Research Bulletin (ARB) No. 51*, "Consolidated Financial Statements" (New York: AICPA, 1959) and FASB, *SFAS No. 94*, "Consolidation of All Majority-Owned Subsidiaries" (Stamford, CT, 1987).

in *APB Opinion No. 18* are met.[29] If the entity does not exert influence, then the investment should be reported at fair value according to *SFAS No. 124.* The FASB's agenda item on "Consolidations and Other Related Matters" may provide more guidance on *control,* and, although it focuses on the for-profit sector, it will apply also to NPOs if a final statement is issued.[30]

Financially Interrelated NPOs	In the case of financially interrelated not-for-profit organizations, an NPO should consolidate another NPO in which it has a controlling financial interest and an economic interest. Control exists if one organization can determine the direction of management policies through ownership, contract, or otherwise. Evidence of control might be majority membership on the Board, a charter granting the ability to dissolve the other organization, or contracts assigning oversight responsibility. An **economic interest** exists if the other entity holds or utilizes significant resources that must be used for the purposes of the NPO; or the reporting organization is responsible for the liabilities of the other entity. Examples of economic interests include:

1. Other entities solicit funds in the name of the reporting organization, and the solicited funds are intended by the contributor to be transferred to the reporting organization or used at it discretion.
2. A reporting organization transfers significant resources to another entity whose resources are held for the benefit of the reporting organization.
3. A reporting organization assigns certain significant functions to another entity.
4. A reporting organization provides funds for another entity or guarantees its debt.

If either control *or* an economic interest exist, but not both, related party disclosures required in *SFAS No. 57* should be made, as well as disclosures that identify the other organization and the nature of the relationship. Contributions made to an organization by its governing board members, officers, or employees need not be disclosed if the contributors do not receive a reciprocal economic benefit in consideration for the contribution. Reasonable amounts of salaries, wages, employee benefits, and reimbursement of expenses incurred in connection with a contributor's duties are not considered reciprocal benefits. If a national or international not-for-profit organization has local organizations that determine their own program activities, are financially independent, and control their own assets, consolidated financial statements are not required.

---

[29]*Accounting Principles Board (APB) Opinion No. 18,* "The Equity Method of Accounting for Investments" (New York, 1971).

[30]When an exposure draft or statement is issued, the publisher will distribute to faculty members who have adopted this text an Update Bulletin describing this issue and its effect on NPOs.

Funds Received as an Agent, Trustee, or Intermediary.   Community, federated fund-raising, and institutionally related foundations (IRFs)[31] asked the FASB to clarify paragraph 4 of *SFAS No. 116*, which declared that the Statement did not apply to transfers of assets in which the reporting entity was acting as an agent, trustee, or intermediary, rather than as a donor or donee. Traditionally these foundations have classified funds received from donors as contributions, and did not want to be viewed merely as agents. *SFAS No. 116* would have required these organizations to report donations made to them for the benefit of another NPO as a liability. The *SFAS No. 116* accounting treatment would have understated the amount of contributions raised and resulted in meaningless comparative financial ratios in the industry. FASB *Interpretation No. 42* provide some relief by permitting NPOs to report the contribution as support and as an asset if the donor grants the unilateral **variance power** to redirect the assets to a beneficiary different than the third party initially indicated.[32] Community foundations and federated fund-raisers (e.g., United Way) that support various charities are presumed to have variance power. However, captive fund-raisers, such as institutionally related foundations, await further guidance from the FASB.

Funds Held in Trust by Others.   Beneficial interests in perpetual trusts held in trust by third parties under a legal trust instrument created by a donor to generate income for an NPO should not be included in the Balance Sheet of the not-for-profit organization if it has no control over the actions of the trustee, and if the organization is not the remainderman under the trust. The existence of the trust may be disclosed either parenthetically in the Balance Sheet or in Notes to the Financial Statements. Income from such trusts, if significant, should be reported separately in the Statement of Activity.

Illustrative Transactions—Voluntary Health and Welfare Organizations

Preceding sections of this chapter point out the fact that there are many differences among NPOs regarding the kinds of program services provided and in the sources of support and revenue utilized. Accordingly, the transactions and accounting entries presented in this section should be taken as illustrative of those considered appropriate for an organization that offers counseling, adoption, and foster home care, but not necessarily typical of other NPOs. The transactions illustrated in this section are assumed to pertain to the year 2000 of a hypothetical organization called the Community Family Service Agency, Inc. The trial balance of the Community Family Service Agency, Inc., as of December 31, 1999 is shown next.

---

[31]According to the Council for the Advancement of Secondary Education, there are almost 800 nongovernmental not-for-profit IRC Sec. 501(c)(3) foundations that are related to public institutions such as universities and handle their fund-raising, manage their endowment, and sometimes manage entrepreneurial activities.

[32]Financial Accounting Standards Board, *Interpretation No. 42*, "Transfers of Assets in Which a Not-for-Profit Organization Acts as an Agent, Trustee, or Intermediary" (Norwalk, CT, 1996).

COMMUNITY FAMILY SERVICE AGENCY, INC.
Trial Balance
As of December 31, 1999

	Debits	*Credits*
Cash	$ 58,711	
Short-term Investments—Unrestricted	22,000	
Short-term Investments—Temporarily Restricted—Plant	20,000	
Accounts Receivable	2,485	
Allowance for Uncollectible Accounts Receivable		$ 135
Contributions Receivable—Unrestricted	5,424	
Allowance for Uncollectible Contributions—Unrestricted		259
Contributions Receivable—Temporarily Restricted	10,470	
Allowance for Uncollectible Contributions—		
Temporarily Restricted for Plant		288
Supplies	23,095	
Prepaid Expense	3,917	
Land—Temporarily Restricted	16,900	
Building—Temporarily Restricted	58,000	
Allowance for Depreciation—Building		4,640
Equipment—Temporarily Restricted	42,824	
Allowance for Depreciation—Equipment		9,136
Long-term Investments—Unrestricted	17,000	
Long-term Investments—Permanently Restricted	230,000	
Accounts Payable and Accrued Expenses		25,911
Mortgage Payable		55,000
Unrestricted Net Assets—Undesignated—Available for Operations		67,302
Unrestricted Net Assets—Designated for Special Outreach Project		30,000
Temporarily Restricted Net Assets—Programs		3,900
Temporarily Restricted Net Assets—Plant		79,130
Temporarily Restricted Net Assets—Time		5,125
Permanently Restricted Net Assets		230,000
Totals	$510,826	$510,826

The trial balance as of December 31, 1999, indicates that the plant assets (land, building, and equipment) are temporarily restricted, either explicitly by the donor or by an organization policy implying that donated fixed assets will be restricted for the term of their useful life. An amount equal to depreciation expense is reclassified from temporarily restricted to unrestricted net assets each year.

It is also apparent from the trial balance that the donors of temporarily restricted gifts for the programs, the plant, or for future periods, have also restricted the specific asset of investments. Donors are more likely to restrict these assets than cash. For simplicity, it is assumed that the investments have not changed in fair value from the prior year. Of course, when there is a change, *SFAS No. 124* requires an adjustment to the asset with the unrealized gain or loss reported in the Statement of Activities.

Contributions received in 1999, but specified by donors for unrestricted use in 2000, were transferred from the temporarily restricted to the unrestricted net asset class, as shown by Entry 1.

1. Net Assets Released—Expiration of Time Restrictions—		
Temporarily Restricted	5,125	
Net Assets Released—Expiration of Time Restrictions—		
Unrestricted		5,125

Pledges receivable resulting from the 2000 fund drive were recorded. Pledges of $69,500 were unrestricted; in addition, pledges of $16,500 were donor-restricted for a special outreach project to be undertaken in 2000.

2a. Contributions Receivable—Unrestricted	69,500	
Contributions—Unrestricted		69,500
2b. Contributions Receivable—Temporarily Restricted	16,500	
Contributions—Temporarily Restricted—Program		16,500

Cash collected for unrestricted pledges totaled $68,500; collection of accounts receivable amounted to $2,200. Cash collected for restricted pledges made this year totaled $16,500. Cash in the amount of $9,200 was collected for pledges given during a building fund drive in the preceding year.

3a. Cash	70,700	
Contributions Receivable—Unrestricted		68,500
Accounts Receivable		2,200
3b. Cash	16,500	
Contributions Receivable—Temporarily Restricted		16,500
3c. Cash	9,200	
Contributions Receivable—Temporarily Restricted		9,200

The organization sponsored a bazaar to raise funds for the Special Outreach Project. Direct costs of $3,000, considered peripheral or incidental in nature, incurred for this event were paid in cash; the event yielded cash contributions of $10,000.

4a. Cash	10,000	
Contributions—Temporarily Restricted—Program		10,000
4b. Contributions—Temporarily Restricted—Program	3,000	
Cash		3,000

The FY2000 allocation from the United Way of Fairshare Bay amounted, in gross, to $317,000. Related fund-raising expenses to be borne by the Community Family Service Agency totaled $13,200; the net allocation was received in cash.

5. Cash	303,800	
Fund-raising Support Expenses	13,200	
Contributions—Unrestricted		317,000

Salaries expense for the year totaled $265,000; employee benefits expense totaled $51,000; and payroll taxes expense was $20,300. As of year-end, $15,100 of these expenses were unpaid; the balance had been paid in cash.

6.	Salaries Expense	265,000	
	Employee Benefits Expense	51,000	
	Payroll Taxes Expense	20,300	
	Cash		321,200
	Accounts Payable and Accrued Expenses		15,100

Expenses incurred for the Special Outreach Project were professional fees, $17,000; supplies, $4,500; and printing and publications, $1,600. All amounts were paid in cash.

7.	Professional Fees Expense	17,000	
	Supplies Expense	4,500	
	Printing and Publications Expense	1,600	
	Cash		23,100

Expenses for program services and supporting services were professional fees, $43,000; supplies, $7,800; telephone, $9,800; postage and shipping, $7,800; occupancy, $23,900; rental and maintenance of equipment, $8,700; printing and publications, $7,900; travel, $22,000; conferences, conventions, and meetings, $13,800; specific assistance to individuals, $30,000; membership dues, $700; awards and grants to national headquarters, $5,500; costs of sales to the public, $900; and miscellaneous, $4,200. All expenses were credited to Accounts Payable and Accrued Expenses.

8.	Professional Fees Expense	43,000	
	Supplies Expense	7,800	
	Telephone Expense	9,800	
	Postage and Shipping Expense	7,800	
	Occupancy Expense	23,900	
	Rental and Maintenance of Equipment Expense	8,700	
	Printing and Publications Expense	7,900	
	Travel Expense	22,000	
	Conferences, Conventions, and Meetings	13,800	
	Specific Assistance to Individuals	30,000	
	Membership Dues	700	
	Awards and Grants to National Headquarters	5,500	
	Cost of Sales to the Public	900	
	Miscellaneous Expense	4,200	
	Accounts Payable and Accrued Expenses		186,000

Unrestricted support and revenue were received in cash during 2000 from the following sources: legacies and bequests, $15,000; membership dues from individuals, $1,000; program service fees, $55,000; net incidental revenue, $250; investment income, $2,900; and miscellaneous, $1,500.

9.	Cash	75,650	
	Contributions—Unrestricted		15,000
	Membership Dues		1,000
	Program Service Fees		55,000
	Net Incidental Revenue		250
	Investment Income—Unrestricted		2,900
	Miscellaneous Revenue		1,500

Sales to the public amounted to $1,000 gross for the year. None of this amount was collected by year-end.

| 10. | Accounts Receivable | 1,000 | |
| | Sales to the Public | | 1,000 |

Accounts payable and accrued expenses paid in cash during 2000 totaled $182,864.

| 11. | Accounts Payable and Accrued Expenses | 182,864 | |
| | Cash | | 182,864 |

Contributions received in cash in 2000 but specified by donors for use in 2001 amounted to $20,000. Of this total, $10,000 was unrestricted as to purpose; $6,000 was for restricted program purposes; and $4,000 was for the purchase of equipment. The Agency chooses to report one Contributions Revenue account for temporarily restricted support and keep a subsidiary ledger for time, program, and plant restrictions.

12.	Cash	20,000	
	Contributions—Temporarily Restricted—Time		10,000
	Contributions—Temporarily Restricted—Program		6,000
	Contributions—Temporarily Restricted—Plant		4,000

Interest of $4,540 and $6,500 on the principal of the mortgage were paid in cash. Short-term investments that were restricted for the plant were sold at par, $5,000; the proceeds were used to purchase equipment. The Agency has a policy that there is an implied restriction on plant assets and that this restriction is satisfied as the assets are used (measured by depreciation expense).

13a.	Miscellaneous Expense	4,540	
	Mortgage Payable	6,500	
	Cash		11,040
13b.	Cash	5,000	
	Short-Term Investments—Temporarily Restricted—		
	Plant		5,000
13c.	Equipment	5,000	
	Cash		5,000

Interest received in cash on short-term investments restricted for the plant amounted to $1,390. Interest received in cash on investments of endowment funds amounted to $12,780. This income was not restricted by the donor.

14a.	Cash	1,390	
	Investment Income—Temporarily Restricted—Plant		1,390
14b.	Cash	12,780	
	Investment Income—Unrestricted		12,780

The Community Family Service Agency paid its national affiliates in accord with the affiliation agreements; the amount of the payment in 2000 was $8,574.

15. Payments to Affiliated Organizations	8,574	
Cash		8,574

End-of-the-Year Adjusting Journal Entries. A physical count of supplies, valued at the lower of cost or market, indicated the proper balance sheet value should be $19,100. Prepaid expenses at year-end were $3,600; the decrease is chargeable to postage and shipping expense.

16a. Supplies Expense	3,995	
Supplies		3,995
16b. Postage and Shipping	317	
Prepaid Expense		317

An analysis of the investment accounts indicated that the fair value of the long-term investments was equal to the cost. The allowance for uncollectible accounts receivable appeared adequate and not excessive, but the allowance for uncollectible unrestricted pledges should be increased by $104.

17. Uncollectible Contributions Expense	104	
Allowance for Uncollectible Contributions—		
Unrestricted		104

Depreciation on buildings and equipment belonging to the Community Family Service Agency is recorded in the amounts shown in entry 18. Since the depreciation reduced the carrying value of the fixed assets, a reclassification is made for the net assets temporarily restricted for plant released from restriction.

18a. Depreciation of Buildings and Equipment	4,185	
Allowance for Depreciation—Building		1,145
Allowance for Depreciation—Equipment		3,040
18b. Net Assets Released—Satisfaction of Plant Restrictions—		
Temporarily Restricted	4,185	
Net Assets Released—Satisfaction of Plant Restrictions—		
Unrestricted		4,185

End-of-the-Year Reclassification Journal Entries. Miscellaneous expenses for mortgage interest (in entry 13a) and depreciation expense (in entry 18a) were allocated to program services and supporting services. The allocation is assumed to be as shown in entry 19.

19. Counseling Program Expenses	2,480	
Adoption Program Expenses	990	
Foster Home Care Program Expenses	2,510	
Special Outreach Project Program Expenses	2,050	
Management and General Support Expenses	530	
Fund-raising Support Expenses	165	
Miscellaneous Expense		4,540
Depreciation of Buildings and Equipment		4,185

The natural classification of expenses in entry 7 were allocated to the Special Outreach Project.

20. Special Outreach Project Program Expenses   23,100
        Professional Fees Expense   17,000
        Supplies Expense   4,500
        Printing and Publications Expense   1,600

The remaining natural classification of expenses (in entries 6, 8, and 16b) were allocated to the various program and support categories as shown in entry 21, except Costs of Sales to the Public (entry 8), which will be netted with Sales to the Public.

21. Counseling Program Expenses   183,033
    Adoption Program Expenses   68,570
    Foster Home Care Program Expenses   170,021
    Special Outreach Project Program Expenses   37,720
    Management and General Support Expenses   52,555
    Fund-raising Support Expenses   13,813
        Salaries Expense   265,000
        Employee Benefits Expense   51,000
        Payroll Taxes Expense   20,300
        Professional Fees Expense   43,000
        Supplies Expense   11,795
        Telephone Expense   9,800
        Postage and Shipping Expense   8,117
        Occupancy Expense   23,900
        Rental and Maintenance of Equipment   8,700
        Printing and Publications Expense   7,900
        Travel Expense   22,000
        Conferences, Conventions, and Meetings   13,800
        Specific Assistance to Individuals   30,000
        Membership Dues   700
        Awards and Grants to National Headquarters   5,500
        Miscellaneous Expense   4,200

Unrestricted net assets that were designated by the Board for the Special Outreach Project were deemed no longer necessary; the Board authorized the return of the amount, $30,000, to Unrestricted Net Assets—Undesignated. $27,400 ($3,900 + $23,500) of temporarily restricted funds were spent on the programs this year.

22. Unrestricted Net Assets—Designated for Special
      Outreach Project   30,000
        Unrestricted Net Assets—Undesignated—
          Available for Operations   30,000

    Net Assets Released—Satisfaction of Program Restrictions—
      Temporarily Restricted   27,400
        Net Assets Released—Satisfaction of Program Restrictions—
          Unrestricted   27,400

End-of-the-Year Closing Journal Entries.   The following closing journal entries are made: (*a*) reclassifications for net assets released are closed into the appropriate categories of net assets, (*b*) unrestricted support and revenue are closed to unrestricted net assets, (*c*) program and support expenses as well as payments to affiliated organizations are closed to unrestricted net assets, (*d*) temporarily restricted support for programs, plant, and time are closed to temporarily restricted net assets, and (*e*) permanently restricted support is closed to permanently restricted net assets, if any.

23a.	Temporarily Restricted Net Assets—Time	5,125	
	Net Assets Released—Expiration of Time Restrictions—		
	Unrestricted	5,125	
	Net Assets Released—Expiration of Time Restriction—		
	Temporarily Restricted		5,125
	Unrestricted Net Assets—Undesignated—		
	Available for Operations		5,125
	Temporarily Restricted Net Assets—Plant	4,185	
	Net Assets Released—Satisfaction of Plant Restrictions—		
	Unrestricted	4,185	
	Net Assets Released—Satisfaction of Plant Restrictions—		
	Temporarily Restricted		4,185
	Unrestricted Net Assets—Undesignated—		
	Available for Operations		4,185
	Temporarily Restricted Net Assets—Program	27,400	
	Net Assets Released—Satisfaction of Program Restrictions—		
	Unrestricted	27,400	
	Net Assets Released—Satisfaction of Program		
	Restrictions—Temporarily Restricted		27,400
	Unrestricted Net Assets—Undesignated—Available		
	for Operations		27,400
23b.	Contributions—Unrestricted	401,500	
	Sales to the Public	1,000	
	Membership Dues—Individuals	1,000	
	Program Service Fees	55,000	
	Net Incidental Revenue	250	
	Investment Income—Unrestricted	15,680	
	Miscellaneous Revenue	1,500	
	Unrestricted Net Assets—Undesignated—Available		
	for Operations		475,930
23c.	Unrestricted Net Assets—Undesignated—Available		
	for Operations	580,315	
	Counseling Program Expenses		185,513
	Adoption Program Expenses		69,560
	Foster Home Care Program Expenses		172,531
	Special Outreach Project Program Expenses		62,870
	Cost of Sales to Public		900
	Uncollectible Contributions Expense		104
	Management and General Support Expenses		53,085
	Fund-raising Support Expenses		27,178
	Payments to Affiliated Organizations		8,574

23d. Contributions—Temporarily Restricted—Program	29,500	
Contributions—Temporarily Restricted—Time	10,000	
Contributions—Temporarily Restricted—Plant	4,000	
Investment Income—Temporarily Restricted—Plant	1,390	
Temporarily Restricted Net Assets—Program		23,500
Temporarily Restricted Net Assets—Plant		1,390
Temporarily Restricted Net Assets—Time		20,000

Note: There were no changes to Permanently Restricted Net Assets.

The effects of the preceding journal entries are reflected in Illustrations 16–2 through 16–5. Illustration 16–7 presents a Statement of Activities prepared according to Format B in *SFAS No. 117*. That is, there are columns displaying the changes in the three categories of net assets, which makes it clear that as donor restrictions expire, net assets are reclassified from the temporarily restricted column to the unrestricted net asset column. Illustration 16–3 follows Format A in *SFAS No. 117*, which is a single column and is most useful for multiyear comparisons. *SFAS No. 117* also displays Format C, which reports information in two statements: The first summarizes detailed changes in unrestricted net assets to focus attention on operating activities; and the second reconciles changes in all three categories of net assets.

NPOs other than VHWOs may have transactions not illustrated here. For example, deferred revenue arises from exchange transactions, such as subscriptions in a performing arts organization; and long-term debt from a construction project may exist in larger not-for-profit organizations.

Selected References

American Institute of Certified Public Accountants. Audit and Accounting Guide, *Not-for-Profit Organizations*. New York: AICPA, 1997.

———. 1997 Audit Risk Alert. *Not-for-Profit Organizations Industry Developments*. New York: AICPA, 1997.

Financial Accounting Standards Board. *Statement of Financial Accounting Standards No. 93*, "Recognition of Depreciation by Not-for-Profit Organizations." Norwalk, CT: FASB, 1987.

———. *Statement of Financial Accounting Standards No. 116*, "Accounting for Contributions Received and Made." Norwalk, CT: FASB, 1993.

———. *Statement of Financial Accounting Standards No. 117*, "Financial Statements of Not-for-Profit Organizations." Norwalk, CT: FASB, 1993.

———. *Statement of Financial Accounting Standards No. 124*, "Accounting for Certain Investments Held by Not-for-Profit Organizations." Norwalk, CT: FASB, 1995.

Oleck, Howard L., and Martha E. Stewart. *Nonprofit Corporations, Organizations, & Associations*. 6th ed. 1997–98 Supplement. Englewood Cliffs, NJ: Prentice Hall, 1994.

United Way of America. *Accounting & Financial Reporting: A Guide for United Ways and Not-for-Profit Human Service Organizations*. Alexandria, VA: 1989.

Illustration 16–7

COMMUNITY FAMILY SERVICE AGENCY, INC.
Statement of Activities
For the year ended December 31, 2000

	Unrestricted	Temporarily Restricted	Permanently Restricted	Total 2000
Revenues, gains, and other support:				
Contributions (Note A)	$388,196	$ 43,500		$431,696
Program service fees (Note B)	55,250			55,250
Membership dues	1,000			1,000
Sales to the public (net)	100			100
Investment income	15,680	1,390		17,070
Miscellaneous	1,500			1,500
Net assets released from restrictions:				
Satisfaction of program requirements	27,400	(27,400)		
Satisfaction of equipment acquisition restrictions	4,185	(4,185)		
Expiration of time restrictions	5,125	(5,125)		
Total revenues, gains, and other support	498,436	8,180		506,616
Expenses and losses:				
Program services:				
Counseling	185,513			185,513
Adoption	69,560			69,560
Foster home care	172,531			172,531
Special outreach project	62,870			62,870
Total program expenses	490,474			490,474
Support expenses:				
Management and general	53,085			53,085
Fund-raising	13,978			13,978
Total support expenses	67,063			67,063
Payments to affiliated organizations	8,574			8,574
Total expenses and losses	566,111			566,111
Change in net assets	(67,675)	8,180		(59,495)
Net assets, December 31, 1999	97,302	88,155	$230,000	415,457
Net assets, December 31, 2000	$ 29,627	$ 96,335	$230,000	$355,962

Note A: Reduced by Special Event fund-raising expense of $13,200 and uncollectible accounts expense of $104.
Note B: Includes $250 net incidental revenue.

Key Terms

Board-designated net assets, 654
Collections, 668
Conditional promise to give, 661
Contribution, 661
Economic interest, 671
Endowment, 654
Exchange transactions, 659
Gains, 659
Gifts in kind, 662
Human service organization, 650
Net assets, 654
Nonexchange transactions, 661

Not-for-profit organization, 650
Permanently restricted net assets, 654
Promise to give, 661
Revenue, 659
Support, 661
Temporarily restricted net assets, 654
Unconditional promise to give, 661
Unrestricted net assets, 654
Variance power, 672
Voluntary health and welfare organizations,
  650

Questions

16–1. Identify the key characteristics that distinguish an entity in the not-for-profit sector from one in the public sector or private sector.

16–2. A university has a collection of rare books that it has never recorded as assets. As an independent CPA, under what conditions would you require that the university capitalize these books? Would they then be depreciated?

16–3. Distinguish between *public support* and *revenue*.

16–4. Health and welfare organizations typically rely heavily on the efforts of volunteer workers. Under what conditions should donated services be recognized in the financial statements as contributions and as expenses, assuming the organization is subject to FASB jurisdiction?

16–5. Distinguish between *program services* and *supporting services* as the terms are used in financial reports recommended for use by not-for-profit organizations.

16–6. Why is a Statement of Functional Expenses considered an important financial statement for a voluntary health or welfare organization? How does a Statement of Functional Expenses relate to a Statement of Activities?

16–7. "The financial statements required for voluntary health and welfare organizations are (1) a Balance Sheet, (2) a Statement of Revenue and Expenses and Changes in Fund Balance, (3) a Statement of Functional Expenses, and (4) a Statement of Cash Flows." Do you agree or disagree? Explain.

16–8. "Responsibility for setting financial reporting standards for not-for-profit organizations is vested in the FASB." Do you agree or disagree? Explain.

16–9. "All not-for-profit organizations must use fund accounting to account for their activities." Do you agree or disagree? Why?

16–10. A privately endowed museum reports all investments at market, even if market is in excess of cost. As an independent CPA, would you be required to take exception to this practice?

16–11. How do you determine if one NPO "controls" another for purposes of combining the financial statements of the two organizations?

Cases

16–1. Compass State University Foundation (CSUF), a not-for-profit organization, was created in 1992 to support a public university in its fund-raising efforts and management of its endowment. The Foundation has a self-perpetuating Board of which one-third of its members are selected by the University's President. Under a joint operating agreement, the University agrees to provide the Foundation with staff, computer and mail services, and office space until such time as the Foundation can be self-sufficient; and to pay the Foundation management fees of 2 percent of the endowment balance, 5 percent of cash gifts received, $.22 per dollar raised, and $1.84 per donor record per year.

From 1986 through 1992, the average donations to the University (both unrestricted and restricted) were $2.2 million and the University Endowment Fund grew very slowly from $5.2 million to $8.3 million. In 1992, the University transferred its entire $8.3 million endowment fund to the Foundation to manage. By 1999, average donations to the Foundation were $8 million and permanently restricted net assets, or endowments, had grown to $24 million. The Foundation's fund-raising and management and general expenses in 1999 totaled $1.5 million and $3 million was returned to the University in the form of scholarships to students and support to faculty.

Required

a. Identify the costs of creating and operating a separate organization, such as the CSUF (e.g., attorney fees to incorporate).

b. Who are the stakeholders in the foundation and what are their accountability concerns?

c. Assume the role of the President of the University and discuss the advantages and disadvantages of transferring $8.3 million of the University's endowment funds to the Foundation.

d. Referring to item c above, assume the role of a donor who established a scholarship endowment with the University 15 years ago. What would you ask about the transfer?

e. Calculate the percentage of total expenses spent on the program and that spent on supporting the programs. Do these ratios seem reasonable?

f. Evaluate the performance of the Foundation based on the information provided. Is the University better off because of the Foundation? Why or why not?

g. From an accounting (not legal) point of view, is the Foundation a separate entity or a component unit of the related public institution?

This case is based on "Compass State University: Managerial Accounting Issues in a Nonprofit Entity," by S. Ravenscroft and S. Kattelus, *Issues in Accounting Education*, Vol. 13, no. 3, 1998.

16–2. The Shelter Association of Gogebic County receives the majority of its funding from the local chapter of the United Way. That federated fund-raising organization has a policy that if a member agency reports unrestricted net assets in excess of one year's budgeted revenues and support, then the excess will be deducted from the next year's allocation. The Association's reporting year ends December 31, and unrestricted net assets are just about equal to last year's revenues and support.

On December 30, Bill Olson contacts the Shelter Association about making a large contribution. It is important to Bill that the gift be made in the current calendar year so that he can deduct the charitable contribution on his personal federal income tax return. However, Bill has heard that the Treasurer of the Association and several Board members recently left due to allegations of financial mismanagement. He is considering restricting his gift for the direct purposes of acquiring food, clothing, and supplies for the homeless over the next several years so that none of the money could be used by the management for overhead expenses.

Required

Take the position of the certified public accountant for the Association.

a. Do you recommend that the Association persuade Mr. Olson to make the gift unrestricted or restricted? Give your reasons.

b. Mr. Olson asks you how he can be assured that the Association spends his contribution as he intends, assuming that he restricts the purpose of his gift. Explain to Mr. Olson what kind of public information is available to him. Do you consider that information adequate to assess whether the not-for-profit agency was efficient and effective in its use of public donations?

16–3. **Internet Case.** Look for the homepage of a nongovernmental not-for-profit entity on the Internet. For example, United Way's address is http://www.unitedway.org. ".Org" indicates that this organization is nonprofit rather than commercial (.com), governmental (.gov), or a university (.edu). Answer the following questions: Are audited financial statements provided on their homepage? What other kind of financial information do they make available? Take the position of a potential donor to this organization. Find some "benchmarks" (or industry averages) for this type of NPO and evaluate their performance compared to similar organizations. Performance measures may include financial ones, such as percentage of program or support expenses to total expenses, rate of return on investment, and payout rates. Output measures or service efforts and accomplishment (SEA) measures may include number of people served, improvement in test scores, or reduction in crimes. [Hint: Try the National Charities Information Bureau (http://www.give.org) or the Council of Better Business Bureau (CBBB) Philanthropic Advisory Service (PAS) (http://www.bbb.org) for comparisons of not-for-profit agencies.]

Exercises and Problems

16–1. Write the numbers 1 through 10 on a sheet of paper. Beside each number, write the letter corresponding with the best answer to each of the following questions:

1. In a Statement of Activities of a voluntary health and welfare organization, depreciation expense should:

   a. Not be included.

   b. Be included as an element of support.

   c. Be included as an element of changes in fund balances.

   d. Be included as an element of expense.

2. Which of the following funds of a voluntary health and welfare organization does *not* have a counterpart *fund* in governmental accounting?
   a. Current Unrestricted.
   b. Land, Building, and Equipment.
   c. Custodian.
   d. Endowment.

3. Securities donated to voluntary health and welfare organizations should be recorded:
   a. At the donor's recorded amount.
   b. At fair market value at the date of the gift.
   c. At fair market value at the date of the gift, or the donor's recorded amount, whichever is lower.
   d. At fair market value at the date of the gift, or the donor's recorded amount, whichever is higher.

4. Which of the following is *not* a criterion that must be met under *SFAS No. 116* for contributed services to be recorded?
   a. They create or enhance nonfinancial assets.
   b. They are provided by licensed professionals.
   c. They are provided by individuals possessing required skills.
   d. They would typically need to be bought if not provided by donation.

5. Which of the following factors, if present, would indicate that a transaction is *not* a contribution under *SFAS No. 116*?
   a. The resource provider entered into the transaction voluntarily.
   b. The resource provider received value in exchange.
   c. The transfer of assets was unconditional.
   d. The organization has discretion in the use of the assets received.

6. Which of the following criteria would suggest that an NPO capitalize its works of art, historical treasures, or similar assets?
   a. They are held for public inspection, education, or research in furtherance of public service rather than financial gain.
   b. They are protected, kept unencumbered, cared for, and preserved.
   c. They are subject to be used to acquire other items for the collection.
   d. They are held primarily to be resold for financial gain.

Items 7 and 8 are based on the following information:
Expenditures incurred by a not-for-profit botanical society during 1999 were as follows:

Printing of annual report	$10,000
Unsolicited merchandise sent to encourage contributions	$20,000

7. What amount should be classified as Fund-Raising Costs in the Society's Statement of Activity?
   a. $0.
   b. $10,000.
   c. $20,000.
   d. $30,000.

8. What amount should be classified as Supporting Services in the Society's Statement of Activity?
   a. $0.
   b. $10,000.
   c. $20,000.
   d. $30,000.

9. Under *SFAS No. 117*, which of the following statements is true?
   a. All nonprofit organizations must include a Statement of Functional Expenses.
   b. Donor-restricted contributions whose restrictions have been met in the reporting period may be reported as unrestricted support.
   c. Statements should focus on the individual unrestricted and restricted funds of the organization.
   d. *SFAS No. 117* contains requirements that are generally more stringent than those for for-profit organizations.

10. Funds held in trust by others under a legal trust instrument created by a donor to generate income for a not-for-profit organization, and over which the not-for-profit organization has no control, should be:
    a. Included with the amounts reported in the Balance Sheet of the not-for-profit organization.
    b. Excluded from the amounts reported in the Balance Sheet of the not-for-profit organization.
    c. Disclosed either parenthetically in the permanently restricted net assets section of the Balance Sheet or in the Notes to the Financial Statements.
    d. Both *b* and *c* are correct.

(Items 1–3, 7–8, and 10, AICPA, adapted)

16–2. The characteristics of voluntary health and welfare organizations differ in certain respects from the characteristics of state or local governmental units. As an example, voluntary health and welfare organizations derive their revenues primarily from voluntary contributions from the general public, while governmental units derive their revenues from taxes and services provided to their jurisdictions.

Required

a. Distinguish between accrual accounting as it should be applied to the recognition of revenues of a voluntary health and welfare organization and accrual accounting as it is applied to the recognition of governmental fund revenues.
b. Discuss how methods used to account for fixed assets differ between voluntary health and welfare organizations and governmental units.

(AICPA, adapted)

16–3. Listed below are four independent transactions or events that relate to a local government and to a voluntary health and welfare organization:

1. $25,000 was disbursed from the General Fund (or its equivalent) for the cash purchase of new equipment.
2. An unrestricted cash gift of $100,000 was received from a donor.
3. Listed common stocks with a total carrying value of $50,000, exclusive of any allowance, were sold by an endowment fund for $55,000, before any dividends were earned on these stocks. There are no restrictions on the gain.
4. $1,000,000 face amount of general obligation bonds payable were sold at par, with the proceeds required to be used solely for construction of a new building. This building was completed at a total cost of $1,000,000, and the total amount of bond issue proceeds was disbursed in connection therewith. Disregard interest capitalization.

Required

   a. For each of the above-listed transactions or events, prepare journal entries, without explanations, and show how these transactions or events should be recorded by a local government whose debt is serviced by general tax revenues.
   b. For each of the above-listed transactions or events, prepare journal entries, without explanations, and show how these transactions or events should be recorded by a nongovernmental NPO.

(AICPA, adapted)

16–4. The Rural Human Services Association had the following expenses for the year ended September 30, 1999.

Salaries and fringe benefits	$ 850,000
Professional fees and contract services	50,000
Supplies	38,000
Telephone	40,000
Postage and shipping	75,000
Occupancy costs	100,000
Travel and meetings	80,000
Printing and publications	100,000
Depreciation of buildings and equipment	17,000
Total expenses	$1,350,000

Required

   a. The programs offered by this Association during that year were Counseling, Outreach, Meals, and Public Education. Supporting services were Management and General, and Fund-Raising. The governing board wants to know the cost of each program service and each supporting service for the year. After discussion with persons engaged in offering each service, and perusal of records of the Association, you determine that the following distribution would be reasonably realistic. Prepare a statement of functional expenses for the year.

	Program Services				Supporting Services	
	Coun-seling	Out-reach	Meals	Public Education	Management and General	Fund-Raising
Salaries and fringes	20%	16%	3%	19%	22%	20%
Professional fees, etc.	10	10	20	20	10	30
Supplies	10	15	5	25	25	20
Telephone	10	20	5	20	15	30
Postage and shipping	5	23	15	15	7	35
Occupancy costs	20	10	10	20	20	20
Travel and meetings	25	10	15	15	25	10
Printing and publications	15	5	2	33	20	25
Depreciation	33	15	5	15	20	12

b. If the Rural Human Services Association approached you as a potential contributor, and presented the statement prepared as the solution to part *a* of this problem as evidence of its merit for your contribution, what would be your reaction and why?

16–5. Helping Hand Agency of America, Inc., was incorporated as a nongovernmental not-for-profit voluntary health and welfare organization on July 1, 1999. The adjusted trial balance as of June 30, 2000, is provided below:

	Debits	Credits
Cash	$ 24,000	
Pledges Receivable—Unrestricted	54,000	
Estimated Uncollectible Pledges		$ 9,000
Inventory	1,000	
Pledges Receivable—Temporarily Restricted	51,000	
Investments—Temporarily Restricted	61,100	
Furniture and Equipment—Temporarily Restricted	3,000	
Accumulated Depreciation		300
Accounts Payable		1,200
Unrestricted Net Assets		–0–
Temporarily Restricted Net Assets		–0–
Permanently Restricted Net Assets		–0–
Contributions—Unrestricted		188,100
Contributions—Temporarily Restricted		121,700
Uncollectible Contributions Expense—Temporarily Restricted	9,000	
Investment Income—Temporarily Restricted		2,100
Salaries Expense	80,000	
Fringe Benefits Expense	5,000	
Occupancy Expense	4,800	
Supplies Expense	8,000	
Printing and Publishing Expense	15,000	
Telephone and Utility Expense	5,200	
Postage and Shipping Expense	1,000	
Depreciation Expense	300	
Totals	$322,400	$322,400

1. Salaries and fringe benefits were allocated to program services and supporting services in the following percentages: public health education, 20 percent; professional education and training, 30 percent; community services, 10 percent; management and general, 15 percent; and fund-raising, 25 percent. All other expenses were allocated in the following percentages: public health education, 15 percent; professional education and training, 20 percent; community services, 10 percent; management and general, 35 percent; and fund-raising, 20 percent.

2. Helping Hand Agency received cash during the year from contributors: $126,000 that was unrestricted and $59,000 that was restricted for investment in the plant. $2,100 of income was earned and received on long-term

investments. The Agency spent cash on salaries $70,000; purchase of goods, $29,000; purchase of furniture and equipment $3,000; and purchase of investments $59,000.

Required

Prepare a Statement of Financial Position, Statement of Activities, Statement of Cash Flows, and a Statement of Functional Expenses for Helping Hand Agency of America, Inc., as of and for the year ended June 30, 2000. Follow the format in Illustrations 16–2 through 16–5.

16–6. The Professional Persons Association of Middleton is a not-for-profit organization subject to the provisions of the AICPA Audit and Accounting Guide, *Not-for-Profit Organizations*. The dues for members are $50 per year; the fiscal year ends on August 31. Prior to September 1, 1999, 410 members had paid their dues for the year ended August 31, 2000. Prior to September 1, 2000, 457 members had paid their dues for the year ended August 31, 2001; one of these died suddenly on August 30, 2000, and the governing Board decided to return his check to his widow. During the fiscal year ended on August 31, 2000, 36 other members died; 15 members were dropped for nonpayment of dues; and one member was expelled—no dues refunds were made to the estates of the 36 decedents; a $25 refund was made to the person expelled. Offsetting these membership decreases, 123 new members joined in fiscal 2000; membership as of September 1, 1999, had been 2,980 persons. Members admitted during a year are charged dues for the full year.

The Association has reported membership dues revenue on the cash basis in prior years. You bring to the attention of the governing Board the requirement that financial statements should be on the accrual basis, unless cash basis statements are not materially different. Since you are so knowledgeable, the Board asks you to compute membership dues revenue for fiscal 2000 on both the cash basis and on the accrual basis and to report to them the amount on each basis *and* your conclusion as to whether the difference between the two is material.

(AICPA, adapted)

16–7. A group of civic-minded merchants in Albury City organized the "Committee of 100" for the purpose of establishing the Community Sports Club, a not-for-profit sports organization for local youth. Each of the Committee's 100 members contributed $1,000 toward the Club's capital and in turn received a participation certificate. In addition, each participant agreed to pay dues of $200 a year for the Club's operations. All dues have been collected in full by the end of each fiscal year ending March 31. Members who have discontinued their participation have been replaced by an equal number of new members through transfer of the participation certificates from the former members to the new ones. Following is the Club's trial balance at April 1, 1999:

	Debits	Credits
Cash	$ 9,000	
Investments (at market equal to cost)	58,000	
Inventories	5,000	
Land	10,000	
Building	164,000	
Accumulated Depreciation—Building		$130,000
Furniture and Equipment	54,000	
Accumulated Depreciation—Furniture and Equipment		46,000
Accounts Payable		12,000
Participation Certificates (100 at $1,000 each)		100,000
Cumulative Excess of Revenue over Expenses		12,000
	$300,000	$300,000

Transactions for the year ended March 31, 2000, were as follows:

1. Collections from participants for dues $20,000
2. Snack bar and soda fountain sales   28,000
3. Interest and dividends received   6,000
4. Additions to voucher register:
   House expenses   17,000
   Snack bar and soda fountain   26,000
   General and administrative   11,000
5. Vouchers paid   55,000
6. Assessments for capital improvements not yet incurred (assessed on March 20, 2000, none collected by March 31, 2000; deemed 100% collectible during year ending March 31, 2001)   10,000
7. Unrestricted bequest received   5,000

Adjustment data:

1. Investments are valued at market, which amounted to $65,000 at March 31, 2000. There were no investment transactions during the year.
2. Depreciation for the year:
   Building $ 4,000
   Furniture and equipment   8,000
3. Allocation of depreciation:
   House expenses   9,000
   Snack bar and soda fountain   2,000
   General and administrative   1,000
4. Actual physical inventory at March 31, 2000, was $1,000, and pertains to the snack bar and soda fountain.

Required

On a functional basis:

a. Record the transactions and adjustments in journal entry form for the year ended March 31, 2000. Omit explanations.

b. Prepare the activity statement illustrated in *SFAS No. 117* for the year ended March 31, 2000.

(AICPA, adapted)

16–8. The University City Art League, Inc., is a nongovernmental not-for-profit organization dedicated to promotion of the arts within the community. The Art League conducts two programs: (1) exhibition and sales of members' art (referred to as "Exhibition") and (2) community art education. Activities of the Art League are administered by a full-time administrator, assisted by a secretary-bookkeeper, and several part-time volunteer receptionists. The volunteer receptionists greet visitors, monitor the security of the exhibit hall, and conduct sales of art to the public. Art on exhibit is considered the property of the member artists, not the Art League.

The post-closing trial balance for the University City Art League as of June 30, 1999, the end of its fiscal year, is shown below.

UNIVERSITY CITY ART LEAGUE, INC.
Post-Closing Trial Balance
As of June 30, 1999

Account Title	Debits	Credits
Cash—unrestricted	$ 1,051	
Cash—temporarily restricted for plant	164	
Cash—temporarily restricted for programs	2,800	
Investments—unrestricted	9,462	
Grants receivable	4,600	
Prepaid expenses	1,060	
Equipment	9,345	
Accumulated depreciation—equipment		$ 2,426
Investments—temporarily restricted for plant	12,649	
Investments—permanently restricted for endowment	4,767	
Accounts payable		1,893
Accrued expenses		756
Long-term notes payable		2,000
Net assets—unrestricted		13,524
Net assets—temporarily restricted		20,532
Net assets—permanently restricted		4,767
Totals	$45,898	$45,898

Following is information summarizing the transactions of the University City Art League, Inc., for the year ended June 30, 2000.

1. During the year unrestricted cash was received from the following sources: grants, $11,600, of which $4,600 had been reported as receivable on June 30, 1999, annual giving from fund drives and other unrestricted gifts, $13,861; membership dues, $16,285; sales of members' art, $12,010, of which 20 percent, or $2,402, represents commissions earned by the Art League; tuition and fees for educational courses and workshops, $6,974; and interest on unrestricted investments, $686. Grants receivable as of June 30, 2000, totaled $5,020, of which $3,120 was recognized as current-year revenue and $1,900 was reported as temporarily restricted.

2. Investment earnings were received in cash in the amounts of $925 on plant investments and $344 on endowment investments. (These investment earnings are temporarily restricted as to use.)

3. Expenses incurred for unrestricted activities of the unrestricted fund during the year were as follows: salaries and fringe benefits, $36,300; occupancy, $9,600; utilities, $2,680; postage and supplies, $2,313; and miscellaneous, $1,037. Included in miscellaneous was interest expense of $160, which was paid in cash during the year. As of June 30, 2000, the balances of the following balance sheet accounts were: Prepaid Expenses, $970; Accounts Payable, $2,019; and Accrued Expenses, $727.

4. During the year $2,900 of matured CDs were sold from plant investments to purchase a new computer. The computer was purchased at a cost of $2,835.

5. In accordance with the terms of the Art League endowment, endowment cash in the amount of $825 was used to provide free art instruction for handicapped children. This amount was allocated $500 to Community Art Education and $325 to General and Administrative Expenses.

6. Expenses for the year were allocated 20 percent to the Exhibition Program, 25 percent to the Community Art Education Program, 30 percent to General and Administrative Expenses, and 25 percent to Fund-Raising. (Round all amounts to the nearest whole dollar.)

7. Depreciation on equipment in the amount of $1,642 was recorded on the plant assets. This amount was allocated to programs, General and Administrative Expenses, and Fund-Raising in the same proportions as in item 6 above. (Round all amounts to the nearest whole dollar.)

8. $9,608, representing the proceeds of art sales, net of commissions, charged by the Art League, was paid to member artists during the year.

9. In order to prepare financial statements as of year-end, all temporary accounts were closed.

Required

a. Prepare in general journal form all required journal entries to record the transactions summarized above for the year ending June 30, 2000.

b. On the advice of their independent auditor, the Art League does not include support and expenses related to the value of services donated by their volunteer receptionists. Discuss the criteria for recognition of donated services and comment on the auditor's likely rationale for not recognizing them in this specific case.

c. Prepare a Statement of Financial Position in the FASB *Statement No. 117* format shown in Illustration 16–2.

d. Prepare a Statement of Activities in the FASB *Statement No. 117* format shown in Illustration 16–3.

e. Prepare a Statement of Cash Flows in the FASB *Statement No. 117* format shown in Illustration 16–4.

CHAPTER 17

Nonprofit Organizations— Regulatory and Taxation Issues

Learning Objectives

After studying this chapter, you should be able to:

~ Identify oversight bodies and the source of their authority over not-for-profit organizations (NPOs).

~ Describe how and why states regulate NPOs and describe the following:

> Nonprofit incorporation laws.
> Registration, licenses, and tax exemption.
> Lobbying and political influence.

~ Identify how the federal government regulates NPOs and describe the following:

> Tax-exempt status—public charities and private foundations.
> Unrelated business income tax.
> Restricting political activity.
> Intermediate sanctions.
> Reorganization and dissolution.

~ Describe governance issues of NPO Boards including incorporating documents and Board membership.

~ Identify how benchmarks and performance measures can be used to evaluate NPOs.

Oversight Authority

The 1990s brought a dramatic increase in the number of nongovernmental not-for-profit organizations (NPOs) in the United States. Along with this growth came very public revelations of financial impropriety and fraud in some of those entities. Managers were fined and sent to jail for personally profiting from the charities they operated; politicians faced allegations that they used charitable foundations to skirt political contribution laws; and NPOs were converted to for-profit entities before distributing the assets to other charities.[1] Because of well-publicized instances of impropriety and fraud, there has been a growing demand for better accountability by NPOs. Demands for accountability by NPOs will increase further as the not-for-profit sector grows in number and dollars to meet the demand brought about by *devolution*—the shifting of responsibility for social programs from the federal government to local levels.[2] NPOs are accountable to the state government that grants them their legal existence, the federal government for granting them tax-exempt status, their own governing board, individual donors and grantors, and the public at large.

Accountants and auditors play a critical role in assuring stakeholders that NPOs have complied with applicable laws and regulations, and, in the process, have efficiently and effectively used the assets with which they were entrusted. The purpose of this chapter is to provide an overview of regulations over NPOs by oversight bodies, such as state governments, federal government, and governing boards. Many of these topics have complex legal aspects that are beyond the scope of this book. For the interested reader, additional references are provided at the end of the chapter.

State Regulation

Oversight responsibility derives from a state's power to give legal life to a nonprofit organization. In the absence of stockholders, the state monitors nonprofit managers whom the public entrusts with funds and grants economic privileges, such as exemption from taxes. The state has responsibility to represent public beneficiaries of charities and to detect cases when managers or directors have mismanaged, diverted, or defrauded the charity and the public.

Legislation regulating NPOs, of course, varies greatly across states; and few states are alike. However, there are some common methods used by states, and sometimes adopted by local governments, to ensure that the public good is protected as NPOs solicit charitable contributions and conduct business. The audited

---

[1]Steve Stecklow, "New Era Foundation Founder Bennett Is Scheduled for Sentencing This Week," *The Wall Street Journal*, September 15, 1997, B2; Leslie Lenkowsky, "Newt Violation Hard to Find," *The Wall Street Journal*, January 3, 1997; "California Blue Cross to Make Payback for Conversion," *National Underwriter* 97, September 6, 1993, pp. 37–41.

[2]Carol J. DeVita, "Viewing Nonprofits across the States," in *Charting Civil Society* (Washington, DC: The Urban Institute, August 1997).

annual financial statements are not always sufficient to satisfy the oversight body that the NPO complied with laws. The accountant often serves the NPO client in preparing specialized reports required by the oversight body.

Nonprofit
Incorporation Laws

A group of individuals who share a philanthropic or other vision may operate as an unincorporated association if they are small or expect their endeavor to have a limited life; however, organizers are treated as partners and share liability for any debts incurred by the association. If the organization plans to grow into a long-lived operation, organizers may choose to file articles of incorporation with a state under the nonprofit corporation statutes or charitable trust laws to create a legal entity and limit the liability of the incorporators and directors. These laws differ across the 50 states, but states generally have built into the nonprofit corporation laws the requirement that organizers: (1) choose a name that is not misleading or in use by another corporation; (2) designate a resident agent and address, (3) state a clear purpose for the entity, (4) appoint a Board of Directors, (5) write by-laws that delineate Board responsibilities and operating structure, (6) call at least one Board meeting a year, and (7) require management to report on financial condition and operations at least once a year. Nonprofit incorporation statutes also state the extent to which directors are individually liable for the misapplication of assets through neglect or failure to exercise reasonable care and prudence in administration of the affairs of the corporation. Upon conferring the NPO legal status separate from the incorporators, the state bears oversight responsibility over the NPO.

Registration,
Licenses, and
Tax Exemption

State regulation of nonprofit corporations has increased since the State of New York established an Office of Charitable Registration in 1955 to administer fund-raising regulations for not-for-profit organizations.[3] Some states require NPOs to register with a specified department of the state (e.g., Attorney General, Secretary of State, Consumer, Regulatory Affairs, or Commerce) or apply for a license in order to solicit funds, hold property, do business in the state, or lobby. For the most part, state and local governments require fees to accompany registration and licenses in order to defray the cost of regulation and monitoring. Failure to file required reports may result in automatic dissolution of the NPO.

License to Solicit Contributions.   Some states protect citizens from competitive fund-raising requests by requiring the NPO to obtain a license to solicit charitable contributions. **Charitable solicitation** is the direct or indirect request for money, credit, property, financial assistance, or other things of value on the representation that these assets will be used for a charitable purpose. The Model Act Concerning the Solicitation of Funds for Charitable Purposes was promulgated in 1986 by the National Association of Attorneys General, the National Association of State Charity Officials, and a private-sector advisory group to guide states in designing this type of legislation. Although regulation has been challenged by some charities that argue soliciting is protected free speech, most legislation stands as an efficient way to protect the public from fraud.

---

[3]Seth Perlman, *Fund-Raising Regulation* (New York: John Wiley & Sons, 1997).

States granting licenses usually impose annual compliance reporting on NPOs. A few states require audited annual financial reports to be filed when the level of public support exceeds a certain threshold, such as $100,000. Some states require a license when an NPO compensates someone for fund-raising, such as a professional fund-raiser or solicitor, and a fee may be required of the organization for the right for each fund-raiser to solicit. Many states also require specific disclosures be put on all written materials mailed to potential donors to indicate that financial information about the organization may be on file with the state. In addition to the state, local governments may regulate charitable solicitation, although sometimes more for its fee revenue potential than for regulatory purposes.

Other Licenses.   States or local governments may require a not-for-profit organization to get a license or permit for bingo, raffles, and charity games with maximum prizes. Often licenses or permits are granted for one-day beer, wine, and liquor sales for events.

Taxes.   NPOs are often exempted from the taxes levied by state and local governments, such as sales, real or personal property, transfer, employment, or excise taxes. Of course, this privilege varies across the country and, in the case of property taxes, is being challenged by interest groups suspicious of some NPOs' charitable mission and defended by nonprofit coalitions.[4] To be relieved from the tax, the NPO may have to file for specific tax exemption and document that the property is *in use* for charitable purposes. Fund-raising events often give rise to sales tax reporting, both collection of tax from customers and exemption from sales tax paid on the purchase of goods. Often overlooked by the NPO are the excise taxes on telephone and utility bills for which they may not be liable and could recover by filing for a refund.

Lobbying and Political Influence

For the most part, a nonprofit organization cannot be organized primarily to attempt to influence legislation or participate in any political campaigns. Two primary ways that states regulate lobbying and political activity for all organizations are through lobbying acts and campaign finance acts. These laws require organizations to register with the state and then account for lobbying or campaign financing activities. The NPO must determine if it, or someone it hires, is a lobbyist or lobbyist agent and, consequently, subject to these regulations. **Lobbying** is communicating directly with a public official in either the executive or legislative branch of the state government for the purpose of influencing legislation. **Influencing** means to promote, support, affect, modify, oppose, or delay by any means. In one state, the amount of money spent on lobbying each year determines whether the NPO must register with a specified state agency. For example, if more than $1,650 is spent on lobbying or more than $425 contributed to any single public official in any 12-month period, the NPO must register, file annual reports detailing its lobbying activity, and specify the amounts contributed to public officials. In

---

[4]Citizen Action for Colorado Nonprofits, *Position Paper on Proposed Taxation of Nonprofits* (Denver, CO: May 2, 1996).

addition to registering and reporting, certain prohibitions may exist. For example, compensation of lobbyists cannot be contingent upon certain legal outcomes; no gifts or honorariums can be paid to public officials; and no contributions can be made to campaigns to support (or defeat) ballot questions.

The impact of excessive political activity on NPOs can be significant due to the harsh sanctions for violating these laws, as well as negative publicity that may harm future fund-raising efforts. The ultimate penalty is revocation of exemption from taxes, but more often fines are imposed for engaging in prohibited behavior.

Illustration 17–1 presents a chart that summarizes typical regulation of non-governmental not-for-profit organizations at the state as well as the federal level.

Illustration 17–1   Regulations over Not-for-Profit Organizations (varies by state)

State and/or Local Government Regulations

Application to operate under an assumed name
Application to incorporate as a nonprofit corporation or a charitable trust
Annual compliance reporting
Special licenses with particular state departments to operate a health care facility (public health), housing corporation (housing authority), residential care facility (social service), school (education), or to handle food
Application for exemption from income, franchise, sales, use, real and personal property taxes
Employer registration including payroll tax returns, withholding of state taxes, and unemployment
License to solicit charitable contributions
Registration of political lobbyists, lobbying agents, or lobbying activities
License for one-day beer, wine, and liquor sales
License to conduct charitable games (e.g., bingo, raffles, millionaires parties)
Policies on conflict of interest and self-dealing with directors
License to collect sales and use taxes as a vendor
Freedom of Information Act (FOIA) (if a substantial amount of funds are public)
Open Meetings Act (if governmental in nature)
Notice of plans to merge with another agency
Notice of plans to dissolve, including tax clearance

Federal Government Regulations	*Federal Forms*
Application for a taxpayer/employer identification number	SS-4
Application for tax exempt status	1023 or 1024
Application for exemption from certain excise taxes	637
Annual reporting	990 or 990-PF
Excise taxes on private foundations	4720
Reporting on unrelated business income tax	990-T
Reporting on lobbying and political contributions	990, 4720, 1120-POL
Election to make expenditures to influence legislation	5786
Payroll employment taxes	W-2, W-4, W-9, 940, 941
Statements to independent contractors earning more than $600 per year	1099
Appraisals for noncash contributions over $5,000 (the donor has primary responsibility for this regulation)	8283, 8282
Substantiation of gifts of cash over $250	
Application for bulk postal permit	Local post office
Financial reporting, audit, cost, and administrative requirements under OMB Circulars	

Federal Regulation

The federal government has encouraged nonprofit associations and charitable contributions since the first revenue act in 1894 and income tax law in 1913 because they serve the common good. The public, then, expects the federal government to monitor those organizations receiving tax benefits to ensure that these privileges are not abused. Of course, NPOs must follow general laws that govern businesses (such as fair labor standards, older workers' benefits protection, equal employment opportunities acts, disabilities acts, civil rights laws, drug-free workplace laws, immigration laws, antidiscrimination and harassment laws, and veterans and whistleblowers' protection), unless they are specifically exempted. This section describes federal laws that are unique to NPOs.

Tax-Exempt Status

Even though a state may have conferred nonprofit corporation status on an organization, that NPO must still apply to the Internal Revenue Service (IRS) for exemption from federal income tax.[5] As shown in Illustration 16–1, not all not-for-profit organizations are tax-exempt. A common reason why an NPO is not exempt from income taxes is that its mission is primarily to influence legislation. The stated purpose of the NPO and the services it will perform determine under which section of the Internal Revenue Code (IRC) of 1986 the NPO requests exemption. The most common classification under IRC Section 501 is Sec. 501(c)(3), which is an organization operated for philanthropic purposes. The **organizational test** for tax-exempt status is that the articles of incorporation must limit the organization's purposes to those described in the categories in IRC Sec. 501 and must not empower it to engage in activities that are not in furtherance of those purposes. Nonprofit hospitals have been criticized for not providing an adequate amount of free services as a benefit to society, as stated in their application for tax-exempt status and required by tax law. Illustration 17–2 shows some of the common classifications of statutory exemptions under which tax-exempt organizations fall.

An individual can receive a charitable contribution deduction by making a donation to a Sec. 501(c)(3) organization and other exempt organizations but only if the gift is used for charitable purposes. Many categories of tax-exempt organizations, such as business leagues, social clubs, and cooperatives, cannot offer donors the advantage of a charitable deduction from income taxes because they operate primarily for the benefit of members and not the public at large. Another advantage of tax exemption under Sec. 501(c)(3) is the opportunity to apply for grants from foundations and government agencies, which often limit funding to public charities. An organization that is not a Sec. 501(c)(3) organization must disclose to donors that contributions are *not* tax-deductible. Independent charitable organizations may voluntarily join together as a **federated fund-raising organization** to raise and distribute money among themselves. Examples of such federations are the United Way and community chests.

---

[5]Application for income tax exemption is made on Form 1023 for public charities and Form 1024 for all other organizations. NPOs may also qualify for exemption from certain federal excise taxes (e.g., communications, manufacturers, diesel and motor fuels taxes).

Illustration 17–2 Tax-Exempt Status According to the Internal Revenue Code (selected)

Section of 1986 Internal Revenue Code	Description of Organization and Its Activities
501(c)(3)	Religious, charitable, scientific, literary, educational, testing for public safety, to foster national or international amateur sports competition, or prevention of cruelty to children or animals organizations
501(c)(4)	Civic leagues, social welfare organizations, and local associations of employees: to promote community welfare
501(c)(5)	Labor unions, agricultural, and horticultural organizations: to educate to improve conditions of work
501(c)(6)	Business leagues, chambers of commerce, real estate boards: to improve business conditions
501(c)(7)	Social and recreational clubs: for pleasure and social activities
501(c)(8)	Fraternal beneficiary society and associations: lodges providing for payment of insurance benefits to members
501(c)(9)	Voluntary employees' beneficiary associations: to provide insurance benefits to members
501(c)(13)	Cemetery companies: burial activities
501(c)(14)	State-chartered credit unions, mutual reserve funds: loans to members
501(c)(20)	Group legal service plans: provided by a corporation for its members
501(d)	Religious and apostolic associations: religious communities
501(e)	Cooperative hospital service organizations: to perform cooperative services for hospitals
501(f)	Cooperative service organizations: operating educational organizations
501(k)	Child care organizations
521(a)	Farmers' cooperative associations: marketing and purchasing for agricultural producers

Annual Compliance Reporting. Form 990 is the primary tool the federal government uses to collect information about the NPO and its activities. The IRS expands the form as Congress requires more information to be furnished by tax-exempt organizations. The form must be made available to the public for three years.[6] Failure to file this form brings significant penalties, unless an extension is granted. Annual reporting requirements do not apply to federal agencies, churches and their affiliates, and NPOs with gross receipts less than $25,000.

Form 990 provides useful information for donors, grantors, regulators, and researchers. Among the information included on Form 990 is identification of the four largest program services; a list of directors and officers and their compensation;

---

[6]The 1996 Taxpayer Bill of Rights 2 requires that tax-exempt organizations provide a copy of Form 990 to persons who request one within 30 days for a reasonable copying fee. However, penalties for failing to do so will not be assessed until 60 days from the time the IRS issues regulations on this issue, which it had not done as of the time of this printing.

a report of expenses segregated into the functional categories of unrelated business income, program, and support; and a list of major contributors, although the latter item need not necessarily be public information. Illustration 17–3 delineates the kinds of information that are required on the annual reporting Form 990.

Public Charities versus Private Foundations.   Tax-exempt status brings with it potential liability for penalties in the form of excise taxes, such as those for certain activities of private foundations, unrelated business income, some activity of feeder organizations, and excess lobbying. IRC Sec. 501(c)(3) encompasses private foundations and public charities. A **private foundation** is one that receives its support from a small number of individuals or corporations and investment income, rather than from the public at large; and it exists to make grants to public charities. These tax-exempt organizations file an annual Form 990-PF and are subject to several excise taxes for (1) failure to take certain actions (such as distribute a minimum amount to public charities); (2) prohibited behavior (such as speculative investing, self-dealing transactions with disqualified persons, and excess business holdings); and (3) net investment income, which is used to support the costs of auditing

---

Illustration 17–3   Parts of the IRS Form 990

Top of Page 1	Descriptive information: name, address, employer identification number (EIN), type of organization, accounting method
Part I	Statement of Revenue, Expenses, and Changes in Net Assets
Part II	Statement of Functional Expenses with Joint Costs
Part III	Statement of Program Service Accomplishments
Part IV	Balance Sheets (for two years)
Part V	List of officers, directors, trustees, and key employees (with compensation)
Part VI	Other information (e.g., amount of political expenditures, compliance with other regulations, location of the books)
Part VII	Analysis of income-producing activities
Part VIII	Relationship of activities to the accomplishment of exempt purpose
Part IX	Information regarding taxable subsidiaries
Schedule A	
Part I	Compensation of the five highest paid employees other than officers, directors, and trustees
Part II	Compensation of the five highest paid independent contractors for professional services
Part III	Statement about activities (e.g., political activity, leasing, making grants)
Part IV	Reason for nonprivate foundation status (and four-year support schedule)
Part V	Private school questionnaire
Part VI-A	Lobbying expenditures by electing public charities
Part VI-B	Lobbying activity by nonelecting public charities
Part VII	Information regarding transfers to and transactions and relationships with noncharitable exempt organizations
Attachments	Exhibits detailing information from above (e.g., list of all Board members)
990-T	Exempt organization business income tax return

tax-exempt organizations. Another disadvantage of private foundation status is that donors are limited in the amount of their charitable deductions. A tax-exempt organization is presumed to be a private foundation unless it meets a specific exclusion allowing it to be considered a public charity.[7]

Public charities receive preferential tax treatment over private foundations because they are funded, operated, and monitored by the public at large, rather than by a limited number of donors. An IRC Sec. 501(c)(3) organization is considered to be a public charity if it notifies the IRS that it meets one of the exclusions to the private foundation definition: For example, it is broadly supported by the public, government, or other public charities; it operates to support another public charity; or it tests products for public safety.

Two parts of the *broad public support test* must be satisfied. The **external support test** is met if at least one-third of the organization's total revenue comes from the government or general public (e.g., individuals, private foundations, corporations) in the form of contributions, grants, membership dues, charges for services, or sales of merchandise. If 2 percent of total support is from any one individual, corporation, or private foundation, then that amount is excluded from public support. Investment income and gains from sales of capital assets are *not* considered public support. Private foundations try not to give a grant to a not-for-profit organization that exceeds 2 percent of its total support because that gift might cause the public charity to fail the support test and be reclassified as a private foundation. If that happens, the foundation must exercise **expenditure responsibility** and monitor whether the grant was used exclusively for the purpose for which it was made. The private foundation can require the grantee to assure them that the grant will not *tip* the grantee into private foundation status before it is granted. The **internal support test** requires that the NPO *not* receive more than one-third of its total support from investment income and unrelated business income. Classification as a public charity must be redetermined each year.

Unrelated Business Income Tax	Owners of small businesses have long complained that NPOs compete with them in businesslike activities with the unfair advantage of lower costs due to exemption from income taxes. For example, college bookstores sell clothing, credit unions operate travel agencies, YMCAs run health clubs, and universities operate veterinary clinics.[8] In 1950 Congress passed the first unrelated business income tax (UBIT), which assesses tax at corporate rates on income that NPOs derive from activities not substantially related to their charitable or tax-exempt mission.[9] UBIT requirements apply to all not-for-profit organizations and state colleges and universities, except federal corporations and certain charitable trusts.

The IRS is primarily interested in how the unrelated business income was earned, not in how it is used, even if it is used to further the organization's

---

[7]IRC Sec. 509(a).

[8]General Accounting Office, *Competition Between Tax-Exempt Organizations and Taxable Businesses*, GGD/T-GGD-88-43 (Washington, DC: Government Printing Office), June 28, 1988.

[9]IRC Secs. 511–513. Unrelated business income is also subject to the alternative minimum tax.

tax-exempt purpose. **Unrelated business income** (UBI) is calculated as the gross income from an unrelated trade or business *regularly* carried on less directly connected expenses, certain net operating losses, and qualified charitable contributions. The first $1,000 of net unrelated business income is excluded from taxation. Unrelated trade or business activities are those that are *substantially* unrelated to carrying out the organization's exempt purpose. The activities that must be carefully examined include sponsorships, advertising, affinity credit card arrangements, sale of mailing lists, travel services, and fund-raising events.

To determine whether the business activity is substantially related to the organization's exempt purpose, the relationship between the business activity and the exempt purpose is examined. Unrelated business income does not include dividends, interest, royalties, fees for use of intangible property, and gains on the sale of property (unless that property was used in an unrelated trade or business), or income from activities in which substantially all of the work is done by volunteers, income from the sale of donated merchandise, income from legally conducted games of chance, rents from real property, or when the trade is conducted primarily for the convenience of its members, such as laundry in a college dorm. However, rents from debt-financed property, rents based on a percentage of net income rather than gross income, and rents on personal property are considered to be unrelated business income. Excluded from UBI is income from advertising done in the form of corporate sponsorships for particular events if (1) the corporate sponsor does not get any substantial benefit in return for its payment, other than the promotion of its name, (2) the display does not advertise the company's products or services, and (3) the amount of payment is not contingent on the level of attendance at the event.[10] Corporate sponsorships that appear in regularly published periodicals are still UBI. Special rules apply to bingo and distribution of low-cost items, such as pens or stickers.

Feeder Organizations.   NPOs may control a **feeder organization** that is organized to carry on a trade or business for the benefit of the exempt organization and remit its profits to the NPO. The income passed from the feeder to the not-for-profit in the form of interest, rents, royalties, and annuities is subject to unrelated business income tax. In 1997, Congress redefined *control* as more than 50 percent of the voting stock of a feeder organization, down from 80 percent, effectively classifying more income of NPOs as unrelated. Some activities not subject to the feeder organization rules are those that (1) generate rental income that would be excluded from rent for UBIT, (2) use volunteers for substantially all the work, and (3) sell merchandise that was substantially all received as contributions.

Unrelated Debt-Financed Income.   If an NPO has income from an asset that is mortgaged or **debt-financed income,** for example, rental of real estate, then that income is UBI. The unrelated business income is the total income times the

---

[10]This change came about in the Taxpayer Relief Act of 1997 and was a codification of proposed IRS regulations from three prior years.

proportion to which the property is financed by debt. There are many exceptions to this general rule, such as property for which substantially all is used to achieve the organization's exempt purpose.

Political Activity

Early legislative attempts at restricting political activity of public charities were intended to deny a charitable contribution income tax deduction for a selfish contribution made merely to advance the personal interests of the donor. The general rule is that no substantial part of a charity's activities may constitute carrying on propaganda or otherwise attempting to influence legislation. **Propaganda** is information skewed toward a particular belief with a tendency to have little or no factual basis. **Legislation** is generally action by Congress, a state legislative body, or a local council to establish laws, statutes, and ordinances. If any of the activities of the NPO consists of participating in any political campaign on behalf of (or in opposition to) any candidate for public office, the organization will not qualify for tax-exempt status. This includes publishing or distributing political statements. However, the facts and circumstances on the amount of money, time, and energy spent on each case determine whether the organization can be tax-exempt. For example, certain voter education activities or public forums conducted in a nonpartisan manner may not be considered prohibited political activity.

If an organization passes the "no *substantial* amount of propaganda or influencing legislation" hurdle and is granted tax-exempt status, it still faces limitations on the amount of political activity it can conduct. The severest penalty is loss of tax-exempt status. Less extreme is a tax on excessive political expenditures.[11] An exempt organization, other than a church, is allowed to make limited expenditures to influence legislation, if properly elected on Form 5786.[12] A permissible amount of **direct lobbying** (i.e., testifying at legislative hearings, corresponding or conferring with legislators or their staffs, or publishing documents advocating specific legislative action) is allowed, up to a ceiling calculated to allow for **grass-roots lobbying** (i.e., an appeal to the general public to contact legislators or to take other action regarding a legislative matter), but not to exceed $1 million in any one year. "Influencing legislation" does not include distributing nonpartisan studies, providing technical advice to a governmental body, opposing legislation that negatively affects the organization, exchanging information among organization members, and communicating on routine matters with governmental officials. The annual Form 990 contains a significant amount of information on legislative and political activities. Federal penalties for excess political activity are in addition to those that might be assessed by a state for lobbying.

Intermediate Sanctions

The preceding sections identified sanctions for specific prohibited or excessive activities by exempt organizations, but until recently, the only sanction for excessive economic benefits received by officers of NPOs was revocation of the organization's tax-exempt status. This drastic measure was seldom used. In 1996 Congress

---

[11]IRC Sec. 4955.
[12]IRC Sec. 501(h).

gave the IRS a new weapon in the Taxpayer Bill of Rights 2.[13] **Intermediate sanctions** for private inurement resulting from excess economic benefit transactions are penalties assessed when a transaction confers a substantial benefit on a disqualified person. A **disqualified person** is one who has substantial influence over the organization's affairs. Examples of **excess benefit transactions** include unreasonable compensation, sales of assets at bargain prices, and lease arrangements.[14] The law applies to public charities, but may be extended to other classifications of exempt organizations. The first-tier penalty is a tax of 25 percent of the excess benefit on the disqualified person, in addition to repayment of the excess benefit. If the organization's managers are aware the transaction is improper, then the NPO is assessed a tax of 10 percent of the excess benefit (up to a maximum of $10,000 per transaction). A second-tier penalty of 200 percent of the excess benefit is assessed on the disqualified person if the transaction is not corrected within the taxable period. Careful structuring of management compensation contracts, along with documentation of comparable salaries of similar positions, is critical in avoiding intermediate sanctions.

Reorganization and Dissolution

If an NPO finds that the social needs initially described in the tax-exemption application are met, then they may redefine their mission, merge, or choose to dissolve the organization. Many not-for-profit entities, particularly in the health care industry, are redefining their mission and then merging with other NPOs or associating with for-profit organizations. Mergers may be to achieve optimal **economic size** (i.e., the minimum possible size to be able to provide services without long-term damage to its financial base) or to integrate services. Many grantors fund only pilot programs that result in NPOs looking for financial resources after the start-up phase of the organization.[15] Accounting issues involved in a reorganization include the merging of two information systems, measuring costs and benefits, **due diligence** (i.e., the formal disclosing and discovery of all relevant information, particularly about risks), and the surviving audit firm's reliance on the work of the former auditor. Accountants play a key role, along with legal and financial consultants, in the process of reorganizing or dissolving an NPO.

The accounting issues involved in a dissolution include ensuring that (1) all creditors are paid, (2) all federal, state, and local taxes are paid, and (3) all assets held in trust for the benefit of society are transferred to another public charity or given to a government. If the incorporating documents are silent about the distribution of assets, then state law or IRS regulations dictate. The IRS has said that if an NPO liquidates, dissolves, or terminates, its assets have to be distributed for another exempt purpose or be given to the federal or a state or local government.[16] Involuntary dissolution may come for failure to file an annual report or as a result of a State Attorney General's determination of fraud or unlawful conduct.

---

[13]U.S. Congress, H.R. 2337, July 30, 1996.
[14]IRC Sec. 4958.
[15]Thomas A. McLaughlin, *Seven Steps to a Successful Nonprofit Merger* (Washington, DC: National Center for Nonprofit Boards, 1996).
[16]Rev. Proc. 82-2 CB 367 1982-1.

Other Issues

The federal government has passed other legislation that impacts NPOs. For example, the Volunteer Protection Act of 1997 holds that a volunteer of a nonprofit organization or governmental entity is relieved of liability for harm in simple negligence cases. An NPO that receives federal grants or contracts must abide by the spending rules found in various OMB Circulars (see Chapter 14 of this text for discussion of cost principles and administrative guidelines for federal assistance recipients). In particular, tax-exempt organizations cannot use federal funds to lobby Congress or state legislatures. Federal legislation also allows tax-exempt entities to apply for reduced postal rates for bulk mailings, as long as mailings do not include excessive for-profit advertising or promotional language describing member benefits, such as affinity credit cards.

Governance

Managers of tax-exempt, not-for-profit organizations are directly accountable to the Board of the organization, which in turn is ultimately responsible to the public and governmental oversight bodies. This relationship is not different from that among corporate managers, Boards of Directors, and stockholders. What is different, however, is the importance of incorporating documents that define the philanthropic or nonprofit mission of the organization and the (sometimes underestimated) responsibilities of Board members who may be invited to serve on the Board more for their fund-raising ability than their financial management expertise.

Incorporating Documents

The incorporating documents include the articles of incorporation, which have an external focus and describe the purpose of the organization without being too restrictive, and the by-laws, which have an internal focus and describe the functional rules of the organization. Other important documents to the accountant include minutes of Board meetings (i.e., the legal history of the organization) and written policies. They establish the charitable or exempt purpose for which the organization was organized and for which it should be held accountable. Expectations of resource providers, such as donors and grantors, as well as federal and state governments requiring reporting on the financial management of assets devoted to the exempt purpose, are revealed in these documents. State laws may govern the type of information that must be included in some of these documents; for example, the articles of incorporation are required to list name, purpose, activities to be engaged in, registered office, and the incorporators.

Nonprofit corporations can take the form of (1) membership, in which there is voting or nonvoting stock (for example, property owners association); or (2) directorship, where the Board is self-perpetuating (i.e., it elects itself). In the case of a directorship there is little threat of removal by the membership at large. The significance of the form of the nonprofit corporation for accountants is that the stakeholders or users of financial information and their needs may differ depending on the organizational form.

Board Membership   Board members are responsible for all authorized activities generating financial support on the organization's behalf.[17] They set policy and provide fiscal guidance and ongoing governance. Characteristics of a quality Board include diversity, leadership, sensitivity, direction, and, probably the most important, the ability of each member to contribute and attract funds. Treasurers of Boards have specific duties articulated in the incorporating documents that require they have custody of corporate funds and securities, keep full and accurate records of all receipts and disbursements, and deposit money and valuables in designated depositories until funds are authorized to be disbursed. Internal Board members, managers and employees of the organization, may have competing objectives from those of external Board members who are outside of the daily operations of the organization and who have no financial stake in the organization. Board members may carry errors and omissions insurance and require that indemnification clauses be included in the articles of incorporation to protect them from lawsuits.

To satisfy its fiduciary responsibilities, the Board should require managers to regularly summarize the activities of administering the entity. It should regularly review the organization's policies, programs, and operations.[18] Incentive performance contracts can be made with managers to encourage certain goals and outcomes. By-laws or policies may call for continuous quality improvement so Boards may assess performance against benchmarks and predetermined performance goals.

Benchmarking and Performance Measures

Oversight bodies, such as Boards of Directors, nonprofit watchdog agencies, and an increasing number of states are tracking performance measures of exempt organizations. Financial and operational outcomes are compared to specified performance targets as well as benchmarked to comparable organizations in the industry. Nonprofit agencies collecting information about entities in the not-for-profit sector include the National Charities Information Bureau (NCIB), Philanthropic Advisory Service (PAS) of the Council of the Better Business Bureau, American Institute of Philanthropy (AIP), Exempt Organizations Division of the Internal Revenue Service (EO), Independent Sector, and Urban Institute.[19]

Generally, financial goals include ensuring that the organization is liquid and can pay its debts, its revenues are sufficient to cover expenses, its expenses are reasonable and primarily spent on the programs rather than supporting the programs, there is intergenerational equity (i.e., future years' revenues are not needed to pay for current services), and there is financial stability and sustained growth in the organization. Donors may incorrectly assume that federal and state laws govern

---

[17]Richard T. Ingram, *Ten Basic Responsibilities of Nonprofit Boards* (Washington, DC: National Center for Nonprofit Boards, 1996).

[18]Regina E. Herzlinger, "Effective Oversight: A Guide for Nonprofit Directors," *Harvard Business Review*, July–August 1994, pp. 52–60.

[19]More information about these groups and the annual reports they produce is available on their Internet homepages, which can be reached through the authors' homepages (see Preface for address).

the percentage of annual revenue that a charity must spend on its programs, or that there are limits on the percentage of revenue that is spent on fund-raising.

Specific financial performance objectives that may be stated in Board policies include maintaining a specified current ratio, a balanced budget, spending such that there is neither an excess of expenses over revenues nor a deficit in net assets, program expenses greater than a specified percent of total expenses, a specified ceiling on long-term debt, a targeted balance between current contributions and planned giving or endowment funds, program spending as a specified percentage of current income, fund-raising costs (and efforts) that are never more than a specific percentage of the contributions that result, investment income equal to the market rate, a targeted percent of endowment income spent on the programs (payout rate), and/or that net assets available for the following year are not more than a certain multiple of current year's expenses or next year's budget, whichever is higher.

The watchdog groups mentioned earlier have some published benchmarks, or averages, they use to rank the performance of public charities. For example, the NCIB uses nine basic standards in evaluating charities and specifies that the program/support expense ratio must be greater than 60/40 in order to receive the highest rating.[20] The PAS of the Better Business Bureau's criteria for a similar standard is 50/50. Some states' Attorney General Offices recommend that an organization spend less than 33 percent of total income on fund-raising and administrative support expenses.[21]

The percentage of total expenses spent on supporting the program as opposed to the program itself is such a publicized measure of effectiveness that organizations are quite careful to allocate as much to the program category as possible. At issue has been the joint costs of advocacy or educational materials that have a fund-raising appeal. As explained in Chapter 16, the AICPA's *SOP 98-2* restricts the amount of such costs that can be classified as program expenses. Another way to increase the proportion of program expenses to total expenses is to recognize the fair value of **gifts in kind** (i.e., contributions of tangible items) and contributed services used in the operations of the program as expenses. Generally accepted accounting principles do require that this type of gift be recognized as both income and expense, if fair value can be objectively determined, expenses would have been incurred even without the donation, nonfinancial assets are enhanced, and amounts are material.[22] At issue is whether fair market value is objective, particularly for corporate contributions of obsolete inventory. If it is overstated, then the public interest is not served.

Form 990 provides a substantial amount of information that can be used in evaluating tax-exempt entities. In addition to financial information, the form asks questions about self-dealing by key officers and for a description of significant program service accomplishments in the charity's own words. Illustration 17–4 provides three performance measures for some of the nation's largest public charities.

---

[20]National Charities Information Bureau, *Standards in Philanthropy* (New York: NCIB, 1997).

[21]Daniel E. Lungren, *Attorney General's Charity Spending Profiles* (San Francisco: California Department of Justice, April 1995).

[22]AICPA, Accounting and Audit Guide, *Not-for-Profit Organizations*, pars. 5.39–5.42.

Illustration 17–4   Ten Largest NPOs and Selected Performance Measures (1996)

	Size = Public Support (in millions)	Program Spending as a Percent of Income	Program Spending as a Percent of of Total Expenses	Fund-Raising Costs as a Percent of Public Support
1. Salvation Army	$816	86	86	4.46
2. American Red Cross	472	89	91	4.03
3. American Cancer Society	427	69	63	17.82
4. United Jewish Appeal, Inc.	359	88	92	7.32
5. Second Harvest	351	99	99	0.14
6. YMCAs of the USA	340	81	84	1.14
7. Catholic Charities USA	336	89	91	1.36
8. Habitat for Humanity International	325	84	81	7.51
9. American Heart Association	274	73	78	12.69
10. World Vision	252	77	79	11.08
Average		**83.5**	**84.4**	**6.76**

Source: "NonProfit Times 100 America's Biggest Nonprofits," *The NonProfit Times*, November 1997, pp. 31–32.

As the federal government requires outcome and performance measures of its agencies, we should expect those agencies to require the same information from the organizations that receive public funds. Many NPOs are voluntarily reporting some type of service efforts and accomplishments in their annual reports. As this practice becomes more widespread, NPOs will report similar statistics to stay competitive for charitable gifts.

Summary

This chapter provides a general description of tax laws and other state and federal regulations so that accountants and decision makers using financial information are familiar with the environment within which tax-exempt organizations operate. It should be clear that a thorough understanding of current case law about exempt organizations is also important, but outside the scope of this text. More specific details are available in Internal Revenue Service literature and books on taxation of tax-exempt organizations. In the future, NPOs can expect increased scrutiny and accountability for performance outcomes as a more well-informed public demands it and as technology enables government agencies, such as the IRS, to audit and monitor tax-exempt organizations.

Key Terms

Selected References

Accounting Aid Society. *Michigan Nonprofit Management Manual*. Detroit, MI: Accounting Aid Society, 1996.

Gross, Malvern J. Jr.; Richard F. Larkin; Roger S. Bruttomesso; and John J. McNally. *Financial and Accounting Guide for Not-for-Profit Organizations*. 5th ed. with annual Cumulative Supplements. New York: John Wiley & Sons, 1997.

Internal Revenue Service, Department of Treasury. *Application for Recognition of Exemption Under Sec. 501(c)(3) of the Internal Revenue Code*. Package 1023.

_____ . Pub. 557. *Tax-Exempt Status for Your Organization*.

Oleck, Howard L.; and Martha E. Stewart. *Nonprofit Corporations, Organizations, and Associations*. 6th ed. and annual Cumulative Supplements. Englewood Cliffs, NJ: Prentice Hall, 1997.

Perlman, Seth. *Fund-Raising Regulation*, and annual Supplements. New York: John Wiley & Sons, 1996.

Stevenson, David R.; Thomas H. Pollak; and Linda M. Lampkin. *State Nonprofit Almanac 1997: Profiles of Charitable Organizations*. Washington, DC: Urban Institute Press, 1997.

Periodicals:

Chronicle of Philanthropy. Washington, DC.

Foundation News. New York: Foundation Center.

The Journal of Taxation of Exempt Organizations. New York: Faulkner & Gray.

Statistics of Income Bulletins. Washington, DC: U.S. Government, Department of Treasury.

Questions

17–1. Why should an auditor understand the laws and regulations that apply to the activities of not-for-profit organizations?

17–2. What are some of the reasons a government has the power and responsibility to regulate a nongovernmental not-for-profit organization?

17–3. Under which statutory authority are these public charities exempt from federal income tax?

   a. Pine Ridge Cemetery.
   b. American Institute of Certified Public Accountants.
   c. Elks Lodge.
   d. Big Oak Country Club.
   e. American Diabetes Association.
   f. Parent Teacher Organization.
   g. Health Maintenance Organization.
   h. Tender Care Child Care Center.
   i. League of Women Voters.
   j. National Hockey League.

17–4. Why might a not-for-profit organization fail to qualify for exemption from federal income taxes?

17–5. Describe the basic differences between public charities and private foundations. Which status receives the most preferential tax treatment under federal laws? Why?

17–6. Describe the limitations on political activity and lobbying that are placed on tax-exempt organizations by the federal government.

17–7. A museum is considering opening a gift shop to sell novelty items related to the exhibits. A committee has been formed to evaluate the costs and benefits of such an operation. What issues should they consider with respect to unrelated business income?

17–8. Define the term *intermediate sanctions* and explain why this is an important tool for the IRS to use in curbing abuses such as excessive management compensation.

17–9. What types of information must be reported to the IRS annually on Form 990? How can a potential donor get this information and use it for evaluating the organization in making his or her decision to make a contribution?

17–10. Discuss the role of inside and outside Board members. How would an incentive compensation plan help ensure the Board that the manager is accountable for the assets with which the agency is entrusted?

Cases

17–1. John Martinez is a newly elected Representative to the United States Congress. He does not come from a wealthy family, but has a large group of people who supported his candidacy and provided funds for his campaign. In appreciation, he always accepts their invitations to speak to groups back in his home state. He has recently been asked to teach a course by one of these supporters at the local community college. In preparation for this opportunity he prepared a 100-page handout that describes the political system in the United States, and in particular the process that is taken to pass a bill. He uses examples from bills that he cosponsored including his reasons for supporting that legislation. John is aware that other Representatives have recently been under attack by the media and Internal Revenue Service for similar educational activities. He has asked your advice.

Required

    a. In general, what type of regulations should John be aware of?

    b. Should John establish a not-for-profit corporation to accept the payments he will receive for his speaking and teaching assignments?

17–2. Linda Brown is a certified internal auditor for the Walnut Hills Country Club, a nonprofit corporation that owns a private members-only country club. The club recently has experienced declining revenues and decided to allow nonmembers to use the restaurant and banquet room facilities. The accountant offset net losses on nonmember sales against the earnings from its investments and reported no unrelated business taxable income. In computing the losses from the unrelated business activities, the club identified two categories of expenses incurred in nonmember sales (1) variable or direct expenses, such as the cost of food that was exceeded by income from nonmember sales, and (2) fixed overhead expenses, which would have been incurred whether or not sales had been made to nonmembers. Linda is aware that the IRS has recently questioned cost allocation methods used by country clubs in the computation of unrelated business taxable income. She has been asked to make sure the Club is following proper procedures.

Required

    a. Is the revenue from sales to nonmembers unrelated business income?

    b. Determine a method of allocating indirect costs in computing the net loss from sales to nonmembers and defend your position. (Hint: See the Supreme Court case: *Portland Golf Club* v. *Commissioner of Internal Revenue*, S. Ct. 89-530; 65 AFTR 2d 90-503, June 21, 1990).

Based on a case in "Accounting for the 'Invisible' Nonprofit Sector: Five Mini-Cases," by J. Young and S. Kattelus, *Journal of Accounting Education*, Vol. 13, no. 3, 1995, pp. 319–42.

17–3. **Internet Case.** See if five of the largest tax-exempt charitable organizations identified in Illustration 17–4 have homepages on the Internet. What financial information and performance measures do they disclose? Locate a comparable organization for each of these five NPOs, perhaps a competitor. Calculate the amount that each spent on its program (as a percent of income and as a percent of total expenses) as well as how many dollars were raised for each dollar spent on fund-raising from information provided on their homepages. Do you have enough information to compare each pair of organizations? Where could you get other useful information? Prepare a table showing the five charities, their counterparts, and performance measures for each. Which charity would you consider the most efficient and effective? Why?

Exercises and Problems

17–1. Write the numbers 1 through 10 on a sheet of paper. Beside each number, write the letter corresponding with the best answer to each of the following questions:

    1. Accountants should be knowledgeable about laws and regulations impacting not-for-profit entities because:

        a. They may be asked by the organization to assist in completing annual compliance reports.

     b. Donors may ask for their help in evaluating a not-for-profit organization.

     c. Auditors are expected to attest to whether the organization complied with all laws and regulations.

     d. All of the above.

2. To qualify as an exempt organization, the applicant:

     a. Need *not* be specifically identified in one of the categories of tax exemption allowed by the Internal Revenue Code, provided that the organization's purposes and activities are of a charitable nature.

     b. Must *not* be classified as a professional organization.

     c. Must *not* be a public charity organized and operated exclusively to influence legislation pertaining to protection of the environment.

     d. May be organized and operated for the primary purpose of carrying on a business for profit, provided that all of the organization's net earnings are turned over to one or more tax-exempt organizations.

3. An organization that tests products for public safety will fail to meet the organizational test to qualify as an exempt organization if:

	The Organization Engages in Insubstantial Nonexempt Activities	The Organization Directly Participates in Any Political Campaign
a.	Yes	Yes
b.	Yes	No
c.	No	Yes
d.	No	No

4. Which of the following organizations is most likely to qualify for tax-exempt status as a not-for-profit organization?

     a. Royal Oak Chamber of Commerce.

     b. Disneyland.

     c. Detroit Red Wings.

     d. City of Huron.

5. Which of the following is a characteristic of public charities but *not* private foundations?

     a. They are subject to excise taxes on certain prohibited transactions, such as self-dealing.

     b. They are supported by a broad set of donors organized to meet the common good.

     c. They are exempt from federal income taxes under IRC Sec. 501(c)(3).

     d. They may not participate in any political campaign on behalf of a candidate for public office.

6. Which of the following activities regularly conducted by a tax-exempt organization will result in unrelated business income?
   I. Operating a thrift store staffed by developmentally disabled persons as part of a sheltered workshop program.
   II. Selling goods made by disabled persons as part of their rehabilitation, when the organization is organized exclusively for rehabilitation.
      a. I only.
      b. II only.
      c. Both I and II.
      d. Neither I or II.

7. New Beginnings, Inc., is an exempt organization that owns an office building and leases it to the Auto Parts Corporation for $120,000 per year. The remaining mortgage on the building is $300,000, and the book value of the building is $500,000. Since the office building is debt-financed property, the unrelated debt-financed income, for purposes of the UBIT, is:
   a. $200,000.
   b. $120,000.
   c. $72,000.
   d. $0.

8. Which of the following statements is correct with regard to unrelated business income of an exempt organization?
   a. An exempt organization that earns any unrelated business income in excess of $100,000 during a particular year will lose its exempt status for that particular year.
   b. An exempt organization is not taxed on the unrelated business income of less than $1,000.
   c. The tax on unrelated business income can be imposed even if the unrelated business activity is intermittent and is carried on once a year.
   d. An unrelated trade or business activity that results in a loss is excluded from the definition of unrelated business.

9. The percentage of total expenses a nonprofit organization spends on its programs as opposed to supporting the programs is a performance measure that can be used in evaluating:
   a. Efficiency or effectiveness.
   b. Liquidity.
   c. Intergenerational equity.
   d. Profitability.

10. Which of the following is an important reason why Board members of a nonprofit agency should be familiar with the laws and regulations that impact the organization?
   a. They have a fiduciary responsibility to ensure that the not-for-profit organization complies with all laws and regulations.
   b. They have a legal responsibility to ensure that the not-for-profit organization complies with all laws and regulations.
   c. They have a responsibility to management to provide on-going fiscal governance, as well as direction.
   d. All of the above.

17–2. The Family Services Agency of Oakville County is a nongovernmental public charity under IRC Sec. 501(c)(3). It had total support last year of the following:

United Way support	$70,000
Grant from Oakville County	50,000
Contributions	330,000
Dividend and interest income	450,000
	$900,000

Of the $330,000 in contributions, five large contributions were each in excess of 2 percent of the total support. These contributions totaled $230,000 and the other $100,000 is comprised of small individual contributions.

Required

a. Calculate the total amount of support that qualifies as "public support" in meeting the support test to escape private foundation status.
b. Is the organization considered a public charity or a private foundation? Why or why not?
c. If the organization received an additional $135,000 grant from one foundation during the year, would the NPO still be classified the same as your response to part *b* (assuming that the previous five gifts are still greater than 2 percent of the new total)?

17–3. LearnMore, Inc., an IRC Sec. 501(c)(3) organization, incurred lobbying expenses of $250,000 and exempt purpose expenditures of $1.1 million in carrying out its exempt mission.

Required

a. What are the tax consequences if the organization *does not* elect to participate in lobbying activities on a limited basis?
b. Discuss the factors involved in the association's decision to elect to participate in lobbying activities under IRC Sec. 501(h).

17–4. The Lewis and Clark Association has a mailing list of 15,000 members, donors, catalog purchasers, and other supporters of the association and its mission—to educate the public about the historic expedition to the West from the eastern United States in the early 1800s. In prior years, revenue from the sale of this list to for-profit companies for use in their promotional activities averaged $5,000. This year, because of a television special about the historic journey, revenue from sales of the list jumped to $86,000. The accountant recently attended a workshop on tax issues in not-for-profit organizations and learned about unrelated business income tax. She is now concerned that this revenue is subject to that tax.

Required

a. Apply the facts of this case to the unrelated business income tax rules. Is the Association liable for unrelated business income tax?
b. What if next year the revenue from sales of the mailing list increases to $286,000? Would the Association then have unrelated business income?

17–5. An exempt organization operates a gift shop and has an operations budget of $2,000,000 for the year. Gift shop sales result in a profit of $50,000. Another $100,000 of endowment income is earned. Both the income from the gift shop and the endowment income are used to support the exempt purpose of the organization. The balance of $1,850,000 required for annual operations is provided through membership dues and charges for services.

Required

    a. Calculate the UBIT if the corporate tax rate is 15 percent on the first $50,000 of net income and 25 percent on the next $25,000 of income.

    b. Assume that the endowment income is reinvested rather than being used to support annual operations. Calculate the amount of unrelated business income.

17–6. For the following independent situations, determine if the organization is at risk for receiving *intermediate sanctions* from the Internal Revenue Service for conferring excess economic benefits on disqualified persons. If so, indicate how the organization can minimize those sanctions.

    1. Jane is the president of an IRC Sec. 501(c)(3) public charity and personally owns a building that she has decided to sell to the not-for-profit organization. The appraisal value is $200,000 and the agreed upon selling price is $250,000.

    2. A large public charity is very happy with its president's performance and offers him a new compensation agreement for the coming year. It reads that he will receive a base salary, plus a percentage of the increase in the gross revenues of the organization, with no limitation as to a maximum amount.

    3. Ann is a member and director of a symphony association and receives 20 free admission tickets as a member of the organization.

    4. The local chapter of the United Way recently hired Joe Curtis as its new president at a salary of $200,000. The outgoing president was paid $150,000. Mr. Curtis had other offers that ranged from $95,000 to $190,000. The minutes of the meeting reflected that he was exceptionally talented and would not have accepted the position for a lower salary.

17–7. Two large human service organizations in an urban area have decided to collaborate in order to reduce administrative costs resulting in more funds available for charitable programs. What financial and accounting issues should they consider in their decision to dissolve one entity or merge the two together?

17–8. Information from the audited financial statements for the American Heart Association for the fiscal year ending June 30, 1996, is presented on the following pages. Notes to the Financial Statements are not included and some line items have been consolidated to simplify the presentation. Compute the following performance measures and comment on what information they convey to a potential donor, without comparing them to prior years or other comparable agencies.

    a. Current ratio—liquidity.

    b. Excess of revenues over expenses.

    c. Percentage of total expenses spent on the programs as opposed to supporting the programs.

    d. Cost of fund-raising.

    e. Intergenerational equity: extent to which future generations have to pay for services offered currently.

American Heart Association, Inc. (National Center)
and all Affiliated Heart Associations
Combined Statement of Financial Position
As of June 30, 1996
(Dollars in Thousands)

	Unrestricted	Temporarily Restricted	Permanently Restricted	Total
Assets				
Current assets:				
Cash and cash equivalents	$ 42,316	$ 6,591	$ 198	$ 49,105
Short-term investments	182,686	6,212	1,680	190,578
Accrued investment income	3,664	4		3,668
Accounts receivable	6,465	40,671	1,000	48,136
Education and campaign materials inventory	10,996			10,996
Prepaid expenses and other assets	5,050			5,050
Total current assets	251,177	53,478	2,878	307,533
Noncurrent assets:				
Long-term investments	139,585	3,868	5,043	148,496
Beneficial interest in perpetual trusts			48,479	48,479
Land, building and equipment (net)	73,051	617		73,668
Accounts receivable	346	28,063		28,409
Other assets	897			897
Total noncurrent assets	213,879	32,548	53,522	299,949
Total assets	$465,056	$86,026	$56,400	$607,482
Liabilities and Net Assets				
Current liabilities:				
Accounts payable and accrued expenses	$ 21,330	$ 713		$ 22,043
Mortgage notes payable	676			676
Research awards payable within one year, net of discount of $960	89,423	4,629		94,052
Deferred revenue and support	5,974			5,974
Other liabilities	1,746			1,746
Total current liabilities	119,149	5,342		124,491
Noncurrent liabilities:				
Other accrued expenses and liabilities	4,513			4,513
Mortgage notes payable	5,154			5,154
Research awards payable after one year, net of discount of $11,562	85,090	3,508		88,598
Deferred revenue and support	1,739			1,739
Total noncurrent liabilities	96,496	3,508		100,004
Total liabilities	215,645	8,850		224,495
Net assets:				
Net investment in land, building and equipment	67,143	617		67,760
Designated by the governing board or restricted for:				
Programs and operations for the ensuing fiscal year	179,498	76,559		256,057
Endowment			$56,400	56,400
Undesignated	2,770			2,770
Total net assets	249,411	77,176	56,400	382,987
Total liabilities and assets	$465,056	$86,026	$56,400	$607,482

Note: These statements are adapted from the American Heart Association's audited financial statements.

**American Heart Association, Inc. (National Center)
and all Affiliated Heart Associations**
Combined Statement of Activities
Year Ended June 30, 1996
(Dollars in Thousands)

	Unrestricted	Temporarily Restricted	Permanently Restricted	Total
Revenue:				
Public support:				
Received directly:				
Contributions and capital campaigns	$ 68,398	$17,246	$1,072	$ 86,716
Contributed services	2,399			2,399
Special events	104,594	1,269		105,863
Special events incentives	(22,482)			(22,482)
Net special events	82,112	1,269		83,381
Legacies and bequests	51,138	27,159	373	78,670
Total received directly	204,047	45,674	1,445	251,166
Received indirectly:				
Federated fund-raising organizations	7,670	11,361		19,031
Unassociated fund-raising organizations	2,669	1,123		3,792
Total received indirectly	10,339	12,484		22,823
Total public support	214,386	58,158	1,445	273,989
Other revenue	65,415	1,253	4,573	71,241
Net assets released from restrictions:				
Satisfaction of research restrictions	16,559	(16,559)		
Satisfaction of program restrictions	11,927	(11,927)		
Expiration of time restrictions	8,601	(8,601)		
Satisfaction of equipment acquisition restrictions	521	(521)		
Satisfaction of geographic restrictions	1,923	(1,923)		
Total net assets released from restrictions	39,531	(39,531)		
Total public support and other revenue	$319,332	$19,880	$6,018	$345,230
Expenses:				
Program services:				
Research	$100,365			$100,365
Public health education	72,424			72,424
Professional education and training	35,250			35,250
Community services	43,561			43,561
Total program services	251,600			251,600
Supporting services:				
Management and general	26,280			26,280
Fund-raising	43,819			43,819
Total supporting services	70,099			70,099
Total program and supporting services	321,699			321,699
Change in net assets before cumulative effect of change in accounting principles	(2,367)	19,880	6,018	23,531
Cumulative effect of change in accounting principles	20,139	34,227	44,134	98,500
Change in net assets	17,772	54,107	50,152	122,031
Net assets, beginning of year	231,639	23,069	6,248	260,956
Net assets, end of year	$249,411	$77,176	$56,400	$382,987

American Heart Association, Inc. (National Center)
and all Affiliated Heart Associations
Combined Statement of Functional Expenses
Year Ended June 30, 1996
(Dollars in Thousands)

	Program Services					Supporting Services			Total
	Research	Public Health Education	Professional Education and Training	Community Services	Subtotal	Management and General	Fund Raising	Subtotal	1996
Salaries	$ 1,971	$31,008	$ 9,987	$20,032	$ 62,998	$12,509	$17,400	$29,909	$ 92,907
Payroll taxes	177	2,581	806	1,691	5,255	974	1,414	2,388	7,643
Employee benefits	404	5,265	1,896	3,393	10,958	2,041	2,844	4,885	15,843
Occupancy	222	3,992	1,281	2,618	8,113	1,344	1,906	3,250	11,363
Telephone	140	1,970	569	1,222	3,901	642	1,181	1,823	5,724
Supplies	94	1,399	422	1,066	2,981	463	952	1,415	4,396
Rental and maintenance of equipment	139	1,240	525	916	2,820	815	677	1,492	4,312
Printing and publications	141	6,520	7,102	5,120	18,883	46	5,536	5,582	24,465
Postage and shipping	103	4,887	3,054	1,153	9,197	474	4,000	4,474	13,671
Visual aids, films and media	8	379	69	174	630	64	183	247	877
Conferences and meetings	691	2,617	5,033	1,449	9,790	1,640	1,050	2,690	12,480
Other travel	109	1,909	582	1,382	3,982	700	1,362	2,062	6,044
Professional fees	2,300	4,609	1,363	918	9,190	2,603	2,864	5,467	14,657
Awards and grants	93,567	448	479	182	94,676	120	310	430	95,106
Other expenses	74	1,178	1,157	830	3,239	693	971	1,664	4,903
Depreciation and amortization	225	2,422	925	1,415	4,987	1,152	1,169	2,321	7,308
Special events incentives					22,482				22,482
Total functional expenses	$100,365	$72,424	$35,250	$43,561	$274,082	$26,280	$43,819	$70,099	$344,181

CHAPTER 18

Accounting for Colleges and Universities

Learning Objectives

After studying this chapter, you should be able to:

~ Distinguish between generally accepted accounting principles for public and private colleges and universities.

~ Describe fund accounting for governmentally owned colleges and universities.

~ Journalize transactions for governmentally owned colleges and universities under the AICPA College Guide model.

~ Prepare financial statements for governmentally owned colleges and universities under the AICPA College Guide model.

~ Prepare financial statements for private colleges and universities following *SFAS No. 117.*

~ Discuss the following accounting issues that relate to colleges and universities:

   Performance measures.
   Auditing.
   Federal financial assistance.
   Related entities.

~ Describe the reporting model changes proposed by the GASB.

Institutions of higher learning have long been dichotomized into public colleges and universities, which are governmental in nature, and private colleges and universities, which are nongovernmental not-for-profit organizations. In comparison, public institutions receive a higher share of their total revenues from state appropriations, whereas private institutions depend to a larger extent upon student tuition and fees, private gifts, and research grants. More recently, community colleges have joined the higher education industry, supported in large part by local property tax assessments, as well as a few for-profit corporations that may receive corporate subsidies. The National Center for Education Statistics estimates that in 1996 there were over 3,700 institutions of higher learning with $189 billion of gross revenue and enrollment of 14.2 million students in the United States.[1] Higher education is one of the most diverse industries in terms of organizational forms, funding sources, missions, and size of its constituents.

Accounting and Financial Reporting Standards

Prior to the formation of the GASB in 1984, and, for practical purposes, until the issuance of FASB *Statement Nos. 116* and *117* in 1993, there had been a single set of accounting and financial reporting standards applicable to all colleges and universities, without regard to their ownership or sources of financing. The standards were set by the American Institute of Certified Public Accountants (AICPA) in cooperation with committees of the National Association of College and University Business Officers (NACUBO) and task forces of groups related to the U.S. Department of Education.[2]

In 1984, the GASB was given jurisdiction over accounting and financial reporting standards for public colleges and universities, as well as state and local governmental units and public schools. The FASB retained jurisdiction over accounting and financial reporting standards for private colleges and universities, and, of course, for for-profit businesses providing higher education. In 1991, the GASB issued a statement that allows public colleges and universities to continue using the AICPA College Guide model until comprehensive studies of governmental reporting models are completed.[3] Public institutions do have the option of reporting using the governmental model, described in Chapters 2 through 10, which is often chosen by community colleges that are funded primarily through local taxes.

FASB *Statement Nos. 116* and *117* now require private colleges and universities to report on the net assets of the entity as a whole, rather than reporting on fund groups. This change was made to standardize the way all nongovernmental not-for-profit entities report to the public, and make them report more like busi-

---

[1]National Center for Education Statistics (NCES), *Digest of Education Statistics* (Washington, DC: Department of Education, 1997).

[2]American Institute of Certified Public Accountants, Audit and Accounting Guide, *Audits of Colleges and Universities* (New York: AICPA, 1973, reprinted in 1994).

[3]GASB, *Codification*, Sec. Co5.101.

nesses and less like governments. An important presumption was that decision makers would find this format more useful, even though comparability between public and private universities would be made more difficult.[4] After much study, the GASB issued an exposure draft in 1997 that would require *public* colleges and universities to report on a dual perspective: on the entity as a whole and on a fund perspective. This change is similar to the financial reporting model proposed for state and local governments and discussed in Chapter 1.[5] The present jurisdictional split between the GASB and FASB for colleges and universities seems to ensure that financial reporting for public and private colleges and universities will not be comparable in the foreseeable future.[6] Standards and the fund structure applicable to public (governmental) colleges and universities are discussed next, including a presentation of illustrative transactions and financial statements. Standards and financial reporting requirements unique to private colleges and universities are discussed later in this chapter.

Public (Governmentally Owned) Colleges and Universities

The fund structure and accounting principles applicable to the AICPA model are set forth in the AICPA Audit Guide *Audits of Colleges and Universities* and in the NACUBO publication *Financial Accounting and Reporting Manual for Higher Education* (FARM). The audit guide was issued for the use of Certified Public Accountants who audit colleges and universities whereas the NACUBO publication is intended to provide guidance for accountants, managers, and others who work for colleges and universities. Fund categories generally needed by colleges and universities are:

- Current funds (unrestricted and restricted).
- Loan funds.
- Endowment and similar funds.
- Annuity and life income funds.
- Plant funds.
- Agency funds.

Current Funds

Current resources available for use in carrying out operations directly related to the institution's educational objectives are accounted for in the Current Funds category. "Directly related" operations include residence halls, food services,

---

[4]Rita Hartung Cheng, Ken W. Brown, and Mary L. Fischer, "Response to the GASB Discussion Document 'Invitation to Comment: College and University Financial Reporting Model'," *Accounting Horizons* 9 (September 1995), pp. 104–110.

[5]The publishers will provide an update bulletin to adopters of this text when the GASB issues a final statement on public college and university financial reporting.

[6]John H. Engstrom and Connie Esmond-Kiger, "Different Formats, Same User Needs: Do the FASB and GASB College and University Reporting Models Meet User Needs?" *Accounting Horizons* 11 (September 1997), pp. 16–34.

intercollegiate athletics, student stores, and other auxiliary enterprises, as well as the instruction, research, and public service activities of the college or university. In NACUBO terminology, Current Funds is referred to as a *fund group* because it includes two subgroups: Unrestricted Current Funds and Restricted Current Funds. (The association of the word *group* with the word *fund* will seem strange to the reader who is familiar with the distinction made between the two terms in state and local governmental accounting, discussed in the first 10 chapters of this text. The confusion may be clarified by reference to the practice discussed in Chapter 7 of maintaining a number of subfunds within an enterprise fund of a governmental unit.) Assets that are available for all purposes of the institution at the discretion of the governing board are *unrestricted*. Examples of unrestricted current funds include general funds, designated funds, and auxiliary funds. Assets that are available for current operating purposes subject to limitations placed on them by persons or organizations outside the institution are *restricted*. For financial reporting purposes, unrestricted assets and related liabilities and fund balances should be reported separately from restricted assets, liabilities, and fund balances. In addition, revenues, expenditures, and transfers must be classified as being related to restricted or unrestricted current funds. Restricted current funds are used to account for federal and other sponsored research grants, scholarship gifts, and other expendable restricted monies.

It might be helpful at this point, and periodically during the discussion of the other fund groups, to refer to the illustrative financial statements for Midwest University presented later in this chapter. These statements are formatted as recommended by NACUBO and the AICPA. The three required financial statements are a Balance Sheet (Illustrations 18–1 and 18–2), a Statement of Current Funds Revenues, Expenditures, and Other Changes (Illustration 18–3), and a Statement of Changes in Fund Balances (Illustration 18–4).

Current Funds Revenues. Governmentally owned colleges and universities should recognize revenues of unrestricted current funds on the accrual basis to the extent practicable. Restricted assets are not considered earned until all of the terms of the agreement under which they were given to the institution have been met; authoritative bodies agree that the terms are met only when the monies are expended in accordance with donor or grantor restrictions. For that reason, restricted assets are initially reported as additions in the Statement of Changes in Fund Balances when they are received and are recognized as revenues in the periods when required expenditures are made and in amounts equal to the expenditures. It may be observed that the recognition of Restricted Current Funds revenue in the amount of donor- and grantor-specified expenditures and in the fiscal period in which those expenditures take place is conceptually similar to the use of the "measurable and available" criterion currently used for the recognition of revenue by governmental fund types of state and local governments.

The term *revenues* is properly used only in relation to Current Funds and not in relation to any of the other categories of funds utilized by colleges and universities. Increases in the fund balances of all funds other than Current Funds are considered *additions* rather than *revenues*.

Current funds revenues accounts provided in the NACUBO chart of accounts include:

Tuition and Fees
Federal Appropriations
State Appropriations
Local Appropriations
Federal Grants and Contracts
State Grants and Contracts
Local Grants and Contracts
Private Gifts, Grants, and Contracts
Endowment Income
Sales and Services of Educational Activities
Sales and Services of Auxiliary Enterprises
Sales and Services of Hospitals
Other Sources
Independent Operations

All of the account titles listed are control accounts and should be supported by appropriately named subsidiary accounts. For example, Tuition and Fees may be supported by subsidiary accounts for the regular session, summer school, extension, continuing education, and any other accounts providing useful information for a given educational institution. Gross tuition and fees should be recorded as a revenue even though some will be offset by fee remissions, scholarships, and fellowships. Actual refunds should be charged to the Tuition and Fees account, but remissions, scholarships, and fellowships should be recorded as Expenditures.

Also in regard to Tuition and Fees, it should be noted that because college fiscal years and academic years rarely coincide, it is common for tuition and fees collected near the end of a fiscal year to relate in large portion to services to be rendered by the institution during the ensuing fiscal year. Current recommendations of the AICPA and NACUBO indicate that revenues and related expenditures that apply to an academic term encompassing two fiscal years should be recognized within the fiscal year in which the term is predominantly conducted.[7] At the end of the year in which revenue is received but not earned, it is reported in the year-end balance sheet as *Deferred Revenue*.

Current Funds Expenditures and Transfers.   The term *expenditures* is properly used only in relation to Current Funds. Current funds expenditures should be recognized on a full accrual basis. Expenditures may be identified as to program functions, organizational units, projects, and object classes. Functional classifications

---

[7]NACUBO, *Financial Accounting and Reporting Manual for Higher Education* (FARM), ¶311; Published in loose-leaf form with bimonthly updates. Also AICPA, *Audits of Colleges and Universities*, p. 7.

provided in the NACUBO chart of accounts for educational and general expenditures include:

Instruction
Research
Public Service
Academic Support
Student Services
Institutional Support
Operation and Maintenance of Plant
Scholarships and Fellowships

Functional expenditure accounts are also provided for auxiliary enterprises, hospitals, and independent operations. Transfers between Current Funds and other funds of the college or university are recorded and reported separately from expenditures, but since transfers out of Current Funds are expected to exceed transfers into Current Funds, the major heading in the Statement of Revenues, Expenditures, and Other Changes is "Expenditures and Mandatory Transfers." Note that in college and university financial reporting, a distinction is made between mandatory transfers and nonmandatory transfers rather than between operating transfers and equity transfers, as is the case in governmental financial reports. **Mandatory transfers** are transfers made from one fund to another in order to comply with legally enforceable agreements, such as bond indentures and grant agreements. **Nonmandatory transfers** are made at the discretion of the governing board to serve whatever purpose the board agrees is desirable.

Within each of the functional expenditure account categories listed above, accounts are kept by organizational unit, project, or other classification that provides useful information for internal or external users of the financial statements. A third level of analysis of expenditures is provided by an object classification— personnel compensation, supplies and expense, and capital expenditures are suggested as object classifications in the NACUBO chart of accounts. Further detail under each of these object classifications is usually kept to facilitate planning and control. For example, "personnel compensation" may be subdivided into "salaries," "other personnel services," and "personnel benefits," with each of these further subdivided as desired by the administrators of a given college or university.

Assets, Liabilities, and Fund Balances. Asset and liability accounts in both the unrestricted and restricted Current Funds groups are similar to those discussed in relation to the general funds of state and local governmental units and public schools; the most significant difference is that current funds of colleges and universities include prepaid expenses and deferred charges as assets, as do enterprise funds of governmental units. Also similar to the practice of governmental enterprise funds is the provision in the NACUBO chart of accounts for the segregation of fund balances into Fund Balances—Allocated and Fund Balances—Unallocated. Allocated fund balances include the equity in auxiliary enterprises, the Reserve for

Encumbrances, and any other reserves established in accord with the action of the governing board (for Unrestricted Current Funds) or in accord with the requirements of external agencies (for Restricted Current Funds).

Loan Funds

Assets that are loanable to students, faculty, and staff of an educational institution are provided by gifts, by grants, by income from endowment funds, by transfers from other funds, and, in some cases, from loans made to the institution for that purpose. The intent is that the **loan fund** be operated on a revolving basis: Repayment of loans and interest received on the loans are deposited in the loan fund and are then available for lending to other eligible persons. Interest earned on loans and interest earned on temporary investments of loan fund cash are expected to offset wholly or partially the cost of administration of the loan fund and the loss from uncollectible loans.

Assets may be given to the institution under very specific restrictions as to who may receive loans; other assets may be used in accord with policies set by the governing board of the institution. Loan funds of the first kind are restricted; loan funds of the second kind are unrestricted. In each case, accounts and reports must be in detail sufficient to demonstrate that the donor's restrictions and board policies are being adhered to. Accordingly, separate fund balance accounts should be kept to show the amounts the loan funds have received from the various sources. Interest on loans should be credited on the full accrual basis to appropriate specific fund balance accounts. Costs of administration of the loan funds, losses on investments of loan funds, and provision for losses on loans (either estimated or actual) should be reported as deductions from loan funds fund balances. Some institutions utilize income and expense accounts to facilitate management of the loan funds, but ultimately these items are reported as additions to and deductions from loan fund balances and are reported in the Statement of Changes in Fund Balances because the terms *revenues* and *expenditures* pertain only to Current Funds.

Endowment and Similar Funds

Funds whose principal is nonexpendable as of the date of reporting and is invested, or is available for investment, for the purpose of producing income are classified as "endowment and similar funds." Endowment funds are defined by NACUBO as funds for which donors or other external agencies have stipulated, as a condition of the gift, that the principal is to be maintained intact. The principal is invested in order to earn income. The use of the income may be restricted by the donor; if so, the income is considered as an addition to the fund balance of the appropriate restricted fund. If the use of the income is unrestricted, the income is considered to be revenue of the Unrestricted Current Funds.

"And similar" in the fund title refers to term endowment funds and funds functioning as endowment. **Term Endowment Funds** are defined in the same manner as Endowment Funds, with the exception that the conditions of the gift provide that the assets are released from inviolability to permit all or a part of them to be expended on the happening of a particular event or the passage of a stated period of time. **Funds functioning as endowment,** sometimes called **quasi-endowment funds,** are funds established by the governing board of the institution to account for assets to be retained and invested. Since they are board-designated funds, the principal as well as the income may be utilized at the discretion of the board; therefore, the quasi-endowment funds generally are unrestricted. In the event the assets of a quasi-endowment fund are taken from restricted funds, the quasi-endowment fund is restricted.

Accounts and reports of endowment and similar funds should disclose separately each subgroup within the category, as is done in Illustration 18–1 and 18–2. Reports should disclose funds in this category for which the income is unrestricted in use and those for which the income is restricted to specific uses if the distinction exists in a given situation.

Earlier in this chapter, under the heading "Current Funds Revenues," *Endowment Income* is listed as one of the current funds revenues control accounts. Endowment fund income that may be expended at the discretion of the governing board of the college or university is credited on the accrual basis to the Endowment Income account of the Unrestricted Current Funds. Endowment income that may be expended only for purposes specified by donors is initially reported under the caption "Additions" in the Restricted Current Funds column of the Statement of Changes in Fund Balance, which in Illustration 18–4 is combined as "Revenues and other additions." As amounts are expended from restricted endowment income, equal amounts are credited to the Endowment income account of Restricted Current Funds. Amounts of unexpended restricted endowment income remain in the restricted current fund Fund Balance until the period when they are expended. Endowment income is recognized as an addition to the endowment fund balance only if the provisions of the gift require the addition of the income to the principal. Note that state institutional investment laws may supersede GAAP guidance. Note also that if the governing board or management decides to *save* all or part of the income on an endowment, then these funds are properly classified as "funds functioning as endowment."

Problems encountered in accounting for endowment and similar funds of educational institutions are much like those discussed in Chapter 9 of this text in relation to nonexpendable trust funds of a governmental unit. Statements and schedules illustrated in Chapter 9 are appropriate for use in reporting the condition and results of operations of Endowment and Similar Funds of educational institutions.

Traditionally, the investment objective of most educational institutions has been the preservation of principal and the production of dividend and interest income. More recently, a broadened concept of return on investments has developed that assumes that changes in market value of portfolio securities are also a part of return on assets. This concept is known as **total return,** the sum of net realized and unrealized appreciation or shrinkage in portfolio value plus dividend and interest yield. Total return has another aspect; this is the determination of **spending rate,** the proportion of total return that may prudently be used by an institution for current purposes. The adoption of total return as a policy requires the approval of legal counsel and formal approval of its governing board. The total return concept appears to be used by an increasing number of colleges and universities.

The AICPA College Audit Guide permits use of the total return concept, provided that gains included in spendable return are reported as a nonmandatory transfer rather than endowment income. In terms of balance sheet valuation, public colleges and universities are required to report investments of all funds at fair value, following GASB *Statement No. 31*.

Annuity and Life Income Funds

Split-interest agreements, as described in Chapters 15 and 16, are common forms of planned giving by donors, who are often alumni, to colleges and universities. The 1973 AICPA Audit Guide for Colleges and Universities is still in effect and uses the terms Annuity and Life Income Funds.

Annuity Funds are used to account for assets given to an institution under agreements binding the institution to pay stipulated amounts periodically to the donors, or other designated individuals, for a period of time specified in the agreements, or for the lifetime of the donor or other designated individual. **Life Income Funds** are used to account for assets given to an institution under agreements that bind the institution to pay periodically to the donors, or other designated individuals, the total income earned by the donated assets for a period of time, usually the lifetimes of the income beneficiaries.

Annuity Funds. The acceptance of annuity funds by a nonprofit organization is subject to regulation by the Internal Revenue Service and, in many jurisdictions, by agencies of the appropriate state government. The Internal Revenue Code and Regulations state the conditions under which (for IRS purposes) an annuity trust may be established and administered. State agencies may specify the types of investments that may be made by annuity funds. Investments received by the institution as a part of the principal of an annuity fund should be recorded at fair value as of the date of receipt; any assets acquired subsequently by purchase should, of course, be recorded by the annuity fund at cost. Liabilities of the fund would include any indebtedness against the assets and also the present value of "all expected annuity payments using appropriate actuarial assumptions."[8] If the liabilities recorded in this manner exceed the initial assets of the annuity fund, it will start operations with a deficit Fund Balance; if the initial assets exceed the liabilities to the annuitants, the annuity fund will have a positive Fund Balance. Accepting an annuity fund that would have an initial deficit Fund Balance would not appear to be in the institution's best interests. Agreements with potential donors of annuity funds should be carefully drawn by competent attorneys in consultation with competent accountants and investment managers in order to protect the interests of the receiving institution as well as the donor. The definition of *income* is one of the matters needing most careful attention. From the accounting point of view, *income* should be defined in accrual terms so that the principal of the gift will not be eroded by failure to deduct appropriate depreciation and

---

[8]Ibid., ¶366.

amortization charges. It is also in the interest of the institution that an equitable allocation of indirect administrative expenses be permitted, as well as a deduction for direct expenses of administering each annuity fund. Definitions and discussion of direct and indirect costs, and methods for assigning them, are covered in Chapter 14 of this text.

Annuity payments are charged to the liability account. Periodically, an adjustment is made between the liability and Fund Balance to record the actuarial gain or loss due to recomputation of the liability based on revised life expectancy and anticipated return on investments. On termination of an annuity agreement, the principal of the annuity fund is transferred to the fund category specified in the agreement; if the agreement is silent on the point, the principal of the terminated annuity fund should be transferred to unrestricted current funds and identified so readers of the financial statements will not infer that a new gift has been received.

Life Income Funds.   Life income funds differ from annuity funds principally in that the life income fund agreement provides that the income earned by the assets donated will be paid to the donors over the specified period, rather than a stipulated amount. Since the amount to be paid periodically by a life income fund will vary from period to period as the income of the fund varies, it is not practicable or necessary to compute the present value of the stream of unknown future payments. Accordingly, the liabilities of life income funds consist of life income payments currently due, amounts due to other funds for advances to income beneficiaries, and any indebtedness against the fund assets. Assets are recorded on the basis of fair market value on the date of receipt of donated assets, or cost, in the case of purchased assets. The amount credited to Fund Balance initially is, of course, the difference between the amount recorded for the assets and the amount recorded for the liabilities when the fund is established. Income from investments, computed as defined in the agreement under which the fund was established, should be credited to liability accounts during the term of the agreement. Gains and losses on sales of investments, however, are considered changes in Fund Balance unless the agreement with the donor provides differently. On termination of a life income agreement, the principal of the fund is handled in the manner described for terminated annuity funds.

The Internal Revenue Code and regulations provide for three variations of the life income "unitrust"—straight, net income, and net plus makeup. The technicalities of income tax law must be complied with by educational institutions with life income agreements in order to qualify for and maintain tax-exempt status. It is not possible in this brief treatment of life income funds to do more than alert the interested reader to the existence of IRS requirements.

Financial Statement Presentation.   Each annuity fund and each life income fund should be accounted for separately to the extent required to enable the college or university to be able to demonstrate that it is in compliance with each annuity agreement and each life income agreement. In practice, good investment management would often dictate that assets of the individual funds be pooled for investment purposes. (Accounting for pooled investments is discussed and illustrated in Chapters 8 and 15 in the context of state and local government investment pools.) Although each of the annuity and life income funds should be accounted for separately, all of the funds should be combined for Balance Sheet presentation in the Annuity and Life Income Funds category, as shown in Illustration 18–1. If the combined total of annuity and life income funds is not material, this category may be further combined with the funds in the Endowment and Similar Funds category.

If operations of annuity and life income funds involve businesses or firms, it is appropriate that income statements be prepared. If operations of these funds are less complex, a Statement of Changes in Fund Balances, supported by appropriate schedules, may provide adequate disclosure.

Plant Funds

The **Plant Funds Group** consists of four self-balancing subgroups:

1. **Unexpended Plant Funds.** The assets of this subgroup are set aside for the acquisition of long-lived assets for institutional purposes.
2. **Funds for Renewals and Replacements.** The assets of this subgroup are set aside for the renewal and replacement of existing institutional properties.
3. **Funds for Retirement of Indebtedness.** This is a subgroup similar to Debt Service Funds of state and local governmental units.
4. **Investment in Plant.** This is a subgroup that accounts for all property, plant, and equipment utilized by the college or university, except when the accounts are held as investments by endowment and similar funds and annuity and life income funds.

Although authoritative publications agree that the Plant Funds Group consists of the four subgroups itemized above, they also agree the assets and liabilities of the four subgroups may be combined in the Balance Sheet as long as separate Fund Balance accounts are reported for each subgroup. An additional alternative that is considered acceptable is the combination of the assets and of the liabilities of the first three subgroups (i.e., Unexpended Plant Funds, Funds for Renewals and Replacements, and Funds for Retirement of Indebtedness), and the reporting of each of the Fund Balance accounts pertaining to the three subgroups. Under the latter alternative, the Investment in Plant subgroup is presented separately in the Balance Sheet. A third acceptable alternative is to present each subgroup separately.

Authoritative publications are also ambivalent as to accounting for construction in progress; both the AICPA and NACUBO provide explicitly that the Construction in Progress account may be carried in either the Unexpended Plant Funds or the Investment in Plant subgroups. The NACUBO *Financial Accounting and Reporting Manual* (FARM) also states that the Construction in Progress account may be carried in the Funds for Renewals and Replacements subgroup, but implies a preference for reporting all Construction in Progress in the Investment in Plant subgroup.[9]

---

[9]NACUBO, FARM, ¶382 and 383.

Sources of Assets.   The general sources of assets of Unexpended Plant Funds, Funds for Renewals and Replacements, and Funds for Retirement of Indebtedness are:

1. Funds from external agencies.
2. Student fees and assessments for debt service or other plant purposes, which create an obligation equivalent to an externally imposed restriction and which are not subject to the discretionary right of the governing board to use for other purposes.
3. Transfers, both mandatory and nonmandatory, from other fund groups.
4. Borrowings from external sources for plant purposes.
5. Borrowings by advances from other fund groups.
6. Income and net gains from investments in the unrestricted and restricted elements of each of the subgroups.
7. Gifts restricted for the plant.[10]

Liquid assets restricted by donors and other outside individuals and agencies for plant purposes, including student fees of the nature specified in the second item listed above, should be recorded directly in the proper plant funds subgroup and should not be passed through the current funds. Liquid assets transferred to plant funds for purposes designated by the governing board of the institution are considered unrestricted, because the board may change the designated purposes or transfer the assets to another fund category at its pleasure. The distinction between restricted and unrestricted assets should be maintained in the accounts of the plant funds so that appropriate disposition may be made of any portion of assets received in excess of the amount needed to accomplish a specified purpose. Some authorities consider that the restrictions under which liquid assets are received may be so binding as to apply to the proceeds from the eventual disposition of plant assets acquired from restricted sources. *Audits of Colleges and Universities* suggests that "the educational institution should consider obtaining a legal opinion" in regard to the proper accounting for the proceeds from the disposition of plant assets acquired from restricted sources.[11]

Unexpended Plant Funds.   Assets of the Unexpended Plant Funds subgroup may consist of cash, investments, receivables, and construction in progress. Liabilities may consist of accounts payable; and bonds, notes, mortgages, leaseholds, and any other payables issued to finance the acquisition of long-lived assets. Separate Fund Balance accounts should be maintained to indicate equity attributable to restricted sources and equity attributable to unrestricted sources.

If construction activities are accounted for within this subgroup rather than within the Investment in Plant subgroup, encumbrances outstanding at the end of a fiscal period may be reported as allocations of the appropriate Fund Balance; or,

---

[10]Ibid., ¶381.
[11]AICPA, *Audits of Colleges and Universities*, p. 44.

alternatively, disclosure may be made in the Notes to the Financial Statements. Subsidiary records should be kept for each project in order to accumulate project costs for accounting and control purposes. Capital expenditures and related liabilities and fund balances preferably are transferred to the Investment in Plant subgroup at the end of each fiscal period, although it is allowable for the transfer to take place on completion of the project. If any project expenditures are not to be capitalized, they should be written off against the Fund Balance of the Unexpended plant funds subgroup; any related liabilities should be transferred to the Investment in Plant subgroup. Readers may recall that liabilities are accounted for in the same fund as the related assets in trust funds and enterprise funds of state and local governmental units, but not in other funds of governmental units.

Funds for Renewals and Replacements.   The distinction between additions and improvements (accounted for in Unexpended Plant Funds) and renewal and replacement of plant fund assets (accounted for in Funds for Renewals and Replacements) is obvious in some cases but nebulous in others. Some portion of renewals and replacements may be capitalized as additions to plant. A thorough treatment of all these distinctions is found in intermediate accounting texts and need not be reproduced here. The discussion of assets, liabilities, fund balances, construction in progress, and encumbrances of Unexpended Plant Funds is also applicable to Funds for Renewals and Replacements.

Funds for Retirement of Indebtedness.   Assets of this subgroup of plant funds may include cash, investments, deposits with fiscal agents, accounts and notes receivable, and amounts due from other funds, all of which are restricted or designated for the purpose of servicing plant fund indebtedness. Liabilities consist of accruals and accounts payable for fiscal agents' fees and other debt service charges, as well as amounts due to other funds. Fund balances should be designated as restricted or as unrestricted for reasons previously discussed. Expenditures of this subgroup that reduce debt principal represent an increase in the institution's investment in plant and will require recognition in the Investment in Plant subgroup as a reduction in the liability accounts of that subgroup and as an increase in the Net Investment in Plant (or Fund Balance of the Investment in Plant subgroup).

Investment in Plant.   The Investment in Plant subgroup accounts for all property, plant, and equipment except that held by endowment and similar funds, and by annuity and life income funds as investments. Long-lived assets are carried at cost, or at fair value at date of acquisition in the case of assets acquired by gift. In the absence of historical cost records, the assets may be stated at historically based appraised values. The basis of valuation should be disclosed in the financial statements or in the Notes to the Financial Statements. As discussed later in this chapter, FASB *Statement No.* 93 requires all not-for-profit organizations subject to its jurisdiction to recognize in general purpose financial statements depreciation of long-lived tangible assets. The GASB *Codification*, Section Co5.103 provides that government-related colleges and universities should not change their accounting and reporting as a result of FASB *Statement No. 93*, since the GASB has projects under way that may affect reporting of depreciation by public colleges and universities. The "AICPA model" and "governmental model" (either of which remains effective for government-related colleges and universities until superseded by some future GASB pronouncement) do not require the computation of depreciation for plant assets of the college or university. However, the governmental model may result in depreciation being recorded on the fixed assets of auxiliary enterprises, whereas even the latter assets are not required to be depreciated under the AICPA model. The AICPA model does allow annual depreciation charges to be debited to the Net Investment in Plant account and credited to appropriate Allowance for Depreciation accounts of the Investment in Plant subgroup. Liability accounts of this subgroup may consist of all liabilities related to the fixed assets: accounts, bonds, notes, mortgages, and leaseholds payable, and amounts due other funds if associated with the acquisition, renewal, or replacement of plant assets. Net Investment in Plant instead of Fund Balance is the account title recommended for use in this subgroup to record the excess of the carrying value of plant assets over associated liabilities. The Net Investment in Plant account may be subdivided to show the sources from which plant assets were acquired, such as appropriations and gifts.

Agency Funds

As is true of general governmental units and public schools, colleges and universities often act as agents of others for the collection, custodianship, and disbursement of assets. If agency assets are immaterial in amount, the assets and liabilities may be reported as assets and liabilities of the Current Funds. If they are material, however, they should be accounted for in separate agency funds. Inasmuch as assets are commonly held in a college agency fund for longer periods of time than is true of general governmental agency funds, assets may include temporary investments, as well as cash, receivables, and amounts due other fund categories, and amounts due individuals and organizations for which the institution is acting as fiscal agent, custodian, or depository. Earnings on temporary investments are added to the appropriate liability accounts. Total liabilities, therefore, equal total assets, and no Fund Balance exists.

Agency funds assets and liabilities are reported to the public and the college or university governing board in the Balance Sheet. Since there are no fund balances of funds in the agency category, present generally accepted accounting principles indicate it is not proper to report additions and deductions to agency funds during a fiscal period in the Statement of Changes in Fund Balances. Accordingly, the changes in agency funds during a fiscal period are not reported in any of the basic financial statements; this is considered adequate disclosure because agency funds do not "belong" to the educational institution. Special periodic reports should be prepared for each agency fund for submission to individuals or organizations owning the assets in custody of the institution so that transactions and balances are disclosed to parties with a legitimate interest.

Transactions involving the fund groups used by Midwest University are illustrated in the next section of this chapter.

Illustrative Transactions (AICPA Model)

This section presents for each fund group a beginning trial balance, followed by journal entries for selected illustrative transactions for the fiscal year ending June 30, 2000. This information is then summarized in the financial statements presented in Illustrations 18–1 through 18–4 (presented later in this chapter).

Unrestricted Current Funds

Account balances for the Unrestricted Current Funds of Midwest University as of July 1, 1999, are given as follows:

	Debits	Credits
Cash	$ 60,000	
Investments	300,000	
Accounts Receivable	148,000	
Allowance for Doubtful Accounts		$ 18,000
Inventories	80,000	
Prepaid Expenses and Deferred Charges	20,000	
Accounts Payable		100,000
Accrued Liabilities		15,000
Students Deposits		35,000
Deferred Revenues		20,000
Fund Balance		420,000
	$608,000	$608,000

During the fiscal year ended June 30, 2000, Accounts Receivable were recorded for the following revenue items:

Tuition and Fees	$2,670,000
Federal Appropriations	230,000
State Appropriations	2,150,000
Federal Grants and Contracts	35,000
Private Gifts, Grants, and Contracts	40,000
Endowment Income	880,000
Sales and Services of Auxiliary Enterprises	2,300,000
Total	$8,305,000

In addition, Deferred Revenues in the amount of $20,000 reported in the beginning trial balance is reclassified as Revenues—Tuition and Fees, as that amount was collected in the preceding year from students for summer classes offered predominantly in the current year.

Entry 1 records the total amount of $8,325,000 to the Revenues control account, assuming that the existing balance of Allowance for Doubtful Accounts is adequate to cover the estimated uncollectibles. In addition, a subsidiary ledger, as explained in Chapters 3 and 4, should be used to record the detail of each revenue type. Alternatively, the detail of revenues could be recorded in general ledger accounts, or several Revenues control accounts could be used, along with a subsidiary ledger for as much detail as needed.

1. Accounts Receivable	8,305,000	
Deferred Revenues	20,000	
Revenues		8,325,000

Entry 2 records the collections of cash for accounts receivable amounting to $8,348,000 during the current year.

2. Cash	8,348,000	
Accounts Receivable		8,348,000

Entry 3 records the incurring of expenditures of Unrestricted Current Funds. This entry illustrates the use of two Expenditures control accounts; the necessary detail for the functional, organizational unit, and object subclassifications, described earlier in this chapter, could be recorded in general ledger accounts or in subsidiary ledger accounts. Although the expenditure detail is omitted here for simplicity, it is included, for illustrative purposes, in the Statement of Current Funds Revenues, Expenditures, and Other Changes presented at the end of this section as Illustration 18–3.

3. Expenditures—Educational and General	5,100,000	
Expenditures—Auxiliary Enterprises	2,022,000	
Accounts Payable		7,122,000

Mandatory transfers from Unrestricted Current Funds to other funds are recorded by Entry 4a; nonmandatory transfers from Unrestricted Current Funds to other funds by Entry 4b; and nonmandatory transfers to Unrestricted Current Funds by Entry 4c. Entry 4d records the accompanying transfer of cash from and to Unrestricted Current Funds arising from these transfers. Again, subsidiary ledger accounts should be used to record the detail necessary for internal management and financial reporting. Illustration 18–3 provides additional detail on both mandatory and nonmandatory transfers. For example, mandatory transfers in the Educational and General category are reported separately from those in the Auxiliary Enterprises category.

4a. Mandatory Transfers—Principal and Interest	360,000	
Mandatory Transfers—Renewals and Replacements	185,000	
Mandatory Transfers—Loan Fund Matching Grant	3,000	
Due to Funds for Retirement of Indebtedness		360,000
Due to Funds for Renewals and Replacements		185,000
Due to Loan Funds		3,000
4b. Nonmandatory Transfers—Unrestricted Gifts Allocated to Other Funds	580,000	
Due to Loan Funds		40,000
Due to Endowment and Similar Funds		510,000
Due to Unexpended Plant Funds		30,000

4c. Due from Endowment and Similar Funds	25,000	
Nonmandatory Transfers—Funds Functioning as		
Endowments-Gains Appropriated		25,000
4d. Due to Funds for the Retirement of Indebtedness	360,000	
Due to Funds for Renewals and Replacements	185,000	
Due to Loan Funds	43,000	
Due to Endowment and Similar Funds	510,000	
Due to Unexpended Plant Funds	30,000	
Due from Endowment and Similar Funds		25,000
Cash		1,103,000

Accounts payable and accrued liabilities were paid in the amounts of $7,070,000 and $15,000, respectively. Refunds of students' deposits amounted to $5,000.

5. Accounts Payable	7,070,000	
Accrued Liabilities	15,000	
Students' Deposits	5,000	
Cash		7,090,000

Inventories and prepaid expenses and deferred charges for Unrestricted Current Funds increased during the year in the amounts shown in Entry 6. These increases reduced Expenditures as shown.

6. Inventories	15,000	
Prepaid Expenses and Deferred Charges	9,000	
Expenditures—Educational and General		16,000
Expenditures—Auxiliary Enterprises		8,000

Investments in the amount of $100,000 were purchased during the year. The investments account was increased by an additional $28,000 for interest earnings accrued at June 30, 2000 (note that the interest earnings is reported as revenues from "other sources" in the Statement of Current Funds Revenues, Expenditures, and Other Changes presented in Illustration 18–3).

7. Investments	128,000	
Cash		100,000
Revenues		28,000

Entry 8 records the accrual of educational and general expenditures, $51,000, and auxiliary enterprises expenditures, $21,000, at June 30, 2000.

8. Expenditures—Educational and General	51,000	
Expenditures—Auxiliary Enterprises	21,000	
Accounts Payable		65,000
Accrued Liabilities		7,000

Near the end of the current year, the university collected tuition and fees in the amount of $35,000 for classes to be offered in a term to be held predominantly in the following year. In conformity with present standards, the university recognizes a liability of $35,000 and will recognize the entire amount as revenue in the following year.

9. Cash	....	35,000	
	Deferred Revenues		35,000

Revenues, Expenditures, and Transfers accounts were closed.

10. Revenues	8,353,000	
Nonmandatory Transfers—Funds Functioning as Endowment-		
Gains Appropriated	25,000	
Expenditures—Educational and General		5,135,000
Expenditures—Auxiliary Enterprises		2,035,000
Mandatory Transfers—Principal and Interest		360,000
Mandatory Transfers—Renewals and Replacements		185,000
Mandatory Transfers—Loan Fund Matching Grant		3,000
Nonmandatory Transfers—Unrestricted Gifts Allocated		
to Other Funds		580,000
Fund Balance		80,000

Restricted Current Funds

Since Restricted Current Funds revenues are not considered to be earned until authorized expenditures take place, increases in assets of Restricted Current Funds are recorded as additions to the Fund Balance account. In order that the accounting system provide detail needed for the Statement of Changes in Fund Balances (shown in Illustration 18–4), it is desirable to maintain a Fund Balance subsidiary ledger for all college and university funds except Unrestricted Current Funds (which recognizes revenues and expenditures on the accrual basis). The Restricted Current Funds had the following account balances as of July 1, 1999:

	Debits	Credits
Cash	$ 90,000	
Investments	250,000	
Accounts Receivable	50,000	
Accounts Payable		$ 40,000
Fund Balances		350,000
	$390,000	$390,000

Entry 11 records the additions to the Restricted Current Funds that occurred during the current year. (Only the general ledger accounts, assuming the use of a Fund Balances control account, are shown here and in the subsequent entries for the remaining fund groups; subsidiary ledger accounts should be used to record the details of fund balance additions and deductions needed for internal management and financial reporting. For the fund groups that have both restricted and unrestricted fund balances, two control accounts are used: Fund Balances—Restricted and Fund Balances—Unrestricted. The Statement of Changes in Fund Balances presented in Illustration 18–4 illustrates the level of detail typically reported for fund balance changes of all funds.)

11. Cash	1,034,000	
Accounts Receivable	75,000	
Fund Balances		1,109,000

Expenditures for authorized purposes during the period amounted to $1,025,000.

12. Expenditures—Educational and General	1,025,000	
Accounts Payable		10,000
Cash		1,015,000

As noted previously, when expenditures of Restricted Current Funds are incurred for purposes specified by donors and grantors, revenue is considered earned in an equal amount. Entry 13 records the earned revenues.

13. Fund Balances	1,025,000	
Revenues		1,025,000

Many granting agencies, including the federal government, allow colleges and universities to include overhead charges, including depreciation, as a part of grant expenditures. In this example, $35,000 has been allowed as indirect cost recoveries. Since that amount is now available for unrestricted purposes (this amount corresponds to the $35,000 unrestricted revenues from Federal Grants and Contracts included in Entry 1), the entry in Restricted Current Funds would be:

14. Fund Balances	35,000	
Cash		35,000

Cash was received in the amount of $102,000 from various grantors, including the $55,000 billed in the previous year.

15. Cash	102,000	
Accounts Receivable		102,000

Investments were purchased in the amount of $15,000:

16. Investments	15,000	
Cash		15,000

Revenues and Expenditures were closed as shown in Entry 17.

17. Revenues	1,025,000	
Expenditures—Educational and General		1,025,000

Loan Funds

Loan funds' assets consist primarily of cash, investments, and receivables resulting from loans to students, faculty, and staff. Fund balances are assumed to relate to, refundable grants from the federal government and to university funds, both restricted and unrestricted. Loan Fund account balances for Midwest University as of July 1, 1999, are as follows:

	Debits	*Credits*
Cash	$ 20,000	
Investments	98,000	
Loans to Students, Faculty and Staff	460,000	
Allowance for Uncollectible Loans		$ 10,000
Fund Balances:		
University Funds—Restricted		38,000
University Funds—Unrestricted		325,000
U.S. Government Grants Refundable		205,000
	$578,000	$578,000

Entry 18 records the additions to the Loan Funds Fund Balances accounts, including the transfers from the Unrestricted Current Funds.

18. Cash	208,000	
Fund Balances—University Funds—Restricted		130,000
Fund Balances—University Funds—Unrestricted		43,000
Fund Balances—U.S. Government Grants Refundable		35,000

Separate subsidiary Fund Balances accounts should be kept for the individual restricted loan funds in order to facilitate the preparation of periodic reports to the grantors, and to provide for appropriate compliance audits.

Deductions from the Fund Balances accounts of the loan funds for amounts refunded to grantors are summarized in the following entry:

19. Fund Balances—U.S. Government Grants Refundable	20,000	
Cash		20,000

Loans were made during the year in the amount of $260,000, and other loans were repaid in the amount of $95,000. Additionally, a year-end adjusting entry was made to increase the Allowance for Uncollectible Loans for expected write-offs in the amount of $2,000. These transactions and events are recorded by Entries 20a, 20b, and 20c.

20a. Loans to Students, Faculty, and Staff	260,000	
Cash		260,000
20b. Cash	95,000	
Loans to Students, Faculty, and Staff		95,000
20c. Fund Balances—U.S. Government Grants Refundable	2,000	
Allowance for Uncollectible Loans		2,000

Endowment and Similar Funds

Midwest University records and reports separately the Fund Balances for Endowment, Term Endowment, Funds Functioning as Endowment (FFAE)—Unrestricted, and Funds Functioning as Endowment (FFAE)—Restricted funds in the endowment and similar funds category. Each category of Fund Balance should, of course, be supported by subsidiary records to show the balance for each individual endowment. The account balances of Midwest University's endowment and similar funds as of July 1, 1999, are as follows:

	Debits	Credits
Cash	$ 60,000	
Investments	8,250,000	
Fund Balances—Endowment		$6,150,000
Fund Balances—Term Endowment		1,180,000
Fund Balances—Funds Functioning as Endowment—Restricted		350,000
Fund Balances—Funds Functioning as Endowment—Unrestricted		630,000
	$8,310,000	$8,310,000

The additions to the Fund Balances of this fund group and unrestricted transfers to the group are summarized by the following entries.

21. Cash	2,150,000	
Fund Balances—Endowment		1,090,000
Fund Balances—Term Endowment		550,000
Fund Balances—Funds Functioning as Endowment—		
Unrestricted		510,000

Fund Balances—Term Endowment was reduced in the amount of $98,000 for an expired term endowment restricted for use in the Unexpended Plant Funds. The effect of this transaction is shown in Entry 32 under Unexpended Plant Funds.

22. Fund Balances—Term Endowment	98,000	
Cash		98,000

Investments with a carrying value of $2,000,000 were sold for $2,159,000; the increase in value was allocated $109,000 to Fund Balances—Endowment and $50,000 to Fund Balances—Funds Functioning as Endowment—Unrestricted. Of the latter amount, $25,000 was appropriated for use in Unrestricted Current Funds. Investments costing $4,200,000 were purchased:

23a. Cash	2,159,000	
Fund Balances—Endowment		109,000
Fund Balances—Funds Functioning as Endowment—		
Unrestricted		50,000
Investments		2,000,000
23b. Fund Balances—Funds Functioning as Endowment—		
Unrestricted	25,000	
Cash		25,000
23c. Investments	4,200,000	
Cash		4,200,000

It should be noted that many public universities maintain separate foundations that have the objective of obtaining contributions and endowments. In those cases, note disclosure should disclose the existence of those foundations, and the amount of investment income or other monies received from them. Related entities are discussed later in this chapter.

Annuity and Life Income Funds

The annuity and life income funds had the following account balances as of July 1, 1999:

	Debits	Credits
Annuity Funds:		
Cash	$ 40,000	
Investments	2,600,000	
Annuities Payable		$1,700,000
Fund Balances		940,000
Life Income Funds:		
Cash	30,000	
Investments	2,040,000	
Income Payable		20,000
Fund Balances		2,050,000
	$4,710,000	$4,710,000

Note that Midwest University's annuity funds have a large balance in the Annuities Payable account. That amount represents the present value of future payments due under the annuity agreements. The liability in the life income funds reflects only the currently unpaid portion of income due contributors, as explained in a previous section. During the fiscal year ended June 30, 2000, cash in the amount of $487,000 was received from new annuity fund contributors. The actuarial annuities payable relating to these annuities were $385,000; the remainder added to Fund Balance. Also, during the year, annuitants were paid $250,000 and additional investments were purchased in the amount of $225,000. The effects of these transactions are summarized by the following entries.

24. Cash—Annuity Funds	487,000	
Annuities Payable		385,000
Fund Balances—Annuity Funds		102,000
25. Annuities Payable	250,000	
Cash—Annuity Funds		250,000
26. Investments	225,000	
Cash—Annuity Funds		225,000

Transactions for the life income funds are summarized by the following entries:

27. Cash—Life Income Funds	325,000	
Fund Balances—Life Income Funds		325,000

28. Investments	325,000	
Cash—Life Income Funds		325,000

Additional entries would be required for the receipt of investment income and the simultaneous recording of liabilities to the life income recipients. These transactions do not flow through the Statement of Changes in Fund Balances because the income is a liability, not a resource of the fund.

Plant Funds

Recall that the Plant Funds group consists of four distinct subgroups: (1) Unexpended Plant Funds, (2) Funds for Renewals and Replacements, (3) Funds for Retirement of Indebtedness, and (4) Investment in Plant. Account balances for the four plant fund subgroups as of July 1, 1999, are as follows:

	Debits	*Credits*
Unexpended Plant Funds:		
Cash	$ 250,000	
Investments	1,400,000	
Fund Balances—Restricted		$ 1,300,000
Fund Balances—Unrestricted		350,000
	$ 1,650,000	$ 1,650,000
Funds for Renewals and Replacements:		
Cash	$ 10,000	
Investments	305,000	
Fund Balances—Restricted		$ 275,000
Fund Balances—Unrestricted		40,000
	$ 315,000	$ 315,000
Funds for Retirement of Indebtedness:		
Cash	$ 35,000	
Deposits with Trustees	350,000	
Fund Balances—Restricted		$ 300,000
Fund Balances—Unrestricted		85,000
	$ 385,000	$ 385,000
Investment in Plant:		
Land	$ 650,000	
Land Improvements	1,300,000	
Buildings	50,000,000	
Equipment	11,000,000	
Library Books	2,000,000	
Notes Payable		$ 700,000
Bonds Payable		25,000,000
Net Investment in Plant		39,250,000
	$64,950,000	$64,950,000

Unexpended Plant Funds account for assets held for the acquisition or construction of property, plant, and equipment. Although the beginning trial balance does not show the account Construction in Progress in either the Unexpended

Plant Funds or the Investment in Plant Funds, financial reporting standards allow it to be reported in either. Entries relating to transactions of the Unexpended Plant Funds are as follows:

Cash for construction of a new laboratory building was received from a state grant in the amount of $220,000, a nonmandatory transfer from Unrestricted Current Funds in the amount of $30,000, and issuance of 8 percent term bonds maturing in five years in the amount of $500,000.

29. Cash	750,000	
Fund Balances—Restricted		220,000
Fund Balances—Unrestricted		30,000
Bonds Payable		500,000

Investments with a carrying value of $330,000 were sold for $350,000. These investments had been purchased with restricted cash.

30. Cash	350,000	
Investments		330,000
Fund Balances—Restricted		20,000

Investment income received in cash was added to the restricted fund balance in the amount of $50,000.

| 31. Cash | 50,000 | |
| Fund Balances—Restricted | | 50,000 |

A term endowment expired in the amount of $98,000 that specified use in the Unexpended Plant Funds.

| 32. Cash | 98,000 | |
| Fund Balances—Restricted | | 98,000 |

During the year, construction expenditures for the laboratory building and other projects amounted to $1,200,000.

| 33. Construction in Progress | 1,200,000 | |
| Cash | | 1,200,000 |

The projects accounted for in Entry 33 were completed at year-end, and the related asset, liability, and Fund Balance accounts were closed in the following assumed amounts in order to transfer accountability for the asset and liability to the Investment in Plant Funds.

34. Fund Balances—Restricted	500,000	
Fund Balances—Unrestricted	200,000	
Bonds Payable	500,000	
Construction in Progress		1,200,000

Funds for Renewals and Replacements exist to provide a mechanism to accumulate resources for rehabilitation and replacement of existing facilities. Often, in practice, this subgroup is used to account for construction (mainly remodeling) activities, as is the case for Midwest University in the transactions recorded below.

Investment income in the amount of $10,000 and a mandatory transfer from the Unrestricted Current Funds (see Entry 4a) in the amount of $185,000 were received and added to Fund Balances—Restricted.

35. Cash	195,000	
Fund Balances—Restricted		195,000

Restricted investments with a carrying value of $145,000 were sold for $155,000.

36. Cash	155,000	
Investments		145,000
Fund Balances—Restricted		10,000

Restricted fund balances used for renovations and replacements totaled $300,000; none of this amount was capitalized.

37. Fund Balances—Restricted	300,000	
Cash		300,000

Funds for Retirement of Indebtedness are accounted for in a manner similar to debt service funds of state and local governmental units (except that resource inflows and outflows are additions to and deductions from fund balance rather than revenues and expenditures). Midwest University deposits investments of this subgroup with trustees. The following entries summarize the activities of this subgroup:

Cash in the amount of $2,065,000 was received from a state appropriation, a private gift, investment earnings, and in the amount of $360,000 from a mandatory transfer from the Unrestricted Current Funds. The total amount was added to Fund Balances—Restricted.

38. Cash	2,425,000	
Fund Balances—Restricted		2,425,000

Interest and principal payments were made on notes and bonds payable; $50,000 was from previously accumulated unrestricted funds. (See Entry 42 for the related effect on bond principal in the Investment in Plant Funds.)

39. Fund Balances—Restricted	2,350,000	
Fund Balances—Unrestricted	50,000	
Cash		2,400,000

During the year, there was a net increase in cash deposited with trustees in the amount of $23,000.

40. Deposits with Trustees	23,000	
Cash		23,000

The Investment in Plant subgroup of plant funds consists of fixed asset accounts; debt related to the fixed assets; and an equity account, Net Investment in Plant. As mentioned earlier in this chapter, governmentally owned colleges and universities may choose, under GASB standards, either to record, or not to record, depreciation. FASB standards, on the other hand, require nongovernmentally owned colleges and universities to record depreciation on fixed assets. Governmentally owned colleges and universities that opt to record depreciation will make the entry in the Investment in Plant subgroup as follows:

Net Investment in Plant	xx,xxx	
Allowance for Depreciation		xx,xxx

Midwest University is a state university and chooses not to record depreciation. The entries below record transactions affecting the Investment in Plant subgroup.

During the year, the following plant acquisitions were made from all funds, including current funds acquisition of equipment, library books, and so on. Note the additions to the Buildings and Bonds Payable accounts related to completion of the projects in Entry 34. The $250,000 for equipment and $40,000 for library books shown in the following entry were included in Entries 3 and 8 of the Unrestricted Current Funds.

41. Buildings	1,200,000	
Equipment	250,000	
Library Books	40,000	
Bonds Payable		500,000
Net Investment in Plant		990,000

Principal was paid on notes and bonds as shown in Entry 39. This action increases the equity account.

42. Notes Payable	50,000	
Bonds Payable	500,000	
Net Investment in Plant		550,000

Certain facilities were scrapped or sold:

43. Net Investment in Plant	210,000	
Land Improvements		110,000
Equipment		100,000

It should be emphasized that, unlike state and local governments in which proprietary fund fixed assets and long-term debt are accounted for differently from general fixed assets and long-term debt, college and university accounting, under the AICPA model, does not distinguish between the fixed assets and related long-term debt of auxiliary enterprises and those of educational and general activities; both are accounted for in the same manner in the Investment in Plant subgroup.

Agency Funds

Agency funds do not have fund balance accounts; therefore, additions to and deductions from agency funds should not be reported in the Statement of Changes in Fund Balances. A Statement of Changes in Assets and Liabilities of Agency Funds could be reported, as illustrated in Chapter 8 (Illustration 8–3), but this is not generally done by colleges and universities. Assets and offsetting liabilities of Agency Funds are reported in the Balance Sheet (see Illustrations 18–1 and 18–2) as a matter of disclosure of the existence of the agency relationship. Account balances for the agency funds as of July 1, 1999, were as follows:

	Debits	Credits
Cash	$ 80,000	
Investments	220,000	
Deposits Held in Custody for Others		$300,000
	$300,000	$300,000

Assume student groups and others deposited $130,000; $110,000 in withdrawals were made; and $60,000 in cash was invested:

44. Cash	130,000	
Deposits Held in Custody for Others		130,000
45. Deposits Held in Custody for Others	110,000	
Cash		110,000
46. Investments	60,000	
Cash		60,000

Detailed records should be kept for each student group and for others for which the college or university is acting as agent.

Illustrative Financial Statements (AICPA Model)

Illustrations 18–1 through 18–4 present the three required financial statements for governmentally owned colleges and universities that follow the AICPA model.

The Balance Sheet (Illustration 18–1) presents funds arranged sequentially in vertical order ("pancake" format); a columnar approach is presented in Illustration 18–2. Note that in all cases, restricted and unrestricted fund balance accounts are disclosed separately. Some colleges and universities choose, as permitted by current standards, to present combined information for the Plant Funds group, with separate disclosure of the Fund Balance amounts for the four subgroups.

The Statement of Current Funds Revenues, Expenditures, and Other Changes (Illustration 18–3) presents those revenues and expenditures that have been recognized, as well as other Fund Balance changes, separately, for the unrestricted and restricted portions. Note that the revenues equal the expenditures for the Restricted Current Funds; remember that revenues are recognized only after the expenditures are recognized. The $49,000 "Excess of Restricted Receipts over Transfers to Revenues" represents the total additions to Fund Balance (see Illustration 18–4) of $1,109,000 less the indirect cost recoveries of $35,000 less the revenues recognized of $1,025,000. Note also that Mandatory Transfers are reported together with Expenditures, while "other changes" are reported separately.

Illustration 18–1

MIDWEST UNIVERSITY
Balance Sheet
June 30, 2000
(with comparative figures at June 30, 1999)

Assets

	Current Year	Prior Year
Current funds:		
Unrestricted:		
Cash	$ 150,000	$ 60,000
Investments	428,000	300,000
Accounts receivable, less allowance of $18,000 both years	87,000	130,000
Inventories, at lower of cost (first-in, first-out basis) or market	95,000	80,000
Prepaid expenses and deferred charges	29,000	20,000
Total unrestricted	789,000	590,000
Restricted:		
Cash	161,000	90,000
Investments	265,000	250,000
Accounts receivable	23,000	50,000
Total restricted	449,000	390,000
Total current funds	$ 1,238,000	$ 980,000
Loan funds:		
Cash	$ 43,000	$ 20,000
Investments	98,000	98,000
Loans to students, faculty, and staff, less allowance of $12,000 current year and $10,000 prior year	613,000	450,000
Total loan funds	$ 754,000	$ 568,000
Endowment and similar funds:		
Cash	$ 46,000	$ 60,000
Investments	10,450,000	8,250,000
Total endowment and similar funds	$10,496,000	$ 8,310,000

Liabilities and Fund Balances

	Current Year	Prior Year
Current Funds:		
Unrestricted:		
Accounts payable	$ 217,000	$ 100,000
Accrued liabilities	7,000	15,000
Students deposits	30,000	35,000
Deferred revenues	35,000	20,000
Fund balance	500,000	420,000
Total unrestricted	789,000	590,000
Restricted:		
Accounts payable	50,000	40,000
Fund balances	399,000	350,000
Total restricted	499,000	390,000
Total current funds	$ 1,238,000	$ 980,000
Loan funds:		
Fund balances:		
U.S. government grants refundable	$ 218,000	$ 205,000
University funds		
Restricted	168,000	38,000
Unrestricted	368,000	325,000
Total loan funds	$ 754,000	$ 568,000
Endowment and similar funds:		
Fund balances:		
Endowment	$ 7,349,000	$ 6,150,000
Term endowment	1,632,000	1,180,000
Funds functioning as endowment— unrestricted	1,165,000	630,000
Funds functioning as endowment— restricted	350,000	350,000
Total endowment and similar funds	$10,496,000	$ 8,310,000

Assets

Annuity funds:		
Cash	$ 52,000	$ 40,000
Investments	2,825,000	2,600,000
Total annuity funds	2,877,000	2,640,000
Life income funds:		
Cash	30,000	30,000
Investments	2,365,000	2,040,000
Total life income funds	2,395,000	2,070,000
Total annuity and life income funds	$ 5,272,000	$ 4,710,000
Plant funds:		
Unexpended:		
Cash	$ 298,000	$ 250,000
Investments	1,070,000	1,400,000
Total unexpended	1,368,000	1,650,000
Renewals and replacements:		
Cash	60,000	10,000
Investments	160,000	305,000
Total renewals and replacements	220,000	315,000
Retirement of indebtedness:		
Cash	37,000	35,000
Deposits with trustees	373,000	350,000
Total retirement of indebtedness	410,000	385,000
Investment in plant:		
Land	650,000	650,000
Land improvements	1,190,000	1,300,000
Buildings	51,200,000	50,000,000
Equipment	11,150,000	11,000,000
Library books	2,040,000	2,000,000
Total investment in plant	66,230,000	64,950,000
Total plant funds	$68,228,000	$67,300,000
Agency funds:		
Cash	$ 40,000	$ 80,000
Investments	280,000	220,000
Total agency funds	$ 320,000	$ 300,000

Liabilities and Fund Balances

Annuity funds:		
Annuities payable	$ 1,835,000	$ 1,700,000
Fund balances	1,042,000	940,000
Total annuity funds	2,877,000	2,640,000
Life income funds:		
Income payable	20,000	20,000
Fund balances	2,375,000	2,050,000
Total life income funds	2,395,000	2,070,000
Total annuity and life income funds	$ 5,272,000	$ 4,710,000
Plant funds:		
Unexpended:		
Fund balances:		
Restricted	$ 1,188,000	$ 1,300,000
Unrestricted	180,000	350,000
Total unexpended	1,368,000	1,650,000
Renewals and replacements:		
Fund balances:		
Restricted	180,000	275,000
Unrestricted	40,000	40,000
Total renewals and replacements	220,000	315,000
Retirement of indebtedness:		
Fund balances:		
Restricted	375,000	300,000
Unrestricted	35,000	85,000
Total retirement of indebtedness	410,000	385,000
Investment in plant:		
Notes payable	650,000	700,000
Bonds payable	25,000,000	25,000,000
Net investment in plant	40,580,000	39,250,000
Total investment in plant	66,230,000	64,950,000
Total plant funds	$68,228,000	$67,300,000
Agency funds:		
Deposits held in custody for others	$ 320,000	$ 300,000
Total agency funds	$ 320,000	$ 300,000

Illustration 18–2

MIDWEST UNIVERSITY
Balance Sheet (Alternate Form)
As of June 30, 2000, with comparative totals at June 30, 1999
(in thousands)

	Unrestricted	Restricted	Loan Funds	Endowment and Similar Funds	Annuity and Life Income Funds	Plant Funds	Agency Funds	Totals FY 2000	Totals FY 1999
Assets									
Cash	$150	$161	$43	$46	$82	$395	$40	$917	$675
Deposits with trustees						373		373	350
Investments	428	265	98	10,450	5,190	1,230	280	17,941	15,463
Accounts receivable (net)	87	23						110	180
Loans receivable			613					613	450
Inventories	95							95	80
Prepaid expenses and deferred charges	29							29	20
Total current assets	789	449	754	10,496	5,272	1,998	320	20,078	17,233
Land						650		650	650
Land improvements						1,190		1,190	1,300
Buildings						51,200		51,200	50,000
Equipment						11,150		11,150	11,000
Library books						2,040		2,040	2,000
Total assets	$789	$449	$754	$10,496	$5,272	$68,228	$320	$86,308	$82,168
Liabilities and Fund Balances									
Liabilities:									
Accounts payable	$217	$50						$267	$140
Accrued liabilities	7							7	15
Students' deposits	30							30	35
Deferred revenues	35							35	20
Annuities payable					$1,835			1,835	1,700
Income payable					20			20	20
Deposits held in custody for others							$320	320	300
Total current liabilities	289	50			1,855		320	2,514	2,230
Notes payable						$ 650		650	700
Bonds payable						25,000		25,000	25,000
Total liabilities	289	1,905				25,650	320	28,164	27,930
Fund Balances:									
Current	500	399						899	770
Loan			$754					754	568
Endowment and similar				$10,496				10,496	8,310
Annuity and life income					3,417			3,417	2,990
Plant Funds:									
Unexpended						1,368		1,368	1,650
Renewals and replacements						220		220	315
Retirement of indebtedness						410		410	385
Net investment in plant						40,580		40,580	39,250
Total fund balances	500	399	754	10,496	3,417	42,578		58,144	54,238
Total liabilities and fund balances	$789	$449	$754	$10,496	$5,272	$68,228	$320	$86,308	$82,168

Illustration 18–3

MIDWEST UNIVERSITY
Statement of Current Funds Revenues, Expenditures, and Other Changes
Year Ended June 30, 2000

	Current Year			Prior-Year Total
	Unrestricted	*Restricted*	*Total*	
Revenues:				
Tuition and fees	$2,690,000		$2,690,000	$2,300,000
Federal appropriations	230,000		230,000	200,000
State appropriations	2,150,000		2,150,000	2,050,000
Federal grants and contracts	35,000	$ 400,000	435,000	430,000
Private gifts, grants, and contracts	40,000	410,000	450,000	445,000
Endowment income	880,000	215,000	1,095,000	950,000
Sales and services of auxiliary enterprises	2,300,000		2,300,000	1,975,000
Other sources	28,000		28,000	23,000
Total current revenues	8,353,000	1,025,000	9,378,000	8,373,000
Expenditures and mandatory transfers:				
Educational and general:				
Instruction	3,298,000	496,000	3,794,000	3,282,000
Research	220,000	404,000	624,000	701,000
Public service	146,000	25,000	171,000	180,000
Academic support	232,000		232,000	231,000
Student services	207,000		207,000	204,000
Institutional support	425,000		425,000	410,000
Operation and maintenance of plant	230,000		230,000	227,000
Scholarships and fellowships	377,000	100,000	477,000	456,000
Educational and general expenditures	5,135,000	1,025,000	6,160,000	5,691,000
Mandatory transfers for:				
Principal and interest	120,000		120,000	116,000
Renewals and replacements	100,000		100,000	97,000
Loan fund matching grant	3,000		3,000	2,000
Total educational and general	5,358,000	1,025,000	6,383,000	5,906,000
Auxiliary enterprises:				
Expenditures	2,035,000		2,035,000	1,698,000
Mandatory transfers for:				
Principal and interest	240,000		240,000	246,000
Renewals and replacements	85,000		85,000	85,000
Total auxiliary enterprises	2,360,000		2,360,000	2,029,000
Total expenditures and mandatory transfers	7,718,000	1,025,000	8,743,000	7,935,000
Other transfers and additions (deductions):				
Excess of restricted receipts over transfers to revenues		49,000	49,000	40,000
Unrestricted gifts allocated to other funds	(580,000)		(580,000)	(400,000)
Portion of funds functioning as endowment gains appropriated	25,000		25,000	
Net increase in fund balances	$ 80,000	$ 49,000	$ 129,000	$ 78,000

Illustration 18–4

MIDWEST UNIVERSITY
Statement of Changes in Fund Balances
Year Ended June 30, 2000

	Current Funds		Loan Funds	Endowment and Similar Funds	Annuity and Life Income Funds	Plant Funds			
	Unrestricted	Restricted				Unexpended	Renewals and Replacements	Retirement of Indebtedness	Investment in Plant
Revenues and other additions:									
Unrestricted current fund revenues	$8,353,000								
Expired term endowment—restricted						$ 98,000			
State appropriations—restricted		$ 525,000						$1,800,000	
Federal grants and contracts—restricted						220,000			
State grants and contracts—restricted									
Private gifts, grants, and contracts—restricted		400,000	$115,000	$1,640,000	$ 427,000				
Investment income—restricted		184,000	8,000			50,000	$10,000	260,000	
Realized gains on investments—unrestricted				50,000					
Realized gains on investments—restricted				109,000		20,000	10,000	5,000	
Interest on loans receivable			7,000						
U.S. government advances			35,000						
Expended for plant facilities (including $290,000 charged to current funds expenditures)									$ 990,000
Retirement of indebtedness									550,000
Total revenues and other additions	8,353,000	1,109,000	165,000	1,799,000	427,000	388,000	20,000	2,065,000	1,540,000
Expenditures and other deductions:									
Educational and general expenditures	5,135,000	1,025,000							
Auxiliary enterprises	2,035,000								
Indirect costs recovered		35,000							
Refunded to grantors			20,000						
Loan cancellations and write-offs			2,000						
Expended for plant facilities (including noncapitalized expenditures of $300,000)						700,000	300,000		
Retirement of indebtedness								550,000	
Interest on indebtedness								1,850,000	
Disposal of plant facilities									210,000
Expired term endowments ($98,000 restricted to plant)				98,000					
Total expenditures and other deductions	7,170,000	1,060,000	22,000	98,000		700,000	300,000	2,400,000	210,000
Transfers among funds—additions (deductions):									
Mandatory:									
Principal and interest	(360,000)							360,000	
Renewals and replacements	(185,000)						185,000		
Loan fund matching grant	(3,000)		3,000						
Unrestricted gifts allocated	(580,000)		40,000	510,000		30,000			
Portion of unrestricted funds functioning as endowment funds investment gains appropriated	25,000			(25,000)					
Total transfers	(1,103,000)		43,000	485,000		30,000	185,000	360,000	
Net increase (decrease) for the year	80,000	49,000	186,000	2,186,000	427,000	(282,000)	(95,000)	25,000	1,330,000
Fund balance at beginning of year	420,000	350,000	568,000	8,310,000	2,990,000	1,650,000	315,000	385,000	39,250,000
Fund balance at end of year	$ 500,000	$ 399,000	$754,000	$10,496,000	$3,417,000	$1,368,000	$220,000	$ 410,000	$40,580,000

The Statement of Changes in Fund Balances (Illustration 18–4) presents *all* of the changes in the Fund Balance accounts of all except the agency funds. The only "Revenues" in this statement are reported in the Unrestricted Current Funds. All other amounts represent direct credits to the Fund Balance accounts. Similarly, the only "Expenditures" in this statement are reported in the Current Funds, both Unrestricted and Restricted. All other amounts represent direct debits to Fund Balances, as described in this chapter. Students should compare how the net increases in Fund Balance for the current funds are presented in Illustrations 18–3 and 18–4.

Private (Nongovernmentally Owned) Colleges and Universities

Setting accounting and financial reporting standards for private colleges and universities, as noted at the beginning of this chapter, is the responsibility of the FASB. Until 1993, with the exception that private colleges and universities were required by FASB *Statement No. 93* to report depreciation of their plant assets, most colleges and universities, both public and private, used the AICPA College Guide model—the model for which illustrative transactions and financial statements have been provided earlier in this chapter. The issuance of FASB *Statement No. 116*, "Accounting for Contributions Received and Contributions Made," and FASB *Statement No. 117*, "Financial Statements of Not-for-Profit Organizations," in 1993, marked a significant divergence in the accounting and reporting standards applicable to public and private colleges and universities.

Private colleges and universities now report on the changes in unrestricted, temporarily restricted, and permanently restricted net assets of the entity as a whole, as do the other nongovernmental not-for-profit organizations described in Chapter 16. The reader is directed back to that chapter for more information on the definitions of net asset classifications and the considerable discretion that is allowed by *SFAS No. 117* in presenting financial information, including optional display of supplementary fund accounting information, if desired. Some of the major differences that now exist between the financial statements of private and public institutions of higher education are in the areas of contributions, tuition revenue, and functional expenses. These issues are discussed next, as well as some accounting issues in the AICPA Audit and Accounting Guide *Not-for-Profit Organizations* and *SFAS No. 116* that are particularly relevant to private colleges and universities.

Contributions

Private colleges and universities may depend more on contributions from alumni and other supporters and research grants to keep tuition costs reasonable than do public institutions that receive relatively more state funding. However, this distinction is becoming less evident as public universities recognize the benefits of increasing endowments to decrease reliance on volatile state funding and constrained tuition support. For example, recent capital campaigns have brought the endowment balances at public universities (e.g., University of Texas System,

$5.7 billion; and University of California, $2.6 billion) much closer to that of private colleges and universities (e.g., Harvard University, $8.8 billion; and Yale University, $4.9 billion).[12] Endowments are permanently restricted net assets that result from nonexchange transactions.

Nonexchange Transactions.   *SFAS No. 116* and the AICPA Audit and Accounting Guide *Not-for-Profit Organizations* distinguish between (1) nonexchange transactions, such as contributions in which the donor does not expect anything of value in return, and (2) exchange transactions in which there is *quid pro quo* or expectation by each party that goods or services will be exchanged between the parties at fair values. Contributions by donors are considered nonexchange transactions as long as the donor does not receive any direct benefits from the donation. Contributions are recognized as income in the period in which they are made, and then reported as increases in either unrestricted, temporarily restricted, or permanently restricted net assets, depending on the stipulation of the donor. If a contribution is conditioned upon a future event, such as obtaining matching funds, then the university waits until the condition has been met before recording the contribution revenue. This discussion applies to promises to give, even though they may not be legally enforceable; however, *intentions to give*, such as naming a university in a will, are not recognized as revenue or considered a promise because the potential donor can change the will at any time.

Grants, Awards, and Scholarships.   Grants and other assistance given by governments, foundations, or corporations may be nonexchange or exchange transactions, depending upon whether the resource provider directly benefits by receiving something of value through the transaction. For example, a federal research grant given to a university in which the value received by the agency is incidental to the public benefit from using the assets transferred is considered a *nonexchange* transaction; consequently, it is recognized as revenue in the period in which the contribution is made and classified as an increase to temporarily restricted net assets. On the other hand, if a federal agency enters into a contract in which the university tests a product and any patent or other results of the activity are retained by the federal agency, then that transaction would be considered an *exchange* transaction and not a contribution; consequently, this transaction results in an increase to unrestricted net assets because only donors in exchange transactions can restrict net assets.[13]

Public universities record restricted grant, gift, and scholarships that are nonexchange transactions as *additions* to current restricted fund balances until the appropriate expenditures are made as the resource provider intends.[14] At the point of expenditure, an equal amount is credited to revenue and debited to fund balance in the current restricted fund. If a grant or contract is considered an exchange

---

[12]*NACUBO Endowment Study* (Washington, DC: NACUBO, 1996), p. 15.

[13]AICPA, Audit and Accounting Guide *Not-for-Profit Organizations* (AAG-NPO) (New York: AICPA, 1996), 5.16.

[14]These funds are often called **Expendable Restricted Funds** or Sponsored Research Funds.

transaction, then *deferred revenue* is credited when the funds are received, and revenue is recognized (and deferred revenue is decreased) as the appropriate expenditures are made. As can be seen, both the timing and method of recognizing revenue from restricted grants, awards, and scholarships differ significantly between public and private institutions.

Tuition Revenue

The AICPA Guide *Not-for-Profit Organizations*, which applies to private colleges and universities, departs from the AICPA Guide *Audits of Colleges and Universities* by requiring that tuition revenue be reported net of tuition discounts and scholarships.[15] Public institutions continue to deduct only tuition refunds from gross tuition revenue and report scholarships and discounts as expenditures.

Functional Expenses

The AICPA Guide *Not-for-Profit Organizations* also requires that expenses that relate to more than one function, such as occupancy costs, including operation and maintenance of the plant, repairs and renovations, retirement of the plant, and interest and other expenses, be allocated to the programs or functional expenses to which they pertain.[16] It is not difficult to assign direct expenses, such as travel, to various functions; however, in order to allocate indirect expenses, such as occupancy costs or interest expense, a reasonable allocation basis must be employed. That basis may be square footage of space occupied by each program, or personnel costs. There appears to be a difference of opinion as to whether CPA firms consider the language in the AICPA Audit and Accounting Guide prescriptive or suggestive. For example, for fiscal years ending June 30, 1997, several institutions audited by large CPA firms reported plant and interest costs as separate line or object items, rather than allocating them across programs.

Other Reporting Issues

Split-Interest Gifts. Colleges and universities are often parties to split-interest agreements, such as charitable lead and remainder trusts, charitable gift annuities, and pooled life income funds. In these cases the institution shares either the income from an investment or the investment itself with the donor and sometimes other beneficiaries. These gifts may be established as trusts with the assets held by a third party. If the institution has an interest in an irrevocable split-interest agreement, then the assets received should be recorded at their fair value when received, or the present value of the interest in future income or assets should be recorded.[17] Any liabilities agreed to, such as to pay the donor-stipulated amounts, should also be recorded at the time of the agreement. Chapter 6 of the AICPA Audit and Accounting Guide *Not-for-Profit Organizations* presents more detailed information on accounting for split-interest agreements.

Collections. Many colleges and universities have historical archives, libraries, and museums containing valuable works of art, historical treasures, and similar

---

[15]AICPA, AAG-NPO, 12.05.
[16]Ibid., 13.42–45.
[17]Ibid., 6.04.

assets. As is the case under the AICPA model, FASB *Statement No. 116* provides for note disclosure of such assets rather than reporting them on the Balance Sheet; however, *Statement No. 116* permits nonrecognition only if the donated items are added to **collections** that meet the conditions given below:

a. Are held for public exhibition, education, or research in furtherance of public service rather than financial gain.
b. Are protected, kept unencumbered, cared for, and preserved.
c. Are subject to an organizational policy that requires the proceeds from sales of collection items to be used to acquire other items for collections.

The clear intent of the *Statement No. 116* criteria is to permit nonrecognition of contributions of valuable collections *only* if the collection is to be maintained to serve the public interest rather than to achieve financial gain from trading in collectible items.

Gifts in Kind.   Contributions of noncash, tangible assets to a college or university are called **gifts in kind.**[18] If these gifts can be used or sold by the institution, they should be recorded in the period received at their fair value. If the donor has stipulated that the assets should be distributed to a third party and the school does not have discretion over the disposition of the assets, then the university is acting as an agent and the gift should not be recorded as a contribution. The university may also receive items, such as tickets or merchandise, that are to be given to the ultimate resource provider at a fund-raising event, for example, an auction for the university's public radio station. In these cases, the value of the contribution to be recognized is initially the fair value of the gift in kind plus any additional amount paid by the ultimate donor (i.e., the listener to the radio station). Of course, if the item is auctioned off for less than the initial fair value, then the contribution revenue should be decreased for the difference between the ultimate amount paid and fair value at the date of the gift to the university.

Contributed Services.   Although contributed service by unpaid volunteers is generally less important for colleges and universities than for other not-for-profit organizations, such as community service organizations and churches, some colleges and universities do utilize volunteers extensively for fund-raising and other activities, and, in the case of religious colleges, for instruction. *Statement No. 116* permits recognition of contributed services at their fair value if the services received create or enhance a nonfinancial asset (e.g., property and equipment) or (1) would need to be purchased by the organization, (2) require specialized skills, and (3) are provided by professionals with those skills. If these criteria are met, then the fair value of the services should be reported as both a contribution and as a salary expense. In any case, reporting the fair value of contributed services is encouraged, if practicable.[19]

---

[18]Ibid., 5.06–5.08.
[19]Ibid., 5.39–5.40.

Illustrations 18–5, 18–6, and 18–7 present the Statement of Financial Position, Statement of Activities, and Statement of Cash Flows, respectively, for Valley College, a hypothetical private not-for-profit college.

Illustration 18–5

VALLEY COLLEGE
Statement of Financial Position
June 30, 2000

Assets

Cash and cash equivalents	$ 1,590,953
Accrued interest on investments	1,344,201
Accounts receivable, less allowance for doubtful accounts of $8,833	588,840
Inventories, at average cost	969,287
Prepaid expenses	415,556
Loans receivable, less allowance for doubtful loans of $52,600	1,906,535
Pledges receivable, less allowance for doubtful pledges of $50,000	5,550,000
Long-term investments, at market, cost of $150,645,430	161,785,400
Property, plant, and equipment, net of accumulated depreciation of $10,174,082	23,417,628
Total Assets	$197,568,400

Liabilities and Net Assets

Liabilities:	
Accounts payable and accrued expenses	$ 1,481,908
Deposits and agency funds	385,476
Annuities payable	1,408,550
Deferred revenue	62,237
Advances from federal government for student loans	124,557
Notes payable	889,934
Bonds payable	5,500,000
Total Liabilities	9,852,662
Net Assets:	
Unrestricted	73,690,687
Temporarily restricted	23,279,442
Permanently restricted	90,745,609
Total Net Assets	187,715,738
Total Liabilities and Net Assets	$197,568,400

Illustration 18–6

VALLEY COLLEGE
Statement of Activities
Year Ended June 30, 2000

	Unrestricted	Temporarily Restricted	Permanently Restricted	Total
Operating Revenues and Gains:				
Student tuition and fees (net)	$ 1,348,685	$ —	$ —	$ 1,348,685
Government grants for student aid	1,166,566	—	—	1,166,566
Endowment income	6,112,895	—	—	6,112,895
Gifts and donations	2,341,276	—	—	2,341,276
Sales and services of auxiliary enterprises	7,440,722	—	—	7,440,722
Capital gains on investments utilized	258,002	—	—	258,002
Net assets released from restriction	756,194	(756,194)	—	—
Total operating revenues and gains	19,424,340	(756,194)		18,668,146
Operating Expenses and Losses:				
Educational and general expense:				
Instruction	4,581,405	—	—	4,581,405
Public service	1,236,283	—	—	1,236,283
Academic support	149,158	—	—	149,158
Student services	2,830,384	—	—	2,830,384
Institutional support	3,045,734	—	—	3,045,734
Total educational and general expense	11,842,964			11,842,964
Auxiliary enterprises	7,435,036	—	—	7,435,036
Annuity and life income payments	412,648	—	—	412,648
Total operating expenses and losses	19,690,648			19,690,648
Excess of operating expenses and losses over operating revenues and gains	(266,308)	(756,194)		(1,022,502)
Nonoperating Activities:				
Gifts and bequests	2,255,736	1,247,639	892,464	4,395,839
Investment income	587,223	407,481	110,515	1,105,219
Capital gains utilized	3,717,237	173,025	5,389,703	9,279,965
Net assets reclassified from temporarily restricted net assets	—	(28,741)	28,741	—
Matured annuity and life income funds	21,746	(57,346)	35,600	—
Refunds to federal government	—	—	(10,458)	(10,458)
Change in net assets from nonoperating activities	6,581,942	1,742,058	6,446,565	14,770,565
Total change in net assets	6,315,634	985,864	6,446,565	13,748,063
Net assets at beginning of year	67,375,053	22,293,578	84,299,044	173,967,675
Net assets at end of year	$73,690,687	$23,279,442	$90,745,609	$187,715,738

Illustration 18–7

VALLEY COLLEGE
Statement of Cash Flows
Year Ended June 30, 2000

Cash Flows from Operating Activities:

Increase in net assets	$13,748,063
Adjustments to reconcile increase in net assets to net cash provided by operating activities:	
Depreciation	878,843
Decrease in pledges receivable	207,500
Decrease in accounts receivable	52,701
Increase in accounts payable and accrued expenses	110,987
Increase in deposits and agency funds	22,366
Increase in annuities payable	355,300
Decrease in deferred revenue	(10,621)
Decrease in advances from federal government	(15,177)
Increase in accrued interest receivable	(922,455)
Increase in prepaid expenses	(161,492)
Increase in inventories	(60,534)
Net capital gains used	(9,537,967)
Interest and dividends restricted for long-term investment	(804,467)
Contributions restricted for long-term investment	(4,603,338)
Adjustment of actuarial liability for annuities payable	(25,395)
Net cash used for operating activities	(765,686)

Cash Flows from Investing Activities:

Proceeds from sale of investments	136,802,105
Purchases of investments	(141,199,838)
Purchases of property, plant, and equipment	(1,380,016)
Loans to students and faculty	(283,781)
Collections of loans to students and faculty	132,725
Net cash used for investing activities	(5,928,805)

Cash Flows from Financing Activities:

Proceeds from contributions restricted for long-term investment	4,603,338
Issuance of long-term debt	3,000,000
Repayment of long-term debt	(3,021,687)
Interest and dividends restricted for long-term investment	804,467
Increase in long-term loans receivable	(151,043)
Net cash provided by financing activities	5,235,075
Net increase in cash and cash equivalents	(1,459,416)
Cash and cash equivalents, beginning of year	3,050,369
Cash and cash equivalents, end of year	$ 1,590,953

Other Accounting Issues

Performance Measures

The performance of the organization is monitored by decision makers, such as internal management (e.g., administrators), oversight bodies (e.g., governing boards, accrediting agencies), funding sources (e.g., governments, donors, grantors, investors), and constituents with a beneficial interest in the school (e.g., students, faculty, alumni). The extent to which these stakeholders use financial information to make their decisions, and the most useful form of financial reporting, continue to be accounting research questions. The objective of audited annual financial statements that conform to generally accepted accounting principles, however, is not to document whether the organization performed efficiently. Consequently, other methods of measuring and reporting performance are being developed.

Public colleges and universities are encouraged to present nonfinancial and nonquantitative information, such as service efforts and accomplishments information, that document how well the organization accomplished its mission.[20] However, many accrediting agencies, and a few states, are requiring assessment of student outcomes, sometimes as a determining factor in funding levels. Some states are requiring standardized norm-based objective exams, although more often the institution is allowed to develop its own measure of outcomes based on mission-based objectives. This approach recognizes that the mission of higher education institutions differs in the weight each one places on instruction, research, and service. Outputs, for example, might be faculty productivity, number of graduates, satisfaction of alumni, or job placements.[21] Outcomes differ from outputs in that they measure the benefits derived by constituents, such as increased knowledge of students. NACUBO, as well as many universities, have projects on benchmarking for process improvement. The best measures would be those that capture the "value added" to the student through the educational process. Although difficult, many universities are measuring the knowledge and skills of students through pretesting upon entering school, and posttesting as the student reaches graduation.[22] There is more discussion about performance evaluation in Chapter 14.

The financial community, through bond-rating agencies, financial analysts, underwriters, and investors, has always evaluated financial performance and the creditworthiness of public institutions that issue tax-exempt debt. Some key ratios they use to evaluate viability, return, and leverage are (1) expendable resources to debt, (2) unrestricted resources to operations, (3) expendable resources to total net assets, (4) total resources per full-time-equivalent student, and (5) maximum debt service coverage.[23]

---

[20]Governmental Accounting Standards Board, *Concepts Statement No. 2*, "Service Efforts and Accomplishments" (Norwalk, CT: GASB, 1994).

[21]Ken Brown and Mary Fischer, "Assessment Measures: Management's Yardstick," *Assessment and Evaluation in Higher Education* 19, no. 3 (1994), pp. 163–74.

[22]J. Gainen and P. Locatelli, *Assessment in the Accounting Curriculum* (Sarasota, FL: AAA, 1995).

[23]See Engstrom and Esmond-Kiger, "Different Formats," pp. 24–25.

Auditing of Colleges and Universities

Most colleges and universities, whether private or public, publish audited financial statements. At a minimum, audits of colleges and universities will be performed in conformity with the generally accepted auditing standards (GAAS) promulgated by the AICPA, as discussed in Chapter 12. Additionally, many colleges and universities, as a condition of accepting federal financial awards, are audited under the auditing standards established by the U.S. General Accounting Office in its publication *Government Auditing Standards* (GAS), also known as the "yellow book," as discussed in Chapter 12. Specifically, if a college or university expends $300,000 or more in federal awards in a given fiscal year, it must have a "single audit" in accordance with the provisions of Office of Management and Budget (OMB) *Circular A-133*, "Audits of States, Local Governments and Nonprofit Organizations." Since the audit requirements for the single audit are described in considerable detail in Chapter 12, they need not be reiterated here.

An item of special emphasis in auditing colleges and universities is to ensure that costs that are unallowable under OMB *Circular A-21*, "Cost Principles for Educational Institutions," are not charged, either as direct costs or indirect costs, to federal grants or contracts. Since 1993, the federal government has devoted an increasing amount of resources to auditing educational institutions that receive federal assistance, in particular their compliance with OMB *Circular A-21*, as well as unrelated business income. The cost principles and administrative requirements under OMB *Circular A-110* are discussed more fully in Chapter 14. Unrelated business income is discussed in Chapter 17. As with single audits of state and local governments, *Circular A-133* audits place heavy emphasis on evaluating the system of internal controls and compliance with applicable laws and regulations, in addition to the traditional audit of the financial statements.

Federal Financial Assistance

The federal government, and sometimes state governments, supports institutions of higher learning in the form of research grants and student loan funds. As mentioned in the previous section on auditing issues, acceptance of federal funds requires reporting back to the grantor and conformance with various cost accounting rules as well as administrative requirements.

Sponsored Research Funds. Research funds received from the federal government are most likely to be in the form of nonexchange transactions, in which the government is not expecting a direct benefit, but rather a report at the end of the grant period as to how the funds were used. In some instances, the organization may contract with the federal government in the form of an exchange transaction, in which the government requires a specific product for the funds paid.

Student Grants and Loans. Student assistance takes various forms: loans or grants, subsidized or unsubsidized, held by the institution or given directly to the student. A Pell grant is one in which the federal government provides funds to the institution, which then selects the recipient.[24] GASB *Statement No. 19* requires that public colleges and universities that follow the AICPA College Guide model must report Pell grants in a restricted current fund rather than an agency fund, as was previously the practice. Additional guidance is available to the auditor in U.S. Department of Education documents, such as *Compliance Audits (Attestation Engagements) of the Federal Student Financial Assistance Program at Participating Institutions* (1997).

Related Entities

Public and private colleges and universities can be complex in their organizational structure, including majority-owned subsidiaries for intellectual property and businesslike enterprises; medical and research facilities; and controlled affiliates for fund-raising, alumni relations, and management of assets. At issue is whether there is sufficient control of one organization over another to combine their financial information under one reporting entity.

Most institutionally related fund-raising and medical foundations are legally separate organizations independent of the public university they serve and, under the criterion established in GASB standards, would not be reported as a component entity of the university.[25] However, it may be misleading to exclude the foundation from the public university's reports if the foundation operates essentially as an agent of the university and is not fiscally independent. At a minimum, note disclosures should be made in the public university's financial report of the existence of these affiliated organizations. Private colleges and universities, although less likely to have independent fund-raising foundations, often have affiliated organizations that should be disclosed in the Notes to the Financial Statements. The FASB's project on consolidations and related entities applies to nongovernmental nonprofit organizations, such as private schools, as well as for-profit entities. The GASB also has a project on affiliated organizations.

Proposed Dual Perspective Model

In the 1997 exposure draft *Basic Financial Statements—and Management's Discussion and Analysis—for Public Colleges and Universities*, the GASB proposed that public colleges and universities report using a dual perspective model. Much like the proposed financial reporting model for state and local governments discussed in Chapter 1, the dual perspective model includes basic financial statements from an entitywide perspective as well as from a fund group perspective. A Management Discussion and Analysis section is also required under the proposal.

---

[24]Pell grants, renamed in 1980 from Basic Educational Opportunity Grants (BEOG) which were first issued in 1973, are covered in Catalog of Federal Domestic Assistance (CFDA) 84.063.

[25]GASB, *Codification*, Sec. 2100.119.

The basic financial statements proposed under the **entitywide perspective** include statements of net assets, changes in net assets, and cash flows designed to give the reader information about the primary institution and its discretely presented component units using accrual accounting (i.e., an economic resources measurement focus). The statements proposed under the **fund group perspective** would give the reader the traditional look at inflows, outflows, and balances of distinctly presented funds in a Balance Sheet and Statement of Revenues, Expenditures, and Other Changes in Fund Balances. Accrual accounting would continue to be used. Among the proposed changes would be the aggregation of the four plant subfunds into a single plant fund. Of course, Notes to the Financial Statements and required supplemental information would still be required. The purpose of the Management Discussion and Analysis is to give the reader more information about why the organization performed as it did the previous year and management's analysis of the financial position at the end of the year.

The proposed reporting model would not be required until fiscal years beginning after June 15, 2000. This recommendation is similar to that presented in the GASB's earlier *Preliminary View*, but different from any of the three models initially proposed in the *Invitation to Comment* (the AICPA model, a consolidated fund balance model, and the *SFAS No. 117* model).[26] Proponents of the GASB dual perspective model believe that there is value in focusing on the entity as a whole, and in providing traditional fund accounting information to decision makers. There seems to be a consensus that the public perceives the higher education industry as a homogenous one in which private and public colleges and universities have more in common than not. Each competes for the same pool of students, faculty, research grants, and federal student loan money. Opponents (for example, the AICPA) believe that the dual perspective model is confusing and presenting statements on the entitywide basis only will allow for more comparability across all organizations in the higher education industry. They have concern about the increased auditing and reporting costs outweighing any benefits of requiring fund basis statements. A compromise might be to make fund-basis financial information **required supplementary information (RSI)** with reconciliations to the entitywide statements. Whatever the near-term outcome, the governmental reporting model project and its public college and university component has certainly shown that accounting standards setting is a dynamic, political process impacted tremendously by technological advances that allow information to be shared among members of constituencies.

---

[26]Governmental Accounting Standards Board, *Preliminary Views of the GASB on Major Issues Related to College and University Reporting Model: Core Financial Statements* (Norwalk, CT: GASB, 1995); *Invitation to Comment College and University Reporting Model* (Norwalk, CT: GASB, 1994).

Key Terms

Annuity funds,   727
Collections,   754
Entitywide perspective,   761
Expendable restricted funds,   752
Fund group perspective,   761
Funds functioning as endowments,   725
Funds for renewals and replacements,   729
Funds for retirement of indebtedness,   729
Gifts in kind,   754
Investment in plant fund,   729
Life income funds,   727

Loan funds,   725
Mandatory transfers,   724
Nonmandatory transfers,   724
Plant funds group,   729
Quasi-endowment funds,   725
Required supplemental information,   761
Spending rate,   726
Split-interest agreements, 727
Term endowment funds,   725
Total return,   726
Unexpended plant funds,   729

Selected References

American Institute of Certified Public Accountants. *Audits of Colleges and Universities,* New York: AICPA, 1973, reprinted in 1994.
_____ . *Statement of Position 74-8.* New York, 1974.
Financial Accounting Standards Board. *Statement of Financial Accounting Standards No. 93.* "Recognition of Depreciation by Not-for-Profit Organizations." Norwalk, CT, 1987.
_____ . *Statement of Financial Accounting Standards No. 116.* "Accounting for Contributions Received and Contributions Made." Norwalk, CT, 1993.
_____ . *Statement of Financial Accounting Standards No. 117.* "Financial Statements of Not-for-Profit Organizations." Norwalk, CT, 1993.
Governmental Accounting Standards Board. *Codification of Governmental Accounting and Financial Reporting Standards as of June 30, 1997.* Norwalk, CT, 1997.
_____ . *Financial Accounting and Reporting Manual for Higher Education* (FARM). Washington, DC. In loose-leaf form with bimonthly updates.
National Center for Higher Education Management Systems. *Higher Education Finance Manual.* Washington, DC: U.S. Government Printing Office, 1980.

Periodicals:
Business Officer. Washington, DC: NACUBO.
The Chronicle of Higher Education. Washington, DC.
Higher Education Director. Falls Church, VA: Higher Education Publications, Inc.

Questions

18–1. Many colleges and universities are governmentally owned; others are privately supported not-for-profit organizations. What bearing does this situation have on the determination of authoritative financial reporting standards for colleges and universities?

18–2. Explain how restricted gifts and grants are accounted for in the Current Funds group of a public college or university that follows the AICPA model. How would such restricted gifts and grants be accounted for and reported by a private college or university that follows FASB *Statement Nos. 116* and *117*?

18–3. "Since revenues and expenditures should not be recognized in Restricted Current Funds, resource inflows and outflows should be accounted for as additions to and deductions from Fund Balance—Restricted." Do you agree? Why or why not?

18–4. Distinguish between expenditures and transfers. How do *mandatory transfers* differ from *nonmandatory transfers*?

18–5. "Colleges and universities are deemed to be presenting financial statements in conformity with GAAP if they report temporary investments of Current Funds at market value and long-term investments of Endowment Funds at cost or amortized cost." Do you agree? Why or why not?

18–6. "Endowment funds of public colleges and universities should be accounted for in the same manner as nonexpendable trust funds of state and local governments." Do you agree? Why or why not?

18–7. Explain fully how the plant fund accounts of a public college or university differ from the General Fixed Assets Account Group of a state or local government.

18–8. "Under FASB standards applicable to private colleges and universities, *all* contributions must be recognized as revenues or gains in the period received." Do you agree? Why or why not?

18–9. Explain the conditions that must exist for a private college or university to avoid accounting recognition of the value of its collections of art, historical treasures, and similar assets.

18–10. Contrast and compare the financial statements required by the FASB for private colleges and universities with those required for public colleges and universities that follow the AICPA model.

18–11. Describe some measures of performance that can be used in assessing whether a university operates effectively.

Cases

18–1. The following is a section taken from the Notes to the Comprehensive Annual Financial Report of the State of Michigan for the fiscal year ended September 30, 1996:

Note 1—Summary of Significant Accounting Policies

A. *Reporting Entity* (selected)

Ten of the State's public universities are considered component units because they have boards appointed by the primary government. These universities all follow the American Institute of Certified Public Accountants Industry Audit Guide, *Audits of Colleges and Universities* (the AICPA model). The universities' operating results are reflected in the Combined Statement of Changes in Fund Balances and the Combined Statement of Current Funds Revenues, Expenditures, Transfers, and Changes in Fund Balances. These statements are unique to the AICPA model and only a "Component Units" column appears on these statements because the State has no institutions of higher education that are part of the primary government. Michigan State University, the University of Michigan, and Wayne State University are *not* included in the State's reporting entity because they have separately elected governing boards and are legally separate. The State provides significant funding to support these institutions; however, under the GASB *Statement No. 14* criteria they are considered fiscally independent special purpose governments. All of the State's component units issue their own separately issued audited financial statements.

Required

    a. Which criteria under GASB *Statement No. 14* do you expect that the three universities *not* included in the State's CAFR fail to meet? (Hint: Review the GASB *Statement No. 14* criteria in Chapter 10.)

    b. What other relationships between states and their public institutions of higher learning might you expect to find (for example, between the State of California and the University of California and California State University systems)?

    c. How useful is the *discrete* method of presenting college and university component units (as opposed to *blending* component units with the State's financial information) if the column in the general purpose financial statements entitled "Component Units" includes the 10 institutions of higher learning and authorities for the bridges, state parks, housing development, and higher education student loans?

18–2. You have recently been hired as the financial manager of Marywood University, a private university in an urban area. Your previous experience has been with Southern State University, a public university in the area. In order to familiarize yourself with the differences between the audited financial statements of this private university, which follows *SFAS No. 117,* and the public university, which follows the AICPA College Audit Guide model, you are comparing Marywood University's Statement of Activities to the Southern State University's Statement of Revenues and Expenditures and Changes in Fund Balances shown on the next page. Student enrollment at the private university is approximately 4,100 and at the public university approximately 23,000.

Required

    a. List some of the differences between the format of the two statements of operations for the year that are immediately evident.

    b. What proportion of the total revenues of Marywood University come from tuition and fees versus state appropriations versus other income? How does that compare to Southern University?

    c. What proportion of all the private gifts, grants, and contracts are in the form of endowments? How does that compare to the public university? Can you tell how much each earns on their endowments?

    d. What proportion of all the expenses are spent for the educational programs as opposed to that spent on supporting the programs (e.g., general and administrative and fund-raising expenses)? How does that compare with the public university?

    e. Which university appears to have had a better year from the perspective of financial activities? Why?

MARYWOOD UNIVERSITY
Statement of Activities
Year ended June 30, 1999
(in thousands)

	Unrestricted	Temporarily Restricted	Permanently Restricted	Totals
Revenues, gains, and other support:				
Tuition and fees (net of scholarships of $805,113)	$15,359	$ —	$ —	$15,359
State appropriation	525	—	—	525
Government grants and contracts	748	—	—	748
Private gifts, grants, and contracts	952	630	257	1,839
Pledges	40	458	63	561
Investment income	1,196	3	—	1,199
Realized gain from investments	3,310	—	—	3,310
Auxiliary enterprises	689	—	—	689
Other sources	384	93	—	477
Net assets released from restrictions	1,643	(1,632)	(11)	—
Total revenues and other support	24,846	(448)	309	24,707
Net appreciation on investments	314	—	—	314
Total revenues, gains, and other support	25,160	(448)	309	25,021
Expenses and losses:				
Instruction	9,391	—	—	9,391
Public service	86	—	—	86
Academic support	2,301	—	—	2,301
Student services	2,056	—	—	2,056
Management and general	2,388	—	—	2,388
Fund-raising	442	—	—	442
Auxiliary enterprises	448	—	—	448
Operations and maintenance of plant	2,768	—	—	2,768
Repairs and renovations	992	—	—	992
Retirement of plant	152	—	—	152
Interest	253	—	—	253
Other	15	—	—	15
Total expenses and losses	21,292	—	—	21,292
Change in net assets	3,868	(448)	309	3,729
Net assets at beginning of year	41,422	891	3,548	45,861
Net assets at end of year	$45,290	$ 443	$3,857	$49,590

SOUTHERN STATE UNIVERSITY
Statement of Revenues, Expenditures,
and Changes in Fund Balance
For the Year Ended June 30, 1999
(in thousands)

	Unrestricted	*Restricted*
Revenues:		
Student tuition and fees	$ 66,974	
State appropriations	69,086	
Federal grants and contracts		$ 9,068
State grants and contracts		2,129
Gifts and other grants	1,048	6,002
Interest income	2,601	93
Departmental activities	3,579	
Auxiliary activities, less internal service billings	25,495	
Other	807	
Decrease in restricted revenue held for future expenditures	429	(429)
Total revenues	170,019	16,863
Expenditures:		
Instruction	61,498	
Research	1,411	1,000
Public service	8,005	
Academic support	9,998	4,932
Student services	14,949	
Institutional support	20,002	1,046
Scholarships and fellowships	5,002	8,301
Operation and maintenance of plant	11,289	
Auxiliary activities, less internal service billings	24,998	
Interest expense	3,428	
Student loan provision	199	
Depreciation	7,837	
Capital additions, net of retirements	(4,787)	
Other	442	
Total expenditures	164,271	15,279
Excess of Revenues over Expenditures	5,748	1,584
Fund Balance, Beginning of year	100,018	17,700
Fund Balance, End of year	$105,766	$19,284

18–3. **Internet Case.** Assume you are a newly hired accountant in the Office of Financial Operations of a large public university. You will be involved in two major initiatives for the coming year: (1) revising the university's chart of accounts, and (2) assisting in a response to the GASB's most recent exposure draft on the financial reporting model for public colleges and universities.

Required

   a. What type of information is available on the Internet to assist you in understanding the chart of accounts of a public university? For example, look at the Accounting Tutorials at the NACUBO homepage (http://www.nacubo.org) and search under "university accounting."

   b. Use the Internet to identify whether other organizations have taken a position on the GASB's dual perspective financial reporting model. For example, try the AICPA (http://www.aicpa.org), Council for the Advancement of Secondary Education (CASE) (http://www.case.org), NACUBO (http://www.nacubo.org), and other public colleges and universities. Try to find organizations that support and that do not support the exposure draft. Describe the constituency of each organization so that you can evaluate the organization's position based on its perspective.

Exercises and Problems

18–1. Write the numbers 1 through 10 on a sheet of paper. Beside each number, write the letter corresponding with the best answer to each of the following questions:

   1. Funds that the governing board of a public university, rather than a donor or other outside agency, has determined are to be retained and invested for purposes other than loan or plant would be accounted for in the:
      a. Endowment Fund.
      b. Funds Functioning as Endowment.
      c. Agency Fund.
      d. Restricted Current Fund.
   2. Which of the following is utilized for current expenditures by a public university?

	Unrestricted Current Funds	Restricted Current Funds
a.	Yes	Yes
b.	Yes	No
c.	No	No
d.	No	Yes

3. Oakville College, a public college, has a 10-week summer session that starts on June 15. During the fiscal year ending June 30, 2000, tuition and fees in the amount of $800,000 were collected from students for classes to be conducted in this session. What amount should Oakville College recognize as Unrestricted Current Funds Revenue in each of the years ended June 30, 2000 and June 30, 2001?

	Year Ended June 30, 2000	Year Ended June 30, 2001
a.	$160,000	$640,000
b.	$ 0	$800,000
c.	$800,000	$ 0

d. Either a or c is allowed, provided the same pattern of recognition is applied consistently in successive years.

4. Tuition scholarships for which there is *no* intention of collection from the student should be classified by a private university as:
   a. Revenues and Expenditures.
   b. Revenues and Expenses.
   c. A reduction of gross revenue to arrive at net revenue.
   d. Any of the above.

5. An alumnus donates securities to Rex College and stipulates that the principal be held in perpetuity and income from the securities be used for faculty travel. Dividends received from the securities should be recognized as revenues in:
   a. Endowment Funds.
   b. Funds Functioning as Endowment.
   c. Restricted Current Funds.
   d. Unrestricted Current Funds.

6. During the years ended June 30, 2000, and 2001, Small University, a public university, conducted a cancer research project financed by a $1,000,000 gift from an alumnus. This entire amount was pledged by the donor on July 10, 1999, although she paid only $500,000 at that date. The gift was restricted to the financing of this particular research project. During the two-year research period, Small's related gift receipts and research expenditures were as follows:

	Year Ended June 30	
	2000	2001
Gift receipts	$200,000	$800,000
Cancer research expenditures	100,000	900,000

How much gift revenue should Small report in the restricted column of its Statement of Current Funds Revenues, Expenditures, and Other Changes for the year ended June 30, 2001?
   a. $0.
   b. $800,000.
   c. $900,000.
   d. $1,000,000.

7. Are public and private colleges and universities required to report depreciation expense in their financial statements?

	Public	Private
a.	Yes	Yes
b.	Yes	No
c.	No	No
d.	No	Yes

8. During the year ended June 30, 2001, Gaudior College, a private college, received a federal government grant of $600,000 for research on the homeless. Expenditures for this research amounted to $200,000 during the same year. Under applicable FASB standards, Gaudior College would report what amount(s) as revenues or support for the year ended June 30, 2001?

	Unrestricted	Temporarily Restricted	Permanently Restricted
a.	$ 0	$200,000	$ 0
b.	$ 0	$200,000	$100,000
c.	$200,000	$400,000	$ 0
d.	$600,000	$ 0	$ 0

9. Which of the following is *not* a condition that would permit a private college or university to avoid accounting recognition of the value of its collections of art, historical treasures, and similar assets?
   a. The assets are held for public exhibition, education, or research in furtherance of public service rather than financial gain.
   b. The assets are protected, kept unencumbered, cared for, and preserved.
   c. The assets are subject to an organizational policy that ensures the proceeds of sales of collectible assets are used for operations of the organization.
   d. None of above; all three items are conditions that will avoid accounting recognition.

10. Which of the following is required as part of a complete set of financial statements for a private college or university?
   a. Statement of Changes in Financial Position.
   b. Statement of Activities.
   c. Statement of Current Funds Revenues, Expenditures, and Other Changes.
   d. Statement of Changes in Fund Balances.

18–2. The Balance Sheet for Caribou College as of June 30, 2000, is shown on the next page. Caribou College is a state-supported institution that follows the AICPA model for accounting and financial reporting purposes. Current Funds transactions during the year 2000–2001 are given. You are required to prepare journal entries for the transactions given and to prepare a Current Funds Balance Sheet as of June 30, 2001. For each entry, indicate whether it affects Unrestricted Current Funds or Restricted Current Funds.

CARIBOU COLLEGE
Balance Sheet
June 30, 2000

Assets

Current Funds:		
Unrestricted:		
Cash		$ 70,000
Accounts receivable—student fees	$25,000	
Less: Allowance for doubtful accounts	1,000	24,000
Due from restricted funds		8,000
State appropriation receivable		182,000
Inventory, at cost		14,000
Total Unrestricted		298,000
Restricted:		
Cash	3,000	
Investments	24,000	
Total Restricted		27,000
Total Current Funds		$325,000

Liabilities and Fund Balances

Current Funds:		
Unrestricted:		
Accounts payable		$ 20,000
Deferred revenue		148,000
Fund balance		130,000
Total Unrestricted		298,000
Restricted:		
Due to unrestricted funds	$ 8,000	
Fund balance	19,000	
Total Restricted		27,000
Total Current Funds		$325,000

---

1. Fees charged to students for the fall and spring semesters of fiscal 2000–2001 totaled $2,200,000 of which $2,100,000 was collected in cash. The Allowance for Doubtful Accounts was increased by $4,000.
2. Collections of accounts receivable totaled $20,000. Accounts amounting to $1,000 were written off.
3. The Deferred Revenue of $148,000 shown in the Balance Sheet resulted from student fees charged for the summer term, which began in fiscal 1999–2000 but was predominantly conducted in 2000–2001.
4. Fees charged to students for summer school totaled $144,000, all of which was collected in cash. The summer term will be predominantly conducted in fiscal 2001–2002.
5. Temporary investments in the amount of $10,000 held at the beginning of the year were sold for $10,500. Restricted current funds cash spent for authorized purposes amounted to $2,500; an additional $8,000 was transferred to unrestricted funds in payment of the liability existing on June 30, 2000.

6. During the year, accounts payable for purchases, salaries and wages, utility bills, and other expenditures totaling $1,750,000 were recorded. Accounts payable at the end of the year amounted to $70,000.
7. Supplies inventory at the end of the year amounted to $25,000, according to physical count.
8. During the year, the state appropriation of $182,000 was received. A further appropriation for current general purposes of $192,000 was made by the state but had not been paid to the college by year-end.
9. Unrestricted fund cash in the amount of $160,000 was transferred to Funds for Retirement of Debt, and $500,000 of unrestricted fund cash was invested in short-term U.S. Treasury notes.
10. Income received in cash from investments of restricted current funds amounted to $1,050; an additional $160 interest was accrued at year-end.
11. All nominal accounts were closed.

18–3. A partial Balance Sheet of Rapapo State University as of the end of its fiscal year ended July 31, 2000, is presented below:

RAPAPO STATE UNIVERSITY
Current Funds Balance Sheet
July 31, 2000

Assets		*Liabilities and Fund Balances*	
Unrestricted:		Unrestricted:	
Cash	$200,000	Accounts payable	$100,000
Accounts receivable—tuition and		Due to other funds	40,000
fees, less allowance for doubtful		Deferred revenue—tuition and	
accounts of $15,000	370,000	fees	25,000
Prepaid expenses	40,000	Fund balance	445,000
Total unrestricted	610,000	Total unrestricted	610,000
Restricted:		Restricted:	
Cash	10,000	Accounts payable	5,000
Investments	210,000	Fund balance	215,000
Total restricted	220,000	Total restricted	220,000
Total current funds	$830,000	Total current funds	$830,000

The following information pertains to the year ended July 31, 2001:

1. Cash collected from students' tuition totaled $3,000,000. Of this $3,000,000, $362,000 represented accounts receivable outstanding at July 31, 2000; $2,500,000 was for current-year tuition; and $138,000 was for tuition applicable to the semester beginning in August 2001.
2. Deferred revenue at July 31, 2000 was earned during the year ended July 31, 2001.
3. Accounts receivable in the amount of $13,000 were determined uncollectible and were written off against the allowance account. At July 31, 2001, the allowance account was estimated at $10,000.

4. During the year, an unrestricted appropriation of $60,000 was made by the state. This state appropriation was to be paid to Rapapo sometime in August 2001.
5. During the year, unrestricted cash gifts of $80,000 were received from alumni. Rapapo's board of trustees allocated $30,000 of these gifts to the student loan fund.
6. During the year, investments with a carrying value of $25,000 were sold for $31,000. Restricted fund investments were purchased at a cost of $40,000. Investment income of $18,000 was earned and collected during the year.
7. Unrestricted general expenses of $2,500,000 were recorded in the voucher system. At July 31, 2001, the unrestricted accounts payable balance was $75,000.
8. The restricted accounts payable balance at July 31, 2000, was paid.
9. The $40,000 due to other funds at July 31, 2000, was paid to the plant fund as required.
10. One-quarter of the prepaid expenses at July 31, 2000, expired during the current year, and pertained to general education expense. There was no addition to prepaid expenses during the year.

Required

a. Prepare journal entries in summary form to record the foregoing transactions for the year ended July 31, 2001, assuming Rapapo State University is a public university. Number each entry to correspond with the number indicated in the description of its respective transaction. Your answer sheet should be organized as follows:

		Current Funds			
		Unrestricted		Restricted	
Entry No.	Accounts	Debits	Credits	Debits	Credits

b. Prepare a Statement of Changes in Fund Balances for the year ended July 31, 2001.

(AICPA, adapted)

18–4. The Balance Sheet of Everglades University as of June 30, 2000, indicated the following with respect to the loan funds:

Loan Funds:			
Cash		$61,000	
Investments		30,000	
Loans to Students, Faculty, and Staff	$100,000		
Accrued Interest Receivable	1,000		
	101,000		
Less: Allowance for Doubtful Loans and Interest	2,000	99,000	
Total Loan Funds			$190,000
Loan Funds:			
Fund Balances—Unrestricted			$190,000
Total Loan Funds			$190,000

You are required to prepare loan funds journal entries for the following transactions, which occurred in the year 2000–2001. You are also required to prepare a loan funds Balance Sheet as of June 30, 2001, assuming that Everglades University is a public university.

1. A bequest of $23,000 in securities was received by Everglades University. The decedent specified that both principal and interest were to be used for student loans.
2. Loans receivable of prior years in the amount of $31,000 were collected during the year. Interest collected on loans receivable in cash during the year amounted to $4,150, $900 of which was accrued at June 30, 2000, and $3,250 of which was earned in 2000–2001.
3. One loan of $600 and accrued interest of $50 (as of balance sheet date) was written off as uncollectible.
4. Loans made to students during the year totaled $42,000. All loans were secured by notes; repayments on these loans during the year amounted to $4,100 ($4,000 principal and $100 interest).
5. Dividends and interest on loan fund investments collected in cash during the year amounted to $2,150. Accrued interest receivable at the end of the year amounted to $640. The Allowance for Doubtful Loans and Interest was increased to $1,900.

18–5. The Balance Sheet of Lockhart University as of June 30, 1999, indicated the following with respect to endowment and similar funds:

Endowment and similar funds:	
Cash	$ 130,000
Securities	800,000
Real estate	270,000
Cash held by trustee	200,000
Total Endowment and Similar Funds	$1,400,000
Endowment and similar funds:	
Accounts Payable	$ 120,000
Endowment fund balances:	
Reserve for replacement of real estate	220,000
Fund balances—income unrestricted	750,000
Fund balances—income restricted	200,000
Funds Functioning as Endowment	110,000
Total Endowment and Similar Funds	$1,400,000

You are required to prepare journal entries to record the following transactions, which relate to the fiscal year 1999–2000; you are also required to prepare a Balance Sheet as of June 30, 2000, assuming Lockhart University is a public university.

1. Cash held by a trustee in the amount of $50,000 was transferred by the trustee to the Endowment Fund Cash Account.
2. Accounts payable on June 30, 1999, were paid.
3. Securities of Funds Functioning as Endowment carried at $55,000 were sold for $51,000 and the proceeds reinvested in other securities.
4. The Reserve for Replacement of Real Estate was increased by $10,000; cash in this amount was received from Unrestricted Current Funds.

18–6. The Balance Sheet of Cougar University as of June 30, 1999, indicated the following with respect to annuity and life income funds. From the transactions that follow, prepare journal entries and a Balance Sheet as of June 30, 2000, assuming Cougar University is a public university.

Annuity and life income funds:		
Cash	$ 30,000	
Investments	135,000	
Total Annuity and Life Income Funds		$165,000
Annuity and life income funds:		
Annuity funds:		
Annuities payable	$ 62,000	
Fund balances	30,000	$ 92,000
Life income funds:		
Fund balances		73,000
Total Annuity and Life Income Funds		$165,000

1. On August 1, 1999, a tract of land with fair market value of $600,000 was received under an agreement that Cougar University would pay the donor $30,000 each year on the anniversary date of the agreement as long as the donor lived. No restrictions were placed on the use of the principal of the fund or any income in excess of $30,000 per year. The present value of the liability to the annuitant is $342,000.
2. Cash income received from annuity fund investments during the year totaled $34,000, of which $11,400 was disbursed to annuitant during the year.
3. During the year, one life income recipient died, her contribution, investments with a fair value of $42,000, was transferred to the loan funds.

18–7. The Balance Sheet of Bronco University as of June 30, 2000, indicated the following with respect to plant funds. From the transactions given below, prepare journal entries and a Plant Funds Balance Sheet as of the end of the year, using subgroups shown below and assuming Bronco University is a public university.

Plant funds:		
Unexpended:		
Cash	$ 20,000	
Investments	276,000	
Due from other funds	4,000	
Total Unexpended Plant Funds		$ 300,000
Retirement of indebtedness:		
Cash	5,000	
Investments	125,000	
Total Retirement of Indebtedness		130,000
Investment in plant:		
Land	115,000	
Buildings	5,260,000	

Equipment	983,000	
Construction in progress	212,000	
Total Investment in Plant		6,570,000
Total Plant Funds		$7,000,000

Plant funds:
Unexpended:

Accounts payable	82,000	
Fund balance	218,000	
Total Unexpended Plant Funds		$ 300,000

Retirement of indebtedness:

Fund balance—unrestricted	130,000

Investment in plant:

Bonds payable	260,000	
Investment in plant:		
From operations	3,075,000	
From gifts	1,410,000	
From governmental appropriations	1,825,000	
Total Investment in Plant		6,570,000
Total Plant Funds		$7,000,000

Transactions during the fiscal year ended June 30, 2001, were:

1. Retirement of Indebtedness Fund investments with a carrying value of $125,000 were sold for $127,000 cash; bonds payable of the plant funds in the amount of $130,000 were retired by use of Retirement of Indebtedness Fund cash.
2. The amount due Unexpended Plant Funds from other funds at the beginning of the year was received.
3. A grant of $800,000 was made to Bronco University by the Bronco Foundation to be used for the acquisition of buildings and equipment. The grant was to be paid to the university in equal installments over an eight-year period; the sum for the current year was received in cash.
4. Invoices and payrolls amounting to $50,000 for the construction in progress were recorded as accounts payable. Accounts payable in the amount of $102,000 were paid during the year. The assets of the Unexpended Plant Funds had been obtained from gifts.
5. The construction in progress, an addition to the School of Business building, was considered completed. It was determined that 80 percent of the total cost was to be charged to Buildings and 20 percent to Equipment.
6. A firm of architects engaged to prepare plans for a new residence hall submitted an invoice for $40,000 for services performed by them this year. (You may credit Accounts Payable.)
7. Unrestricted Current Funds transferred $65,000 cash to the Retirement of Indebtedness Fund. The latter fund invested that amount in certificates of deposit.

18–8. Zenith College had always kept its accounts on a so-called commercial basis and not in the form ordinarily used by educational institutions. The Balance Sheet as of June 30, 2001 was as follows:

ZENITH COLLEGE
Balance Sheet
June 30, 2001

Assets

Current assets:		
Cash	$ 1,180	
Tuition fees receivable	8,000	
Inventory of supplies	2,000	$ 11,180
Endowment fund investments:		
Rented real estate—at cost	75,000	
Less: Allowance for depreciation	15,000	
	60,000	
Mortgages, 7 percent—at cost	145,000	
5 percent public utility bonds—at fair value	220,000	425,000
Plant and equipment, net of allowance for depreciation of $166,000		830,000
		$1,266,180

Liabilities

Current liabilities:		
Bank loans	$ 15,000	
Accounts payable	9,000	$ 24,000
First-mortgage bonds, 7 percent, maturing at the rate of $15,000 semi-annually on June 30 and December 31 of each year		300,000
Endowment fund balance		540,000
Capital:		
Balance at July 1, 2000	400,000	
Excess of income over expenses for the year ended June 30, 2001, per annexed statement	2,180	402,180
		$1,266,180

Required

a. Prepare a written report for the Controller of Zenith College to set forth the changes that must be made to bring the College's financial statement into conformity with FASB financial reporting standards for a private college, as described in Chapter 18.

b. Prepare a Statement of Financial Position for Zenith College, as of June 30, 2001, in conformity with FASB financial reporting standards for a private college. Use the format for these statements shown in Illustration 18–5 earlier in this chapter.

(AICPA, adapted)

Accounting for Health Care Organizations

Learning Objectives

After studying this chapter, you should be able to:

~ Describe different organizational forms for providing health care services.

~ Identify the authoritative accounting literature that governs health care entities.

~ Describe financial reporting for health care organizations.

~ Explain unique accounting and measurement issues in health care organizations including accounting for revenues, assets, expenses, and liabilities.

~ Journalize transactions and prepare the basic financial statements for not-for-profit health care providers.

~ Prepare the basic financial statements for governmental health care providers.

~ Describe other accounting issues in the health care industry:
  Budgeting and costs.
  Auditing.
  Taxation and regulation.

~ Discuss unique issues with certain types of health care organizations, such as prepaid health care services and continuing care retirement communities.

~ Explain financial and operational analysis of health care organizations.

Health Care Industry

The health care industry in the United States has changed dramatically over the last century. In the early 1900s health care was provided primarily by nonprofit hospitals affiliated with communities or religious organizations; acute care was provided at reasonable costs; major projects were funded by donations; and hospital managers had little financial expertise and faced few regulations. Today, health care organizations are complex entities that cross the private, public, and not-for-profit sectors; spiraling costs outpace inflation; capital construction requires extensive financing; and professional managers face increasing public scrutiny and governmental oversight. Technological advances brought dramatic changes in the delivery and quality of health care services, but also contributed greatly to rising costs. Health care is now a $1 trillion industry representing 15 percent of gross national product.[1]

There are political, social, and economic factors that explain the tremendous change in the health care industry. For example, in the 1940s and 1950s, health insurance coverage became a common employee fringe benefit, and health care providers began to look to employers and third parties for payment for services. The Hill Burton Program in 1944 encouraged growth in the industry by making federal funds available for the construction of health care facilities.[2] The initiation of entitlement programs, such as Medicare and Medicaid in the 1960s, reflected public policy efforts to make health care a basic right to be regulated at the federal level. In the 1980s employers and insurance companies initiated managed care systems in an attempt to bring down the cost of providing health care coverage. In the 1990s, comprehensive health care reform became a political issue at the federal level. Today, roughly half of *hospital* health care is provided by not-for-profit organizations, although most *providers* of health care are for-profit groups of medical professionals who are associated with governmental or not-for-profit health care organizations.

Illustration 19–1 shows classifications of health care organizations by legal structure as well as by the nature of services they provide. This chapter focuses on the financial reporting and accounting issues of these organizations that charge patients or third parties for the services provided. Voluntary health and welfare organizations, which are nonbusiness-oriented, and which provide more general social services funded primarily by contributions and grants rather than charges for services, are discussed in Chapter 16.

GAAP for Health Care Providers

Generally accepted accounting principles (GAAP) for hospitals and other health care organizations have evolved through the efforts of the American Hospital Association (AHA), the Healthcare Financial Management Association (HFMA),

---

[1] U.S. Department of Health and Human Services, *Health U.S.*, Pub. No. 96-1232, 1995, Table 114, p. 239.

[2] The Hospital Survey and Construction Act of 1946 (P.L. 79-725).

Illustration 19–1   Classification of Health Care Organizations

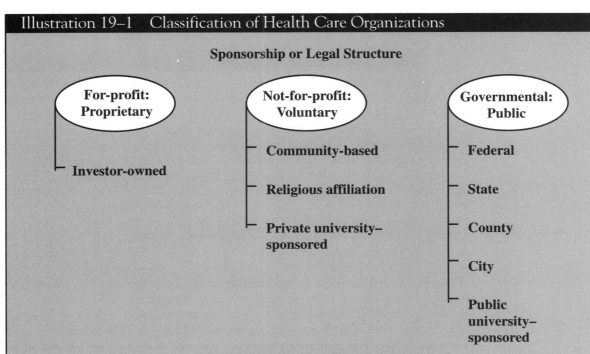

Sponsorship or Legal Structure

**For-profit:
Proprietary**

— **Investor-owned**

**Not-for-profit:
Voluntary**

— **Community-based**

— **Religious affiliation**

— **Private university–
sponsored**

**Governmental:
Public**

— **Federal**

— **State**

— **County**

— **City**

— **Public
university–
sponsored**

Types of Health Care Organizations

Clinics, medical group practices, individual practice associations, individual practitioners, emergency care facilities, laboratories, surgery centers, and other ambulatory care organizations

Continuing care retirement communities (CCRCs)

Health maintenance organizations (HMOs) and similar prepaid health care plans

Home health agencies

Hospitals

Nursing homes that provide skilled, intermediate, and a less-intensive level of health care

Drug and alcohol rehabilitation centers and other rehabilitation facilities

Source: American Institute of Certified Public Accountants, Audit and Accounting Guide *Health Care Organizations* (New York: AICPA, 1997), p. vii.

and the American Institute of Certified Public Accountants (AICPA). More recently, Statements of the Financial Accounting Standards Board and the Governmental Accounting Standards Board directly impact accounting and reporting for health care providers. The AICPA Audit and Accounting Guide *Health Care Organizations* applies to health care organizations that are either (1) investor-owned businesses, (2) not-for-profit enterprises that, although they have no ownership interests, are essentially business-oriented and self-sustaining from fees charged for goods and services, or (3) governmental entities. These organizations are often classified by the nature of the services provided, as listed in Illustration 19–1. Since 1990, the AICPA Audit and Accounting Guide has covered *all* providers of health care services, not just hospitals. The Guide covers *governmental* providers that use enterprise accounting, as well as private and not-for-profit health care organizations; and it integrates *SFAS Nos. 116* and *117* for not-for-profit organizations, which focus on net assets of the entity as a whole, rather than on fund balances.[3]

The GASB gives governmental health care entities that use proprietary or enterprise fund accounting the option of following all applicable FASB pronouncements issued after November 30, 1989 ("the FASB option"), unless they conflict with GASB pronouncements.[4] Governmentally owned and operated hospitals that are financed primarily from appropriations, rather than user charges, are accounted for as a general or special revenue fund as discussed in Chapters 3 and 4 of this text. The AICPA Audit Guide is considered Category (b) authority for both governmental and nongovernmental entities, which means that GASB and FASB statements take precedence.[5] Consequently, even though there is only one Audit Guide for all health care entities, accounting and reporting rules may differ depending on whether the health care provider is legally structured as an investor-owned, not-for-profit, or governmental organization. Some of the differences relate to accounting and reporting for contributions and financial reporting display, cash flows, and investments, as seen in Illustration 19–2.

As discussed in Chapter 18, the FASB statements on not-for-profit organizations create a substantial divergence in the accounting and financial reporting standards applicable to public (governmental) and private (nongovernmental) colleges and universities. However, they have much less impact on standards for health care entities since contributions are not as important to the operations of health care entities as they usually are to higher education institutions. In addition, GAAP for all health care organizations specifies the use of the accrual basis of accounting, including reporting of depreciation expense. This chapter illustrates financial accounting and reporting for not-for-profit, nongovernmental health care

---

[3]American Institute of Certified Public Accountants, Audit and Accounting Guide *Health Care Organizations* (AAG-HCO) (New York: AICPA, 1997).

[4]GASB, *Codification*, Sec. P80.105 (i.e., par. 7 of GASB *Statement No. 20*); and AAG-HCO 1.08.

[5]American Institute of Certified Public Accountants, *SAS No. 69* "The Meaning of 'Present Fairly in Conformity with Generally Accepted Accounting Principles' in the Independent Auditor's Report" (New York: AICPA, 1991).

Illustration 19–2 GAAP for Health Care Entities in Different Sectors

Accounting and Reporting Issue	Health Care Providers		
	Investor-Owned	Not-for-Profit	Governmental
Reporting entity	APB *Opinion No. 18,* SFAS *No. 94*	AICPA SOP 94-3	GASB *Statement No. 14*
Contributions and financial statement display	SFAS *No. 116*	SFAS *Nos. 116* and *117*	GASB *Statement No. 29* prohibits following SFAS *Nos. 116* and *117.* GASB requires entities to follow the AAG-HCO.
Cash flows	SFAS *No. 95*	SFAS *No. 95*	GASB *Statement No. 9*
Deposits with financial institutions	SFAS *No. 105*	SFAS *No. 105*	GASB *Statement No. 3*
Investments	SFAS *No. 115* and AAG-HCO, Chapter 4	SFAS *No. 124*	GASB *Statement Nos. 3* and *31*
Operating leases	SFAS *No. 13*	SFAS *No. 13*	GASB *Statement No. 13*
Prepaid health care arrangements and self-insurance programs	AAG-HCO, Chapters 8 and 14	AAG-HCO, Chapters 8 and 14	GASB *Statement No. 10* as amended by GASB *Statement No. 30.* AAG-HCO, Chapter 14 if following "the FASB Option"
Compensated absences	SFAS *Nos. 43* and *112*	SFAS *Nos. 43* and *112*	GASB *Statement No. 16*
Debt refundings	APB *Opinion No. 26,* SFAS *Nos. 4* and *125*	APB *Opinion No. 26,* SFAS *Nos. 4* and *125*	GASB *Statements No. 7* and *23*
Pensions	SFAS *No. 87*	SFAS *No. 87*	GASB *Statement No. 27*
Risks and uncertainties	AICPA SOP 94-6	AICPA SOP 94-6	GASB *Statements No. 10* and *30*
Post retirement benefits	SFAS *No. 106*	SFAS *No. 106*	GASB *Statements No. 12* and *27*

Source: Adapted from AICPA, *Audit Risk Alert, Health Care Industry Developments—1997–98* (New York: AICPA, 1998), pp. 39–41.

organizations, the largest segment of the in-patient health care industry, and points out particular differences for investor-owned and governmental health care providers. The reader is directed to Chapter 16 for a more thorough discussion of SFAS *Nos. 116* and *117* for not-for-profit organizations, and to Chapter 7 for a discussion of business-type enterprises of governmental entities.

Financial Reporting

The information needs of users of financial statements differ depending upon whether they are giving, paying, or loaning money to the health care organization. The basic financial statements of a health care entity created to serve a broad set of users include a (1) Balance Sheet, (2) Statement of Operations, (3) Statements of Changes in Equity (net assets/fund balances), and (4) Statement of Cash Flows, as well as Notes to the Financial Statements. The FASB and AICPA allow considerable flexibility in displaying financial information; for example, the Statements of Changes in Equity and Operations may be combined. A health care organization may choose to use fund accounting for internal purposes, in part, to account for revenues and expenses associated with grants (or because it is a governmental entity). For organizations using fund accounting, the fund structure should include general unrestricted funds and donor-restricted funds (e.g., Specific Purpose, Plant Replacement and Expansion, and Endowment). Comparative statements for a hypothetical not-for-profit hospital are presented in Illustrations 19–3 through 19–5. Statements for a governmental entity are presented in Illustrations 19–6 through 19–9.

Balance Sheet

The Balance Sheet presented in Illustration 19–3 shows assets classified into current assets, assets limited as to use, and noncurrent assets, such as property, plant, and equipment. Not-for-profit organizations are required to present information about the liquidity of their assets and liabilities. The equity section of an investor-owned health care provider would show stockholders' equity separated into capital stock and retained earnings. The fund equity section of a governmental organization reports unrestricted and donor-restricted fund balances. Not-for-profit organizations classify net assets into unrestricted, temporarily restricted, and permanently restricted in their equity sections.

Statement of Operations

The principal sources of revenue for a hospital are (1) patient service revenue; (2) premium revenue derived from **capitation fees,** which are the fixed fees per person paid periodically regardless of services provided; (3) resident service revenue, such as maintenance or rental fees; (4) other revenue; and (5) net assets released from restrictions used for operations. Service revenue is shown net of contractual adjustments. Other revenue includes sales (e.g., medical supplies and cafeteria meals), fees (e.g., for educational programs or transcripts), rental of facilities other than to residents, investment income and gains, and unrestricted contributions. Some governmental health care organizations may be supported, at least in part, by taxes. Research grants or contracts may be considered exchange transactions (i.e., sales) or nonexchange transactions (i.e., contributions), as discussed in earlier chapters. Net assets released from temporary restrictions are shown as increases to unrestricted net assets if they were used for operations, otherwise they are reported along with other contributions for property purchases. Bloomfield Hospital, as shown in Illustration 19–4, reports some of these sources of income. Considerable flexibility is allowed in displaying the results of operations, such as classification by operating and nonoperating, expendable and nonexpendable, earned and unearned, or recurring and nonrecurring. FASB Concepts Statements provide guidance on distinguishing operating items (i.e., those arising from ongoing major activities, such as service revenue) from nonoperating items (i.e., those arising from transactions peripheral or incidental to the delivery of health care, such as investment income and unrestricted contributions).[6]

---

[6]Financial Accounting Standards Board, *Concepts Statement No. 6*, "Elements of Financial Statements" (Norwalk, CT: FASB, 1985).

Illustration 19–3

BLOOMFIELD HOSPITAL
Balance Sheet
As of September 30, 2000

Assets		Liabilities and Net Assets	
Current Assets:		**Current Liabilities:**	
Cash	$ 172,100	Accounts payable	$ 259,000
Accounts and notes receivable, net of allowance for		Accrued expenses payable	173,500
uncollectibles of $135,000	353,000		
Pledges receivable, net of allowance for uncollectibles			
of $114,300	1,048,700		
Accrued interest receivable	44,000		
Inventory	160,000		
Prepaid expenses	8,000		
Short-term investments	1,278,000		
Total Current Assets	3,063,800	Total Current Liabilities	432,500
Assets Limited as to Use:		**Long-Term Debt:**	
By Board for expansion of facilities—cash	6,500	Mortgages payable	6,000,000
By Board for expansion of facilities—investments	778,000	Total Liabilities	6,432,500
Total Assets Limited as to Use	784,500	**Net Assets:**	
Long-Term Investments	146,000	Unrestricted—Undesignated	8,536,600
Property, Plant, and Equipment:		Unrestricted—Designated	784,500
Land	1,080,000	Temporarily restricted	2,417,700
Buildings, net of accumulated depreciation of $1,365,000	9,685,000	Permanently restricted	178,000
Equipment, net of accumulated depreciation		Total Net Assets	11,916,800
of $1,702,000	3,590,000		
Total Property, Plant, and Equipment	14,355,000		
Total Assets	$18,349,300	Total Liabilities and Net Assets	$18,349,300

Illustration 19–4   Illustration of a Two-Part Statement of Operations

BLOOMFIELD HOSPITAL
Statement of Operations
Year Ended September 30, 2000

Unrestricted revenues and gains:		
Net patient service revenue		$ 9,161,000
Other revenue		48,800
Contributions		297,900
Investment income		36,100
Total unrestricted revenues and gains		9,543,800
Net assets released from restrictions:		
Satisfaction of equipment acquisition restrictions		100,000
Total unrestricted revenues, gains, and other support		9,643,800
Unrestricted expenses and losses:		
Nursing services	$4,667,500	
Other professional services	1,311,620	
General services	2,056,260	
Fiscal and administrative services	1,332,320	
Total expenses		9,367,700
Loss on disposal of equipment		1,500
Total unrestricted expenses and losses		9,369,200
Increase in unrestricted net assets		$ 274,600

Statement of Changes in Net Assets
Year Ended September 30, 2000

Unrestricted net assets (see Part 1)	
Total unrestricted revenues and gains	$ 9,543,800
Net assets released from restrictions	100,000
Total unrestricted expenses and losses	(9,369,200)
Increase in unrestricted net assets	274,600
Temporarily restricted net assets:	
Contributions	25,000
Investment income	77,000
Increase in provision for uncollectible pledges	(66,300)
Loss on sale of investments	(26,000)
Net assets released from restrictions	(100,000)
Decrease in temporarily restricted net assets	(90,300)
Permanently restricted net assets:	
Contributions	24,000
Increase in permanently restricted net assets	24,000
Increase in net assets	208,300
Net assets at beginning of year	11,708,500
Net assets at end of year	$11,916,800

Of course, this not-for-profit hospital reports all expenses as decreases in unrestricted assets. Functional expenses must be displayed or disclosed in the notes and can be as simple as distinguishing between health care services and general/administrative. If functional expenses are displayed, then all natural expenses (e.g., depreciation, interest, and provision for bad debts), must be allocated to the functional expenses.

Health care organizations should include a **performance indicator** to report the results of operations. The principal components of a performance indicator are unrestricted revenues, gains, and other support; expenses; and other income. Examples include excess of revenues over expenses, revenues and gains over expenses and losses, earned income, and performance earnings. Investment income, realized gains and losses, and unrealized gains and losses on trading securities should be reported in the performance indicator; however, the following items should be reported separately from the performance indicator:

- Transactions with owners acting in that capacity.
- Equity transfers involving other related entities.
- Receipt of temporarily and permanently restricted contributions.
- Contributions of (and assets released from donor restrictions related to) long-lived assets.
- Unrealized gains and losses on investments not restricted by donors or by law, except for those investments classified as trading securities.
- Investment returns restricted by donors or by law.
- Other items that are required by GAAP to be reported separately, such as extraordinary items, the effect of discontinued operations, or the cumulative effect of accounting changes.[7]

Statement of Changes in Equity

Illustration 19–4 shows increases and decreases in the three classes of net assets for a not-for-profit organization: unrestricted, temporarily restricted, and permanently restricted. Net assets released from restrictions increase unrestricted net assets and decrease temporarily restricted net assets. Net gains on permanently restricted endowments are shown as increases to the permanently restricted net assets in Illustration 19–4; however, the accounting treatment of net gains will depend on donor stipulations, state law, and organizational policy. Illustration 19–8 shows changes in restricted and unrestricted fund balances for a governmental organization.

Statement of Cash Flows

The Statement of Cash Flows in Illustration 19–5 is that required by *SFAS No. 95* (as amended) for not-for-profit organizations and investor-owned entities.[8] The direct method is presented with a reconciliation of changes in net assets to net cash provided by operating activities, although the direct method is also acceptable.

---

[7]AAG-HCO, 10.05, 10.16, 10.17.

[8]Financial Accounting Standards Board, *Statement No. 95*, "Statement of Cash Flows" (Norwalk, CT: FASB, 1987), as amended by *SFAS No. 117*, "Financial Statements of Not-for-Profit Organizations" (Norwalk, CT: FASB, 1993).

Illustration 19–5   Illustration of Statement of Cash Flows— Not-for-Profit and Investor-Owned Organizations

BLOOMFIELD HOSPITAL
Statement of Cash Flows
Year Ended September 30, 2000

Cash flows from operating activities:	
Cash received from patients and third-party payors	$ 8,842,000
Other receipts from operations	48,800
Interest received on assets limited as to use	36,100
Receipts from unrestricted gifts	297,900
Cash paid to employees and suppliers	(8,014,200)
Interest paid	(160,000)
Net cash provided by operating activities	1,050,600
Cash flows from investing activities:	
Purchase of property and equipment	(400,000)
Purchase of long-term investments	(737,000)
Proceeds from sale of securities	59,000
Proceeds from sale of equipment	500
Net cash used by investing activities	(1,077,500)
Cash flows from financing activities:	
Proceeds from contributions restricted for:	
Investment in plant	292,000
Future operations	5,000
	297,000
Other financing activities:	
Interest and dividends restricted to endowment	69,000
Repayment of long-term debt	(400,000)
	(331,000)
Net cash used by financing activities	(34,000)
Net increase (decrease) in cash	(60,900)
Cash and cash equivalents, September 30, 1999	239,500
Cash and cash equivalents, September 30, 2000	$ 178,600

Reconciliation of Changes in Net Assets to Net Cash Provided by Operating Activities

Changes in net assets	$ 208,300
Adjustments to reconcile change in net assets to net cash	
provided by operating activities:	
Depreciation	783,000
Loss on disposal of equipment	1,500
Increase in patient accounts receivable, net	(139,000)
Increase in supplies	(80,000)
Increase in accounts payable and accrued expenses	306,500
Decrease in prepaid expenses	4,000
Gifts, grants, and bequests restricted for long-term investment	(49,000)
Interest restricted for long-term investment	(77,000)
Loss on sale of investments	26,000
Increase in provision for uncollectible pledges	66,300
Net cash provided by operating activities	$ 1,050,600

Illustration 19–9 shows the Statement of Cash Flows required by GASB *Statement No. 9* for a governmental organization.[9]

The Statement of Cash Flows under GASB jurisdiction and the Statement of Cash Flows under FASB jurisdiction are similar in some respects. Both, for example, present cash inflows, outflows, and net cash flows related to operating activities, investing activities, and financing activities, although financing activities in the GASB statement are subdivided into noncapital financing activities and capital and related financing activities. Both the GASB statement and the FASB statement can be prepared using either the direct method or the indirect method.

The statements differ primarily in terms of which cash flows are reported as part of each activity. In the GASB statement, interest paid and interest received are reported as investing activities, whereas the same items are reported as operating activities in the FASB statement, except for interest and dividend income added to temporarily or permanently restricted net assets. Such restricted income is reported in the FASB statement as a financing activity. Acquisitions of property and equipment are reported as capital and related financing activities in the GASB statement but as investing activities in the FASB statement. Unrestricted gifts are reported as cash flows from noncapital financing activities in the GASB statement but as cash flows from operating activities in the FASB statement. A final, and major, difference is that the reconciliation schedule in the GASB statement reconciles operating income (loss) to cash flows from operating activities, whereas in the FASB statement the schedule reconciles changes in net assets to cash flows from operating activities. In preparing either cash flow statement, the worksheet or T-account approaches explained in most intermediate accounting texts may be useful.

Accounting and Measurement Issues

Revenues

Sources of Revenue.   Health care organizations receive the majority of their revenue in the form of fees for services. These fees may come from the patient; the government in the form of Medicare or Medicaid payments; third-party payors, such as Blue Cross/Blue Shield or other private insurance companies; or contracts with other private health care companies. This service revenue is recorded at the gross amount when services are rendered. **Contractual adjustments (or allowances)** are recorded as contra-revenue accounts (i.e., reduction of receivables) for the difference between the gross patient service revenue and the negotiated payment by third-party payors in arriving at net patient service revenue. Prepaid health care plans that earn revenues from *agreements to provide* services record revenue at the point agreements are made, and not when services are rendered. The variety of payment plans with third-party payors makes accounting for patient service revenue a complicated accounting task. For example, payments can be made on a per case, per service performed, per diem, or per person (capitated) basis. In addition, interim payments are often received with final settlement at a later point in time.

---

[9]GASB, *Codification*, Sec. 2450.

Charity Service.   Tax-exempt entities are expected to provide **charity care,** services to persons with a demonstrated inability to pay. Since charity service is never expected to result in cash flows, it is neither recognized as revenue nor receivables nor bad debt expense.[10] In practice, it is often difficult to distinguish bad debt expense from charity service. However, it is important to disclose management's charity care policies and the level of care provided for several reasons. The Hill Burton Act of 1946 requires that hospitals receiving federal assistance for construction projects perform some charity care. The IRS and local tax authorities question the tax-exempt status of some not-for-profit health care providers that do not appear to deliver an adequate amount of charity service to justify their tax exemption. Some third-party payors reimburse for a portion of bad debts, but not charity service.

Third-Party Payors.   Contracts with Medicare, Medicaid, Blue Cross plans, insurance companies, and state and local welfare agencies customarily provide for payment by **third-party payors** according to allowable costs or a predetermined (prospective) contractual rate rather than paying the service rates billed by the health care provider. For example, under Medicare's **Prospective Payment System** (PPS), payments are based on allowable service costs for medical procedures within the same diagnosis-related group (DRG) rather than on the length of the patient's hospital stay or actual cost of services rendered. Some payment methods, such as capitation fees in prepaid health care plans, shift a considerable amount of risk to the provider. That is, the fixed amount of revenue received per patient may not cover the costs of providing the service.

Other Revenue and Support.   Donated services and noncash assets generally are recorded at their fair value when received, if the criteria described in Chapter 16 and the AICPA Audit and Accounting Guide are met.[11] Noncash assets could be supplies used in operations or long-lived items, such as land, buildings, or equipment. Donors may make these gifts in kind unrestricted or restricted, either temporarily or permanently.

Assets

Assets Limited as to Use.   The phrase **Assets Limited as to Use** refers to assets whose use is limited by contracts or agreements with outside parties other than donors or grantors. Examples include proceeds of debt issues; funds deposited with a trustee; self-insurance funding arrangements, such as medical malpractice funding arrangements; and statutory reserve requirements (i.e., those required under state law for health maintenance organizations). The term can also refer to limitations placed on the assets by the Board of Directors or Trustees, such as for capital acquisition. Information about significant contractual limits should be disclosed in the Notes to the Financial Statements. Internally designated funds should be reported

---

[10]AAG-HCO, 10.03.
[11]Ibid., 10.08–10.12.

separately from externally designated funds on the Balance Sheet.[12] Assets that are held in trust by other parties are not reported on the Balance Sheet of the health care entity; however, their existence should be disclosed in the Notes.

Investments. Generally, health care organizations report their investments at fair value, although exact treatment of specific assets depends on the legal structure of the organization, as seen in Illustration 19–2. Not-for-profit organizations follow *SFAS No. 124*, which requires that all investments in equity securities with readily determinable values and all debt securities be reported at fair value, with the realized and unrealized gains and losses reported as changes in net assets. Governmental entities follow GASB *Statement No. 31*, which requires that changes in the fair value of certain investments be reported in the Statement of Operations. Investor-owned entities follow *SFAS No. 115*, which is the most complicated set of rules in that investments are separated into three categories and the accounting treatment differs for each category.[13]

Receivables. Amounts due from patients and third-party payors result in several asset and contra-asset accounts on the Balance Sheet: Accounts Receivable, Allowance for Uncollectible Accounts, Allowance for Contractual Adjustments, Clearing accounts, Interim Payments, and Settlement accounts. **Settlement accounts** are the receivables (or payables) arising from differences between original reimbursement estimates by third-party payors, cash received and paid, and final determinations.

The rate-setting process in the health care industry is complex and beyond the scope of this text. However, an understanding of the relationship between accrual accounting revenue recognition principles and alternative payment methods, such as prospective and retrospective, is critical in properly accounting for revenues and receivables in a health care organization. These organizations may also have pledges receivable that arise from donations and loans receivable that result from loans to employees or physicians' groups.

Expenses

All health care providers use full accrual accounting, and the accrual of expenses is the same as for any business organization. Bad debts is an expense, not a reduction of gross revenue to arrive at net revenue (as it had been in previous Audit Guides). Depreciation is recorded on all fixed assets other than land, including donated buildings and equipment. Expenses can be reported using either a natural presentation (e.g., salaries, supplies, and occupancy costs) or a functional presentation (e.g., inpatient services, ancillary outpatient services, and fiscal and administrative services). Functional expenses, if reported, should be based on full cost allocations.

---

[12]AAG-HCO, pars. 1.13–1.14.
[13]Financial Accounting Standards Board, *Statement No. 115*, "Accounting for Certain Investments in Debt and Equity Securities" (Norwalk, CT: FASB, 1993), and *Statement No. 124*, "Accounting for Certain Investments Held by Not-for-Profit Organizations" (Norwalk, CT: FASB, 1996). GASB, *Statement No. 31*, "Accounting and Financial Reporting for Certain Investments and for External Investment Pools" (Norwalk, CT: GASB, 1996).

Public companies that are registered with the SEC and governmental entities that use proprietary fund accounting must report segment information.[14]

Liabilities

Commitments and Contingencies.   Contingencies that are unique to health care providers arise from malpractice claims, risk contracting, third-party payor payment programs, obligations to provide uncompensated care, and contractual agreements with physicians. Other commitments and contingencies found in most business enterprises also apply to health care organizations, such as those that arise from construction contracts, pension plans, operating leases, purchase commitments, and loan guarantees. The cost of these claims against the health care organization should be accrued if they can be reasonably estimated, and it is probable they will have to be paid.[15] Accruals should be made for unasserted claims at the best estimates based on industry experience.

Long-Term Debt.   The high cost and critical nature of facilities and equipment in the delivery of health care lead to significant amounts of long-term debt. Very often, health care providers are entitled to financing assistance through tax-exempt debt or governmental financing authorities, such as the federal Health and Education Financing Authority, without regard to their legal structure. Financing agreements often include requirements to set aside funds for repayment of the interest on and principal of the debt. These funds are reported as *Assets Limited as to Use*.

Illustrative Case for a Not-for-Profit Health Care Organization

The illustrative transactions provided in this section are for a hypothetical non-governmentally owned not-for-profit hospital—the Bloomfield Hospital. Hospitals continue to be the dominant form of health care organization and usually exhibit a greater range of operating activities and transactions than other forms of health care organizations. Typical hospital transactions are illustrated below, following the post-closing trial balance as of September 30, 1999, for Bloomfield Hospital, the end of its fiscal year.

---

[14]AAG-HCO, par. 10.21.
[15]Financial Accounting Standards Board, *SFAS No. 5*, "Accounting for Contingencies" (Norwalk, CT: FASB, 1975); Financial Accounting Standards Board, *Interpretation No. 14*, "Reasonable Estimation of the Amount of a Loss" (Norwalk, CT: FASB, 1976); and GASB, *Codification*, Sec. C50.

BLOOMFIELD HOSPITAL
(a not-for-profit organization)
Post-Closing Trial Balance
As of September 30, 1999

	Debits	Credits
Cash	$ 233,000	
Short-Term Investments	980,000	
Accrued Interest Receivable	36,000	
Accounts and Notes Receivable	300,000	
Allowance for Uncollectible Receivables		$ 86,000
Pledges Receivable	1,460,000	
Allowance for Uncollectible Pledges		73,000
Inventory	80,000	
Prepaid Expenses	12,000	
Assets Limited as to Use—Cash	6,500	
Assets Limited as to Use—Investments	400,000	
Long-Term Investments	146,000	
Land	1,080,000	
Buildings	11,050,000	
Equipment	4,920,000	
Accumulated Depreciation—Buildings		1,050,000
Accumulated Depreciation—Equipment		1,260,000
Accounts Payable		110,000
Accrued Expenses Payable		16,000
Mortgages Payable		6,400,000
Net Assets—Unrestricted, Undesignated		8,640,000
Net Assets—Unrestricted, Designated		406,500
Net Assets—Temporarily Restricted—Plant		2,508,000
Net Assets—Permanently Restricted		154,000
	$20,703,500	$20,703,500

During fiscal year 2000, the gross revenues for patient services from all responsibility centers totaled $9,261,000. It is the practice of Bloomfield Hospital to debit receivable accounts for the gross charges for all services rendered to patients, except for charity care patients; the AICPA Audit and Accounting Guide requires that charity care services be excluded both from receivables and revenues. The following entry should be made:

1. Accounts and Notes Receivable 9,261,000
   Patient Service Revenue 9,261,000

The preceding entry recorded the revenues the hospital would have earned if all services rendered to each patient (other than charity care patients) were to be collected from the patients, or from third-party payors, as billed. Customers of profit-seeking businesses do not all pay their bills in full, and neither do hospital patients nor patients' insurance companies. The variety of third-party payment policies makes estimation of net patient service revenue difficult but obviously necessary for sound financial management and proper financial reporting. For the FY2000, it is assumed the estimated provision for bad debts is $180,000 and actual contractual adjustments from third-party payors is $100,000. The entry to record this information is:

2. Provision for Bad Debts	180,000	
Contractual Adjustments	100,000	
Allowance for Uncollectible Receivables		180,000
Accounts and Notes Receivable		100,000

Provision for Bad Debts is another name for Bad Debts Expense and is reported as an operating expense. Contractual Adjustments, however, is deducted from Patient Service Revenue and only the net amount is reported as revenues of the period.

Examples of other revenues for hospitals include tuition from nursing students, interns, or residents; cafeteria and gift shop revenues; parking fees; fees for copies of medical records; and other activities related to the ongoing major or central operations of the hospital. Similarly, unrestricted gifts, grants, and endowment income restricted by donors to finance charity care would appropriately be classified as *other revenue* of a hospital. If a total of $48,800 was received in cash during FY2000 from sources classified as other revenue, Entry 3 is appropriate:

3. Cash	48,800	
Other Revenue		48,800

Apart from items previously described, hospitals may receive unrestricted donations of money or services. Ordinarily such donations should be classified as nonoperating gains rather than revenues. Hospitals often receive donated medicines and other materials. If such medicines and materials would otherwise have to be purchased, it is appropriate to record these donations at fair value as other revenue. Hospitals also routinely receive benefits from the services of volunteer workers; however, it is only rarely that the value of such services is recorded as a revenue or gain (and as an expense) since the restrictive conditions required by the AICPA Audit and Accounting Guide for recognition are seldom met. (See related discussions in Chapters 16 and 18.)

Assume total contributions were received in cash in the amount of $297,900 and unrestricted endowment income was $8,100.

4. Cash	306,000	
Contributions—Unrestricted		297,900
Investment Income—Unrestricted		8,100

One piece of fixed equipment, which had a historical cost of $28,000 and a book value of $2,000 as of September 30, 1999, was sold early in the 2000 fiscal year for $500 cash. The entry to record the disposal of the asset at a loss is:

5. Cash	500	
Loss on Disposal of Equipment	1,500	
Accumulated Depreciation—Equipment	26,000	
Equipment		28,000

New fixed equipment costing $400,000 was purchased during FY2000 by the Bloomfield Hospital; $100,000 with temporarily restricted net assets and $300,000 with unrestricted net assets. The entries should be:

6a. Equipment	400,000	
Cash		400,000

6b. Net Assets Released from Restrictions—		
Temporarily Restricted	100,000	
Net Assets Released from Restrictions—Unrestricted		100,000

During the year, the following items were recorded as Accounts Payable: the $16,000 accrued expenses payable as of September 30, 1999; nursing services expenses, $4,026,000; other professional services expenses, $947,200; general services expenses, $1,650,000; fiscal and administrative services expenses, $1,124,000; and supplies added to inventory, $400,000. The following entry summarizes that activity:

7. Accrued Expenses Payable	16,000	
Nursing Services Expenses	4,026,000	
Other Professional Services Expenses	947,200	
General Services Expenses	1,650,000	
Fiscal and Administrative Services Expenses	1,124,000	
Inventory	400,000	
Accounts Payable		8,163,200

Collections on accounts and notes receivable during the year amounted to $8,842,000; accounts and notes receivable totaling $131,000 were written off:

8. Cash	8,842,000	
Allowance for Uncollectible Receivables	131,000	
Accounts and Notes Receivable		8,973,000

The following cash disbursements were made during FY2000: Accounts Payable, $8,014,200; a principal payment in the amount of $400,000 was made to reduce the mortgage liability; and interest amounting to $160,000 on mortgages was paid:

9. Accounts Payable	8,014,200	
Mortgages Payable	400,000	
Interest Expense	160,000	
Cash		8,574,200

Supplies issued during the year cost $320,000 ($20,000 of the total was for use by fiscal and administrative services; $120,000 for use by general services; and the remainder by other professional services):

10. Other Professional Services Expenses	180,000	
General Services Expenses	120,000	
Fiscal and Administrative Services Expenses	20,000	
Inventory		320,000

Accrued expenses as of September 30, 2000, included $160,000 interest on mortgages; fiscal and administrative service expenses, $8,700; and other professional services expenses, $4,800. Prepaid expenses, consisting of general services expense items, declined $4,000 during the year:

11.	Interest Expense	160,000	
	Fiscal and Administrative Service Expenses	8,700	
	Other Professional Services Expenses	4,800	
	General Services Expenses	4,000	
	Accrued Expenses Payable		173,500
	Prepaid Expenses		4,000

Depreciation of plant and equipment for FY2000 was in the amounts shown in the following journal entry:

12.	Depreciation Expense	783,000	
	Accumulated Depreciation—Buildings		315,000
	Accumulated Depreciation—Equipment		468,000

The hospital received cash of $28,000 for interest on investments held in the Assets Limited as to Use—Investments account. Entry 13 records the receipt of cash and the corresponding credit.

13.	Cash	28,000	
	Investment Income—Unrestricted		28,000

The $28,000 received in cash for interest (see Entry 13) was reinvested in investments to be held for eventual use for expansion of facilities; the hospital governing board decided to purchase an additional $350,000 of investments for the same purpose. Entries 14a and 14b reflect the purchase of the investments and the increase in unrestricted designated net assets.

14a.	Assets Limited as to Use—Investments	378,000	
	Cash		378,000
14b.	Net Assets—Unrestricted, Undesignated	378,000	
	Net Assets—Unrestricted—Designated		378,000

Individual philanthropists and civic and charitable groups have donated money and securities to Bloomfield Hospital subject to the restriction that the assets may be utilized only for plant replacement and expansion. Cash was received during FY2000 from the following sources: Interest on marketable securities (including the amount accrued at the end of the 1999 fiscal year), $69,000; collections of pledges receivable, $292,000;

15.	Cash	361,000	
	Pledges Receivable		292,000
	Accrued Interest Receivable		36,000
	Investment Income—Temporarily Restricted		33,000

Marketable securities carried in the accounts at $85,000 were sold for $59,000. The proceeds were reinvested in marketable securities, and $300,000 additional marketable securities were purchased from cash received during the year:

16a.	Cash	59,000	
	Loss on Sale of Investments	26,000	
	Short-Term Investments		85,000
16b.	Short-Term Investments	359,000	
	Cash		359,000

A review of pledges receivable indicated pledges in the amount of $25,000 should be written off, and the allowance for uncollectible pledges should be increased to a total of 10 percent of the outstanding pledges, or $114,300. (Computation: September 30, 1999, balance, $1,460,000, less collections of $292,000 and write-offs of $25,000 = $1,143,000 balance at time of review.)

17a.	Allowance for Uncollectible Pledges	25,000	
	Pledges Receivable		25,000
17b.	Provision for Uncollectible Pledges	66,300	
	Allowance for Uncollectible Pledges		66,300

The fair values of short-term investments and assets limited as to use have not changed during the year. At the end of FY2000, the amount of interest accrued on marketable securities is computed to be $44,000:

18.	Accrued Interest Receivable	44,000	
	Investment Income—Temporarily Restricted		44,000

Bloomfield Hospital did not have any net assets temporarily restricted for programs as of September 30, 1999. In September 2000, however, a civic organization donated $5,000 to the hospital to be used to augment the physician residency program. The organization pledged an additional sum of $20,000 to be paid at the rate of $5,000 per year for the same purpose.

19.	Cash	5,000	
	Pledges Receivable	20,000	
	Contributions—Temporarily Restricted		25,000

The governing board and administration of Bloomfield Hospital expect the civic organization to honor its pledge; therefore, no Allowance for Uncollectible Pledges is created. Because the gift was received shortly before the end of FY2000, no expenses for the program were incurred during the year.

The hospital endowment consists of donated assets, the principal of which must be retained intact. The income from hospital endowment assets is expendable as the donor directed—either for general operating purposes or for named items or projects. The discussion in Chapters 9, 16, and 18 concerning the problems involved in distinguishing between principal and income are relevant, also, to hospital endowments. In order to be able to show that the terms of each endowment have been complied with, it is desirable to keep records for each separate endowment. As of September 30, 1999, Bloomfield Hospital is assumed to have only one endowment.

During FY2000, the hospital received marketable securities with a market value at the date of the gift of $24,000. The securities are to be held for the production of income; the income from these securities is for unrestricted use. The endowment may be accounted for as shown in the following entry:

20. Short-Term Investments   24,000
      Contributions—Permanently Restricted   24,000

Natural expenses of depreciation, interest, and provision for bad debts were allocated to the functional expenses based on an allocation basis established by the hospital.

21. Nursing Services Expenses   641,500
    Other Professional Services Expenses   179,620
    General Services Expenses   282,260
    Fiscal and Administrative Services Expenses   179,620
        Provision for Bad Debts   180,000
        Depreciation Expense   783,000
        Interest Expense   320,000

End-of-the-Year Closing Journal Entries.

Unrestricted revenues and expenses that pertain to FY2000 are closed to the Unrestricted, Undesignated Net Asset account as shown below:

22. Patient Service Revenue   9,261,000
    Other Revenue   48,800
    Contributions—Unrestricted   297,900
    Investment Income—Unrestricted   36,100
        Contractual Adjustments   100,000
        Nursing Services Expenses   4,667,500
        Other Professional Services Expenses   1,311,620
        General Services Expenses   2,056,260
        Fiscal and Administrative Services Expenses   1,332,320
        Loss on Disposal of Equipment   1,500
        Net Assets—Unrestricted, Undesignated   174,600

Restricted revenues that pertain to FY2000 are closed to the restricted net asset accounts as shown below:

23. Contributions—Temporarily Restricted—Programs   25,000
    Contributions—Permanently Restricted   24,000
    Investment Income—Temporarily Restricted   77,000
    Net Assets—Temporarily Restricted—Plant   15,300
        Provision for Uncollectible Pledges   66,300
        Loss on Sale of Investments   26,000
        Net Assets—Temporarily Restricted—Programs   25,000
        Net Assets—Permanently Restricted   24,000

Net Assets Released from Restrictions are closed out in the following entry:

24. Net Assets Released from Restrictions—Unrestricted   100,000
    Net Assets—Temporarily Restricted—Plant   100,000
        Net Assets Released from Restrictions—
          Temporarily Restricted   100,000
        Net Assets—Unrestricted, Undesignated   100,000

The pre-closing trial balance for Bloomfield Hospital as of September 30, 2000, is shown below. Financial statements reflecting the preceding transactions for Bloomfield Hospital were shown earlier in this chapter as Illustrations 19–3, 19–4, and 19–5.

BLOOMFIELD HOSPITAL
Pre-Closing Trial Balance
As of September 30, 2000

	Debits	Credits
Cash	$ 172,100	
Short-Term Investments	1,278,000	
Accrued Interest Receivable	44,000	
Accounts and Notes Receivable	488,000	
Allowance for Uncollectible Receivables		$ 135,000
Pledges Receivable	1,163,000	
Allowance for Uncollectible Pledges		114,300
Inventory	160,000	
Prepaid Expenses	8,000	
Assets Limited as to Use—Cash	6,500	
Assets Limited as to Use—Investments	778,000	
Long-Term Investments	146,000	
Land	1,080,000	
Buildings	11,050,000	
Equipment	5,292,000	
Accumulated Depreciation—Buildings		1,365,000
Accumulated Depreciation—Equipment		1,702,000
Accounts Payable		259,000
Accrued Expenses Payable		173,500
Mortgages Payable		6,000,000
Net Assets—Unrestricted, Undesignated		8,262,000
Net Assets—Unrestricted, Designated		784,500
Net Assets—Temporarily Restricted—Plant		2,508,000
Net Assets—Permanently Restricted		154,000
Patient Service Revenue		9,261,000
Contractual Adjustments	100,000	
Other Revenue		48,800
Contributions—Unrestricted		297,900
Contributions—Temporarily Restricted		25,000
Contributions—Permanently Restricted		24,000
Investment Income—Unrestricted		36,100
Investment Income—Temporarily Restricted		77,000
Net Assets Released from Restrictions—Unrestricted		100,000
Net Assets Released from Restrictions—Temporarily Restricted	100,000	
Nursing Services Expenses	4,667,500	
Other Professional Services Expenses	1,311,620	
General Services Expenses	2,056,260	
Fiscal and Administrative Services Expenses	1,332,320	
Loss on Disposal of Equipment	1,500	
Provision for Uncollectible Pledges	66,300	
Loss on Sale of Investments	26,000	
	$31,327,100	$31,327,100

Illustrative Statements for a Governmental Health Care Organization

The differences between governmental health care entities and not-for-profit and investor-owned organizations have been discussed throughout the preceding sections of this chapter. Illustrations 19–6 through 19–9 show the financial statements of the hypothetical Bloomfield Hospital, whose transactions for a typical year were illustrated in the preceding section, assuming it is a *governmental* entity rather than a not-for-profit entity. One reason the Balance Sheet in Illustration 19–6 is different than the one in Illustration 19–3 is that the organization has separated activity into four *funds*, which are self-balancing accounting and fiscal entities. The presentation that is shown *stacks* the funds in a *pancake* presentation, although the funds could have been presented in columns as shown in Chapter 18 on colleges and universities. The AICPA Audit and Accounting Guide requires only an aggregated Balance Sheet for governmental health care entities, similar to that reported in Illustration 19–3. However, reporting by funds is not prohibited. The Statement of Operations in Illustration 19–7 is only appropriate for the General Funds because the restricted funds will report changes throughout the year as additions and deductions from fund balances as seen in Illustration 19–8. The Statement of Cash Flows shown in Illustration 19–9 is presented according to GASB standards and differs from that in Illustration 19–5, in part, because there are four sections of cash flows on the GASB statement. The additional section required by GASB relates to cash flows from noncapital financing activities, such as unrestricted gifts and gifts restricted for future periods.

Related Entities

Health care organizations have long been associated with separate fund-raising foundations, medical research foundations, auxiliaries, and guilds. More recently, organizations are networking with other organizations in an effort to integrate health care services, control costs, increase efficiency, and ultimately improve the quality of health care. Some independent organizations combine for a specific purpose, for example, to obtaining financing, in which case they become an **obligated group.** These joint ventures include every combination of legal structure: for-profit, not-for-profit, and governmental organizations. Financial reporting guidance comes from the FASB in existing statements on consolidations and affiliated organizations and the GASB in statements on the reporting entity.[16] If one entity controls another, then the financial statements of the two organizations should be consolidated in order to be most useful to the decision maker. At a minimum, any economic interest between the organizations should be disclosed in each other's Notes to the Financial Statements. At issue is a working definition of *control* and *agency*. The FASB is expected to provide further guidance as part of its consolidations project.[17]

---

[16]FASB, Exposure Draft, *Consolidated Financial Statements: Policy and Procedures* (Norwalk, CT: FASB, 1995); GASB, *Codification*, Sec. 2100.

[17]When the FASB completes its projects on consolidations and affiliated organizations, the authors will make an Update Bulletin available to adopters of this book.

Illustration 19–6   Illustration of "Layered" Balance Sheet

BLOOMFIELD HOSPITAL
Balance Sheet
As of September 30, 2000

General Funds

Assets			Liabilities and Fund Balances		
Current Assets:			Current Liabilities:		
Cash		$ 93,100	Accounts payable	$ 259,000	
Accounts and notes receivable	$ 488,000		Accrued expenses payable	173,500	
Less: Allowance for uncollectible receivables	135,000	353,000			
Inventory		160,000			
Prepaid expenses		8,000			
Total Current Assets		614,100	Total Current Liabilities		$ 432,500
Assets Limited as to Use		784,500	Long-Term Debt:		
Property, Plant, and Equipment:			Mortgages payable		6,000,000
Land	11,050,000		Total Liabilities		6,432,500
Buildings	1,365,000		Fund Balance:		
Less: Accumulated depreciation	5,292,000	1,080,000	Designated	784,500	
Equipment	1,702,000	9,685,000	Undesignated	8,536,600	
Less: Accumulated depreciation		3,590,000	Total		9,321,100
Total Property, Plant, and Equipment		14,355,000			
Total General Funds		$15,753,600	Total General Funds		$15,753,600

Donor-Restricted Funds

Plant Replacement and Expansion Fund

Cash		$ 66,000	Fund balance	$ 2,392,700
Short-term investments		1,254,000		
Accrued interest receivable		44,000		
Pledges receivable	$ 1,143,000			
Less: Allowance for uncollectible pledges	114,300	1,028,700		
Total Plant Replacement and Expansion Funds		$ 2,392,700	Total Plant Replacement and Expansion Funds	$ 2,392,700

Specific Purpose Funds

Cash	$ 5,000	Fund balance	$ 25,000
Pledges receivable	20,000		
Total Specific Purpose Funds	$ 25,000	Total Specific Purpose Funds	$ 25,000

Endowment Funds

Cash	$ 8,000	Fund balance—Income unrestricted	$ 178,000
Short-term investments	24,000		
Long-term investments	146,000		
Total Endowment Funds	$ 178,000	Total Endowment Funds	$ 178,000

Illustration 19–7   Illustration of Statement of Operations

BLOOMFIELD HOSPITAL
Statement of Operations—Unrestricted Funds
Year Ended September 30, 2000

Net patient service revenue		$9,161,000
Other revenue		48,800
Total revenue		9,209,800
Expenses:		
Nursing services	$4,026,000	
Other professional services	1,132,000	
General services	1,774,000	
Fiscal and administrative services	1,152,700	
Depreciation expense	783,000	
Interest	320,000	
Provision for bad debts	180,000	
Total expenses		9,367,700
Income (loss) from operations		(157,900)
Nonoperating gains (losses):		
Unrestricted gifts	297,900	
Investment income	36,100	
Loss on disposal of equipment	(1,500)	
Total nonoperating gains (losses)		332,500
Revenues and gains in excess of expenses and losses		$ 174,600

Illustration 19–8   Illustration of Statement of Changes in Fund Balances

BLOOMFIELD HOSPITAL
Statement of Changes in Fund Balances
Year Ended September 30, 2000

	General Funds	Specific Purpose Funds	Plant Replacement and Expansion Funds	Endowment Funds
			Donor-Restricted Funds	
Balances, September 30, 1999	$9,046,500	$ –0–	$2,508,000	$154,000
Additions:				
Revenue and gains in excess of expenses	174,600			
Investment income			77,000	
Gifts, grants, and bequests		25,000		24,000
Transfer for capital outlay	100,000		(100,000)	
	274,600	25,000	(23,000)	24,000
Deductions:				
Provision for uncollectible pledges			66,300	
Loss on sale of investments			26,000	
Balances, September 30, 2000	$9,321,100	$25,000	$2,392,700	$178,000

Illustration 19–9 Illustration of Statement of Cash Flows— GASB Jurisdiction

BLOOMFIELD HOSPITAL
Statement of Cash Flows
Year Ended September 30, 2000

Cash flows from operating activities:	
Cash received from patients and third-party payors	$8,842,000
Cash paid to employees and suppliers	(8,014,200)
Other receipts from operations	48,800
Net cash provided by operating activities	876,600
Cash flows from noncapital financing activities:	
Unrestricted gifts and income from endowments	306,000
Gifts restricted for future operations	5,000
Net cash provided by noncapital financing activities	311,000
Cash flows from capital and related financing activities:	
Purchase of property and equipment	(400,000)
Principal paid on mortgage	(400,000)
Interest paid	(160,000)
Collection of pledges receivable	292,000
Proceeds from sale of equipment	500
Net cash used for capital and related financing activities	(667,500)
Cash flows from investing activities:	
Proceeds from sale of securities	59,000
Interest received on assets limited as to use	28,000
Interest received on donor-restricted assets	69,000
Cash invested in assets limited as to use	(378,000)
Cash invested in donor-restricted assets	(359,000)
Net cash used by investing activities	(581,000)
Net increase (decrease) in cash	(60,900)
Cash and cash equivalents, September 30, 1999	239,500
Cash and cash equivalents, September 30, 2000	$ 178,600

Reconciliation of Operating Income to Net Cash
Provided by Operating Activities

Operating income (loss)	$ (157,900)
Adjustments:	
Depreciation	783,000
Increase in patient accounts receivable, net	(139,000)
Increase in inventory	(80,000)
Increase in accounts payable	149,000
Increase in accrued expenses	157,500
Decrease in prepaid expenses	4,000
Interest paid in cash (Note 1)	160,000
Net cash provided by operating activities and gains and losses	$ 876,600

Note 1: Interest was classified as an operating expense on the income statement but as cash flows from capital and related activities on the cash flows statement prepared in conformity with GASB standards.

Other Accounting Issues

Budgeting and Costs   Governmental and other not-for-profit hospitals and other health care entities, even though they are service institutions, must have an inflow of funds at least equal to their outflow of funds. Since this is the case, prudent management will attempt to forecast the outlays for a definite period and forecast the income for the same period. Equating anticipated income and outgo means future operations must be planned. "Planning future operations" is a phrase that defines budgeting as it is thought of today in successful businesses. Budgeting is not merely planning financial affairs, but developing an integrated plan for all phases of the operations of the organizations. If this is done properly, each department knows the objectives of the organization and has determined to what extent and in what manner the department will contribute to them. The predetermination of the role each department is to play in achieving the organization's objectives enables management to measure the success each department has in attaining its objectives. Frequent measurement helps keep each department on the proper path. Thus, budgeting is of considerable usefulness to management.

Most hospitals use comprehensive budgets for managerial purposes but do not incorporate the budgetary provision in the accounts. Other hospitals, principally governmental hospitals, do record their budgets in the ledger. Nevertheless, it is important that every hospital and other health care entity have an annual budget and that the budget be administered intelligently. For a hospital, or for any other enterprise, good financial management requires outlays to be evaluated in terms of results achieved. Insistence on rigid adherence to a budget not related to actual workload (as is the case in some governmental agencies) tends to make the budget useless as a management tool. Generally budgetary accounts are used only if required by law.

Until the 1980s, it was customary for hospitals to determine costs of services rendered during a fiscal year by rearranging financial accounting data generated during that year. Although never satisfactory for financial management purposes, the procedure for cost determination was acceptable for purposes of reporting costs to third-party payors, which reimbursed hospitals on a retrospective (after-the-fact) basis. Since 1983, however, the largest purchaser of hospital services, Medicare, in an attempt to establish better control over hospital costs, has utilized a system of prospective payment. The Medicare system pays health care providers standardized rates for services rendered to patients in each **diagnosis-related group (DRG).** Health care providers, therefore, have an incentive to determine actual costs of services rendered, by DRG, in order to keep their costs commensurate with Medicare's payments for services rendered to Medicare patients. It is now common for most hospitals to have sophisticated systems to capture costs by procedure or DRG.

The DRG is a case-mix classification scheme that is used to determine the payment provided to the hospital for inpatient services, regardless of how much the hospital spends to treat a patient. For example, the DRG for maternity patients may provide payment at 0.8 relative to a norm of 1.0, while the DRG for a heart transplant patient may provide 1.3 times the average payment. These relative numbers are multiplied by the federal standard rate as determined by the Healthcare Financing Administration (HCFA). There are approximately 470 DRGs and the average reimbursement was $6,029 in 1997.

Auditing

Auditing issues of particular significance to the health care industry relate to contingencies, third-party payors, related entities, and restructuring. Renewed efforts on the part of the federal government to curb health care fraud and illegal acts also affect auditors and their clients. Congress instituted new civil and criminal penalties in the Health Insurance Portability and Accountability Act of 1996, False Claims Act, and Stark Laws I and II that are designed to penalize individuals and organizations that contribute to the estimated $100 billion losses due to fraud and abuse in the health care industry. Investigations center on improper billing and coding, improper care, and kickbacks. Many health care providers are proactively implementing voluntary compliance programs.[18] Another important auditing issue relates to the revision of OMB *Circular A-133* and its application to hospitals and health care organizations, as described in Chapter 12 of this text.

Taxation and Regulatory Issues

Since a large share of health care providers are legally structured as tax-exempt organizations under IRC Sec. 501(c)(3), the regulations and activities of the Internal Revenue Service should be of concern to the accountant working with health care organizations. For example, the penalties for private inurement or excess economic benefits to individuals, introduced in the Taxpayer Bill of Rights 2 of 1996 and Chapter 17 of this text, apply to health care administrators and persons with substantial influence over the organization. The IRS has increased its review of physician recruiting incentives, joint operating agreements for exemption applications, unrelated business income (such as hospital pharmacy sales to the general public), private-activity bonds, and independent contractor (versus employee) status. Congressional and public scrutiny over the distributions of assets of not-for-profit organizations that change legal status and the amount of charity care delivery by tax-exempt hospitals is at its highest point in the century. Sanctions are economically significant and may involve loss of tax-exempt status or eligibility for tax-exempt financing.

Certain Types of Health Care Organizations

Prepaid health care plans, such as **health maintenance organizations (HMO)** or **preferred provider organizations (PPO),** function as brokers between the consumer or patient demanding the services and the providers of health care, such as health care professionals or hospitals. Contractual arrangements among these parties,

---

[18]AICPA, Audit Risk Alert, *Health Care Industry Developments* 1997–98 (New York: AICPA, 1998), p. 7.

including employers, are complex and varied. If the premium revenue from contracts is not expected to cover the agreed-upon health care costs, then the prepaid plan may transfer some of its risk to an insurance company under *stop-loss insurance*, or a **risk contract.** In any case, the costs of future services to be rendered, net of anticipated revenue, should be recorded as a liability if it meets the criteria of a contingent liability. Certain contract acquisition costs, such as commissions paid to agents based on new enrollments or subscriber contracts, should be expensed as incurred, although there is some theoretical support for deferring these costs.[19]

There are more than 1,000 **continuing care retirement communities (CCRCs)** in the United States which are operated primarily by not-for-profit organizations. CCRCs provide residential care in a facility, along with some level of long-term medical care that is less intensive than hospital care. There are many ways to structure contracts between the patient/resident and the CCRC; however, most plans require advance payment of an entrance fee and periodic fees to cover operating costs in exchange for current use of the facilities and the promise to provide some level of health and residential services in the future. The advance fee may be refundable if certain future events occur, such as the death of the resident. Accounting issues relate to the refundable and nonrefundable advance fees, the obligation to provide future services, and the costs of acquiring initial care contracts.

Financial and Operational Analysis

The goal of financial and operational analysis depends, of course, on the needs of the decision maker. For example, managers are directly accountable for performance; financial analysts determine the creditworthiness of organizations issuing debt; and third parties determine appropriate payment based on costs. Consumers may want nonfinancial performance and quality measures, such as the success rate for various procedures or the value received for the money spent.

Health care entities are evaluated using a variety of ratios and benchmarks, some of which are unique to hospitals and others that are similar to those applied to other businesses. These analyses can be categorized into those that measure:

1. Capacity utilization (e.g., occupancy rate or daily census and average length of stay).
2. Profitability (e.g., gross patient service revenue per discharge or operating profit margin or cash flow per bed).
3. Patient and payout mix (e.g., Medicare case-mix index or Medicaid acute care days as a percentage of total acute care days).
4. Pricing strategy (e.g., markup ratio for ancillary or laboratory services).

---

[19]AAG-HCO, Sec. 13.10.

5. Productivity and efficiency (e.g., full-time-equivalent personnel per average daily census or overhead expenses as a percentage of operating expenses).

6. Capital and liquidity (e.g., plant, property, and equipment per bed or debt per bed and current ratio and number of days in accounts receivable).[20]

Once ratios are computed, they are compared to industry benchmarks. Hospitals are compared based upon bed size, geographic location, and teaching designation. Further analysis is done according to the type of patient care. Organizations that accumulate information about health care norms include the American Hospital Association (AHA); the Institute for Health Care Improvement (IHI); bond-rating agencies, such as Moody's and Standard & Poor's; Health Care Investment Analysts, Inc. (HCIA); and the Center for Health Care Industry Performance Studies (CHIPS).

Conclusion

A single chapter on accounting for health care entities can touch on only the most outstanding features. Variations in the operating and accounting procedures for individual health care entities exist due to the variety in the type and size of health care providers, the range of services offered, the dependence of these entities on third-party payors, and the financial sophistication of the governing board, administrator, and finance director. For further information, the references cited in the Selected References section are recommended.

Key Terms

Assets limited as to use,   788
Capitation fees,   782
Charity care,   788
Continuing care retirement community
   (CCRC),   804
Contractual adjustments
   (or allowances),   787
Diagnosis-related groups (DRGs),   802
Health maintenance organization
   (HMO),   803

Obligated group,   798
Performance indicator,   785
Preferred provider organization
   (PPO),   803
Prospective payment system (PPS),   788
Risk contract,   804
Settlement accounts,   789
Third-party payor,   788

---

[20]Nadia A. Perry, *Introduction to the Health Care Industry* (Englewood, CO: Micromash, 1997).

Selected References

American Institute of Certified Public Accountants. Audit and Accounting Guide *Health Care Organizations*. New York, 1997.

Financial Accounting Standards Board. *Statement No. 116*. "Accounting for Contributions Received and Contributions Made." Norwalk, CT, 1993.

————. *Statement No. 117*. "Financial Statements of Not-for-Profit Organizations." Norwalk, CT, 1993.

Periodicals

Healthcare Financial Management. The journal of the Healthcare Financial Management Association, Oak Brook, IL.

Hospital Progress. The journal of the Catholic Hospital Association, St. Louis, MO.

Hospitals. The journal of the American Hospital Association, Chicago, IL.

Questions

19–1. "All providers of health care services must use fund accounting." True or false? Explain your answer.

19–2. What are the required financial statements under the provisions of the AICPA Audit and Accounting Guide *Health Care Organizations*?

19–3. What are the major differences between the accounting treatment of hospital property, plant, and equipment used in rendering hospital services and the accounting treatment of general fixed assets of state and local governmental units?

19–4. How do the accounting treatments for charity services, patient discounts, contractual adjustments, and provision for bad debts differ in terms of their effects on patient service revenues and related receivables?

19–5. What is the difference in accounting for investments among investor-owned, not-for-profit, and governmental health care organizations?

19–6. Breyer Memorial Hospital received a $100,000 gift that was restricted by the donor for heart research. At fiscal year-end Breyer had incurred $25,000 in expenses related to this project. Explain how these transactions would be reported in Breyer's balance sheet and operating statement under the independent assumptions that (a) Breyer is a *governmentally* owned not-for-profit hospital and (b) Breyer is a *nongovernmentally* owned not-for-profit hospital.

19–7. "FASB standards applicable to nongovernmentally owned not-for-profit health care entities preclude such entities from distinguishing 'Assets Limited as to Use' from other unrestricted assets." Do you agree? Explain fully.

19–8. What contingent liabilities arise from a health care organization's relations with third-party payors?

19–9. Explain the importance of diagnosis-related groups (DRGs) in the cost accounting systems of a health care provider.

19–10. What are some particular accounting issues in continuing care retirement communities (CCRCs)?

Cases

19–1. The local newspaper of a large urban area printed a story entitled "Charity Care by Hospitals Stirs Debate." The story quotes one legislator who wants "to ensure that the state's nonprofit hospitals are fulfilling their obligation; that is to provide charity care at least equal to the tax exemption they receive as a nonprofit entity." The following chart is provided:

Comparison of Selected Factors in Three Nonprofit Hospitals
(dollars in millions)

	Hope Hospital	St. Pat's Hospital	Capitol Hospital
Estimated taxes the hospitals would pay if they were not tax-exempt	$6.8	$2.2	$4.5
Charity and other uncompensated care	$17.79 of which $3.8 is bad debts	$3.1 not including bad debts	$6.7
Community service programs*	$1.6	$1.0	n.a.
Unpaid cost of Medicaid and Medicare	$3.4	$0.6	n.a.
Nonreimbursed research and graduate medical education	$2.0	$0.7	n.a.

n.a. = Not available.
*Including such programs as activity sponsorships, playground equipment, neighborhood summits, and scholarships for at-risk students.

Required

    a. What are the obligations of nongovernmental IRC Sec. 501(c)(3) organizations to provide charity care?

    b. Do you agree that the hospitals are not fulfilling their obligations? Why or why not?

    c. What additional information would you like to have? Do you expect to find this information in the audited annual financial statements?

19–2. You are an accountant with a large public hospital. The Hospital Board recently decided to horizontally integrate by purchasing other health care organizations that provide specialized services. You have been asked to review Arbor Community Hospital's Statement of Operations (presented on the next page) in order to determine if it is a "profitable" organization. It is a not-for-profit hospital with a self-perpetuating board comprised of community leaders. Arbor Community offers specialized services including an inpatient headache clinic and a substance abuse clinic.

Required

    a. Write a concise, professional report to your superior identifying some ratios you find relevant from the Statement of Operations that support your position as to whether the hospital is profitable.

    b. What other factors do you consider critical in a decision to purchase an existing health care facility?

    c. What other financial information would you like to review in order to form an opinion as to the performance of this hospital?

ARBOR COMMUNITY HOSPITAL
Statements of Operations
Years Ended December 31

	2000			1999		
	Unrestricted	Temporarily Restricted	Total	Unrestricted	Temporarily Restricted	Total
Revenue, gains, and other support:						
Net patient service revenue	$39,408,595	—	$39,408,595	$36,655,677	—	$36,655,677
Other revenue	2,701,284	—	2,701,284	2,411,442	—	2,411,442
Investment income	980,244	$ 32,752	1,012,996	514,844	$ 14,183	529,027
Net assets released from restrictions used for operations	44,034	(44,034)	—	20,086	(20,086)	—
Total revenue, gains, and other support	43,134,157	(11,282)	43,122,875	39,602,049	(5,903)	39,596,146
Expenses:						
Inpatient nursing services	5,035,376	—	5,035,376	5,219,917	—	5,219,917
Outpatient and ancillary services	18,468,238	—	18,468,238	16,236,239	—	16,236,239
Physician offices	1,928,224	—	1,928,224	1,933,725	—	1,933,725
General services	5,692,281	—	5,692,281	5,677,606	—	5,677,606
Fiscal services	1,585,042	—	1,585,042	1,621,436	—	1,621,436
Administrative services	4,967,417	—	4,967,417	4,381,216	—	4,381,216
Interest	809,895	—	809,895	510,008	—	510,008
Depreciation and amortization	2,752,519	—	2,752,519	2,459,604	—	2,459,604
Bad debts	994,506	—	994,506	858,790	—	858,790
Total expenses	42,233,498	—	42,233,498	38,898,541	—	38,898,541
Excess of revenue, gains, and other support over (under) expenses:	900,659	(11,282)	889,377	703,508	(5,903)	697,605
Net gain on investments reported at fair value	48,674	—	48,674	433,446	—	433,446
Contributions	952	158,068	159,020	4,566	135,267	139,833
Net assets released from restrictions used for purchase of property and equipment	36,540	(36,540)	—	488,524	(488,524)	—
Change in net assets before extraordinary item	986,825	110,246	1,097,071	1,630,044	(359,160)	1,270,844
Extraordinary loss on refinancing of debt	—	—	—	(140,129)	—	(140,129)
Increase (decrease) in net assets	$ 986,825	$ 110,246	$ 1,097,071	$ 1,489,915	$(359,160)	$ 1,130,755

19–3.   **Internet Case.** Many professional associations of health care professionals and providers have published position papers on health care reform. Identify the organizations that have large and/or influential constituencies and find their home-pages on the Internet. See if they have a position paper, publication, or letter to a federal oversight body that articulates their position on proposed changes in the delivery and payment of health care in the United States. List the accounting issues that they discuss (e.g., financial reporting, managerial accounting, taxation, information systems, and auditing) as opposed to financing issues. For example, the American Hospital Association (http://www.aha.org) wrote a letter to Senator William Roth on July 1, 1997, that was available through their homepage. (Note: Web pages change frequently, so this letter may not still be on the web site when you look at it.)

Exercises and Problems

19–1. Write the numbers 1 through 10 on a sheet of paper. Beside each number, write the letter corresponding with the best answer to each of the following questions:

1. Not-for-profit health care organizations are typically sponsored by:
   a. Community organizations.
   b. Religious organizations.
   c. Universities.
   d. Any of the above.

2. Revenue from the gift shop of a hospital would normally be included in:
   a. Nonoperating gains.
   b. Other revenue.
   c. Patient service revenue.
   d. Professional services revenue.

3. Donated medicine that normally would be purchased by a hospital should be recorded at fair market value and should be credited directly to:
   a. Other Revenue.
   b. Nonoperating Gains.
   c. Fund Balance.
   d. Deferred Revenue.

4. A not-for-profit hospital that follows FASB standards and the AICPA Audit and Accounting Guide *Health Care Organizations* should report investment income from endowments that is restricted to a specific operating purpose as:
   a. General Fund revenue.
   b. Endowment Fund revenue.
   c. Unrestricted revenue.
   d. Temporarily restricted revenue.

5. A $50,000 donation is held by a bank in perpetuity with the investment income dedicated for use by a hospital for operating purposes. The $50,000 principal should be:
   a. Reported as assets limited as to use by the hospital.
   b. Reported as nonoperating revenue of the hospital.
   c. Reported as permanently restricted assets of the hospital.
   d. Disclosed in Notes to the Financial Statements of the hospital.

6. If a governmental hospital uses fund accounting, then restricted funds are:
   a. Not available unless the board of directors removes the restrictions.
   b. Restricted as to use by the donor, grantor, or other source of the resources.
   c. Not available for current operating use; however, the income earned on the funds is available.
   d. Restricted as to use only for board-designated purposes.

7. Depreciation should be recognized in the financial statements of:
   a. Proprietary (for-profit) hospitals only.
   b. Both proprietary (for-profit) and not-for-profit hospitals.
   c. Both proprietary (for-profit) and not-for-profit hospitals, only when they are affiliated with a college or university.
   d. All hospitals, as a memorandum entry not affecting the statement of revenues and expenses.

8. The financial statements of a nongovernmental not-for-profit hospital and its related medical research foundation should be consolidated if:
   a. The hospital "controls" the Foundation by appointing all the directors to its Board.
   b. The hospital has a significant economic interest in the activities and assets of the Foundation.
   c. The assets of the Foundation were contributed by donors who stipulated that they could only be used for the benefit of the Hospital.
   d. All of the above are factors to consider in the determination of whether to consolidate two reporting entities, or merely disclose the existence of each other.

9. Which of the following sets of financial statements is required by GAAP for nongovernmentally owned hospitals?
   a. Balance Sheet, Statement of Revenues and Expenses of General Funds, and Statement of Changes in Fund Balances.
   b. Balance Sheet, Statement of Revenues and Expenses of General Funds, and Statement of Cash Flows.
   c. Balance Sheet, Statement of Changes in Fund Balances, and Statement of Cash Flows.
   d. Balance Sheet, Statement of Operations, and Statement of Cash Flows.

10. A possible contingency that might have to be disclosed in the Notes to the Financial Statements of a health care organization is:
    a. An agreed-upon settlement between a third-party payor and the health care provider.
    b. Premiums received for prepaid health care by a health maintenance organization.
    c. An uncertain result of ongoing negotiations for reimbursement with a third-party payor for services rendered to patients.
    d. None of the above.

19–2. The Clearwater Community Hospital Balance Sheet as of December 31, 1999, is presented on the next page.

CLEARWATER COMMUNITY HOSPITAL
Balance Sheet
December 31, 1999

Assets			*Liabilities and Fund Balance*		
Current:			Current:		
Cash		$ 65,000	Accounts payable		$ 65,000
Accounts and notes receivable	$ 140,000		Accrued payroll		110,000
Less: Allowance for					
uncollectibles	12,000	128,000			
Inventory		71,000			
Total Current Assets		264,000	Total Current Liabilities		175,000
Assets Limited as to Use:					
Cash	11,500		Long-Term Debt:		
Investments	210,000		Mortgage payable		3,500,000
Total Assets Limited			Total Liabilities		3,675,000
as to Use		221,500			
Property, Plant, and Equipment:			Net Assets:		
Land		208,000	Unrestricted, Undesignated		1,782,000
Buildings, at cost	4,516,000		Unrestricted, Designated for		
Less: Accumulated			Plant Replacements		221,500
depreciation	1,506,000	3,010,000	Total Net Assets		2,003,500
Equipment, at cost	2,871,000				
Less: Accumulated depreciation	896,000	1,975,000			
Total Property, Plant,					
and Equipment		5,193,000			
Total Assets		$5,678,500	Total Liabilities and Net Assets		$5,678,500

Required

a. Record in general journal form the effect of the following transactions during the fiscal year ended December 31, 2000 assuming Clearwater Community Hospital is a nongovernmental, not-for-profit hospital.

(1) Summary of revenue journal:

Patient services revenue, gross	$3,497,500
Adjustments and allowances:	
Contracting agencies	122,600

(2) Summary of cash receipts journal:

Interest on Investments in Assets	
Limited as to Use	20,000
Unrestricted grant from United Fund	160,000
Collections of receivables	3,373,600

(3) Purchases journal:

Administration	163,900
General services expenses	176,800
Nursing services expenses	269,400
Other professional services expenses	256,600

(4) Payroll journal:

Administration	247,600
General services expenses	175,000
Nursing services expenses	540,300
Other professional services expenses	412,200

(5) Summary of cash payments journal:

Interest expense	280,000
Payment on mortgage principal	500,000
Accounts payable for purchases	839,500
Accrued payroll	1,370,000
Transfer to Assets Limited as to Use	30,000

(6) Fixed equipment that cost $6,560, and for which accumulated depreciation totaled $4,920, was traded for similar new equipment costing $9,840; the payment in cash amounted to $8,800 (the cash was paid from Assets Limited as to Use—Cash).

(7) Depreciation charges for the year amounted to $117,000 for the buildings; $58,000 for fixed equipment; and $70,500 for major movable equipment.

(8) Other information:

    (*a*) Provision for uncollectible receivables, $29,000.

    (*b*) Supplies inventory:

	12/31/1999	12/31/2000
Administration	$ 8,000	$ 7,300
General services expenses	8,700	9,000
Nursing services expenses	17,000	17,200
Other professional services expenses	37,300	40,000
Totals	$71,000	$73,500

    (*c*) Portion of Mortgage Payable due within one year, $500,000.

(9) Assume there was no change in fair value of investments at year-end.

(10) Provisions for bad debts, interest expense, and depreciation expense were allocated to functional expense accounts in proportion to their pre-allocation balances. Nominal accounts were closed.

  b. Prepare a Balance Sheet as of December 31, 2000.

  c. Prepare a Statement of Operations for the year ended December 31, 2000.

19–3.   The following transactions occurred in the Jackson Hospital:

1. Under the will of Samuel H. Samuels, a bequest of $100,000 was received for research on gerontology. The investment income is to be used for research purposes.

2. Pending the need of the money for the designated purpose, part of it was invested in $95,000 of par value City of Jackson 6 percent bonds, at 103 and accrued interest of $823.
3. An interest payment of $2,850 was received on the City of Jackson bonds.
4. The bonds were sold at 104 and accrued interest of $443.
5. The income from the Samuels gift was used for the stipulated purpose.

Required

Make journal entries for the above transactions assuming this is a nongovernmental, not-for-profit hospital.

19–4. The following transactions took place in the Brady Memorial Hospital during the fiscal year 2000.

1. Gross revenues of $78,000,000 were earned for service to Medicare patients.
2. Expected contractual adjustments with Medicare, a third-party payor, are $36,050,000; an "Allowance for Contractual Adjustments" account is used to record these contractual adjustments.
3. Medicare "cleared charges" of $78,000,000 with payments of $39,608,000 and contractual allowances of $38,392,000.
4. Interim payments received from Medicare amounted to $2,600,000.
5. The Hospital made a lump-sum payment back to Medicare of $1,000,000.

The Hospital uses an Interim Payments account to keep track of the payments made between Medicare and the Hospital until final settlement is determined.

Required

a. Record the transactions in the general journal.
b. Calculate the amount of net patient service revenue.
c. What is the net cash flow from transactions with Medicare?
d. What adjustments must be made at the end of the year to "settle" up with Medicare and properly report the net patient service revenue after this settlement?

19–5. The Dexter City Hospital Combined Balance Sheet as of December 31, 1999, is shown on the next page. The Controller asks you to prepare an aggregated Balance Sheet in accord with current financial reporting standards according to the AICPA Audit and Accounting Guide *Health Care Organizations*. You determine that (1) the cash and investments of the Plant Fund are restricted under the terms of several gifts to use for plant replacement or expansion; income from Plant Fund investments is restricted to the same purposes. (2) Income from Endowment Fund investments may be used at the discretion of the hospital governing board.

DEXTER CITY HOSPITAL
Balance Sheet
As of December 31, 1999

Assets			*Liabilities and Fund Balances*		
		Operating Fund			
Cash		$ 20,000	Accounts payable		$ 16,000
Accounts receivable	$ 37,000		Accrued expense—payable		6,000
Less: Allowance for					
uncollectible accounts	7,000	30,000	Total Liabilities		22,000
Inventory of supplies		14,000	Fund balance		42,000
Total		$ 64,000	Total		$ 64,000
		Plant Fund			
Cash		$ 53,800	Mortgage bonds payable		$ 150,000
Investments		71,200			
Land		400,000			
Buildings	$1,750,000				
Less: Accumulated			Fund balance:		
depreciation	430,000	1,320,000	Investment in plant		2,021,000
			Reserved for plant improvement		
Equipment	680,000		and replacement		220,000
Less: Accumulated					
depreciation	134,000	546,000			2,241,000
Total		$2,391,000	Total		$2,391,000
		Endowment Fund			
Cash		$ 6,000	Fund balance—income		
Investments		260,000	unrestricted		$ 266,000
Total		$ 266,000	Total		$ 266,000

19–6. During 1999, the following events and transactions were recorded by Blackpool City Hospital. Show in general journal form the entries that should be made for each of the 12 transactions and the closing entries in accord with the standards for a governmental health care entity discussed in this chapter.

1. Gross charges for hospital services, all charged to accounts and notes receivable, were as follows:

> Patient service revenues $1,086,000

2. Additional information relating to current-year receivables and revenues were as follows:

> Contractual adjustments $30,000
> Provision for bad debts   15,000

3. Paid $18,000 to retire mortgage bonds payable with an equivalent face value.

4. During the year, the General Fund received in cash unrestricted contributions of $50,000 and unrestricted income from endowment investments of $6,500.

5. New equipment costing $26,000 was acquired from donor-restricted cash. An X-ray machine that cost $24,000 and had an undepreciated cost of $2,400 was sold for $500 cash.

6. Vouchers totaling $1,191,000 were issued for the following items:

Fiscal and administrative services expenses	$215,000
General services expenses	225,000
Nursing services expenses	520,000
Other professional services expenses	165,000
Inventory	60,000
Expenses accrued at December 31, 1998	6,000

7. Collections of accounts receivable totaled $985,000. Accounts written off as uncollectible amounted to $11,000.

8. Cash payments on vouchers payable (paid to employers and suppliers) during the year were $825,000.

9. Supplies of $37,000 were issued to nursing services.

10. On December 31, 1999, accrued interest income on investments was $800.

11. Depreciation of buildings and equipment was as follows:

Buildings	$44,000
Equipment	73,000

12. On December 31, 1999, an accrual of $6,100 was made for interest on mortgage bonds payable.

13. On December 31, 1999, closing entries were made in the General Funds general journal.

19–7. The following selected information was taken from the books and records of Glendora Hospital (a nongovernmental, not-for-profit hospital) as of and for the year ended June 30, 2000.

- Patient service revenue totaled $16,000,000, with the allowance for uncollectible accounts and contractual adjustments amounting to $1,800,000 and $1,600,000, respectively. Other revenue aggregated $346,000 and included $160,000 from specific purpose funds. Revenue of $6,000,000 recognized under cost-reimbursement agreements is subject to audit and retroactive adjustment by third-party payors (other than Medicare). Estimated retroactive adjustments under these agreements have been included in allowances.

- Unrestricted gifts and bequests of $410,000 were received.

- Unrestricted income from endowments totaled $160,000.

- Income from investments aggregated $82,000.

- Operating expenses totaled $13,370,000 and included $500,000 for depreciation computed on the straight-line basis. However, accelerated depreciation is used to determine reimbursable costs under certain third-party reimbursement agreements. Net cost reimbursement revenue amounting to $220,000, resulting from the difference in depreciation methods, was deferred to future years.

- Also included in operating expenses are pension costs of $100,000, in connection with a noncontributory pension plan covering substantially all of Glendora's employees. Accrued pension costs are funded currently. Prior service cost is being amortized over a period of 20 years. The actuarially computed value of vested and nonvested benefits at year-end amounted to

$3,000,000 and $350,000, respectively. The assumed rate of return used in determining the actuarial present value of accumulated plan benefits was 8 percent. The plan's net assets available for benefits at year-end was $3,050,000.
- Gifts and bequests are recorded at fair market values when received.
- Patient service revenue is accounted for at established rates on the accrual basis.

Required

    a. Prepare a formal Statement of Operations for Glendora Hospital for the year ended June 30, 2000.

    b. Draft the appropriate disclosures in separate notes accompanying the Statement of Operations referencing each note to its respective item in the statement.

                                           (AICPA, adapted)

19–8. Esperanza Hospital's post-closing trial balance at December 31, 1999, appears as follows:

ESPERANZA HOSPITAL
Trial Balance
December 31, 1999

	Debits	Credits
Cash	$ 60,000	
Investment in U.S. Treasury Bills	400,000	
Investment in Corporate Bonds	500,000	
Interest Receivable	10,000	
Accounts Receivable	50,000	
Inventory	30,000	
Land	100,000	
Building	800,000	
Equipment	170,000	
Allowance for Depreciation		$ 410,000
Accounts Payable		20,000
Notes Payable		70,000
Endowment Fund Balance		520,000
Other Fund Balances		1,100,000
Totals	$2,120,000	$2,120,000

Esperanza, which is a nongovernmentally affiliated not-for-profit hospital, did not maintain its books in conformity with the principles of the AICPA Audit and Accounting Guide *Health Care Organizations.* Effective January 1, 2000, Esperanza's Board of Trustees voted to adjust the December 31, 2000, general ledger balances to conform to the Guide.

Additional Account Information

- *Investment in corporate bonds* pertains to the amount required to be accumulated under a board policy to invest cash equal to accumulated depreciation until the funds are needed for asset replacement. The $500,000 balance at December 31,

1999, is less than the full amount required because of errors in computation of building depreciation for past years. Included in the allowance for depreciation is a correctly computed amount of $90,000 applicable to equipment.

- *Endowment balance* has been credited with the following:

Donor's bequest of cash	$300,000
Gains on sales of securities	100,000
Interest and dividends earned in 1997, 1998, and 1999	120,000
Total	$520,000

The terms of the bequest specify that the principal, plus all gains on sales of investments, is to remain fully invested in U.S. government or corporate securities. At December 31, 1999, $400,000 was invested in U.S. Treasury bills. The bequest further specifies that interest and dividends earned on investments are to be used for payment of current operating expenses.

- *Land* comprises the following:

Donation of land in 1990, at appraised value	$ 40,000
Appreciation in fair value of land as determined by independent appraiser in 1999	60,000
Total	$100,000

- *Building* comprises the following:

Hospital building completed 40 years ago, when operations were started (estimated useful life, 50 years), at cost	$720,000
Installation of elevator 20 years ago (estimated useful life, 20 years), at cost	80,000
Total	$800,000

Required

- *a.* Prepare in general journal form adjusting entries necessary to restate the accounts given in the trial balance properly. Show all supporting computations in good form.
- *b.* Prepare in general journal form entries to distribute the adjusted account balances to funds that Esperanza Hospital should report in financial statements prepared in conformity with generally accepted accounting principles as set forth in the AICPA Audit and Accounting Guide.

(AICPA, adapted)

Glossary

Some of these definitions were taken with permission from publications of the Government Finance Officers Association. Others were taken from specialized publications cited in the text; the remainder were supplied by the authors. The letters "q.v." signify "which see"; that is, the preceding word is defined elsewhere in the glossary.

Abatement A complete or partial cancellation of a levy imposed by a governmental unit. Abatements usually apply to tax levies, special assessments, and service charges.

Account Group A self-balancing set of accounts, but not a fiscal entity, therefore not a fund. See General Fixed Assets Account Group, and General Long-Term Debt Account Group.

Accountability Being obliged to explain one's actions, to justify what one does; the requirement for government to answer to its citizenry—to justify the raising of public resources and expenditure of those resources. Also, in the GASB's view, the obligation to report whether the government operated within appropriate legal constraints; whether resources were used efficiently, economically, and effectively; whether current-year revenues were sufficient to pay for the services provided in the current year; and whether the burden for services previously provided will be shifted to future taxpayers.

Accounting Period A period at the end of which, and for which, financial statements are prepared. See also Fiscal Period.

Accounting System The total structure of records and procedures that discover, record, classify, and report information on the financial position and operations of a governmental unit or any of its funds, account groups, and organizational components.

Accounts Receivable Amounts owing on open account from private persons, firms, or corporations for goods and services furnished by a governmental unit. Taxes Receivable and Special Assessments Receivable are recorded separately. Amounts due from other funds or from other governmental units should be reported separately.

Accrual Basis The basis of accounting under which revenues are recorded when earned and expenditures (or expenses) are recorded as soon as they result in liabilities for benefits received, notwithstanding that the receipt of cash or the payment of cash may take place, in whole or in part, in another accounting period. See also Accrue and Levy.

Accrue To record revenues when earned and to record expenditures (or expenses) as soon as they result in liabilities for benefits received, notwithstanding that the receipt of cash or payment of cash may take place, in whole or in part, in another accounting period. See also Accrual Basis, Accrued Expenses, and Accrued Revenue.

Accrued Expenses   Expenses incurred during the current accounting period but not payable until a subsequent accounting period. See also Accrual Basis and Accrue.

Accrued Income   See Accrued Revenue.

Accrued Interest on Investments Purchased   Interest accrued on investments between the last interest payment date and the date of purchase.

Accrued Interest Payable   A liability account that represents the amount of interest expense accrued at the balance sheet date but not due until a later date.

Accrued Revenue   Revenue earned during the current accounting period but not to be collected until a subsequent accounting period. See also Accrual Basis and Accrue.

Accrued Taxes Payable   A liability for taxes that have accrued since the last payment date.

Accrued Wages Payable   A liability for wages earned by employees between the last payment date and the balance sheet date.

Accumulated Depreciation   See Allowance for Depreciation.

Acquisition Adjustment   Difference between amount paid by a utility for plant assets acquired from another utility and the original cost (q.v.) of those assets less depreciation to date of acquisition. Similar to goodwill in nonmonopolistic enterprises.

Activity   A specific and distinguishable line of work performed by one or more organizational components of a governmental unit for the purpose of accomplishing a function for which the governmental unit is responsible. For example, Food Inspection is an activity performed in the discharge of the Health function. See also Function, Subfunction, and Subactivity.

Activity-Based Costing (ABC)   A cost accounting system that identifies specific factors (cost drivers) that drive the costs of service or production activities, and tracks the consumption of cost drivers in producing outputs of goods or services. See also Cost Determination.

Activity Classification   A grouping of expenditures on the basis of specific lines of work performed by organization units. For example, sewage treatment and disposal, solid waste collection, solid waste disposal, and street cleaning are activities performed in carrying out the function of sanitation, and the segregation of the expenditures made for each of these activities constitutes an activity classification.

Actuarial Accrued Liability (AAL)   A liability arising from past unfunding and ad hoc changes in pension plan provisions. AAL is determined by using any of several generally accepted actuarial methods, for example, entry age method.

Actuarial Basis   A basis used in computing the amount of contributions to be made periodically to a fund so that the total contributions plus the compounded earnings thereon will equal the required payments to be made out of the fund. The factors taken into account in arriving at the amount of these contributions include the length of time over which each contribution is to be held and the rate of return compounded on such contribution over its life. A trust fund for a public employee retirement system is an example of a fund set up on an actuarial basis.

Actuarial Present Value of Total Projected Benefits   A component of the annual required contribution that allows for projected salary increases and additional statutory or contractual agreements.

Actuarial Value of Assets   The value of a pension plan's assets used by an actuary for purposes of determining annual required contributions and other actuarial aspects of a defined benefit pension plan.

Ad Valorem   In proportion to value. A basis for levy of taxes on property.

Advance Refunding   The issuance of debt instruments to refund existing debt before the existing debt matures or is callable.

Agency Fund   A fund consisting of resources received and held by the governmental unit as an agent for others; for example, taxes collected and held by a municipality for a school district. Note: sometimes resources held by one fund of a governmental unit for other funds of the unit are handled through an agency fund known as a *pass-through agency fund*. An example would be taxes held by an agency fund for redistribution among other funds. See also Allocation.

Allocate   To divide a lump-sum appropriation into parts that are designated for expenditure by specific organization units and/or for specific purposes, activities, or objects. See also Allocation.

Allocation   A part of a lump-sum appropriation that is designated for expenditure by specific organization units and/or for special purposes, activities, or objects. In federal usage, a transfer of obligational authority from one agency to another. See also Allocate.

Allot   To divide an appropriation into amounts that may be encumbered or expended during an allotment period. See also Allotment and Allotment Period.

Allotment   A part of an appropriation (or, in federal usage, parts of an apportionment) that may be encumbered (obligated) or expended during an allotment period. See also Allot and Allotment Period.

Allotment Period   A period of time less than one fiscal year in length during which an allotment is effective. Bimonthly and quarterly allotment periods are most common. See also Allot and Allotment.

Allotments Available for Commitment/Obligation   The portion of a federal agency's allotments not yet obligated by issuance of purchase orders, contracts, or other evidence of commitment.

Allowable Costs   Costs that meet specific criteria determined by the resource provider, generally used in the context of federal financial assistance.

Allowance for Amortization   The account in which the amounts recorded as amortization of the intangible asset are accumulated.

Allowance for Depreciation   The account in which the amounts of cost of the related asset that have been charged to expense are accumulated.

Amortization   (1) Gradual reduction, redemption, or liquidation of the balance of an account according to a specified schedule of times and amounts. (2) Provision for the extinguishment of a debt by means of a debt service fund (q.v.).

Annual Pension Cost   The annual expense to an employer for a pension plan, which is a function of annual required contribution (ARC), net pension obligation (NPO), interest, and adjustments.

Annual Required Contribution (ARC)   An actuarially determined amount that the employer should contribute each year to a defined benefit pension plan to ensure full actuarial funding of the plan.

Annuities Payable   A liability account that records the amount of annuities due and payable to retired employees in a public employee retirement system.

Annuity   A series of equal money payments made at equal intervals during a designated period of time. In governmental accounting, the most frequent annuities are accumulations of debt service funds for term bonds and payments to retired employees or their beneficiaries under public employee retirement systems.

Annuity, Amount of   The total amount of money accumulated or paid during an annuity period from an annuity and compound interest at a designated rate.

Annuity Funds   Funds established to account for assets given to an organization subject to an agreement that binds the organization to pay stipulated amounts periodically to the donor(s).

Annuity Period   The designated length of time during which an amount of annuity is accumulated or paid.

Apportionment   A distribution made of a federal appropriation by the Office of Management and Budget into amounts available for specified time periods.

Appropriation   An authorization granted by a legislative body to incur liabilities for purposes specified in the Appropriation Act (q.v.). Note: an appropriation is usually limited in amount and as to the time when it may be expended. See, however, Indeterminate Appropriation.

Appropriation Act, Bill, Ordinance, Resolution, or Order   A legal action giving the administration of a governmental unit authorization to incur on behalf of the unit liabilities for the acquisition of goods, services, or facilities to be used for purposes specified in the Act, Ordinance, or so on, in amounts not to exceed those specified for each purpose. The authorization usually expires at the end of a specified term, most often one year.

Appropriation Expenditure   See Expenditures.

Appropriations Budget   Appropriations requested by departments or by the central administration of a governmental unit for a budget period. When the Appropriations budget has been adopted in accord with procedures specified by relevant law, the budget becomes legally binding on the administration of the governmental unit for which the budget has been adopted.

Appropriations Used   An account used in federal government accounting to indicate resources provided by current- or prior-period appropriations that were consumed during the current fiscal period.

Arbitrage   Earning a higher interest rate from investing borrowed funds than is applicable to the entity's tax-exempt debt. Federal tax regulations require governments to rebate the investment earnings in excess of that permitted. See also Arbitrage Rebate.

Arbitrage Rebate   Required repayment to the federal government arising from the arbitrage rules that prohibit the governmental entity from investing bond proceeds at interest rates higher than that applicable to the entity's tax-exempt debt.

Assess   To value property officially for the purpose of taxation. Note: The term is also sometimes used to denote the levy of taxes, but such usage is not correct because it fails to distinguish between the valuation process and the tax levy process.

Assessed Valuation   A valuation set on real estate or other property by a government as a basis for levying taxes.

Assessment   (1) The process of making the official valuation of property for purposes of taxation. (2) The valuation placed on property as a result of this process.

Assets   Probable future economic benefits obtained or controlled by a particular entity as a result of past transactions or events.

Assets Limited as to Use   Assets whose use is limited by contracts or agreements with outside parties (such as proceeds of debt issues; funds deposited with a trustee; self-insurance funding arrangements; and statutory reserve requirements) other than donors or grantors. The term also includes limitations placed on assets by the Board of Directors or trustees.

Audit   The examination of documents, records, reports, systems of internal control, accounting and financial procedures, and other evidence for one or more of the following purposes:

1. To determine whether the financial statements, or other financial reports and related items, are fairly presented in accordance with generally accepted accounting principles or other established or stated criteria.
2. To determine whether the entity has complied with laws and regulations and other specific financial compliance requirements that may have a material effect on the financial statements, or that may affect other financial reports or the economy, efficiency, or effectiveness of program activities.
3. To determine whether the entity is acquiring, protecting, and using its resources economically and efficiently.
4. To determine whether the desired program results or benefits established by the legislature or other authorizing body are being achieved.

Audit Committee   A committee of the governing board whose function it is to help select the auditor, monitor the audit process, review results of the audit, assist the governing board in understanding the results of the audit, and participate with both management and the independent auditor in resolving internal control or other deficiencies identified during the audit.

Audit Findings   Items identified by the auditors in the course of the audit, such as internal control weaknesses, instances of noncompliance, questioned costs, fraud, and material misrepresentations (by the auditee).

Auditor's Opinion or Report   A statement signed by an auditor stating that he or she has examined the financial statements in accordance with generally accepted auditing standards (with exceptions, if any) and expressing his or her opinion on the financial condition and results of operations of some or all of the fund types and account groups of the reporting entity, as appropriate.

Authority   A governmental unit or public agency created to perform a single function or a restricted group of related activities. Usually such units are financed from service charges, fees, and tolls, but in some instances they also have taxing powers. An authority may be completely independent of other governmental units, or in some cases it may be partially dependent on other governments for its creation, its financing, or the exercise of certain powers.

Authority Bonds   Bonds payable from the revenues of a specific authority (q.v.). Since such authorities usually have no revenue other than charges for services, their bonds are ordinarily revenue bonds (q.v.).

Auxiliary Enterprises   Activities of a college or university that furnish a service to students, faculty, or staff on a user-charge basis. The charge is directly related to, but not necessarily equal to, the cost of the service. Examples include college unions, residence halls, stores, faculty clubs, and intercollegiate athletics.

Available   Collectible within the current period or soon enough thereafter to be used to pay liabilities of the current period.

Balance Sheet   A statement that reports the balances of assets, liabilities, reserves, and equities of a fund, governmental unit, or nonprofit entity at a specified date, properly classified to exhibit financial position of the fund or unit at that date.

Basis of Accounting   The standard (or standards) used to determine the point in time when assets, liabilities, revenues, and expenses (expenditures) should be measured and recorded as such in the accounts of an entity. See Accrual Basis, Cash Basis, and Modified Accrual Basis.

Bearer Bond   A bond that requires the holder to present matured interest coupons or matured bonds to the issuer or a designated paying agent for payment. Payments are made to the bearer since the issuer maintains no record of current bond ownership. Note: Federal law requires that all tax-exempt bonds issued since June 15, 1983, must be in registered form (see also Registered Bonds). However, some long-term bearer bonds remain outstanding.

Benchmark A number that represents a target to which actual results are compared, or a basis for comparison; for example, industry averages.

Betterment An addition made to, or change made in, a fixed asset that is expected to prolong its life or to increase its efficiency over and above that arising from maintenance (q.v.) and the cost of which is therefore added to the book value of the asset. Note: The term is sometimes applied to sidewalks, sewers, and highways, but these should preferably be designated as "improvements" or "infrastructure assets" (q.v.).

Blended Presentation The method of reporting the financial data of a component unit in a manner similar to that in which the financial data of the primary government are presented. Under this method the component unit data are usually combined with the appropriate fund types of the primary government and reported in the same columns as the data for the primary government except general funds. See Discrete Presentation.

Block Grants Federal monies given to state or local governments along with the discretion to administer for many projects and to many recipients, and for which no matching requirement exists.

Board-Designated Funds Funds created to account for assets set aside by the governing board of an organization for specified purposes.

Board-Designated Net Assets Unrestricted net assets that the not-for-profit organization's Board decided to set aside or "designate" for specific purposes.

Bond A written promise to pay a specified sum of money, called the *face value* or *principal* amount, at a specified date or dates in the future, called the *maturity date(s)*, together with periodic interest at a specified rate. Note: The difference between a note and a bond is that the latter runs for a longer period of time and requires greater legal formality.

Bond Anticipation Notes (BANs) Short-term interest-bearing notes issued by a governmental unit in anticipation of bonds to be issued at a later date. The notes are retired from proceeds of the bond issue to which they are related. See also Interim Borrowing.

Bond Discount The excess of the face value of a bond over the price for which it is acquired or sold. Note: The price does not include accrued interest at the date of acquisition or sale.

Bond Fund A fund formerly used to account for the proceeds of general obligation bond issues to be used for construction or acquisition of capital assets. Such proceeds are now accounted for in a capital projects fund (q.v.).

Bond Indenture The contract between a corporation issuing bonds and the trustees or other body representing prospective and actual holders of the bonds.

Bond Ordinance or Resolution An ordinance (q.v.) or resolution (q.v.) authorizing a bond issue.

Bond Premium The excess of the price at which a bond is acquired or sold over its face value. Note: The price does not include accrued interest at the date of acquisition or sale.

Bonded Debt That portion of indebtedness represented by outstanding bonds. See Gross Bonded Debt and Net Bonded Debt.

Bonded Indebtedness See Bonded Debt.

Bonds Authorized and Unissued Bonds that have been legally authorized but not issued and that can be issued and sold without further authorization. Note: This term must not be confused with the terms *margin of borrowing power* or *legal debt margin*, either one of which represents the difference between the legal debt limit of a governmental unit and the debt outstanding against it.

Book Value Value (q.v.) as shown by books of account. Note: In the case of assets subject to reduction by valuation allowances, *book value* refers to cost or stated value less the appropriate allowance. Sometimes a distinction is made between *gross* book value and *net* book value, the former designating value before deduction of related allowances and the latter after their deduction. In the absence of any modifier, however, the term *book value* is understood to be synonymous with net book value.

Budget A plan of financial operation embodying an estimate of proposed expenditures for a given period and the proposed means of financing them. Used without any modifier, the term usually indicates a financial plan for a single fiscal year.

Budget Accounts Accounts used in federal agencies that are broad in scope, for which appropriations are made, and that are not the same as the Standard General Ledger accounts used for accounting purposes. Budget accounts may cover an entire organization or a group of budget accounts may be aggregated to cover an organization.

Budget Calendar A schedule of certain steps to be followed in the budgeting process and the dates by which each step must be completed.

Budget Document The instrument used by the budget-making authority to present a comprehensive financial program to the appropriating body. The budget document usually consists of three parts. The first part contains a message from the budget-making authority, together with a summary of the proposed expenditures and the means of financing them. The second consists of schedules supporting the summary. These schedules show in detail the information as to past years' actual revenues, expenditures, and other data used in making the estimates. The third part is composed of drafts of the appropriation, revenue, and borrowing measures necessary to put the budget into effect.

Budget Message A general discussion of the proposed budget as presented in writing by the budget-making authority to the legislative body. The budget message should contain an explanation of the principal budget items, an outline of the governmental unit's experience during the past period and its financial status at the time of the message, and recommendations regarding the financial policy for the coming period.

Budget Officer A person, usually in the central administrative office, designated to ensure that administrative policies are actually used in budget preparation and that the budget calendar and other legal requirements are met.

Budgetary Accounts Those accounts that reflect budgetary operations and condition, such as estimated revenues, appropriations, and encumbrances, as distinguished from proprietary accounts. See also Proprietary Accounts.

Budgetary Control The control or management of a governmental unit or enterprise in accordance with an approved budget for the purpose of keeping expenditures within the limitations of available appropriations and available revenues.

Budgetary Resources A term that includes new budgetary authority for the period plus unobligated budgetary authority carried over from the prior period and offsetting collections, if any, plus or minus any budgetary adjustments in a federal agency.

Buildings A fixed asset account that reflects the acquisition value of permanent structures used to house persons and property owned by a governmental unit. If buildings are purchased or constructed, this account includes the purchase or contract price of all permanent buildings and fixtures attached to and forming a permanent part of such buildings. If buildings are acquired by gift, the account reflects their appraised value at time of acquisition.

Business-Type Activities Commercial-type activities of a government, such as, public utilities (e.g., electric, water, gas, and sewer utilities), transportation systems, toll roads, toll bridges, hospitals, parking garages and lots, liquor stores, golf courses, and swimming pools.

Callable Bond A type of bond that permits the issuer to pay the obligation before the stated maturity date by giving notice of redemption in a manner specified in the bond contract. Also called Optional Bond.

Capital Assets See Fixed Assets.

Capital Budget A plan of proposed capital outlays and the means of financing them for the current fiscal period. It is usually a part of the current budget. If a Capital Program is in operation, it will be the first year thereof. A Capital Program is sometimes referred to as a Capital Budget. See also Capital Program.

Capital Expenditures See Capital Outlays.

Capital Improvement Fund A fund to accumulate revenues from current taxes levied for major repairs and maintenance to fixed assets of a nature not specified at the time the revenues are levied. Appropriations of this fund are made in accord with state law at the time specific projects become necessary.

Capital Lease A lease that substantively transfers the benefits and risks of ownership of property to the lessee. Any lease that meets certain criteria specified in applicable accounting and reporting standards is a capital lease. See also Operating Lease.

Capital Outlays Expenditures that result in the acquisition of or addition to fixed assets.

Capital Program A plan for capital expenditures to be incurred each year over a fixed period of years to meet capital needs arising from a long-term work program or otherwise. It sets forth each project or other contemplated expenditure in which the government is to have a part and specifies the full resources estimated to be available to finance the projected expenditures.

Capital Projects Fund (CPF) A fund created to account for all resources to be used for the construction or acquisition of designated fixed assets by a governmental unit except those financed by proprietary or fiduciary funds. See also Bond Fund.

Capitation Fee Fixed dollar amount of fees per person paid periodically by a third-party payor to a health care organization, regardless of services provided.

Cash Currency, coin, checks, money orders, and bankers' drafts on hand or on deposit with an official or agent designated as custodian of cash and bank deposits. Note: All cash must be accounted for as a part of the fund to which it belongs. Any restrictions or limitations as to its availability must be indicated in the records and statements. It is not necessary, however, to have a separate bank account for each fund unless required by law.

Cash Basis   The basis of accounting under which revenues are recorded when received in cash and expenditures (or expenses) are recorded when cash is disbursed.

Cash Discount   An allowance received or given if payment is completed within a stated period of time.

Cash Equivalent   Short-term, highly liquid investments that are both readily convertible into known amounts of cash and so near their maturity that they present insignificant risk of changes in value due to changes in interest rates.

Certificate of Participation (COP)   A long-term debt instrument authorized for construction of municipal facilities, typically issued by a quasi-independent authority but secured by a long-term lease with a general purpose local government.

Character   A basis for distinguishing expenditures according to the periods they are presumed to benefit. See also Character Classification.

Character Classification   A grouping of expenditures on the basis of the fiscal periods they are presumed to benefit. The three groupings are: (1) current expenditures, presumed to benefit the current fiscal period; (2) debt service, presumed to benefit prior fiscal periods primarily but also present and future periods; and (3) capital outlays, presumed to benefit the current and future fiscal periods. See also Activity, Activity Classification, Function, Functional Classification, Object, Object Classification, and Expenses.

Charitable Solicitation   The direct or indirect request for money, credit, property, financial assistance or other things of value on the representation that these assets will be used for a charitable purpose.

Charity Care   Service provided by a health care organization to persons with a demonstrated inability to pay.

Check   A bill of exchange drawn on a bank and payable on demand; a written order on a bank to pay on demand a specified sum of money to a named person, to his or her order, or to the bearer, out of money on deposit to the credit of the maker. Note: A check differs from a warrant in that the latter is not necessarily payable on demand and may not be negotiable. It differs from a voucher in that the latter is not an order to pay.

Clearing Account   An account used to accumulate total charges or credits for the purpose of distributing them later among the accounts to which they are allocable or for the purpose of transferring the net differences to the proper account. Also called Suspense Account.

Cognizant Agency for Audit Responsibilities   The federal awarding agency that provides the predominant amount of direct funding to a nonfederal entity expending more than $25 million in federal awards, as provided by the OMB *Circular A-133*, unless the OMB designates a different cognizant agency.

Collateralized   Secured with the pledge of assets to minimize the risk of loss. Deposits, investments, or loans are often required to be collateralized.

Collections   Works of art, historical treasures, or similar assets that are (1) held for public exhibition, education, or research in furtherance of public service rather than financial gain; (2) protected, kept unencumbered, cared for, and preserved; and (3) subject to an organizational policy that requires the proceeds of items that are sold to be used to acquire other items for collection.

Combined Financial Statement   A single financial statement that displays the combined financial data for various fund types and, if applicable, account groups and discretely presented component units in separate adjacent columns. See Combining Financial Statement.

Combining Financial Statement   A financial statement that displays the financial data for each of the funds of a given fund type (e.g., special revenue funds) in separate adjacent columns. The totals reported for that fund type should agree with those reported in the column for that fund type in the combined financial statements. See Combined Financial Statement.

Commitments   In federal government usage, a reservation of an agency's allotment in the estimated amount of orders for goods or services, prior to actually placing the orders. See also Obligations.

Compliance Audit   An audit designed to provide reasonable assurance that a governmental entity has complied with applicable laws and regulations. Required for every audit performed in conformity with generally accepted governmental auditing standards.

Component Unit (CU)   A separate governmental unit, agency, or nonprofit corporation that, pursuant to the criteria in the GASB *Codification*, Section 2100, is combined with other component units to constitute the reporting entity (q.v.).

Comprehensive Annual Financial Report (CAFR) A governmental unit's official annual report prepared and published as a matter of public record. In addition to the general purpose financial statements, the CAFR should contain introductory material, schedules to demonstrate legal compliance, and statistical tables specified in the GASB *Codification*.

Conditional Promise to Give A promise to make a contribution to an organization that depends on the occurrence of a specified future and uncertain event to bind the promisor, such as, obtaining matching gifts by the recipient.

Conscience Money Money received by governmental units in payment of previously undisclosed debts, usually based on embezzlement, tax evasion, or theft.

Construction Work in Progress The cost of construction work that has been started but not yet completed.

Consumption Method A method of recording supplies as Inventory when purchased and as Expenditures when used or consumed. The alternative method is called the *purchases method.*

Contingency Fund Assets or other resources set aside to provide for unforeseen expenditures or for anticipated expenditures or uncertain amount.

Contingent Liabilities Items that may become liabilities as a result of conditions undetermined at a given date, such as guarantees, pending lawsuits, judgments under appeal, unsettled disputed claims, unfilled purchase orders, and uncompleted contracts. Contingent liabilities of the latter two types are disclosed in Balance Sheets of governmental funds as Reserve for Encumbrances; other contingent liabilities are disclosed in Notes to the Financial Statements.

Continuing Appropriation An appropriation that, once established, is automatically renewed without further legislative action, period after period, until altered or revoked. Note: The term should not be confused with Indeterminate Appropriation (q.v.).

Continuing Care Retirement Community (CCRC) A facility that provides residential care along with some level of long-term nursing or medical care, generally to elderly or retired persons.

Contractual Adjustments (or allowances) The difference between the gross patient service revenue and the negotiated payment by third-party payors in arriving at net patient service revenue.

Contributed equity Equity in an enterprise fund that results from the contribution of assets by another fund within the governmental unit, or another governmental unit, or private donations as distinguished from the equity that results from retained earnings.

Contributions Amounts given to an individual or to an organization for which the donor receives no direct private benefits. Contributions may be in the form of pledges, cash, securities, materials, services, or fixed assets.

Control Account An account in the general ledger in which are recorded the aggregate of debit and credit postings to a number of identical or related accounts called *subsidiary accounts.* For example, the Taxes Receivable account is a control account supported by the aggregate of individual balances in individual property taxpayers' accounts.

Cost The amount of money or money's worth exchanged for property or services. Note: Costs may be incurred even before money is paid, that is, as soon as a liability is incurred. Ultimately, however, money or money's worth must be given in exchange. Again, the cost of some property or service may, in turn, become a part of the cost of another property or service. For example, the cost of part or all of the materials purchased at a certain time will be reflected in the cost of articles made from such materials or in the cost of those services in the rendering of which the materials were used.

Cost Accounting The branch of accounting that provides for the assembling and recording of all the elements of cost incurred to accomplish a purpose, to carry on an activity or operation, or to complete a unit of work or a specific job.

Cost Determination The use of statistical procedures to determine or estimate the cost of goods or services, as opposed to accumulating such costs in a formal cost accounting system.

Cost Objective In federal terminology, an organization unit, function, activity, project, cost center, or pool established for the accumulation of costs.

Cost Unit A term used in cost accounting to designate the unit of product or service whose cost is computed. These units are selected for the purpose of comparing the actual cost with a standard cost or with actual costs of units produced under different circumstances or at different places and times. See also Unit Cost and Work Unit.

Coupon Rate The interest rate specified on interest coupons attached to a bond. The term is synonymous with nominal interest rate (q.v.) for coupon bonds.

Credit Risk The risk that a debt issuer will not pay interest and principal when due. See also Default.

Cumulative Results of Operations The net difference between expenses/losses and financing sources, including appropriations, revenues, and gains, since the inception of the activity. A term generally used in federal agencies.

Current A term that, applied to budgeting and accounting, designates the operations of the present fiscal period as opposed to past or future periods.

Current Assets Those assets that are available or can be made readily available to meet the cost of operations or to pay current liabilities. Some examples are cash, temporary investments, and taxes receivable that will be collected within 60 days from the balance sheet date.

Current Fund In governmental accounting sometimes used as a synonym for General Fund.

Current Funds Funds the resources of which may be expended for operating purposes during the current fiscal period. Colleges and universities and voluntary health and welfare organizations often use fund types called Current Fund—Unrestricted and Current Funds—Restricted.

Current Liabilities Liabilities payable within a relatively short period of time, usually no longer than a year. See also Floating Debt.

Current Resources Resources (q.v.) to which recourse can be had to meet current obligations and expenditures. Examples are estimated revenues of a particular period not yet realized, transfers from other funds authorized but not received, and, in the case of certain funds, bonds authorized and unissued.

Current Revenue Revenues of a governmental unit available to meet expenditures of the current fiscal year. See Revenue.

Current Special Assessments (1) Special assessments levied and becoming due during the current fiscal period, from the date special assessment rolls are approved by the proper authority to the date on which a penalty for nonpayment is attached. (2) Special assessments levied in a prior fiscal period but becoming due in the current fiscal period, from the time they become due to the date on which a penalty for nonpayment is attached.

Current Taxes (1) Taxes levied and becoming due during the current fiscal period, from the time the amount of tax levy is first established to the date on which a penalty for nonpayment is attached. (2) Taxes levied in the preceding fiscal period but becoming due in the current fiscal period, from the time they become due until a penalty for nonpayment is attached.

Current-Year's Tax Levy Taxes levied for the current fiscal period.

Customer Advances for Construction Amounts required to be deposited by a customer for construction projects undertaken by the utility at the request of the customer.

Cycle Billing A practice followed by utilities, retail stores, and other organizations with a large number of credit customers of billing part of the customers each working day during a month, instead of billing all customers as of a certain day of the month.

Data Processing (1) The preparation and handling of information and data from source media through prescribed procedures to obtain such end results as classification, problem solution, summarization, and reports. (2) Preparation and handling of financial information wholly or partially by use of computers.

Debt A liability resulting from the borrowing of money or from the purchase of goods and services. Debts of governmental units include bonds, time warrants, notes, and floating debt. See also Bond, Notes Payable, Time Warrant, Floating Debt, Long-Term Debt, and General Long-Term Debt.

Debt-Financed Income Income from property that is subject to debt, such as, rental income from a building that has been financed with a mortgage.

Debt Limit The maximum amount of gross or net debt that is legally permitted.

Debt Margin The difference between the amount of the debt limit (q.v.) and the net amount of outstanding indebtedness subject to the limitation.

Debt Service Fund (DSF) A fund established to finance and account for the payment of interest and principal on all tax-supported debt, serial and term, including that payable from special assessments.

Default Failure of a debtor to pay interest or repay the principal of debt when legally due.

Defeasance A transaction in which the liability for a debt is substantively settled, and the liability is removed from the accounts, even though the debt has not actually been paid. See also Legal Defeasance and In-Substance Defeasance.

Deferred Revenues or Deferred Credits In governmental accounting, items that may not be recognized as revenues of the period in which received because they are not "available" until a subsequent period.

Deferred Serial Bonds   Serial bonds (q.v.) in which the first installment does not fall due for two or more years from the date of issue.

Deficiency   A general term indicating the amount by which anything falls short of some requirement or expectation. The term should not be used without qualification.

Deficit   (1) The excess of liabilities and reserved equity of a fund over its assets. (2) The excess of expenditures over revenues during an accounting period; or in the case of enterprise and internal service funds, the excess of expense over revenue during an accounting period.

Defined Benefit Pension Plan   A pension plan that provides a specified amount of benefits based on a formula that may include such factors as age, salary, and years of employment.

Defined Contribution Pension Plan   A pension plan that specifies the amount or rate of contribution, often a percentage of covered salary, that the employer and employees must contribute to the members' accounts.

Delinquent Special Assessments   Special assessments remaining unpaid on and after the date on which a penalty for nonpayment is attached.

Delinquent Taxes   Taxes remaining unpaid on and after the date on which a penalty for nonpayment is attached. Even though the penalty may be subsequently waived and a portion of the taxes may be abated or canceled, the unpaid balances continue to be delinquent taxes until abated, canceled, paid, or converted into tax liens. Note: The term is sometimes limited to taxes levied for the fiscal period or periods preceding the current one, but such usage is not entirely correct. See also Current Taxes, Current-Year's Tax Levy, and Prior-Years' Tax Levies.

Deposit Warrant   A financial document prepared by a designated accounting or finance officer authorizing the treasurer of a governmental unit to accept for deposit sums of money collected by various departments and agencies of the governmental unit.

Deposits   Money deposited with a financial institution that must be released upon the "demand" of the depositor; for example, demand deposits (checking) and time deposits (savings accounts). These funds are generally insured by the Federal Deposit Insurance Corporation (up to a limit) and are distinguished from investments.

Depreciation   (1) Expiration of the service life of fixed assets, other than wasting assets, attributable to wear and tear, deterioration, action of the physical elements, inadequacy, and obsolescence. (2) The portion of the cost of a fixed asset, other than a wasting asset, that is charged as an expense during a particular period. Note: In accounting for depreciation, the cost of a fixed asset, less any salvage value, is prorated over the estimated service life of such an asset, and each period is charged with a portion of such cost. Through this process, the cost of the asset less salvage value is ultimately charged off as an expense.

Designated   Assets, or equity, set aside by action of the governing board are designated; as distinguished from assets or equity set aside in conformity with requirements of donors, grantors, or creditors, which are properly referred to as *restricted*.

Diagnosis-Related Groups (DRGs)   A case-mix classification scheme instituted by Congress in 1983 in relation to the Medicare program that is used to determine the reimbursement received by a hospital for inpatient services. Payment is made based on the patient's diagnosis regardless of how much the hospital spends to treat a patient.

Dimension   Groupings of expenditure classifications specified by the National Center for Education Statistics (NCES) for public school accounting. Dimensions consist of two main groups: those essential for financial reporting to the federal government and those available optionally for management use.

Direct Cost   A cost incurred because of some definite action by or for an organization unit, function, activity, project, cost center, or pool; a cost identified specifically with a cost objective (q.v.).

Direct Debt   The debt that a governmental unit has incurred in its own name or assumed through the annexation of territory or consolidation with another governmental unit. See also Overlapping Debt.

Direct Expenses   Those expenses that can be charged directly as a part of the cost of a product or service, or of a department or operating unit, as distinguished from overhead and other indirect costs that must be prorated among several products or services, departments, or operating units.

Direct Lobbying   Testifying at legislative hearings, corresponding or conferring with legislators or their staffs, and publishing documents advocating specific legislative action.

Disbursements   Payments in cash.

Discount on Taxes   A cash discount offered to taxpayers to encourage early payment of taxes.

Discrete Presentation   The method of reporting financial data of component units in a column(s) separate from the financial data of the primary government.

Disqualified Person A person who has substantial influences over the affairs of a nonprofit organization; such as, an officer or manager.

Donated Assets Noncash contributions (q.v.). Donated assets may be in the form of securities, land, buildings, equipment, or materials.

Donated Materials See Donated Assets.

Donated Services The services of volunteer workers who are unpaid, or who are paid less than the market value of their services.

Double Entry A system of bookkeeping that requires, for every entry made to the debit side of an account or accounts, an entry for a corresponding amount or amounts to the credit side of another account or accounts. Note: Double-entry bookkeeping involves the maintaining of a balance between assets on the one hand and liabilities and fund equities on the other.

Due Diligence Formal disclosure and discovery of all relevant information about a transaction or organization, particularly about risks.

Earnings See Income and Revenue.

Economic Interest An interest in another organization because it holds or utilizes significant resources that must be used for the purposes of the reporting organization, or the reporting organization is responsible for the liabilities of the other entity.

Economic Size The minimum possible size to be able to provide services without long-term damage to the organization's financial base.

Effective Interest Rate The rate of earning on a bond investment based on the actual price paid for the bond, the maturity date, and the length of time between interest dates, in contrast with the nominal interest rate (q.v.).

Encumbrances An account used to record the estimated amount of purchase orders, contracts, or salary commitments chargeable to an appropriation. The account is credited when goods or services are received and the actual expenditure of the appropriation is known.

Endowment Fund A fund whose principal must be maintained inviolate but whose income may be expended.

Enterprise Debt Debt that is to be retired primarily from the earnings of governmentally owned and operated enterprises. See also Revenue Bonds.

Enterprise Fund (EF) A fund established to finance and account for the acquisition, operation, and maintenance of governmental facilities and services that are entirely or predominantly self-supporting by user charges; or where the governing body of the governmental unit has decided periodic determination of revenues earned, expenses incurred, and/or net income is appropriate. Governmentally owned utilities and hospitals are ordinarily accounted for by enterprise funds.

Entitlement The amount of payment to which a state or local government is entitled as determined by the federal government pursuant to an allocation formula contained in applicable statutes.

Entity Assets Those assets of a federal agency that the reporting entity has authority to use in its operations, as opposed to holding but not available to spend.

Entitywide Perspective A view of the net assets of the organization as a whole, rather than as a collection of separate funds.

Entry (1) The record of a financial transaction in its appropriate book of account. (2) The act of recording a transaction in the books of account.

Equipment Tangible property of a more or less permanent nature (other than land, buildings, or improvements other than buildings) that is useful in carrying on operations. Examples are machinery, tools, trucks, cars, furniture, and furnishings.

Equity Transfer Nonrecurring or nonroutine transfers of equity between funds. Also referred to as Residual Equity Transfer (q.v.).

Escheat Property Private property that reverts to government ownership upon the death of the owner if there are no legal claimants or heirs.

Estimated Expenditures The estimated amounts of expenditures included in budgeted appropriations. See also Appropriations.

Estimated Other Financing Sources Amounts of financial resources estimated to be received or accrued during a period by a governmental or similar type fund from interfund transfers or from the proceeds of noncurrent debt issuance.

Estimated Other Financing Uses Amounts of financial resources estimated to be disbursed or accrued during a period by a governmental or similar type fund for transfer to other funds.

Estimated Revenue For revenue accounts kept on an accrual basis (q.v.), this term designates the amount of revenue estimated to accrue during a given period regardless of whether or not it is all to be collected during the period. For revenue accounts kept on a cash basis (q.v.), the term designates the amount of revenue estimated to be collected during a given period. Under the modified accrual basis (q.v.), estimated revenues include both cash and accrual basis revenues. See also Revenue, Revenue Receipts, Cash Basis, Accrual Basis, and Modified Accrual Basis.

Estimated Revenue Receipts   A term used synonymously with estimated revenue (q.v.) by some governmental units reporting their revenues on a cash basis. See also Revenue and Revenue Receipts.

Estimated Uncollectible Accounts Receivable (Credit) That portion of accounts receivable that it is estimated will never be collected. The account is deducted from the Accounts Receivable account on the balance sheet in order to arrive at the net amount of accounts receivable.

Estimated Uncollectible Current Taxes (Credit)   A provision out of tax revenues for that portion of current taxes receivable that is estimated will never be collected. The amount is shown on the balance sheet as a deduction from the Taxes Receivable—Current account in order to arrive at the net taxes receivable.

Estimated Uncollectible Delinquent Taxes (Credit) That portion of delinquent taxes receivable that it is estimated will never be collected. The account is shown on the balance sheet as a deduction from the Taxes Receivable—Delinquent account to arrive at the net delinquent taxes receivable.

Estimated Uncollectible Interest and Penalties on Taxes (Credit)   That portion of interest and penalties receivable that is estimated will never be collected. The account is shown as a deduction from the Interest and Penalties Receivable account on the balance sheet in order to arrive at the net interest and penalties receivable.

Estimated Uncollectible Tax Liens   That portion of tax liens receivable that it is estimated will never be collected. The account is shown as a deduction from the Tax Liens Receivable account on the balance sheet in order to arrive at the net amount of tax liens receivable.

Excess Benefit Transaction   A transaction that results in unfair benefits to a person who has substantial influence over a not-for-profit organization, for example, unreasonable compensation, sales of assets at bargain prices, and lease arrangements.

Exchange Transactions   Transactions in which each party receives direct tangible benefits commensurate with the resources provided, for example, sales between a buyer and a seller.

Exemption   A statutory reduction in the assessed valuation of taxable property accorded to certain taxpayers, such as, senior citizens and war veterans.

Exhibit   (1) A balance sheet or other principal financial statement. (2) Any statement or other document that accompanies or is a part of a financial or audit report. See also Schedules and Statements.

Expendable Fund   A fund whose assets and resources may be converted into cash and used in their entirety for purposes of the fund.

Expendable Restricted Funds   Current funds in a college or university that are restricted by external donors or resource providers, but that can be spent in full (e.g., scholarships or federal research grants).

Expendable Trust Fund   A trust fund in which the fund balance can be expended for a purpose specified in the trust agreement. Typically used to account for the expendable income of a Nonexpendable Trust Fund (q.v.).

Expended Appropriation   A charge against an appropriation for the actual cost of items received; the appropriation is no longer available to acquire additional goods and services.

Expenditure Disbursements   A term sometimes used by governmental units operating on a cash basis (q.v.) as a synonym for expenditures (q.v.). It is not recommended terminology.

Expenditure Responsibility   The responsibility of one public charity over another to which it has given a grant to ensure that the grant was used exclusively for the purpose for which it was made.

Expenditures   Expenditures are recorded when liabilities are incurred pursuant to authority given in an appropriation (q.v.). If the accounts are kept on the accrual basis (q.v.) or the modified accrual basis (q.v.), this term designates the cost of goods delivered or services rendered, whether paid or unpaid, including expenses, provision for debt retirement not reported as a liability of the fund from which retired, and capital outlays. Where the accounts are kept on the cash basis (q.v.), the term designates only actual cash disbursements for these purposes. Note: Encumbrances are not expenditures.

Expenditures Budget   See Appropriations Budget.

Expenses   Charges incurred, whether paid or unpaid, for operation, maintenance, interest, and other charges presumed to benefit the current fiscal period.

External Investment Pool   Centrally managed investment portfolios (pools) that manage the investments of participants (e.g., other governmental units and not-for-profit organizations) outside the reporting entity of the government that administers the pool.

External Support Test   One of two parts of the broad public support test to determine if an organization is a public charity, rather than a private foundation. It is met if at least one-third of the organization's total revenue comes from the government or general public in the form of contributions, grants, membership dues, charges for services, or sales of merchandise.

Face Value   As applied to securities, the amount of liability stated in the security document.

Facilities and Administrative Costs (F&A)   Costs that are not readily assignable to one program or cost objective in a college or university, but rather are incurred for a joint purpose. These costs are called *indirect costs* in some OMB *Circulars*. See also Indirect Costs.

Fair Value   The amount at which a financial instrument could be exchanged in a current transaction between willing parties, other than in a forced or liquidation sale.

Federal Financial Management Improvement Act   Act of Congress in 1990 that requires that each federal agency maintain a financial management system that applies federal accounting standards and provides the information necessary to report whether the agency is in compliance with those standards.

Federated Fund-Raising Organization   An organization comprised of independent charitable organizations that have voluntarily joined together to raise and distribute money among themselves.

Feeder Organization   An organization controlled by a not-for-profit organization and organized to carry on a trade or business for the benefit of an exempt organization and remit its profits to the exempt organization.

Fidelity Bond   A written promise to indemnify against losses from theft, defalcation, and misappropriation of public finds by government officers and employees. See also Surety Bond.

Fiduciary Activities   Activities in which the government acts in a fiduciary capacity, either as an agent or trustee, for parties outside the government, for example in the collection of taxes, or amounts bequeathed from private citizens, as well as assets held for employee pension plans.

Fiduciary Funds   Any fund held by a governmental unit in a fiduciary capacity, ordinarily as agent or trustee. Also called Trust and Agency Funds.

Financial Accountability   The obligation of government to justify the raising of public resources and what those resources were expended for. See Accountability.

Financial Audit   One of the two major types of audits defined by the U.S. General Accounting Office (see Performance Audit for the other major type). A financial audit provides an auditor's opinion that financial statements present fairly an entity's financial position and results of operations in conformity with generally accepted accounting principles or that other financial reports comply with specified finance-related criteria.

Financial Condition   The probability that a government will meet its financial obligations as they become due and its service obligations to constituencies, both currently and in the future. See Financial Position.

Financial Position   The adequacy of cash and short-term claims to cash to meet current obligations and those expected in the near future. See Financial Condition.

Fiscal Accountability   Current-period financial position and budgetary compliance reported in fund-type financial statements of governments. See also Financial Accountability.

Fiscal Agent   A bank or other corporate fiduciary that performs the function of paying, on behalf of the governmental unit, or other debtor, interest on debt or principal of debt when due.

Fiscal Period   Any period at the end of which a governmental unit determines its financial position and the results of its operations.

Fiscal Year   A 12-month period of time to which the annual budget applies and at the end of which a governmental unit determines its financial position and the results of its operations. For example, FY99 refers to the year that ends in 1999 (e.g., 7-1-98 to 6-30-99).

Fixed Assets   Assets of a long-term character that are intended to continue to be held or used, such as land, buildings, machinery, furniture, and other equipment. Note: The term does not indicate the immobility of an asset, which is the distinctive character of "fixture" (q.v.).

Fixed Charges   Expenses (q.v.) the amount of which is set by agreement. Examples are interest, insurance, and contributions to pension funds.

Fixed Liabilities   See Long-Term Debt.

Fixtures   Attachments to buildings that are not intended to be removed and that cannot be removed without damage to the latter. Note: Those fixtures with a useful life presumed to be as long as that of the building itself are considered a part of the building; all others are classed as equipment.

Flexible Budgeting   Budgeting method that provides for alternative levels of activity, such as separate budgets for high, medium, and low levels of activity.

Floating Debt   Liabilities other than bonded debt and time warrants that are payable on demand or at an early date. Examples are accounts payable, notes, and bank loans. See also Current Liabilities.

Force Account   Construction of buildings and improvements by some agency of the governmental unit.

Forfeiture   The automatic loss of cash or other property as a punishment for not complying with legal provisions and as compensation for the resulting damages or losses. Note: The term should not be confused with confiscation. The latter term designates the actual taking over of the forfeited property by the government. Even after property has been forfeited, it cannot be said to be confiscated until the governmental unit claims it.

Franchise   A special privilege granted by a government permitting the continuing use of public property, such as city streets, and usually involving the elements of monopoly and regulation.

Full Cost   The total cost of providing a service or producing a good; the sum of both direct costs (q.v.) and indirect costs (q.v.).

Full Faith and Credit   A pledge of the general taxing power for the payment of debt obligations. Note: Bonds carrying such pledges are usually referred to as *general obligation bonds*.

Function   A group of related activities aimed at accomplishing a major service or regulatory responsibility for which a governmental unit is responsible. For example, public health is a function. See also Subfunction, Activity, Character, and Object.

Functional Classification   A grouping of expenditures on the basis of the principal purposes for which they are made. Examples are public safety, public health, and public welfare. See also Activity, Character, and Object Classification.

Fund   A fiscal and accounting entity with a self-balancing set of accounts recording cash and other financial resources, together with all related liabilities, and residual equities or balances, and changes therein, which are segregated for the purpose of carrying on specific activities or attaining certain objectives in accordance with special reg-

ulations, restrictions, or limitations. See General Fixed Assets Account Group and General Long-Term Debt Account Group.

Fund Accounting   An accounting system organized on the basis of funds, each of which is considered a separate accounting entity. The operations of each fund are accounted for with a separate set of self-balancing accounts that comprise its assets, liabilities, fund equity, revenues, and expenditures, or expenses, as appropriate. Resources are allocated to and accounted for in individual funds based upon purposes for which they are to be spent and the means by which spending activities are controlled. Fund accounting is used by states and local governments and by not-for-profit organizations that need to account for resources the use of which is restricted by donors or grantors.

Fund Balance   The portion of Fund Equity (q.v.) available for appropriation.

Fund Balance Sheet   A Balance Sheet for a single fund. See Fund and Balance Sheet.

Fund Balance with Treasury   An asset account of a federal agency representing cash balances held by the U.S. Treasury upon which the agency can draw. The Treasury will disburse cash on behalf of and at the request of the agency to pay for authorized goods and services.

Fund Equity   The excess of fund assets and resources over fund liabilities. A portion of the equity of a governmental fund may be reserved (q.v.) or designated (q.v.); the remainder is referred to as *Fund Balance*.

Fund Group Perspective   The traditional view of a college or university as a collection of separate groups of funds, rather than viewing the entity as a whole.

Fund Type   A classification of funds that are similar in purpose and character.

Funded Debt   Same as Bonded Debt, which is the preferred term.

Funded Deficit   A deficit eliminated through the sale of bonds issued for that purpose. See also Funding Bonds.

Funded Ratio   The ratio of actuarial value of assets to actuarial accrued liability (AAL) of a pension plan.

Funding   The conversion of floating debt or time warrants into bonded debt (q.v.).

Funding Bonds   See Refunding Bonds.

Funds for Renewals and Replacements   One of the four subgroups that make up the Plant Funds Group in a governmental college or university. This fund accounts for assets set aside for the renewal and replacement of existing institutional properties.

Funds for Retirement of Indebtedness   One of the four subgroups that make up the Plant Funds Group in a governmental college or university. This fund accounts for repayment of debt similar to the Debt Service Fund of a state or local government unit.

Funds Functioning as Endowments (FFAE)   See Quasi-Endowment Funds.

General Fixed Assets (GFA)   Those fixed assets of a governmental unit that are not accounted for by a proprietary or fiduciary fund.

General Fixed Assets Account Group (GFAAG)   A self-balancing group of accounts set up to account for the general fixed assets of a governmental unit. See General Fixed Assets.

General Fund (GF)   A fund used to account for all transactions of a governmental unit that are not accounted for in another fund. Note: The General Fund is used to account for the ordinary operations of a governmental unit that are financed from taxes and other general revenues.

General Long-Term Debt (GLTD)   Long-term debt legally payable from general revenues and backed by the full faith and credit of a governmental unit. See Long-Term Debt.

General Long-Term Debt Account Group (GLTDAG)   A self-balancing group of accounts set up to account for the general long-term debt of a governmental unit. See General Long-Term Debt.

General Obligation (GO) Bonds   Bonds for whose payment the full faith and credit of the issuing body is pledged. More commonly, but not necessarily, general obligation bonds are considered to be those payable from taxes and other general revenues. In some states, these bonds are called *tax-supported bonds*. See also Full Faith and Credit.

General Obligation Special Assessment Bonds   See Special Assessment Bonds.

General Property, Plant, and Equipment   Property, plant, and equipment used to provide general government goods and services in a federal agency.

General Purpose Financial Statements (GPFS)   The five combined financial statements of a reporting entity that are required for conformity with generally accepted accounting principles.

General Purpose Governments   Governments that provide many categories of services to their residents, such as states, counties, municipalities, and townships.

General Revenue   The revenues (q.v.) of a governmental unit other than those derived from and retained in an enterprise. Note: If a portion of the net income in an enterprise fund is contributed to another nonenterprise fund, such as the General Fund, the amounts transferred constitute general revenue of the governmental unit.

Generally Accepted Accounting Principles (GAAP)   The body of accounting and financial reporting standards, conventions, and practices that have authoritative support from standards-setting bodies such as the Governmental Accounting Standards Board and the Financial Accounting Standards Board, or for which a degree of consensus exists among accounting professionals at a given point in time. Generally accepted accounting principles are continually evolving as changes occur in the reporting environment.

Generally Accepted Auditing Standards (GAAS)   Standards prescribed by the American Institute of Certified Public Accountants to provide guidance for planning, conducting, and reporting on audits by Certified Public Accountants.

Generally Accepted Governmental Auditing Standards (GAGAS)   Auditing standards set forth by the Comptroller General of the United States to provide guidance for federal auditors and state and local governmental auditors and public accountants who audit federal organizations, programs, activities, and functions. See also GAS.

Gifts in kind   Contributions of tangible items to a tax-exempt organization.

Government Auditing Standards (GAS)   Auditing standards set forth by the Comptroller General of the United States to provide guidance for federal auditors, state and local governmental auditors, and public accountants who audit federal organizations, programs, activities, and functions. Also referred to as *generally accepted governmental auditing standards (GAGAS)*.

Governmental Accounting   The composite activity of analyzing, recording, summarizing, reporting, and interpreting the financial transactions of governmental units and agencies. The term generally is used to refer to accounting for state and local governments, rather than the U.S. federal government.

Governmental Activities   Core governmental services, such as protection of life and property (e.g., police and fire protection), public works (e.g., streets and highways, bridges, and public buildings), parks and recreation facilities and programs, and cultural and social services. Also includes general administrative support, such as data processing, finance, and personnel.

Governmental Assets (Liabilities)   Assets (or liabilities) that arise from transactions of the federal government, or an entity of the federal government, with nonfederal entities.

Governmental Funds   A generic classification used by the GASB to refer to all funds other than proprietary and fiduciary funds. The General Fund, special revenue funds, capital projects funds, and debt service funds are the types of funds referred to as governmental funds.

Grant   A contribution by one governmental unit to another unit. The contribution is usually made to aid in the support of a specified function (for example, education), but it is sometimes also for general purposes, or for the acquisition or construction of fixed assets.

Grants in Aid   See Grant.

Grass-Roots Lobbying   An appeal to the general public to contact legislators or to take other action regarding a legislative matter.

Gross Bonded Debt   The total amount of direct debt of a governmental unit represented by outstanding bonds before deduction of any assets available and earmarked for their retirement. See also Direct Debt.

Gross Revenue   See Revenue.

Gross Tax Levy   The amount of the tax bill sent to the taxpayer without regard for any estimate of uncollectible taxes.

Health Maintenance Organization (HMO)   A prepaid health care plan that functions as a broker of health care between the consumer/patient requiring services and health care providers. HMOs differ depending, in part, on whether or not the health care provider is an employee of the HMO. Also called *preferred provider organizations (PPOs)*.

Historical Cost   The amount paid, or liability incurred, by an accounting entity to acquire an asset and make it ready to render the services for which it was acquired.

Human Service Organizations   See Voluntary Health and Welfare Organizations.

Improvements   Buildings, other structures, and other attachments or annexations to land that are intended to remain so attached or annexed, such as sidewalks, trees, drives, tunnels, drains, and sewers. Note: Sidewalks, curbing, sewers, and highways are sometimes referred to as *betterments*, but the term *improvements other than buildings* is preferred. *Infrastructure assets* is also a term used.

Improvements Other than Buildings   A fixed asset account that reflects the acquisition value of permanent improvements, other than buildings, that add value to land. Examples of such improvements are fences, retaining walls, sidewalks, pavements, gutters, tunnels, and bridges. If the improvements are purchased or constructed, this account contains the purchase or contract price. If improvements are obtained by gift, it reflects fair value at time of acquisition.

Income   A term used in accounting for governmental enterprises to represent the excess of revenues earned over the expenses incurred in carrying on the enterprise's operations. It should not be used without an appropriate modifier, such as operating, nonoperating, or net. See also Operating Income, Nonoperating Income, and Net Income. Note: The term *income* should not be used in lieu of *revenue* (q.v.) in nonenterprise funds.

Income Bonds   See Revenue Bonds.

Incremental Budgeting   A budgeting approach that is simply derived from the current-year's budget by multiplying by a factor (i.e., an incremental increase equal to inflation), or by adding amounts expected to be required by salary and other cost increases and deducting expenses not needed when the scope of operations is reduced.

Indenture   See Bond Indenture.

Indeterminate Appropriation   An appropriation that is not limited either to any definite period of time or to any definite amount, or to both time and amount. Note: A distinction must be made between an indeterminate appropriation and a continuing appropriation. A continuing appropriation is indefinite only as to time, an indeterminate appropriation is indefinite as to both time and amount. Even indeterminate appropriations that are indefinite only as to time are to be distinguished from continuing appropriations in that such indeterminate appropriations may eventually lapse.

Indirect Charges   See Overhead.

Indirect Cost   A cost incurred that cannot be identified specifically with a cost objective (q.v.), but rather benefits multiple cost objectives (e.g., a hospital cafeteria, central data processing department, and general management costs).

Industrial Aid Bonds   Bonds issued by governmental units, the proceeds of which are used to construct plant facilities for private industrial concerns. Lease payments made by the industrial concern to the governmental unit are used to service the bonds. Such bonds may be in the form of general obligation bonds (q.v.) or revenue bonds (q.v.). Also called Industrial Development Bonds, (IDBs).

Influence Promote, support, affect, modify, oppose, or delay by any means. Often used in the context of "influencing" legislation or political candidates.

Infrastructure Assets Roads, bridges, curbs and gutters, streets, sidewalks, drainage systems, and lighting systems installed for the common good. See also Improvements.

In-Substance Defeasance A transaction in which low-risk U.S. Government securities are placed into an irrevocable trust for the benefit of debtholders, and the liability for the debt is removed from the accounts of the entity even though the debt has not been repaid. See Defeasance and Legal Defeasance.

Interest and Penalties Receivable on Taxes The uncollected portion of interest and penalties receivable on taxes.

Interest Receivable on Investments The amount of interest receivable on investments, exclusive of interest purchased. Interest purchased should be shown in a separate account.

Interest Receivable—Special Assessments The amount of interest receivable on unpaid installments of special assessments.

Interfund Accounts Accounts in which transactions between funds are reflected. See Interfund Transfers.

Interfund Loans Loans made by one fund to another.

Interfund Transfers Amounts transferred from one fund to another.

Intergovernmental Revenue Revenue from other governments. Grants, shared revenue, and entitlements are types of intergovernmental revenue.

Interim Borrowing (1) Short-term loans to be repaid from general revenues during the course of a fiscal year. (2) Short-term loans in anticipation of tax collections or bonds issuance. See Bond Anticipation Notes, Tax Anticipation Notes, and Revenue Anticipation Notes.

Interim Statement A financial statement prepared before the end of the current fiscal year and covering only financial transactions during the current year to date. See also Statements.

Intermediate Sanctions Penalties imposed by the IRS in the form of excise taxes on private inurement to disqualified persons resulting from excess economic benefit transactions. For example, excessive salaries paid to a manager of a not-for-profit organization or rents greater than fair market value paid to a Board member who owns the building the organization occupies.

Internal Control A plan of organization under which employees' duties are so arranged and records and procedures so designed as to make it possible to exercise effective accounting control over assets, liabilities, revenues, and expenditures. Under such a system, the work of employees is subdivided so that no single employee performs a complete cycle of operations. Thus, for example, an employee handling cash would not post the accounts receivable records. Moreover, under such a system, the procedures to be followed are definitely laid down and require proper authorizations by designated officials for all actions to be taken.

Internal Service Fund (ISF) A fund established to finance and account for services and commodities furnished by a designated department or agency to other departments and agencies within a single governmental unit, or to other governmental units. Amounts expended by the fund are restored thereto either from operating earnings or by transfers from other funds, so that the original fund capital is kept intact. Formerly called a *Working Capital Fund* or *Intragovernmental Service Fund*.

Internal Support Test One of two tests of broad public support to determine if an organization is a public charity, rather than a private foundation. The test is met if the not-for-profit organization does not receive more than one-third of its total support from investment income and unrelated business income.

Interperiod Equity A term coined by the Governmental Accounting Standards Board indicating the extent to which current-period revenues are adequate to pay for current-period services.

Inventory A detailed list showing quantities, descriptions, and values of property and frequently also units of measure and unit prices.

Investment in General Fixed Assets An account in the General Fixed Assets Group of accounts that represents the governmental unit's equity in general fixed assets (q.v.). The balance of this account is subdivided according to the source of funds that financed the asset acquisition, such as general fund revenues and special assessments.

Investment in Plant One of the four subgroups of funds that make up the Plant Funds Group in a governmental college or university. This fund accounts for all property, plant, and equipment utilized by the institution, except when the accounts are held as investments by endowment and similar funds and annuity and life income funds.

Investments Securities and real estate held for the production of income in the form of interest, dividends, rentals, or lease payments. The term does not include fixed assets used in governmental operations.

Irregular Serial Bonds　Bonds payable in which the total principal is repayable, but the repayment plan does not fit the definitions of regular serial bonds, deferred serial bonds, or term bonds.

Job Order Cost　Cost accounting system most appropriate for recording costs chargeable to specific jobs, grants, programs, projects, activities, or departments.

Judgment　An amount to be paid or collected by a governmental unit as the result of a court decision, including a condemnation award in payment for private property taken for public use.

Judgment Bonds　Bonds issued to pay judgments (q.v.). See also Funding.

Judgments Payable　Amounts due to be paid by a governmental unit as the result of court decisions, including condemnation awards in payment for private property taken for public use.

Land　A fixed asset account that reflects the carrying value of land owned by a governmental unit. If land is purchased, this account shows the purchase price and costs such as legal fees and filling and excavation costs that are incurred to put the land in condition for its intended use. If land is acquired by gift, the account reflects its appraised value at time of acquisition.

Lapse　(Verb) As applied to appropriations, this term denotes the automatic termination of an appropriation. Note: Except for indeterminate appropriations (q.v.) and continuing appropriations (q.v.), an appropriation is made for a certain period of time. At the end of this period, any unexpended and unencumbered balance thereof lapses, unless otherwise provided by law.

Leasehold　The right to the use of real estate by virtue of a lease, usually for a specified term of years, for which a consideration is paid.

Legal Defeasance　A transaction in which debt is legally satisfied based on certain provisions in the debt instrument (e.g., third-party guarantor assumes the debt) even though the debt has not been repaid. See also Defeasance and In-Substance Defeasance.

Legal Investments　(1) Investments that public employee retirement systems, savings banks, insurance companies, trustees, and other fiduciaries (individual or corporate) are permitted to make by the laws of the state in which they are domiciled, or under the jurisdiction of which they operate or serve. The investments that meet the conditions imposed by law constitute the legal investment list. (2) Investments that governmental units are permitted to make by law.

Legal Opinion　(1) The opinion of an official authorized to render it, such as an attorney general or city attorney, as to legality. (2) In the case of municipal bonds, the opinion of a specialized bond attorney as to the legality of a bond issue.

Legislation　Action by Congress, a state legislative body, or a local council to establish laws, statues, and ordinances.

Levy　(Verb) To impose taxes, special assessments, or service charges for the support of governmental activities. (Noun) The total amount of taxes, special assessments, or service charges imposed by a governmental unit.

Liabilities　Probable future sacrifices of economic benefits arising from present obligations of a particular entity to transfer assets or provide services to other entities in the future as a result of past transactions or events. Note: The term does not include encumbrances (q.v.).

Life Income Funds　Funds, ordinarily of colleges and universities and other nonprofit organizations, established to account for assets given to the organization subject to an agreement to pay to the donor or designee the income earned by the assets over a specified period of time.

Limited Obligation Debt　Debt secured by a pledge of the collections off a certain specified tax (rather than by all general revenues).

Limited Purpose Governments　Governments that provide only a single function, or a limited number of functions, such as independent school districts and special districts.

Line Item Budget　A detailed expense or expenditure budget, generally classified by object within each organizational unit, and, often, classified within each object as to authorized number of employees at each salary level within each job classification, and so on.

Loan Fund　A fund whose principal and/or interest is loaned to individuals in accordance with the legal requirements and agreements setting up the fund. Such a fund is accounted for as a trust fund. See also Trust Fund.

Loans Receivable　Amounts that have been loaned to persons or organizations, including notes taken as security for such loans.

Lobbying   Communicating directly with a public official in either the executive or legislative branch of the state government for the purpose of influencing legislation.

Local Education Agency (LEA)   A broad term that is used to include school districts, public schools, intermediate education agencies, and school systems.

Local Improvement Fund   See Special Assessment Fund.

Local Improvement Tax   See Special Assessment.

Long-Term Budget   A budget prepared for a period longer than a fiscal year, or, in the case of some state governments, a budget prepared for a period longer than a biennium. If the long-term budget is restricted to capital expenditures, it is called a *Capital Program* (q.v.) or a *Capital Improvement Program*.

Long-Term Debt   Debt with a maturity of more than one year after the date of issuance.

Lump-Sum Appropriation   An appropriation made for a stated purpose, or for a named department, without specifying further the amounts that may be spent for specific activities or for particular objects of expenditure. An example of such an appropriation would be one for the police department that does not specify the amount to be spent for uniform patrol, traffic control, and so on, or for salaries and wages, materials and supplies, travel, and so on.

Machinery and Equipment   See Equipment.

Maintenance   The upkeep of physical properties in condition for use or occupancy. Examples are the inspection of equipment to detect defects and the making of repairs.

Major Programs   All federal programs identified by the auditor through a risk-based process that will be audited as part of a Single Audit.

Management's Discussion and Analysis (MD&A)   Narrative information, in addition to the basic financial statements, in which management provides a brief, objective, and easily readable analysis of the government's financial performance for the year and its financial position at year-end. The MD&A proposed in the GASB's Exposure Draft on the Basic Financial Statements for State and Local Governments.

Mandatory Transfers   Transfers made in a college or university from one fund to another in order to comply with legally enforceable agreements, such as bond indentures and grant agreements.

Market risk   The risk of loss arising from increases in market rates of interest or other factors that reduce market value of securities.

Material Weakness   A reportable condition of such magnitude that the internal control structure elements do not reduce the risk of material noncompliance to an acceptably low level.

Matured Bonds Payable   Bonds that have reached their maturity date but remain unpaid.

Matured Interest Payable   Interest on bonds that has matured but remains unpaid.

Measurable   Capable of being expressed in monetary terms.

Measurement Focus   The nature of the resources, claims against resources, and flows of resources that are measured and reported by a fund or other entity. For example, governmental funds and certain fiduciary funds currently measure and report available financial resources, whereas proprietary and certain other fiduciary funds measure and report economic resources.

Modified Accrual Basis   Under the modified accrual basis of accounting, required for use by governmental funds (q.v.), revenues are recognized in the period in which they become available and measurable, and expenditures are recognized at the time a liability is incurred pursuant to appropriation authority.

Modified Cash Basis   Sometimes same as Modified Accrual Basis, sometimes a plan under which revenues are recognized on the cash basis, but expenditures are recognized on the accrual basis.

Mortgage Bonds   Bonds secured by a mortgage against specific properties of a governmental unit, usually its public utilities or other enterprises. If primarily payable from enterprise revenues, they are also classed as revenue bonds. See also Revenue Bonds.

Municipal   In its broadest sense, an adjective that denotes the state and all subordinate units of government. As defined for census statistics, the term denotes a city, town, or village as opposed to other units of local government.

Municipal Bond   A bond (q.v.) issued by a state or local governmental unit.

Municipal Corporation   A body politic and corporate established pursuant to state authorization for the purpose of providing governmental services and regulations for its inhabitants. A municipal corporation has defined boundaries and a population and is usually organized with the consent of its residents. It usually has a seal and may sue and be sued. Cities and towns are examples of municipal corporations. See also Quasi-Municipal Corporations.

Municipal Improvement Certificates   Certificates issued in lieu of bonds for the financing of special improvements. Note: As a rule, these certificates are placed in the contractor's hands for collection from the special assessment payors.

Net Assets   The difference between total assets and total liabilities. Equivalent to the fund equity of a fund, the equity of not-for-profit organization, or the owners' equity of a business. Net assets are classified as unrestricted, temporarily restricted, or permanently restricted.

Net Bonded Debt   Gross bonded debt (q.v.) less cash or other assets available and earmarked for its retirement.

Net Income   A term used in accounting for governmental enterprises to designate the excess of total revenues (q.v.) over total expenses (q.v.) for an accounting period. See also Income, Operating Revenues, Operating Expenses, Nonoperating Income, and Nonoperating Expenses.

Net Pension Obligation (NPO)   A component of annual pension cost that is comprised of (1) the transition pension liability (or asset), if any, and (2) the cumulative difference from the implementation date of GASB *Statement No. 27* to the current balance sheet date between the annual pension cost and the employer's actual contributions.

Net Position   Net assets of a federal agency.

Net Profit   See Net Income.

Net Revenue   See Net Income.

Net Revenue Available for Debt Service   Gross operating revenues of an enterprise less operating and maintenance expenses but exclusive of depreciation and bond interest. *Net revenue* as thus defined is used to compute "coverage" of revenue bond issues. Note: Under the laws of some states and the provisions of some revenue bond indentures, net revenues used for computation of coverage are required to be on a cash basis rather than an accrual basis.

Nominal Interest Rate   The contractual interest rate shown on the face and in the body of a bond and representing the amount of interest to be paid, in contrast to the effective interest rate (q.v.). See also Coupon Rate.

Nonentity Assets   Those assets of a federal agency that the reporting entity is holding but are not available for the entity to spend.

Nonexchange Transactions   Transactions in which the donor derives no direct tangible benefits from the recipient agency, for example, a contribution to or support for a not-for-profit organization.

Nonexpendable Trust Fund   A fund, the principal, and sometimes also the earnings, of which may not be expended. See also Endowment Fund.

Nonexpenditure Disbursements   Disbursements not chargeable as expenditures; for example, a disbursement made for the purpose of paying a liability previously recorded on the books.

Nonmandatory Transfers   Transfers made in a college or university from one fund to another at the discretion of the governing board to serve whatever purpose the board agrees is desirable.

Nonoperating Expenses   Expenses (q.v.) incurred for nonoperating properties or in the performance of activities not directly related to supplying the basic service by a governmental enterprise. An example of a nonoperating expense is interest paid on outstanding revenue bonds. See also Nonoperating Properties.

Nonoperating Income   Income of governmental enterprises that is not derived from the basic operations of such enterprises. An example is interest on investments or on bank time deposits.

Nonoperating Properties   Properties owned by a governmental enterprise but not used in the provision of basic services for which the enterprise exists.

Nonoperating Revenue   Revenue arising from transactions peripheral or incidental to the delivery of health care, including investment income, gains and losses, and unrestricted contributions.

Nonrevenue Receipts   Collections other than revenue (q.v.), such as receipts from loans where the liability is recorded in the fund in which the proceeds are placed and receipts on account of recoverable expenditures. See also Revenue Receipts.

Normal Cost   The present value of benefits allocated to the current year by the actuarial cost method being used.

Not-for-Profit Organizations (NPO)   An entity that is distinguished from a business enterprise by these characteristics: (1) contributions by providers who do not expect commensurate returns, (2) operating purposes other than to earn a profit, and (3) absence of ownership interests.

Notes Payable   In general, an unconditional written promise signed by the maker to pay a certain sum in money on demand or at a fixed or determinable time either to the bearer or to the order of a person designated therein. See also Temporary Loans.

Notes Receivable   A note payable held by a governmental unit.

Object   As used in expenditure classification, this term applies to the article purchased or the service obtained (as distinguished from the results obtained from expenditures). Examples are personal services, contractual services, materials, and supplies. See also Activity, Character, Function, and Object Classification.

Object Classification   A grouping of expenditures on the basis of goods or services purchased, for example, personal services, materials, supplies, and equipment. See also Functional Classification, Activity Classification, and Character Classification.

Objects of Expenditure   See Object.

Obligated Group   A group of independent organizations that have joined together for a specific purpose, for example, to obtain financing in which case all parties are obligated in some way to repay the debt.

Obligations   Generally amounts that a governmental unit may be required legally to meet out of its resources. They include not only actual liabilities but also unliquidated encumbrances. In federal usage, obligation has essentially the same meaning as encumbrance in state and local government accounting.

Obsolescence   The decrease in the value of fixed assets resulting from economic, social, technological, or legal changes.

Operating Budget   A budget that applies to all outlays other than capital outlays. See Budget.

Operating Cycle   The cycle of an organization that includes forecasts of cash flows; collections of revenues; investment of excess cash; tracking the performance and security of investments; making disbursements for various purposes; and monitoring, evaluating, and auditing cash flows.

Operating Expenses   (1) As used in the accounts of governmental enterprises, the term means those costs that are necessary to the maintenance of the enterprise, the rendering of services, the sale of merchandise, the production and disposition of commodities produced, and the collection of enterprise revenues. (2) The term is also sometimes used to describe expenses for general governmental purposes.

Operating Fund   The fund used to account for all assets and related liabilities used in the routine activities of a hospital. Also sometimes used by governmental units as a synonym for General Fund.

Operating Income   Income of a governmental enterprise derived from the sale of its goods and/or services. For example, income from the sale of water by a municipal water utility is operating income. See also Operating Revenues.

Operating Lease   A rental-type lease in which the risks and benefits of ownership are substantively retained by the lessor, and that does not meet the criteria defined in applicable accounting and reporting standards as a capital lease. See also Capital Lease.

Operating Revenues   Revenues derived from the operation of governmental enterprises of a business character.

Operating Statement   A statement summarizing the financial operations of a governmental unit for an accounting period as contrasted with a Balance Sheet (q.v.) that shows financial position at a given moment in time.

Operating Transfers   Legally authorized interfund transfers (from a fund receiving revenue to the fund that is to make the expenditures). See also Residual Equity Transfer.

Operational Accountability   Information useful in assessing operating results and short- and long-term financial position and the cost of providing services from an economic perspective reported in entitywide financial statements.

Order   A formal legislative enactment by the governing body of certain local governmental units that has the full force and effect of law. For example, county governing bodies in some states pass orders rather than laws or ordinances.

Ordinance   A formal legislative enactment by the council or governing body of a municipality. If it is not in conflict with any higher form of law, such as a state statute or constitutional provision, it has the full force and effect of law within the boundaries of the municipality to which it applies. Note: The difference between an ordinance and a resolution (q.v.) is that the latter requires less legal formality and has a lower legal status. Ordinarily, the statutes or charter will specify or imply those legislative actions that must be by ordinance and those that must be by resolution. Revenue-raising measures, such as the imposition of taxes, special assessments, and service charges, universally require ordinances.

Organizational Test   A nonprofit organization meets the organizational test if its articles of incorporation limit the organization's purposes to those described in IRC Sec. 501 and does not empower it to engage in activities that are not in furtherance of those purposes.

Original Cost   The total of assets given and/or liabilities assumed to acquire an asset. In utility accounting, the original cost is the cost to the first owner who dedicated the plant to service of the public.

Other Appropriations Realized   A budgetary account used in federal government accounting to record an agency's basic operating appropriations for a fiscal period.

Other Financing Sources   An operating statement classification in which financial inflows other than revenues are reported, for example, proceeds of long-term debt and operating transfers-in.

Other Financing Uses   An operating statement classification in which financial outflows other than expenditures are reported, for example, operating transfers-out.

Outlays   Sometimes synonymous with disbursements. See also Capital Outlays.

Overdraft   (1) The amount by which checks, drafts, or other demands for payment on the Treasury or on a bank exceed the amount of the credit against which they are drawn. (2) The amount by which requisitions, purchase orders, or audited vouchers exceed the appropriation or other credit to which they are chargeable.

Overhead   Those elements of cost necessary in the production of an article or the performance of a service that are of such a nature that the amount applicable to the product or service cannot be determined accurately or readily. Usually they relate to those objects of expenditure that do not become an integral part of the finished product or service, such as rent, heat, light, supplies, management, or supervision.

Overlapping Debt   The proportionate share of the debts of local governmental units located wholly or in part within the limits of the government reporting entity that must be borne by property within each governmental unit. Note: Except for special assessment debt, the amount of debt of each unit applicable to the reporting unit is arrived at by (1) determining what percentage of the total assessed value of the overlapping jurisdiction lies within the limits of the reporting unit and (2) applying this percentage to the total debt of the overlapping jurisdiction. Special assessment debt is allocated on the basis of the ratio of assessments receivable in each jurisdiction that will be used wholly or in part to pay off the debt to total assessments receivable that will be used wholly or in part for this purpose.

Oversight Agency   The federal agency that makes the predominant amount of direct funding to the nonfederal entity receiving less than $25 million in federal awards. An oversight agency's responsibilities are similar to those of a cognizant agency, but less extensive.

Pay-As-You-Go Basis   A term used to describe the financial policy of a governmental unit that finances all of its capital outlays from current revenues rather than by borrowing. A governmental unit that pays for some improvements from current revenues and others by borrowing is said to be on a *partial* or *modified pay-as-you-go basis*.

Pay-In Warrant   See Deposit Warrant.

Payment Warrant   See Warrant.

Penalty   A legally mandated addition to a tax on the day it became delinquent (generally, the day after the day the tax is due).

Pension Trust Fund (PTS)   See Public Employee Retirement Systems.

Performance Audit   One of the two major types of audits defined by the U.S. General Accounting Office (see Financial Audit for the other type). A performance audit provides an auditor's independent determination (but not an opinion) of the extent to which government officials are efficiently, economically, and effectively carrying out their responsibilities.

Performance Budget   A budget format that relates the input of resources and the output of services for each organizational unit individually. Sometimes used synonymously with program budget (q.v.).

Performance Indicator   A measure of how well a health care organization "performed." Examples include "excess of revenues over expenses," "revenues and gains over expenses and losses," "earned income," and "performance earnings."

Permanently Restricted Assets   A term used in accounting for not-for-profit organizations indicating assets whose use is permanently restricted by an external donor. See Endowment Fund and Permanently Restricted Net Assets.

Permanently Restricted Net Assets   A term used in accounting for not-for-profit organizations indicating the amount of net assets whose use is permanently restricted by an external donor. See Endowment Fund, Net Assets, and Permanently Restricted Assets.

Perpetual Inventory   A system whereby the inventory of units of property at any date may be obtained directly from the records without resorting to an actual physical count. A record is provided for each item or group of items to be inventoried and is so divided as to provide a running record of goods ordered, received, and withdrawn, and the balance on hand, in units and frequently also in value.

Petty Cash   A sum of money set aside for the purpose of making change or paying small obligations for which the issuance of a formal voucher and check would be too expensive and time consuming. Sometimes called a *petty cash fund*, with the term *fund* here being used in the commercial sense of earmarked liquid assets.

Planning-Programming-Budgeting System (PPBS)   A budgeting approach that integrates planning, programming, and budgeting into one system; most popular in the federal government during the 1960s.

Plant   Acquisition   Adjustment   See   Acquisition Adjustment.

Plant Replacement and Expansion Fund   A fund classification provided for hospitals to account for assets restricted by donors or grantors for plant replacement or expansion.

Pooled Investments   In order to simplify portfolio management, obtain a greater degree of investment diversification for individual endowment or trusts, and reduce brokerage, taxes, and bookkeeping expenses, investments may be merged, or pooled.

Postaudit   An audit made after the transactions to be audited have taken place and have been recorded or have been approved for recording by designated officials if such approval is required. See also Preaudit.

Posting   The act of transferring to an account in a ledger the data, either detailed or summarized, contained in a book or documentary of original entry.

Preaudit   An examination for the purpose of determining the propriety of proposed financial transactions and financial transactions that have already taken place but have not yet been recorded, or, if such approval is required, before the approval of the financial transactions by designated officials for recording.

Preferred Provider Organization (PPO)   See Health Maintenance Organization.

Prepaid Expenses   Expenses entered in the accounts for benefits not yet received. Prepaid expenses differ from

deferred charges in that they are spread over a shorter period of time than deferred charges and are regularly recurring costs of operations. Examples of prepaid expenses are prepaid rent, prepaid interest, and premiums on unexpired insurance.

Prepayment of Taxes   The deposit of money with a governmental unit on condition that the amount deposited is to be applied against the tax liability of a designated taxpayer after the taxes have been levied and such liability has been established. See also Taxes Collected in Advance, and Deferred Revenues.

Primary Government   A state government or general purpose local government. Also, a special purpose government that has a separately elected governing body, is legally separate, and is fiscally independent of other state or local governments.

Prior-Years' Encumbrances   See Reserve for Encumbrances—Prior Year.

Prior-Years' Tax Levies   Taxes levied for fiscal periods preceding the current one.

Private Foundation   An organization exempt from federal income taxes under IRC Sec. 501(a) that (1) receives its support from a small number of individuals or corporations and investment income, rather than from the public at large, and (2) exists to make grants to public charities.

Private Trust Fund   A trust fund (q.v.) that will ordinarily revert to private individuals or will be used for private purposes, for example, a fund that consists of guarantee deposits.

Pro Forma   For form's sake; an indication of form; an example. The term is used in conjunction with a noun to denote merely a sample form, document, statement, certificate, or presentation, the contents of which may be either wholly or partially hypothetical, actual facts, estimates, or proposals.

Process Cost   Cost accounting system most appropriate for recording costs of continuous activities or processes; such as, governmental services, health care services, or higher education.

Program Budget   A budget wherein inputs of resources and outputs of services are identified by programs without regard to the number of organizational units involved in performing various aspects of the program. See also Performance Budget and Traditional Budget.

Program-specific Audit   An audit of one specific federal program as opposed to a single audit of the whole entity.

Project   A plan of work, job, assignment, or task. Also refers to a job or task.

Promise to Give   A pledge or promise to make a contribution that may be unconditional or conditional.

Propaganda   Information that is skewed toward a particular belief with a tendency to have little or no factual basis.

Property Assessment   A process by which each parcel of taxable real and personal property owned by each taxpayer is assigned a valuation.

Property Taxes   Taxes levied by a legislative body against agricultural, commercial, residential, or personal property pursuant to law and in proportion to the assessed valuation of said property, or other appropriate basis. See Ad Valorem.

Proprietary Accounts   Those accounts that show actual financial position and operations, such as actual assets, liabilities, reserves, fund balances, revenues, and expenditures, as distinguished from budgetary accounts (q.v.).

Proprietary Fund   Sometimes referred to as *income-determination*, *business-like*, or *commercial-type* funds of a state or local governmental unit. Examples are enterprise funds and internal service funds.

Prospective Payment System (PPS)   Medicare's system in which payments are based on allowed service costs for medical procedures within the same diagnosis-related group, rather than on the length of the patient's hospital stay or actual cost of services rendered.

Public Authority   See Authority.

Public Charity   An organization exempt from taxes under IRC Sec. 501(a) that receives its support from the public at large, rather than from a limited number of donors. Most often public charities are exempt from federal income taxes under IRC Sec. 501(c)(3).

Public Corporation   See Municipal Corporation and Quasi-Municipal Corporation.

Public Employee Retirement Systems (PERS)   The organizations that collect retirement and other employee benefit contributions from government employers and employees, manage assets, and make payments to qualified retirants, beneficiaries, and disabled employees.

Public Enterprise Fund   See Enterprise Fund.

Public Improvement Fund   See Special Assessment Fund.

Public Trust Fund   A trust fund (q.v.) whose principal, earnings, or both, must be used for a public purpose, for example, a pension or retirement fund.

Purchases Method   A method of recording supplies as Expenditures when purchased. If inventory levels have risen at the end of the month, the asset, Supplies Inventory, is debited and Fund Balance—Reserve for Inventory is credited. An alternative method is called the *Consumption Method*.

Purchase Order   A document that authorizes the delivery of specified merchandise or the rendering of certain services and the making of a charge for them.

Quasi-Endowment Funds   Funds established by a governing board of an institution to account for assets to be retained and invested as if they were endowments. Also called Funds Functioning as Endowments.

Quasi-External Transaction   Transactions between funds that are similar to and accounted for the same as if the other party to the transaction had been an external entity. An example is the purchase of supplies by the General Fund from an internal service fund. This transaction results in an expenditure by the General Fund and a revenue to the Internal Service Fund.

Quasi-Municipal Corporation   An agency established by the state primarily for the purpose of helping to carry out its functions, for example, a county or school district. Note: Some counties and other agencies ordinarily classified as quasi-municipal corporations have been granted the powers of municipal corporations by the state in which they are located. See also Municipal Corporations.

Questioned Cost   A cost identified by an auditor in an audit finding that generally relates to noncompliance with a law, regulation, or agreement, where the costs are either not supported by adequate documentation or appear unreasonable. OMB cost Circulars identify, for different kinds of organizations, which costs are allowable and unallowable.

Rate Base   The value of utility property used in computing an authorized rate of return as authorized by law or a regulatory commission.

Realize   To convert goods or services into cash or receivables. Also to exchange for property that is a current asset or can be converted immediately into a current asset. Sometimes applied to conversion of noncash assets into cash.

Rebates   Abatements (q.v.) or refunds (q.v.).

Receipts This term, unless otherwise qualified, means cash received.

Recoverable Expenditure An expenditure made for or on behalf of another governmental unit, fund, or department, or for a private individual, firm, or corporation, that will subsequently be recovered in cash or its equivalent.

Refund (Noun) An amount paid back or credit allowed because of an overcollection or on account of the return of an object sold. (Verb) To pay back or allow credit for an amount because of an overcollection or because of the return of an object sold. (Verb) To provide for the payment of a loan through cash or credit secured by a new loan.

Refunding Bonds Bonds issued to retire bonds already outstanding. The refunding bonds may be sold for cash and outstanding bonds redeemed in cash, or the refunding bonds may be exchanged with holders of outstanding bonds.

Registered Bond A bond the owner of which is registered with the issuing governmental unit, and that cannot be sold or exchanged without a change of registration.

Registered Warrant A warrant that is registered by the paying officer for future payment on account of present lack of funds and that is to be paid in the order of its registration. In some cases, such warrants are registered when issued; in others, they are registered when first presented to the paying officer by the holders. See also Warrant.

Regular Serial Bonds Bonds payable in which the total principal is repayable in a specified number of equal annual installments.

Regulatory Accounting Principles (RAP) The accounting principles prescribed by federal or state regulatory commissions for investor-owned and some governmentally owned utilities. Also called *statutory accounting principles* (SAP). RAP or some SAP may differ from GAAP.

Reimbursement Cash or other assets received as a repayment of the cost of work or services performed or of other expenditures made for or on behalf of another governmental unit or department or for an individual, firm, or corporation.

Replacement Cost The cost as of a certain date of a property that can render similar service (but need not be of the same structural form) as the property to be replaced. See also Reproduction Cost.

Reportable Condition A significant deficiency in the design or operation of the internal control structure that could adversely affect the entity's ability to administer federal financial assistance programs in accordance with laws and regulations.

Reporting Entity The primary government and all related component units, if any, combined in accordance with GASB *Codification* Section 2100 constitute the governmental reporting entity.

Reproduction Cost The cost as of a certain date of reproducing an exactly similar new property in the same place.

Repurchase Agreement An agreement wherein a governmental unit transfers cash to a financial institution in exchange for securities, and the financial institution agrees to repurchase the same securities at an agreed-upon price.

Required Supplemental Information (RSI) Information that is required by generally accepted accounting principles to be included with the audited annual financial statements, usually directly following the notes to the general purpose financial statements.

Requisition A written demand or request, usually from one department to the purchasing officer or to another department, for specified articles or services.

Reserve An account that records a portion of the fund equity that must be segregated for some future use and that is, therefore, not available for further appropriation or expenditure. See Reserve for Inventory or Reserve for Encumbrances.

Reserve for Advance to _____ Fund A reserve that represents the segregation of a portion of a fund equity to indicate that assets equal to the amount of the reserve are invested in a long-term loan to another fund and are, therefore, not available for appropriation.

Reserve for Encumbrances A segregation of a portion of fund equity in the amount of encumbrances outstanding. See also Reserve.

Reserve for Encumbrances—Prior Year Encumbrances outstanding at the end of a fiscal year are designated as pertaining to appropriations of a year prior to the current year in order that related expenditures may be matched with the appropriations of the prior year rather than an appropriation of the current year.

Reserve for Inventory A segregation of a portion of fund equity to indicate that assets equal to the amount of the reserve are invested in inventories and are, therefore, not available for appropriation.

844   *Glossary*

Reserve for Realized Gains and Losses An account used by a cash and investment pool to accumulate realized gains and losses on sales of investments pending distribution to pool participants. See Undistributed Earnings.

Reserve for Revenue Bond Contingency A reserve in an Enterprise Fund that represents the segregation of a portion of retained earnings equal to current assets that are restricted for meeting various contingencies, as may be specified and defined in the revenue bond indenture.

Reserve for Revenue Bond Debt Service A reserve in an Enterprise Fund that represents the segregation of a portion of retained earnings equal to current assets that are restricted to current servicing of revenue bonds in accordance with the terms of a bond indenture.

Reserve for Revenue Bond Retirement A reserve in an Enterprise Fund that represents the segregation of a portion of retained earnings equal to current assets that are restricted for future servicing of revenue bonds in accordance with the terms of a bond indenture.

Reserve for Uncollected Taxes A reserve equal to the amount of taxes receivable by a fund. The reserve is deducted from Taxes Receivable, thus effectively placing the fund on the cash basis of revenue recognition.

Residual Equity Transfer Nonrecurring or nonroutine transfers of equity between funds (e.g., transfers of residual balances of discontinued funds to the General Fund or a debt service fund). See also Equity Transfer.

Resolution A special or temporary order of a legislative body; an order of a legislative body requiring less legal formality than an ordinance or statute. See also Ordinance.

Resources Legally budgeted revenues of a state or local government that have not been recognized as revenues under the modified accrual basis of accounting as of the date of an interim Balance Sheet.

Restricted Assets Assets (usually of an enterprise fund) that may not be used for normal operating purposes because of the requirements of regulatory authorities, provisions in bond indentures, or other legal agreements, but that need not be accounted for in a separate fund.

Restricted Fund A fund established to account for assets the use of which is limited by the requirements of donors or grantors. Hospitals may have three types of restricted funds: specific purpose funds, endowment funds, and plant replacement and expansion funds. The governing body or administration cannot restrict the use of assets, they may only designate the use of assets. See Board-Designated Funds.

Retained Earnings The accumulated earnings of an Enterprise or Internal Service Fund that have been retained in the fund and are not reserved for any specific purpose.

Retirement Allowances Amounts paid to government employees who have retired from active service or to their survivors. See Annuity.

Retirement Fund A fund out of which retirement annuities and/or other benefits are paid to authorized and designated public employees. A retirement fund is accounted for as a Trust Fund (q.v.).

Revenue Additions to fund financial resources other than from interfund transfers (q.v.) and debt issue proceeds.

Revenue Anticipation Notes (RANS) Notes issued in anticipation of the collection of revenues, usually from specified sources, and to be repaid upon the collection of the revenues.

Revenue Bonds Bonds whose principal and interest are payable exclusively from earnings of a public enterprise. In addition to a pledge of revenues, such bonds sometimes contain a mortgage on the enterprise's property and are then known as *mortgage revenue bonds*.

Revenue Receipts A term used synonymously with *revenue* (q.v.) by some governmental units that account for their revenues on a cash basis (q.v.). See also Nonrevenue Receipts.

Revenues Budget A legally adopted budget authorizing the collection of revenues from specified sources and estimating the amounts to be collected during the period from each source.

Revenues Collected in Advance A liability account that represents revenues collected before they are earned.

Revolving Fund See Internal Service Fund.

Risk-Based Approach This approach, used by auditors to determine which programs will be audited as part of the single audit, is a five-step process designed to select federal programs that are relatively large as well as likely to have problems. The auditors can use their professional judgment to classify programs that have been audited recently without audit findings, have had no significant changes in personnel or systems, or have a high level of oversight by awarding agencies as "low risk."

Risk Contract An insurance policy used to protect a prepaid health care plan from losses arising from excess of actual cost of providing health care over the fixed (capitation) fee.

Schedules (1) The explanatory or supplementary statements that accompany the Balance Sheet or other principal statements periodically prepared from the accounts. (2) The accountant's or auditor's principal work papers covering their examination of the books and accounts. (3) A written enumeration or detailed list in orderly form. See also Exhibit and Statements.

Scrip An evidence of indebtedness, usually in small denomination, secured or unsecured, interest-bearing or noninterest-bearing, stating that the governmental unit, under conditions set forth, will pay the face value of the certificate or accept it in payment of certain obligations.

Securities Bonds, notes, mortgages, or other forms of negotiable or nonnegotiable instruments. See also Investments.

Self-Supporting or Self-Liquidating Debt Debt obligations whose principal and interest are payable solely from the earnings of the enterprise for the construction or improvement of which they were originally issued. See also Revenue Bonds.

Serial Annuity Bonds Serial bonds in which the annual installments of bond principal are so arranged that the combined payments for principal and interest are approximately the same each year.

Serial Bonds Bonds the principal of which is repaid in periodic installments over the life of the issue. See Serial Annuity Bonds and Deferred Serial Bonds.

Service Efforts and Accomplishments A conceptualization of the resources consumed (inputs), tasks performed (outputs), and goals attained (outcomes), and the relationship among these items, in providing services in selected areas (e.g., police protection, solid waste garbage collection, and elementary and secondary education).

Shared Revenue Revenue levied by one governmental unit but shared, usually on a predetermined basis, with another unit of government or class of governments.

Shared Tax See Shared Revenue.

Short-Term Debt Debt with a maturity of one year or less after the date of issuance. Short-term debt usually includes floating debt, bond anticipation notes, tax anticipation notes, and interim warrants.

Single Audit An audit prescribed by federal law for state and local governmental units and nonprofit organizations that receive federal financial assistance above a specified amount. Such an audit is to be conducted in conformity with the Office of Management and Budget *Circular A-133*. Such an audit is conducted on an organizationwide basis rather than on the former grant-by-grant basis. The Single Audit Act of 1984, as amended in 1996, and the circular cited above impose uniform, and rigorous, requirements for conducting and reporting on single audits.

Sinking Fund See Debt Service Fund.

Sinking Fund Bonds Bonds issued under an agreement that requires the governmental unit to set aside periodically out of its revenues a sum that, with compound earnings thereon, will be sufficient to redeem the bonds at their stated date of maturity. Sinking fund bonds are usually also term bonds (q.v.).

Special Assessment A compulsory levy made against certain properties to defray part or all of the cost of a specific improvement or service that is presumed to be a general benefit to the public and of special benefit to such properties.

Special Assessment Bonds Bonds payable from the proceeds of special assessments (q.v.). If the bonds are payable only from the collections of special assessments, they are known as *special-special assessment bonds*. If, in addition to the assessments, the full faith and credit of the governmental unit is pledged, they are known as *general obligation special assessment bonds*.

Special Assessment Fund A fund type no longer authorized for use in the GPFS.

Special Assessment Liens Receivable Claims that a governmental unit has on properties until special assessments (q.v.) levied against them have been paid. The term normally applies to those delinquent special assessments for the collection of which legal action has been taken through the filing of claims.

Special Assessment Roll The official list showing the amount of special assessments (q.v.) levied against each property presumed to be benefited by an improvement or service.

Special District An independent unit of local government organized to perform a single governmental function or a restricted number of related functions. Special districts usually have the power to incur debt and levy taxes; however, certain types of special districts are entirely dependent on enterprise earnings and cannot impose taxes. Examples of special districts are water districts, drainage districts, flood control districts, hospital districts, fire protection districts, transit authorities, port authorities, and electric power authorities.

Special District Bonds Bonds issued by a special district. See Special District.

Special Fund　Any fund that must be devoted to some special use in accordance with specific regulations and restrictions. Generally, the term applies to all funds other than the General Fund (q.v.).

Special Revenue Fund (SRF)　A fund used to account for revenues from specific taxes or other earmarked revenue sources that by law are designated to finance particular functions or activities of government. After the fund is established, it usually continues year after year until discontinued or revised by properly legislative authority. An example is a motor fuel tax fund used to finance highway and road construction.

Special-Special Assessment Bonds　See Special Assessment Bonds.

Specific Purpose Fund　A fund classification provided for hospitals to record the principal and income of assets that may be used only for purposes specified by the donor.

Spending Rate　The proportion of total return that may prudently be used by an institution for current purposes.

Statements　(1) Used in a general sense, statements are all of those formal written presentations that set forth financial information. (2) In technical accounting usage, statements are those presentations of financial data that show the financial position and the results of financial operations of a fund, a group of accounts, or an entire governmental reporting entity, or component unit thereof, for a particular accounting period. See also Exhibit and Schedule.

Statute　A written law enacted by a duly organized and constituted legislative body. See also Ordinance, Resolution, and Order.

Statutory Accounting Principles　See regulatory accounting principles.

Stewardship Investments　Beneficial investments of the federal government in such items as nonfederal physical property (property financed by the federal government but owned by state or local governments), human capital, and research and development.

Stewardship Land　Federal land other than that included in general property, plant, and equipment (e.g., national parks).

Stores　Materials and supplies on hand in storerooms, subject to requisition and use.

Straight Serial Bonds　Serial bonds (q.v.) in which the annual installments of a bond principal are approximately equal.

Subactivity　A specific line of work performed in carrying out a governmental activity. For example, replacing defective street lamps would be a subactivity under the activity of street light maintenance.

Subfunction　A grouping of related activities within a particular governmental function. For example, "police" is a subfunction of the function "public safety."

Subsidiary Account　One of a group of related accounts that support in detail the debit and credit summaries recorded in a control account. An example is the individual property taxpayers' accounts for taxes receivable in the general ledger. See also Control Account and Subsidiary Ledger.

Subsidiary Ledger　A group of subsidiary accounts (q.v.) the sum of the balances of which is equal to the balance of the related control account. See also Control Account and Subsidiary Account.

Subvention　A grant (q.v.).

Support　The increase in net assets arising from contributions of resources or nonexchange transactions and includes only amounts for which the donor receives no direct tangible benefits from the recipient agency.

Surety Bond　A written promise to pay damages or to indemnify against losses caused by the party or parties named in the document, through nonperformance or through defalcation. An example is a surety bond given by a contractor or by an official handling cash or securities.

Surplus　Now generally obsolete in accounting usage. See Fund Balance, Retained Earnings, and Investment in General Fixed Assets.

Surplus Receipts　A term sometimes applied to receipts that increase the balance of a fund but are not a part of its normal revenue, for example, collection of accounts previously written off. Sometimes used as an account title.

Suspense Account　An account that carries charges or credits temporarily, pending the determination of the proper account or accounts to which they are to be posted. See Suspense Fund, Clearing Account.

Suspense Fund　A fund established to account separately for certain receipts pending the distribution or disposal thereof. See also Agency Fund.

Sweep Accounts　Arrangements in which a bank automatically "sweeps" cash that exceeds the target balance into short-term cash investments.

Syndicate, Underwriting　A group formed for the marketing of a given security issue too large for one member to handle expeditiously, after which the group is dissolved.

Tax Anticipation Notes (TANs) Notes (sometimes called *warrants*) issued in anticipation of collection of taxes, usually retirable only from tax collections, and frequently only from the proceeds of the tax levy whose collection they anticipate.

Tax Anticipation Warrants See Tax Anticipation Notes.

Tax Certificate A certificate issued by a governmental unit as evidence of the conditional transfer of title to tax-delinquent property from the original owner to the holder of the certificate. If the owner does not pay the amount of the tax arrearage and other charges required by law during the special period of redemption, the holder can foreclose to obtain title. Also called *tax sale certificate* and *tax lien certificate* in some jurisdictions. See also Tax Deed.

Tax Deed A written instrument by which title to property sold for taxes is transferred unconditionally to the purchaser. A tax deed is issued on foreclosure of the tax lien (q.v.) obtained by the purchaser at the tax sale. The tax lien cannot be foreclosed until the expiration of the period during which the owner may redeem his property through paying the delinquent taxes and other charges. See also Tax Certificate.

Tax Expenditure A revenue loss attributable to provisions of federal tax laws that allow a special exclusion, exemption, or deduction from gross income, or that provide a special credit, a preferential rate of tax, or a deferral of tax liability.

Tax Increment Debt Debt secured by an incremental tax earmarked for servicing the debt, such as a half-cent sales tax, or payable from taxes derived from incremental growth in the tax base that was financed by the tax increment debt.

Tax Levy See Levy.

Tax Levy Ordinance An ordinance (q.v.) by means of which taxes are levied.

Tax Liens Claims that governmental units have on properties until taxes levied against them have been paid. Note: The term is sometimes limited to those delinquent taxes for the collection of which legal action has been taken through the filing of liens.

Tax Liens Receivable Legal claims against property that have been exercised because of nonpayment of delinquent taxes, interest, and penalties. The account includes delinquent taxes, interest, and penalties receivable up to the date the lien becomes effective, and the cost of holding the sale.

Tax Notes See Tax Anticipation Notes.

Tax Rate The amount of tax stated in terms of a unit of the tax base, for example, 25 mills per dollar of assessed valuation of taxable property.

Tax Rate Limit The maximum rate at which a governmental unit may levy a tax. The limit may apply to taxes raised for a particular purpose, or to taxes imposed for all purposes; and may apply to a single government, to a class of governments, or to all governmental units operating in a particular area. Overall tax rate limits usually restrict levies for all purposes and of all governments, state and local, having jurisdiction in a given area.

Tax Roll The official list showing the amount of taxes levied against each taxpayer or property. Frequently, the tax roll and the assessment roll are combined, but even in these cases the two can be distinguished.

Tax Sale Certificate See Tax Certificate.

Tax Supplement A tax levied by a local unit of government that has the same base as a similar tax levied by a higher level of government, such as a state or province. The local tax supplement is frequently administered by the higher level of government along with its own tax. A locally imposed, state-administered sales tax is an example of a tax supplement.

Tax-Supported Debt All debt secured by pledges of tax revenues.

Tax Title Notes Obligations secured by pledges of the governmental unit's interest in certain tax liens or tax titles.

Taxable Property All property except that which is exempt from taxation–examples are property owned by governmental units and property used by some religious and charitable organizations.

Taxes Compulsory charges levied by a governmental unit for the purpose of financing services performed for the common benefit. Note: The term does not include specific charges made against particular persons or property for current or permanent benefits such as special assessments. Neither does the term include charges for services rendered only to those paying such charges as, for example, sewer service charges.

Taxes Collected in Advance A liability for taxes collected before the tax levy has been made or before the amount of taxpayer liability has been established.

Taxes Levied for Other Governmental Units Taxes levied by the reporting governmental unit for other governmental units, which, when collected, are to be paid over to these units.

Taxes Paid in Advance　Same as Taxes Collected in Advance. Also called *Prepaid Taxes*.

Taxes Receivable—Current　The uncollected portion of taxes that a governmental unit has levied but that are not yet delinquent.

Taxes Receivable—Delinquent　Taxes remaining unpaid on and after the date on which a penalty for nonpayment is attached. Even though the penalty may be subsequently waived and a portion of the taxes may be abated or canceled, the unpaid balances continue to be delinquent taxes until paid, abated, canceled, or converted into tax liens.

Temporarily Restricted Assets　A term used in accounting for not-for-profit organizations indicating assets temporarily restricted by an external donor for use in a future period or for a particular purpose. See Temporarily Restricted Net Assets.

Temporarily Restricted Net Assets　A term used in accounting for not-for-profit organizations indicating the amount of net assets temporarily restricted by an external donor for use in a future period or for a particular purpose. See Net Assets and Temporarily Restricted Assets.

Temporary Loans　Short-term obligations representing amounts borrowed for short periods of time and usually evidenced by notes payable (q.v.) or warrants payable (q.v.). They may be unsecured, or secured by specific revenues to be collected. See also Tax Anticipation Notes.

Term Bonds　Bonds the entire principal of which matures on one date.

Term Bonds Payable　A liability account that records the face value of general obligation term bonds issued and outstanding.

Term Endowment Funds　Funds for which donors or other external agencies have stipulated, as a condition of the gift, that the principal is to be maintained intact for a stated period of time (or term).

Time Warrant　A negotiable obligation of a governmental unit having a term shorter than bonds, and frequently tendered to individuals and firms in exchange for contractual services, capital acquisitions, or equipment purchases.

Time Warrants Payable　The amount of time warrants outstanding and unpaid.

Total Quality Management (TQM)　A management approach in which an organization seeks to continuously improve its ability to meet or exceed customer demands, where *customer*, in government or not-for-profit organiza-

tion usage, may be broadly defined to include such parties as taxpayers, service recipients, students, and members.

Total Return　A comprehensive measure of rate of investment return in which the sum of net realized and unrealized appreciation or shrinkage in portfolio value is added to dividend and interest yield.

Traditional Budget　A term sometimes applied to the budget of a governmental unit wherein appropriations are based entirely or primarily on objects of expenditure. The focus of a traditional budget is on input of resources, rather than on the relationship between input of resources and output of services. For budgets focusing on the latter, see Program Budget and Performance Budget.

Transfers　See Operating Transfers and Residual Equity Transfers.

Trial Balance　A list of the balances of the accounts in a ledger kept by double entry (q.v.), with the debit and credit balances shown in separate columns. If the totals of the debit and credit columns are equal or their net balance agrees with a control account, the ledger from which the figures are taken is said to be "in balance."

Trust and Agency Funds　See Agency Fund, Trust Fund, and Fiduciary Fund.

Trust Fund　A fund consisting of resources received and held by the governmental unit as trustee, to be expended or invested in accordance with the conditions of the trust. See also Endowment Fund, Private Trust Fund, and Public Trust Fund.

2a7 Pool　An external investment pool that is not registered with the Securities and Exchange Commission as an investment company, but has a policy that it will, and does, operate in a manner consistent with the SEC's Rule 2a7 of the Investment Company Act of 1940.

Unallotted Balance of Appropriation　An appropriation balance available for allotment (q.v.).

Unamortized Discounts on Bonds Sold　That portion of the excess of the face value of bonds over the amount received from their sale that remains to be written off periodically over the life of the bonds.

Unamortized Premiums on Bonds Sold　An account in an Enterprise Fund that represents that portion of the excess of bond proceeds over par value and that remains to be amortized over the remaining life of such bonds.

Unapportioned Authority　The amount of a federal appropriation made by the Congress and approved by the

President, but not yet apportioned by the Office of Management and Budget. See Other Appropriations Realized and Apportionments.

Unbilled Accounts Receivable An account that designates the estimated amount of accounts receivable for services or commodities sold but not billed. For example, if a utility bills its customers bimonthly but prepares monthly financial statements, the amount of services rendered or commodities sold during the first month of the bimonthly period would be reflected in the Balance Sheet under this account title.

Unconditional Promise to Give A promise to make contributions to an organization that depends only on the passage of time or demand by the promisee for performance.

Underwriting Syndicate See Syndicate, Underwriting.

Undistributed Earnings An account used by a cash and investment pool to accumulate investment earnings pending distribution to pool participants. See also Reserve for Realized Gains and Losses.

Unearned Income See Deferred Revenues.

Unencumbered Allotment That portion of an allotment not yet expended or encumbered.

Unencumbered Appropriation That portion of an appropriation not yet expended or encumbered.

Unexpended Allotment That portion of an allotment that has not been expended.

Unexpended Appropriations The equity of a federal agency provided by an appropriation that has not yet been expended.

Unexpended Plant Funds One of the four subgroups that make up the Plant Funds Group in a governmental college or university. This fund accounts for assets set aside for the acquisition of long-lived assets for institutional purposes.

Unfunded Actuarial Liability See actuarial accrued liability (AAL).

Unit Cost A term used in cost accounting to denote the cost of producing a unit of product or rendering a unit of service, for example, the cost of treating and purifying a thousand gallons of sewage.

Unliquidated Encumbrances Encumbrances outstanding.

Unrealized Revenue See Accrued Revenue.

Unrelated Business Income (UBI) Gross income from trade or business regularly carried on by a tax-exempt organization less directly connected expenses, certain net operating losses, and qualified charitable contributions that is not related to its exempt purpose. UBI greater than $1,000 is subject to federal income tax at corporate tax rates.

Unrestricted Assets Assets that may be utilized at the discretion of the governing board of a nonprofit entity.

Unrestricted Funds Funds established to account for assets or resources that may be utilized at the discretion of the governing board.

Unrestricted Net Assets The portion of the excess of total assets over total liabilities that may be utilized at the discretion of the governing board of a governmental or not-for-profit entity. See Net Assets, Temporarily Restricted Net Assets, and Permanently Restricted Net Assets.

User Charge A charge levied against users of a service or purchasers of a product of an enterprise fund or an internal service fund.

Utility Fund See Enterprise Fund.

Utility Plant Acquisition Adjustment The premium paid on a utility plant purchased by a governmental unit. Similar to Goodwill in that it is the difference between the purchase price and fair value of the assets acquired; however, it is different because utilities do not capitalize the value of excess earnings.

Value As used in governmental accounting, this term designates (1) the act of describing anything in terms of money or (2) the measure of a thing in terms of money. The term should not be used without further qualification. See also Book Value and Face Value.

Variance Power The unilateral power of an organization to redirect donated assets to a beneficiary different than the third party initially indicated by the donor.

Voluntary Health and Welfare Organization Not-for-profit organizations that receive contributions from the public at large and provide health and welfare services for a nominal or no fee. Also known as Human Service Organizations.

Voucher A written document that evidences the propriety of transactions and usually indicates the accounts in which they are to be recorded.

Voucher Check A document combining a check and a brief description of the transaction covered by the check.

Voucher System A system that calls for the preparation of vouchers (q.v.) for transactions involving payments and for the recording of such vouchers in a special book of original entry (q.v.), known as a *voucher register,* in the order in which payment is approved.

Vouchers Payable   Liabilities for goods and services evidenced by vouchers that have been preaudited and approved for payment but not been paid.

Warrant   An order drawn by the legislative body or an officer of a governmental unit on its treasurer, directing the latter to pay a specified amount to the person named or to the bearer. It may be payable on demand, in which case it usually circulates the same as a bank check, or it may be payable only out of certain revenues when and if received, in which case it does not circulate as freely. See also Registered Warrant and Deposit Warrant.

Warrants for Disbursements   A formal certification of the validity of the debt, with authorization or direction to a financial agent to pay the debt. One step beyond a voucher in the payment process.

Warrants Payable   The amount of warrants outstanding and unpaid.

Work Order   A written order authorizing and directing the performance of a certain task and issued to the person who is to direct the work. Among the items of information shown on the order are the nature and location of the job, specifications of the work to be performed, and a job number that is referred to in reporting the amount of labor, materials, and equipment used.

Work Program   A plan of work proposed to be done during a particular period by an administrative agency in carrying out its assigned activities.

Work Unit   A fixed quantity that will consistently measure work effort expended in the performance of an activity or the production of a commodity.

Working Capital Fund   See Internal Service Fund.

Yield Rate   See Effective Interest Rate.

Zero-Based Budget (ZBB)   A budget based on the concept that the very existence of each activity must be justified each year, as well as the amounts of resources requested to be allocated to each activity.

Governmental and Not-for-Profit Organizations

AAA	**American Accounting Association** An organization of accounting educators and practitioners involved in education whose objectives are to contribute to the development of accounting theory, to encourage and sponsor accounting research, and to improve the quality of accounting education.
ACE	**American Council on Education** A not-for-profit organization founded in 1918 with members from institutions of all sectors of higher education and other education-related organizations. It provides leadership and advocacy on adult and higher education issues, represents the views of the higher education community to policy makers, and offers services to its members.
AHA	**American Hospital Association** An association organized in the early 1900s by hospital administrators to promote economy and efficiency in hospital management. It current mission is to take a leadership role in public policy, representation and advocacy, and health services.
AICPA	**American Institute of Certified Public Accountants** The professional organization to which certified public accountants (CPAs) belong. In addition to providing educational and lobbying services on behalf of its members, the AICPA is responsible for promulgating auditing standards.
AGA	**Association of Government Accountants** An association formed in 1950 to serve the professional interests of governmental financial managers by providing education, encouraging professional development, influencing governmental financial management policies and practices, and serving as an advocate for the profession.
ASBO	**Association of School Business Officials International** A professional association that provides programs and services to employees of public and private schools (including community and junior colleges and state departments of education) that promote the highest standards of school business management practices, professional growth, and the effective use of educational resources.

CBO   **Congressional Budget Office**   An office of the legislative branch of the federal government established in 1974 that gathers information for the House and Senate budget committees with respect to the budget submitted to the executive branch, appropriations bills, other bills providing budget authority, tax expenditures, and other analysis.

CSG   **Council of State Governments**   An association of state financial officers formed in 1933 to assist states with multistate and regional solutions to problems.

FAF   **Financial Accounting Foundation**   The organization that finances and appoints members of the Financial Accounting Standards Board and Governmental Accounting Standards Board.

FASAB   **Federal Accounting Standards Advisory Board**   The nine-member standards-setting body that recommends federal governmental accounting and financial reporting standards to the U.S. Comptroller General, Secretary of the Treasury, and Director of the Office of Management and Budget.

FASAC   **Financial Accounting Standards Advisory Council**   The council that advises the Financial Accounting Standards Board on policy matters, agenda items, project priorities, technical issues, and task forces.

FASB   **Financial Accounting Standards Board**   An independent, nongovernmental, privately funded entity that is responsible to the public at large and the public accounting profession for developing concepts, standards, and guidance on financial accounting and reporting for commercial entity as well as nongovernmental, not-for-profit organizations. The organization was established in 1973 and replaced the Accounting Principles Board.

GAO   **General Accounting Office**   An agency of the legislative branch of the federal government responsible for prescribing accounting principles for federal agencies. The auditing arm of Congress.

GASAC   **Governmental Accounting Standards Advisory Council**   The council that advises the Governmental Accounting Standards Board on policy matters, agenda items, project priorities, technical issues, and task forces.

GASB   **Governmental Accounting Standards Board**   The independent agency established under the Financial Accounting Foundation in 1984 as the official body designated to set accounting and financial reporting standards for state and local governments.

GFOA   **Government Finance Officers Association**   A professional association of government finance managers founded in 1906 (formerly the Municipal Finance Officers Association) to help establish uniformity in state and local government accounting practices. The GFOA administers the Certificate of Achievement program to reward excellence in financial reporting, budgeting, and other areas.

HFMA   **Healthcare Financial Management Association**   A nonprofit organization of financial management professionals employed by hospitals and other health care providers established in 1946 to provide professional development opportunities, influence health care policy, and communicate information and technical data.

ICMA   **International City/County Management Association**   An organization founded in 1914 (formerly International City Management Association) that is the professional and educational association of appointed administrators serving cities, counties, other local governments, and regional entities around the world.

NACo   **National Association of Counties**   An organization created in 1935 by county officials to provide legislative, research, technical, and public affairs assistance to members, and ensure that the concerns of over 3,000 counties in the United States are heard at the federal level of government.

NACUBO   **National Association of College & University Business Officers**   A nonprofit professional organization founded in 1962 representing chief administrative and financial officers at colleges and universities whose mission is to promote sound management and financial practices at institutions of higher education.

NASACT   **National Association of State Auditors, Comptrollers, and Treasurers**   An organization formed in 1915 to represent the states' views on financial management issues and to provide leadership and training in meeting state fiscal and financial management challenges in order to improve the financial management of state government.

NCSL   **National Conference of State Legislatures**   A national association of state legislatures that includes many sections offering services to member legislatures, such as the NCSL Leadership Staff Section for leaders and party caucuses and the National Legislative Services and Security Association, which produces a manual to enable legislatures to cope with the problems of maintaining order and normal operations.

NCGA   **National Council on Governmental Accounting**   The body that established accounting and financial reporting standards for state and local governments prior to the formation of the Governmental Accounting Standards Board.

NLC   **National League of Cities**   An organization founded in 1924 (formerly the American Municipal Association) by state municipal leagues to serve and represent municipal governments by establishing unified policy positions, advocating these policies, and sharing information that strengthens municipal government throughout the nation.

OMB   **Office of Management and Budget**   An office of the executive branch of the federal government that has responsibility for establishing policies and procedures for approving and publishing financial accounting principles and standards to be followed by executive branch agencies. It also has the authority to control the size and nature of appropriations requested of each Congress.

PCIE   **President's Council on Integrity and Efficiency**   A federal agency established by executive order that is comprised of all presidentially appointed Inspectors General, as well as other federal agency members. Its charge is to conduct interagency and interentity audits, and inspection and investigation projects in order to effectively and efficiently deal with government-wide issues of fraud, waste, and abuse.

SEC   **Securities and Exchange Commission**   An independent, quasi-judicial federal agency formed in 1934 to protect investors in publicly traded securities by ensuring that there is full and fair disclosure of all material facts concerning securities offered for sale across state lines.

USCM   **U.S. Conference of Mayors**   A nonpartisan organization established in 1932 representing U.S. cities with populations of 30,000 or more. The conference aids the development of effective national urban policy, strengthens federal-city relationships, ensures that federal policy meets urban needs, and provides mayors with leadership and management tools of value in their cities.

For the address, phone number, FAX number, Internet address, and journal of each of these organizations, see the author's homepage: http://www.online.emich.edu/~acc_kattelus under "Government and Nonprofit Resources."

Index